World Resources

1998–99

World Resources

1998–99

A joint publication by

The World Resources Institute

The United Nations
Environment Programme

The United Nations
Development Programme

The World Bank

New York   Oxford
Oxford University Press
1998

On the cover: *Aedes aegypti,* the mosquito that carries dengue fever and yellow fever.

The World Resources Institute, the United Nations Environment Programme, the United Nations Development Programme, and the World Bank gratefully acknowledge permission to reprint from the following sources:

Part I:
Figure 2.2, Box 3.2, Table 3.2, Box 3.7, Figure China.1, Table China.2, Figure China.3, Table China.4, The World Bank; Box 1.1, Figure 1.10, Table 1.5, Table 2.1, Table 3.1, Oxford University Press; Table 1.3, Table 1.4, Earthscan Publications, Ltd.; Table 1.1, Figure 1.7a and Figure 1.7b, Box 1.3, Table 1.2, Figure 1.12, Figure 1.13, Table 2.3, Table 2.7, Figure 2.10, Table 2.8, Figure 2.11, Table 2.9, Table China.3, World Health Organization; Figure 3.3, Annual Reviews, Inc.; Figure 1.9, International Institute for Environment and Development; Figure 1.5a and Figure 1.5b, Academic Press, Inc.; Table 2.2, Foundation for Advancements in Science and Education; Table 2.6, Journal of the American Medical Association; Figure 2.7 American Association for the Advancement of Science; Table 2.4, United Nations Environment Programme.

Part II:
Figure HW.6, The World Bank; Figure FW.4, Table FW.2, Table RR.3, Food and Agriculture Organization of the United Nations; Table FW.4, International Society for Mangrove Ecosystems; Table PC.1, Smithsonian Migratory Bird Center and Natural Resources Defense Council; Table RR.4, SCOPE, John Wiley & Sons, Ltd.; Table GC.1, Organisation for Economic Co-Operation and Development; Figure GC.4, University Corporation for Atmospheric Research; Figure GC.8, *Nature,* Macmillan Magazines, Ltd.; Figure GC.11, U.S. National Office for Marine Biotoxins and Harmful Algae; Map of domesticated lands, United Nations Environment Programme.

Oxford University Press

Oxford   New York
Athens   Auckland   Bangkok   Bogota   Bombay   Buenos Aires
Calcutta   Cape Town   Dar es Salaam   Delhi   Florence
Hong Kong   Istanbul   Karachi   Kuala Lumpur
Madras   Madrid   Melbourne   Mexico City
Nairobi   Paris   Singapore   Taipei   Tokyo   Toronto   Warsaw

and associated companies in
Berlin   Ibadan

Copyright © 1998 by the World Resources Institute

Published by Oxford University Press, Inc.
198 Madison Avenue, New York, New York, 10016

Oxford is a registered trademark of Oxford University Press.

ISBN 0-19-521407-2
ISBN (PBK) 0-19-521408-0
Library of Congress Cataloging Number: 86-659504
ISSN 0887-0403

World Resources is a biennial publication of
The World Resources Institute,
1709 New York Avenue, N.W.
Washington, D.C. 20006

Printed in the United States of America on recycled paper.

Printing (last digit): 9 8 7 6 5 4 3 2 1

Contents

Part III   Data Tables

Editor's Note

The *World Resources* series is published to meet the need for accessible, accurate information on the environment and development. Wise management of natural resources and protection of the global environment are essential to achieve sustainable development and hence to alleviate poverty, improve the human condition, and preserve the biological systems on which all life depends. The series is published as a collaborative product of four international organizations: the World Resources Institute (WRI), the United Nations Environment Programme (UNEP), the United Nations Development Programme (UNDP), and the World Bank. The continued and expanded collaboration of these four organizations ensures that the *World Resources* series will provide the most objective and up-to-date report of conditions and trends in the world's natural resources and global environment.

With *World Resources 1998–99*, the eighth report in this series, we introduce a new design and format that we believe will better meet the need for informed data and analysis on global environment and development issues. Part I of this volume focuses in depth on the critical issue of Environmental Change and Human Health. Chapter 1 explores the links between environmental quality and human health, looking both at the environmental threats associated with poverty and those associated with unwise development. This chapter introduces new indicators that estimate a country's potential exposure to environmental risks that can undermine health. Chapter 2 examines three trends that are changing the face of the planet—and also influencing human health: agricultural intensification, industrialization, and rising energy use, in particular, use of fossil fuels. It examines the potential of these three trends to improve human health and well-being and also, if not well managed, to degrade the environment and create risks to human health, both from exposure to infectious agents and chemical pollutants. Chapter 3 describes a range of environmental interventions, from local to international, that can safeguard both environmental quality and human health. Following these overview chapters is a collection of signed essays that reflects a diversity of opinions concerning the links between environment and health. The section ends with two regional profiles—one of the Senegal River Basin in West Africa; the other of China—that illustrate many of the tensions and opportunities explored in this section.

This volume introduces a new section, entitled Global Environmental Trends, which highlights critical trends in a graphic and easy-to-read format. The section features some 30 stories in five broad areas: Population and Human Well-Being, Feeding the World, Production and Consumption, the Global Commons, and Resources at Risk. Together, this collection provides both an overview of progress to date on sustainable development and an in-depth look at certain especially critical issues, such as the extent of threats to the world's forests. Coverage is not exhaustive; topics will change with each volume to call attention to emerging issues. Also, within this section, we introduce a new chapter that highlights key trends in each of the world's geographic regions. Entitled Regions at a Glance, this chapter aims to better serve the needs for regional policy analysis. The chapter also features eight global maps highlighting key environment and development indicators the world over. (We are interested in your opinion of these changes and the report overall. Please take a few minutes to complete the reader survey at the back of this volume.)

Part III, Data Tables, continues and expands the tradition of providing relevant data on most countries of the world. Complementary data are available in the *Human Development Report*, published annually by UNDP, and the World Bank's annual *World Development Indicators,* and a new report by UNEP, *Global Environmental Outlook.* To make an expanded set of data accessible to policymakers, scholars, and nongovernmental organizations, WRI also publishes on diskette the World Resources Database—expanded to include additional countries, variables, and where possible, 20-year time series.

The audience for the *World Resources* series has steadily expanded, with English, French, Spanish, Arabic, German, Japanese, and Chinese editions now in print, as well as an Indian edition published in English but printed in New Delhi. A *Teacher's Guide to World Resources* is also available to make the series more useful to teachers and students.

As always, the effort to put together this report was enormous. The book itself would not be possible without the collaboration of many institutions and individuals who freely shared both data and ideas. (See Acknowledgments.) The book was edited and assembled by the World Resources staff, who drew heavily upon the expertise within the four partner organizations: WRI, UNEP, UNDP, and the World Bank. The Editorial Advisory Board, chaired by M.S. Swaminathan, provided active advice and support at all stages of the project. We wish to thank the Netherlands Ministry of Foreign Affairs for its support of the preparation of the report and the distribution of the report in developing countries.

For the special section on Environmental Change and Human Health, we wish to thank the U.S. Agency for International Development and the Environmental Health Project for their financial and intellectual support. Through its offices in both Geneva and Rome, the World Health Organization provided invaluable assistance, as did our Special Advisors to this special section. We also wish to thank the Risk Science Institute of the International Life Sciences Institute for its financial contribution.

Leslie Roberts

Editorial: Environment and Health

An examination of trends in human health at the end of the 20th Century reveals a great deal of good news. In many world regions today, more people are living longer, reflecting many of the advances of human ingenuity and modern life. Better food and housing, fewer instances of child labor, more efficient and safer workplaces, improved access to health care, and reduced levels of pollution are all factors contributing to these gains in public health. Yet, the relative role any of these factors plays in influencing health is difficult to determine, because many of them work in combination. For example, improved nutrition reduces people's vulnerability to pollution. Better housing enhances people's capacity to work more efficiently and productively. The multiplicative effects of these advances show our capacity to change conditions that affect people's lives for the better through many different paths.

Not all regions share equally in these improvements, however. Progress has been slow in sub-Saharan Africa, the world's poorest region, where life expectancy lags some 25 years behind that of the wealthiest nations. Life expectancy has declined in some parts of Eastern Europe and the former Soviet Union as well, reflecting a combination of social, political, behavioral, and environmental factors. Thus, although global health trends are positive, they tend to obscure the serious and profound disparities that occur throughout the world between the more and the less advantaged members of any given society.

A huge gap in health status exists between rich and poor nations. Similarly, within countries—even the richest countries in the world—the poor suffer far worse health than do the wealthy. Although the United States ranks as one of the healthiest countries in the world, infants born in parts of the Mississippi Delta region or the inner cities of Washington, D.C., or Baltimore, Maryland, have life expectancies similar to those in such developing countries as Namibia, Lesotho, or India. Although new cases of asthma have increased in many industrialized countries in the past decade, in the United States, at least, African-American children have a four times greater risk of dying from asthma than do white children, who are comparatively wealthier.

A principal factor driving these disparities is that environment-based health risks—from mosquito-borne diseases to chemical contaminants to indoor air pollution—still play a large role in creating ill health in many regions. Conditions in both the global and the local environment are critical to our health and well-being. Indeed, environment-related risks can be deadly: each year, infectious diseases linked to environmental conditions kill one out of every five children in the poorest regions of the world. Government reports from China confirm that much of the limited groundwater in heavily industrialized and populated northern China is seriously contaminated with both human wastes and industrial pollutants, posing a clear threat to human health. During the forest fires in Southeast Asia in 1997, air pollution sometimes exceeded the levels believed to have occurred during the London smog, which killed some 4,000 people during the winter of 1952–53. Even before the forest fires, populations in many of Asia's megacities faced intolerably high exposures to air pollution.

Understanding the complex links between the environment and health is important. Humans are exposed to multiple health risks on a daily basis. Identifying which exposures or combination of exposures undermine health, and to what degree, is a challenge. To date, however, little research has been conducted on how much environmental factors add to the world's burden of ill health. However, it is inarguable that many environment-related risks can be reduced through preventive action, and that this approach provides a clear and achievable route to better public health in both developing and developed nations. Globally, millions of preventable deaths and millions more cases of illness appear to be either directly caused or worsened by environmental contamination and degradation. Diarrhea and acute respiratory infections, linked with water contaminated from human wastes and air filled with smoky fumes, respectively, are two of the top killers of children in the developing world today. Thus, addressing these two risks alone would provide health benefits of global proportions.

Implementing preventive actions to reduce environmental threats to health risks will entail devising public policies and making financial investments that explicitly recognize the relationship between environment and health. Many actions can be taken now that are practical, sensible, and cost-effective—and are not now being done. One of the best opportunities to improve health through preventive action is through efforts to improve the household and community environment in developing countries. Such actions include expanding access to water, sanitation, and hygiene education; ensuring that garbage is collected and disposed of properly; promoting the use of clean household fuels; and controlling the insect and animal vectors that carry diseases—especially the mosquitoes that transmit malaria, dengue fever, yellow fever, and other tropical illnesses. Such improvements would greatly contribute to reducing the 17 million deaths each year from infectious diseases. The failure to undertake such basic measures as providing clean water and waste management for all people is an unnecessary and continuing blight on humanity.

The unprecedented pace of development underway throughout much of the world offers a wealth of opportunities for cost-effective environmental interventions. To date, in too many places, rapid industrial and commercial growth has resulted in environmental degradation and increased threats to human health. Yet, this growth also contains the seeds of solutions. In Asia, some 70 percent of the energy infrastructure and 90 percent of the cars projected to be in service in 2010 have yet to be built. Ensuring that the most efficient and least polluting technologies are adopted is an excellent way to safeguard both environmental quality and human health.

Encouraging the phaseout of lead in gasoline is a clear example of prudent and affordable prevention. The damaging effects of lead on child development and adult health have been well documented through the past three decades of research. Evidence from numerous countries reveals that although the health benefits of phasing lead out of gasoline are great, the cost is relatively low. On average, countries can recover 5 to 10 times the cost of converting to unleaded gas in health and economic savings. The United States, for instance, saved more than US$10 for every US$1 it invested in the conversion to unleaded gasoline. Accordingly, there is no rationale for new vehicles to be built that require leaded gasoline, nor for additional refineries to manufacture leaded fuel. Despite this evidence, many nations persist in manufacturing or importing vehicles that use leaded fuel.

Devising uniform practices for international trade in toxics offers another opportunity for preventive actions that will greatly benefit both developed and developing countries. Despite growing evidence that toxic exposures do not remain neatly within regional or national boundaries, the export of hazardous substances has not abated. "Environmental degradation tends to follow the path of least resistance," as Michael Dorsey writes in this volume. Between 1989 and 1994, countries in the Organisation for Economic Co-Operation and Development (OECD) exported an estimated 2.6 million metric tons of hazardous waste to non-OECD countries. Although the United States has reduced the use of many toxic pesticides domestically, it still exports them to developing countries—some 108 million kilograms of banned or restricted compounds between 1992 and 1994. While developed countries are generally phasing out most uses of asbestos, Brazil will double its use of this dangerous material within the decade and is exporting about 70,000 metric tons of it to India, Nigeria, Thailand, and other rapidly developing nations.

Finally, actions to prevent or reduce environmental risks often yield multiple benefits, sometimes in both the short and longer terms. For instance, after greatly reducing pesticide subsidies and implementing Integrated Pest Management, Indonesia has increased crop yields and reduced insect-resistance problems even as it reduced overall pesticide use and pesticide-related health risks. In the realm of global climate change, a recent analysis by the World Resources Institute and the World Health Organization suggests that reducing the use of fossil fuels and increasing energy efficiency could save an estimated 700,000 lives a year globally by 2020—for a cumulative total of 8 million lives worldwide by 2020—and lower the global burden of illnesses, all while helping to curtail the buildup of greenhouse gases in the atmosphere. Many other opportunities exist to reduce environmental risks, save resources, and protect public health. To ignore such options will impose on yet another generation an unacceptably high—and preventable—health burden and will deny the promise of sustainable global development.

Jonathan Lash
President
World Resources Institute

Klaus Töpfer
Executive Director
United Nations Environment Programme

James Gustave Speth
Administrator
United Nations Development Programme

James D. Wolfensohn
President
The World Bank

PART I

Environmental Change and Human Health

OVERVIEW

Despite vast improvements in health globally over the past several decades, environmental factors remain a major cause of sickness and death in many regions of the world. In the poorest regions, one in five children do not live to see their fifth birthday, largely because of environmentally related—and preventable—diseases. That number translates into 11 million childhood deaths each year, mostly due to illnesses such as diarrhea and acute respiratory infections. Insect-borne diseases also exact a heavy toll; malaria alone claims 1 to 3 million lives a year, again, most of them children.

Environmental threats to health are by no means limited to developing countries. In the United States, some 80 million people are exposed to levels of air pollution that can impair health. In China, which has one of the world's fastest growing economies, 2 million people die each year from the effects of air and water pollution, according to one recent estimate. Nearly 100 countries, both developed and developing, still use leaded gasoline, unnecessarily exposing their citizens to a pollutant long known to cause permanent brain damage.

Environmental health problems vary dramatically from region to region, reflecting geography, climate, and perhaps most important, a country's level of economic development and policy choices. Many environmental health problems are associated with poverty and a lack of essential resources, chief among them sufficient and clean water, food, shelter, fuel, and air. Indeed, the World Health Organization has called poverty the world's biggest killer. These environmental problems underlie the 17 million deaths each year from infectious diseases.

Other environmental threats to health are associated with development itself, when it is pursued without proper safeguards for the environment. Without

question, economic growth and social development are critical for improving human health and well-being. Yet, if not well managed, economic growth can exact a major toll on environment and health. It is not a coincidence that some of the booming Asian economies also have some of the worst air pollution in the world.

In many developing countries today, populations are in double jeopardy, facing both the unfinished agenda of traditional environmental health problems, such as insufficient clean water and sanitation, as well as the emerging problems of industrial pollution. In these countries, both pesticides and feces may contaminate drinking water; likewise, air pollution may stem both from the household burning of dirty fuels and the industrial use of fossil fuels.

New indexes developed for this report attempt to capture the geography of environmental threats to health. Portrayed in maps, these indexes highlight those countries where traditional risks are high, and also vast areas such as India and China where traditional and modern risks coincide. In the more developed countries, the indexes show that many populations still face threats from avoidable hazards such as leaded gasoline. Although preliminary, these indexes suggest where policy interventions could improve both environmental quality and human health.

Although useful for painting a picture in broad strokes, these indicators cannot capture serious disparities in risk that occur within countries. For example, although the United States overall faces low environmental risks to health, the prevalence of asthma is increasing among poor and minority populations, and environmental factors are believed to be contributing to that increase. Similarly, lead exposures are typically far higher among poor, inner-city children than other groups. This unequal burden of risk, closely tied to poverty, is described in detail in the text. Nor do country-level indicators reveal another inequity: the disproportionate share of global environmental threats created by the wealthiest countries, who consume more energy and resources per capita than do poorer countries. The wealthy countries, for instance, bear the greatest responsibility for releasing the greenhouse gases that threaten to change global climate, with myriad potential health effects.

This special section describes the complex links between the environment, development, and health. It explores the ways in which environmental factors, and particularly environmental change, can degrade health—either directly, by exposing people to harmful agents, or indirectly, by disrupting the ecosystems that sustain life. The section then examines how improved environmental management can preserve both human health and environmental quality.

Why focus on the role of environment in health? Admittedly, environmental factors are by no means the only, or even the major, cause of ill health globally. Environmental factors predominate in poorer countries, for instance, but play a much smaller role in undermining health in the wealthier countries, where voluntary behaviors such as diet and smoking are larger determinants of health. In both settings, however, environmental factors deserve increased policy attention because they are avoidable causes of ill health.

Much has been done globally in the past few decades to improve health. Governments, communities, international agencies, donors, and nongovernmental groups have worked together to make widely available such life-saving interventions as vaccines and oral rehydration therapy. Many millions of dollars have been spent on medical research, although arguably not enough on tropical diseases that cause so much misery and claim so many lives throughout the developing world. These health-care strategies are essential and deserve increased support. However, supplementing these approaches with preventive strategies that intervene earlier in the disease process and stop harmful exposures from occurring in the first place would bring additional gains, often at relatively modest cost.

This report attempts to illuminate these points of intervention by exploring the driving forces and trends that underlie many of today's environmental health problems. Three trends stand out in terms of their profound impact on the physical environment and their enormous potential for influencing human health: the intensification of agriculture, industrialization, and rising energy use—in particular, fossil fuel consumption.

All of these trends play a vital role in economic development patterns worldwide, yet all can be a source of avoidable ill health as well. For instance, agricultural intensification can expose workers and communities to toxic pesticides. Land clearing and irrigation projects can facilitate increases in vector-borne diseases such as malaria and schistosomiasis. Industrialization, which is so critical to economic growth, can also bring exposure to heavy metals and other toxic contaminants. Rising energy use is largely responsible for air pollution that blankets many of the world's cities and also has the potential to alter the Earth's climate.

This report then describes a range of environmental interventions—from simple and local to complex and international—that can mitigate these problems. Many of these problems are hard to address. Indeed, the question of how to expand access to water and sanitation has defied simple solution for decades. Yet, tackling fundamental problems will yield myriad benefits, not just in terms of health. The provision of water and sanitation and associated interventions, for instance, would not only reduce disease and improve human dignity but could also help combat poverty if the time formerly spent collecting water or caring for sick children could be devoted to education or income-generating activities.

Other interventions, too, promise multiple benefits beyond the health arena. Curbing fossil fuel consumption could save lives immediately by reducing levels of ambient air pollution. In addition, the same strategy could help avert long-term climate change and its predicted ecological, economic, and health costs. Similarly, adopting more environmentally benign forms of agriculture—approaches that use fewer agricultural chemicals and cause less ecological disruption—would help to reduce both acute and chronic health risks associated with exposure to harmful pesticides. At the same time, reducing the use of fertilizer and improving watershed management could lessen agriculture's toll on coastal waters—particularly the harmful algal blooms and fish kills that threaten not only ecosystem health but human health as well.

In addition to these large-scale changes, the report calls attention to situations in which the problems and solutions are relatively well understood. Removing lead from gasoline, for instance, could immediately reduce environmental threats to health. Similarly, the report illustrates the many benefits possible if concerns about environmental threats to health are incorporated into development planning at the outset. Experience has shown it is possible to anticipate and prevent some of the problems associated with development. Dams can be built so that they do not provide habitat for disease vectors. Factories can be sited so that they do not contaminate groundwater. But achieving such results requires coordination and communication among agencies that do not often interact, such as government ministries of health, agriculture, economics, and the environment, and also international aid agencies. Making the environment a central component in public health strategies is essential to ensure health for everyone in the 21st Century.

Chapter 1

Linking Environment and Health

Edwin Huffman/World Bank

The environment, which sustains human life, is also a profound source of ill health for many of the world's people. In the least developed countries, one in five children do not live to see their fifth birthday—mostly because of avoidable environmental threats to health (1). That translates into roughly 11 million avoidable childhood deaths each year. Hundreds of millions of others, both children and adults, suffer ill health and disability that undermine their quality of life and hopes for the future. These environmental health threats—arguably the most serious environmental health threats facing the world's population today—stem mostly from traditional problems long since solved in the wealthier countries, such as a lack of clean water, sanitation, adequate housing, and protection from mosquitoes and other insect and animal disease vectors.

Indeed:

● Contaminated water—contaminated by feces, not chemicals—remains one of the biggest killers worldwide. Lack of adequate water, sanitation, and hygiene is responsible for an estimated 7 percent of all deaths and disease globally, according to one recent estimate (2). Diarrhea alone claims the lives of some 2.5 million children a year (3).

● Overcrowding and smoky indoor air—from burning biomass fuels for cooking or heating—contribute to acute respiratory infections that kill 4 million people a year, again, mostly children younger than age 5. The World Bank estimates that between 400 million and 700 million women and children are exposed to severe air pollution, in most instances, from cooking fires (4).

● Malaria kills 1 million to 3 million people a year (5), approximately 80 percent of them children (6). Other mosquito-borne diseases, such as dengue and yellow fever, affect millions more each year and are on the rise, prompting the World Health Organization (WHO) to declare the mosquito "Public Enemy Number One" (7).

What's more, in many newly and rapidly industrializing regions of the developing world, the populations are in double jeopardy, facing both this unfinished agenda of traditional environmental health problems as well as emerging problems of industrial pollution. Cottage industries, such as backyard tanneries, can place workers and residents in direct contact with hazardous chemicals. In those areas where the use of pesticides and other agricultural chemicals is increasing and safeguards are lax—or risks poorly understood—high exposures can ensue, leading to acute poisonings and even death.

Box 1.1 Demographic Regions Used in this Report

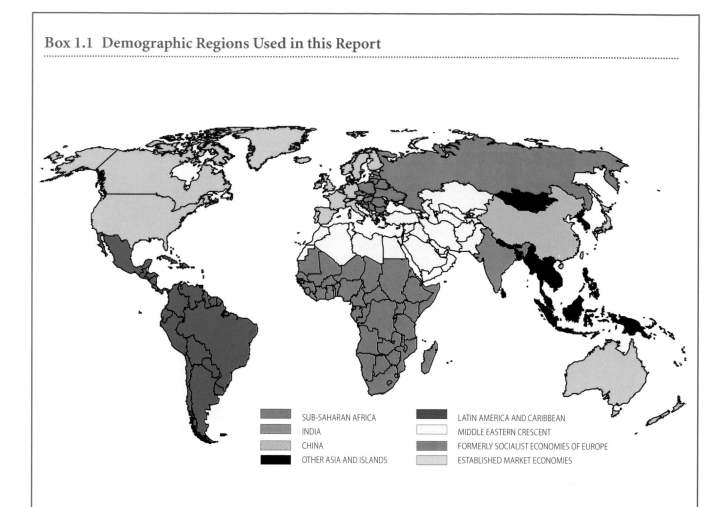

SUB-SAHARAN AFRICA

INDIA

CHINA

OTHER ASIA AND ISLANDS

LATIN AMERICA AND CARIBBEAN

MIDDLE EASTERN CRESCENT

FORMERLY SOCIALIST ECONOMIES OF EUROPE

ESTABLISHED MARKET ECONOMIES

Population, Economic Indicators, and Progress in Health by Demographic Region, 1975–1990

REGION	POPULATION, 1990 (millions)	DEATHS, 1990 (millions)	INCOME PER CAPITA DOLLARS, 1990	INCOME PER CAPITA GROWTH RATE, 1975–90 (percent per year)	CHILD MORTALITY 1975	CHILD MORTALITY 1990	LIFE EXPECTANCY AT BIRTH (years) 1975	LIFE EXPECTANCY AT BIRTH (years) 1990
Sub-Saharan Africa	510	7.9	510	-1.0	212	175	48	52
India	850	9.3	360	2.5	195	127	53	58
China	1,134	8.9	370	7.4	85	43	56	69
Other Asia and Islands	683	5.5	1,320	4.6	135	97	56	62
Latin America and the Caribbean	444	3.0	2,190	-0.1	104	60	62	70
Middle Eastern Crescent	503	4.4	1,720	-1.3	174	111	52	61
Formerly Socialist Economies of Europe (FSE)	346	3.8	2,850	0.5	36	22	70	72
Established Market Economies (EME)	798	7.1	19,900	2.2	21	11	73	76
Demographically Developing Group [a]	4,123	39.1	900	3.0	152	106	56	63
FSE and EME	1,144	10.9	14,690	1.7	25	15	72	75
World	**5,267**	**50.0**	**4,000**	**1.2**	**135**	**96**	**60**	**65**

Source: The World Bank, *World Development Report 1993: Investing in Health, World Development Indicators* (Oxford University Press, New York, 1993), p. 2.

Note: Child mortality is the probability of dying between birth and age 5, expressed per 1,000 live births; life expectancy at birth is the average number of years that a person would expect to live at the prevailing age-specific mortality rates.
a. Includes the countries of the demographic regions Sub-Saharan Africa, India, China, Other Asia and Islands, Latin America and the Caribbean, and Middle Eastern Crescent.

Environmental Change and Human Health

For countries in the early stages of development, both pesticides and feces may contaminate drinking-water supplies, and air pollution may stem both from traditional biomass fuels and industrial use of fossil fuels (8). Such problems are increasingly pronounced in the slum settlements that ring many of the world's cities.

Problems can be particularly acute where economic growth is extremely rapid. In many of the most rapidly developing countries in Asia, industrialization is occurring at triple the pace of the industrial revolution in the West (9). Many of those regions are also experiencing industrial pollution on a scale not seen in the developed world for the past 40 years—not since the London fog of 1952 caused some 4,000 excess deaths in the weeks subsequent to the episode (10). According to the United Nations, 13 of the 15 cities with the worst air pollution in the world are in Asia (11). A recent World Bank study estimates that more than 2 million people die each year in China alone from the effects of air and water pollution (12).

In the world's wealthiest regions, such as Europe, North America, and Japan, although environmental risks overall tend to be lower, they have by no means disappeared.

- Asthma is rising dramatically throughout the developed countries, and environmental factors appear to be at least partly to blame.

- Millions of people in Europe and North America are still exposed to unsafe air, and some air pollutants are proving more recalcitrant to control than many expected.

- Meanwhile, biological contamination is by no means a thing of the past, as shown by the 1993 outbreak of *Cryptosporidium* in the United States.

- The extension of travel and trade is providing new opportunities for the spread or re-emergence of infectious diseases. In the past two decades, some 30 "new" infectious diseases have emerged (13).

In all regions of the world, populations face the threat of climate change and other global environmental problems, such as stratospheric ozone depletion. Worldwide, fossil fuel emissions continue to rise, bringing with them the risk of climate change and both immediate and long-term health effects. However, it is important to note that although the activities that are driving these changes, such as intense fossil fuel consumption, have largely been concentrated among the wealthiest nations, the impacts are likely to be greatest in the poorest regions that do not have the resources to adapt to them (14). Similarly, in the wealthiest countries, disadvantaged populations often endure the highest exposures and have the fewest resources to deal with them.

As these examples reveal, despite considerable progress in addressing environmental problems, environmental degradation still poses a huge threat to human health in many regions. The exact nature and scale of environmental risks to health vary dramatically according to where and how one lives. The distribution of risks reflects a number of factors, including the level of socioeconomic development, distribution of wealth, a region's geography and climate (heat and humidity are major killers), and equally important, policy choices and investments. (The regional breakdowns used in this section and in calculating the WRI indicators that follow can be found in Box 1.1.)

The Geography of Risk

The maps on page 5 portray the geographic distribution of various environmental threats to health. These maps, the outcome of new indicators developed by the World Resources Institute (WRI), suggest both the level and type of environmental risks individual countries face. Because environmental threats to health emanate from many sources and vary dramatically by region and level of economic development, WRI calculated risks to health separately for developed and developing countries.

Figure 1.1 conveys the extent of environmental threats to health in the developing countries. In these countries, environmental threats to health are broad, stemming from both biological risks associated with poverty and chemical risks associated with industrialization. Threats in the former category include inadequate water and sanitation and exposure to vector-borne diseases that thrive in tropical climates. In some countries, the effects of ambient air pollution, from both conventional air pollutants and lead in gasoline, are compounded by the burning of smoky fuels indoors. The effects of pollutants and infectious agents are exacerbated by inadequate nutrition, as will be discussed later. For these reasons, the developing country index examines risks in three categories: air, water, and food. Some countries, such as poorer countries in Africa, may face high risks from indoor air pollution but low risks from outdoor air pollution; other countries such as India and China face both. In areas where these threats coincide with poor nutrition and/or water-related diseases, the environmental risks to health are likely to be high. Generally, countries in Africa and parts of Asia face the highest environmental threats to health. In much of Central and South America, environmental risks are moderate to low. Many of these countries have expanded water and sanitation coverage in recent years and have also removed lead from gasoline. (For details on how these indexes were constructed and additional data on each country, see Box 1.2 and the Appendix at the end of Part I.)

In most developed countries, by contrast, environmental threats stem primarily from industrial pollution—either conventional air pollutants, air toxics, or hazardous chemicals. Because data on chemical releases or exposures are generally

Box 1.2 Indicators of Environmental Threats to Health

WRI has developed new indicators to assess the extent of risks to health that people face from environmental threats in different countries of the world. Creating such indicators is fraught with difficulty, because national-level data are often lacking, necessitating the use of surrogate measures. For instance, most countries do not report information on how many of their population are exposed to potentially harmful levels of indoor air pollution from the use of smoky fuels. A rough surrogate can be constructed using the amount of biomass fuel used per household. Thus, these indicators are not precise measures of actual risk but rather rough gauges based on data availability and quality.

As described in the text, WRI developed separate indicators for developing and developed countries. For the developing country indicator, WRI selected several measures that represent potential environmental threats to health and then aggregated them, in a procedure described below. Because environmental threats to health are many and varied in developing countries, this indicator attempts to measure risks from three sources: air, water, and food. The air component for the developing country indicator includes three measures representing potential exposure to poor quality air: exposure to polluted indoor air, exposure to polluted ambient air, and exposure to air polluted with lead from gasoline.

The water component for the developing country indicator includes measures of percent of population without access to safe water, with-out adequate sanitation, and potential exposure to malaria (as a surrogate for a number of insect-borne diseases). The nutrition component includes three measures representing potential exposure to poor nutrition: percent of children under 5 years of age who are underweight, total number of available calories per person, and percent of population at risk of either vitamin A or iodine deficiency (whichever micronutrient deficiency was higher).

The three measures within each component of the developing country indicator were ranked from lowest (lowest relative risk) to highest (highest relative risk). If the number of countries with data available differed among the three measures, the ranks were standardized, or spread, to match the maximum number of ranks for any of the three measures. The three ranks from the three measures were then averaged (each country must have at least two measures to be included in the calculation), and the final average rank was ranked again from lowest to highest risk.

The next level of aggregation was to combine the ranks of the three components. Here again, when the number of countries with available data differ, the ranks were standardized to match the maximum number or ranks for any of the three measures. The ranks of the three components were then averaged (each country must have at least two measures to be included in the final ranking), and the final average rank was ranked again. The final result was a list of developing countries ranked according to potential exposure to the three components and associ-ated measures. The final rank was separated into high, medium, and low categories of potential, relative risk by dividing the countries into three equal groups.

For developed countries, WRI developed two indicators rather than a single aggregated index. One indicator suggests potential exposure to polluted ambient air; the other suggests potential exposure to air polluted with lead used in gasoline. The lead indicator is shown in Figure 1.2; the ambient air pollution indicator is included in the Appendix but is not mapped because of insufficient data. In both of these indicators, countries were ranked from lowest to highest exposures. To determine the final rank, the countries were divided into three equal groups, reflecting high, medium, and low potential risk.

In these preliminary indicators, the final rankings for each country should be considered suggestive, to be used as a basis for exploring environmental health threats in greater detail. WRI used the best available data to construct the indicator, but still, the data were often incomplete or unreliable. Dividing nations into thirds to designate the three risk categories is, admittedly, arbitrary. There may be very little difference between countries at the cut-off points between high and medium risk or medium and low risk. The broad categories, however, suggest differences in relative risks, and the indicator maps serve as preliminary tools for identifying countries with different potential for exposure to environmental health threats. (For additional information, see the Appendix at the end of Part I.)

---

lacking or of poor quality, WRI's preliminary indicators for developed countries focus solely on air pollution. Countries are ranked both according to their potential exposure to polluted ambient air and their potential exposure to lead in gasoline. Figure 1.2 shows countries where the populations face an elevated risk from potential exposure to air polluted with lead from gasoline. (For data on country-level risk of exposure to outdoor air pollution, see the Appendix.) The former Soviet Union and parts of Eastern Europe face high risks from exposure to lead in gasoline. Perhaps more unexpected, France, Germany, the Netherlands, and the United Kingdom, among others, also face high risks because of their continued use of leaded gasoline and dense urban populations.

As with any indicator, a number of caveats are warranted. First, these indicators do not measure adverse health effects; rather, they identify where risks are high, based on exposure to harmful agents. It is not possible to translate the risks identified in these indicators into estimates of excess sickness or death. Even so, one can safely assume that lower risk generally translates into better health. Nor do these indicators capture variations in risks within countries, which are known to be substantial, as will be discussed later in this chapter.

Shortcomings aside, the developing world indicator does serve as a rough guide to the severity and types of potentially harmful environmental exposures people face in various countries. Many of these exposures and their adverse effects can be prevented through policy actions at the local, national, or international level. As the indicator suggests, countries need not be wealthy to reduce environmental threats to health. Many actions can improve both environmental quality and public health for relatively low cost. These and other preventive policies are the focus of Chapter 3.

Potential Exposure to Health Risks from Environmental Threats

FIGURE 1.1 Developing Countries

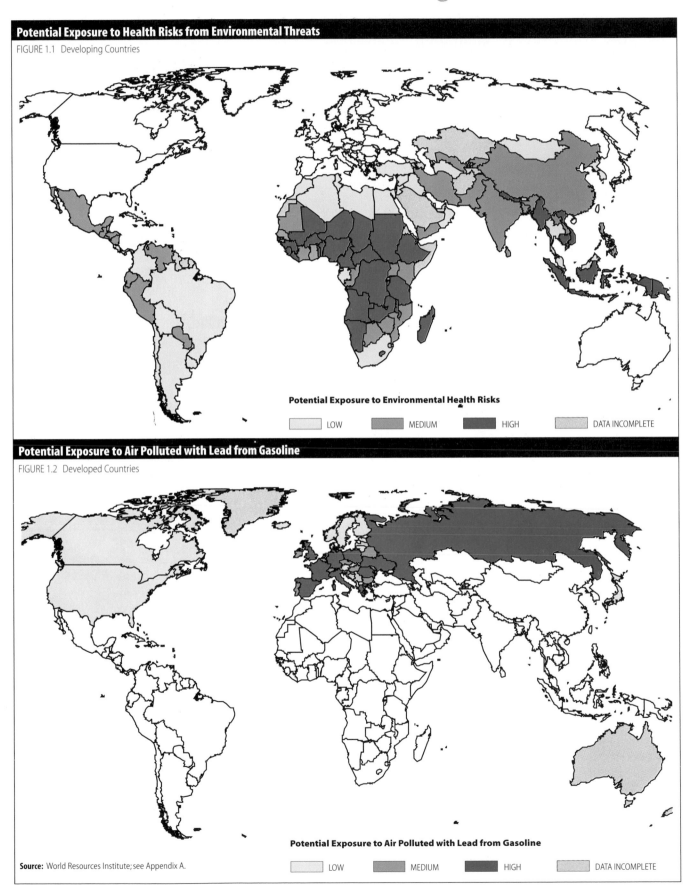

Potential Exposure to Environmental Health Risks

| | LOW | | MEDIUM | | HIGH | | DATA INCOMPLETE |

Potential Exposure to Air Polluted with Lead from Gasoline

FIGURE 1.2 Developed Countries

Potential Exposure to Air Polluted with Lead from Gasoline

| | LOW | | MEDIUM | | HIGH | | DATA INCOMPLETE |

Source: World Resources Institute; see Appendix A.

Changing Environment, Changing Health Threats

This report examines the myriad ways in which environmental conditions, and especially environmental change, affect human health. Here "environment" is defined as the physical, chemical, and biological setting in which people live—in other words, the condition of the air, water, soil, and climate. Not included are the social environment; lifestyle and behavioral choices such as smoking, alcohol consumption, and diet; or the workplace. Although these factors have enormous influences on health, they are beyond the scope of this report.

Environmental hazards to health fall into two broad categories. The first is a lack of access to essential environmental resources—chief among them sufficient and clean water, food, shelter, fuel, and air. The second broad category is exposure to hazards in the environment. These hazards include biological agents—microorganisms such as bacteria and viruses and parasites—that contribute to the huge global burden of infectious diseases. Biological agents are implicated in diseases from diarrhea to acute respiratory infections, to malaria, to ulcers, and to some cancers. Also included are noxious chemical and physical hazards in the environment. Some pollutants, such as pesticides and industrial solvents, are created by human activities. Others, including arsenic or ultraviolet (UV) radiation, occur naturally in the environment, although exposure can be exacerbated by human activities. These pollutants can undermine health in various ways, by contributing to cancer or birth defects or perhaps by damaging the body's immune system, which renders people more susceptible to a variety of other health risks.

In the past several years, scientists have become increasingly aware that environmental changes, locally and regionally, as well as globally, can exacerbate both types of environmental health problems. Development projects such as the building of dams and roads can displace local populations, for instance, altering agricultural practices, undermining nutrition, and increasing the spread of infectious diseases. On a global scale, greenhouse warming threatens to render certain land unsuitable for agriculture or even habitation and may also increase the range of disease-carrying mosquitoes.

This report is concerned not just with today's environmental health threats, which are clearly substantial, but also with the extent to which human activities are altering the environment and what those changes portend for human health. Environmental change is an inevitable consequence of economic development and people's desires to improve their quality of life. In pursuit of a better life, forests and grasslands are converted to farms, homes, and commercial spaces; raw materials are extracted for energy and commerce; and waterways dammed and diverted. Pollutants are dispersed into air, water, and soil. In the process, the face of the planet has been transformed.

Without question, the benefits of economic development have been enormous. Economic growth and social progress of the past several decades have ushered in an era of untold prosperity and health in most regions of the world. Globally, per capita gross domestic product (GDP) has jumped from US$2,257 to US$3,168 in the past 25 years; life expectancy has climbed from 57.9 to 65.6 (15). Yet, economic development has had unintended consequences as well—namely, environmental degradation and increased threats to human health. Unless consideration is given in advance to the consequences of economic growth—especially the rapid growth now underway in many parts of the world—environmental threats to human health will surely intensify, undermining the gains in welfare that development typically brings.

The Drivers of Change

Environmental change and its attendant health impacts are driven by many factors, including economic growth, population growth and movements, urbanization, transportation, and war, to name just a few. Here we focus on three broad trends—the intensification of agriculture, industrialization, and rising energy use—which stand out in terms of their profound impacts on the physical environment and their enormous potential for influencing human health. Given current development patterns, all are essential for economic development and improved welfare. Yet, all lead to pressures on the environment, such as pollutant emissions and resource depletion, that in turn can increase human exposure to threats in the environment.

Intensification of agriculture is essential for producing more food but, when not well managed, creates substantial risks, such as exposing workers and communities to toxic pesticides, contaminating groundwater supplies, and creating pesticide-resistant pests. Land clearing, irrigation, and dams can bring increases in vector-borne diseases such as malaria and schistosomiasis, both of which exact a huge toll in rural areas of the developing world.

Industrialization is the linchpin of economic growth and, like urbanization to which it is closely related, is associated with major gains in health. Yet, along with rising standards of living—at least for a majority of the population—industrialization often means increased exposure to heavy metals, persistent chemicals such as polychlorinated biphenyls (PCBs), and other toxic chemicals. This is especially true for workers and the poor who often live close to factories. Such exposures are likely to be increasingly pronounced in the developing world, where the most rapid industrialization is occurring.

Rising energy use is needed to fuel industrial growth but brings many attendant problems. Local air pollution from in-

*E*nvironmental Change and Human Health

dustrial and vehicle emissions has proved difficult to manage even in developed economies. Fossil fuel use also has the potential to alter the Earth's climate, with a predicted range of health impacts from severe storms, to drought, to flooding, to an increase in insect-borne diseases such as malaria. Energy demand, which is already huge in the developed countries, is rising fastest in the developing world.

Although these trends are discussed separately here, in the real world they rarely occur in isolation. Rising energy use, for instance, is part and parcel of industrialization and agriculture. The effects of industrialization are often difficult to disentangle from those of urbanization. Many of the effects of these trends are well known and predictable (for example, increased air pollution that accompanies rising use of fossil fuels, or exposure to toxic chemicals through improper disposal of industrial wastes). Others, however, are far less certain, though potentially large, such as those associated with global climate change and wide-scale ecological disruption.

Until recently, discussions of environmental threats to health have tended to focus on direct toxicological effects of specific insults or exposures. Now, awareness is growing that changes in the environment can affect health in indirect and often unexpected ways as well, by disrupting local or global ecosystems (16). For instance, soil erosion stemming from poor agricultural practices can result in reduced crop yields; this could have important consequences for nutrition. Farm animal wastes in the eastern United States are suspected of causing toxic algal blooms, leading to massive fish kills and potential harm to humans (17). Even well-intended development projects can have unexpected outcomes, as occurred in Africa's Senegal River Valley, where the construction of two dams set off a cascade of events that ultimately contributed to nutritional problems for the population and a dramatic increase in schistosomiasis. (See Regional Profile on Damming the Senegal River.)

Although agricultural intensification, industrialization, and rising energy use hold considerable potential for harming both the environment and public health, these negative impacts are by no means inevitable. Experience has shown that it is possible to manage economic growth in ways that preserve environmental quality and enhance human health. But this will not come from the random interaction of market forces alone (18). Achieving the benefits of economic development while minimizing its deleterious impacts will require an increased awareness of links between environment and health and a broader approach to strategies to improve public health.

In particular, achieving these benefits will depend on a greater emphasis on prevention, either by managing the environment so that health risks do not occur, or by intervening before these risks lead to illness. Prevention is essential because the health risks associated with environmental degradation and change—such as the impacts of increasing fossil

fuel use or the lack of sanitation in burgeoning slums—are simply too big for the health sector to tackle alone. Typically, health strategies focus on individual cases, attempting to prevent a person from contracting a disease and, when that is not possible, treating the disease. Although such approaches have been enormously successful in improving public health, it is clearly possible to do even more by pursuing strategies that intervene earlier in the pathway toward illness.

Environmental interventions seek to do that by preventing exposure to the pathogens that cause disease or eliminating conditions that enable vectors to breed. For instance, rather than just treating diarrhea with oral rehydration therapy, which saves lives but does not reduce the incidence of the disease and the suffering it causes, an environmentally based approach would seek to increase access to water and sanitation and hygiene education.

In the past few years, several organizations have called for broadening health strategies by factoring in environmental considerations as well (19). In a recent report for instance, WHO made the case for pursuing "upstream" policy actions—in other words, actions removed from the immediate hazards that instead address the underlying pressure or driving force (20). Health improvements from upstream interventions, such as the provision of water and sanitation or a shift away from fossil fuel use, may be slower in coming than improvements from clinical intervention, notes WHO. For this reason, environmental approaches must be combined with clinical strategies to treat immediate health problems. But in the long run, the benefits of prevention are more enduring in terms of improved public health, a cleaner and safer environment, and stronger socioeconomic development.

A key challenge of this approach is that it requires coordination among many sectors—for instance, environment, energy, transportation, and health—that often don't interact. But on the positive side, the benefits will reach far beyond the health sector as well. An increased emphasis on public transportation versus the private car will reduce air pollution and associated respiratory illnesses. But such a shift might not be justified on the basis of health improvements alone. However, when the potential economic savings from reduced urban congestion are factored in, not to mention reduced pollution damage to regional ecosystems, the case becomes more compelling.

Improving both health and the environment will also require increased consideration of equity issues, or how risks are distributed among populations. All too often, as the following chapters document, environmental risks are borne disproportionately by the poor and disenfranchised—not just in developing countries but in affluent nations as well. This issue warrants increased attention because economic disparities are increasing both within and among countries. One consequence of these disparities is that the rich can often

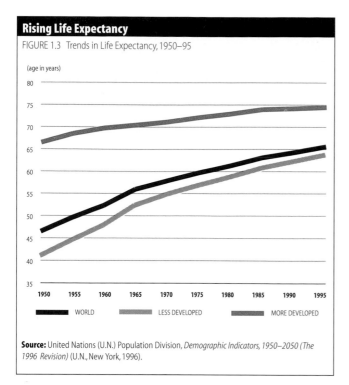

Rising Life Expectancy

FIGURE 1.3 Trends in Life Expectancy, 1950–95

(age in years)

Legend:
WORLD   LESS DEVELOPED   MORE DEVELOPED

Source: United Nations (U.N.) Population Division, *Demographic Indicators, 1950–2050 (The 1996 Revision)* (U.N., New York, 1996).

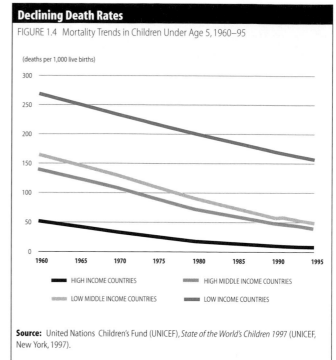

Declining Death Rates

FIGURE 1.4 Mortality Trends in Children Under Age 5, 1960–95

(deaths per 1,000 live births)

Legend:
HIGH INCOME COUNTRIES   HIGH MIDDLE INCOME COUNTRIES
LOW MIDDLE INCOME COUNTRIES   LOW INCOME COUNTRIES

Source: United Nations Children's Fund (UNICEF), *State of the World's Children 1997* (UNICEF, New York, 1997).

protect themselves from environmental threats to health, while the poor usually cannot.

Before turning to an examination of the health implications of the three trends, the remainder of this chapter describes the major patterns of death and disease worldwide and their links with the environment.

Global Health Patterns

Global health conditions improved more in the past half-century than in all of the years before (21). Worldwide, life expectancy has risen to an average of 65 years and death rates have declined, especially among young children (22). (See Figures 1.3 and 1.4.)

In the wealthiest countries, average life expectancy climbed from roughly 67 years in 1950 to 77 years in 1995; in the developing countries, life expectancy jumped from 40 to 64 years. Even in the least developed regions, such as sub-Saharan Africa, average life expectancy has climbed from 36 to 52 years. The only exception to these positive regional trends occurred in the transitional economies of Eastern Europe, where life expectancy for men declined from 1989 to 1993. Major strides have also been made in reducing child mortality. As recently as 1950, 287 children out of every 1,000 born in the developing countries would die before reaching age 5. By 1995, that number had dropped to 90 (23).

Yet, this incredible progress should not mask the fact that health conditions remain dismal in many parts of the world, creating huge disparities between the richest and the poorest

countries, and indeed, between the rich and the poor within the same country or even city. Today, nearly one fifth of all people in the developing countries are not expected to survive until age 40 (24). Sierra Leone has the lowest life expectancy in the world—roughly 38 years—less than half that of Japan, which boasts the highest at nearly 80 years (25). Similarly, without diminishing the huge improvements in child survival, it must be noted that more than 20 percent of children born in the least developed countries will die before reaching age 5; in the richest countries, less than 1 percent will (26).

Just a century ago, health conditions in Europe, North America, and Japan were similar to those of the least developed countries today, as was environmental quality. Conditions in London and other major centers were squalid; sewage-filled rivers, garbage-strewn streets, and overcrowded and dank housing were the norm. Much of the population lacked access to fresh water or adequate sanitation. Epidemics of typhus, cholera, dysentery, tuberculosis, and measles swept these cities. Indeed, in the world's most prosperous cities at the time, the infant mortality rate—the number of children who die before their first birthday—was more than 100 per 1,000 live births, and in some places it exceeded 200 (27). Diarrheal and respiratory diseases and other infections were the major causes of death.

By 1950, life expectancy in the most developed countries had climbed to 67 years, and infant mortality had dropped to 58 per 1,000 live births. This remarkable improvement in public health was related to several factors, but chief among them was a concerted effort by both government and nongovern-

Environmental Change and Human Health

The Sanitary Revolution and Changing Patterns of Disease

FIGURE 1.5a Death Rates for Respiratory Tuberculosis (TB) in England and Wales, 1840–1968

FIGURE 1.5b Death Rates for Measles in Children Under Age 15, England and Wales, 1850–1970

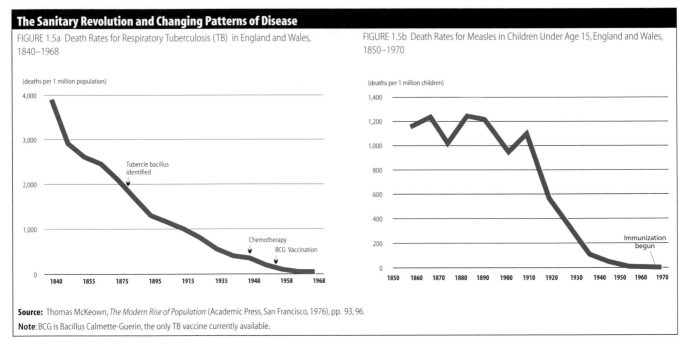

Source: Thomas McKeown, *The Modern Rise of Population* (Academic Press, San Francisco, 1976), pp. 93, 96.

Note: BCG is Bacillus Calmette-Guerin, the only TB vaccine currently available.

mental organizations to improve the environmental conditions of the poor. Appalled by the health conditions of the poor, and increasingly aware that infectious diseases could infect the rich as well, reformers at the end of the 19th Century instituted a series of improvements, known as the Sanitary Revolution (28). Perhaps the most important of these changes was the provision of water and sewage systems for removing human wastes. These fundamental improvements did much to quell the epidemic of infectious disease and contribute to overall improvements in human health and well-being.

Other factors were also at work to improve health over the past century, including rising prosperity, improved nutrition, safer workplace conditions, better housing, and advances in health care—all important determinants of health. Indeed, some 100 years later, the exact contribution of each is still the subject of considerable debate (29). Environmental interventions clearly played a major role, however, as the most dramatic drops in infectious disease occurred before the widespread availability of vaccines and antibiotics (30)(31)(32). (See Figures 1.5a and 1.5b.)

Today, it is widely assumed that with increasing economic growth, the developing countries will follow the same path as Europe and North America and experience what has become known as the "epidemiologic transition." This term describes the changing patterns of disease that accompanied overall improvements in health in the late 19th and early 20th Century. As mortality rates declined and life expectancy rose, these populations experienced a shift in the pattern of disease, from one dominated by infectious diseases to one dominated by chronic disorders such as heart disease and cancer. The shift

to chronic diseases can be partly explained by the fact that many more people were living to the age when chronic diseases strike. Even so, this transition represented not just a simple substitution of one set of problems for another but an overall improvement in health.

Elements of this epidemiologic transition are in fact occurring now, to varying degrees, throughout much of the developing world. In some of the middle-income countries of Latin America and Asia, for instance, chronic diseases now take as great or an even greater toll than infectious diseases (33). But this transition is by no means complete. Many countries, especially the poorest, still have a huge burden of infectious diseases along with a growing problem of chronic diseases. These populations have not traded one set of problems for another; instead, they are suffering from both, in what is known as the "double burden" of disease (34). Nor is the transition inevitable. As the history of the Sanitary Revolution illustrates, concerted policies and investments are necessary to improve both environmental quality and public health.

Where countries are in this epidemiologic transition can be discerned in today's patterns of death and disease, discussed next.

CURRENT PATTERNS OF DEATH AND DISEASE

About 52 million people of all ages died in 1996—the last year for which the WHO has estimates (35). Beyond these gross numbers, however, it is difficult to discern the exact causes of death. Data are abundant and reliable on causes of mortality in the developed countries but are sorely lacking in the developing world. Of those 52 million deaths, for instance, WHO had reliable records of cause of death for approximately 13

Relative Toll of Infectious and Chronic Diseases

FIGURE 1.6   Main Causes of Mortality, 1990

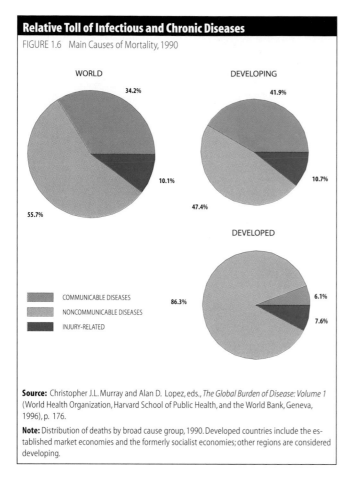

WORLD

34.2%
10.1%
55.7%

DEVELOPING

41.9%
10.7%
47.4%

DEVELOPED

86.3%
6.1%
7.6%

COMMUNICABLE DISEASES
NONCOMMUNICABLE DISEASES
INJURY-RELATED

Source: Christopher J.L. Murray and Alan D. Lopez, eds., *The Global Burden of Disease: Volume 1* (World Health Organization, Harvard School of Public Health, and the World Bank, Geneva, 1996), p. 176.

Note: Distribution of deaths by broad cause group, 1990. Developed countries include the established market economies and the formerly socialist economies; other regions are considered developing.

Top Ten Causes of Death by Region

TABLE 1.1   Leading Causes of Death, 1990

WORLD	DEATHS (000)	PERCENTAGE OF TOTAL DEATHS
All causes	**50,467**	–
Ischemic heart disease	6,260	12.4
Cerebrovascular disease	4,381	8.7
Lower respiratory infections	4,299	8.5
Diarrheal diseases	2,946	5.8
Conditions arising during the perinatal period	2,443	4.8
Chronic obstructive pulmonary disease	2,211	4.4
Tuberculosis	1,960	3.9
Measles	1,058	2.1
Road traffic accidents	999	2.0
Trachea, bronchus, and lung cancers	945	1.9
DEVELOPED REGIONS		
All causes	**10,912**	–
Ischemic heart disease	2,695	24.7
Cerebrovascular disease	1,427	13.1
Trachea, bronchus, and lung cancers	523	4.8
Lower respiratory infections	385	3.5
Chronic obstructive pulmonary disease	324	3.0
Colon and rectum cancers	277	2.5
Stomach cancer	241	2.2
Road traffic accidents	222	2.0
Self-inflicted injuries	193	1.8
Diabetes mellitus	176	1.6
DEVELOPING REGIONS		
All causes	**39,554**	–
Lower respiratory infections	3,915	9.9
Ischemic heart disease	3,565	9.0
Cerebrovascular disease	2,954	7.5
Diarrheal diseases	2,940	7.4
Conditions arising during the perinatal period	2,361	6.0
Tuberculosis	1,922	4.9
Chronic obstructive pulmonary disease	1,887	4.8
Measles	1,058	2.7
Malaria	856	2.2
Road traffic accidents	777	2.0

Source: Christopher J.L. Murray and Alan D. Lopez, eds., *The Global Burden of Disease: Volume 1* (World Health Organization, Harvard School of Public Health, and the World Bank, Geneva, 1996), pp. 179–180.

million—most of those from the developed countries (36). That means that the exact cause of death is known in only about one case out of four; the rest are estimated according to a series of well-established, if imperfect, procedures. Even less is known about sickness, or morbidity, because most illnesses are not reported.

Different methods used to tally the toll of sickness and death produce different pictures, sparking intense debate over whose numbers are "right" and generally underscoring the sorry state of global health data (37)(38).(See Box 1.3.) With these caveats in mind, the global estimates reported here are sufficient to paint a broad picture of the relative importance of various diseases, but exact numbers should be viewed with caution. Data for this section are drawn from estimates in a 1996 study, the *Global Burden of Disease* (GBD) (39). Performed by researchers at Harvard University and WHO, this

study provides comprehensive and comparable estimates for death and disease in 1990 in different regions of the world. In later sections that discuss individual diseases, this report relies on the most recent WHO statistics and attempts to note when they vary significantly from the GBD study.

What do these estimates reveal about patterns of death in 1990? (See Figure 1.6.) They show clearly that the epidemic of chronic, or noncommunicable, diseases is no longer limited

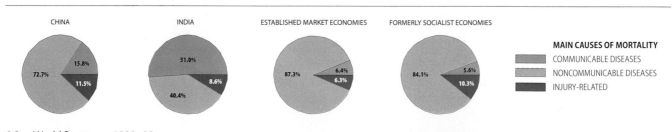

CHINA
15.8%
72.7%
11.5%

INDIA
51.0%
40.4%
8.6%

ESTABLISHED MARKET ECONOMIES
87.3%
6.4%
6.3%

FORMERLY SOCIALIST ECONOMIES
84.1%
5.6%
10.3%

MAIN CAUSES OF MORTALITY
COMMUNICABLE DISEASES
NONCOMMUNICABLE DISEASES
INJURY-RELATED

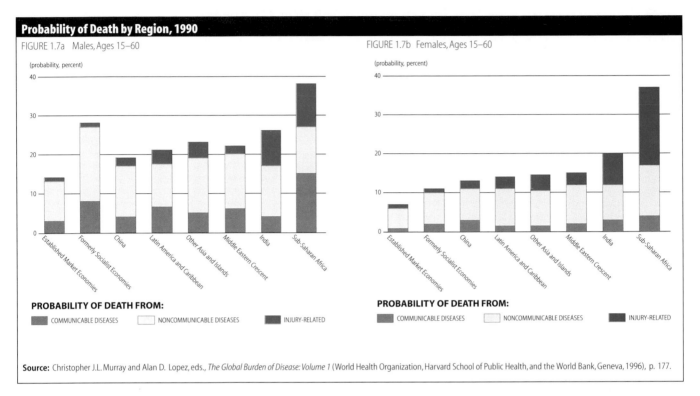

Probability of Death by Region, 1990

FIGURE 1.7a   Males, Ages 15–60

(probability, percent)

FIGURE 1.7b   Females, Ages 15–60

(probability, percent)

PROBABILITY OF DEATH FROM:

COMMUNICABLE DISEASES   NONCOMMUNICABLE DISEASES   INJURY-RELATED

PROBABILITY OF DEATH FROM:

COMMUNICABLE DISEASES   NONCOMMUNICABLE DISEASES   INJURY-RELATED

Source: Christopher J.L. Murray and Alan D. Lopez, eds., *The Global Burden of Disease: Volume 1* (World Health Organization, Harvard School of Public Health, and the World Bank, Geneva, 1996), p. 177.

to the developed world. Indeed, chronic diseases, which include cancers, heart disease, and stroke, accounted for 56 percent of all deaths globally in 1990. Infectious (communicable) diseases have by no means disappeared, however; in fact, they account for a considerable 34 percent of all deaths in 1990 (40). (The GBD study includes in the communicable disease category deaths from maternal, perinatal, and nutritional conditions.) Injuries accounted for roughly 10 percent of all deaths in the GBD study.

When these categories are viewed by comparing developed and developing countries, a startlingly different picture emerges, however. (Note: In keeping with the GBD study, "developed" countries include the established market economies and the former socialist economies; other regions are considered "developing.") Chronic diseases are nearly twice as important in the developed countries, where they account for about 86 percent of all deaths. By contrast, in the poorer countries, they account for approximately 47 percent of all deaths. The biggest contrast, however, can be seen in the patterns for communicable diseases, which account for just over 6 percent of all deaths in the developed countries and nearly 42 percent in the developing world. Injuries account for a slightly smaller

share in the developed world—7.6 percent—as opposed to 10.7 percent in the developing countries (41). Table 1.1 shows the 10 leading causes of death globally and by developed and developing regions.

Even within the developing world, however, the picture is far from homogeneous. A country's economic development, investment in health care, and social policies can make an enormous difference. In the world's poorest region, sub-Saharan Africa, deaths from communicable diseases take the largest toll, at 64 percent. But marked differences exist between India and China as well, which have roughly comparable wealth. In India, communicable diseases account for nearly 51 percent of all deaths; in China, just 16 percent (42).

Nor is the pattern in the developed world homogenous. When the probability of dying is examined by gender, the precarious position of adult men in the former socialist economies becomes strikingly evident. (See Figures 1.7a and 1.7b.) Indeed, men between the ages of 15 and 60 in this region face a 28.4 percent risk of dying before age 60, second only to men in sub-Saharan Africa, where the odds are 39.1 percent (43). This remarkable increase in deaths in the former socialist economies is due to much higher risks from both chronic diseases

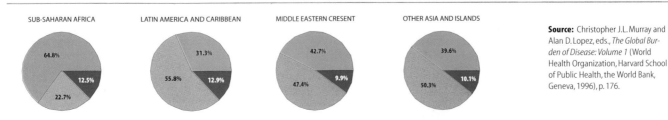

SUB-SAHARAN AFRICA

64.8%

12.5%

22.7%

LATIN AMERICA AND CARIBBEAN

31.3%

55.8%   12.9%

MIDDLE EASTERN CRESENT

42.7%

47.4%   9.9%

OTHER ASIA AND ISLANDS

39.6%

50.3%   10.1%

Source: Christopher J.L. Murray and Alan D. Lopez, eds., *The Global Burden of Disease: Volume 1* (World Health Organization, Harvard School of Public Health, the World Bank, Geneva, 1996), p. 176.

Box 1.3 Counting Deaths Differently

Different methods of estimating mortality yield different results, making it difficult to know which methods are preferable. Because actual mortality data are hard to come by for developing countries, the World Health Organization (WHO) has historically estimated these global numbers using a range of techniques, including modeling and extrapolation from local studies. Using these well-accepted techniques, WHO estimates that for 1993, infectious diseases accounted for 40 percent of the 51 million deaths, while noncommunicable diseases such as heart disease and cancer accounted for 36 percent, and injuries another 8 percent. WHO attributed fully 16 percent of all deaths in 1993 to unknown causes (1).

Using a different approach, other scientists within WHO and Harvard University have recently generated quite different estimates, published in a 1996 book *The Global Burden of Disease* (2). In this study, the researchers strived to avoid double-counting deaths. (In other words, they ensured that the sum of all childhood deaths of specific diseases did not exceed the number of childhood deaths.) The Global Burden of Disease (GBD) team also developed a technique to assign deaths from unknown causes to a specific cause, distributing those that occurred among children younger than age 5 to infectious diseases, and those that occurred to children older than age 5 to chronic diseases. The result? Noncommunicable diseases, rather than infectious diseases, top the list as the world's largest killer, accounting for 56 percent of all deaths. The infectious disease toll is 34 percent, and injuries account for 10 percent. In all, this study provides a very different snapshot of the world, showing developing countries to be much farther along in the demographic transition than previously expected. The table below shows global estimates for specific diseases from these two different studies, one for 1993 and the other for 1990. (Because disease trends vary only slightly from year to year, the fact that these two studies took place in different years is not believed to have a bearing on results.)

Each estimate has its own, often vociferous, advocates and detractors. Alan Lopez of WHO, one of the GBD study coauthors, along with Christopher Murray of Harvard, concedes that "there is large room for error in global mortality estimates"—both theirs and WHO's. "We might well be off by a factor of 2, but I doubt that we are off by a factor of 10" (3). These differences, and the debate over them, underscore the tentative nature of all global mortality estimates, which should be seen as approximate ranges, not absolutes. It also reinforces the need for better data collection.

The controversy over mortality estimates pales in comparison to that engendered by a new

indicator the same team developed to measure both death and disability attributable to a particular disease—the Disability-Adjusted Life Year, or DALY. This indicator, originally published in the 1993 *World Development Report* and updated in the 1996 study, combines both premature mortality and years lived with disability, adjusted for the severity of the disability, to come up with an index of the total burden of a particular disease, such as heart disease or malaria. Malaria, for instance, is responsible for 31,706,000 DALYs per year (4). These estimates, which Lopez, Murray, and their colleagues developed for hundreds of diseases, can then be tallied to provide the global burden of disease or the burden borne by a particular region.

Since it was first published, the DALY indicator has been widely heralded as a bold new approach that provides the most comprehensive estimates to date of the global burden of disease. But it has also been dismissed as incomplete and misleading. Critics, which include WHO's own Committee on Health Research, claim that the indicator obscures more than it conceals because it aggregates data across a country, without reflecting the regional differences within a country that may be quite pronounced—a problem of all such summary indicators (5). Critics also question some of the assumptions used in constructing the indicator—for example, about the value of a life at different ages or the severity of a particular disability. Although the committee commended the effort to examine both sickness and death in assessing the total burden of disease, it has "serious reservations" about how the DALY approach should be applied to health policy decisionmak-

ing (6). At the same time, the advisory committee has created a new subcommittee to explore additional indicators of global health.

Harvard's Murray and WHO's Lopez concede that the indicator is a work in progress. "We have not necessarily got it right," they readily admit, while positing that it is nonetheless useful even at this stage. Indeed, some 30 countries are now using this new method to assess the burden of disease within their own countries, says Lopez (7). Meanwhile, anyone curious about the underlying assumptions and calculations used to create the DALY can find them in the authors' updated 10-volume study, the first two volumes of which were published in 1996.

References and Notes

1. World Health Organization (WHO), *The World Health Report 1995: Bridging the Gaps* (WHO, Geneva, 1995), p. 20.
2. Christopher J. L. Murray and Alan D. Lopez, eds., *The Global Burden of Disease: Volume 1* (World Health Organization, Harvard School of Public Health, the World Bank, Geneva, 1996).
3. Alan D. Lopez, Scientist, Programme on Substance Abuse at the World Health Organization, Geneva, 1997 (personal communication).
4. *Op. cit.* 2, p. 573.
5. B.G. Mansourian, "ACHR News," *Bulletin of the World Health Organization,* Vol. 74, No. 3 (1996), p. 333.
6. World Health Organization (WHO), *The World Health Report 1997: Conquering Suffering, Enriching Humanity* (WHO, Geneva, 1997), p. 23.
7. *Op. cit.* 3.

Estimated Global Number of Deaths, 1990–93

DISEASE	1990 DEATHS ACCORDING TO GLOBAL BURDEN OF DISEASE		1993 DEATHS ACCORDING TO 1995 WORLD HEALTH REPORT	
	(000)	PERCENT	(000)	PERCENT
Cardiovascular Diseases	14,327	28.0	9,676	19.0
Cancer	6,024	12.0	6,013	12.0
Acute Respiratory Infections	4,380	8.7	4,110	8.1
Unintentional Injuries	3,233	6.4	2,915	5.7
Diarrheal Diseases	2,946	5.8	3,010	5.9
Chronic Respiratory Diseases	2,935	5.8	2,888	5.7
Perinatal Conditions	2,443	4.8	3,180	6.2
Vaccine-Preventable Infections	1,985	3.9	1,677	3.3
Tuberculosis	1,960	3.9	2,709	5.3
Intentional Injuries	1,851	3.7	1,082	2.1
Malaria	856	1.7	2,000	3.9
Mental Health Conditions	700	1.4	–	–
Other Identified Diseases	6,827	13.5	3,616	7.1
Unknown Causes	–	–	8,214	16.0
Total	**50,467**	**100.0**	**51,000**	**100.0**

Source: World Health Organization (WHO), *Health and Environment in Sustainable Development: Five Years After the Earth Summit* (WHO, Geneva, 1997), p. 134.

Environmental Change and Human Health

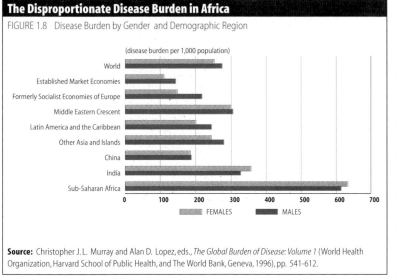

The Disproportionate Disease Burden in Africa

FIGURE 1.8 Disease Burden by Gender and Demographic Region

(disease burden per 1,000 population)

World
Established Market Economies
Formerly Socialist Economies of Europe
Middle Eastern Crescent
Latin America and the Caribbean
Other Asia and Islands
China
India
Sub-Saharan Africa

0   100   200   300   400   500   600   700

■ FEMALES   ■ MALES

Source: Christopher J. L. Murray and Alan D. Lopez, eds., *The Global Burden of Disease: Volume 1* (World Health Organization, Harvard School of Public Health, and The World Bank, Geneva, 1996), pp. 541-612.

and injuries, though the underlying causes remain the subject of considerable speculation. (See Guest Commentary by Clyde Hertzman.)

A New Metric: Factoring in Sickness and Disability

But what about sickness? For all their relative benefits, mortality figures do not capture the huge toll of sickness and disability caused by diseases that stop this side of death, keeping workers off the job and children out of school and generally slowing both economic and social development. Yet statistics on disease incidence, or morbidity, are even harder to come by than are mortality numbers. In addition, the few figures that do exist tend to be biased because wealthier people seek medical care much more often than the poor.

Over the years various investigators have attempted to overcome these limitations by developing new metrics that factor in disability or quality of life along with mortality. One of the most recent—and still controversial—measures is the Disability-Adjusted Life Year, or DALY. DALYs combine losses from premature death (defined as the difference between the actual age of death and life expectancy at that age in a low-mortality population), and loss of healthy life resulting from disability. In simple terms, a DALY strives to tally the complete burden that a particular disease exacts. Key elements to consider include the age at which disease or disability occurs, how long its effects linger, and its impact on quality of life. Losing one's sight at age 7, for instance, is a greater loss than losing one's sight at 67. Similarly, a bout of acute illness that is over quickly counts less in the DALY calculation than one that leaves lingering weakness, such as persistent worm infections.

This new indicator can be used in different ways to compute the total burden of a particular disease, such as malaria

(which accounts for some 65,578,000 DALYs per year), or to tally up the total global burden of disease (in 1990 the world's population lost 2,480,237,000 DALYs), or to compare the relative burden of disease among different regions of the world (44).

Looked at from this perspective—which considers not just premature death but disability as well—the huge toll of ill health in developing countries stands out even more starkly. Nearly nine tenths of the global burden of disease occurs in developing regions where only 1 in 10 health care dollars are spent (45). As Figure 1.8 shows, sub-Saharan Africa suffers twice the burden of ill health as the global average and nearly five times more than the richest countries.

Using this new metric, communicable diseases are the single most important cause of ill health globally, accounting for 44 percent of the total. (Table 1.2 compares the 10 leading causes of death with the 10 leading causes of DALYS.) This increase in the relative importance of infectious diseases reflects in large part the early age at which they strike. Of the top 10 causes of DALYs globally, communicable diseases account for 7, with lower respiratory infections and diarrheal diseases heading the list (46). DALYs also underscore the disproportionate burden of ill health borne by the world's children. Children under age 15 account for almost one half of all lost DALYs worldwide. As the following discussion makes clear, the diseases that most affect children tend to be heavily influenced by environmental factors.

Deaths versus DALYs

TABLE 1.2 Comparing Causes of Death Worldwide with DALYs

	TOP 10 CAUSES OF DISABILITY-ADJUSTED LIFE YEARS, 1990	TOP 10 CAUSES OF DEATH, 1990
1.	Lower respiratory infections	Ischemic heart disease
2.	Diarrheal diseases	Cerebrovascular disease
3.	Conditions arising during the perinatal period	Lower respiratory infections
4.	Unipolar major depression	Diarrheal diseases
5.	Ischemic heart disease	Conditions arising during the perinatal period
6.	Cerebrovascular disease	Chronic obstructive pulmonary disease
7.	Tuberculosis	Tuberculosis
8.	Measles	Measles
9.	Road traffic accidents	Road traffic accidents
10.	Congenital anomalies	Trachea, bronchus, and lung cancers

Source: Christopher J.L. Murray and Alan D. Lopez, eds., *The Global Burden of Disease: Volume 1* (World Health Organization, Harvard School of Public Health, and the World Bank, Geneva, 1996), p. 179 and 262.

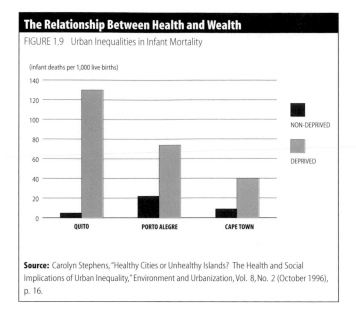

The Relationship Between Health and Wealth

FIGURE 1.9 Urban Inequalities in Infant Mortality

(infant deaths per 1,000 live births)

NON-DEPRIVED

DEPRIVED

QUITO   PORTO ALEGRE   CAPE TOWN

Source: Carolyn Stephens, "Healthy Cities or Unhealthy Islands? The Health and Social Implications of Urban Inequality," Environment and Urbanization, Vol. 8, No. 2 (October 1996), p. 16.

Poverty, Health, and the Environment

What accounts for the strikingly different health profiles in various regions of the world? Access to adequate health care, for both prevention and treatment, is vital. Individual behavior and lifestyle choices also matter; they go far in explaining the rising incidence of chronic diseases and injuries. Sedentary lifestyles, high-fat diets, and consumption of alcohol and tobacco—and particularly these factors in combination—all contribute substantially to the increasing incidence of cancer, heart disease, and stroke.

In addition, individual susceptibility determines how one reacts to various health threats. Genetics, for instance, renders some people more susceptible to the effects of certain cancer-causing agents than others. Beyond an individual's particular characteristics or behaviors, one's age also affects health. Both the very young and the very old tend to be more vulnerable to a host of diseases—getting sick more often and dying more often when they are sick.

Disease and death are thus abetted by many factors. Yet, of all factors that combine to degrade health, poverty stands out for its overwhelming role. Indeed, WHO has called poverty the world's biggest killer (47). Statistically, poverty affects health in its own right: just being poor increases one's risk of ill health. Poverty also contributes to disease and death through its second-order effects; poor people, for instance, are more likely to live in an unhealthy environment. The interactions of disease agents, individual susceptibility, behavior (which often reflects education), and local environmental conditions all bear heavily on health outcomes. Efforts to reduce extreme poverty and increase disposable income levels around the world continue. But this objective will not be achieved quickly or easily. In the interim, understanding how

poverty affects both the environment and health can enable policymakers to identify new strategies for action.

HEALTH AND WEALTH

As the disproportionate burden of ill health in the poorest countries shows, a clear correlation exists between health and wealth. By and large, the wealthier a country becomes, or the higher its average per capita income, the healthier its population becomes, by several measures. This connection can be tracked historically by reviewing the health gains in 19th Century Europe, and can also be seen in the current differences in health status among countries at different stages of development.

This relationship between health and wealth holds true for individuals as well as countries. Regardless of the overall level of a country's wealth, the rich are, as a whole, in better health than the poor (48). Figure 1.9 shows child mortality for rich and poor neighborhoods in selected metropolitan areas in the late 1980s. Life expectancy, a well-established indicator of national health, rises with per capita GDP and continues to climb until per capita GDP reaches about US$5,000 per year—enough, perhaps, to provide a minimal standard of living (49). Child mortality rates also decline with rising income.

Why is the link between health and wealth so strong? At the most fundamental level, many of the world's poorest poor, the 1.3 billion who live on less than US$1 a day (50), are unable to secure even the bare necessities for a healthy life—adequate food, water, clothing, shelter, and health care. One of the major causes of ill health globally is malnutrition, which is an issue of poverty and rarely an indicator of actual food shortages. Most recent estimates indicate that globally there are 158 million children under age 5 who are malnourished (51). By one estimate, malnutrition accounted for roughly 12 percent of all deaths in 1990 (52). But it plays a much more insidious role as well, rendering people more susceptible to both infectious and chronic diseases. When calculated for this effect, malnutrition is believed to contribute to up to one half of deaths among children in developing countries (53). (See Box 1.4.)

So, rising incomes may mean more and better food, housing, and clothing—all relatively well-understood pathways to better health. Growing prosperity typically means improved access to health care. The wealthier also tend to be better educated and thus more informed about the disease process and prevention. Study after study has revealed that households with more education enjoy better health (54). In addition, wealthier groups usually have sufficient income to act upon this knowledge. Actions may include improving hygiene, immunizing children against common diseases, or seeking oral rehydration therapy to treat diarrhea. Even independent of wealth, improvements in education, particularly the mother's education, are strongly linked with improvements in the family's health. Data from 25 developing countries have shown

Environmental Change and Human Health

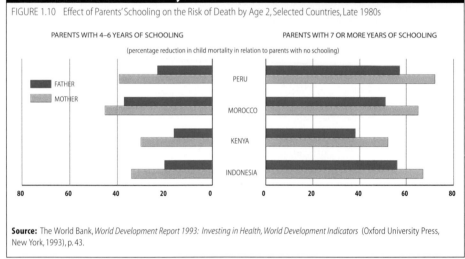

Education and the Link with Family Health

FIGURE 1.10   Effect of Parents' Schooling on the Risk of Death by Age 2, Selected Countries, Late 1980s

PARENTS WITH 4–6 YEARS OF SCHOOLING   PARENTS WITH 7 OR MORE YEARS OF SCHOOLING

(percentage reduction in child mortality in relation to parents with no schooling)

FATHER
MOTHER

PERU
MOROCCO
KENYA
INDONESIA

80   60   40   20   0   0   20   40   60   80

Source: The World Bank, *World Development Report 1993: Investing in Health, World Development Indicators* (Oxford University Press, New York, 1993), p. 43.

tween rich and poor, both among and within nations, are increasing (60).

In all countries, income and equity, though important, are not the only factors. A country's economic development approach, investment in health care, and social policies can make an enormous difference in the health of its population. Figure 1.11 shows the link between a nation's average income (shown here in purchasing power parity) and life expectancy. Although income generally corresponds to life expectancy, what is most interesting are the exceptions: those countries, such as Costa Rica, Cuba, China, and others that have a much longer life expectancy than

that, all else being equal, even 1 to 3 years of maternal education can reduce child mortality by up to 15 percent (55). Improvements increase with more schooling. (See Figure 1.10.) Apparently, education enables primary caregivers, who are almost always women, to avoid health threats and deal with illness more easily, even when they lack extra income.

In wealthy countries, the links between health and wealth are more complex. Poverty in this context does not entail severe material deprivation, as it does in the least developed countries. What seems to be important in wealthy countries instead is relative poverty—how one fares in relation to the rest of society—rather than absolute poverty (56). Indeed, evidence from numerous studies, such as data on government workers in England, suggests that even at higher income levels, it is not wealth *per se* but how that wealth is distributed among groups within the country—that is, a country's income equality—that is the best predictor of health status. "The countries with the longest life expectancy are not the wealthiest but those with the smallest spread of incomes, and the smallest proportion of the population in relative poverty," explains noted researcher Richard Wilkinson of the University of Sussex, England (57). This theory explains some of the puzzling discrepancies among life expectancy in the more developed nations. The United States, for instance, does considerably worse at ensuring the health of all its citizens than income alone would predict. In 1970, Japan and the United States had roughly similar income distributions and life expectancy. Since then, however, Japan has leapfrogged ahead and now boasts the longest life expectancy in the world (nearly 80 years) along with the most egalitarian income distribution. By contrast, income inequality has actually increased in the United States, which now ranks 21st out of 157 countries in life expectancy (58)(59). This finding has important implications for future health trends because gaps be-

would be predicted on the basis of income alone. The success of these and other countries in reducing child mortality and increasing life expectancy clearly shows that a high level of economic activity is not essential for successful programs to improve health. It also demonstrates the enormous potential for targeted policy interventions. Examples of wise policy steps that have raised health levels for the poor include agrarian reform programs to generate employment and income, attention to primary health care systems carefully aligned with traditional health care practices, a focus on upgrading sewer

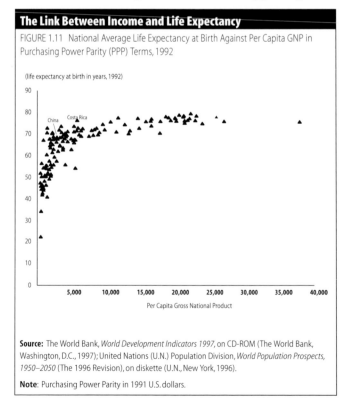

The Link Between Income and Life Expectancy

FIGURE 1.11   National Average Life Expectancy at Birth Against Per Capita GNP in Purchasing Power Parity (PPP) Terms, 1992

(life expectancy at birth in years, 1992)

China   Costa Rica

5,000   10,000   15,000   20,000   25,000   30,000   35,000   40,000

Per Capita Gross National Product

Source: The World Bank, *World Development Indicators 1997*, on CD-ROM (The World Bank, Washington, D.C., 1997); United Nations (U.N.) Population Division, *World Population Prospects, 1950–2050* (The 1996 Revision), on diskette (U.N., New York, 1996).

Note: Purchasing Power Parity in 1991 U.S. dollars.

Box 1.4 Malnutrition

Poverty—not insufficient global food production—is the root cause of malnutrition. Poor families lack the economic, environmental, or social resources to purchase or produce enough food. In rural areas, land scarcity and degradation, water salinity due to overirrigation, soil erosion, droughts, and flooding can all undermine a family's ability to grow enough food. In urban areas, low wages, lack of work and underemployment, and rapid changes in food prices often place food supplies out of the reach of poor households. War and civil strife almost always cause upheaval in the food system and often result in widespread famine, as with the civil wars in Rwanda and Somalia.

Although overall trends are positive, with the proportion of people with malnutrition declining, many remain at risk, and some regions are hit especially hard. (See Figure 1.) Between 1990 and 1992, approximately 841 million people—or 1 out of every 5 people in the developing world—did not have access to enough food for healthy living (1).

The health consequences of inadequate nutrition are enormous. According to one estimate, malnutrition contributed to roughly 12 percent of all deaths in 1990 (2). Although much of this toll stems from underconsumption of protein and energy, deficiencies in key micronutrients such as iodine, vitamin A, and iron also undermine health (3).

When poverty limits an adequate and varied diet, deficiencies of iron, iodine, and vitamin A often occur simultaneously with protein-energy malnutrition. Geography and soil characteristics also influence the amount of these nutrients commonly found in food. Mountainous areas are often deficient in io-

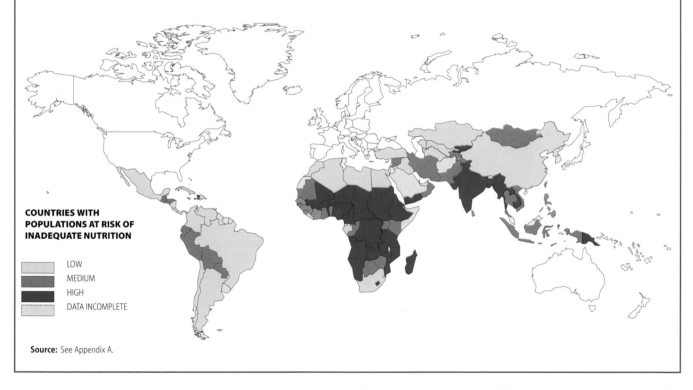

COUNTRIES WITH POPULATIONS AT RISK OF INADEQUATE NUTRITION

- LOW
- MEDIUM
- HIGH
- DATA INCOMPLETE

Source: See Appendix A.

and water systems, and concerted efforts to address infectious diseases while improving nutrition. Countries or states that have achieved these unusual health results with poor populations, which include Kerala State in India and Sri Lanka, also have long-standing commitments to education and equity (61)(62).

Costa Rica, for instance, added 15 to 20 years to life expectancy in little more than two decades without significant gains in wealth. It did so through a number of policy actions, including a targeted program to control infectious diseases through improved sanitation, immunization, and the extension of primary health care to a wider population (63). These changes were accompanied by a national commitment to education for all, as well as Costa Rica's first national health plan and law of universal social security, both passed in 1971 (64).

POVERTY AND ENVIRONMENTAL RISKS

Poverty also influences health because it largely determines an individual's environmental risks, as well as access to resources to deal with those risks (65).

Throughout the developing world, the greatest environmental health threats tend to be those closest to home (66). Many in these countries live in situations that imperil their health through steady exposure to biological pathogens in the immediate environment. More than 1 billion people in devel-

*E*nvironmental Change and Human Health

Box 1.4 continued

dine; the most severely deficient regions are the Himalayas, Andes, European alps, and mountains of China (4). Areas with arid, infertile land or heavy rainfall and humidity may be deficient in vitamin A (5). Africa, the Andean region of South America, and many parts of Asia are at risk from not only protein energy malnutrition, but also from all three main micronutrient deficiencies because of both poverty and environmental factors.

Iron deficiency is the most common micronutrient disorder. In developing countries, 40 percent of nonpregnant women and 50 percent of pregnant women are anemic, and 3.6 billion people suffer from iron deficiencies (6). The problem is most severe in India, where 88 percent of pregnant women are anemic. Anemia increases the risk of death from hemorrhage in childbirth. Iron deficiencies can also reduce physical productivity and affect a child's capacity to learn (7).

Globally, some 42 million children under age 6 have mild to moderate vitamin A deficiency. In its severe form, vitamin A deficiency can cause blindness; indeed, it is the single most important cause of childhood blindness in developing countries. About 250,000 to 300,000 children go blind annually, and 50 to 80 percent of those die within 1 year (8). Up to 3 million more children suffer lesser but still serious effects, such as loss of night vision. An estimated 254 million children of preschool age are at risk of vitamin A deficiency (9).

Iodine deficiency is the world's leading single cause of preventable brain damage and mental retardation. In 1990, some 26 million people suffered from brain damage associated with iodine deficiency (10). An estimated 1.5 billion people are at risk of iodine deficiency disorders (IDD), and 655 million people are affected by goiter, which is the enlargement of the thyroid gland, an

indicator of IDD (11). Where this deficiency is endemic, the entire population may be affected, with different symptoms appearing in different age groups. In pregnant women, for instance, iodine deficiency may cause irreversible brain damage in the developing fetus (12).

The combination of malnutrition and infectious disease can be particularly pernicious. Protein-energy malnutrition can impair the immune system, leaving malnourished children less able to battle common diseases such as measles, diarrhea, respiratory infections, tuberculosis, pertussis, and malaria. Vitamin A deficiencies are often worsened by infectious disease; and reciprocally, poor vitamin A status is likely to prolong or exacerbate the course of an illness such as measles (13). Similarly, malaria parasites, which require iron in order to multiply in blood, can cause or exacerbate anemia (14). Malnutrition can also heighten the adverse impacts of toxic substances. Deficiencies of protein and some minerals, for example, can significantly influence the absorption of lead and cadmium into the body (15)(16).

The consequences of food and nutrition shortfalls are enormous. Africa and Southeast Asia confront problems of both malnutrition and such diseases as diarrhea, malaria, and measles—a combination that is likely to increase the toll that either problem would take alone. In rapidly industrializing cities with high levels of malnutrition as well as disease and growing industrial pollution, residents may confront a triple burden of malnutrition, infection, and toxic pollution.

References and Notes

1. Food and Agriculture Organization of the United Nations (FAO), *The Sixth World Food Survey* (FAO, Rome, 1996), pp. v–vi.
2. Christopher J.L. Murray and Alan D. Lopez, eds. *The Global Burden of Disease: Volume 1* (World Health Organization, Harvard School of Public Health, and The World Bank, Geneva, 1996), p. 311.
3. The World Bank, *World Development Report 1993: Investing in Health* (The World Bank, Washington, D.C., 1993), p. 75.
4. World Health Organization (WHO), United Nations Children's Fund (UNICEF), and the International Council for the Control of Iodine Deficiency Disorders, "Global Prevalence of Iodine Deficiency Disorders," Micronutrient Deficiency Information System Working Paper No. 1 (WHO, Geneva, 1993), p. 7.
5. World Health Organization (WHO) and the United Nations Children's Fund (UNICEF), "Global Prevalence of Vitamin A Deficiency," Micronutrient Deficiency Information System Working Paper No. 2 (WHO, Geneva, 1995), p. 5.
6. World Health Organization (WHO), *The World Health Report 1997: Conquering Suffering, Enriching Humanity* (WHO, Geneva, 1997), p. 51.
7. *Op. cit.* 3.
8. Henry M. Levin *et al.*, "Micronutrient Deficiency Disorders," in *Disease Control Priorities in Developing Countries*, Dean T. Jamison *et al.*, eds. (Oxford University Press, New York, 1993), p. 424.
9. *Op. cit.* 5, pp. ix, 16.
10. *Op. cit.* 4, pp. 5, 8.
11. *Op. cit.* 4, p. 5.
12. *Op. cit.* 4, p. 5.
13. Andrew Tomkins and Fiona Watson, *Malnutrition and Infection: A Review* (United Nations Administrative Committee on Coordination/Subcommittee on Nutrition, WHO, Geneva, 1989), pp. 5–6.
14. *Ibid.*, p. 7.
15. Howard Hu, Sudha Kotha, and Troyen Brennan, "The Role of Nutrition in Mitigating Environmental Insults: Policy and Ethical Issues," *Environmental Health Perspectives*, Vol. 103, Supplement No. 6 (1995), p. 186.
16. Kathryn R. Mahaffey, "Nutrition and Lead: Strategies for Public Health," *Environmental Health Perspectives*, Vol. 103, Supplement No. 6 (1995), p. 193.

---

oping countries live without adequate shelter or in unacceptable housing (67), more than 1.4 billion lack access to safe water (68), and more than 2.9 billion people have no access to adequate sanitation (69)—all of which are essential for good hygiene. Unable to afford clean fuels, the poor rely instead on biomass fuels for cooking and heating. Inside the smoky dwellings of developing countries, air pollution is often higher than it is outdoors in the world's most congested cities (70).

Such problems, historically considered rural, have now become urban as well, as sprawling slum settlements surround the world's major cities (71). Risks are compounded in these peri-urban settlements, where garbage collection is often nonexistent and drainage tends to be poor, creating ideal conditions for insects and other disease vectors. Overcrowding increases the risk of disease transmission. Even among the poor, certain groups are more at risk than others. Women and children are more likely than men to be exposed to indoor air pollution from biomass fuels, because women spend many hours a day indoors near an open fire, often cooking with a child strapped on their backs. (See Chapter 2 for a discussion of indoor air pollution.)

In developing countries, the poorest strata are often excluded from the benefits of emerging prosperity and may also face a disproportionate share of health risks related to economic growth. Urban slums may be located near major roads, factories, or dumpsites, for instance, exposing residents to higher levels of air pollution or to the risks of industrial accidents. The chief victims of the accident at Bhopal, India, for example, were not just workers but slum dwellers who had settled near the factory.

Even in wealthier countries where environmental threats to the general population may be relatively small, they are likely to be greater for poor and minority populations. The distribution of lead toxicity in the United States is grossly unequal, for instance, with poor, minority, inner-city children bearing much higher burdens of exposure and effects (72). Similarly, asthma, which has been linked with poor household environmental conditions such as the presence of cockroaches and other allergens, occurs most often among poor, inner-city children in the United States (73). (See Chapter 2.)

Concern about unequal exposure to hazardous pollutants in the United States has sparked what is known as the environmental justice movement. The precipitating event was the landmark 1987 study by the United Church of Christ, which concluded that hazardous waste sites were disproportionately located in minority neighborhoods (74). Since then, several studies have shown that hazardous waste sites or polluting industries are indeed concentrated in low-income or minority areas (75)(76)(77). Other studies suggest that low-income and minority groups also tend to face greater exposures to selected air pollutants and contaminated fish, by virtue of their diets (78)(79)(80). (See Guest Commentary by Michael Dorsey.)

Looking ahead at development, environment, and health, then, it seems vital to consider distribution of wealth as well as rising income. Economic growth in and of itself is not sufficient to improve health for all, especially if rising income disparities mean that millions of people will not participate in these advances. As this income gap increases, the health gap is also likely to grow, leading to what some have dubbed "epidemiologic polarization." Unlike the more optimistic scenario of a smooth transition to better health, with a dramatic decline in infectious disease, this polarization scenario foresees a future in which mortality from infectious disease and malnutrition remains high but is increasingly concentrated among the poor (81)(82). As WHO reported in 1997, many countries are already experiencing this polarization (83)(84).

Characterizing Environmental Hazards

Improving health requires understanding how environmental conditions foster disease. While the causal connections are clear for some diseases and conditions, for others scientific evidence can only identify associations and likely contributors. This section focuses on both biological and chemical hazards in the environment. Biological factors lead to infectious diseases. Although many of these diseases have proven difficult to eradicate, enough is known about them to identify actions that will drastically reduce their incidence.

Chemical hazards in the environment can cause immediate, dangerous health effects and can also contribute to chronic, or long-term, problems. In contrast to infectious diseases, our understanding of how chemical exposures influence health, especially very low-level exposures typically found in the environment, remains incomplete.

BIOLOGICAL HAZARDS

Of all the environmental hazards humans encounter, the most formidable adversaries remain the microorganisms—viruses, bacteria, protozoa, and helminths (parasitic worms.) Up to 17 million deaths per year are attributable to these infectious and parasitic agents, almost all in the developing world, along with hundreds of millions of cases of sickness (85). Indeed, the history of humankind has been a struggle between humans and microbes (86)(87). Years of concerted efforts have revealed that while it is very difficult to eradicate microbial threats, it is possible to live in balance with them. However, human activities that change the environment and disrupt natural ecosystems can tip the scales in favor of the microbes (88).

Why consider infectious diseases "environmental" in origin? Because most, though certainly not all, are intimately connected with conditions in the physical environment. (See Table 1.3.) Cholera and other diarrheal diseases, for instance, are associated with inadequate access to clean water and sanitation and poor hygiene. Intestinal worms, which debilitate hundreds of millions at any given time, are associated with contaminated or undercooked food—which in turn arise from inadequate water supplies and improper food preparation or storage. Malaria, schistosomiasis, and other vector-borne diseases require certain ecological conditions for the vector—mosquito, fly, or snail—to persist. Environmental conditions increase the biological organisms' ability to thrive or spread. Although some supporting conditions exist in the natural environment, many are created or enhanced by human activities, as will be described more fully in Chapter 2. Other diseases, such as acute respiratory infections or tuberculosis or measles, are linked with poor conditions within the household environment, including overcrowding, soot and smoke, and air pollution. The role of environmental factors here seems to be to weaken the body's natural defenses to organisms that are often present.

The agents that cause infectious disease require not only favorable environmental conditions but also a susceptible host. The most vulnerable people tend to be those with low or reduced immunity, such as those weakened by malnutrition or other infections. Children are particularly vulnerable, especially infants who are not breast-fed and thus do not have the advantage of the mother's immunity. (See Box 1.5.) For some infectious diseases, new migrants to an area are also at heightened risk because they have not been previously exposed to diseases endemic in the area and thus have not built up any

*E*nvironmental Change and Human Health

Environmental Hazards and Disease

TABLE 1.3 Links Between Disease/Injury and the Environment

DISEASES	NOTES
Strong relationship between disease/injury and environment	
Most insect-borne diseases (including malaria, Chagas disease, dengue fever, yellow fever, leishmaniasis) and schistosomiasis	Modifying the environment to reduce the breeding, feedings or resting places for the vector is often a major part of disease control; in addition, for schistosomiasis, improved sanitation reduces the cycle of infection as schistosome eggs are no longer released into the environment.
Most diarrheal diseases, cholera, hepatitis A, most intestinal worms	Adequate provision for water, sanitation, drainage, and hygienic food preparation and storage can greatly reduce their incidence; overcrowded housing is also a risk factor.
Most of the common eye and skin infections and louse-borne diseases	Large reductions in their incidence are possible through improved water supply (including provision for washing) and sanitation.
Accidental burns, scalds and other injuries within the home and its surroundings, including those from road accidents	The incidence of such injuries is strongly associated with the size and quality of the home and the settlement or neighborhood in which it is located.
Diseases and injuries in the workplace	Most are related to toxic chemicals and/or dust in the workplace, as well as inadequate protection of workers from heat, machinery, and noise.
Important relationships between disease and environment but other factors also important	
Acute respiratory infections	Overcrowding, inadequate ventilation, dampness, and indoor air pollution influence their incidence and severity; so do high levels of ambient air pollution.
Tuberculosis; also meningococcal meningitis and rheumatic fever	Overcrowding and poor ventilation increase the risk of disease transmission.
Many psychosocial disorders	There is a strong association with poor quality housing and stressors associated with it, although many nonenvironmental factors are also important.
Relationship between disease and environment but other factors more important	
Maternal and perinatal health	Most of the above health problems affect the health of mothers, but improved health care and provision for safe delivery are more important in reducing maternal and perinatal deaths.
Important relationship between disease and environment but most cost-effective means of addressing it is through nonenvironmental means	
Measles and pertussis	Both are transmitted through aerosols, with increased transmission in overcrowded dwellings. Immunization against the diseases is the most cost-effective way of reducing their health impact.
Tetanus	Often caused by an accidental injury as the pathogen enters the human body through any cut or wound; rapid treatment and immunization against it are the most effective means to control tetanus because the pathogen that causes the disease cannot be controlled through environmental modification.
Certain forms of under-nutrition (e.g. those linked to iodine, iron, and vitamin A deficiency)	Iodine and vitamin A deficiency are particular problems in regions where foods rich in iodine and vitamin A are limited; provision of supplements, fortification of food, and, for vitamin A and iron deficiency, dietary modification is the most effective ways of preventing these deficiencies.

Reprinted from: David Satterthwaite *et al.*, *The Environment for Children: Understanding and Acting on the Environmental Hazards that Threaten Children and Their Parents* (Earthscan Publications, Ltd., London, 1996), pp. 8–9.

defenses against them. The next section reviews the major infectious diseases and the environmental conditions that influence their incidence.

Water-, Food-, and Soilborne Diseases

Of all the infectious diseases, diarrhea has perhaps the clearest links to the environment and some of the most deadly repercussions. Diarrhea is spread by both bacteria and viruses through contaminated food or water, and these disease-causing agents represent one of the most widespread health problems in the contemporary world. Diarrhea killed roughly 2.5 million people in 1996, according to WHO, most of whom were children under age 5 (89). In 1990, diarrhea accounted for 8 percent of DALYs globally (90). Diarrhea kills through dehydration. Fortunately, it is easily and fairly inexpensively managed with oral rehydration therapy (ORT), for those who have access to adequate medical care. Despite concerted efforts to make ORT widely available, the huge death toll from diarrhea clearly shows that much more remains to be done. Short of death, the roughly 4 billion episodes of diarrhea each year cause widespread debilitation (91). Diarrhea is intimately connected to malnutrition, which increases the frequency and severity of diarrheal episodes; repeated bouts of diarrhea, in turn, exacerbate malnutrition (92). Among causative agents, one of the most common is the intestinal bacteria *E. coli*, although a variety of other pathogens can cause diarrhea.

Box 1.5 Children's Special Vulnerability

Worldwide, as much as two thirds of all preventable ill health due to environmental conditions occurs among children (1). Children most affected belong to impoverished populations living in rural and peri-urban areas in developing countries. Currently, many of these children are exposed not only to biological hazards associated with lack of access to a clean environment, but also to toxic chemicals and other pollutants that stem from uncontrolled development. These pollutants include agrochemicals, industrial chemicals such as polychlorinated biphenyls (PCBs), heavy metals such as lead and arsenic, and a variety of air pollutants. These substances have been linked with birth defects, cancer, and weakening of the immune system.

The risk for contracting environmentally related illness is altered by several factors including a person's genetic background, nutritional status, age, lifestyle, and income level. Age is a major determinant of risk because the processes that determine exposure, absorption, metabolism, excretion, and tissue vulnerability are all age-related. The metabolism of infants and children differs from those of adults, as do their physiological and biochemical processes (2).

Susceptibility—the capacity to be affected—is a key factor in determining environmental risks to children. It also varies among different populations, ethnic groups, and genetic backgrounds, as well as by age, experience, and development. The combination of increased susceptibility and increased opportunity for exposure to a particular set of environmental threats—such as some pesticides and air pollutants—can increase health hazards for children (3).

Exposure to environmental agents is the first step in the sequence of environmentally related health effects. Exposures to these agents can occur even before conception, if the mother is exposed to certain pollutants that cross the placenta, such as lead or mercury. Exposures vary depending on one's physical location, breathing zones, oxygen consumption, and behavioral and eating patterns, all of which can change several times before an individual reaches adulthood.

The sources and routes of exposure to toxic substances for children are multiple. Some exposures are occupationally related— when children work in fields sprayed with pesticides, for instance, or when parents carry home chemical residues on clothing, or when chemicals to which the mother is exposed at work are transferred via breast milk to the child. Still other exposures can come from discharges to the air and water, certain waste sites, and on occasion, industrial accidents (4).

Because they have higher metabolic rates than adults, children breathe more air—twice as much per pound of body weight—than adults. In addition, children breathe air that is closer to the ground, where concentrations of contaminated dust can be higher. When children are more active, they inhale more deeply and may deposit pollutants deeper into their lungs than adults. These particles are more readily retained in the lungs and absorbed (5).

The maximum concentration of air pollutants recommended by the World Health Organization (WHO) is routinely exceeded in many Latin American cities including São Paulo and Rio de Janeiro, Brazil; Santiago, Chile; and Mexico City. Approximately 76 million people in Latin American cities are exposed to levels of suspended particulates well beyond maximum allowable levels. Annually in this region, as many as 3 million cases of chronic coughing in children have been attributed to this cause (6).

Poor indoor air quality is a major contributor to disease in the developing world, especially among low-income women and children whose families cook with biomass fuels. Worldwide, an estimated 3 million premature deaths, mostly due to acute and chronic respiratory infections, have been attributed to foul air; of these deaths, 2.8 million are due to indoor air pollution and 90 percent occur in developing countries (7).

Exposure of children to lead and persistent organic pollutants is another particular concern. Although mounting evidence shows that many developed countries have reduced human exposure and health risks of toxic chemicals such as lead, cadmium, mercury, DDT, and PCBs, in other parts of the world these problems have yet to be addressed (8).

Children are also likely to be exposed to higher levels of toxics from agrochemicals than are adults. Children are particularly vulnerable to health damage from some agrochemicals. A child's susceptibility is greater between conception and age 5, before organ systems and other functions mature, such as the liver's detoxification potential and the kidneys' filtration potential. Because those body cells are reproducing rapidly, children may be especially vulnerable to carcinogens. Likewise, children may be more susceptible to loss of brain function if exposed to neurotoxins during critical periods of development, as suggested by studies on lead, methyl mercury, PCBs, and dioxin (9).

Because the dietary diversity of most very young children is low—consisting of breast milk, infant formula and/or cow's milk first, and then fruit juices together with pureed fruits and vegetables before finally switching to the table foods of their parents—their exposure to agrochemical residues in both water and foods may often be higher than that of adults. For example, children in the United States eat up to seven times more of certain fruits in proportion to their body weight (10).

Children of farmworkers are believed to be at elevated risk of pesticide exposure. Particularly in developing countries, peasant children may work in the fields alongside their parents, and infants are sometimes carried and breastfed by their mothers while at work. Pesticide contamination of breast milk has been found even in remote villages in Papua New Guinea and India. Studies have shown that women in developing countries suffer the greatest exposure to pesticide residues (11).

It is clear that children are exposed to certain chemicals more than adults and that certain of their organs and biological functions are more susceptible to damage during specific phases of their development. However, the poor quality of information on food consumption, plus the inconclusive data on pesticide residues and toxicity, make it impossible to establish with any certainty the health risks for children. It is likely, however, that where general standards for pesticide exposure levels have been set, they may be inadequate for protecting children.

References and Notes

1. World Health Organization (WHO), *Health and Environment in Sustainable Development: 5 Years After the Earth Summit* (WHO, Geneva, 1997), p. 199.
2. Cynthia F. Bearer, "How Are Children Different From Adults?" in National Institutes of Health/National Institute of Environmental Health Sciences *Environmental Health Perspectives Supplements*, Vol. 103, Supplement 6 (1995), pp. 7–12.
3. Lynn R. Goldman, "Children—Unique and Vulnerable: Environmental Risks Facing Children and Recommendations for Response," in National Institutes of Health/National Institute of Environmental Health Sciences *Environmental Health Perspectives Supplements*, Vol. 103, Supplement 6 (1995), pp. 13–18.
4. *Ibid.*, p. 16.
5. Robin Meadows, "Growing Pains," in National Institutes of Health/National Institute of Environmental Health Sciences *Environmental Health Perspectives Supplements*, Vol. 104, No. 2 (1996), p. 147.
6. Henyk Weitzenfeld, "Contaminación atmosférica y salud en América Latina, *Bolétin de la Oficina Sanitaria Panamericana,* Vol. 112, No. 2 (1992), pp. 97–109.
7. *Op cit.* 1, p. 87.
8. *Op cit.* 1, p. 201.
9. John Wargo, *Our Children's Toxic Legacy: How Science and Law Fail to Protect Us from Pesticides* (Yale University Press, New Haven, Connecticut, 1996), pp. 11–12.
10. *Op cit* 5.
11. Pratap Chatterjee, "Pesticide Poison Circles the Globe, *Panoscope,* No. 39 (April 1994), p. 24.

Environmental Change and Human Health

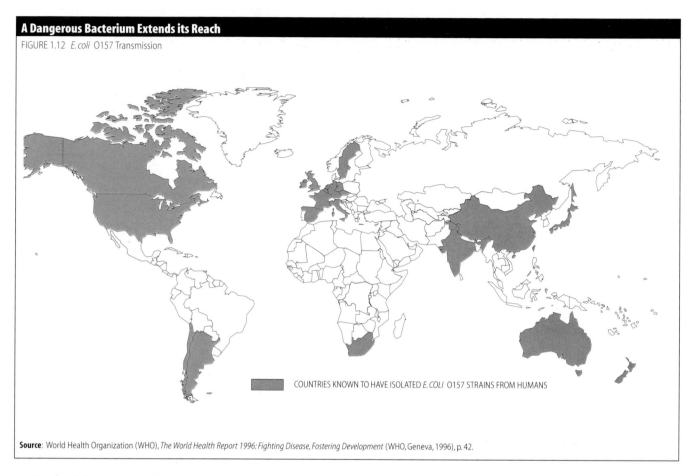

A Dangerous Bacterium Extends its Reach

FIGURE 1.12 *E. coli* O157 Transmission

COUNTRIES KNOWN TO HAVE ISOLATED *E. COLI* O157 STRAINS FROM HUMANS

Source: World Health Organization (WHO), *The World Health Report 1996: Fighting Disease, Fostering Development* (WHO, Geneva, 1996), p. 42.

Diarrheal diseases arise through contact with feces and are spread by what is known as the fecal-oral route. Until recently, contaminated water supplies were thought to be the chief culprit, but now the pathway is known to be more complex. An even greater factor appears to be insufficient water for washing, especially hand-washing, which makes proper hygiene impossible (93). When inadequate water supplies are coupled with shared latrines—or none at all—it creates conditions rife for transmitting diarrhea. Today, an estimated 2.9 billion people lack access to adequate sanitation and roughly 1.4 billion people do not have access to safe drinking water (94). This situation has persisted despite investments of more than US$100 billion during the International Water and Sanitation Decade.

Improvements in coverage continue to be overtaken by rapid population growth and even more explosive urban growth (95)(96). Ensuring access to adequate supplies of good-quality water and some form of sanitation—coupled with hygiene education and general socioeconomic development—remain critical factors in reducing the toll of diarrheal diseases.

Diarrheal diseases are by no means limited to the developing world, although they are most deadly there. In the developed world, where diarrhea is a major cause of sickness but rarely death, *Salmonella* and *Campylobacter jejuni*, spread through tainted chicken or milk, are among the most common agents (97). In addition, new microbial agents are increasingly implicated in human disease. *Campylobacter jejuni*, for instance, was once found only in animals, but now it is among the most common causes of foodborne illness in humans (98). Public health officials in the United States and elsewhere warn of an epidemic of foodborne pathogens (99). Several recent outbreaks of food poisoning in the United States, Canada, Europe, and Japan have been linked with *Cyclospora* and a new, particularly vicious form of *E. coli* (100). (See Figure 1.12.) To avert any possibility of a considerable outbreak, such as occurred in Japan in 1996 from *E. coli* O157 (101), the U.S. Government in 1997 recalled more than 11 million kilograms of beef suspected to be contaminated with the organism (102).

In 1993, the United States experienced the largest outbreak of diarrhea in recent history—affecting more than 400,000 people—when the municipal water supply of Milwaukee, Wisconsin, was contaminated by *Cryptosporidium parvum* from farm animal wastes (103). This protozoan parasite has been wreaking havoc in countries across Europe as well, raising new concerns about the safety of drinking water in some of the world's most affluent countries.

Box 1.6 Cholera Returns

In 1991, a cholera epidemic swept down the west coast of South America—the first such outbreak in nearly a century in the New World. Between 1991 and 1995, a disease long thought to have been vanquished in the Americas had infected more than 1 million people and killed 11,000 (1). Africa experienced a similar cholera surge in 1991, with the number of cases rising fourfold in a single year (from 38,683 in 1990 to 153,367 in 1991) and deaths mounting to 14,000 (2)(3). Three years later, the cholera epidemic hit Russia and cholera cases jumped from just 23 the year before to 1,048 (4)(5).

Why has cholera reemerged as a global health threat, after virtually disappearing from the Americas and most of Africa and Europe for more than a century? (6) The answer may lie in how changing environmental conditions—from both natural and human causes—can affect the spread of an infectious disease.

Cholera is generally spread by contact with water or food contaminated with human waste containing cholera bacteria. That is why the disease has long been associated with the unsanitary conditions often found in urban slums, or in connection with war, natural disasters, and other dislocations. But cholera also has a traditional link with the sea. In nature, the cholera organism (*Vibrio cholerae*) thrives best in moderately salty waters such as coastal estuaries, though it can also tolerate the open ocean. It generally only inhabits rivers and other freshwater sources if nutrient levels from organic pollution such as human feces are quite high (7).

These two environmental links—with the sea and with unsanitary conditions—do much to explain the pattern of cholera epidemics throughout history. Global epidemics (pandemics) of cholera often hit first in coastal cities and have clearly been associated with unhygienic conditions. Originally restricted to the Indian subcontinent, cholera spread from India to Europe between 1817 and 1823, launching the first global cholera pandemic (8). Since then, six more pan-

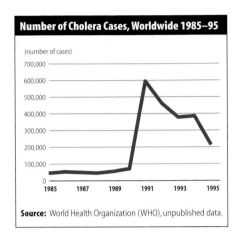

Number of Cholera Cases, Worldwide 1985–95

(number of cases)

Source: World Health Organization (WHO), unpublished data.

demics have washed, wavelike, across the continents, receding for a time between each pulse.

By the end of the 19th Century, cholera appeared to retreat as a global health threat. After 1900, it disappeared from the Americas and most of Europe; and by 1950 it was largely confined to the Indian subcontinent, where it had originated, and the Asian countries west of India (9). But in 1961, a new pulse of the disease—the seventh pandemic—began to spread from Asia, eventually emerging with a vengeance in 1991 in Latin America and Africa. Though this latest pandemic has peaked, the disease remains endemic throughout these regions (10).

Part of the blame for the dramatic rise in cholera cases in Latin America and Africa rests with obvious causes: deteriorating water and sanitation systems, poor living conditions, malnutrition, crowding, and political and economic turmoil. For example, studies of the 1991 cholera epidemic in Peru suggest that the lack of effective water treatment measures contributed to the rapid spread of the disease. Engineers of the public water supply system in the coastal city of Trujillo believed that no water treatment would be necessary. The fear of the carcinogenic risk associated with chlorine disinfection byproducts superceded the fear of cholera infection (11). And,

testimony of health workers in Iquitos, a jungle city in Peru, suggests that even home-based chlorination could have been key in arresting further dissemination of the disease (12). Rapid population growth and lack of investment in public services had led to serious declines in Lima's sanitation coverage, and between 5 million and 6 million city residents had no access to acceptable latrines (13). In Africa, civil strife and drought in the 1980s had led to unusually large migrations and concentrations of people in urban slums and refugee camps (14). About 50,000 Rwandan refugees contracted cholera in such camps after the 1991 outbreak, and many thousands died (15).

Other factors played a role as well in cholera's resurgence. Some cholera cases in Latin America were traced to the growing use of wastewater to irrigate crops near urban areas (16). In addition, food-handling practices, especially by street vendors, may have added to the global outbreak. Street vendors are a central feature of poor urban communities throughout the developing world, but their lack of refrigeration and clean water often increases the risk of contamination (17). In Latin America, uncooked seafood, such as ceviche, was also an important route of cholera transmission because seafood is often caught or processed in unhygienic conditions (18).

But these factors don't fully explain how cholera reemerged in Latin America so suddenly after more than a century's absence. Moreover, the 1991 pandemic struck nearly simultaneously over a wide area, appearing in ports from the Chilean to the Ecuadorean border within a few weeks. What event or series of events had so effectively reintroduced cholera over huge stretches of open coastline?

One possibility is that the cholera organism was carried by ship from Asian to Latin American ports in ballast water—a well-known vehicle for transporting foreign organisms, ranging from microscopic bacteria and viruses to mollusks and small crabs (19). DNA testing of the Latin American cholera strain

---

Other familiar and dangerous infectious diseases, such as cholera and hepatitis A and E, can also be transmitted by fecally contaminated food and water. This is most common in developing countries, but frequently occurs elsewhere. In the United States, for instance, 151 students and staff in four different school districts in Michigan developed hepatitis A in March 1997. The cases have been associated with the consumption of frozen strawberries imported from Mexico (104). Cholera sweeps around the globe periodically in major pandemics. Annual death rates fluctuate wildly, ranging in recent years from several thousand up to hundreds of thousands. Most deaths occur in Africa, often among displaced or refugee populations; overall, some 79 million people in Africa alone are at risk for the disease, according to WHO (105). Recent outbreaks in Latin America and the appearance of a new strain of cholera in India and Bangladesh provide examples of how changing environmental conditions can accelerate disease transmission. (See Box 1.6.)

Among the food-, water-, and soilborne diseases, those caused by parasitic worms are noted for the debilitation they

Box 1.6 continued

shows that it is genetically similar—although not identical—to a cholera strain common in Bangladesh [20], and this strain has been isolated in samples of ballast, bilge, and sewage from cargo ships active in the area [21]. Still, the speed with which the epidemic spread to points so widely dispersed casts some doubt on whether shipping traffic alone can explain the disease's reemergence [22].

A second theory is that cholera never really disappeared from the Americas at all, but merely went into a dormant, noninfective state in coastal waters, from which it reemerged when the right combination of favorable environmental conditions appeared. Evidence for this theory of ocean waters as a reservoir of cholera comes from the recent discovery that some species of plankton can act as hosts for the dormant cholera organism, allowing the organism to persist in coastal waters for long periods, and then "reappear" after years of seeming absence [23]. This theory also helps explain why cholera epidemics in Bangladesh occur seasonally, often coinciding with plankton blooms in the Bay of Bengal.

The cholera-plankton connection probably also offers the disease a means of long-distance travel, hitchhiking with the plankton on ocean currents across thousands of kilometers and over periods of months and years. This might explain how an Asian cholera strain could find its way to several points along the coast of South America without stowing away in ballast water.

El Niño, a periodic change in weather patterns that can profoundly affect local environmental conditions, may also have played a key role in cholera's return. El Niño heats surface water currents that start in the eastern Pacific Ocean near the coast of Central and South America and then spread throughout the tropics and subtropics. The warm sea surface temperatures that El Niño brings can encourage large plankton blooms, especially in coastal waters with high levels of nutrients from sewage and stormwater runoff [24].

These blooms can awaken the cholera organism, bringing it back to its infectious state [25]. The Latin American cholera epidemic occurred in tandem with the coming of the last El Niño, which began in 1991 and lasted until mid-1995—the longest El Niño on record [26].

Cholera's dependence on environmental factors such as sea surface temperatures, nutrient levels in coastal waters, and plankton blooms may have some important implications for the future of the disease. For one, the frequency of plankton blooms is increasing worldwide and is likely to rise even more in the future due to a combination of factors. These include higher ocean temperatures from global warming, increased nutrient runoff from expanding urban populations, and an additional plankton fertilizing effect from high carbon dioxide levels in the atmosphere. More frequent plankton blooms will very likely put more coastal areas at risk of cholera outbreaks [27]. This means that tackling urban poverty and providing for adequate water and sanitation services—the front lines in the fight against cholera—will only become more important in the years ahead. [28].

References and Notes

1. Integrated Management of Childhood Illness Communicable Disease Program, Division of Disease Prevention and Control, Pan American Health Organization (PAHO)/World Health Organization (WHO), "Cholera Situation in the Americas," Update Number 14, (PAHO/WHO, Washington, D.C., April 1996), p. 1.
2. World Health Organization (WHO), unpublished data (WHO, Geneva, 1996).
3. World Health Organization (WHO), *Weekly Epidemiological Record*, Vol. 67, No. 34 (August 21, 1992), p. 258.
4. *Op. cit.* 2.
5. *Op. cit.* 2.
6. Robert Tauxe *et al.*, "The Future of Cholera: Persistence, Change, and an Expanding Research Agenda," in Vibrio cholerae *and Cholera: Molecular to Global Perspectives*, I. Kaye Wachsmuth, Paul A. Blake, and Orjan Olsvik, eds. (American Society

for Microbiology, Washington, D.C., 1994), p. 443.
7. Rita R. Colwell, "Global Climate and Infectious Disease: The Cholera Paradigm," *Science*, Vol. 274 (December 20, 1996), p. 2027.
8. *Op. cit.* 6.
9. *Op.cit.*6.
10. *Op.cit.*7, pp. 2027–2028.
11. Eduardo Salazar-Lindo *et al.*, "The Peruvian Cholera Epidemic and the Role of Chlorination in its Control and Prevention," in *Safety of Water Disinfection: Balancing Chemical and Microbial Risks*, Gunther F. Craun, ed. (ILSI Press, Washington, D.C., 1993), pp. 403–404.
12. *Ibid.*, p. 412.
13. Joseph Haratani and Donald Hernandez, "El Colera en El Perú: Una Evaluación Rápida de la Infrastructura de Abasteciemiento de Agua y Saneamiento del País y su Papel en la Epidemia," Field Report No. 331 (Environmental Health Project, U.S. Agency for International Development, Washington, D.C., May 1991), p. 32.
14. *Op. cit.* 3.
15. *Op. cit.* 7, p. 2028.
16. Robert Tauxe *et al.*, "The Latin American Epidemic," in Vibrio cholerae *and Cholera: Molecular to Global Perspectives*, I. Kaye Wachsmuth, Paul A. Blake, and Orjan Olsvik, eds. (Amercan Society for Microbiology, Washington, D.C., 1994), p. 339.
17. *Ibid*, p. 338..
18. *Op. cit.* 16, p. 338.
19. Mary E. Wilson, "Travel and the Emergence of Infectious Diseases," *Emerging Infectious Diseases*, Vol. 1, No. 2 (April–June 1995), p. 43.
20. *Op. cit.* 7, p. 2026.
21. S.A. McArthy, R.M. McPhearson, and A.M. Guarino, "Toxigenic *Vibrio cholerae* 01 and Cargo Ships Entering Gulf of Mexico," *Lancet*, Vol. 339, No. 8793 (March 7, 1992), p. 624.
22. *Op. cit.* 7.
23. *Op. cit.* 7, p. 2029.
24. John Tibbets, "Oceans," *Environmental Health Perspectives*, Vol. 104, No. 4 (April 1996), p. 384.
25. *Op. cit.* 7.
26. *Op. cit.* 24, pp. 383–384.
27. A.J. McMichael, *Planetary Overload: Global Environmental Change and the Health of the Human Species* (Cambridge University Press, Cambridge, U.K. 1993), p. 281.
28. *Op. cit.* 6.

cause [106]. At any one time, roughly 3.5 billion people are infected with one or several species of parasitic worms—making these among the most prevalent human infections—and some 450 million people are ill as a result [107].

The chief transmission route is the familiar trail through human feces, via either contaminated food or soil. When an infected person defecates in the open, the soil becomes a breeding ground. The contaminated soil is then carried into homes on the soles of the feet. Not surprisingly, worm infections are on the rise in urban slums and shanty towns of the developing world, according to WHO [108].

Rarely fatal, worm infections nonetheless exact a tremendous and diverse toll. Infection takes place repeatedly, and the disease becomes more serious as the worm burden in the body builds up. The most vulnerable group is school-aged children, who may harbor multiple infections simultaneously. The effects on children are especially pernicious because chronic infections impair both physical and intellectual growth and development.

The worm infection that is most deadly is schistosomiasis; it kills some 20,000 people a year and causes chronic ill health among hundreds of millions more. Safe and effective drugs

Malaria Distribution and Problem Areas

FIGURE 1.13 Main Areas of Malaria Transmission Worldwide

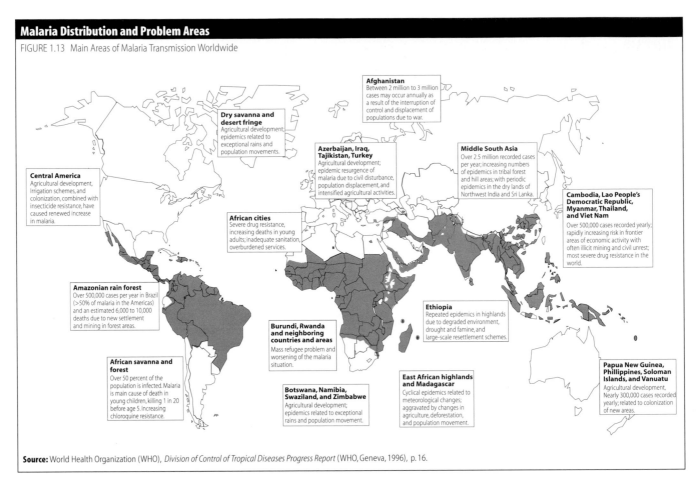

Afghanistan
Between 2 million to 3 million cases may occur annually as a result of the interruption of control and displacement of populations due to war.

Dry savanna and desert fringe
Agricultural development; epidemics related to exceptional rains and population movements.

Azerbaijan, Iraq, Tajikistan, Turkey
Agricultural development; epidemic resurgence of malaria due to civil disturbance, population displacement, and intensified agricultural activities.

Middle South Asia
Over 2.5 million recorded cases per year; increasing numbers of epidemics in tribal forest and hill areas; with periodic epidemics in the dry lands of Northwest India and Sri Lanka.

Cambodia, Lao People's Democratic Republic, Myanmar, Thailand, and Viet Nam
Over 500,000 cases recorded yearly; rapidly increasing risk in frontier areas of economic activity with often illicit mining and civil unrest; most severe drug resistance in the world.

Central America
Agricultural development, Irrigation schemes, and colonization, combined with insecticide resistance, have caused renewed increase in malaria.

African cities
Severe drug resistance, increasing deaths in young adults; inadequate sanitation, overburdened services.

Amazonian rain forest
Over 500,000 cases per year in Brazil (>50% of malaria in the Americas) and an estimated 6,000 to 10,000 deaths due to new settlement and mining in forest areas.

Burundi, Rwanda and neighboring countries and areas
Mass refugee problem and worsening of the malaria situation.

Ethiopia
Repeated epidemics in highlands due to degraded environment, drought and famine, and large-scale resettlement schemes.

African savanna and forest
Over 50 percent of the population is infected. Malaria is main cause of death in young children, killing 1 in 20 before age 5. Increasing chloroquine resistance.

Botswana, Namibia, Swaziland, and Zimbabwe
Agricultural development; epidemics related to exceptional rains and population movement.

East African highlands and Madagascar
Cyclical epidemics related to meteorological changes; aggravated by changes in agriculture, deforestation, and population movement.

Papua New Guinea, Phillippines, Soloman Islands, and Vanuatu
Agricultural development, Nearly 300,000 cases recorded yearly; related to colonization of new areas.

Source: World Health Organization (WHO), *Division of Control of Tropical Diseases Progress Report* (WHO, Geneva, 1996), p. 16.

---

cost 30 cents to treat one patient, but this cost is prohibitive in many countries (109). The disease is caused by parasitic flatworms, called flukes, of the genus *Schistosoma*, whose intermediate hosts are snails common throughout Asia, Africa, and other tropical regions. These snails flourish in relatively calm supplies of fresh water. WHO estimates that about 200 million people in tropical countries have acquired the disease from bathing or wading in infested rivers, lakes, and irrigation systems, and as many as 500 million to 600 million more are at risk (110). Schistosomiasis is on the upswing in developing countries, in part because it spreads to previously unaffected areas through water development projects, such as dams or irrigation. (See Chapter 2.)

As with diarrhea, providing for the sanitary disposal of feces would do much to prevent the transmission of schistosomiasis and other worm infections. The gains from improved sanitation may take years to materialize, however; in the near term, experts recommend a combined strategy that includes snail control, sanitary improvements, education, and repeated treatment with medicines to keep the worm burden low (111).

Insect-Borne Diseases

Malaria is the most deadly of the insect-borne diseases, claiming the lives of some 1 million to 3 million people each year—90 percent of them in Africa, and most of them children (112). (Because of different calculation methods, the *Global Burden of Disease* study estimates malaria mortality at roughly 800,000 per year (113).) WHO estimates that some 300 million to 500 million cases of malaria occur each year—and the number is on the rise—and that 40 percent of the world's population is at risk for malaria (114). Malaria has been called the "laziness" disease because it is so debilitating. The most prevalent disease in poor rural regions, malaria produces recurrent infections with attacks of fever in warm and rainy seasons, just when workers are needed to collect crops (115).

Caused by four different species of protozoal parasites, malaria is transmitted through the bite of the *Anopheles* mosquito, which harbors the parasites. Thus, the geographic range of the disease is determined by the environmental conditions that the mosquito in question requires—a particular combination of altitude, rainfall, heat, and humidity, and available surface water. Because ideal conditions vary for the 60 or so species of *Anopheles* that transmit the disease, strategies designed to control one vector won't necessarily work for another.

Environmental Change and Human Health

In the tropics, where malaria is most entrenched and deadly, spread of the disease is abetted by conditions of heat, humidity, poverty, and inadequate waste disposal. (See Figure 1.13.) Malaria is a particular problem in newly cultivated or frontier areas such as Amazonia (See Box 2.4.) and areas of recent agricultural expansion. Once targeted for global eradication, malaria has turned out to be more than a worthy adversary. A more realistic goal is simply to control the disease (116).

WHO has declared the mosquito "Public Enemy Number One" because it is involved in so many deadly or debilitating diseases—not just malaria but also dengue fever, yellow fever, filariasis (elephantiasis), and Japanese encephalitis (117). These diseases, too, are exquisitely attuned to changing environmental conditions. The *Aedes aegypti* mosquitoes that carry dengue and yellow fever, for instance, thrive in urban settings, where they lay their eggs in water storage containers or in discarded plastic bottles or tires. (See Box 1.7.)

In other vector-borne diseases, flies and other insects transmit the infectious parasite. Sleeping sickness (African trypanosomiasis) for instance, is transmitted by the bite of the tsetse fly. Leishmaniasis is transmitted by the sandfly, again through a parasite-contaminated bite. This disease is a major problem in parts of Africa, Latin America, and the Middle East, where some 2 million cases occur each year (118). In its deadliest form, visceral leishmaniasis, fatality rates can reach 100 percent if untreated. In its more common form, the disease produces painful ulcers on the face, arms, and legs. WHO estimates that some 350 million people are at risk of contracting the leishmaniasis(119). As with other vector-borne diseases, its spread is accelerated by development projects such as road building or forest exploitation, which bring people into contact with the disease vector. Leishmaniasis is reappearing in some areas where it had once been controlled, in part because of the cessation of insecticide spraying to control malaria. A beneficial side effect of DDT, it turns out, was that it kept sandflies in check.

Chagas disease, also known as American trypanosomiasis, is unique to the Americas, where housing conditions pose the biggest risk factor. In this case the culprit, the parasite *T. cruzi*, is carried by both wild and domesticated animals. It is usually transmitted, however, by a blood-sucking bug that lives in thatched roofs. About one third of those infected develop a chronic form of the disease, which can lead to heart damage and death. WHO estimates that Chagas disease is the leading cause of cardiac death among young adults in parts of South America (120).

Airborne Diseases

Commonly known as ARI, acute respiratory infections kill more than 4 million people per year and are the leading cause of death among children under age 5 (121). This range of infections, which includes pneumonia in its most serious form, ac-

counts for more than 8 percent of the global burden of disease (122). ARI's reach is global: it is the most frequent disease worldwide and a common causes of visits to pediatricians in the industrialized countries, although essentially all deaths from ARI occur in the developing world.

The risk factors for ARI are numerous and difficult to sort out. Caused by different viruses or bacteria, ARI is closely associated with poverty. Overcrowding and unsanitary household conditions favor the transmission of the disease, which is spread by droplets from a cough or a sneeze or unwashed hands. Death most often strikes those children who are already weakened by low birth weight, other infections, and malnutrition (123).

Several other factors seem to exacerbate the disease. Exposure to tobacco smoke increases the risk of contracting these infections, and many studies implicate both indoor and outdoor air pollution. Indoor air pollution has been the focus of particular concern, specifically, the soot and smoke associated with the burning of biomass fuels such as wood, coal, or dung. Many people in the developing world, mostly in rural areas, rely on biomass fuels for heating or cooking. (See Chapter 2.) A cause-and-effect relationship between indoor air pollution and ARI has been difficult to prove, however, in part because people who use biomass fuels tend to be poor and exposed to multiple risks such as overcrowding, tobacco smoke, and malnutrition. Even so, the World Bank estimated in 1992 that switching to better fuels could halve the number of pneumonia deaths (124).

Other airborne diseases also thrive in conditions of poverty, exploiting enclosed spaces, crowding, and poor hygienic conditions. Tuberculosis (TB), to name just one, killed an estimated 3 million people in 1996, and nearly 7.5 million others developed the disease (125). TB is the single largest cause of adult death from infectious diseases. Roughly 95 percent of all TB sufferers are in the developing world, mostly in Southeast Asia, Western Pacific, and Africa—many in the slums of poor cities. In recent years, however, TB has resurfaced in developed countries, where it is concentrated among poor populations. (See Chapter 2.)

Measles and diphtheria, also diseases of crowding and poverty, have been all but eliminated in the developed world since the advent of successful vaccines. In the developing world, however, measles still affects 42 million children per year who lack access to the vaccine; roughly 1 million of these children die (126). Since 1990, diphtheria has resurfaced in the former Soviet Union, triggered by social disruption and a drop in immunization rates (127).

Measles and diphtheria are just two of a cluster known as childhood (or vaccine-preventable) diseases. Other familiar diseases in this group are neonatal tetanus, poliomyelitis, and pertussis. This cluster, all linked with environmental conditions, accounts for nearly 15 percent of the total disease bur-

Box 1.7 The Spread of Dengue Hemorrhagic Fever

In the last 20 years, the incidence of dengue and its more severe, often lethal, form—dengue hemorrhagic fever (DHF)—has increased dramatically, especially in the tropical regions of the world. During the 1960s, dengue typically averaged about 30,000 cases per year (1). Some 30 years later, though, in 1995, 592,000 cases of dengue were reported, and the true number of people afflicted is believed to be several fold higher (2). The World Health Organization (WHO) estimates that 20 million cases occur each year, requiring 500,000 hospitalizations (3), and researchers estimate that 2.5 billion people live in urban tropical centers, placing them at risk of contracting the disease (4).

Also known as "break-bone" fever, dengue is the Swahili term for "a sudden overtaking by a spirit." Caused by four distinct virus serotypes,

the disease's symptoms include fever, severe headaches, and disabling muscle and joint pain. Although classical dengue is relatively benign, the more serious hemorrhagic form causes breathing difficulties and bleeding from the nose, mouth, and gums (5). Multiple infections are possible because immunity to one virus serotype does not provide immunity to the others. In fact, previous infection from one dengue serotype or a sequence of infections can contribute to the risk of contracting the more severe DHF (6). Approximately 5 percent of all DHF cases are fatal, mostly among children (7). Although dengue is still rarely lethal, its contribution to disease and ill health, especially among young children, should make dengue control a primary public health concern.

The reemergence of dengue as a public health threat illustrates how human-directed changes in

the environment can influence the patterns of infectious disease. Although the various factors responsible for this worldwide increase in dengue are not fully understood, it is believed that rapid urbanization, the wide use of non-biodegradable plastic packaging and cellophane, increased travel and trade, and the lack of effective mosquito control efforts contribute in important ways to the spread of the disease (8).

Demographic changes—in particular, rapid, unplanned urbanization—have resulted in conditions that encourage the spread of dengue. The two primary mosquito vectors of dengue, *Aedes aegypti* and *Aedes albopictus*, have adapted from their natural forest environs (where they breed in tree holes containing rainwater) to the urban environment (where they breed in pots, pitchers, water cans,

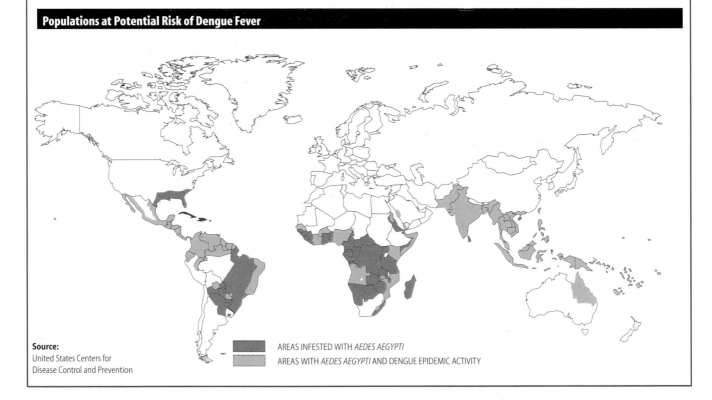

Populations at Potential Risk of Dengue Fever

Source:
United States Centers for
Disease Control and Prevention

▮ AREAS INFESTED WITH *AEDES AEGYPTI*
▮ AREAS WITH *AEDES AEGYPTI* AND DENGUE EPIDEMIC ACTIVITY

den globally for children under age 5. Despite widespread immunization programs, these diseases nonetheless claimed the lives of 1,985,000 children in 1990 (128).

CHEMICAL HAZARDS IN THE ENVIRONMENT

Exposure to chemical agents in the environment—in air, water, food, and soil—has been implicated in numerous adverse effects, from cancer to lung disease to brain damage to birth

defects. Some evidence is ironclad; some is suggestive at best. Although the acute effects such as poisonings are the best understood, it seems clear that hazardous pollutants contribute to the large and growing toll of chronic conditions, such as cancers and heart disease. Chemical pollutants can also play a role in infectious diseases, perhaps by rendering the body less able to ward off infections. The exact magnitude of the risk they pose, however, is difficult to quantify. This has fueled an

Environmental Change and Human Health

drains, bottles, and discarded tires). This fact makes dengue particularly troublesome in cities of the developing world, where between one third and two thirds of solid waste is not collected, but left on streets, in drains, or dumped in open landfills (9). In addition to waste usage problems, crowding, inadequate water and sanitation systems, and poor housing conditions can further facilitate the spread of the disease (10).

Especially in Southeast Asia, for example, rapid population growth and urbanization after World War II has resulted in endemic dengue. An insufficient supply of piped water in this region makes it necessary to store water for drinking and washing; this situation, along with poor sanitation and crowding, helps to create conditions that favor the breeding of *Aedes aegypti*. Between 1970 and 1987, attack rates of severe DHF in Southeast Asia increased from 15 people per 100,000 population to 170 per 100,000 (11). In cities like Delhi, the storage of drinking water in pots as well as in open water room coolers provides perfect breeding sites for the disease-carrying mosquitoes (12).

Similarly, in Latin America, rapid urbanization spurred by intensive industrialization and social and economic changes, has led to rapid reinfestation of the mosquito that carries dengue. The *Aedes aegypti* mosquito was almost eradicated from most Central and South American countries in the 1950s and 1960s as a result of an extensive campaign to end yellow fever, which is carried by the same mosquito. After 1972, however, government complacency and the shift of economic resources to meet the increasing demands imposed by rapid urbanization and inadequate health-care systems dramatically curtailed mosquito control efforts (13)(14). By 1995, *Aedes aegypti* had returned to the same level of distribution as before the eradication program, and 14 countries in the region reported confirmed cases of DHF (15). In Mexico, for instance, 358 cases of DHF (with a case fatality rate of 7.8 percent) were confirmed in 1995 compared with only 30 cases in 1994 and only 26 cases between 1984 and 1993 (16)(17).

Tourism and travel have also become important mechanisms for facilitating the dengue virus and its vectors. *Aedes albopictus*, for instance, was

introduced from Asia into the Americas as the result of increased tire trade. Used truck tires in Asia, destined for the United States for recapping, were stored in the open before export, where they collected rainwater and became breeding sites. During the 1980s, more than 1 million tires per year were imported into the United States from Asia of which approximately 20 percent were simply discarded in the environment (18). In these breeding grounds, the mosquito spread rapidly and has established itself in at least 17 American states (19). Overall, however, the risk for dengue outbreaks in the United States is small, because most U.S. homes have running water, window and door screens, and air conditioning. In addition, public health surveillance and prevention and control programs tend to be better developed.

Because effective dengue vaccines are not likely to exist for at least 5 to 10 years, the only way to prevent dengue is to eliminate or reduce the mosquito vectors, either by direct control efforts or by improving housing conditions to reduce the number of potential breeding sites. Integrated prevention strategies need to be developed, and high-technology, quick-fix solutions should not be relied upon to combat the virus (20)(21). (See Chapter 3.) Without nationwide vector-control programs, however, the absolute number of dengue cases will continue to expand with population growth and the growth of cities (22).

References and Notes

1. Thomas P. Monath, "Dengue: The Risk to Developed and Developing Countries," *Proceedings of the National Academy of Sciences*, Vol. 91 (March 1994), p. 2397.
2. World Health Organization (WHO), *The World Health Report 1996: Fighting Disease, Fostering Development* (WHO, Geneva, 1996), p. 24.
3. *Ibid.*, p. 48.
4. Duane J. Gubler and Gary G. Clark, "Community Involvement in the Control of *Aedes aegypti*," *Acta Tropica*, Vol. 61 (1996), p. 170.
5. *Op cit.* 2, p. 48.
6. Duane J. Gubler, "Vigilancia Activa Del Dengue y de la Fiebre hemorrágica del Dengue," *Boletín de la Oficina Sanitaria Panamericana*, Vol. 107 (1989), pp. 22-30, cited in Baltasar Briseño-García et al.,

7. "Potential Risk for Dengue Hemorrhagic Fever: The Isolation of Serotype Dengue-3 in Mexico," *Emerging Infectious Diseases*, Vol. 2, No. 2 (April-June 1996).
7. Duane J. Gubler and Gary G. Clark, "Dengue/Dengue Hemorrhagic Fever: The Emergence of a Global Health Problem," *Emerging Infectious Diseases*, Vol. 1, No. 2 (1995), pp. 55–57.
8. *Op. cit.* 4.
9. World Resources Institute in collaboration with the United Nations Environment Programme, the United Nations Development Programme, and The World Bank, *World Resources 1996-97: The Urban Environment* (Oxford University Press, New York, 1996), pp. 23 and 70.
10. Duane J. Gubler and Gary G. Clark, "Community-Based Integrated Control of *Aedes aegypti*: A Brief Overview of Current Programs," *American Journal of Tropical Medicine and Hygiene*, Vol. 50, No. 6 (1994), p. 50.
11. Donald S. Shepard and Scott B. Halstead, "Dengue (with Notes on Yellow Fever and Japanese Encephalitis)," in *Disease Control Priorities in Developing Countries*, Dean T. Jamison et al., eds. (Oxford University Press, New York, 1993), p. 304.
12. Tara Patel, "Dengue Fever Outbreak Angers Indian Judges," *New Scientist*, Vol. 152, No. 2053 (October 26, 1996), p. 10.
13. Edward B. Hayes and Duane J. Gubler, "Dengue and Dengue Hemorrhagic Fever," *Pediatric Infectious Disease Journal*, Vol. 11, No. 4 (1992), p. 315.
14. *Op. cit.* 1, p. 2398.
15. *Op. cit.* 7, pp. 55–57.
16. Baltasar Briseño-García et al., "Potential Risk for Dengue Hemorrhagic Fever: The Isolation of Serotype Dengue-3 in Mexico," *Emerging Infectious Diseases*, Vol. 2, No. 2 (April-June 1996).
17. R. J. Narro and H. Gómez-Dantés, "El dengue en México: un problema prioritario de salud pública," *Salud Publica Mexico*, Vol. 37 (1995), S12-S20 as cited in Baltasar Briseño-García et al., "Potential Risk for Dengue Hemorrhagic Fever: The Isolation of Serotype Dengue-3 in Mexico," *Emerging Infectious Diseases*, Vol. 2, No. 2 (April-June 1996).
18. *Op. cit.* 1, p. 2396.
19. Stephen S. Morse and Ann Schlueberg, "Emerging Viruses: The Evolution of Viruses and Viral Diseases," *The Journal of Infectious Diseases*, Vol. 162 (July 1990), p. 2.
20. *Op. cit.* 10, pp. 50–52.
21. *Op. cit.* 4, pp. 177–178.
22. *Op. cit.* 11, p. 304.

intense debate over what constitutes safe use and disposal of toxic substances. This debate has occurred mostly in the affluent countries but is increasingly occurring in the developing world as well.

Although cause-and-effect relationships for most infectious diseases are well known, the links between chemical pollutants and disease are murkier. A person contracting cholera, for instance, clearly has been exposed to the *cholera vibrio*. The circumstances of that exposure may remain mysterious—and other contributing factors may be involved—but exposure to the bacterium is an established causal factor. The same pathway

cannot be traced for a disease such as lung cancer. Cancers may take 10 to 40 years to develop, and many factors may contribute to the appearance of the disease in a particular person. Accordingly, chemical risks tend to be described in terms of the numbers of people exposed—for instance, 1.4 billion urban dwellers exposed to air quality that exceeds health guidelines, as WHO estimates (129). (See Chapter 2.) Such estimates reveal little about how many people will actually suffer the adverse effects from these exposures. (See Box 1.8.)

On a global scale, the health risk from chemical agents in the environment is considerably smaller than that from bio-

Box 1.8 From Exposure To Effect

People are exposed to toxic substances through a variety of routes by ingesting contaminated food and water, by breathing contaminated air, or by contact with the skin. Other paths to exposure are indirect, for example, parental exposures that harm a fetus developing in the womb. Exposure *per se* does not necessarily result in an adverse impact. The level of impact depends on several factors; key among them is dose. *Exposure* is defined as the amount of a substance that reaches a person, whereas *dose* is the amount actually absorbed by the target organ. The timing and duration of the dose, as well as the amount absorbed, are all important in determining impact. For some toxic substances, there appears to be a threshold level below which no effects occur. Others, by contrast, may exert effects at the lowest possible doses.

Further complicating the connection between exposure and effect is the fact that the same dose will not necessarily elicit the same effect in two different people. As is true with infectious diseases, some people are more sensitive to the ill effects of chemical or physical pollutants than others. Children are particularly at risk, for a number of reasons, including their rapid growth rate, the amount they ingest in relation to their body weight, and the manner in which they are exposed. (See Box 1.5.) The developing fetus is also exquisitely sensitive to a number of chemical agents, especially in the first several months of development. Beyond age, genetics plays a key role, as does an individual's general state of health and nutritional status. Children deficient in iron or zinc, for instance, absorb more lead than well-nourished children with identical exposures (Bowen and Hu, 1993).

In addition, a given chemical can have a variety of ill effects, or endpoints, ranging from minor irritation to death. These effects may show up immediately (acute effects), as is the case with pesticide poisonings, in several years (chronic effects), or in subsequent generations, as is the case with birth defects. For some effects, similar to certain cancers, the routes and mechanisms of action are relatively well understood because they have been studied extensively. For others, such as substances thought to disrupt the endocrine system, scientific understanding is rudimentary at best.

Adapted from D. Briggs, C. Corvalán, and M. Nurminen, eds., Linkage Methods for Environment and Health Analysis, Office of Global and Integrated Environmental Health, World Health Organization (WHO) (WHO, Geneva, 1996). Also cited: Elizabeth L. Bowen and Howard Hu, "Food Contamination Due to Environmental Pollution," in *Critical Condition: Human Health and the Environment*, Eric Chivian et al., eds. (The MIT Press, Cambridge, Massachusetts, 1993), p. 50.

logical pathogens described in the previous section. In some heavily polluted areas, however, chemical risks can be quite high. Risks are likely to be higher in less developed as opposed to more developed countries, because fewer safeguards are typically in place there, either to reduce emissions or to protect people from exposure. Equally important, regardless of their magnitude, the risks from chemical pollutants are preventable.

Body of Evidence

Environmental pollutants arise from many sources, and exposures may occur through many different routes. (See Table 1.4.) Many occur on the job, where workers are exposed to doses typically much higher than those encountered in the ambient environment. Although occupational exposures are a major source of ill health globally, this subject is outside the purview of this section, which focuses on chemicals in the ambient environment.

Some pollutants of particular concern are airborne substances—primarily suspended particulates, sulfur dioxide, nitrogen oxides, ozone, and carbon monoxide—emitted as byproducts of energy production, industry, and transportation (130). While most scientific attention and policy debate has focused on outdoor air pollutants, indoor air pollutants such as smoke and soot, arising from the burning of biomass fuels such as dung and wood, appear to pose an even greater risk to human health, because indoor exposures tend to be many times higher than those encountered outdoors. Hundreds of millions of people in the developing world are regularly exposed to potentially harmful indoor emissions, which are believed to contribute to chronic lung disease, cancer, and ARI.

Exposure to pesticides can occur directly, typically to agricultural workers and their families and those who live near farms where pesticides are heavily used. Exposures can also be indirect, when pesticides contaminate surface waters or groundwater or soil, or when pesticide residues on food or contaminated fish or wildlife are ingested. Some of the most problematic pesticides are organic compounds that are slow to degrade and thus persist in the environment for years, accumulating in animal and human tissues.

Some industrial chemicals, such as PCBs, also persist in the environment and have caused widespread environmental contamination. Exposure to industrial chemicals can result from intentional releases to either air or water, from accidents, or from the leaching of these substances from disposal sites into surrounding soil or water.

Heavy metals are used for a variety of agricultural and industrial purposes and are frequent contaminants in industrial wastes. Many are toxic: mercury, for instance, is a known neurotoxin; arsenic can cause skin and other cancers. One of the most important environmental pollutants is lead, which at even very low doses can cause significant neurological impairment and loss of intelligence. Major sources of lead in the environment include exhaust from vehicles using leaded gasoline, lead-based paints, and some types of water pipes.

Not surprisingly, much evidence of the harmful effects of industrial chemicals has come from the workplace, where exposures tend to be high and sustained relative to those in the ambient environment. For instance, studies of British textile workers alerted researchers to the link between asbestos and lung cancer (131). The reproductive toxicity of the pesticide DBCP (1, 2-dibromo-3-chloropropane) became startlingly clear in the late 1970s and early 1980s when male farm workers in the banana-growing region of Costa Rica were found to

Environmental Change and Human Health

be sterile. By the mid-1990s, some 1,500 male workers had been medically diagnosed with sterility from exposure to DBCP (132). While these examples illuminate the risks of high-level exposures, they do not indicate the extent of risk posed by lower levels of exposures that are typically encountered in the environment.

One difficulty in determining the exact magnitude of the potential health risk is that epidemiologic studies, which look at differences between exposed and nonexposed groups, generally show a statistical association between an environmental exposure and adverse effects. They do not attempt to demonstrate cause and effect. In many cases, studies cannot reveal links between an exposure and an adverse effect unless the particular risk is quite high or the effect is unusual (133), as was the case with vinyl chloride and angiosarcoma, a relatively rare form of liver cancer (134). Given these difficulties, some studies will find an association, others will refute it. Thus, proof of a causal relationship often takes years to amass—as with smoking and lung cancer—if it is ever established.

Calculating how much of a specific pollutant a person is exposed to can be daunting. For example, to assess air quality, a city might have only a few monitors dispersed throughout a wide geographic area. The direction of the wind on any given day will do much to determine who is exposed, as will whether that person spent most of the day indoors or out. In addition, air pollution monitors are usually installed on rooftops, so recorded pollutant levels do not describe the exposure of a commuter stuck in traffic, or, say, a small child on a playground. So, although it is widely agreed that ambient air pollution at levels normally encountered in many cities can damage health and even kill, the magnitude of the effect remains controversial. (Estimates range from 200,000 to 570,000 excess deaths per year (135)).

In the absence of definitive human data, investigators often must rely on animal studies and quantitative risk assessment models to estimate the toxicity of a particular substance. In some instances, health effects in wildlife have first alerted researchers to potential dangers of a class of environmental pollutants. For example, reproductive damages in seagulls and other wildlife presented some of the first clues about the adverse effects of DDT (136). More recently, reproductive anomalies in wildlife have sparked concern about the ability of some chemicals to cause ill effects by disrupting the body's normal hormonal system. Translating effects in wildlife to risks in humans, however, remains difficult. Even laboratory experiments in animals are less than definitive, because it is difficult to extrapolate from effects seen when high doses are given to animals to probable results from the low doses common to human exposure.

Despite widespread public concern over chemical safety, toxicity testing remains inadequate. For the vast majority of

---

Chemicals in the Environment

TABLE 1.4   Chemical Pollutants within the Human Environment that are Hazardous to Human Health

Chemicals found in food and water:
- lead (in food and drinking water, especially where there is a combination of lead water pipes and acidic water);
- aflatoxins and other natural food toxicants;
- nitrates in drinking water (and their conversion into nitrites in the body);
- trace pollutants in water supply, many from agrochemicals (for instance, various halogenated organic chemicals);
- aluminum (food and drinking water);
- arsenic and mercury.

Chemicals commonly found in the indoor environment (home/workplace):
- carbon monoxide (incomplete combustion of fossil fuels);
- lead (paint ingested by children);
- asbestos (usually from roofing insulation or air conditioning conduits);
- smoke from combustion of coal and wood (or other biomass fuel);
- tobacco smoke;
- potentially dangerous chemicals used without health and safety safeguards (by homeworkers and in occupational settings);
- formaldehyde (mostly from insulation; also some in wood preservatives and adhesives).

Chemicals found outdoors in urban areas in the air (ambient):
- lead (exhausts of motor vehicles using gasoline with lead additive, from external paint, some industrial emissions);
- sulphur dioxide, sulphates, and smoke/suspended particles (mainly from coal or heavy oil combustion by industries, power stations, and, in some cities, households);
- oxides of nitrogen (in most cities, mostly from motor vehicle emissions; also some industries);
- hydrocarbons (motor vehicles, petrol stations, some industries);
- ozone (secondary pollutant formed by reaction of nitrogen dioxide and hydrocarbons in sunlight);
- carbon monoxide (incomplete combustion of fossil fuels, mostly by motor vehicles);
- volatile organic compounds (VOCs) (a considerable range of such compounds are, or may be, hazardous).

Chemicals that may contaminate land sites:
- cadmium and mercury compounds and other heavy metal compounds (industrial wastes);
- Dioxins, PCBs, arsenic, organochlorine pesticides (industrial wastes).

Also in both indoor and outdoor settings:
- micropollutants;
- mixtures of each at trace level (with possible additive effects).

Reprinted from: David Satterthwaite *et al., The Environment for Children: Understanding and Acting on the Environmental Hazards that Threaten Children and Their Parents* (Earthscan Publications, Ltd., London, 1996), p. 41.

Box 1.9 Why the Increase in Asthma?

Over the past two decades, researchers have reported a startling rise in the prevalence of asthma among children and young adults. This trend persists today, mostly in affluent countries, leading some to call asthma a disease of the industrialized 20th Century (1). Indeed, asthma appears to be rare in developing countries, although some evidence suggests that the disease is emerging in urban centers in parts of Africa and Asia as well (2).

In many affluent countries where asthma is common today, its prevalence has climbed nearly 50 percent in just a 10-year span (3). Rates of hospitalization for asthma are also rising in these countries, a fact that suggests the disease is becoming more severe (4). Particularly disturbing is the rise in the number of deaths attributed to asthma. Asthma deaths among people 5 to 34 years of age increased more than 40 percent between the mid-1970s and mid-1980s in most countries studied (5).

Improved diagnosis and greater awareness of asthma may partly account for the rising number of cases (6). Similarly, changes in health insurance and medical practice may contribute to the rise in hospitalization rates for asthma. Even considering these factors, many researchers are convinced that the increase is real (7). This recognition has prompted a large-scale effort to find out what could be driving the increase. Although a definitive answer remains elusive, environmental factors have emerged as key.

A Hunt for Clues

Asthma is a complex disease whose development is influenced by both host susceptibility and environmental or lifestyle factors (8). Some people are genetically predisposed to develop asthma. Other people acquire asthma, often in early childhood, for reasons that are still unclear but seem to involve early and repeated exposure to a variety of factors in the environment, including allergens and viruses.

People with asthma are exquisitely sensitive to certain external triggers, typically allergens like pollen or cat dander but also viral infections, exercise, cold air, tobacco smoke, and air pollution. When exposed to one of these triggers, someone with a common allergy, such as hay fever, may develop a runny nose or sneezing. For an asthmatic, however, exposure triggers a cascade of events in which certain immune cells marshal other cells that then launch an inflammatory attack on the respiratory system, causing the airways to constrict and making breathing difficult.

Evidence that environmental factors play a major role in prevalence of asthma comes from a number of investigations. First, although genetics clearly influences the development of asthma, studies of twins suggest genetic tendencies might

account for 20 to 75 percent of asthma cases, leaving a substantial number unexplained (9)(10). Still other studies show that when people migrate to new areas, their risk of developing asthma often changes (11). Other clues can be discerned from looking at the variable distribution of asthma prevalence across the globe.

Asthma is generally more prevalent in urban areas, although South Australia is an important exception (12). Mortality rates from asthma are also higher in urban areas for some countries (13). In most countries, asthma is most pronounced among the higher socioeconomic classes (14). However, in the United States, poor and minority populations are disproportionately affected. In the United States, increases in asthma prevalence have been found among all groups of children and youths, but they are highest among poor, black, and Hispanic children (15)(16). Poverty and race also appear to be important risk factors in asthma mortality. In the United States in 1993, black children were four times more likely than white children to die from asthma (17). In New York City's East Harlem, the mortality rate is 10 times the national average (18).

Outdoor Air Pollution

Numerous studies have shown that episodes of air pollution can exacerbate existing asthma conditions—by either triggering or worsening an attack (19). Emergency room visits for asthma often increase after a bout of air pollution, as do hospitalizations. However, because air pollution is composed of a mix of pollutants that vary from location to location, it is difficult to tease apart which pollutants are to blame.

The urban pollutant with perhaps the worst record for provoking asthma or exacerbating its symptoms is ozone, a principal component of smog. Low levels of ozone trigger coughing, hampered and painful breathing, and inflammation of the airways in both healthy and asthmatic people (20). Ozone exposure also seems to render people more susceptible to other irritants, either pollutants or allergens such as dust mites (21)(22).

Evidence is conflicting regarding the links between sulfur dioxide and nitrogen oxide and asthma. Recent attention has turned to fine particulate pollution, or PM_{10}. Several studies have linked fine particulate pollution with increased asthma symptoms and emergency room visits (23). But opinion remains divided on whether air pollution is contributing to the increase in asthma prevalence. What confounds some researchers is that many developed countries are showing a rise in the prevalence of asthma, yet an overall decline in air pollution.

Overall, the body of evidence suggests that although air pollution may play a role, it alone is

not the driving force behind the increase in asthma prevalence and mortality. Asthma researcher David Bates of the University of British Columbia in Vancouver summarized the situation recently: "We have good reason to be suspicious of the contemporary role of air pollutants, but proof is something else" (24).

Indoor Air Pollution

Asthma in children and young adults is strongly associated with sensitization to allergens found in homes. Tobacco smoke, for one, is known to increase the risk of asthma. Children have about twice the risk of developing asthma if one or both parents are cigarette smokers (25). Beyond tobacco smoke, the chief culprits indoors appear to be microscopic dust mites that inhabit bedding, furniture, and carpets, and also cockroach parts and animal dander. Toxic cleaning agents and pesticides may also be involved, although their role is less clear (26).

Increasingly, attention is focused on bio-allergens such as dust mites and cockroaches. Dust mites have long been known to increase the risk of asthma. Indeed, high exposures to them in infancy seem to lead to early onset of asthma (27). In general, children who become allergic to foreign proteins—such as insect parts or animal dander in the home—have an increased risk of developing asthma, and continued exposure contributes to the disease. Increasing numbers of homes and buildings are now "air tight," which can lock in bio-allergens and also cigarette smoke and other pollutants.

A number of recent changes in the indoor environment—such as carpeting, upholstered furniture, mattresses, humidifiers, and central air conditioning or heating—make it easier for dust mites and molds, another potent allergen, to thrive. For example, one study in Denver, Colorado, found that although the city is located in a dry climate not conducive to dust mites, the air conditioning in homes nonetheless fostered significant dust mite levels (28).

In the United States, some of the strongest evidence to date implicates a well-known urban denizen, the cockroach. Indeed, early and continued exposure to cockroaches appears to shed light upon the disproportionate prevalence of asthma among poor, inner-city children, as studies suggest that the degree to which people are exposed to cockroaches correlates with their socioeconomic status (29).

Evidence from a 1997 study suggests that cockroaches play an even larger role than previously believed (30). This large study of eight urban areas in the United States found that asthma was most pronounced among children

Box 1.9 continued

who are allergic to cockroach allergens and are exposed to a high level of that allergen in bedroom dust. Specifically, those who were allergic to cockroaches and heavily exposed to them at home were 3.4 times more likely to be hospitalized than other poor, asthmatic youth. They also lost more sleep and school days because of asthma problems. Although roughly the same proportion of the youth tested as allergic to both cockroaches and dust mites (roughly 35 percent) and 23 percent were allergic to cat dander, cockroach allergen was far more prevalent in their bedrooms (31).

Exposure to allergens alone is not sufficient to account for increased severity of asthma among poor and minority populations. Social factors are clearly at play, chief among them limited access to appropriate medical care. One study found fewer medications were prescribed to control asthma in adolescents from low-income homes compared to their peers in more affluent homes (32).

Changing Lifestyles

What is more, many people in developed countries are spending an increasing amount of time indoors. In many affluent countries, indoor sources of entertainment, such as computer games, television shows, and videos, are rapidly replacing outdoor playgrounds. This scenario has led several asthma experts to postulate that the rise of the "indoor amusement culture," perhaps coupled with a lack of exercise, may contribute to the increase in asthma seen in developed countries (33).

Numerous changes related to medical practice in the more developed nations, from the availability of asthma medicines to the changing patterns of childhood infections, may also play a role. Overuse of bronchodilator inhalers has been implicated in the rise in asthma mortality in several countries (34). However, as elevated mortality rates among poor populations suggest, undermedication is likely to be a greater problem (35).

Other researchers hypothesize that some of the benefits of modern medicine may in fact be reducing immunologic protection, rendering some people more susceptible to asthma (36). Although viral infections are known to exacerbate asthma, some studies suggest that having certain infections during early childhood can protect a child from later developing the disease, perhaps by stimulating an immune response that suppresses later allergic reactions (37)(38). Similarly, the rise in asthma in developed nations might also be due, in part, to an increase in the number of surviving premature babies, as these infants are more prone to developing asthma (39).

If any consensus exists in the rapidly changing field of asthma research, it is that no single factor is sufficient to explain current trends in asthma. More likely, suggest researchers such as Woolcock and Peat, "a number of lifestyle changes may have combined to cause the disease to be expressed in children who, in previous times, were immunologically protected from developing asthma—or were not exposed to high allergen levels"(40). Sorting out the role of environmental and lifestyle factors will be key in devising strategies to prevent this debilitating disease.

References and Notes

1. Thomas A.E. Platts-Mills and Melody C. Carter, "Asthma and Indoor Exposure to Allergens," *The New England Journal of Medicine*, Vol. 336, No. 19 (May 8, 1997), p. 1384.
2. Ann J. Woolcock and Jennifer K. Peat, "Evidence for the Increase in Asthma Worldwide," in *The Rising Trends in Asthma*, Ciba Foundation Symposium 206 (John Wiley & Sons, Chichester, U.K., 1997), pp. 123–125.
3. Kevin Weiss, Peter Gergen, and Diane Wagener, "Breathing Better or Wheezing Worse? The Changing Epidemiology of Asthma Morbidity and Mortality," *Annual Review of Public Health*, Vol. 14 (1993), pp. 493–494.
4. Richard Beasley, Neil Pearce, and Julian Crane, "International Trends in Asthma Mortality," in *The Rising Trends in Asthma*, Ciba Foundation Symposium 206 (John Wiley & Sons, Chichester, U.K., 1997), p. 147.
5. M.R. Sears, "Worldwide Trends in Asthma Mortality," *Bulletin of the International Union of Tubercule Lung Disease*, Vol. 66 (1991), p. 80.
6. *Op. cit.* 3, pp. 500–501.
7. *Op. cit.* 4, pp. 142–143.
8. Eugene R. Bleecker, Dirkje S. Postma, and Deborah A. Meyers, "Genetic Susceptibility to Asthma in a Changing Environment," in *The Rising Trends in Asthma*, Ciba Foundation Symposium 206 (John Wiley & Sons, Chichester, U.K., 1997), p. 91.
9. M.L. Edfors-Lubs, "Allergy in 7,000 Twin Pairs," *Acta Allergologica*, Vol. 26 (1971), pp. 249–285.
10. Peter Gergen, National Institute of Allergy and Infectious Diseases, national Institutes of Health, Rockville, Maryland, January 14, 1998 (personal communication).
11. C.H. van Niererk *et al.*, "Prevalence of Asthma: A Community Study of Urban and Rural Xhosa," *Clinical Allergy*, Vol. 9 (1979), pp. 319–24, cited in Anthony Newman-Taylor, "Environmental Determinants of Asthma," *Lancet*, Vol. 345 (February 4, 1995), p. 296.
12. Kevin B. Weiss, Peter J. Gergen, and Ellen F. Crain, "Inner-City Asthma: The Epidemiology of an Emerging U.S. Public Health Concern," *Chest*, Vol. 101, No. 6, Supplement (June 1992), p. 362S.
13. Kevin B. Weiss and Diane K. Wagener, "Changing Patterns of Asthma Mortality: Identifying Target Populations at High Risk," *Journal of the American Medical Association*, Vol. 264, No. 13 (October 3, 1990), p. 1687.
14. *Op. cit.* 2, pp. 122–131.
15. Elaine Friebele, "The Attack of Asthma," *Environmental Health Perspectives*, Vol. 104, No. 1 (January 1996), p. 23.
16. Michael Weitzman *et al.* "Recent Trends in Prevalence and Severity of Childhood Asthma," *Journal of the American Medical Association*, Vol. 268, No. 19 (1992), p. 2673.
17. Centers for Disease Control, "Asthma Mortality and Hospitalization Among Children and Young Adults—United States, 1980–1993," *Morbidity and Mortality Weekly Report*, Vol. 45, No. 17 (May 3, 1996), p. 351.
18. *Op. cit.* 12, p. 362S.
19. Hillel S. Koren and Mark J. Utell, "Asthma and the Environment," *Environmental Health Perspectives*, Vol. 105, No. 5 (May 1997), p. 534.
20. Hillel S. Koren, "Associations between Criteria Air Pollutants and Asthma," *Environmental Health Perspectives*, Vol. 103, Supplement 6 (1995), p. 238.
21. David V. Bates, "Observations on Asthma," *Environmental Health Perspectives*, Vol. 103, Supplement 6 (1995), p. 245.
22. Rebecca Bascom, "Environmental Factors and Respiratory Hypersensitivity: The Americas," *Toxicology Letters*, Vol. 86 (1996), pp. 122–124.
23. David V. Bates, "The Effects of Air Pollution on Children," *Environmental Health Perspectives*, Vol. 103, Supplement 6 (1995), p. 50.
24. *Op. cit.* 21, p. 246.
25. National Institutes of Health: Heart, Lung, and Blood Institute (NHLBI), *Global Initiative for Asthma: Global Strategy for Asthma Management and Prevention* (NHLBI/World Health Organization (WHO) Workshop Report, 1995), p. 65.
26. *Op. cit.* 3, pp. 503–504.
27. *Op. cit.* 3, p. 504.
28. *Op. cit.* 22, p. 119.
29. Alkis Togias *et al.*, "Evaluating the Factors that Relate to Asthma Severity in Adolescents," *International Archives of Allergy and Clinical Immunology*, Vol. 113 (1997), pp. 87–95.
30. Curt Suplee, "Most Serious Youth Asthma Cases Linked to Roaches, Study Finds," *The Washington Post* (May 8, 1997), p. A12.
31. David L. Rosenreich *et al.*, "The Role of Cockroach Allergy and Exposure to Cockroach Allergen in Causing Morbidity Among Inner-City Children With Asthma," *The New England Journal of Medicine*, Vol. 336, No. 19 (1997), pp. 1358–1359.
32. *Op. cit.* 29, pp. 87–95.
33. Thomas A.E. Platts-Mills and Judith Woodfolk, "Rise in Asthma Cases," *Science*, Vol. 278 (November 1997), p. 1001.
34. Malcolm Sears and D. Robin Taylor, "The β2-agonist Controversy: Observations, Explanations, and Relationship to Asthma Epidemiology," *Drug Safety*, Vol. 11, No. 4 (1994), pp. 264–265.
35. *Op. cit.* 10.
36. *Op. cit.* 2, p. 130.
37. Ttaro Shirakawa *et al.*, "The Inverse Association between Tuberculin Responses and Atopic Disorder," *Science*, Vol. 275, No. 3 (1997), p. 77.
38. Erika von Mutius *et al.*, "Prevalence of Asthma and Atopy in Two Areas of West and East Germany," *American Journal of Respiratory and Critical Care Medicine*, Vol. 149 (1994), p. 363.
39. Peter Gergen and Kevin Weiss, "The Increasing Problem of Asthma in the United States," *American Review of Respiratory Disease*, Vol. 146 (1992), p. 824.
40. *Op. cit.* 2, p. 122.

chemicals in widespread use, no toxicity testing results are available in the public record (137)(138). Most of the testing for chronic effects that has occurred has focused on cancer. To date, about 74 chemicals or mixtures have been found to cause cancer in humans (139). Hundreds of others, however, cause cancer or mutations in cells or in animals, which raises concerns about their effects in humans.

Of the other potential effects of chemical hazards, such as infertility, birth defects, immune system impairment, or brain damage, even less is known. In the United States, for instance, the chief agency for chemical evaluation spent nearly US$29 million on testing chemicals for cancer in 1991, but just about $6 million for both genetic and reproductive effects (140). Testing for other health concerns, such as immune system effects or endocrine disruption, lags even further behind. Again, the United States provides an apt example: according to a recent study, 86 percent of chemicals in widespread use have not been tested for immunotoxicity, and 67 percent have not been tested for neurotoxicity (141). This focus on cancer means that other important and preventable risks may be overlooked. Standard methods of toxicity testing, for instance, would not have identified lead as a significant hazard—even though the U.S. Centers for Disease Control and Prevention has called lead poisoning the single, most significant preventable disease associated with environmental and occupational exposures (142).

More precise techniques to evaluate chemical safety are under development, including mechanistic studies to illuminate exactly what changes a chemical exerts within a cell. Such methods, however, tend to be time-consuming and expensive and thus are not widely applicable in large-scale studies (143).

Meanwhile, policymakers must rely on the best available data—often from animal studies and risk assessments—in setting policies to protect the public from suspected risks. Because chemical products are so widely used and evidence suggests they may damage the environment and human health, governments face increasing pressure to adopt the "precautionary principle." This principle affirms that when harm is strongly suspected, it is best to take action to prevent exposure, even if absolute proof of harm is missing.

Such prudent policies are by no means the norm. As described in more detail in Chapter 2, many chemicals banned in developed countries are still in widespread use throughout the developing world, despite their known hazards, because they are cheap and effective. Among them is a class of particularly hazardous products known as persistent organic pollutants, or POPs. Similarly, roughly two decades after the United States began to phase out the use of lead in gasoline because of its well-known health effects, it remains ubiquitous throughout much of Asia and Latin America.

Efforts to minimize pollutants' harmful impacts are complicated by the increasing realization that they can harm human health not just through direct toxicological routes but also indirectly, through large-scale ecological disruptions. This realization hit home with the unexpected discovery in 1985 of a "hole" in the stratospheric ozone layer, caused by human activity leading to chlorofluorocarbon emissions (144). The health impacts of this thinning ozone layer, which protects the Earth from harmful ultraviolet radiation, range from skin cancer to cataracts to immune system depression to disruption of the food chain. None of these results was anticipated a mere 15 years ago. Similarly, the combustion of fossil fuels not only causes urban air pollution but also disrupts atmospheric chemistry and may lead to global warming. Plausible health impacts include increased deaths from excessive heat episodes and violent storms, and a greater toll from malaria and other vector-borne diseases in developing countries.

The Environmental Contribution

So, all told, how much do these environmental hazards contribute to the global burden of ill health? The answer is impossible to pin down with any precision because of the complex etiology of most diseases. Asthma is a case in point. Although the disease is on the upswing and environmental factors appear to be involved, their exact contribution is difficult to discern. (See Box 1.9.) Clearly, however, the risk posed by environmental factors varies enormously depending upon where one lives. A major portion of death and disease in developing countries can be directly tied to poor environmental conditions, especially at the household or local level. Indeed, the two major sources of death and disability in the developing world—ARI and diarrhea—have their origins in poverty and degraded household environments. Together, these two diseases account for up to 7 million deaths per year (145). The Global Burden of Disease study calculates that they contribute more than 21 percent to the burden of disease in developing countries. Similarly, malaria accounts for 2.6 percent, and the tropical disease cluster, which includes trypanosomiasis, Chagas disease, schistosomiasis, leishmaniasis, filariasis, and onchocerciasis, accounts for 0.87 percent (146). Improving the household environment—providing improved housing, clean fuels, improved access to water and sanitation, and better waste removal—would do much to reduce the burden of these diseases. But because these diseases are influenced by multiple factors, including nutrition, hygiene, and education, it would be simplistic to think environmental interventions could eliminate them entirely. (See Chapter 3.)

The environmental contribution to health risks is less clear in the developed countries, where many of the most obvious and immediate threats, such as fecal contamination or lack of water, have been virtually eliminated, and the burden of infec-

Box 1.10 Smoking-Related Deaths

The current death toll attributable to tobacco-related illnesses is estimated at one in eight in the developing world, one in four in developed countries, and one in six for the world as a whole. In 1993 alone, tobacco use was responsible for 3 million deaths (1). In the mid-1990s, about 25 percent of all male deaths in developed countries were due to smoking (2). In the United States and other industrialized countries where smoking has been prevalent for decades, lung cancer and ischemic heart disease are the leading causes of tobacco-related deaths. The total number of deaths caused by tobacco in these nations was more than 1.8 million in 1990 and is expected to reach 20 million during the last decade of this century (3). However, the rate of increase in the epidemic of smoking-caused mortality is slowing somewhat among men, but continues to increase rapidly among women in the industrialized world (4).

In most of the developing world, smoking has only more recently become a widespread habit, but medical researchers expect that within the next 25 to 30 years the mortality pattern associated with smoking will approximate that of the industrialized countries. This trend has already become apparent in countries such as China, where unpublished evidence in a nationwide study suggests that tobacco is already causing half a million deaths annually, of which about one half are due to chronic lung disease. The effects of the smoking epidemic on mortality rates in China will certainly worsen substantially during the next century, given the fact that between 1978 and 1992, consumption of manufactured cigarettes in that country more than tripled, from

500 billion to 1,700 billion (about 30 percent of the world total) (5).

According to the World Health Organization (WHO), there are about 1.1 billion smokers worldwide, or about one third of the population 15 years and older. The vast majority—800 million smokers—are in developing countries; 700 million of these smokers are men. In the developed countries, an estimated 42 percent of men and 24 percent of women smoke; corresponding figures for the developing world are about 48 percent of men and 7 percent of women (6). In China, however, where most of the world's smokers now reside, 63 percent of men and 3.8 percent of women are current smokers (7).

The number of deaths annually attributable to tobacco is expected to increase from 3 million in 1993 to 8.4 million in 2020, of which 6 million are projected to occur in the developing world (8)(9). In fact, within 25 years, tobacco will surpass infectious diseases to become the leading threat to human health worldwide (10). Currently, the global cost of tobacco-related illnesses is nearly $200 billion a year in direct health-care expenses and lost productivity related to morbidity and premature mortality. One third of this loss occurs in the developing world (11).

The Food and Agricultural Organization of the United Nations (FAO) estimates that tobacco consumption in developing nations has increased at a rate of 2.1 percent annually during 1985–90 and is increasing at a rate of 1.9 percent during 1995–2000 (12). Various factors may explain this increase, including larger than ever amounts of disposable income coupled with widespread advertising and promotion of tobacco products, and insufficient legislation regarding product

warning labels and smoke-free workplaces and public areas. This scenario reflects a lack of awareness of the health risks that tobacco presents, and this ignorance may relate to the approximate 25- to 30-year lag time between the onset of persistent tobacco use and the actual deaths attributable to smoking. Thus, policymakers and health officials in the developing world may not yet focus on tobacco as a source of preventable mortality and morbidity.

References and Notes

1. Howard Barnum, "The Economic Burden of the Global Trade in Tobacco," *Tobacco Control* , Vol. 3 (1994), p. 359.
2. World Health Organization (WHO), *Tobacco Alert 1996* (WHO, Geneva, 1996), pp. 16–19.
3. Richard Peto, *et al.,* "Mortality from Smoking Worldwide," *British Medical Bulletin* , Vol. 52, No. 1 (1996), p. 19.
4. *Op. cit.* 2.
5. *Op. cit.* 3, p. 20.
6. *Op. cit.* 2, p. 4.
7. Chinese Academy of Preventive Medicine, "Prevalence of Smoking and Related Behavior," in *Smoking and Health in China: 1996 National Prevalence Survey of Smoking Patterns* (China Science and Technology Press, Beijing, 1997), p. 22.
8. *Op. cit* . 1, p. 359.
9. Christopher Murray and Alan Lopez, "Evidence-Based Health Policy—Lessons from the Global Burden of Disease Study," *Science,* Vol. 274 (November 1, 1996), p. 742.
10. Christopher Murray and Alan Lopez, "Evidence-Based Health Policy—Lessons from the Global Burden of Disease Study," *Science,* Vol. 274 (November 1, 1996), p. 742.
11. *Op. cit* . 1, pp. 359–360.
12. *Op. cit.* 1, p. 360.

tious diseases is relatively small. (AIDS and TB are important exceptions.) Environmental factors clearly play a role in chronic conditions such as cancer and heart disease, which predominate in the wealthier countries. The question is: how large a role?

The debate over cancer illuminates some of these difficulties. Cancers of all types claimed some 6 million lives in 1996 including 3.8 million in developing countries (147). Moreover, cancer's links to the environment are unequivocal, as increasing evidence about the process of carcinogenesis has made clear. Cancer arises through a multistep process of accumulated damage to genes in a single cell. Several distinct mutations (genetic alterations) are required—some to start the process, some to release the normal controls on cell growth. In a small number of cases, perhaps 5 percent of breast cancers, for instance, one or more mutations may be inherited. But additional mutations are still required before cancer ensues, and

many of these can be triggered by external agents. The list of known carcinogens is long and includes radiation, natural or synthetic chemicals, tobacco smoke, some viruses, agents in the diet, and sunlight. Whether any agent contributes to cancer depends not just on the timing of the exposure but also on the effectiveness of the body's defenses.

Based on this same understanding, estimates of the environmental contribution to cancer vary widely. In their classic 1981 study, epidemiologists Richard Doll and Richard Peto estimated that 1 to 5 percent of cancers derive from environmental pollutants in air, water, and food. They estimated that behavioral factors such as tobacco use and unhealthy diets play a much larger role, accounting for 30 and 35 percent, respectively (148). (See Box 1.10.) Similarly, a 1996 study estimated that just 2 percent of all cancers arise from exposure to air pollution (149). In contrast, WHO recently estimated the

Disease Burden Associated with Poor Household Environments

TABLE 1.5   Estimated Burden of Disease from Poor Household Environments in Demographically Developing Countries, 1990, and Potential Reduction through Improved Household Services

PRINCIPAL DISEASES RELATED TO POOR HOUSEHOLD ENVIRONMENTS[a]	RELEVANT ENVIRONMENTAL PROBLEM	BURDEN FROM THESE DISEASES IN DEVELOPING COUNTRIES (millions of DALYS per year)[b]	REDUCTION ACHIEVABLE THROUGH FEASIBLE INTERVENTIONS (percent)[c]	BURDEN AVERTED BY FEASIBLE INTERVENTIONS (millions of DALYs per year)	BURDEN AVERTED PER 1,000 POPULATION (DALYs per year)
Tuberculosis	Crowding	46	10	5	1.2
Diarrhea[d]	Sanitation, water supply, hygiene	99	40	40	9.7
Trachoma	Water supply, hygiene	3	30	1	0.3
Tropical cluster[e]	Sanitation, garbage disposal, vector breeding around the home	8	30	2	0.5
Intestinal worms	Sanitation, water supply, hygiene	18	40	7	1.7
Respiratory infections	Indoor air pollution, crowding	119	15	18	4.4
Chronic respiratory diseases	Indoor air pollution	41	15	6	1.5
Respiratory tract cancers	Indoor air pollution	4	10[f]	*	0.1
All the above		**338**	**—**	**79**	**19.4**

Source: The World Bank, *World Development Report 1993: Investing in Health, World Development Indicators* (Oxford University Press, Oxford, U.K., 1993), p. 90.

Notes: * Less than 1. The demographically developing group consists of the demographic regions of Sub-Saharan Africa, India, China, Other Asia islands, Latin America and the Caribbean, and the Middle Eastern crescent. a. The diseases listed are those for which there is substantial evidence of a relationship with the household environment. Examples of excluded conditions are violence related to crowding (because of lack of evidence) and guinea worm infection related to poor water supply. b. DALYs are disability-adjusted life years. c. Estimates derived from the product of the efficacy of the interventions and the proportion of the burden of disease that occurs among the exposed. The efficacy estimates assume the implementation of improvements in sanitation, water supply, hygiene, drainage, garbage disposal, indoor air pollution, and crowding of the kind being made in poor communities in developing countries. d. Includes diarrhea, dysentery, cholera, and typhoid. e. Diseases within the tropical cluster most affected by the domestic environment are schistosomiasis, South American trypanosomiasis, and Bancroftian filariasis. f. Based on very inadequate data on efficacy.

---

contribution of environment—including the workplace—to cancer at 25 percent (150).

ATTRIBUTABLE RISK

Investigators are experimenting with approaches to better assess the environment's contribution to human death and disease. Some estimates are reported here, with the caveat that they are all only crude approximations. Even so, these estimates can provide useful guides in designing policies to improve public health (151).

One approach is to estimate the attributable risk of certain factors in disease. The 1996 Global Burden of Disease study tried to tease apart the contribution of 10 different risk factors, including some key environmental hazards, by determining what proportion of the disease burden would not have occurred in the absence of specified exposures. In the interest of scientific caution, the study authors have interpreted their analysis conservatively, so these estimates are more likely to be underestimates than overestimates(152).

● At the top of the list is malnutrition, which, estimates reveal, is responsible for 11.7 percent of total deaths and 15.9 percent of total DALYs. In sub-Saharan Africa, however, it accounts for a staggering 33 percent of the global burden of disease; in India, 22 percent (153). As described earlier, malnutrition is not an environmental problem *per se* but interacts strongly with environmental factors to cause disease.

● The combination of poor water supply, sanitation, and personal and domestic hygiene is the next biggest risk factor, accounting for 5.3 percent of total deaths and 6.8 percent of

total DALYs. Like malnutrition, these factors in combination contribute to significantly more of the burden in the poorer regions; 10 percent in sub-Saharan Africa, 9.5 percent in India, and 8.8 percent in the Middle East (154).

● Outdoor air pollution accounts for 1.1 percent of total deaths and 0.5 percent of total DALYs, according to GBD estimates. In the developed regions, these numbers rise to 2.5 percent of deaths and 1.5 percent of DALYS, and in the former socialist economies, this factor climbs to 5.5 percent of all deaths and 3.1 percent of DALYs (155).

Using a different approach, the World Bank in 1993 calculated the total burden of disease that could be attributed to the household environment. The Bank defined household environmental problems to include crowding, lack of sanitation and garbage disposal, indoor air pollution, and vector-breeding grounds (156). (See Table 1.5.) Their conclusion: 30 percent, 20 percent of which could be averted by modest improvements in the household environment (157).

Most recently, a 1997 study by WHO, *Health and Environment in Sustainable Development,* estimated the proportion of major disease categories that could be attributed to environmental factors. (The WHO study defines the environmental contribution as the specific fraction of disease occurrence that could be prevented through "feasible environmental interventions" (158).) WHO estimated that although virtually all cases have an environmental cause, 90 percent of diarrheal diseases could be averted through feasible environmental interventions (159). The same study attributes the likely environmental contribution to malaria also at 90 percent, to ARI

*E*nvironmental Change and Human Health

at 60 percent, and to cancer at 25 percent. All told, WHO estimates that environmental factors—which in their definition includes occupational exposures—account for 23 percent of the global burden of disease.

Implications for Prevention

Whatever the exact contribution of environmental factors to disease, reducing environmental threats will clearly improve human health and well-being. In taking these actions, however, policymakers must make decisions armed with only imperfect information. The speed and magnitude of environmental changes are great, dollars are few, and development will not stop until more research takes place. Poverty and income disparity continue to plague many countries and millions of people. Needed development, however, may bring not only increased incomes but also unintended negative health consequences. Choosing the safest path through the jungle of choices is not obvious nor easy.

Chapter 2 traces in detail how agricultural intensification, industrialization, and rising energy use may create conditions that increase both acute and chronic health problems. Examples illustrate how poor development choices can exacerbate health problems, while development policies designed with health impacts in mind can lead to positive outcomes.

Chapter 3 explores environmental interventions that can prevent exposure to disease-causing agents in the first place, whether they are feces, mosquitoes, or particulates in the air. Preventing illness reduces suffering, improves economic outlooks, and can save enormous costs for health care. Such an approach encompasses a range of interventions, from simple to complex. Strategies for preventing infectious diseases, for instance, vary from providing basic hygiene education and bed nets to supplying clean water and sanitation. Efforts to reduce the toll of chronic disease related to air pollution range from distributing improved stoves to adopting better national energy choices. Phasing lead out of gasoline could prevent brain damage, improving the quality of life for many thousands of individuals and boosting societal productivity.

Preventive actions focused on environmental factors are not a remedy for global health problems, nor can they substitute for research on and treatment of disease. But because they eliminate harmful exposures rather than leave society to deal with the consequences, they are a vital component of any realistic strategy for achieving development that improves the quality of life.

Chapter 2

Changing Environments, Changing Health

Mark Edwards/Still Pictures

Chapter 1 describes in detail the environment's role as an important determinant of human health. Given this role, changes in the environment will influence health in the future, for better or for worse. The three trends discussed in this chapter—the intensification of agriculture, industrialization, and rising energy use—stand out in terms of their profound impact on the physical environment and their enormous potential to influence human health. While each trend has the potential to bring about dramatic health improvements, each also shares the potential to degrade the physical environment and increase human exposure to environmental threats through pollutant emissions and resource depletion.

Predicting the global environmental changes that will occur because of human-directed activities in the future—and how these changes might affect human health—is difficult at best. Even the most sophisticated models describing future interactions among environmental, economic, technical, and social developments are simplistic and often misleading (1). In addition, these three trends are interdependent (2). Looking forward is necessary, however, because doing so enables one to anticipate where future health problems might arise. Future energy demand in China and India provides an apt example.

By the year 2015, commercial energy use in these two countries alone is expected to more than double as the result of population growth, economic growth, and consumer demand for modern products, although per capita energy consumption will remain well below that of developed nations (3). The magnitude of air pollutants and greenhouse gases emitted by these countries will depend largely on how energy demand is met, with attendant consequences for human and indeed for planetary health. Foresight can help development experts identify preventive steps that could improve human health as well as protect the environment; some of these interventions are identified in Chapter 3.

To understand these three trends, one must first understand the context in which they are occurring. All three trends discussed in this chapter are influenced by the following driving forces: population growth and urbanization, economic growth and consumption, and the persistence of poverty and economic inequalities (4).

Population growth is a fundamental force underlying all others. On a positive note, recent estimates suggest that population growth rates are slowing faster than demographers had projected. The number of people added to the world's population each year is thought to have dropped from a peak of 87 million in the late 1980s to 81 million in the first half of the

FIGURE 2.1 Gross World Product, 1970–95

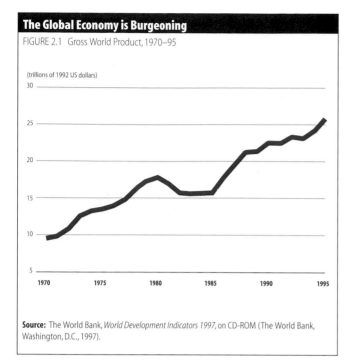

(trillions of 1992 US dollars)

Source: The World Bank, *World Development Indicators 1997,* on CD-ROM (The World Bank, Washington, D.C., 1997).

1990s; demographers project that the world's population in 2050 will reach about 9.4 billion people (5).

The global economy is burgeoning. In the past three decades, global GDP has expanded from roughly US$9.4 trillion to more than US$25 trillion. (See Figure 2.1.) Average per capita incomes have more than tripled (6). Although the developed countries account for the lion's share of this wealth, economic growth in developing countries has nonetheless been enormous, with per capita incomes growing nearly 3.5 percent per year during this period (7). This growth is expected to continue well into the middle of the next century.

Despite Economic Growth, Poverty Remains Pervasive

FIGURE 2.2 Number of Persons Living on Less Than One Dollar Per Day, 1987–93

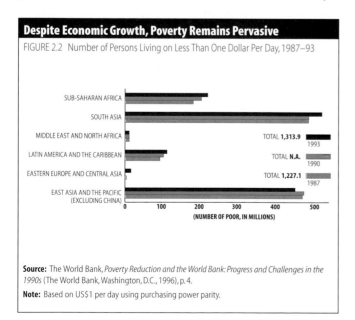

Source: The World Bank, *Poverty Reduction and the World Bank: Progress and Challenges in the 1990s* (The World Bank, Washington, D.C., 1996), p. 4.

Note: Based on US$1 per day using purchasing power parity.

The liberalization of both trade and investment across borders has helped fuel this economic growth (8). Global trade rose an estimated 45 percent in nominal terms between 1990 and 1995, from US$4,345 billion to US$6,255 billion (9). Liberalization has also greatly increased the flow of private capital into developing countries. In 1995 alone, the flow of net private capital into low-income and middle-income countries totaled about US$180 billion, roughly 4 times more than in 1990 (10). Official flows amounted to just US$64 billion in 1995. The nature of private capital flows is also changing, moving away from investments in emerging stock markets and toward direct investments in projects such as factories, power plants, and roads (11). Between 1988 and 1995, multinational corporations invested nearly US$422 billion in new factories, supplies, and equipment in developing countries (12).

Such economic growth creates resources and opportunities for improving the quality of living conditions, which, of course, is essential to good health (13). Indeed, global health conditions have improved more in the past half century than in all of previous history (14), demonstrated through rising life expectancy and declining child mortality rates (15). Yet, this generally positive picture is still colored by regional differences and growing disparities between rich and poor. In some developing countries, continued population growth and poverty have impeded economic and social progress. The most rapid population growth rates are concentrated in the poorest regions. Africa continues to have the highest population growth rate (2.7 percent), well above the average rate (1.8 percent) for developing countries as a whole (16).

As Chapter 1 describes in detail, poverty and inequity are two critical determinants of human health. Despite economic progress, it appears that the health problems linked with economic stagnation, poverty, and environmental degradation are likely to continue well into the future. Global economic growth has failed to alleviate poverty for a large share of the world's people. Despite an overall rising global economy, the absolute scale of poverty continues to grow. Large parts of the developing world have been bypassed by the past three decades of economic growth. Three fourths of the least developed countries, home to more than 400 million people, suffered negative economic growth during the 1980s and early 1990s (17).

A recent analysis by the World Bank found that, although the percentage of poor decreased slightly between 1987 and 1993, approximately 1.3 billion people in the developing world still subsisted on less than US$1 a day in 1993. Indeed, in each of the world regions except East Asia, the absolute number of poor increased (18). (See Figure 2.2.) Poverty continues to be concentrated in rural areas. Some 30 million people in developing countries are landless, and an additional 138

Environmental Change and Human Health

Urban Populations Could Double By 2030

FIGURE 2.3 Urban Population Growth by Region, 1950–2030

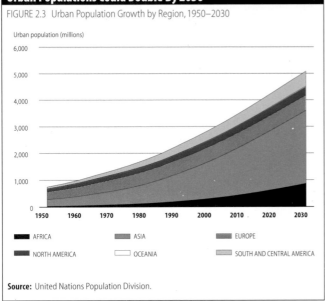

Source: United Nations Population Division.

million are near-landless; these numbers appear to be growing, especially in South Asia (19).

Many experts believe that urban poverty will soon overtake rural poverty in significance. By the year 2025, 5 billion people are expected to live in urban areas, 4 billion of them in cities in the developing world. The highest rates of urban growth are in Africa and Southeast Asia. (See Figure 2.3.) In general, urbanization brings improvements in human health because of improved access to education and health services in cities (20). In urban areas of Indonesia, for instance, the mortality rate of children younger than age 5 is 84 per 1,000 live births, as compared with 116 in rural areas (21).

But statistical averages hide the health impacts associated with poverty in urban slums or squatter shantytowns where growing proportions—up to one half in some cases—of urban populations live. Estimates suggest that, depending on the definition used, between 25 and 50 percent of the world's urban population now live in extreme poverty (22)(23). While the exact definitions of urban poverty vary, inadequate housing—lacking water, sanitation, or garbage collection—is a primary characteristic or urban poverty (24). The links between urban poverty and health are illustrated by the resurgence of tuberculosis among the poor in cities of the developed world as well. (See Box 2.1.)

In addition, the gap between rich and poor is widening, both within and among countries (25). In 1960, the richest 20 percent of the world's population controlled 70 percent of global income. By 1993, they controlled 85 percent, and the share of the poorest 20 percent had decreased from 2.3 to 1.4 percent. These disparities are likely to increase for the next half century—even if real economic growth rates in most developing regions significantly outpace those in the developed

regions (26). Within many countries, income is also distributed inequitably. Table 2.1 shows how the poor compare in income with the national average income of several countries (27). The differences are striking: in Brazil, the poor earn only one tenth as much as the average person.

As poverty continues to degrade health in much of the world, serious concerns have arisen over the long-term viability of consumption patterns in the developed world, which are now appearing in the rapidly industrializing countries. Paralleling growth of the world economy, resource and material consumption has accelerated at a rate unprecedented in human history. Over the past 45 years, the richest one fifth of the world's population has doubled its per capita consumption of energy, meat, timber, steel, and copper, and quadrupled its rate of car ownership. By contrast, the per capita consumption of the poorest one fifth has barely increased (28). One byproduct of this increased consumption is that developed countries account for about 70 percent of carbon dioxide (CO_2) emissions (29) with less than 20 percent of global population.

New technologies can help to increase the efficiency of resources, delivering equivalent or improved services while substantially reducing environmental and health burdens (30). This was the case in the 1970s and 1980s, when energy intensity (the energy required per unit of economic output) fell by about 2 percent per year. It has since leveled off (31). However, even with conservation efforts and more efficient technologies, some believe that if long-term environmental protection is to be achieved, consumption patterns themselves will need to change.

The Gap Between Rich and Poor Is Widening

TABLE 2.1 Per Capita Income of the Poorest 20 Percent, 1993 [a]

COUNTRY	AVERAGE PER CAPITA INCOME	PER CAPITA INCOME OF THE POOREST 20 PERCENT
United States	24,240	5,814
Japan	20,850	9,070
The Netherlands	17,330	7,105
United Kingdom	17,210	3,958
Republic of Korea	9,630	3,563
Chile	8,400	1,386
Hungary	6,050	3,297
Brazil	5,370	564
Guatemala	3,350	352
Indonesia	3,150	1,370
Nigeria	1,400	357
India	1,220	537
Bangladesh	1,290	613
Nepal	1,020	464
Guinea-Bissau	840	88
Tanzania	580	70

Source: United Nations Development Programme (UNDP), *Human Development Report 1996* (UNDP, New York, 1996), p. 13.

Note: a. Values are in 1993 International dollars using purchasing power parity.

Against this backdrop, this chapter explores the health consequences of the intensification of agriculture, industrialization, and rising energy use, paying particular attention to their effects on the poor in developing countries. The chapter examines the ways in which all three of these trends can increase exposure to hazards in the environment—to both biological and chemical agents. Strategies for preventing some of these harmful exposures are explored in Chapter 3.

Box 2.1 Tuberculosis and Urban Inequality

In the early 1600s, the development of cities and the spread of poverty in feudal Europe produced the necessary environmental changes to set off the first tuberculosis (TB) epidemic in humans. Dubbed "the Great White Plague," TB ran rampant in the crowded, unsanitary slums of early industrial cities (1). At its apex in the 17th and 18th Centuries, tuberculosis took the lives of one in five adults (2).

Contrary to the belief that tuberculosis is a disease of the past, nearly 3 million people died of TB in 1995 (3). Although the disease appears to have leveled off in 1996 as the result of concerted government action, and a control program launched by the World Health Organization (WHO), the TB epidemic is expected to continue to pose a serious threat to human health, especially in developing countries. Global implementation of WHO's strategy could reduce these numbers dramatically, but without interventions, as many as 90 million people could contract TB in the next 10 years (4).

The global emergence of HIV/AIDS has been an important factor driving the prevalence of TB, especially in Africa and Asia. The HIV virus damages the immune system and accelerates the speed at which tuberculosis progresses from a harmless infection to a life-threatening condition. About one third of the estimated 1 million AIDS-related deaths in 1995 were the result of a secondary infection with TB (5).

Increasing poverty and homelessness in cities also seems to be linked with the reemergence of TB (6). Associations among tuberculosis, urbanization, and poverty have been noted in studies from countries as diverse as Denmark and Puerto Rico (7). It is clear that growing numbers of poor, malnourished people living in unhygienic, overcrowded conditions can facilitate the transmission of TB. In poor neighborhoods, the combination of overcrowding and poor ventilation often means that one person with TB, if not properly treated, will transmit the infection to between 10 to 15 other people each year (8).

In the United States, the number of tuberculosis cases increased by 20 percent between 1985 and 1992, with most of these cases concentrated in inner cities (9). Since then, the numbers have dropped, but rates in cities such as Washington,

D.C., and New York remain high (10). In Russia, the number of TB cases climbed 42 percent between 1991 and 1994, and the death rate soared 87 percent in the same 3-year period. After experiencing nearly 40 years of a steady decline of TB, Eastern Europe now shows an increase in TB deaths, which is linked to the impact of recent political, social, and economic changes that have dramatically reduced living standards and incomes (11).

Multidrug resistance has become an important factor, impeding the effort to control and prevent TB in large urban centers. New York, London, Milan, Paris, Atlanta, Chicago, as well as cities throughout the developing world—especially in Asia—have reported increasing numbers of multidrug-resistant TB cases (12). In some countries of the developing world where resources are limited, it is estimated that drug-resistant rates exceed 30 percent (13). The implications are profound: for individuals infected with multidrug-resistant strains of TB, the fatality rate is greater than 50 percent. In addition, the average cost of treating an antibiotic-susceptible case of TB in New York City is around US$2,000, but for a multidrug-resistant case, the number soars to around US$250,000, placing effective treatment well beyond the reach of impoverished nations and people (14).

The social and economic costs of TB are enormous, particularly because the incidence of TB is concentrated in adults between the ages of 15 and 54, who are the primary producers and wage earners. Of avoidable adult deaths globally, 26 percent may be due to TB (15). One estimate projects that the Thai economy will lose the equivalent of US$7 billion by the year 2015, solely to TB sickness and death. In India, the estimated loss of economic output due to TB deaths reaches more than US$370 million every year (16). Overall, the death or disability of an adult wage earner can severely affect the ability of a household to survive, especially because TB tends to strike households least able to cope without those earnings. Studies have shown that in households where one parent suffers from a serious debilitating disease, such as TB, children are 2.5 times more likely to be severely malnourished (17). The combination of the enormous burden of TB as well as the inconsistent availability of cost-effective interventions,

such as chemotherapy and immunization, make TB one of the highest priorities for action in international health (18).

References and Notes

1. Joseph H. Bates and William W. Stead, "The History of Tuberculosis as a Global Epidemic," *Medical Clinics of North America*, Vol. 77, No. 6 (November 1993), p. 1207.
2. Michael D. Iseman, "Evolution of Drug-Resistant Tuberculosis: A Tale of Two Species," *Proceedings of the National Academy of Sciences*, Vol. 91 (March 1994), p. 2428.
3. World Health Organization (WHO), "TB Deaths Reach Historic Levels," March 21, 1996 (WHO press release no. 22).
4. World Health Organization (WHO), *Groups at Risk: WHO Report on the Tuberculosis Epidemic 1996*, (WHO, Geneva, 1996), p. 1.
5. *Ibid.*, pp. 2–3, 12.
6. Carolyn Stephens, "Healthy Cities or Unhealthy Island? The Health and Social Implications of Urban Inequality," *Environment and Urbanization*, Vol. 8, No. 2 (October 1996), p. 23.
7. Donald Enarson, Jie-Siu Wang, and John M. Dirks, "The Incidence of Active Tuberculosis in a Large Urban Area," *The American Journal of Epidemiology*, Vol. 129, No. 6 (June 1989), p. 1274.
8. *Op. cit.* 4.
9. World Health Organization (WHO), *TB: A Global Emergency, WHO Report on the TB Epidemic* (WHO, Geneva, 1994), p. 2.
10. "Tuberculosis Morbidity–United States, 1996," *Morbidity and Mortality Weekly Report*, Vol. 46, No. 30 (1997), p. 695.
11. Mary E. Wilson, "Disease in Evolution: Introduction," *Disease in Evolution: Global Changes and Emergence of Infectious Diseases*, Annals of the New York Academy of Sciences, Vol. 740, Mary E. Wilson, Richard Levins, and Andrew Spielman, eds. (New York Academy of Sciences, New York, 1994), p. 8.
12. *Op. cit.* 3.
13. *Op. cit.* 2.
14. World Health Organization (WHO), *The TB Epidemic is Getting Worse*," (WHO, Geneva, 1995), available online at: http:// www.who.ch/programmes/gtb/tbrep_95/worse.htm (December 11, 1997).
15. Christopher Murray, Karel Styblo, and Annik Rouillon, "Tuberculosis," in *Disease Control Priorities in Developing Countries*, Dean T. Jamison et al., eds. (Oxford University Press, Oxford and New York, 1993), p. 245.
16. *Op. cit.* 4, p. 14.
17. *Op. cit.* 15, p. 245.
18. *Op. cit.* 15, p. 256.

*E*nvironmental Change and Human Health

Intensification of Agriculture

Throughout human history, increasing population growth and changing dietary patterns have resulted in more and more land moving from forest or grasslands into agricultural production. Over the past few decades, the greatly increased use of chemical fertilizers and pesticides, plus changes in irrigation practices and improved seed stock, have enabled land already under cultivation to be farmed much more intensively. Given current population trends—United Nations' projections anticipate as much as a doubling of world population by 2050 (32)—substantial intensification of agriculture on hectares now in cropland is certain, and conversion of more land to agricultural use is likely, especially in developing countries. Both actions will have far-reaching implications for environmental quality and human health.

Over the long term, increased food production is a prerequisite for a healthy world population. More people will be seeking better diets; and as incomes rise, dietary patterns shift to include more animal protein. The methods used to grow this additional food, as well as the nature and extent of land conversion, will determine whether significant negative health impacts will arise.

Health concerns related to agricultural intensification stem from increased exposure to toxic substances such as pesticides, a higher incidence of infectious diseases associated with expansion of irrigation systems and the use of wastewater for irrigation, and increased human exposure to infectious agents as tropical forests and other ecosystems are converted to agricultural land. Agricultural intensification could undermine health in less direct ways as well. If practices now common in some parts of the world persist or spread, basic agricultural resources could be degraded through soil erosion, loss of soil fertility, loss of genetic variability in crops, and depletion of water resources. This would eventually deplete agriculture's global productive capacity.

Chemical Inputs

Synthetic fertilizers and pesticides have played a dominant role in agricultural intensification in industrialized and developing countries for decades. Although both have become widely distributed in the environment, most of the concern related to the health consequences of agriculture now centers around pesticides.

WORLD PESTICIDE USE

By any measure—volume used, hectares treated, or market value—global pesticide use is large and still climbing (33). In 1995, world pesticide consumption reached 2.6 million metric tons of so-called active ingredients, the biologically active

Nigel Dickinson/Still Pictures

chemicals at the heart of commercial pesticide formulations, with a market value of US$38 billion (34). Roughly 85 percent of this consumption was used in agriculture (35).

About three quarters of pesticide use occurs in developed countries, mostly in North America, Western Europe, and Japan, where high pesticide application rates are common. In these regions, the pesticide market is dominated by herbicides, which tend to have lower acute, or immediate, toxicity than insecticides. In most developing nations, the situation is reversed, and insecticide use predominates, with a correspondingly higher level of acute risk. Although the volume of pesticides that developing countries use is small relative to that in developed countries, it is nonetheless substantial and is growing steadily. (See Figures 2.4 and 2.5.) Pesticide use is particularly intense where such export crops as cotton, bananas, coffee, vegetables, and flowers predominate. (See Box 2.2.)

Insecticides of choice in the developing world are often older, broad-spectrum compounds belonging to the organophosphate and carbamate classes—chemical families noted for their acute toxicity. These products are popular partly be-

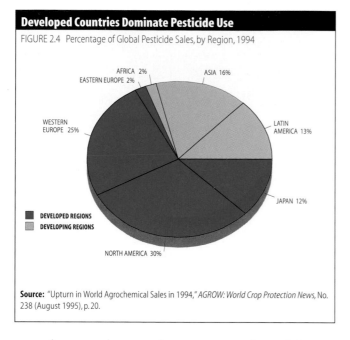

Developed Countries Dominate Pesticide Use

FIGURE 2.4   Percentage of Global Pesticide Sales, by Region, 1994

AFRICA 2%
EASTERN EUROPE 2%
ASIA 16%
WESTERN EUROPE 25%
LATIN AMERICA 13%
JAPAN 12%
NORTH AMERICA 30%

■ DEVELOPED REGIONS
▨ DEVELOPING REGIONS

Source: "Upturn in World Agrochemical Sales in 1994," *AGROW: World Crop Protection News*, No. 238 (August 1995), p. 20.

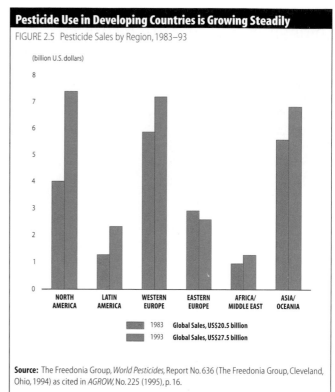

Pesticide Use in Developing Countries is Growing Steadily

FIGURE 2.5   Pesticide Sales by Region, 1983–93

(billion U.S. dollars)

NORTH AMERICA   LATIN AMERICA   WESTERN EUROPE   EASTERN EUROPE   AFRICA/MIDDLE EAST   ASIA/OCEANIA

▨ 1983   **Global Sales, US$20.5 billion**
■ 1993   **Global Sales, US$27.5 billion**

Source: The Freedonia Group, *World Pesticides*, Report No. 636 (The Freedonia Group, Cleveland, Ohio, 1994) as cited in *AGROW*, No. 225 (1995), p. 16.

cause they are no longer under patent protection and thus are considerably cheaper than the newer, still-proprietary pesticides increasingly used in more developed countries. Organochlorine insecticides such as DDT, lindane, and toxaphene are still widely used in the developing world, although their danger to humans and animals is well known. Many developed countries have banned or severely restricted the most toxic of these compounds but continue to manufacture and sell them. Trade in restricted and banned pesticides is almost impossible to track, but customs records for shipments from the United States show that at least 108,000 metric tons of banned, restricted, or discontinued pesticides were exported from U.S. ports from 1992 to 1994 (36). (See Table 2.2.) A critical policy issue is to determine how to remove these older pesticides from circulation and use. (See Chapter 3.)

PESTICIDE HEALTH RISKS

Global use of pesticides creates substantial health impacts in all parts of the world, although the exact toll is difficult to pinpoint, given both the various chemicals and types of exposure. In short, not all pesticides are equally risky, and not all people are equally at risk. Effects can be divided broadly into two categories: acute effects, which appear immediately or very soon after exposure; and chronic effects, which may manifest themselves many years later and whose origins are often difficult to trace.

Acute Effects

Exposure to pesticides can lead to an array of acute effects, depending on the pesticide's toxicity and the dose absorbed by the body. For pesticides with high acute toxicity, exposure can produce symptoms within minutes or hours, most of which

diminish in time. These acute effects—known as poisonings or intoxications—run from mild headaches and flu-like symptoms, to skin rashes, to blurred vision, and other neurological disorders (37). For example, a fieldworker who gets a few drops of methyl parathion on his skin might experience severe sweating, headache, and nausea, and even an inability to walk. Other acute responses include chemical burns, paralysis, blindness, and even death (38).

Air temperature and the exposed person's general health condition influence the severity of these symptoms. Toxic reactions may be worse for those suffering from poor nutrition or dehydration, and warmer temperatures also may increase the toxic effects. These factors mean that field laborers working in the heat may be more susceptible to poisoning (39).

The majority of pesticide poisonings and deaths occur in the developing world, although far greater quantities of pesticides are used in the developed world. Reasons for this include the following: developing countries have a higher proportion of the populace involved in agriculture, they have poorer pesticide handling practices, they commonly use unsafe equipment (such as leaky backpack sprayers), and they generally employ more toxic pesticides than those used in developed countries. A 1991 survey of farmworkers involved in export agriculture in Ecuador revealed that more than 60 percent of farmworkers participating in the study suffered from one or more symptoms of acute pesticide poisoning such as headaches, allergies, dizziness, dermatitis, or blurred vision (40).

Environmental Change and Human Health

Box 2.2 Bittersweet Harvest: Pesticide Exposures In Latin America's Flower Export Trade

The year-round demand in North America for fresh vegetables, fruits, and flowers has fueled a booming export trade from Latin America and the Caribbean. But this economic success has come with a price: serious pesticide exposure for many workers who raise and handle these export crops. There is no better example of this than the flower industry, where remarkably high amounts of pesticides are applied, usually inside greenhouses.

Rose and carnation producers in Ecuador, for example, use an average of six fungicides, four insecticides, and three nematicides (nematode poisons), along with several herbicides. Many of these compounds are applied frequently, some daily, in order to chemically "sanitize" the greenhouses, which are particularly vulnerable to pest or disease epidemics. Moreover, since flowers are not edible, importers do not inspect them for pesticide residues, and producers thus have little incentive to minimize their use of pesticides.

The flower industry in Ecuador—which has grown dramatically in the last decade—is concentrated in the highland region, near Quito and the airport. Plantations have a sophisticated infrastructure that includes complex irrigation and drainage systems and electricity for night lighting. Production cycles, which are very labor intensive, are planned, timed, and executed to meet the high-quality standards and periodic demand of the North American market, with exports peaking during U.S. holidays like Valentine's Day and Mother's Day.

Colombian and Costa Rican flower plantations show similar patterns. In Costa Rica, for instance, greenhouse workers treat flowers and ornamental plants with extremely toxic insecticides and nematicides that include methyl parathion, terbufos, and aldicarb—all compounds whose use in North America is restricted because of the health hazard they pose. A wide array of other pesticides with known health risks is also used. These include fungicides such as mancozeb and captan, which are both suspected carcinogens, and herbicides such as paraquat, which is extremely toxic through any route of exposure, whether absorbed through the skin, inhaled, or inadvertently ingested.

The danger of exposure to these substances is compounded by the type of setting in which they are applied and the frequency of application. Many of these chemicals are applied daily in the warm, poorly ventilated greenhouses, where high levels of toxic vapors can accumulate, and contact with pesticide residues on treated plants is hard to avoid.

Women are particularly subject to pesticide poisoning in Latin America's export flower business because they often make up as much as 70 to 80 percent of the labor force. In addition to the direct threat of pesticide exposure, these workers' health is also jeopardized by inadequate housing, poor diet, and the lack of public health services and education.

A study of 80 women working on flower plantations (and other export crop farms) in Ecuador revealed heavy exposure to organophosphates and carbamates, two classes of pesticides well known for their acute toxicity. The women complained of blurred vision, intolerance to light, headaches, and nausea, all typical symptoms of organophosphate and carbamate poisoning. Often, workers were expected to continue their tasks while pesticides were being applied near them—a serious breach of safe practices.

The majority of women workers in this study received no training or information on pesticide use and the need for protective equipment. Some 40 percent of the workers interviewed received no protective equipment, and the rest only occasionally received gloves, boots, and, rarely, glasses. Even when they were given protective equipment, it was either inadequate or poorly maintained. Health and hygiene facilities on these plantations were also deficient. Only 5 per-cent of the workers interviewed received company-paid medical examinations.

In Colombia, conditions are similar, yet probably more serious, partly because the scale is multiplied. A study of some 8,900 workers on flower plantations near Bogota showed that they were exposed to 127 different types of pesticides. An estimated 20 percent of these pesticides were banned or unregistered in the United Kingdom or the United States. The surveyed workers suffered a variety of acute effects: nearly two thirds of the workers suffered from headaches, nausea, impaired vision, conjunctivitis, rashes, and asthma. They also suffered serious chronic effects, such as stillbirths, miscarriages, and respiratory and neurological problems.

Pressures to maximize output and speed exacerbate these problems, encouraging management to push workers beyond the limits of safety. Inadequate or below-minimum wages, poor living conditions, and lack of respect for laws governing maternity leave are also common. Workers' attempts to organize and assert their rights have generally been met with reprimands and dismissals, because replacement workers are easy to find.

Some flower farms have improved occupational health conditions, partly in response to negative media attention or pressure from workers and environmental groups. In both Ecuador and Colombia, several flower companies now take workers' blood samples to check for pesticide exposure, and some have improved medical services and provide masks and gloves for workers. However, many producers have not yet begun to take even these minimal steps, and the industry has yet to make worker safety a clear priority.

Adapted from: Lori Ann Thrupp, *Bittersweet Harvests for Global Supermarkets: Challenges in Latin America's Agricultural Export Boom* (World Resources Institute, Washington, D.C., 1995).

More typical estimates for the percentage of workers experiencing acute pesticide toxicity range from 7 to 13 percent (41)(42).

A high percentage of pesticide poisonings worldwide is attributable to two particularly toxic classes of pesticides: organophosphates and carbamates, many of which are banned or restricted in the developed countries. The toxicity of these compounds stems from their ability to inhibit the action of cholinesterase, an enzyme essential to nervous system functioning (43)(44)(45).

Worker exposure can often be prevented if proper application methods are used and protective clothing is worn (46).

However, farm managers often fail to make such equipment available or do not insist that it be used. A complicating factor is that field conditions may be too hot for protective clothing to be worn comfortably. Even in developed countries where equipment is more routinely provided, studies show that farmers and farm laborers do not diligently use protective clothing, especially in hot weather (47).

Although occupational exposures account for the majority of serious pesticide poisonings, workers are not the only ones at risk from acute pesticide effects. People who live adjacent to farms or plantations can also experience significant pesticide exposures from wind drift from aerial spraying, from volatili-

Trade in Restricted Pesticides

TABLE 2.2 Banned and Restricted Pesticide Exports From United States Ports, 1992–94

CATEGORY	(metric tons)			
	1992	1993	1994	TOTAL
Banned, suspended, or discontinued	2,063	1,708	3,008	**6,779**
Severely restricted	3,361	4,136	2,612	**10,109**
Restricted use	26,096	32,066	32,732	**90,894**
Total	**31,520**	**37,910**	**38,352**	**107,782**

Source: Foundation for Advancements in Science and Education (FASE), *FASE Research Report* (Spring 1996), p. 4.

zation and redeposition of applied pesticides, from use of empty pesticide containers as drinking water storage, or from contamination from spills or the dumping of pesticide wastes. One study in Nicaragua found that residents living next to cotton fields regularly sprayed with insecticides had depressed cholinesterase levels—an effect typical of exposure to organophosphate or carbamate pesticides (48). Children living near treated fields are especially vulnerable, because they may spend considerable time playing among contaminated soil or plants, or they may help out in the field work. In Colombia, 18 percent of recorded pesticide poisonings from 1978 to 1989 occurred in children younger than age 14 (49).

The number of people exposed to damaging doses of pesticides through their association with agriculture is not clear, because only the most serious poisoning incidents are usually recorded. One estimate—admittedly uncertain—shows that between 50 million and 100 million people in the developing world may receive intensive pesticide exposure, and another 500 million receive lower exposures; these exposures may result in some 3.5 million to 5 million acute pesticide poisonings per year, with a much larger number of people suffering from subacute effects (50).

Even in developed countries where regulations are stricter and protective gear more available, occupational exposures can be significant. In the United States, the U.S. Environmental Protection Agency (U.S. EPA) estimates that nearly 4 million people in the agricultural workforce are at risk of significant occupational exposure because they handle or apply pesticides, and that these exposures result in about 10,000 to 20,000 pesticide poisonings medically treated per year (51)(52). U.S. EPA estimates that at least that number of cases probably goes untreated, because studies show that exposure is greatly underreported (53). For example, a study of 98 Nebraska farmers and pesticide applicators who routinely handled organophosphate pesticides found that 30 percent of the group had reduced levels of blood cholinesterase, an indication of significant exposure, and 22 percent actually exhibited

symptoms including headache, nausea, or diarrhea. None of the affected workers sought medical treatment (54).

Chronic Effects

The acute effects of pesticide exposure are relatively well understood. By contrast, much more uncertainty surrounds long-term or chronic effects, especially those believed to arise from low-level exposures to pesticide residues in food or water. There is little dispute regarding the nature of some chronic effects, such as those that follow high-dose exposures. Several studies have shown that many people who experience acute pesticide poisoning from organophosphates later suffer neurological damage. Symptoms of this problem include weakness, tingling, or even paralysis in the legs due to dieback of some nerve endings, and reduced memory and attentiveness (55)(56). Because organophosphates may account for as many as 70 percent of occupational pesticide poisonings, the number of people suffering such neurological damage could be substantial (57).

Chronic dermatitis, which includes rashes and enhanced sun sensitivity, is one of the most common effects of pesticide exposure seen in farmworkers (58). In California, where agricultural pesticide use is substantial, a 1990 study found that dermatitis accounted for one third of reported pesticide-related illnesses (59).

Pesticide exposure may cause reproductive damage as well. Male sterility has been definitely linked to heavy exposure to dibromochloropropane (DBCP), once commonly used to control nematodes. Several epidemiological studies suggest that exposure to certain pesticides—particularly the herbicide 2,4-D, which is widely used on crops, pastureland, rights-of-way, and lawns—heightens the risk of birth defects. However, other studies of 2,4-D have not produced conclusive findings (60)(61).

Recently, pesticide exposure has been implicated in cases of immune system suppression as well (62). A compromised immune system makes it more difficult to fight off infectious diseases, parasites, or tumors, and could increase the toll these threats exact on one's health. This combination could be particularly significant in developing countries, where the population's exposures to both pesticides and infectious agents may be high and their immune systems may already be compromised by other factors. (See Box 2.3.)

Of all the possible health impacts from pesticide exposure, cancer has been the most frequent focus of attention and controversy. Many pesticides show cancer-causing potential in animals; many other pesticides give no indication of causing cancer. Central questions in the debate about pesticides' role in the development of cancer relate to the level of exposure and dose required to affect cells, the possible synergistic effects of chemicals in the body, the manner in which chemicals accumulate in body tissue, the length of time they remain in

*E*nvironmental Change and Human Health

Box 2.3 Pesticides and the Immune System: The Public Health Risks

Health concerns about pesticides have tended to focus on their potential to act as acute poisons or their ability to cause cancer. But pesticides may pose other important risks as well. Recently, evidence has accumulated that many commonly used pesticides can suppress the normal response of the human immune system to invading viruses, bacteria, parasites, and tumors. The immune system is the body's primary line of defense against disease agents, so weakening its response could increase the toll of disease.

Laboratory studies show that a variety of organochlorine, organophosphate, carbamate, and metal-based pesticides (such as those based on arsenic, copper, or mercury) can suppress the immune system of mammals. Because substances toxic to other mammals are usually toxic to humans (since human immune systems are structured similarly to mammals), these laboratory studies indicate the kinds of immunosuppression humans may also experience.

Such tests provide an abundance of evidence. For example, exposure to the organochlorines aldrin and dieldrin reduces mouse resistance to viral infection, while DDT decreases antibody production in mammal and bird species. The organophosphate parathion delays antibody production and suppresses T-cell response in cell cultures, while chronic low-dose exposures of the commonly used organophosphate malathion can depress several different immune responses. Many solvents, inert ingredients, and contaminants that are part of pesticide formulations can also suppress immune responses in laboratory tests.

Epidemiological evidence, though limited, also indicates that pesticides can be toxic to the human immune system. Among Indian factory workers chronically exposed to several pesticides, blood lymphocyte levels—one element of immune system health—decreased by as much as two thirds from baseline levels and returned to normal only after pesticide exposure ceased.

Epidemiologists in the former Soviet Union have long observed that T-cell counts and functions are suppressed after pesticide exposure. For example, residents of agricultural districts in southern Russia where pesticide use was substantial had lower T-cell counts than control groups in the general population, and the former group also had higher rates of infectious diseases.

Likewise, in Moldova—also part of the former Soviet Union—teenagers in villages where pesticide application levels were greatest exhibited rates of infections of the respiratory and digestive tracts several times higher than teenagers from areas of lower pesticide use. From the 1960s through the 1980s, per hectare pesticide application rates in farming regions in central and southern Moldova were almost 20 times the world average.

Immune suppression from pesticide exposure may also play a role in the development of some cancers. As a group, farmers face higher risks than the general population for contracting Hodgkin's disease, melanoma, multiple myeloma, and leukemia—all of which are cancers of the immune system.

Unfortunately, despite current evidence, the study of the immune suppressive potential for most pesticides is still in its infancy, and little work has been done to clarify the relationship between dose and effect. Thus, consensus has not been reached on how much pesticide exposure is required to compromise the immune system enough to affect health, or what kinds of immune-suppressing effects chronic low-dose exposures might cause in the public at large. Nonetheless, it is clear that the potential risk to public health, especially in agricultural communities where exposure is widespread, is significant.

As with other pesticide health risks, the dangers of immune suppression from pesticide exposure may be greatest in parts of the developing world and in countries of the former Soviet Union, where much larger fractions of the populace still live in the countryside and work on farms. In these developing regions, pesticide use is growing rapidly, yet pesticide regulations and handling practices are often grossly inadequate.

To make matters worse, living conditions for many people in the developing world put them at especially high risk for immune suppression. Their immune responses are already weakened by widespread malnutrition; at the same time, contaminated water supplies, lack of sanitation, and poor housing conditions expose them to more disease agents. The result is particularly high fatality rates due to common diseases—measles and whooping cough, for example—diseases from which most patients in wealthy countries recover.

Adding pesticide-induced immune suppression on top of these other risks may substantially increase the burden of common diseases. The consequences could remain undetected because people would not necessarily die of acute pesticide poisoning; rather, deaths would be attributed to such diseases as pneumonia, or gastroenteritis, or to complications of measles. The fact that pesticide exposure weakened their immune responses and increased their vulnerability to illness or death would remain unrecognized.

Adapted from: Robert Repetto and Sanjay Baliga, *Pesticides and the Immune System: The Public Health Risks* (World Resources Institute, Washington, D.C., 1996).

---

the system, and many other issues. Based largely on animal studies, the U.S. EPA reports that of 321 chemicals examined, 146 are probable or possible human carcinogens (63).

Epidemiological studies, too, suggest a link between some pesticides and cancer. For example, epidemiological studies have shown an association between exposure to organochlorines and various cancers, including lymphoma and leukemia, as well as lung, pancreatic, and breast cancer (64). Such findings are significant because organochlorines such as DDT, aldrin, and chlordane are widely dispersed in the environment and can easily accumulate in human tissues.

Additional epidemiological evidence links exposure to several common herbicides with cancer. Several studies have found an association between 2,4-D and non-Hodgkin's lymphoma (65)(66). In one study, farmers exposed to the herbicide

more than 20 days per year had a sixfold higher risk of non-Hodgkin's lymphoma, and those who mixed or applied the herbicide themselves had an eightfold greater risk (67).

Many pesticides that show carcinogenic potential remain in active use in agriculture. Could exposure to these pesticides, under normal conditions of use, actually lead to cancer? For those who work directly with these compounds on a regular basis, the answer may well be yes. Calculations show that for people who are occupationally exposed, the typical lifetime doses of a number of these pesticides would be enough to raise one's risk of contracting cancer substantially (68).

For the general public, the answer is much less clear. Although pesticide residues are nearly ubiquitous in food and water even in developed countries, sampling studies show these residues are generally minute. In 1996, an expert panel

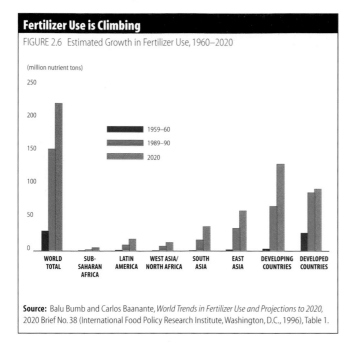

Fertilizer Use is Climbing

FIGURE 2.6 Estimated Growth in Fertilizer Use, 1960–2020

(million nutrient tons)

Legend:
- 1959–60
- 1989–90
- 2020

Categories: WORLD TOTAL, SUB-SAHARAN AFRICA, LATIN AMERICA, WEST ASIA/NORTH AFRICA, SOUTH ASIA, EAST ASIA, DEVELOPING COUNTRIES, DEVELOPED COUNTRIES

Source: Balu Bumb and Carlos Baanante, *World Trends in Fertilizer Use and Projections to 2020*, 2020 Brief No. 38 (International Food Policy Research Institute, Washington, D.C., 1996), Table 1.

of the U.S. National Academy of Sciences concluded that although evidence was limited, consuming such small amounts of pesticides in the diet was unlikely to pose an appreciable cancer risk (69).

Even with minimal exposures, concern has arisen that children may be at greater risk than adults because they often consume more per body weight of certain foods such as fruits that are likely to contain pesticide residues. They are also undergoing rapid tissue growth, allowing for greater concentration of these substances in their systems (70). In addition, pesticides are used widely around the home, for instance, on lawns and gardens and inside for pest control. Thus, pesticide exposure for some portion of the nonfarm population could be significant, even if pesticide residues in food and water are minimal.

In developing countries, exposures to the farm and nonfarm population may be greater, and risks may be higher. A lack of training in, or controls on, pesticide use often means that crops are treated excessively or sprayed too close to harvest and then sent straight to market with little washing (71).

FUTURE TRENDS IN PESTICIDE USE

Will intensification of world agriculture necessarily entail a substantial increase in the use of pesticides? If so, a greater toll on world health may be exacted, unless pesticide application practices improve drastically or less toxic products come into use. Predicting future pesticide use is impossible; however, it is possible to identify some trends and opportunities.

In the developed world, although considerable use of older pesticides persists, the trend is toward using newer pesticides that are more selective, less toxic to humans and the environment, and require less application per hectare to be effective

(72). A small but growing percentage of these are biopesticides, including microbial pesticides like *Bacillus thuringiensis* (Bt), and biochemical pesticides such as pheromones, growth regulators, and hormones—substances that ordinarily pose little danger except to the targeted pest (73). In addition, there is growing acceptance of alternative approaches to pest control such as Integrated Pest Management. (See Chapter 3.)

In the developing world, pesticide sales are on a strong upswing, and many highly toxic insecticides remain popular. Over the next decade at least, a significant increase in pesticide use is likely. Pesticide sales in India rose 5 percent in volume between March 1995 and 1996 (74). Brazil (already the fourth largest pesticide consumer in the world) is experiencing similar growth, as is China, which represents by far the most dynamic market in Asia (75)(76). Even Africa, which has the lowest use rate of any region, has increased its pesticide sales in the past decade (77)(78).

One factor contributing to increasing pesticide use in the developing world is a growing local production capacity. Brazil and India have become regional pesticide exporters; China's production capacity increased 40 percent from 1995 to 1996 (79). Most of this growth in sales and manufacture has been in older, highly toxic insecticides. The top-selling pesticide in India is monocrotophos, a highly toxic insecticide whose registration was canceled in the United States in 1988 (80)(81).

By contrast, some developing countries are paying increasing attention to human health effects in setting regulations for the use and trade of pesticides. In July 1996, regulators in Egypt banned the import and use of all pesticides classified as probable or possible carcinogens (82). In 1987, Indonesia acted similarly to ban a variety of rice pesticides in common use. In addition, several successful Integrated Pest Management programs are underway, especially in Asia and Cuba.

NITRATE CONTAMINATION FROM FERTILIZER AND MANURE

Pesticides are not the only chemical input that may increase with intensifying agriculture. Nitrogen fertilizer is one of the most effective tools for increasing yields, and its use on a global basis grew more than fivefold from 1960 to 1990. It is still climbing today, although at a slower pace (83). Fertilizer consumption in developing countries is projected to double by 2020, with especially rapid growth in Africa and South Asia. (See Figure 2.6.)

This surge in fertilizer use has led to greater contamination of surface and groundwater with nitrates—essentially dissolved nitrogen fertilizer that has not been taken up by plants. This contamination poses threats to both environmental quality and human health. Determining precisely how much and when to fertilize is not easy for farmers, and overfertilization is common. Excess nitrate is water soluble and easily washed through soil by rain or irrigation water, making nitrate contamination a widespread problem where nitrogen fertilizers are used with any frequency. Manure from intensive livestock operations is also a potent nitrate source. Although agricultural sources of nitrate predominate in most rural areas (84), nonagricultural sources such as septic systems and cesspools, and even nitrogen oxide particulates deposited by cars and power plants, all add to the burden.

Public health officials consider nitrate contamination a significant health risk based on both its wide distribution and its effects on infants. In young infants, exposure to high levels of nitrates can result in a disorder whereby the red blood cells cannot function properly, leading to insufficient oxygen or "blue-baby syndrome," which can be fatal (85). In adults, high levels of nitrate exposure may increase the risk of contracting some cancers, although the extent of the risk is unclear (86).

Worldwide, the scale of nitrate contamination is undoubtedly quite large. Although no global assessment exists of how many areas exceed the WHO standard, individual country reports indicate that nitrate is one of the most common chemical contaminants found in drinking water. This finding is not surprising given the huge volume of nitrogen fertilizer used worldwide (87)(88)(89)(90). In the United States, for example, nitrate contamination is the nation's most widespread groundwater pollution problem; in a national survey, 22 percent of wells in U.S. agricultural areas contained nitrate levels in excess of the federal limit (91). Nitrate is also a prime contaminant in Europe (92).

The overuse of nitrates can affect human health indirectly as well. Nitrate runoff from agricultural fields and feedlots can stimulate the growth of toxic algal blooms in estuaries and near-coastal waters, contaminating shellfish and other seafood. More generally, "fertilization" of coastal waters by nitrate runoff—a process called eutrophication—can degrade these waters, resulting in an overall decline in the local seafood catch, which is an important food source. In summary, unless greater attention is given to adjusting agricultural methods to avoid overfertilization, increasing the food supply over the next few decades could mean increased exposure to nitrates, with attendant health effects (93).

Irrigation

Hectare for hectare, irrigated land is far more productive than rainfed land, and the expansion of irrigated acreage over the past 30 years has played an important part in the gains in food production. At the height of the Green Revolution in the 1970s, irrigated land was expanding at a global rate of more than 2 percent per year (94). Since then, annual growth in irrigated hectares has declined to about 1 percent, mostly because of the great expense involved in developing irrigation systems, as well as the increased competition for water supplies.

Despite these barriers of cost and limited water availability, agriculture experts expect continued growth in irrigated land to meet future food needs and expand export agriculture, at least in developing countries. The Food and Agriculture Organization of the United Nations (FAO) projects that irrigated land in developing nations (excluding China) will increase at roughly 0.8 percent per year, expanding from 123 million hectares in 1990 to some 146 million hectares in 2010. Egypt, Mexico, and Turkey anticipate particularly rapid growth in irrigated acreage (95).

Along with the benefits of higher and more reliable yields, irrigation brings risks of increased infectious diseases such as malaria and schistosomiasis through habitat disruption. By providing habitat for disease agents, irrigation channels and the dams or impoundments that supply them can greatly extend the range and transmission of some infectious diseases (96). The association of schistosomiasis with irrigation is a case in point. Worldwide prevalence of the disease has risen over the past five decades, due mostly to the expansion of irrigation systems in hot climates (97). Clear links to increases in schistosomiasis have been documented in irrigation projects such as the Mwea project in Kenya, where schistosomiasis accounts for 18 percent of all deaths (98). The slow-moving water in the irrigation canals and drainage ditches provides ideal habitat for the snail that is the intermediate host of the schistosomiasis organism. Calm waters along reservoir banks, thick with vegetation, are also heavily colonized by these snails and are an ideal transmission site for the disease because human activity is usually centered near the lakeside as well (99)(100). In the upper region of Ghana, schistosomiasis prevalence tripled in the late 1950s and early 1960s when a large number of agricultural impoundments were constructed. In these areas, infection rates were as high as 50 percent (101).

In all, more than 30 diseases have been linked to irrigation, and the health toll from these can be quite significant regionally (102). Asian paddy-rice agriculture is frequently associated with malaria and Japanese encephalitis, in addition to schistosomiasis. In Central and South America, irrigated farming may expose farmers to filariasis as well as malaria and other mosquito-borne diseases (103). In Africa, in addition to the suite of mosquito-borne diseases and schistosomiasis associated with irrigation canals, dam spillways have provided breeding sites for the black fly that carriers river blindness (onchocerciasis) (104). Although it is impossible to quantify the additional toll of diseases related specifically to irrigation systems, it is fair to say that in agricultural areas these systems are important contributing factors to the overall burden of water-related diseases.

Other health risks emerge from the use of wastewater from municipal and industrial sources to irrigate crops. Irrigating

Box 2.4 Malaria in the Brazilian Amazon

Malaria incidence in Brazil rose steadily in the 1970s and 1980s, from just 52,469 cases in 1970 to 577,520 in 1989 (1). By 1994, reported cases still exceeded half a million (2). In 1970, 72 percent of all malaria cases in the country were in the Amazon Basin (3); by 1985, this figure had risen to 99 percent (4). Today, virtually all endemic malaria occurs in the Amazon region (5).

While malaria has long been endemic in Brazil, the dramatic surge in malaria cases over the past two decades in the Amazon can be attributed to a complex set of interrelated factors: rapid population growth, migration and displacement of laborers and indigenous people, the growth of gold mining, environmental destruction, and misguided development. Two subpopulations—gold miners and indigenous Indians—have borne the greatest burden of increased malaria incidence.

The Brazilian Amazon is home to the world's largest remaining tropical forests as well as significant mineral reserves. Since the 1960s, the government has instituted a series of ambitious plans to develop and colonize the Amazon Basin to relieve some of the pressures of urban poverty, crowding, and social unrest in other regions of Brazil. As a result of these efforts, which were heavily subsidized by the government, population growth in the region soared. Between 1970 and 1980, population growth rates in the Amazon region were above 5 percent per year, the highest in Brazil (6). The construction of the Belem-Brasilia highway and the Trans-Amazon highway further spurred the growth of logging, agribusiness, and mining in the region.

More recently, a "gold rush" in the Amazon has made the region a magnet for migrants, in particular from the poverty-stricken northeastern region. Gold prospectors and miners, called "garimpeiros," have flocked to mining sites in the Brazilian Amazon, with the highest proportions

moving to the states of Rondonia, Para, Mato Grosso, and Roraima in search of economic opportunities. By 1991, between 400,000 and 600,000 garimpeiros had moved to the region.

The gold mining boom has had several unintended consequences, including high levels of environmental degradation from mine tailings, deforestation, and deteriorating living conditions. In particular, malaria has swept mining towns across the region. In 1988, for instance, 50 percent of all malaria transmission in Mato Grosso occurred at gold mining sites (7).

Conditions in mining camps provide perfect conditions for malaria infection and transmission. Temporary shelters provide little or no mosquito protection. In addition, the garimpeiros themselves are highly susceptible to malaria because they are often migrants from areas free from malaria, and thus lack immunity to the disease. In their search for gold, miners also routinely destroy the banks of local streams. The widened river beds then become swamplike habitats perfect for mosquito breeding.

The costs of treating malaria are beyond most miners' means, so many infected miners go untreated. Even when infected miners do buy medicine (often paid for with gold), they usually stop taking it once the fever recedes, but before they are entirely cured. As a result, drug-resistant strains of malaria that are much more difficult and expensive to treat have emerged.

The high exposure of miners to the heavy metal mercury, which is commonly used to extract raw gold from mine tailings, is probably also an important factor in the high malaria incidence. From 3 to 5 kilograms (kg) of mercury are used to extract 1 kg of gold (8), and the lack of environmental controls at most mining sites means that exposures to mercury probably exceed limits set by the World Health Organization. Researchers are beginning to suspect that mercury exposure can suppress or damage the im-

mune system, perhaps making the garimpeiros more susceptible to malaria infection (9).

Miners are not the only victims of the Amazon gold rush. In fact, the local Indian population has suffered far worse. The mineral wealth of many Indian reservations makes them a prime target for invasion by garimpeiros. To a great extent, the development of the Brazilian Amazon has been defined by the invasion of traditional Indian territories and the appropriation of their natural resources. Disease transmission and depopulation have been the devastating result.

The Roraima Gold Rush provides a vivid illustration. In 1987, garimpeiros invaded the homeland of 10,000 Yanomami Indians. By 1989, an estimated 40,000 miners were working within the land of the Yanomami, the last large, semi-isolated, and traditional Indian group in the Americas (10). The consequences were immediate: cultural conflicts, violence, epidemics, starvation, and high mortality imperiled the very existence of the Yanomami as a people. Nor was this the first time that development had threatened Indian communities in the region. In the early 1970s, epidemics of measles and influenza brought by workers constructing the Perimetral Norte highway wiped out three Yanomami communities in northern Amazonas State (11).

The Roraima Gold Rush and subsequent immigration by garimpeiros have dramatically increased malaria incidence and deaths among the Indians. A survey at the Indian Hospital in the city of Boa Vista showed that malaria was the main cause of admission of Yanomami Indians from 1987 to 1989. Of the 144 deaths reported during this period, malaria was responsible for over half (51.8 percent) (12). Estimates suggest that nearly 10 percent of the Yanomami population died of malaria between 1987 and 1990. Overall, about 20 per-

---

with raw or partially treated sewage can conserve water and fertilize crops economically by capturing nutrients that would normally be wasted. This irrigation method is also an effective way to prevent contamination of nearby waterways with the disease organisms and nutrients that sewage contains—a considerable health benefit (105). The most serious drawback of using sewage for irrigation is its role in transmitting infectious diseases both to agricultural workers and the general public. Two worm-related infections that are endemic in many developing countries, one from the *Ascaris* worm and the other from the *Trichuris* worm, are commonly associated with wastewater irrigation. Eating uncooked vegetables that have been irrigated with such water can effectively trans-

mit these worms, which colonize the small and large intestines. Farmworkers in fields irrigated with wastewater may also become infected with hookworm, whose debilitating effects include anemia (106).

Wastewater irrigation has also been linked to transmission of enteric diseases such as cholera and typhoid, even in areas where these diseases are not endemic. For example, a 1970 cholera outbreak in Jerusalem was blamed on consumption of vegetables irrigated with wastewater. The seasonal pattern of typhoid infections in Santiago, Chile, in the 1970s and 1980s was tied to consumption of salad crops and vegetables grown outside the city on sewage-irrigated farms. In both instances, sanitation levels were fairly good, so the normal

Box 2.4 continued

cent of the Yanomami population contracted malaria, and in some of the villages the parasite infected more than 90 percent of the community.

Although the Roraima Gold Rush is waning, the legacy of malaria infection continues to pose a risk to Amazonian Indians. Between 1991 and 1995, malaria was responsible for 25 percent of all Yanomami deaths (13). Annual rates of malaria incidence in areas where contact with miners and other immigrants is frequent are as high as 1,350 per 1,000 population, meaning that some individuals have had more than one attack of malaria in just one year. This is in sharp contrast to rates in the villages not affected by the invasion of outsiders, which run around 20 cases per 1,000 population. It is also substantially higher than malaria incidence among the general Amazonian population, estimated to be around 40 per 1,000 (14)(15).

Starting in 1990, the Brazilian government intervened to remove the garimpeiros from the Yanomami territory, but with little apparent effect. Because the lure of gold remained, the garimpeiros simply moved to other mining areas in the state of Roraima. As a consequence, malaria spread to the four ethnic groups of eastern Roraima and became the leading cause of death there between 1991 and 1994 (16).

While the reasons behind the extremely high incidence of malaria among indigenous Indians are not completely understood, many factors, both socioeconomic and environmental, may be playing a role. First, malaria control activities—such as housespraying and case detection and treatment—that had been successful in the southeastern and northeastern regions of Brazil were unsuccessful in the heavily forested areas of the Amazon because of logistical and organizational difficulties and population mobility (17). In addition, most mosquito bites occur outdoors, making domestic indoor spraying for malaria

control ineffective. Second, the physical isolation of many of the groups in the Amazon may increase their susceptibility to malaria. Third, because most of these communities are in remote areas, the people have only limited access to health services. Virtually all of the 350 Yanomami villages can be reached only by plane.

In addition, culturally determined behaviors may increase the risk of malaria transmission or make treatment difficult. For example, the custom of bathing in rivers early in the morning and late in the afternoon coincides with the peak hours of mosquito activity. Also, the mobility associated with subsistence fishing and hunting can be a problem, because some cases of malaria need an uninterrupted two-week course of drugs, which is difficult to administer in the face of frequent travel. On the other hand, the structure of Yanomami huts may offer some protection from malaria; the cone-shaped and closed huts are often filled with dense smoke from cookfires inside, which tends to repel mosquitoes.

The outlook for the future is guarded. As long as profits from mining appear to be lucrative, mining will probably continue to play a role in malaria transmission in the Amazon region. At the same time, continued high rates of deforestation could also increase the population of malaria-carrying mosquitoes and facilitate the spread of the disease (18).

Ulisses Confalonieri, Professor of Public Health, Fundación Oswaldo Cruz, Rio de Janeiro.

References and Notes

1. Donald Rolfe Sawyer, "Malaria and the Environment," Documento de Trabalho, No. 13 (Instituto Sociedade, Populacão e Natureza, Brasília, Brazil, March 1992), p. 2.

2. Pedro Luiz Tauil, "Comments on the Epidemiology and Control of Malaria in Brazil," *Mem. Inst. Oswaldo Cruz,* Vol. 81, Supplement II (1986), p. 39.

3. *Op. cit.* 1.

4. Pedro L. Tauil, "Malária: Agrava-Se O Quadro Da Doença No Brasil," *Ciência Hoje,* Vol. 2, No. 12 (May–June 1984), pp. 58–59.

5. *Op. cit.* 1.

6. Agostinho Cruz Marques, "Migrations and the Dissemination of Malaria in Brazil," *Mem. Inst. Oswaldo Cruz,* Vol. 81, Supplement II (1986), p. 17.

7. *Ibid.,* p. 28.

8. Steven G. Gilbert and Kimberly S. Grant-Webster, "Neurobehavioral Effects of Developmental Methyl Mercury Exposure," *Environmental Health Perspectives,* Vol. 103, Supplement 6 (1995), p. 136.

9. J. Bernier, "Immunotoxicity of Heavy Metals in Relation to Great Lakes," *Environmental Health Perspectives,* Vol. 103, Supplement 9 (December 1995), pp. 23–24.

10. Margareth Marmori, "A Historia Do Conflito," *Ciência Hoje,* Vol. II, No.64, (July 1990), p. 75.

11. Alcida R. Ramos, "Yanomami Indians in North Brazil Threatened by Highway," (November 1978), pp. 1–30.

12. Oneron A. Pithan *et al.,* "A Situacao de Saude dos Indios Yanomami: Diagnostico a Partir da Casa do Indio de Boa Vista, Roraima, 1987-1989. PESQUISA. Cadernos de Saude Publica, RJ, 7(4): 563-580, out/dez, 1991.

13. Maria Stella de Castro Lobo, "O Caso Yanomami Do Brasil: Uma Proposta Estrategica De Vigilancia Epidemiologica," Rio de Janeiro, 1996. Escola Nacional de Saude Publica, Mestrado em Saude Publica, Area de Concentracao: Epidemiologia Geral, p. 50.

14. *Ibid.*

15. *Op. cit.* 6.

16. Ulisses Confalonieri, "Amazon Health Report: Indigenous People's of Brazil," draft paper (The World Bank, Washington, D.C., 1994).

17. *Op. cit.* 1, p. 12.

18. J.F. Walsh *et al.,* "Deforestation: Effects on Vector-borne Disease," *Parasitology,* Vol. 106 (1993) (Cambridge University Press), p. S58.

routes of cholera and typhoid transmission (contaminated drinking water and poor personal hygiene) were not the culprits (107). Other gastrointestinal diseases such as dysentery, giardiasis, and even infectious hepatitis may be similarly transmitted through contaminated vegetables (108).

Land Conversion

Conversion of land to agriculture is still proceeding in many developing countries and is likely to continue. The United Nations Environment Programme (UNEP) predicts that agricultural land area could nearly double in Africa and West Asia by 2050 and climb by 25 percent in the Asia-Pacific region, although greater investment in agricultural management and

technology on existing cropland could lower these numbers considerably (109). Much of this conversion will target forested areas. Indeed, conversion of forestland to agriculture is already a prime force driving forest loss in the tropics and even in some temperate areas, including China (110). One fifth of the world's remaining large blocks of forest may well become cropland and pasture (111).

Unfortunately, land conversion—especially forest conversion—is associated with a higher incidence of certain infectious diseases, including malaria and leishmaniasis. Forest clearance often creates new habitats, such as depressions where water can collect and mosquitoes, ticks, and fleas can breed. Often, the forest fringe at the edge of converted forestland provides a potent contact point between disease organisms from the forest and human populations. For example, the mosquito *Anopheles dirus*, which breeds in sunlit pools along the partially cleared forest margin, is a very effective malaria vector. Intense malaria transmission by this mosquito occurs along forest fringes in large portions of South and Southeast Asia (112). The clearing of forests for cattle grazing in parts of southern India's Shimoga district caused a different problem. It led to an upsurge in the local tick population and an outbreak of Kyasanur forest disease in the 1980s, the product of a rare virus from the forest (113).

In Africa, deforestation favors malaria transmission by the mosquito *Anopheles gambiae*, which prefers to breed in the open rather than in the dense forest. The rise in surface temperatures that clearing of forests brings can also help in spreading malaria by speeding both the life cycle of the mosquito and the development of the malaria parasite it harbors. In the Usambara mountains in northeastern Tanzania, forest-clearing activities along the mountaintops are considered one cause of the introduction and spread of malaria (114). A combination of altered natural conditions plus migration has created a particularly deadly situation in Brazil's Amazon basin. (See Box 2.4.)

At times, the influence of agricultural conversion on disease can be complex and can extend over large regions. In southern Honduras, conversion of forest to cotton and sugarcane culture and cattle pasture altered the region's hydrological cycle, making it drier and hotter and less hospitable to the mosquito species responsible for malaria in the area. Malaria incidence declined accordingly. However, the semidesertification in the south prompted the population's migration to the newer factories and plantations of the north; many relocated on cleared forestland where malaria was still present. The migrants carried no immunity to malaria, and so a sharp rise of the disease in the north began in 1987. Heavy pesticide use on export crops also played a part in the outbreak by encouraging widespread pesticide resistance among the anopheline mosquitoes (115).

As with irrigation-related illnesses, it is difficult to quantify the additional burden of illness associated with land conversion. The complex relationships among habitat modification, the functioning of ecosystems, and the transmission of disease mean that it is difficult to predict exactly how land use changes will affect disease rates, especially when the vulnerability of exposed populations varies so widely with income, access to health care, and proper nutrition.

*E*nvironmental *Change and Human Health*

Industrialization

Industrialization is central to economic development and improved prospects for human well-being (116). The benefits of industrial production can be seen in all aspects of life—from the range of consumer goods available, to the efficiency of transportation systems, to the astounding advances made in computers and communications technology. Since the 18th Century, wealth in the developed countries has paralleled industrial growth, and developed countries continue to produce the lion's share of manufactured goods—indeed, about 74 percent of the world's industrial output takes place in the developed world (117).

Today, many developing countries are experiencing an Industrial Revolution of their own, capturing an ever-increasing share of industrial growth. The pace of this newest cycle—particularly in Asia—far exceeds that of developed countries. In China, for instance, industrial growth between 1990 and 1995 reached 18.1 percent a year; East Asia and the Pacific and South Asia experienced growth rates of approximately 15 percent and 6.4 percent a year, respectively (118). By comparison, North America's industrial output grew by only about 2.6 percent a year during the same period.

The positive economic and social results of industrial growth have been accompanied by serious environmental degradation, however, as well as growing threats to health from occupational hazards. To some extent, these problems are analogous to those of early industrial Europe. In the 19th Century, the shift from a rural, agrarian society to an urban, industrial society initially involved widespread social and economic disruption, unemployment, homelessness, pollution, and increased exposure to health hazards both at work and at home (119). Many of these same problems characterize cities in the developing world today.

Despite the similarities between earlier European industrialization and current changes in the developing world, important differences exist in the scale and pace of industrial growth. The earlier Industrial Revolution spanned nearly 200 years; recently, countries like Thailand and Indonesia have been undergoing similar changes in just a couple of decades. As part of this growth, industrial wastes are growing in quantity and becoming more varied, more toxic, and more difficult to dispose of or degrade (120). Densities in cities where much of the industrial production is located far surpass those in developed countries, so the number of people exposed to pollutants is potentially much greater.

Furthermore, a substantial share of industrial growth in developing countries revolves around the transformation of raw materials into industrial products such as steel, paper, and chemicals. The production of industrial chemicals, for instance, has been shifting to the developing world. Between

Julio Etchart/Still Pictures

1990 and 1994, this industry's annual rate of growth was 5.6 percent in developing countries, compared with a mere 1 percent in the developed world (121). Not only are these processes resource-intensive, but also industries such as electricity generation, chemicals and petroleum refining, mining, paper production, and leather tanning tend to produce a disproportionately large amount of hazardous and toxic wastes. As Table 2.3 shows, a wide range of pollutants is associated with these industries. In contrast, much of economic growth in developed countries is now in the service sector (e.g., education, entertainment, defense, and finance) and communication sector (e.g., computers, cellular phones, and electronics), which are inherently less polluting.

This rapid industrial growth has made water pollution, air pollution, and hazardous wastes pressing environmental problems in many areas of the developing world. Industrial emissions combine with vehicle exhausts to cause air pollution, while concentrations of heavy metals and ammonia loads are often high enough to cause major fish kills downriver from industrial areas (122). The lack of hazardous waste facilities compounds the problem, with industrial wastes of-

TABLE 2.3 Environmental Impacts of Selected Industries

SECTOR	AIR	WATER	SOIL/LAND
Chemicals (industrial inorganic and organic compounds, excluding petroleum products)	• Many and varied emissions depending on processes used and chemicals manufactured • Emissions of particulate matter, SO_2, NO_x, CO, CFCs, VOCs and other organic chemicals, odors • Risk of explosions and fires	• Use of process water and cooling water • Emissions of organic chemicals, heavy metals (cadmium, mercury), suspended solids, organic matter, PCBs • Risk of spills	• Chemical process wastes disposal problems • Sludges from air and water pollution treatment disposal problems
Paper and pulp	• Emissions of SO_2, NO_x, CH_4, CO_2, CO, hydrogen sulphide, mercaptans, chlorine compounds, dioxins	• Use of process water • Emissions of suspended solids, organic matter, chlorinated organic substances, toxins (dioxins)	
Cement, glass, ceramics	• Cement emissions of dust, NO_x, CO_2, chromium, lead, CO • Glass emissions of lead, arsenic, SO_2, vanadium, CO, hydrofluoric acid, soda ash, potash, specialty constituents (e.g., chromium) • Ceramics emissions of silica, SO_2, NO_x, fluorine compounds	• Emissions of process water contaminated by oils and heavy metals	• Extraction of raw materials • Soil contamination with metals and waste disposal problems
Mining of metals and minerals	• Emissions of dust from extraction, storage, and transport of ore and concentrate • Emissions of metals (e.g., mercury) from drying of ore concentrate	• Contamination of surface water and groundwater by highly acidic mine water containing toxic metals (e.g., arsenic, lead, cadmium) • Contamination by chemicals used in metal extraction (e.g., cyanide)	• Major surface disturbance and erosion • Land degradation by large slag heaps
Iron and steel	• Emissions of SO_2, NO_x, hydrogen sulphide, PAHs, lead, arsenic, cadmium, chromium, copper, mercury, nickel, selenium, zinc, organic compounds, PCDDs/PCDFs, PCBs, dust, particulate matter, hydrocarbons, acid mists • Exposure to ultraviolet and infrared radiation, ionizing radiation • Risks of explosions and fires	• Use of process water • Emissions of organic matter, tars and oil, suspended solids, metals, benzene, phenols, acids, sulphides, sulphates, ammonia, cyanides, thiocyanates, thiosulphates, fluorides, lead, zinc (scrubber effluent)	• Slag, sludges, oil and grease residues, hydrocarbons, salts, sulphur compounds, heavy metals, soil contamination and waste disposal problems
Nonferrous metals	• Emissions of particulate matter, SO_2, NO_x, CO, hydrogen sulphide, hydrogen chloride, hydrogen fluoride, chlorine, aluminum, arsenic, cadmium, chromium, copper, zinc, mercury, nickel, lead, magnesium, PAHs, fluorides, silica, manganese, carbon black, hydrocarbons, aerosols	• Scrubber water containing metals • Gas-scrubber effluents containing solids, fluorine, hydrocarbons	• Sludges from effluent treatment, coatings from electrolysis cells (containing carbon and fluorine) soil contamination and waste disposal problems
Coal mining and production	• Emissions of dust from extraction, storage, and transport of coal • Emissions of CO and SO_2 from burning slag heaps • CH_4 emissions from underground formations • Risk of explosions and fires	• Contamination of surface water and groundwater by highly saline or acidic mine water	• Major surface disturbance and erosion • Subsidence of ground above mines • Land degradation by large slag heaps
Refineries, petroleum products	• Emissions of SO_2, NO_x, hydrogen sulphide, HCs, benzene, CO, CO_2, particulate matter, PAHs, mercaptans, toxic organic coumpounds, odors • Risk of explosions and fires	• Use of cooling water • Emissions of HCs, mercaptans, caustics, oil, phenols, chromium, effluent from gas scrubbers	• Hazardous waste, sludges from effluent treatment, spent catalysts, tars
Leather and tanning	• Emissions including leather dust, hydrogen sulphide, CO_2, chromium compounds	• Use of process water • Effluents from the many toxic solutions used, containing suspended solids, sulphates, chromium	• Chromium sludges

Source: Adapted from World Health Organization (WHO), *Health and Environment in Sustainable Development: Five Years after the Earth Summit* (WHO, Geneva, 1997), Table 3.10, p. 64.

Environmental Change and Human Health

ten discarded on fallow or public lands, in rivers, or in sewers designed to carry only municipal wastes.

The future scale of environmental and health problems from industrialization in developing countries will depend greatly on policy actions taken today. In Asia, for instance, up to 70 percent of the power-generating capacity and 90 percent of the cars in use in 2010 will be added in the next 12 years (123). If current production practices remain the norm, air pollution and toxic effluents from industrial production are likely to increase rapidly. If, however, choices are made to invest in more efficient and less-polluting technologies, many of industrialization's negative impacts on health could be avoided. The potential the developing countries have to leap-frog to cleaner production is enormous, given gains in technology as well as the levels of private capital now flowing into these countries. In Indonesia, for instance, in the first half of 1997, petrochemicals represented almost one half of the US$16.2 billion in foreign investments (124). Decisions regarding the location sites of those industries, the technologies used, and the type of precautions for occupational safety could have a tremendous impact on the future health of the people who live and work there.

Part of this industrial growth has been spurred by globalization, a term coined to describe the rapid spread of free trade, the development of free markets, and the growth of private investment across borders. Advances in production and communication technologies permit companies to locate their operations far from both raw material supplies and markets. For many companies, this freedom means locating operations in developing countries, where labor costs are significantly lower. In 1992, for example, the hourly wage in Malaysia's manufacturing sector was five times lower than in the United States, whereas in the Philippines, it was eight times lower, and in Mexico and Nicaragua, more than 10 times lower (125). Between 1988 and 1995, multinational corporations invested nearly US$422 billion worth of new factories, supplies, and equipment in developing countries. In 1995 alone, the flow of private capital into the developing world totaled close to US$180 billion (126).

Yet, globalization also carries the risk that in order to compete for valuable industries, countries will neglect measures to restrict child labor, to protect the environment, or to ensure worker safety (127). One of the most disturbing aspects of the growth of the global market is the increasing number of export-processing zones—also known as free trade zones, maquiladoras, or special economic zones. In these often unregulated areas, employees, many of them young women and sometimes children, work long hours for low pay, under sometimes hazardous conditions (128)(129).

Another concern is that industries heavily regulated in the developed world because of their harmful environmental and health impacts are migrating to the developing world. The asbestos industry is a good example. Production of asbestos, known to cause lung cancer, has shifted from developed countries such as the United States to countries such as Brazil, India, Pakistan, Indonesia, and the Republic of Korea (130). Although developed countries are phasing out asbestos, consumption in Brazil is increasing at an annual rate of about 7 percent. What is not used domestically (about 70,000 metric tons per year) is exported principally to Angola, Argentina, India, Mexico, Nigeria, Thailand, and Uruguay (131).

The export of hazardous wastes is another pressing issue. More than 350 million metric tons of hazardous waste are generated worldwide each year (132). Of this amount, approximately 1.9 million metric tons are traded among Organisation for Economic Co-Operation and Development (OECD) countries for treatment and disposal, representing an important economic industry. Officially, fewer than 1,000 metric tons are traded to developing countries (133).

Despite these official figures, illegal traffic in hazardous wastes likely represents a serious threat to the environment and human health, affecting mostly the developing world. Although no reliable figures exist for the volume of hazardous waste exported illegally, the U.S. EPA has estimated that illegal shipments outnumber legal ones by 8 to 1. Illegal shipments from the United States have been intercepted en route to Ecuador, Guinea, Haiti, Malaysia, Mexico, Panama, and Sri Lanka (134). Africa, given its financial situation and poor regulatory capacity, has become a prime target for the illegal dumping of toxic waste. As the costs of disposal continue to increase in the more developed countries—in the United States, it can cost anywhere from US$200 to US$2,300 to incinerate 1 metric ton of polychlorinated biphenyls (PCBs)—companies have a significant financial incentive to resort to illegal practices (135).

Industrialization and Health

While many of the products of industrial processes are known toxins, it is difficult to determine how these chemicals affect public health at the levels found in the environment. To what extent does environmental pollution from industrial wastes contribute to the observed increases in, for instance, birth defects and some cancers (136)?

Studies of the adverse health effects of industrial chemicals and metals are rife with complications, as described in Chapter 1. People are often exposed to a variety of environmental insults—unsafe drinking water, air pollution, and tobacco smoke, to name just a few—making it difficult to firmly link exposure to a specific chemical with an adverse health effect. In addition, health effects may take years or even decades to emerge (137). Finally, industrial pollution may act in concert with other threats such as malnutrition and infectious diseases to undermine health, particularly in the industrial slums of developing countries.

Despite these complications, toxicology, epidemiology, and occupational health studies are providing new insights into how industrial chemicals affect health. Studies show that health risks from industrial production can occur in three ways: direct physical injury from accidents in industrial production; acute chemical poisoning in the workplace or surrounding neighborhoods; and long-term exposure to chemicals released into the general environment.

Physical injury and chemical poisoning generally fall within the field of occupational health, and their health impacts are relatively well understood. Since the 1700s when Sir Percival Pott first established a link between chimney sweeps and a higher incidence of scrotal cancer, occupational exposures to hazardous chemicals provided initial warning of potential harm to the wider public. They remain a serious problem today.

The health impacts of chronic, long-term exposures are less clear. Until recently, most of the concern surrounding possible links among chemicals and long-term health effects has focused on cancers. Although numerous examples have linked occupational exposures with specific types of cancer, such as asbestos with malignant mesothelioma, it is unclear to what extent environmental exposures to chemicals contribute to the overall cancer rate (138).

Concern now encompasses other health effects as well, such as damage to the immune, nervous, and reproductive systems. Recent evidence suggests that a variety of chemicals, including PCBs, dioxins, pesticides, and heavy metals, can compromise the immune system. The immune system plays a crucial role in protecting the body from viruses, bacteria, and other invaders (139).

Although the health effects emanating from exposure to these chemicals are likely to be small compared to the toll ex-

acted from factors such as smoking, diet, and infectious disease, concern is nonetheless warranted. Industrial chemicals can persist in the environment for many decades and accumulate in marine and terrestrial food chains, thus posing health risks years after these chemicals are no longer used. Evidence also suggests the effects of exposure to toxic substances could be transgenerational. Medical history also shows that caution is appropriate; some chemicals, such as asbestos and PCBs, were used for years before they were found to cause adverse health effects.

The range of industrial processes, industrial wastes, and possible health impacts is too vast to cover in this chapter. Instead, this section focuses on two categories of ubiquitous pollutants—persistent organic pollutants (POPs) and heavy metals—to illustrate the various sources, routes of exposure, and possible health impacts resulting from exposure to industrial pollutants. In particular, this section examines the health effects of PCBs and lead in the environment. The chapter then looks at how industrial chemicals can affect human health in unsuspected ways through global ecological disruption, by looking at chlorofluorocarbons (CFCs) and the health consequences of ozone depletion. Air pollution, to which industrial production contributes significantly, is discussed in the next section, Rising Energy Use.

Persistent Organic Pollutants

The wide dissemination of POPs in the environment is generating increasing international concern. POPs, long-lived organic compounds that become more concentrated as they move up the food chain, can travel thousands of kilometers from their point of release (140).

Although POPs include a wide range of chemicals, much of the research revolves around 12 chemicals (or chemical classes) that include the industrial PCBs, polychlorinated dioxins and furans (unwanted by- products of various industrial processes), and pesticides such as DDT, chlordane, and heptachlor (141)(142). Although their use is restricted or banned in most developed countries, many POPs are still manufactured in the United States and other developed nations for export and remain widely used in developing countries (143). A recent survey of

Toxic Chemicals Are Widely Used Despite Known Risks

TABLE 2.4 Global Legal Status of Nine Persistent Organic Pollutants , 1996

	NUMBER OF COUNTRIES THAT HAVE BANNED COMPLETELY					
CHEMICAL	AFRICA (53 countries included)	NORTH AMERICA AND CENTRAL AMERICA (24 countries included)	SOUTH AMERICA (12 countries included)	ASIA (46 countries included)	EUROPE (39 countries included)	OCEANIA (10 countries included)
Aldrin	1	4	2	9.0	10.0	x
Chlordane	2	2	2	7	9	x
DDT	1	3	4	10	9	3
Dieldrin	2	5	3	10	10	3
Endrin	3	3	4	9	8	1
Heptachlor	2	2	3	9		x
Hexachlorobenzene	1	1	1	2	6	2
PCBs	x	x	x	x	2	x
Toxaphene	2	3	x	8	5	x

Source: United Nations Environment Programme (UNEP), "UNEP Survey on Sources of POPs," prepared for Intergovernmental Forum on Chemical Safety Experts Meeting on Persistent Organic Pollutants, Manila, the Philippines, June 17–19, 1996.

*E*nvironmental Change and Human Health

60 countries found that the majority were still producing, importing, or exporting the nine POPs studied. In Africa, for instance, only two countries have banned the use of chlordane, dieldrin, or heptachlor (144). (See Table 2.4.)

The health risks posed by industrial POPs can perhaps best be illustrated by PCBs, a large family of more than 200 compounds. First manufactured in the United States in 1929, PCBs quickly became ubiquitous in industrial production because of their capacity to conduct heat without conducting electricity. As electricity came into widespread use during the first half of this century, PCBs were used as insulators in refrigerators, capacitors, and in the manufacture of electrical insulation and hydraulic fluids (145). By 1989, total world production of PCBs (excluding the Soviet Union) had reached 1.5 million metric tons (146). As of 1994, only two countries reported having entirely banned PCBs, and only six reported having restricted their use (147).

As with many chemicals, high-level exposures to PCBs have been shown to be extremely dangerous to human health. In 1968, a serious mass intoxication occurred in Japan from a large-scale PCB contamination of rice-bran oil. More than 1,700 people became ill, and about 20 died. A similar mass poisoning, called Yu-Chen, occurred in Taiwan in 1979, with more than 2,000 identified victims (148). For the lower exposures typically encountered in the environment, evidence of health effects is less clear. Even so, laboratory and field observations on animals, as well as clinical and epidemiological studies in humans, suggest that adverse health effects from PCB exposure may include immune dysfunction, neurological deficits, reproductive anomalies, behavioral abnormalities, and cancer.

THE GREAT LAKES

Much of the evidence supporting low-level health effects from PCBs and other POPs in humans has been collected around the Great Lakes region in the United States. Home to roughly 36 million people, the Great Lakes basin has been a major industrial and agricultural area for many years. Until the 1970s, POPs, heavy metals, polyaromatic hydrocarbons (PAHs), and other pollutants were routinely disposed of in the lakes (149). In the 1970s and 1980s, people began to observe ill effects in fish, birds, and mammals, including signs of reproductive failure, biochemical changes, congenital malformations, and population declines (150).

These findings prompted extensive clean-up efforts, and since the early 1970s, levels of many pollutants have dropped significantly—by as much as 90 percent (151)(152). Some of the most damaging compounds still persist at significant concentrations, however. The U.S. and Canadian governments are jointly studying whether these contaminants have resulted in adverse health effects for the populations living around the lakes (153).

A primary finding of the Great Lakes research is that the major route of exposure to these chemicals is through contaminated food, such as locally raised meat and locally caught fish. Preliminary results have shown that a greater than average consumption of Great Lakes fish contaminated with PCBs and mercury compounds can damage the neurological system in the developing fetus (154).

Children are clearly at greater risk from PCBs than adults because primary exposure can occur not only during development in the womb but also through the mother's breast milk. *In utero* exposure to PCBs has been linked with deficits in fetal and postnatal growth, neurological anomalies at birth, delays in developing gross motor functions, and reduced short-term memory in infants (155). A recent study in the Great Lakes region has shown that those effects can continue into school age, leading to diminished IQ and short- and long-term memory deficits, and shortened attention span (156). Similar findings have been documented among Taiwanese children whose mothers had ingested rice oil contaminated with PCBs and dibenzofurans (157). These chemicals have also been implicated in damage to the immune system.

Because researchers have documented substantial reproductive effects in wildlife populations exposed to Great Lakes contaminants, concern has arisen over possible reproductive effects in humans. To date, evidence is inadequate to conclude that environmental contaminants damage human reproductive functions at the levels currently measured in the general population around the Great Lakes (158). (See Box 2.5.)

So far, studies do not show that the general public living near the lakes is at elevated risk from chemical contamination (159). Certain groups, however, such as Native Americans, poor urban families, Southeast Asian immigrants, and anglers may be at higher risk because these groups tend to rely on fish for a greater part of their diets, increasing their exposure to contaminants (160)(161)(162)(163). In some cases, these chemical exposures may compound the health risks these groups already face, for instance, from low nutritional status and lack of prenatal care (164). In addition, nursing infants, as well as the developing fetus, may be at special risk because of the intrinsic sensitivity of developing organisms and organ systems and the elevated exposures of nursing infants. U.S. EPA estimates that nursing infants may face exposures 40 to 50 times higher than adults (165).

FUTURE IMPLICATIONS

The lack of data in developing countries makes it difficult to assess the global scale of POP pollution and its health consequences, but it is possible to make some inferences. Incinerators equipped to deal with POPs are expensive, and the few that exist are almost all located in developed countries (166). In many developing countries, industrial wastes are burned in open dumpsites, which can release high levels of POPs into the

Box 2.5 Are Hormone Mimics Affecting Our Health?

The March 1996 publication of *Our Stolen Future* brought into full public view a debate that had been simmering in the scientific literature for several years. In this widely publicized book, zoologist Theo Colborn of the World Wildlife Fund and two coauthors hypothesize that some industrial chemicals commonly found in the environment could be wreaking havoc with human health by disrupting the body's hormonal system. Specifically, the authors suggest that these substances—dubbed "endocrine disruptors" because they interact with the endocrine, or hormone system—may be playing a role in a range of problems, from reproductive and developmental abnormalities to neurological and immunological defects to cancer (1). Evidence suggests that, at high exposures, some of these substances, which include DDT and PCBs and some pesticides, can cause reproductive and developmental problems in wildlife. The question is whether these substances can exert similar effects on humans at the relatively low doses typically found in the environment.

A lack of definitive evidence of adverse health effects in humans, yet abundant suggestive evidence associating these chemicals with problems in animals, has provided tinder for a volatile debate. Colborn and others believe that the weight of evidence in animals and people provides warning that these contaminants are threatening our fertility, intelligence, and basic survival (2). Others, such as Stephen Safe of Texas A&M University, believe these concerns are overstated, claiming they are based on findings that are contradictory at best or not relevant to the human situation (3)(4). Although many of these chemicals have been banned by developed countries because of other documented adverse effects, their widespread dispersal and persistence in the environment makes them potential health menaces for a long time to come.

So far, at least 45 chemical compounds have been proposed to be endocrine disruptors. Many are long-lived organic compounds that can persist in the environment for decades and bioaccumulate in body tissue. The list includes: certain herbicides, fungicides, and insecticides (e.g., atrazine and chlordane); industrial chemicals and byproducts such as polychlorinated biphenyls (PCBs) and dioxin; and a number of compounds found in plastics, such as phthalates and styrenes, that are used to package foods and beverages (5).

The Endocrine System

The problems attributed to endocrine disruptors are thought to arise mainly from the ability of these compounds to mimic or interfere with the normal functioning of sex hormones such as estrogen, testosterone, and progester-

one, or thyroid hormones integral to the development of the brain and other organs and tissues. Natural sex hormones play a crucial role in governing normal development. Estrogen, for example, not only helps orchestrate the sexual development of the human embryo and fetus, but it is also needed for the normal development of the brain, bone, muscles, immune system, and other organs or tissues (6). Prenatal and/or lifetime exposures to sex hormones are also hypothesized to influence the risk of developing various cancers (7).

These hormones travel in the blood and exert their effects by binding to molecules in cells known as hormone receptors. This in turn activates genes in the nucleus of the cell to produce a range of biological responses. Under normal conditions, the body carefully controls the amount of active hormones to ensure that the system runs smoothly. For instance, the body produces specific proteins that can latch onto the hormones and regulate their access to cells. The body also protects itself from excessive amounts of potent hormones by putting the reins on hormone production or by damping cells' sensitivity to hormones. Endocrine disruptors can work as both hormone mimics and hormone blockers, in both cases with a potential to disrupt normal cellular activity. Scientists are still a long way from knowing at what levels of exposure these effects can be seen (8)(9).

Clues from Wildlife

The first evidence of the effects of endocrine disruptors on reproduction was prompted by dramatic findings in wildlife. During the 1970s and 1980s, PCBs, DDT, dioxin, and other endocrine disruptors were linked with reproductive abnormalities including reduced penis size and hampered fertility of Florida alligators, and abnormal mating behavior and reproductive organs in Western gulls in the United States (10).

These findings prompted researchers to look at the possible role of these substances in human health problems as well. Results have been conflicting, with some studies suggesting harm while others do not. Sorting out these scientific questions is complicated because many of these substances, such as DDT, are known to have adverse effects on both animals and humans, whether or not they disrupt the endocrine system. In other words, their adverse health effects could be unrelated to the compound's influence on hormones. Complicating matters further, many of the recent epidemiologic studies have been preliminary, or "ecological," in nature. That means that a study may find that a rise in cancer, for instance, coincides with a rise in the use of a suspect chemical—but there may be no evidence that people

exposed to the chemical develop cancer. As one researcher points out, data can show that the stork population has declined and that the number of births has declined, but that doesn't mean storks bring babies.

Human Health Effects

Some of the strongest evidence on the reproductive effects of endocrine disruptors in humans comes from long-term studies of the potent synthetic estrogen diethylstilbestrol (DES), which was given to thousands of women in the 1950s and 1960s to prevent miscarriage. Studies tracking DES-exposed sons and daughters since the 1970s have found a significant number of abnormalities in the structure and function of reproductive organs (11). Some studies have documented that men exposed to DES prenatally are significantly more likely to have smaller testicles and penises, undescended testicles, and poor semen quality (12). Other studies contradict those findings. In addition, because the men were exposed prenatally to much larger quantities of an estrogen-like substance than they would be likely to encounter in normal environmental settings, these findings cannot be easily extrapolated to the general population.

Nevertheless, some researchers have suggested that endocrine disruptors may be associated with a decline in sperm counts in the general population. This hypothesis emerged when Danish, French, Belgian, and British researchers noted as much as a 50 percent decline in sperm counts over the past 20 to 60 years—roughly the same time during which the use of these endocrine disruptors became widespread (13). Studies in the United States, France, and Finland, however, have not seen a decline in sperm counts; some have even reported an increase (14)(15). That leaves researchers uncertain about, first, whether a decline in sperm counts has actually occurred in some parts of the world; and second, if it has, whether such a decline can be attributed to the influence of endocrine disruptors.

Similar uncertainties abound over whether exposure to endocrine disruptors could be affecting the ratio of male-to-female births in humans. Animal studies suggest that exposure to certain pesticides can affect the sex ratio of gulls, alligators, and turtles, resulting in a decline in male births (16)(17). In humans, some studies have suggested a minor decline in the proportion of male births in the Netherlands from 1950 to 1994 and in Denmark from 1951 to 1995 (18)(19). Many other factors are known to affect the proportion of female births, in-

Box 2.5 continued

cluding the age of parents, the time in their cycles during which women conceive, or the introduction of hormonally induced ovulation in the 1980s (20).

Concern that endocrine disruptors might cause cancer has arisen in part from the clear role of DES in cancers in female reproductive organs. In addition, a number of epidemiologic studies have shown that elevated lifetime exposure to the body's own estrogens, (from, say, early onset of menses or late menopause) increases a woman's risk of developing breast cancer (21). Could exposure to endocrine disruptors also boost the risk of developing such cancers? (See the Guest Commentary by Devra Davis.) Trend data suggest that the incidence of hormonally mediated cancers, which include breast, testicular, and prostate cancer, are on the rise in some parts of the world (22).

Some of the increase in breast and prostate cancer is thought to stem from better screening techniques, earlier diagnosis, and the effect of an aging population. Some researchers have posited that environmental and occupational exposure to endocrine disruptors may also explain some of the rise. Indeed, some studies have found that farmers exposed to certain pesticides and herbicides have an increased risk of developing prostate cancer or testicular cancer. Other studies have not found such a link, although in some cases other chemicals were examined (23)(24).

Another potentially serious effect of exposure to endocrine disruptors is neurological impairment. Much of the concern stems from a study conducted in the Great Lakes region of the United States, which found that children exposed to PCBs prenatally suffered small but significant intellectual impairment. The most highly exposed children were three times as likely to have lowered IQ scores and were twice as likely to be at least two years behind in reading comprehension. The exposed children were also more likely to have problems with attention span and memory. What's more, the levels of PCBs that these children were exposed to were only slightly higher than those found in the general population (25).

As for a possible mechanism, laboratory studies have suggested that exposure to PCBs prenatally or through breast milk can lower blood levels of thyroid hormones needed to stimulate the growth and maturation of brain cells (26). However, the mechanism has yet to be determined, and it is also possible that PCBs are impairing intelligence through a mechanism unrelated to endocrine disruption (27).

Natural hormones also have a hand in shaping the prenatal development of the immune system and influencing its actions in children and adults (28), sparking concern that endocrine disruptors might affect the immune system to some degree

and put people more at risk of developing infections.

The role of endocrine disruptors in causing these and other effects is now under active investigation worldwide. At this stage, the general consensus among most experts is that many more studies need to be done to assess whether the synthetic chemicals that have helped shape agriculture and industry are also shaping the health fates of individuals, or even the population at large. At the international level, the World Health Organization and the Organisation for Economic Co-Operation and Development (OECD) are undertaking an international inventory of research. National governments, other international organizations, and even private companies are funding and/or conducting research to fill in the current knowledge gaps (29)(30). In the interim, countries are struggling with whether and how to regulate these substances as scientific understanding evolves.

References and Notes

1. Theo Colborn, Dianne Dumanoski, and John Peterson Myers, *Our Stolen Future* (Penguin Books, New York, 1996), pp. 26, 81, 133–134, 199.

2. *Ibid.,* pp. 260–268.

3. Stephen H. Safe, "Is There an Association Between Exposure to Environmental Estrogens and Breast Cancer?" *Environmental Health Perspectives* (in press) pp. 2–8.

4. Ronald Bailey, "Hormones and Humbug," *The Washington Post* (March 31, 1996), p. C3.

5. Theo Colborn, Frederick S. Vom Saal, and Ana M. Soto, "Developmental Effects of Endocrine Disrupting Chemicals in Wildlife and Humans," *Environmental Health Perspectives*, Vol. 101, No. 5, (1993), p. 379.

6. *Op. cit.* 1, p. 46.

7. Brian Henderson, Ronald Ross, and Malcolm Pike, "Toward the Primary Prevention of Cancer," *Science*, Vol. 254 (Nov. 22, 1991), pp. 1135–36.

8. Stephen H. Safe and Timothy Zacharewski, "Organochlorine Exposure and Risk for Breast Cancer," in *Etiology of Breast and Gynecological Cancers*, (John Wiley and Sons, New York, in press).

9. Louis Guillette, Jr., D. Andrew Crain, Andrew Rooney, and Daniel Pickford, "Organization versus Activation: The Role of Endocrine-Disrupting Contaminants during Embryonic Development in Wildlife," *Environmental Health Perspectives*, Vol. 103, Supplement 7 (1995), p. 161.

10. *Op. cit.* 1, pp. 21–23, 131–132, 150–156.

11. R.J. Stillman "*Inutero* exposure to diethylstilbestrol: adverse effects on the reproductive tract and reproductive performance in male and female offspring," *American Journal of Obstetrics and Gynecology*, Vol. 142 (1982), pp. 905–921.

12. Jorma Toppari *et al.*, "Male Reproductive Health and Environmental Xenoestrogens," *Environmental Health Perspectives*, Vol. 104, Suppl. 4 (1996), pp. 753–754.

13. *Ibid.*, pp. 742–743.

14. *Op. cit.* 12, p. 743.

15. Larry Lipshultz, "The Debate Continues—the Continuing Debate over the Possible Decline in Semen

Quality," *Fertility and Sterility*, Vol. 65, No. 5 (1996), p. 910.

16. *Op. cit.* 9, pp. 157–158.

17. *Op. cit.* 12, p. 751.

18. Karin van der Pal-de-Bruin, S. Pauline Verloove-Vanhorick and Nel Roeleveld, "Change in male:female ratio among newborn babies in Netherlands," *The Lancet*, Vol. 349 (January 4, 1997), p. 62.

19. Henrik Moller, "Change in male-female ratio among newborn infants in Denmark," *Lancet*, Vol. 348, Sept 21 (1996), p. 828–29.

20. *Ibid.*

21. *Op. cit.* 7.

22. Kate Cahow, "The Cancer Conundrum," in *Environmental Health Perspectives*, Vol. 103, No. 11 (November 1995), p. 999.

23. K. Wiklund and J. Dich, "Cancer Risks Among Male Farmers in Sweden," *European Journal of Cancer Prevention*, Vol. 4, No. 1 (February 1995), p. 81.

24. *Ibid.*, pp. 81–90.

25. Joseph Jacobson and Sandra Jacobson, "Intellectual Impairment in Children Exposed to Polychlorinated Biphenyls in Utero," *New England Journal of Medicine*, Vol. 335, No. 11 (1996), p. 783.

26. Susan P. Porterfield, "Vulnerability of the Developing Brain to Thyroid Abnormalities: Environmental Insults to the Thyroid System," *Environmental Health Perspectives* (June 1994), pp. 125–130.

27. Committee on Environment and Natural Resources, National Science and Technology Council (CENR), *The Health and Ecological Effects of Endocrine Disrupting Chemicals: A Framework for Planning* (CENR, Washington, D.C., November 22, 1996), p. 4.

28. U.S. Environmental Protection Agency (U.S.EPA), *Special Report on Environmental Endocrine Disruption: An Effects Assessment and Analysis* (U.S.EPA, Washington, D.C., 1997), p. 55.

29. European Environment Agency (EEA), "Call for Action to Reduce Uncertainties and Risks Concerning Reproductive Health Due to Endocrine Disruptors," Copenhagen, April 17 (press release). Available online at: http://www.eea.dk/document/NLetPR/PressRel/enocr.htm (January 22, 1998).

30. Society of Organic Chemical Manufacturers Association (SOCMA), *SOCMA Response on Endocrine Modulators.* Available online at http://www.socma.com/endopos.html (December 1997).

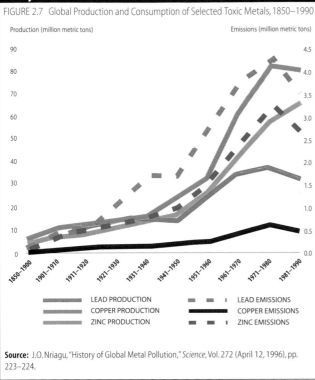

Heavy Metal Production Has Soared Since 1850

FIGURE 2.7 Global Production and Consumption of Selected Toxic Metals, 1850–1990

Production (million metric tons)   Emissions (million metric tons)

LEAD PRODUCTION — — LEAD EMISSIONS
COPPER PRODUCTION — — COPPER EMISSIONS
ZINC PRODUCTION — — ZINC EMISSIONS

Source: J.O. Nriagu, "History of Global Metal Pollution," *Science*, Vol. 272 (April 12, 1996), pp. 223–224.

immediate vicinity. Concern is mounting that the history of environmental contamination in the Great Lakes region is repeating itself in many industrial and agricultural areas of the developing world. In Cameroon, for instance, growth in industries such as oil refineries, electroplating, and power generation is creating large quantities of wastes contaminated with metals and POPs. Scientists have measured extremely high PCB loads in the surrounding area (167).

Furthermore, as the experience with the Great Lakes has shown, even after decades of expensive cleanup, concentrations of many pollutants, including dioxins, PCBs, and methyl mercury, can remain unacceptably high in some fish species (168)(169). In many parts of the world, fish represent an important source of protein, so levels of PCBs are an important health concern.

Heavy Metals and Health

Since the Industrial Revolution, the production of heavy metals such as lead, copper, and zinc has increased exponentially. Between 1850 and 1990, production of these three metals increased nearly 10-fold, with emissions rising in tandem (170). (See Figure 2.7.) Heavy metals have been used in a variety of ways for at least 2 millennia. For example, lead has been used in plumbing, and lead arsenate has been used to control in-

sects in apple orchards. The Romans added lead to wine to improve its taste, and mercury was used as a salve to alleviate teething pain in infants (171)(172).

The toxicity of these metals has also been documented throughout history: Greek and Roman physicians diagnosed symptoms of acute lead poisoning long before toxicology became a science. Today, much more is known about the health effects of heavy metals. Exposure to heavy metals has been linked with developmental retardation, various cancers, kidney damage, and even death in some instances of exposure to very high concentrations. Exposure to high levels of mercury, gold, and lead has also been associated with the development of autoimmunity, in which the immune system starts to attack its own cells, mistaking them for foreign invaders (173). Autoimmunity can lead to the development of diseases of the joints and kidneys, such as rheumatoid arthritis, or diseases of the circulatory or central nervous systems (174).

Despite abundant evidence of these deleterious health effects, exposure to heavy metals continues and may increase in the absence of concerted policy actions. Mercury is still extensively used in gold mining in many parts of Latin America. Arsenic, along with copper and chromium compounds, is a common ingredient in wood preservatives. Lead is still widely used as an additive in gasoline. Increased use of coal in the future will increase metal exposures because coal ash contains many toxic metals and can be breathed deeply into the lungs. For countries such as China and India, which continue to rely on high-ash coal as a primary energy source, the health implications are ominous (175).

Once emitted, metals can reside in the environment for hundreds of years or more. Evidence of human exploitation of heavy metals has been found in the ice cores in Greenland and sea water in the Antarctic. The lead contents of ice layers deposited annually in Greenland show a steady rise that parallels the mining renaissance in Europe, reaching values 100 times the natural background level in the mid-1990s (176).

Mining itself, not only of heavy metals but also of coal and other minerals, is another major route of exposure. Despite some noted improvements in worker safety and cleaner production, mining remains one of the most hazardous and environmentally damaging industries. In Bolivia, toxic sludge from a zinc mine in the Andes had killed aquatic life along a 300-kilometer stretch of river systems as of 1996. It also threatened the livelihood and health of 50,000 of the region's subsistence farmers (177). Uncontrolled smelters have produced some of the world's only environmental "dead zones," where little or no vegetation survives. For instance, toxic emissions from the Sudbury, Ontario, nickel smelter have devastated 10,400 hectares of forests downwind of the smelter (178).

Environmental Change and Human Health

LEAD

Aside from smoke, lead is probably the oldest human-made atmospheric and occupational toxin, dating back at least 8,000 years to the first lead-smelting furnaces (179). Today, lead poisoning remains the single most significant preventable disease associated with an environmental and occupational toxin (180).

The risks of lead exposure vary greatly depending upon where one lives. In Bangkok, Mexico City, and Jakarta, exposure largely stems from automotive exhausts; however, in inner-city Chicago and Washington, D.C., exposure is mostly associated

Lead Pollution Poses a Special Hazard to Children

TABLE 2.5 Selected Studies Showing High Blood Lead Levels Among Children, 1988–95

COUNTRY (city/region)	YEAR	RANGE OF BLOOD LEAD LEVELS (micrograms per deciliter)	MEAN	PERCENTAGE OF CHILDREN WITH LEVELS >10 MICROGRAMS PER DECILITER
Argentina (urban)	1989	7–42	22.1±7	NA
Bulgaria				
Haskovo	1995	5.5–19.8		NA
Kritehim	1991	4.1–15.1		NA
Kourtove-Kon	1991	6.5–41.3		NA
China				
Shenyang (polluted urban)	1991	NA	30.5	99.5
Shenyang (nonpolluted urban)	1991	NA	12.2	67.9
Beijing (polluted suburban)	1992	NA	22.4	64.9
Shanghai (polluted urban)	1988	5.0–55.0	23.4	85.6
Shanghai (nonpolluted suburban)	1988	0–55.0	18.4	88.2
Mexico (urban)	1995	1–31	9.0±5.8	27.8
Poland				
Town with no industrial emitters	1992–94	2.25–2.39		NA
Town with copper and zinc mills	1992–94	7.37–11.40		NA
Romania				
Bucharest	1995	17.10–21.93		NA
Uruguay	1994	1–31	9.5	NA

Sources: Argentina, Mexico, and Uruguay: Isabelle Romieu *et al.*, "Lead Exposure in Latin America and the Caribbean," *Environmental Health Perspectives*, Vol. 105, Number 4 (April 1997), p. 404. Bulgaria and Romania: Danish Environmental Protection Agency, "Second Meeting of the Task Force on the Phaseout of Lead in Gasoline," Working Document Presenting the Preliminary Results of Country Surveys, Part I (May 1997), p. 25. China: Xiao-ming Shen *et al.*, "Childhood Lead Poisoning in China," *The Science of the Total Environment*, Vol. 181 (1996), p. 103.

Note: NA = not available.

with lead in house paint (181). Generally, human exposure to lead comes from the following main sources: using leaded gasoline; using lead-based paint; having lead pipes in water supply systems; and exposure to industrial sources from processes such as lead mining, smelting, and coal combustion. Additional sources of lead include soldered seams in food cans, ceramic glazes, batteries, and cosmetics (182).

Lead is particularly toxic to the brain, kidneys, reproductive system, and cardiovascular system. Exposures can cause impairments in intellectual functioning, kidney damage, infertility, miscarriage, and hypertension (183). Lead is a special hazard for young children. Several studies have shown that lead exposures can significantly reduce the IQ of school-aged children; some estimates suggest that every 10-microgram-per-deciliter increase in lead levels in the blood is associated with a 1- to 5-point decrease in the IQ of exposed children (184). Lead exposures have also been associated with aggressive behavior, delinquency, and attention disorders in boys between the ages of 7 and 11 (185). In adults, lead exposure has been related to increased blood pressure and hypertension, conditions known to increase the risk of cardiovascular disease.

Unlike most chemicals for which health impacts of low-level doses are still uncertain, exposure to lead, even at very low levels, is highly toxic (186). Although 10 micrograms of lead per 1 deciliter of blood is generally used as the level above

which health impacts are known to be substantial, scientists have not yet identified a level below which no adverse effects of lead occur (187)(188). Several studies have found detectable learning problems in children whose blood lead levels are as low as 5 to 10 micrograms per deciliter (189).

Exposures to unhealthy levels of lead remain common throughout both developed and developing countries. (See Table 2.5.) Among urban children in developing countries, the majority of children younger than 2 years of age have average blood lead levels greater than 10 micrograms per deciliter, estimates suggest (190). A review of 17 studies from different parts of China found that between 65 and 99.5 percent of children living in industrial and heavy traffic areas had blood lead levels above 10 micrograms per deciliter. Even outside of those high-risk areas, as many as 50 percent of China's children had unacceptably high blood lead levels (191). Even in Africa, despite comparatively low levels of industrialization and car usage, lead exposure is a serious problem. In Nigeria, for instance, it is estimated that 15 to 30 percent of the children in urban areas have blood lead levels greater than 25 micrograms per deciliter (192).

The health toll of lead exposure is particularly high among poor populations of developed and developing countries alike, both because exposures are typically higher and because the populations may be more susceptible. In urban areas, for instance, the poor may live near major roadways where exposure to vehicle emissions is high. They also tend to live in older housing, where the risks from lead-based paint are greater. In addition, lead is believed to be absorbed from the stomach more completely when the stomach is empty and when the diet lacks essential trace elements, such as iron, calcium, and zinc (193).

LEAD IN GASOLINE

Although lead in gasoline represents only 2.2 percent of total global lead use, leaded gasoline remains by far the single largest source of lead exposure in urban areas. Approximately 90 percent of all lead emissions into the atmosphere are due to the use of leaded gasoline (194). Populations in at least 100 countries are still exposed to air polluted with lead from gasoline. (See Appendix.) Besides posing an immediate health risk through inhalation, vehicular lead emissions can also accumulate in soil, contaminate drinking water, and enter the food chain (195).

The use of lead in gasoline has a long history. In 1922, auto manufacturers realized that adding lead to gasoline could boost its octane rating and produce more power. Concerns over the health effects of lead in gasoline surfaced just two years later, when, in the experimental laboratories of the Standard Oil Company, 5 out of 49 workers died and 35 experienced severe neurological symptoms from organic lead poisoning. Soon thereafter, the state of New York, the city of Philadelphia, and some other municipalities briefly banned the sale of leaded gasoline. However, once the immediate furor subsided, the use of lead in gasoline resumed (196). The amount of lead additives increased quickly, rising to 375,000 metric tons annually by early 1970s (197).

By 1970, however, concerns about tailpipe emissions led to the introduction of catalytic converters in the United States and Canada. Because leaded gasoline is incompatible with catalytic converters, cars with converters required unleaded gasoline (198). In 1985, the U.S. EPA decided to accelerate its gradual phaseout of leaded gasoline and implemented legislation designed to slash the use of lead in gasoline by more than an order of magnitude in less than 1 year (199). (See Chapter 3.) The public health benefits of these reductions have been dramatic. Between 1976 and 1990, average blood lead levels in the U.S. population declined from 14.5 to 2.8 micrograms per deciliter, paralleling the phaseout of leaded gasoline (200). This finding suggests that as much as 40 to 60 percent of blood lead levels in the U.S. population were associated with leaded gasoline (201). Similarly, after unleaded gasoline was introduced in Mexico City in 1990, mean blood lead level concentrations in schoolchildren dropped from 16.5 to 11.14 micrograms per deciliter in 1992 (202).

Despite these remarkably successful programs, by the end of 1996, only 14 countries had completely phased out the use of leaded gasoline (203)(204). In many countries in Africa and Southeast Asia, unleaded gasoline is scarce, and the maximum allowed lead content of gasoline may reach or exceed 0.8 grams per liter (205). Although fuel consumption in these countries is considerably lower than in the rest of the world, lead emissions represent a serious health hazard because of the increasing pace of urbanization and the increased use of motor vehicles (206). Even in Latin America, where several countries are making concerted efforts to reduce the lead in gasoline, increased gasoline consumption associated with urban growth and car ownership is nevertheless forcing large increases in the total amount of lead emissions (207). In most European countries, roughly one half of the cars use unleaded gasoline, while the other half still use gas containing 0.15 grams of lead per liter (208).

OTHER SOURCES

For some populations, other sources of lead may be more important than gasoline. The most acute and even fatal lead poisoning cases are associated with lead mining and processing. In a 1992 study of the Baia Mare (Big Mine), Romania, lead smelter workers had mean blood lead levels of 77.4 micrograms per deciliter. In children living near the lead smelter, mean blood lead levels of 63.3 micrograms per deciliter were measured (209).

Battery recycling is also an important source of lead exposures. On a global scale, 63 percent of all processed lead is used in the manufacturing of batteries (210). In Mexico, the Caribbean, and India, family-based industries use open furnaces in their backyards to recover lead from batteries by crude smelting. These cottage industries can result in extremely high lead exposures for the whole family. In Jamaica, children living near backyard smelter sites had mean blood lead levels nearly three times those of children from communities with no backyard smelting activities, according to a recent study (211). In 1991, an outbreak of lead poisoning occurred in Trinidad and Tobago where the soil was contaminated by wastes from battery recycling. Blood lead concentrations in children living in this area varied between 17 and 235 micrograms per deciliter, with an average of 72.1 micrograms per deciliter (212).

Lead-glazed pottery and lead pigments in children's toys and pencils are other routes of exposure (213). Approximately 30 percent of the population in Mexico uses glazed pottery regularly, placing nearly 24 million people at risk of exposure to lead from this single source (214). Lead solder in aluminum cans can also pose significant risks; in Honduras, for instance, studies have shown that lead residues in canned food range from 0.13 to 14.8 milligrams per kilogram, far above WHO guidelines (215).

In the United States, despite much progress in reducing mean blood lead levels and eliminating lead from gasoline, lead poisoning remains a major health hazard for children under the age of 6. Approximately 1.7 million children in the

*E*nvironmental Change and Human Health

United States have blood lead levels that exceed the recommended level of 10 micrograms per deciliter (216), with the highest average blood lead levels found among poor, urban, African-American, and Hispanic children (217). (See Table 2.6.) Lead-based paint is a major exposure route. Although lead has been banned from residential paint since 1978, about three quarters of all housing units built before 1980 contain some lead-based paint (218). Because lead-based paint is still used throughout Latin America and the Caribbean, this threatens to become a major route of exposure in those countries as well (219).

CFCs, the Ozone Hole, and Health

Until recently, concern about industrial pollution has centered on its direct toxicological effects. Yet, researchers have begun to understand that pollutants can also affect humans indirectly, through large-scale ecological disruptions.

Like PCBs, chlorofluorocarbons (CFCs) were first synthesized in 1930 and were quickly hailed as safe alternatives to ammonia and other coolants prone to leaks and explosions (220). CFCs were used extensively as refrigeration and air-conditioning fluids, aerosol propellants, solvents, and fire suppressants. Since then, however, it has become evident that these long-lived chemicals are primarily responsible for the progressive depletion of the stratospheric ozone layer. The most dramatic manifestation of ozone depletion is the springtime ozone hole over Antarctica, first discovered in 1985.

In response to stratospheric ozone depletion, the international community negotiated the Montreal Protocol in 1987 to phase out production of ozone-depleting substances. The treaty required developed countries to end the production of most ozone-depleting substances by January 1996. Developing countries were allowed to increase the production of CFCs until 1999, after which their production must be cut progressively until it ends in 2010. However, even assuming that the Montreal Protocol is fully implemented, the concentration of stratospheric ozone is not expected to return to its normal level until the second half of the next century (221). (See Stratospheric Ozone Depletion in Chapter 4.)

The major significance of stratospheric ozone depletion for health is reduced shielding of the Earth's surface against incoming solar ultraviolet radiation, in particular UV-B (222). Efforts to measure the associated increase in ground-level UV radiation are just beginning, but models provide some insight into the expected changes. Under existing conditions, the World Meteorological Association has projected that ground-level UV-B radiation will increase by around 15 percent in winter and spring and 8 percent in summer and autumn in the northern midlatitudes (including countries in North America and Europe). Southern temperate areas are expected to experience ground-level UV-B increases of 13 percent (223). Increased UV-B levels have been documented in some studies for mid- and high-latitude locations. In the Swiss Alps, for instance, scientists recently concluded that ground-level UV-B has increased by 7 ($\pm$ 4 percent) between 1981 and 1991 (224).

The extent to which skin cancer incidence will rise in response is uncertain. Assuming no change occurs in the behavior of the general population, a sustained 10 to 15 percent depletion of stratospheric ozone over several decades, as projected, could result in an estimated 15- to 20-percent increase in the incidence of skin cancer in fair-skinned populations, or about 250,000 additional cases each year (225). This figure is rough, however, since the model does not take into account individual susceptibility and personal behavior, such as wearing sunscreen to minimize exposures. In addition to its link with skin cancer, UV light can cause cataracts. The best current estimate shows that for each 1-percent depletion in stratospheric ozone, cataract incidence would increase by 0.6 to 0.8 percent (226).

Over the past 15 years, animal studies have identified several immunosuppressive effects of UV-B; the few studies that have been conducted on humans lend support to these results (227). Other studies suggest that although dark-skinned people are at less risk of skin cancer, pigmentation does not seem to be protective against UV's effects on the immune system (228). A compromised immune system makes it more difficult to fight off infectious diseases, making UV's immunosuppressive effects potentially some of the most dangerous (229).

Lead Poisoning Threatens Many U.S. Children

TABLE 2.6   Differences in Blood Lead Levels Based on Race/Ethnicity, Income Level, and Urban Status, 1988–91

	PERCENTAGE OF CHILDREN 1 TO 5 YEARS OF AGE WITH BLOOD LEAD LEVELS $\geq$10 MICROGRAMS PER DECILITER			
INCOME LEVEL	**ALL**	**NON-HISPANIC WHITE**	**NON-HISPANIC BLACK**	**MEXICAN AMERICAN**
Low	16.3	9.8	28.4	8.8
Mid	5.4	4.8	8.9	5.6
High	4.0	4.3	5.8	0 [a]
Urban status				
Central city, > 1 million	21.0	6.1 [a]	36.7	17.0
Central city, < 1 million	16.4	8.1	22.5	9.5
Noncentral city	5.8	52.0	11.2	7.0

Source: Debra Brody *et al.,* "Blood Lead Levels in the U.S. Population: Phase I of the Third National Health and Nutrition Examination Survey (NHANES III, 1988 to 1991)," *Journal of the American Medical Association,* Vol. 272, Number 4 (July 27, 1994), p. 282, Table 5.

Note: a. Estimate may be unstable due to small sample size.

Rising Energy Use

Energy is central to our economies, our lifestyles, and our health. It powers industrial production, transportation, and increasingly, agricultural production. It provides services such as heating, refrigeration, and lighting, which raise the quality of life and provide tangible health benefits such as unspoiled food and relief from the stresses of heat or cold.

Global energy use has climbed steadily over the years as industrial economies have expanded; this rapid rise is expected to continue over the next several decades. According to one model, energy use could increase roughly 40 percent between 1993 and 2010 (230). Even if anticipated gains in energy efficiency from the adoption of new technology are factored in, energy use is likely to continue to surge beyond 2010 as well (231). (Of course, aggressive steps to reduce energy use could change the course of these trends.)

Today, developed nations consume nearly three quarters of all commercial energy; however, much of the additional energy demand in the next few decades will come from developing nations. Indeed, developing nations are expected to increase their share of world energy use to almost 40 percent by 2010 (232), reflecting rapid economic expansion, high population growth, and the substitution of fossil fuels for traditional biomass fuels. (See Figure 2.8.) Growth will be particularly dramatic in East and South Asia (exclusive of Japan).

The health implications of rising energy use are profound. To the extent that rising energy use contributes to services

Jorgen Schytte/Still Pictures

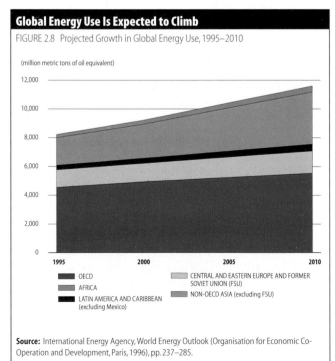

Global Energy Use Is Expected to Climb

FIGURE 2.8 Projected Growth in Global Energy Use, 1995–2010

(million metric tons of oil equivalent)

- OECD
- AFRICA
- LATIN AMERICA AND CARIBBEAN (excluding Mexico)
- CENTRAL AND EASTERN EUROPE AND FORMER SOVIET UNION (FSU)
- NON-OECD ASIA (excluding FSU)

Source: International Energy Agency, World Energy Outlook (Organisation for Economic Co-Operation and Development, Paris, 1996), pp. 237–285.

Note: Assumes current energy use patterns continue to dominate future consumption.

such as heating or refrigeration, to a more stable food supply, or to greater per capita income through economic expansion, it could bring considerable health benefits, especially in developing nations. However, it will undoubtedly bring about substantial health risks as well, since it will involve a major increase in the use of fossil fuels, despite some anticipated growth in the use of less-polluting forms of renewable energy (233).

The most direct impact of higher fossil fuel use could be an increase in air pollution levels, especially in urban areas. At the same time, rapid urbanization in the developing world will be exposing greater numbers of people to dirty urban air. Without greater attention to pollution control, some cities in the developing world could see as much as a doubling of their current air pollution levels in the next decade or so (234).

Greater coal use and a rapidly expanding fleet of cars and trucks worldwide are the two most serious threats to air quality as fossil fuel consumption rises. Coal, as a potent source of sulfur dioxide and particulates, is notorious for its impact on air quality. Global coal use over the next two decades is expected to rise more than 50 percent, mostly in the developing

*E*nvironmental Change and Human Health

world and especially in Asia (235). Meanwhile, the vehicle fleet will continue to grow, particularly in areas like China, India, and Thailand, where vehicle density is still relatively low and per capita income—and consumer appetites—are on the rise. The energy used for transportation of all types is predicted to rise about 50 percent from 1993 to 2010, an average rise of a little more than 2 percent per year. By comparison, transport-related energy will grow twice that fast in the developing world as a whole, and three times that fast in south Asia (236).

Increasing energy use will not necessarily result in a one-for-one increase in pollution levels, because attention to pollution control will likely increase as well. Much is possible through the adoption of new technologies to clean up power plant emissions, auto exhaust, and other pollution sources, or a switch to cleaner fuels. But in areas like Asia, the growth in energy use is likely to outpace efforts at pollution control. In China, for instance, the government has achieved some success in reducing residential coal use and thus indoor air pollution, but increased auto traffic on congested roadways offers a new and growing threat to air quality. (See Regional Profile on China.) Even in industrialized countries, where air quality standards may well get stricter in light of concerns over health effects, trends toward higher energy use and greater traffic congestion will make it hard to meet national air quality goals.

Looking beyond immediate impacts on air quality, rising fossil fuel use will produce higher greenhouse gas emissions, increasing the threat of global warming. Without a major global effort to curtail carbon dioxide emissions, they are expected to double from pre-industrial levels before 2100 (237). In response, the Earth's average surface temperature is expected to warm by 1.0° C to 3.5° C over the coming century (238) —a more rapid change in climate than has occurred for the last 10,000 years. Although health impacts are uncertain, most are likely to be negative, according to the Intergovernmental Panel on Climate Change (IPCC) (239).

Health Effects of Air Pollution

OUTDOOR AIR AND HEALTH

For more than a century, severe air pollution incidents in cities such as London have shown that breathing dirty air can be dangerous and, at times, deadly. In 1880, 2,200 Londoners died in one such incident when coal smoke from home heating and industry combined to form a toxic smog of sulfur dioxide gas and airborne combustion particles (240). But concern about the health effects of outdoor air pollution did not effectively coalesce until the late 1940s and early 1950s, when air pollution disasters on two continents raised an alarm. Both the 1948 "killer fog" in the small town of Denora, Pennsylva-

nia, that killed 50, and the particularly virulent London "fog" of 1952, in which some 4,000 died, were associated with widespread use of dirty fuels and were catalysts for government efforts to tackle urban air pollution.

Since then, many nations have adopted ambient air quality standards to safeguard the public against the most common and damaging pollutants. These include sulfur dioxide, suspended particulate matter, ground-level ozone, nitrogen dioxide, carbon monoxide, and lead—all of which are tied directly or indirectly to the combustion of fossil fuels. Although substantial investments in pollution control in some industrialized countries have lowered the levels of these pollutants in many cities, poor air quality is still a major concern throughout the industrialized world. A recent assessment by the European Environment Agency found that 70 to 80 percent of 105 European cities surveyed exceeded WHO air quality standards for at least one pollutant (241). In the United States, an estimated 80 million people live in areas that do not meet U.S. air quality standards, which are roughly similar to WHO standards (242).

Meanwhile, urban air pollution has worsened in most large cities in the developing world, a situation driven by population growth, industrialization, and increased vehicle use. Despite pollution control effects, air quality has approached the dangerous levels recorded in London in the 1950s in a number of megacities, such as Beijing, Delhi, Jakarta, and Mexico City (243). In these cities, pollutant levels sometimes exceed WHO air quality standards by a factor of three or more. In some of China's major cities, particulate levels are as much as six times the WHO guidelines (244). Worldwide, WHO estimates that as many as 1.4 billion urban residents breathe air exceeding the WHO air guidelines (245).

The health consequences of exposure to dirty air are considerable. On a global basis, estimates of mortality due to outdoor air pollution run from around 200,000 to 570,000, representing about 0.4 to 1.1 percent of total annual deaths (246) (247). As the range of these estimates indicates, it is difficult to quantify the toll of outdoor air pollution. The health impacts of urban air pollution seem likely to be greater in some of the rapidly developing countries where pollution levels are higher. The World Bank has estimated that exposure to particulate levels exceeding the WHO health standard accounts for roughly 2 to 5 percent of all deaths in urban areas in the developing world (248).

However, these mortality estimates alone do not capture the huge toll of illness and disability that exposure to air pollution brings at a global level. Health effects span a wide range of severity from coughing and bronchitis to heart disease and lung cancer. Vulnerable groups include infants, the elderly, and those suffering from chronic respiratory conditions including asthma, bronchitis, or emphysema. For example, air pollution in developing world cities is responsible for some 50

Box 2.6 Urban Air: Health Effects of Particulates, Sulfur Dioxide, and Ozone

Of the suite of pollutants that taint urban air, fine suspended particulate matter, sulfur dioxide (SO_2), and ozone pose the most widespread and acute risks; however, airborne lead pollution is a critical concern in many cities as well. Recent studies on the effects of chronic exposure to air pollution have singled out particulate matter as the pollutant most responsible for the life-shortening effect of dirty air, although other pollutants may also play an important role.

Particulate Pollution

Suspended particulate matter is a nearly ubiquitous urban pollutant. Although particulate levels in North America and Western Europe rarely exceed 50 micrograms of particulate matter per cubic meter ($\mu g/m^3$) of air, levels in many Central and Eastern European cities and in many developing nations are much higher, often exceeding 100 $\mu g/m^3$ (1).

Particulate air pollution is a complex mixture of small and large particles of varying origin and chemical composition. Larger particles, ranging from about 2.5 microns to 100 microns in diameter, usually comprise smoke and dust from industrial processes, agriculture, construction, and road traffic, as well as plant pollen and other natural sources. Smaller particles—those less than 2.5 microns in diameter—generally come from combustion of fossil fuels. These particles include soot from vehicle exhaust, which is often coated with various chemical contaminants or metals, and fine sulfate and nitrate aerosols that form when SO_2 and nitrogen oxides condense in the atmosphere. The largest source of fine particles is coal-fired power plants, but auto and diesel exhaust are also prime contributors, especially along busy transportation corridors.

The health effects of particulates are strongly linked to particle size. Small particles, such as those from fossil fuel combustion, are likely to be most dangerous, because they can be inhaled deeply into the lungs, settling in areas where the body's natural clearance mechanisms can't remove them. The constituents in small particulates also tend to be more chemically active and may be acidic as well and therefore more damaging (2).

Numerous studies associate particulate pollution with acute changes in lung function and respiratory illness (3)(4), resulting in increased hospital admissions for respiratory disease and heart disease, school and job absences from respiratory infections, or aggravation of chronic conditions such as asthma and bronchitis (5)(6). But the more demonstrative—and sometimes controversial—evidence comes from a number of recent epidemiological studies. Many of these studies have linked short-term increases in particulate levels, such as the ones that occur during pollution episodes, with immediate (within 24 hours) increases in mortality. This pollution-induced spike in the death rate ranges from 2 to 8 percent for every 50-$\mu g/m^3$ increase in particulate levels. These basic findings have been replicated on several continents, in cities as widely divergent as Athens, São Paulo, Beijing, and Philadelphia (7)(8)(9). During major pollution events, such as those involving a 200-μg increase in particulate levels, an expert panel at the World Health Organization (WHO) estimated that daily mortality rates could increase as much as 20 percent (10). These estimates should be viewed with caution, however, because some of those who die during a pollution episode were already sick, and the pollution may have hastened the death by only a few days.

In the aggregate, pollution-related effects like these can have a significant impact on community health. WHO has identified particulate pollution as one of the most important contributors to ill health within Europe. In those cities where data on particulates were available, WHO estimated that short-term pollution episodes accounted for 7 to 10 percent of all lower respiratory illnesses in children, with the number rising to 21 percent in the most polluted cities. Furthermore, 0.6 to 1.6 percent of deaths were attributable to short-term pollution events, climbing to 3.4 percent in the cities with the dirtiest air (11).

Nor are health effects restricted to occasional episodes when pollutant levels are particularly high. Numerous studies suggest that health effects can occur at particulate levels that are at or below the levels permitted under national and international air quality standards. In fact, according to the WHO and other organizations, no evidence so far shows there is a threshold below which particle pollution does not induce some adverse health effects, especially for the more susceptible populations (12)(13). This situation has prompted a vigorous debate about whether current air quality standards are sufficient to protect public health.

Sulfur Dioxide

SO_2 is emitted largely from burning coal, high-sulfur oil, and diesel fuel. Because this gas is usually found in association with particulate pollution—as SO_2 is the precursor for fine sulfate particles—separating the health effects of these two pollutants is difficult. Together, SO_2 and particulates make up a major portion of the pollutant load in many cities, acting both separately and in concert to damage health.

Although ambient concentrations of SO_2 have declined in many cities in Western Europe and North America, they remain higher—often by a factor of 5 to 10—in a number of cities in Eastern Europe, Asia, and South America, where residential or industrial coal use is still prevalent and diesel traffic is heavy (14).

SO_2 affects people quickly, usually within the first few minutes of exposure. Epidemiol-

---

million cases per year of chronic coughing in children younger than 14 years of age (249). However, even healthy adults can suffer negative effects (250). (See Box 2.6.)

Many of air pollution's health effects, such as bronchitis, tightness in the chest, and wheezing, are acute, or short term, and can be reversed if air pollution exposures decline. Other effects appear to be chronic, such as lung cancer and cardiopulmonary disease. In fact, in the United States, two long-term epidemiological studies—representing some of the most significant recent research on air pollution effects—documented an increase in the death rate of those chronically exposed to dirty air. These studies, which compared death rates among many U.S. cities with widely varying pollution levels, found that mortality rates were 17 to 26 percent higher in cities with the dirtiest air compared with those with the cleanest air, and those with the dirtiest air had significantly higher rates of lung cancer and cardiopulmonary disease (251)(252). These increased risks translate roughly to a 1- to 2-year shorter life span for residents of the most polluted cities (253)(254). Higher infant mortality rates have also been associated with high particulate levels (255).

Fewer studies have been done in developing countries, and those that have been done have relied on calculations of health impacts in developed countries. These calculations may not

Box 2.6 continued

ogical studies indicate that SO_2 exposure can lead to the kind of acute health effects typical of particulate pollution. Exposure is linked to an increase in hospitalizations and deaths from respiratory and cardiovascular causes, especially among asthmatics and those with preexisting respiratory diseases (15)(16)(17)(18). The severity of these effects increases with rising SO_2 levels, and exercise enhances the severity by increasing the volume of SO_2 inhaled and allowing SO_2 to penetrate deeper into the respiratory tract (19). Asthmatics may experience wheezing and other symptoms at much lower SO_2 levels than those without asthma. When ozone pollution is also present, asthmatics become even more sensitive to SO_2—a good reminder that air pollutants generally do not occur in isolation, but in complex mixtures that create the potential for synergistic effects among pollutants (20)(21).

Ozone

Ground-level ozone is the major component of the photochemical smog that blankets many urban areas. It is not emitted directly but is formed when nitrogen oxides from fuel combustion react with so-called volatile organic compounds (VOCs) such as unburned gasoline or paint solvents in the atmosphere. Sunlight and heat stimulate ozone formation, so peak ozone levels generally occur in the summer.

Ozone pollution has become widespread in cities in Europe, North America, and Japan as auto and industrial emissions have increased. Many cities in developing countries also suffer from high ozone levels, although few monitoring data exist (22)(23).

A powerful oxidant, ozone can react with nearly any biological tissue. Breathing ozone concentrations of 0.012 ppm—levels typical in many cities—can irritate the respiratory tract and impair lung function, causing coughing, shortness of breath, and chest pain. Exercise increases these effects, and heavy exercise can bring on symp-

toms even at low ozone levels (0.08 ppm). Evidence also suggests ozone exposure lowers the body's defenses, increasing susceptibility to respiratory infections (24)(25).

As ozone levels rise, hospital admissions and emergency room visits for respiratory illnesses such as asthma also increase. On average, studies show that hospital admissions rise roughly 7 to 10 percent for a 0.05 ppm increase in ozone levels. In its recent analysis of ozone health impacts in 13 cities where ozone levels exceeded U.S. air standards, the American Lung Association estimated that high ozone levels were responsible for approximately 10,000 to 15,000 extra hospital admissions and 30,000 to 50,000 additional emergency room visits during the 1993–94 ozone season (26)(27).

References and Notes

1. World Health Organization (WHO), *Update and Revision of the Air Quality Guidelines for Europe*, WHO Regional Office for Europe, Report No. EUR/ICP/EHAZ 94-05/PB01 (WHO, Copenhagen, 1994), p. 14.
2. *Ibid.*, p. 15.
3. Douglas Dockery *et al.*, "Health Effects of Acid Aerosols on North American Children: Respiratory Symptoms," *Environmental Health Perspectives*, Vol. 104, No. 5 (1996), p. 503.
4. U.S. Environmental Protection Agency (USEPA), Office of Air Quality Planning and Standards, *Review of National Ambient Air Quality Standards for Particulate Matter: Policy Assessment of Scientific and Technical Information*, Report No. EPA-452/R-96-013 (USEPA, Washington, D.C., 1996), pp. V-23–V-24, V-27–V-28, V-71.
5. Deborah Shprentz, *Breathtaking: Premature Mortality Due to Particulate Air Pollution in 239 American Cities* (Natural Resources Defense Council, New York, 1996), p. 14–15.
6. *Op. cit.* 4, pp. V-20–V-22.
7. *Op. cit.* 4, pp. V-11 to V-14.
8. Bart Ostro, "The Association of Air Pollution and Mortality: Examining the Case for Inference," *Archives of Environmental Health*, Vol. 48, No. 5 (1993), p. 336.
9. Health Effects Institute (HEI), *Particulate Air Pollution and Daily Mortality: Replication and Validation*

of Selected Studies (HEI, Cambridge, MA, 1995), p. 4.
10. *Op. cit.* 4, pp. v–18.
11. R. Bertollini *et al.*, *Environment and Health 1: Overview and Main European Issues*, WHO Regional Publications, European Series, No. 68 (World Health Organization, Copenhagen, 1996), pp. 34–38.
12. *Op. cit.* 1, p. 15.
13. *Op. cit.* 5, p. 14.
14. *Op. cit.* 1, p. 11.
15. A. Peters *et al.*, "Acute Effects of Exposure to High Levels of Air Pollution in Eastern Europe," *American Journal of Epidemiology*, Vol. 144, No. 6 (1996), pp. 570, 578–80.
16. J. Sunyer *et al.*, "Air Pollution and Mortality in Barcelona," *Journal of Epidemiology and Community Health*, Vol. 50 (Supplement 1) (April 1996), p. S76.
17. M. Vigotti *et al.*, "Short-Term Effects of Urban Air Pollution on Respiratory Health in Milan, Italy, 1980–1989," *Journal of Epidemiology and Community Health*, Vol. 50 (Supplement 1) (April 1996), p. S71.
18. G. Touloumi, E. Samoli, and K. Katsouyanni, "Daily Mortality and 'Winter type' Air Pollution In Athens, Greece–A Time Series Analysis Within the APHEA Project," *Journal of Epidemiology and Community Health*, Vol. 50 (Supplement 1) (April 1996), p. S47.
19. *Op. cit.* 1, p. 11.
20. Lawrence Folinsbee, "Human Health Effects of Air Pollution," *Environmental Health Perspectives*, Vol. 100 (1992), pp. 47–48.
21. Derek Elsom, *Smog Alert: Managing Urban Air Quality* (Earthscan Publications Limited, London, 1996), p. 48.
22. *Op. cit.* 1, p. 3.
23. World Health Organization and the United Nations Environment Programme, *Urban Air Pollution in Megacities of the World* (Blackwell Publishers, Oxford, UK, 1992), pp. 10–11.
24. Halûk Özkaynak *et al.*, *Ambient Ozone Exposure and Emergency Hospital Admissions and Emergency Room Visits for Respiratory Problems in 13 U.S. Cities* (American Lung Association, Washington, D.C., 1996), pp. 2–7.
25. *Op. cit.* 4, pp. 37–38, 58.
26. *Op. cit.* 24, pp. 1–10.
27. *Op. cit.* 4, pp. 24, 46–51, 61.

be directly transferable, however, given differences in pollutant exposures and baseline health (both nutrition and general health status may be lower in some developing countries) (256). Nonetheless, studies performed in developing countries suggest that urban air pollution may have a tremendous impact on health. For example, one recent analysis of Jakarta estimated that some 1,400 deaths, 49,000 emergency room visits, and 600,000 asthma attacks could be avoided each year if particulate levels were brought down to WHO standards (257). Meanwhile, in Latin America, exposure of some 81 mil-

lion city residents—more than one quarter of all city dwellers in the region — to high air pollution levels is believed to cause an estimated 65 million days of illness each year (258).

INDOOR AIR: STILL A MAJOR THREAT

As dangerous as polluted outdoor air can be to health, indoor air pollution actually poses a greater health risk on a global level. Indoor air pollution is a concern in developed countries, where, for example, energy efficiency improvements sometimes make houses relatively airtight, reducing ventilation and raising indoor pollutant levels. In such circumstances,

Biomass Use, While Declining, Will Remain High

FIGURE 2.9 Current and Projected Use of Biomass by Region, Selected Years

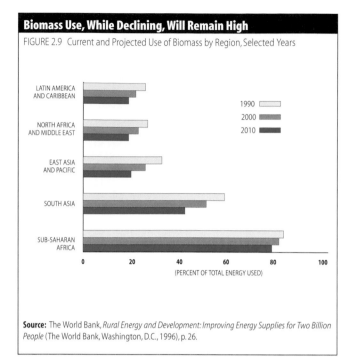

Source: The World Bank, *Rural Energy and Development: Improving Energy Supplies for Two Billion People* (The World Bank, Washington, D.C., 1996), p. 26.

even small pollution sources — emanating from a furnace, a new carpet, or from naturally occurring radon gas—can lead to significant human exposures.

By far the greatest threat of indoor pollution, however, still occurs in the developing countries, where some 3.5 billion people — mostly in rural areas, but also in many cities — continue to rely on traditional fuels for cooking and heating. (See Figure 2.9.) Burning such fuels produces large amounts of smoke and other air pollutants in the confined space of the home—a perfect recipe for high exposures. (Liquid and gaseous fuels such as kerosene and bottled gas, although not completely pollution-free, are many times less polluting than these unprocessed solid fuels.) In these circumstances, exposure to pollutants is often far higher indoors than outdoors. Indeed, the World Bank has designated indoor air pollution in developing countries as one of the four most critical global environmental problems (259).

As Table 2.7 shows, concentrations of indoor pollutants in households burning dirty fuels are excessive. These estimates must be viewed with some caution, however, because monitoring in developing countries has been limited. Daily averages often exceed current WHO guidelines by factors of 10, 20, or even more. Peak levels during cooking may exceed these levels by a further factor of five or so. Indeed, these data suggest that many tens of millions of people in developing countries routinely encounter pollution levels reached during the infamous London killer fog of 1952, leading to a huge estimated toll in disease and premature death. One researcher estimates that as many as 2.8 million deaths per year result from breathing elevated levels of indoor smoke from dirty fuels

(i.e., in excess of the WHO particulate standard). This finding translates to about 6 percent of all deaths each year (260). If this kind of effect is confirmed, indoor air pollution would be one of the largest single risk factors for ill health in the world.

Epidemiological studies in developing countries have linked exposure to indoor air pollution from dirty fuels with at least four major categories of illness: acute respiratory infections (ARI) in children; chronic obstructive lung diseases such as asthma and chronic bronchitis; lung cancer; and stillbirths and other problems at birth. Of these, ARI appears to have the greatest health impact in terms of the number of people affected and the time lost due to illness, especially in children younger than age 5.

Studies in a number of different countries and settings have examined the link between exposure to smoke from cookstoves with the development of ARI in children. In South Africa, investigators found that Zulu children living in homes with woodstoves were almost five times more likely to develop a respiratory infection severe enough to require hospitalization (261). In Nepal, researchers observed a significant relationship between the number of hours spent near the fire and the incidence of moderate and severe cases among 2-year-olds (262). Likewise, a recent study in the Gambia found that children carried on their mother's backs as they cooked over smoky cookstoves contracted pneumococcal infections—one of the most serious kinds of respiratory infections—at a rate 2.5 times higher than nonexposed children (263).

Many respiratory infections in the developing world result in death, and evidence shows that exposure to cookstove

Burning Biomass Fuels Pollutes Indoor Air

TABLE 2.7 Indoor Particulate Concentrations from Biomass Combustion in Developing Countries

REGION	NUMBER OF STUDIES	DURATION	MICROGRAMS PER CUBIC METER
Pacific	2	12 h	1,300–5,200
South Asia	15	Cooking period	850–4,400[a]
		Cooking	630–820
		Non-cooking	880[a]
		24 h	2,000–2,800[a]
		Various	2,000–6,800[a]
		Urban infants, 24 h	400–520[a]
China	8	Various	2,600–2,900[a]
		Various	1,100–11,000[a]
Africa	8	Cooking/heating	800–1,700
		Cooking/heating 24 h	1,300[a]
		Urban area, 24 h	1,300–2,100[a]
			400–590[a]
Latin America	5	Cooking/heating 24 h	440–1,100[a]
			720–1,200[a]

Source: Adapted from World Health Organization (WHO), *Health and Environment in Sustainable Development: Five Years after the Earth Summit* (WHO, Geneva, 1997), Table 4.4, p. 87.

Note: a. Particles less than 10 μm in diameter.

smoke may contribute to higher mortality rates. For example, a study in Tanzania found that children younger than 5 years of age who died of ARI were 2.8 times more likely to have been sleeping in a room with an open cookstove than healthy children (264). Overall, studies indicate that exposure to wood smoke from cook fires in poorly ventilated conditions may increase the risk of a young child contracting a serious respiratory infection from two to six times.

Adults suffer the ill effects of severe indoor pollution as well. Several studies found strong links between chronic lung diseases in women and exposure to smoke from open cookstoves (265)(266). One recent Colombian study found women exposed to smoke during cooking were more than three times more likely to suffer chronic lung disease (267). Other studies suggest that this risk increases in response to the years of exposure to smoke. A study in Mexico showed that women who had been exposed to wood smoke for many years faced 75 times more risk of acquiring chronic lung disease than unexposed women—about the level of risk that heavy cigarette smokers face (268). Lung cancer, too, is associated with high levels of smoke—especially coal smoke, which contains a plethora of carcinogenic compounds. Most studies of coal-smoke exposures have been conducted in China, where residential use of coal is still common (269). More than 20 studies suggest that urban women who use coal for cooking and heating over many years are subject to a risk of lung cancer two to six times higher than women who use gas. Rural coal-smoke exposures, which tend to be higher, seem to increase lung cancer risks by a factor of nine or more (270).

Exposure to high indoor smoke levels has also been linked with pregnancy-related problems like stillbirths and low birth weight. One study in western India found a 50-percent increase in stillbirths associated with the exposure of pregnant women to indoor smoke (271). Indoor air pollution most likely contributes to excess heart disease in developing countries as well. In developed countries, outdoor pollution at levels far below those found in smoky indoor environments has been linked with heart disease.

When it happens, the well-documented transition up the energy ladder from dirty to clean fuel will greatly reduce the threat from indoor air pollution in developing countries. The speed of this transition will depend on several factors, including energy prices, trends in personal income, and national policies targeting the indoor air problem. Continued low oil prices and strong government action promoting cleaner stoves and cleaner fuels such as kerosene or gas could result in a much faster transition, but these favorable conditions are far from assured. In fact, even though investments in cleaning up indoor air can be very cost-efficient in terms of health, nations have historically spent little on the indoor air problem.

Climate Change and Health

Climate influences many of the key determinants of health: temperature extremes and violent weather events; the geographical range of disease organisms and vectors; the quantity of air, food, and water; and the stability of the ecosystems on which we depend.

Because climate affects us in so many ways and because the details of how the global climate may change are so uncertain, predicting the health effects of climate change is an inexact science at best. But given what is already known about the connection between climate and health and the magnitude of the global warming that scientists project, future health effects could be substantial. These effects are likely to vary widely from region to region, because climate itself is predicted to change differently in various regions. For instance, temperatures are expected to rise more in some areas than others; some places likely will get drier, while others will get more rain than they do today.

Likely health impacts of climate change include direct effects from temperature and weather extremes and from sea-level rise. A number of indirect impacts are also likely to arise from changes in precipitation and temperature patterns, which may disturb natural ecosystems, change the ecology of infectious diseases, harm agriculture and freshwater supplies, exacerbate air pollution levels, and cause large-scale reorganization of plant and animal communities. (See Figure 2.10.) These indirect effects may, in the long run, have greater cumulative impacts on human health than the direct effects (272).

DIRECT IMPACTS

One of the most easily imagined impacts of global warming is an increase in the number and severity of heat waves. Heat stress is a well-known danger during prolonged bouts of hot weather, especially in cities, which tend to trap heat. In both New York and Shanghai, for instance, records show that daily mortality rates increase sharply once temperatures exceed a certain threshold (273). During intense heat waves, the death toll attributed to heat stress can be surprisingly high, as occurred in Chicago in July 1995, when heat stress killed 726 people during a 4-day heat wave (274)(275).

Midlatitude cities including Washington, D.C., Athens, and Shanghai seem to be at greatest risk for deadly heat waves. In these cities, residents (especially the elderly, the very young, and the poor) are not acclimatized to extremely hot weather and are thus more vulnerable to heat stress. Among these vulnerable groups, the existence of previous health problems, greater heat exposure due to substandard housing, and lack of access to air conditioning are all factors leading to higher heat-related mortality. By the middle of the next century, climate change could increase the frequency of very hot days severalfold in a city similar to Washington, D.C., according to

Climate Change Could Profoundly Affect Health

FIGURE 2.10   Direct and Indirect Health Impacts of Climate Change

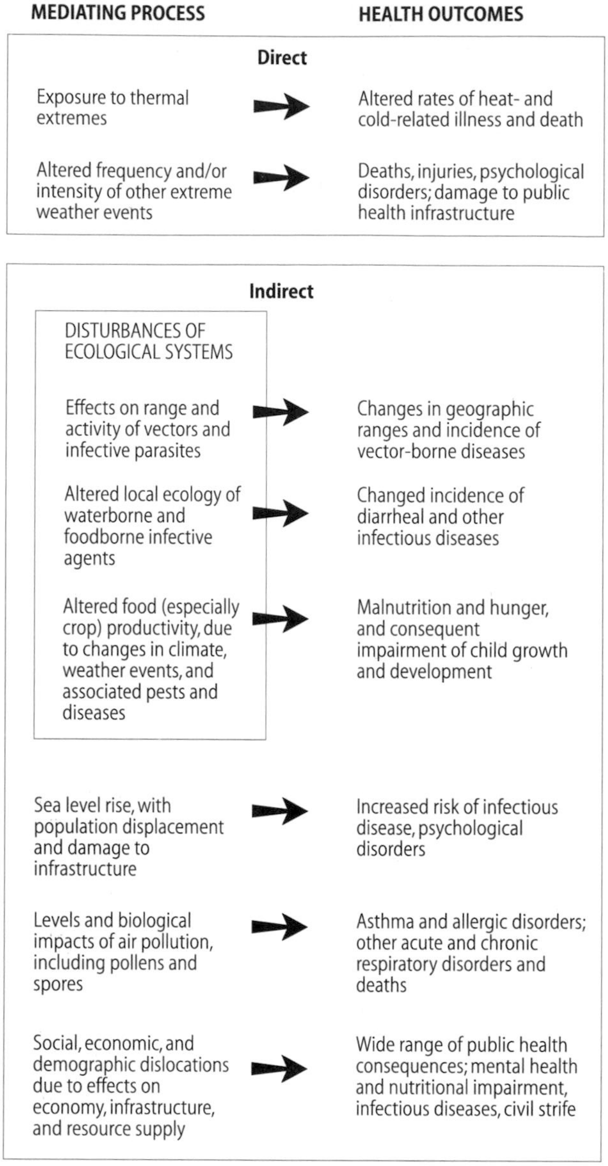

MEDIATING PROCESS	HEALTH OUTCOMES

Direct

Exposure to thermal extremes	→	Altered rates of heat- and cold-related illness and death
Altered frequency and/or intensity of other extreme weather events	→	Deaths, injuries, psychological disorders; damage to public health infrastructure

Indirect

DISTURBANCES OF ECOLOGICAL SYSTEMS

Effects on range and activity of vectors and infective parasites	→	Changes in geographic ranges and incidence of vector-borne diseases
Altered local ecology of waterborne and foodborne infective agents	→	Changed incidence of diarrheal and other infectious diseases
Altered food (especially crop) productivity, due to changes in climate, weather events, and associated pests and diseases	→	Malnutrition and hunger, and consequent impairment of child growth and development

Sea level rise, with population displacement and damage to infrastructure	→	Increased risk of infectious disease, psychological disorders
Levels and biological impacts of air pollution, including pollens and spores	→	Asthma and allergic disorders; other acute and chronic respiratory disorders and deaths
Social, economic, and demographic dislocations due to effects on economy, infrastructure, and resource supply	→	Wide range of public health consequences; mental health and nutritional impairment, infectious diseases, civil strife

Source: Adapted from: World Health Organization (WHO), *Climate Change and Human Health,* A.J. McMichael *et al.,* eds. (WHO, Geneva, 1996), Figure 1.1, p. 12.

one estimate (276). The normally hotter average temperatures in tropical and subtropical cities seem to help residents accommodate heat waves better, so they suffer fewer heat-stress problems, although heat-related deaths during a 1995 heat wave in New Delhi indicate that even residents in the tropics can be susceptible to extreme temperatures (277).

Conversely, a potential health benefit of warmer global temperatures could be fewer cold-related deaths as winters become milder. A recent British study estimated that by 2050,

an increase in the average wintertime temperature by 2.0° C to 2.5° C, as predicted by some climate models, might result in as many as 9,000 fewer cold-related deaths per year in England and Wales. Yet, this decrease in winter mortality would probably only partially offset additional heat-related deaths; studies indicate that higher mortality is generally associated with heat waves than cold spells (278). (See Table 2.8.)

In addition to more frequent heat waves, global climate change is expected to result in greater weather variability overall. In particular, climatologists believe that relatively small changes in the average global climate in the future could produce large changes in the frequency of extreme weather events (279), such as hurricanes (cyclones), violent thunderstorms, and windstorms. Through flood and wind damage, these natural disasters already exact a heavy burden in the destruction of lives and property (280).

Rising sea levels, another expected consequence of global warming, could adversely affect the health and well-being of coastal inhabitants. Sixteen of the world's largest cities with populations of more than 10 million are located in coastal zones, and coastal populations are increasing rapidly worldwide. The IPCC projects that sea level will rise between 0.3 and 1.0 meter by 2100, with a best-guess estimate of 0.5 meter (281).

The most immediate threat from such a rise would be to those who live directly on the coast, in low-lying areas such as

Deaths From Heat Waves Could Rise

TABLE 2.8   Estimates of Summer Heat-Related Deaths in 2020 in Selected Cities Under a Climate Change Scenario[a]

CITY	PRESENT MORTALITY[b]	POPULATION NOT ACCLIMATIZED	POPULATION ACCLIMATIZED
United States			
Atlanta	78	191	96
Dallas	19	35	28
Detroit	118	264	131
Los Angeles	84	205	102
New York	320	356	190
Philadelphia	145	190	142
San Francisco	27	49	40
Canada			
Montreal	69	121	61
Toronto	19	36	0
China			
Shanghai	418	1,104	833
Egypt			
Cairo	281	476	N.A.

Source: World Health Organization (WHO), *Climate Change and Human Health,* A.J. McMichael, *et al.,* eds. (WHO, Geneva, 1996), Table 3.5, p. 57.

Notes:

a. Numbers represent average summer-season heat-related deaths for each city under the GFDL89 climate change scenario. For example, during a typical summer today, 78 extra deaths occur in Atlanta from heat-related causes and, assuming no acclimatization, this number rises to 191 deaths. Numbers assume no change in population size and age distribution.

b. Raw mortality data.

N.A. = Not applicable.

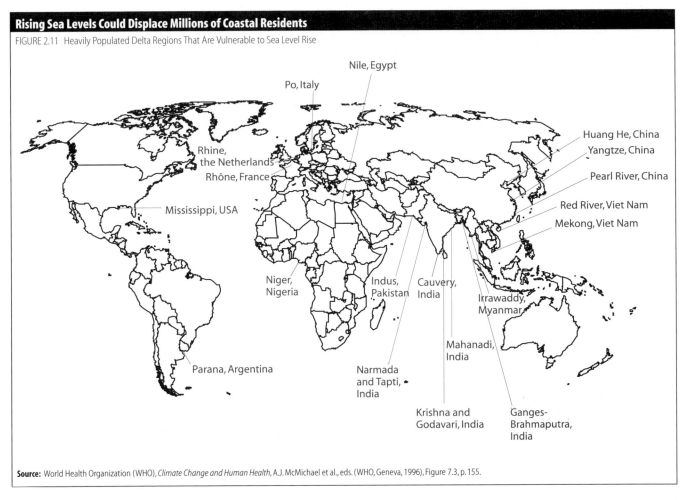

Rising Sea Levels Could Displace Millions of Coastal Residents

FIGURE 2.11 Heavily Populated Delta Regions That Are Vulnerable to Sea Level Rise

Source: World Health Organization (WHO), *Climate Change and Human Health*, A.J. McMichael et al., eds. (WHO, Geneva, 1996), Figure 7.3, p. 155.

river deltas, or on small island nations such as the Maldives, the Marshall Islands, Kiribati, and Tonga, where land is virtually all within a few meters of sea level already. Rising seas would inundate many of these islands, increase storm damage to the remaining land, and contaminate the freshwater supplies found in island aquifers (282).

Delta regions such as the Ganges-Bramaputra delta in Bangladesh, the Nile delta in Egypt, or the Niger delta in Nigeria could also suffer a similar fate. The situation in Bangladesh's densely settled Ganges-Bramaputra delta is probably the most serious. A recent study projects that a 1-meter sea rise could inundate 17 percent of Bangladesh's total land area and displace some 11 million people (at current population densities). In the Nile delta, a 1-meter rise would displace around 6 million people unless costly protection efforts were mounted; and in the Niger delta, a similar rise would inundate 15,000 square kilometers of land and force about one half million people to relocate (283). (See Figure 2.11.)

Beyond actual inundation, a rising sea level would put millions of people at greater risk of occasional storm-related flooding. Under current conditions, about 46 million coastal residents experience some flooding from storms each year.

The number at risk from flooding would double if sea level rises 0.5 meters and nearly triple with a 1-meter rise, according to one study. In an area like Bangladesh, where storm surges can reach as far as 200 kilometers inland during some intense cyclones, the increase in flood risk could greatly magnify the already high toll associated with such storms. Coastal erosion would also increase substantially, endangering natural protective features such as sand dunes, mangroves, and barrier islands, and exacerbating the flood risk (284).

Climate change could influence air pollution profiles—and the health effects that come from exposure to polluted air—by altering the rate of chemical reactions in the atmosphere that form or destroy pollutants, or by influencing the factors such as wind and precipitation that regulate how pollutants accumulate or disperse. For example, higher temperatures favor the formation of pollutants like ground-level ozone—the main constituent of smog. Preliminary calculations by U.S. EPA show that a 4° C increase in ambient air temperatures in the San Francisco Bay area would likely increase ozone levels by 20 percent and double the size of the area that does not meet national air quality standards (285). Higher temperatures would also increase the evaporation of volatile liquids such as gasoline or organic solvents, again adding to the urban smog problem.

Changes in regional wind and rainfall patterns accompanying climate change could also affect air pollution levels. If winds increase in a given area, they would tend to disperse and dilute air pollutants, thereby lowering human exposures. By contrast, a decrease in winds with an increased tendency to form local inversion layers—where warm, still air aloft traps pollutants close to the surface—would increase pollution exposures. Likewise, in areas where rainfall increases, pollutant loads may decline, since precipitation scours many pollutants from the air. A decrease in rainfall, on the other hand, may increase pollution levels since fewer pollutants are washed out of the atmosphere (286)(287).

INDIRECT IMPACTS

Climate change will likely raise the already considerable toll of infectious diseases worldwide. This impact is likely to occur because factors such as temperature and rainfall can affect the abundance and distribution of disease vectors or disease-causing microbes, as well as the vulnerability of populations to these diseases. It is impossible to predict exactly how disease rates will change in response to climate change because the interactions between environment and disease are so complex, and the effects of climate change will vary so much from location to location. But considerable evidence shows that many diseases are quite sensitive to variations in climate and are likely to increase their range and incidence as temperatures rise and precipitation patterns change.

Mosquitoes are quite sensitive to changes in temperature and rainfall and are among the first organisms to extend their range when environmental conditions become favorable (288). Thus, higher temperatures could influence the incidence of diseases such as malaria, dengue fever, yellow fever, and several types of encephalitis. Cold temperatures are often the limiting factor in mosquito survival, so any increase in minimum winter temperatures would likely extend mosquito ranges into temperate regions or higher altitudes where they do not survive now.

Higher temperatures also speed the life cycles of both the mosquito and the disease organisms they harbor and make adult mosquitoes bite more often. At 30° C, the dengue virus takes 12 days to incubate in the *Aedes aegypti* mosquito, but only 7 days at 32° C. The shorter incubation period translates to a potential threefold higher transmission rate of the disease. Higher temperatures also produce smaller adult mosquitoes that must feed more often to develop an egg batch, which in turn increases the chances for disease transmission (289).

Although temperature most determines the potential range of the mosquito and the disease organism, precipitation principally governs the availability of breeding sites and the over-

all population of mosquitoes. Thus, the combination of temperature and rainfall changes—modified by many other factors such as land use changes, human population densities, and whether exposed populations have any built-in disease immunity—will determine how the patterns of mosquito-borne diseases change (290). In some areas, the interplay of these factors will increase disease incidence; in other areas, incidence may decline.

Argentina provides an example of the complex changes in malaria distribution that climate change could bring. Currently, most of Argentina lies just south of the zone in which malaria occurs. But if global warming increases rainfall in central Argentina and makes it semitropical, as models project, the malaria-carrying mosquitoes might be able to expand south into the pampas and savanna regions, introducing malaria to these areas. On the other hand, northwestern Argentina, where malaria mosquitoes can now be found, might well become drier with global warming, making it less conducive to mosquito survival and reducing malaria outbreaks there (291).

The most pronounced effects of climate change on vector-borne diseases such as malaria or dengue fever will undoubtedly occur where the diseases are newly introduced at the edges of the vector range and people have little resistance built up. In Africa, this will often be at higher elevations that were formerly too cold to support these diseases. Increasing numbers of malaria cases have already been reported in the highlands of Madagascar and Ethiopia as a result of warming; in Rwanda, record high temperatures and rainfall in 1987 brought malaria into the highlands where local residents had no immunity. These incidents have led public health officials to fear that relatively small increases in temperature from global warming could spread malaria into large urban centers such as Nairobi, Kenya, and Harare, Zimbabwe, that currently lie just outside of the malaria range (292)(293).

Under a similar scenario, malaria and dengue fever could spread into large swaths of the temperate zone where populations now lack resistance. Rough models of the spread of malaria affected by global warming show that malaria prevalence may increase by 50 million to 80 million cases per year with an associated 3° C rise in average global temperature by the year 2100 (294).

Other vector-borne diseases such as schistosomiasis, Chagas disease, sleeping sickness, river blindness, and various strains of encephalitis all could change their ranges and patterns of infection in the course of climate change. For example, recent modeling of the response of schistosomiasis to current global warming trends suggests that an additional 5 million cases will appear per year by 2050 (295). Another recent study predicted that the population of black flies that carry river blindness could increase as much as 25 percent if temperature and precipitation patterns change in the manner

Altered Temperature and Rainfall Patterns Will Change Infectious Disease Patterns

TABLE 2.9 Major Tropical Vector-Borne Diseases and the Likelihood of Change in Their Distribution as a Result of Climate Change

DISEASE	VECTOR	NUMBER AT RISK (millions) [a]	NUMBER INFECTED OR NEW CASES PER YEAR	PRESENT DISTRIBUTION	LIKELIHOOD OF ALTERED DISTRIBUTION WITH CLIMATE CHANGE
Malaria	Mosquito	2400	300 million to 500 million	Tropics/subtropics	Highly likely
Schistosomiasis	Water snail	600	200 million	Tropics/subtropics	Very likely
Lymphatic filariasis	Mosquito	1094	117 million	Tropics/subtropics	Likely
African trypanosomiasis	Tsetse fly	55	250,000 to 300,000 cases/year	Tropical Africa	Likely
Dracunculiasis	Crustacean (copepod)	100	100,000/year	South Asia/Middle East/ Central and West Africa	Unknown
Leishmaniasis	Phlebotomine sandfly	350	12 million infected, 500,000 new cases/year [b]	Asia/South Europe/ Africa/Americas	Likely
Onchocerciasis	Blackfly	123	17.5 million	Africa/Latin America	Very likely
American trypanosomiasis	Triatomine bug	100	18 million to 20 million	Central and South America	Likely
Dengue fever	Mosquito	2500	50 million/year	Tropics/subtropics	Very likely
Yellow fever	Mosquito	450	<5,000 cases/year	Tropical South America and Africa	Very likely

Source: World Health Organization (WHO), *Climate Change and Human Health*, A. J. McMichael, *et al.*, eds. (WHO, Geneva, 1996), Table 4.1, p. 75.

Notes:

a. Top 3 entries are population-pro-rated projections, based on 1989 estimates.

b. Annual incidence of visceral leishmaniasis; annual incidence of cutaneous leishmaniasis is 1 to 1.5 million cases per year.

predicted by some climate models (296). Waterborne diseases including cholera and the suite of diarrheal diseases caused by organisms such as giardia, salmonella, and cryptosporidium could also be affected as precipitation patterns change, altering the dynamics of water courses and human access to water supplies and sanitation (297). (See Table 2.9.)

In addition, the changing temperature and rainfall patterns and the increasing CO_2 levels projected to accompany climate change will undoubtedly have important effects on global agriculture, and thus on human nutrition. Determining how climate change will affect world agriculture is every bit as complex as determining its effects on infectious disease, and every bit as speculative. A variety of effects will inevitably occur, and these will vary greatly by region, resulting in more favorable agricultural conditions in some areas and less favorable conditions in others.

On the positive side, higher atmospheric CO_2 levels are expected to have a "fertilizing" effect on some plants, increasing their growth rate and cutting transpiration rates, reducing their water demand. Increasing temperatures may bring longer growing seasons to some high-latitude farming regions, increasing yields and expanding the range of crops that can grow there. Higher rainfall in some areas might enable higher production from unirrigated land and more water for irrigation in these areas (298).

On the other hand, higher temperatures and diminished rainfall could reduce soil moisture in many areas, particularly in some tropical and midcontinental regions, reducing the water available for irrigation and impairing crop growth in nonirrigated regions. For example, drier summers and more frequent hot spells in the North American corn belt might reduce yields substantially, although it might extend the corn-growing region northward. Reduced rainfall in already arid regions like sub-Saharan Africa could have very negative consequences for agriculture in areas that can ill afford to lose production (299).

Climate change will affect plant pests and diseases in the same way it affects infectious disease agents. In other words, the range of many insects will expand or change, and new combinations of pests and diseases may emerge as natural ecosystems respond to altered temperature and precipitation profiles. Any increase in the frequency or severity of extreme weather events, including droughts, heat waves, windstorms, or floods, could also disrupt the predator-prey relationships that normally keep pest populations in check. An explosion of the rodent population that damaged the grain crop in Zimbabwe in 1994, after 6 years of drought had eliminated many rodent predators, shows how altered climate conditions can intensify pest problems. The effect of climate on pests may add to the effect of other factors such as the overuse of pesticides and the loss of biodiversity that already contribute to plant pest and disease outbreaks (300).

The ingenuity of farmers, breeders, and agricultural engineers, and the natural resilience of biological systems, will help buffer many of the negative effects of climate change on agriculture. However, experts believe that over the longer term, the accumulated stresses of sustained climate change stand a good chance of disrupting agro-ecosystems and reducing global food productivity.

The regions thought to be most vulnerable to productivity declines are semiarid and arid areas where rain-fed, nonirrigated agriculture predominates. Unfortunately, many of these areas—as in sub-Saharan Africa, South and East Asia, and on some Pacific islands—are already hard-pressed agriculturally and suffer from high rates of malnutrition. In Senegal, for example, one study predicts a 30-percent yield decline with a 4°C rise in temperatures and no change in rainfall from current levels. The effect of this kind of agricultural decline on local food security would be severe. The negative effects of climate change on agriculture in poor countries could put an additional 40 to 300 million people at risk of hunger by 2060 (301).

Perhaps the greatest long-term danger to human health from climate change will be the disruption of natural ecosystems, which provide an array of services that ultimately support human health. Biotic systems—whether in forests, rangelands, aquatic environments, or elsewhere—provide food, materials, and medicines; store and release fresh water; absorb and detoxify wastes; and satisfy human needs for recreation and wilderness. They are also intimately involved in sustaining the genetic basis of agriculture.

These systems will likely undergo major reorganization as global temperatures rise and rainfall patterns change more rapidly than they have in the past 10,000 years. Rough estimates of the effects of a doubling of atmospheric CO_2 levels show a major redistribution of Earth's vegetation. As much as one third to one half of all plant communities—and the animals that depend on them—might shift in response to changing ecological conditions.

Chapter 3

*C*hapter 3

Improving Health Through Environmental Action

Mark Edwards/Still Pictures

T he message that emerges from Chapters 1 and 2 is clear: a clean environment supports good health, while a degraded environment increases the likelihood of death and disease. The toll environmental degradation exacts on human health is heavy, especially for children in the poor regions of the world. In the poorest countries, one out of every five children dies before reaching his or her fifth birthday, usually because of environmentally related—and largely preventable—diseases (1). Improving environmental conditions could thus do much to reduce both death and disease.

Environmental threats to health come from myriad sources, as Chapter 1 describes. Many of these threats go hand in hand with poverty and a lack of development; these threats tend to be most pronounced at the household or community level. For instance, in impoverished areas, inadequate access to water and sanitation contribute to the 2.5 million childhood deaths each year from diarrhea. Poor drainage and uncollected garbage encourage the proliferation of insect and rodent vectors that carry disease. Household exposure to

smoke from burning biomass fuels for heating and cooking contributes to both acute and chronic respiratory disease.

Other environmental risks stem from the processes of economic development and industrialization, when they occur without sufficient safeguards for environmental quality and human health. The three trends discussed in this report—agricultural intensification, industrialization, and rising energy use—are all intimately associated with economic development today. All can contribute enormously to increased prosperity and improved quality of life. Yet, if not properly managed, these trends can also increase risks to human health. Health risks arise not only from direct exposure to polluted air, water, and soil but also indirectly when human activities disrupt ecosystems in unexpected ways. Twenty years ago, for instance, few would have guessed that emissions of chlorofluorocarbons (CFCs) were already damaging the Earth's protective ozone layer, increasing the risks of developing skin cancer, cataracts, or damage to the immune system (2).

Although the exact contribution of environmental factors to the development of death and disease cannot be precisely determined, the World Health Organization (WHO) has estimated that as much as 23 percent of the global burden of disease is associated with environmental factors (3). Indeed, many of the diseases that each year claim the lives of 11 million children younger than 5 years of age could be prevented by reducing hazards in the environment (4).

Environmental health problems also place significant economic and social burdens on both individuals and societies. In some large urban areas of the developing world, the estimated economic losses each year from air pollution and congestion alone range from US$500 million to US$3.5 billion (5). Exposure to infectious and chemical agents can stunt physical growth, impair cognitive skills, and hamper educational participation and performance, thereby reducing the future potential of individuals and, perhaps, of society as a whole. Preventing these impacts from occurring in the first place is an urgent need because certain impacts, such as lowered IQ known to result from exposure to some heavy metals, cannot be remedied.

Because environment and health are so intimately linked, so too should be strategies for improving public health. Yet, with the advent of increasingly sophisticated medical technologies over the past several decades, medical treatment and other clinical interventions have generally received priority over environmental strategies to improve health. Without question, vaccines and drugs have made it possible to prevent or treat diseases that once were certain killers. Indeed, seven major childhood killers—smallpox, diphtheria, tetanus, yellow fever, whooping cough, polio, and measles—have all been brought under varying degrees of control thanks to the development of vaccines (6). Every year, immunization can be credited with saving 9 million lives worldwide (7).

Yet, even in situations where a vaccine or drug exists (and for many environmental threats to human health, one does not), many benefits can be gained by supplementing clinical interventions with environmental management. The rising problem of antibiotic resistance underscores the value of multiple strategies for disease control (See Box 3.1.) Although a specific exposure to an environmental hazard may be the immediate cause of ill health, addressing and correcting the driving forces and pressures contributing to environmental degradation may offer more effective and enduring avenues for improving health over the long term (8). Broad environmental interventions such as ensuring clean air and water will address multiple health conditions and, indeed, may yield other benefits outside of the health arena. Reducing use of fossil fuels, for example, will not only improve air quality for human health today but also may help avert damages from acid rain and mitigate the prospects of future climate change.

Reducing the environmental contribution to ill health will require addressing the links among environment, development, and health at the outset. Infectious diseases are a case in point. Clearly, governments should continue to offer incentives to pharmaceutical companies to develop and market at reasonable prices new drugs and vaccines for diseases such as malaria, dengue fever, and cholera. Steps to improve monitoring and surveillance systems to track newly emerging or reemerging infectious diseases are also critical (9)(10). But these initiatives alone will not alleviate the infectious disease burden because they do not address the myriad factors that contribute to emerging infections (11). For instance, despite these efforts, land use changes resulting from development—including deforestation, dam building, and irrigation schemes—will continue to lead to shifts in disease vectors as well as bring workers into areas where they may encounter infectious agents for which they lack immunity. Uncontrolled pollution of water resources from domestic, agricultural, and industrial wastes will continue to challenge the health of marine ecosystems and increase risks of cholera and/or shellfish poisoning. Unwise chemical use may alter the delicate balance between predators and insects as well as foster chemical resistance. Even rising energy use, which seems far removed from a case of malaria, could influence disease transmission through its effects on global climate.

The advantage of looking beyond the traditional focus on disease agents toward broader environmental issues is that doing so illuminates new places to initiate preventive actions and policy reforms. Specifically, this chapter focuses on environmental strategies to prevent disease and improve public health; it does not address the important reforms needed within the health sector. First, the chapter explores the longstanding environmental health problems related to poverty and lack of development. It examines a range of interventions and technologies, many of which can be applied at the household or community level, and some of which require broad government reforms. Next, the chapter explores those problems that emerge as countries begin to develop—as they begin to industrialize, intensify their agriculture, and consume more fossil fuels. As described in Chapter 1, many countries face both types of problems, traditional and modern, simultaneously; they are separated here simply for ease of discussion. Solutions to these problems typically require policy actions at the national or international level. Because it is impossible to describe these policies in great detail within one chapter, the discussion that follows makes the case more broadly for ensuring that health and environment concerns receive greater prominence in policy decisions facing industrialized and developing countries alike. This discussion is by no means exhaustive but outlines the variety of possible interventions, as well as the different actors who will be critical to finding solutions.

Local Environmental Improvements Can Save Lives

TABLE 3.1 Improving The Household Environment: The Benefits To Health

DISEASE	DALYs (millions per year)	RELEVANT ENVIRONMENTAL PROBLEM	PERCENTAGE OF DALYs THAT WOULD BE AVERTED BY FEASIBLE ENVIRON- MENTAL INTERVENTIONS	PREVENTIVE STRATEGIES
Acute Respiratory Infections	119	Indoor air pollution, crowding	15	● improve ventilation ● improve cookstoves ● provide electricity to rural households and urban poor
Diarrhea	99	Sanitation, water supply, hygiene	40	● improve quality of drinking water ● increase the quantity of water used by improving accessibility and reliability of water supply ● improve sanitation improve hygiene (behavior changes include washing hands, boiling water, preventing casual use of unprotected sources)
Intestinal Worms	18	Sanitation, water supply, hygiene	40	● same as for diarrhea ● reduce need for contact with infected water
Malaria	X	Water supply	X	● improve surface water management ● destroy breeding sites of insects ● reduce need to visit breeding site ● use mosquito netting
Dengue Fever	X	Water supply, garbage collection	X	● improve surface water management ● destroy breeding sites of insects ● reduce need to visit breeding site ● use mosquito netting
Tropical Cluster (includes schistosomiasis, trypanosomiasis, and filariasis)	8	Sanitation, garbage disposal, vector breeding around the home	30	● reduce need for contact with infected water ● control snail population ● filter water
Tuberculosis	46	Crowding	10	● improve housing quality and quantity
Chronic Respiratory Diseases	41	Indoor air pollution	15	● same as for acute respiratory infections

Source: Adapted from The World Bank, *World Development Report 1993: Investing in Health* (The World Bank, Washington, D.C., 1993), p. 90.

Tackling the Problems of Poverty, Environment, and Health

The most pressing environmental health problems today, in terms of deaths and illness worldwide, are those associated with poor households and communities in the developing world. (See Guest Commentary by Roberto Bertollini.) In rural areas and in the peri-urban slums of the developing world, inadequate shelter, overcrowding, lack of adequate safe water and sanitation, contaminated food, and indoor air pollution are by far the greatest environmental threats to human health (12). These conditions are often compounded by poor nutrition and lack of education, which make people more vulnerable to, and less able to cope with, environmental threats.

According to WHO and the World Bank, environmental improvements at the household and community level would make the greatest difference for global health (13)(14). Specifically, the World Bank has calculated that improvements in local environmental conditions facing the poor could lower the incidence of major killer diseases by up to 40 percent (15). (See Table 3.1.)

Given the strong correlation between environmental health risks and poverty, one strategy to reduce these risks is to raise incomes and improve the distribution of wealth (16). Without question, reducing poverty and closing the gap between rich and poor would drastically lower the toll of death and disability from many diseases. Implementing policies to eradicate poverty remains a top priority for improving health, and many organizations—including national governments, the United Nations (U.N.), numerous nongovernmental organizations (NGOs), and foundations—have marshaled considerable force toward this end. The United Nations Development Programme (UNDP) *Human Development Report 1997*, for instance, outlines six priorities for action—ranging from empowering the poor to carefully managing globalization trends to ensure fair terms of trade and more equal economic growth (17).

Box 3.1   Antibiotic Resistance Undermines Treatment

Antibiotics are the cornerstone of treatment for infectious disease (1). Since 1928, when the English microbiologist Alexander Fleming discovered penicillin, antibiotics have greatly reduced morbidity and mortality from bacterial infections. The use of antibiotics, along with improved hygiene, sanitation, better housing, nutrition, and vaccines, dramatically curtailed deaths from diseases such as tuberculosis (TB) and pneumonia in the developed world (2)(3).

Recently, however, public health officials and scientists have become concerned that the increased use as well as misuse of antibiotics is leading to a surge of drug-resistant bacteria. This trend has disturbing implications for public health, because resistance can impede the treatment of many common infections, contributing to more serious illness and increased deaths, as well as raising costs of treatment.

Drug resistance is not a new phenomenon. Indeed, as early as 1945, only shortly after penicillin's debut into hospitals, scientists discovered that staphylococci were already resistant to treatment with penicillin (4). Today, however, resistant pathogens are emerging and spreading more rapidly than in previous decades (5). Moreover, resistance is not unique to bacteria; it has also been detected among fungi, parasites, viruses, cancers, and insects (6). The malaria parasite, for instance, has become resistant to chloroquine as well as to other drugs used to treat the disease (7).

Even more worrisome, single-drug resistance has been replaced by multidrug resistance, which further complicates treatment by eliminating the usefulness of numerous antibiotics and reducing treatment options (8)(9). The first warning that resistant TB strains had emerged in the industrialized countries was the dramatic outbreaks of multidrug-resistant cases among patients infected with the HIV virus in the United States and Europe. These cases, which occurred mostly in hospitals, were associated with high fatality rates (10). A recent global survey found that among first-time TB patients the prevalence of drug resistance ranged from 2 to 40 percent; this prevalence was higher in countries with poor TB control (11). Because TB is highly infectious, drug resistance could have serious repercussions for the spread and control of this disease worldwide.

The number of drug-resistant bacteria continues to grow each year, a reality that hampers the treatment of a variety of infections including dysentery, gonorrhea, herpes, pneumonia, meningitis, and ear infections in children (12)(13)(14). Antibiotic resistance is a particular problem in hospitals; in both Europe and the United States, many strains of staphylococci are resistant to all antibiotics except the expensive intravenous drug vancomycin (15)(16).

Factors that Contribute to the Emergence or Spread of Resistance

Antibiotic resistance is a human amplification of a natural phenomenon (17). Resistant genes occur and replicate in the natural microbial world (18). When antibiotics are used judiciously, the effect on the microbial world is small. However, the current misuse of antibiotics is affecting the natural balance between susceptible and resistant bacteria (19)(20).

Indeed, by one estimate, as much as 50 percent of antibiotic use in medical treatment is inappropriate because it does not benefit the patient (21). The heavy use of antibiotics in hospitals to prevent possible infections, for instance, exerts enormous selective pressure for the emergence and spread of antibiotic-resistant bacteria (22). Patients, who often believe that antibiotics are "miracle" drugs designed to cure any cough or fever, demand antibiotics from their physicians, even though antibiotics are powerless against viruses (23). Even if antibiotics are properly prescribed, patients often disregard prescription labels and do not take the full regimen, stopping once they feel better. However, when treatment is cut short, only the most susceptible members of a bacterial population are killed, and the more resistant variants are left behind, increasing the number of resistant bacteria in the population (24). The fact that antibiotics to treat TB are often taken only intermittently by poor patients, the homeless, and prison populations also fosters drug resistance (25). These conditions are aggravated in many developing countries, where many medications are bought and sold without prescriptions; this situation can contribute to improper therapy (26).

The use of antibiotics in agriculture is also a concern. Estimates suggest that at least one half of all antibiotics produced are used in farm animals, in fish farming, and in fruit and vegetable cultivation in industrialized countries (27). Approximately 90 percent of these antibiotics are not used to treat infections but rather to promote or stimulate animal growth or reduce the amount of feed necessary to help animals reach their marketable weights (28)(29). Because most of these "growth promoters" are members of the classes of antibiotics used to treat people, and because they are used at low dosages and for long periods, scientists are concerned that antibiotic use in animal feeding can foster the development of resistance in bacterial pathogens that affect humans as well as animals (30). In Europe, for instance, the growth promoter avoparcin—which is related to the human drug vancomycin—seems to be associated with the emergence of a large reservoir of vancomycin-resistant enterococci among animals (31). Moreover, the resistant strain of the species that infects humans has been found in poultry sold in retail markets and in communities surrounding agricultural areas (32).

The Costs of Antibiotic Resistance

Antibiotic resistance greatly raises the costs of disease. Results of a number of studies show that mortality, morbidity, likelihood of hospitalization, and length of hospitalization are twice as great for infections that are resistant (33)(34). Furthermore, when treatment fails because of resistance, the infection persists, increasing the opportunity of spreading the infection (35).

Treating a single case of multidrug-resistant TB in the industrialized countries, for example, can cost as much as US$250,000 (36). By contrast, treating a person with nonresistant TB can cost as little as US$13 and rarely more than US$100 in developing countries (37). Antibiotic resistance can also culminate in additional costs as a result of time spent in a hospital, extra doctor visits, and lost work days. Antibiotic resistance is a particularly difficult problem in developing countries, where the ability to obtain costlier and more effective antibiotics is compromised by the lack of financial resources (38).

Policy Actions

On the positive side, it is possible to reduce antibiotic resistance by removing the pressures that foster its emergence. The most

---

Environmental management need not wait until economic development reaches a certain level, however; it is a critical tool for improving public health both today and in the future. By targeting policies that help to reduce environmental threats that contribute both to ill health and poverty, it is possible to produce good health long before income growth could do so on its own. Improving the conditions of daily life may by itself help to reduce poverty. In other words, removing the environmental hazards that make people sick could keep people working and raise incomes (18).

Box 3.1 continued

effective and least expensive way to prevent and curb resistance is to use antibiotics appropriately (39). In this regard, some steps have taken place. Because of the concern over the use of antibiotics in agriculture and animal husbandry, the European Community has recently stopped the use of avoparcin as a feed additive (40). However, avoparcin's replacement, tylosin, still selects for vancomycin resistance. WHO has recommended that all countries stop using "human" antibiotics in animal husbandry; however, many countries, including the United States, have not heeded these recommendations. Other countries, such as Sweden, have banned the use of all growth-promoting antibiotics (41).

National campaigns that educate policymakers, prescribers, health care professionals, and the general public about how to avoid the misuse of antibiotics can also be effective. Surveillance is key (42). In Iceland, government officials, who were alarmed by the number of resistant *S. pneumoniae* strains, instituted a nationwide effort to screen for *S. pneumoniae* infections, monitor drug use, and educate the public about the safe use of antibiotics. After 3 years, the number of drug-resistant strains fell by 15 percent (43). In Hungary, sharp drops in penicillin use have also helped to reduce drug resistance (44). In Greece, Laiko General Hospital reduced its antibiotic consumption by more than 80 percent between 1989 and 1995 without reducing the efficacy of treatment. Resistance rates of several classes of antibiotics dropped in tandem (45).

Surveillance systems, such as those implemented by the Alliance for Prudent Use of Antibiotics and WHO, can map where drug-resistant strains are prevalent. This information should help clinicians select the correct antibiotic, which in turn would not only help ensure good patient care but would also help curb the spread of drug resistance, reduce costs, and save lives (46). Another action should be to reserve newer antibiotics only for the treatment of those patients harboring otherwise untreatable antibiotic infections. This would extend the usefulness of these newer antibiotics. Finally, pharmaceutical companies need incentives to develop new antibiotics and vaccines (47).

Antibiotic resistance requires global attention. Even if one country is successful in curtailing resistance, the potential for resistant organisms to spread across boundaries should encourage international cooperation (48). Controlling the rise in antibiotic resistance by promoting the wise use of antibiotics can ensure continued success in treating infectious diseases.

References and Notes

1. Stuart B. Levy, "Antibiotic Availability and Use: Consequences to Man and His Environment," *Journal of Clinical Epidemiology,* Vol. 44, Supplement II (1991), pp. 83S–87S.
2. United States Office of Technology Assessment, *Impacts of Antibiotic-Resistant Bacteria* (U.S. Government Printing Office, Washington, D.C., 1995), p. 39.
3. Mitchell L. Cohen, "Epidemiological Factors Influencing the Emergence of Antimicrobial Resistance," in *Ciba Foundation Symposium 207: Antibiotic Resistance: Origins, Evolution, Selection and Spread* (John Wiley & Sons, Chichester, U.K., 1997), pp. 223–224.
4. *Op. cit.* 2, p. 3.
5. World Health Organization, "Resistance to Antimicrobial Agents," *Weekly Epidemiological Record,* Vol. 72, No. 45 (1997), pp. 1–4.
6. *Ibid.*
7. Stuart B. Levy, *The Antibiotic Paradox: How Miracle Drugs Are Destroying the Miracle* (Plenum Press, New York, 1992), p. 101.
8. Stuart B. Levy, "Confronting Multidrug Resistance: A Role for Each of Us," *Journal of the American Medical Association,* Vol. 269, No. 14 (1993), p. 1840.
9. *Op. cit.* 1.
10. World Health Organization (WHO), *Anti-Tuberculosis Drug Resistance in the World* (WHO, Geneva, 1997), p. 17.
11. *Ibid.*, p. 91.
12. Stuart B. Levy, "Antimicrobial Resistance: A Global Perspective," in *Antimicrobial Resistance: A Crisis in Health Care,* Donald L. Jungkind *et al.*, eds. (Plenum Press, New York, 1995), p. 5.
13. *Op. cit.* 8.
14. Scott Dowell and Benjamin Schwartz, "Resistant Pneumococci: Protecting Patients Through Judicious Use of Antibiotics," *American Family Physician,* Vol. 55, No. 5 (1997), p. 1648.
15. *Op. cit.* 2, pp. 3, 34.
16. Sharon Kingman, "Resistance: A European Problem, Too," *Science,* Vol. 264 (April 15, 1994), pp. 363–365.
17. *Op. cit.* 10.
18. Joelle E. Gabay, "Ubiquitous Natural Antibiotics," *Science,* Vol. 264 (April 15, 1994), p. 373.
19. Julian Davies, "Inactivation of Antibiotics and the Dissemination of Resistance Genes," *Science,* Vol. 264 (April 15, 1994), pp. 375–381.
20. *Op. cit.* 1.
21. *Op. cit.* 2, p. 4.

22. *Op. cit.* 2, p. 69.
23. Stuart B. Levy, "Editorial Response: Antibiotic Resistance Worldwide—A Spanish Task Force Responds," *Clinical Infectious Diseases,* Vol. 23 (1996), p. 824.
24. *Op. cit.* 8, p. 1841.
25. *Op. cit.* 12, p. 8.
26. *Op. cit.* 1.
27. *Op. cit.* 5.
28. *Op. cit.* 2.
29. *Op. cit.* 2.
30. Wolfgang Witte, "Impact of Antibiotic Use in Animal Feeding on Resistance of Bacterial Pathogens in Animals," in *Ciba Foundation Symposium 207: Antibiotic Resistance: Origins, Evolution, Selection, and Spread* (John Wiley & Sons, Chichester, U.K., 1997), p. 69.
31. *Op. cit.* 23.
32. *Op. cit.* 2, p. 159.
33. *Op. cit.* 12, p. 10.
34. Scott D. Holmberg, Steven L. Solomon, and Paul A. Blake, "Health and Economic Impacts on Antimicrobial Resistance," *Review of Infectious Disease,* Vol. 9 (1987), pp. 1065–1078.
35. *Op. cit.* 5.
36. World Health Organization (WHO), *Anti-Tuberculosis Drug Resistance in the World* (WHO, Geneva, 1997).
37. World Health Organization (WHO), *TB: A Global Emergency,* WHO Report on the TB Epidemic (WHO, Geneva, 1994), p. 6.
38. *Op. cit.* 1.
39. *Op. cit.* 1.
40. *Op. cit.* 30, p. 69.
41. *Op. cit.* 2, p. 159.
42. Ruth L. Berkelman *et al.*, "Infectious Disease Surveillance: A Crumbling Foundation," *Science,* Vol. 264 (April 15, 1994), pp. 368–370.
43. Joan Stephenson, "Icelandic Researchers Are Showing the Way to Bring Down Rates of Antibiotic-Resistant Bacteria," *Journal of the American Medical Association Medical News & Perspectives* (January 17, 1996), pp. 6–8.
44. Rachel Novak, "Hungary Sees an Improvement in Penicillin Resistance," *Science,* Vol. 264 (April 15, 1994), p. 364.
45. Helen Giamarellou and Anastasia Antoniadou, "The Effect of Monitoring of Antibiotic Use on Decreasing Antibiotic Resistance in the Hospital," *Ciba Foundation Symposium 207: Antibiotic Resistance: Origins, Evolution, Selection, and Spread* (John Wiley & Sons, Chichester, U.K., 1997), pp. 82–84.
46. Mitchell L. Cohen, "Antimicrobial Resistance: Prognosis for Public Health," *Trends in Microbiology,* Vol. 2, No. 10 (October 1994), p. 424.
47. John Travis, "Reviving the Antibiotic Miracle?" *Science,* Vol. 264 (April 15, 1994), p. 361.
48. *Op. cit.* 8, p. 1841.

Many of the interventions described in the following sections rely on changes in behavior and improvements in the environment at the household level, because a large share of disease is incurred in or around the home environment. For instance, even if water supplies are clean at the public tap, they can become contaminated if stored in an unhygienic manner. This reality makes the role of public policy difficult, since policies are generally directed toward the public domain (19). One key role for public action is investment in health and hygiene education. Several studies have shown that the promotion of hand washing, for instance, can drastically reduce the incidence of diarrheal diseases (20). In addition, abundant evidence has made clear that educating women more broadly has an immediate, positive effect on health. (See Box 3.2.)

Policy actions should not be limited to education alone. Governments can also help facilitate changes at the household level by removing many of the institutional and financial barriers that keep poor households from protecting themselves (21). As one scholar has explained, "The poor do not lack healthy water systems only because they cannot afford them, but also because they lack the local political space to organize, and the political leverage to make the public sector respond to their needs" (22). To remove such barriers, governments can develop financing schemes that offset the initial investments needed to improve coverage of basic infrastructure for low-income communities. In addition, both governmental and development agencies should ensure that primary health care packages include environmental interventions as a key component. In other words, health care packages should provide access to water filters, polystyrene beads, and bed nets—all useful to prevent exposure to infectious agents—as well as to vaccines and drugs.

EXPANDING WATER AND SANITATION COVERAGE

In 1977, the United Nations Water Conference declared that all people, regardless of their stage of development or their social and economic conditions, have the right of access to drinking water in quantities and quality equal to their basic needs (23). Two decades later, however, an estimated 1.4 billion people still do not have access to safe drinking water, and 2.9 billion do not have access to adequate sanitation (24).

Improved water supply and sanitation services for those who lack them would do much to reduce the global burden of water-related diseases and to improve quality of life. Studies have consistently shown that improvements in water and sanitation coverage—including the implementation of low-cost, simple technology systems—can reduce the incidence of

---

Box 3.2 Improving Female Education

The link between female education and child health is strong. Studies have consistently shown that improvements in women's education can dramatically improve child health. On average, child mortality falls by about 8 percent for each additional year of parental schooling, for at least the first 8 to 10 years of schooling. (See figure.) Indeed, the link between a mother's education and a child's chances of living past the age of 2 may even be stronger than the link between wealth and health. Parental education influences child mortality because it provides parents with the tools to make use of medical services and to introduce changes in household health behavior such as washing hands and boiling water.

The case for educating girls becomes even stronger when other benefits are included, such as reduced fertility rates and higher household incomes. Women, as the "gatekeepers of their homes and communities," have traditionally had frontline responsibility in protecting the health of their families (Davis, 1997). As such, there are major opportunities to promote and protect environmental health if the status of women is improved.

Encouragingly, the percentage of girls in school has grown dramatically in the past 20 years; however, the battle toward achieving female literacy is far from won. In 1990 in developing countries, 77 million girls between the ages of 6 and 11 were not in school. Unless these countries commit to investing in the education of girls, it is projected that by the year 2015, 92 million girls, or 27 percent, will not have access to an education. Although investments in education are important throughout the entire world, a commitment to improving education in Africa should be considered a development and investment priority. Africa is the only region that has experienced a decline in education since the 1980s; without intervention, it is projected that by 2015, 55 percent of girls between the ages of 6 and 11 will still not be in school.

Source: Adapted from The World Bank, *Priorities and Strategies for Education: A World Bank Review* (The World Bank, Washington, D.C., 1995); also cited: Devra Davis, "Chemicals and the Environment," in *The Convergence of U.S. National Security and the Global Environment* (The Aspen Institute, Washington, D.C., 1997).

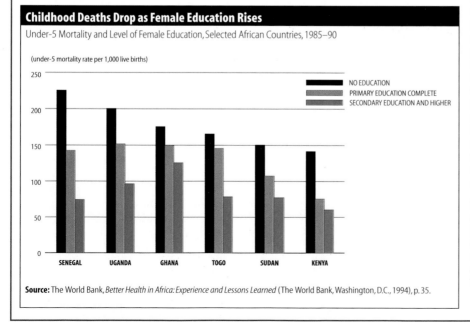

Childhood Deaths Drop as Female Education Rises

Under-5 Mortality and Level of Female Education, Selected African Countries, 1985–90

(under-5 mortality rate per 1,000 live births)

Legend:
- NO EDUCATION
- PRIMARY EDUCATION COMPLETE
- SECONDARY EDUCATION AND HIGHER

(Countries: SENEGAL, UGANDA, GHANA, TOGO, SUDAN, KENYA)

Source: The World Bank, *Better Health in Africa: Experience and Lessons Learned* (The World Bank, Washington, D.C., 1994), p. 35.

Environmental Change and Human Health

diarrhea, ascariasis, guinea worm, schistosomiasis, and other water-related diseases (25)(26)(27)(28)(29). Furthermore, providing water and sanitation confers multiple benefits beyond reducing water-related diseases, including alleviating the time and economic burden of having to collect water. As one researcher put it, "Most investments by government and aid donors in water and sanitation are fully justified irrespective of their health benefits; because they save drudgery and expense, contribute to human dignity and the emancipation of women, and offer many other benefits" (30).

Expanding access to water and sanitation, however, will not be easy. Much has been written about how to improve water and sanitation coverage; indeed, a whole decade was devoted to the effort (31)(32). The inability of the efforts undertaken during the International Drinking Water Supply and Sanitation Decade to do more than keep up with population growth provides sobering proof of the difficulty of finding effective solutions when the objective is clear but situations vary greatly and are extremely complex (33). A critical component of success, therefore, is to tailor solutions to individual circumstances rather than to search for simple, universal fixes.

Because one of the largest obstacles to providing water and sanitation coverage results from the huge cost of the initial installation of the system (and not necessarily the price of the water), assisting poor communities in financing simple connections may provide good near-term results. In Rufisque, Senegal, for example, nine low-income communities worked in partnership with an international NGO (ENDA-Tiers Monde) and the local authorities to set up a revolving community fund that helps pay for initial sanitation and sewage pipe connections. Grants from international agencies provided the initial jumpstart for the fund and covered initial management expenses; now community members contribute small amounts of money each month and provide the bulk of the US$50,000 fund. In addition, using narrow pipes (as opposed to thicker sewer pipes needed to withstand freezing in colder climes) has reduced the cost of sewage installation to 5 percent of conventional systems, increasing the number of families that can afford connection. Since the project's inception in 1990, community members have noticed a decrease in illnesses related to local environmental conditions (34).

Although community involvement in providing water and sanitation can help expand coverage at low cost, it should not be considered a panacea. Well-organized community groups do not simply emerge from the complex terrain of local politics because planners say they should; often outside support is necessary (35). NGOs can help mobilize residents or strengthen existing leadership functions and roles in the community. Local governments can also help foster organization by explicitly recognizing the rights of communities to organize and by encouraging women's education.

Equally important, governments have a major role to play in providing safe water and sanitation because these essentials confer benefits to not just the individual but to the broader public as well. If fecal material from one home is swept or washed into a street-side gutter because of lack of sanitation facilities, it is not only one household that is affected (36). For this reason, water and sanitation services have traditionally been highly subsidized by governments. However, these subsidies rarely reach the urban poor. As a result, in many cities, the poor often pay proportionately more for less water than do the rich. For example, in Onitsha, Nigeria, poor households spend an estimated 18 percent of their income on water during the dry season, compared with upper-income households, who pay a mere 2 to 3 percent (37). Conversely, the rich tend to waste water because they are not charged the full price of the water they receive. Utilities therefore cannot generate sufficient revenue to expand coverage to new peri-urban settlements or to perform routine maintenance (38).

Because of this situation, government efforts to adjust subsidies or to otherwise alter water pricing can be an effective tool in improving water services, if measures are taken to ensure equity. Recovering a greater percentage of the costs of water services would provide funds to expand coverage into new areas or to maintain and improve existing facilities. To address equity concerns, fees could be structured so that all consumers receive a basic amount of water at low cost and pay a proportionately greater amount for any additional water.

Involving the private sector, by either shifting management of water services to the private sector or by creating public-private partnerships, can also improve water delivery. Privatization schemes are being tried in Latin America (Argentina, Colombia, and Mexico); Asia (Bangladesh, Indonesia, Nepal, Pakistan, the Philippines, and Sri Lanka); and Africa (Côte d'Ivoire, Madagascar, Morocco, Niger, Senegal, and Tunisia) (39). For instance, in Abidjan, Côte d'Ivoire, the privately run SODECI has been providing water to the city for more than 30 years. By regularly collecting fees from its customers and using profits to extend coverage, the company has been able to provide water to 7 out of 10 urban dwellers. It has made a conscious and consistent effort to serve poor neighborhoods, even waiving—for three out of four such households—its usual charges for hooking up consumers to its pipelines (40).

Neither water pricing nor public-private partnerships will be effective without strong governments and sufficient political will. Many of the same circumstances that prevent the public sector from providing services to low-income settlements (including governance problems, low public-sector wages, public utility financing shortfalls, illegal land settlement, and politically powerless residents) also threaten the viability of public-private partnerships (41). There is no guarantee, for instance, that a financially motivated utility will invest

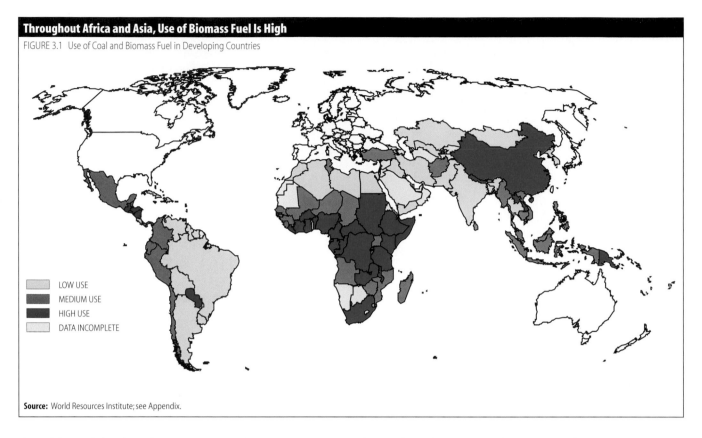

Throughout Africa and Asia, Use of Biomass Fuel Is High

FIGURE 3.1 Use of Coal and Biomass Fuel in Developing Countries

LOW USE
MEDIUM USE
HIGH USE
DATA INCOMPLETE

Source: World Resources Institute; see Appendix.

the additional funds in low-income neighborhoods rather than high-income suburbs (42).

However, placing water and sanitation programs—in addition to oral rehydration therapy (ORT) and health education—firmly on the political agenda can achieve dramatic improvements in health. Mexico in the early 1990s provides an apt example. In 1984, Mexico had begun to tackle childhood diarrheal deaths through the widespread promotion of ORT, with some success. In 1991, however, prompted by the fear of cholera that was sweeping over Latin America, the government deliberately went about improving basic sanitation, initiating widespread chlorination of water for human consumption, and prohibiting the irrigation of fruit and vegetables with sewage water—in addition to continuing measles immunization efforts and ORT use. The results of the more comprehensive package were marked: between 1991 and 1993, the annual mean number of episodes of diarrhea among children younger than 5 years of age decreased from 4.5 to 2.2, while the corresponding mortality rate fell from 101.6 to 62.9 per 100,000 (43).

TACKLING INDOOR AIR POLLUTION

The burning of solid fuels in the home is another major contributor to ill health globally. In 1992, the World Bank classified indoor air pollution as one of the four most critical environmental problems in developing countries (44). Indoor air pollution can weaken the body's defenses and damage the lungs; these factors contribute to acute lower respiratory infections, chronic lung disease, lung cancer, asthma, low birth weight, blindness, and heart disease (45)(46). Nearly 100 developing countries rely on biomass fuels for some of their residential energy needs, according to a new World Resources Institute (WRI) estimate. (See Figure 3.1.) In countries where use of smoky fuels is high, risks to health are likely to be high as well. Indeed, WHO recently estimated that indoor air pollution may be responsible for as many as 2.8 million deaths each year, making it one of the largest environmental risk factors of any kind (47).

In the short term, one way to reduce indoor air pollution is to improve household ventilation, but this strategy has obvious limitations and often worsens outdoor air quality. A more effective approach is to promote the use of improved stoves that remove the smoke from the house through a flue or chimney. In the past 20 years, hundreds of improved stove programs have been implemented throughout the developing world (48).

Although most of these programs had as their chief objective improved fuel efficiency rather than smoke removal, studies have shown that a well-designed, well-built, and well-maintained stove can reliably lower indoor air pollutants from cooking to levels 10 to 40 percent of those in kitchens with open fires (49). However, it is difficult to design and disseminate improved stoves that are affordable to the families who need them most. Furthermore, these improved stoves mainly serve to put the smoke outdoors, which can result in high levels of neighborhood air pollution.

Thus, improved stoves should be seen as an interim solution in the transition to less polluting and more efficient liquid fuels—such as kerosene and liquefied petroleum gas (LPG)—and electricity. This move up the energy ladder to fossil fuels for domestic uses typically occurs as incomes grow. But this transition to cleaner fuels may be impeded by the scale of poverty today and the number of people who rely on biomass fuels. Indeed, even in east Asia and the Pacific, a region that has experienced rapid economic growth, biomass fuels still account for 33 percent of energy supplies; use is expected to decrease by only 50 percent over the next 15 to 25 years (50).

National governments can help facilitate this transition to cleaner household fuels. Poor families can benefit from policies that reduce the upfront cash costs of new appliances (such as improved stoves or LPG bottles) or of obtaining electricity connections. Such policies can be implemented through programs that provide innovative credit; offer simple, low-cost service connection for electricity and LPG; and spread connection costs over a long period to reduce monthly outlay. In the electricity sector, the urban poor can benefit from "lifeline" rates—charging consumers who use very little energy less than those who use more. Thailand, for instance, has adopted this approach. As a result, the urban poor pay less than wealthier households for lighting, and the country has near-universal electricity service, although many people still rely on biomass fuels for cooking (51).

The benefits of encouraging this energy transition extend beyond reductions in indoor air pollution. The time that would have been spent collecting fuelwood could instead be devoted to child care, agriculture, and income-generating activities. In addition, reduced use of wood fuels might also result in less deforestation, soil erosion, and accompanying losses in soil fertility (52).

CONTROLLING DISEASE VECTORS IN THE LOCAL ENVIRONMENT

As Chapter 1 illustrated, vector-borne diseases such as malaria, dengue fever, yellow fever, and schistosomiasis cause enormous suffering and death throughout the developing world. Vaccines to prevent these diseases, or drugs to treat those diseases that cannot be prevented, hold out promise for future disease control. At this stage, however, vaccines and drugs are lacking for many of the major vector-borne diseases, in part because the disease organisms are formidable adversaries. Perhaps a greater reason is that these diseases are generally not a priority to large pharmaceutical companies, although there are important exceptions (53).

Even when drugs to combat diseases like dengue fever and malaria become available, vector control should remain a pri-

ority. Environmental interventions to contain the insects that transmit disease can occur at a range of levels, such as household, community, or region. Improvements in and around the home, for instance, can often make a tremendous difference in controlling vector populations and reducing the incidence of infectious diseases. In areas where Chagas disease remains high, for example, helping low-income families finance home improvements that remove the thatched roofs where the reduviid bugs hide can be a more effective use of public funds than investing in costly pesticide applications. In Brazil and Venezuela, replacing palm-thatched roofs with tiles or corrugated tin and repairing walls and floors were instrumental in reducing human contact with the disease vector and ultimately in reducing Chagas disease (54). These housing improvements also provided the added benefits of better ventilation, which improved indoor air quality at the same time (55).

Household water storage, used to make up for intermittent or inadequate piped water supplies, can also provide reservoirs for disease-bearing mosquitoes and other insects. Giving families fitted lids or screens to place over water containers can be a cheap, interim way to lower the risk of disease by reducing mosquito-breeding sites (56). Septic tanks and latrine pits can also be made mosquito-proof at low cost with polystyrene beads. These beads form a floating layer through which female mosquitoes cannot lay their eggs and mosquito larvae cannot breathe. Experience in Brazil, India, and Tanzania has shown that the layer will remain in place for more than 4 years (57). Similarly, providing nylon gauze with which to filter water drawn from shallow wells or surface water has proven successful in reducing the incidence of guinea worm (58). Making these types of interventions more widely available through primary health-care clinics or local health-care workers can help reduce disease incidence at low cost.

Community programs are an effective, often inexpensive, means of vector control. In such programs, community members take measures to improve the environmental conditions in and around their homes, thereby reducing reservoirs for mosquitoes, flies, and rats. Mass media campaigns can educate residents about the importance of removing garbage and other mosquito habitats from the community—creating a community "police" force against the disease (59). Other approaches tie vector control to income generation. In India, for example, several communities have controlled *Anopheles* mosquito breeding in shallow coastal lagoons by removing algae from larval breeding places and using it as manure or in papermaking. Other strategies involve introducing fish and shrimp that eat mosquito larvae into pools where mosquitoes might breed; these fish can later be sold (60).

The success of household or community interventions does not imply that governments can abdicate their responsibility in vector control. Clearly, many of these simple interventions would not be necessary if longer-term strategies were imple-

Box 3.3 Malaria: The Continuing Struggle

In 1955, the World Health Organization (WHO) began a campaign to eradicate malaria (1). By 1970, a huge malaria-ridden area that sheltered nearly 700 million people was virtually free from the disease (2). These gains were short-lived, however. Today, malaria claims the lives of some 1 to 3 million people each year, and the number is on the rise. In India, for example, new cases of malaria jumped from 100,000 in the early 1960s to almost 3 million in 1996 (3)(4).

The global "reemergence" of malaria has several underlying causes. Population and demographic changes have resulted in more people moving into densely populated areas, thereby increasing transmission. Human environmental changes such as road building, mining, deforestation, and new agricultural and irrigation projects—particularly in tropical regions such as the Amazon basin—have created new breeding sites. (See Box 2.4 in Chapter 2.)

Controlling malaria has also become more complicated, since the mosquitoes that carry malaria have developed resistance to the insecticides used for their control. In Africa, where 90 percent of malaria cases occur, the three main mosquito vectors are resistant to one or more insecticides (5). This is often due to the excessive use of the same or similar insecticides for control of agricultural pests. In addition, malaria parasites have developed resistance to chloroquine, the most commonly used and least expensive antimalaria drug. Another contributing factor is that in many

regions, malaria control programs have deteriorated or been abandoned (6).

Considering these diverse underlying factors makes it clear that no single strategy will be effective in reducing the burden of malaria. A comprehensive malaria control strategy requires three interdependent and complementary components: disease management, surveillance, and prevention, including environmental management.

Disease management includes strengthening health care to ensure access to accurate diagnosis, care, and treatment. It can dramatically reduce malaria mortality, as well as reduce the severity and duration of the illness. Indeed, accurate diagnosis and prompt, appropriate treatment are fundamental to any malaria control program.

Surveillance, at both the international and local level, is also crucial if malaria is to be controlled. National, continental, or global data make it possible to observe large-scale trends. Surveillance and assessment should also include monitoring of underlying risk factors, either human behaviors or environmental conditions. Collecting and mapping this information would enable the delineation of risk areas at national and regional levels, a critical step in long-term disease management as well as in epidemic control.

Prevention is critical to reducing malaria disease rates and also reducing the associated burden on the health-care system. Malaria prevention is often viewed as personal protection, such as use of bed nets, protective clothes, and insect repellents. However, a variety of other preventive measures have been successfully applied around

the world. The full range of preventive activities includes not only personal protection but also:

- environmental management, especially to eliminate the aquatic breeding sites of mosquito vectors near human habitations;
- targeted residual spraying;
- the use of larvicides, biological control agents, and predators of larval vectors; and
- education.

Strategies for environmental management involve modifying habitat to reduce breeding sites for the mosquito. Actions can include: changing water levels at dams or other water bodies, either permanently or at strategic times; creating channels in marshy areas; planting water-intensive trees; and adequately disposing of wastewater. Large-scale draining of marshes can also successfully control mosquito populations, but such measures may damage valuable wetlands.

In contrast to large-scale wetland clearing, malaria can be stemmed by relatively simple measures such as changing the water levels in irrigation ditches at strategic times. A number of other simple measures include covering water storage tanks, street drains, and latrines; making sure there are no objects such as discarded tires or flower pots that can collect rainwater outside of residences; and screening windows and closing the eaves of houses. These strategies clearly require community involvement to succeed. In addition, the princi-

---

mented, such as providing water and sanitation and improving garbage collection and disposal. Reliable piped water would reduce the need to store water in the first place, with the added benefit of reducing the burden of diarrheal diseases.

Furthermore, coordinated efforts among multinational agencies, national governments, and private companies can reduce disease incidence much more effectively, and on a larger scale, than communities can on their own. The Onchocerciasis Control Programme in West Africa, for instance, has dramatically reduced the threat of river blindness. A multinational effort by the Food and Agriculture Organization of the United Nations (FAO), the United Nations Development Programme (UNDP), the World Bank, and WHO has controlled the blackfly by destroying its larvae with insecticides sprayed from the air. The environmental impact of the insecticides is continuously monitored. In addition, the U.S. pharmaceutical manufacturer Merck & Co. has committed to providing ivermectin—a drug that safely and effectively kills the larvae in the body—free of charge as long as river blindness exists. This program protects about 30 million people from river blind-

ness, at an annual cost of less than US$1 per person (61). As part of a WHO-coordinated program to eliminate another tropical disease, lymphatic filariasis or elephantiasis, Smith-Kline Beecham announced in early 1998 that it would supply free of charge an antiparasitic drug to roughly one fifth of the world's population (62).

For many other vectors—most notably the mosquito—both community involvement and government investment are needed to successfully reduce the burden of disease. (See Box 3.3.) A tremendous and often overlooked opportunity also exists to control disease vectors on a larger scale through careful planning of development projects and land use changes, as will be described below.

Addressing the Unintended Consequences of Development

Beyond the environmental problems associated with poverty are those that can arise from economic growth itself, as countries industrialize, intensify their agricultural production, and

Box 3.3 continued

ples of environmental management can be incorporated into development planning to ensure that malaria problems do not arise, particularly as a consequence of water resource development projects. In the United States, for example, planned fluctuations of the water level in reservoirs were used to control local malaria vectors in the areas around the Tennessee Valley Authority (TVA), a large hydroelectric project in the southeastern part of the country.

Urban and peri-urban malaria is a special case requiring alternative assessment and control options. Urbanization is proceeding rapidly in sub-Saharan Africa and other malaria-endemic regions of the world. By the year 2000, an estimated 43 percent of the population may live in urban areas. Increasing evidence suggests that urbanization is already having a significant impact on malaria epidemiology. Although formal urban development typically reduces mosquito densities, the kind of informal development occurring in sub-Saharan Africa often simply changes the vector species to those such as the culicines (*Culex sps.*) that breed in polluted water, as has been well documented in Dar es Salaam, Tanzania, and other cities (7). Other studies indicate that in urban and peri-urban areas of sub-Saharan Africa, transmission is often intense but seasonal, occurring for shorter times than in rural areas (8).

This preliminary evidence indicates that cost-effective malaria control in urban and peri-urban areas of sub-Saharan Africa will likely include well-targeted environmental management in pri-

ority areas. In Mozambique, for instance, in areas of high human density, mosquito and parasite dispersion is very limited, suggesting that malaria control strategies could, therefore, be specifically targeted to local environmental conditions, including housing construction (9).

The use of environmental versus chemical vector control remains a subject of intense debate. In India, a team of researchers compared the costs of achieving malaria control by four means: using the pesticides DDT, lindane (HCH), or malathion, or using a combination of environmental management and biological control. The combination of environmental management and biological control, referred to as bioenvironmental control, was found to be the least costly in achieving malaria control for the district's 350,000 people. The bioenvironmental control measures relied extensively on donated community labor. Actions included a combination of filling and leveling burrow pits; installing permanent underground drains (French drains); repairing leaks in water systems; cleaning ponds and cement tanks and stocking them with larvivorous fishes; and planting eucalyptus trees to increase evapotranspiration in water-logged soils (10).

Health education is essential to the success of any malaria prevention program. This can include programs in the community and the schools, the training of control staff, and efforts to raise community awareness. Equally critical is the development of supportive government policies and long-term financing. Such cross-sector,

community-based approaches are key to the long-term prevention of many environmentally related diseases, including malaria.

References and Notes.

1. Laurie Garrett, *The Coming Plague* (Farrar Straus and Giroux, New York, 1994), p. 31.
2. John Wargo, *Our Children's Toxic Legacy* (Yale University Press, New Haven, Connecticut, 1996), p. 46.
3. Declan Butler, "Time to put Malaria Control on the Global Agenda," *Nature,* Vol. 386 (April 10, 1997), p. 535.
4. K.S. Jaryarman, "India Plans $200-Million Attack on Malaria," *Nature,* Vol. 386 (April 10, 1997), p. 536.
5. *Op. cit.* 2, p. 50.
6. *Op. cit.* 4.
7. David J. Bradley, "Malaria," in *Disease and Mortality in Sub-Saharan Africa,* Richard G. Feachem and Dean T. Jamison, eds. (Oxford University Press, Oxford, U.K., 1991), p. 199.
8. M. Alogbeto, J.P.L. Chippaux, and M. Colluzi, "Le Paludisme Urbain Côtier à Cotonou (République du Bénin), Étude Entomologique," *Revue d'Epidémiologie et de Santé Publique,* Vol. 40, No. 4 (1992), pp. 233–239.
9. R. Thompson *et al.,* "The Matola Malaria Project: A Temporal and Spatial Study of Malaria Transmission and Disease in a Suburban Area of Maputo, Mozambique," *American Journal of Tropical Medicine and Hygiene,* Vol. 57, No. 5 (November 1997), pp. 550–559.
10. P. K. Ranjagopalan *et al.,* "Environmental and Water Management for Mosquito Control," in *Appropriate Technology in Vector Control,* C.F. Curtis, ed. (CRC Press, Boca Raton, Florida, 1989), pp. 121–138.

consume greater amounts of fossil fuels. The challenge facing policymakers worldwide is to manage economic growth in a way that maximizes its benefits and reduces its costs, in terms of damage to both the environment and to public health.

Accomplishing this task is not easy. Resources, both institutional and financial, are limited, and pressures for development are strong. Often, competing risks exist, and deciding which to tackle first is never easy. (See Guest Commentary by K.J. Nath.)

Policymakers must often weigh immediate benefits—of using a pesticide to increase agricultural yields, for instance—against uncertain and longer-term health risks. Questions of equity among different social groups and even generations can further complicate decisionmaking. Often, the evidence for future health or environmental impacts is speculative or uncertain. Issues of cost are also often raised, such as: Why not wait for economic growth and technology improvements before acting, since both would reduce the costs of cleanup?

This wait-and-see approach is in itself costly, however. Some of the health effects of environmental degradation—such as lowered IQ as a result of lead exposures, or reproductive damages—cannot be reversed no matter how high the future investments. Furthermore, experience in the developed economies has shown that preventing or controlling pollution is often cheaper than cleaning up later. Clear policy signals today are necessary in order to avoid the negative impacts of economic growth and to reap the full benefits of development.

Policymakers have a much richer variety of tools at their disposal than they did 20 years ago, many of which could improve environmental protection at relatively low cost. In the past, the typical approach was to regulate behavior, often through what are known as command-and-control approaches. Although these approaches are important, they can also be costly and difficult to enforce. More recently, policymakers have been using market-based incentives as a way to achieve environmental health goals. These incentives can take the form of subsidy reforms, taxes to increase prices to reflect social costs, or the establishment of new markets in which pollution permits can be traded (63). Information, too, is a powerful tool for facilitating change. Public education campaigns explaining the links between environmental hazards and human health can influence individual behavior, as well as provide pressure for broader environmental action.

Other steps are also necessary. Development planners in national governments and international agencies need to understand the possible health impacts of their projects. Environmental impact assessments are now commonplace. What is lacking in many cases, however, are environmental *health* impact assessments. Often, the deleterious health impacts of a particular project, such as a dam, can be anticipated and prevented (64). (See Box 3.4.)

Techniques for assessing risk can also be broadened. An approach to risk analysis that incorporates ecosystem impacts would help clarify where long-term or indirect risks might emerge. This approach could include using biological indicators, such as plant, rodent, and insect populations, as well as monitoring of environmental and climatological changes. Existing tests may show that a new pesticide under development is not directly toxic to humans. But if these tests do not investigate whether or not that pesticide may cause ecological damages, over the long term, populations may be exposed to new health risks emanating from environmental change. Data gathered from public health, ecology, and other scientific disciplines might enable risk assessors to better predict the more unexpected health implications of environmental changes (65).

Each of the policy approaches described above has its strengths and weaknesses; policymakers must select among them to find the appropriate mix of instruments that will achieve both environmental and health protection. The rest of this chapter explores various strategies for addressing the unintended health consequences of the three trends described in Chapter 2—the intensification of agriculture, industrialization, and rising energy use. The chapter examines strategies for remediation, where environmental degradation has already occurred, and also discusses strategies to prevent environmental degradation and risks to human health.

INTENSIFICATION OF AGRICULTURE

In addition to its clear benefits, agricultural intensification can lead to adverse health effects. Risks include exposure to

---

Box 3.4 Putting Health On The Map

Strategies that incorporate health concerns into development projects can have multiple and overlapping benefits. Anticipating health effects in the project planning stage saves time, money, and lives. This can be as simple as thinking about snail habitat when designing irrigation canals, or as complex as designing new communities in a way that will reduce the use of vehicles.

Although it may be easy to recognize the value of integrating preventive health measures into policy and project planning, accomplishing this goal is far from easy. Resources are always constrained, educated and trained personnel may not be available, and pressures to proceed with development are great. Moreover, the health and environment communities do not have the benefit of many years of experience in working together. Nevertheless, a number of international bodies, such as the World Health Organization (WHO), are encouraging such interaction. Other organizations that bring together the health and environment communities include the U.N. Commission on Sustainable Development (CSD), the Inter-Agency Committee on Sustainable Development, and the Inter-Agency Environment Coordination Group, which is an advisory and consultative body to the United Nations Environment Programme (UNEP).

Several regional and country initiatives show that it is possible to broaden the perspective of those responsible for development decisions. Many countries have established intersectoral committees, partly to follow up on the *Agenda 21* recommendations of the Rio Summit.

● In Jordan, the Ministry of Health set up an intersectoral working group, and a national health and environment action plan was prepared.

● In Guatemala, a working team was established with representation from the Health Ministry, planning, and environment sectors; and a national plan for environmental health and sustainable development was produced, along with an institutional analysis of national sectors associated with health and the environment.

● In Guinea-Bissau, a national interministerial committee on health and the environment was formed to foster a national process of coordination among agencies, government, and civil society; the committee addresses ways of integrating health and environment concerns into overall national sustainable development planning. A national plan of action on health and environment for sustainable development was produced.

● In Iran, a draft strategy document on health and the environment was developed, to be incorporated ultimately into a national strategy on sustainable development. The draft strategy included a situation analysis and proposals for structural and institutional reform.

● In Nepal, a health perspective was added to the draft Nepal Environmental Policy and Action Plan. Initially, the plan did not incorporate a public health component. Through the Nepal Environmental Health Initiative, a comprehensive health and environment strategy was developed, and most of the resulting recommendations were incorporated into the final Environmental Policy and Action Plan.

● In the Philippines, collaboration was strengthened between health agencies and the Philippine Council for Sustainable Development. The latter oversees implementation of activities in support of commitments to sustainable development principles made at the Earth Summit. An Interagency Committee on Environmental Health, organized by the Ministry of Health and the Council, jointly sponsored a detailed analysis with case studies of the best approaches for integrating health and environment issues into the development and implementation of national plans for sustainable development.

Adapted from: World Health Organization (WHO), *Health and Environment in Sustainable Development: Five Years After the Earth Summit* (WHO, Geneva, 1997).

agricultural chemicals and also to infectious disease agents associated with agricultural practices. Less directly, hazards can also arise from soil degradation when it undermines local capacity to produce food.

For a variety of reasons—health, environmental, and economic—it is clearly in society's long-term interest to develop and implement more environmentally benign forms of agriculture—forms that use fewer agricultural chemicals, less water, less energy, and cause less ecosystem disruption while maintaining agricultural biodiversity. This shift, now underway in some parts of the world, will take some time to accomplish and will not be driven by health concerns alone. In the near term, however, considerable health benefits can be gained by reducing the threat of acute pesticide poisonings among agricultural workers, their families, and communities. The toll of death and disease from pesticide poisonings is both large and preventable with interventions available today.

Reducing Acute Risks from Pesticide Use

In developing countries, pesticides may poison as many as 5 million people, and many millions more may suffer lesser, but nonetheless unhealthy pesticide exposures (66). Even in the developed world, where safety regulations are stricter and pesticides are generally safer, tens of thousands of farmworkers are affected (67). The number of acute pesticide poisonings could be greatly reduced if countries and pesticide manufacturers agreed to phase out the use of the most toxic pesticides and enact other reforms to increase the safety of pesticide handling.

As described in Chapter 2, some extremely toxic pesticides that are banned in developed countries are still widely used in the developing world. Many of the pesticides of the 1990s are more selective in what they kill, less toxic to humans and the environment, and require less per hectare to be effective, thus reducing risks to human health (68). Because price and availability largely determine the type of pesticide used, national governments can encourage the shift toward safer pesticides by using a combination of taxes and financial incentives. For instance, a tax or fee that falls more heavily on older pesticides would provide the farmer an incentive to switch to newer compounds that are applied sparingly (69).

To boost agricultural production, many governments heavily subsidize pesticides. These subsidies often result in excessive and inefficient use of pesticides and provide a disincentive to try alternative pest control methods, such as Integrated Pest Management (IPM). Removing or adjusting these subsidies can greatly influence pesticide use. In Indonesia, for

Yields Rise Despite Declines in Pesticide Subsidies

TABLE 3.2   Pesticide Subsidies in Indonesia, 1985–90

	1985	1986	1987	1988	1989	1990
Pesticide subsidy (1995 million U.S. dollars)	141	179	134	85	2	0
Subsidy rate (percent)	85	75	45	40	0	0
Pesticide production (thousand metric tons)	53	46	58	48	29	22
Milled rice production (million metric tons)	26.5	26.8	27.3	28.3	29.4	30.3

Source: The World Bank, *Five Years After Rio: Innovations in Environmental Policy* (The World Bank, Washington, D.C., 1997), p. 26.

instance, a combined strategy of phasing out pesticide subsidies and implementing IPM has reduced pesticide use without compromising rice production. The policy shift has not only saved more than US$100 million per year in government subsidies but also has reduced pesticide production from 53,000 to 22,000 tons over 5 years (70). (See Table 3.2.)

Market incentives need to be coupled with a strong regulatory and enforcement system; unfortunately, such systems are lacking in many developing and developed countries alike. In Africa, for instance, 76 percent of countries lack pesticide control statutes (71). Even where regulations do exist, statutes are often not enforced and practices are not monitored. Building capacity for improved environmental management—for example, by ensuring that the environmental ministry within a country has both financial and political power, or by providing adequate technical support—is an important long-term goal (72).

As part of the effort to reduce exposures to and use of some of the most dangerous pesticides, several international conventions have been established to help control the trade of hazardous pesticides and other chemicals. Although they do not regulate use directly, these conventions hope to address the problem of exporting dangerous compounds to countries with less stringent regulations where they would either be used or disposed of unsafely. One example is the Prior Informed Consent (PIC) mechanism (73). This procedure was designed to ensure that countries have accurate and detailed information on specific pesticides and industrial chemicals that have been found to be hazardous. Based on this information, countries can then make informed decisions about whether to import or use these chemicals.

The PIC procedure was first implemented for six pesticides in 1990. By 1997, 154 countries had agreed to participate in the procedure, which then covered 27 pesticides and industrial chemicals. One weakness of this procedure, however, is that it is voluntary. FAO and UNEP are now facilitating international negotiations to develop a legally binding instrument; agreement is expected during 1998 (74).

Several international bodies, private corporations, and nonprofit organizations are also working with communities to educate them about the safe use of pesticides. Some pesticide manufacturers are also trying to reduce risks through improved packaging and labeling. Some companies have developed water-soluble packaging. This eliminates the need to rinse the original container to dispose of it safely (75). Public right-to-know laws can also provide an incentive for change. Once information is available on pesticide use and its hazards, health advocates, citizen groups, and others can bring pressure on growers and individuals using the products.

Adopting Less Disruptive Agricultural Practices

Ultimately, reducing health risks from agriculture will require a shift to a more environmentally benign form of agriculture, one that uses fewer agricultural chemicals overall, minimizes ecological disruption, and reduces agriculture's heavy demand for water.

Managing Pests Strategically. Over the long term, IPM promises to reduce the use of pesticides greatly. This strategy encourages natural control of pest populations by anticipating problems and preventing them from reaching economically damaging levels. Techniques include enhancing natural enemies, planting pest-resistant crops, and, as a last resort, judicious use of pesticides.

In a number of cases, IPM has proven not only better for health but more economical than pest control based solely on agrochemicals. In Brazil, about 40 percent of commercial soybean farmers have switched to IPM since the 1970s, saving more than US$200 million dollars a year as the result of reduced use of insecticides, labor, machinery, and fuel. In the early 1970s, five insecticide applications per season were needed to control soybean pests; now one or two yearly applications are sufficient (76). Pesticide use has been reduced by 80 to 90 percent (77).

Although IPM use has increased steadily over the past two decades, the proportion of farmers using it remains small. Part of the difficulty is that in each case, specific techniques must be identified for local conditions. Governments often offer little support, such as funding or education, to encourage growers to invest in this new approach. In addition, pesticides continue to be attractive to most farmers and governments because their use is simple and economic returns are predictable. Promoting a switch to IPM will require more education and training at the farm level, along with continuing research. In addition, promoting IPM will require adjusting those subsidies and policies that encourage extensive pesticide use.

Reducing Fertilizer Use. Excessive fertilization of agricultural crops can damage both ecosystems and human health. Excess fertilizer can leach through soil where porosity is high, leading to nitrate contamination of groundwater, which poses a direct threat to infant health. Runoff from heavily fertilized fields is also a prime contributor to the eutrophication of surface waters and coastal estuaries—one of the most critical threats to aquatic ecosystems today and therefore to the harvest of fish and shellfish that constitute an important human food source.

Reducing the risks of fertilizer use will require a combination of better agricultural practices that raise fertilizer efficiency and increased efforts to trap agricultural runoff before it leaches into waterways. Better timing of fertilizer applications, for instance, can reduce the amount of fertilizer wasted in the field. In Hawaii, one sugar cane plantation was able to cut nitrogen fertilizer use by one third and reduce losses of nitrous oxide and nitric oxide 10-fold by dissolving the fertilizer in irrigation water, delivering it below the soil surface, and timing multiple applications to meet the needs of the growing crop (78). Other strategies to keep excess fertilizer from contaminating local waterways include establishing vegetation buffer strips around crop and pasturelands and restoring natural wetlands. Over the long term, controlling water pollution from agriculture will require more coordination between agricultural and environmental objectives. (See Box 3.5.)

Rational Irrigation. Although the spread of irrigation has been a major contributor to the remarkable increases in agricultural output, current irrigation practices can cause much damage. Problems include excessive consumption of fresh water, which can contribute to local water scarcity and also indirectly undermine health by harming the agricultural resource base. Irrigation projects can also create breeding sites for mosquitoes and other vectors, increasing the transmission of these diseases. And when wastewater is used for irrigation, it can increase the risk of cholera, hepatitis, and other diseases associated with human sewage.

Even relatively simple improvements in irrigation projects and planning can bring high short-term rewards in terms of reduced water consumption and improved health. Careful scheduling of irrigation, matching crops to local climatic conditions, and modest improvements to inefficient systems can result in large water savings (79). Coordination between water development planners and health authorities could substantially lower the incidence of vector-borne diseases. If health concerns and costs are analyzed and factored into planning, controlling vectors through environmental management can be relatively inexpensive and effective, with long-term benefits—in contrast to having to implement a chemical control strategy or establish treatment centers after the disease vector has taken hold (80). Changing dam water levels at strategic times, or digging channels to ensure proper water flow, for instance, can reduce the risks of vector-borne disease.

The risks associated with using wastewater for irrigation can also be greatly reduced through simple interventions. For example, irrigation with wastewater during planting is less risky than application during the growing cycle; risks drop if wastewater irrigation ceases several weeks before the harvest.

Box 3.5 Overcoming Agricultural Water Pollution in the European Union

Until the mid-1980s, the European Community generally had separate sets of policies for agriculture and the environment. The Common Agricultural Policy (CAP), which encouraged the intensification of agricultural practices, did not take into account water quality or any other environmental implications. Environmental policy rarely addressed the negative side effects of agriculture. As a result, agriculture became a major source of water pollution and, in some areas, a threat to drinking water supplies.

As incorporated into the 1957 Treaty of Rome, the CAP was designed to increase agricultural productivity and to ensure farmers a fair standard of living. To achieve this, the European Community adopted market price support measures and subsidies. Together with technological advances, this policy stimulated intensive agricultural practices and production. Between 1960 and 1985, agricultural production, in monetary terms, climbed dramatically, with increases ranging from 50 percent in France to about 85 percent in the Netherlands.

Resulting pressure on water resources from the intensity of inorganic nitrogen fertilizer use rose in tandem. From 1970 to the mid-1980s, inorganic nitrogen use on agricultural land grew by 42 percent in the Netherlands and by 135 percent in the United Kingdom. As a result, agriculture became a major source of nitrate and phosphorus pollution of water during this period, while industrial and municipal discharges of these substances continued to decline. By the end of the 1980s, agriculture accounted for 70 to 85 percent of the nitrogen pollution, and more than 30 percent of the phosphorus pollution, of the surface water in rural areas.

In 1980, environmental policies on drinking water required member countries to ensure that they met certain quality objectives for drinking water supplies by 1985. During the second half of the 1980s, it became obvious that most member countries had not achieved these quality objectives. In particular, the maximum pollutant level for nitrate, set at 50 milligrams per liter, was exceeded in many areas.

As a result of these problems, in the last decade, the European Union (EU) countries have made efforts to reconcile their policies for agriculture and the environment. At the EU level, agricultural policy is expanding subsidies for less-intensive and less-polluting methods of production, and environmental policy has begun to directly target agricultural pollution of water.

In individual member countries, policies for controlling agricultural water pollution have gradually been extended to incorporate a mix of voluntary, regulatory, and incentive-based measures. In 1984, the French Ministries of Agriculture and the Environment created a new organization that was solely responsible for promoting education, information, and research on agricultural water pollution control. When it became clear that education and voluntary measures alone were not sufficient to induce broad changes in agricultural practices, the member countries gradually introduced regulatory measures. For instance, in 1984, the Dutch Government forbade new "factory farms" for pigs and poultry, and in 1986 the German Government imposed greater restrictions on the use of pesticides.

Incentive-based measures, mainly subsidies, have been adopted since the late 1980s. For example, a program for environmentally sensitive areas in the United Kingdom provides grants to farmers to induce them to reduce the application

of fertilizers and pesticides or to convert to organic farming. Another incentive-based approach has been adopted by the Dutch Government for controlling manure production and disposal. It establishes manure quotas for individual farms and a national manure bank to stimulate the distribution of manure supplies. From 1990 to 1994, manure quotas were gradually tightened, and in 1994 they became tradable.

Overall, there has been a great reluctance to use other than voluntary measures. In cases where regulatory or incentive-based measures have been used, they were usually accompanied by payments to farmers. The implicit assumption seems to have been that farmers have a right to use land as they see fit, and if the public wants less intensive land use, it must provide monetary compensation. The irony is that the public is also paying for the agricultural support prices that encourage intensification.

A recent Agreement on Agriculture, along with the planned enlargement of the EU to include countries of central and Eastern Europe, makes additional reforms of the EU's agricultural policy likely. In particular, direct income support is expected to increasingly replace agricultural price supports. This change should provide efficient incentives for agricultural pollution abatement.

Adapted from: Susanne M. Scheierling, "Overcoming Agricultural Pollution of Water: The Challenge of Integrating Agricultural and Environmental Policies in the European Union," World Bank Technical Paper No. 269 (The World Bank, Washington, D.C., 1995). Available online at http://www.worldbank.org/fandd/english/0996/articles/0100996.htm (January 6, 1998).

Using wastewater to irrigate cotton or animal fodder, rather than fruits and vegetables, is another good choice (81).

INDUSTRIALIZATION

Industrialization can impose pressures on the environment and human health from several sources, including the extraction and consumption of raw materials, emissions of industrial pollutants, and increased energy demand. In most developed countries, decades of strong regulations have brought some of the worst pollution problems under control, although serious problems still remain. In the less developed countries, where regulations and enforcement tend to be more lax and pressures for economic growth are intense, pollution abatement remains a critical challenge. Problems of resource consumption remain prominent across the world, especially in the wealthiest countries, which consume vast quantities of

raw resources to support their quality of life. Implementing changes to make industry both cleaner and more efficient could greatly influence health, both today and in the future.

Pollution Abatement

Despite substantial progress, continuing efforts are warranted in both developed and developing countries to reduce exposure to industrial pollutants. Command-and-control strategies remain an important component of pollution control strategies, especially in developing countries. In addition, market strategies can provide financial incentives for industry to adopt less polluting behavior or technology. Such strategies tend to be flexible, enabling the polluter to choose the most economical option for reaching a desired target. Examples of market strategies include environmental taxes, pollution levies, and tradeable permit systems.

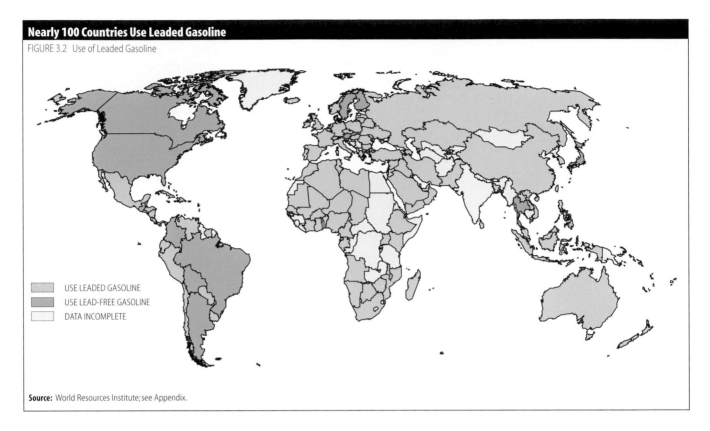

Nearly 100 Countries Use Leaded Gasoline

FIGURE 3.2 Use of Leaded Gasoline

USE LEADED GASOLINE
USE LEAD-FREE GASOLINE
DATA INCOMPLETE

Source: World Resources Institute; see Appendix.

In the United States, emissions trading has successfully reduced overall industrial sulfur dioxide (SO_2) emissions. Under this program, companies can meet emissions reduction targets by reducing pollution themselves, by purchasing reductions from another company that was able to cut more emissions at lower cost, or by employing a combination of both methods. Public disclosure of environmental performance can also encourage pollution reduction. Indonesia has recently initiated an overall environmental performance rating system for factories, rating plants according to five categories. Preliminary evidence suggests that this program is having a significant impact on pollution abatement (82). In both Rio de Janeiro and São Paulo, Brazil, pollution control agencies have also experimented with programs that involve public disclosure of poor environmental performance of large industries (83).

Reducing Exposure to the Worst Offenders

When faced with numerous and uncertain health risks and limited resources to combat pollution, it makes sense for governments to focus control efforts on the worst offenders. Scientific debate continues regarding the exact health effects related to low-level exposures of some industrial pollutants. But for other pollutants—in particular heavy metals such as lead—no such subtleties remain. Heavy metals are extremely hazardous to human health, and there is no justification for the human exposures that continue today, causing avoidable

and sometimes irreversible damage to human health. Long-lived chemical pollutants, known as persistent organic pollutants (POPs), are another case in point. (See Box 3.6.) Removing substances such as heavy metals and POPs from use and trade is both urgent and feasible.

Getting Lead Out of Gasoline. Lead poisoning remains the single most significant and easily preventable condition associated with an environmental and occupational toxin (84). As Figure 3.2 shows, many countries are still placing their populations—in particular, their children—at risk by allowing the use of lead in gasoline.

Evidence from the United States, Japan, Europe, and Mexico suggests that phasing out leaded gasoline will be the most effective way to reduce the general population's exposure to lead, although other sources of lead exposure are also important (85). (See Figure 3.3.) Phasing out lead is not a policy action limited to wealthy or middle-income countries; indeed, Honduras and Nicaragua, both low-income countries, have made dramatic strides in phasing out leaded gasoline (86).

Although the technical process of phasing out lead from gasoline is simple and the costs are modest, rapid phaseout is nevertheless complex. At the core of any successful campaign to eliminate leaded gasoline is the need to raise public awareness of the risks of using leaded gasoline (87). Misconceptions are still widespread that high octane, and therefore highly leaded, fuels provide better vehicle performance. Changing this perception and informing citizens about the health im-

Box 3.6 The Problem of POPs

Because of their high toxicity, ability to be transported long distances, and persistence in the environment, persistent organic pollutants (POPs) have engendered considerable alarm. At the international level, The United Nations Environment Programme (UNEP) has identified POPs as prime candidates for international phaseout. Many of these chemicals are pesticides, described earlier in this chapter. A few are industrial pollutants or byproducts, such as polychlorinated biphenyls (PCBs), dioxin and furans.

In 1997, the governing council of UNEP concluded that international action, including a global legally binding instrument (e.g., treaty or convention), was needed in order to reduce the risks of POPs to human health and the environment. An intergovernmental negotiating committee (INC) was established with a mandate to prepare this international legally binding instrument for implementing international action. The first meeting of the INC is scheduled for early 1998. The INC will also establish an expert group that will help develop science-based criteria and a procedure for identifying additional POPs as candidates for future international action. In the short term, UNEP has initiated a number of immediate actions involving development and sharing of information about the hazards of POPs (1).

At the national level, policies regarding disposal and cleanup will vary greatly depending on the types of POPs in use or storage. Policies will also be shaped with consideration of whether or not the existing waste treatment and disposal infrastructure can be used or easily modified for POPs management, and the relative cost of various management options (2). A key priority for all countries is to identify those areas where POPs contamination is a concern. Because the majority of human exposures to POPs arise through the food chain, warning the public of possible contamination of fish or other wildlife can also help minimize health risks (3).

References and Notes

1. United Nations Environment Programme (UNEP), *UNEP Chemicals Newsletter,* Vol. 1, No. 2 (UNEP, Nairobi, 1997). Available online at: http://irptc.unep.ch/irpte/docs/newslt12.html (January 21, 1998).
2. U.S. Environmental Protection Agency, Office of Pollution Prevention and Toxics, "Management of Polychlorinated Biphenyls in the United States," January 30, 1997 paper available online at http://www.irptc.unep.ch.
3. The Council on Environmental Quality, *Environmental Quality: 25th Anniversary Report* (U.S. Government Printing Office, Washington, D.C., 1997), p. 118.

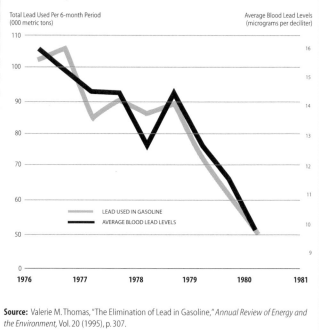

Benefits of Reducing Lead in Gasoline

FIGURE 3.3 Decreases in Blood Lead Values and Amounts of Lead Used in Gasoline in the United States, 1976–80

Total Lead Used Per 6-month Period (000 metric tons)

Average Blood Lead Levels (micrograms per deciliter)

LEAD USED IN GASOLINE
AVERAGE BLOOD LEAD LEVELS

Source: Valerie M. Thomas, "The Elimination of Lead in Gasoline," *Annual Review of Energy and the Environment,* Vol. 20 (1995), p. 307.

pacts of lead—especially on children—can be powerful tools for getting the public to support difficult policy decisions and change consumer behavior.

Refineries shoulder the greatest cost in a switch to unleaded gasoline. However, governments can offset some of these costs by helping companies finance the initial modifications needed to produce unleaded gasoline. Market-based policy incentives that allow the refineries some flexibility can also help reduce the costs of lead phaseout. In the United States, for example, interrefinery trading and the banking of lead credits—similar to today's SO$_2$ emissions trading program—accelerated the ability of refineries to respond to more stringent

environmental regulations about lead content. Large refineries, which could afford the costs of adjustment, achieved higher-than-required lead reductions, earning credits that could then be sold to smaller refineries (which have fewer resources to make adjustments), or banked against future reduction requirements (88). In addition, refinery investments necessary to reduce the lead content of gasoline often pay for themselves over time as a result of improved productivity and refining efficiency (89).

During the phaseout period, when both unleaded and leaded gasoline are available, pricing leaded gasoline higher than unleaded can increase consumer demand for unleaded gasoline. In most Western European countries, for example, the initial small difference in the price of leaded versus unleaded fuel was gradually increased; in the United Kingdom, leaded gasoline now costs 11 percent more than unleaded gasoline (90).

Generally, countries can recover 5 to 10 times the cost of converting to unleaded gas in health and economic savings. The United States, for example, saved more than US$10 for every US$1 it invested in the conversion due to reduced health costs, savings on engine maintenance, and improved fuel efficiency (91). Because leaded gasoline contains lead salts and halogen acids, it causes greater corrosion of automobile exhaust systems and requires more frequent oil and spark-plug changes. Switching from leaded to unleaded gasoline may increase engine life by as much as 150 percent. Indeed, the U.S. experience showed that it pays to remove lead from gasoline solely in terms of vehicle maintenance costs; the substantial health benefits are an additional benefit.

The Future: Clean Production

A long-term strategy for preventing exposure to hazardous industrial pollutants is to reduce their use in the first place through cleaner production. Moving toward eco-efficiency, as this goal is often defined, means that industry must reduce raw material inputs—chemicals, natural resources, energy, water—and at the same time reduce air, water, and solid pollutants for each unit of production (92). This push toward cleaner production is typically driven by environmental and economic concerns rather than by health concerns, although it seems certain that cleaner production would benefit public health as well.

Unlike the industrialized countries, developing countries have the opportunity to leapfrog over some polluting industries and technologies into cleaner production. Recent advances in information systems, telecommunications, biotechnology, new materials, and miniaturization portend dramatic reductions in material and energy inputs (93). Pollution monitoring and control technologies have also improved over the past 20 years. If proper incentives are in place, developing countries need not build or import yesterday's dirty technology, as all too often occurs today. The key to spurring this technological change and transfer is to send clear social, economic, and regulatory signals to companies and to ensure that markets for environmentally benign technologies will continue to grow (94).

The potential for improved investments is enormous. The current trend toward globalization, with its accompanying investment flows, means that private companies are increasingly influencing industrial change, much more so than public investments or development assistance. Indeed, roughly 70 percent of net resource flows to the developing world now derive from the private sector (95). Especially in the newly industrializing, fast-growth economies—those facing the greatest risks from unchecked industrial pollution—conditions are conducive for financing environmentally sound technology. The World Bank estimates, for example, that firms that have yet to be established will account for more than 80 percent of industrial output by 2010 (96). Indonesia has already made strides in this direction. For instance, the new pulp and paper mills being built there have pulping and bleaching technologies on par with those now being proposed as the U.S. environmental standard (97). Although the initial costs of cleaner technologies may be higher than those of older technologies, the provision of financial and technical assistance can encourage their adoption. Such a strategy will offer economic savings and environmental and health benefits long into the future.

RISING ENERGY USE

Along with tackling the environmental and health problems at the household and community level, perhaps the next greatest opportunity for improving both environmental quality and human health is to reduce air pollution and carbon dioxide (CO_2) emissions from the burning of fossil fuels. Energy-related environmental pollution figures prominently as a contributor to a number of diseases, including acute respiratory infections, chronic respiratory diseases, cardiovascular diseases, and cancer. Exposure to urban air pollution remains a widespread and serious environmental problem worldwide (98). Less certain but no less pressing, the potential health impacts resulting from global climate change loom on the horizon. On the positive side, tremendous health benefits and economic savings may be gained if the links among energy, air pollution, and climate change are dealt with in a coordinated way.

Clearing the Air

An estimated 1.4 billion people are exposed to unhealthy outdoor air (99). Especially in the developing world, where maximum particulate and SO_2 concentrations in many cities still exceed WHO guidelines 10-fold, air pollution poses a clear danger to public health. In the developed world, although levels of pollution tend to be lower and episodes of extremely severe air pollution have been relegated to the history books, air pollution still remains a problem in many cities. In the United States, for instance, particulate air pollution is believed to contribute to about 50,000 to 60,000 deaths each year, primarily through respiratory or cardiovascular disease (100)(101).

Improved monitoring and tightening of air quality standards and regulations remain top priorities for developed and developing countries alike. In the United States, the Environmental Protection Agency (U.S. EPA) recently tightened the national air quality standards. Although the United States has seen dramatic improvements in air quality over the past 20 years, these standards are designed to further reduce the health risks of small particulates and ozone, especially for children, the elderly, and people with asthma or other respiratory diseases (102). Several cities in the developing world, including Bangkok, Santiago, and Bombay, are all in the process of tightening air quality standards and improving monitoring and enforcement efforts (103)(104)(105).

Nevertheless, these regulatory approaches will likely be inadequate to address the energy-related problems of air pollution and climate change. What is needed, instead, in countries of all levels of development, are ambitious, forward-looking strategies to reduce energy consumption. Avenues for intervention range from energy pricing, to curbing urban sprawl, to investing in alternative transportation options, to increasing the energy efficiency of products and processes.

Given the complexity of the problem, strategies for reducing air pollution must be tailored to a particular city, bearing in mind both the key contributors and the city's priorities and resources. In those cities that are still industrial centers, for example, controlling industrial emissions of SO_2 and particulates should be a high priority. The Bangkok metropolitan region alone, for instance, is home to nearly three quarters of Thailand's manufacturing industries. Similarly, industry is concentrated in many large cities in India, Indonesia, Mexico, the Philippines, and the Republic of Korea (106).

In other cities, reducing emissions from the use of coal for domestic heating and power generation should be of greatest concern. In Central and Eastern Europe, China, and India, for example, the use of coal contributes a large share to outdoor air pollution, especially in terms of SO_2 and particulates. Emissions of SO_2 and particulates can be reduced by as much as 99 percent and nitrous oxide (N_2O) emissions can be reduced by as much as 90 percent though the use of clean coal technologies (107). Coal preparation—which consists of processes that range from mechanical sorting that yields pieces of uniform size to treating the coal to remove ash, sulfur, and moisture—can also help to reduce emissions at relatively low cost (108).

Switching from coal to natural gas can also improve local air quality. In the Czech Republic, for example, Czech Energy Works reduced SO_2 emissions by 36 percent, dust and particulate emissions by 49 percent, and N_2O emissions by 50 percent between 1989 and 1995. These reductions were accomplished by installing scrubbers on coal power utilities and switching to natural gas and oil for home heating (109). Although air pollution still exceeds WHO health guidelines, the Czech Republic believes that within 7 or 8 years it can achieve levels of air quality that Western Europe took 20 years to achieve (110).

Cars and other vehicles are another major contributor to urban air pollution. The problems associated with using leaded gasoline were discussed earlier. Motor vehicles also emit a variety of other pollutants, including particulates and SO_2. As the demand for cars grows, emissions can be expected to worsen unless there are dramatic improvements in fuel efficiency and vehicle technology. Indeed, the number of vehicles in China has been growing at an annual rate of almost 13 percent for 30 years, nearly doubling every 5 years. India's fleet has been expanding at more than 7 percent per year (111).

Especially in developing countries, where cars tend to be old and polluting, tackling the problems of motor vehicle emissions can have immediate and positive impacts on health. Investments in cleaning up the worst offenders can reduce pollution significantly at relatively low cost. In Manila, for instance, cleaning up the dirtiest vehicles alone could save an estimated 160 deaths and 4 million respiratory symptom days each year (112). Similar benefits have been estimated for

Bombay and Jakarta (113)(114). Cutting the sulfur content of diesel and gasoline can also greatly reduce both SO_2 and fine particle concentrations (115).

Although these measures can significantly reduce concentrations of conventional pollutants, they do not address the inherent problems of a transportation system that is based on the private car. After more than 30 years of rigorous regulation of automobile emissions and fuels, the U.S. Government estimates that, by 2005, automobile emissions in the United States will begin to rise again as the result of increased travel and the switch to gas-guzzling minivans (116). One of the greatest opportunities for developing countries—where car ownership is still relatively low—is to implement policies that encourage alternative transportation systems. Policies that raise the price of auto fuel or car ownership, for instance, would help curb urban sprawl and make public transportation, bicycles, and walking more attractive options. As the experience of many developed cities has shown, once automobile ownership drives out these alternatives, they are almost impossible to institute (117).

Reducing CO_2 Emissions

In 1995, the International Panel on Climate Change (IPCC) concluded that the cumulative effects of anthropogenic CO_2 emissions were having a discernable impact on the environment (118). As Chapter 2 described, changes in the global climate may affect human health in myriad ways, ranging from deaths and injuries linked with an increased frequency of severe storms to increases in vector-borne diseases. Although the exact health effects remain uncertain, their potential scale provides added weight to the case for reducing CO_2 emissions.

Scientists estimate that global emissions of CO_2 need to be reduced to well below 1990 levels to eventually stabilize the atmospheric concentrations of greenhouse gases at a safe level (119). This task will require a major restructuring of the global energy supply, away from the use of coal and oil and toward natural gas and renewable energy sources. Buildings and transportation systems, as well as industrial processes, will need to be redesigned to use energy much more efficiently. Undertaking these measures will entail difficult political decisions and economic costs. As negotiations in Kyoto in late 1997 made abundantly clear, these issues are not easily solved. Intense debate continues not only about desirable goals and timetables, but also about the relative roles of developed and developing nations in the effort to curb emissions. (See Global Commons in Chapter 4.)

Without question, reducing fossil fuel consumption will require raising the price of these fuels. Fossil fuel prices remain unreasonably low in most parts of the world. Electricity, natural gas, and coal are subsidized in most countries; petroleum consumption is subsidized in oil-exporting developing nations. Until prices more truly reflect the costs of using fossil

Box 3.7 Effects of Energy Taxes and Subsidies on the Economy and the Environment

Some people worry about the negative impact of energy taxation on economic growth, but removing energy subsidies and taxing environmentally adverse energy use can be an economically and environmentally sound policy for a country.

Germany and Japan have heavily taxed energy for years. Their percentages of gasoline prices accounted for by taxes in 1995, for example, were 78 percent and 53 percent, respectively. (See table.) The energy productivity (measured by gross domestic product (GDP) per kilogram of energy

used) in Germany and Japan, however, is about 10 times higher than in Russia and China where energy is still subsidized. Also, carbon dioxide emission intensity is much lower in Japan and Germany (0.30 and 0.49 metric tons per thousand U.S. dollars, respectively) than in Russia and China (5.43 and 5.27 metric tons per thousand U.S. dollars, respectively).

Germany provides an example of a country where the link between economic growth and energy consumption growth can be broken by improving efficiency in the use of energy. Between

1990 and 1994, Germany's economy grew at 1.1 percent per year, while its energy consumption dropped by 1.5 percent per year. Similar results can also be seen in China. From 1990 to 1994, China's GDP grew annually by 12.9 percent, while the country's growth rate of energy consumption was only 4 percent per year.

Adapted from: The World Bank, *Five Years After Rio: Innovations in Environmental Policy* (The World Bank, Washington, D.C., 1997), p. 32.

Taxing Energy Use Can Be Good for the Economy

Effects of Energy Taxes or Subsidies: Cross-Country Comparison

COUNTRY	AVERAGE TAX (SUBSIDY) RATES[a] (1995) (percent)	PER CAPITA ENERGY USE[b] (1994) (kilograms)	GDP PER KILOGRAM OF ENERGY (1994) (US$/kg)	CARBON DIOXIDE EMISSIONS PER DOLLAR OF GDP (1992) (metric tons per US$1,000)	AVERAGE ANNUAL ENERGY GROWTH RATE (1990–94) (percent)	AVERAGE ANNUAL GDP GROWTH RATE (1990–94) (percent)
China	(7)	647	0.7	5.27	4.0	12.9
Germany	78.4	4097	6.1	0.49	-1.5	1.1
Japan	52.8	3825	9.6	0.30	2.3	1.2
Russia	(20)	4038	0.6	5.43	-8.9	-10.6
United States	33.3	7905	3.2	0.82	1.8	2.5

Source: The World Bank, *Five Years After Rio: Innovations in Environmental Policy* (The World Bank, Washington, D.C., 1997), p. 32.

Notes: a. For Germany, Japan, and the United States, average tax rates on regular unleaded gasoline; for China and Russia, average subsidy rates. b. Measured in oil equivalents.

fuel—including the health costs from air pollution and costs of environmental degradation—few policy measures will stem the growing use. (See Box 3.7.)

Such changes are neither simple nor straightforward, however. Energy, like water, is a vital resource that is essential to human well-being and economic development. That recognition underlies policies that subsidize its use. Providing power to a remote area brings enormous opportunities to people, which is one reason energy has historically been subsidized. Refrigeration, to use just one example, can save many lives from foodborne illness. If prices are to be changed, these immediate benefits must be weighed against the more hidden costs of environmental degradation and future health damages.

In addition, once energy prices have been set in a particular range, they can be difficult to alter. Although economists and consumers may agree in principle that energy prices should better reflect the true costs, consensus breaks down rapidly in setting a specific goal—such as raising the price of gasoline. Reducing energy subsidies and adjusting energy prices may cause negative short-term consequences for some, and perhaps substantial economic impact, so political opposition seems certain.

Even so, some countries have made considerable progress in reducing energy subsidies over the past several years. Between 1990 and 1996, total fossil fuel subsidies in 14 developing countries declined by 45 percent, from US$60 billion to about US$33 billion. Brazil, China, India, Mexico, Saudi Arabia, and South Africa all cut fossil fuel subsidies significantly. During this same period, subsidies in developed countries declined by 20.5 percent, from US$12.5 billion to US$9.9 billion. In China, price reform has led to significant energy efficiency gains—gains that, according to the World Bank, have the potential to yield savings of 1 to 1.7 billion metric tons of coal equivalents per year by 2020, an amount greater than China's total energy consumption in 1990 (120). Although these cuts were made to meet economic, social, and public health needs, they nevertheless have contributed to significant carbon savings (121).

A carbon tax is currently the subject of heated debate. A carbon tax would reduce emissions of certain air pollutants by increasing the costs of fuels according to their carbon content, carbon being a proxy for emissions. For example, coal would be taxed more heavily than natural gas, because coal's carbon content per British thermal unit (Btu) is higher than that of natural gas. Advocates of the carbon tax believe it would be a strong tool for preventing global climate change and would also reduce energy consumption and lower conventional pollutants. So far, only five countries—Denmark, Finland, the Netherlands, Norway, and Sweden—have implemented carbon taxes (122).

To date, the benefits of reducing greenhouse gas emissions have been generally considered in the context of long-term gains. In other words, investments now can avert harmful effects later. What has often been overlooked, however, is the immediate improvement that would occur in terms of reductions of ambient air pollution—with benefits to ecosystems, economies, and human health. Indeed, efforts to reduce CO_2 emissions will lead to measurable reductions in particulates, SO_2, and other airborne toxic compounds, with consequent and immediate improvements in air quality and human health, according to a recent analysis by a working group established by WRI and WHO. This study suggests that the same policies that will avert greenhouse warming in the long term will save hundreds of thousands of lives. Specifically, the study found that under a relatively stringent climate policy scenario—a 15 percent reduction in developed country emissions by 2010, with smaller reductions in developing na-

tions—an estimated 700,000 deaths per year could be avoided by 2020 (123).

Because the exact effects of a warming planet remain uncertain, it can be difficult for nations to take actions that cause economic pain today. Yet, this recent study illustrates how preventive environmental strategies can yield multiple payoffs—not only in terms of reducing immediate and long-term health damages from air pollution but also in averting ecological disruption and the economic costs predicted to accompany a warming planet.

In summary, the range of interventions and policies described in this chapter is by no means exhaustive. Nor does this chapter attempt to describe the complex choices and trade-offs that will be necessary to implement policies on a local level. Effecting change, admittedly, is difficult. Policymakers typically confront competing demands and priorities and are handicapped by myriad financial and technical constraints. At the same time, however, the benefits of the changes outlined here promise to be substantial, not only in terms of improving public health but also in preserving environmental quality and ensuring equitable development.

GUEST COMMENTARIES

Environmental Health In the 21st Century: Challenges for Researchers and Decisionmakers

ROBERTO BERTOLLINI, M.D., M.P.H.

The first principle of the 1992 Declaration of the United Nations Conference on the Environment and Development affirms that human beings are entitled to a healthy life. At the close of the 20th Century, the world situation with respect to the effects of the environment on health is complex and full of contrasts. In the developed world, concern for environmental influences on health is mainly focused on chronic diseases associated with pollution. Yet a large part of the global population—both in the developing world and in the inner cities of the developed world—is still struggling with traditional environmental health problems. These problems include a lack of clean drinking water, decent housing, and proper sanitation. In the 1996 *World Health Report*, these issues are described as "old diseases—old problems" (1). As Chapter 1 describes, at least 2.9 billion people in developing countries, or two thirds of the developing world's population, lack an adequate system for disposing of their feces. About 25 percent do not have access to safe drinking water. Overall, some 3.7 million deaths each year are due to food-, water-, and soilborne diseases, representing about 22 percent of all deaths due to infectious diseases each year.

At the same time, economic growth and massive urbanization in many developing countries are changing the picture. Adding to the traditional environmental health issues noted above are those associated with chemical pollution and occupational exposures to hazardous substances (2). Many countries are going through a so-called environmental health transition, a situation in which traditional risks remain important health threats for many, particularly the poor and disadvantaged, while modern risks associated with economic development increase (3).

There is no question in my mind that the most important priority for public health decisionmakers around the world is to find an effective way to accomplish the unfinished business of providing every citizen of the world with the basic conditions needed to ensure their health and well-being. This is *the* issue for international organizations, national governments, and nongovernmental organizations; it should be seen as a major goal for the first years or decades of the next century. Most of these longstanding problems are relatively well known, solutions are feasible—though by no means simple—and measures of progress are available to monitor results and achievements. The real question is whether the governments and major economic groups of the world have the necessary commitment to reach this goal. The answer is neither easy nor straightforward, because the positions and policies of many government and international bodies are contradictory and unclear. In this context, I am convinced that one of the most important roles of public health professionals will be to concentrate the attention of governments, local authorities, and the public on the issue of providing basic necessities for all.

The priority I place on traditional issues does not mean that today's pollution-related problems do not require appropriate attention. True, uncertainties remain in the scientific understanding of the overall role of pollution in ill health, as well as on more specific issues such as dose-response relationships, biological mechanisms, and so forth. Because of problems related to the quality and type of data used to assess the impacts of pollution, relevant questions often remain unanswered.

For example, several important studies have used a new indicator, the disability-adjusted life year, or DALY, to quantify the burden of disease attributable to a number of known risk factors (4). One study suggests that only 0.5 percent of the global disease burden is actually attributable to air pollution—1.5 percent of the disease burden in the developed world and 0.4 percent in developing countries (5). Yet how accurately do these figures reflect the real impact of air pollution on human health? DALYs portray mortality and long-term disability; they do not capture short-term illness. Moreover, exposure to air pollution varies dramatically by location, so while DALYs and other indicators might be useful in global evaluations, they may not be good guides for policy at the local level.

What is needed, then, are additional methods that incorporate appropriate data on sickness as well as death into evaluations and decisionmaking. This will require opening the field of environmental health to what might be considered unconventional approaches. Most approaches to assessing environmental health effects focus on well-defined diseases or causes of death as classified in internal medicine textbooks. Perhaps there is also another class of effects—more subtle and difficult to classify but more frequently associated with the presence of environmental hazards. These might include symptoms like headache, nausea, or skin rashes, which are not easy to measure but are frequently reported by populations exposed to potential environmental hazards; these symptoms may pose a major burden on well-being. These effects can-

Environmental Change and Human Health

not be dismissed as unmeasurable or biologically implausible. The limitations of existing knowledge are not sufficient reason for the public health community to deny the existence of ailments affecting the people's lives.

This last point raises another dimension of the environmental influence on health, the so-called psychosocial effects that began attracting scientific attention after the Chernobyl accident. Following that accident, epidemiologists and public health scientists searched for the expected effects of radiation on the thyroid, growing brain, or hematopoietic system. The incidence of thyroid cancer in children increased remarkably, but no major effects have been observed so far on the incidence of leukemia (6)(7). However, the population affected by the accident suffers from a variety of other diseases—a mixture of minor disturbances of several organs and systems, psychiatric disorders, and stress-related diseases. It is generally agreed that, apart from the increase in thyroid cancer, these psychosocial effects are the most important public health effects of the accident (8).

This concept contrasts with the prevailing conceptual model, in which the environment is seen mostly as a vehicle for toxic or hazardous substances. But this prevailing model fails to fully account for the role of environment in human health and well-being. It can be argued that living conditions more broadly might help to explain differences in health among selected populations through their impact on psychology and behavior. Thus, the environment has not only a direct "toxicological" role but also an indirect role, together with the work, social, and living conditions, in influencing health. In this new conceptual framework, the role of environment is much broader than traditionally understood. Lifestyle, for instance, may be partly dependent on environmental conditions.

This approach has been used in attempts to explain the East-West life expectancy gap observed in Europe over the past few decades. In 1994, males in Eastern Europe died on average almost 7 years sooner than their counterparts in the European Union (9). As Clyde Hertzman points out in his commentary in this volume, there is probably an upper limit to pollution's contribution in traditional terms to the life expectancy gap. However, pollutants may interact with other factors in the social environment to undermine health. The fact that people have to live in communities with polluted skies and bad odors may contribute to a sense of powerlessness. Thus, pollution becomes an element of the psychosocial environment, influencing lifestyle or behavior.

Adopting this new conceptual framework will require the development of new research methodologies, for instance, establishing an effective interaction among the fields of public health, demography, sociology, behavioral science, economy, and business management. The development of methods for studying the underlying societal determinants of health, as well as their interaction with environmental and other factors, is one of the major challenges for the next generation of epidemiologists and public health scientists (10).

Interdisciplinary research and predictive models are also needed if the environmental health community is to anticipate the likely impact of future changes, such as global warming. This is a new area for environmental health impact assessment that must be added to the standard after-the-fact assessment. For example, environmental health scientists should be able to use information about shifts in distribution of key indicator species (e.g., rodents, insects, algae) as early warnings of climate change. These shifts might presage changes in human health risks, including the emergence or reemergence of unexpected infectious diseases (11).

In summary, the environment remains a major source of hazards for human health and well-being, and the world's poor are the most vulnerable group. Much needs to be done to raise awareness of these hazards and to promote policy and concrete action, particularly at the local level. We need a better understanding of the link between environment and health to support decisionmaking. We also need stronger partnerships among experts in the different sectors of society, particularly health, the environment, and the economy. Environmental and health scientists must increase their role as advocates, constantly highlighting the links among health, environment, and sustainable development—particularly when policies are being developed and actions planned. We must pursue all these steps urgently to ensure a sustainable, healthy environment for future generations.

References and Notes

1. World Health Organization (WHO), *The World Health Report 1996: Fighting Disease, Fostering Development* (WHO, Geneva, 1996).
2. World Health Organization (WHO), *Health and Environment in Sustainable Development* (WHO, Geneva, 1997).
3. K.R. Smith, "Development, Health and the Environmental Risk Transition," in *International Perspectives on Environment, Development, and Health: Toward a Sustainable World*, G.S. Shahi *et al.*, eds. (Springer, New York, 1997), pp. 51–62.
4. Christopher J.L. Murray and Alan D. Lopez, "Global Mortality, Disability, and the Contribution of Risk Factors: Global Burden of Disease Study," *Lancet*, Vol. 349 (1997), pp. 1436–1442.
5. Christopher J.L. Murray and Alan D. Lopez, eds., *The Global Burden of Disease: Volume 1* (World Health Organization, Harvard School of Public Health, and The World Bank, Geneva, 1996), p. 315.
6. V.A. Stsjazhko *et al.*, "Childhood Thyroid Cancer Since the Accident at Chernobyl," *British Medical Journal*, Vol. 310 (1995), p. 801.
7. D.M. Parkin *et al.*, "Childhood Laeukaemia in Europe after Chernobyl: 5-Year Follow Up," *British Journal of Cancer*, Vol. 73 (1996), pp. 1006–1012.
8. WHO European Centre for Environment and Health, *Concern for Europe's Tomorrow: Health and Environment in the WHO European Region* (Wissenschaftliche Verlaggesellschaft mbH, Stuttgart, Germany, 1995).
9. World Health Organization (WHO), *Health in Europe*, WHO Regional Publications European Series, No. 56 (WHO, Copenhagen, 1994).
10. C.M. Shy, "The Failure of Academic Epidemiology: Witness for the Prosecution," *American Journal of Epidemiology*, Vol. 145 (1997), pp. 479–484.
11. World Health Organization, World Meterological Organization, and the United Nations Environment Programme, *Climate Change and Human Health* (WHO, Geneva, 1996).

Roberto Bertollini is the director of the World Health Organization (WHO), European Centre for Environment and Health, Rome Division. This paper is a summary of the views expressed by the author and does not necessarily represent the decisions or the stated policy of WHO.

What Accounts for the Life Expectancy Gap in Central and Eastern Europe?

CLYDE HERTZMAN

In the early 1990s prospects for living a long and healthy life in Central and Eastern Europe dimmed considerably (1). In the late 1980s, life expectancy in the region was already 4 to 6 years lower than it was in Western Europe, and that gap widened in the early 1990s. For males in Russia, life expectancy peaked at 64.9 years in 1987 then fell to 62 in 1992 and to 57.3 by 1994 (2). Similar, though generally less extreme, declines occurred in other nations in Central and Eastern Europe. Mortality rates increased sharply in this region between 1989 and 1993, followed by a gradual stabilization thereafter (3). Now, male life expectancy in Western Europe hovers around 73 or 74 (73.7 in France, 74.1 in Italy, 73.2 in Spain, 74.2 in the United Kingdom). In Central Europe, it is generally in the mid- to upper-60s: 64.8 in Hungary, 67.6 in Poland, and 69.5 in the Czech Republic. There is over a 9-year difference in male life expectancy between Hungary and the United Kingdom (4).

This significant decline in life expectancy followed a period of severe and extended pollution. From the late 1960s to the early 1990s, the region's reliance on poor-quality brown coal inflicted a terrible toll on the atmosphere, especially in the northern Bohemia region of Czechoslovakia and the Silesian industrial region in southwest Poland (5). These environmental "hot spots" contained much of Central Europe's heavy industry—especially steel, cement, chemical, and petrochemical works—and a phalanx of inefficient coal-burning power plants spewing forth copious amounts of sulfur dioxide and soot.

The contrast with trends in Western Europe, North America, and Japan was striking. By 1985, for example, sulfur dioxide concentrations in urban air among Western cities

had dropped to 33 micrograms per cubic meter, or about one fourth the 1970 level (6). In some areas of Poland during the same period, concentrations had reached 636 micrograms per cubic meter, or nearly 20 times the Canadian average (7). Levels of particulates, lead, and toxic wastes were exceptionally high in some parts of Central Europe. In parts of the Katowice area in Poland, lead levels in soil were as high as 19,000 parts per million, about 38 times the acceptable level.

The causes of the environmental crisis were complex. Under Communist regimes, governments set prices of energy and natural resources at relatively low levels, which led to inefficient consumption. Incentives were weak for state enterprises to control pollutants or use resources more efficiently. There was a continuing emphasis on heavy industry, but a lack of hard currency to invest in new technology. Furthermore, antipollution fees were set too low and were only weakly enforced, and local communities and citizens had little chance to force improvements in environmental quality (8). Environmental pollution began to decline rapidly following the political upheavals in 1989—not because of planned interventions, but because of declines in industrial production that accompanied the political turmoil (9).

Does pollution account for the gap in life expectancy and the region's morbidity and mortality rates, as some researchers have posited? From 1989 to 1992 a team of investigators from the World Bank began collecting and evaluating environmental health data from 10 countries in Central and Eastern Europe, looking particularly at well-known pollution-health relationships such as air pollution and lead exposures. Among their findings:

- In 37 locations in 7 countries, exposures to lead from industrial and vehicular sources occurred among children at levels that could lead to deficits in learning and behavior. In several locations, including Katowice, Poland, and Copsa Mica, Romania, these effects were well documented.

- In 53 locations in 10 countries, increased rates of acute eye, nose, throat, and lung problems were associated with high airborne concentrations of dust, sulfur dioxide, and other gases. In 35 locations, chronic lung conditions (primarily bronchitis and asthma) were associated with these exposures.

- In 19 locations in 7 countries where air pollution was severe, rates of abnormal physiological development among children were unusually high.

- In the rural areas of 6 countries, nitrate concentrations in drinking water were high enough to put newborns at risk of blue-baby syndrome, or methemoglobinemia, which can lead to illness and death.

These findings suggest that environmental pollution, especially air pollution, was a major cause of disease in locations throughout Central and Eastern Europe in the early 1990s. But can pollution account for the overall decline in life expectancy in the region? It seems unlikely, because the most serious environmental problems were confined largely to a small number of regional hot spots—either old industrial areas where nearby populations numbering in the several thousands were exposed to heavy emissions from point sources; or areas where housing or farms had been placed right

*E*nvironmental Change and Human Health

next to an offending factory. By contrast, the relative decline in life expectancy took place more or less equally in both heavily polluted and unpolluted parts of Central and Eastern Europe. Thus, pollution does not seem to have been the principal cause of the life expectancy gap with the West, though it clearly contributed to it.

If pollution was not the principal factor explaining the life expectancy gap, what was? Several other theories, in addition to pollution, have been suggested. One is that, for a variety of economic and political reasons, the public health care system in the region was to blame. Yet, if ineffective health care services were a major contributor, then the difference between the West and Central Europe in the rate of "medically avoidable deaths" (i.e., causes of death for which effective life-saving medical treatment exists) would have increased sharply over the time period when the life expectancy gap emerged. The available evidence shows that it did not.

A third theory posits that the life expectancy gap can be explained by high-risk behaviors displayed by Central European populations as opposed to Western populations, especially in terms of their tobacco smoking, blood pressure control, and dietary habits, reflected in cholesterol levels and obesity rates. These are the established risk factors for heart disease and stroke. Yet even though these risk factors can explain individual differences in the risk of death from heart disease, stroke, and injuries, they do not contribute a great deal to explaining differences in mortality among societies. In fact, a recent global study found that differential exposure to these risk factors did not explain societal differences in mortality from heart disease (10). Rather, a country's gross domestic product (GDP) per capita does a better job of predicting mortality from heart disease. This seems a highly unlikely conclusion—after all, how could factors that explain differences in risk within a society not explain differences in risk among societies? The answer appears to be that the effects of specific risk factors differ from one society to another. For example, a 30-cigarette per day smoking habit creates a 17-fold increased risk of lung cancer among smokers in

Britain, but only an 8-fold increased risk in Japan.

A final theory is that political, economic, and social change is to blame. According to this theory, conditions in Central and Eastern Europe in the 1970s and 1980s created a climate of powerlessness, deprivation, and isolation that undermined the region's health. It is well known that socioeconomic factors such as material deprivation, a perception of lack of control over one's life, and insufficient levels of social support all undermine health status. These socioeconomic factors differ markedly between Western society and Central and Eastern Europe, and since 1989, socioeconomic conditions have worsened in the latter region (11).

No doubt, the transition from Communism has proven traumatic for large numbers of people. Indeed, opinion polls in several Central and Eastern European countries after the transition showed that trust in the political structures of democracy was low, and most people had a negative view of free market reforms. In the 3 years following the dramatic changes in 1989, real wages in former Warsaw Pact countries fell between 15 and 35 percent. Social disruption was widespread, as witnessed by an almost 35 percent decline in crude marriage rates and marked reductions in preprimary school enrollment (12). Survey research showed that citizens of the region lacked a sense of control over their lives (13).

By 1993, sufficient life expectancy data were available to determine more precisely the trends in mortality since the end of the Cold War. Throughout the region, death rates indeed rose dramatically, with the greatest increase occurring among people in midlife (25 to 59 years) (14). Premature mortality afflicted more single and divorced people than married ones (15). This pattern strongly suggests that the life expectancy gap reflects changing socioeconomic conditions. What has not been determined, however, is how this broad range of factors can undermine a population's health to the extent it has in Central and Eastern Europe. Set out below is our best hypothesis:

Much more so than the West, societies in Central and Eastern Europe have long resem-

bled an hourglass. The top represented the elite who gleaned all the available economic and social benefits. The narrow middle section consisted of a failed or nonexistent civil society, the lack of which makes daily life terribly difficult for the average person. And those at the bottom of the hourglass relied strongly on family and personal support to compensate for the lack of a civil society and the indifference of the elite (16).

Before the political changes of 1989, those at the top of the hourglass, or the elites, "bought off" those at the bottom. After 1989, the twin ideologies of individualism and capitalism gave those at the top license to abandon those at the bottom. With a negligible civil society to fall back upon, life became nastier, more brutish, and, for some, a great deal shorter than before. The pattern of mortality in the region fits this model well. In an hourglass society, those with the weakest social support systems will be the most vulnerable. Moreover, the same plight befalls those in midadulthood in the short run; in other words, those who depend upon civil society functions to earn a living and support families.

Environmental pollution, inadequate health care, and poor health habits have all contributed to the declining health of people in Central and Eastern Europe. But above all, the political, social, and economic conditions in the region created a climate of powerlessness, deprivation, and isolation during the period in Soviet history that ultimately undermined the health status of the people. The declines in health status that occurred during the initial years of the recent transition to capitalism show that the free market, too, can be dangerous to one's health.

References and Notes

1. Unless otherwise noted, this discussion is largely drawn from The World Bank, *Setting Environmental Priorities in Central and Eastern Europe: Discussion Document on Analytical Approaches*, Report 11099-ECA, Europe, Central Asia, Middle East and North Africa Regions, Environment Division (The World Bank, Washington, D.C., 1992).

2. World Resources Institute in collaboration with the United Nations Environment Programme, the United Nations Development Programme, and the World Bank, *World Resources 1996–97* (Oxford University Press, New York, 1996).

3. UNICEF, *Crisis in Mortality, Health and Nutrition*, Economies in Transition Studies, Regional Monitoring Report No. 2 (UNICEF International Child Development Centre, Florence, Italy, 1994), p. 40.

4. Council of Europe, *Recent Demographic Developments in Europe* (Council of Europe Press, Strasbourg, France, 1996), p. 57.

5. *Op. cit.* 1, pp. 19, 28.

6. Organisation for Economic Co-Operation and Development (OECD), *Environmental Data Compendium 1997* (OECD, Paris, 1997), pp 50–52.

7. Clyde Hertzman, "Poland: Health and Environment in the Context of Socioeconomic Decline," Health Services and Policy Research Unit Discussion Paper 90:2D (Centre for Health Services and Policy Research, University of British Columbia, 1990).

8. World Resources Institute in collaboration with the United Nations Environment Programme and the United Nations Development Programme, *World Resources 1992-93* (Oxford University Press, New York, 1992), pp. 57–74.

9. Organisation for Economic Co-Operation and Development (OECD), *Environmental Indicators: A Review of Selected Central and Eastern European Countries*, OECD Working Papers, Vol. IV (OECD, Paris, 1996), pp. 14–31.

10. The World Health Organization MONICA Project, "Ecological Analysis of the Association between Mortality and Major Risk Factors of Cardiovascular Disease," *International Journal of Epidemiology*, Vol. 23, No. 3 (1994), pp. 505–515.

11. *Op. cit.* 3, pp. 1–8.

12. *Op. cit.* 3, pp. 92, 106.

13. Richard Rose, *New Russia Barometer IV: Survey Results*, Studies in Public Policy No. 250 (Centre for the Study of Public Policy, University of Strathclyde, Glasgow, Scotland, 1995), pp. 1–72.

14. *Op. cit.* 3, pp. 1–8.

15. *Op. cit.* 3, p. 68.

16. Richard Rose, "Russia as an Hour-Glass Society: A Constitution Without Citizens," *East European Constitutional Review*, Vol. 4, No. 3 (1995), p. 34–42.

Clyde Hertzman is a professor in the Department of Health Care and Epidemiology at the University of British Columbia and director of the Population Health Program at the Canadian Institute for Advanced Research.

Environmental Change and Human Health

Toward an Idea of International Environmental Justice

MICHAEL K. DORSEY

The idea that pollution is equitably distributed pervades the rhetoric and policies of many institutions charged with protecting the global environment. Notions like "we are all in this together," "the circle of poison," and "Our Common Future" distract policymakers and scholars from realizing that there is a pattern of disproportionate exposure to environmental hazards and degradation among marginalized people. Globally, those on the margins tend to be racial and ethnic minorities, poor, less educated, politically powerless, or all of the above. The fact that marginalized people bear the brunt of environmental degradation should come as no surprise (1). Yet, the idea that those on the margins are intentionally targeted for pollution and purposely forgotten during mitigation efforts is a relatively new and, for some, a controversial notion. In the United States, scholars, policymakers, and activists have referred to this phenomenon as "environmental racism." It is defined most succinctly by Benjamin Chavis as:

> racial discrimination in environmental policymaking and the enforcement of regulations and laws, the deliberate targeting of people of color communities for toxic and hazardous waste facilities, the official sanctioning of the life-threatening presence of poisons and pollutants in [those] communities, and the history of excluding people of color from the leadership of the environmental movement (2).

Attempts to address environmental racism have come largely under the rubric of the U.S.-based movement for environmental justice. This movement has been principally led by researchers, scholars, activists, and policy-makers, who have argued in countless studies, reports, congressional testimonies, theoretical and lay books and journals—as well as in print and broadcast media—that environmental racism is a real problem that must be addressed (3). Despite this legacy of painstaking scholarship, heartfelt campaigns, and the painful loss of health and life by survivors of environmental racism, countervailing studies—some funded by polluting industries deemed perpetrators—have attempted to discredit the existence of environmental racism (4). These studies, as well as those who quibble over the facts, miss the crucial point: that the movement to end environmental racism is the first broad-based effort by marginalized people to fundamentally redefine and reshape one of the largest social movements of modern time: the environmental movement. Accordingly, it seems appropriate to examine how responses to environmental racism took shape in the United States and what the international implications might be.

Resolving Environmental Racism: Toward Environmental Justice

Since the turn of the century, the environmental movement in the United States has been dominated by predominantly white organizations (5). The movement's whiteness was premised and fortified upon a legacy of overt racism that evolved into institutionalized racism (6). At the turn of the century, it was unthinkable that ethnic minorities would be granted access to fishing and hunting clubs that were featured in the early wilderness preservation and conservation movements—precursors to modern-day environmentalism (7). Considered one of the most progressive of the early environmental organizations (and currently the largest), the Sierra Club deliberately excluded African Americans, Jews, and other minorities through a policy of "sponsorship" that allowed established members to exclude nonwhites and non-Christians (8). National parks and public beaches, created through the efforts of early environmental campaigns, banned access based on race (9).

In the midst of the *de facto*, institutionalized racism of mainstream environmental organizations, the United States was accumulating a toxic legacy of catastrophic proportions. This legacy was partly the result of unfettered industrialization and a consequence of poorly understood effects of chemical pollutants. It was widely assumed that everyone shared the burden of hazardous and toxic wastes equally. This assumption was found to be untrue.

In 1982, U.S. Congressional Delegate Walter Fauntroy—arrested during protests that year to stop the siting of a hazardous waste landfill in predominantly African-American Warren County, North Carolina—asked the U.S. General Accounting Office (GAO) to "determine the correlation between the location of hazardous waste landfills and the racial and economic status of the surrounding communities in the Environmental Protection Agency's Region IV (which includes North Carolina)." The GAO results were startling. It concluded: "Blacks make up the majority of the population in three out of four communities where landfills are located" (10). The GAO study, while important, was limited by its regional focus. Thus, the United Church of Christ Commission for Racial Justice (UCC-CRJ) attempted to ascertain whether the GAO results had national implications. The 1987 UCC-CRJ report—*Toxic Wastes and Race in the United States*—revealed that race was the most significant factor in determining the location of commercial hazardous waste facilities. The report noted that communities with the greatest number of commercial hazardous waste facilities had the highest composition of racial and ethnic residents; in addition, the study found that three out of every five African-American and Hispanic-American citizens lived in communities with uncontrolled waste sites. It also reported that minority communities were disproportionately targeted for hazardous waste facilities (11). Several years later, in 1992, the *National Law Journal* issued a special report, *Unequal Protection: The Racial Divide in Environmental Law*, which stated that "there is a racial divide in the way the U.S. Government cleans up toxic waste sites and punishes polluters. White communities see faster action, better results, and stiffer penalties than communities where blacks, Hispanics, and other minorities live ... unequal protection often occurs whether the community is wealthy or poor" (12). These findings, coupled with the legacy of *de facto* racism within the U.S. Green movement, inspired UCC–CRJ Director Ben Chavis' concept of environmental racism.

This particular racism was the genesis moment for a broad-based, grassroots movement for environmental justice. Proponents of the movement have argued for the need to eliminate biased, unjust, and inequitable conditions and decisions long rooted in a broad array of domains including land use planning, transportation policy, housing, and public health—all of which can have adverse, discriminatory environmental consequences (13). The movement's principal champions have worked to (re)conceptualize racial and ethnic dimensions of environmental problems and the environmental facets of economic and social justice concerns; in these efforts, they have worked to redefine and expand the notion of what represents an environmental problem (14). They are addressing social and economic injustice simultaneously with the environmental concerns. Those arguing for environmental justice maintain that while all people have a right to be protected from environmental degradation, communities disproportionately burdened by pollution and benefiting last from cleanup efforts by government agencies should be disproportionately targeted for remediation efforts and resources (15). The focus on resolving the discriminatory aspects of environmental degradation and mitigation efforts, however, compels us to rethink our understanding of global environmental problems and existing proposals to solve them.

Environmental Injustice in International Context

Internationally, environmental degradation follows the paths of least resistance. Between 1989 and 1994, it is estimated that the Organisation for Economic Co-Operation and Development (OECD) countries exported 2,611,677 metric tons of hazardous wastes to non-OECD countries (16). Yet these exports should come as no surprise in light of the comments of the current U.S. Under Secretary of the Treasury and former World Bank official Lawrence Summers. In a December 12, 1991, World Bank memo, Summers opined: "Just between you and me, shouldn't the World Bank be encouraging *more* migration of the dirty industries to the LDCs?" (17). As Summers' logic would have it, lives in developing nations are of less value; thus, it makes economic sense to export pollution to those nations. Whatever the economic logic, the in-country effects of hazardous wastes can be serious. The negative effects of these exports are exacerbated because many of the recipient countries lack the technology to adequately contain and monitor these wastes to protect public health.

Beyond the waste trade, environmental injustices manifest themselves in numerous ways globally. Ethnic and racial minorities have borne the brunt of nuclear testing (18). The Western Shoshone in the United States, ethnic minorities in the Central Asian Republics, Australian Aborigines, ethnic minorities in Algeria, and indigenous people in the South Pacific have all suffered acute and prolonged health problems caused by radiation from testing (19). In another example of environmental injustice, the benefits of biodiversity conservation in protected areas tend to be lowest at the local level and highest at the national and global level; while the costs are the highest at the local level and the lowest at the national and international levels (20). Similarly, in the context of determining national contributions to global climate change, methane emissions of draft animals and naturally decaying areas are unjustly given parity with carbon dioxide emissions from luxury automobiles and inefficient power plants (21).

Toward International Environmental Justice

Realizing the inequitable distribution of environmental degradation and mitigation efforts compels us to propose *just solutions* to environmental problems in lieu of *equitable solutions*. Such a proposal has serious implications for institutions that work on global environmental problems. Equitable benefit-sharing schemes—within the Convention on Biological Diversity and the Framework Convention on Climate Change—become questionable and perpetuate injustice when we recognize historical patterns of injustice. If local communities benefit the least and incur the greatest costs from biodiversity conservation, "fair and equitable" sharing of "the benefits arising from the commercial and other utilization of genetic resources" *ex post facto* may only serve to maintain inequalities.

In the context of the waste trade, environmental justice argues for prior-informed-consent (PIC) mechanisms in agreements that regulate the trade between exporters and importers. Beyond PIC, a comprehensive ban on the trade of

*E*nvironmental Change and Human Health

waste from wealthier countries to poorer ones is long overdue. Further still, chemicals must be stripped of human rights deeming them innocent (i.e., safe) until proven guilty (i.e., unsafe, carcinogenic, or deadly). Viewing chemicals as inherently unsafe would drastically alter the associated regulatory frameworks that dictate their production and introduction into the biosphere. More important, it would shift the burden of proof to polluters who harm, discriminate, or fail to equally protect marginalized people.

An environmental justice analysis, in the United States and globally, attempts to identify and eliminate legacies of systematic, harmful, and disproportionate effects of environmental degradation and mitigation efforts. It is not about redistributing or transferring benefits and burdens after environmental harm is done to particular communities—this is environmental equity, not justice. In an unjust world, environmental benefits, such as those from conservation programs, need to be disproportionately remitted to those who incurred past, disproportionate harm. Simultaneously, the means to "cost sharing" must be radically reconceptualized. Treating environmental problems after communities have been harmed has to be replaced by moves to prevent environmental problems from occurring in the first place.

References and Notes

1. For a good list of cases studies, see the "Suggested Reading" in K. Danaher, ed., *50 Years Is Enough: The Case Against the World Bank and the International Monetary Fund* (South End Press, Boston, 1994), pp. 188–89.
2. Benjamin Chavis, "The Historical Significance and Challenges of the First National People of Color Environmental Leadership Summit," in *Proceedings of the First National People of Color Environmental Leadership Summit* (United Church of Christ Commission for Racial Justice, Washington, D.C., 1991).
3. For detailed evidence of the existence of environmental racism beyond the U.S. Government Accounting Office (GAO) 1983 study *Siting of Haz-* *ardous Waste Landfills and Their Correlation with Racial and Economic Status of Surrounding Communities (GAO/RCED-83-168)* (U.S. Government Printing Office, Washington, D.C., 1983) and the 1987 United Church of Christ Commission for Racial Justice study *Toxic Waste and Race in the United States: A National Report on the Racial and Socioeconomic Characteristics of Communities with Hazardous Wastes Sites* (Public Access, New York, 1987), see also: Bunyan Bryant and Paul Mohai, eds., *Race and the Incidence of Environmental Hazards: A Time for Discourse* (Westview, Boulder, Colorado, 1992); Michel Gelobter, *The Distribution of Outdoor Air Pollution by Income and Race: 1970–1984*, Master's Thesis, Energy and Resources Group (University of California, Berkeley, California, 1987). For a discussion on how and why environmental racism, not classicism, has worsened since initial studies in the late 1980s identifying the problem, see Benjamin Goldman and Laura J. Fitton, *Toxic Waste and Race Revisited* (Center for Policy Alternatives, Washington, D.C., 1993).
4. For criticisms, see Vicki Been, "Market Dynamics and the Siting of LULUs: Questions to Raise in the Classroom About Existing Research," *West Virginia Law Review* 96, No. 4 (1994), pp. 1069–78; Christopher Boerner and Thomas Lambert, "Environmental Injustice," *The Public Interest,* No. 118 (Winter 1995), pp. 61–82; Douglas Anderson *et al.*, "Hazardous Waste Facilities: 'Environmental Equity' Issues in Metropolitan Areas," *Evaluation Review,* Vol. 18, No. 2 (April 1994), pp. 123–40. Note also that Anderson *et al.* was funded by a grant from Waste Management Incorporated, the largest waste management corporation in the United States.
5. Donald Snow, ed., *Voices From the Environmental Movement: Perspectives for a New Era* (Island Press, Washington, D.C., 1992), p. 75.
6. For more on this topic, see Dorceta Taylor, "Can the Environmental Movement Attract and Maintain the Support of Minorities," in *Race and the Incidence of Environmental Hazards: A Time for Discourse,* Bunyan Bryant, ed. (Westview, Boulder, Colorado, 1992), pp. 28–54.
7. Stephen Fox, *John Muir and His Legacy: The American Conservation Movement* (Little Brown, Boston, 1981), p. 351.
8. *Op. cit.* 5, p. 76. Many Sierra Club chapters maintained this policy well into the 1960s.
9. Marc R. Poirier, "Environmental Justice and the Beach Access Movements of the 1970s in Connecticut and New Jersey: Stories of Property and Civil Rights," *28 Connecticut Law Review 719* (1996), pp. 741–742.
10. U.S. Government Accounting Office (GAO), *Siting of Hazardous Waste Landfills and Their Correlation with Racial and Economic Status of Surrounding Communities (GAO/RCED-83-168)* (U.S. Government Printing Office, Washington, D.C., 1983), p. 1.
11. United Church of Christ Commission for Racial Justice, *Toxic Waste and Race in the United States: A National Report on the Racial and Socioeconomic Characteristics of Communities with Hazardous Wastes Sites* (Public Access, New York, 1987), p. 9.
12. National Law Journal (NLJ), *Unequal Protection: The Racial Divide in Environmental Law, A Special Investigation* (NLJ, Washington, D.C., 1992), p. S1.
13. For environmental justice responses to (a) land use planning and housing, see R. Bullard *et al.*, eds., *Residential Apartheid: The American Legacy* (UCLA Center for African Studies Publications, Los Angeles, 1994), p. l; (b) transportation, see E. Mann, *Driving the Bus of History—The Bus Riders Union Models a New Theory of Urban Insurgency in the Age of Transnational Capitalism* (Verso, London, forthcoming, 1998); (c) public health, see National Institute of Environmental Health Sciences (NIEHS), NIH, *Symposium on Health Research Needs to Ensure Environmental Justice: Executive Summary and Proceedings, February 10-12, 1994, Arlington, Virginia* (NIEHS: Research Triangle Park, North Carolina, 1994).
14. For a thorough presentation of "Principles of Environmental Justice" and their ramifications for many aspects of environmentalism, see Charles Lee, ed., *Proceedings: The First National People of Color Environmental Leadership Summit* (United Church of Christ Commission for Racial Justice, Washington, D.C., 1991).
15. Robert Bullard, "Conclusion: Environmentalism with Justice," in *Confronting Environmental Racism: Voices from the Grassroots,* Robert Bullard, ed. (South End Press, Boston, 1993).
16. Greenpeace, *The Database of Known Hazardous Waste Exports from OECD to Non-OECD Countries, 1989–March 1994* (Greenpeace, Washington, D.C., 1994).
17. The World Bank, Memorandum, Lawrence H. Summers, December 12, 1991.
18. Minority Rights Group, *The Pacific: Nuclear Testing and Minorities* (Minority Rights Group, London, 1991), p. 5; or Arjun Makhijani, Howard Hu, and Katherine Yih, *Nuclear Wastelands: A Global Guide to Nuclear Weapons Production and Its Health and Environmental Effects* (MIT Press, Cambridge, Massachusetts, 1997).
19. Dana Alston and Nicole Brown, "Global Threats to People of Color," in *Confronting Environmental Racism: Voices from the Grassroots,* Robert Bullard, ed. (South End Press, Boston, 1993), p. 183.
20. Michael Wells, "Biodiversity Conservation, Affluence, and Poverty: Mismatched Costs and Benefits and Efforts to Remedy Them," *Ambio,* Vol. 21 (1992), pp. 237–43.
21. Steven Yearley, *Sociology, Environmentalism, Globalization: Reinventing the Globe* (Sage Publications, London, 1996), pp. 103–107.

Michael K. Dorsey, a member of the U.S. Delegation to UNCED, is currently a director of the Sierra Club, and an associate of the newly formed Center for Justice and Sustainability in Oxon Hill, Maryland.

Breast Cancer and the Environment

DEVRA LEE DAVIS

Devra Lee Davis

Breast cancer is a disease of enormous public health importance. According to the World Health Organization's International Agency for Research on Cancer, breast cancer is now the most common form of cancer in women in the world. Rates of new cases are highest in industrial nations but are rising rapidly in some developing countries (1). In those few developed countries where widespread screening programs have recently become routine, some of the growth in incidence reflects improved detection by mammography, which can spot small breast tumors years before they would otherwise be detected. Although increased use of mammography can explain part of the increase in new cases in the United States and a few other developed countries, it cannot account for the recent, substantial increases in certain regions in Central Europe and Asia where no screening is conducted (2).

For more than three decades, scientists have consistently identified a number of risk factors that are generally believed to account for up to 40 percent of all cases of breast cancer. Among the established risk factors for breast cancer are: having menstrual periods that begin before age 12 and end after age 55, having no children or bearing children late in life, not nursing children, early and repeated exposures to relatively high doses of radiation, obesity after menopause, and a family history of breast cancer occurring in a close relative before age 40 (3). Other factors are suspected of increasing risk, although the data are less clear. These include: drinking alcohol daily, lack of vigorous exercise, low intake of vitamin D and fiber, active and passive smoking, and living near chemical facilities (4).

Despite the continued public attention to inherited breast cancer genes, fewer than 1 in 10 cases develops in a woman born with defects in the major breast cancer genes identified thus far—BRCA1, BRCA2, and ATM (5). Breast cancer, like all cancers, is thought to arise from a multistep process that involves sequential or simultaneous damage to several genes that control cell growth and maturation. Genetic damage can also occur when a cell miscopies its own DNA during cell division and fails to repair such mistakes. Metabolic differences in the way the body processes compounds that are affected by genetic factors can also affect the risk of cancer developing (6).

So, although certain risk factors for breast cancer, such as age at menarche, diet, and genetic predisposition, have been well known for years, many breast cancer cases occur in women with no known risk factors for disease (7). Scientists cannot explain why there are more new cases of breast cancer today. However, a growing and complex array of evidence suggests that the general external environment—including behavior, diet, and physical and chemical exposures—plays a major role in fostering breast cancer. The general environment can induce breast cancer by two distinct mechanisms. Environmental exposures may damage genes directly or they may affect the overall production of growth-regulating hormones, such as estrogen, progesterone, and other such naturally produced substances (8).

Timing of exposure may be just as important as the degree of exposure to one or more of these risk factors in the development of disease, with exposures that occur prenatally being especially important.

Further evidence that environmental factors generally play a role in the development of breast cancer comes from the observations of considerable geographic variation in breast cancer cases both among and within ethnic groups. Studies have shown that Asian women living in the United States have higher rates of breast cancer than women living in their countries of origin (9).

Abundant evidence exists that a woman's cumulative exposure to estrogen plays a role in increasing breast cancer risk. The longer a woman is exposed to estrogen over the course of her lifetime, the greater her risk for developing breast cancer. Women who start menstruating at an earlier age and enter menopause at a late age, for example, are more vulnerable to breast cancer than women who are menstrual for a shorter period of time. Reduction of estrogen by surgical removal of ovaries can lower cancer risk substantially; breast-feeding, which lowers cumulative estrogen exposure by disrupting regular menses, also reduces the risk of breast cancer somewhat (10). In addition, women who have toxemia during pregnancy have lower hormone levels. One recent study suggests that their daughters have a reduced risk of breast cancer, possibly because their developing breast cells were subjected to lower prenatal levels of circulating hormones (11).

How might estrogens and other hormones be affecting the risk of breast cancer? Hormones, especially those that are not bound and excreted rapidly through normal metabolism, are thought to foster the growth of genetically damaged breast cells, causing them to develop into clinically significant cancers. Those periods when cells are rapidly dividing, as in the prenatal period and during puberty, are also times of greater vulnerability to genetic damages that can cause disease, because repair mecha-

*E*nvironmental Change and Human Health

nisms may not be up to speed at the rate of cell growth. Studies suggest that elevated prenatal estrogen exposure affects breast cancer risk in offspring, perhaps by permanently affecting the sensitivity of breast cells to estrogen.

Such evidence of the role of naturally occurring hormones in cancer risk has led to the hypothesis that synthetic hormones could be involved as well. Over the past three decades, several lines of evidence have converged indicating that a number of commonly used synthetic compounds can modify or mimic the actions of natural estrogen in the body. (See Box on hormone mimics in Chapter 2.) Some of these hormone-mimicking compounds may be beneficial, such as those generally found in plants and fish. In contrast, other hormone-mimicking compounds appear to be generally harmful, such as those often found in pesticides, plastics, and fuels. Experimental, wildlife, and some human studies have found higher levels of some of these damaging compounds in organisms with altered hormonal functioning or other health problems, including developmental and behavioral defects (12).

Based on these observations, my colleagues at the Strang–Cornell Cancer Research Laboratory in New York City and I have hypothesized that these same hormone disrupting environmental exposures can play a role in the development of breast cancer, if they perturb the effects of natural estrogen. We theorize that certain of these synthetic xenoestrogens may increase the risk of breast cancer by adversely affecting the metabolism of estrogen, while other xenoestrogens in plants such as soy may protect against the disease. Natural estrogens and xenoestrogens can lead to breast cancer through the same mechanism. Both the body's own natural estrogen as well as xenoestrogens can bind to estrogen receptors and alter how much and what types of estrogen the body produces. Estradiol, the main type of estrogen generated by women, is metabolized in the body into different forms that have markedly different effects in the body. There are thought to be "good" and "bad" forms of these estrogen metabolites. The good estrogen appears to

promote cell repair and prevent cancer from arising by enhancing protective factors in the cell cycle that discourage cancer. In contrast, the bad estrogen appears to stimulate cancer-causing damage of protective genes and to increase overall amounts of unbound hormones, either one of which can prompt the accelerated growth of breast cells. Such enhanced growth increases the chance that genetic damage will occur and be sustained (13). Animal and human studies suggest that high levels of the bad estrogen are tied to an increased risk of breast cancer (14).

While evidence for this hypothesis remains incomplete, experimental analyses have recently provided increased support for the theory. My colleagues at Strang and I found that human breast cancer cells had levels of the bad estrogen that were more than four times higher than those of normal breast cells. When organochlorine pesticides were added to breast cancer cells, the ratio of the amounts of bad to good estrogen significantly jumped (15). These pesticides, which tend to accumulate in fat cells may somehow have influenced the formation of different estrogen metabolites. These and other findings led us to postulate that exposures to certain xenoestrogens in the environment might account for some of the current rise in breast cancer incidence by increasing the ratio of bad and good estrogens in breast tissue. Several small studies conducted in the 1970s and 1980s found that women with higher levels of DDT metabolites in their blood had higher risks of breast cancer (16).

In contrast to these experimental studies of hormone-disrupting potential in environmental chemicals, human studies have not consistently found an association between some fat-seeking pesticide residues and breast cancer. Three recent studies have found no link between breast cancer risk and metabolites of DDT, a suspected estrogen mimic, in the body (17) (18). In these studies, however, both women with breast cancer and those with whom they were compared had levels of DDT pesticide metabolites that were nearly one sixth of those measured in the United States in the late 1960s (19). Moreover, in all these studies information could not be

obtained on possible prenatal exposures to harmful xenoestrogens, nor on the history of long-term use or exposure to possible bad or good xenoestrogens, such as those in plants, fish, and fiber. In short, the jury is still out.

Documenting the role of potentially harmful xenoestrogens, such as some long-lived organochlorine pesticides, provides a major challenge to epidemiologic research. In part, this is because other contributing factors, both positive or negative, cannot be easily measured and may be of relatively greater importance. For instance, some relevant sources of bad estrogens for breast cancer could include exposures that occurred two or three decades earlier to widely used materials such as plastics, fuels, and pharmaceuticals, none of which could be detected years later because they do not accumulate in fat. Consistent with this idea is one recent study that found that post-menopausal women who had never breast-fed had a much higher risk of breast cancer compared with those who had breast-fed. Breast-feeding can release materials, such as organochlorines, from the breast into nursing infants. While this may lower a woman's risk for breast cancer, the long-term consequences for children exposed to higher levels of such contaminants in breast milk is of concern (20).

How might harmful xenoestrogens get into the body to act on breast cells or the developing brain? One highly likely route is through animal fat in the diet. Harmful synthetic xenoestrogens tend to accumulate in fatty tissue and move up the food chain. Some synthetic xenoestrogens wind up in food because once they enter the environment, they can persist and accumulate for more than 50 years. People who live in polluted areas might be directly exposed to harmful xenoestrogens simply by breathing the air or drinking contaminated water. Occupational exposures to xenoestrogens can also occur, such as in chemical laboratories and industrial plants.

Some investigators, such as Stephen Safe of Texas A&M University, question whether synthetic xenoestrogens can play any role in breast cancer. They point out that people are exposed to minute quantities of individual chemicals in the environment that are far less potent than natural estrogen, such as those produced in the body itself or derived from plant products. In addition, dietary plant estrogens like soy appear to diminish harmful estrogenic effects, canceling out the influences of the bad estrogens. These observations are correct, but incomplete. It is true that any given synthetic xenoestrogen may enter the body in very small amounts, compared with the body's own natural hormones. However, once in the body, many fat-seeking synthetic xenoestrogens tend to persist for decades in tissues and are not readily excreted. In contrast, plant estrogens are usually degraded rapidly in the body. Thus, it is unlikely that natural estrogens consumed in most people's diets can completely negate the activity of persistent, cumulative synthetic compounds.

We realize that xenoestrogens cannot account for all breast cancer cases that occur. Recent findings of low levels of some organochlorines in blood and fat are welcome indications of the success of past environmental control efforts to reduce or ban the use of many such compounds. But the variety of materials that can alter hormone metabolism appears extensive and not well characterized at this time. The combined effect on human and ecological health remains a matter of serious concern. In contrast to many established risk factors for breast cancer, such as early onset of menstruation and late menopause, exposure to synthetic xenoestrogens can be reduced or controlled through public policies. In addition, beneficial xenoestrogens, such as those in broccoli, soy, and fish, may prove useful in preventing the disease from occurring or recurring. If reducing avoidable exposures to harmful xenoestrogens and encouraging the use of beneficial materials made it possible to avert only one fifth of breast cancers every year, millions of women—and those who care about them—would be spared the burden of this difficult disease, and the public would be spared the burgeoning costs of treatment and care. Such prospects are too tantalizing to ignore.

References and Notes

1. D.M. Parkin *et al.*, eds., *Cancer Incidence in Five Continents*, Vol. VII, IARC (International Agency for Research on Cancer) Scientific Publications No. 143 (World Health Organization/IARC, Lyon, France), on CD-ROM.

2. Devra Lee Davis *et al.*, "Environmental Influences on Breast Cancer Risk," *Science and Medicine*, Vol. 4, No. 3 (May–June 1997), p. 56.

3. M.P. Madigan *et al.*, "Proportion of Breast Cancer Cases in the United States Explained by Well-Established Risk Factors," *Journal of the National Cancer Institute*, Vol. 87, No. 22 (1995), pp. 1681–1685.

4. *Op. cit.* 2, p. 58.

5. *Op. cit.* 2.

6. Christine B. Ambrosone *et al.*, "Cigarette Smoking, N-Acetyltransferase 2 Genetic Polymorphisms, and Breast Cancer Risk," *Journal of the American Medical Association*, Vol. 276, No. 18 (November 13, 1996), p. 1494.

7. Devra Lee Davis *et al.* "Recent Developments on the Avoidable Causes of Breast Cancer," in *Preventive Strategies for Living in a Chemical World: A Symposium in Honor of Irving J. Selikoff*, Annals of the New York Academy of Sciences, Vol. 837, Eula Bingham and David P. Rall, eds. (New York Academy of Sciences, New York, 1997), p. 514.

8. *Ibid.*, p. 520.

9. Regina G. Ziegler *et al.*, "Migration Patterns and Breast Cancer Risk in Asian-American Women," *Journal of the National Cancer Institute*, Vol. 85, No. 22 (November 17, 1993), pp. 1819–1827.

10. *Op. cit.* 2.

11. Anders Ekbom *et al.*, "Intrauterine Environment and Breast Cancer Risk in Women: A Population-Based Study," *Journal of the National Cancer Institute*, Vol. 89, No. 1 (January 1, 1997), pp. 71–72.

12. Theo Colborn, Dianne Dumanoski, and John Peterson Myers, *Our Stolen Future: Are We Threatening Our Fertility, Intelligence, and Survival?—A Scientific Detective Story* (Penguin Books, New York, 1996), pp. 47–67.

13. H. Leon Bradlow *et al.*, "Effects of Pesticides on the Ratio of 16∝/2-Hydroxyestrone: A Biologic Marker of Breast Cancer Risk," *Environmental Health Perspectives*, Vol. 103, Supplement 7 (October 1995), pp. 147–150.

14. Devra Lee Davis *et al.*, "Medical Hypothesis: Xenoestrogens as Preventable Causes of Breast Cancer," *Environmental Health Perspectives*, Vol. 101, No. 5 (October 1993), pp. 372–377.

15. *Op. cit.* 13.

16. *Op. cit.* 2, pp. 60–61.

17. David J. Hunter *et al.*, "Plasma Organochlorine Levels and the Risk of Breast Cancer," *The New England Journal of Medicine*, Vol. 337, No. 18 (October 2, 1997), pp. 1253–1258.

18. Nancy Krieger *et al.*, "Breast Cancer and Serum Organochlorines: A Prospective Study Among White, Black, and Asian Women," *Journal of the National Cancer Institute*, Vol. 86, No. 8 (April 20, 1994), pp. 589–599.

19. *Op. cit.* 17.

20. Joseph L. Jacobson and Sandra W. Jacobson, "Intellectual Impairment in Children Exposed to Polychlorinated Biphenyls in Utero," *New England Journal of Medicine*, Vol. 335, No. 11 (1996), pp. 783–789.

Devra Lee Davis is the director of the Health, Environment, and Development Program at the World Resources Institute and a Presidential appointee of the National Chemical Safety and Hazard Investigation Board.

*E*nvironmental Change and Human Health

Weighing Risks in West Bengal

PROFESSOR K.J. NATH

Development decisions can result in unanticipated health consequences. In West Bengal, this tragedy can be seen in the growing problem of arsenic poisoning.

From the 1950s through the 1970s, the Indian Government actively encouraged the building of tube wells, which tap water from 150 meters or more below ground. Historically, villagers had used surface water for drinking. However, surface waters such as ponds and rivers had become grossly polluted by bacterial contaminants due to the lack of sanitation in the area. In addition, the new tube wells provided abundant water to irrigate the high-yield varieties of rice that were being promoted as part of the Green Revolution. As a result, farmers were suddenly able to grow three or four crops, continuing cultivations right through the 6-month dry season, whereas before farmers grew only a single rain-watered rice crop each year (1)(2).

The cost of these development decisions is only now becoming clear. The underground strata, from which the tube-well water is drawn, contains natural arsenic. The first cases of arsenic poisoning surfaced as early as the 1980s. But by late 1995, according to West Bengal Government health authorities, more than 1,500 people had reported for treatment in government health centers and hospitals. There is no doubt that the actual number of people suffering was substantially higher. (Some unofficial reports estimated that about 200,000 people may have suffered from skin lesions, pigmentation abnormalities, and keratoses on the palms and soles of their feet caused by arsenic poisoning.) However, without a comprehensive epidemiological survey with adequate sample size, it was not possible to conduct a realistic assessment of the problem. So far, scientists have found widespread

poisoning in at least six districts, where average arsenic levels in a substantial number of tube wells exceed the WHO permissible limit alarmingly (by 5–50 times). Some individual wells show even higher concentrations. However, it would be difficult to estimate the exact number of wells contaminated with arsenic without comprehensive water quality monitoring in all these districts. Scientists estimate that one million people might be at risk of drinking arsenic-contaminated water (3)(4).

Finding a solution will not be easy. First, while there are control programs for known diseases like malaria, filariasis, and tuberculosis—however inefficient and short sighted these programs might be—there does not appear to be a comprehensive action plan for the emerging challenges that are directly related to the processes let loose by economic, ecological, and development policies. So far, health authorities have taken a typical medical view of the situation and have stressed curative rather than preventive actions under the compulsion of crisis management.

Second, considerable uncertainty persists among the scientists as to the extent and magnitude of the arsenic problem. Arsenic is a cumulative poison, and health effects may not be fully manifested for 10 to 20 years. As one WHO researcher commented, "[The] question is whether or not only the tip of the iceberg now has been identified, or if the majority of the most seriously affected villages are already evident."

Third, without diluting the gravity of the arsenic situation, policymakers must weigh the competing environmental health risks in the region. While the thousands of cases of arsenic poisoning created an uproar in national and international media, the millions of cases of diarrhea, tuberculosis, and malaria

each year in West Bengal have caused barely a stir. More than one third of all deaths in the urban areas of the state can be attributed to preventable risks in the environment, and almost two thirds of the rural sicknesses are due to lack of sanitation and safe water. While it is not applicable to make a precise comparison among the competing risks of malaria, diarrhea, and other communicable diseases and those posed by arsenic contamination of groundwater, in terms of the number of people affected, there is no doubt that the former is much greater. As such, any decision with respect to large-scale investments in the health and environmental sector need to be based on an objective risk-to-risk trade-off. One should not forget these fundamental realities in dealing with the arsenic problem.

Finally, we must not overlook the fact that, in any scarcity-based economy like that of West Bengal, optimizing return from public expenditure has to be the major goal of policymakers. Until health authorities understand and appreciate social and environmental routes of disease, the health problems plaguing West Bengal, and many other developing regions, will continue.

References and Notes

1. Fred Pierce, "Death and the Devil's Water," *New Scientist*, Vol. 147 (September 16, 1995), p. 14.
2. Pavalla Bagla and Jocelyn Kaiser, "India's Spreading Health Crisis Draws Global Arsenic Experts," *Science*, Vol. 274 (October 1996), p. 174.
3. *Op. cit.* 1.
4. *Op. cit.* 2.

K.J. Nath is the director of the All India Institute of Hygiene and Public Health, Calcutta.

Environmental Health and Environmental Equity

CAROLYN STEPHENS

It is hard to be optimistic about environmental change and improved human health for everyone in the face of massive poverty and massive inequity around the world. It is even harder to maintain optimism in light of evidence that shows current policy decisions are contributing to an increase, rather than a decrease, in the inequitable distribution and control of environmental, economic, and political resources internationally (1)(2).

The shuffling Northern and impatient Southern feet of the world's political leaders at Rio Plus Five provide testimony to how far from reality the hopes of Rio remain. There is talk about sustainability, social justice, environmental equity, and overconsumption. Yet, we haven't even begun to conquer old-fashioned poverty.

Is it all gloom? Certainly health statistics over the past century suggest that some major achievements have occurred, most as the result of what now seem like simple and obvious environmental interventions, such as the provision of ample and potable water, sanitation, nutritious food, and decent housing. Significantly, these goods were achieved through social and political processes, and came with societal structures that placed education on the agenda and promoted remunerative and healthy work conditions for all (3)(4).

Most people in Europe and North America, some in South America, and a minority in most Asian and African countries now have these basic environmental goods that support life. Since the end of the last century, these basics have no longer been considered health goods but are seen as clear rights and universal necessities.

Why then, as we move into the 21st Century, do we need another report on environmental change and human health, arguing the case for sharing basic environmental goods that presage life for the majority? It feels, eerily, as though we are having to repeat the same arguments used by our 19th Century colleagues when they saw the awful conditions in the slums of Europe (5) (6). To our 19th Century colleagues, the process they saw was not development; this exploitative, dirty, unfair process was "murder" (7).

Today, by contrast, the international society that controls access to resources seems to choose to ignore the reality faced by the world's majority. But if one looks, the conditions faced by the majority are similar to, or perhaps worse than, those faced by our 19th Century counterparts. For one thing, the distance between the rich and the poor's experience is enormous, and the scale of the health problems faced by the latter is dauntingly large.

It was urban poverty that provoked the last century's conscience. By 2025, three out of four of us will live in towns and cities, the majority in conditions that undermine good health. The majority is in a trap that the minority does not seem to see, let alone feel (8).

I say this from the perspective of a health professional—an environmental epidemiologist. I started working on poverty and health in India 18 years ago. More recently, in Accra in 1992, I worked with colleagues to identify the city's most deprived communities in terms of the environmental burdens to health. We located areas that experienced death rates two to four times higher than rates overall and five to six times higher than rates in the most privileged areas (9). Directly, the inflated death rates were due to infectious and parasitic diseases, linked with the very poor access to basic water and sanitation. Less directly, people did not have the economic resources to improve their conditions. Even less directly, they had no control over their opportunities or their access to resources. And finally, decisions over resources were made by the city's privileged who did not *feel* their link with the city's poverty, nor did they *see* the health problems to which they contributed by their professional decisions and personal actions. Thus, although the poor communities had intermittent (or nonexistent) water supplies for which they paid dearly, the wealthy watered their lawns and filled swimming pools with scarce potable water. The wealthy paid less than the poor for the water they did consume. To state it bluntly, the poor paid more for their cholera, a pattern repeated internationally (10)(11). Under the circumstances, it seems disingenuous to simply suggest that the solution to the urban health problem in Accra was only to improve water and sanitation conditions in the poor areas—rather than to plan a careful redistribution of resources through progressive policies.

Accra is not an extreme example. London, Washington, and Paris show the same dynamic (12); local, national, and international statistics show the same pattern (13). Few, if any, environmental, social, or health inequalities are, at root, a matter of chance or a reflection of one group's inability to live in a healthy manner versus another's. Today's inequalities reflect how human beings see and act, based on their mutual connection and their mutual responsibility to share resources—within a city or within the world.

In a guest editorial, I can speak personally. As a technical professional who interacts routinely with policymakers, I have long been aware that environmental health for the majority will only be achieved if those with power in the global society seriously address how environmental, economic, and political resources are distributed and managed at all levels. Discomfort has yet to impinge personally on the minority of world citizens who consume and control most of the world's environmental resources. Lacking discomfort, these citizens have yet to lobby for or produce any tangible change.

Naturally, change cannot come from the minority alone (14). In reality, even if they wished to, the international technical and policy community cannot shift policies toward sustainability without mass changes in the attitudes and actions of the majority (15). Action toward solving such a complex problem requires that more people recognize that the problem—increasing inequity—exists, and that everyone has a role in changing the situation. Gradually, but rapidly, the debate on sustainability and equity must move from the rarified atmosphere of United Nations summits, United Nations agencies, and academic

discussions until the world's citizens feel again our mutual connection and responsibility for each other's well-being.

References and Notes

1. United Nations Development Programme (UNDP), *Human Development Report 1992* (Oxford University Press, New York, 1992), pp. 1–216.

2. United Nations Development Programme (UNDP), *Human Development Report 1997* (Oxford University Press, New York, 1997), pp. 1–216.

3. C. Stephens, *Urban Health for the Future: From Descriptions of Health Inequality to Policies for Equity*, technical paper for the World Health Organization Working Group Meeting on Determinants and Indicators of Urban Health, Kobe, Japan, August 20–23 1997.

4. D. Acheson, "The Road to Rio: Paved with Good Intentions," *British Medical Journal*, Vol. 304 (May 1992), pp. 1391–1392.

5. *Ibid.*

6. S. Wing, "Limits of Epidemiology," *Medicine and Global Survival*, Vols. 1 and 2 (1994), pp. 74–86.

7. F. Engels, *The Conditions of the Working Classes in England* (Penguin, London, 4th edition, 1987), pp. 1–293.

8. D. Korten, "Sustainability and the Global Economy: Beyond Bretton Woods," *Forest, Trees and People* (June 1996).

9. C. Stephens *et al.*, *Environment and Health in Developing Countries: An Analysis of Intra-urban Differentials Using Existing Data*. Collaborative Studies in Accra and São Paulo and Analysis of Urban Data of Four Demographic and Health Surveys (London School of Hygiene and Tropical Medicine, London, 1994).

10. G. Benneh *et al.*, *Environmental Problems and the Urban Household in the Greater Accra Metropolitan Area (GAMA)—Ghana* (Stockholm Environment Institute, Stockholm, Sweden, 1993).

11. S. Cairncross and J. Kinnear, "Elasticity of Demand for Water in Khartoum, Sudan," *Social Science and Medicine*, Vol. 34, No. 2 (1992), pp. 183–189.

12. C. Stephens, "Review Article: Healthy Cities or Unhealthy Islands? The Health and Social Implications of Urban Inequalities," *Environment and Urbanization*, Vol. 8, No. 2 (1996), pp. 9–30.

13. M. Wolfe, "Globalization and Social Exclusion: Some Paradoxes," in *Social Exclusion; Rhetoric, Reality, Responses*, G. Rodgers, C. Gore and J.B. Figueiredo, eds., (International Labour Organization, Geneva, 1995), pp. 81–103.

14. C. Short, Secretary of State Speech on Equity, Sustainability and Development for the UNED-UK Annual Conference on the Way Forward: Beyond Agenda 21 (1997).

15. *Op. cit.* 8.

Carolyn Stephens is a senior lecturer in Environmental Health and Policy at the London School of Hygiene and Tropical Medicine, London.

A regional effort to harness the waters of the Senegal River for hydropower, irrigation, and transportation has resulted in profound environmental changes in the river basin. These environmental changes have, in turn, caused severe health and general welfare problems for the river basin's residents. This case study illustrates the complex relationships that can unfold between people and their environment as societies work to meet their growing needs for energy, agricultural production, and industrial development. Although many of the harmful effects were predicted before the project began, the project's purported benefits—water storage for irrigation, drought, and domestic supply; electrical power for urban areas and industry; and a transportation channel to the sea for land-locked Mali—were deemed too important to forgo. Now, years later, the river basin management authority, national ministries in three riparian countries (Mali, Mauritania, and Senegal), and international agencies financing the project are trying to mitigate some of the most severe problems as they continue work to realize the project's potential benefits.

Background

The Senegal River is the second longest river in West Africa (1). Its principal tributary, the Bafing River, rises in the highlands of Guinea's Fouta Djallon and runs north into Mali, where it joins the Bakoye River at Bafoulabe to form the Senegal River. From Bafoulabe, the Senegal River flows northwest through Mali and down to Kayes, receives waters from the Faleme River, and then flows onto the flood plain starting at Bakel in Senegal. For its remaining length from Bakel to the Atlantic Ocean, the Senegal River forms the border between Mauritania to the north and Senegal to the south.

The upland areas above Bakel, and particularly those in Guinea, receive 700 to

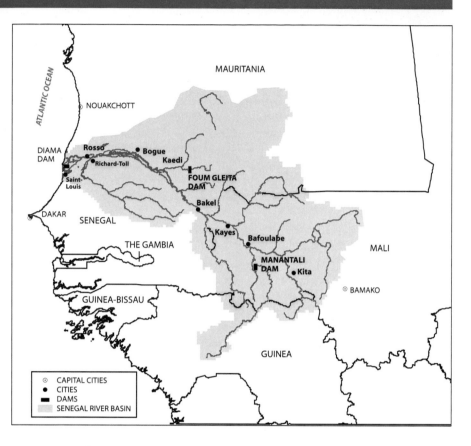

2,000 millimeters of rainfall annually and provide virtually all of the flow in the Senegal River. Annual rainfall below Bakel is typically between 150 and 300 millimeters. Tributaries to the Senegal River are temporary, seasonal systems that function as distributaries when flow is high in the main channel. In its natural state, the Senegal River's annual flood inundated approximately 150,000 hectares in an average year and up to 350,000 hectares in high-flow years. In the dry season, freshwater flow stopped in the lower reaches of the river, and saltwater flow traveling upstream created estuarine conditions from the Atlantic coast to Dagana, approximately 250 kilometers inland. These conditions created a natural division of the river basin into three zones: an upper basin above Bakel; the middle valley from Bakel to Dagana; and the delta, or lower valley, from Dagana to the Atlantic coast.

Approximately 2 million people of several ethnic groups live in the river basin. The predominant groups are the Malinke in the upper basin, the Soninke around Bakel, the Pulaar and Maures in the middle valley, and the Wolof in the delta. All of these groups are agropastoralists, relying for their livelihood on a combination of agriculture, small animal husbandry, and fishing. Herders have historically traveled with their cattle from the valley floor in the dry season to the adjacent Sahelian fringe areas in the rainy season and floods.

Because of their dependence on the river, residents' fortunes have risen and fallen through the years in relation to the availability of water from rainfall and floods. From 1968 to 1973, the region experienced a prolonged and severe great drought that caused extensive famine and focused international attention on the Sahel region.

*E*nvironmental Change and Human Health

Development Projects on the Senegal River

Because of its size and regional importance, the Senegal River has long been a target for development projects. There were two international efforts to develop agriculture, navigation, and hydroelectric projects in the four riparian states (including Guinea) during the colonial period in the 1930s and early 1940s. In the 1960s, after gaining independence, the riparian countries created an Inter-Country Committee and a successor organization to pursue an integrated development program for the river basin. However, most of the early attempts at developing the river's resources failed, either for technical reasons or because of tension among the participating states.

In the early 1970s, circumstances finally combined to favor mounting several large-scale projects. In 1970, a U.N.-sponsored study identified several potential sites for hydroelectric dams in western Mali and northeastern Guinea. In 1972, partially in response to the great drought and the resulting attention from international agencies, the governments of Mali, Mauritania, and Senegal created a regional river basin authority, the Organisation pour la Mise en Valeur du Fleuve Senegal (OMVS). Guinea was not included in the OMVS because of its lack of interest and effective participation in the earlier regional organizations. The three member states of the OMVS thought a regional organization would be the best way to prioritize economic objectives for developing resources in the basin, to organize a cooperative effort, and to reach agreement on common responsibilities for financing and managing the major works. Arab oil states also took an interest in financing projects on the Senegal River, a reflection of their prosperity during the oil boom of the 1970s and of their desire to assist other members of the Islamic community and increase Islamic economic and cultural influence in the region.

The OMVS members developed an integrated plan for development of the Senegal River, designed to stimulate economic growth in the three member countries and to moderate the effects of drought on people living in the basin. The plan had six components:

● an upland hydroelectric dam on the Bafing River at Manantali, Mali, for water storage and power production;

● a lowland dam on the Senegal River near Diama, Senegal, to limit saltwater intrusion, regulate water levels in the middle valley, and store water for domestic water supplies;

● facilities and conditions (i.e., locks, channel dredging, and water-level management) to ensure navigability from the Atlantic coast at Saint-Louis, Senegal, to Kayes, Mali;

● irrigation projects and agricultural development in the middle and lower valley;

● urban water supplies using the reservoir created by Diama Dam; and

● development of agroindustry.

The OMVS was given direct authority for building and operating the two dams and responsibility for developing the navigation project. The member states retained responsibility for developing irrigation, water supply, and agroindustrial projects within their own territories.

Politically, the major selling points of the plan were that it would lessen the impact of future droughts and help close the food gap that was emerging as rapid population growth outpaced domestic food production. The OMVS was directed to manage the river's water resources to achieve two objectives that related primarily to agriculture: first, to reduce the large seasonal and annual fluctuations in water availability; and second, to control flooding so that land in the valley could be developed for irrigated agriculture. Senegal and Mauritania would realize most of the benefits from meeting these objectives: of the 375,000 hectares of land that were to be developed for irrigation, all but 9,000 hectares were in these two countries. The hydropower and navigation components were included in the plan primarily to meet Mali's interests.

The expectations of mutual benefit and accelerated development, coupled with the crisis conditions created by the great drought and realistic prospects of international financing, enabled the three countries to overcome entrenched suspicions and proceed with the project. The three member states have maintained a level of cooperation sufficient to complete construction of both dams. Diama Dam was completed and began storing water in 1986. The reservoir behind Manantali Dam began filling in 1987 and reached spillway level in 1991. Other portions of the plan have developed more slowly than first envisioned. Irrigation projects have been completed in the middle valley, and rice and sugar cane production have increased, although not as rapidly as originally predicted. Financing was recently arranged for the hydropower component, which involves installation of turbines and generators at Manantali Dam and building transmission lines to the three capitals (Dakar, Nouakchott, and Bamako) and several points in the basin. Plans for the navigation component have been modified to reflect more realistic water management conditions, shipping systems, and associated development of sea and river ports. Some critics maintain that the navigation project is still unrealistic and will likely never be built. Plans are being developed for water supply projects in Senegal. Most recently, a small amount of industrial development has occurred in the valley, primarily connected with the agricultural sector.

Although the OMVS has implemented portions of its development plan, the projects have not yet generated substantial economic benefits for the member states. Agricultural development has proceeded more slowly than expected, in part because of inappropriate plans for irrigation projects, low yields being experienced in existing projects, and (until recently) centralized control over agricultural planning, production, distribution, and marketing. The power and navigation projects have not yet been implemented. There is some question whether the full plan, even if completed, will ever generate the level of economic benefit originally predicted. The Senegal River dams were initiated in a global economic climate that favored large development projects and a political climate in which the major donors exerted little influence—too little, maintain some critics—over project planning and implementation (2)(3)(4).

Whatever balance may eventually be realized between the economic benefits and costs of the projects for the region and for each country, it is also important to consider the distribution of those costs and benefits and, particularly, the situation of people most directly affected by the projects— those living in the river basin. The completed projects and the OMVS' practices to date in managing water levels in the basin have provided few benefits and serious negative consequences for the basin's residents—some anticipated, and some unanticipated. The ecological, health, and social consequences will be explored in the following sections.

Ecosystem Changes in the Senegal River Basin

The Manantali and Diama dams have changed the river basin ecosystem in several obvious and profound ways. The annual flood has been reduced substantially, because the flow from the Bafing River has been impounded at Manantali Dam. The amount of water available from other tributaries is considerably less than that from the Bafing River. Water has been released from Manantali Dam to provide a managed flood every year since 1987. Unfortunately, the volume of water released each year has been far less than would have been available under natural conditions. And during several years, the period chosen for a water release was poorly timed.

The Senegal River now flows yearround. The region above Diama Dam is now a stable freshwater lake and no longer shifts to estuarine conditions during the dry season. The area below Diama Dam now has a relatively constant estuarine status, as opposed to the previous shifts between freshwater and estuarine

conditions that occurred as a result of high freshwater flows in the flood season and low-to-nonexistent freshwater flows in the dry season. The shoreline is increasing as irrigation canals are developed. Weeds and grasses characteristic of a freshwater lake are growing along the banks of the river and canals from Diama Dam to Dagana and could eventually reach another 100 kilometers inland to Bogué. The vegetation, partially submerged along the river's edge, is favorable habitat for the snails that carry schistosomiasis; increasing vegetation is the primary cause of the growing disease problem among the population of the lower basin.

The changes in aquatic habitat and the physical barrier of Diama Dam have greatly affected fisheries in the lower valley, delta, and coastal waters. Before the dams were built, the sediments carried by the annual flood were an important source of nutrients for coastal fisheries, and the flood plains in the upper delta were spawning and feeding grounds for saltwater and freshwater species. A major coastal fishing industry was centered around Saint-Louis, and fish were an important source of protein for people living in the valley. Although the prolonged drought had already reduced annual catches in the valley before the dams were built, a study in 1994 concluded that the dams have generally had a detrimental effect on fish production both in the valley and in the upper part of the delta. People living in the valley maintain that fish consumption has decreased since 1988. They say that the fish now consumed are almost exclusively saltwater species, trucked in from the Senegalese and Mauritanian coastal areas.

Above Manantali Dam, a large, deep freshwater lake now exists in what was previously a forested valley. The dam was designed to store 11 billion cubic meters of water, enough to supply 2 years' flow during a drought. The surface of Lake Manantali now covers 447 square kilometers; its shoreline is approximately 150 kilometers, and it is 65 meters deep at the dam. Studies conducted before the dams

were built predicted that fish populations would increase in the lake behind Manantali Dam (stabilizing at around 3,000 metric tons annual production) and decrease below the dam (5). Although the fish population in Lake Manantali did increase after the reservoir was filled, the annual catch has never reached predicted levels and has fallen sharply in subsequent years, to 420 metric tons in 1991 and 285 metric tons in 1993. The decreased catch reflects in part the techniques and equipment used by the fisherman, who were accustomed to fishing in rivers rather than in a deep lake, and also the movement of people away from the area.

Environmental Changes and Health Problems

People living in the Senegal River basin have long suffered from schistosomiasis, malaria, and other infectious and vector-borne diseases endemic in large areas of sub-Saharan Africa. Before dams were constructed, malnutrition was widespread in the valley, and infant and child mortality rates were high, especially during the extended drought. The development plan endorsed by the member states of the OMVS predicted that residents' well-being would improve as agriculture and transportation expanded and people had more income and greater access to food, water, and health care.

The reality has been different. Agriculture is developing, but more slowly than anticipated and in a manner that stretches the financial and human resources of existing landholders. Transportation has not improved. Although some indicators of health have improved in the region, health risks from certain diseases—most notably schistosomiasis, diarrheal diseases, and malaria—have increased, in some cases dramatically. The net impact of the Senegal River development projects on people's health has clearly been negative to this point.

*E*nvironmental Change and Human Health

SCHISTOSOMIASIS

Schistosomiasis results from infection by species of the trematode *Schistosoma*. The parasite has a complex life cycle with a stage that infects freshwater snails, which then release larvae into the water. Humans come into contact with the larvae when they wade in shallow waters (for example, when collecting water, washing clothes, or, for children, playing); they become infected when larvae penetrate the skin. Larvae migrate through the host's circulatory system and lungs while developing into mature male and female worms; they eventually migrate to blood vessels in the abdomen and form permanent reproductive pairs, after which the females may produce large numbers of eggs for many years.

There are two main species of *Schistosoma* that infect humans in Africa; they rely on different snail hosts, settle in different tissues of their human hosts, and produce different forms of the disease. *S. mansoni* settle in blood vessels near the liver or intestines and cause intestinal schistosomiasis; *S. haematobium* settle near the bladder and cause urinary schistosomiasis. The severity of the disease in each individual depends on the position and size of the egg load and the host's cellular response to it. Intestinal schistosomiasis causes diarrhea and bloody stools in moderate cases and, in heavy infections, permanent organ damage that can lead to death. Urinary schistosomiasis causes blood in the urine; severe cases involve serious damage to the urinary tract, sometimes leading to bladder cancer.

Before 1986, urinary schistosomiasis was endemic in the Senegal River basin, with relatively low rates of infection in the lower valley and moderate to high rates in the middle and upper valleys. Since the construction of Diama Dam, the snail hosts of *S. haematobium* have extended their range and increased their number in the lower valley, especially along the Lampsar River (a southern branch of the Senegal River in Senegal). Infection rates in humans have also increased. A 1994 survey found the prevalence of urinary schistosomiasis was moderate (11 to 12 percent) among schoolchildren surveyed along the Mauritanian shore of the Senegal River at Rosso, Baghdad, and Jidrel Moghuen. That year, the snail host was found for the first time in the Taouey canal in Senegal, near its outfall to Lake Guiers. There was no evidence at that time of infection among schoolchildren in Mbane, a town on the eastern shore of the lake, although the presence of the snail host suggests that future increases in disease rates in this area are possible.

The net impact of the Senegal River development projects on people's health has clearly been negative to this point.

In the upper valley around Lake Manantali, the prevalence of urinary schistosomiasis was high (69 to 95 percent) in several lake shore villages and in a village just downstream of the dam, according to the 1994 survey. Prevalence decreased with greater distance from the dam (to 49 percent and 7 percent in two villages further downstream). In at least one place in the middle valley, in the irrigation projects around the Foum Gleita Dam in Mauritania, the prevalence of urinary schistosomiasis has been reduced to less than 5 percent by a combination of mitigation measures and natural conditions. The former includes switching from rice to other crops on some of the land and keeping irrigation canals free of weeds. These efforts are aided by the naturally flat terrain of the lake bed behind the dam, which results in large fluctuations in the location of the water line along the shore as water levels fluctuate in the lake. These fluctuations disturb the growth of marginal vegetation along the lake shore and reduce the amount of favorable habitat for snails.

The most dramatic health impact of the Diama and Manantali dams and the new water management regime has been the introduction and rapid spread of intestinal schistosomiasis in the lower valley. Before 1986, *S. mansoni* was not present in the lower and middle valleys and had been reported at only a few locations in the upper valley. In 1988, soon after the completion of Diama Dam, a new focus of intestinal schistosomiasis was reported in a sugar cane project area in Richard-Toll, on the Senegal side of the river. Prevalence reached epidemic levels the following year in Richard-Toll and, by 1993, had climbed to nearly 100 percent in the nearby village of Ndombo and 70 percent in Ngnith, a village on Lake Guiers. In 1994, disease prevalence was 82 percent among schoolchildren at Mbane on Lake Guiers and 47 percent at Dagana, the easternmost boundary of Lake Diama. These Senegalese children had heavy infections with very high egg counts.

In the Mauritanian portion of the lower valley, intestinal schistosomiasis was first reported in 1994 with prevalence rates of 25 to 32 percent in children in three towns from Rosso to Jidrel Moghuen; these children had infections of light to moderate severity. However, the snail host of *S. mansoni* was found in large numbers with high infection rates along the Mauritanian shore of the Senegal River and spreading northward into the Garak canal at Tougene and the Sokam canal near Lake Rkiz. These findings suggest that the extent and intensity of the epidemic will likely increase in Mauritania, possibly following the same course as in Senegal.

As of 1994, the problem with intestinal schistosomiasis had not extended into the middle valley and had not increased greatly in the upper valley. Under the current operating regime, Lake Diama ends at Dagana; above Dagana, the Senegal River is still within its original banks. There is little or no growth of marginal weeds in this region and, therefore, no habitat for the snails.

The introduction of intestinal schistosomiasis and the increases in urinary schistosomiasis are due to a combination of human factors. First, Diama Dam eliminated saltwater intrusion into the lower river and maintained nearly constant water levels, creating conditions favoring the growth of marginal vegetation along the river edges and the spread of the snail hosts of *Schistosoma* species. Second, *S. mansoni* was probably introduced to the lower valley by people migrating into the region, possibly from the upper valley. Population in the region has increased rapidly, especially around the irrigation projects at Richard-Toll, as people move there to take advantage of new jobs. Water supply and sanitation facilities have not kept up with this rapid growth. As a result, the increased contamination of surface waters, and their greater use by residents, has contributed to higher transmission rates for schistosomiasis and increased risks for other waterborne diseases as well. The increased prevalence of urinary schistosomiasis around Lake Manantali—as well as the increased number of the type of snails associated with intestinal schistosomiasis—are due to the year-round presence of water in the lake and its nearly constant water level.

RIFT VALLEY FEVER

Rift Valley Fever is a mosquito-borne viral disease that is most often benign in humans but can occasionally lead to blindness, encephalitis, and fatal hemorrhagic fever. Epidemics are common in livestock and can cause high rates of stillbirths and abortions. The virus is transmitted to humans by biting insects (mosquitoes, sand flies, and, possibly, ticks) or by direct contact with blood or organs of infected animals after slaughter.

An outbreak of Rift Valley Fever occurred near Rosso, Mauritania, in 1987 soon after the completion of Diama Dam and the initial filling of Lake Diama. It began during the rainy season in pastoralist groups in Mauritania and spread to Rosso, eventually appearing on both sides of the river. The outbreak was the first known epidemic of Rift Valley Fever in humans west of Uganda and reportedly killed more than 200 people (6). The disease had been observed only once before in epidemic form in humans, in Egypt in 1977 near the Aswan High Dam on the Nile River. Although the exact ecological

conditions conducive to rapid transmission of Rift Valley Fever remain unclear, the initial filling of a nearby reservoir may be a factor, since this was a common condition in the events at Aswan in 1977 and Mauritania in 1987 (7). Filling the Diama reservoir created more standing water—a location preferred by the *Aedes* mosquito, the probable vector of Rift Valley Fever in Mauritania (8).

The potential for such an outbreak in the Senegal River basin had been identified in pre-dam construction health assessments in 1980, 1984, and just before the onset of the rainy season in 1987 (9). Despite these warnings, authorities in the basin did not take necessary precautions to prevent an outbreak.

MALARIA

Malaria occurs in most parts of the Senegal River basin. Most reported cases are due to malaria tropica (*Plasmodium falciparum*), which can cause severe disease and death. The risk of infection is greater in the upper valley than in the lower areas because the rainy season is longer and the amount of rainfall is higher, creating better conditions for the mosquito vector (*Anopheles* species). *Falciparum* malaria has become a serious concern in Africa because of the parasite's growing resistance to antimalarial drugs.

Evidence is conflicting regarding whether the new water management regime on the Senegal River and the expansion of irrigated areas in the lower valley are causing an increase in malaria infection rates. Reliable evidence shows that *A. gambiae* population densities have increased during the rainy season (August to December) in the middle valley, and that malaria transmission is continuing later into the dry season (December to April). Routine surveillance data from health service facilities in Rosso, Richard-Toll, and Podor reflect an overall increase in the number of malaria cases, although most of the reported cases were not confirmed by microscopic analysis. In contrast, longitudinal studies conducted in the delta region at Kasak-Nord and the middle valley at Podor, and an unpub-

lished study performed in 1991 by the OMVS throughout the basin, do not show increased malaria.

MALNUTRITION

Malnutrition has been widespread in the Senegal River valley for a long time; it was particularly severe during the droughts before construction of the dams. The Senegal River development projects were expected to improve the nutritional status of valley residents as irrigated agriculture catalyzed economic development and brought significant improvements in peoples' socioeconomic status, giving them more income to spend on nutrition and health. Although the situation is complex and no authoritative studies exist with which to compare nutritional status before and after dam construction, the available information suggests that overall, the quality of peoples' diet and their nutritional status have not improved significantly, and may have declined, since construction of the dams.

Before the dams were built, valley residents grew and consumed a wide variety of food crops grown in family plots and small fields in the river's flood plain. Construction of the dams, interruption of the annual flood, and expansion of irrigation projects has reduced traditional agriculture and has increased rice and sugar cane cultivation. In the lower and middle valley, residents' diets now appear to include more rice, a smaller variety of vegetables in most villages, and lower consumption of meat, dairy products, and freshwater fish. This change may reflect the financial strain on family resources caused by low rice yields and farmers' attempts to grow two crops of rice each year, and also the reduced livestock production and fish catch in the valley. For rice-producing families, rice is the predominant food in the diet and is usually eaten at least once or twice a day. Rice is less nutritious than millet and sorghum, which used to be staples in the diet but are now more difficult to find in the markets.

Several studies of nutritional status in towns along the Senegalese shore of the Senegal River in 1990–91 found the

Environmental Change and Human Health

prevalence of chronic malnutrition in children at levels between 20 percent and 36 percent. One study concluded that levels of malnutrition observed in 1992 were comparable to those in 1983, before construction of the dams (10). The same study found the prevalence of nutritional stunting to be 22 percent and wasting to be 11 percent in 1990 among children aged 0 to 5 years old, with somewhat lower levels observed in 1992 (16 percent and 5 percent, respectively). On the Mauritanian side of the river, a 1986 study in the Trarza district (around Rosso) found chronic malnutrition to exist among 25 percent of children younger than 5 years of age. In a 1994 study, rates of chronic malnutrition among children in the same region were estimated at 36 percent, with 11 percent of children showing evidence of nutritional wasting.

DIARRHEAL DISEASES

Changes in water management practices and voluntary migration into the lower valley have affected the rates of diarrheal diseases in basin residents. Development plans for the region called for improvements in water supply, sanitation, and health services, but few improvements have been made to date.

In the lower valley, modest improvements have been insufficient to deal with population movements. In Richard-Toll, an influx of workers to serve the sugar cane industry added an additional 50,000 people to the population, overwhelming improvements in the town's water supply and sanitation facilities. There is an increased risk of cholera and other waterborne diseases in the Richard-Toll area, and there was a cholera epidemic near Rosso, Mauritania, in 1987. Because future improvements to the water supply systems of Dakar and Saint-Louis will draw on water from Lake Diama and Lake Guiers, the quality of those water bodies may soon affect these large population centers as well.

In the middle valley, the regulation of water levels in the river has allowed the development of wind-powered water pumps. These pumps draw water from aq-

uifers bordering the river, resulting in an improvement of water supplies for these villages. Further away from the river, however, the absence of the annual flood has interrupted the previous cycle of aquifer recharging, resulting in a gradual decline in the water table and reduced water availability. The result has been a rise in the reported rates of diarrheal disease. Along the river in the upper valley, diarrheal disease has continued to be a severe problem despite regulation of the river, and health authorities in Kayes, Mali, report that conditions have worsened.

Social Changes and Conflict

The environmental and health changes seen in the Senegal River basin have not happened in isolation; the change in water management and the growth of irrigated agriculture have also brought broad-based social changes, including tensions between pastoralists and farmers and among ethnic groups as well. The dam projects resulted in the relocation of roughly 10,000 people in more than 40 villages and hamlets in Mali. The Malian government, the U.S. Agency for International Development (USAID), and the World Health Organization moved these populations from the area inundated by the Manantali Dam and resettled them in new sites on the plateau above the lake and downstream along the Bafing River. One year after being resettled, villagers reported in a 1989 USAID study that they had insufficient land for cultivation and grazing and insufficient water for gardening. Housing and personal water supplies were considered adequate at that time, because the additional external funding that accompanied the dam projects ensured that these basic items were supplied to the displaced populations. Health problems are common in resettled populations, and increases in diarrheal illnesses and allergies, a measles epidemic, and an outbreak of livestock disease were reported among some of the resettled villages. Some health indicators did improve for the residents of some resettled villages, where

residents had been guaranteed health centers and one water point for every 100 inhabitants. Two years after their displacement, residents continued to receive additional support, such as supplemental nutrition programs funded by the donor governments.

Traditional systems of livestock production have been altered in the middle valley. Construction of the dams was expected to foster an increase in livestock production, but herders have had to cope with a decrease in pastureland due to the persistent drought, the reduction in the annual flood, and the expansion of irrigated land. The increased difficulty of gaining access to the river for watering animals and the reduction in grazing land has led to tensions between pastoralists and farmers.

The development of irrigation along the Senegal River also disturbed patterns of land use and land tenure, exacerbating ethnic conflict among groups in the region. Tens of thousands of people lost their property rights, and massacres occurred in both Mauritania and Senegal (11).

Looking Forward

Dam building will continue to be an important element of economic development plans in many countries. The potential benefits for agriculture, water supply, power production, transportation, industrial development, and flood control are obvious and desirable. Given this expectation, what lessons can be drawn from the experience of Mali, Mauritania, and Senegal in developing the Senegal River?

This case study illustrates the many secondary impacts that a dam project may have on the health, livelihood, social structure, and general welfare of people living in the area. Many of these impacts can be predicted—indeed, most of the impacts of the Senegal River dams were predicted in preconstruction studies.

If many of the negative impacts of the Senegal River dams were predicted, then why were they not avoided? The answer is complicated. First, the financing consortium could have required changes in the project's design but did not. The financing agreements for the dams were reached in the late 1970s, at a time when most participants were not especially sensitive to environmental impacts and, in any case, were eager to participate in the project and would not have been inclined to force changes to which the borrowing countries objected.

Second, the people who have been hurt by the project lack political power and were not represented effectively either in the project design or in its operation. Measures that would have reduced the project's negative impacts on valley residents were not implemented because they were perceived to be adverse to the project's objectives. In the Senegal River basin, more attention should have been paid to how benefits and costs would be distributed among various groups. Generally speaking, even when the overall balance of benefits to risks is positive and a project is justifiable at the level of national interest, the distribution of benefits and costs may be quite unfair. This situation was certainly apparent with the Senegal River dams project. The benefits of the project—income from irrigated agriculture and electrical power from Manantali Dam—will be enjoyed primarily by the people living in the capital cities, while people living in the valley pay the price for the project in terms of poorer health, changed livelihoods, relocation, and disrupted social relationships.

Third, even if the OMVS had the political will to reduce the negative impacts resulting from construction of the Senegal River dams, the organization does not have the technical capability to do so. Many of the negative impacts could be reduced even now by making operational changes in the project. For example, more water could be released to restore an annual flood. Planned variations in the water levels of Lake Manantali and Lake Diama could be used to control snail populations and reduce the spread of schistosomiasis. Yet, if the OMVS were to decide that such measures have merit, it would need greater capabilities in terms of water resource modeling, planning, and operations; genuine expertise in other disciplines (e.g., health and social sciences); and improved mechanisms for communicating with national agencies of its member states.

The experience with the Senegal River dams, therefore, points to at least the following five lessons:

- More effort is needed to evaluate the environmental, health, and social impacts of dams systematically in order to predict their varied impacts more accurately and with greater certainty.

- The design reviews and evaluations conducted by international funding agencies represent a critical juncture at which to make modifications that would reduce negative impacts.

- Dam projects should include funding for measures needed to mitigate their environmental, health, and social impacts as an integral part of the project.

- Institutional arrangements created for managing such projects should include representatives of affected populations in positions of real authority.

- These institutions need funding and technical assistance to develop adequate technical capacity and a multidisciplinary staff that understands and can address the broad range of potential negative impacts.

There is some hope that conditions will improve in the Senegal River valley as a result of international attention to the problems. An international consortium has recently concluded negotiations with the OMVS for the purchase and installation of turbines and hydroelectric generators at Manantali Dam and power distribution lines from Manantali to the national capitals and several locations in the valley. The project includes funding for a study of alternative water management regimes at Manantali Dam and, specifically, for evaluating options for manipulating water levels to reduce schistosomiasis transmission and other impacts. The World Bank, which is a member of the power project consortium, is also developing health sector projects in Senegal and Mauritania that will improve health services and disease surveillance. The World Bank is also developing water supply and sanitation projects in Senegal that will improve facilities and reduce the population's exposure to schistosomiasis.

References and Notes

1. Unless noted otherwise, information in this article is taken from Diop *et al.*, *Senegal River Basin Health Master Plan Study* (Water and Sanitation for Health (WASH) Field Report No. 453, December 1994, reprint ed.).
2. Construction costs for the two dams amounted to US$637 million. The funds came principally from the governments of Saudi Arabia, Kuwait, Abu Dhabi, the Federal Republic of Germany, France, Iran, and the African Development Bank. The United States (U.S. Agency for International Development) and the World Bank declined to provide capital funds for the projects, but supported environmental assessments and other research related to the projects and provided financial and technical assistance for relocating villages that were displaced by the Manantali Dam.
3. Anne Guest, "Conflict and Cooperation in a Context of Change: A Case Study of the Senegal River Basin," in *Boundaries in Question: New Directions in International Relations*, John Macmillan and Andrew Linklater, eds. (Pinter Publishers, London, 1993), pp. 163–173.
4. *Ibid.*
5. Gannett Fleming Corddry and Carpenter, Inc., "Assessment of Environmental Effects of Proposed Developments in the Senegal River Basin," prepared for the Organisation Pour La Mise en Valeur du Fleuve Senegal, 1977.
6. John Walsh, "Rift Valley Fever Rears Its Head," *Science*, Vol. 240 (June 10, 1988), pp. 1397–1399.
7. William R. Jobin, "Rift Valley Fever: A Problem for Dam Builders in Africa," *Water Power and Dam Construction* (August 1989), pp. 32–34.
8. *Op. cit.* 3.
9. J.P. Digoutte and C.J. Peters, "General Aspects of the 1987 Rift Valley Fever Epidemic in Mauritania," *Research in Virology*, Vol. 140, No. 1 (1989), pp. 27–30.
10. E. Benefice and K. Simondon, "Agricultural Development and Nutrition Among Rural Populations: A Case Study of the Middle Valley in Senegal, 1993," *Ecology of Food and Nutrition*, Vol. 31, No. 1–2 (1993), pp. 45–66.
11. Thomas Homer Dixon, *Environmental Scarcity and Violent Conflict: Evidence from Cases*, Peace and Conflict Studies Program, University of Toronto. Available online at: http://ut1.library.utoronto.ca/disk1/www/documents/pcs/evid1.htm (January 1998).

Eugene P. Brantly and Karen E. Ramsey, Environmental Health Project of the U.S. Agency for International Development, Washington, D.C.

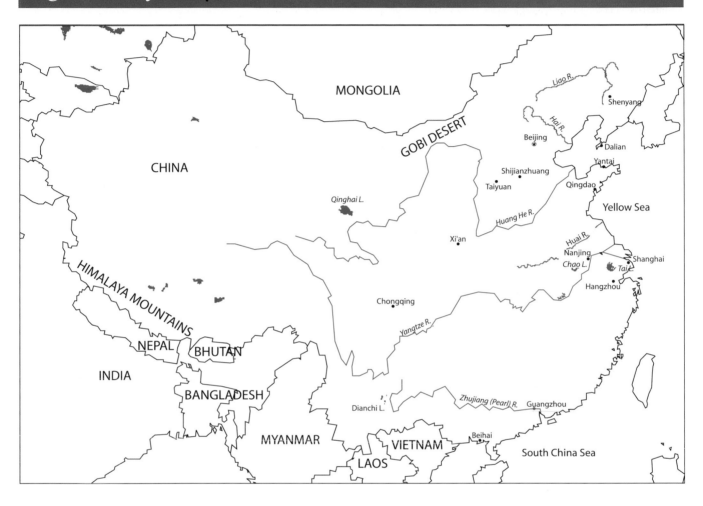

No country better typifies the confluence of trends discussed in this report—nor the challenges they pose to environmental quality and public health—than does modern China. Since the economic reforms of 1978, China has experienced dramatic industrialization and rising energy use against a backdrop of population growth and unprecedented urbanization. China's astounding industrial growth over the past two decades has created a country poised to become a major economic power in the 21st Century. Per capita, China is still one of the world's poorest countries, yet the future looks promising—incomes are rising, poverty rates are falling, and life expectancy is up. Yet, along with these gains, China is grappling with some of the most serious environ-

mental problems on the planet, which in turn could prevent China from sustaining high levels of economic growth in the coming decades.

Recognizing the urgency of these problems, the Chinese Government has endorsed a suite of policies to curb air and water pollution. The extent to which these policies are successful has direct bearing on not only the health of the Chinese people and the local environment but the global environment as well.

Encompassing a geographically vast area with a number of distinct ecological zones, China extends from the massive and sparsely populated Gobi Desert and the mountains of the southwestern Himalayas to the densely inhabited valleys of the eastern coast. As the world's most

populous country, with more than 1.2 billion people, China's economic growth is the fastest and most sustained of any major country in the world, rising an average of 10 percent annually over more than a decade (1). In fact, some autonomous regions in the golden southeastern coastal zones have grown nearly 20 percent annually, doubling in less than 4 years (2).

Industry is China's largest productive sector, accounting for 48 percent of its gross domestic product (GDP) and employing 15 percent of the country's total labor force (3). In the 1990s, the output of China's 10 million industrial enterprises has increased by 18 percent annually (4). Without a doubt, Chinese industry is largely responsible for lifting many millions of people out of poverty. It also underlies a huge and growing demand for energy.

China's demand for high-grade energy such as oil and natural gas will increase rapidly, although coal will continue to dominate the energy structure, accounting for more than 75 percent of total energy production. From 1990 to 1995, China's oil demand grew at 4.3 percent annually, while oil production increased only 1.2 percent each year. As a result of these trends, China has become a net oil importer (5).

Along with industrialization has come rapid urbanization, especially in what is known as the southern coastal crescent that runs from Guangzhou to Shanghai. The proportion of the population living in cities has grown about 50 percent since 1980. Some 370 million people now live in cities, and this number is expected to grow to 440 million by the turn of the century (6). A World Bank model predicts that by the year 2020, 42 percent of China's population, more than 600 million people, will live in urban areas overwhelmingly concentrated in the eastern and southern coastal provinces (7).

Since the political transformation of 1949, dramatic and extensive social improvements have accompanied China's growth. In 1949, the new People's Republic of China faced a massive burden of nutritional deficiency and infectious and parasitic diseases. More than half the population died as a result of infectious and other nondegenerative diseases before reaching middle age—a pattern still common throughout much of the developing world. Since 1949, the average life span in China has risen from 35 years to the current 70. The infant mortality rate has dropped from 200 per 1,000 to 31 per 1,000. Infectious diseases, while still a serious problem in some parts of the country, claim the lives of a mere 0.0004 percent of the population each year (8). The decrease in morbidity and mortality rates associated with infectious diseases in China is a remarkable achievement for the world's most populous country. This decline can be attributed to an aggressive

campaign to improve primary health care and tackle infectious diseases (9).

However, over the coming decades, China's deteriorating environment threatens to undermine the gains that rising incomes would otherwise bring. China's rapid industrialization, urbanization, and economic growth are contributing to respiratory diseases and chronic illnesses such as cancer. Levels of particulate air pollution from energy and industrial production in several of China's megacities, such as Shanghai and Shenyang, are among the highest in the world, leading to corresponding problems of lung disease in their populations. Water pollution in some regions, such as in the Huai River Valley, is also without parallel.

In 1996, the government annual report, *State of the Environment,* noted that environmental pollution was expanding into the countryside, and that ecological destruction was intensifying (10). Environmental problems are seriously affecting overall social and economic development in the country. *China Environment News,* a national newspaper of the National Environmental Protection Agency (NEPA), reported that in recent years, economic costs associated with ecological destruction and environmental pollution have reached as high as 14 percent of the country's gross national product (GNP) (11). More recently, the World Bank estimated that air and water pollution cost China nearly 8 percent of its GNP, around US$54 billion (12). Although solid scientific data are lacking, the government has identified environmental factors as one of the four leading factors influencing the morbidity and mortality of China's people today (13). The importance of environmental factors is well understood by some, as shown by a 1994 opinion survey about risks. Respondents who hold science or engineering degrees ranked risk from pollution ahead of natural disasters (14).

Responding to growing public concerns about the environment, the Chinese Government has officially named the environment as one of its top priorities and has committed itself to reversing the trend of environmental deterioration (15). Over the

past decade, China has increased environmental spending, adopted market incentives, strengthened lawmaking and enforcement, and promoted nationwide environmental education. Decisions made in the next decade or two about energy, transportation, and agricultural technologies will largely determine how successful China will be in achieving its goal of sustainable development.

This case study describes the initial findings of an ongoing project between the World Resources Institute (WRI) and the Chinese Government to evaluate the links between environment and health in China. The goal of this collaborative project is to develop information and indicators that will enable decisionmakers to make informed choices about the environment, energy, infrastructure, and related issues.

The first section of this profile focuses on air pollution trends and the impact of air pollution on human health. Routine monitoring of air pollution and good hospital and health records have enabled researchers to gain a fairly clear picture of air pollution's impact on human health and what the future will hold if air pollution continues to worsen. Water pollution also presents a major threat to public health, although data in this area are less complete. Although data limitations prevent a comprehensive review, the second section reviews the most recent evidence concerning the extent of health problems associated with water pollution. The third section reviews China's laws and policies to protect the environment and health.

Air Pollution and Health Effects

POOR AMBIENT AIR QUALITY PREVAILS

"The residents of many of China's largest cities are living under long-term, harmful air quality conditions," Zhao Weijun, deputy director of the air pollution department of NEPA, reported in 1997 in *China Environment News* (16). China has long recognized air pollution as a critical prob-

Environmental Change and Human Health

lem. Ambient concentrations of total suspended particulates (TSP) and sulfur dioxide (SO_2) are among the world's highest. (See Figure China.1.) In 1995, more than one half of the 88 cities monitored for SO_2 were above the World Health Organization (WHO) guideline. All but two of the 87 cities monitored for TSP far exceeded WHO's guideline. Some cities such as Taiyuan and Lanzhou had SO_2 levels almost 10 times the WHO guideline (17).

Largely because of controls at power plants and within households, particulate emissions have not risen as much as might have been expected with the doubling of coal consumption. Overall, particulate emissions in China have remained relatively level since the early 1980s (18). In fact, in some large cities, ambient particulate concentrations have decreased markedly since the 1980s (19). In contrast, SO_2 emissions have roughly paralleled the increase in coal consumption, reflecting heavy coal burning and inadequate sulfur control measures.

Coal burning, the primary source of China's high SO_2 emissions, accounts for more than three quarters of the country's commercial energy needs, compared with 17 percent in Japan and a world average of 27 percent (20). China's consumption of raw coal increased annually by 2 percent between 1989 and 1993 (21). (See Figure China.2.) Meanwhile, SO_2 emissions increased by more than 20 percent and TSP increased by approximately 10 percent (22). The country is expected to burn 1.5 billion metric tons of coal annually by the year 2000, up from 0.99 billion metric tons in 1990 (23). Without even more dramatic measures to control emissions than are currently in place, the deterioration of air quality seems inevitable.

Particulates and SO_2 are the ambient air pollutants of greatest concern; both are byproducts of coal combustion. While industrial emissions of heavy metals and toxics are also significant contributors to air pollution in China, they are not routinely monitored and will not be addressed in this section.

The extent and type of air pollution in China vary dramatically by geographic re-

gion. SO_2 and particulate emissions are highest in the northern half of China, where coal is used to heat homes and other buildings for several months of the year and where industrial centers also depend heavily on coal burning. Yet, air pollution in the North would be much worse if not for the higher quality, cleaner coal that is available there. By contrast, the coal mined in the South is high in sulfur and extremely polluting, contributing to

serious problems with acid precipitation, especially in the southwest provinces of Sichuan, Guizhou, Guangxi, and Hunan (24) (25).

Industry accounts for two thirds of China's coal use—industrial boilers alone consume 30 percent of China's coal. These boilers are usually highly inefficient and emit through low smoke stacks, contributing to much of China's ground-level air pollution, especially small particulates

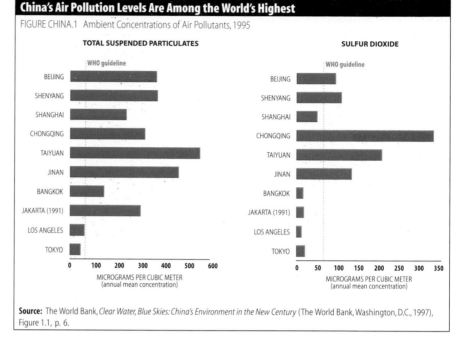

China's Air Pollution Levels Are Among the World's Highest

FIGURE CHINA.1 Ambient Concentrations of Air Pollutants, 1995

Source: The World Bank, *Clear Water, Blue Skies: China's Environment in the New Century* (The World Bank, Washington, D.C., 1997), Figure 1.1, p. 6.

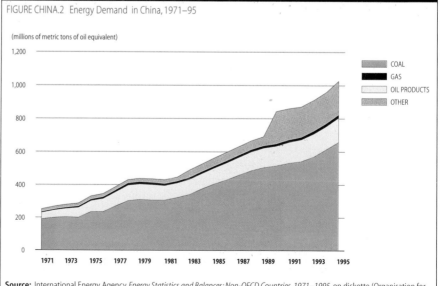

China's Growing Consumption of Coal

FIGURE CHINA.2 Energy Demand in China, 1971–95

Source: International Energy Agency, *Energy Statistics and Balances: Non-OECD Countries, 1971–1995,* on diskette (Organisation for Economic Co-Operation and Development, Paris, 1997).

Outdated Vehicles Degrade Urban Air Quality

TABLE CHINA.1 Percentage of Emissions in Selected Chinese Cities Attributable to Motor Vehicles

| | PERCENTAGE ATTRIBUTABLE TO MOTOR VEHICLES | | | |
	CARBON MONOXIDE	HYDROCARBONS	NITROUS OXIDES	CATEGORIES
Beijing	48–64	60–74	10–22	District
Shanghai	69	37		District
Shenyang	27–38		45–53	District
Jinan	28		4–6	District
Hangzhou	24–70			Road
Urumqi	12–50			Road
Guangzhou	70		43	

Source: He *et al.*, "Status and Development of Vehicular Pollution in China," *Environmental Science,* Vol. 7, No. 4 (August 1996).

and SO₂. Inefficient and dirty boilers are particularly problematic because many of the industries that use them are located in densely populated metropolitan areas, placing populations in these areas at high risk of exposure. The residential sector accounts for approximately 15 percent of total coal use, yet is estimated to contribute to more than 30 percent of urban ground-level air pollution (26)(27).

Although the energy and industrial sectors are now the biggest contributors to urban air pollution in China, the transportation sector is becoming increasingly important. The number of motor vehicles on China's roads has tripled since 1984, climbing from less than 2.4 million in 1984 to 9.4 million in 1994 (28). By 2020, the urban vehicle population is expected to be 13 to 22 times greater than it is today (29). This trend will likely have a major influence on the future of China's air quality. The shift toward vehicle use is most apparent in China's big cities. For example, from 1986 to 1996, the number of vehicles in Beijing increased fourfold, from 260,000 to 1.1 million. Although this is only one tenth of the number of vehicles in Tokyo or Los Angeles, the pollution generated by Beijing motor vehicles equals that in each of the two other cities (30).

The problem stems not just from the growing size of the vehicle fleet but also from low emissions standards, poor road infrastructure, and outdated technology, which combine to make Chinese vehicles among the most polluting in the world

(31). Vehicle emissions standards in China are equivalent to the standards of the developed world during the 1970s, and some domestic companies are manufacturing vehicles modeled after vehicles from 20 years ago. Actual emissions often exceed these standards: Chinese vehicles emit 2.5 to 7.5 times more hydrocarbons, 2 to 7 times more nitrous oxides (N₂O), and 6 to 12 times more carbon monoxide (CO) than foreign vehicles (32). In Beijing, Shanghai, Hangzhou, and Guangzhou, up to 70 percent of CO emissions have been attributed to motor vehicles. Cars also contribute a large share of hydrocarbons and N₂O in the cities where data are available (33). (See Table China.1.) As a result, although China's vehicle fleet is small compared with the developed countries, its large cities are already blanketed with smog.

A recent study in Beijing revealed that at all monitoring points within the Third Ring Road—a rough boundary separating downtown Beijing and its outskirts—the CO levels exceeded the national standard (4 micrograms per cubic meter per day). During the summer, ozone concentrations repeatedly exceeded the national standard, which is set on an hourly basis—often several times per day. In addition, concentrations of N₂O have almost doubled over the past decade (34).

Compounding these pollution problems is the fact that the burgeoning Chinese motor vehicle fleet is largely fueled by leaded gasoline. Although lead exposure is known to be a significant health

hazard in China, no routine monitoring of environmental concentrations or blood-lead levels is performed. A few studies have been conducted and are described below. These scanty data suggest that ambient lead levels in the urban area of major cities such as Beijing are usually 1 to 1.5 micrograms per cubic meter—the national standard is 1 microgram per cubic meter. In some areas, ambient lead levels can reach as high as 14 to 25 micrograms per cubic meter (35). The health effects, described below, are significant, although recent and dramatic government actions to phase out leaded gasoline will likely have a major impact on this problem. Beijing and Shanghai as well as other cities have already begun to act, and the countrywide phaseout is expected to be complete by the year 2000.

HEALTH EFFECTS FROM AMBIENT AND INDOOR AIR POLLUTION

Air pollution is thought to be one of the leading risk factors for respiratory diseases, such as chronic obstructive pulmonary disease (COPD), lung cancer, pulmonary heart disease, and bronchitis, diseases that are the leading causes of death in China. The fact that men and woman have similar rates of these diseases, despite women's much lower smoking rates, provides evidence that this high disease burden is related to pollution (36).

Although only a limited number of epidemiologic studies have been conducted, air pollution has clearly contributed to both excess mortality and morbidity in China. At this stage, however, it is extremely difficult to tease apart which sources of air pollution have the greatest impact on human health, indoor or outdoor. In urban areas, there is a great deal of exchange between outdoor and indoor air, both of which are polluted from different sources—indoor primarily from the burning of coal for cooking and heating. Summaries of selected recent estimates of health impacts are presented to provide a more complete understanding of the complex relationship between air pollution and human health.

Environmental Change and Human Health

Based on dose-response functions from studies conducted within China and in other countries, the World Bank has estimated the number of deaths and diseases associated with air pollution among urban populations. Using the Chinese standards as a benchmark, they estimate the number of deaths that could be prevented if air pollution were reduced to those levels. According to their calculations, approximately 178,000 deaths, or 7 percent of all deaths in urban areas, could be prevented each year. Another measure of air pollution's impact on health is the number of hospital admissions from respiratory diseases. This study found 346,000 hospitalizations associated with the excess levels of air pollution in urban areas. Table China.2 summarizes the estimated health impact of both ambient and indoor air pollution in China (37).

In China, the effects of outdoor air pollution are compounded by those of indoor air pollution. Households using coal for domestic cooking and heating are especially at risk because coal emits very high levels of indoor particulate matter less than 2.5 microns in size—the size believed to be most hazardous to health. (These concentrations can be more than 100 times the proposed U.S. ambient air 24-hour standard.) Exposure to these small-sized particles is especially harmful because they persist in the environment and reach deep into the lungs (38).

Indoor air pollution affects both urban and rural populations. Nor is it simply a problem indoors: numerous studies have shown that intense indoor coal burning can affect ambient air quality as well. For instance, rural neighborhoods are generally unaffected by urban sources of air pollutants but can be extremely polluted from the burning of coal indoors. Table China.3 shows the extremely high levels of particulates in both rural and urban indoor environments (39). Indoor air pollution causes as many health problems as smoking, with the effects concentrated among women and children (40).

Although the proportion of China's households that burn polluting biomass fuels indoors for cooking and heating remains significant, it has been declining with the proliferation of alternative energy sources. Largely as a result of government investments, about one third of urban Chinese now have access to gas for cooking, and coal-burning households are increasingly turning to the use of cleaner, more efficient briquettes (41).

Perhaps the most compelling example of the health impact from indoor air pollution is the extremely high lung cancer rates among nonsmoking women in rural Xuan Wei County. Studies conducted by the United States Environmental Protection Agency (U.S. EPA) report that in the three communes with the highest mortality rates, the age-adjusted lung cancer mortality rate between 1973 and 1979 was 125.6 per 100,000 women, compared with

Air Quality May Be Worse Indoors

TABLE CHINA.3 Indoor Particulate Air Pollution from Coal Burning in China (Sample Studies)

PLACE	URBAN/ RURAL	PARTICULATES (micrograms per cubic meter)
Shanghai	Urban	500–1,000
Beijing	Urban	17–1,100[a]
Shenyang	Urban	125–270
Taiyuan	Urban	300–1,000
Harbin	Urban	390–610[a]
Guangzhou	Urban	460
Chengde	Urban	270–700[a]
Yunnan	Rural	270–5,100
Beijing	Rural	400–1,300
Jilin	Rural	1,000–1,200[a]
Hebei	Rural	1,900–2,500
Inner Mongolia	Rural	400–1,600[a]

Source: World Health Organization (WHO), *Health and Environment in Sustainable Development: Five Years after the Earth Summit* (WHO, Geneva, 1997), p. 86.

Note: a. Particles less than 10 micrometers in size.

average rates of 3.2 and 6.3 for Chinese and U.S. women, respectively, for the same time. Because surveys showed that virtually no women (in the county) smoked tobacco products, other sources of potent exposure must have contributed to these troubling rates. Analyses of indoor air and blood samples from the women indicate that fuel burning inside the home was largely responsible for the lung cancers. The U.S. EPA studies found a strong association between the existence of lung cancer in females and the duration of time spent cooking food indoors. The levels of carcinogenic compounds present in smoky coal (a local type of coal that smokes copiously) were found to be much higher in the women who used smoky coal for cooking (42)(43).

Since the 1980s, a number of studies examining the relationship between ambient air pollution and health effects in China have been conducted. It is important to remember that although the studies measured only ambient air pollution levels, in reality people are exposed to a combination of indoor and outdoor air. One of most definitive of these studies examined the relationship between air pollution and mortality in two residential areas of Beijing. According to this study, the risk of mortality was estimated to in-

Air Pollution's Toll

TABLE CHINA.2 Estimates of Respiratory Damage That Could Be Avoided by Meeting Class 2 Air Quality Standards in China

PROBLEM	NUMBER OF CASES AVERTED
Urban air pollution	
Premature deaths	178,000
Respiratory hospital admissions	346,000
Emergency room visits	6,779,000
Lower respiratory infections or child asthma	661,000
Asthma attacks	75,107,000
Chronic bronchitis	1,762,000
Respiratory symptoms	5,270,175,000
Restricted activity days (years)	4,537,000
Indoor air pollution	
Premature deaths	111,000
Respiratory hospital admissions	220,000
Emergency room visits	4,310,000
Lower respiratory infections or child asthma	420,000
Asthma attacks	47,755
Chronic bronchitis	1,121,000
Respiratory symptoms	3,322,631,000
Restricted activity days (years)	2,885,000

Source: The World Bank, *Clear Water, Blue Skies: China's Environment in the New Century* (The World Bank, Washington, D.C., 1997), Table 2.1, p. 19.

crease by 11 percent with each doubling of SO_2 concentration, and by 4 percent with each doubling of TSP. When the specific causes of mortality were examined, mortality from COPD increased 38 percent with a doubling of particulate levels and 29 percent with doubling of SO_2. Pulmonary heart disease mortality also increased significantly with higher pollution levels. Levels of air pollution measured often exceeded WHO guidelines, particularly in winter when ambient air pollution was exacerbated by indoor fuel burning and climatic conditions. Yet, what was striking is that excess mortality was associated with pollutant levels below WHO guidelines, suggesting that the guidelines cannot be perceived as a safe limit [44].

Respiratory diseases, hospitalization, or doctor visits are often a more sensitive measure of the impact of air pollution on human health than mortality. One recent study confirmed that as concentrations of SO_2 and TSP rose in Beijing, so did visits to the emergency room. This increase in unscheduled hospital visits occurred both when air pollution levels were extremely high (primarily in the winter) and when the levels were below WHO's recommended guidelines, bolstering studies in developed countries that have shown excess respiratory disease and mortality at lower doses [45]. Although Beijing has been the focus of many studies, it has no monopoly on bad air. Chongqing, the largest and most recently declared autonomous zone, has a higher concentration of SO_2 than any of China's five other largest cities [46]. A recent study found that several symptoms of compromised health, including reduced pulmonary function and increased mortality, hospital admissions, and emergency room visits, were correlated with higher levels of air pollution in Chongqing [47]. A study conducted in another of China's largest cities, Shenyang, estimated total mortality increased by 2 percent with each 100 micrograms per cubic meter increase in SO_2 concentration, and by 1 percent for each 100 micrograms per cubic meter in TSP [48].

Respiratory diseases are not the only health impacts of concern associated with air pollution. Lead exposure, for instance, leads to neurological damage, particularly in children. China has no comprehensive national data on blood-lead levels, a reliable biomarker of exposure, but some studies show that blood-lead levels are far above the threshold associated with impaired intelligence, neurobehavioral development, and physical growth. (The U.S. standard is 10 micrograms per deciliter.) Between 65 and 100 percent of children in Shanghai have blood-lead levels greater than 10 micrograms per deciliter. Those in industrialized or congested areas had levels averaging between 21 and 67 deciliters [49]. In Shanghai, prenatal exposures to lead from urban air were associated with adverse development in the children during their first year of life [50].

Water Scarcity, Water Pollution, and Health

China's rapid economic growth, industrialization, and urbanization—accompanied by inadequate infrastructure investment and management capacity—have all contributed to widespread problems of water scarcity and water pollution throughout the country. China has some of the most extreme water shortages in the world. Of the 640 major cities in China, more than 300 face water shortages, with 100 facing severe scarcities [51]. As discharges of both domestic and industrial effluents have increased, clean water has become increasingly scarce. The impact of China's dual problem of water scarcity and water pollution exacts a costly toll on productivity. Water shortages in cities cause a loss of an estimated 120 billion yuan (US$11.2 billion) in industrial output each year. The impact of water pollution on human health has been valued at approximately 41.73 billion yuan per year (US$3.9 billion), which is almost certainly an underestimate [52]. Although Chinese decisionmakers are increasingly concerned about the damages associated with water pollution, years of neglect and a lack of funding for research

have resulted in limited data on water pollution and even fewer epidemiologic studies on the links between water pollution and human health effects.

China has a total of 2,800 billion cubic meters of annually renewed fresh water; the world's most populous country is fourth in the world in terms of total water resources [53]. Considering per capita water resources, China has the second lowest per capita water resources in the world, less than one third the world average. Northern China is especially water-poor, with only 750 cubic meters per capita; this geographic region has one fifth the per capita water resources of southern China and just 10 percent of the world average [54].

The distribution of groundwater is similarly skewed: average groundwater resources in the South are more than four times greater than in the North. Dramatic shifts in annual and monthly precipitation cause floods and droughts, which further threaten economic growth.

As surface water quality has worsened, the Chinese have increased their extraction of groundwater to meet water demand. As a result, overextraction of groundwater has become a serious problem in a number of cities including Nanjing, Taiyuan, Shijiazhuang, and Xi'an. Groundwater depletion is most problematic in coastal cities, including Dalian, Qingdao, Yantai, and Beihai, where saltwater intrusion is on the rise [55]. Although there is no comprehensive monitoring of China's groundwater, studies suggest that groundwater quality, not just quantity, is severely threatened in many regions. According to one estimate, one half the groundwater in Chinese cities has been contaminated [56].

INDUSTRIAL AND MUNICIPAL WASTEWATER THREATENS CHINA'S WATER QUALITY

Each year, large amounts of pollutants are dumped into China's water bodies from municipal, industrial, and agricultural sources. China is the world's largest consumer of synthetic nitrogen fertilizers [57]. As a result of these activities, pollu-

Environmental Change and Human Health

tion is widespread in China's rivers, lakes, and reservoirs. Except for some inland rivers and large reservoirs, water pollution trends in China have worsened in recent years, with the pollution adjacent to industrially developed cities and towns being particularly severe (58).

Some of the major threats to water quality stem from inadequate treatment of both municipal and industrial wastewater. In 1995, China discharged a total of 37.29 billion cubic tons of wastewater, not including wastewater from township-and-village enterprises (TVEs), into lakes, rivers, and reservoirs. Approximately 60 percent was released from industrial sources, the rest from municipal. With only 77 percent of industrial wastewater receiving any treatment in 1995, nearly one half of the industrial wastewater discharged failed to meet government standards (59). Industrial discharges usually contain a range of toxic pollutants including petroleum, cyanide, arsenic, solvents, and heavy metals (60).

Although the amount of wastewater discharged from regulated industries has leveled off since the early 1990s, discharges from TVEs and municipal sources have increased rapidly (61). The increase from TVEs can be traced to the rising proportion of total industrial output from these enterprises and to a lack of pollution control over these enterprises because of their widely scattered geographical distribution. In addition, local authorities are reluctant to tighten control over pollution when pursuit of economic benefits is their first goal.

Treatment of municipal sewage lags far behind that of industrial wastewater. In 1995, China had only 100 modern wastewater treatment plants (62). Beijing had only one secondary sewage treatment plant, with a capacity of 500,000 metric tons, which cannot keep pace with the increasing amounts of sewage in the city (63). Treatment should improve rapidly, however, following the amendment of the Water Pollution Prevention and Control Law (64), which set more restrictive regulations, as well as a recent government de-

cision requiring all cities with a population of more than 500,000 to have at least one sewage treatment plant (65).

Water bodies near urban areas are generally the most severely polluted, and the situation is deteriorating. Many urban sections of rivers are polluted by toxic and even carcinogenic compounds, such as arsenic. Although most Chinese attempt to protect themselves from bad water by boiling it, boiling does not affect many of the toxins.

Biological contamination remains a problem as well. Indeed, fecal coliform, mostly from sewage, has become the most challenging drinking water pollutant in the country. In 1994, 54 out of 134 rivers tested did not meet Grade 4 and 5 surface water standards, indicating that the water was deemed unsuitable for even industrial or agricultural use. About 90 percent of the sections of rivers around urban areas were found to be seriously polluted. Because heavy industry is concentrated in northern China, the major river systems in the North are more heavily polluted than those in the South (66). (See Figure China.3.)

HEALTH IMPLICATIONS

Access to Safe Drinking Water is Key to Protecting Public Health

The health of China's people depends, to a great extent, on the quantity and quality of its drinking water supply. Drinking water quality is largely determined by sources of incoming water, modes of water supply, and the level of water treatment. The majority of Chinese urban and some suburban residents now have access to tap water, while the largest portion of the rural population still relies on hand- or motor-pumped wells, or they fetch water directly from rivers, lakes, ponds, or wells, with little or no treatment at all. Large rivers are the most common source of urban drinking water, as well as the major source for rural residents in many parts of the country.

In only 6 of China's 27 largest cities does drinking water quality meet state standards, according to one recent study.

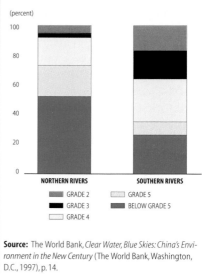

Polluted Rivers

FIGURE CHINA.3   Water Quality Is Low at 135 Monitored Urban River Sections, 1995

(percent)

NORTHERN RIVERS   SOUTHERN RIVERS

GRADE 2   GRADE 5
GRADE 3   BELOW GRADE 5
GRADE 4

Source: The World Bank, *Clear Water, Blue Skies: China's Environment in the New Century* (The World Bank, Washington, D.C., 1997), p. 14.
Note: Grades 4 and 5 are deemed unsuitable for direct human contact.

Groundwater did not meet state standards in 23 of these cities (67). The problem is more pronounced in rural China. In some rural areas, the fecal coliform in the drinking water supply exceeds the maximum level by as much as 86 percent; in towns and small cities, the rate is about 28 percent. Currently, around 700 million people in China drink water that fails to meet state standards for fecal coliform (68).

Over the past decade, the government has launched a major initiative to improve access to safe drinking water in rural areas. From 1991 to 1995, the government spent 14.45 billion yuan (US$1.35 billion) to improve the drinking water supply in rural regions (69). Although the rural population with access to tap water more than doubled between 1987 and 1995, when it reached 47 percent, more than one half of those people still drank water that failed to meet safety standards (70).

Infectious Diseases Associated with Poor Water Quality

Despite an overall decline in mortality from infectious diseases in China, the population still suffers from a number of diseases associated with inadequate drinking water quality and sanitation. For the past two decades, diarrheal diseases and viral hepatitis, both diseases associated with fecal pollution, have been the two leading infectious diseases in China. In 1995, the incidence of hepatitis was 63 per 100,000, a 46 percent decrease from 1991. After a sharp drop from 1991 and 1992, the incidence of dysentery has risen since 1994, in part because of the deterioration of water quality. A sudden upswing in the incidence of typhoid fever in 1991 and a large outbreak in some provinces in 1992 were also partly attributed to the poor drinking water quality in rural areas. In 1991, typhoid fever incidence reached as high as 10.6 per 100,000. Although the incidence of waterborne diseases is still high compared with many other countries, effective medical care has kept mortality low, averaging less than 0.1 per 100,000 (71).

It is more difficult to establish the impacts of industrial and chemical water pollution on human health than pollution by human waste. However, recent epidemiological studies suggest that exposure to organic and inorganic chemicals in drinking water may significantly contribute to chronic disease. Liver and stomach cancers are the leading causes of cancer mortality in rural China. Many studies in China and abroad have shown a strong association between drinking water pollution and cancer incidence and mortality. An example is a study conducted in Lujiang County, Anhui Province, where mortality rates for stomach and liver cancers were associated with the high levels of inorganic substances in surface water (72). Although diet and alcohol consumption may play some role in the increases of these cancers, environmental causes cannot be dismissed (73). Since the 1970s, deaths from liver cancer have doubled—China now has the highest liver cancer death rate in the world (74).

In southern China, where some of the population has long depended on ponds for drinking water, the rates of digestive-system cancers are very high. An investigation of 560,000 people in 23 villages and towns showed that between 1987 and 1989, cancer mortality was 172 per

100,000, which is much greater than the average mortality rates in rural China (75). Gastric, esophageal, and liver cancers accounted for 85 percent of all cancers. Other studies reported that the high incidence of liver cancer in Jiangsu's Qidong and Guangxi's Fushun regions is highly correlated with drinking water pollution (76)(77). Further research is needed to confirm this link and identify the specific pollutants at fault.

Impact of Wastewater Irrigation on Health

Irrigation with wastewater has been a common practice in many parts of China throughout its 2,000-year-old agricultural history. In the past several decades, however, the age-old practice of using night soil has been supplemented by the use of industrial wastewater as well, leading to problems with both biological and chemical contaminants. Irrigation with industrial wastes is especially common in the northern regions, where water is scarce. Pollutants, including some organic pollutants, heavy metals, and carcinogens, enter the food chain in the irrigation process and can affect human health.

Numerous studies since the 1970s have shown significant increases in cancer rates and deaths, as well as birth defects, in areas that rely on wastewater for irrigation. For example, research in Shenyang and Fushun showed that the incidence of intestinal infections and enlargement of the liver was, respectively, 49 percent and 36 percent higher in the irrigated areas than in the control area. There were twice as many cancer patients in the sewage-irrigated area. In Fushun, in Liaoning Province, more than 13,000 hectares of farmland are irrigated with water polluted with oil. The adjusted rate of malignant tumor mortality was almost twice that of the control area, and the incidence of congenital malformation was double the rate in the control area (78). Although these associations raise alarms, they do not prove that wastewater is to blame.

Township-and-Village Enterprises: Lack of Regulation Poses Major Threat to Health and Environment

The rapid development of TVEs will have an enormous impact on China's water quality in the coming years. Although their development can be traced back to the late 1950s, these enterprises boomed in the past 10 years. The economic success of the TVEs has reduced poverty for millions of farmers, but they have also inflicted severe damage on the environment in rural China. Even though the Chinese Government has enacted a number of laws and policies to control and regulate industrial discharges (79), the government has not yet effectively regulated TVEs (80).

By 1995, more than 7 million TVEs existed throughout China, with a total output of 5.126 trillion yuan (US$671 billion), accounting for 56 percent of the total industrial GDP—considerably more than the contribution of state-owned enterprises. The number of TVEs is expected to continue to grow. A conservative estimate holds that the TVEs discharge more than half of all industrial wastewater in China—more than 10 billion metric tons. Most TVEs have no wastewater or hazardous waste treatment facilities, and since TVEs are widely scattered across vast rural areas, wastes from TVEs have the potential to affect the health of many people (81).

A 1989–1991 investigation of the 10 leading TVE industries in seven provinces and municipalities showed that industrial wastes were discharged without any treatment and control. An analysis of the health of 860,000 people in the area revealed that the incidence rate of chronic diseases was between 12 and 29 percent, much higher than the national average for rural areas, which is approximately 9 percent. The total mortality in polluted areas averaged 4.7 per 1,000, higher than the average 3.6 in the control area. Life expectancy in the polluted areas was 2 years lower than in the control area. Although not definitive, evidence suggests that industrial pollution from TVEs could become a major threat to human health in China (82).

Environmental Change and Human Health

Laws and Policies to Protect the Environment and Health

China's achievements in health and life expectancy over the past four decades have far exceeded what could be expected for a country at its stage of economic development, according to a recent World Bank evaluation. Behind these dramatic gains in public health was an extraordinary campaign for the Chinese people carried out by the central government, which provided family planning, childhood immunization, accessible primary health care (particularly for mothers and children), improved nutrition, infectious disease control, better education, and improvements in housing and sanitation. (See Table China.4.) Morbidity and mortality from infectious diseases continue to decline on average in most areas of China, although in remote and poor regions, the levels of communicable disease remain much higher than the national averages. The overall success of these programs can be attributed to the central government's approach of adopting the best of traditional methods and wedding these with modern methods. For instance, a campaign to eradicate major public health scourges, such as diphtheria and syphilis, succeeded in large part because it involved vast numbers of traditional doctors in the rural areas (83).

Along with rising income and improved literacy rates, the era of reform has brought more environmental awareness to the Chinese people. A few recent studies in China showed that as communities have become wealthier and better educated, the public has begun to push for stronger regulations and enforcement (84). The increase in media coverage of pollution accidents has contributed to the public's awareness. A popular saying in China's developed eastern region is, "The house is new, the money is enough, but the water is foul and the life is short" (85).

How will China set priorities to prevent environmental exposures and protect public health? Although the government has already begun to address particulate

Most Chinese Have Safe Water and Sanitation

TABLE CHINA.4 Access to Safe Drinking Water and Sanitation Among Selected Countries in Asia, 1990

| | PERCENTAGE OF THE POPULATION WITH ACCESS TO | | | | | |
| | SAFE DRINKING WATER | | | SANITATION [a] | | |
COUNTRY	URBAN	RURAL	TOTAL	URBAN	RURAL	TOTAL
China	87	68	72	100	81	85
India	86	69	73	44	3	14
Indonesia	35	33	34	79	30	45
Sri Lanka	80	55	60	68	45	50
Japan	100	85	96	100	100	100

Source: The World Bank, *Clear Water, Blue Skies: China's Environment in the New Century* (The World Bank, Washington, D.C., 1997), Table 2.2, p. 20.

Notes: a. Assumes that residents have access to water for washing and that sewage is removed from the house through outdoor latrines, night-soil collection systems, or flush toilets.

and SO_2 emissions, much remains to be done. While regulatory standards will likely reduce emissions from power plants and state-regulated industries, smaller residential sources and TVE industries will continue to threaten air quality. Residential coal burning for cooking and heating will continue to be a major source of exposure until there is more universal adoption of cleaner fuels. Even though the government has focused some attention on mobile source pollution, it will be a difficult problem to address, given the rapid expansion of the fleet of vehicles.

ENVIRONMENTAL LAWS AND REGULATIONS

Since the promulgation of the Environmental Protection Law in 1979, the first of its kind in China, 5 pollution-control statutes and 10 natural resource conservation statutes have been enacted. The Environmental Protection and Natural Resources Conservation Committee of the National People's Congress, the lawmaking arm, submitted a 5-Year Legislative Plan to the National People's Congress in 1993. According to the plan, approximately 7 key environment and natural resource statutes will be created or amended by 1998, and more than 17 such statutes will be created or amended by the end of this century. The United States, by comparison, has passed approximately 21 major environmental acts in the last four decades.

The Energy Conservation Law was passed on November 1, 1997, and came

into force on January 1, 1998. The scope of this law extends to energy from coal, crude oil, natural gas, electric power, coke, coal gas, thermal power, biomass power, and other energy sources. This law may be the harbinger of strengthened efforts by the Chinese Government to prohibit certain new industrial projects that seriously waste energy and employ outmoded technologies.

Despite the complex system of legislative and policy tools in place and the network of environmental officials throughout China, compliance with environmental regulations remains low, essentially because economic development remains the country's priority at all levels of society.

As part of its efforts to strengthen environmental law enforcement, the government revised its criminal code to punish violations against the environment and resources. This step may provide law enforcement agencies with some power. However, the vagueness of standards in many laws and regulations, coupled with the lack of a comprehensive enforcement regime, has led to a situation where many environmental laws still reflect deals cut between the local environmental protection agencies, NEPA, other ministries, local government bodies, and the polluting enterprises. Thus, the degree of actual compliance and enforcement depends on the region concerned and the personalities involved. Often, the richer the potential investor, the more strictly environmental policy will be applied (86).

For the next decade or so, China's rapid development will likely lead to further uncertainty in the regulatory regime. In the meantime, an increasing array of resources are being devoted to enforcement, and discussions are currently underway to elevate NEPA to ministerial status, which may give NEPA more leverage and authority in law enforcement. Nonetheless, many Chinese officials adamantly hold that economic development must come before environmental protection. They also disagree about how stringent environmental initiatives need to be to protect the health of billions of citizens while maintaining economic growth. This internal struggle enhances the paradoxical quality of Chinese environmental law, which may at once appear both simple and complex, or lenient and severe (87).

USING ECONOMIC INSTRUMENTS— HARNESSING THE MARKET

In its transition from a command to a market economy, China is trying to harness the market to work for the environment rather than against it. Continued and accelerated economic reform is a prerequisite to reorient state enterprises so that they respond to environmental penalties. Liberating international trade will give Chinese industry access to the latest environmental technology. The development of capital markets is necessary to provide financing to firms and municipalities supplying environmental infrastructure. Adjustments of the pricing system are needed to ensure that it reflects true environmental costs.

Despite the fact that China is resource-poor, it prices its energy and water far lower than the actual costs. However, great strides are being made to rectify this situation. Over the past 3 years, the government has raised and partly deregulated coal prices; in most areas, coal prices now cover the costs of production and delivery. In addition, many cities and provinces are currently preparing to increase sewage and water charges to consumers and industries. In Taiyuan of Shanxi Province, for instance, the price bureau has announced that water prices will quadruple over the next 5 years

in order to recover supply costs (88). Shanghai recently increased tap water prices by between 25 and 40 percent to fund water quality improvement programs and to make sewage self-financing. Guangzhou and Chongqing are eager to do the same (89).

The increasing market orientation of the industrial sector offers an opportunity to use market-based pollution controls more effectively. Achieving pollution control objectives will require increasing pollution charges. NEPA has proposed a 10-fold increase in the air pollution levy; this increase would go a long way toward reducing air pollutant emissions. Higher levies are needed both to lower current emissions and to finance the large investment required to achieve desired ambient air quality in Chinese cities. Currently, the pollution levies are assessed only on discharges that exceed the standard; in other words, emissions cost the polluter nothing until the standards are breached. Moreover, effluent charges are based on the pollutant that exceeds the standard by the greatest amount and do not reflect the risks posed by other pollutants. The World Bank has been working with NEPA to overcome these shortcomings. These two organizations are developing a system that incorporates both maximum discharge rates for all pollutants as well as incentives to encourage emissions at levels below the maximum allowed (90).

INCREASING ENVIRONMENTAL INVESTMENT

Environmental protection demands more spending. The Chinese Government has attributed the continued deterioration of the environment largely to lack of funding. Despite extremely ambitious 5-year plans to control environmental pollution in the past, insufficient investment has prevented realization of these goals. Now in its Ninth 5-Year Plan period, the government has adopted the Trans-Century Green Plan, which sets targets for environmental protection for the year 2010. In conjunction with other environmental protection plans, NEPA is striving to stabilize the emissions of several pollutants

at 1995 levels by the year 2000. The percentage of SO_2, particulates, untreated sewage, and heavy metals sewage treated would be increased from its current 19 percent to 25 percent, and treatment of industrial wastewater would be expanded by about 70 million metric tons. This ambitious plan, which NEPA estimates will cost 450 billion yuan (1.3 percent of China's GNP) to achieve, accords top priority to certain areas, especially along the east coast and in some parts of its inner land: the Hai, Huai, and Liao rivers; the Chao, Dianchi, and Tai lakes; and two areas in southwest China with pronounced problems with SO_2 levels and acid rain (91).

Industries and local governments are increasingly looking for new sources of funding, through the "polluter pays" principle, urban environmental infrastructure funds, and even bank loans. The central government is playing a more supportive role in seeking loans and foreign investment and implementing economic policies. The government intends to increase the proportion of GNP spent on controlling pollution from the current 0.8 percent to more than 1 percent at the turn of the century, or approximately 188 billion yuan (US$17.5 billion) (92). Some cities are investing in an even higher proportion. For instance, Beijing, Shanghai, and Xiamen have decided to allocate up to 3 percent of their GDP to pollution control. Tianjin will set aside up to 2 percent (93). In the meantime, China also hopes that foreign investment will continue to provide funds supporting its ambitious plans to address pollution. A recent World Bank report noted that investing about 1 percent of GDP each year gradually rising to 2.5 percent over the next 25 years—divided roughly equally between air and water investment—would greatly reduce pollution in China by 2020 (94). The report also noted that the operating and the average investment costs each year of such a program would gradually rise to about 2.5 percent of GDP by the end of the period. According to the World Bank, the benefits of these measures exceed the costs by large margins, and these measures are es-

*E*nvironmental Change and Human Health

sential if China is to redirect its development toward a more sustainable path.

---

*Changhua Wu, Michelle Gottlieb, and **Devra Davis**,
Health, Environment, and Development Program,
World Resources Institute, Washington, D.C.*

References and Notes

1. The World Bank, *World Development Indicators 1997*, on CD-ROM (The World Bank, Washington, D.C., 1997).

2. Jonathan Sinton, ed., *China Energy Databook, 1996 Revision* (University of California at Berkeley, Berkeley, 1996), p. x-12.

3. International Labour Organization (ILO), *Economically Active Population, 1950–2010: Vol. 1, Asia* (ILO, Geneva, 1996), p. 205.

4. The World Bank, *World Development Indicators 1997* (The World Bank, Washington, D.C., 1997), p. 130.

5. International Energy Agency, *Energy Statistics and Balances: Non-OECD Countries, 1971–1995*, on diskette (Organisation for Economic Co-Operation and Development, Paris, 1997).

6. United Nations (U.N.) Population Division, *Urban and Rural Areas 1950–2030 (The 1996 Revision)*, on diskette, (U.N., New York, 1997).

7. Li Junfeng et al., *Energy Demand in China: Overview Report, Issues and Options in Greenhouse Gas Emissions Control Subreport Number 2* (The World Bank, Washington, D.C., 1995), p. 17.

8. China Ministry of Public Health, *Selected Edition on Health Statistics of China 1991–1995* (China Ministry of Public Health, Beijing, 1996), p. 3.

9. Chen Junshi et al., *Diet, Lifestyle, and Mortality in China: A Study of the Characteristics of 65 Chinese Counties*, published in the U.K. by Oxford University Press, Oxford; in the United States by Cornell University Press, Ithaca; and in China by the People's Medical Publishing House, Beijing (Oxford University Press, Oxford, 1990), p. 73.

10. National Environmental Protection Agency (NEPA), *1996 Report on the State of the Environment* (NEPA, Beijing, 1997) (Chinese language edition).

11. Qian Chen, "Improve the Eco-Environment and Rebuild the Beautiful Mountains and Rivers," *China Environment News* (September 13, 1997), p. A.

12. The World Bank, *Clear Water, Blue Skies: China's Environment in the New Century* (The World Bank, Washington, D.C., 1997), p. 23.

13. *Op. cit.* 10.

14. Zhang Jianguang, "Environmental Hazards in the Chinese Public's Eyes," *Risk Analysis*, Vol. 14, No. 2 (1994), p. 165.

15. Outlined in National Environmental Protection Agency (NEPA), *The National Ninth 5-Year Plan for Environmental Protection and the Long-Term Targets for the Year 2010* (NEPA, Beijing, 1996).

16. Fang Cai, "Stare Into the Sky—When Will It be Clear?," *China Environment News* (January 21, 1997), p. 1.

17. National Environmental Protection Agency (NEPA), *National Environmental Quality Report, 1991–1995* (NEPA, Beijing, 1996), pp. 5, 15.

18. *Op cit.* 12, pp. 8–9.

19. China Environment Yearbook, *China Environment Yearbook*, various issues (China Environment Yearbook Press, Beijing, various years) (Chinese language editions).

20. International Energy Agency, *Energy Statistics and Balances: Non-OECD Countries, 1971–1995*, and *Energy Statistics and Balances: OECD Countries,* *1960–1995*, both on diskette (Organisation for Economic Co-Operation and Development, Paris, 1997).

21. *Op. cit.* 2, p. iv-11.

22. *Op. cit.* 19.

23. *Op. cit.* 7, p. 43.

24. *Op. cit.* 2, p. viii-2.

25. *Op. cit.* 12, pp. 21–22, map 1.

26. *Op. cit.* 12, pp. 8, 46.

27. *Op. cit.* 2, p. v-4.

28. American Automobile Manufacturers Association (AAMA), *Motor Vehicle Facts and Figures* (AAMA, Washington, D.C., 1996), pp. 44–47.

29. Stephen Stares and Liu Zhi, "Motorization in Chinese Cities: Issues and Actions," in *China's Urban Transport Development Strategy: Proceedings of a Symposium in Beijing, November 8–10, 1995*, World Bank Discussion Paper No. 352 (The World Bank, Washington, D.C., 1996), p. 50.

30. Liu Xianshu and Xiao Yunxiang, "How to Enjoy and Use Automobiles," *China Environment News* (January 28, 1997), p. 1.

31. Michael Walsh, "Motor Vehicle Pollution in China: An Urban Challenge," in *China's Urban Transport Development Strategy: Proceedings of a Symposium in Beijing, November 8–10, 1995*, World Bank Discussion Paper No. 352 (The World Bank, Washington, D.C., 1996), pp. 118–122.

32. He Kebin et al., "The Status and Trend of Urban Vehicular Pollution," *Environmental Science*, Vol. 17, No. 4 (1996), pp. 80–83 (in Chinese).

33. He Kebin et al., "Status and Developments in China's Vehicle Emissions Pollution," *Environmental Science*, Vol. 7, No. 4 (1996), pp. 15–17 (in Chinese).

34. *Ibid.*

35. *Op. cit.* 31, p. 120.

36. *Op. cit.* 12, pp. 17–18.

37. *Op. cit.* 12, Table 2.1, p. 19.

38. World Health Organization (WHO), *Health and Environment in Sustainable Development: Five Years After the Earth Summit* (WHO, Geneva, 1997), p. 82.

39. *Ibid.*, pp. 83–86.

40. *Op. cit.* 12, p. 19.

41. *Op. cit.* 12, p. 19.

42. Robert S. Chapman et al., "Assessing Indoor Air Pollution Exposure and Lung Cancer Risk in Xuan Wei, China," *Journal of the American College of Toxicology*, Vol. 8, No. 5 (1989), pp. 941–948.

43. Judy L. Mumford et al., "DNA Adducts As Biomarkers for Assessing Exposure to Polycyclic Aromatic Hydrocarbons in Tissues from Xuan Wei Women with High Exposure to Coal Combustion Emissions and High Lung Cancer Mortality," *Environmental Health Perspectives*, Vol. 99 (1993), pp. 83–87.

44. Xu Xiping et al., "Air Pollution and Daily Mortality in Residential Areas of Beijing, China," *Archives of Environmental Health*, Vol. 49, No. 4 (1994), pp. 216–222.

45. Xu Xiping, Li Bauluo, and Huang Huying, "Air Pollution and Unscheduled Hospital Outpatient and Emergency Room Visits," *Archives of Environmental Health*, Vol. 103, No. 3 (1995), pp. 286–289.

46. China Environment Yearbook, *China Environment Yearbook, 1996* (China Environment Yearbook Press, Beijing, 1997), p. 193 (Chinese language edition).

47. *Op. cit.* 12, p. 18.

48. Xu Zhaoyi et al., "The Effect of Air Pollution on Mortality in Shenyang City," *Journal of Public Health in China*, Vol. 15, No. 1 (1996), p. 61.

49. *Op. cit.* 12, p. 20.

50. Shen Xiao-Ming et al., "Prenatal Low-Level Lead Exposure and Infant Development in the First Year: A Prospective Study in Shanghai, China," paper presented to the International Society for Environmental Epidemiology, University of Alberta, Edmunton, Canada, August 1996.

51. *Op. cit.* 10.

52. *Op. cit.* 12, pp. 23, 87–88.

53. See Data Table 12.1.

54. *Op. cit.* 12, p. 88.

55. *Op. cit.* 10.

56. Zhang Weiping et al., eds., *Twenty Years of China's Environmental Protection Administrative Management* (China Environmental Sciences Press, Beijing, 1994), pp. 215–217.

57. Food and Agriculture Organization of the United Nations (FAO), *FAOSTAT Statistical Database* (FAO, Rome, 1996–1997).

58. Vaclav Smil, "China Shoulders the Cost of Environmental Change," *Environment*, Vol. 39, No. 6 (1996), p. 33.

59. *Op. cit.* 10.

60. *Op. cit.* 46.

61. *Op. cit.* 10.

62. China Environment Yearbook, *China Environment Yearbook, 1996* (China Environment Yearbook Press, Beijing, 1997), p. 215 (English language edition).

63. Xiaoke Jiang, Former Director, Beijing's Environmental Protection Bureau, Beijing, 1998 (personal communication).

64. The Water Pollution Prevention and Control Law, initially adopted in 1984, was amended in 1996.

65. This is a decision announced at the 4th National Conference on Environmental Protection, which was convened in Beijing in September 1996.

66. *Op. cit.* 10.

67. Vaclav Smil, *Environmental Problems in China: Estimates of Economic Costs*, East-West Center Special Report No. 5 (East-West Center, Honolulu, 1996), pp. 2, 24.

68. Cai Shiwen, "China's Environmental Pollution and Health Problem," paper presented at the Second Conference of the China Council of International Cooperation and Development, Beijing, 1993.

69. China Ministry of Public Health, *China Yearbook of Public Health 1996* (People's Medical Publishing House, Beijing, 1997), pp. 416–417.

70. Zhang Feng et al., "Status and Analysis of Rural Drinking Water Quality," *Journal of Hygiene Research*, Vol. 26, No. 1 (1997), pp. 30–32.

71. China Ministry of Public Health, *Selected Edition on Health Statistics of China, 1991–95* (China Ministry of Public Health, Beijing, 1996), pp. 69–70.

72. Guili Chen, "The Warning of Huai River," *Contemporary Magazine*, Vol. 2 (1996).

73. Howard Frumpkin, "Cancer of the Liver and Gastrointestinal Tract," in *Textbook of Clinical Occupational and Environmental Medicine* (W.B. Saunders Co., Philadelphia, 1994), p. 576.

74. Feng Rukang, "China Maps Out Geographical Belt of Liver Cancer," *China Environment News* (October 15, 1997), p. 8.

75. Su Delong, "Drinking Water and Liver Cancer," *Journal of Chinese Preventative Medicine*, Vol. 14, No. 2 (1990), pp. 65–73.

76. Liang et al., "Epidemiologic Investigation of Relationships Between Drinking Water Types and Liver Cancer," *Cancers*, Vol. 6, No. 3 (1987), p. 177 (in Chinese).

77. Tang He and Lin Nianfeng, "The Relationship Between Organic Water Pollution and Liver Cancer at Fushui in Guangxi," *Journal of Environment and Health*, Vol. 12, No. 5 (1995), pp. 193–195 (in Chinese).

78. Yuan, "Etiologic Study of High Stomach Cancer Incidence Among Residents in Wastewater Irrigated

Areas," *Environmental Protection Science*, Vol. 19, No. 1 (1993), pp. 70–73 (in Chinese).

79. Such policies include pollution levies and permits.

80. Cao Fenzhong, "Air and Water Pollution Problems in TVEs," a policy paper prepared for the Chinese National Environmental Protection Agency (NEPA) (NEPA, Beijing, 1997), p. 1.

81. *Ibid.*, pp. 1–5.

82. Xu Fang *et al.*, "Economic Analysis and Counter-measure Study of TVEs Pollution's Damage to Human Health," *Journal of Hygiene Research*, Vol. 21, Supplement (1992), pp. 1–23.

83. "Decision on Public Health Reform and Development by the Central Committee of the Chinese Communist Party and the State Council," *People's Daily* (February 18, 1997, Beijing), p. 1.

84. *Op. cit.* 12, p. 13.

85. *Report of the 4th National Conference on Environmental Protection* (China Environmental Sciences Press, Beijing, 1996), p. 32.

86. *Op. cit.* 83.

87. Richard J. Ferris Jr., "The People's Republic of China: An Environmental Law Briefing for Corporate Council," *The Metropolitan Corporate Counsel* (December 1997), p. 13.

88. *Op. cit.* 12, pp. 95–96.

89. Shuping Lu, Director, Shanghai Environmental Protection Agency, 1998 (personal communication).

90. Dr. Hua Wang, Consultant and Principal Economist in the Environment, Infrastructure, and Agriculture Division, Policy Research Department, The World Bank, Washington, D.C., 1997 (personal communication).

91. *Op. cit.* 15, p. 12.

92. *Op. cit.* 15, p. 4.

93. Wang Yi, Professor/Senior Scientist, Eco-Environment Research Center of the Chinese Academy of Sciences, 1997 (personal communication).

94. The World Bank, *Can the Environment Wait? Priorities for East Asia* (The World Bank, Washington, D.C., 1997), p. 1.

Environmental Risks to Human Health: New Indicators

As presented in Chapter 1, the World Resources Institute (WRI) has developed new environmental health indicators that describe environmental risks to human health in both developing and developed countries. The indicators rank countries according to potential environmental threats to human health. Set out below is a description of the methods used to compile the maps shown in Chapter 1. (Supporting data are available online at: http://www.wri.org/wri/.)

Developing Countries

For developing countries, the indicator aggregates measures of environmental risks to human health from three categories: air, water, and nutrition. Each category includes three variables described below. In some cases, selected variables for the indicator were simply added, averaged, and ranked from lowest to highest. In other cases, the variables were constructed using several data sets that were combined in a way to represent potential exposure to an environmental health threat.

AIR QUALITY

The air portion of the indicator for developing countries includes three variables representing potential exposure to poor quality air: exposure to polluted indoor air, exposure to polluted ambient air, and exposure to air polluted with lead from gasoline. Each of these three variables was estimated using the best available data. For example, exposure to polluted indoor air was calculated using the amount of residential coal and biomass fuel consumed per household in each country. WRI divided the total amount of residential coal and biomass fuel consumed per country by the total number of households within that country.

When the amount of residential coal and biomass fuel burned per country was not available from the International Energy Agency, WRI used data from the United Nations (*Energy Yearbook*) on total traditional fuel consumed. WRI subtracted the amount of bagasse produced by each country from the total biomass fuel consumed, assuming that the remainder was used exclusively for residential use. (Bagasse is a residue left after sugar is extracted from sugar cane and is often used as a fuel in the sugar milling industry.) This indicator of exposure to indoor air pollution does not account for confounding factors that can reduce exposure to biomass fuel used indoors such as cooking methods, stove and heater design, house and kitchen design, and ventilation systems.

Potential exposure to polluted ambient air was calculated using the number of cities with air concentration levels of pollutants exceeding World Health Organization (WHO) guidelines (for several gases and particles) and the population of those cities. Pollutants considered include total suspended particulates (TSP), black smoke (BS), particulate matter (PM-10), sulfur dioxide (SO_2), and nitrogen dioxide (NO_2). The final estimate, representing potential exposure to polluted outdoor air, shows the population living in cities with air quality data exceeding WHO guidelines as a percentage of the total population of all cities for which WRI had both air quality and population data. (The city's entire population was considered at risk if any pollutants listed previously exceeded WHO guidelines, using the most recently reported air quality data.)

Data shortcomings complicate the task of estimating potential exposure to polluted air. Consistent and reliable data on air quality for most cities of the world are lacking. In constructing these indicators, bear in mind that the urban population in some countries is represented with data from only one city and that many countries do not have any cities with air quality data and thus could not be included in the indicator. Ambient air quality, however, is important to consider when examining human health and the environment. Even though the data are not comprehensive, they are important to include as one measure of comparing relative environmental health threats among countries.

Exposure to air polluted with lead from gasoline is derived using three variables: the market share of leaded gasoline used in a country, the total amount of gasoline consumed, and the maximum lead content of the gasoline. The leaded gas emission level obtained from multiplying these variables was then weighted with the urban population density to arrive at the final lead exposure measure.

The market share of leaded gasoline and the maximum lead concentration of the gasoline are rapidly changing in many countries of the world. Generally, countries are moving away from using leaded gasoline with high concentrations of lead to either gasoline with lower concentrations of lead or to all lead-free gasoline. Exceptions do occur, however. Between 1995 and 1997, Bulgaria increased its use of leaded gasoline from 87 to 95 percent (1).

To estimate population density of urban areas, WRI combined a database that determines the builtup areas in countries from satellite images of city lights at night with data on urban population from the U.N. Population Division. The *Nighttime Lights of the World* database is a 1 kilometer by 1 kilometer resolution map derived from nighttime imagery from the Defense Meteorological Satellite Program (DMSP) Operational Linescan System (OLS) of the United States. This database contains the locations of stable lights, including frequently observed light sources such as gas flares at oil drilling sites. Time series analysis is used to exclude temporary light sources such as fires and lightning.

Although the lights database provides the best available source for data on builtup areas for countries of the world, it may underestimate the builtup area for countries with densely populated but low-lit areas, such as squatter settlements. This type of underestimation could have the effect of showing an inflated value for exposure to leaded gasoline (the leaded gas would be emitted over a smaller, more densely populated area). However, WRI used the database because it is the best source of information for calculating a relative estimate of urban populations potentially exposed to leaded gas emissions.

WATER QUALITY

The water portion of the indicator for developing countries includes three variables: two represent potential exposure to poor quality water (i.e., percentage of the population without access to safe water and without adequate sanitation), and one represents exposure to insect-borne diseases (i.e., the percentage of the population with malaria). Data regarding access to safe water and adequate sanitation are problematic (as is often pointed out by UNICEF, the agency that publishes these data). Definitions of these situations may vary within and among countries over time; they may be based on descriptive reports of water sources or installed sewage systems, rather than on quantitative measures regarding water quality or distance to the facility for the population served. In addition, although WHO provides recommended values for distance to water supply and sanitation and for quantities available, countries revise these standards. For example, Brazil reports that only toilets on a sewage system are considered an adequate means of excreta disposal. Conversely, many sub-Saharan African countries report access to any kind of pit latrine as access to an adequate means of excreta disposal.

The water portion of the environmental health indicator for developing countries includes a surrogate measure for potential exposure to insect-borne diseases. WRI combined two variables: the number of cases of malaria per country and the country's total population. The final ranked measure is the percentage of the country's total population with malaria. Many environmental factors, including fluctuations in temperature, precipitation, and humidity, are linked with the spread of insect-borne diseases. Although many insect-borne diseases have major impacts on human health (e.g., dengue, leishmaniasis, trypanosomiasis, and schistosomiasis), few comprehensive databases exist. Shortcomings aside, malaria data are one of the better data sets available worldwide for an insect-borne disease.

NUTRITION

The nutrition portion of the developing country indicator includes three variables that represent potential exposure to poor nutrition: percentage of children younger than 5 years of age who are underweight, total number of available calories per person, and percentage of population at risk of developing either vitamin A or iodine deficiency (whichever micronutri-

ent deficiency was higher). These variables are included to underscore the important correlation between adequate food and nutrition and environmental factors.

Underweight children refers to those younger than age 5 whose weight-for-age is below minus 2 standard deviations (for moderate underweight) or below minus 3 standard deviations (for severe underweight) from the median weight-for-age of the reference population. WRI included the number of calories available per person and populations at risk of developing micronutrient deficiencies as potential measures of an adequate diet. The percentage of the population at risk of developing vitamin A deficiency is estimated by WHO using extrapolations from subnational surveys of the proportion of the total country likely to be affected considering similar ecological conditions. The percentage of the population at risk of developing iodine deficiency is estimated by WHO based on the presence of goiter: persons are considered at risk of developing an iodine deficiency disorder if they reside in a geographical region where the total goiter rate in school-aged children (i.e., children 6 to 11 years of age) is equal to, or greater than, 5 percent. WRI divided WHO's estimate for the population at risk by the corresponding population data for the country from the U.N. Population Division.

FINAL RANKING: DEVELOPING COUNTRIES

The three variables within the air, water, and nutrition portions of the developing country indicator were ranked from lowest (lowest relative risk) to highest (highest relative risk). If data were not available for the same number of countries for all of the variables, the ranks of the variables were standardized, or spread, to match the maximum number of ranks for any of the variables within air, water, or nutrition. The three ranks (replaced with a standardized rank when appropriate) were then averaged, and the final average rank was ranked again from lowest to highest risk. To be included in the calculation, each country must have data for at least two variables for air, water, and nutrition.

These calculations were then used to determine a relative rank for the air, water, and nutrition portions of the developing country indicator. The ranks for each portion were then separated into three equal groupings: the first one third represent countries at low relative risk from potential exposure to the environmental health threats, the middle one third represent countries at moderate relative risk of exposure, and the last one third, countries at high relative risk of exposure. Table A.1 shows the low-, medium-, or high-risk scores for each country for each of the air, water, and nutrition portions of the indicator for developing countries.

The next level of aggregation was to combine the ranks of the three portions. Here again, if data were not available for the same number of countries for all of the variables, the ranks of the variables were standardized to match the maximum

*E*nvironmental Change and Human Health

TABLE A.1 Developing Countries

AFRICA / CENTRAL AMERICA

	AIR	WATER	NUTRITION	FINAL RANK
AFRICA				
Algeria	moderate	low	low	low
Angola	X	high	high	high
Benin	high	high	moderate	high
Botswana	X	moderate	moderate	moderate
Burkina Faso	moderate	high	high	high
Burundi	X	high	high	high
Cameroon	high	high	high	high
Central African Rep	X	high	high	high
Chad	low	high	high	high
Congo, Dem Rep	X	high	high	high
Congo, Rep	X	high	moderate	moderate
Côte d'Ivoire	high	moderate	moderate	moderate
Egypt	moderate	moderate	low	low
Equatorial Guinea	X	X	X	X
Eritrea	X	X	X	X
Ethiopia	high	high	high	high
Gabon	X	moderate	low	low
Gambia, The	X	high	high	high
Ghana	high	moderate	moderate	moderate
Guinea	X	high	moderate	high
Guinea-Bissau	X	high	moderate	moderate
Kenya	moderate	moderate	moderate	moderate
Lesotho	X	high	high	high
Liberia	high	high	X	high
Libya	low	low	low	low
Madagascar	X	high	high	high
Malawi	X	high	high	high
Mali	low	high	high	high
Mauritania	X	moderate	moderate	moderate
Mauritius	X	low	low	low
Morocco	low	moderate	low	low
Mozambique	X	moderate	high	moderate
Namibia	X	high	high	high
Niger	low	high	high	high
Nigeria	high	moderate	high	high
Rwanda	X	X	high	X
Senegal	moderate	moderate	moderate	moderate
Sierra Leone	X	high	moderate	high
Somalia	X	high	X	X
South Africa	high	low	low	low
Sudan	X	high	high	high
Swaziland	X	X	low	X
Tanzania	X	high	high	high
Togo	X	high	high	high
Tunisia	low	low	low	low
Uganda	high	moderate	moderate	moderate
Zambia	X	high	high	high
Zimbabwe	X	moderate	moderate	moderate
CENTRAL AMERICA				
Belize	X	X	low	X
Costa Rica	low	low	low	low
Cuba	low	low	low	low
Dominican Rep	low	low	low	low
El Salvador	moderate	low	low	moderate
Guatemala	moderate	moderate	moderate	moderate
Haiti	X	high	high	high
Honduras	X	low	moderate	moderate
Jamaica	low	low	low	low
Mexico	high	low	low	moderate
Nicaragua	X	moderate	low	moderate
Panama	low	low	low	low
Trinidad and Tobago	X	low	X	X

SOUTH AMERICA / ASIA / OCEANIA

	AIR	WATER	NUTRITION	FINAL RANK
SOUTH AMERICA				
Argentina	low	low	low	low
Bolivia	low	moderate	moderate	low
Brazil	low	moderate	low	low
Chile	high	low	low	low
Colombia	moderate	low	low	low
Ecuador	high	moderate	moderate	moderate
Guyana	X	X	X	X
Paraguay	moderate	moderate	moderate	moderate
Peru	moderate	moderate	moderate	moderate
Suriname	X	X	X	X
Uruguay	low	moderate	X	low
Venezuela	high	moderate	low	moderate
ASIA				
Afghanistan, Islamic State	X	X	X	X
Armenia, Rep	X	X	moderate	X
Azerbaijan	X	X	high	X
Bangladesh	moderate	moderate	high	moderate
Bhutan	X	moderate	X	X
Cambodia	X	high	high	high
China	high	moderate	low	moderate
Georgia	X	X	moderate	X
India	moderate	moderate	high	moderate
Indonesia	high	moderate	moderate	high
Iran, Islamic Rep	high	low	moderate	moderate
Iraq	moderate	moderate	low	low
Israel	X	low	X	X
Jordan	X	low	low	low
Kazakstan, Rep	low	X	low	X
Korea, Dem People's Rep	X	low	low	low
Korea, Rep	moderate	low	X	low
Kuwait	X	X	X	X
Kyrgyz Rep	X	moderate	high	moderate
Lao People's Dem Rep	moderate	high	high	moderate
Lebanon	moderate	low	low	low
Malaysia	moderate	low	low	low
Mongolia	X	low	moderate	low
Myanmar	X	high	high	high
Nepal	X	moderate	high	high
Oman	X	low	moderate	low
Pakistan	moderate	moderate	moderate	moderate
Philippines	high	low	moderate	moderate
Saudi Arabia	X	low	X	X
Singapore	low	low	X	low
Sri Lanka	low	moderate	moderate	moderate
Syrian Arab Rep	X	low	moderate	low
Tajikistan, Rep	X	X	moderate	X
Thailand	moderate	low	moderate	low
Turkey	high	low	low	low
Turkmenistan, Rep	X	low	low	low
United Arab Emirates	X	low	X	X
Uzbekistan, Rep	X	high	low	moderate
Vietnam	high	high	moderate	high
Yemen	low	moderate	high	moderate
OCEANIA				
Fiji	X	X	low	X
Papua New Guinea	X	high	moderate	high
Solomon Islands	X	X	high	X

number of ranks for any of the three portions. The ranks (replaced with a standardized rank when appropriate) were then averaged, and the final average rank was ranked again. To be included in the final ranking, each country had to have data for at least two of the three portions. The final result was a list of developing countries ranked according to potential exposure to the environmental health threats. The final rank was separated into high, medium, and low categories of potential relative risk by dividing the countries into three equal groups.

Developed Countries

For developed countries, WRI constructed two variables (or indicators) representing potential exposure to polluted air: potential exposure to polluted ambient air and potential exposure to air polluted with lead from gasoline. These two variables (also used in the developing country indicator discussed previously) were ranked from lowest to highest exposure. The ranks were then separated into three equal categories to represent low-, medium-, and high-relative risk. These ranks were not aggregated as in the developing country indicator, but rather are shown separately in Table A.2.

Refining the Indicators

These preliminary indicators are a work in progress that can be improved with additional data. The final rankings for each country are suggestive, not definitive, and should be considered a starting point for exploring environmental health threats in greater detail. Although WRI used the best available data to construct the indicators, data were often incomplete or unreliable. Dividing nations into thirds, to create the three risk categories, is admittedly arbitrary. For instance, there may be very little difference between countries at the cutoff points, between high and medium risk or medium and low risk. The broad categories, however, suggest differences in relative risks, and the indicator maps serve as preliminary tools for identifying countries with different potential for exposure to environmental health threats.

References and Notes

1. Magda Lovei, The World Bank, Washington, D.C., January 1998 (personal communication).

TABLE A.2 Developed Countries	POTENTIAL RISK OF EXPOSURE TO POLLUTED OUTDOOR AIR	POTENTIAL RISK OF EXPOSURE TO AIR POLLUTED WITH LEAD FROM GASOLINE
EUROPE		
Albania	X	X
Austria	low	low
Belarus, Rep	X	moderate
Belgium	low	moderate
Bosnia and Herzegovina	X	X
Bulgaria	high	moderate
Croatia, Rep	low	moderate
Czech Rep	low	moderate
Denmark	high	low
Estonia, Rep	X	low
Finland	moderate	low
France	high	high
Germany	moderate	high
Greece	high	high
Hungary	high	moderate
Iceland	low	low
Ireland	low	moderate
Italy	moderate	high
Latvia, Rep	X	X
Lithuania, Rep	X	low
Macedonia, FYR	X	X
Moldova, Rep	X	moderate
Netherlands	high	high
Norway	moderate	low
Poland, Rep	moderate	high
Portugal	high	moderate
Romania	high	high
Russian Federation	high	high
Slovak Rep	low	low
Slovenia, Rep	X	moderate
Spain	moderate	high
Sweden	low	low
Switzerland	moderate	moderate
Ukraine	high	high
United Kingdom	moderate	high
Yugoslavia, Fed Rep	X	X
NORTH AMERICA		
Canada	low	low
United States	moderate	low
ASIA		
Japan	high	low
OCEANIA		
Australia	moderate	X
New Zealand	low	X

Environmental Change and Human Health

Part I: Environmental Change and Human Health

Chapter 1: Linking Environment and Health

1. World Health Organization (WHO), *Health and Environment in Sustainable Development: Five Years After the Earth Summit* (WHO, Geneva, 1997), p. 1.

2. Christopher J. L. Murray and Alan D. Lopez, eds., *The Global Burden of Disease: Volume 1* (World Health Organization, Harvard School of Public Health, and The World Bank, Geneva, 1996), p. 311.

3. World Health Organization (WHO), *The World Health Report 1997: Conquering Suffering, Enriching Humanity* (WHO, Geneva, 1997), p. 15.

4. The World Bank, *World Development Report 1992: Development and the Environment* (The World Bank, Washington, D.C., 1992), p. 53.

5. *Op. cit.* 3, p. 15.

6. *Op. cit.* 1, p. 136.

7. World Health Organization (WHO), *The World Health Report 1996: Fighting Disease, Fostering Development* (WHO, Geneva, 1996), p. 4.

8. Kirk R. Smith, "Development, Health and the Environmental Risk Transition" in G.S. Shahi *et al.*, eds., *International Perspectives on Environment, Development and Health* (Springer Publishing Company, New York, 1997), pp. 51–62.

9. Nicholas D. Kristof, "Across Asia, a Pollution Disaster Hovers," *The New York Times* (November 28, 1997), p. A14.

10. *Op. cit.* 1, p. 159.

11. *Op. cit.* 9.

12. The World Bank, *Clear Water, Blue Skies* (The World Bank, Washington, D.C., 1997), p. 21.

13. Anne E. Platt, "Infecting Ourselves: How Environmental and Social Disruptions Trigger Disease," Worldwatch Paper 129 (Worldwatch Institute, Washington, D.C., 1996), p. 6.

14. James P. Bruce, Hoesung Lee, and Erik F. Haites, eds., *Climate Change 1995: Economic and Social Dimensions of Climate Change* (Cambridge University Press, Cambridge, U.K., 1996), pp. 97–99.

15. United Nations (U.N.) Population Division, *World Population Prospects, 1950-2050 (The 1996 Revision)*, on diskette (U.N., New York, 1996), using median estimates of five-year intervals.

16. A.J. McMichael, *Planetary Overload: Global Environmental Change and the Health of the Human Species* (Cambridge University Press, Cambridge, U.K., 1993).

17. Joby Warrick and Todd Shields, "Maryland Counties Awash in Pollution-Causing Nutrients Reports Suggest State Faces Battle Controlling Agricultural Runoff into the Bay," *The Washington Post* (October 3, 1997), p. A1.

18. David Bradley, "Health, Environment, and Tropical Development," *Health and the Environment: The Linacre Lectures*, Bryan Cartledge, ed. (Oxford University Press, Oxford, U.K.,1994), p. 147.

19. See *Op. cit.* 1 and Helen Murphy, Bonnie Stanton, and Jennifer Galbraith, "Prevention: Environmental Health Interventions to Sustain Child Survival," Applied Study No. 3 (Environmental Health Project, Washington, D.C., 1997).

20. *Op. cit.* 1.

21. The World Bank, *World Development Report 1993: Investing in Health* (The World Bank, Washington, D.C., 1993), p. 21.

22. *Op. cit.* 7, p. 12.

23. *Op. cit.* 7, p. 14.

24. United Nations Development Programme (UNDP), *Human Development Report 1997* (UNDP, New York, 1997), p. 28.

25. *Op. cit.* 15.

26. *Op. cit.* 1.

27. David Satterthwaite *et al.*, *The Environment for Children: Understanding and Acting on the Environmental Hazards that Threaten Children and their Parents* (Earthscan Publications, Ltd., London, 1996), p. 4.

28. World Resources Institute in collaboration with the United Nations Environment Programme, the United Nations Development Programme, and The World Bank, *World Resources Report 1996–97* (Oxford University Press, New York, 1996), p. 37.

29. John W. Frank and J. Fraser Mustard, "The Determinants of Health from a Historical Perspective," *Daedalus*, Vol. 123, No. 4 (Fall 1994), pp. 5–6.

30. *Op. cit.* 21, pp. 90–98.

31. Richard G. Wilkinson, "The Epidemiological Transition: From Material Scarcity to Social Disadvantage?" *Daedalus*, Vol. 123, No. 4 (Fall 1994), p. 65.

32. Thomas McKeown, *The Modern Rise of Population* (Academic Press, New York, 1976), pp. 108–109.

33. *Op. cit.* 2, p. 18.

34. A. Rossi-Espagnet, G.B. Goldstein, and I. Tabibzadeh, "Urbanization and Health in Developing Countries: A Challenge for Health for All," *World Health Statistics Quarterly*, Vol. 44, No. 4 (1991), p. 208.

35. *Op. cit.* 3.

36. Christopher J.L. Murray, and Alan D. Lopez, "Evidence-Based Health Policy—Lessons from the Global Burden of Disease Study," *Science*, Vol. 274 (November 1, 1996), p. 740.

37. Barbara J. Culliton, "Numbers Game Fuels Debate on International Health Priorities," *Nature Medicine*, Vol. 3, No. 6 (June 1997), p. 599.

38. *Op. cit.* 3, p. 23.

39. *Op. cit.* 2.

40. *Op. cit.* 2, p.176.

41. *Op. cit.* 2, p. 176.

42. *Op. cit.* 2, p. 176.

43. *Op. cit.* 2, p. 178.

44. *Op. cit.* 2, p. 609.

45. *Op. cit.* 2, p. 254.

46. *Op. cit.* 2, p. 175.

47. World Health Organization (WHO), *The World Health Report 1995: Bridging the Gaps* (WHO, Geneva, 1995), p. 1.

48. Bonita Stanton, "Child Health: Equity in the Non-Industrialized Countries," *Social Science Medicine*, Vol. 38, No. 10 (1994), p. 1375.

49. *Op. cit.* 31, pp. 62–63.

50. United Nations (U.N. Department for Policy Coordination and Sustainable Development), *Critical Trends: Global Change and Sustainable Development* (U.N., New York, 1997), p. 59.

51. *Op. cit.* 24, p. 27.

52. *Op. cit.* 2, p. 312.

53. *Op. cit.* 3, p. 50.

54. *Op. cit.* 21, p. 42.

55. *Op. cit.* 21, p. 42.

56. *Op. cit.* 31, pp. 61–77.

57. *Op. cit.* 31, p. 68.

58. *Op. cit.* 31, p. 70.

59. *Op. cit.* 21, p.40.

60. *Op. cit.* 24, p. 38.

61. World Health Organization (WHO), *Our Planet, Our Health: Report of the WHO Commission on Health and Environment* (WHO, Geneva, 1992), p. 10.

62. Scott B. Halstead, Julia A. Walsh, and Kenneth S. Warren, eds., *Good Health at Low Cost: Proceedings of a Conference Held at the Bellagio Conference Center, Bellagio, Italy* (The Rockefeller Foundation, New York, 1985), p. 184.

63. *Ibid.*, p. 129.

64. *Op. cit.* 62, p. 128.

65. *Op. cit.* 28, p. 48.

66. Gordon McGranahan, "Household Environmental Problems in Low-Income Cities: An Overview of Problems and Prospects for Improvement," *Habitat International*, Vol. 17, No. 2 (1993), p. 105.

67. *Op. cit.* 24, p. 29.

68. United Nations Children's Fund (UNICEF), *The Progress of Nations 1997* (UNICEF, New York, 1997).

69. *Ibid.*

70. *Op. cit.* 1, p. 85.

71. *Op. cit.* 28, pp. 43, 58.

72. Ellen Silbergeld and Kevin Tonat, "Investing in Prevention: Opportunities to Prevent Disease and Reduce Health Care Costs by Identifying Environmental and Occupational Causes of Noncancer Disease," *Toxicology and Industrial Health: An International Journal*, Vol. 10, No. 6 (1994), p. 681.

73. Thomas A.E. Platts-Mills and Melody C. Carter, "Asthma and Indoor Exposure to Allergens," *The New England Journal of Medicine*, Vol. 336, No. 19 (May 8, 1997), p. 1383.

74. United Church of Christ, *Toxic Wastes and Race in the United States* (United Church of Christ, New York, 1987).

75. Benjamin A. Goldman and Laura J. Fitton, *Toxic Wastes and Race Revisited: An Update of the 1987 Report on the Racial and Socioeconomic Characteristics of Communities with Hazardous Waste Sites* (Center for Policy Alternatives, Washington, D.C., 1994).

76. U.S. Environmental Protection Agency (U.S. EPA), *Environmental Justice 1994 Annual Report: Focusing on Environmental Protection for All People* (U.S. EPA, Washington, D.C., April 1995).

77. U.S. General Accounting Office (GAO), *Hazardous and Nonhazardous Waste: Demographics of People Living Near Waste Facilities* (GAO, Washington, D.C., 1995).

78. John E. Vena *et al.*, "The New York Angler Cohort Study: Exposure Characterization and Reproductive and Developmental Health," *Toxicology and Industrial Health*, Vol. 12, No. 3/4 (1996), pp. 327–334.

79. Jeanne M. Courval *et al.*, "Fish Consumption and Other Characteristics of Reproductive-Aged Michigan Anglers—A Potential Population for Studying the Effects of Consumption of Great Lakes Fish on Reproductive Health," *Toxicology and Industrial Health*, Vol. 12, No. 3/4 (1996), pp. 347–359.

80. Donald P. Waller *et al.*, "Great Lakes Fish as a Source of Maternal and Fetal Exposure to Chlorinated Hydrocarbons," *Toxicology and Industrial Health*, Vol. 12, No. 3/4 (1996), pp. 335–345.

81. José Luis Bobadilla *et al.*, "The Epidemiologic Transition and Health Priorities," in *Disease Control Pri-*

orities in Developing Countries, Dean T. Jamison, *et al.*, eds. (Oxford University Press, Oxford, U.K., 1993), p. 53.

82. W. Henry Mosley, *et al.*, "The Health Transition: Implications for Health Policy in Developing Countries," *Disease Control Priorities in Developing Countries*, Dean T. Jamison, *et al.*, eds. (Oxford University Press, Oxford, U.K., 1993), p. 679.

83. *Op. cit.* 47, p. 40.

84. *Op. cit.* 3, p. vi.

85. *Op. cit.* 3, p. 20.

86. *Op. cit.* 13, p. 21.

87. William H. McNeill, *Plagues and Peoples* (Anchor Books, Garden City, New York, 1976).

88. *Op. cit.* 13, p. 21.

89. *Op. cit.* 3, p. 15.

90. *Op. cit.* 2, p. 573.

91. *Op. cit.* 7, p. 24.

92. José Martines, Margaret Phillips, and Richard G.A. Feachem, "Diarrheal Diseases," in *Disease Control Priorities in Developing Countries*, Dean T. Jamison *et al.*, eds. (Oxford University Press, Oxford, U.K. and New York, 1993), p. 91.

93. James Van Derslice and John Briscoe, "Environmental Interventions in Developing Countries: Interactions and Their Implications," *American Journal of Epidemiology*, Vol. 141, No. 2 (1995), p. 143.

94. *Op. cit.* 68.

95. Diane B. Bendahmene, ed., *Lessons Learned in Water, Sanitation and Health: Thirteen Years of Experience in Developing Countries* (Water and Sanitation for Health Project, Arlington, Virginia, 1993), p. 79.

96. *Ibid.*

97. *Op. cit.* 92.

98. International Life Sciences Institute (ILSI), "Global Approach to Prevent, Detect, and Treat Foodborne Disease," *ILSI News*, Vol. 15, No. 2 (March/April 1997), p. 9.

99. "Foodborne Pathogens: Implications and Control," *Emerging Infectious Diseases*, Vol. 3, No. 2 (April–June 1997).

100. *Op. cit.* 98, p. 2.

101. "Food Safety: Enterohaemorrhagic Eschericha Coli Infection, Japan," *Weekly Epidemiological Record*, Vol. 71, No. 35 (August 30, 1996), p. 267.

102. Cindy Skrzycki, "The *E. coli* Aftermath—For Meat Recalls, USDA Choice Isn't to Industry's Taste," *The Washington Post* (September 12, 1997), p. EO1.

103 . *Op. cit.* 7, p. 38.

104. "Hepatitis A Associated with Consumption of Frozen Strawberries—Michigan, March 1997," *Morbidity and Mortality Weekly Report*, Vol. 46, No. 13 (April 4, 1997), p. 288.

105. *Op. cit.* 7, p. 38.

106. *Op. cit.* 27, p. 35.

107. *Op. cit.* 7, p. 43.

108. *Op. cit.* 7, p. 43.

109. *Op. cit.* 47, p. 28.

110. *Op. cit.* 7, p. 39.

111. Kenneth S. Warren, *et al.*, "Helminth Infection" in *Disease Control Priorities in Developing Countries*, Dean T. Jamison, *et al.*, eds. (Oxford University Press, Oxford, U.K., 1993), pp. 141, 156.

112. *Op. cit.* 3, p. 15.

113. *Op. cit.* 2, p. 465.

114. *Op. cit.* 7, p. 47.

115. Jose A. Najera, Bernhard H. Liese, and Jeffrey Hammer, "Malaria," in *Disease Control Priorities in Developing Countries*, Dean T. Jamison *et al.*, eds. (Oxford University Press, Oxford, U.K., 1993), p. 281.

116. *Op. cit.* 3, p. 122.

117. *Op. cit.* 7, p. 46.

118. *Op. cit.* 112, p. 11.

119. *Op. cit.* 112, p. 11.

120. *Op. cit.* 7, p. 53.

121. *Op. cit.* 7, p. 25.

122. *Op. cit.* 2, p. 262.

123. Sally K. Stansfield and Donald S. Shepard, "Acute Respiratory Infection," in *Disease Control Priorities in Developing Countries*, Dean T. Jamison *et al.*, eds. (Oxford University Press, Oxford, U.K., 1993), pp. 68–70.

124. The World Bank, *World Development Report 1992: Development and the Environment* (The World Bank, Washington, D.C., 1992).

125. *Op. cit.* 3, p. 15.

126. *Op. cit.* 7, p. 25.

127. *Op. cit.* 7, p. 26.

128. *Op. cit.* 2, p. 465.

129. *Op. cit.* 27, p. 44.

130. *Op. cit.* 27, p. 44.

131. John C. Scatarige and Frederick P. Stitik, "Induction of Thoracic Malignancy in Inorganic Dust Pneumoconiosis," *Journal of Thoracic Imagery*, Vol. 3, No. 4 (1988), p. 71.

132. Lori Ann Thrupp, "Sterilization of Workers from Pesticide Exposure: The Causes and Consequences of DBCP-Induced Damage in Costa Rica and Beyond," *International Journal of Health Services*, Vol. 21, No. 4 (1991), p. 734.

133. National Research Council, *Science and Judgement in Risk Assessment* (National Academy Press, Washington, D.C., 1994), p. 2.

134 . L. Tomatis, *et al.*, eds, *Cancer: Causes, Occurrence and Control* (International Agency for Research on Cancer, Lyon, France, 1990), p. 128.

135. *Op. cit.* 2, p. 311; and *op. cit.* 1, p. 87.

136. U.S. Environmental Protection Agency (U.S. EPA), *Special Report on Environmental Endocrine Disruption: An Effects Assessment and Analysis* (U.S. EPA, Washington, D.C., 1997), p. 72.

137. Environmental Defense Fund (EDF), *Toxic Ignorance: The Continuing Absence of Basic Health Testing for Top-Selling Chemicals in the United States* (EDF, Washington, D.C., 1997), p. 15.

138. Dian Turnheim, "Evaluating Chemical Risks," *OECD Observer*, No. 189 (August/September, 1994), pp. 12–15.

139. International Agency for Research on Cancer (IARC), "Overall Evaluations of Carcinogenicity to Humans." Available online at: http://www.iarc.fr/monoeval/crthall.htm.

140. *Op. cit.* 72, p. 676.

141. *Op. cit.* 137, p. 16.

142. Op. cit. 72, pp. 676–677.

143. D. Briggs, C. Corvalán, and M. Nurminen, eds., *Linkage Methods for Environment and Health Analysis: General Guidelines* (Office of Global and Integrated Environmental Health, WHO, Geneva, 1996), p. 10.

144. F. Sherwood Rowland, "Stratospheric Ozone Depletion by Chlorofluorocarbons," *Ambio*, Vol. 19, No. 6–7 (October 1990), p. 291.

145. *Op. cit.* 2, p. 464.

146. *Op. cit.* 2, pp. 549–572.

147. Dr. Annie J. Sasco, Head, Programme of Epidemiology for Cancer Prevention, International Agency for Research on Cancer, September 1997 (personal communication).

148. Richard Doll and Richard Peto, *The Causes of Cancers: Quantitative Estimates of Avoidable Risks of Cancer in the United States Today* (Oxford University Press, Oxford, U.K., 1981), p. 1256.

149. *Op. cit.* 1, p. 161.

150. *Op. cit.* 1, p. 173.

151. *Op. cit.* 2, p. 321.

152. *Op. cit.* 2, p. 321.

153. *Op. cit.* 2, p. 312.

154. *Op. cit.* 2, p. 312.

155. *Op. cit.* 2, pp. 311, 315.

156. *Op. cit.* 21, p. 90.

157. *Op. cit.* 21, p. 90.

158. *Op. cit.* 1, p. 173.

159. *Op. cit.* 1, p. 173.

Chapter 2: Changing Environments; Changing Health

1. Vaclav Smil, *Global Ecology: Environmental Change and Social Flexibility* (Routledge, London and New York, 1993), p. 35.

2. United States Environmental Protection Agency (U.S. EPA), *Beyond the Horizon: Using Foresight to Protect the Environmental Future* (U.S. EPA, Washington, D.C., January 1995), p. 7.

3. Energy Information Administration, *International Energy Outlook 1997* (U.S. Department of Energy, Washington, D.C., April 1997), p. 115.

4. World Health Organization (WHO), *Health and Environment in Sustainable Development: Five Years After the Earth Summit* (WHO, Geneva, 1997), p. 19.

5. United Nations (U.N.) Population Division, *World Population Prospects 1950–2050* (*The 1996 Revision*), on diskette (U.N., New York, 1996).

6. United Nations Development Programme (UNDP), *Human Development Report 1997* (UNDP, New York, 1997), p. 2.

7. United Nations Development Programme (UNDP), *Human Development Report 1996* (UNDP, New York, 1996), p. 12.

8. United Nations (U.N.), *Critical Trends: Global Change and Sustainable Development* (U.N., New York, 1997), p. 58.

9. The World Bank, *World Development Indicators 1997*, on CD-ROM (The World Bank, Washington, D.C., 1997).

10. The World Bank, *World Development Indicators 1997* (The World Bank, Washington, D.C., 1997), p. 238.

11. Hilary F. French, "Private Finance Flows to Third World," in *Vital Signs 1996* (Worldwatch Institute, Washington, D.C., 1996), p. 116.

12. Keith B. Richburg, "Free Trade Helps Lift World Poor," *The Washington Post* (December 29, 1996), p. AO1.

13. *Op. cit.* 4, p. 20.

Environmental Change and Human Health

14. The World Bank, *World Development Report 1993: Investing in Health* (The World Bank, Washington, D.C., 1993), p. 21.

15. World Health Organization (WHO), *The World Health Report 1997* (WHO, Geneva, 1997), p. 14.

16. *Op. cit.* 5, using median estimates of 5-year intervals.

17. *Op. cit.* 7, p. 12

18. Martin Ravallion and Shaohua Chen, "What Can New Survey Data Tell Us About Recent Changes in Distribution and Poverty?" World Bank paper (The World Bank, Washington, D.C., 1996), Table 5.

19. Food and Agriculture Organization of the United Nations (FAO), "Social and Political Changes and Food Security," background paper prepared for the World Food Summit, Rome, 1996 (FAO, Rome, 1996), p. 8.

20. Michael McCally, "Human Health and Population Growth," in *Critical Condition: Human Health and the Environment,* Eric Chivian *et al.,* eds. (The MIT Press, Cambridge and London, 1993), p. 181.

21. World Resources Institute in collaboration with the United Nations Environment Programme, the United Nations Development Programme and the World Bank, *World Resources Report 1996–97* (Oxford University Press, New York, 1996), p. 32.

22. *Op. cit.* 4, p. 198.

23. D.R. Phillips, "Urbanization and Human Health," in *Parasitology,* Vol. 106, Supplement (1993), p. S93.

24. *Op. cit.* 4, pp. 230, 237.

25. *Op. cit.* 7, p. 13.

26. David Morawetz, "The Gap Between Rich and Poor Countries," in *Development and Underdevelopment: The Political Economy of Inequality,* Mitchell A. Seligson and John T. Passe-Smith, eds. (Lynne Rienner Publishers, Boulder and London, 1993), pp. 10–11.

27. *Op. cit.* 7, p. 13.

28. *Op. cit.* 4, p. 34.

29. *Op. cit.* 8, p. 22.

30. *Op. cit.* 8, p. 23.

31. *Op. cit.* 8, p. 23

32. *Op. cit.* 8, p. 12.

33. World consumption of pesticides has grown markedly since it started to surge in the 1960s, with production increasing tenfold from 1955 to 1985. Although consumption leveled off in the early 1990s, it has resumed its growth since then, and the volume of pesticides used is currently rising at about 1 percent per year. The Freedonia Group, Inc., Freedonia Study No. 768, *Pesticides* (The Freedonia Group, Inc., Cleveland, Ohio, 1996).

34. Arnold L. Aspelin, *Pesticides Industry Sales and Usage: 1994–95 Market Estimates* (U.S. Environmental Protection Agency, Washington, D.C., 1997), p. 8.

35. S. Henao *et al., Pesticides and Health in the Americas* (Pan American Health Organization, Washington, D.C., 1993), p. 7.

36. Foundation for Advancements in Science and Education (FASE), "Exporting Risk: Pesticide Exports from U.S. Ports, 1992–1994," *FASE Research Report* (FASE, Los Angeles, 1996), p. 4.

37. United States General Accounting Office (GAO), *Pesticides on Farms: Limited Capability Exists to Monitor Occupational Illnesses and Injuries* (GAO, Washington, D.C., 1994), p. 3.

38. Extension Toxicology Network (EXTOXNET), "Methyl Parathion," EXTOXNET, p. 54. Available online at http://ace.ace.orst.edu/info/extoxnet pips/methylp.

39. World Health Organization (WHO), *Public Health Impacts of Pesticides Used in Agriculture* (WHO, Geneva, 1990), p. 36.

40. Lori Ann Thrupp, "Challenges in Latin America's Recent Agroexport Boom: Sustainability and Equity of Nontraditional Export Policies in Ecuador," World Resources Institute Issues in Development Series (World Resources Institute, Washington, D.C., 1994), p. 12.

41. *Op. cit.* 39, p. 86.

42. J. Finkelman, G. Corey, and R. Calderon, eds., *Environmental Epidemiology: A Project for Latin America and the Caribbean* (Pan American Health Organization, Washington, D.C., 1993), p. 7.

43. *Op. cit.* 39, pp. 36–37.

44. Robert Repetto and Sanjay Baliga, *Pesticides and the Immune System: The Public Health Risks* (World Resources Institute, Washington, D.C., 1996), pp. 3–5.

45. *Op. cit.* 35, pp. 2–3.

46. Tracy Woodruff, Amy Kyle, and Frederic Bois, "Evaluating Health Risks from Occupational Exposure to Pesticides and the Regulatory Response," *Environmental Health Perspectives,* Vol. 102, No. 12 (1994), p. 1090.

47. Kenneth Abrams, Daniel Hogan, and Howard Maibach, "Pesticide-Related Dermatoses in Agricultural Workers," *Occupational Medicine: State-of-the-Art Reviews,* Vol. 6, No. 3 (1991), p. 468.

48. *Op. cit.* 44, p. 11.

49. *Op. cit.* 42, p. 155.

50. *Op. cit.* 39, pp. 84–86.

51. U.S. Environmental Protection Agency (U.S. EPA), Office of Pesticide Programs, *Regulatory Impact of the Worker Protection Standard for Agricultural Pesticides,* U.S. EPA contract No. 68-D1-0134 (U.S. EPA, Washington, D.C., 1992), pp. v –2.

52. Jerome Blondell, "Epidemiology of Pesticide Poisonings in the U.S., With Special Reference to Occupational Cases," draft paper (U.S. EPA, Washington, D.C., 1996), p. 23.

53. *Ibid.,* p. 24.

54. *Op. cit.* 51, p. v–19.

55. M. Ruijten *et al.,* "Effect of Chronic Mixed Pesticide Exposure on Peripheral and Autonomic Nerve Function," *Archives of Environmental Health,* Vol. 49, No. 3 (1994), p. 188.

56. R. Ames *et al.,* "Chronic Neurologic Sequelae to Cholinesterase Inhibition Among Agricultural Pesticide Applicators," *Archives of Environmental Health,* Vol. 50, No. 6 (1995), pp. 440–444.

57. *Op. cit.* 39, pp. 87–88.

58. *Op. cit.* 39, p. 56.

59. *Op. cit.* 35, p. 175.

60. V. Garry *et al.,* "Pesticide Appliers, Biocides, and Birth Defects in Rural Minnesota," *Environmental Health Perspectives,* Vol. 104, No. 4 (1996), pp. 394–399.

61. *Op. cit.* 35, pp. 172–173.

62. *Op. cit.* 44, pp. 1–2.

63. U.S. Environmental Protection Agency (U.S. EPA), "Office of Pesticide Programs List of Chemicals Evaluated for Carcinogenic Potential" (U.S. EPA, Washington, D.C., 1997).

64. Sheila Zahm and Susan Devesa, "Childhood Cancer: Overview of Incidence Trends and Environmental Carcinogens," *Environmental Health Perspectives,* Vol. 103, Supplement 6 (1995), p. 180.

65. Sheila Zahm and Aaron Blair, "Pesticides and Non-Hodgkin's Lymphoma" *Cancer Research,* Vol. 52 (Supplement) (1992), pp. 5485s–5488s.

66. Aaron Blair and Sheila Zahm, "Carcinogenic Risks From Pesticides," in *1992 Accomplishments in Cancer Research,* General Motors Cancer Research Foundation, J. Fortner and J. Rhoades, eds. (Lippincott, Philadelphia, 1993), pp. 266–272.

67. Sheila Hoar *et al.,* "Agricultural Herbicide Use and Risk of Lymphoma and Soft-Tissue Sarcoma," *Journal of the American Medical Association,* Vol. 256, No. 9 (1986), p. 1141.

68. *Op. cit.* 46, pp. 1089–1090.

69. National Research Council, *Carcinogens and Anticarcinogens in the Human Diet* (National Academy Press, Washington, D.C., 1996), pp. 5–10.

70. National Research Council, *Pesticides in the Diets of Infants and Children* (National Academy Press, Washington, D.C., 1993), p. 359.

71. *Op. cit.* 39, p. 67.

72. "World Pesticide Market to Grow 4.4% Per Annum to 1998," *Agrow: World Crop Protection News,* No. 225 (February 3, 1995), p. 16.

73. U.S. Environmental Protection Agency (U.S. EPA), *Office of Pesticide Programs Annual Report for 1995* (U.S. EPA, Washington, D.C., 1995), p. 2.

74. "Indian Pesticide Sales Up 24%," *Agrow: World Crop Protection News,* No. 260 (July 12, 1996), p. 18.

75. "Brazilian Pesticide Sales Up 34%," *Agrow: World Crop Protection News,* No. 232 (May 12, 1995), p. 18.

76. *Op. cit.* 72, pp. 16–17.

77. *Op. cit.* 39, p. 29.

78. *Op. cit.* 2, p. 16.

79. "Chinese First-Half A.I. Production," *Agrow: World Crop Protection News,* No. 263 (August 30, 1996), p. 18.

80. *Op. cit.* 74, p. 18.

81. Shirley Briggs *et al., Basic Guide to Pesticides: Their Characteristics and Hazards* (Hemisphere Publishing Corp., Washington, D.C., 1992), p. 167.

82. "Egyptian Pesticide Ban in Place," *Agrow: World Crop Protection News,* No. 262 (August 16, 1996), p. 14.

83. Balu Bumb and Carlos Baanante, "World Trends in Fertilizer Use and Projections to 2020," 2020 Brief No. 38 (International Food Policy Research Institute, Washington, D.C., 1996), pp. 1–2.

84. David Stanners and Philippe Bourdeau, eds., *Europe's Environment: The Dobris Assessment* (European Environment Agency, Copenhagen, 1995), p. 455.

85. Gordon Conway and Jules Pretty, *Unwelcome Harvest* (Earthscan Publications, Ltd., London, 1991), pp. 225–228.

86. *Ibid.,* pp. 232–251, 261–262.

87. United States Environmental Protection Agency (U.S. EPA), *National Water Quality Inventory, 1994 Report to Congress,* Report No. EPA 841-R-95-005 (U.S. EPA, Washington, D.C., 1995), pp. 109, 114–115.

88. Clyde Hertzman, *Environment and Health In Central and Eastern Europe* (The World Bank, Washington, D.C., 1995), pp. 34, 41–42.

89. Anna Bellisari, "Public Health and the Water Crisis in the Occupied Palestinian Territories," *Journal of Palestine Studies,* Vol. 23, No. 2 (1994), p. 56.

90. *Op. cit.* 84, pp. 103–104, 455.

91. *Op. cit.* 87, p. 115.

92. *Op. cit.* 84, pp. 103–104, 455.

93. *Op. cit.* 84, p. 104.

94. United Nations Economic and Social Council, "Review of Progress on Water-Related Issues," Committee on Natural Resources (United Nations, New York, 1994), pp. 10–14.

95. Nikos Alexandratos, ed., *World Agriculture: Towards 2010* (United Nations Food and Agriculture Organization, Rome, 1995), pp. 159–160, 160–167.

96. David Bradley, "Health, Environment, and Tropical Development," in *Health and the Environment: The Linacre Lectures* (Oxford University Press, Oxford, U.K., 1994), pp. 137–139.

97. A. McMichael *et al.,* eds., *Climate Change and Human Health* (World Health Organization, Geneva, 1996), p. 93.

98. Panel of Experts on Environmental Management for Vector Control, *Promotion of Environmental Management for Disease Vector Control Through Agricultural Extension Programmes* (World Health Organization, Geneva, 1995), pp. 58, 66.

99. *Op. cit.* 96, pp. 137–139.

100. World Health Organization (WHO) Commission on Health and the Environment, *Report of the Panel on Food and Agriculture* (WHO, Geneva, 1992), pp. 127–128.

101. World Health Organization (WHO), *Our Planet, Our Health* (WHO, Geneva, 1992), pp. 83–87.

102. *Ibid.*, p. 86.

103. *Op. cit.* 100, p. 129.

104. *Op. cit.* 101, p. 85.

105. H. Shuval *et al.*, *Wastewater Irrigation in Developing Countries: Health Effects and Technical Solutions* (The World Bank, Washington, D.C., 1986), p. 296.

106. *Ibid.*, pp. 116, 131–133, 299–300.

107. *Op. cit.* 105, pp. 77–84, 117, 299–300.

108. *Op. cit.* 105, p. 84.

109. United Nations Environment Programme, *Global Environmental Outlook* (Oxford University Press, New York, 1997), pp. 232–234.

110. United Nations Food and Agricultural Organization (FAO), *Forest Resources Assessment 1990: A Global Synthesis* (FAO, Rome, 1995), pp. 8–9.

111. Dirk Bryant, Daniel Nielsen, and Laura Tangley, *The Last Frontier Forests: Ecosystems and Economies on the Edge* (World Resources Institute, Washington, D.C., 1997), p. 16.

112. *Op. cit.* 100, p. 130.

113. A. Dobson, M. Campbell, and J. Bell, "Fatal Synergisms: Interactions Between Infectious Diseases, Human Population Growth, and Loss of Biodiversity," in *Biodiversity and Human Health*, F. Grifo and J. Rosenthal, eds. (Island Press, Washington, D.C., 1997), p. 98.

114. S.W. Lindsay and M.H. Birley, "Climate Change and Malaria Transmission," *Annals of Tropical Medicine and Parasitology*, Vol. 90, No. 6 (1996), p. 582.

115. J. Almendares *et al.*, "Critical Regions, a Profile of Honduras," *The Lancet*, Vol. 342, No. 8884 (December 4, 1993), p. 1400.

116. *Op. cit.* 4, p. 62.

117. *Op. cit.* 4, p. 71.

118. *Op. cit.* 10, pp. 130–132.

119. N. Pearce *et al.*, "Industrialization and Health," in *Occupational Cancer in Developing Countries*, International Agency for Research on Cancer (IARC), Scientific Publications No. 129, N. Pearce *et al.*, eds. (World Health Organization, IARC, Lyon, France, 1994), p. 7.

120. Daniel R. Headrick, "Technological Change," in *The Earth as Transformed by Human Action: Global and Regional Changes in the Biosphere over the Past 300 Years*, B.L. Turner II *et al.*, eds. (Cambridge University Press with Clark University, Cambridge, U.K., 1990), p. 65.

121. United Nations Industrial Development Organization (UNIDO), *International Yearbook of Industrial Statistics 1997* (UNIDO, Vienna, Austria, 1997), Table 1.10.

122. David Taylor, "Trade-Offs in Thailand," *Environmental Health Perspectives*, Vol. 104, No. 12 (December 1996), p. 1288.

123. Carter Brandon, "Reversing Pollution Trends in Asia," *Finance and Development*, No. 3 (1994), pp. 21–23.

124. Jean-François Tremblay, "Chemical Boom in Indonesia," *Chemical and Engineering News*, Vol. 75, No. 32 (August 11, 1997), p. 16.

125. International Labour Office (ILO), *1996 Yearbook of Labour Statistics* (ILO, Geneva, 1996), Table 5B.

126. *Op. cit.* 12.

127. M.E. Conroy, "Regional Dimensions of Economic Integration and Global Restructuring," paper presented at the 1997 American Association for the Advancement of Science (AAAS) Annual Meeting and Science Innovation Exposition, Seattle, Washington, February 13–18, pp. 4–5.

128. Jason Abott, "Export Processing Zones and the Developing World," *Contemporary Review*, Vol. 270, No. 1576 (May 1997), pp. 232–238.

129. Bob Herbert, "Children of the Dark Ages," *The New York Times* (July 21, 1995), p. A11.

130. Barry I. Castleman, "The Migration of Industrial Hazards," *International Journal of Occupational and Environmental Health*, Vol. 1, No. 2 (April–June 1995), pp. 87–89.

131. Joseph LaDou, "International Occupational and Environmental Health," in William N. Rom., ed., *Environmental and Occupational Medicine*, Third Edition (forthcoming), p. 5.

132. Cristina Cortinas de Nava, "Worldwide Overview of Hazardous Wastes," *Toxicology and Industrial Health*, Vol. 12, No. 2 (1996), p. 129.

133. *Ibid.*

134. *Op. cit.* 132, p. 135.

135. U.S. Environmental Protection Agency (U.S. EPA), *Final Report: Costs of Compliance with the Proposed Amendments to the PCB Regulation* (U.S., EPA, Office of Pollution Prevention and Toxics, Washington, D.C., 1994), cited in U.S. EPA Office of Pollution Prevention and Toxics, *Management of Polychlorinated Biphenyls in the United States* (U.S. EPA, Washington, D.C., 1997).

136. A.B. Miller, "Review of Extant Community-Based Epidemiological Studies on Health Effects of Hazardous Wastes," *Toxicology and Industrial Health*, Vol. 12, No. 2 (1996), p. 226.

137. *Ibid*, pp. 226–227.

138. Kate Cahow, "The Cancer Conundrum," *Environmental Health Perspectives*, Vol 103, No. 11 (November 1995), p. 999.

139. Krzysztof Krzystyniak, Helen Tryphonas, and Michael Fournier, "Approaches to the Evaluation of Chemical-Induced Immunotoxicity," *Environmental Health Perspectives*, Vol. 103, Supplement 9 (December 1995), p. 17.

140. Frank Wania and Donald Mackay, "Tracking the Distribution of Persistent Organic Pollutants," *Environmental Science & Technology*, Vol. 30, No. 9 (1996), p. 394A.

141. *Ibid.*, p. 390A.

142. Programme for the Promotion of Chemical Safety, the Division of Control of Tropical Diseases, and the Food Safety Unit of the World Health Organization (WHO), "Persistent Organic Pollutants," paper prepared for the Intergovernmental Forum on Chemical Safety Experts Meeting on Persistent Organic Pollutants, June 17–19, 1996, Manila, The Philippines (WHO, Geneva, 1996).

143. Foundation for Advancements in Science and Education (FASE), "Exporting Risk, Pesticide Exports from U.S. Ports, 1992–1994," *FASE Research Report* (FASE, Los Angeles, 1996), pp. 1–12.

144. United Nations Environment Programme (UNEP), "UNEP Survey on Sources of POPs," prepared for Intergovernmental Forum on Chemical Safety Experts Meeting on Persistent Organic Pollutants, Manila, The Philippines, June 17–19, 1996. Available online at: irptc.unep.ch/pops/indxhtms/manexp3.html.

145. Helmut F. van Emden and David B. Peakall, *Beyond Silent Spring: Integrated Pest Management and Chemical Safety* (Chapman & Hall, London, 1996), p. 30.

146. Carol W. Bason and Theo Colborn, "U.S. Application and Distribution of Pesticides and Industrial Chemicals Capable of Disrupting Endocrine and Immune Systems," in *Chemically-Induced Alterations in Sexual and Functional Development: The Wildlife/Human Connection*, Theo Colborn and Coralie Clement, eds., Advances in Modern Environmental Toxicology, Vol. XXI (Princeton Scientific Publishing Co., Inc., Princeton, New Jersey, 1992), p. 342.

147. *Op. cit.* 140.

148. Babasaheb R. Sonawane, "Chemical Contaminants in Human Milk: An Overview," *Environmental Health Perspectives*, Vol. 103, Supplement 6 (1995), p. 199.

149. Neil W. Tremblay and Andrew P. Gilman, "Introduction: Human Health, the Great Lakes, and Environmental Pollution: A 1994 Perspective," *Environmental Health Perspectives*, Vol. 103, Supplement 9 (December 1995), p. 3.

150. *Ibid.*

151. *Op. cit.* 149.

152. Dieter Riedel and Neil W. Tremblay, "Progress on Research into Great Lakes Pollution and Health Risks," *Health and Environment Digest*, Vol. 10, No. 3 (July 1996), p. 19.

153. Christopher T. DeRosa and Barry L. Johnson, "Strategic Elements of ATSDR's Great Lakes Human Health Effects Research Program," *Toxicology and Industrial Health*, Vol. 12, No. 3/4 (1996), p. 315.

154. *Op. cit.* 152, p. 20.

155. Joseph L. Jacobson and Sandra W. Jacobson, "Intellectual Impairment in Children Exposed to Polychlorinated Biphenyls in Utero," *The New England Journal of Medicine*, Vol. 335, No. 11 (September 12, 1996), p. 788.

156. *Ibid.*

157. Y.C. Chen *et al.*, "Cognitive Development of Hu-Cheng ("Oil Disease") Children Prenatally Exposed to Heat-Degraded PCBs," *Journal of the American Medical Association*, Vol. 268, No. 22 (December 9, 1992), p. 3213.

158. *Op. cit.* 149, p. 4.

159. *Op. cit.* 149, p. 4.

160. John E. Vena *et al.*, "The New York Angler Cohort Study: Exposure Characterization and Reproductive and Developmental Health," *Toxicology and Industrial Health*, Vol. 12, No. 3/4 (1996), pp. 327–334.

161. Jeanne M. Courval *et al.*, "Fish Consumption and Other Characteristics of Reproductive-Aged Michigan Anglers—A Potential Population for Studying the Effects of Consumption of Great Lakes Fish on Reproductive Health," *Toxicology and Industrial Health*, Vol. 12, No. 3/4 (1996), pp. 347–359.

162. Donald P. Waller *et al.*, "Great Lakes Fish as a Source of Maternal and Fetal Exposure to Chlorinated Hydrocarbons," *Toxicology and Industrial Health*, Vol. 12, No. 3/4 (1996), pp. 335–345.

163. Edward F. Fitzgerald *et al.*, "Polychlorinated Biphenyl (PCB) and Dichlorodiphenyl Dichloroethylene (DDE) Exposure Among Native American Men from Contaminated Great Lakes Fish and Wildlife," *Toxicology and Industrial Health*, Vol. 12, No. 3/4 (1996), pp. 361–368.

164. *Op. cit.* 162, p. 338.

165. Christopher T. DeRosa, Director, Division of Toxicology, Agency for Toxic Substances and Disease Registry, Atlanta, Georgia, August 1997 (personal communication).

166. Programme for the Promotion of Chemical Safety, the Division of Control of Tropical Diseases, and the Food Safety Unit of the World Health Organization (WHO), "Persistent Organic Pollutants," paper prepared for the Intergovernmental Forum on Chemical Safety Experts Meeting on Persistent Organic Pollutants, June 17–19, 1996, Manila, The Philippines (WHO, Geneva, 1996).

167. Dudley Achu Sama, "The Constraints in Managing the Pathways of Persistent Organic Pollutants into the Large Marine Ecosystem of the Gulf of Guinea: The Case of Cameroon," paper prepared for the Intergovernmental Forum on Chemical Safety Ex-

Environmental Change and Human Health

perts Meeting on Persistent Organic Pollutants, June 17–19, 1996, Manila, The Philippines (WHO, Geneva, 1996).

168. *Op. cit.* 149, p. 4.

169. *Op. cit.* 152, p. 19.

170. Jerome O. Nriagu, "A History of Global Metal Pollution," *Science*, Vol. 272, No. 5259 (April 12, 1996), p. 223.

171. David L. Eaton and William O. Robertson, "Toxicology," in *Textbook of Clinical Occupational and Environmental Medicine*, Linda Rosenstick and Mark R. Cullen, eds. (W.B. Saunders Company, Philadelphia, 1994), pp. 116–117.

172. Cheryl Simon Silver and Dale S. Rothman, *Toxics and Health: The Potential Long-Term Effects of Industrial Activity* (World Resources Institute, Washington, D.C., 1995), p. 7.

173. Janet Glover-Kerkvliet, "Environmental Assault on Immunity," *Environmental Health Perspectives*, Vol. 103, No. 3 (March 1995), pp. 236–237.

174. *Ibid.*, p. 237.

175. *Op. cit.* 172, p. 7.

176. *Op. cit.* 170.

177. Rob Edwards, "Toxic Sludge Flows Through the Andes," *New Scientist* (November 23, 1996), p. 4.

178. John E. Young, "Mining the Earth," Worldwatch Paper No. 109 (Worldwatch Institute, Washington, D.C., July 1992), p. 21.

179. Josef Elsinger, "Sweet Poison," *Natural History*, Vol. 105, No. 7 (July 1996), p. 50.

180. Ellen Silbergeld and Kevin Tonat, "Investing in Prevention: Opportunities to Prevent Disease and Reduce Health Care Costs By Identifying Environmental and Occupational Causes of Noncancer Disease," *Toxicology and Industrial Health*, Vol. 10, No. 6 (1994), p. 677.

181. A.J. McMichael, *Planetary Overload: Global Environmental Change and the Health of the Human Species* (Cambridge University Press, Cambridge, 1993), p. 279.

182. Ellen K. Silbergeld, "The International Dimensions of Lead Exposure," *International Journal of Occupational and Environmental Health*, Vol. 1, No. 4 (Oct./Dec. 1995), pp. 338, 340.

183. Ellen Silbergeld, "The Elimination of Lead from Gasoline: Impacts of Lead in Gasoline on Human Health, and the Costs and Benefits of Eliminating Lead Additives," draft paper (The World Bank, Washington, D.C., 1996), p. 3.

184. Robert A. Goyer, "Results of Lead Research: Prenatal Exposure and Neurological Consequences," *Environmental Health Perspectives*, Vol. 104, No. 10 (October 1996), p. 1050.

185. Herbert L. Needleman *et al.*, "Bone Lead Levels and Delinquent Behavior," *Journal of the American Medical Association*, Vol. 275, No. 5 (February 7, 1996), pp. 363–369.

186. *Op. cit.* 182, p. 336.

187. J. Schwartz, "Low Level Lead Exposure and Children's IQ: A Meta-Analysis and Search for a Threshold," *Environmental Research*, Vol. 65, No. 1 (1994), pp. 42–55.

188. *Op. cit.* 183.

189. *Op. cit.* 183.

190. Alliance to End Childhood Lead Poisoning (Alliance) and the Environmental Defense Fund (EDF), *The Global Dimensions of Lead Poisoning: An Initial Analysis* (Alliance and EDF, Washington, D.C., 1994), p. 35.

191. "Preventing Lead Poisoning in China," *Environmental Health Perspectives*, Vol. 104, No. 10 (October 1996), p. 1025.

192. Jerome O. Nriagu, Mary L. Blankson, and Kwamena Ocran, "Childhood Lead Poisoning in Africa: A Growing Public Health Problem" *The Science of the Total Environment*, Vol. 181 (1996), p. 99.

193. Robert A. Goyer, "Results of Lead Research: Prenatal Exposure and Neurological Consequences," *Environmental Health Perspectives*, Vol. 104, No. 10 (October 1996), p. 1051.

194. Magda Lovei, "Phasing Out Lead From Gasoline: World-Wide Experience and Policy Implications," draft paper (The World Bank, Washington, D.C., May 1996), p. 2.

195. *Op. cit.* 183, p. 7.

196. George M. Gray, Laury Saligman, and John D. Graham, "The Demise of Lead in Gasoline," in *The Greening of Industry: A Risk Management Approach*, John D. Graham and Jennifer Kassalow Hartwell, eds. (Harvard University Press, Cambridge, Massachusetts, 1997), p. 18.

197. Jerome Nriagu, "The Rise and Fall of Leaded Gasoline," in *The Science of the Total Environment*, Vol. 92 (1990), pp. 13–28.

198. *Op. cit.* 194, p. 8.

199. Albert L. Nichols, "Lead in Gasoline," in Richard Morgenstern, ed., *Economic Analyses at EPA: Assessing Regulatory Impact* (Resources for the Future, Washington, D.C., 1997), p. 1.

200. James L. Pirkle *et al.*, "The Decline in Blood Lead Levels in the United States," *Journal of the American Medical Association*, Vol. 272, No. 4 (July 27, 1994), pp. 284–291.

201. *Op. cit.* 183, p. 9.

202. Jacobo Finkelman, "Phasing Out Leaded Gasoline Will Not End Lead Poisoning in Developing Countries," *Environmental Health Perspectives*, Vol. 104, No. 1 (January 1996), p. 1.

203. Magda Lovei, *Phasing Out Lead From Gasoline in Central and Eastern Europe* (The World Bank, Washington, D.C., 1997).

204. The World Bank, *Elimination of Lead in Gasoline in Latin America and the Caribbean*, Report No. 194197EN, Energy Management Assistance Programme (The World Bank, Washington, D.C., 1996).

205. *Op. cit.* 203.

206. *Op. cit.* 194, p. 20.

207. *Op. cit.* 202.

208. *Op. cit.* 194, p. 19.

209. M.M. Verberk *et al.*, "Environmental Pollution and Health," *The Lancet*, Vol. 340, No. 8829 (November 14, 1992), p. 1221.

210. *Op. cit.* 190, p. 9.

211. T.D. Matte *et al.*, "Lead Exposure from Conventional and Cottage Lead Smelting in Jamaica," Archives of Environmental Contamination and Toxicology, Vol. 21 (1991), pp. 65–71.

212. Isabelle Romieu *et al.*, "Lead Exposure in Latin America and the Caribbean," *Environmental Health Perspectives*, Vol. 105, No. 4 (April 1997), p. 399.

213. *Op. cit.* 202.

214. Lizbeth López-Carillo *et al.*, "Prevalence and Determinants of Lead Intoxication in Mexican Children of Low Socioeconomic Status," *Environmental Health Perspectives*, Vol. 104, No. 11 (November 1996), p. 1210.

215. *Op. cit.* 202.

216. Debra J. Brody *et al.*, "Blood Lead Levels in the U.S. Population: Phase 1 of the Third National Health and Nutrition Examination Survey (NHANES III, 1988 to 1991)," *Journal of the American Medical Association*, Vol. 272, No. 4 (July 27, 1994), p. 277.

217. Lynn Goldman, "Childhood Lead Poisoning in 1994," *Journal of the American Medical Association*, Vol. 272, No. 4 (July 27, 1994), p. 315.

218. *Ibid.*

219. *Op. cit.* 202.

220. *Op. cit.* 172, p. 6.

221. M. Prather *et al.*, "The Ozone Layer: The Road Not Taken," *Nature*, Vol. 381 (1996), p. 554.

222. Steven A. Lloyd, "Stratospheric Ozone Depletion," *The Lancet*, Vol. 342 (November 6, 1993), p. 1156.

223. *Op. cit.* 97, p. 38.

224. S. Madronich *et al.*, "Changes in Ultraviolet Radiation Reaching the Earth's Surface," *Ambio*, Vol. 24, No. 3 (May 1995), p. 148.

225. *Op. cit.* 97, p. 166.

226. *Op. cit.* 97, p. 167.

227. Amminikutty Jeevan and Margaret L. Kripke, "Ozone Depletion and the Immune System," *The Lancet*, Vol. 342 (November 6, 1993), pp. 1159–1160.

228. M. Vermeer *et al.*, "Effects of Ultraviolet B Light on Cutaneous Immune Responses of Humans with Deeply Pigmented Skin," *Journal of Investigative Dermatology*, Vol. 97 (1991), pp. 732–733.

229. *Op. cit.* 227.

230. International Energy Agency, *World Energy Outlook*, 1996 (Organisation for Economic Co-Operation and Development, Paris, 1996), p. 3.

231. *Op. cit.* 21, pp. 280–281.

232. *Op. cit.* 230, p. 2.

233. *Op. cit.* 230, p. 237, Table A-5.

234. A. Faiz, K. Sinha, S. Gautam, *Air Pollution Characteristics and Trends, World Bank Discussion Paper* (The World Bank, Washington, D.C., 1994), p.1.

235. United States Energy Information Administration, *International Energy Outlook, 1996* (U.S. Department of Energy, Washington, D.C., 1996), pp. 5, 49, 94 (Table A-4).

236. *Op. cit.* 230, p. 45.

237. *Op. cit.* 21, p. 320.

238. *Op. cit.* 97, p. 32.

239. *Op. cit.* 97, pp. vii, 1, 6–7.

240. United Nations Environment Programme (UNEP), *Urban Air Pollution*, UNEP/GEMS Environment Library Report No. 4 (UNEP, Nairobi, 1991), p. 6.

241. Derek Elsom, *Smog Alert: Managing Urban Air Quality* (Earthscan Publications, Ltd., London, 1996), p. 1

242. U.S. Environmental Protection Agency (U.S. EPA), *National Air Quality and Emissions Trends Report*, 1995 Report No. EPA-454/R-96-005 (U.S. EPA, Washington, D.C., 1996), p. 2.

243. World Health Organization and the United Nations Environment Programme, *Urban Air Pollution in Megacities of the World* (Blackwell Publishers, Oxford, U.K., 1992), pp. 43–44.

244. T. Johnson, F. Liu, and R. Newfarmer, *Clear Water, Blue Skies: China's Environment in the 21st Century*, draft report No. 16481-CHA (The World Bank, Washington, D.C., May 1997), p. 3.

245. David Satterthwaite *et al.*, *The Environment for Children: Understanding and Acting on the Environmental Hazards that Threaten Children and Their Parents* (Earthscan Publications, Ltd., London, 1996), p. 44.

246. *Op. cit.* 4, p. 87.

247. Christopher J.L. Murray and Alan D. Lopez, eds., *The Global Burden of Disease: Volume I* (World Health Organization, Harvard School of Public Health, and the World Bank, Geneva, 1996), pp. 311–315, Tables 6.2 and 6.12.

248. The World Bank, *World Development Report 1992: Development and the Environment* (Oxford University Press, New York, 1992), pp. 51–52.

249. *Ibid.*

250. Lawrence Folinsbee, "Human Health Effects of Air Pollution," *Environmental Health Perspectives*, Vol. 100 (1992), p. 46.

251. D. Dockery *et al.*, "An Association Between Air Pollution and Mortality in Six U.S. Cities," *The New England Journal of Medicine*, Vol. 329, No. 24 (1993), p. 1753.

252. C.A. Pope *et al.*, "Particulate Air Pollution as a Predictor of Mortality in a Prospective Study of U.S.

Adults," *American Journal of Respiratory and Critical Care Medicine*, Vol. 151 (1995), p. 672.

253. Deborah Shprentz, *Breathtaking: Premature Mortality Due to Particulate Air Pollution in 239 American Cities* (Natural Resources Defense Council, New York, 1996), p. 7.

254. R. Bertollini *et al.*, *Environment and Health 1: Overview and Main European Issues*, WHO Regional Publications, European Series, No. 68 (World Health Organization, Copenhagen, 1996), p. 36.

255. T. Woodruff, J. Grillo, and K. Schoendorf, *The Relationship Between Selected Causes of Postneonatal Infant Mortality and Particulate Air Pollution in the United States*, draft 1996, pp. 16–19.

256. Bart Ostro, *Estimating the Health Effects of Air Pollutants: A Method with an Application to Jakarta*, World Bank Policy Research Working Paper No. 1301 (The World Bank, Washington, D.C., 1994), pp. 48–49.

257. *Ibid.*, p. 47.

258. Isabelle Romieu, Henyk Weitzenfeld, and Jacobo Finkelman, "Urban Air Pollution in Latin America and the Caribbean: Health Perspectives," *World Health Statistics Quarterly*, Vol. 43 (1990), p. 162.

259. Along with clean water, urban air pollution, and deforestation. The World Bank, *World Development Report* (Oxford University Press, New York, 1992).

260. *Op. cit.* 4, pp. 81–87.

261. D. Kossove, "Smoke-Filled Rooms and Respiratory Disease in Infants," *South African Medical Journal*, Vol. 63 (1982), pp. 622–624.

262. M.R. Pandey *et al.*, "Domestic Smoke Pollution and Acute Respiratory Infections in a Rural Community of the Hill Region of Nepal," *Environment International*, Vol. 15 (1989), pp. 337–340.

263. T.J.D. O'Dempsey *et al.*, "A Study of Risk Factors for Pneumococcal Disease Among Children in a Rural Area of West Africa," *International Journal of Epidemiology*, Vol. 25, No. 4 (1996), pp. 885–893.

264. F.D.E. Mtango *et al.*, "Risk Factors for Deaths in Children Under 5 Years Old in Babamoyo District, Tanzania," *Tropical Medicine and Parasitology*, Vol. 43 (1992), pp. 229–233.

265. *Op. cit.* 263, pp. 337–339.

266. M. Døssing, J. Khan, and F. al-Rabiah, "Risk Factors for Chronic Obstructive Lung Disease in Saudi Arabia," *Respiratory Medicine*, Vol. 88, No. 7 (1994), pp. 519–522.

267. Rudolfo J. Dennis *et al.*, "Woodsmoke Exposure and Risk for Obstructive Airways Disease Among Women," *Chest*, Vol. 109, No. 1 (1996), pp. 115–119.

268. R. Perez-Padilla *et al.*, "Exposure to Biomass Smoke and Chronic Airway Disease Among Mexican Women," *American Journal of Respiratory and Critical Care Medicine*, Vol. 154 (1996), pp. 701–706.

269. Kirk R. Smith and Youcheng Liu, "Indoor Air Pollution in Developing Countries," in *The Epidemiology of Lung Cancer*, J. Samet, ed. (Marcell Dekker, New York, 1994), pp. 151–175.

270. P.G. Shields, G.X. Xu, and W.J. Blot, "Mutagens from Heated Chinese and U.S. Cooking Oils," *Journal of the National Cancer Institute*, Vol. 87, No. 11 (1995), pp. 836–841.

271. D.V. Mavalankar, C.R. Trivedi, and R.H. Gray, "Levels and Risk Factors for Perinatal Mortality in Ahmedabad, India," *Bulletin of the World Health Organization*, Vol. 69, No. 4 (1991), pp. 435–442.

272. Valerie Setlow and Andrew Pope, eds., *Conference on Human Health and Global Climate Change: Summary of the Proceedings*, from a conference sponsored by the National Academy of Science, Institute of Medicine on Sept. 11–12, 1995 (National Academy Press, Washington, D.C., 1996), p. 7.

273. *Op. cit.* 97, pp. 43–44.

274. *Op. cit.* 273, p. 9.

275. "Heat Related Mortality—Chicago, July, 1995," *Morbidity and Mortality Weekly Report*, Vol. 44, No. 31 (August 11, 1995).

276. *Op. cit.* 97, pp. 50–52, 54.

277. *Op. cit.* 273, p. 9.

278. *Op. cit.* 97, pp. 53–54.

279. *Op. cit.* 97, pp. 123–124.

280. *Op. cit.* 97, pp. 33–34, 123.

281. *Op. cit.* 97, pp. 145, 148.

282. *Op. cit.* 97, pp. 152–153.

283. *Op. cit.* 97, pp. 153–156.

284. *Op. cit.* 97, pp. 146, 149–150, 154.

285. U.S. Environmental Protection Agency (U.S. EPA), *The Potential Effects of Global Climate Change on the United States*, EPA Report No. EPA-230-05-89-050 (U.S. EPA, Washington, D.C., 1989), p. 199.

286. *Op. cit.* 97, p. 65.

287. John Balbus, Assistant Professor of Medicine, The George Washington University, "Air Pollution and Climate Change," presentation at the Annual Meeting of the Society for Occupational and Environmental Health (SOEH), National Institutes of Health, March 6, 1997.

288. S. Lindsay and M. Birley, "Climate Change and Malaria Transmission," *Annals of Tropical Medicine and Parasitology*, Vol. 90, No. 6 (1996), p. 580.

289. J. Patz *et al.*, "Global Climate Change and Emerging Infectious Diseases," *Journal of the American Medical Association*, Vol. 275, No. 3 (1996), p. 218.

290. *Op. cit.* 97, p. 81.

291. *Op. cit.* 97, pp. 84–86.

292. *Op. cit.* 290, p. 218.

293. *Op. cit.* 289, p. 580.

294. *Op. cit.* 97, p. 82.

295. *Op. cit.* 290, p. 220.

296. *Op. cit.* 290, p. 220.

297. *Op. cit.* 97, pp. 96–100.

298. *Op. cit.* 97, pp. 110–111.

299. *Op. cit.* 97, pp. 110, 111, 114.

300. *Op. cit.* 97, pp. 111–113.

301. *Op. cit.* 97, pp. 115–121.

Chapter 3: Improving Health Through Environmental Action

1. World Health Organization (WHO), *Health and Environment in Sustainable Development: Five Years After the Earth Summit* (WHO, Geneva, 1997), p. 1.

2. A.J. McMichael *et al.*, eds., *Climate Change and Human Health: An Assessment Prepared by a Task Group on Behalf of the World Health Organization, the World Meteorological Organization, and the United Nations Environment Programme* (World Health Organization, Geneva, 1996), pp. 163–170.

3. *Op. cit.* 1, p. 172.

4. World Health Organization (WHO), *The World Health Report 1996: Fighting Disease, Fostering Development* (WHO, Geneva, 1996), p. 13.

5. Carter Brandon and Ramesh Ramankutty, *Toward an Environmental Strategy for Asia* (The World Bank, Washington, D.C., 1993), p. 52.

6. United Nations Children's Fund (UNICEF), *The Progress of Nations* (UNICEF, New York, 1996), p. 26.

7. *Ibid.*

8. *Op. cit.* 1, p. 8.

9. *Op. cit.* 4, pp. 64–65.

10. Institute of Medicine, *Emerging Infections: Microbial Threats to Health in the United States,* Joshua Lederberg, Robert E. Shope, and Stanley C. Oaks, Jr., eds. (National Academy Press, Washington, D.C., 1992).

11. Paul R. Epstein, "Emerging Diseases and Ecosystem Instability: New Threats to Public Health," *American Journal of Public Health*, Vol. 85, No. 2 (February 1995), pp. 168–170.

12. *Op. cit.* 1, p. 198.

13. The World Bank, *World Development Report 1993: Investing in Health* (The World Bank, Washington, D.C., 1993).

14. *Op. cit.* 1.

15. *Op.cit.* 13, p. 90.

16. *Op. cit.* 13, p. 92.

17. United Nations Development Programme (UNDP), *Human Development Report 1997* (UNDP, New York, 1997).

18. Marianne Kjellen and Gordon McGranahan, *Urban Water—Towards Health and Sustainability* (Stockholm Environment Institute, Stockholm, 1997), p. 17.

19. Sandy Cairncross *et al.*, "The Public and Domestic Domains in the Transmission of Disease," *Tropical Medicine and International Health*, Vol. 1, No. 1 (February 1996), pp. 27–34.

20. S.R.A. Huttly, S.S. Morris, and V. Pisani, "Prevention of Diarrhea in Young Children in Developing Countries," *Bulletin of the World Health Organization*, Vol. 75, No. 2 (1997), pp. 166–167.

21. *Op. cit.* 19, pp. 27–34.

22. *Op. cit.* 18, p. 17.

23. World Health Organization (WHO), *The International Drinking Water Supply and Sanitation Decade* (WHO, Geneva, 1992), p. iii.

24. *Op. cit.* 6, p. 49.

25. Steven A. Esrey *et al.*, *Health Benefits from Improvements in Water Supply and Sanitation* (Water and Sanitation for Health Project, United States Agency for International Development [U.S. AID], Washington, D.C., 1989).

26. Steven A. Esrey, "Water, Waste, and Well-Being: A Multicountry Study," *American Journal of Epidemiology,* Vol. 143, No. 6 (1996), pp. 608–623.

27. *Op. cit.* 20, p. 167.

28. Sandy Cairncross and Peter J. Kolsky, "Re: 'Water, Waste, and Well-Being: A Multicountry Study,'"

American Journal of Epidemiology, Vol. 146, No. 4 (1997), pp. 359–360.

29. Steven A. Esrey, "The Author Replies," *American Journal of Epidemiology,* Vol. 146, No. 4 (1997), pp. 360–361.

30. *Op. cit.* 28, p. 359.

31. *Op. cit.* 23.

32. Sandy Cairncross, *Sanitation and Water Supply: Practical Lessons from The Decade* (The World Bank, Washington, D.C., 1992).

33. *Op. cit.* 23.

34. Malick Gaye and Fodé Diallo, "Community Participation in the Management of Urban Environment in Rufisque (Senegal)," *Environment and Urbanization,* Vol. 9, No. 1 (April 1997), pp. 9–30.

35. *Op. cit.* 18, p. 16.

36. *Op. cit.* 18, p. 15.

37. The World Bank, *Water Resources Management* (The World Bank, Washington, D.C., 1993), p. 31.

38. David Haarmeyer and Ashoka Mody, "Private Capital in Water and Sanitation," *Finance and Development,* Vol. 34, No. 1 (March 1997), pp. 34–37.

39. *Op. cit.* 37, pp. 54–55.

40. Patricia Annez and Alfred Friendly, "Cities in the Developing World: Agenda for Action Following Habitat II," *Finance and Development,* Vol. 33, No. 4 (December 1996), p. 14.

41. *Op. cit.* 18, p. 17.

42. World Resources Institute in collaboration with the United Nations Environment Programme, the United Nations Development Programme, and The World Bank, *World Resources 1996–97* (Oxford University Press, New York, 1996), pp. 108–109.

43. G. Gutiérrez *et al.,* "Impact of Oral Rehydration and Selected Public Health Interventions on Reduction of Mortality from Childhood Diarrhoeal Diseases in Mexico," *Bulletin of the World Health Organization,* Vol. 74, No. 2 (1996), p. 194.

44. The World Bank, *World Development Report 1992: Development and the Environment* (The World Bank, Washington, D.C., 1992), p. 2.

45. H.W. de Koning, K.R. Smith, and J.M. Last, "Biomass Fuel Combustion and Health," *Bulletin of the World Health Organization,* Vol. 63, No. 1 (1985), pp. 11–26.

46. Kirk R. Smith, "Indoor Air Pollution in Developing Countries: Growing Evidence of Its Role in the Global Disease Burden," paper presented at Indoor Air '96: The 7th International Conference on Indoor Air Quality and Climate, Nagoya, Japan (July 21–26, 1996), pp. 1–12.

47. *Op. cit.* 1, p. 87.

48. Douglas F. Barnes *et al., What Makes People Cook with Improved Biomass Stoves? A Comparative International Review of Stove Programs* (The World Bank, Washington, D.C., 1994), p. 3.

49. M.R. Pandey *et al.,* "The Effectiveness of Smokeless Stoves in Reducing Indoor Air Pollution in a Rural Hill Region of Nepal," *Mountain Research and Development,* Vol. 10, No. 4 (1990), p. 319.

50. Douglas F. Barnes, Robert van der Plas, and Willem Floor, "Tackling the Rural Energy Problem in Developing Countries," *Finance and Development,* Vol. 34, No. 2 (June 1997), pp. 11–15.

51. Douglas Barnes, "Consequences of Energy Policies for the Urban Poor," *FDP Energy Note No. 7* (The World Bank, Washington, D.C., 1995).

52. *Op. cit.* 50, pp. 11–15.

53. Daniel S. Greenberg, "A Pittance to Fight Malaria," *The Washington Post* (January 4, 1998), p. C7.

54. Steven K. Ault, "Environmental Management: A Reemerging Vector Control Strategy," *American Journal of Tropical Medicine and Hygiene,* Vol. 50, No. 6 (1994), pp. 38–39.

55. Gilles Forget, *Health and the Environment: A People-Centred Research Strategy* (International Development Research Centre, Ottawa, 1992), p. 11.

56. *Op. cit.* 54, p. 37.

57. Sandy Cairncross and Richard G. Feachem, *Environmental Health Engineering in the Tropics: An Introductory Text,* 2nd edition (John Wiley & Sons, Chichester, U.K., 1993), p. 229.

58. Sandy Cairncross, E.I. Braide, and Sam Z. Bugri, "Community Participation in the Eradication of Guinea Worm Disease," *Acta Tropica,* Vol. 61 (1996), pp. 121–136.

59. Duane J. Gubler and Gary G. Clark, "Community Involvement in the Control of *Aedes aegypti,*" *Acta Tropica,* Vol. 61, No. 2 (1996), pp. 169–179.

60. M.W. Service, "Community Participation in Vectorborne Disease Control," *Annals of Tropical Medicine and Parasitology,* Vol. 87, No. 2 (1993), p. 229.

61. *Op. cit.* 13, p. 19.

62. David Brown, "Company Will Donate Drug to Fight Disfiguring Disease," *The Washington Post* (January 27, 1998).

63. The World Bank, *Five Years After Rio: Innovations in Environmental Policy* (The World Bank, Washington, D.C., 1997), p. 5.

64. Robert Goodland, "Environmental Sustainability in the Hydro Industry: Disaggregating the Debate," in *Large Dams: Learning from the Past, Looking at the Future. Workshop Proceedings* (International Union for Conservation of Nature and Natural Resources, Gland, Switzerland and Cambridge, U.K., and The World Bank, Washington, D.C., 1997), pp. 89–93.

65. "Reform Bill 'Dead Wrong' on Risk; Integrated Analysis Needed," *Environmental Health Letter* (July 3, 1995), p. 118.

66. World Health Organization (WHO), *Public Health Impact of Pesticides Used in Agriculture* (WHO, Geneva, 1990), pp. 84–86.

67. Tim Flood, "Occupational Exposure to Toxic Materials: Farm Worker Exposures to Pesticides from Application," draft paper (United States Environmental Protection Agency, Washington, D.C., 1996). Available online at: http://www.epa.gov/oppeinet/oppe/futures/risk/ crexamples/examples/Arizona/humhlth/farmwrkr.txt.html.

68. "World Pesticide Market to Grow 4.4% Per Annum to 1998," *Agrow: World Crop Protection News,* No. 225 (February 3, 1995), p. 16.

69. Robert Repetto and Sanjay S. Baliga, *Pesticides and the Immune System: The Public Health Risks* (World Resources Institute, Washington, D.C., 1996), p. 63.

70. *Op. cit.* 63, p. 26.

71. Tjaart W. Schillhorn van Veen *et al., Integrated Pest Management: Strategies and Policies for Effective Implementation* (The World Bank, Washington, D.C., 1997), p. 24.

72. *Op. cit.* 63, p. 16.

73. PIC incorporated into the *International Code of Conduct on the Distribution and Use of Pesticides* (Food and Agriculture Organization of the United Nations [FAO], Rome, 1989) and the *London Guidelines for the Exchange of Information on Chemicals in International Trade* (United Nations Environment Programme, Nairobi, 1989).

74. United Nations Environment Programme (UNEP), "PIC-Update on Implementation as of June 1997," "PIC—A Brief Overview of What It Is and How It Operates," and "Development of an Internationally Legally Binding Instrument." Available online at: http://irptc.unep.ch/pic/ (January 21, 1997).

75. United States Environmental Protection Agency (U.S. EPA), *Office of Pesticide Programs Annual Report for 1995* (U.S. EPA, Washington, D.C., 1995), p. 7.

76. United Nations Environment Programme (UNEP), *Integrated Pest Management in the Tropics: Current Status and Future Prospects* (John Wiley & Sons, Chichester, U.K., 1995), p. 138.

77. *Op. cit.* 1, p. 63.

78. *Issues in Ecology,* No. 1 (February 1997), pp. 13–14.

79. Vaclav Smil, *Global Ecology: Environmental Change and Social Flexibility* (Routledge, London, 1993), pp. 138–139.

80. *Op. cit.* 54, p. 43.

81. *Op. cit.* 57, p. 207.

82. *Op. cit.* 63, p. 46.

83. The World Bank, *Brazil: Managing Environmental Pollution in the State of Rio de Janeiro* (The World Bank, Washington, D.C., August 1996), p. 94.

84. Ellen Silbergeld and Kevin Tonat, "Investing in Prevention: Opportunities to Prevent Disease and Reduce Health Care Costs By Identifying Environmental and Occupation Causes of Noncancer Disease," *Toxicology and Industrial Health,* Vol. 10, No. 6 (1994), p. 677.

85. Ellen K. Silbergeld, "The International Dimensions of Lead Exposure," *International Journal of Occupational and Environmental Health,* Vol. 1, No. 4 (October/December 1995), p. 336.

86. Magda Lovei, "Phasing Out Lead From Gasoline: Worldwide Experience and Policy Implications," draft paper (The World Bank, Washington, D.C., May 1996), p. 20.

87. Magda Lovei, *Phasing Out Lead from Gasoline: Worldwide Experience and Policy Implications* (The World Bank, Washington, D.C., August 1996), p. 28.

88. Albert L. Nichols, "Lead in Gasoline," in *Economic Analyses at EPA: Assessing Regulatory Impact,* Richard Morganstern, ed. (Resources for the Future, Washington, D.C., 1997), pp. 5–6.

89. *Op. cit.* 86, p. 13.

90. *Op. cit.* 87, p. 23.

91. Magda Lovei, *Phasing Out Lead from Gasoline: Worldwide Experience and Policy Implications,* World Bank Technical Paper No. 397 (The World Bank, Washington, D.C., 1998), p. 6.

92. United Nations Environment Programme (UNEP), *Global Environment Outlook* (UNEP, Nairobi, 1996), p. 134.

93. George R. Heaton, Jr., R. Darryl Banks, and Daryl W. Ditz, *Missing Links: Technology and Environmental Improvement in the Industrializing World* (World Resources Institute, Washington, D.C., 1994), p. 25.

94. *Ibid.,* p. 26.

95. Lester R. Brown, Christopher Flavin, and Hal Kane, eds., *Vital Signs 1996: The Trends that Are Shaping Our Future* (Worldwatch Institute, Washington, D.C., 1996), p. 116.

96. The World Bank, *Indonesia: Environment and Development* (The World Bank, Washington, D.C., 1994), p. 130.

97. David Sonnenfeld, "Ecological Modernization? The Case of the Pulp and Paper Industry in Indonesia," paper presented at the University of Washington, Seattle, Washington, October 1997.

98. *Op. cit.* 1, p. 200.

99. D. Satterthwaite *et al., The Environment for Children: Understanding and Acting on the Environmental Hazards that Threaten Children and Their Parents* (Earthscan Publications, Ltd., London, 1996), p. 44.

100. C. Arden Pope II *et al.,* "Particulate Air Pollution as a Predictor of Mortality in a Prospective Study of U.S. Adults," *American Journal of Respiratory and Critical Care Medicine,* Vol. 151, No. 3 (March 1995), pp. 669–674.

101. Philip J. Hilts, "Studies Say Soot Kills Up to 60,000 in U.S. Each Year," *The New York Times* (July 19, 1993), p. A1.

102. Council on Environmental Quality, *Environmental Quality: 25th Anniversary Report* (U.S. Government

Printing Office, Washington, D.C., 1995), pp. 87–89.

103. Michael Walsh and Jitendra J. Shah, *Clean Fuels for Asia: Technical Options for Moving Toward Unleaded Gasoline and Low-Sulfur Diesel* (The World Bank, Washington, D.C., 1997), p. 45.

104. The World Bank, *Chile: Managing Environmental Problems: Economic Analysis of Selected Issues* (The World Bank, Washington, D.C., 1994), p. 14.

105. Urban Air Quality Management Strategy in Asia (URBAIR), *Greater Mumbai Report* (The World Bank, Washington, D.C., 1996), p. 62.

106. Lakdasa Wijetilleke and Suhashini A.R. Karunaratne, *Air Quality Management: Considerations for Developing Countries* (The World Bank, Washington, D.C., 1995), p. 81.

107. E. Stratos Tavoulareas and Jean-Pierre Charpentier, *Clean Coal Technologies for Developing Countries* (The World Bank, Washington, D.C., 1995), p. 5.

108. Peter van der Veen and Cynthia Wilson, "A New Initiative to Promote Clean Coal," *Finance and Development,* Vol. 34, No. 4 (December 1997), p. 38.

109. Peter Havlicek, "The Czech Republic: First Steps Toward a Cleaner Future," *Environment,* Vol. 39, No. 3 (April 1997), pp. 38–39.

110. *Ibid.,* p. 41.

111. American Automobile Manufacturers Association (AAMA), *World Motor Vehicle Data 1993 (AAMA, Washington, D.C., 1993), pp. 40, 46; and various editions of American Automobile Manufacturers Association (AAMA), Motor Vehicle Facts and Figures* (AAMA, Washington, D.C.).

112. Urban Air Quality Management Strategy in Asia (URBAIR), *Metro Manila Report* (The World Bank, Washington, D.C., 1997), p. 3.

113. *Op. cit.* 105, p. 3.

114. Urban Air Quality Management Strategy in Asia (URBAIR), *Jakarta Report* (The World Bank, Washington, D.C., 1996), p. 3.

115. Winston Harrington and Alan Krupnick, *Energy, Transportation, and Environment: Policy Options for Environmental Improvements* (The World Bank, Washington, D.C., 1997), p. 21.

116. United States Environmental Protection Agency (U.S. EPA), "Automobiles and Ozone," EPA Fact Sheet, EPA 400-F-92-006 (U.S. EPA, Washington, D.C., 1993). Available online at: http://www.epa.gov/omswww/04-ozone.htm (January 21, 1998).

117. For a more detailed description of urban transportation policies, see World Resources Institute in collaboration with the United Nations Environment Programme, the United Nations Development Programme, and the World Bank, *World Resources 1996–97* (Oxford University Press, New York, 1996), pp. 81–102.

118. Intergovernmental Panel on Climate Change, *Climate Change 1995: The Science of Climate Change* (Cambridge University Press, Cambridge, U.K., 1996), p. 4.

119. *Ibid.,* p. 3.

120. Walter V. Reid and José Goldemberg, "Are Developing Countries Already Doing as Much as Industrialized Countries to Slow Climate Change?" *Climate Notes* (World Resources Institute, Washington, D.C., 1997).

121. *Ibid.*

122. Roger C. Dower and Mary Beth Zimmerman, *The Right Climate for Carbon Taxes: Creating Economic Incentives to Protect the Atmosphere* (World Resources Institute, Washington, D.C., 1992), p. 32.

123. Working Group on Public Health and Fossil-Fuel Combustion, "Short-Term Improvements in Public Health from Global-Climate Policies on Fossil-Fuel Combustion: An Interim Report," *The Lancet,* Vol. 350, No. 9088 (November 8, 1997), pp. 1341–1348.

PART II

Global Environmental Trends

OVERVIEW

The past 100 years have brought unprecedented gains in many of the indicators that we use to gauge progress in human development, from life expectancy to per capita income to education. During the same period, however, human impact on the natural world has risen dramatically as the scope and intensity of human activities have increased. Although there has been progress recently in tackling air and water pollution problems in some countries, many negative trends, such as the loss of tropical forests and the buildup of greenhouse gases in the atmosphere, continue unabated.

An overview of environment and development trends yields the following snapshot:

• World population—now at nearly 6 billion—is growing more slowly than predicted just a few years ago but is still expected to increase substantially before stabilizing. Projections put world population at between 8 and 12 billion in 2050, with nearly all of this growth expected in the developing world.

• The economic fortunes of a number of developing nations have risen steadily in the past two decades, but many other nations have experienced economic decline and falling per capita incomes since 1980. The disparity in incomes between the rich and poor within nations and between wealthy and poorer nations in general continues to widen.

• During the past 30 years, a higher proportion of children have been attending school, and adult literacy has climbed steadily.

• Global food production is generally adequate to meet human nutritional needs, but problems with distribution mean that some 800 million people remain undernourished. World food production is still rising, but yields of the major grain crops are rising more slowly now than in the past. In addition,

postharvest losses remain high, and soil degradation from erosion and poor irrigation practices continues to harm agricultural lands, jeopardizing production in some regions.

• Consumption of natural resources by modern industrial economies remains very high—in the range of 45 to 85 metric tons per person annually when all materials (including soil erosion, mining wastes, and other ancillary materials) are counted. It currently requires about 300 kilograms of natural resources to generate US$100 of income in the world's most advanced economies. Given the size of these economies, this represents a truly massive scale of environmental alteration.

• Global energy use, which has increased nearly 70 percent since 1971, is projected to increase at more than 2 percent annually for the next 15 years. This will raise greenhouse gas emissions about 50 percent higher than current levels unless a concerted effort takes place to increase energy efficiency and move away from today's heavy reliance on fossil fuels.

• Nations have cut consumption of ozone-depleting substances some 70 percent since 1987. However, the ozone layer is still not safe. Phaseout of chlorofluorocarbons (CFCs) and other ozone-destroying chemicals is not complete, and a significant black market in illegal CFCs has sprung up, endangering some of the gains already made.

• In the past 50 years, excess nitrogen, principally from fertilizers, human sewage, and the burning of fossil fuels, has begun to overwhelm the global nitrogen cycle, with a variety of ill effects ranging from reduced soil fertility to eutrophication in lakes, rivers, and coastal estuaries. The amount of biologically available nitrogen may double over the next 25 years.

• Acid rain is a growing problem in Asia, with sulfur dioxide emissions expected to triple there by 2010 if current trends continue.

• Deforestation continues to shrink world forests, with deforestation rates in many countries increasing from 1990 to 1995 despite a surge of public awareness about the loss of forests, especially in the tropics. Deforestation in the Amazon doubled from 1994 to 1995 before declining in 1996, and forest fires in both Indonesia and the Amazon took a heavy toll in 1997.

• Competition from nonnative plant and animal species—"bioinvasions"—represents a relentless and growing threat to ecosystems, with some 20 percent of all endangered vertebrate species threatened by exotic invaders.

• Risks to the world's ecosystems are nowhere greater than in aquatic environments such as coral reefs and freshwater habitats in rivers, lakes, and wetlands. Some 58 percent of the world's reefs and 34 percent of all fish species may be at risk from human activities.

• Global water consumption is rising quickly, and water availability is likely to become one of the most pressing resource issues of the 21st Century. One third of the world's population lives in countries already experiencing moderate to high water stress, and that number could rise to two thirds in the next 30 years without serious water conservation measures.

What do these trends portend for the global environment? On the surface, they paint a troubling picture of the future, with many critical environmental indicators continuing to decline at their current pace or at increasing speed. Although global food supply and economic growth appear robust in the short term, such accumulating environmental harm ultimately puts at risk the ecosystems and environmental processes such as climate that form the basis of human health and well-being. Yet, interpreting environmental trends requires care. Environmental threats are not always comparable or additive, since they differ greatly in terms of scale, effect, and the time frame in which they act, from the local and immediate threats of overfishing or deforestation, to long-acting and global-scale threats such as climate change and ozone depletion.

Overall, the trends sketched above and detailed in the following pages support some important conclusions. First, changes to natural ecosystems are occurring on a larger scale than ever before, involving entire landscapes. Such large-scale landscape changes—through deforestation, expansion of agricultural land, and urban and suburban growth—will likely dictate the physical condition and extent of terrestrial ecosystems in the next several decades. Fragmentation of the world's remaining forest blocks; buildup in coastal areas; and the spread of cities, suburbs, and infrastructure over once-rural tracts will do much to degrade the habitat and watershed values of these areas.

Second, the very scale of these landscape-level changes, as well as the increasing intensity of industrial and agricultural processes, are inducing changes in the global systems and cycles—such as the atmosphere and the nitrogen cycle—that underpin the functioning of ecosystems. These changes in what can be called the "global commons" represent long-term environmental threats of a profound and far-reaching nature. Global warming from the buildup of

greenhouse gases is the best-known example, with the potential for large-scale disruption of natural ecosystems, agriculture, and human settlements due to changes in rainfall and temperature patterns and rising sea levels.

Third, threats to biodiversity from all sources are quickly reaching a critical level that may precipitate widespread changes in the number and distribution of species, as well as the functioning of ecosystems. Current extinction rates are 100 to 1,000 times higher than prehuman levels, and projected losses of habitat from land conversion, as well as increasing competition from nonnative species, will probably push this rate higher still.

Even as these trends indicate the environmental challenges ahead, it is important to remember that they can be modified with human resolve. Already, the transition to more environmentally benign ways of growing food, producing goods and services, managing watersheds, and accommodating urban growth has begun in many far-sighted communities and companies. How fast this transition to more "sustainable" forms of production and environmental management will proceed, and whether it can effectively mitigate the effects of large-scale environmental change, is the real question.

The following two chapters explore in greater detail these and other environmental trends. Chapter 4 reports on current conditions and critical trends in five broad areas—Population and Human Well-Being, Feeding the World, Production and Consumption, The Global Commons, and Resources at Risk—and tries to illuminate the forces driving these changes, be they population growth and demographic changes, consumption patterns, government policies, or other factors. Chapter 5 offers a regional perspective to the topics addressed in Chapter 4, with data on a variety of environmental and human development indicators for each of seven major regions.

POPULATION AND HUMAN WELL-BEING

Although the world's population is still growing, it is doing so at a slower rate than demographers had projected only a few years ago. Recent major gains in average life expectancy, reduced rates of child and infant mortality, and the increasing proportion of children now attending school all provide grounds for optimism about human well-being. Many of these gains have been made possible by unprecedented rates of economic growth in many countries. Some 3 billion to 4 billion people are expected to experience substantial improvements in their standard of living by the end of the 20th Century.

Yet these global successes mask urgent, sometimes worsening problems at the local or regional level, especially among developing countries. More than one quarter of the world's population has not shared in the economic and social progress experienced by the majority and still lives in poverty. Hunger, disease, illiteracy, and restricted freedom of choice or action are persistent problems in many of the least developed countries of sub-Saharan Africa and south Asia, as well as in parts of central Asia and South America. The pressure of population growth can contribute to human deprivation, especially in poor rural areas where competition for land and water can strain the capacity of local environments. Rapid population growth is also fueling problems in many cities, where it can overwhelm the capacity of municipal authorities to provide even elementary services.

Yet the interaction between population growth and human well-being is complex and not a matter of numbers alone. The capacity of countries to support growing populations is enhanced when those countries achieve a sufficient, equitable distribution of wealth, technological development, effective government, strong institutions, and social stability. This section explores some recent trends in population growth and demographic change, as well as in key indicators of human prosperity and social development.

Population Growth—Stabilization?

The world population is still increasing and has now reached more than 5.9 billion, according to the most recent United Nations (U.N.) estimates (1). (See Data Table 7.1.) However, the global annual increment—that is, the number of people added to the world's population each year—is thought to have peaked between 1985 and 1990 at about 87 million per year. Estimates for 1990–95 are that 81 million persons were added to the population each year

(2). Thanks to long life expectancy and low fertility rates, the populations of most developed countries are now stable or even in decline. Developing countries, however, have not yet achieved that goal. Indeed, the youthful age structure of most developing countries means that their *absolute populations* continue to grow, even where the *rate* of increase has declined significantly. (See Figure HW.1.)

Some regions are therefore closer than others to completing the demographic transition—the point at which death rates and birth rates are approximately equal and population growth

levels off. (See Figure HW.2.) Based on current demographic trends, the world population is projected to reach 9.4 billion by 2050 (3).

Estimates of future population size, however, are highly uncertain. The U.N. projections for 2050 range from a low of 7.7 billion to a high of 11.2 billion. (See Figure HW.3.) The latest "medium-variant" U.N. projection of 9.37 billion is nearly 500 million (4.7 percent) lower than the 9.83 billion medium variant projected in 1994 (4).

The medium-variant projection depends on a number of important assumptions:

- Fertility rates will continue to decline.

- Life expectancy will continue to increase.

- Developing countries will broadly follow the demographic transition already experienced in the industrialized world.

Fertility rates. The most rapid fertility declines have so far occurred in countries that have achieved major improvements in child survival rates and educational levels and have implemented family planning programs (for example, Colombia and Kenya). These developments, in turn, are often associated with economic growth and social changes including improved reproductive rights, rural–urban shifts, new family structures, and new employment patterns, especially changes in female labor force participation rates. Striking fertility declines are evident in rapidly developing countries such as Bangladesh, the Republic of Korea, and Singapore in Asia, and Colombia in Latin America (5). (See Figure HW.4.)

Today, the total fertility rate in developed countries is 1.6 children per woman; however, it is still 3.1 children per woman in developing countries. To realize the U.N.'s medium-variant population projection, the world total fertility rate must be lowered from 2.8

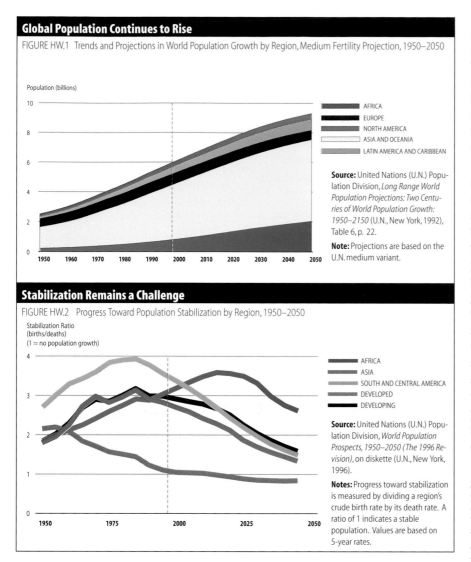

Global Population Continues to Rise

FIGURE HW.1 Trends and Projections in World Population Growth by Region, Medium Fertility Projection, 1950–2050

Population (billions)

AFRICA
EUROPE
NORTH AMERICA
ASIA AND OCEANIA
LATIN AMERICA AND CARIBBEAN

Source: United Nations (U.N.) Population Division, *Long Range World Population Projections: Two Centuries of World Population Growth: 1950–2150* (U.N., New York, 1992), Table 6, p. 22.

Note: Projections are based on the U.N. medium variant.

Stabilization Remains a Challenge

FIGURE HW.2 Progress Toward Population Stabilization by Region, 1950–2050

Stabilization Ratio
(births/deaths)
(1 = no population growth)

AFRICA
ASIA
SOUTH AND CENTRAL AMERICA
DEVELOPED
DEVELOPING

Source: United Nations (U.N.) Population Division, *World Population Prospects, 1950–2050 (The 1996 Revision)*, on diskette (U.N., New York, 1996).

Notes: Progress toward stabilization is measured by dividing a region's crude birth rate by its death rate. A ratio of 1 indicates a stable population. Values are based on 5-year rates.

(the current rate) to 2.1 children per woman (replacement level) by 2050 (6). (See Data Table 7.2.) Clearly, Africa is the region in which the future trend in fertility is significantly different from that of the past, and for this reason, its projection must be considered the most speculative.

Thailand has experienced one of the strongest rates of economic development—and one of the steepest declines in fertility—in the world. Thailand's total fertility rate declined from 6.59 children per woman during 1955–60 to 1.94 during 1990–95 (7). In 1960, the government launched a vigorous family planning program and made contraceptives freely available all over the

country. As a result, the population growth rate has fallen from a high of 3.1 percent to its current level of 0.9 percent. In poorer countries, duplicating this kind of experience would be a formidable challenge. Even so, population programs and social change are beginning to reduce fertility rates in many of the least developed countries as well. For example, Tanzania experienced a small but significant decline in total fertility rate, which dropped from 6.8 children per woman in the 1960s and 1970s to just under 6 children per woman in 1990–95 (8). The continued support of donor countries and institutions for the country's family planning program, as well as economic and educational devel-

opment, are likely to be critical in maintaining progress. The government of Tanzania has estimated that, if it is to meet its target of universal access to family planning services by 2015, it must provide for 5.6 million contraceptive users by 2015, almost a sixfold increase over the 1995 demand (9).

Life expectancy. Low death rates primarily reflect improved child survival rates, and child survival is a key determinant in family size. Developing countries have halved the life expectancy gap with industrialized countries over the past 40 years. The least developed countries, however, have experienced smaller gains, and life expectancy in these countries lags at about 50 years. In the medium-variant projection, life expectancy rates are assumed to rise to 81, 76, and 72 years in developed, developing, and least developed countries, respectively, by 2050. This increase presupposes, among other things, major progress in the fight against infectious diseases (10). (See Chapter 1.)

Demographic transition. Demographic experts believe that the shift from high to low birth rates, and from low to high life expectancy, is brought about by "social modernization." This complex of changes involves improved health care and access to family planning; higher educational attainment, especially among women; economic growth and rising per capita income levels; and urbanization and growing employment opportunities. Stabilization of the world's population will therefore depend on continuing or accelerating socioeconomic development in the great majority of the world's developing countries. A number of factors could impede the demographic transition, including stagnating economic growth, persistent poverty, or cultural factors that encourage large family size despite rising prosperity. If the transition is stalled, global population would presumably continue to rise throughout the next century.

Population projections carried out recently by another institution, Austria's International Institute for Applied Systems Analysis (IIASA), explicitly address some of the uncertainties underlying population forecasts. IIASA's projections make use of a probability model, reflecting expert opinion on the future courses of fertility, mortality, and migration, and the extent of their uncertainty. This model leads to a somewhat broader range of estimates than those from the U.N.; according to IIASA, world population in 2050 will probably number between 8.1 billion and almost 12 billion (11).

What are the implications of an approximately doubled world population? Population growth is of most concern where countries appear least able to deal with its consequences. Key issues in providing for increased populations will include the achievement of adequate income levels, food security, employment, and the provision of basic social services. Also critical is the sound management of natural resources that, in many developing countries, still directly support the livelihoods of a majority of their inhabitants. These and other issues are discussed throughout this section.

A significant number of the world's people already face critical shortfalls of the essentials needed for a healthy life. Some 1.3 billion live in absolute poverty, 840 million are undernourished (12), roughly 1.4 billion lack safe drinking water (13), and about 900 million are illiterate (14). In many areas, population growth is accelerating the rate of degradation of forests, fisheries, and productive soils. (See Resources at Risk.) Populations at direct risk from environmental degradation are concentrated in the least developed countries of sub-Saharan Africa and south Asia, and in parts of Latin America. Population growth, together with continued economic expansion, also presents risks at the global level. If the world's popula-

tion approximately doubles and average incomes continue to rise, it is likely that the production and consumption patterns characteristic of middle- and upper-income social groups will be adopted more widely throughout the developing world. The environmental impacts of the economic activity re-

quired to support modern consumer societies are already immense. (See Production and Consumption.) If tomorrow's consumers use and waste resources in the same manner as today's, the consequences in terms of global climate change, loss of vital renewable resources, and toxic pollution will be severe.

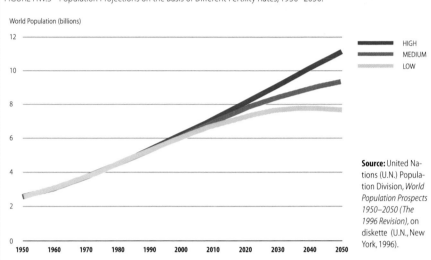

Different Assumptions, Different Projections

FIGURE HW.3   Population Projections on the Basis of Different Fertility Rates, 1950–2050.

World Population (billions)

Legend: HIGH, MEDIUM, LOW

Source: United Nations (U.N.) Population Division, *World Population Prospects 1950–2050 (The 1996 Revision),* on diskette (U.N., New York, 1996).

Notes: Under the high fertility rate projection, which assumes that high fertility countries will stabilize at 2.6, and low fertility countries will rise to stabilize at 2.1, world population would reach 11.2 billion in 2050. Under the medium fertility rate projection, which assumes that the fertility rate ultimately will stabilize at a replacement level of about 2.1, the global population would reach about 9.4 billion in 2050. The low fertility rate projection assumes that countries currently with higher-than-replacement fertility rates will stabilize at 1.6, and that countries currently with lower-than-replacement rates will either stabilize at 1.5 or remain constant. Under these assumptions, world population would stabilize at 7.7 billion in 2050.

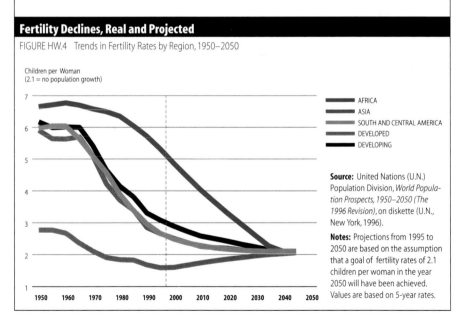

Fertility Declines, Real and Projected

FIGURE HW.4   Trends in Fertility Rates by Region, 1950–2050

Children per Woman (2.1 = no population growth)

Legend: AFRICA, ASIA, SOUTH AND CENTRAL AMERICA, DEVELOPED, DEVELOPING

Source: United Nations (U.N.) Population Division, *World Population Prospects, 1950–2050 (The 1996 Revision),* on diskette (U.N., New York, 1996).

Notes: Projections from 1995 to 2050 are based on the assumption that a goal of fertility rates of 2.1 children per woman in the year 2050 will have been achieved. Values are based on 5-year rates.

Economic Growth and Human Development

Economic growth is an important factor in reducing poverty and generating the resources necessary for human development and environmental protection. There is a strong correlation between gross domestic product (GDP) per capita and indicators of development such as life expectancy, infant mortality, adult literacy, political and civil rights, and some indicators of environmental quality. However, economic growth alone does not guarantee human development. Well-functioning civil institutions, secure individual and property rights, and broad-based health and educational services are also vital to raising overall living standards. Despite its shortcomings, though, GDP remains a useful proxy measure of human well-being.

The world economy has grown approximately fivefold since 1950, an unprecedented rate of increase. The industrialized economies still dominate economic activity, accounting for US$22.5 trillion of the US$27.7 trillion global GDP in 1993 (1). Yet a remarkable trend over the past 25 years has been the burgeoning role played by developing countries, in particular the populous economies of east and south Asia. (See Figure HW.5.)

A major factor in this development has been the steady integration of the global economy. Since the Second World War, international trade has grown consistently faster than output and now accounts for approximately 25 percent of world GDP. Other measures of globalization include the enormous expansion of international financial markets, the spread of new technologies that have revolutionized international communications and encouraged the development of transnational patterns of production and consumption, and the fourfold increase in foreign direct

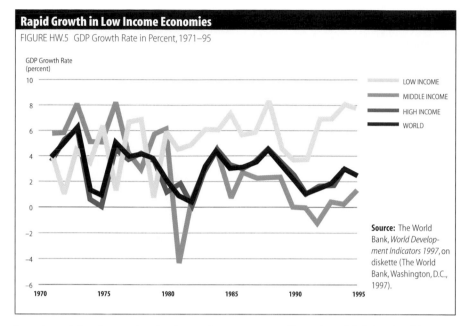

Rapid Growth in Low Income Economies

FIGURE HW.5 GDP Growth Rate in Percent, 1971–95

Source: The World Bank, *World Development Indicators 1997,* on diskette (The World Bank, Washington, D.C., 1997).

investment flowing to developing and transition economies over the past decade (2)(3).

However, this overall picture masks large, growing disparities among the developing countries; not all countries have been able to take advantage of the benefits of globalization. Since about 1980, the fastest-growing economies of Asia and Latin America have been characterized by high rates of domestic savings, declining dependence on agriculture, and a rapid growth in trade, especially of manufactured exports. The emerging economies of the developing world—such as Brazil, China, Indonesia, and Mexico—have been increasingly attractive to private finance; two thirds of the US$95.5 billion foreign direct investment flows in 1995 went to just six developing countries (4). In addition, of the estimated 12 million jobs created by transnational corporations' investment in developing countries, about half are in China (5).

Alongside this unprecedented economic surge, some 100 countries have experienced economic decline or stagnation; in 70 of these countries, average incomes are lower today than they were in 1980 (6). Factors in this decline include continued dependence on exports of primary commodities and falling

commodity prices, high levels of indebtedness, slow progress with political and macroeconomic reform, and, in some countries, political instability and armed conflict. These circumstances have discouraged foreign direct investment and contributed to a continuing decline in the real level of official development assistance from the industrialized countries. This is a critical development, given that such assistance constitutes nearly two thirds of net monetary flows to low-income countries. In the case of the transition economies (Russia and central and Eastern Europe), political and economic turmoil following the fall of Communist regimes has led to sharp declines in income and standards of living since 1990 (7).

The net result of these contrasting trends is that more than 3.8 billion people have seen their incomes rise by 3 percent or more from 1980 levels, but some 1 billion others—more than one fifth of the world's population—are worse off (8).

In the developing countries as a whole, broad-based, balanced economic growth has enabled giant strides in key indicators of human development since 1960: infant mortality rates have been reduced by one half and adult illiteracy rates by nearly one half. Since 1975, the rate of underweight children under 5 years of age declined by almost one half. At the same time, whole regions remain sunk in poverty; they are sidelined from the global economy and are in danger of falling further behind in coming decades (9).

POVERTY AND INCOME INEQUITY

Poverty remains an enormous problem worldwide, despite major reductions over the past 50 years. Within the developing countries, about one third of the population lives on less than US$1 a day. (The World Bank defines poverty as an income of less than US$1 per day, using purchasing power parity—in other words, exchange rates adjusted to the local currency.) By this measure, although the percentage of the world's population living in poverty declined slightly between 1987 and 1993 (from 30.1 percent to 29.4 percent) (10), the absolute number of people living in poverty increased from 1.2 billion to 1.3 billion people (11). (See Figure HW.6.) Although some Asian countries, such as Indonesia, have made considerable progress in reducing poverty, in south Asia, progress has been slow. In sub-Saharan Africa and in Latin America and the Caribbean, the percentage of the population living in poverty actually increased slightly between 1987 and 1993 (12).

Poverty can also be defined more broadly than by income alone. The Human Poverty Index, developed recently by the United Nations Development Programme (UNDP), is an aggregate index that measures other forms of deprivation, including low life expectancy, illiteracy, and measures of access to health services, safe water, and adequate nutrition. More than one quarter of the world's population lives in this condition of "human poverty," according to UNDP. Both types of poverty—income and human—usually coincide, but not always. Human poverty is most widespread in sub-Saharan Africa and south Asia. By contrast, in Latin America and the Caribbean, income poverty remains at 24 percent, but human poverty is significantly lower, at 15 percent. That means, in brief, that the poor are better off, thanks to expanding choices and opportunities—especially access to basic education and health services (13).

Perhaps the most glaring economic trend to emerge in the past 30 years is the growing gap between rich and poor. Disparities have widened at the international level, despite a boom in much of the developing world. (See Figure HW.7.) The difference between average per capita income in the industrialized and developing countries tripled between 1960 and 1993 (14). The poorest 20 percent of the world's population now claims just 1.1 percent of global income, while the richest 20 percent claims 86 percent. Between 1960 and 1994, the ratio of the income of the richest 20 percent to the poorest 20 percent increased from 30:1 to 78:1 (15).

Within some regions and countries, the gap is increasing as well. In Latin America and the Caribbean, the richest 20 percent of the population has average

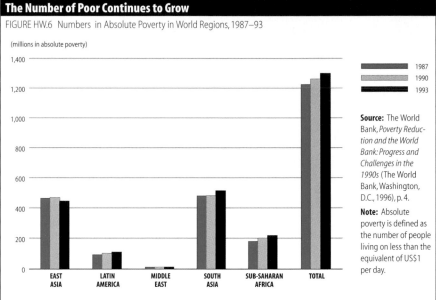

The Number of Poor Continues to Grow

FIGURE HW.6 Numbers in Absolute Poverty in World Regions, 1987–93

(millions in absolute poverty)

Source: The World Bank, *Poverty Reduction and the World Bank: Progress and Challenges in the 1990s* (The World Bank, Washington, D.C., 1996), p. 4.

Note: Absolute poverty is defined as the number of people living on less than the equivalent of US$1 per day.

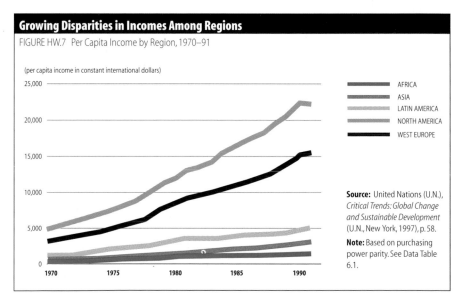

Growing Disparities in Incomes Among Regions

FIGURE HW.7 Per Capita Income by Region, 1970–91

(per capita income in constant international dollars)

Source: United Nations (U.N.), *Critical Trends: Global Change and Sustainable Development* (U.N., New York, 1997), p. 58.

Note: Based on purchasing power parity. See Data Table 6.1.

incomes of more than US$17,000; for the poorest 20 percent, the average income is US$930 (16). Even in relatively more equitable east and Southeast Asia, income gaps appear to be widening. Wealth disparities between urban and rural areas are growing in China, Indonesia, and the Philippines; data for Thailand are controversial, but one estimate claims the wealth gap in that country more than doubled between 1981 and 1992 (17).

In the industrialized countries, income disparities grew during the 1980s and early 1990s. The biggest changes in disparity were recorded in the United Kingdom and the United States (18). Overall in the industrialized countries, according to UNDP, the average income of the richest 20 percent is seven times higher than that of the poorest 20 percent (19).

INEQUITY AND CONFLICT

Inequities hamper economic development and lead to other problems as well, such as social instability. In recent years, social instability and armed conflict have been associated with rising income inequality and growing resource scarcity. In Indonesia, mobs have burned factories and cars to protest grievances ranging from land disputes to pollution from shrimp ponds. In the Philippines, Muslim rebels are most active in western Mindanao, where the wealth gap between that region and the capital Manila is as great as that between the Republic of Korea and Bangladesh (20). There is a close correlation between the stronghold areas of the guerrilla movement in Peru and the areas suffering greatest poverty. Further, the Zapatista rebellion in the southern Mexican state of Chiapas is largely attributable to grossly inequitable patterns of land tenure and the inability of peasant farmers to subsist on their small, degraded land holdings (21).

Many governments are responding to the economic and security threats

posed by growing income inequities. In the early 1990s, for example, the Chinese government targeted 80 million people living in poverty, mostly in villages in the western areas of the country. It gave priority to ensuring adequate supplies of food and clothing. By 1996, 22 million people had been lifted above the national poverty line (22). In the longer term, reducing income inequality and ensuring adequate human development for all is likely to depend on greater commitment to the implementation of policies for broader-based economic growth and poverty reduction through increased investment in public education and health. (See section below.)

Urban Growth

The world's urban population is currently growing at four times the rate of the rural population (1). Between 1990 and 2025, the number of people living in urban areas is projected to double to more than 5 billion; if it does, then almost two thirds of the world's population will be living in towns and cities. An estimated 90 percent of the increase will occur in developing countries (2). (See Figure HW.8.) Urbanization is rapid in the fast-growing economies of the Asia-Pacific region, where the average annual urban growth rate is more than 4 percent. Yet the fastest urbanization rates are now occurring in some of the least developed countries. Africa has the highest urban growth rate of all world regions: 5 percent per year (3). (See Figure HW.9.)

One feature of today's urbanization is the continuing trend of ever larger metropolitan areas. The number of megacities (cities with at least 8 million inhabitants) rose from just 2 in 1950 (New York and London) to 23 in 1995, with 17 of them in the developing world. By 2015, the number is projected to grow to 36; 23 of these megacities will be located in Asia (4). (See Table HW.1.)

As described at length in the 1996–97 volume of *World Resources*, urbanization presents both opportunities and challenges. The current pace and scale of change—over 60 million people are added to urban populations each year

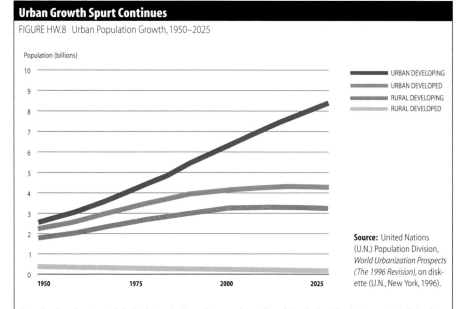

Urban Growth Spurt Continues

FIGURE HW.8 Urban Population Growth, 1950–2025

Population (billions)

URBAN DEVELOPING
URBAN DEVELOPED
RURAL DEVELOPING
RURAL DEVELOPED

Source: United Nations (U.N.) Population Division, *World Urbanization Prospects (The 1996 Revision)*, on diskette (U.N., New York, 1996).

Note: Developed regions include North America, Japan, Europe, and Australia and New Zealand; developing regions include Africa, Asia (excluding Japan), South America and Central America, and Oceania (excluding Australia and New Zealand). The European successor states of the former Soviet Union are classified as developed regions, while the Asian successor states are classified as developing regions.

Megacities

TABLE HW.1 Expected Growth in Cities with Populations of 8 Million or More, 1995 and 2015

CITY	POPULATION (millions)	
	1995	2015
Tokyo, Japan	26.96	28.89
Mexico City, Mexico	16.56	19.18
São Paulo, Brazil	16.53	20.32
New York, United States	16.33	17.60
Bombay, India *	15.14	26.22
Shanghai, China	13.58	17.97
Los Angeles, United States	12.41	14.22
Calcutta, India	11.92	17.31
Buenos Aires, Argentina	11.80	13.86
Seoul, Korea, Rep.	11.61	12.98
Beijing, China	11.30	15.57
Osaka, Japan	10.61	10.61
Lagos, Nigeria *	10.29	24.61
Rio de Janeiro, Brazil	10.18	11.86
Delhi, India *	9.95	16.86
Karachi, Pakistan *	9.73	19.38
Cairo, Egypt	9.69	14.42
Paris, France	9.52	9.69
Tianjin, China	9.42	13.53
Metro Manila, Philippines *	9.29	14.66
Moscow, Russian Fed.	9.27	9.30
Jakarta, Indonesia *	8.62	13.92
Dhaka, Bangladesh	8.55	19.49

Source: United Nations (U.N.) Population Division, *Urban Agglomerations, 1950–2015 (The 1996 Revision)*, on diskette (U.N., New York, 1996).

Note: * Cities expected to grow by >50% by 2015.

Africa and Asia are Urbanizing Fastest

FIGURE HW.9 Percentage of Population Residing in Urban Areas, by Region, 1970–2025

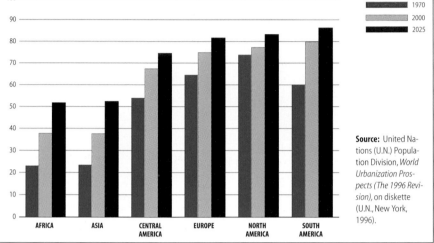

Source: United Nations (U.N.) Population Division, *World Urbanization Prospects (The 1996 Revision)*, on diskette (U.N., New York, 1996).

(5)—often strain the capacity of local and national governments to provide even the most basic services to urban residents. An estimated 25 to 50 percent of urban inhabitants in developing countries live in impoverished slums and squatter settlements, with little or no access to adequate water, sanitation, or refuse collection (6). In such situations, both environmental quality and human health and well-being are at risk. (See Chapter 3.)

Many countries are developing policies that try to address the new de-mands created by the increasing concentration of people in cities while capitalizing on the benefits of urbanization, such as economic growth and efficient delivery of services. Indonesia is a case in point. During the 1980s, Indonesian cities expanded at the rate of 5.4 percent per year, fueled by declining prospects for agriculture in the outer islands and high levels of foreign direct investment in export-oriented manufacturing on the island of Java. Indeed, Indonesia's 10 largest metropolitan areas—each with more than 1 million inhabitants—are all on Java; 60 percent of Java's population now lives in urban corridor developments along the northern coast. Although basic infrastructure and services are lacking in many areas, urban migration is expected to continue. In 1992, the government of Indonesia introduced the Spatial Use Management Act, one of a suite of laws intended to ensure the provision of adequate public services and to minimize adverse effects on surrounding communities and ecosystems. Among other reforms, the act provides for the identification of environmentally sensitive areas, where development activities would be restricted, and for improved planning for the location and support of activities such as industrial development (7).

International Migration

International migration, which includes both voluntary migration for economic or other reasons as well as the involuntary movement of refugees, is on the rise. Data are uncertain and trends are difficult to track, but, according to the U.N., at least 120 million people (excluding refugees) lived or worked outside of their own country in 1990, an increase from about 75 million in 1965. The annual growth rate of immigration has been steepest in developing countries, and approximately half of all international migration takes place within the developing world. Nevertheless, foreign-born residents accounted for only 1.6 percent of the total population of developing countries in 1990 but 4.5 percent of the population of developed countries. Today, for instance, population growth in member countries of the Organisation for Economic Co-Operation and Development (OECD) is being driven not by natural rates of increase but largely by immigration (1) (2). Between 1990 and 1995, 45 percent of

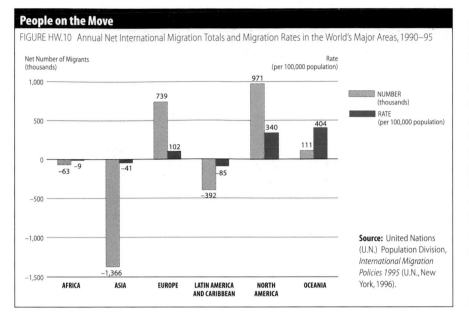

FIGURE HW.10 Annual Net International Migration Totals and Migration Rates in the World's Major Areas, 1990–95

Net Number of Migrants (thousands)

Rate (per 100,000 population)

NUMBER (thousands)

RATE (per 100,000 population)

1,000

971

739

500

340

404

102

111

0

−63 −9

−41

−85

−392

−500

−1,000

−1,366

−1,500

AFRICA ASIA EUROPE LATIN AMERICA AND CARIBBEAN NORTH AMERICA OCEANIA

Source: United Nations (U.N.) Population Division, *International Migration Policies 1995* (U.N., New York, 1996).

part of the country, has destroyed local grain stores and forced people from their grazing and fishing grounds (7).

Environmental degradation and resource scarcity can help to trigger mass migration. Population growth, land scarcity, and a cycle of droughts and floods has encouraged the illegal immigration of more than 10 million Bengalis—perhaps 20 million including their descendants—to neighboring Indian states from Bangladesh. The influx has prompted local resentments, and more than 4,000 people were killed in a series of violent clashes in the early 1980s. Tensions continue today (8).

Many governments increasingly view immigration as a problem, despite the

overall population growth in developed countries was due to immigration; in Europe, the proportion was 88 percent (3). (See Figure HW.10.)

Considering involuntary movements, the number of refugees worldwide doubled between 1984 and 1991, although it has since fallen from a high of about 18 million in 1993 to just about 14 million in 1996, partly as a result of resettlement programs (4). However, the number of refugees is overshadowed by the increase in the number of internally displaced persons—those who have been forced to flee their homes by armed conflict, persecution, or natural or manmade disasters, but who remain within their national borders. Because of the rising number of civil wars and local conflicts, the number of internally displaced persons now totals an estimated 30 million worldwide, mostly concentrated in some 35 countries. Africa is the worst-affected region, with up to 16 million people having been internally displaced (5) (6). Sudan, where a civil war is now entering its 15th year, has the highest number of displaced people in the world, estimated at from 3.5 million to 4 million. Fighting between rival rebel armies, as well as between rebels and the government in the northern

Progress Toward Democracy

As a new report from the World Bank makes clear, the quality of government remains a crucial factor in promoting economic growth, social well-being, and sound environmental management. Government accountability through democratic elections is central to achieving these basic goods. Trends in the spread of democracy are encouraging. In 1974, only 39 countries (about 25 percent) were independent democracies; today, 117 countries are (about 60 percent). The spread of democracy has been driven by new communication technologies, which make clear a government's failings in relation to other countries, and also by increased levels of education among citizens, who are less tolerant of such failure.

Democratically Elected Governments by Region, 1960–94

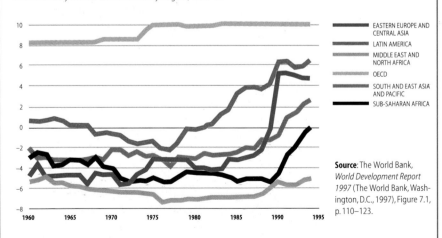

EASTERN EUROPE AND CENTRAL ASIA

LATIN AMERICA

MIDDLE EAST AND NORTH AFRICA

OECD

SOUTH AND EAST ASIA AND PACIFIC

SUB-SAHARAN AFRICA

Source: The World Bank, *World Development Report 1997* (The World Bank, Washington, D.C., 1997), Figure 7.1, p. 110–123.

Note: This particular index of democracy is based on Polity III data developed by Keith Jaggers and Ted Robert Gurr. It is calculated for 177 countries from scores on five component indicators: (1) competitiveness of political participation, (2) regulation of political participation, (3) competitiveness of executive recruitment, (4) openness of executive recruitment, and (5) constraints on the chief executive. For more information, see Keith Jaggers and Ted Robert Gurr, "Tracking Democracy's Third Wave with the Polity III Data," *Journal of Peace Research*, Vol. 32, No. 4 (1995), pp. 469–482.

fact that immigrant labor often benefits both the home and host countries (9). Perceptions of national identity, cultural differences, and fears of unemployment are all contributing to actual and potential hostilities between immigrants and nationals. The percentage of governments that view their country's immigration level as too high rose from 6 to 21 percent between 1976 and 1996; in the developed countries, 29 percent consider immigration too high (10). Nonetheless, immigration, either legal or illegal, seems certain to continue.

Rx For Health: Education

Well-educated, healthy populations are of fundamental importance in raising levels of socioeconomic development. Numerous studies now document the positive correlations among, for example, women's education, reduced fertility, and improved child health, and also between literacy rates and average per capita incomes. The World Bank argues that human resources—which include labor, the returns on educational investments, and social organizations—are one of the most important components of the wealth of most nations (1).

Good education and health do not follow as an automatic consequence of economic growth but depend on government action, especially policies that target primary-level education and health care. The provision of high-quality basic social services benefits the poorer members of society, who cannot afford private alternatives, as well as the economy as a whole.

One multicountry study has indicated that a 10-percent increase in life expectancy raises the national economic growth rate by about 1 percent per year (2). Other research suggests that increasing the average education of the labor force by 1 year raises the GDP by 9 per-

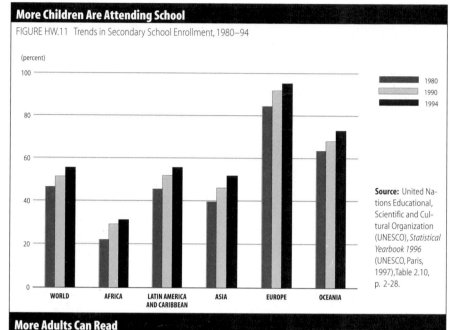

More Children Are Attending School

FIGURE HW.11 Trends in Secondary School Enrollment, 1980–94

(percent)

Legend: 1980, 1990, 1994

Categories: WORLD, AFRICA, LATIN AMERICA AND CARIBBEAN, ASIA, EUROPE, OCEANIA

Source: United Nations Educational, Scientific and Cultural Organization (UNESCO), *Statistical Yearbook 1996* (UNESCO, Paris, 1997), Table 2.10, p. 2-28.

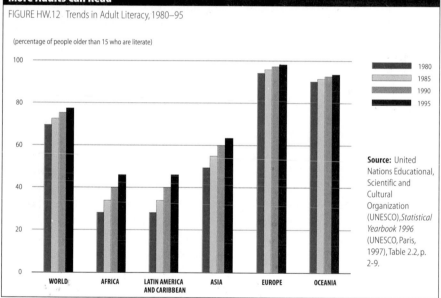

More Adults Can Read

FIGURE HW.12 Trends in Adult Literacy, 1980–95

(percentage of people older than 15 who are literate)

Legend: 1980, 1985, 1990, 1995

Categories: WORLD, AFRICA, LATIN AMERICA AND CARIBBEAN, ASIA, EUROPE, OCEANIA

Source: United Nations Educational, Scientific and Cultural Organization (UNESCO), *Statistical Yearbook 1996* (UNESCO, Paris, 1997), Table 2.2, p. 2-9.

cent, although this holds true only for the first 3 years of extra education, with diminishing returns thereafter (3).

Investment in basic social services usually has more impact on human development and economic growth than does spending on higher education or advanced medical facilities. It has been estimated that the social rate of return for all developing countries averages 24 percent for primary schooling, 15 percent for secondary schooling, and 12 percent for postsecondary education

(4). Many economists now attribute much of the economic success of the "Asian tigers" to their governments' commitment to public funding of primary education as the foundation for development. In 1960, Pakistan and the Republic of Korea had similar incomes but quite different school enrollment ratios—30 percent in Pakistan and 94 percent in Korea. Over the next 25 years, per capita GDP in Korea grew to three times that of Pakistan. It has been estimated that if Korea's enrollment ratio had stayed the same as Pakistan's, its per capita GDP would be about 40 percent less than it is today (5).

Educational achievements worldwide have improved significantly over the past 30 years; the proportion of children attending school has risen, and adult literacy programs have helped to spread basic reading skills. (See Figures HW.11 and HW.12.)

The gender gap (the difference in educational attainment between boys and girls) has also narrowed at all educational levels, with the greatest progress being made in the Arab states, followed by Southeast Asia and Latin America (6). However, nearly two thirds of the world's 840 million illiterate adults are women (7). In sub-Saharan Africa, the gender gaps in adult literacy and higher education rates are still widening. This situation has serious implications for child health and food security, given that women in rural areas of the region are almost solely responsible for child nutrition and produce up to 80 percent of basic foodstuffs (8)(9).

Human health has also improved significantly in recent decades. Globally, average life expectancy has risen to 65 years, and the life expectancy gap between the industrialized and developing countries has almost halved since 1960 (10). Deadly diseases such as polio, leprosy, and neonatal tetanus may be eradicated in the near future (11). Infant and child mortality rates have fallen in all regions. Despite this progress, infectious diseases remain the leading cause of death of children under age 5 worldwide, and new diseases such as acquired immune deficiency syndrome (AIDS) and new varieties of hemorrhagic fevers have emerged (12). Unfortunately, the least developed countries have experienced the smallest gains in key indicators of human health, and the gap between them and developing countries as a whole is widening.

INVESTMENT IN PUBLIC EDUCATION AND HEALTH

Despite the evidence that public and private expenditures on basic social services appear to bring the greatest returns on capital in terms of promoting GDP growth, investment levels have risen slowly or erratically in recent decades. Public expenditures on education have fallen, as a proportion of gross national product, in many world regions since the 1980s. Military budgets have also fallen in much of the developing world but are still comparable with those for education (13).

Public financing of health and education is increasingly augmented by private investment. In many industrialized countries, governments are faced with looming fiscal crises brought on by the expanding demands of comprehensive welfare systems. Individuals are therefore being required either to contribute more to state education and health systems or to seek private alternatives. Citizens in many developing countries are also required to foot much of the bill for social services, but far fewer of them are in a position to do so. Among low-income countries, for example, private sources account for 80 percent of total education spending in Haiti and nearly 60 percent in Uganda and Vietnam (14). In such situations, the poor majority of the population have quite limited educational opportunities.

There is, as yet, no evidence of a significant trend to shift spending toward basic social service provision in sub-Saharan Africa, where public expenditures are most skewed (15). Raising the level of investment in human capital there, and in parts of south Asia and Latin America, will be essential if the current downward spiral of poverty, underemployment, and resource degradation is to be reversed. However, some governments in these regions are beginning to spend more on primary education and health care, and these programs provide encouraging examples for others to follow. A number of countries have achieved far greater improvements in human development than are usual for their income level, thanks to enlightened policies that address the needs of the broad majority of their citizens.

Kerala State, in India, is an apt example. Despite quite low income and productivity growth since 1970, Kerala's citizens enjoy a life expectancy on a par with Hungary and literacy rates comparable with those in Norway. By 1991, the fertility rate had dropped to 1.8 children per woman, below the replacement rate (16). Almost all villagers now have access to a school and a modern health clinic within a radius of 2.5 kilometers. Newspapers and telecommunication facilities are also available in the great majority of villages. These successes are the result of a strong political commitment to mass education and health care dating back to the 19th Century. Important support has come from social policies that have achieved relatively equitable land distribution, an efficient food distribution system, and a breakdown of the restrictive caste system. Attitudes toward women are enlightened; girls outnumber boys in higher education, and Kerala has appointed the first female chief justice, surgeon general, and chief engineer in India. Social investment appears to be paying off. Kerala's annual growth rate in per capita income was almost twice that of India between 1987 and 1992 (17) (18).

AIDS Toll Climbs

The AIDS epidemic is far larger than previously believed and showed no signs of stabilization at the end of 1997, according to a recent report by the Joint United Nations Programme on HIV/AIDS (UNAIDS) and the World Health Organization (WHO) (1). According to these revised estimates, some 30.6 million people globally are now infected with the human immunodeficiency virus (HIV) that causes AIDS, and 11.7 million have died of the disease—2.3 million in 1997 alone. This estimate of the number of people infected with the virus is almost 30 percent higher than the previous year's estimate, reflecting new ways of extrapolating from figures at the country level rather than the regional level. Roughly 5.8 million people are believed to have become infected with HIV in 1997. Of these new infections, more than 40 percent occurred among women, and more than 50 percent occurred in young adults aged 15 to 24.

The disparities in disease between rich and poor countries are vast and growing. According to the new report, more than 90 percent of all HIV-infected people live in developing countries, and most of them do not know they are infected; thus they are not taking precautions to prevent the spread of the disease. Infection rates are soaring in sub-Saharan Africa, the world's poorest region, whereas in the wealthy regions of Western Europe and North America, rates are slowing dramatically. In Western Europe, according to the latest data, the number of new cases declined roughly 30 percent between 1995 and 1997. What is more, many of those in wealthy countries who are infected with HIV have access to antiviral drugs that delay the disease's progress; these expensive drugs are largely unavailable in poor countries (and to the poor in wealthy countries).

The AIDS epidemic has been particularly devastating in sub-Saharan Africa, where fully two thirds of the total number of people infected with the virus now reside. Although Africa has long been the region with the highest total number of people infected, experts at the World Bank had thought the epidemic was leveling off (2). The latest UNAIDS/WHO estimates challenge those claims, asserting that 7.4 percent of the adult population, aged 15 to 49, is now infected. In the worst-hit areas, the rate is far higher. In Botswana, for instance, nearly 30 percent of the adult population is believed to be infected, double the number from just 5 years ago.

The AIDS epidemic is newer in Asia than in Africa, and many Asian countries have not yet developed comprehensive surveillance systems. Available data suggest that although HIV-infection rates are generally still low, the number of people infected is enormous because the region is so large. In India, for example, less than 1 percent of the adult population is believed to be infected, but that translates into 3 million to 5 million people. The nascent epidemic in China continues to spread through drug use in the south and prostitution in the east. In Southeast Asia, although the picture is bleak in Cambodia and Vietnam, Thailand has successfully decreased the number of new infections as a result of its sustained condom use campaigns and other educational efforts.

In Latin America and the Caribbean, infection rates are relatively low, and the disease has been concentrated mainly among homosexual men and intravenous drug users. It now appears to be spreading among poor and less educated parts of the population, as well as among women. According to UN-AIDS/WHO, a major opportunity exists in this region to slow the spread of AIDS, but it will require special attention to the prevention needs of poor and socially marginalized people.

In Eastern Europe and the former Soviet Union, HIV is spread primarily through intravenous drug use. Experts caution that infection rates may soon rise significantly—a soaring number of cases of sexually transmitted diseases suggest an increase in unprotected sexual activity in this region.

In the wealthier countries, by contrast, aggressive prevention and treatment strategies have led to a declining number of AIDS cases, especially among homosexual men. In the United States, the latest estimates indicate the first-ever annual decrease in new AIDS cases—6 percent in 1996. Among some disadvantaged groups in the United States, however, AIDS is still on the rise. In 1996, new AIDS cases rose by 19 percent among African-American heterosexual men and by 12 percent among African-American heterosexual women. In the Hispanic community, the number of cases rose 13 percent among men and 5 percent among women in just 1 year. These disparate trends reflect, in part, differing access to expensive antiviral drugs and a lower level of success of prevention efforts targeted to minority communities.

FEEDING THE WORLD

In the past 30 years, global agriculture has made remarkable progress in expanding world food supplies. Although world population doubled over this period, food production rose even faster, so that the world's croplands and pasturelands support an additional 1.5 billion people today. Gains have been particularly significant in the developing world. Per capita food supplies there rose from less than 2,000 calories per day in 1962 to more than 2,500 calories in 1995, driven by the combination of better seeds, expanded irrigation, and higher fertilizer and pesticide use—what has become known as the Green Revolution—as well as by the rapid growth in food imports from the rest of the world.

The prospect of feeding an additional 3 billion people over the next 30 years poses an even greater challenge. In the short term, experts predict that there will be adequate global food supplies, but that problems with distribution will result in hundreds of millions of people being malnourished. In the longer term, a number of additional issues raise concerns.

The rate of growth in world food production has started to slow. In addition, high rates of food loss during harvest, storage, and distribution persist, needlessly raising production requirements. Erosion and other types of soil degradation continue to take millions of hectares out of production.

However, none of these obstacles is insurmountable. Progress on all of these fronts will be essential to reach the goal of simultaneously intensifying production while reducing environmental costs, and ensuring that this food bounty is more equitably shared among the people of the world.

Food Production: Have Yields Stopped Rising?

Feeding an ever-larger world population predicted for the future will require an agricultural system that stays apace of population growth. Achieving such a system will not be easy. In fact, although total yields continue to increase on a global basis, there is a disturbing decline in the rate of yield growth (1). If such a slowdown persists, it could prevent production levels from rising as much as is needed in the next few decades.

What has been termed a "yield plateau" or "yield stagnation" has been detected in many of the globe's major crops, especially for the cereals from which people get most of their food energy (2). For wheat, yield growth rates slid from 2.92 percent per year for the period from 1961 to 1979 to 1.78 percent for the period from 1980 to 1997. For maize, the rates slipped from 2.88 percent to 1.29 percent during the same period. For paddy rice, yield growth rates have remained stable at 1.95 percent (3). (See Figure FW.1.) Yet the demand for all cereals is expected to rise substantially in the next two decades (4).

Throughout history, whenever more food has been needed, people have simply cleared more land to plant more crops. However, most high-quality agricultural land is already in production, and the environmental costs of converting remaining forest, grassland, and wetland habitats to cropland are well recognized. Even if such lands were converted to agricultural uses, much of the remaining soil is less productive and more fragile; thus, its contribution to future world food production would likely be limited. The marginal benefit of converting new land increases the importance of continuing to improve crop yields so the existing agricultural lands can produce additional food (5).

Several factors may be contributing to the yield plateau. The most direct ways of increasing yields—planting new varieties, extending irrigation, and using fertilizer—were already exploited in many locations during the Green Revolution of the 1960s and 1970s. In addition, the emphasis of much recent agricultural research has been on achieving goals other than increased yields, such as improving drought tolerance or resistance to insects and disease.

More important, world cereal prices have declined in recent years, and grain farmers who might have justified the expense of additional inputs (e.g., fertilizer and water) to keep yields up have shifted away from cereals to more profitable crops. (See Data Table 6.3.)

Crop intensification may also be a prime culprit in yield stagnation, especially for rice. Today, it is common for farmers to produce two or even three rice crops per year where only one or two were grown in the past. This is possible because some new rice varieties mature more quickly than traditional varieties, in addition to yielding more grain per plant. For example, the rice known as IR-8, one of the early "miracle rice" varieties introduced in 1966 by plant breeders at the International Rice Research Institute (IRRI) in the Philippines, ripens 20 to 30 days ahead of unimproved varieties (6). Yet the extra crops that the newer varieties allow can place a heavy strain on soils, particularly those used in paddy rice production, where the growing medium is under water for long periods. It is not yet

Yields Are Up, But Growth is Slowing

FIGURE FW.1 Global Changes in Cereal Yields and Yield Growth Rates, 1961–96

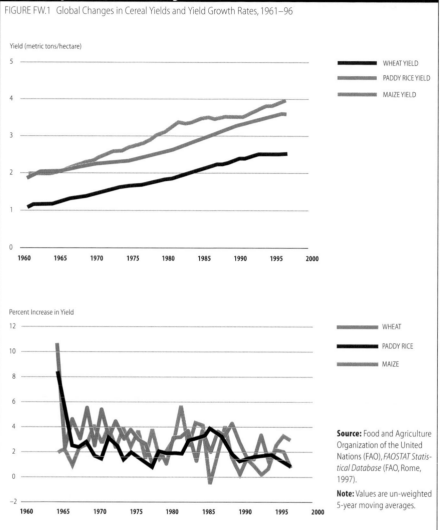

Source: Food and Agriculture Organization of the United Nations (FAO), *FAOSTAT Statistical Database* (FAO, Rome, 1997).

Note: Values are un-weighted 5-year moving averages.

Yields Vary Widely

TABLE FW.1 World Average, Highest, and Lowest Yields of Cereal Crops, 1990–96 Mean Value (metric tons per hectare)

World Average Yield	2.7
Highest Yield (Netherlands)	8.8
Lowest Yield (Botswana)	0.35

Source: Food and Agriculture Organization of the United Nations (FAO), *FAOSTAT Statistical Database* (FAO, Rome, 1997).

For other crops as well, an enormous gap exists between the yields actually achieved on real-world farms and those theoretically possible. For wheat, for example, the average global yield is less than 2 metric tons per hectare. The record yield is said to be 14 metric tons per hectare, and as many as 21 metric tons may be possible (10). There is also a wide variation in yields from country to country. (See Table FW.1.)

How can the world's farmers take advantage of this genetic potential? Both biotechnology and traditional plant breeding techniques still hold great promise for yield increases. For example, scientists at IRRI are currently using both strategies to improve older rice varieties by tailoring them to take advantage of specific local environments. They are also working on an entirely new "super rice" that in trials has achieved up to 25 percent higher yields than current varieties, although this new strain will not be ready for introduction for another 5 years or so (11).

The need for such improvements is urgent. Some projections suggest that roughly 50 percent more people will become rice consumers during the next 25 years, requiring a major increase in rice production (12). This increase will, by necessity, have to be achieved with less land, less water, and less labor (13).

Food Insecurity: A Trend Toward Hunger

The term "food insecurity" may seem technical to some, but when it is defined in its most basic terms—a lack of nutri-

clear how much this strain erodes yields in the long term (7).

Yields of other staples more commonly grown outside the developed world have also declined. Sorghum and millet rate fifth and seventh, respectively, in production among the world's grains. They and a handful of other crops are crucial staples in many regions, especially in Africa and Asia, where drought is commonplace and the populations are among the world's poorest (8).

In recent years, world sorghum and millet production has increased, but only because the cultivated area has grown. Even so, yields per hectare have remained flat or have even declined in

places where production has expanded into more marginal areas. Improved varieties of millet and sorghum exist, but, in general, poor, small-scale farmers commonly achieve only about one fifth of the genetic potential of millet and sorghum because they cannot afford fertilizers, good weed control, timely planting, and the other crop management techniques that these crops require. Yields might decline even further in the future because many small-scale millet and sorghum producers have been shortening their fallow periods in an attempt to increase production levels—a strategy that may eventually lead to declining soil fertility (9).

Progress in Feeding the World Has Varied Widely by Region

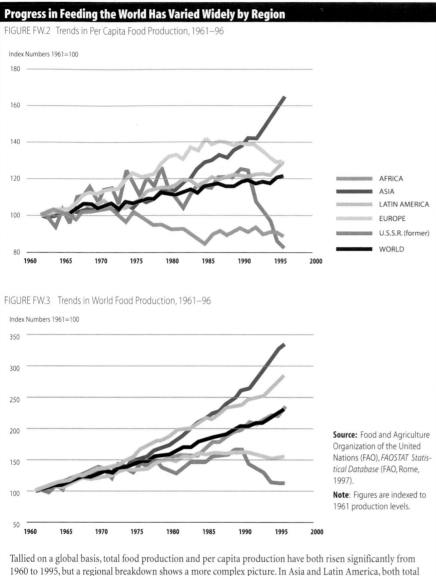

FIGURE FW.2 Trends in Per Capita Food Production, 1961–96

Index Numbers 1961=100

AFRICA
ASIA
LATIN AMERICA
EUROPE
U.S.S.R. (former)
WORLD

FIGURE FW.3 Trends in World Food Production, 1961–96

Index Numbers 1961=100

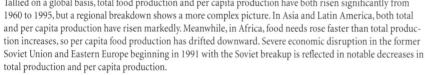

Source: Food and Agriculture Organization of the United Nations (FAO), *FAOSTAT Statistical Database* (FAO, Rome, 1997).

Note: Figures are indexed to 1961 production levels.

Tallied on a global basis, total food production and per capita production have both risen significantly from 1960 to 1995, but a regional breakdown shows a more complex picture. In Asia and Latin America, both total and per capita production have risen markedly. Meanwhile, in Africa, food needs rose faster than total production increases, so per capita food production has drifted downward. Severe economic disruption in the former Soviet Union and Eastern Europe beginning in 1991 with the Soviet breakup is reflected in notable decreases in total production and per capita production.

tious food needed to keep people alive and healthy—it becomes frighteningly human. Some 800 million of the world's people—200 million of them children—suffer from chronic undernutrition (1)(2). (See box on malnutrition in Chapter 1.)

When the global numbers are added up, nutrition seems to be improving. Life expectancy is growing worldwide, and better nutrition is one of the key factors behind this rise (3). On the surface at least, there is plenty of food.

Global supplies of food are in relatively good shape, with surpluses in many areas of the world. (See Figures FW.2 and FW.3) One researcher has calculated that if the global food supply were converted to calories and divided by the world's population, there would be enough food for roughly 12 percent more than the actual population (4).

Yet this simple calculation hides the difficulty of matching global food supply with actual food needs at a local level. Even though the problem might

not be one of production for the world as a whole, production failures at the local level are indeed among the major causes of hunger (5).

The statistics on hunger and malnutrition are discouraging, especially as they concern children. About one third of the children in developing countries are malnourished, according to the World Health Organization (6). In addition, malnutrition is associated with over half the deaths among children in developing countries under the age of 5 (7). Malnutrition in children is generally determined by weight—the percentage of children under age 5 who weigh considerably less than the general population (8). Low-birth-weight babies are children who are born weighing less than 2,500 grams. Their low weight is generally attributed to maternal malnutrition. When children begin life with a low-weight deficit, they are often prone to a shortened lifetime full of troubles, including retarded development and susceptibility to disease (9).

The Food and Agriculture Organization of the United Nations (FAO) organized a World Food Summit in 1996 with the goal of reducing the number of undernourished people to half their current level by no later than 2015. Even though governments made no financial commitments, the summit planners did assemble a mass of data on food and its availability, little of it encouraging. According to FAO projections, the chronically undernourished portion of the Earth's population is expected to decrease over the next decade or so by more than 10 percent from current levels. (See Figure FW.4.) Yet that will still leave some 680 million people with insufficient food in 2010. Sub-Saharan Africa will be particularly hard-hit, with more than 260 million people—about one third of the population—lacking adequate food (10).

The most widely recognized cause of malnutrition is poverty—the lack of money to buy food or the means, land, resources, and knowledge needed to

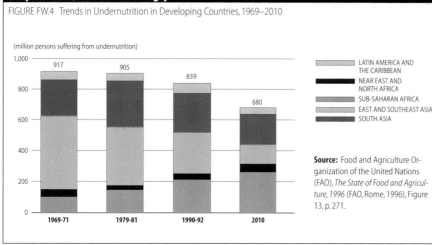

Despite Gains, Millions Go Hungry

FIGURE FW.4 Trends in Undernutrition in Developing Countries, 1969–2010

(million persons suffering from undernutrition)

LATIN AMERICA AND THE CARIBBEAN
NEAR EAST AND NORTH AFRICA
SUB-SAHARAN AFRICA
EAST AND SOUTHEAST ASIA
SOUTH ASIA

Source: Food and Agriculture Organization of the United Nations (FAO), *The State of Food and Agriculture, 1996* (FAO, Rome, 1996), Figure 13, p. 271.

grow it. Yet, there are other factors at work as well, both environmental and social. A shortage of potable water or water for agriculture—a shortage felt by more than one quarter of the world's people—is likely to be reflected in poor child and adult health (11). Local water scarcity can be more devastating than food shortages because it is more difficult and expensive to trade water among regions than it is to trade agricultural products (12).

Famines caused by continent-wide droughts were once considered inevitable occurrences in Earth's cycle of calamities. Dry spells continue, but their effects have been reduced in recent years through good planning and early-warning systems established by international, national, and regional aid agencies, as well as allied nongovernmental aid agencies. Yet famine's destructiveness has not been eliminated. The "natural" famines of the past have been replaced with famines created as a result of localized wars and the consequent displacement of civilians. Often those who foment these wars use starvation intentionally as a weapon. Even countries that are not experiencing conflicts are affected if they are neighbors of areas in upheaval. Hungry refugees quickly become an entire region's problem. Refugees suffer particularly serious effects because they usually have no rights to land or other resources and are

often concentrated in areas that have marginal soils and scarce water resources.

The prognosis for ending world hunger is not encouraging. There is little prospect for stopping the kinds of wars and local upheavals that often cause starvation and malnutrition. Just as troubling, nations in the developed world show less and less interest in sending aid of any sort (other than military) to the less developed world. Figures from the Organisation for Economic Co-Operation and Development document a continuing decline in public aid from well-off nations to developing countries, with a 4 percent drop in aid from 1995 to 1996 (13). Though the United Nations adopted a covenant as far back as 1966 declaring a universal "right to adequate food," this proclamation has a somewhat hollow ring as the world approaches the end of the century with hunger still much in evidence (14).

Despite the discouraging news, the battle against malnutrition continues. Indeed, some countries have succeeded in reducing malnutrition. In the 10-year period ending in 1991, Thailand reduced nutritional deficiency in preschool children by two thirds. It did so by establishing a national goal to increase the amount of protein and calories in children's diets; an educational program stressing breast-feeding, hy-

giene, and home production of nutritious foods; a national surveillance effort that weighed and examined every preschool child at 3-month intervals; and school lunch programs (15).

Thailand's efforts were also aided by significant economic growth during this period, which raised average incomes and increased access to food. Over the longer term, such economic development is one of the most potent tools against continuing malnutrition.

Disappearing Food: How Big Are Postharvest Losses?

Farmers and food sellers have been concerned about losses since agriculture began. Yet the problem of how much food is lost after harvest to processing, spoilage, insects and rodents, or to other factors takes on greater importance as world food demand grows. Cutting postharvest losses could, presumably, add a sizable quantity to the global food supply, thus reducing the need to intensify production in the future.

Yet exactly how much of the world harvest is really lost? Surprisingly little solid information exists on the precise amount and nature of loss. This is partly because losses vary greatly by crop, by country, and by climatic region, and partly because there is no universally applied method of measuring losses (1). As a consequence, estimates of total postharvest food loss are controversial and range widely—generally from about 10 percent to as high as 40 percent (2)(3).

Just how much of that loss can be prevented, and by what degree of effort and expense, is not known. Nor is there clear evidence that if losses were reduced, the food thus rescued would find its way onto the plates of those who need it most.

Lost Bounty

TABLE FW.2 Estimated Postharvest Rice Losses in Southeast Asia

ACTIVITY	ESTIMATED RANGE OF LOSS (PERCENT)
Harvest	1–3
Handling	2–7
Threshing	2–6
Drying	1–5
Storage	2–6
Transport	2–10
Total	**10–37**

Source: Food and Agriculture Organization of the United Nations (FAO). Available online at: http://www.fao.org/News/FACTFILE/FF9712-E.HTM.

Nonetheless, there is little doubt that the problem of food loss is locally significant, especially where it concerns staple crops. Rice is a good example. A study by the International Rice Research Institute (IRRI) in the Philippines has estimated that from 5 to 16 percent of rice is lost in the harvest process, which includes cutting, handling, threshing, and cleaning. During the postharvest period, another 5 to 21 percent disappears in drying, storage, milling, and processing. Total estimated losses, not counting later losses by retailers and consumers, run from 10 to 37 percent of all rice grown (4). The Food and Agriculture Organization of the United Nations reports similar estimates of rice loss in Southeast Asia (5). (See Table FW.2.)

Other recent scientific surveys place rice losses in China at 5 to 23 percent (not counting processing) (6), and in Vietnam at 10 to 25 percent under typical conditions and 40 to 80 percent under more extreme conditions (7).

Although these figures are already high, they do not tell the whole story. Food losses, according to those who study them, cannot be reckoned solely in terms of physical losses. There is a natural inclination to focus on how many hungry people a ton of lost maize or potatoes would feed, but qualitative factors are important, too.

Consumers' demand for cosmetically perfect produce often means that much of the food successfully harvested is wasted. One agricultural researcher notes that the importance of such qualitative factors is growing, and foods that might have been acceptable before may become "lost" now because they do not meet the market's higher standards for acceptability (8). The demand for perfect produce is especially common in the more affluent world. A tiny mark made by a bee early in the life of a pear can disqualify the end product for consumer consideration. A recent review of food waste in the United States reported that some 43 billion kilograms of food, or 27 percent of the food available for people to consume in the United States, were lost in only three stages of the marketing process—retailing, food service, and consumers. The total did not include losses elsewhere in the food harvesting and distribution system (9).

Whatever the source, postharvest losses represent more than just a loss of food. When 20 percent of a harvest is lost, the actual crop loss is just part of the problem. Also wasted is 20 percent of all the factors that contributed to producing the crop—20 percent of the land used to grow the food and 20 percent of the water used to irrigate it, along with the human labor, seeds, fertilizer, and everything else. In other words, postharvest food loss translates not just into human hunger and financial loss to farmers but into tremendous environmental waste as well.

Addressing the problem of postharvest losses is complicated because losses occur in so many different ways; yet some recent efforts have shown promise. For example, a number of strategies have targeted losses during food storage, especially directly after harvest when foods' internal moisture is being reduced and they are prone to attack by insects and other pathogens. In one experiment in Benin, hermetically sealing storage containers of beans and soybeans asphyxiated insect larvae that had infested the beans, cutting losses substantially. Also in Benin, yam losses fell significantly when the tubers were stored in elevated structures that maintained an ideal humidity level (10).

Engineers at IRRI reduced rat damage to rice by rigging a simple plastic fence around paddies, with a hole every 5 meters leading to a trap. A rat, smelling rice, swims along the fence until it finds the hole—and the trap.

Experts believe farmers could cut losses by altering production methods, such as moving from hand gleaning to mechanical harvesting. As with all agricultural decisions, however, the cost of an improvement is a deciding factor in its adoption. IRRI estimates the cost of its rat-catching system at US$400 per hectare, and it lasts just a few seasons. This can equal one third or more of the value of a rice crop, and may be too much for a farmer to pay (11).

Governmental policies, too, are important to minimizing losses, especially where commodity crops like rice and corn are concerned. According to agronomists, policies that promote a stable, sufficient supply of these crops in an open, competitive marketplace stimulate food producers to be more efficient and quality conscious (12).

Disappearing Land: Soil Degradation

The process of raising the world's food has not always been kind to the environment. Many of the adverse environmental impacts resulting from agriculture are connected either to the loss of natural habitat that occurs when land is converted to agricultural purposes or to the use (or misuse) of pesticides and fertilizers. Yet soil degradation has also been a factor, and one with implications for food production as well.

By 1990, poor agricultural practices had contributed to the degradation of 562 million hectares, about 38 percent of the roughly 1.5 billion hectares in cropland worldwide (1). (See Figure FW.5.) Some of this land was only

Degraded Soil Means Less Food

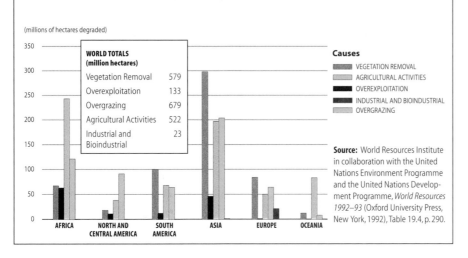

FIGURE FW.5   Human-Induced Soil Degradation by Region and by Cause, 1945 to Late 1980s

(millions of hectares degraded)

WORLD TOTALS (million hectares)

Vegetation Removal	579
Overexploitation	133
Overgrazing	679
Agricultural Activities	522
Industrial and Bioindustrial	23

Causes
- VEGETATION REMOVAL
- AGRICULTURAL ACTIVITIES
- OVEREXPLOITATION
- INDUSTRIAL AND BIOINDUSTRIAL
- OVERGRAZING

Source: World Resources Institute in collaboration with the United Nations Environment Programme and the United Nations Development Programme, *World Resources 1992–93* (Oxford University Press, New York, 1992), Table 19.4, p. 290.

slightly degraded, but an appreciable amount was damaged severely enough to impair its productive capacity or to take it out of production completely. Since 1990, losses have continued to mount year by year, with an additional 5 million to 6 million hectares lost to severe soil degradation annually (2).

Degradation comes in several forms, the best known of which is soil erosion. Most soil erosion—about two thirds—is caused by water washing away topsoil, with another third caused by wind (3). One analysis of global soil erosion estimates that, depending on the region, topsoil is currently being lost 16 to 300 times faster than it can be replaced (4). Soil-making processes are notoriously slow, requiring from 200 to 1,000 years to form 2.5 centimeters of topsoil under normal agricultural conditions (5).

Farmland can be degraded in several other ways besides erosion. Physical degradation from mechanical tilling can lead to soil compaction and crusting. Repeated cropping without sufficient fallow periods or replacement of nutrients with cover crops, manure, or fertilizer can deplete soil nutrients. In addition, overapplication of agricultural chemicals can kill beneficial soil organisms (6).

Poor water management on irrigated cropland is a leading cause of degraded farmland. Inadequate drainage can lead to waterlogging of the soil or to salinization, in which salt levels build up in the soil to toxic levels. With some 10 to 15 percent of all irrigated land suffering some degree of waterlogging and salinization, these two problems alone represent a significant threat to the world's productive capacity (7). (See Figure FW.6.)

Often, when climate and human activities combine to turn once-healthy soil into wasteland, the degradation is seemingly irreversible. However, many forms of degradation can be remedied through painstaking reconstruction of the soil's health (8).

How much has damage to the world's arable lands affected global food supply? Because total global food production has continued to increase over the years even in the face of significant soil degradation, it is tempting to view soil decline as a minor matter. However, factors such as increased fertilizer use, extension of irrigated lands, and higher cropping densities have masked the effects of soil degradation so far. Substantial yield losses have already occurred in certain regions, though few studies have attempted to quantify these losses. One 1994 study estimated that soil degradation between 1945 and 1990 lowered world food production some 17 percent (9). Regional studies have localized these losses. In Africa, production losses from soil erosion alone are estimated at just over 8 percent (10). Data from several different studies indicate that the decline in productivity resulting from soil degradation may exceed 20 percent in a number of Asian and Middle Eastern countries (11).

These losses are predicted to worsen as soil degradation continues. Though the total global harvest may not reflect such losses immediately, they may be noticeable in some areas, especially

Food Supply Increasingly Relies on Irrigation

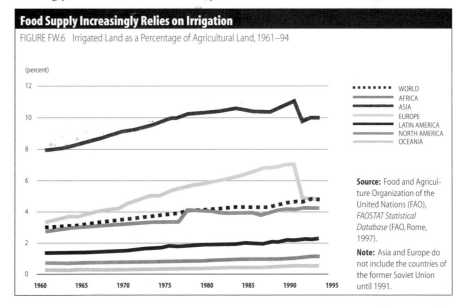

FIGURE FW.6   Irrigated Land as a Percentage of Agricultural Land, 1961–94

(percent)

- ▪▪▪▪▪ WORLD
- AFRICA
- ASIA
- EUROPE
- LATIN AMERICA
- NORTH AMERICA
- OCEANIA

Source: Food and Agriculture Organization of the United Nations (FAO), *FAOSTAT Statistical Database* (FAO, Rome, 1997).

Note: Asia and Europe do not include the countries of the former Soviet Union until 1991.

where degradation is severe and progressing quickly. For example, soil erosion is expected to seriously compromise production in southeast Nigeria, Haiti, and the Himalayan foothills, as well as in some parts of southern China, Southeast Asia, and Central America. Salinization is expected to become a major threat in the irrigation systems of the Indus, Tigris, and Euphrates River basins, as well as in northeastern Thailand and China, in the Nile delta, in northern Mexico, and in the Andean highlands. Nutrient depletion is likely to be a serious problem in large areas of Africa and in a variety of other far-flung locations from Myanmar to the Caribbean Basin (12).

Yet not all the news on soil degradation is bad. More soil-friendly farming practices that minimize tilling and reduce the erosive potential of the tilling that is done are coming into wider use, are spreading into countries such as Morocco, the Philippines, and Thailand, and are expanding regionally in parts of sub-Saharan Africa and South America. These methods include contour farming, terracing, vegetative barriers, and improved land use practices at the farm and landscape levels. Better water management practices that control salinization and lower the amount of irrigation water needed per hectare are also spreading (13).

Agronomists are beginning to realize that erosion and allied concerns are not just local problems but threats to entire watersheds; as such, they can be managed most effectively when approached in this way. Until recently, most researchers studied degradation on almost a farm-by-farm basis and failed to see the big picture. Now the big picture is available, literally, through geographic information systems (GIS). These databases integrate huge amounts of information—elevation, cropping practices, rainfall, slope, water flow patterns, and other factors—and construct custom-made maps that depict a watershed or

farming region in ways in which it could never be seen before.

Where this technology is available, such information can help farmers manage their effect on the soil by identifying those areas that are most amenable to agriculture, as well as those most prone to damage. Researchers in Honduras, for instance, have used GIS to map the hilly Yoro area, where there is pressure to expand cultivation. As expected, the richest soils and highest productivity occur in the valleys, but the maps make clear that high-quality soils exist on some slopes as well.

Farmers and policymakers can use this information to determine which areas are capable of substantial production with the least environmental harm. Also not to be overlooked are other important techniques to improve soil health including increasing organic content and nutrient cycling, as well as soil conservation through use of biologically intensive management practices such as green manures, cover crops, intercropping, agroforestry, and crop rotation.

Farming Fish: The Aquaculture Boom

Aquaculture—the farming of fish, shrimp, shellfish, and seaweeds—has been a source of human protein for nearly 4,000 years, especially in Asia (1). Unprecedented growth in aquaculture production in the last decade, however, has given it increased importance in the modern food supply. From 1984 to 1994, world aquaculture production more than doubled, making it one of the fastest-growing food production activities (2).

Globally, almost 20 percent of all fish and shellfish production in 1995 was attributable to aquaculture, or about 21 million metric tons (not counting seaweeds) out of 112 million metric tons (3). (See Figure FW.7.) Yet this industry's contribution to the human diet is actually greater than the numbers imply. Whereas one third of the conventional fish catch is used to make fishmeal and fish oil, virtually all farmed fish are used as human food. Today, one fourth of the fish consumed by humans is the product of aquaculture, and that percentage will only increase as aquaculture expands and the world's conventional fish

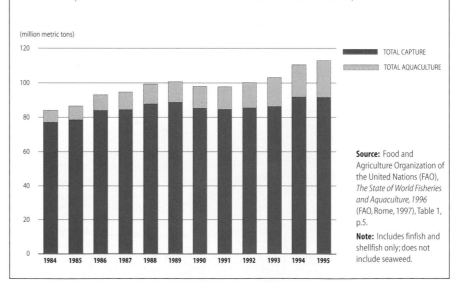

Farmed Fish Are a Growing Share of the Global Fish Harvest

FIGURE FW.7   Aquaculture Production as a Share of Total Marine and Freshwater Fish Harvest, 1984–95

(million metric tons)

TOTAL CAPTURE

TOTAL AQUACULTURE

Source: Food and Agriculture Organization of the United Nations (FAO), *The State of World Fisheries and Aquaculture, 1996* (FAO, Rome, 1997), Table 1, p.5.

Note: Includes finfish and shellfish only; does not include seaweed.

catch from oceans and lakes continues to decline because of overfishing and environmental damage (4). As currently practiced, however, aquaculture also causes environmental damage, raising questions about how best to meet food demands and preserve environmental quality.

Asia dominates world aquaculture, producing four fifths of all farmed fish, shrimp, and shellfish (5). China is by far the leading producer, contributing nearly 60 percent of 1994 world production, or some 15 million metric tons (6). Indeed, aquaculture accounts for more than half of China's total fish production each year. India is the second largest producer, with 9 percent of the world's aquaculture total in 1994 (7). (See Table FW.3.)

Aquaculture products fall into two distinct groups: high-valued species such as shrimp and salmon that are frequently grown for export, and lower-valued species such as carp and tilapia that are consumed primarily locally. China, for instance, raises a substantial amount of shrimp in intensively managed ponds along its coastline for the lucrative export trade (8). Yet China's total aquaculture production is dominated not by shrimp but by carp raised in relatively low-tech inland ponds for local consumption. The four major carp species—silver carp, grass carp, common carp, and bighead carp—account for more than one third of world aquaculture production—nearly all of it in China (9).

These carp are raised primarily as a supplementary activity to regular crop agriculture on Chinese farms. Carp are herbivores and can survive on low-cost, readily available feed material, rather than on the high-cost fishmeal that carnivorous species such as shrimp and salmon require to grow; thus carp farming is both more economical and easier to integrate with other conventional farm activities than are other types of aquaculture. Whereas farmed shrimp tend to grace the tables of consumers in

China Dominates World Aquaculture

TABLE FW.3   Share of Global Aquaculture Production, 1994

COUNTRY	PERCENT SHARE OF GLOBAL PRODUCTION
China	57
India	9
Japan	4
Indonesia	4
Thailand	3
United States	2
Philippines	2
Korea, Republic of	2
Other countries	17

Source: Food and Agriculture Organization of the United Nations (FAO), *The State of World Fisheries and Aquaculture, 1996* (FAO, Rome, 1997), p. 12.

high-income regions like Japan, Europe, and the United States, carp make a direct, significant contribution to the protein needs of less affluent rural Chinese (10)(11).

Can continued expansion of aquaculture increase the global fish catch enough to feed the world's growing need for fish protein? Certainly, some growth in world aquaculture can be expected, but just how much is not clear. One analysis projects that, under favorable conditions, global production could nearly double by 2010 to 39 million metric tons. Several factors are pushing this growth in both intensive aquaculture and in small-scale, farm-based efforts. Global demand for fish is rising even as many ocean stocks are declining, and aquaculture techniques and technology continue to improve. In addition, small-scale aquaculture offers farmers a ready source of both subsistence food and cash, and these benefits are likely to promote expansion

beyond its traditional stronghold in Asia (12).

However, there are also serious constraints on aquaculture's future growth. For one, fish farming requires both land and water—two resources already in short supply in many areas. In Thailand both these resources have been diverted in recent years to fuel the growth of the aquaculture industry. For example, nearly half the land now used for shrimp ponds in Thailand was formerly used for rice paddies; in addition, water diversion for shrimp ponds has lowered groundwater levels noticeably in some coastal areas. In China, the concern over loss of arable land has led to restrictions on any further conversion of farmland to aquaculture ponds (13).

More serious still is concern over the environmental impacts of aquaculture operations, especially the intensive production systems and large-scale facilities used to raise high-value shrimp, salmon, and other premium species. Shrimp farming has taken an especially heavy toll on coastal habitats, with mangrove swamps in Africa and Southeast Asia being cleared at an alarming rate to make room for shrimp ponds (14)(15). In just 6 years, from 1987 to 1993, Thailand lost more than 17 percent of its mangrove forests to shrimp ponds (16). (See Table FW.4.) Destruction of mangroves has left these coastal areas exposed to erosion and flooding, has altered natural drainage patterns, has increased salt intrusion, and has removed a critical habitat for many aquatic species (17).

Thailand Has Lost Mangroves to Shrimp Ponds

TABLE FW.4   Changes in the Distribution of Mangroves in Thailand, 1961–86

REGION	AREA (square kilometers)			
	1961	1975	1979	1986
Gulf of Thailand—eastern coast		490	441	280
Gulf of Thailand—northern coast		273	231	3
Gulf of Thailand—western coast	1,065	447	419	204
Andaman Sea—eastern coast	3,679	3,127	2,873	1,964
Total	**4,744**	**4,337**	**3,964**	**2,451**

Source: M. Spaulding, F. Blasco, and C. Field, eds., *World Mangrove Atlas* (International Society for Mangrove Ecosystems, Okinawa, Japan, 1997), p. 68.

Intensive aquaculture operations can also lead to water pollution, which is also a major concern. When flushed into nearby coastal or river waters, heavy concentrations of fish feces, uneaten food, and other organic debris can lead to oxygen depletion and contribute to harmful algal blooms. In Thailand alone, shrimp ponds discharge some 1.3 billion cubic meters of effluent into coastal waters each year (18).

Paradoxically, some aquaculture production also puts more pressure on ocean fish stocks, rather than relieving pressure. As noted previously, carnivorous species like salmon and shrimp depend on high-protein feed formulated from fishmeal—a blend of sardines, anchovies, pilchard, and other low-value fish. Some 10 to 15 percent of all fishmeal goes to aquaculture feeds, and it takes roughly 2 kilograms of fishmeal to produce a kilogram of farmed fish or shrimp. The result is a net loss of fish protein (19)(20).

The Food and Agriculture Organization of the United Nations asserts that some progress has been made in reducing the environmental impacts of aquaculture. For example, several countries where salmon are farmed have instituted controls on production to ensure that pollution is kept within acceptable limits (21). In some cases, new technology has also helped. In Puget Sound, on the west coast of the United States, one salmon farmer is using a giant, floating, semienclosed tub to raise his fish rather than the usual porous pens made of netting. The tub prevents fish wastes from polluting surrounding waters and also keeps fish from escaping and intermingling with wild salmon, which would contaminate the gene pool of the native fish (22).

Even in the problematic shrimp-farming industry, there are some initial signs of progress. In South Asia, a major shrimp producer has instituted a temporary ban on new ponds until the government adopts an acceptable social

and environmental policy (23). In addition, some shrimp farmers are advocating an "ecolabeling" scheme that would certify shrimp grown by producers using more benign farming practices (24).

Progress in aquaculture research can also be expected to help in the transition to low-impact, high-productivity fish farming in the future. For example, Chinese researchers are developing a protein supplement based on yeast that can substitute for more than half the fishmeal in aquaculture feed preparations. Further, work on fish breeding has already produced a strain of tilapia that grows 60 percent faster and with higher survival rates than native tilapia (25).

In the end, aquaculture's contribution to the global food supply will likely turn on how well these and other innovations can help fish farms more closely mimic natural ecosystems, with better recycling of nutrients and less waste generation (26). That will mean fewer inputs and impacts, without eroding aquaculture's profitability and versatility.

PRODUCTION AND CONSUMPTION

The material requirements of modern industrial economies are enormous, as are the environmental impacts of such consumption. In industrialized societies, an average person consumes many tons of raw materials each year, which must be extracted, processed, and ultimately disposed of as wastes. This section examines some of the repercussions of current production and consumption patterns and explores how companies and governments are beginning to adopt practices to reduce consumption's environmental toll.

One way to measure the "environmental footprint" of industrial societies is to track the volume and kind of materials flowing through their economies. A recent effort to make just such an accounting, reported here, reveals that the environmental footprint of the most highly industrialized economies is surprisingly large, extending well beyond the industrial processes themselves and well past the point of consumption. The continued trend toward greater consumption and wider environmental impacts is apparent in developed and developing countries alike. An analysis of global paper consumption, for instance, shows that use of paper products has tripled over the past three decades and is expected to grow by half again before 2010.

Consumption's environmental profile is affected not just by rising demand, but also by changes in markets and production methods. Coffee is an example. For years, this crop was grown in a mixed forest setting that provided habitat for migratory birds. However, new intensive methods of cultivation are greatly reducing the forest canopy.

Driven by pollution regulations, public pressure, and a growing awareness that better environmental performance can be profitable, efforts to reduce the impacts of industry and agriculture are on the rise. New technologies, redesigned products, and reconfigured processes are increasing the efficiency of resource use and driving down process wastes. New management practices are extending the range of business responsibilities to include the environmental and social impacts of goods and services, even on distant communities or ecosystems.

Yet more remains to be done. Achieving industrial growth that is sustainable—both ecologically and economically viable over the long term—will require more than just cleaner, more efficient industrial processes. Business leaders and analysts acknowledge that it will demand a reorientation of business so that companies can derive traditional business success—higher cash flow, shareholder value, and return on assets—while still contributing to public goods like clean water and air, robust food, and healthy ecosystems. The subset of companies that are actively trying to restructure their businesses along these lines is still quite small.

Wasting the Material World: The Impact of Industrial Economies

What does it take to produce the goods and services that underpin our lives? A detailed study of Germany, Japan, the Netherlands, and the United States shows that for highly industrialized economies, the total volume of natural resources required can be staggering—in the range of 45 to 85 metric tons of material per person each year (1).

That value is relevant today because industrialization is proceeding rapidly in many nations and will play a large part in the four- or fivefold expansion of the global economy expected over the next 50 years. But is it sustainable? The kind of resource-intensive production that is commonplace in developed countries probably cannot be replicated in a large number of other countries without causing serious environmental harm (2).

Specifically, this type of production often requires moving or processing large quantities of primary natural resources that do not end up being used in the final product. (See Figure PC.1.) For example, fabricating the automobiles and other metal-intensive products for which Japan is well known requires mining and processing a yearly per capita equivalent of about 14 metric tons of ore and minerals (3). Growing the food required to feed a single U.S. resident causes about 15 metric tons of soil erosion annually. In Germany, producing the energy used in a year requires removing and replacing more than 29 metric tons of coal overburden for each German citizen, quite apart from the fuel itself or the pollution caused by its combustion (4).

These hidden material flows from mining, earth moving, erosion, and other sources—which together account

FIGURE PC.1 Direct Inputs and Hidden Material Flows as a Proportion of Total Material Requirements of Selected Economies, 1991

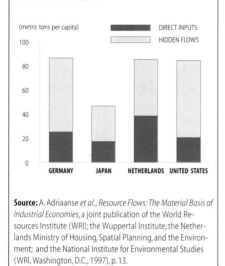

Source: A. Adriaanse *et al., Resource Flows: The Material Basis of Industrial Economies,* a joint publication of the World Resources Institute (WRI); the Wuppertal Institute; the Netherlands Ministry of Housing, Spatial Planning, and the Environment; and the National Institute for Environmental Studies (WRI, Washington, D.C., 1997), p. 13.

for as much as 75 percent of the total materials that industrial economies use—are easy to ignore because they do not enter the economy as commodities bought or sold and thus are not accounted for in a nation's gross domestic product. Hidden material flows like soil or rock may not be as toxic or environmentally harmful on a weight-for-weight basis as many industrial wastes, but they are quite important in terms of the total environmental impact of industrial activities, since they represent a truly massive scale of environmental alteration (5).

Significantly, the resulting impacts from these hidden flows, including water pollution and landscape disturbance, are often felt far from the economies that benefit from them, since industrial economies import many raw materials from afar. More than 70 percent of the materials that flow through the Dutch economy, for example, never touch Dutch soil. This includes the mine tailings, eroded soil, logging debris, and excavated earth and rock associated with extracting the raw materials used in nearly all Dutch industrial processes. Likewise, 50 percent of the mate-

rial flows contributing to the Japanese economy take place offshore (6).

This raises real concerns about environmental equity and the global economy, since the benefits and costs of this kind of industrial production are not equally shared. While these concerns are not new, the scale of the material flows puts them in a new light.

BECOMING LESS MATERIAL INTENSIVE

Progress toward environmentally sustainable industrial economies clearly will require reducing the volume of the hidden material flows that precede industrial processes—the front end of the industrial materials cycle—rather than just cleaning up the wastes that result from actual production. This has important implications for environmental policies. For example, it makes the benefits of recycling quite clear. Every ton of iron recycled not only replaces a ton that would have been mined but also avoids the creation of several tons of mine tailings or overburden, as well as ore-processing wastes.

Yet not everything can be recycled. Coal or oil, for instance, can be burned only once. Unfortunately, fossil fuels and the hidden material flows associated with them make up a large percentage—between 26 and 46 percent—of

the total materials used in the most industrialized countries. (See Figure PC.2.) This means that reducing fossil fuel use is crucial to reducing the total impact of industrial production, in addition to the other global benefits such a reduction would bring in terms of improved air quality and lower greenhouse gas emissions.

Likewise, more sustainable cultivation methods are essential to stem the significant soil loss associated with modern intensive agricultural systems. Erosion, for example, accounts for 17 percent of the total materials requirement of the United States. This number has come down in recent years largely because the United States instituted a policy—embodied in the Conservation Reserve Program—to curtail agricultural production in erosion-prone areas. The program's success shows that policies that reduce hidden resource flows like soil loss can significantly reduce the environmental impacts of industrial society (7).

This and other hopeful signs show that it might be possible to transform industrial economies. Over the past two decades, the overall economies of Germany, Japan, the Netherlands, and the United States grew slightly faster than did their use of natural resources. If this modest trend toward decoupling natural resource use and economic activity

FIGURE PC.2 Primary Contributions to the Total Material Requirements of Selected Economies, 1991

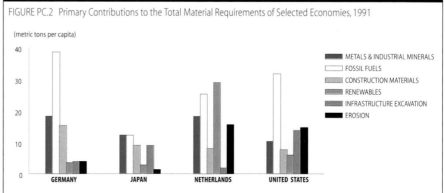

Source: A. Adriaanse *et al., Resource Flows: The Material Basis of Industrial Economies,* a joint publication of the World Resources Institute (WRI); the Wuppertal Institute; the Netherlands Ministry of Housing, Spatial Planning, and the Environment; and the National Institute for Environmental Studies (WRI, Washington, D.C., 1997), p. 12.

were to intensify, it might indicate that future economic growth could take place without increasing the already heavy burden these economies place on the planet.

The realization of this goal is still a long way off, however. At present, it takes about 300 kilograms of natural resources, including hidden material flows, to generate US$100 of income. The member countries of the Organisation for Economic Co-Operation and Development (OECD) (8), which collectively represent a large percentage of the world's industrial base, have set a preliminary target of reducing this ratio by a factor of 10, to 30 kilograms per US$100 income, over the next several decades. Without major progress toward this goal, there seems little prospect for reducing the scale of environmental impacts worldwide, especially as developing nations increase their use of natural resources to expand their economies and improve their lifestyles (9).

No End to Paperwork

Paper remains the dominant and essential vehicle of modern communications. In addition to such traditional products as newspapers, books, magazines, and writing paper, a new world of mail order catalogs, marketing and promotional materials, and household papers has developed in recent years. In addition, far from ushering in a paperless office, the advent of computers and other electronic equipment has fueled paper demand. By one estimate, personal computers alone account for 115 billion sheets of paper per year worldwide (1). Communications, however, makes up less than half of the world's paper use; a bigger share is now taken by the booming packaging industry (2). In many Western countries, high paper consumption has come to be regarded as a symbol of overconsumption and of the wastefulness of modern society.

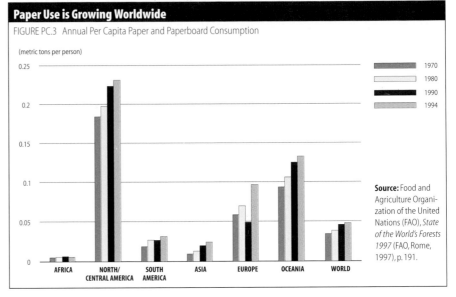

Paper Use is Growing Worldwide

FIGURE PC.3   Annual Per Capita Paper and Paperboard Consumption

(metric tons per person)

Legend: 1970, 1980, 1990, 1994

Source: Food and Agriculture Organization of the United Nations (FAO), *State of the World's Forests 1997* (FAO, Rome, 1997), p. 191.

In the developing world, paper consumption is growing quite rapidly—by more than 7 percent annually between 1980 and 1994—but average per capita consumption remains low, at about 15 kilograms per year (3). This is well below the 30 to 40 kilograms of paper per capita per year considered the minimum level necessary to meet basic needs for communication and literacy. In the industrialized countries, consumption is vastly greater—333 kilograms per capita per year in the United States and 160 in Western Europe (4).

Unlike consumption trends in other mature commodity sectors, paper consumption shows little sign of decoupling from economic growth. Globally, paper consumption has increased by a factor of 20 this century and has tripled over the past several decades (5). (See Figure PC.3.)

Paper consumption is projected to grow by about 50 percent by 2010. The biggest increase—over 80 percent—is expected to occur in developing countries in Asia, where demand is being driven by rapid growth of both incomes and population (6). North America and Europe are expected to be able to maintain their current balance between demand and supply. Asia, however, despite having the world's fastest increases in

local wood production, is likely to experience shortfalls in the supply of all wood products, but especially pulp and paper, soon after the turn of the century (7). The critical questions concern how, and from where, the future demand for paper will be met.

THE PAPER CYCLE

Every stage of the paper production and consumption cycle is associated with a range of potential problems. Most wood fiber, from which pulp and paper are made, comes from natural forests managed for timber production in North America, Europe, and Asia, and from plantations around the world. Only 2 percent of wood fiber comes from tropical rainforests and virgin temperate hardwood forests (8).

As demand rises, pressure on unmanaged forests is likely to increase, especially on the largely untouched boreal forests of the former Soviet Union. Plantations, which in 1993 supplied 29 percent of global wood pulp, may offer one solution (9)(10). In theory, the world's current total demand for wood fiber for pulp could be supplied from high-yielding industrial plantations totaling about 40 million hectares (roughly the size of Sweden or Paraguay)—an area equivalent to about 1.5

Paper Recycling: Rising Volume, Growing Importance

FIGURE PC.4 Paper Recovery as a Percentage of Paper and Paperboard Production

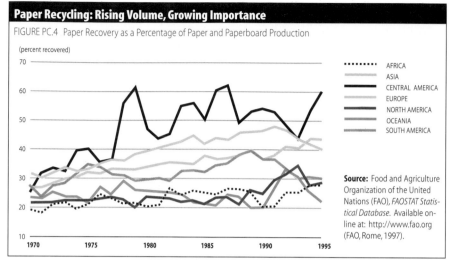

(percent recovered)

Legend:
- ········ AFRICA
- ———— ASIA
- ———— CENTRAL AMERICA
- ———— EUROPE
- ———— NORTH AMERICA
- ———— OCEANIA
- ———— SOUTH AMERICA

Source: Food and Agriculture Organization of the United Nations (FAO), *FAOSTAT Statistical Database.* Available online at: http://www.fao.org (FAO, Rome, 1997).

percent of the world's closed forest area (11). However, intensively managed plantations often involve environmental, social, or aesthetic trade-offs compared with natural forests.

Pulp- and papermaking can be a highly polluting process. Liquid effluents from mills include a range of organic, toxic, and chlorinated organic matter that adversely affects water quality and can be lethal to fish. While large-scale paper producers in some industrialized countries have succeeded in achieving closed-cycle bleaching, in which no effluent is discharged, serious problems are still common in small pulp and paper mills in developing countries (12).

Pollution could actually be worsened by a physical or economic scarcity of wood fiber in the future, particularly in developing countries. Shortages could encourage greater use of nonwood fibers for papermaking—already a significant raw material in China and India. Nonwood fibers from crops like kenaf or from the leftovers of sugarcane pressing, however, are not a perfect sub-

stitute for wood pulp. Agricultural products such as these usually require the use of more fertilizers and pesticides, which can then lead to more pollution. Use of nonwood fibers also makes chemical recovery more difficult because of the material's high silica component. In addition, nonwood fibers are bulky, expensive to transport, and tend to be available only seasonally (13) (14). However, there are encouraging signs that developing countries may be willing to import paper rather than to incur such high environmental costs. China has recently closed nearly 50,000 small paper mills and other factories that cause high levels of pollution (15) (16).

In industrialized countries, concerns have focused equally, if not more so, on the ever-increasing volumes of waste paper being created. Disposal of paper products in landfill sites leads to emissions of the greenhouse gas methane; in addition, there are suspicions that incineration of chlorine-bleached paper causes the release of dioxins into the atmosphere. Disposal facilities of any kind are increasingly difficult to establish due to public hostility. These problems, together with consumers' perceptions of wasteful paper use and excessive packaging, have led to numerous government, private-sector, and voluntary initiatives intended to increase recycling rates. Between 1970 and 1994, worldwide paper recovery rates rose from 23 percent to 37 percent; at the same time, many countries have achieved considerably higher recovery rates (17). (See Figure PC.4.)

The use of paper is generally considered essential for modern living, and the current paper cycle cannot be considered sustainable while the needs of the majority of people in developing countries remain unmet. The Food and Agriculture Organization of the United Nations suggests that no immediate crisis exists in terms of meeting near-term demand for pulp and paper worldwide. Over the longer term, however, antici-

The German Packaging Ordinance

The German Packaging Ordinance of June 1991 imposed requirements on packaging producers and distributors to take back and reuse or recycle packaging materials including paper, cardboard, glass, tinplate, and aluminum. Collection quotas of 80 percent were established for paper and paperboard, recycling quotas were set at 64 percent. Both quotas were to be achieved by July 1, 1995. After sticking at 45 percent for nearly 20 years, Germany's wastepaper recycling rate rose to 54 percent in 1994; the total volume of packaging in the Federal Republic of Germany fell by approximately 1 million metric tons between 1991 and 1993 (1) (2) (3). In a different approach, the U.S. paper industry has set a voluntary goal of a 50 percent recovery rate by 2000. United States paper mills sharply increased their use of recovered paper in 1996,

and the national recovery rate climbed to 44.8 percent (4).

References and Notes

1. International Institute for Environment and Development (IIED), *Towards a Sustainable Paper Cycle: An Independent Study on the Sustainability of the Pulp and Paper Industry,* report prepared for the World Business Council for Sustainable Development (IIED, London, 1996), p. 180.
2. Food and Agriculture Organization of the United Nations (FAO), *State of the World's Forests 1997* (FAO, Rome, 1997), p. 75.
3. Siegbert Schneider, "Waste Management Case Study: Germany," paper presented to the International Workshop on Policy Measures for Changing Consumption Patterns (August 30– September 1, 1995, Seoul, Republic of Korea), pp. III.2.1–5.
4. American Forest and Paper Association, "Paper Recycling Programs." Available online at: http://www.afandpa.org/recycling/paper/programs.html (December 1997).

pated growth in demand for wood products of all types will probably necessitate changes in forest management practices, such as greater reliance on plantations and even the use of wood products grown on smaller scales in farm woodlots and agroforestry systems (18).

Improved operations in pulp and paper mills is an urgent need on both environmental and health grounds. Conservative estimates suggest that bringing all mills worldwide up to a uniform "good" environmental standard could require an investment of about US$20 billion, plus annual operating costs of more than US$8 billion (19). However, forest degradation and pollution are currently most severe in regions where financial and technical resources are limited and demand for paper is projected to rise most steeply. In the developed countries, additional measures, including mandated recycling targets, certification or labeling schemes to promote the use of sustainably produced paper products, and financial incentives for paper recovery, will probably be necessary to secure greater efficiency in current patterns of paper consumption.

Trouble Brewing: The Changing Face of Coffee Production

For well over a century, coffee has been a major export from Latin America, shaping both the economy and the natural landscape of the region. Yet recent changes in coffee production methods, driven by increased demand, the desire to boost yields, and an international trade agreement based on quotas, threaten to erode many of the benefits of traditional coffee culture on small plantations, with wildlife and small farmers paying the price.

In dollar value, coffee is the most important (legal) traded commodity after oil in the world and is the primary export of many developing countries, accounting for as much as one third of export earnings in several Latin American countries (1). It is also a significant source of employment, with some 20 million to 25 million people—most of them small farmers—dependent on income from the world coffee crop (2). More than two thirds of current world coffee production is exported from Latin America and the Caribbean, with much of the rest coming from African and Asian producers such as Cameroon, Côte d'Ivoire, Indonesia, and Papua New Guinea (3). However, most coffee is consumed in the developed world; the United States and the European Community together import two out of every three bags of coffee produced in the world (4).

Coffee production has grown by nearly 200 percent since 1950 (5), and recent years have seen a surge in consumer demand for specialty coffees such as gourmet blends, flavored coffees, and organically grown coffees. (See Table PC.1.) Indeed, fashionable coffee bars in many developed countries today are not unlike the coffeehouses of 18th-Century Europe, which flourished when the drink was first introduced.

Yet new consumer trends in coffee drinking are not the only change in the global coffee business. In a bid to modernize, the coffee industry has begun to shift from its traditional reliance on small coffee producers growing their plants in fairly low-density, diversified plots to industrial cultivation on larger plantations. Much of this shift has been promoted and subsidized by government and international aid organizations as a way of raising the coffee sector's productivity and promoting rural development. However, as with other agricultural modernization efforts this century, changes in coffee production have had broad environmental and social repercussions.

Traditionally, coffee has been grown as a crop within a mixed-shade cover of fruit trees and other hardwood species, which together form a forestlike agroecosystem. Such "shade" coffee plantations—which are more often than not small farms—provide a rich habitat particularly valuable to migratory birds. Biologists in Mexico have found that traditionally managed coffee plantations support at least 180 species of birds, a number exceeded only by undisturbed tropical forest (6). Besides coffee, a typical mixed plantation also provides fruit, firewood, timber, and other products that can be used directly or sold for cash, providing alternative sources of income. This can be especially important to the many small coffee farmers living at or below the poverty level (7).

In the past 20 years, coffee farmers have increasingly converted to more intensive systems, involving high-yielding coffee varieties grown with no shade and high applications of chemical fertilizers and pesticides. About 40 percent of the coffee planted in Colombia, Mexico, Central America, and the Caribbean has been converted to so-called "sun coffee," which is grown in the open (8). While planting sun coffee has increased production, it has involved some significant environmental trade-offs. For one, it provides a largely monocultural habitat and is associated with higher rates of soil degradation and water pollution.

More significantly, because of the importance of traditional coffee plantations as migratory bird habitats, the conversion to industrial coffee production systems may have devastating consequences for migratory bird populations, as well as for other species. This is especially true in Central America and Colombia, where many migratory routes converge. In many parts of Central America, shade coffee plantations account for a large percentage of the remaining forest, as in El Salvador, where they make up 60 percent of the nation's forest area. In effect, sun coffee conversion is a form of deforestation, with consequent effects on species diversity. Studies in Colombia and Mexico show that sun coffee plantations support 90 percent fewer bird species than do shade coffee plantations (9).

Although some farmers and large producers may benefit, especially when coffee prices are high, many small farmers may suffer as a result of the conversion to sun coffee, since it involves considerable use of pesticides under conditions that may lead to unhealthy exposures for farm workers. Loss of the noncoffee products that shade plantations produce can also be an economic blow, making farmers more dependent on the notoriously volatile coffee market for their sole income.

Opposing this trend toward sun coffee cultivation are small but encouraging signs of growing consumer interest in sustainably grown coffee, produced under conditions that are better both for the environment and for small farmers. Sales of certified organic coffee, which generally comes from coffee plants grown under more traditional shaded conditions, are currently growing faster than any other type of specialty coffee, though they still represent only 1 to 2 percent of the $5 billion specialty coffee market. Certified organic coffee beans sell for 10 to 15 percent more than standard gourmet beans, and so can translate into higher returns for

growers, although the costs associated with the certification process itself can be significant (10).

In addition, the so-called "fair trade" movement has taken root in the world coffee market in the past few years. The movement's goal is to achieve a fair price paid to small growers for their coffee, which is distributed through small, democratically run cooperatives, whose principles of shared profits free of middlemen are used as a commercial selling point. While the fair trade criteria under which these cooperatives operate do not explicitly require the use of shade coffee, they encourage sustainable production methods and organic methods as well. Fair trade coffee has been most successful in Europe, capturing between 2 percent (Germany) and 5 percent (Switzerland) of most markets, and it is moving from niche to mainstream outlets. For example, fair trade coffee is available in 90 percent of supermarkets in the United Kingdom (11).

Farmers producing for such cooperatives receive significantly higher prices for their coffee and more secure markets. In some cases, this stability and extra income are being used to support a conversion to fully organic production. Coocafé, a fair trade organization in Costa Rica, is planning to produce only organic coffee beans by 2002. The decision—which will affect 3 percent of Costa Rica's coffee production—was made as part of a long-term economic

and marketing strategy, based on financial, environmental, and health and safety considerations (12).

Are Business and Industry Taking Sustainability Seriously?

Business today is operating in a profoundly different world than it did 30 years ago. Environmental management is no longer a relatively simple matter of controlling local pollution. Today, manufacturing companies may be held responsible for the impacts of their operations at every stage from raw material extraction through distribution to consumer use and final product disposal. These impacts are sometimes distant in space and even in time from each other. Managers must also deal with the expectations of a more environmentally aware public and the realization that reduced environmental impacts must come without sacrificing product quality or function.

This new set of ground rules offers progressive businesses fresh commercial opportunities to distinguish themselves from their competitors on the basis of both product quality and environmental performance. For these companies, cleaner production processes, more recyclable designs, and new ways of delivering services with less material throughput represent aggressive investments in a changing marketplace in which environmental values have greater business currency. Yet these companies are still the exception, not the rule.

Industry analysts recognize a natural progression of phases that companies have passed through in terms of their commitment to environmental concerns since the 1970s. Companies begin with basic compliance with environmental regulations, then move to environmental management aimed at re-

More Coffee, Fewer Birds?

TABLE PC.1 Coffee Production in Northern Latin America, 1950–90

| REGION | PRODUCTION (000 metric tons) | | | | | PERCENT CHANGE |
	1950[a]	1960[b]	1970[c]	1980	1990	1950–90
World	**2,222**	**4,268**	**4,262**	**5,039**	**6,282**	**183**
Central America [d]	189	341	428	605	680	260
Caribbean [e]	107	136	121	134	139	30
Northern Latin America [f]	711	1,102	1,214	1,707	2,104	196

Source: Robert A. Rice and Justin R. Ward, *Coffee, Conservation, and Commerce in the Western Hemisphere* (Smithsonian Migratory Bird Center and Natural Resources Defense Council, Washington D.C., 1996), Table 2, p. 39.

Notes: a. 1948–52 average. b. 1961–65 average. c. 1969–71 average. d. Production figures for Central America include Mexico, Costa Rica, El Salvador, Guatemala, Honduras, Nicaragua, and Panama. e. Production figures for the Caribbean include Cuba, Dominican Republic, Haiti, Jamaica, Puerto Rico, and Trinidad and Tobago. f. Production figures for northern Latin America include all the countries listed above, plus Colombia.

ducing emissions beyond basic compliance, to broader concerns with resource efficiency and waste minimization. The last phase involves proactive goal-setting that embraces environmental, social, and ethical concerns (1). By the mid-1990s, the majority of firms in industrialized nations were still in the compliance phase. One recent estimate is that less than 20 percent of North American and European companies can be described as proactive in their commitment to improving environmental performance in alignment with sustainable development objectives, which hold that today's wealth and lifestyles should not be achieved at the expense of future generations (2).

Those companies that have taken a proactive stance are, nevertheless, influential in developing new concepts and practices to reconcile business and sustainability objectives.

ECO-EFFICIENCY AND PRODUCT STEWARDSHIP

The concept of eco-efficiency merges ecological and economic goals. In practice, eco-efficiency involves improving the productivity of energy and material inputs to reduce resource consumption and cut pollution per unit of output— in essence, making more and better products from the same amount of raw materials with less waste and fewer adverse environmental impacts. As such, it represents a win–win approach that benefits both the bottom line and the environment. An early pioneer, 3M Corporation, now claims that its Pollution Prevention Pays program has prevented more than 750,000 metric tons of polluting emissions since 1975 by cleaning up and redesigning processes and products, saving the company more than US$790 million (3).

Eco-efficiency efforts cover a wide range of activities and often involve reconfiguring a product without degrading its performance. In 1989, Proctor & Gamble introduced concentrated deter-

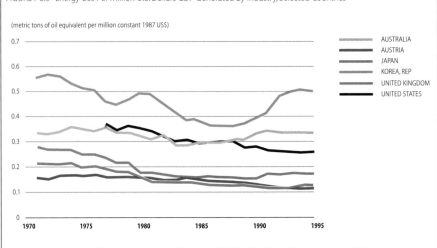

Industry Has Gradually Improved Its Energy Efficiency

FIGURE PC.5 Energy Use Per Million U.S. Dollars GDP Generated By Industry, Selected Countries

(metric tons of oil equivalent per million constant 1987 US$)

AUSTRALIA
AUSTRIA
JAPAN
KOREA, REP
UNITED KINGDOM
UNITED STATES

Sources: World Bank, *World Development Indicators 1997* on CD-ROM (The World Bank, Washington, D.C., 1997); International Energy Agency, *Energy Statistics and Balances: Non-OECD Countries, 1971–1995*, and *Energy Statistics and Balances: OECD Countries, 1960–1995*, both on diskette (Organisation for Economic Co-Operation and Development, Paris, 1997).

Notes: Data for United States not available before 1977. Metric tons of oil equivalent (mtoe) is a measure in which all energy sources are expressed in terms of a metric ton of oil. Countries were selected primarily on data availablility.

gent powders—called Ultra detergents—that took up half the volume of traditional detergents. The products cleaned the same amount of clothes, but were more convenient for consumers to handle, used 30 percent fewer raw materials, required 30 percent less packaging, and substantially cut the energy needed to transport them to market (4).

Overall, resource efficiency has improved by about 2 percent per year in industrialized countries since 1970 (though energy efficiency has barely changed since 1990) (5). (See Figure PC.5.) These gains are due to technological advances and structural economic changes such as the shift away from energy-intensive heavy industry. A key aim of eco-efficiency is to accelerate this process. (See Box on Eco-Efficiency.) Indeed, the Factor 10 Club, a group of prominent figures in environment and development, have called for a 10-fold increase in the average resource productivity of industrialized countries over the long term (6). Many eco-efficiency initiatives to date have been driven by legislated pollution controls, either actual or anticipated. How-

ever, a number of companies are going beyond legal requirements and are attempting to reduce dramatically their raw material requirements and emissions through the development of "closed-loop" processing cycles in which wastes are completely recycled or reused and never enter the environment.

An eco-efficiency program established at SC Johnson Wax in 1990 has cut the company's manufacturing waste by half, reduced virgin packaging waste by 25 percent, and reduced the use of volatile organic compounds by 16 percent; at the same time, production has increased by more than 50 percent. The company's largest plant extracts methane gas from a nearby landfill and recaptures organic vapors from process lines to obtain one third of its energy needs; another plant continuously reuses 95 percent of its wastewater so that it is never discharged. The company has realized more than US$20 million in annual cost savings (7).

There is also a growing trend to hold companies responsible for the environmental impacts of their products and services throughout their entire life cycle, known as product stewardship. A wave of new legislation and industry–government agreements, especially in Europe, has extended the Polluter Pays Principle (which states that the polluting party should be responsible for the financial costs of mitigation or cleanup) from the manufacturing to the use and disposal phases of a product's life. Examples of such measures include material taxes, mandatory recycling targets, and "take-back" requirements that direct manufacturers to collect and process various packaging and consumer products such as batteries, domestic appliances, and even cars at the end of their useful lives. In response, affected companies are redesigning their products by using substitutes for toxic or hazardous materials, reducing packaging, and improving recyclability.

In some cases, as with office equipment, manufacturers are turning to reconditioning or rebuilding old equipment, rather than building every new machine from scratch. Xerox, for example, has developed aggressive product return practices to recapture old copiers for reconditioning (8). The company has found that even recycling low-value items such as toner cartridges can be profitable. In 1994, Xerox saved some US$2 million in raw material costs by reusing toner cartridges—enough to cover the costs of collecting the cartridges, including a cash incentive program to prod customers to join the recycling effort (9) (10).

RESHAPING INCENTIVES, REMAKING INDUSTRIES

Many business leaders have begun to realize that achieving truly sustainable enterprises will require going beyond incremental improvements in product and process efficiency to restructuring markets and changing the economic incentives that drive business and consumer behavior. (See Box on Corporate Responsibility Movement.) One point of entry into this kind of transformation is to begin defining business success more in terms of the services or benefits provided rather than the quantity of products sold. In the United Kingdom, Ford Motor Co. used this approach to reduce costs and environmental impacts associated with painting its new vehicles when it hired DuPont to manage its entire paint shop operation, rather than simply to supply paint. Ford pays DuPont not for the amount of paint it applies, but for the number of vehicles painted. DuPont's incentive now is to use its chemical expertise to minimize the paint used per vehicle and to develop a more durable finish, rather than simply increasing the volume of paint it sells (11).

In other instances, the transformation to sustainability may mean reconfiguring an entire industry. The plastics industry is a good example. Interest is building now in chemical processes that depolymerize, or "unzip," used plastics—a step well beyond traditional recycling technology, since it will yield materials equivalent in quality to virgin plastic that could be used in all the applications of the original material. Polyester can already be unzipped in this way in commercial quantities with a process perfected by DuPont, and work is proceeding with nylon and other common polymers (12).

Widespread use of this kind of recycling process could help close the materials loop in the plastics industry, greatly decreasing the need for virgin materials and ultimately saving on production costs. Yet making this kind of recycling meaningful will mean increasing the collection and return rate of plastics to a level that is much higher than the current one.

DuPont is working toward this goal, at least with polyester, by licensing its recycling process to others in the industry and jointly developing a comprehensive collection system for used polyester. In other words, DuPont is enlisting the help of the entire industry to reshape the polyester business into a more sustainable and profitable form, allowing the business to expand into new applications while trading on polyester's reputation as the "greenest" of polymers (13) (14).

The developments outlined above, and many others, are being incorporated into business culture and daily operations through environmental management systems, voluntary codes of conduct, the use of performance indicators, and regular reports to "stakeholders," including employees, the local community, environmental activists, government authorities, and shareholders. The growth of innovative programs and self-regulation are important indicators of change. Yet it is clear that the steps taken so far represent just the start of a complex, lengthy transition to more sustainable enterprises.

Many environmentalists argue that the voluntary approaches currently prevalent will be too slow to deal with urgent problems of pollution and resource degradation and depletion. This is especially the case in newly industrializing countries where pollution is accelerating, but environmental concerns rank lower among business, government, and public priorities. In addition, in industrialized countries, progress in cleaning up production has not been matched by improvements in resource efficiency, especially when compared with the gains in labor productivity achieved during this century. To date, policy measures intended to improve resource efficiency—notably energy taxes—have been strenuously resisted by industry.

Above all, progress is still generally confined to large companies and multinationals; their achievements are not matched by the vast mass of small- and medium-sized enterprises. Smaller companies often lack the knowledge and resources needed to make significant changes in their organization or technologies. Incentives are also lacking; the financial benefits of "going green" remain controversial. A recent review of 500 firms across industrial sectors suggests that pollution prevention does indeed benefit operating and financial performance (15), but many small companies remain unconvinced (16).

Lingering skepticism suggests the need for a greater focus on ensuring that sustainable industrial development is compatible with profitability. Government's best role may lie in restructuring the ground rules—the environmental and health regulations, tax codes, and other government policies that influence the business environment—to increase incentives for embracing "green" investments and practices.

The Corporate Responsibility Movement

During the 1980s, the "corporate responsibility" movement emerged in response to the retreat of the state from what has been called the "moral domain of the economy" in the wake of widespread deregulation and privatization. Pressure on the private sector to consider its wider social duties also increased from external interest groups such as environmental nongovernmental organizations. The result has been a move toward greater democracy, disclosure, and accountability, particularly in industry sectors with a high public or environmental profile.

The social dimension of sustainable development is still poorly defined from industry's perspective, but it is coming to be identified with responsibilities to local communities affected by corporate operations and to employees and their families. An additional component is a consideration of ethical issues surrounding, for example, conservation, biodiversity, and animal rights. Measurement of a company's social and ethical performance is necessarily difficult and was at first resisted by business. However, "social auditing" is now emerging as a key technique through which companies can demonstrate their openness to key stakeholders, improve staff loyalty, and gauge their wider public standing.

Social audits were undertaken in the early 1990s by a small number of companies with assertive environmental and ethical policies—notably Bodyshop International and Ben & Jerry's Homemade, Inc. Today, there is increasing mainstream interest in such audits: the Co-Operative Movement (wholesale and retail services) in the United Kingdom has completed a first audit, and Shell Oil and British Petroleum announced publicly in 1997 that they would undertake social audits of their operations.

Source: New Economics Foundation, London, August 1997 (personal communication).

THE GLOBAL COMMONS

The impacts of many human activities are experienced, at least initially, at the local or regional level. Urban smog, the degradation of watersheds, and the loss of local wildlife habitat are examples. But some human impacts affect the Earth on a much wider scale. This section looks at developments in the areas of climate change, stratospheric ozone depletion, and the global nitrogen cycle. These trends reflect some of our impacts on the global commons—those natural systems and cycles that underpin the functioning of ecosystems everywhere.

It is the *scale* of human activities, rather than the individual activities themselves, that poses the greatest risk to global resources. Greenhouse gas emissions from a single power plant or automobile hardly threaten the global atmosphere, but multiply these sources by several orders of magnitude and the combined effects become global in their reach. Today, carbon dioxide emissions from human sources—mostly from the burning of fossil fuels—average more than 7 billion metric tons of carbon per year and have begun to alter the dynamics of the world's climate system.

Over the past 25 years, global energy use has risen some 70 percent and is expected to keep climbing. Options, such as renewable energy sources, energy efficiency improvements, and even traditional nuclear energy, are available to keep up with the world's power needs without letting greenhouse gas emissions spiral out of control, but their development and use on a wider scale will require concerted action by the international community.

Other challenges also require the world's attention. The struggle to repair damage to the stratospheric ozone layer is far from over. Acid rain has become a major problem in Asia; and the massive use of fertilizer and the burning of fossil fuels have disrupted the natural cycling of nitrogen compounds that form the basis of plant and animal nutrition everywhere. Again, the scale of these threats is very large, and no single nation's action will suffice to reduce them.

Power Surge: Energy Use and Emissions Continue to Rise

Global energy use has risen nearly 70 percent since 1971 and is poised to continue its steady increase over the next several decades, fueled by economic expansion and development (1)(2). Energy demand has risen at just over 2 percent per year for the past 25 years and will continue to climb at about this same rate over the next 15 years if current energy use patterns persist, according to the International Energy Agency (IEA). Along with rising energy use comes a concomitant increase in greenhouse gas emissions from fossil fuels and an anticipated increase in global warming. Fossil fuels supply roughly 90 percent of the world's commercial energy; energy-related emissions account for more than 80 percent of the carbon dioxide (CO_2) released into the atmosphere each year (3). By 2010, IEA projects that global energy consumption—and annual CO_2 emissions—will have risen by almost 50 percent from 1993 levels (4)(5). (See Figure GC.1.)

Policies to promote greater energy efficiency—in generation, transmission, and at the point of final use in factories, appliances, or cars—could curb this rate of growth significantly. IEA projections that incorporate such policies show just a 34-percent rise in energy use from 1993 to 2010, with emissions increasing 36 percent. (See Table GC.1.) More aggressive policies might be able to cut the growth rate still more. But even with substantial efforts to use energy more efficiently, future economic development will still entail a significant rise in energy use, at least in the developing world (6)(7)(8).

In the developed world, energy use per capita is already extremely high and continues to increase slowly. By contrast, the most rapid growth is now occurring in developing countries, where energy use is still low compared with that in more affluent nations. Developing nations account for more than 80 percent of world population, but consume only about one third of the world's energy.

That will likely change quickly. The developing nations' share of commercial energy consumption is expected to grow to nearly 40 percent by 2010 (9)(10). CO_2 emissions would rise even faster to about 45 percent of global emissions (11). The factors driving this increased energy demand in the developing world include rapid industrial expansion and infrastructure improvement; high population growth and urbanization; and rising incomes that enable families to purchase energy-consuming appliances and cars they could not afford before. Even so, in 30 years, per capita energy consumption in the developing world is still likely to be only one fifth of what it is in the industrialized world today (12).

Increased use of fossil fuels and consequent growth in CO_2 emissions will be particularly intense in China and south Asia, where dependence on coal, which produces the highest CO_2 emis-

Global Energy Use Is Projected to Rise

FIGURE GC.1   Past and Projected Trends in Energy Demand, 1970–2010 [a]

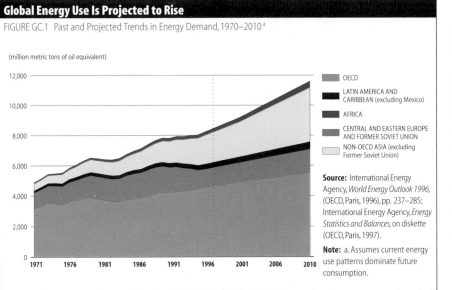

(million metric tons of oil equivalent)

Legend:
- OECD
- LATIN AMERICA AND CARIBBEAN (excluding Mexico)
- AFRICA
- CENTRAL AND EASTERN EUROPE AND FORMER SOVIET UNION
- NON-OECD ASIA (excluding Former Soviet Union)

Source: International Energy Agency, *World Energy Outlook 1996,* (OECD, Paris, 1996), pp. 237–285; International Energy Agency, *Energy Statistics and Balances,* on diskette (OECD, Paris, 1997).

Note: a. Assumes current energy use patterns dominate future consumption.

Saving Energy Cuts CO₂ Emissions

TABLE GC.1   World Carbon Dioxide Emissions Based on Two Scenarios, 1990–2010 [a]

	ENERGY-SAVING SCENARIO [b] (billion metric tons of carbon dioxide)			CURRENT TRENDS SCENARIO [c] (billion metric tons of carbon dioxide)		
	1990	2000	2010	1990	2000	2010
OECD	10.4	11.3	11.8	10.4	11.8	13.3
North America	5.6	6.2	6.6	5.6	6.5	7.3
Europe	3.4	3.5	3.6	3.4	3.6	4.0
Pacific OECD	1.4	1.6	1.7	1.4	1.7	1.9
FSU and CEE [d]	4.4	3.2	3.6	4.4	3.4	4.2
Rest of World	5.9	8.8	12.8	5.9	9.0	13.5
China	2.4	3.4	5.0	2.4	3.5	5.1
East Asia	0.9	1.6	2.4	0.9	1.7	2.5
South Asia	0.7	1.1	1.9	0.7	1.1	2.0
Other	1.9	2.7	3.5	1.9	2.7	3.9
World	**21.1**	**23.7**	**29.0**	**21.1**	**24.7**	**31.5**

Source: Adapted from International Energy Agency, *World Energy Outlook 1996* (Organisation for Economic Co-Operation and Development, Paris, 1996), Table 2.2, p. 59.

Notes: a. From commercial energy sources (not including traditional biomass fuels.) b. Energy-Saving Scenario assumes adoption of significant energy efficiency measures. c. Current Trends Scenario assumes that current energy use patterns dominate future consumption.   d. FSU is the former Soviet Union; CEE is Central and Eastern Europe.

Just how this will affect the global climate is uncertain, but the Intergovernmental Panel on Climate Change (IPCC), which represents the consensus of the international scientific community, estimates that current emission patterns are likely to increase Earth's average temperature 1° C to 3.5°C by 2100, and raise sea levels 15 to 95 centimeters (16). (See Chapter 2.)

IPCC calculations clearly show that the Earth is already committed to some global warming, based on past and current emissions, but it is possible to stabilize atmospheric CO_2 concentrations in the future to try to minimize warming in the centuries ahead. Doing so will require reductions in CO_2 emissions to levels far below today's emissions (17)(18). (See Figure GC.8 in Kyoto Protocol section.) Taking action will not be easy, because current market conditions favor continued reliance on cheap and abundant fossil fuels. But unless actions are taken now to increase energy efficiency, substitute cleaner fuels such as natural gas for coal, and hasten the development and adoption of renewable energy technologies, the accumulated burden of CO_2 will continue to grow.

Proceed With Caution: Growth in the Global Motor Vehicle Fleet

Transportation of all types already accounts for more than one quarter of the world's commercial energy use. That makes the rapid increase in the global transport sector, particularly the world's vehicle fleet, a real concern. Motor vehicles—cars, trucks, buses, and scooters—account for nearly 80 percent of all transport-related energy (1).

Motor vehicles have brought enormous social and economic benefits. They have enabled flexibility in where people live and work, the rapid and timely distribution of manufactured

sions of any fossil fuel, is high. Coal generates more than 70 percent of the electricity in China and more than 60 percent in south Asia; electricity demand is rising at 6 to 7 percent per year in these regions, which may result in a doubling of CO_2 emissions in these nations between 1990 and 2010 (13).

The implications of these emission trends for the global climate are sobering. CO_2 levels in the atmosphere are already rising at an annual rate of about 1.5 parts per million (ppm) from hu-

man activities (14). Even keeping CO_2 emissions roughly at today's levels—hardly a simple task—would result in a doubling of the CO_2 concentration in the atmosphere from its preindustrial level by the end of the 21st Century, with the CO_2 concentration continuing to rise for another century after that before stabilizing (15). With the higher CO_2 emissions projected for the decades ahead, atmospheric CO_2 concentrations are likely to double much sooner and keep rising to much higher levels before stabilizing.

goods, and ready access to a variety of services and leisure options. But the widespread use of vehicles also has real environmental and economic costs, which have ballooned as vehicle numbers have risen sharply in the past few decades. Vehicles are major sources of urban air pollution and greenhouse gas emissions. They also represent an important threat to the economic security of many nations because of the need to import oil to fuel them. Currently, the transport sector consumes about one half of the world's oil production, the bulk of it as motor fuel (2).

The adoption of cars as common items in family life and commerce began after World War II in developed countries. In 1950, there were only 70 million cars, trucks, and buses on the world's roads. By 1994, there were about nine times that number, or 630 million. (See Figure GC.2.) Since about 1970, the global fleet has been growing at the rate of about 16 million vehicles per year. This expansion has been accompanied by a similar linear growth in fuel consumption (3). If this kind of linear growth continues, by the year 2025 there will be well over 1 billion vehicles on the world's roads (4).

Clearly, there is an enormous potential worldwide for increases in vehicle use. Per capita car ownership is high in the wealthy nations of North America, Europe, and Japan, but it is still low in most developing nations. (See Figure GC.3.) Growth potential is especially great in the rapidly developing economies of Asia. In China, for example, there are only about 8 vehicles per 1,000 persons, and in India, only 7 per 1,000 persons; by contrast, there are about 750 motor vehicles per 1,000 persons in the United States (5).

The combination of low vehicle ownership and robust economies has led to very rapid growth in the vehicle fleets in China and India in recent years. The number of vehicles in China has been growing at an annual rate of almost 13 percent for 30 years, nearly doubling every 5 years. India's fleet has been expanding at more than 7 percent per year (6). While together these two countries now account for only a small percentage of the vehicles on the road, that percentage can be expected to grow as these countries continue to industrialize in the years to come.

The growing use of internal combustion vehicles, especially in urban areas, will increase congestion, raise the demand for oil, worsen air pollution, and increase emissions of a variety of greenhouse gases, including methane, ozone, carbon monoxide, nitrous oxide, and, most important, CO_2.

Worldwide, motor vehicles currently emit well over 900 million metric tons of CO_2 each year. These emissions account for more than 15 percent of global fossil fuel CO_2 releases (7). Because of their large vehicle fleets, developed countries are responsible for a commensurately large share of emissions. In 1993, the countries of the Or-

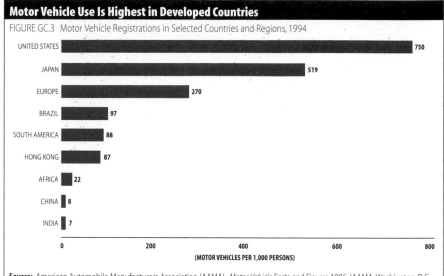

Motor Vehicle Use Is Highest in Developed Countries

FIGURE GC.3 Motor Vehicle Registrations in Selected Countries and Regions, 1994

(MOTOR VEHICLES PER 1,000 PERSONS)

UNITED STATES 750
JAPAN 519
EUROPE 270
BRAZIL 97
SOUTH AMERICA 88
HONG KONG 87
AFRICA 22
CHINA 8
INDIA 7

Source: American Automobile Manufacturers Association (AAMA), *Motor Vehicle Facts and Figures 1996* (AAMA, Washington, D.C., 1996), pp. 44–47.

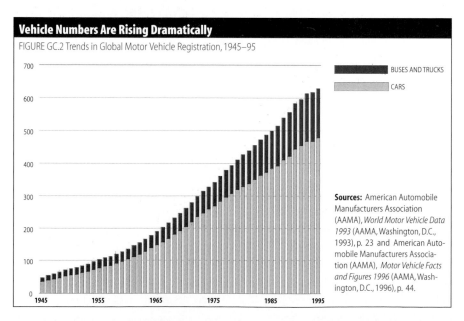

Vehicle Numbers Are Rising Dramatically

FIGURE GC.2 Trends in Global Motor Vehicle Registration, 1945–95

BUSES AND TRUCKS
CARS

Sources: American Automobile Manufacturers Association (AAMA), *World Motor Vehicle Data 1993* (AAMA, Washington, D.C., 1993), p. 23 and American Automobile Manufacturers Association (AAMA), *Motor Vehicle Facts and Figures 1996* (AAMA, Washington, D.C., 1996), p. 44.

ganisation for Economic Co-Operation and Development (OECD) accounted for about two thirds of total world CO_2 emissions from motor vehicles, although these countries represented only 16 percent of the world's population. If the linear growth in emissions characterizing the past 20 years were to continue into the next century, OECD countries would still account for fully 60 percent of global motor vehicle emissions by the year 2050 (8).

Given the likely growth of the world vehicle fleet, the problems of global warming and urban air pollution will almost certainly need to be addressed by making a long-term shift away from oil as the universal energy source for transportation. But designing a new generation of resource-efficient, environmentally friendly vehicles is one of the most challenging technological problems facing the industrialized world. Most of the major automakers around the world are responding to this challenge and are actively developing more efficient conventionally fueled vehicles as well as so-called alternatively fueled vehicles. The latter are variously powered by fossil fuels (called hybrid vehicles), electric batteries, or hydrogen. In all cases, the vehicles have electric drives, meaning they are ultimately driven by electric motors.

In a typical hybrid configuration, a small, clean, internal combustion engine or gas turbine generates electricity that can power the car directly through its motors or charge on-board batteries. In some designs, the gasoline (or other liquid hydrocarbon, such as methanol) is broken down into hydrogen and CO_2, and the hydrogen is then used to power a fuel cell that produces electricity, which in turn powers the vehicle. Hybrid vehicles powered by fossil fuels are much more efficient than today's standard vehicle designs but still emit CO_2. In this sense, they are not a long-term solution.

Battery-powered vehicles are actively being developed by several automakers,

and a small number are currently in use. The driving range of battery-powered vehicles using two of the most promising long-range batteries—nickel-metal hydrid and lithium batteries—is well over 62 kilometers, but battery costs are still very high. In one promising battery system, developed by Electric Fuel, Ltd., of Israel, long-range zinc-air batteries are removed entirely from the vehicles after they run down and replaced by fresh ones, shortening the refueling time. The run-down batteries are then recharged and used again. Large-scale tests of this system in Germany have yielded positive results so far. Fuel-cell vehicles with the hydrogen stored in high pressure tanks have also been tested; the biggest remaining problem is developing a less bulky, low-cost storage system for the hydrogen.

Because developments in car design and propulsion are progressing rapidly, there is no indication yet which combination of hydrogen fuel cells, batteries, or other technologies will power the vehicles of the 21st Century.

Climate Brief: Searching for a Greenhouse Fingerprint

It is generally accepted that the planet has warmed 0.3° C to 0.6° C over the past century or so (1). (See Figure GC.4.) But is this warming due to human activities that have increased greenhouse gas concentrations in the atmosphere, or does it simply reflect the natural variability of the global climate, as some skeptics suggest? In its 1996 report, the IPCC tackled this question directly, concluding that there is "a discernible human influence on global climate" from the buildup of greenhouse gases. The panel acknowledged that uncertainty remains as to the extent and timing of global warming, as well as to how it will affect Earth's ecosystems and people. But the IPCC stressed that,

overall, the scientific case for greenhouse warming from human causes continues to strengthen, further reinforcing the idea that policy steps to address the issue of climate change are necessary now (2).

Within the past few years, scientists have made progress in their search to find a distinctive pattern of response in the atmosphere—a fingerprint—that would clearly indicate that greenhouse gases are changing the climate. Recent studies have detected a greenhouse fingerprint by examining the temperature profiles of the atmosphere—air temperatures measured at different altitudes and different latitudes. These analyses show that since 1950, when CO_2 emissions began to rise sharply, the atmosphere's temperature profile has gradually started to resemble the profile predicted by computer models for a greenhouse-warmed atmosphere—with warmer temperatures in the lower atmosphere and cooler temperatures in the stratosphere. The quality of the match between the predicted greenhouse profile and the actual temperature profile as measured today is quite high, and statistically speaking, it is not likely that the match can be explained by natural climate variability alone (3)(4)(5)(6).

Other lines of evidence also point to a human effect on the climate, including a study showing that several distinct changes in weather patterns observed over North America match well with predicted changes from greenhouse warming (7). While these studies do not constitute proof of greenhouse warming, they were convincing enough to bolster the IPCC's conclusion that human activities were, in fact, playing a role in climate change. Other studies published since the IPCC report have continued to strengthen the evidence tying the current warming to human-caused emissions (8)(9), and the IPCC's conclusion has become one of the driving forces behind international negotiations on reducing greenhouse emis-

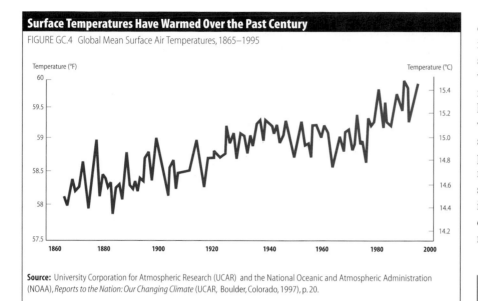

Surface Temperatures Have Warmed Over the Past Century

FIGURE GC.4   Global Mean Surface Air Temperatures, 1865–1995

Source: University Corporation for Atmospheric Research (UCAR) and the National Oceanic and Atmospheric Administration (NOAA), *Reports to the Nation: Our Changing Climate* (UCAR, Boulder, Colorado, 1997), p. 20.

sions. (See the section on the Kyoto Protocol.)

Climate Brief:
Early Spring, Late Winter

The manner in which progressive global warming may affect Earth's ecosystems in the future is difficult to predict. However, recent studies showing how higher CO_2 levels and slightly warmer global temperatures have affected the biosphere so far offer clues about what may lie ahead. Two of these studies have demonstrated that, since the 1960s, warmer average temperatures have brought an earlier spring and a later winter over the higher latitude areas of the Northern Hemisphere, advancing the growing season by about 7 days in the spring and extending it about 2 to 4 days in the fall. This extended growing season, along with elevated levels of CO_2, has spurred greater plant growth over a wide swath of territory, including Alaska, Canada, Scandinavia, northern Europe, and northern sections of Russia and China [1][2][3].

Previous studies have shown about a 10-percent reduction of snow cover as-

sociated with warmer temperatures in higher latitudes, which probably translates to quicker warming of the soil and a faster start to spring growth; the increased CO_2 available probably also adds to photosynthesis rates over the growing season. The increase in plant growth—which may be as great as 10 percent in the affected regions—provides some of the best direct evidence so far of a large-scale ecosystem response to climate change. This response is not likely to be universal, however. Higher temperatures and less rainfall in some areas may decrease soil moisture levels and actually suppress growth and agricultural yields [4][5].

The effects of global warming will not be confined to plants. Field studies of a small North American butterfly, known as Edith's checkerspot butterfly, have shown the first convincing evidence that the geographic range of an animal species has shifted in response to climate change. Scientists have long predicted that as global temperatures get warmer, the geographic ranges of plant and animal species will shift toward the poles or to higher elevations to maintain their preferred temperature conditions. This is precisely what happened to the checkerspot. Over a number of

decades, as global temperature was rising slowly, butterfly colonies on the southern limit of the range failed to survive, while new colonies formed on the northern limit of the range and also at higher elevations. This shift worked out well enough for the checkerspot, but such range migration may not always be possible in the future. Global development and habitat loss will very likely stand in the way of some species, leaving a shrinking range of habitats and increasing the possibility of extinction for many species as temperatures rise [6][7].

Negotiating Climate:
Kyoto Protocol Marks a
Step Forward

How can the international community strike the necessary balance between expanding the pace of economic development—and resultant higher energy use—and responding adequately to concerns about climate change? How can nations gradually but substantially reduce their emissions of greenhouse gases without stalling their economies? And how can we ensure that the burden of protecting the climate is shared most equitably among nations? These are the questions the 167 nations that ratified the 1992 Framework Convention on Climate Change have been grappling with since before they first initialed the treaty at the Rio Earth Summit.

In December 1997, these nations began to address these questions by forging the Kyoto Protocol, which was a follow-on to the original climate treaty, and marks the first international attempt to place legally binding limits on greenhouse gas emissions from developed countries. In addition to CO_2, the primary greenhouse gas, the Protocol focuses on five other greenhouse gases: methane (CH_4), nitrous oxide (N_2O), hydrofluorocarbons (HFCs), perfluorocarbons (PFCs), and sulfur hexafluoride

Greenhouse Gases

FIGURE GC.5 Share of Greenhouse Warming Due to Different Greenhouse Gases

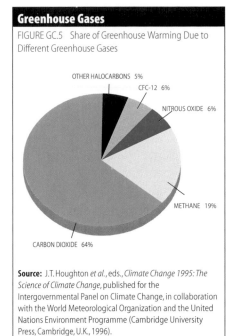

OTHER HALOCARBONS 5%
CFC-12 6%
NITROUS OXIDE 6%
METHANE 19%
CARBON DIOXIDE 64%

Source: J.T. Houghton *et al.*, eds., *Climate Change 1995: The Science of Climate Change*, published for the Intergovernmental Panel on Climate Change, in collaboration with the World Meteorological Organization and the United Nations Environment Programme (Cambridge University Press, Cambridge, U.K., 1996).

Kyoto Goal: Cut Emissions by 5 Percent

TABLE GC.2 Target Greenhouse Gas Emissions Reductions by 2012, Kyoto Protocol

COUNTRY	KYOTO TARGET (percent change from 1990 emissions)
Australia	+8
Bulgaria	–8
Canada	–6
Croatia	–5
Estonia	–8
European Union	–8
Hungary	–6
Iceland	+10
Japan	–6
Latvia	–8
Liechtenstein	–8
Lithuania	–8
Monaco	–8
New Zealand	0
Norway	+1
Poland	–6
Romania	–8
Russian Federation	0
Slovakia	–8
Slovenia	–8
Switzerland	–8
Ukraine	0
United States	–7

Source: United Nations (U.N.), *Kyoto Protocol to the United Nations Framework Convention on Climate Change*, Article 3, Annex B (U.N., New York, 1997). Available online at: http://www.unfccc.de (January 18, 1998).

(SF_6). (See Figure GC.5.) Specifically, the Protocol aims to cut the combined emissions of greenhouse gases from developed countries by roughly 5 percent from their 1990 levels by the 2008–2012 time frame, and it specifies the amount each industrialized nation must contribute toward meeting that reduction goal. Nations with the highest CO_2 emissions—the United States, Japan, and most European nations—are expected to reduce emissions by a range of 6 to 8 percent. (See Tables GC.2 and GC.3.) By 2005, all industrialized nations that ratify the accord must show "demonstrable progress" toward fulfilling their respective commitments under the Protocol. To enter into force, at least 55 nations must ratify the treaty, including enough developed countries to account for 55 percent of the global CO_2 emissions in 1990 (1)(2).

The new treaty represents real progress in bringing to fruition the good intentions of the 1992 agreement. For the most part, developed nations have failed to attain the nonbinding emission reductions they committed to in the original climate treaty (i.e., they had agreed to voluntarily reduce greenhouse gas emissions back to 1990 levels by

2000), and have thus acknowledged the need for the binding emission targets represented in the Kyoto Protocol. Despite this progress, the new agreement contains complex issues to be resolved in future negotiations. One issue is that the Kyoto Protocol officially sanctions the concept of "emissions trading" between industrialized nations. In this scenario, a nation whose emissions fall below its treaty limit can sell credit for its remaining emissions allotment to another nation, which in turn can use the credit to meet its own treaty obligations. Proponents of this market-based approach to pollution control believe an emissions trading program will help curb the cost of controlling greenhouse gases by allowing emissions cuts to occur wherever they are least expensive. Such a trading scheme has been quite successful in the United States in lower-

ing the cost of controlling SO_2 emissions from power plants—the primary source of acid rain. However, the details for implementing such a complex trading plan, involving six different gases across several national borders, will need to be worked out at the next negotiating session in 1998 in Buenos Aires (3)(4). The plan will need to address how reductions are to be counted, verified, and credited.

Another problematic area is that the treaty is ambiguous regarding the extent to which developing nations will participate in the effort to limit global emissions. The original 1992 climate treaty made it clear that, while the developed nations most responsible for the current buildup of greenhouse gases in the atmosphere should take the lead in combating climate change, developing nations also have a role to play in protecting the global climate (5). (See Figures GC.6 and GC.7.) However, the Kyoto Protocol does not set any binding limits on developing nation emissions, nor does it establish a mechanism or

Emissions Reflect Economic Size

TABLE GC.3 Fifteen Countries with the Highest Industrial Emissions of Carbon Dioxide

COUNTRY	TOTAL CO_2 EMISSIONS (000 metric tons)
South Africa	305,805
Poland, Rep	338,044
France	340,085
Mexico	357,834
Korea, Rep	373,592
Italy	409,983
Canada	435,749
Ukraine	438,211
United Kingdom	542,140
Germany	835,099
India	908,734
Japan	1,126,753
Russian Federation	1,818,011
China	3,192,484
United States	5,468,564

Source: Carbon Dioxide Information Analysis Center (CDIAC), Environmental Sciences Division, Oak Ridge National Laboratory, "1995 Estimates of CO_2 Emissions from Fossil Fuel Burning and Cement Manufacturing Based on the United Nations Energy Statistics and the U.S. Bureau of Mines Cement Manufacturing Data," ORNL/CDIAD-25, NDP-030 (an accessible numerical database) (Oak Ridge, Tennessee, November 1997).

timetable for these countries to take on such limits voluntarily. On the other hand, the Protocol does establish a so-called Clean Development Mechanism, which allows developed countries to invest in projects in developing countries that reduce greenhouse gas emissions and receive credit for the reductions. The intent is to help developing nations minimize their emissions even as they develop their energy sectors and expand their economies (6).

Still another issue with the treaty relates to the practicability of achieving the specified level of emissions reductions (5 percent from 1990 levels). This task will present a formidable challenge to many industrialized countries, because greenhouse gas emissions have grown significantly since 1990 and are projected to continue growing at a brisk pace without substantial changes in energy consumption patterns and in the mix of fuels used for energy generation. For example, recent U.S. Department of Energy estimates show that by 2010 U.S. carbon emissions are likely to increase 34 percent from 1990 levels in the absence of any change in energy policies and consumer behavior. Stated another way, the United States, as the leading contributor to the world's greenhouse gas emissions, will need to reduce emissions more than one third from their anticipated level to meet its obligations under the treaty. Higher than expected economic growth, lower energy prices, and slower gains in energy efficiency and in the penetration of renewable energy sources have boosted U.S. emissions more quickly than anticipated even a few years ago (7).

The treaty negotiators in Kyoto acknowledged that the Kyoto Protocol represents only a first step toward achieving the goal set by the original climate treaty: to stabilize greenhouse gas concentrations in the atmosphere "at a level that would prevent dangerous interference with the climate system." Even if the Kyoto Protocol is ratified

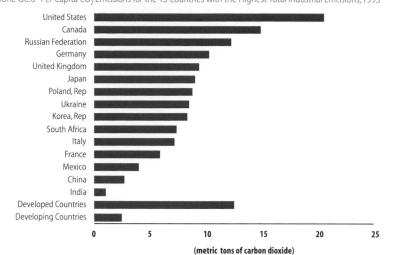

Per Capita CO₂ Emissions Are Small in Developing Countries

FIGURE GC.6   Per Capita CO$_2$ Emissions for the 15 Countries with the Highest Total Industrial Emissions, 1995

(metric tons of carbon dioxide)

Source: Carbon Dioxide Information Analysis Center (CDIAC), Environmental Sciences Division, Oak Ridge National Laboratory, "1995 Estimates of CO$_2$ Emissions from Fossil Fuel Burning and Cement Manufacturing Based on the United Nations Energy Statistics and the U.S. Bureau of Mines Cement Manufacturing Data," ORNL/CDIAD-25, NDP-030 (an accessible numerical database) (Oak Ridge, Tennessee, November 1997); United Nations (U.N.) Population Division, *Annual Populations (The 1996 Revision)*, on diskette (U.N., New York, 1993).

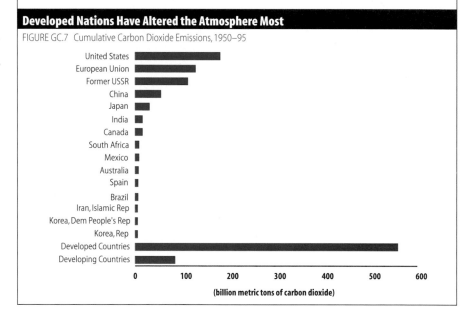

Developed Nations Have Altered the Atmosphere Most

FIGURE GC.7   Cumulative Carbon Dioxide Emissions, 1950–95

(billion metric tons of carbon dioxide)

and nations abide by its terms, neither of which can be taken for granted, its effect will only slow—not halt—the buildup of greenhouse gases. Unlike the Montreal Protocol on Substances That Deplete the Ozone Layer, which will eventually "solve" the problem of ozone depletion if adhered to, the Kyoto Protocol will not "solve" the problem of climate change, but only begin the long

process of weaning the world away from heavy reliance on fossil fuels and other sources of greenhouse gases.

Indeed, although clear consensus has not been reached regarding the level at which greenhouse gas concentrations must be stabilized in order to prevent "dangerous climate interference," calculations by the IPCC make it clear that emission reductions well beyond any

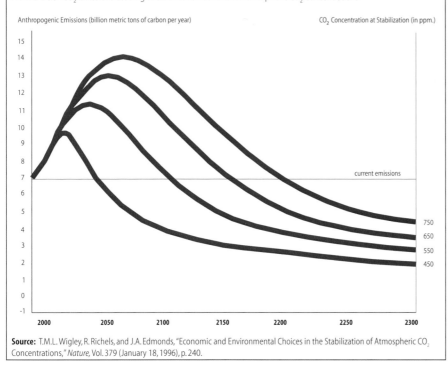

Stabilizing CO₂ Means Steep Emission Cuts Eventually

FIGURE GC.8 CO_2 Emissions Leading to Stabilization at Various Atmospheric CO_2 Concentrations

Anthropogenic Emissions (billion metric tons of carbon per year)

CO₂ Concentration at Stabilization (in ppm.)

current emissions

750
650
550
450

Source: T.M.L. Wigley, R. Richels, and J.A. Edmonds, "Economic and Environmental Choices in the Stabilization of Atmospheric CO₂ Concentrations," *Nature*, Vol. 379 (January 18, 1996), p. 240.

and lower greenhouse gas emissions (12).

Stratospheric Ozone Depletion: Celebrating Too Soon

Since 1987, the international community has made great strides toward eliminating the manufacture, trade, and use of ozone-destroying substances such as chlorofluorocarbons (CFCs), with global consumption of these chemicals dropping more than 70 percent (1). (See Figure GC.9.) In fact, the Montreal Protocol has been held up as a model of international mobilization in the face of a global environmental threat.

Despite these efforts, the stratospheric ozone layer is not safe yet. The conversion process from CFCs to less damaging substances is not complete in developed nations and is still at an early stage in many developing nations. Moreover, the Montreal Protocol's ambitious plan to replace ozone-depleting chemicals is threatened by the recent growth of a black market in CFCs, and by the difficulty a few Eastern European countries have had in phasing out CFC

contemplated in the Kyoto treaty will be needed to stabilize atmospheric CO₂ concentrations (which are a good proxy for all greenhouse gases) at even two or three times their preindustrial level of 280 parts per million (ppm). (See Figure GC.8.) For instance, stabilizing CO₂ concentrations at double their preindustrial level—a common benchmark used in discussions of global warming—would require eventually reducing global carbon emissions (from all nations) by 60 percent from 1990 levels. And there is no guarantee that this would be a safe concentration. As Figure GC.8 shows, higher emissions expected in the next few decades will require concomitantly deeper emissions cuts in the future to achieve the same stabilization (8).

Less ambitious and lower-cost strategies can also cut acid-forming emissions substantially, but the amount of environmental protection these strategies buy is commensurately less and will not protect many areas from serious acid deposition. In the end, perhaps the

most cost-effective option for controlling acid rain will be to adopt energy-efficiency measures that cut overall energy use and thus reduce emissions. If systematically employed, such energy-saving measures could cut control costs from one quarter to one third, according to the World Bank's analysis; in addition, these measures would yield ancillary benefits such as better air quality

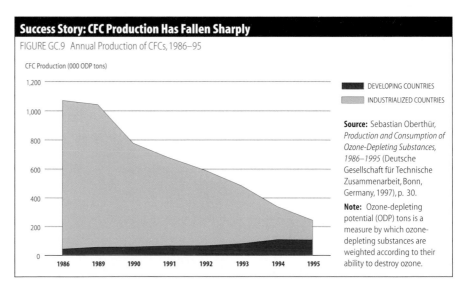

Success Story: CFC Production Has Fallen Sharply

FIGURE GC.9 Annual Production of CFCs, 1986–95

CFC Production (000 ODP tons)

DEVELOPING COUNTRIES

INDUSTRIALIZED COUNTRIES

Source: Sebastian Oberthür, *Production and Consumption of Ozone-Depleting Substances, 1986–1995* (Deutsche Gesellschaft für Technische Zusammenarbeit, Bonn, Germany, 1997), p. 30.

Note: Ozone-depleting potential (ODP) tons is a measure by which ozone-depleting substances are weighted according to their ability to destroy ozone.

production and consumption. Perhaps of most concern is the increasing production and use of CFCs in some rapidly developing nations.

The good news is that the speed of the transition away from CFCs and other ozone-depleting chemicals has been more rapid than many thought possible, given the ubiquity of these chemicals in commerce just a decade ago. As refrigerants, foam-blowing agents, solvents, aerosol propellants, fire retardants, and cleaning agents, these chemicals reached into nearly every household and workplace in the developed world in one product or another. In the United States, which alone accounted for roughly one third of global CFC use in 1987 when the Montreal Protocol was negotiated, CFCs played a role in delivering some US$28 billion in goods and services and were essential to the functioning of some US$130 billion worth of installed equipment such as refrigeration units and air conditioners (2). Despite widespread use, most developed countries were able to meet the Protocol's 1996 deadline to cease CFC production.

Reaching this goal required a remarkable level of cooperation among governments, CFC producers, and various industries. Reluctant at first, but faced with the international community's resolve to meet the problem head on, industry groups accepted the challenge of retooling products and processes to avoid CFC use. Industry estimates of the final price tag for a global phaseout of CFCs and halons are as high as US$40 billion, excluding the costs governments and international organizations have incurred organizing and promoting the transition (3).

In response to these efforts, atmospheric concentrations of CFCs are beginning to level off or decline (4)(5)(6). If the plan to eliminate all ozone-depleting substances proceeds as set forth in the Protocol, the levels of stratospheric chlorine—the CFC breakdown product that actually destroys

ozone—should peak between 1997 and 1999 and then decline gradually for more than a century (7). In turn, ozone loss will diminish gradually as well until, around 2050, the Antarctic ozone hole disappears (8).

The bad news is that several factors, key among them illegal trade, threaten to undermine full compliance in the years ahead (9). Substantial demand for these chemicals still exists in the developed world, mostly to service existing refrigeration and cooling equipment. In most developed countries, servicing requirements for these units can be met legally with either recycled CFCs or new CFCs from preexisting stocks. However, because these sources are limited, there is added incentive to illegally import virgin CFCs.

Estimates of the size of the CFC black market range from 20,000 to 30,000 metric tons annually worldwide (10). In late 1995, the chemical industry estimated that as much as 20 percent of the CFCs then in use in the world had been obtained on the black market (11). A good deal of this illegal trade is focused in the United States, which has imposed a high excise tax on CFCs since 1990 to encourage recycling of CFCs already in use and to spur conversion of equipment away from CFC use. Since the excise tax has substantially increased the cost of CFCs in the U.S. market, it has provided a potent driving force for the illegal trade. Europe has also experienced considerable black market trade, probably in the range of 6,000 to 10,000 metric tons per year (12).

In the United States, enforcement agencies have begun to crack down on illegal trade, with some encouraging results. United States Customs authorities and law enforcement officials had impounded some 1,000 metric tons of smuggled CFCs by the end of 1997, and authorities report some tapering off in the flow of illegal materials (13). In Europe, enforcement has recently taken a significant step forward with the con-

fiscation of about 1,000 metric tons of illegal CFCs in Germany (14).

One possibility is that damage to ecosystems from acid deposition may be more fundamental and long-lasting than was first believed. For example, scientists now report that acid rain leaches as much as 50 percent of the calcium and magnesium from forest soils; these are crucial minerals which buffer or neutralize acids and are essential for plant growth. If soil chemistry is changed dramatically in this way, it may take many decades for all the linked ecosystems to recover (15). A related problem is the continued leaching of heavy metals and other substances that acid rain has mobilized in the soil, providing a persistent source of toxicity to surrounding vegetation and aquatic life.

Even more troubling than black market trade in developed nations is an unexpectedly rapid rise in the use of CFCs and other ozone-depleting chemicals in some developing nations. The Montreal Protocol permits increases in production and use of ozone-depleting chemicals in developing nations until 1999, when production levels are to be frozen at 1995–97 levels; thereafter, production of ozone-destroying chemicals must be cut progressively until it ends in 2010. However, from 1986–95, production of CFCs rose nearly 2.5 times in the developing world, while consumption rose nearly 40 percent (18). Most of this growth has taken place in a few rapidly industrializing nations: Brazil, India, Mexico, and particularly China. For example, China increased its production of halons—typically used as fire retardants—from 4,000 metric tons in 1991 to more than 10,000 metric tons in 1995 (19). (See Figure GC.10.) This increase is particularly worrisome because halons destroy 3 to 10 times more ozone than CFCs and were specifically targeted for early phaseout (1994) in developed countries. Recent measurements show that concentrations of halons continue to rise in the atmosphere, offsetting some of the progress

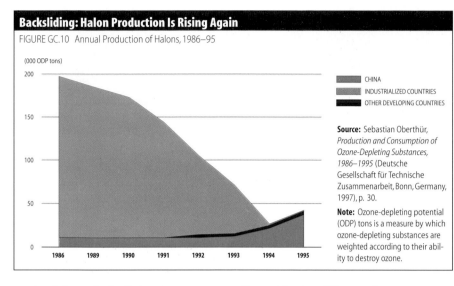

Backsliding: Halon Production Is Rising Again

FIGURE GC.10   Annual Production of Halons, 1986–95

(000 ODP tons)

CHINA
INDUSTRIALIZED COUNTRIES
OTHER DEVELOPING COUNTRIES

Source: Sebastian Oberthür, *Production and Consumption of Ozone-Depleting Substances, 1986–1995* (Deutsche Gesellschaft für Technische Zusammenarbeit, Bonn, Germany, 1997), p. 30.

Note: Ozone-depleting potential (ODP) tons is a measure by which ozone-depleting substances are weighted according to their ability to destroy ozone.

attained through declining CFC use (20).

The international community has already directed considerable attention to helping developing countries switch from CFCs before they become too dependent on them. The Multilateral Fund, which was set up under the Montreal Protocol to help pay for new technologies, equipment conversion projects, and training in developing nations, has so far contributed to some 1,800 separate projects in 106 countries at a cost of US$565 million. When complete, these projects will phase out the equivalent of more than 80,000 metric tons of CFCs (21). A typical example is Venezuela's Plasticos Molanca plastic foam factory, which used Multilateral Fund money to pay for 80 percent of its conversion from the use of CFCs to butane as a foam-blowing agent (22). Similar projects, aided by strong government commitment and substantial private investment, have allowed some developing nations to proceed quickly toward total phaseout.

Less ambitious and lower-cost strategies can also cut acid-forming emissions substantially, but the amount of environmental protection these strategies buy is commensurately less and will not protect many areas from serious acid deposition. In the end, perhaps the most cost-effective option for control-

ling acid rain will be to adopt energy-efficiency measures that cut overall energy use and thus reduce emissions. If systematically employed, such energy-saving measures could cut control costs from one quarter to one third, according to the World Bank's analysis; in addition, these measures would yield ancillary benefits such as better air quality and lower greenhouse gas emissions (12).

Developed nations can help the developing world by continuing to aggressively fund conversion projects through the Multilateral Fund. The United Nations Environment Programme (UNEP) estimates that the US$466 million that developed countries have agreed to add to the fund over the next several years should be sufficient to allow developing nations to meet the 1999 deadline to freeze production levels of ozone-destroying chemicals (23). But additional funds, as well as increased transfer of CFC-free technologies, will be needed in the years after 2000 to complete the phaseout (24).

Other steps could hasten the healing of the ozone layer. Developed nations could encourage faster phaseout of their own remaining CFC use by requiring retirement or retrofit of CFC-using machinery. In addition, more rapid elimination of halon production in the developing world and the destruction of

some or all of the existing halon stocks still in industrialized countries would significantly lower ozone loss (25).

Nutrient Overload: Unbalancing the Global Nitrogen Cycle

As a basic building block of plant and animal proteins, nitrogen is a nutrient essential to all forms of life. But it is possible to have too much of a good thing. Recent studies have shown that excess nitrogen from human activities such as agriculture, energy production, and transport has begun to overwhelm the natural nitrogen cycle with a range of ill effects from diminished soil fertility to toxic algal blooms (1)(2)(3).

Until recently, the supply of nitrogen available to plants—and ultimately to animals—has been quite limited. Although it is the most abundant element in the atmosphere, nitrogen from the air cannot be used by plants until it is chemically transformed, or fixed, into ammonium or nitrate compounds that plants can metabolize. In nature, only certain bacteria and algae (and, to a lesser extent, lightning) have this ability to fix atmospheric nitrogen, and the amount that they make available to plants is comparatively small. Other bacteria break down nitrogen compounds in dead matter and release it to the atmosphere again. As a consequence, nitrogen is a precious commodity—a limiting nutrient—in most undisturbed natural systems.

All that has changed in the past several decades. Driven by a massive increase in the use of fertilizer, the burning of fossil fuels, and an upsurge in land clearing and deforestation, the amount of nitrogen available for uptake at any given time has more than doubled since the 1940s. In other words, human activities now contribute more to the global supply of fixed nitrogen each year than natural processes do, with human-generated nitrogen totaling about 210 million metric tons per year, while natural processes contribute about 140 million metric tons (4). (See Table GC.4.)

This influx of extra nitrogen has caused serious distortions of the natural nutrient cycle, especially where intensive agriculture and high fossil fuel use coincide. In some parts of northern Europe, for example, forests are receiving 10 times the natural levels of nitrogen from airborne deposition (5), while coastal rivers in the northeastern United States and northern Europe are receiving as much as 20 times the natural amount from both agricultural and airborne sources (6). Nitrate levels in many Norwegian lakes have doubled in less than a decade (7). Although many of the nitrogen trouble spots tend to be in North America and Europe, the threat of nitrogen overload is global in scope, as both fertilizer use and energy use are growing quickly in the developing world. In fact, global nitrogen deposition may as much as double in the next 25 years as agriculture and energy use continue to intensify (8).

The effects of this surfeit of nutrients reach into every environmental domain, threatening air and water quality and disrupting the health of terrestrial and aquatic ecosystems. Natural systems may be able to absorb a limited amount of additional nitrogen by producing more plant mass, just as garden vegetables do when fertilized. Atmospheric deposition of nitrogen emissions on some heavily cut forests in North America and Europe seems to have spurred additional growth in this manner. But there is a limit to the amount of nitrogen that natural systems can take up; beyond this level, serious harm can ensue. In terrestrial ecosystems, nitrogen saturation can disrupt soil chemistry, leading to loss of other soil nutrients such as calcium, magnesium, and potassium and ultimately to a decline in fertility (9).

Excess nitrogen can also wreak havoc with the structure of ecosystems, affecting the number and kind of species found. Researchers in the United Kingdom and the United States have found that applying nitrogen fertilizer to grasslands enables a few nitrogen-responsive grass species to dominate, while others disappear. In one British experiment, this effect led to a fivefold reduction in the number of species in the most heavily fertilized plots (10)(11). In the Netherlands, where nitrogen deposition rates are among the highest in the world, whole ecosystems have been altered because of this shift in dominant plants, with species-rich heathlands being converted to species-poor forests and grasslands that better accommodate the nitrogen load (12).

Although terrestrial ecosystems are vulnerable to the global nitrogen glut, aquatic ecosystems in lakes, rivers, and coastal estuaries have probably suffered the most so far. They are the ultimate receptacle of much of the nutrient overload, which tends to accumulate in runoff or to be delivered directly in the form of raw or treated sewage. (Sewage is very high in nitrogen from protein in the human diet.) In these aquatic systems, excess nitrogen often greatly stimulates the growth of algae and other aquatic plants. When this extra plant matter dies and decays, it can rob the water of its dissolved oxygen, suffocating many aquatic organisms.

This overfertilization process, called eutrophication, is one of the most serious threats to aquatic environments today, particularly in coastal estuaries and inshore waters where most commercial fish and shellfish species breed (13)(14). Partially enclosed seas such as the Baltic Sea, the Black Sea, and even the Mediterranean have also been hard hit by nitrogen-caused eutrophication, and an extensive "dead zone" of diminished productivity has developed at the mouth of the Mississippi River in the Gulf of Mexico because of the large in-

A Global Glut of Nitrogen

TABLE GC.4 Global Sources of Biologically Available (Fixed) Nitrogen

ANTHROPOGENIC SOURCES	ANNUAL RELEASE OF FIXED NITROGEN (teragrams)
Fertilizer	80
Legumes and other plants	40
Fossil fuels	20
Biomass burning	40
Wetland draining	10
Land clearing	20
Total from human sources	**210**
NATURAL SOURCES	
Soil bacteria, algae, lightning, etc.	140

Source: Peter M. Vitousek *et al.,* "Human Alteration of the Global Nitrogen Cycle: Causes and Consequences," *Issues in Ecology,* No. 1 (1997), pp. 4–6.

flux of nitrogen from agricultural runoff (15). One of the more troubling aspects of this nutrient assault on aquatic systems has been a steady rise in toxic algal blooms, which can take a heavy toll on fish, seabirds, and marine mammals (16). (See Figure GC.11.)

The nitrogen glut also impinges on the health of the atmosphere when the nitrogen-containing gases nitric oxide and nitrous oxide are released into the air, either from fossil fuel burning, land clearing, or agriculture-related activities. Nitric oxide, for example, is a potent precursor of smog and acid rain, and nitrous oxide is a long-lived greenhouse gas that traps some 200 times more heat than carbon dioxide. Nitrous oxide can also play a role in depleting the stratospheric ozone layer. Nitrous oxide concentrations in the atmosphere are rising rapidly—about 0.2 to 0.3 percent per year (17) (18).

Curbing the world's nitrogen overload will mean acting on several fronts. Making fertilizer applications more efficient is one of the most promising options. Agriculture accounts for by far the largest amount of human-generated nitrogen—some 86 percent (19). Fertilizer use was scant until the 1950s but since then has increased exponentially. (See Figure GC.12.)

Excess Nutrients May Spur Algal Blooms

FIGURE GC.11 Major or Recurring Harmful Algal Blooms, Before and After 1972

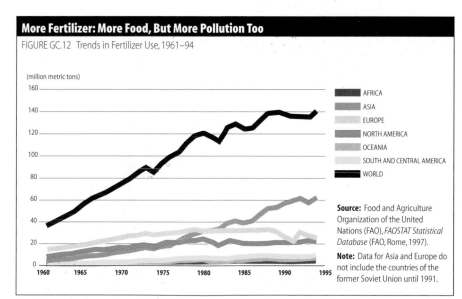

Pre-1972

Post-1972

HI   PR

HI   PR

Source: Donald Anderson, "Expansion of HAB Problems in the U.S.," National Office for Marine Biotoxins and Harmful Algal Blooms, Woods Hole Oceanographic Institution. Available online at: http://habserv1.whoi.edu/hab/HABdistribution/habexpand.html (February 10, 1998).

Note: The increase in algal blooms may be attributable to a number of causes, including an increase in waterborne nutrients from human activities.

In fact, one half of all the commercial fertilizer ever produced has been applied since 1984 (20). The problem is that about one half of every metric ton of fertilizer applied to fields never even makes it into plant tissue but ends up evaporating or being washed into local watercourses (21). A combination of better timing of fertilizer applications, more exact calculation of doses, and more accurate delivery could cut this waste substantially.

Cutting airborne nitrogen emissions from fossil fuels will also be important and will benefit from many of the same strategies used to reduce carbon dioxide emissions, including a greater emphasis on energy efficiency, a gradual shift toward alternative energy sources, and the use of low-nitrogen technology in power plants and cars. Other strategies make sense as well, such as restoration of wetlands, which are natural nutrient traps that sponge up

excess nitrogen before it can damage aquatic systems.

But none of these steps is easy or obvious, and there seems little likelihood of concerted action until the nitrogen threat is elevated to a higher global profile. While the risks of global warming from a buildup of greenhouse gases in the atmosphere are fairly common knowledge today, the dangers of the world's heavy nitrogen habit have gone largely unheralded so far, although this habit may be as pervasive and hard to address as cutting greenhouse gas emissions.

Acid Rain: Downpour in Asia?

Although there has been major progress in controlling acid-forming emissions in some countries, the global threat from acid rain is far from over yet. In fact, the dimensions of the acid rain problem are growing rapidly in Asia, with sulfur dioxide (SO_2) emissions expected to as much as triple from 1990 levels by 2010 if current trends con-

More Fertilizer: More Food, But More Pollution Too

FIGURE GC.12 Trends in Fertilizer Use, 1961–94

(million metric tons)

AFRICA
ASIA
EUROPE
NORTH AMERICA
OCEANIA
SOUTH AND CENTRAL AMERICA
WORLD

Source: Food and Agriculture Organization of the United Nations (FAO), *FAOSTAT Statistical Database* (FAO, Rome, 1997).

Note: Data for Asia and Europe do not include the countries of the former Soviet Union until 1991.

tinue. Curtailing the already substantial acid rain damage in Asia and avoiding much heavier damages in the future will require investments in pollution control on the order of those made in Europe and North America over the past 20 years (1).

Even in developed countries where there have been serious efforts to control acid rain, the story is more complicated than it once appeared. Questions remain in regards to how much damage has been done to forests, lakes, and streams over the years; whether current progress is sufficient to protect the most vulnerable ecosystems; and how soon acid-damaged areas will recover.

Acid rain emerged as a concern in the 1960s with observations of dying lakes and forest damage in northern Europe, the United States, and Canada. It was one of the first environmental issues to demonstrate a large-scale regional scope, with the chief pollutants—oxides of sulfur (SO_x) and nitrogen (NO_x) from combustion of fossil fuels—able to be carried hundreds of miles by winds before being washed out of the atmosphere in rain, fog, and snow.

As evidence grew of the links between air pollution and environmental damage, legislation to curb emissions was put in place. The 1979 Geneva Convention on Long-Range Transboundary Air Pollution and its subsequent amendments set targets for reductions of sulfur and nitrogen emissions in Europe that have largely been achieved. The 1970 and 1990 Clean Air Acts have led to similar improvements in the United States.

Scientific uncertainties about acid rain persist, however. In the case of forest damage, the contribution of acid rain is hard to isolate from other stresses such as drought, fire, and pests that figure heavily in forest health. In Canada, for example, losses to fires and insects exceed the volume of timber harvested for industrial use (2). For this reason, the contribution of air pollution to forest damage is a controversial sub-

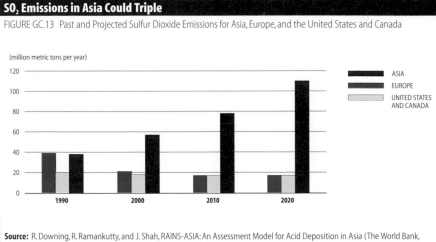

SO₂ Emissions in Asia Could Triple

FIGURE GC.13   Past and Projected Sulfur Dioxide Emissions for Asia, Europe, and the United States and Canada

(million metric tons per year)

Legend:
- ASIA
- EUROPE
- UNITED STATES AND CANADA

Source: R. Downing, R. Ramankutty, and J. Shah, RAINS-ASIA: An Assessment Model for Acid Deposition in Asia (The World Bank, Washington, D.C., 1997), p. 11.

ject, particularly in North America. The most recent and authoritative assessment of forest conditions in Europe reports that 25 percent of trees sampled in more than 30 countries were rated as damaged (having lost more than 25 percent of their leaves). Damage has been increasing over the past 20 years and, while the report notes the difficulty of identifying definitive causes, nearly one half of the countries participating in the survey mentioned air pollution as a cause (3).

Acid rain is now emerging as a major problem in the developing world, especially in parts of Asia and the Pacific region where energy use has surged and the use of sulfur-containing coal and oil—the primary sources of acid emissions—is very high. An estimated 34 million metric tons of SO_2 were emitted in the Asia region in 1990, over 40 percent more than in North America (4)(5). Acid deposition levels were particularly high in areas such as southeast China, northeast India, Thailand, and the Republic of Korea, which are near or downwind from major urban and industrial centers. The effects are already being felt in the agriculture sector. Researchers in India found that wheat growing near a power plant where SO_2 deposition was almost five times greater than the critical load (the amount the soil can safely absorb with-

out harm) suffered a 49-percent reduction in yield compared with wheat growing 22 kilometers away (6). In southwestern China, a study in Guizhou and Sichuan provinces revealed that acid rain fell on some two thirds of the agricultural lands, with 16 percent of the crop area sustaining some level of damage. Other ecosystems are also beginning to suffer. A study of pines and oaks in acid rain-affected areas of the Republic of Korea, both rural and urban, showed significant declines in growth rates since 1970 (7).

One possibility is that damage to ecosystems from acid deposition may be more fundamental and long-lasting than was first believed. For example, scientists now report that acid rain leaches as much as 50 percent of the calcium and magnesium from forest soils; these are crucial minerals which buffer or neutralize acids and are essential for plant growth. If soil chemistry is changed dramatically in this way, it may take many decades for all the linked ecosystems to recover (15). A related problem is the continued leaching of heavy metals and other substances that acid rain has mobilized in the soil, providing a persistent source of toxicity to surrounding vegetation and aquatic life.

As a result, damage to natural ecosystems and crops is likely to increase dramatically. Large regions of southern and

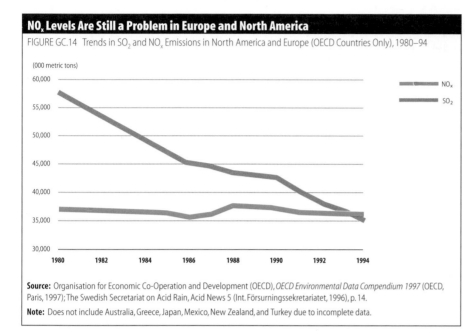

NO$_x$ Levels Are Still a Problem in Europe and North America

FIGURE GC.14   Trends in SO$_2$ and NO$_x$ Emissions in North America and Europe (OECD Countries Only), 1980–94

(000 metric tons)

— NO$_x$
— SO$_2$

Source: Organisation for Economic Co-Operation and Development (OECD), *OECD Environmental Data Compendium 1997* (OECD, Paris, 1997); The Swedish Secretariat on Acid Rain, *Acid News 5* (Int. Försurningssekretariatet, 1996), p. 14.

Note: Does not include Australia, Greece, Japan, Mexico, New Zealand, and Turkey due to incomplete data.

eastern China, northern and central Thailand, and much of the Korean peninsula could experience damaging sulfur deposition levels (9). In some industrialized areas of China, for example, acid deposition levels may some day exceed those experienced in Central Europe's "Black Triangle," a large swath of Poland, the Czech Republic, and southeast Germany where both acid rain levels and forest damage were acute in the 1980s (10).

Damage could be largely avoided if modern pollution control technologies, such as flue-gas scrubbers, are widely adopted and if low-sulfur fuel is substituted where possible. In fact, the World Bank calculates that use of the best available pollution control technologies could cut acid deposition levels in half from 1990 levels by 2020 in Asia, even though energy use is projected to triple during this period. But the price for this level of environmental protection is steep: roughly US$90 billion per year throughout the Asia region, or about 0.6 percent of the region's gross domestic product (11).

Less ambitious and lower-cost strategies can also cut acid-forming emissions substantially, but the amount of environmental protection these strate-

gies buy is commensurately less and will not protect many areas from serious acid deposition. In the end, perhaps the most cost-effective option for controlling acid rain will be to adopt energy-efficiency measures that cut overall energy use and thus reduce emissions. If systematically employed, such energy-saving measures could cut control costs from one quarter to one third, according to the World Bank's analysis; in addition, these measures would yield ancillary benefits such as better air quality and lower greenhouse gas emissions (12).

MORE TO DO IN THE DEVELOPED WORLD

In industrialized countries, environmental regulations restricting sulfur emissions and market forces that favor greater use of natural gas—which contains little sulfur—have proved relatively effective in cutting SO$_2$ emissions. However, even this success may not be enough in some sensitive areas. A recent Canadian report concluded that SO$_2$ emissions might have to fall another three quarters if ecosystems in a large area of southeastern Canada were to be adequately protected (13). In addition,

declines in SO$_2$ emissions are likely to be partially offset in the future by emissions of NO$_x$, which have remained broadly constant in the OECD countries since 1980. (See Figure GC.14.) In much of Europe, NO$_x$ emissions are now creeping up again, due mainly to increased vehicle numbers and usage (14).

Overall, however, acid-forming emissions have been largely decoupled from economic growth, and transboundary pollution has fallen substantially in the past 25 years, resulting in less acid rain. It has therefore been somewhat of a mystery why damaged trees, streams, and lakes have not bounced back in those areas where acid rain has diminished.

One possibility is that damage to ecosystems from acid deposition may be more fundamental and long-lasting than was first believed. For example, scientists now report that acid rain leaches as much as 50 percent of the calcium and magnesium from forest soils; these are crucial minerals which buffer or neutralize acids and are essential for plant growth. If soil chemistry is changed dramatically in this way, it may take many decades for all the linked ecosystems to recover (15). A related problem is the continued leaching of heavy metals and other substances that acid rain has mobilized in the soil, providing a persistent source of toxicity to surrounding vegetation and aquatic life.

It is also becoming clear that the long-term impacts of acidification cannot be studied in isolation from other environmental problems. Climate change and acidification have led to decreases in dissolved organic carbon concentrations in North American lakes. Carbon absorbs ultraviolet (UV) radiation, which has, in turn, increased due to depletion of the ozone layer. In combination, these changes have resulted in much deeper penetration of UV radiation into lake waters and higher death and disease rates among fish and aquatic plants (16). This effect can be compounded by drought when sulfur compounds stored in lake sediments oxidize in response to falling water levels (17). About 140,000 lakes in North America are estimated to have carbon levels low enough to be at risk of deep UV penetration (18).

These data suggest that the problem of acid rain in developed countries does not end with reduced emission. Although important progress has been made, forest recovery is likely to take decades. Acidification of surface waters in some areas is likely to increase despite falling deposition levels, as ozone depletion continues and the climate continues to warm.

RESOURCES AT RISK

Despite growing awareness and increasing investments in environmental protection, pressures on the world's natural resources and ecosystems continue to increase rapidly. The impacts of human activities reach into every corner of the natural world. For instance, between one third and one half of the Earth's land surface has been substantially transformed by agriculture, urbanization, and commercial activities of various kinds; about one quarter of all bird species have been driven to extinction; and more than one half of all accessible surface water, as well as an enormous quantity of groundwater, is diverted for human uses. These uses have brought unquestionable benefits to human welfare. But the upshot of this growing human domination of the planet is that no ecosystem on Earth is free from pervasive human influence.

This section considers some of the more widespread and pressing threats to the planet's physical and biological resources. Global forest cover, for example, faces enormous pressure in both tropical and temperate regions from conversion to agricultural and urban uses, as well as from logging. Deforestation rates in many developing countries continue to increase, even as the condition of many forests in developed countries is degraded by air pollution. Risks to the world's rich array of living species are also climbing. These threats to biodiversity are particularly intense in aquatic systems such as coral reefs and freshwater habitats in rivers, lakes, and wetlands. Bioinvasions from exotic species introduced accidentally through global trade and tourism or by deliberate import for agriculture comprise a kind of "biological pollution" that also poses a growing threat to the world's biodiversity, both aquatic and terrestrial.

Other resources face critical depletion in the near future. In the absence of strict management schemes to reduce fishing pressure, many marine fish stocks continue to decline, endangering an important source of food and employment. Meanwhile, water availability is set to become one of the prime constraints on development in many regions in the near future. This section also reports on recent efforts to put a price tag on the services that natural ecosystems such as forests and wetlands supply the world without charge. This preliminary effort to assign economic values to these essential services is a powerful way to demonstrate the costs of continuing to degrade the world's vital systems.

Deforestation: The Global Assault Continues

Although public awareness of the impact of global deforestation has increased in recent years, it has not slowed the rate of deforestation appreciably. A comprehensive assessment of the state of the world's forests, recently released by the Food and Agriculture Organization of the United Nations (FAO), indicates that total forested area continues to decline significantly. According to the FAO analysis, deforestation was concentrated in the developing world, which lost nearly 200 million hectares between 1980 and 1995. This loss was partially offset by reforestation efforts, new forest plantations, and the gradual regrowth and expansion of forested area in developed countries. The result was a net loss of some 180 million hectares between 1980 and 1995, or an average annual loss of 12 million hectares (1).

According to FAO, the rate of deforestation dropped slightly during its last survey period. Between 1990 and 1995, annual forest loss in developing countries was estimated at 13.7 million hectares. This rate compares with a rate of 15.5 million hectares annually between 1980 and 1990 (2). (See Figure RR.1.) This small decline is largely due to reported decreases in the deforestation rate in the Amazon in the early 1990s. Even this small decline is disputed by some forest experts, who regard FAO's calculations for 1990 to 1995 as underestimates (3).

In any case, there is no dispute that deforestation rates remain high in many countries; indeed, in the majority of countries that FAO surveyed, deforestation rates have actually increased. In addition, evidence from other sources suggests that deforestation rates in some important regions have increased since the assessment.

In the Brazilian Amazon, for example, the annual deforestation rate declined from a peak of more than 20,000 square kilometers in 1988 to just over 11,000 square kilometers in 1991. However, newly released data from the Brazilian Government show that it rebounded to more than 29,000 square kilometers in 1995 before declining to 18,100 square kilometers in 1996 (4). (See Figure RR.2.) Official estimates of Amazon deforestation in 1997 are not available yet, but there are indications that the deforestation rate may have risen again. Satellite data for the Amazon region show a 50-percent increase from 1996 to 1997 in the number of forest fires set by farmers to clear land for cultivation or pasture. Many of the fires are set to clear old cattle pastures or secondary forest

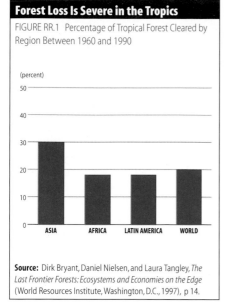
areas, but about one third of the fires are set to clear virgin forest and thus represent one of the principal means of deforestation in the region (5).

Fire-related deforestation also rose sharply in Indonesia in 1997, as severe drought conditions helped spread fires set by plantation workers and farmers into forest areas. Preliminary estimates of the forest area destroyed run from 150,000 to 300,000 hectares (6). Although most of the burning took place in secondary forests rather than virgin

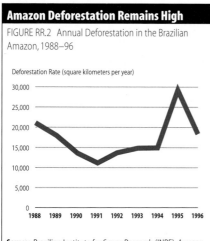
rainforest, the impact has nonetheless been high, destroying habitat for a variety of wildlife species from orangutans to tigers. The fires may increase pressure on adjacent virgin forests by increasing access to formerly remote sites (7).

The FAO analysis concludes that the leading causes of deforestation are the extension of subsistence farming (more common in Africa and Asia), and government-backed conversion of forests to other land uses such as large-scale ranching (most common in Latin America and also Asia). Poverty, joblessness, and inequitable land distribution, which force many landless peasants to invade the forest for lack of other economic means, continue to drive forest clearance for subsistence farming in many regions. Often, people move into forest areas as logging activity creates roads that open formerly inaccessible regions. As for centrally planned forest conversion schemes, these are often used to spur short-term economic development, gain better political control of remote forest regions, and expand agricultural output (8).

The state of the world's forests is not simply a matter of their extent. Increasing attention is focused upon the health, genetic diversity, and age profile of forests, collectively known as forest quality. Measures of total forest area do not reveal the degraded nature of much regrowth forest. For example, in FAO's forest assessment, logging is not counted as deforestation, since logged-over areas can, in theory, regrow to fully functioning forests. But logging often does degrade forest quality, inducing soil and nutrient losses and reducing the forest's value as habitat. Logging pressures in many of the remaining large, virgin rainforest areas continue to increase, with logging activities shifting from the largely deforested areas of Southeast Asia to the rainforests of the Amazon region, Papua New Guinea, and the Congo Basin.

Nor do deforestation numbers reflect the reduced ecological and aesthetic values of plantations that sometimes replace natural forests. Between 1980 and 1995, forest plantations in the developed countries increased from approximately 45 million to 60 million hectares to about 80 million to 100 million hectares (9). In the developing world, the area in forest plantations doubled from about 40 million to about 81 million hectares over the same period. More than 80 percent of plantations in the developing world are found in Asia, where demand for wood-based panels and paper continues to boom.

Forest quality in the developed countries is also of concern. FAO reports that forest cover in Europe (excluding the former Soviet Union) increased by more than 4 percent between 1980 and 1994 (10), but forest conditions worsened. Trees are being damaged by fire, drought, pests, and air pollution. More than 25 percent of trees assessed in a 1995 survey of forest conditions in Europe were suffering significant defoliation. Annual European survey results show the number of completely healthy trees falling from 69 percent in 1988 to 39 percent in 1995 (11).

Overall, the convergence of population growth, rising demand for lumber and fuelwood, and the conversion of forests to agriculture (particularly in Africa) are expected to put increasing pressure on the world's forests in the next few decades. The result will likely be a considerable loss in forest area and quality, with the remaining forest fragmented into smaller isolated tracts (12). (See section on Fragmenting Forests.)

Continued forest loss and degradation will have serious implications at local, regional, and global levels. Exploitation and clearance of natural forests are destroying the environment and way of life for tens of thousands of indigenous people. Disappearing forest cover also represents incalculable losses in biological diversity and ecological services, including nutrient recycling, watershed management, and climate regulation.

Many of Earth's Forests Have Been Cleared or Degraded

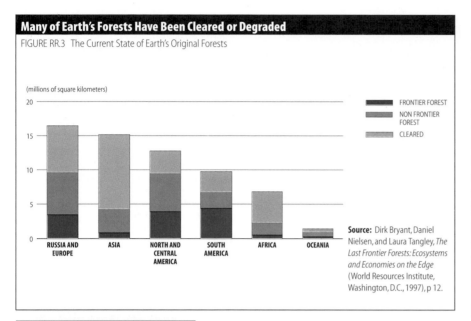

FIGURE RR.3 The Current State of Earth's Original Forests

(millions of square kilometers)

Legend:
- FRONTIER FOREST
- NON FRONTIER FOREST
- CLEARED

Regions: RUSSIA AND EUROPE, ASIA, NORTH AND CENTRAL AMERICA, SOUTH AMERICA, AFRICA, OCEANIA

Source: Dirk Bryant, Daniel Nielsen, and Laura Tangley, *The Last Frontier Forests: Ecosystems and Economies on the Edge* (World Resources Institute, Washington, D.C., 1997), p 12.

Fragmenting Forests: The Loss of Large Frontier Forests

Over the past 8,000 years, nearly one half of the forests that once covered the Earth have been converted to farms, pastures, and other uses. But the human impact on forests did not stop there. Most of the forests that are left have been heavily altered by humans, often rendered into a patchwork of smaller forested areas. According to a 1997 World Resources Institute (WRI) assessment, just one fifth of the Earth's original forest remains in large, relatively natural ecosystems—what are known as frontier forests (1). (See Figure RR.3.).

This fragmentation process is one of the most serious consequences of the current deforestation and degradation of world forests. Frontier forests differ significantly from the dissected, human-modified forests that dominate the planet today. For one thing, frontier forests are large and natural enough to ensure the long-term survival of their plant and animal species, including the biggest mammals with the most extensive home ranges. As secure habitats for native species, frontier forests are invaluable refuges for global biodiversity. Forests are home to between 50 and 90 percent of the world's terrestrial species—plants and animals that have provided much of the food and other basics that humans need to survive (2).

Frontier forests also contribute a large portion of the ecological services that make the planet habitable. They take up tremendous amounts of carbon dioxide (CO_2), for example, and are therefore an important factor in regulating Earth's climate. Recent calculations suggest that frontier forests store approximately 430 billion metric tons of carbon (from CO_2)—more carbon than is likely to be released by fossil fuel burning and cement manufacture over the next 70 years or so (3).

Remaining frontier forests occur either in far northern climes or in the

Frontier Forests Suffer a Variety of Threats

TABLE RR.1 Threats to Frontier Forests

REGION	PERCENTAGE OF FRONTIER FOREST UNDER MODERATE OR HIGH THREAT [a]	PERCENTAGE OF THREATENED FOREST FRONTIERS AT RISK FROM				
		LOGGING	MINING, ROADS, AND OTHER INFRASTRUCTURE	AGRICULTURAL CLEARING	EXCESSIVE VEGETATION REMOVAL	OTHER [b]
Africa	77	79	12	17	8	41
Asia	60	50	10	20	9	24
North and Central America	29	83	27	3	1	14
Central America	87	54	17	23	29	13
North America	26	84	27	2	0	14
South America	54	69	53	32	14	5
Russia and Europe	19	86	51	4	29	18
Europe	100	80	0	0	20	0
Russia	19	86	51	4	29	18
Oceania [c]	76	42	25	15	38	27
World	**39**	**72**	**38**	**20**	**14**	**13**

Source: Dirk Bryant, Daniel Nielsen, and Laura Tangley, *The Last Frontier Forests: Ecosystems and Economies on the Edge* (World Resources Institute, Washington, D.C., 1997), p. 17.

Notes: a. Frontier forests considered under immediate threat, as a percentage of all frontier forest assessed for threat. Threatened frontier forests are places where ongoing or planned human activities are likely, if continued over coming decades, to result in the significant loss of natural qualities associated with all or part of these areas. b. "Other" includes such activities as overhunting, introduction of harmful exotic species, isolation of smaller frontier forest islands through development of surrounding lands, changes in fire regimes, and plantation establishment. c. Oceania consists of Papua New Guinea, Australia, and New Zealand.

tropics: 48 percent of frontier forests are boreal forests (a broad belt of primarily coniferous trees located between Arctic tundra and the temperate zone), while 44 percent are tropical forests. By contrast, only a tiny fraction of Earth's frontier forests are in the temperate zone.

A country-by-country breakdown shows that 76 countries have lost all of their frontier forest. Another 11 nations are close to losing their last remaining frontier forests, having fewer than 5 percent of these forests left, all of which are threatened. More than three quarters of all frontier forests fall within three large tracts that cover parts of seven countries: two blocks of boreal forest (one blanketing much of Canada and Alaska and the other in Russia), and one large tropical forest covering South America's northwestern Amazon Basin and Guyana Shield. Three countries alone—Brazil, Canada, and Russia—contain nearly 70 percent of all frontier forests (4).

A significant number of frontier forests that have survived into the 20th Century are threatened today. WRI's assessment found that 39 percent of Earth's remaining frontier forests are endangered by human activities. One surprising result was that logging represents by far the greatest danger to frontier forests (5). (See Table RR.1.)

The assessment found good news in a few parts of the world. Seven nations (Brazil, Canada, Colombia, Guyana, Russia, Suriname, and Venezuela) and one Overseas Department of France (French Guiana) have kept a large number of their frontier forests, and many of these ecosystems do not face imminent risk. However, these currently unthreatened forests remain vulnerable—particularly in the tropics—because they contain high-value resources such as timber and gold and other minerals (6).

The majority of frontier forests that are not threatened today lie within boreal regions, inhospitable to most developers. Outside of boreal forests, however, 75 percent of the world's frontier

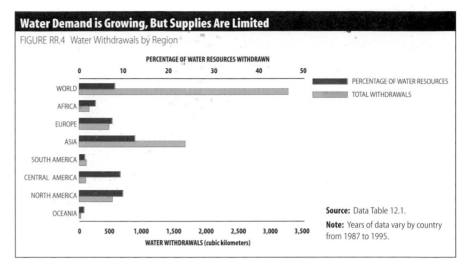

Water Demand is Growing, But Supplies Are Limited

FIGURE RR.4 Water Withdrawals by Region

Source: Data Table 12.1.

Note: Years of data vary by country from 1987 to 1995.

forests—including all temperate frontier forests—are endangered by human activity (7).

Water: Critical Shortages Ahead?

The world's thirst for water is likely to become one of the most pressing resource issues of the 21st Century. Global water consumption rose sixfold between 1900 and 1995—more than double the rate of population growth—and continues to grow rapidly as agricultural, industrial, and domestic demand increases (1).

Globally, water supplies are abundant, but they are unevenly distributed among and within countries. In some areas, water withdrawals are so high, relative to supply, that surface water supplies are literally shrinking and groundwater reserves are being depleted faster than they can be replenished by precipitation (2). (See Figure RR.4.)

This situation has already caused serious water shortages to develop in some regions, shortchanging human water needs and damaging aquatic ecosystems. A 1997 United Nations assessment of freshwater resources found that one third of the world's population lives in countries experiencing moderate to high water stress. To arrive at its esti-

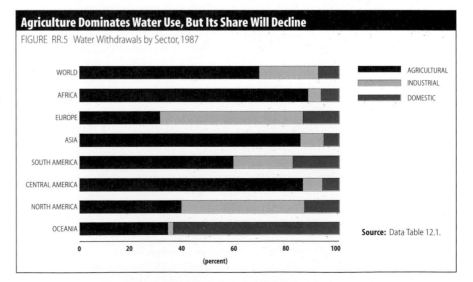

Agriculture Dominates Water Use, But Its Share Will Decline

FIGURE RR.5 Water Withdrawals by Sector, 1987

Source: Data Table 12.1.

mate, the United Nations determined each country's ratio of water consumption to water availability—its use-to-resource index—which is a good gauge of overall pressure on water resources (3). Moderate to high stress translates to consumption levels that exceed 20 percent of available supply (4).

The U.N. assessment makes clear that the global water situation will get considerably worse over the next 30 years without major improvements in the way water is allocated and used. In fact, the United Nations projects that the share of the world's population in countries undergoing moderate or high water stress could rise to two thirds by 2025. Population growth and socioeconomic development are currently driving a rapid increase in water demand, especially from the industrial and household sectors. Industrial water use, for example, is predicted to double by 2025 if current growth trends persist (5).

Water use in agriculture is slated to increase as world food demand rises. Agriculture already accounts for about 70 percent of water consumption worldwide, and the United Nations projects a 50- to 100-percent increase in irrigation water by 2025 (6). (See Figure RR.5.)

Much of the projected increase in water demand will occur in developing countries, where population growth and industrial and agricultural expansion will be greatest. However, per capita consumption continues to rise in the industrialized world as well.

Water pollution adds enormously to existing problems of local and regional water scarcity by removing large volumes of water from the available supply. Water quality in most of the developed countries has steadily improved in recent years, thanks to strict legislation and major investments in new water and sanitation infrastructure. Even in the developed world, however, wastewater is not necessarily treated before discharge. In the southern member states of the European Union, about 50 percent of the population is not

yet connected to sewage treatment operations (7).

The situation is far worse in many developing countries. Water scarcity has been exacerbated and human health gravely damaged by accelerating contamination of usable water supplies, especially in rapidly urbanizing areas.

Many developing countries undergoing rapid industrialization are now faced with the full range of modern toxic pollution problems—eutrophication, heavy metals, acidification, persistent organic pollutants (POPs)—while still struggling to deal with traditional problems of poor water supply and lack of sanitation services (8). The pollution threat is particularly serious when it affects groundwater supplies, where contamination is slow to dilute and purification measures are costly. Groundwater reserves are estimated to provide more than 50 percent of domestic supplies in most Asian countries (9); yet, these countries are currently experiencing rapid growth in the mining and manufacturing sectors—two big sources of groundwater contamination.

As clean water supplies have diminished, competition for them has been growing, usually between expanding urban areas and rural users. Where systems of water law and allocation exist, water markets can operate to transfer supplies between buyers and sellers for an agreed price. Such systems are operating with some success in an increasing number of countries, including the western United States (10) and Australia (11). However, effective water pricing, which sets water prices high enough to discourage waste, remains a highly sensitive issue in low-income countries, where most people depend on irrigated agriculture for their living. Even so, socioeconomic development in water-scarce countries may depend critically on more rational distribution of scarce supplies. Planners in China have estimated that a given amount of water used in industry generates more than 60

times the value of the same water used in agriculture (12).

Better management of water resources is the key to mitigating water scarcities in the future and avoiding further damage to aquatic ecosystems. In the short term, more efficient use of water could dramatically expand available resources. In developing countries, for example, 60 to 75 percent of irrigation water never reaches the crop and is lost to evaporation or runoff (13). Although the use of water-efficient drip irrigation has increased 28-fold since the mid-1970s, it is still employed in less than 1 percent of the world's irrigated areas (14).

In the longer term, however, the U.N. water assessment makes clear that looming water crises in many regions must be addressed through hard policy decisions that reallocate water to the most economically and socially beneficial uses. Far greater emphasis on water-efficient technologies and pollution control is also essential. However, even with measures to contain the growth of demand and use water more efficiently, new supplies will be needed. The World Bank has estimated that the financial and environmental costs of tapping new supplies will be, on average, two or three times those of existing investments, because most of the low-cost, accessible water reserves have already been exploited (15).

The U.N. study also highlights the potentially desperate situation of developing countries that combine high water stress with low per capita income. The majority of these countries are found in the arid or semiarid regions of Africa and Asia. Many use most of their available water supplies for farm irrigation and suffer from a lack of pollution controls. Future development in these countries appears severely constrained because they have neither the extra water nor the financial resources to shift development away from intensive irrigation and into other sectors that would create employment and generate income to import food. Figure RR.6 gives

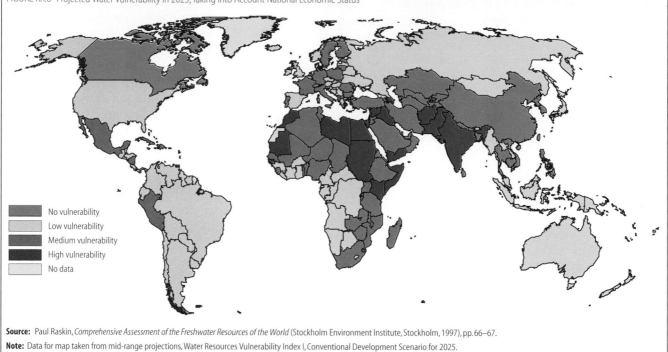

Low-Income Nations Are Especially Vulnerable to Water Scarcity

FIGURE RR.6 Projected Water Vulnerability in 2025, Taking into Account National Economic Status

No vulnerability
Low vulnerability
Medium vulnerability
High vulnerability
No data

Source: Paul Raskin, *Comprehensive Assessment of the Freshwater Resources of the World* (Stockholm Environment Institute, Stockholm, 1997), pp. 66–67.

Note: Data for map taken from mid-range projections, Water Resources Vulnerability Index I, Conventional Development Scenario for 2025.

an idea of the future vulnerability of nations to water scarcity in 2025, taking into account their income level and their ability to cope with water stress both economically and socially.

The Decline of Freshwater Ecosystems

In a world in which it seems that nearly every natural ecosystem is under stress, freshwater ecosystems—the diverse communities found in lakes, rivers, and wetlands—may be the most endangered of all. Some 34 percent of fish species, mostly from fresh water, are threatened with extinction, according to the latest tally of the World Conservation Union (IUCN), which tracks threats to the world's biodiversity (1). Freshwater ecosystems have lost a greater proportion of their species and habitat than ecosystems on land or in the oceans; in addition, they are probably in greater danger of further losses from dams, pollution, overfishing, and other threats (2).

In extent, freshwater ecosystems are quite limited, covering only about 1 percent of the Earth's surface. Yet, they are highly diverse and contain a disproportionately large number of the world's species. The Amazon River, for instance, is home to more than 3,000 fish species. Lake Victoria in Africa has—or had before recent depredations—as many as 350 species of a single family of fish (cichlids) (3). The Mississippi River in North America contains almost 300 freshwater mussel species (4). In all, more than 40 percent of the world's fish species (5) and some 12 percent of animal species in general (6) reside in freshwater habitats, with many of these species restricted to extremely small areas and therefore quite vulnerable to disturbance.

The majority of the world's population lives near and depends on freshwater environments, with most inland cities lying adjacent to a river or lake (7). In addition to being biologically rich, freshwater systems play a vital role in the lives of many people, providing a source of water, food, and employment.

About 6 percent of the world's fish catch, or 7 million metric tons per year, (8) come from rivers and lakes, as well as the bulk of the world's irrigation water. Rivers and lakes are also crucial as transportation and shipping routes, as power sources, and, unfortunately, as waste sinks. All of these human uses take their toll on freshwater ecosystems.

Dams and channelization remain the two most pervasive threats to freshwater ecosystems today, with dramatic effects on species abundance and diversity. Since 1970, when Egypt's Aswan Dam came into operation, the number of commercially harvested fish species on the Nile has dropped by almost two thirds, and the sardine catch in the Mediterranean has fallen by more than 80 percent (9). On the Rhine River, more than 100 years of channelization and riverside development have cut the river off from 90 percent of its original flood plains, and the native salmon run has nearly disappeared (10).

The scale and extent of these human impacts on freshwater systems have risen precipitously in recent years. In

1950, there were 5,270 large dams; today, there are more than 36,500 (11). (See Figure RR.7.) Meanwhile, the number of waterways altered for navigation has grown from fewer than 9,000 in 1900 to almost 500,000 today, with a consequent decline in their viability as habitat (12).

Given their benefits to shipping, agriculture, and power production, dams and channelization projects remain important components of national development strategies, even though their environmental impacts are well known. In Southeast Asia, dozens of dams are being planned along most of the length of the Mekong River and its tributaries. The Mekong River Basin has few dams so far and retains one of the world's richest troves of freshwater biodiversity. Estimates of the number of fish species in the basin run to 500 and higher, and the annual fish catch on the Mekong and its tributaries is a vital part of the local food supply (13)(14). Experience with one of the few dams in the basin shows how vulnerable this resource can be. After the Pak Mun Dam was built in the early 1990s on Thailand's Mun River, a Mekong tributary, all 150 fish species that had inhabited the river virtually disappeared (15).

In South America, the Hidrovia—or Water Highway—project will create a 3,400-kilometer shipping corridor, opening landlocked Paraguay and Bolivia, as well as parts of the Brazilian interior, to river trade. The project involves dredging, widening, and straightening large sections of the Paraguay and Paraná rivers to allow large convoys of barges to pass into the continent's interior. Unfortunately, the Paraguay River runs through the Gran Pantanal, the world's largest and most pristine wetland. Dredging and channelization through the area could lower the water level considerably, imperiling the 600 species of fish, 650 varieties of birds, 80 types of mammals, and more than 90,000 varieties of plants that inhabit the Pantanal (16) (17).

Freshwater ecosystems face many other risks as well:

● Industrial discharges and agricultural and urban runoff are pervasive stresses. By the early 1990s, acid rain had caused a 40-percent decline in fish species in Canadian lakes (18).

● Overfishing, which plagues many freshwater systems, is currently driving various sturgeon species toward extinction in the Caspian Sea and its tributaries (19).

● Water diversions for agriculture and urban water supplies have rendered all native fish species in the lower Colorado River either endangered or extinct (20).

● Siltation from soil erosion has been cited as a major factor in the decline of endemic fishes in Sri Lanka (21).

● Competition from nonnative fishes in Lake Victoria has driven 200 species of native cichlids to extinction and endangered 150 more (22).

In response to these threats, concern for freshwater systems is growing. At the World Bank and other development banks that have traditionally looked favorably on dams and other major water projects, policies have shifted to emphasize a more thorough examination of the full benefits and costs of the these projects. For instance, the Inter-American Development Bank so far has refused requests to bankroll the Hidrovia project in light of its environmental impacts (23).

More positive still is a nascent trend toward restoring some damaged freshwater ecosystems. In Romania, officials at the Danube Delta Biosphere Reserve, with funds from the World Bank's Global Environmental Facility and other foreign donors, are breaching dikes and dams that were built to convert the immense delta wetlands at the mouth of the Danube to farmland. In the United States, engineers are attempting a similar restoration at the

River Habitats Have Been Heavily Altered

FIGURE RR.7 Waterways Altered for Navigation, 1680–1980

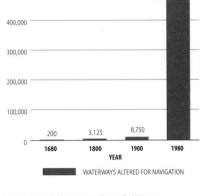

(kilometers)

Year	Value
1680	200
1800	3,125
1900	8,750
1980	498,000

WATERWAYS ALTERED FOR NAVIGATION

Source: Janet N. Abramowitz, "Imperiled Waters, Impoverished Future: The Decline of Freshwater Ecosystems," Worldwatch Paper No. 128 (Worldwatch Institute, Washington, D.C., 1996), p. 13.

Everglades National Park in Florida (24)(25).

To minimize further damage to freshwater ecosystems, the signatory nations to the U.N. Convention on Biological Diversity have agreed to focus on risks to freshwater ecosystems at their next meeting in 1998 (the Fourth Conference of the Parties). With the scale of water developments still growing worldwide, experts stress that the need for coordinated action is urgent.

Valuing Ecosystem Services

What are Mother Nature's life-support services worth? In one sense, their value is infinite. The Earth's economies would soon collapse without fertile soil, fresh water, breathable air, and an amenable climate. But "infinite" too often translates to "zero" in the equations that guide land use and policy decisions. Practitioners in the young field of ecological economics believe more concrete numbers are required to help nations avoid unsustainable economic

FIGURE RR.8 Estimates of Human Economic Activities and Ecosystem Services

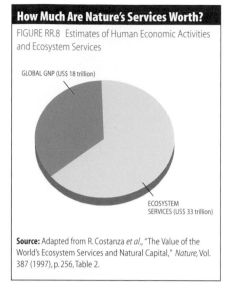

GLOBAL GNP (US$ 18 trillion)

ECOSYSTEM SERVICES (US$ 33 trillion)

Source: Adapted from R. Costanza *et al.,* "The Value of the World's Ecosystem Services and Natural Capital," *Nature,* Vol. 387 (1997), p. 256, Table 2.

choices that degrade both their natural resources and the vital services that healthy natural ecosystems generate.

In one of the first efforts to calculate a global number, a team of researchers from the United States, Argentina, and the Netherlands has put an average price tag of US$33 trillion a year on these fundamental ecosystem services, which are

TABLE RR.2 Estimates of Various Ecosystem Services

ECOSYSTEM SERVICES	VALUE (trillion $US)
Soil formation	17.1
Recreation	3.0
Nutrient cycling	2.3
Water regulation and supply	2.3
Climate regulation (temperature and precipitation)	1.8
Habitat	1.4
Flood and storm protection	1.1
Food and raw materials production	0.8
Genetic resources	0.8
Atmospheric gas balance	0.7
Pollination	0.4
All other services	1.6
Total value of ecosystem services	**33.3**

Source: Adapted from R. Costanza *et al.,* "The Value of the World's Ecosystem Services and Natural Capital," *Nature,* Vol. 387 (1997), p. 256, Table 2.

largely taken for granted because they are free. That is nearly twice the value of the global gross national product(GNP) of US$18 trillion (1).(See Figure RR.8 and Table RR.2.)

Even those involved in the study admit their number is a first approximation, but they consider it an essential starting point for further analysis and debate that will help nations overhaul their economic and environmental decisionmaking. Not everyone agrees with this approach, however. Some critics believe the effort to assign prices to ecosystem services is fundamentally flawed since these services can never be traded in open commerce, which is how prices of conventional goods and services are determined (2). Others believe that, even if such prices can be reasonably calculated, they cannot reflect the full value of these services, which reaches well beyond their importance to the world economy. In fact, the study team also readily acknowledged that there are moral, ethical, and aesthetic reasons to value and protect nature quite apart from its benefits to humanity (3).

But the reality is that human societies put price tags on nature every day. Every land use decision involves implicit assumptions about value, even when no dollar figure is assigned. The problem is that the value of services provided by the Earth's ecological infrastructure does not fit into current economic equations, partly because most of the benefits fall outside the marketplace. Such services are public goods that contribute immeasurably to human welfare without ever being drawn into the money economy. For instance, the cycling of essential nutrients like nitrogen and phosphorus, which is not reflected in any nation's GNP, accounts for US$17 trillion of the US$33 trillion in annual ecosystem services, according to the study team's estimate (4).

Indeed, economic indicators such as GNP are increasingly recognized as flawed measures of both economic progress and sustainability, because

they do not explicitly account for the degradation in ecological services that industry and commerce cause (5). For example, valuing forests only for the marketable timber they produce, which is as much as the GNP can conveniently measure, ignores the many indirect costs that society bears when forests are logged: soil erosion, nutrient loss, increased flooding, declines in fisheries and water quality, reduced carbon storage capacity, changes in regional temperature and rainfall, and diminished wildlife habitat and recreational opportunities.

There have been many attempts in the past few decades to estimate the value of various separate ecological services. The US$33 trillion calculation is a synthesis of results from more than 100 published studies using a variety of different valuation methods. In synthesizing these results, the research team looked at the value of 17 categories of services such as waste treatment, pollination, climate regulation, food production, and recreation in each of 16 types of ecosystems, from coastal estuaries to tropical forests, rangelands, lakes, and deserts. They calculated an average dollar value per hectare for each type of service in each ecosystem, then multiplied that dollar value by the total area each ecosystem type occupies on the globe (6).

This exercise clearly highlighted areas where much more work is needed. For some types of ecosystems, such as deserts, tundra, and croplands, so little is known that the valuation columns under nearly every ecological service remain blank (7). That is one reason the study team considers the US$33 trillion a minimum value; it will likely increase as more ecological services are studied and the complex interactions among ecological processes are better understood. Values are also likely to increase as these services become more degraded and scarce in the future (8).

Whatever the eventual number, ecological economists consider the global dollar figure itself less important to policy than to the potential application of this valuation concept to local and regional land use decisions. Although the average value of wetland services may not be the same per hectare in Brazil, Indonesia, or Uganda, the very existence of the global estimates calculated in the study should broaden the context of local decisionmaking (9). In fact, in a small but growing number of cases around the world, the benefits of proposed projects are being weighed against the social costs of lost ecosystem services.

In some parts of the United States, for instance, attention is now focused on the benefits of protecting natural watersheds to assure safe and plentiful drinking water supplies, rather than on building expensive filtration plants to purify water from degraded watersheds. New York City recently found it could avoid spending US$6 billion to US$8 billion in constructing new water treatment plants by protecting the upstate watershed that has traditionally accomplished these purification services for free. Based on this economic assessment, the city invested US$1.5 billion in buying land around its reservoirs and instituting other protective measures, actions that will not only keep its water pure at a bargain price but also enhance recreation, wildlife habitat, and other ecological benefits (10).

In the traditionally prosperous Hadejia-Jama'are flood plain region in northern Nigeria, where more than one half of the wetlands have already been lost to drought and upstream dams, ecosystem valuation has been used to weigh the costs and benefits of proposals that would divert still more water away for irrigated agriculture. The net benefits of such a diversion priced out at US$29 per hectare. Yet, the intact flood plain already provides US$167 per hectare in benefits to a wider range of local people engaged in farming, fishing, grazing livestock, or gathering fuel-

wood and other wild products—benefits that would be greatly diminished by the project. Thus, even without accounting for such services as wildlife habitat, the wetland is far more valuable to more people in its current state than diverted for irrigation (11).

Although ecological valuations like these are still rare, further development of the concept promises to provide a powerful tool for protection and sustainable use of natural ecosystems and the vital services they provide.

Coral Reefs: Assessing the Threat

Around the world, coral reefs are under assault from a multitude of sources. Depending on their location, reefs have been damaged directly through harmful practices such as coral mining, fishing with dynamite, or overfishing in general; haphazard coastal development; or even careless pleasure diving by tourists. Reefs have also suffered indirectly from sediment from inland deforestation and removal of coastal mangroves; from industrial pollution; and from nutrient pollution contributed by sewage, fertilizers, and urban runoff.

Just how much reefs have suffered from these depredations on a global basis is not yet clear. Both anecdotal and scientific reports of reef damage have increased over the past 20 years, and reef specialists agree there is a serious global decline (1). In 1992, Australian reef ecologist Clive Wilkinson estimated that some 10 percent of the world's reefs were already severely degraded; he predicted that figure would rise to 30 percent within the next two decades, with further losses continuing as populations in the coastal tropics surge (2). But these are just rough estimates, based on expert opinion. To date, no survey of reef conditions has been conducted worldwide, so scientists do

not know the actual condition of the vast majority of the world's reefs. In the Pacific, for example, 90 percent of coral reefs have yet to be assessed (3).

Although definitive data on reef conditions are some years off, a preliminary analysis of current reef threats indicates that a high percentage of the world's coral reefs are at risk of degradation. The ongoing assessment, which is being conducted by the World Resources Institute, the International Centre for Living Marine Aquatic Resources, and the World Conservation Monitoring Centre, looks at four broad categories of potential threat to coral reefs: coastal development, overfishing and destructive fishing practices, land-based pollution (especially sediment) from deforestation and agriculture, and marine pollution from oil spills and the discharge of oily ballast water. The analysis, due to be published in June 1998, does not measure actual reef conditions but estimates the threat to reefs based on the proximity and intensity of known risk factors, such as ports, urban centers, coastal population density, and land use patterns (4).(See Figure RR.9.)

Key findings include the following:

● Globally, 58 percent of the world's reefs are at risk from human activities, with about 27 percent of reefs at high or very high risk.

● Significant regional differences exist regarding the degree of risk that coral reefs face. The reefs of Southeast Asia, which are the most species-diverse in the world, are also the most threatened, with more than 80 percent at risk, including 55 percent at high or very high risk. On the other hand, the reefs in the Pacific region, which contains more reef area than any other region, face comparatively less risk. Forty-one percent of Pacific reefs were classified as threatened, and just 10 percent face a high risk.

This ongoing assessment suggests that overexploitation (overfishing and destructive fishing practices) and coastal development pose the greatest potential threat to reefs, with each of these threats affecting about one third of all reefs (5).(See Figure RR.10.)

Overexploitation of reef resources has several effects. Destructive fishing practices, such as dynamite or cyanide fishing and trawling in deeper waters, cause direct physical damage to corals. The indirect effects of overfishing appear to be more widespread, although poorly understood by scientists. At a minimum, overfishing results in shifts in fish size and species composition within reef communities, which may precipitate large-scale ecosystem changes (6).

In parts of the Caribbean, this process appears to have led to major changes in reef composition, particularly near Jamaica. Widespread overfishing in the region over many decades has led to very low levels of herbivorous fish, which normally play an important part in keeping algae from overgrowing reefs. In the absence of herbivorous fish, the role of keeping algae levels in check fell to a species of grazing sea urchin. When an epidemic nearly wiped out the beneficial urchins on Jamaican reefs in the early 1980s, algae quickly overgrew and killed the corals. Subsequently, hurricanes in the region reduced the now

largely dead reef framework to rubble, with the result that living corals that used to cover half of the seafloor in the shallow nearshore waters off Jamaica now only cover 5 percent of the bottom (7). Some scientists claim this is a harbinger of events to come as reefs around the world continue to be overfished. Others argue that these major ecosystem effects may be reversible (8).

Coastal development also gives rise to several harmful effects. Direct effects come from coral mining, shoreline filling for land reclamation, and harbor dredging. Indirect effects, however, are more pervasive. Algal blooms resulting from nutrient-laden sewage released nearshore can block sunlight in the water column, stunting coral growth and interfering with reproduction. Shoreline construction disturbs sediments, which smother corals. Warm water discharges from power plants and industrial effluents also take their toll (9).

Even tourism, where it is unregulated, can pose a threat. For example, recreational divers in the Gulf of Aqaba, a finger of the Red Sea, have caused considerable coral destruction through trampling and the dropping of dive-boat anchors (10).

The prospect of widespread reef losses is particularly worrisome given

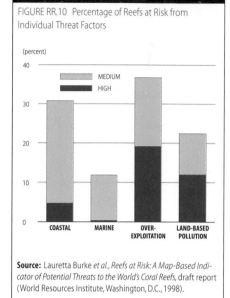

Reef Threats Are Extensive

FIGURE RR.10 Percentage of Reefs at Risk from Individual Threat Factors

Source: Lauretta Burke *et al., Reefs at Risk: A Map-Based Indicator of Potential Threats to the World's Coral Reefs,* draft report (World Resources Institute, Washington, D.C., 1998).

the critical role they play in fostering the productivity of the tropical oceans. Coral reefs are often compared with tropical rainforests in terms of their importance as habitat and the biological diversity they harbor. Some 4,000 species of fish and 800 species of reef-building coral have been described to date, but the total number of species associated with reefs is probably more than 1 million (11)(12).

Reefs are also an integral part of the livelihood and food supply of the human populations that live near them. It has been estimated that about one quarter of the potential fish harvests in developing countries come from coral reefs (13). Properly managed, reefs can yield, on average, 15 tons of fish and other seafood per square kilometer each year (14). Reefs yield tourist dollars as well. Caribbean countries, which attract millions of visitors annually to their beaches and reefs, derive one half of their gross national product (GNP) from the tourism industry, valued at US$8.9 billion in 1990 (15). Reefs also provide essential services like coastal protection, buffering adjacent shorelines from erosive wave action and storm impacts.

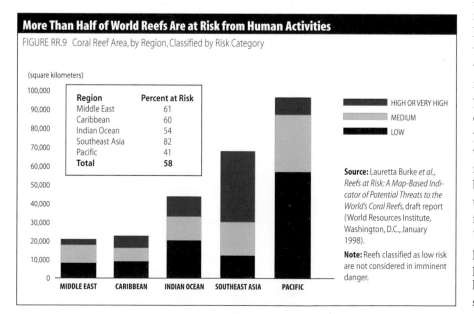

More Than Half of World Reefs Are at Risk from Human Activities

FIGURE RR.9 Coral Reef Area, by Region, Classified by Risk Category

Region	Percent at Risk
Middle East	61
Caribbean	60
Indian Ocean	54
Southeast Asia	82
Pacific	41
Total	**58**

HIGH OR VERY HIGH
MEDIUM
LOW

Source: Lauretta Burke *et al., Reefs at Risk: A Map-Based Indicator of Potential Threats to the World's Coral Reefs,* draft report (World Resources Institute, Washington, D.C., January 1998).

Note: Reefs classified as low risk are not considered in imminent danger.

Because reefs provide so many benefits, degrading them is costly. A recent study found that the costs of destroying just 1 kilometer of reef range from about US$137,000 to almost US$1.2 million over a 25-year period, just counting the economic value of fisheries, tourism, and shoreline protection (16).

The realization that reefs and their many benefits are increasingly in jeopardy has begun to prompt action at many levels. The International Coral Reef Initiative (ICRI), started in 1995, stresses the need for integrated coastal management to minimize the detrimental effects of coastal development. The ICRI now boasts the participation of more than 80 nations and includes a major effort to monitor global reef conditions (the International Coral Reef Monitoring Network)—an essential component of any effort to manage reef impacts (17).

At the national and local levels, a number of governments and communities have taken steps to protect and restore coral reefs. In general, these examples of good stewardship involve a combination of planning, management, law enforcement, environmental education, and legal protection. Approaches range from building sewage and industrial waste treatment facilities, to regulating access and use of reefs (for example, by establishing community ownership over reef fisheries), to restricting development in sensitive coastal areas (18).

Australia's Great Barrier Reef, the largest reef in the world, illustrates the potential of careful reef management. The reef remains in good condition, although sedimentation from runoff is a threat in some localized areas. Careful zoning of the reef—20 percent is protected, the rest is managed for multiple use—along with strict enforcement and environmental education has preserved this globally important resource (19).

Overfishing Has Progressed From Ocean to Ocean

TABLE RR.3 Peak Harvest Year of High-Value (Demersal) Fish by Region

FISHING AREA	YEAR OF MAXIMUM HARVEST	RECENT HARVEST (000 metric tons)	MAXIMUM HARVEST (000 metric tons)
Atlantic, Northwest	1967	1,007	2,588
Antarctic	1971	28	189
Atlantic, Southeast	1972	312	962
Atlantic, Western Central	1974	162	181
Atlantic, Eastern Central	1974	320	481
Pacific, Eastern Central	1975	76	93
Atlantic, Northeast	1976	4,575	5,745
Pacific, Northwest	1987	5,661	6,940
Pacific, Northeast	1988	2,337	2,556
Atlantic, Southwest	1989	967	1,000
Pacific, Southwest	1990	498	498
Pacific, Southeast	1990	459	508
Mediterranean	1991	284	284
Indian Ocean, Western	1991	822	822
Indian Ocean, Eastern	1991	379	379
Pacific, Western Central	1991	833	833

Source: Food and Agriculture Organization of the United Nations (FAO), *The State of World Fisheries and Aquaculture 1996* (FAO, Rome, 1997), p.36.

Diminishing Returns: World Fisheries Under Pressure

World fisheries face a grim forecast. Forty-five years of increasing fishing pressure have left many major fish stocks depleted or in decline. Despite the increasing attention of policymakers and industry representatives, progress toward better management of fish harvests has been slow, and the government policies and market forces behind the trend toward global overfishing remain largely in place.

Overfishing was recognized as an international problem as far back as the early 1900s. However, prior to the 1950s, the problem was confined to relatively few regions such as the North Atlantic, the North Pacific, and the Mediterranean Sea (1)(2). With the expansion of global fishing activities in the 1950s, the exploitation of global fish stocks has followed a predictable pattern, progressing across the oceans as each region in turn reaches its maximum productivity and then begins to decline. (See Table RR.3.) This same boom-and-bust cycle of exploitation has typified the exploitation of other of the world's renewable resources from forests to whales. In effect, fish are the last wild creatures to be hunted on a large scale.

Sixty percent of the world's important fish stocks are "in urgent need of management" to rehabilitate them or keep them from being overfished, according to a recent analysis by the Food and Agriculture Organization of the United Nations (FAO). This analysis, based on fish harvest records from 1950 to 1994, found that 35 percent of the most important commercial fish stocks show a pattern of declining yields and require immediate action to halt overharvesting. Another 25 percent show steady yields but are being fished at their biological limit and are vulnerable to declines if fishing levels increase (3). The harvest of overexploited fish stocks has dropped 40 percent in only 9 years, from 14 million metric tons in 1985 to 8

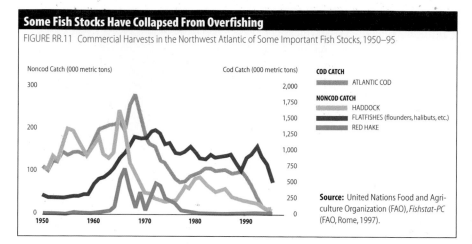

Some Fish Stocks Have Collapsed From Overfishing

FIGURE RR.11 Commercial Harvests in the Northwest Atlantic of Some Important Fish Stocks, 1950–95

Noncod Catch (000 metric tons)

Cod Catch (000 metric tons)

COD CATCH
ATLANTIC COD

NONCOD CATCH
HADDOCK
FLATFISHES (flounders, halibuts, etc.)
RED HAKE

Source: United Nations Food and Agriculture Organization (FAO), *Fishstat-PC* (FAO, Rome, 1997).

million metric tons in 1994. These numbers mask more precipitous drops in certain fish stocks such as Atlantic cod, haddock, and redfish, which have all but collapsed in some areas of the North Atlantic (4). (See Figure RR.11.) Such declines prompted the World Conservation Union in 1996 to add several commercial fish species—including Atlantic cod, haddock, and bluefin tuna—to its influential "red list" of species whose survival is in some degree endangered (5).

Fish are an important element of the human food supply, and fishing is an important factor in global employment. Current harvest trends and fishery conditions put both of these at risk. Fish account for roughly one fifth of all animal protein in the human diet, and around 1 billion people rely on fish as their primary protein source. Indeed, production of fish products is far greater than global production of poultry, beef, or pork. However, new projections suggest that the contribution of fish to the global food supply is likely to decrease in the next two decades as demand for fish increases and production flags (6).

Currently, some 80 million metric tons of fish are available each year for direct human consumption. FAO expects demand to increase to 110 to 120 million metric tons in 2010 as world population grows. By FAO's estimate, such demand could be satisfied only

under the most optimistic scenario, with aquaculture production doubling and overfishing brought under control so that ocean fish stocks can recover. However, it is more likely that aquaculture growth will be moderate and that the ocean catch will plateau at current levels or decline, leaving a substantial gap between supply and demand and also raising fish prices (7)(8).

Any shortfall in fish supplies is likely to affect developing nations more than developed nations. As demand and fish prices rise, exports of fish products from developing nations will tend to rise as well, leaving fewer fish for local consumption and putting fish protein increasingly out of reach for low-income families (9).

Employment within the fisheries sector is also likely to change profoundly, especially for small-scale fishers who fish for the local market or for subsistence. Already, these fishers, who number some 10 million worldwide, have been losing ground over the past two decades as competition from commercial vessels has grown (10). Off the west coast of Africa, for instance, surveys show that fish resources in the shallow inshore waters where these artisanal fishers ply their trade dropped more than half from 1985 to 1990 due to increased fishing by commercial trawlers (11).

Substantial potential exists for increasing the ocean fish harvest with better management of fish stocks, although sound management is neither easy nor obvious. FAO estimates that marine catches could rise some 9 million metric tons if fishing pressure were reduced overall and juvenile fish were allowed to live longer before being caught. Experience in Cyprus and the Philippines shows that substantial increases in catch from better management can sometimes appear in as little as 18 months in tropical waters. Such quick improvements are unlikely in colder waters, however. For instance, cod stocks in the cold waters off the Canadian Atlantic coast have not rebounded quickly since their collapse in the early 1990s, even though the cod fishery has been closed to fishing until very recently (12)(13)(14)(15).

The urgency of the current fisheries decline has begun to galvanize both governments and the private sector, at least in the developed world. Such nations as the United States, Canada, and the members of the European Union have recently adopted tougher fishing controls and have started to shrink the size of their fishing fleets. Unilever, a major fish processor and marketer in Europe and North America, has pledged to purchase fish only from sustainably managed fish stocks by 2005. To develop criteria for what "sustainably managed" means, Unilever has joined with the World Wide Fund for Nature (WWF) to form the Marine Stewardship Council, which will establish industry-wide principles for sustainable fishing and also set standards for individual fish stocks. Fish harvested according to the Council's standards will be eligible for certification, or eco-labeling, which may increase its consumer appeal and provide a market incentive for producers to adopt the Council's recommended fishing practices (16)(17)(18)(19).

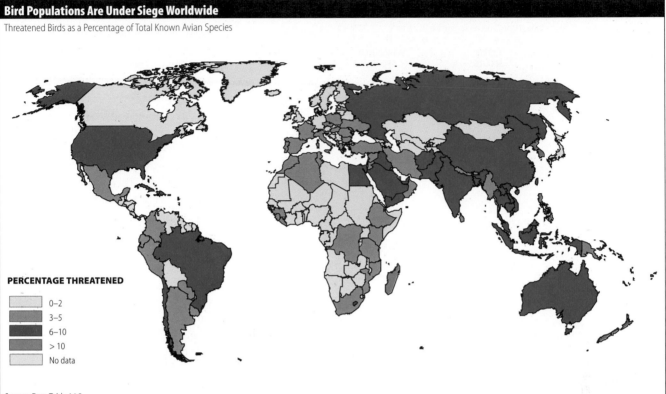

Bird Populations Are Under Siege Worldwide

Threatened Birds as a Percentage of Total Known Avian Species

PERCENTAGE THREATENED

- 0–2
- 3–5
- 6–10
- > 10
- No data

Source: Data Table 14.2

Approximately 11 percent of all known bird species are threatened with extinction. Habitat fragmentation or loss is the principal factor in this decline, but harvesting for food and trade and competition from nonnative species are important as well.

Bioinvasions: Stemming The Tide of Exotic Species

Ever since humans began traveling over land and sea, assorted livestock, crops, pets, pests, and weeds have tagged along. Nearly every region of the globe has benefited economically from introduced species. Yet, new arrivals that become invasive have also created major problems for agriculture and other human enterprises and disrupted distinct communities of native plants and animals. Today, almost 20 percent of the world's endangered vertebrate species are threatened in some way by exotic invaders, including 13 percent of vulnerable mainland vertebrates and 31 percent of those on islands (1).

In fact, invasions of natural ecosystems by nonnative species now rank second to habitat loss as the major threat to biodiversity (2). The sparse data available so far suggest that the pace of invasions is accelerating in parallel with the growth of global trade. In the San Francisco Bay area, for instance, the rate of successful aquatic invasions has climbed from one new species every 36 weeks since the 1850s, to one every 24 weeks since the 1970s, to as many as one every 12 weeks in the past decade (3). Some ecologists predict that as the number of potential invaders increases and the supply of undisturbed natural areas declines, biological pollution by alien invaders may become the leading factor of ecological disintegration (4). (See Table RR.4.)

The Convention on Biological Diversity adopted at the 1992 United Nations environmental summit in Rio de Janeiro recognized this threat. The treaty calls on participating nations "as far as possible and as appropriate [to] prevent the introduction of, [to] control, or [to] eradicate those alien species that threaten ecosystems, habitats, or species" (5). Participating nations are now exploring how to begin implementing this enormous task (6).

A BIOLOGICAL CONVEYOR BELT

Burgeoning world trade poses a particular threat in terms of its potential to increase bioinvasions. Most species introductions are unintentional, and trade opens up major dispersal opportunities. Food- and waterborne disease organisms, agricultural pests and weeds, and other nuisance species hitchhike to new lands aboard ships, airplanes, and

Bioinvasions Represent Broadscale "Biological Pollution"

TABLE RR.4 Percentages of Introduced Plant Species in Selected Countries

COUNTRY/REGION	NATIVE SPECIES	INTRODUCED SPECIES	PERCENTAGE INTRODUCED
Antigua/ Barbuda	900	180	10
Australia	15,000–20,000	1,500–2,000	10
Sydney	1,500	400–500	26–33
Victoria	2,750	850	27.5
Austria	3,000	300	10
Canada	3,160	881	28
Ecuador			
Rio Palenque	1,100	175	15
Finland	1,250	120	10
France	4,400	500	11
Guadeloupe	1,668	149	9
Hawaii	1,200–1,300	228	17.5–19
Java	4,598	313	7
New Zealand	1,790	1,570	47
Spain	4,900	750	15

Source: Vernon H. Heywood, "Patterns, Extents, and Modes of Invasions by Terrestrial Plants," in *Biological Invasions: A Global Perspective,* SCOPE 37, J.A. Drake *et al.,* eds. (John Wiley & Sons Ltd., Chichester, U.K., 1989), p. 40.

trucks, stowing away in shipping containers and packing materials or riding on nursery stock, unprocessed logs, fruits, vegetables, and seeds (7). On any given day, for instance, some 3,000 aquatic species are moving around the globe in the ballast tanks of ships, a biotic conveyor belt that has already altered the ecological makeup of much of the world's coastal waters (8).

Deliberate introductions of exotic plants and animals for commercial and agricultural purposes also can pose risks. The bulk of the diet of most of the world's population comes from crop and livestock species that originated elsewhere (9), and land managers, agricultural scientists, and other sectors of society have clear economic incentives to continue importing exotic species for food, timber, horticultural, and other uses.

But these intentional imports do not always prove benign. The golden apple snail, which was introduced into Asia from South America in 1980 to be cultivated as a high-protein food source, has dispersed into the region's rice paddies, where it feeds voraciously on rice seedlings, causing significant crop damage (10).

Of course, not all newly arriving species become problems, but those that do can cause not only biological damage but also economic damage. In the United States, roughly one fifth of 4,500 established exotic species cause serious economic or ecological harm. Estimates of economic losses, not including damage to native species or to ecological services, range up to several billion dollars per year in the United States alone (11). In the Philippines, estimates of economic losses associated with the golden apple snail alone ranged from US$425 million to US$1.2 billion in 1990 (12).

ERECTING BARRIERS AGAINST INVASIONS

What can be done to stem the tide of bioinvasions? For one, before intentionally introducing an exotic, it would be helpful to thoroughly analyze potential risks and trade-offs of the introduction. However, biologists cannot predict with certainty the invasive potential of any given plant, animal, or microbe (13). For this reason, a few nations such as New Zealand—where 47 percent of the flora is already exotic (14)—have adopted the precautionary principle, banning importation of all exotic species except for a few clean-list species that are known to be benign. In contrast, most nations, if they have any import restrictions at all, use a dirty-list concept, only denying import of known problem pests or weeds (15).

In the case of unintentional introductions, the first line of defense is a system of quarantines and regulations designed to limit the free flow of species through trade, transport, aquaculture, agriculture, forestry, game farming, horticulture, the pet trade, recreation, tourism, and travel (16). Strengthening these barriers will not be easy in light of potential conflicts with treaties such as the General Agreement on Tariffs and Trade (GATT) that promote fewer, rather than more stringent, restrictions on international trade (17).

Yet, some steps are already underway. The 156-nation International Maritime Organization has been developing regulations to control ballast water discharge, which is the source of many exotic species in coastal estuaries (18). In the interim, several countries have acted individually to protect their own waters from invasions. In the Great Lakes bordering the United States and Canada, mandatory controls on ballast water releases from commercial shipping have been in place since 1990, in reaction to the invasion of the zebra mussel (19). More recently, the United States has extended voluntary ballast water controls to other U.S. ports, requesting that ships filter or exchange their ballast water at sea before entering port (20). Chile and the port of Haifa, Israel, have also instituted mandatory ballast water requirements, and Australia has a program to control ballast water releases as well (21)(22).

Other strategies to deal with the larger issues of invasions of both aquatic and terrestrial ecosystems are taking shape at an international level. These strategies include computerized databases of information on known harmful invasives in various regions that can serve as an early warning system for other nations. Other approaches include a global assessment of the status of invasions—such as the land area dominated by exotic plants—as well as techniques for rapid and regular reassessment of the extent of bio-invasions (23)(24).

AFRICA

Population and Human Well-Being

Life Expectancy (1995-00):	**53.8 years**
Total Fertility Rate (1995-00):	**5.3 children per woman**
Infant Mortality (1995-00):	**86 per 1,000 live births**
Crude Death Rate (1995-00):	**12.9 per 1,000 people**
Percentage of Population that is:	
Rural (1995):	**65 percent**
Urban (1995):	**35 percent**
Under Age 15 (2000):	**43 percent**
Over Age 65 (2000):	**3 percent**
Motor Vehicles Per Capita (1991):	**0.02**
Televisions Per 1,000 People (1994):	**40**
Number of Cities with Populations Greater than 750,000 (1995):	**44**

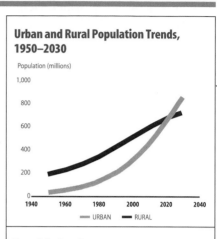

Urban and Rural Population Trends, 1950–2030

Population (millions)

— URBAN   — RURAL

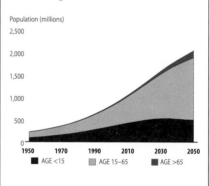

Trends in Age Structure, 1950–2050

Population (millions)

■ AGE <15   ■ AGE 15–65   ■ AGE >65

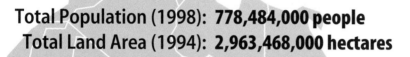

Total Population (1998): 778,484,000 people
Total Land Area (1994): 2,963,468,000 hectares

Economics

Gross Domestic Product Per Capita (current $US)*:	
Exchange-Rate-Based (1994):	**$639**
Purchase-Power-Parity-Based (current $I) (1994):	**$2,174**
Average Annual Growth Rate (1990-95):	**1.3 percent**
Official Development Assistance (1995):	**$20,327 million**
Total External Debt (1993-95)**:	**$301,943 million**

* GDP data for Africa exclude a total of 25 countries,
including the Democratic Republic of Congo, Liberia, Libya, Tanzania, and Uganda.

** Data are collected only for developing countries.

Total and Per Capita GDP in Constant 1987 U.S. Dollars, 1970–95

GDP
(millions of 1987 U.S. dollars)

Per Capita GDP
(1987 U.S. dollars)

— TOTAL GDP   — PER CAPITA GDP

Note: See Data Tables in Part III for regional definitions, data sources, and technical notes.

Agriculture

	Cropland:	
	Total (1994):	**190,022,000 hectares**
	Per Capita (1994):	**0.27 hectares**
	Cereal Production:	
	Total (1996):	**127,583,800 metric tons**
	Per Capita (1996):	**0.17 metric tons**
Hectares of Permanent Pastureland (1994):		**883,812,000**
Annual Fertilizer Use (1994):		**18 kilograms per hectare**
Average Cereals Yield (average 1994-96):		**1,220 kilograms per hectare**
Net Trade in Cereals (average 1993-95):		**31,242,000 metric tons**

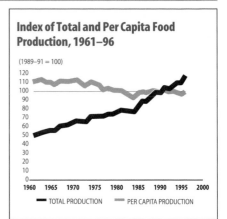

Index of Total and Per Capita Food Production, 1961–96

(1989–91 = 100)

TOTAL PRODUCTION   PER CAPITA PRODUCTION

Energy

Commercial Energy Production (1995):		
	Total:	**22,610 petajoules**
	Per Capita:	**31.4 gigajoules**
Commercial Energy Consumption (1995):		
	Total:	**9,451 petajoules**
	Per Capita:	**13.1 gigajoules**
Traditional Fuels as a Percentage of Commercial Energy (1995):		**71.5 percent**
Percentage of Electricity Supplied by Renewable Sources (1995):		**15.5 percent**
Energy Efficiency (terajoules per million $GDP) (1994):		**24.1**

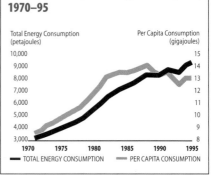

Total and Per Capita Energy Consumption, 1970–95

Total Energy Consumption (petajoules)   Per Capita Consumption (gigajoules)

TOTAL ENERGY CONSUMPTION   PER CAPITA CONSUMPTION

Forests

Total Timber (Roundwood) Production (1995):	**583.5 million cubic meters**
Total Forest Extent (1995):	**520,237,000 hectares**
Natural Forest Extent (1995):	**515,455,000 hectares**
Plantation Forest Extent (1990):	**4,416,000 hectares**
Percent Change in Total Forests from 1990 to 1995:	**–3.5 percent**
Percentage of Original Forest Remaining (1996):	**33.9 percent**
Value of Forest Products Exported ($US) (1995):	**2,819.4 million**

* Represents export trade of each country regardless of destination.

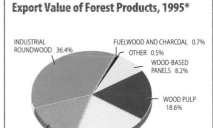

Export Value of Forest Products, 1995*

INDUSTRIAL ROUNDWOOD 36.4%
FUELWOOD AND CHARCOAL 0.7%
OTHER 0.5%
WOOD-BASED PANELS 8.2%
WOOD PULP 18.6%
SAWNWOOD AND SLEEPERS 20.4%
PAPER AND PAPERBOARD 15.2%

Atmosphere

Carbon Dioxide Emissions (1995):		
	Total:	**745,594,000 metric tons**
	Per Capita:	**1.1 metric tons**
Percentage of Emissions from:		
	Solid Fuels:	**36.8 percent**
	Liquid Fuels:	**36.1 percent**
	Gas Fuels:	**13.5 percent**

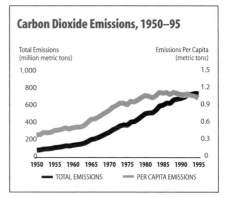

Carbon Dioxide Emissions, 1950–95

Total Emissions (million metric tons)   Emissions Per Capita (metric tons)

TOTAL EMISSIONS   PER CAPITA EMISSIONS

Fresh Water

Renewable Water Supply (1995):	
Total:	**3,996 cubic kilometers**
Per Capita:	**5,554 cubic meters**
Annual Water Withdrawals (1995):	
Total:	**145 cubic kilometers**
Per Capita:	**202 cubic meters**
Percent of Cropland under Irrigation:	**6.0 percent**

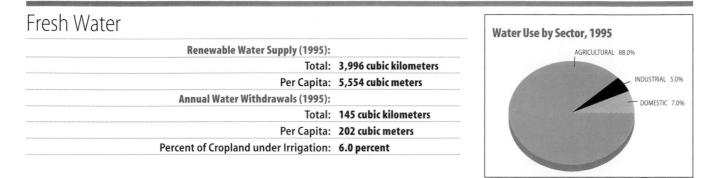

Water Use by Sector, 1995

AGRICULTURAL 88.0%

INDUSTRIAL 5.0%

DOMESTIC 7.0%

Oceans and Fish

Marine Fish Catch (1995)*:	**3,006,300 metric tons**
Aquaculture Production (1995)**:	**82,014 metric tons**
Average Annual Balance of Trade in Fish ($US) (1993-95):	**299.6 million**
Length of Coastline:	**40,142 kilometers**

* Diadromous fish excluded.
** Data exclude plants.

Trends in Marine Fish Catch, 1950–95

Marine Fish Catch (metric tons)

Biodiversity and Protected Areas

Percent of Land Area Protected (1996):	**5.2 percent**
Number of Protected Areas Larger than:	
100,000 hectares:	**209 areas**
1 million hectares:	**36 areas**

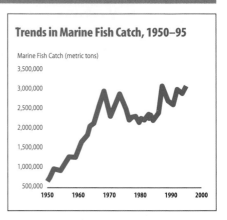

**PERCENTAGE OF MAMMAL
SPECIES THAT ARE THREATENED**

- < 5
- 5–10
- 10–20
- > 20
- No data

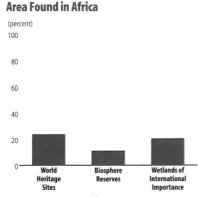

**Percent of Internationally Protected Land
Area Found in Africa**

(percent)

- World Heritage Sites
- Biosphere Reserves
- Wetlands of International Importance

EUROPE

Population and Human Well-Being

Life Expectancy (1995-00):	**72.6 years**
Total Fertility Rate (1995-00):	**1.5 children per woman**
Infant Mortality (1995-00):	**12 per 1,000 live births**
Crude Death Rate (1995-00):	**11.5 per 1,000 people**
Percentage of Population that is:	
Rural (1995):	**26 percent**
Urban (1995):	**74 percent**
Under Age 15 (2000):	**18 percent**
Over Age 65 (2000):	**15 percent**
Motor Vehicles Per Capita (1991):	**0.27**
Televisions Per 1,000 People (1994):	**412**
Number of Cities with Populations Greater than 750,000 (1995):	**84**

Total Population (1998): **729,406,000 people**
Total Land Area (1994): **2,260,320,000 hectares**

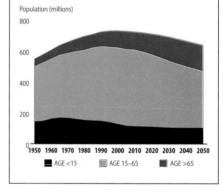

Urban and Rural Population Trends, 1950–2030

Population (millions)

— URBAN   — RURAL

Trends in Age Structure, 1950–2050

Population (millions)

■ AGE <15   ■ AGE 15–65   ■ AGE >65

Economics

Gross Domestic Product Per Capita (current $US):	
Exchange-Rate-Based (1994):	**$11,804**
Purchase-Power-Parity-Based (current $I) (1994):	**$9,643**
Average Annual Growth Rate (1990-95):	**not available for Europe**
Official Development Assistance (1995):	**−$11,866 million**
Total External Debt (1993-95)*:	**$216,556 million**

*   Data are collected only for Eastern Europe and the countries of the former Soviet Union.
** Data do not include Germany or the countries of the former Socialist Republic of Yugoslavia.

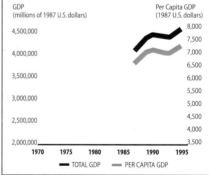

Total and Per Capita GDP in Constant 1987 U.S. Dollars, 1970–95 **

GDP
(millions of 1987 U.S. dollars)

Per Capita GDP
(1987 U.S. dollars)

— TOTAL GDP   — PER CAPITA GDP

Note: Some time series for Europe show a jump because of the inclusion of countries of the former Soviet Union.

Agriculture

	Cropland:	
Total (1994):	**316,378,000 hectares**	
Per Capita (1994):	**0.43 hectares**	
	Cereal Production:	
Total (1996):	**389,960,300 metric tons**	
Per Capita (1996):	**0.54 metric tons**	
Hectares of Permanent Pastureland (1994):	**179,132,000**	
Annual Fertilizer Use (1994):	**157 kilograms per hectare***	
Average Cereals Yield (average 1994-96):	**2,884 kilograms per hectare**	
Net Trade in Cereals (average 1993-95):	**−20,823,000 metric tons**	

* Data do not include countries of the former Soviet Union.

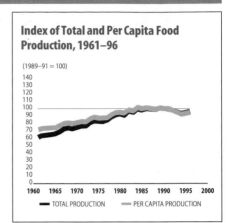

Index of Total and Per Capita Food Production, 1961–96

(1989–91 = 100)

Legend: TOTAL PRODUCTION — PER CAPITA PRODUCTION

Energy

Commercial Energy Production (1995):	
Total:	**9,783 petajoules**
Per Capita:	**124.7 gigajoules**
Commercial Energy Consumption (1995):	
Total:	**105,339 petajoules**
Per Capita:	**144.6 gigajoules**
Traditional Fuels as a Percentage of Commercial Energy (1995):	**1.9 percent**
Percentage of Electricity Supplied by Renewable Sources (1995):	**17.5 percent**
Energy Efficiency (terajoules per million $GDP) (1994):	**20.8**

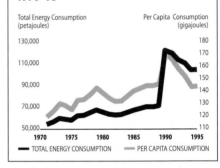

Total and Per Capita Energy Consumption, 1970–95

Legend: TOTAL ENERGY CONSUMPTION — PER CAPITA CONSUMPTION

Forests

Total Timber (Roundwood) Production (1995):	**478.2 million cubic meters**
Total Forest Extent (1995):	**145,988,000 hectares**
Natural Forest Extent (1995):	**not available for Europe**
Plantation Forest Extent (1990):	**not available for Europe**
Percent Change in Total Forests from 1990 to 1995:	**1.3 percent**
Percentage of Original Forest Remaining (1996):	**58.4 percent**
Value of Forest Products Exported ($US) (1995):	**62,501.6 million**

* Represents export trade of each country regardless of destination.

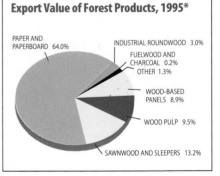

Export Value of Forest Products, 1995*

PAPER AND PAPERBOARD 64.0%
INDUSTRIAL ROUNDWOOD 3.0%
FUELWOOD AND CHARCOAL 0.2%
OTHER 1.3%
WOOD-BASED PANELS 8.9%
WOOD PULP 9.5%
SAWNWOOD AND SLEEPERS 13.2%

Atmosphere

Carbon Dioxide Emissions (1995):	
Total:	**6,247,094,000 metric tons**
Per Capita:	**8.5 metric tons**
Percentage of Emissions from:	
Solid Fuels:	**36.2 percent**
Liquid Fuels:	**33.2 percent**
Gas Fuels:	**27.5 percent**

Carbon Dioxide Emissions, 1950–95

Legend: TOTAL EMISSIONS — PER CAPITA EMISSIONS

Fresh Water

Renewable Water Supply (1995):	
Total:	**6,234 cubic kilometers**
Per Capita:	**8,561 cubic meters**
Annual Water Withdrawals (1995):	
Total:	**455 cubic kilometers**
Per Capita:	**625 cubic meters**
Percent of Cropland under Irrigation:	**8.7 percent**

Water Use by Sector, 1995

DOMESTIC 14.0%

AGRICULTURAL 31.0%

INDUSTRIAL 55.0%

Oceans and Fish

Marine Fish Catch (1995)*:	**14,869,500 metric tons**
Aquaculture Production (1995)**:	**1,535,702 metric tons**
Average Annual Balance of Trade in Fish ($US) (1993-95):	**−504.4 million**
Length of Coastline:	**113,725 kilometers**

*   Diadromous fish excluded.
** Data exclude plants.

Trends in Marine Fish Catch, 1950–95

Marine Fish Catch (metric tons)

22,000,000
20,000,000
18,000,000
16,000,000
14,000,000
12,000,000
10,000,000
8,000,000
6,000,000
4,000,000

1950   1960   1970   1980   1990   2000

Biodiversity and Protected Areas

Percent of Land Area Protected (1996):	**4.7 percent**
Number of Protected Areas Larger than:	
100,000 hectares:	**209 areas**
1 million hectares:	**11 areas**

Percent of Internationally Protected Land Area Found in Europe

(percent)

100

80

60

40

20

0

World Heritage Sites

Biosphere Reserves

Wetlands of International Importance

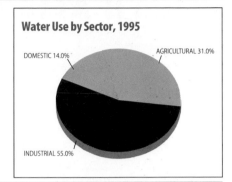

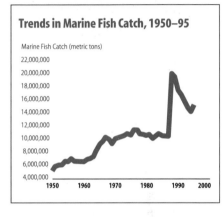

PERCENTAGE OF MAMMAL SPECIES THAT ARE THREATENED

	< 5
	5–10
	10–20
	> 20
	No data

NORTH AMERICA

Population and Human Well-Being

Life Expectancy (1995-00):	**76.9 years**
Total Fertility Rate (1995-00):	**1.9 children per woman**
Infant Mortality (1995-00):	**7 per 1,000 live births**
Crude Death Rate (1995-00):	**8.6 per 1,000 people**
Percentage of Population that is:	
Rural (1995):	**24 percent**
Urban (1995):	**76 percent**
Under Age 15 (2000):	**21 percent**
Over Age 65 (2000):	**12 percent**
Motor Vehicles Per Capita (1991):	**0.72**
Televisions Per 1,000 People (1994):	**793**
Number of Cities with Populations Greater than 750,000 (1995):	**51**

Total Population (1998): 304,078,000 people
Total Land Area (1994): 1,838,009,000 hectares

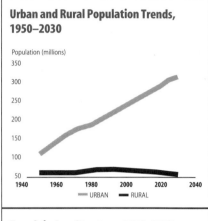

Urban and Rural Population Trends, 1950–2030

Population (millions)

URBAN   RURAL

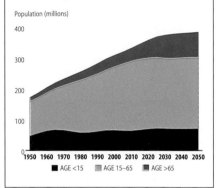

Trends in Age Structure, 1950–2050

Population (millions)

AGE <15   AGE 15–65   AGE >65

Economics

Gross Domestic Product Per Capita (current $US):	
Exchange-Rate-Based (1994):	**$24,479**
Purchase-Power-Parity-Based (current $I) (1994):	**$25,448**
Average Annual Growth Rate (1990-95):	**2.3 percent**
Official Development Assistance (1995):	**–$9,434 million**
Total External Debt (1993-95)*:	**not applicable for N.A.**

* Data are collected only for developing countries.

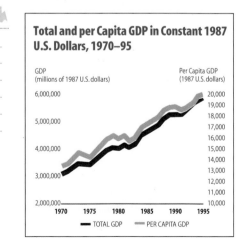

Total and per Capita GDP in Constant 1987 U.S. Dollars, 1970–95

GDP (millions of 1987 U.S. dollars)   Per Capita GDP (1987 U.S. dollars)

TOTAL GDP   PER CAPITA GDP

Agriculture

Cropland:	
Total (1994):	**233,276,000 hectares**
Per Capita (1994):	**0.79 hectares**
Cereal Production:	
Total (1996):	**397,073,300 metric tons**
Per Capita (1996):	**1.33 metric tons**
Hectares of Permanent Pastureland (1994):	**267,072,000**
Annual Fertilizer Use (1994):	**92 kilograms per hectare**
Average Cereals Yield (average 1994-96):	**3,679.5 kilograms per ha**
Net Trade in Cereals (average 1993-95):	**−108,419,000 metric tons**

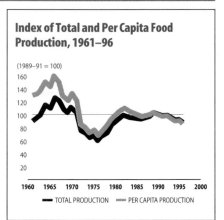

Index of Total and Per Capita Food Production, 1961–96

Energy

Commercial Energy Production (1995):	
Total:	**83,999 petajoules**
Per Capita:	**283.2 gigajoules**
Commercial Energy Consumption (1995):	
Total:	**96,782 petajoules**
Per Capita:	**326.3 gigajoules**
Traditional Fuels as a Percentage of Commercial Energy (1995):	**2.9 percent**
Percentage of Electricity Supplied by Renewable Sources (1995):	**17.9 percent**
Energy Efficiency (terajoules per million $GDP) (1994):	**16.3**

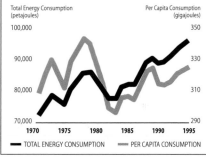

Total and Per Capita Energy Consumption, 1970–95

Forests

Total Timber (Roundwood) Production (1995):	**689.7 million cubic meters**
Total Forest Extent (1995):	**457,086,000 hectares**
Natural Forest Extent (1995):	**not available for N.A.**
Plantation Forest Extent (1990):	**not available for N.A.**
Percent Change in Total Forests from 1990 to 1995:	**0.8 percent**
Percentage of Original Forest Remaining (1996):	**77.3 percent**
Value of Forest Products Exported ($US) (1995):	**45,935.2 million**

* Represents export trade of each country regardless of destination.

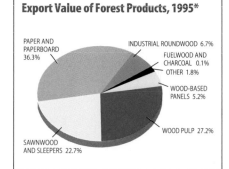

Export Value of Forest Products, 1995*

Atmosphere

Carbon Dioxide Emissions (1995):	
Total:	**5,904,312,000 metric tons**
Per Capita:	**19.9 metric tons**
Percentage of Emissions from:	
Solid Fuels:	**37.9 percent**
Liquid Fuels:	**38.9 percent**
Gas Fuels:	**22.3 percent**

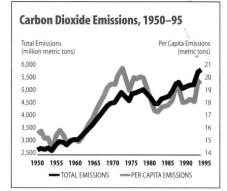

Carbon Dioxide Emissions, 1950–95

Fresh Water

Renewable Water Supply (1995):	
Total:	**5,309 cubic kilometers**
Per Capita:	**17,896 cubic meters**
Annual Water Withdrawals (1995):	
Total:	**512 cubic kilometers**
Per Capita:	**1,798 cubic meters**
Percent of Cropland under Irrigation:	**7.4 percent**

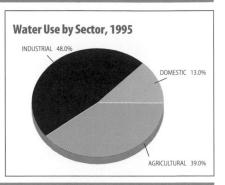

Water Use by Sector, 1995

INDUSTRIAL 48.0%

DOMESTIC 13.0%

AGRICULTURAL 39.0%

Oceans and Fish

Marine Fish Catch (1995)*:	**3,939,100 metric tons**
Aquaculture Production (1995)**:	**479,580 metric tons**
Average Annual Balance of Trade in Fish ($US) (1993-95):	**10.7 million**
Length of Coastline:	**110,832 kilometers**

* Diadromous fish excluded.
** Data exclude plants.

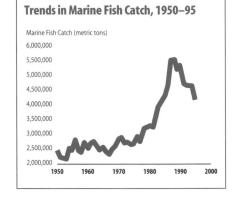

Trends in Marine Fish Catch, 1950–95

Marine Fish Catch (metric tons)

Biodiversity and Protected Areas

Percent of Land Area Protected (1996):	**11.7 percent**
Number of Protected Areas Larger than:	
100,000 hectares:	**262 areas**
1 million hectares:	**47 areas**

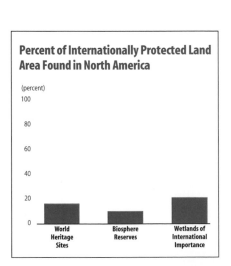

Percent of Internationally Protected Land Area Found in North America

(percent)

| World Heritage Sites | Biosphere Reserves | Wetlands of International Importance |

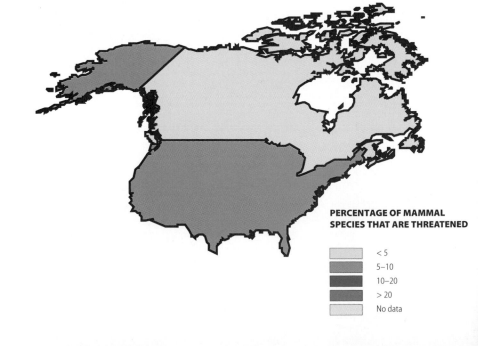

PERCENTAGE OF MAMMAL SPECIES THAT ARE THREATENED

- < 5
- 5–10
- 10–20
- > 20
- No data

CENTRAL AMERICA

Population and Human Well-Being

Life Expectancy (1995-00):	**71.7 years**
Total Fertility Rate (1995-00):	**3.0 children per woman**
Infant Mortality (1995-00):	**33 per 1,000 live births**
Crude Death Rate (1995-00):	**5.3 per 1,000 people**
Percentage of Population that is:	
Rural (1995):	**34 percent**
Urban (1995):	**66 percent**
Under Age 15 (2000):	**35 percent**
Over Age 65 (2000):	**5 percent**
Motor Vehicles Per Capita (1991):	**0.11**
Televisions Per 1,000 People (1994)*:	**171**
Number of Cities with Populations Greater than 750,000 (1995):	**21**

* Value is for Central and South America combined.

Total Population (1998): 130,710,000 people
Total Land Area (1994): 264,835,000 hectares

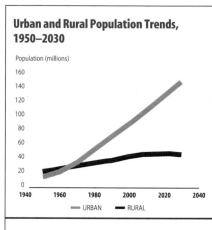

Urban and Rural Population Trends, 1950–2030

Population (millions)

— URBAN   — RURAL

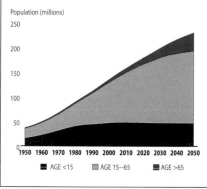

Trends in Age Structure, 1950–2050

Population (millions)

■ AGE <15   ■ AGE 15--65   ■ AGE >65

Economics

Gross Domestic Product Per Capita (current $US):	
Exchange-Rate-Based (1994):	**$3,354**
Purchase-Power-Parity-Based (current $I) (1994):	**$6,704**
Average Annual Growth Rate (1990-95):	**1.4 percent**
Official Development Assistance (1995):	**$3,205 million**
Total External Debt (1993-95)*:	**$146,888 million**

* Data are collected only for developing countries.

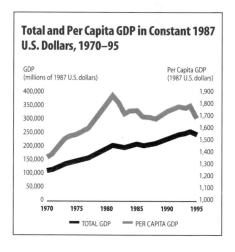

Total and Per Capita GDP in Constant 1987 U.S. Dollars, 1970–95

GDP (millions of 1987 U.S. dollars)   Per Capita GDP (1987 U.S. dollars)

— TOTAL GDP   — PER CAPITA GDP

Agriculture

Cropland:	
Total (1994):	**41,112,000 hectares**
Per Capita (1994):	**0.34 hectares**
Cereal Production:	
Total (1996):	**32,304,700 metric tons**
Per Capita (1996):	**0.26 metric tons**
Hectares of Permanent Pastureland (1994):	**98,472,000**
Annual Fertilizer Use (1994):	**58 kilograms per hectare**
Average Cereals Yield (average 1994-96):	**not available for C.A.**
Net Trade in Cereals (average 1993-95):	**12,216 metric tons**

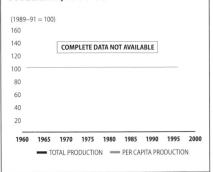

Index of Total and Per Capita Food Production, 1961–96

(1989–91 = 100)

COMPLETE DATA NOT AVAILABLE

TOTAL PRODUCTION PER CAPITA PRODUCTION

Energy

Commercial Energy Production (1995):	
Total:	**9,160 petajoules**
Per Capita:	**74.2 gigajoules**
Commercial Energy Consumption (1995):	
Total:	**7,063 petajoules**
Per Capita:	**57.2 gigajoules**
Traditional Fuels as a Percentage of Commercial Energy (1995):	**14.6 percent**
Percentage of Electricity Supplied by Renewable Sources (1995):	**25.8 percent**
Energy Efficiency (terajoules per million $GDP) (1994):	**28.6**

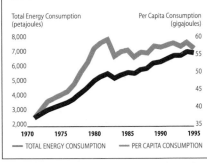

Total and Per Capita Energy Consumption, 1970–95

Total Energy Consumption (petajoules) Per Capita Consumption (gigajoules)

TOTAL ENERGY CONSUMPTION PER CAPITA CONSUMPTION

Forests

Total Timber (Roundwood) Production (1995):	**71.1 million cubic meters**
Total Forest Extent (1995):	**79,443,000 hectares**
Natural Forest Extent (1995):	**78,958,000 hectares**
Plantation Forest Extent (1990):	**501,000 hectares**
Percent Change in Total Forests from 1990 to 1995:	**–6.1 percent**
Percentage of Original Forest Remaining (1996):	**54.5 percent**
Value of Forest Products Exported ($US) (1995):	**410.8 million**

* Represents export trade of each country regardless of destination.

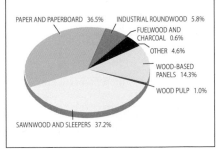

Export Value of Forest Products, 1995*

PAPER AND PAPERBOARD 36.5% INDUSTRIAL ROUNDWOOD 5.8%
FUELWOOD AND CHARCOAL 0.6%
OTHER 4.6%
WOOD-BASED PANELS 14.3%
WOOD PULP 1.0%
SAWNWOOD AND SLEEPERS 37.2%

Atmosphere

Carbon Dioxide Emissions (1995):	
Total:	**477,045,000 metric tons**
Per Capita:	**3.6 metric tons**
Percentage of Emissions from:	
Solid Fuels:	**5.0 percent**
Liquid Fuels:	**74.7 percent**
Gas Fuels:	**15.5 percent**

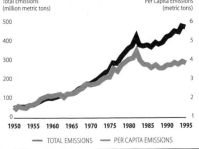

Carbon Dioxide Emissions, 1950–95

Total Emissions (million metric tons) Per Capita Emissions (metric tons)

TOTAL EMISSIONS PER CAPITA EMISSIONS

Fresh Water

Renewable Water Supply (1995):	
Total:	**1,057 cubic kilometers**
Per Capita:	**8,558 cubic meters**
Annual Water Withdrawals (1995):	
Total:	**96 cubic kilometers**
Per Capita:	**916 cubic meters**
Percent of Cropland under Irrigation:	**16.3 percent**

Water Use by Sector, 1995

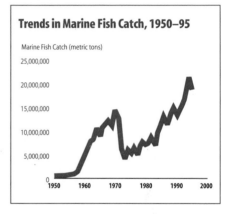

INDUSTRIAL 8.0%
DOMESTIC 6.0%
AGRICULTURAL 86.0%

Oceans and Fish

Marine Fish Catch (1995)*:	**18,311,300 metric tons**
Aquaculture Production (1995)**:	**120,625 metric tons**
Average Annual Balance of Trade in Fish ($US) (1993-95):	**−39.0 million**
Length of Coastline:	**28,172 kilometers**

* Diadromous fish excluded.
** Data exclude plants.

Trends in Marine Fish Catch, 1950–95

Marine Fish Catch (metric tons)

25,000,000

20,000,000

15,000,000

10,000,000

5,000,000

0

1950 1960 1970 1980 1990 2000

Biodiversity and Protected Areas

Percent of Land Area Protected (1996):	**5.6 percent**
Number of Protected Areas Larger than:	
100,000 hectares:	**34 areas**
1 million hectares:	**3 areas**

Percent of Internationally Protected Land Area Found in Central America

(percent)

100

80

60

40

20

0

World Heritage Sites | Biosphere Reserves | Wetlands of International Importance

PERCENTAGE OF MAMMAL SPECIES THAT ARE THREATENED

	< 5
	5–10
	10–20
	> 20
	No data

SOUTH AMERICA

Population and Human Well-Being

Life Expectancy (1995-00):	**69.0 years**
Total Fertility Rate (1995-00):	**2.5 children per woman**
Infant Mortality (1995-00):	**36 per 1,000 live births**
Crude Death Rate (1995-00):	**6.8 per 1,000 people**
Percentage of Population that is:	
Rural (1995):	**23 percent**
Urban (1995):	**77 percent**
Under Age 15 (2000):	**30 percent**
Over Age 65 (2000):	**6 percent**
Motor Vehicles Per Capita (1991):	**0.09**
Televisions Per 1,000 People (1994)*:	**171**
Number of Cities with Populations Greater than 750,000 (1995):	**38**

* Value is for Central and South America combined.

Total Population (1998): 331,889,000 people
Total Land Area (1994): 1,752,925,000 hectares

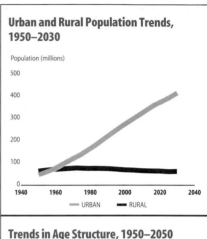

Urban and Rural Population Trends, 1950–2030

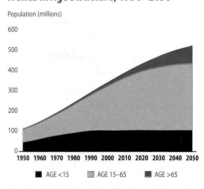

Trends in Age Structure, 1950–2050

Economics

Gross Domestic Product Per Capita (current $US):	
Exchange-Rate-Based (1994):	**$3,562**
Purchase-Power-Parity-Based (current $I) (1994):	**$5,822**
Average Annual Growth Rate (1990-95):	**3.6 percent**
Official Development Assistance (1995):	**$2,775 million**
Total External Debt (1993-95)*:	**$311,140.0 million**

* Data are collected only for developing countries.

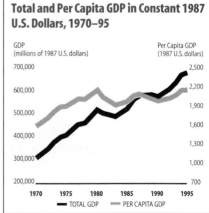

Total and Per Capita GDP in Constant 1987 U.S. Dollars, 1970–95

*R*egions at a Glance

Agriculture

Cropland:	
Total (1994):	**114,901,000 hectares**
Per Capita (1994):	**0.37 hectares**
Cereal Production:	
Total (1996):	**94,049,200 metric tons**
Per Capita (1996):	**0.29 metric tons**
Hectares of Permanent Pastureland (1994):	**494,727,000**
Annual Fertilizer Use (1994):	**60 kilograms per hectare**
Average Cereals Yield (average 1994-96):	**2,547 kilograms per hectare**
Net Trade in Cereals (average 1993-95):	**4,361,000 metric tons**

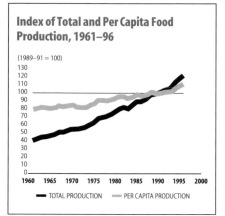

Index of Total and Per Capita Food Production, 1961–96

(1989–91 = 100)

TOTAL PRODUCTION — PER CAPITA PRODUCTION

Energy

Commercial Energy Production (1995):	
Total:	**17,724 petajoules**
Per Capita:	**55.8 gigajoules**
Commercial Energy Consumption (1995):	
Total:	**11,939 petajoules**
Per Capita:	**37.6 gigajoules**
Traditional Fuels as a Percentage of Commercial Energy (1995):	**19.8 percent**
Percentage of Electricity Supplied by Renewable Sources (1995):	**81.4 percent**
Energy Efficiency (terajoules per million $GDP) (1994):	**18.6**

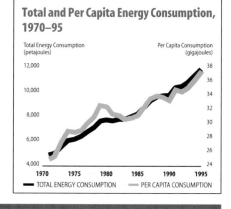

Total and Per Capita Energy Consumption, 1970–95

Total Energy Consumption (petajoules) — Per Capita Consumption (gigajoules)

TOTAL ENERGY CONSUMPTION — PER CAPITA CONSUMPTION

Forests

Total Timber (Roundwood) Production (1995):	**392.0 million cubic meters**
Total Forest Extent (1995):	**870,594,000 hectares**
Natural Forest Extent (1995):	**863,315,000 hectares**
Plantation Forest Extent (1990):	**7,264,000 hectares**
Percent Change in Total Forests from 1990 to 1995:	**–2.7 percent**
Percentage of Original Forest Remaining (1996):	**69.1 percent**
Value of Forest Products Exported ($US) (1995):	**6,343.9 million**

* Represents export trade of each country regardless of destination.

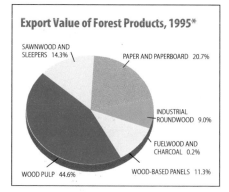

Export Value of Forest Products, 1995*

SAWNWOOD AND SLEEPERS 14.3%
PAPER AND PAPERBOARD 20.7%
INDUSTRIAL ROUNDWOOD 9.0%
FUELWOOD AND CHARCOAL 0.2%
WOOD-BASED PANELS 11.3%
WOOD PULP 44.6%

Atmosphere

Carbon Dioxide Emissions (1995):	
Total:	**747,331,000 metric tons**
Per Capita:	**2.4 metric tons**
Percentage of Emissions from:	
Solid Fuels:	**10.3 percent**
Liquid Fuels:	**60.8 percent**
Gas Fuels:	**21.5 percent**

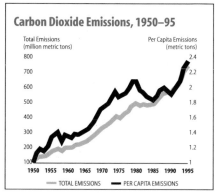

Carbon Dioxide Emissions, 1950–95

Total Emissions (million metric tons) — Per Capita Emissions (metric tons)

TOTAL EMISSIONS — PER CAPITA EMISSIONS

Fresh Water

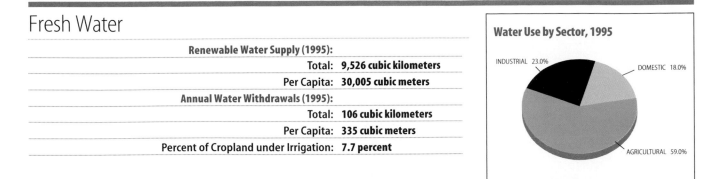

Renewable Water Supply (1995):

Total: **9,526 cubic kilometers**

Per Capita: **30,005 cubic meters**

Annual Water Withdrawals (1995):

Total: **106 cubic kilometers**

Per Capita: **335 cubic meters**

Percent of Cropland under Irrigation: **7.7 percent**

Water Use by Sector, 1995

INDUSTRIAL 23.0%
DOMESTIC 18.0%
AGRICULTURAL 59.0%

Oceans and Fish

Marine Fish Catch (1995)*: **933,852 metric tons**

Aquaculture Production (1995)**: **328,931 metric tons**

Average Annual Balance of Trade in Fish ($US) (1993-95): **1,211.9 million**

Length of Coastline: **30,663 kilometers**

* Diadromous fish excluded.
** Data exclude plants.

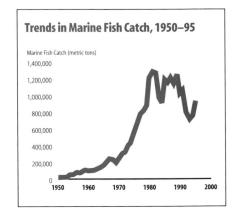

Trends in Marine Fish Catch, 1950–95

Marine Fish Catch (metric tons)

Biodiversity and Protected Areas

Percent of Land Area Protected (1996): **7.4 percent**

Number of Protected Areas Larger than:

100,000 hectares: **198 areas**

1 million hectares: **24 areas**

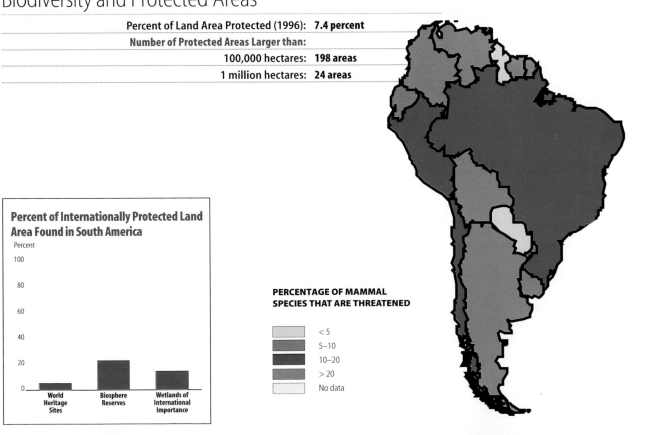

Percent of Internationally Protected Land Area Found in South America

Percent

World Heritage Sites / Biosphere Reserves / Wetlands of International Importance

PERCENTAGE OF MAMMAL SPECIES THAT ARE THREATENED

< 5
5–10
10–20
> 20
No data

Regions at a Glance

ASIA

Population and Human Well-Being

Life Expectancy (1995-00):	**66.2 years**
Total Fertility Rate (1995-00):	**2.7 children per woman**
Infant Mortality (1995-00):	**56 per 1,000 live births**
Crude Death Rate (1995-00):	**7.9 per 1,000 people**
Percentage of Population that is:	
Rural (1995):	**65 percent**
Urban (1995):	**35 percent**
Under Age 15 (2000):	**30 percent**
Over Age 65 (2000):	**6 percent**
Motor Vehicles Per Capita (1991):	**0.03**
Televisions Per 1,000 People (1994):	**130**
Number of Cities with Populations Greater than 750,000 (1995):	**184**

Total Population (1998): 3,588,877,000 people
Total Land Area (1994): 3,085,414,000 hectares

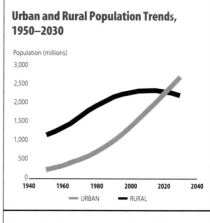

Urban and Rural Population Trends, 1950–2030

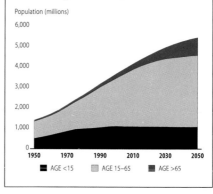

Trends in Age Structure, 1950–2050

Economics

Gross Domestic Product Per Capita (current $US):	
Exchange-Rate-Based (1994):	**$2,241**
Purchase-Power-Parity-Based (current $I) (1994):	**$3,430**
Average Annual Growth Rate (1990-95):	**not available for Asia**
Official Development Assistance (1995):	**$3,092 million**
Total External Debt (1993-95)*:	**$564,986 million**

*   Data are collected only for developing countries.

** Total GDP figures for Asia are not available before 1988 because of insufficient data.

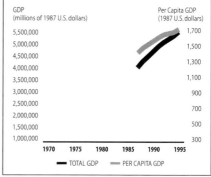

Total and Per Capita GDP in Constant 1987 U.S. Dollars, 1970–95 **

Agriculture

Cropland:	
Total (1994):	**621,590,000 hectares**
Per Capita (1994):	**0.18 hectares**
Cereal Production:	
Total (1996):	**973,121,600 metric tons**
Per Capita (1996):	**0.28 metric tons**
Hectares of Permanent Pastureland (1994):	**1,046,888,000**
Annual Fertilizer Use (1994):	**129 kilograms per hectare ***
Average Cereals Yield (average 1994-96):	**2,895 kilograms per hectare**
Net Trade in Cereals (average 1993-95):	**77,933,000 metric tons**

* Data do not include countries of the former Soviet Union.

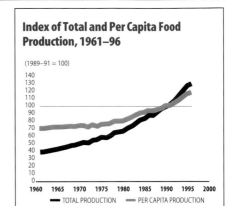

Index of Total and Per Capita Food Production, 1961–96

(1989–91 = 100)

TOTAL PRODUCTION — PER CAPITA PRODUCTION

Energy

Commercial Energy Production (1995):	
Total:	**111,998 petajoules**
Per Capita:	**32.6 gigajoules**
Commercial Energy Consumption (1995):	
Total:	**120,967 petajoules**
Per Capita:	**35.6 gigajoules**
Traditional Fuels as a Percentage of Commercial Energy (1995):	**21.6 percent**
Percentage of Electricity Supplied by Renewable Sources (1995):	**17.7 percent**
Energy Efficiency (terajoules per million $GDP) (1994):	**19.4**

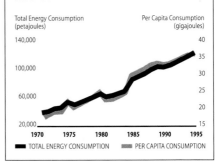

Total and Per Capita Energy Consumption, 1970–95

Total Energy Consumption (petajoules) — Per Capita Consumption (gigajoules)

TOTAL ENERGY CONSUMPTION — PER CAPITA CONSUMPTION

Forests

Total Timber (Roundwood) Production (1995):	**1,146.6 million cubic meters**
Total Forest Extent (1995):	**474,172,000 hectares**
Natural Forest Extent (1995):	**255,751,000 hectares**
Plantation Forest Extent (1990):	**56,115,000 hectares**
Percent Change in Total Forests from 1990 to 1995:	**–3.4 percent**
Percentage of Original Forest Remaining (1996):	**28.2 percent**
Value of Forest Products Exported ($US) (1995):	**16,515 million**

* Represents export trade of each country regardless of destination.

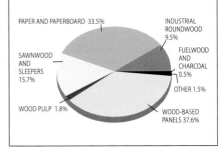

Export Value of Forest Products, 1995*

PAPER AND PAPERBOARD 33.5%
INDUSTRIAL ROUNDWOOD 9.5%
FUELWOOD AND CHARCOAL 0.5%
OTHER 1.5%
WOOD-BASED PANELS 37.6%
WOOD PULP 1.8%
SAWNWOOD AND SLEEPERS 15.7%

Atmosphere

Carbon Dioxide Emissions (1995):	
Total:	**8,270,648,000 metric tons**
Per Capita:	**2.3 metric tons**
Percentage of Emissions from:	
Solid Fuels:	**47.9 percent**
Liquid Fuels:	**33.9 percent**
Gas Fuels:	**9.3 percent**

Note: CO$_2$ and per capita CO$_2$ emissions do not include countries of the former Soviet Union until 1992.

Carbon Dioxide Emissions, 1950–95

Total Emissions (million metric tons) — Per Capita Emissions (metric tons)

TOTAL EMISSIONS — PER CAPITA EMISSIONS

Fresh Water

Renewable Water Supply (1995):

Total: **13,207 cubic kilometers**

Per Capita: **3,841 cubic meters**

Annual Water Withdrawals (1995):

Total: **1,634 cubic kilometers**

Per Capita: **542 cubic meters**

Percent of Cropland under Irrigation: **25.1 percent**

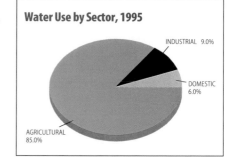

Water Use by Sector, 1995

INDUSTRIAL 9.0%

DOMESTIC 6.0%

AGRICULTURAL 85.0%

Oceans and Fish

Marine Fish Catch (1995)*: **20,124,900 metric tons**

Aquaculture Production (1995)**: **18,239,947 metric tons**

Average Annual Balance of Trade in Fish ($US) (1993-95): **–3,635.0 million**

Length of Coastline: **252,776 kilometers**

* Diadromous fish excluded.
** Data exclude plants.

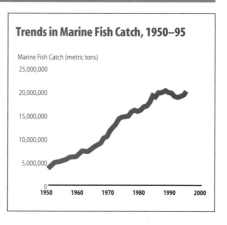

Trends in Marine Fish Catch, 1950–95

Marine Fish Catch (metric tons)

25,000,000

20,000,000

15,000,000

10,000,000

5,000,000

0

1950   1960   1970   1980   1990   2000

Biodiversity and Protected Areas

Percent of Land Area Protected (1996): **5.3 percent**

Number of Protected Areas Larger than:

100,000 hectares: **227 areas**

1 million hectares: **25 areas**

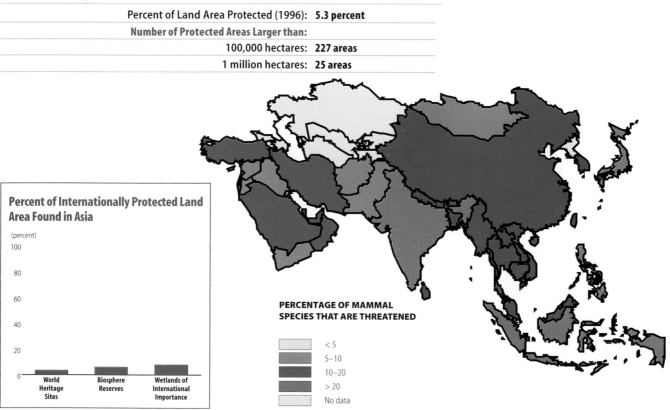

Percent of Internationally Protected Land Area Found in Asia

(percent)

100

80

60

40

20

0

World Heritage Sites | Biosphere Reserves | Wetlands of International Importance

PERCENTAGE OF MAMMAL SPECIES THAT ARE THREATENED

< 5
5–10
10–20
> 20
No data

OCEANIA

Population and Human Well-Being

Life Expectancy (1995-00):	**73.9 years**
Total Fertility Rate (1995-00):	**2.5 children per woman**
Infant Mortality (1995-00):	**24 per 1,000 live births**
Crude Death Rate (1995-00):	**7.7 per 1,000 people**
Percentage of Population that is:	
Rural (1995):	**30 percent**
Urban (1995):	**70 percent**
Under Age 15 (2000):	**26 percent**
Over Age 65 (2000):	**10 percent**
Motor Vehicles Per Capita (1991):	**0.43**
Televisions Per 1,000 People (1994):	**386**
Number of Cities with Populations Greater than 750,000 (1995):	**6**

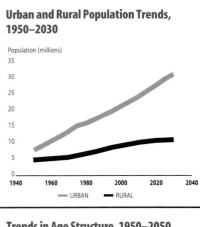

Urban and Rural Population Trends, 1950–2030

Trends in Age Structure, 1950–2050

Total Population (1998): 29,460,000 people
Total Land Area (1994): 849,135,000 hectares

Economics

Gross Domestic Product Per Capita (current $US):	
Exchange-Rate-Based (1994):	**$14,686**
Purchase-Power-Parity-Based (current $I) (1994):	**$15,181**
Average Annual Growth Rate (1990-95):	**3.6 percent**
Official Development Assistance (1995):	**–$316 million**
Total External Debt (1993-95)*:	**2,891 million**

* Data are collected only for developing countries.

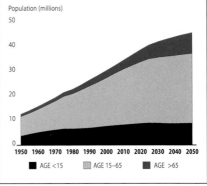

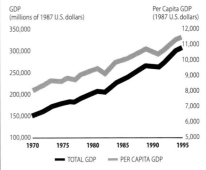

Total and Per Capita GDP in Constant 1987 U.S. Dollars, 1970–95

Regions at a Glance

Agriculture

Cropland:	
Total (1994):	**51,515,000 hectares**
Per Capita (1994):	**1.84 hectares**
Cereal Production:	
Total (1996):	**35,485,100 metric tons**
Per Capita (1996):	**1.24 metric tons**
Hectares of Permanent Pastureland (1994):	**428,638,000**
Annual Fertilizer Use (1994):	**46 kilograms per hectare**
Average Cereals Yield (average 1994-96):	**1,779 kilograms per hectare**
Net Trade in Cereals (average 1993-95):	**−13,382,000 metric tons**

Index of Total and Per Capita Food Production, 1961–96

Energy

Commercial Energy Production (1995):	
Total:	**8,334 petajoules**
Per Capita:	**294.4 gigajoules**
Commercial Energy Consumption (1995):	
Total:	**5,282 petajoules**
Per Capita:	**186.6 gigajoules**
Traditional Fuels as a Percentage of Commercial Energy (1995):	**4.5 percent**
Percentage of Electricity Supplied by Renewable Sources (1995):	**23.6 percent**
Energy Efficiency (terajoules per million $GDP) (1994):	**14.7**

Total and Per Capita Energy Consumption, 1970–95

Forests

Total Timber (Roundwood) Production (1995):	**50.1 million cubic meters**
Total Forest Extent (1995):	**90,695,000 hectares**
Natural Forest Extent (1995):	**41,752,000 hectares**
Plantation Forest Extent (1990):	**149,000 hectares**
Percent Change in Total Forests from 1990 to 1995:	**−0.5 percent**
Percentage of Original Forest Remaining (1996):	**64.9 percent**
Value of Forest Products Exported ($US) (1995):	**3,071.9 million**

* Represents export trade of each country regardless of destination.

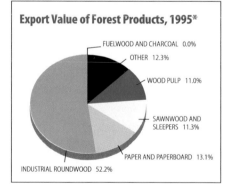

Export Value of Forest Products, 1995*

Atmosphere

Carbon Dioxide Emissions (1995):	
Total:	**322,535,000 metric tons**
Per Capita:	**11.3 metric tons**
Percentage of Emissions from:	
Solid Fuels:	**57.2 percent**
Liquid Fuels:	**29.2 percent**
Gas Fuels:	**12.5 percent**

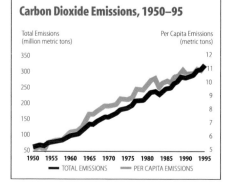

Carbon Dioxide Emissions, 1950–95

Fresh Water

Renewable Water Supply (1995):	
Total:	**1,614 cubic kilometers**
Per Capita:	**57,031 cubic meters**
Annual Water Withdrawals (1995):	
Total:	**17 cubic kilometers**
Per Capita:	**591 cubic meters**
Percent of Cropland under Irrigation:	**4.8 percent**

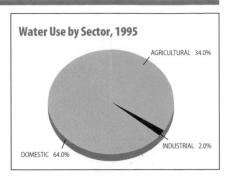

Water Use by Sector, 1995

AGRICULTURAL 34.0%
DOMESTIC 64.0%
INDUSTRIAL 2.0%

Oceans and Fish

Marine Fish Catch (1995)*:	**598,277 metric tons**
Aquaculture Production (1995)**:	**95,974 metric tons**
Average Annual Balance of Trade in Fish ($US) (1993-95):	**294.0 million**
Length of Coastline:	**30,663 kilometers**

* Diadromous fish excluded.
** Data exclude plants.

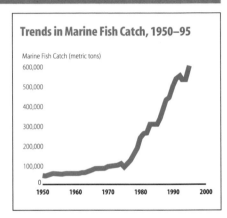

Trends in Marine Fish Catch, 1950–95

Marine Fish Catch (metric tons)

Biodiversity and Protected Areas

Percent of Land Area Protected (1996):	**7.1 percent**
Number of Protected Areas Larger than:	
100,000 hectares:	**124 areas**
1 million hectares:	**13 areas**

Percent of Internationally Protected Land Area Found in Oceania

(percent)

World Heritage Sites   Biosphere Reserves   Wetlands of International Importance

PERCENTAGE OF MAMMAL SPECIES THAT ARE THREATENED

< 5
5–10
10–20
> 20
No data

The World's Wealth Is Not Evenly Distributed

WORLD BANK INCOME GROUPS

- Low income
- Lower middle income
- Upper middle income
- High income
- No data

Source: The World Bank, *World Development Indicators, 1997.*

Per capita income in the industrialized countries of North America, Europe, and Australia exceeds per capita income in the largely agriculture-based economies of much of Africa, South America, and Asia. (See Data Table 6.1.)

Human Impact Is High in Densely Populated Regions

POPULATION DENSITY (persons per square kilometer)

- <2
- 2–10
- 10–40
- 40–100
- 100–500
- 500–35,000
- No data

Source: Consortium for International Earth Science Information Network.

Historically, humans have significantly transformed the natural landscape in areas of high population density through agricultural conversion, water diversion and extraction, urbanization, and industrialization.

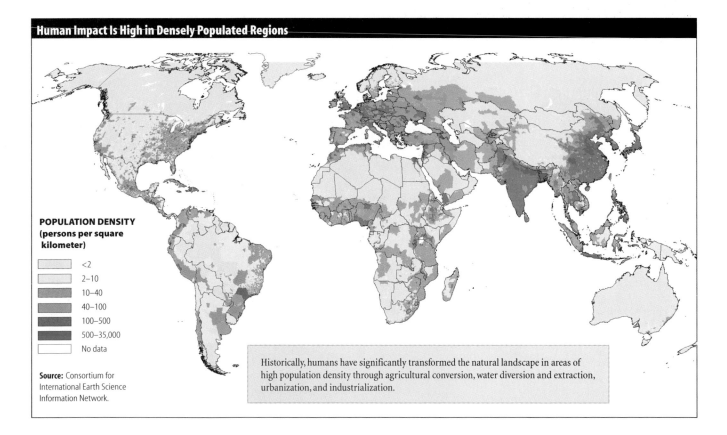

Wealth Is Not the Only Measure of Human Well-Being

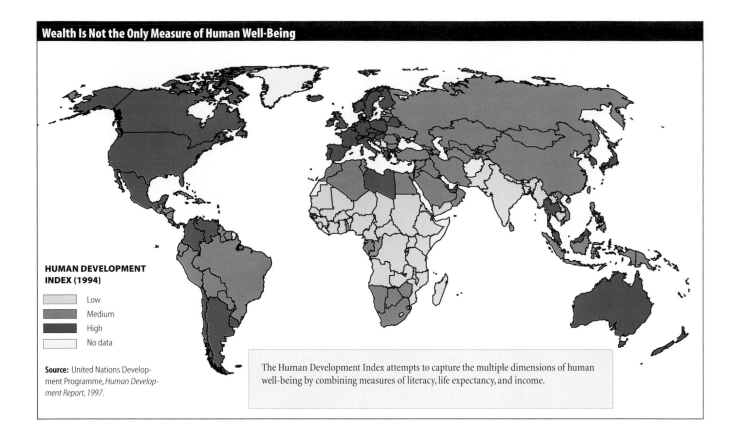

HUMAN DEVELOPMENT INDEX (1994)

- Low
- Medium
- High
- No data

Source: United Nations Development ment Programme, *Human Development Report, 1997.*

The Human Development Index attempts to capture the multiple dimensions of human well-being by combining measures of literacy, life expectancy, and income.

Domesticated Land Has Replaced Much of Earth's Original Land Cover

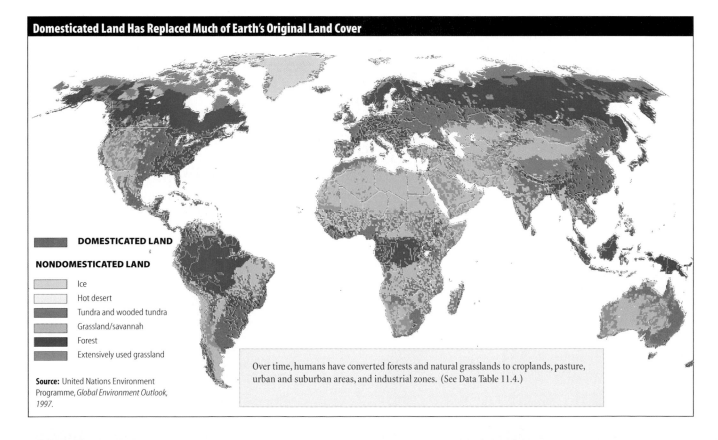

DOMESTICATED LAND

NONDOMESTICATED LAND

- Ice
- Hot desert
- Tundra and wooded tundra
- Grassland/savannah
- Forest
- Extensively used grassland

Source: United Nations Environment Programme, *Global Environment Outlook, 1997.*

Over time, humans have converted forests and natural grasslands to croplands, pasture, urban and suburban areas, and industrial zones. (See Data Table 11.4.)

The World's Forests Have Shrunk by Nearly Half

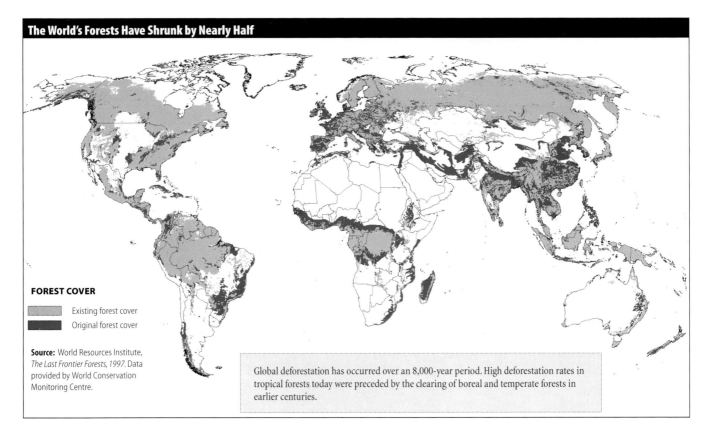

FOREST COVER

Existing forest cover
Original forest cover

Source: World Resources Institute, *The Last Frontier Forests, 1997*. Data provided by World Conservation Monitoring Centre.

Global deforestation has occurred over an 8,000-year period. High deforestation rates in tropical forests today were preceded by the clearing of boreal and temperate forests in earlier centuries.

Water Scarcity Is A Critical Resource Issue

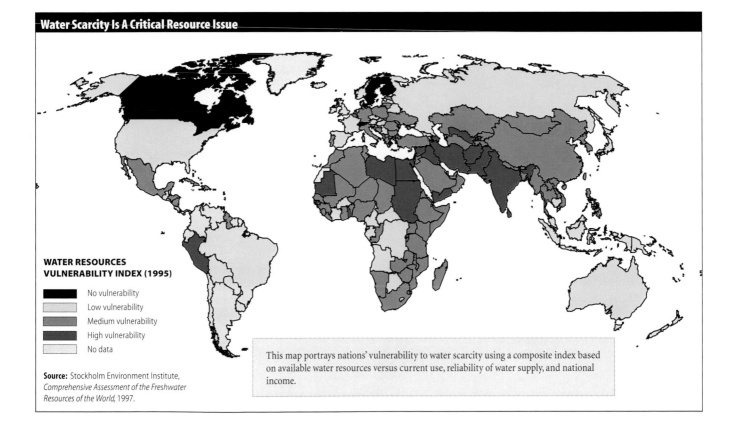

WATER RESOURCES VULNERABILITY INDEX (1995)

No vulnerability
Low vulnerability
Medium vulnerability
High vulnerability
No data

Source: Stockholm Environment Institute, *Comprehensive Assessment of the Freshwater Resources of the World, 1997.*

This map portrays nations' vulnerability to water scarcity using a composite index based on available water resources versus current use, reliability of water supply, and national income.

Many Major Watersheds Cross National Boundaries

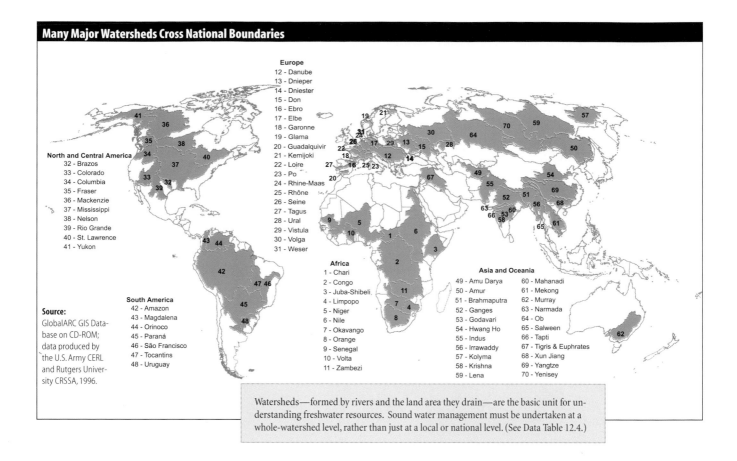

Europe
12 - Danube
13 - Dnieper
14 - Dniester
15 - Don
16 - Ebro
17 - Elbe
18 - Garonne
19 - Glama
20 - Guadalquivir
21 - Kemijoki
22 - Loire
23 - Po
24 - Rhine-Maas
25 - Rhône
26 - Seine
27 - Tagus
28 - Ural
29 - Vistula
30 - Volga
31 - Weser

North and Central America
32 - Brazos
33 - Colorado
34 - Columbia
35 - Fraser
36 - Mackenzie
37 - Mississippi
38 - Nelson
39 - Rio Grande
40 - St. Lawrence
41 - Yukon

South America
42 - Amazon
43 - Magdalena
44 - Orinoco
45 - Paraná
46 - São Francisco
47 - Tocantins
48 - Uruguay

Africa
1 - Chari
2 - Congo
3 - Juba-Shibeli
4 - Limpopo
5 - Niger
6 - Nile
7 - Okavango
8 - Orange
9 - Senegal
10 - Volta
11 - Zambezi

Asia and Oceania
49 - Amu Darya
50 - Amur
51 - Brahmaputra
52 - Ganges
53 - Godavari
54 - Hwang Ho
55 - Indus
56 - Irrawaddy
57 - Kolyma
58 - Krishna
59 - Lena
60 - Mahanadi
61 - Mekong
62 - Murray
63 - Narmada
64 - Ob
65 - Salween
66 - Tapti
67 - Tigris & Euphrates
68 - Xun Jiang
69 - Yangtze
70 - Yenisey

Source:
GlobalARC GIS Database on CD-ROM; data produced by the U.S. Army CERL and Rutgers University CRSSA, 1996.

Watersheds—formed by rivers and the land area they drain—are the basic unit for understanding freshwater resources. Sound water management must be undertaken at a whole-watershed level, rather than just at a local or national level. (See Data Table 12.4.)

Nighttime Lights Show the Distribution of Settlements and Infrastructure

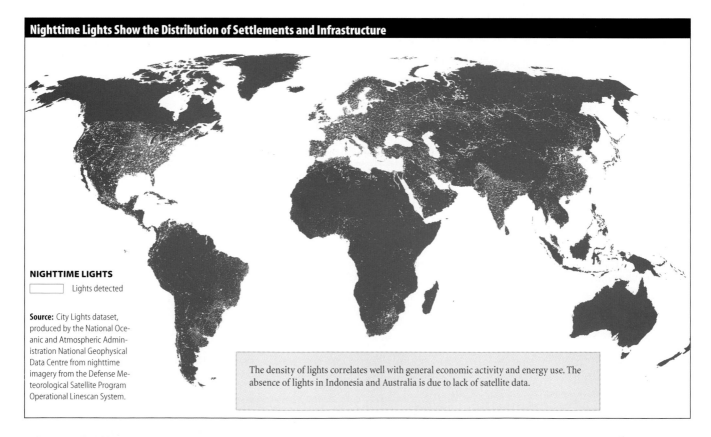

NIGHTTIME LIGHTS

☐ Lights detected

Source: City Lights dataset, produced by the National Oceanic and Atmospheric Administration National Geophysical Data Centre from nighttime imagery from the Defense Meteorological Satellite Program Operational Linescan System.

The density of lights correlates well with general economic activity and energy use. The absence of lights in Indonesia and Australia is due to lack of satellite data.

Global Environmental Trends

PART II: GLOBAL ENVIRONMENTAL TRENDS

Chapter 4: Critical Trends/Population and Human Well-Being

Population Growth—Stabilization?

1. United Nations (U.N.) Population Division, *World Population Prospects 1950-2050 (The 1996 Revision)*, on diskette (U.N., New York, 1996).
2. *Ibid.*
3. *Op. cit.* 1.
4. United Nations (U.N.) Population Division, *World Population Prospects 1950-2050: The 1996 Revision*, Annex 1: Demographic Indicators (U.N., New York, 1997), pp. 11–45.
5. *Ibid.*, p. 121.
6. *Op. cit.* 4, pp. 124–125.
7. *Op. cit.* 1.
8. *Op. cit.* 4, Table A.18, pp. 120–122.
9. United Nations Fund for Population Activities (UNFPA), *Country Profile: United Republic of Tanzania* (UNFPA, New York, 1992).
10. *Op. cit.* 4, pp. 164, 179.
11. Wolfgang Lutz, Warren Sanderson, and Sergei Scherbov, *Probability World Population Projections Based on Expert Opinion,* Working Paper (WP-96-17) (International Institute for Applied Systems Analysis, Laxenburg, Austria, 1996), p. 20.
12. United Nations Development Program (UNDP), *Human Development Report 1997* (Oxford University Press, New York, 1997), pp. 3–4.
13. United Nations Children's Fund (UNICEF), *The Progress of Nations 1997* (UNICEF, New York, 1997).
14. United Nations Educational, Scientific and Cultural Organization (UNESCO), *Statistical Yearbook 1996* (UNESCO, Paris, 1996), Table 2.2, p. 2-9.

Economic Growth and Human Development

1. World Resources Institute in collaboration with the United Nations Environment Programme, the United Nations Development Programme, and the World Bank, *World Resources 1996–97* (Oxford University Press, New York, 1996), p. 223.
2. The World Bank, *World Development Indicators 1997* (The World Bank, Washington, D.C., 1997), p. 289.
3. *Ibid.*, p. 235.
4. *Op. cit.* 2, pp. 235–238.
5. The Norwegian Forum for Environment and Development, *An Unwanted Child Has Grown Up*, report from the New Development Options Conference (The Norwegian Forum for Environment and Development, Oslo, 1995), p. 27.
6. United Nations Development Programme (UNDP), *Human Development Report 1996* (UNDP, New York, 1996), p. 1.
7. *Op. cit.* 2, pp. 127, 291.
8. The World Bank, *World Development Indicators 1996* (The World Bank, Washington, D.C., 1996), pp. 11–12.
9. United Nations Development Programme (UNDP), *Human Development Report 1997* (UNDP, New York, 1997), pp. 28–29.
10. *Op. cit.* 2, p. 31.
11. *Op. cit.* 2, p. 31.
12. *Op. cit.* 2, p. 31.

13. *Op. cit.* 9, p. 23.
14. *Op. cit.* 6, p. 2.
15. *Op. cit.* 9, p. 9.
16. *Op. cit.* 9, p. 7.
17. Japanese economist Jukio Ikemoto, quoted in Johanna San, "Widening Wealth Gaps Stoke Social Tensions in South East Asia," *Interpress Service (IPS Terraviva)*, Vol. 4, No. 151 (August 8, 1996).
18. *Op. cit.* 9, p. 1.
19. *Op. cit.* 9, p. 38.
20. Johanna San, "Widening Wealth Gaps Stoke Social Tensions in South East Asia," *Interpress Service (IPS Terraviva)*, Vol. 4, No. 151 (August 8, 1996).
21. Thomas Homer-Dixon and Valerie Percival, *Environmental Scarcity and Violent Conflict: Briefing Book* (American Association for the Advancement of Science and University College, University of Toronto, 1996), p. 17.
22. Government of the People's Republic of China, *The People's Republic of China: National Report on Sustainable Development* (Government of the People's Republic of China, Beijing, 1997), pp. 41–42.

Urban Growth

1. United Nations (U.N.) Population Division, *World Urbanization Prospects: The 1996 Revision,* Annex Tables (U.N., New York, 1997), pp. 44, 48.
2. World Resources Institute in collaboration with the United Nations Environment Programme, the United Nations Development Programme, and the World Bank, *World Resources Report 1996–97* (Oxford University Press, New York, 1996), p. 3.
3. The World Bank, *World Development Report 1997* (The World Bank, Washington, D.C., 1997), p. 231.
4. *Op. cit.* 1, pp. 66–71.
5. United Nations (U.N.) Population Division, *Concise Report on the World Population Situation in 1995* (U.N., New York, 1995), p. 26.
6. United Nations General Assembly, *Fourth Review and Appraisal of the World Population Plan of Action*, A/CONF.171/PC/3, March 1, 1994 (Preparatory Committee for the International Conference on Population and Development, Third Session, Item 4), p. 19. For further discussion of the social and environmental implications of urbanization, see World Resources Institute in collaboration with the United Nations Environment Programme, the United Nations Development Programme, and the World Bank, *World Resources Report 1996–97* (Oxford University Press, New York, 1996), Chapters 1–6.
7. Arie D. Djoekardi, "Urban Land Use Planning Policy in Indonesia," paper presented at the International Workshop on Policy Measures for Changing Consumption Patterns, Seoul, Republic of Korea, August 30–September 1, 1995, pp. 3–4, 12–13.

International Migration

1. United Nations (U.N.) Population Division, "World Population Prospects: The 1996 Revision," *Population Newsletter,* No. 62 (December 1996), pp. 9–10.
2. The OECD member countries are Australia, Austria, Belgium, Canada, Denmark, Finland, France, Germany, Greece, Iceland, Ireland, Italy, Japan, Lux-

embourg, Mexico, the Netherlands, New Zealand, Norway, Portugal, Spain, Sweden, Switzerland, Turkey, the United Kingdom, and the United States.
3. *Op. cit.* 1, p. 9.
4. The U.S. Committee for Refugees, *World Refugee Survey 1997* (The U.S. Committee for Refugees, Washington, D.C., 1997), pp. 3, 12.
5. *Ibid.*, p. 6.
6. United Nations High Commission for Refugees (UNHCR), "Home is Where the Hurt Is," *Internally Displaced Persons,* Issue 103 (UNHCR, Geneva). Available online at: http://www.unhcr.ch/pubs/rm103/rm10307.htm (July 26, 1997).
7. United Nations High Commission for Refugees (UNHCR), "Out of Sight, Out of Mind," *Internally Displaced Persons,* Issue 103 (UNHCR, Geneva). Available online at: http://www.unhcr.ch/pubs/rm103/rm10307.htm (July 26, 1997).
8. Thomas Homer-Dixon and Valerie Percival, *Environmental Scarcity and Violent Conflict: Briefing Book* (American Association for the Advancement of Science and University College, Toronto, 1996), p. 13.
9. The World Bank, *World Development Indicators 1997* (The World Bank, Washington, D.C., 1997), pp. 326–327.
10. *Op. cit.* 1, p. 12.

R_x For Health: Education

1. The World Bank, "Expanding the Measure of Wealth: Indicators of Sustainable Development," CSD Edition, Draft for Discussion (The World Bank, Washington, D.C., 1997), pp. 5–15.
2. United Nations Development Programme (UNDP), *Human Development Report 1997* (UNDP, New York, 1997), p. 76.
3. *Ibid.*
4. United Nations Development Programme (UNDP), *Human Development Report 1996* (UNDP, New York, 1996), p. 74.
5. *Ibid.*, p. 76.
6. United Nations Development Programme (UNDP), *Human Development Report 1995* (UNDP, New York, 1995), p. 29.
7. *Op. cit.* 2, p. 30.
8. *Op. cit.* 2, p. 30.
9. Food and Agriculture Organization of the United Nations (FAO), *Women Feed the World,* FAO Factsheet for World Food Summit (FAO, Rome, 1996).
10. World Resources Institute (WRI), *World Resources Database 1998-99,* on diskette (WRI, Washington, D.C., 1998).
11. World Health Organization (WHO), *The World Health Report 1996* (WHO, Geneva, 1996), p. v.
12. *Ibid.*, pp. 14–16.
13. *Op. cit.* 2, pp. 226–227.
14. The World Bank, *World Development Report 1997* (The World Bank, Washington, D.C., 1997), p. 55.
15. Hans P. Binswanger and Pierre Landell-Mills, *The World Bank's Strategy for Reducing Poverty and Hunger: A Report to the Development Community,* Environmentally Sustainable Development Studies and Monographs Series No. 4 (The World Bank, Washington, D.C., 1995), p. 22.

16. Leela Visaria and Pravin Visaria, "India's Population in Transition," *Population Bulletin*, Vol. 50, No. 3 (1995), p. 22.

17. *Op. cit.* 4, p. 81.

18. Mohammad Basheer, "Kerala: Health and Education Progress Despite Poverty," in The Norwegian Forum for Environment and Development, *An Un-* *wanted Child Has Grown Up*, report from the New Development Options Conference (The Norwegian Forum for Environment and Development, Oslo, 1995), pp. 14–17.

AIDS Toll Climbs

1. The Joint United Nations Programme on HIV/AIDS (UNAIDS) and the World Health Organization (WHO), *Report on the Global HIV/AIDS Epidemic* (UNAIDS/WHO, Geneva, 1997).

2. The World Bank, *Confronting AIDS: Public Priorities in a Global Epidemic* (Oxford University Press, New York, 1997), p. 13.

Chapter 4: Critical Trends/Feeding The World

Food Production: Have Yields Stopped Rising?

1. World Resources Institute calculation using data from Food and Agriculture Organization of the United Nations (FAO), *FAOSTAT Statistical Database* (FAO, Rome, 1997).

2. Mark D. Winslow, special assistant to the associate director general (research), International Crops Research Institute for the Semi-Arid Tropics, July 16, 1997 (personal communication).

3. *Op. cit.* 1.

4. Nikos Alexandratos, ed., *World Agriculture: Towards 2010* (Food and Agriculture Organization of the United Nations and John Wiley and Sons, Chichester, 1995), pp. 168–169.

5. International Rice Research Institute (IRRI), *Program Report for 1995* (IRRI, Los Baños, Philippines, 1996), p. 3.

6. Agnes C. Rola and Prabhu L. Pingali, *Pesticides, Rice Productivity, and Farmers' Health* (International Rice Research Institute and World Resources Institute, Los Baños, Philippines, and Washington, D.C., 1993), p. 21.

7. Osamu Ito, International Rice Research Institute, July 10, 1997 (personal communication).

8. International Crops Research Institute for the Semi-Arid Tropics and Food and Agriculture Organization of the United Nations, *The World Sorghum and Millet Economies: Facts, Trends, and Outlook* (International Crops Research Institute for the Semi-Arid Tropics, Andhra Pradesh, India, 1996), p. 1.

9. *Op. cit.* 2.

10. Nurul Islam, ed., *Population and Food in the Early Twenty-First Century: Meeting Future Food Demand of an Increasing Population* (International Food Policy Research Institute, Washington, D.C., 1995), pp. 208–209.

11. Mark Rosegrant and Robert Livernash, "Growing More Food, Doing Less Damage," *Environment*, Vol. 38, No. 7 (1996), p. 30.

12. *Op. cit.* 7.

13. *Op. cit.* 7.

Food Insecurity: A Trend Toward Hunger

1. Even though in general parlance the words "hunger," "starvation," "undernutrition," and "malnutrition" are often used interchangeably, FAO makes some distinctions among them. Individuals experiencing "undernutrition" have an insufficient intake of energy for normal growth and physical development, body maintenance, and for pursuing ordinary human activities. "Malnutrition" is more strictly defined as a nutritional disorder resulting from faulty or inadequate nutrition. It is also used to describe dietary deficiencies (e.g., micronutrient deficiencies such as vitamin A, iodine, or iron).

2. Food and Agriculture Organization of the United Nations (FAO), *Agriculture and Food Security: The Situation Today—Hunger Amid Plenty.* Available online at: http://www.fao.org/wfs/fs/e/agricult/AgSit-e.htm (September 25, 1997).

3. United Nations Development Programme, *Human Development Report 1997* (Oxford University Press, New York, 1997), p. 148.

4. Peter Uvin, "The State of World Hunger," in *The Hunger Report: 1995,* Ellen Messer and Peter Uvin, eds. (Gordon and Breach Publishers SA, Amsterdam, 1996), p. 1. Uvin uses 1993 FAO figures compiled in 1994 and assumes the average per capita caloric requirement is 2,350 kilocalories per day.

5. Nikos Alexandratos, ed., *World Agriculture: Toward 2010* (Food and Agriculture Organization of the United Nations and John Wiley & Sons, New York, 1995), p. 44.

6. The World Bank, *World Development Indicators 1997* (The World Bank, Washington, D.C., 1997), p. 83.

7. World Health Organization (WHO), *The World Health Report 1997* (WHO, Geneva, 1997), pp. 13–14.

8. According to the World Health Organization (WHO), underweight is defined as more than 2 standard deviations below the median weight of a reference population. WHO, *World Health Statistics Annual 1995* (WHO, Geneva, 1996), p. xi.

9. *Op. cit.* 6, p. 85.

10. Food and Agriculture Organization of the United Nations, *Agriculture and Food Security: Looking Forward—Continued Gain, Continued Pain.* Available online at: http://www.fao.org/wfs/fs/e/agricult/AgLoo-e.htm (September 25, 1997).

11. United Nations (U.N.) Department of Policy Coordination and Sustainable Development, *Critical Trends: Global Change and Sustainable Development* (U.N., New York, 1997), p. 49.

12. World Meteorological Organization (WMO), *A Comprehensive Assessment of the Freshwater Resources of the World* (WMO, Geneva, 1997), p. 28.

13. Organisation for Economic Co-Operation and Development, "Aid and Other Resource Flows in 1996," June 18, 1997 (press release). Available online at: http://www.oecdwash.org/PRESS/PRESRELS/news9757.htm (September 8, 1997).

14. The United Nations first spoke of a human right to food in its 1948 Universal Declaration of Human Rights. In 1966, the body adopted an International Covenant on Economic, Social, and Cultural Rights, recognizing "the right of everyone to an adequate standard of living for himself and his family, including adequate food" (Per Pinstrup-Andersen, David Nygaard, and Annu Ratta, "The Right to Food: Widely Acknowledged and Poorly Protected," International Food Policy Research Institute (IFPRI) 2020 Brief 22 (IFPRI, Washington, D.C., 1995). The United States did not sign the covenant because policymakers feared it might encourage lawsuits by malnourished citizens; U.S. General Accounting Office, *Food Security: Preparations for the 1996 World Food Summit*, GAO/NSIAD-97-44 (GAO, Washington, D.C., 1996), pp. 6–7.

15. *Op. cit.* 3, p. 30.

Disappearing Food: How Big Are Postharvest Losses?

1. François Mazaud, Food and Agriculture Organization of the United Nations (FAO), Agro-Industries and Postharvest Management Service, Rome, July 1997 (personal communication).

2. Morton Satin, Food and Agriculture Organization of the United Nations (FAO), Agro-Industries and Postharvest Management Service, Rome, July 1997 (personal communication).

3. Food and Agriculture Organization of the United Nations, "Estimated Post-Harvest Losses of Rice in Southeast Asia." Available online at: http://www.fao.org/News/FACT-FILE/FF9712-E.HTM (July 16, 1997).

4. Dante De Padua, "Rice Post-Production and Processing: Its Significance to Agricultural Development," in *Accelerated Agricultural Development*, J.D. Drillon and D.F. Sangit, eds. (SERCA College, Laguna, Philippines, 1978).

5. *Op. cit.* 3.

6. H. Yong *et al.*, "Grain Post-Production Practices and Loss Estimates in South China," *Agricultural Mechanization in Asia, Africa, and Latin America*, Vol. 28, No. 2 (1997), pp. 37–40.

7. H.H. Phan and L.H. Nguyen, "Drying Research and Application in the Mekong Delta of Vietnam," in Proceedings of the 17th ASEAN Technical Seminar on Grain Postharvest Technology, July 25–27, 1995.

8. Mark Bell, International Rice Research Institute, July 1997 (personal communication).

9. Linda Scott Kantor *et al.*, "Estimating and Addressing America's Food Losses," *FoodReview*, Vol. 20, No. 1, (1997).

10. Michel Grolleaud, "Post-Harvest Losses: Discovering the Full Story," draft paper (Food and Agriculture Organization of the United Nations, Rome, 1997), pp. 49–52.

11. Graeme Quick, scientist, International Rice Research Institute, Los Baños, Philippines, 1993 (personal communication).

12. Dante De Padua, scientist, International Rice Research Institute, Los Baños, Philippines, July 1997 (personal communication).

Disappearing Land: Soil Degradation

1. L.R. Oldeman, "The Global Extent of Soil Degradation," in *Soil Resilience and Sustainable Land Use* (CAB International, Oxon, U.K., 1994), p. 115.
2. United Nations Environment Programme (UNEP), *Global Environment Outlook* (Oxford University Press, New York, 1997), p. 236.
3. World Resources Institute in collaboration with the United Nations Environment Programme and the United Nations Development Programme, *World Resources 1992–93* (Oxford University Press, New York, 1992), p. 114.
4. C. Barrow, *Land Degradation* (Cambridge University Press, Cambridge, U.K., 1991), cited in Henry Kendall and David Pimentel, "Constraints on the Expansion of the Global Food Supply," *Ambio*, Vol. 23, No. 3 (1994), p. 200.
5. Henry Kendall and David Pimentel, "Constraints on the Expansion of the Global Food Supply," *Ambio*, Vol. 23, No. 3 (1994), p. 200.
6. *Op. cit.* 3, p. 115.
7. Nikos Alexandratos, ed., *World Agriculture: Towards 2010* (Food and Agriculture Organization of the United Nations and John Wiley and Sons, Chichester, U.K., 1995), p. 359.

8. Sara Scherr and Satya Yadav, *Land Degradation in the Developing World: Implications for Food, Agriculture, and the Environment to 2020*, a synthesis of recommendations from an international workshop; Food, Agriculture, and the Environment Discussion Paper No. 14 (International Food Policy Research Institute, Washington, D.C., 1996), p. 3.
9. Pierre Crosson, "Degradation of Resources as a Threat to Sustainable Agriculture," paper presented at the first World Congress of Professionals in Agronomy, Santiago, Chile, September 5–8, 1994.
10. Rattan Lal, "Erosion-Crop Productivity Relationships for Soils of Africa," *Soil Science Society of America Journal*, Vol. 59, No. 3 (1995), pp. 661–667.
11. *Op. cit.* 8, pp. 1–2.
12. Sara Scherr and Satya Yadav, *Land Degradation in the Developing World: Issues and Policy Options for 2020*, 2020 Vision Policy Brief No. 44 (International Food Policy Research Institute, Washington, D.C., 1997), p. 2.
13. *Ibid.*

Farming Fish: The Aquaculture Boom

1. George K. Iwama, "Interactions between Aquaculture and the Environment," *Critical Reviews in Environmental Control*, Vol. 21, No. 2 (1991), pp. 177–216.
2. Food and Agriculture Organization of the United Nations (FAO), *The State of World Fisheries and Aquaculture, 1996* (FAO, Rome, 1997), p. 11.

3. *Ibid.*, p. 5, Table 1.
4. *Op. cit.* 2, pp. 4–5.
5. *Op. cit.* 2, p. 12, Figure 12.
6. *Op. cit.* 2, p. 59.
7. *Op. cit.* 2, pp. 11–13; p. 14, Figure 14.
8. Biksham Gujja and Andrea Finger-Stich, "What Price Prawn? Shrimp Aquaculture's Impact in Asia," *Environment*, Vol. 38, No. 7 (1996), pp. 12–14, 33.
9. *Op. cit.* 2, pp. 11–12.
10. *Op. cit.* 2, p. 59.
11. Bob Holmes, "Blue Revolutionaries," *New Scientist* (December 7, 1996), p. 34.
12. *Op. cit.* 2, pp. 24–25.
13. *Op. cit.* 11, pp. 35–36.
14. *Op. cit.* 8, pp. 12–15, 33–39.
15. *Op. cit.* 1, pp. 192–216.
16. *Op. cit.* 11, p. 36.
17. *Op. cit.* 1, pp. 177–216.
18. *Op. cit.* 11, pp. 34–35.
19. *Op. cit.* 2, p. 22.
20. *Op. cit.* 11, pp. 34–35.
21. *Op. cit.* 2, p. 22.
22. Jon Christensen, "Cultivating the World's Demand for Seafood," *New York Times* (March 1, 1997), pp. 27–29.
23. *Op. cit.* 2, p. 22.
24. *Op. cit.* 22, p. 29.
25. *Op. cit.* 11, pp. 34–35.
26. Carl Folke and Nils Kautsky, "Aquaculture with Its Environment: Prospects for Sustainability," *Ocean and Coastal Management*, Vol. 17, No. 1 (1992), pp. 5–24.

Chapter 4: Critical Trends/Production And Consumption

Wasting the Material World: The Impact of Industrial Economies

1. A. Adriaanse *et al.*, *Resource Flows: The Material Basis of Industrial Economies*, a joint publication of the World Resources Institute (WRI); the Wuppertal Institute; the Netherlands Ministry of Housing, Spatial Planning, and the Environment; and the National Institute for Environmental Studies (WRI, Washington, D.C., 1997), p. iv.
2. *Ibid.*, pp. iv–v.
3. *Op. cit.* 1, p. 15. Further, a typical car contains nearly 900 kg of metals, according to Jim Beard, ed. *The Environmental Impact of the Car* (Greenpeace, Seattle, Washington, 1992), p. 42.
4. *Op. cit.* 1, p. 15.
5. *Op. cit.* 1, pp. 1, 6.
6. *Op. cit.* 1, p. 13.
7. *Op. cit.* 1, pp. 11, 17.
8. The member countries of the OECD include: Australia, Austria, Belgium, Canada, Denmark, Finland, France, Germany, Greece, Iceland, Ireland, Italy, Japan, Luxembourg, Mexico, the Netherlands, New Zealand, Norway, Portugal, Spain, Sweden, Switzerland, Turkey, the United Kingdom, and the United States.
9. *Op. cit.* 1, p. 2.

No End to Paperwork

1. Steven Anzovin, *The Green PC: Making Choices That Make a Difference* (McGraw-Hill, Toronto, 1993), cited in John Young, *Global Network: Computers in a Sustainable Society*, Worldwatch Paper 115 (Worldwatch Institute, Washington, D.C., 1993), p. 42.
2. International Institute for Environment and Development (IIED), *Towards a Sustainable Paper Cycle: An Independent Study on the Sustainability of the Pulp and Paper Industry*, report prepared for the World Business Council for Sustainable Development (IIED, London, 1996), p. 16.
3. Food and Agriculture Organization of the United Nations (FAO), *State of the World's Forests 1997* (FAO, Rome, 1997), pp. 47, 51.
4. R. Robins *et al.*, "Rethinking Paper Consumption," International Institute for Environment and Development (IIED) Discussion Paper (IIED, London, September 1996), cited in Organisation for Economic Co-Operation and Development (OECD), *Sustainable Consumption and Production* (OECD, Paris, 1997), p. 32.
5. *Ibid.*
6. *Op. cit.* 3, p. 78.
7. *Op. cit.* 3, pp. 80–81.
8. *Op. cit.* 2, pp. 33–34.
9. *Op. cit.* 2, p. 34.
10. Roger Sedjo and Daniel Botkin, "Forest Plantations to Spare Natural Forests," *Environment*, Vol. 39, No. 10 (1997), pp. 15–20.
11. *Op. cit.* 2, p. 36.
12. *Op. cit.* 2, pp. 117–124.
13. *Op. cit.* 3, p. 74.
14. *Op. cit.* 10, pp. 16, 20.
15. *Associated Press News Beijing*, October 23, cited in *op. cit.* 3, p. 75.

16. *Op. cit.* 2, pp. 75–78.
17. *Op. cit.* 2, pp. 186–210.
18. *Op. cit.* 3, pp. 6, 74.
19. *Op. cit.* 2, pp. 126–127.

Trouble Brewing: The Changing Face of Coffee Production

1. Robert A. Rice and Justin R. Ward, *Coffee, Conservation, and Commerce in the Western Hemisphere* (Smithsonian Migratory Bird Center and Natural Resources Defense Council, Washington, D.C., 1996), p. 41.
2. International Institute for Environment and Development (IIED), *Unlocking Trade Opportunities: Changing Consumption and Production Patterns*, report for the U.N. Department of Policy Coordination and Sustainable Development (IIED, London, 1997), p. 36.
3. International Coffee Organization, "Global Coffee Production and Exports." Available online at: http://ico.org/ico_data0.html (March 24, 1997).
4. *Ibid.*
5. Food and Agriculture Organization of the United Nations (FAO), *Production Yearbook* (various years), cited in *op. cit.* 1, p. 39.
6. Russell Greenberg, "Phenomena, Comment and Notes," *Smithsonian*, Vol. 25, No. 8 (1994), p. 25, cited in *op. cit.* 1, p. 17.
7. *Op. cit.* 1, p. 5.
8. *Op. cit.* 1, p. 12.
9. *Op. cit.* 1, pp. 1, 17.

10. *Op. cit.* 1, pp. 22–24.
11. *Op. cit.* 2, p. 36.
12. *Op. cit.* 2, p. 37.

Are Business and Industry Taking Sustainability Seriously?

1. John R. Ehrenfeld and Jennifer Howard, "Setting Environmental Goals: The View from Industry: A Review of Practices from the '60s to the Present," paper commissioned by the National Research Council for the National Forum on Science and Technology Goals—No. 1: Environment, October 1995.
2. Arthur D. Little International, Inc., "Sustainable Industrial Development: Sharing Responsibilities in a Competitive World," conference paper prepared for the Dutch Ministries of Housing, Spatial Planning and Environment, and Economic Affairs, February 1996, pp. 20–21.

3. 3M Inc., "Pollution Prevention Pays, The 3P Program." Available online at: http://www.3m.com/profile/envt/3p.html (December 22, 1997).
4. Livio D. DeSimone and Frank Popoff with the World Business Council for Sustainable Development, *Eco-Efficiency: The Business Link to Sustainable Development* (MIT Press, Cambridge, Massachusetts, 1997), p. 61.
5. Andrew Glyn, "Northern Growth and Environmental Constraints," in V. Bhaskar and Andrew Glyn, eds., *The North, The South: Ecological Constraints and the Global Economy* (Earthscan Publications, Ltd., London, 1995), p. 49.
6. *Op. cit.* 4, p. 6.
7. Stephan Schmidheiny, Rodney Chase, and Livio D. DeSimone, *Signals of Change* (World Business Council for Sustainable Development, Geneva, 1997), p. 20.
8. Xerox's European affiliate now recovers roughly two thirds of the 120,000 Xerox copiers discarded yearly in Europe, remanufacturing most of them and using some for spare parts.
9. *Op. cit.* 4, p. 75.

10. "Rank Xerox: Towards Waste-Free Products from Waste-Free Factories," *ENDS Report*, Vol. 261 (October 1996), p. 19.
11. Matt Arnold, "The Road to Sustainablilty," draft paper (World Resources Institute, Washington, D.C., 1997), pp. 6–7.
12. Susan Warren, "Polyester Trash is Pure Plastic After an 'Unzip,'" *Wall Street Journal* (November 6, 1997), p. B-1.
13. *Ibid.*
14. Robert Day, "DuPont Films: Sustainability as a Business Strategy," draft case study (World Resources Institute, Washington, D.C., 1997), p. 10.
15. Stuart L. Hart and Gautum Ahuja, "Does It Pay to Be Green? An Empirical Examination of the Relationship Between Emission Reduction and Firm Performance," *Business Strategy and the Environment*, Vol. 5, No. 1 (March 1996), pp. 30–37.
16. Groundwork Trust, "Small Firms and the Environment: A Groundwork Status Report," cited in *Financial Times* (November 15, 1995, London), p. 16. This Gallup survey of 300 small- and medium-sized enterprises in the U.K. revealed quite low levels of environmental awareness and deep scepticism over the benefits of environmental action.

Chapter 4: Critical Trends/Global Commons

Power Surge: Energy Use and Emissions Continue to Rise

1. International Energy Agency, *Energy Statistics and Balances,* on diskette (Organisation for Economic Co-Operation and Development, Paris, 1997).
2. International Energy Agency, *World Energy Outlook 1996* (Organisation for Economic Co-Operation and Development, Paris, 1996), pp. 18–19; p. 237, Table A-5.
3. World Resources Institute in collaboration with the United Nations Environment Programme, the United Nations Development Programme, and the World Bank, *World Resources 1996–97* (Oxford University Press, New York, 1996), pp. 328–330, Tables 14.2 and 14.4. For more on commercial energy production, see Data Table 15.3, Energy Production and Consumption, 1985–95.
4. *Op. cit.* 2.
5. International Energy Agency tracks world energy trends and uses this information, along with predictions of economic and population growth and the rate of new technology development, to model future energy use and carbon dioxide emissions.
6. Energy Sector Management Assistance Programme, *Annual Report 1995* (The World Bank, Washington, D.C., 1996), p. 1.
7. Jose Goldemberg, "Energy Needs in Developing Countries and Sustainability," *Science*, Vol. 269 (1995), pp. 1058–59.
8. *Op. cit.* 2, pp. 18–19, 58.
9. *Op. cit.* 2, p. 2.
10. In addition to their consumption of commercial energy, developing nations also use considerable quantities of traditional biomass fuels such as wood, crop residues, and dung. Roughly 85 percent of all biomass fuels are consumed in the developing world.
11. *Op. cit.* 2, p. 59, Table 2.2.
12. *Op. cit.* 6.
13. *Op. cit.* 2, p. 59, Table 2.2; p. 60.

14. J.T. Houghton *et al.*, eds., *Climate Change 1995: The Science of Climate Change*, published for Intergovernmental Panel on Climate Change, in collaboration with the World Meteorological Organization and the United Nations Environment Programme (Cambridge University Press, Cambridge, U.K., 1996), p. 15, Table 1.
15. *Ibid.*, p. 25.
16. *Op. cit.* 14, p. 6.
17. *Op. cit.* 14, pp. 3, 25.
18. T. Wigley, R. Richels, and J. Edmonds, "Economic and Environmental Choices in the Stabilization of Atmospheric CO_2 Concentrations," *Nature*, Vol. 379 (1996), pp. 240–243.

Proceed With Caution: Growth in The Global Motor Vehicle Fleet

1. See **Data Table 15.3**, **Energy Balances, 1985–95**.
2. International Energy Agency, *World Energy Outlook 1995* (Organisation for Economic Co-Operation and Development, Paris, 1995), p. 245.
3. WRI calculation based on compiled data from various editions of: International Energy Agency, *Energy Statistics and Balances of Non-OECD Countries* and *Energy Statistics and Balances of OECD Countries* (Organisation for Economic Co-Operation and Development, Paris, various editions).
4. American Automobile Manufacturers Association (AAMA), *World Motor Vehicle Data 1993 (AAMA, Washington, D.C., 1993)*, p. 23, and American Automobile Manufacturers Association (AAMA), *Motor Vehicle Facts and Figures 1996* (AAMA, Washington, D.C., 1996), p. 44.
5. American Automobile Manufacturers Association (AAMA), *Motor Vehicle Facts and Figures 1996* (AAMA, Washington, D.C., 1996), pp. 44–47.
6. *Op. cit.* 3.
7. *Op. cit.* 3.
8. *Op. cit.* 3.

Climate Brief: Searching for a Greenhouse Fingerprint

1. J.T. Houghton *et al.*, eds., *Climate Change 1995: The Science of Climate Change*, published for the Intergovernmental Panel on Climate Change, in collaboration with the World Meteorological Organization and the United Nations Environment Programme (Cambridge University Press, Cambridge, U.K. 1996), p. 4.
2. *Ibid.*, pp. 4–5.
3. B.D. Santer *et al.*, "A Search for Human Influences on the Thermal Structure of the Atmosphere," *Nature*, Vol. 382 (1996), pp. 39–45.
4. Richard A. Kerr, "Studies Say—Tentatively—That Greenhouse Warming is Here," *Science*, Vol. 268 (1995), pp. 1567–1568.
5. B.D. Santer *et al.*, in "Human Effect on Global Climate?" *Nature*, Vol. 384 (1996), pp. 522–524.
6. *Op. cit.* 1, pp. 427, 430, 434.
7. Thomas R. Karl *et al.*, "Indices of Climate Change for the United States," *Bulletin of the American Meteorological Society*, Vol. 77, No. 2 (1996), pp. 279–292.
8. Simon F.B. Tett *et al.*, "Human Influence on the Atmospheric Vertical Temperature Structure: Detection and Observations," *Science*, Vol. 274 (1996), pp. 1170–1173.
9. Robert Kaufmann and David Stearn, "Evidence for Human Influence on Climate From Hemispheric Temperature Relations," *Nature*, Vol. 388 (1997), pp. 39–44.

Climate Brief: Early Spring, Late Winter

1. R. Monastersky, "Warming Reaps Earlier Spring Growth," *Science News*, Vol. 150 (1996), p. 21.
2. R.B. Myneni *et al.*, "Increased Plant Growth in the Northern High Latitudes From 1981 to 1991," *Nature*, Vol. 386 (1997), pp. 698–702.

3. Inez Fung, "A Greener North," *Nature*, Vol. 386 (1997), p. 659.
4. *Op. cit.* 2.
5. William Stevens, "Greener Green Belt Bears Witness to Warming Trend," *New York Times* (April 22, 1997), p. C-3.
6. Camille Parmesan, "Climate and Species Range," *Nature*, Vol. 382 (1996), pp. 765–766.
7. William Stevens, "Western Butterfly Shifting North as Global Climate Warms," *New York Times* (September 3, 1996), p. C-4.

Negotiating Climate: Kyoto Protocol Marks a Step Forward

1. United Nations (U.N.), *Kyoto Protocol to the United Nations Framework Convention on Climate Change*, Articles 3 and 24, (U.N., New York, 1997). Available online at: http://www.unfcc.de (January 8, 1998).
2. Lelani Arris, ed., "A Brief Analysis of the Kyoto Protocol," *Global Environmental Change Report*, Vol. 9, No. 24 (1997), pp. 1–3, 6.
3. *Op. cit.* 1, Article 16.
4. *Op. cit.* 2.
5. United Nations (U.N.), United Nations Framework Convention on Climate Change, Articles 3 and 4 (U.N., New York, 1992). Available online at: http://www.unfcc.de/fccc/conv/conv.htm (January 8, 1998).
6. *Op. cit.* 1, Article 12.
7. U.S. Department of Energy, Energy Information Administration, November 12, 1997 (press release).
8. J.T. Houghton *et al.*, eds., *Climate Change 1995: The Science of Climate Change*, published for the Intergovernmental Panel on Climate Change, in collaboration with the World Meteorological Organization and the United Nations Environment Programme (Cambridge University Press, Cambridge, U.K., 1996), p. 25.

Stratospheric Ozone Depletion: Celebrating Too Soon

1. Sebastian Oberthür, *Production and Consumption of Ozone-Depleting Substances, 1986–1995* (Deutsche Gesellschaft für Technische Zusammenarbeit, Bonn, Germany, 1997), p. 65.
2. Elizabeth Cook, ed., *Ozone Protection in the United States* (World Resources Institute, Washington, D.C., 1996), p. 1.
3. F.A. Vogelsberg, "An Industry Perspective: Lessons Learned and the Cost of the CFC Phaseout," paper presented at the International Conference on Ozone Protection Technologies, Washington, D.C., October 1996, p. 1.
4. R.G. Prinn *et al.*, "Atmospheric Trends and Lifetime of CH_3CCl_3 and Global OH Concentrations," *Science*, Vol. 269 (1995), p. 187–191.
5. J.H. Butler *et al.*, "A Decrease in the Growth Rates of Atmospheric Halon Concentrations," *Nature*, Vol. 359 (1992), pp. 403–405.
6. J.W. Elkins *et al.*, "Decrease in the Growth Rates of Atmospheric Chlorofluorocarbons 11 and 12," *Nature*, Vol. 364 (1993), p. 780.
7. D.J. Hofmann, "Recovery of Antarctic Ozone Hole," *Nature*, Vol. 384 (1996), pp. 222–223.
8. M. Prather *et al.*, "The Ozone Layer: The Road Not Taken," *Nature*, Vol. 381 (1996), p. 554.
9. Duncan Brack, *International Trade and the Montreal Protocol* (Royal Institute of International Affairs, London, 1996), pp. 105–114.

10. Duncan Brack, Senior Research Fellow, Royal Institute of International Affairs, London, November 1997 (personal communication).
11. *Op. cit.* 9, p. 105.
12. *Op. cit.* 10.
13. Thomas Land, Stratospheric Ozone Protection Division, U.S. Environmental Protection Agency, Washington, D.C., November 1997 (personal communication).
14. *Op. cit.* 10.
15. *Op. cit.* 10.
16. *Op. cit.* 13.
17. *Op. cit.* 10.
18. *Op. cit.* 1, pp. vi, 35.
19. United Nations Environment Programme (UNEP), *Plan for Halon Phaseout in China*, Working paper submitted to the Executive Committee of the Multilateral Fund for the Implementation of the Montreal Protocol 20th meeting, Montreal, Canada, October 16–18, 1996, p. 8, Table 1-1.
20. J. Butler, S. Montzka, and J. Lobert, "Growth and Distribution of Halons in the Atmosphere," *Journal of Geophysical Research: Atmospheres*, Vol. 103, No. 1 (1998), p. 1503.
21. Sheng Shuo Lang, Deputy Chief Officer, Multilateral Fund for the Implementation of the Montreal Protocol, Montreal, Canada, February 1997 (personal communication).
22. United Nations Environment Programme (UNEP), OzonAction Programme, "Plasticos Molanca: A Multilateral Fund Phaseout Project," *OzonAction*, Special Supplement No. 3 (UNEP, Nairobi, 1995), p. 9.
23. *Op. cit.* 21.
24. United Nations Environment Programme (UNEP), *June 1996 Report of the Technology and Economic Assessment Panel of the Montreal Protocol on Substances That Deplete the Ozone Layer* (UNEP, Nairobi, 1996), pp. 17–19.
25. United Nations Environment Programme (UNEP), *Report of the Ninth Meeting of the Parties to the Montreal Protocol on Substances That Deplete the Ozone Layer* (UNEP, Nairobi, 1995), Item 21.

Nutrient Overload: Unbalancing the Global Nitrogen Cycle

1. Peter M. Vitousek *et al.*, "Human Alteration of the Global Nitrogen Cycle: Causes and Consequences," *Issues In Ecology*, No. 1 (February 1997), p. 2.
2. Thomas E. Jordan and Donald E. Weller, "Human Contributions to Terrestrial Nitrogen Flux: Assessing the Sources and Fates of Anthropogenic Fixed Nitrogen," *BioScience*, Vol. 46, No. 9 (1996), p. 665.
3. Gregory P. Asner, Timothy R. Seastedt, and Alan R. Townsend, "The Decoupling of Terrestrial Carbon and Nitrogen Cycles: Human Influences on Land Cover and Nitrogen Supply Are Altering Natural Biogeochemical Links in the Biosphere," *BioScience*, Vol. 47, No. 4 (1997), p. 232.
4. *Op. cit.* 1, pp. 5–6.
5. Fred Pearce, "Planet Earth Is Drowning in Nitrogen," *New Scientist* (April 12, 1997), p. 10.
6. *Op. cit.* 1, p. 10.
7. *Op. cit.* 1, p. 10.
8. *Op. cit.* 3, p. 228.
9. *Op. cit.* 1, pp. 7–9.
10. *Op. cit.* 1, pp. 9–10.
11. David Wedin and David Tilman, "Influence of Nitrogen Loading and Species Composition on Carbon Balance of Grasslands," *Science*, Vol. 274 (1996), pp. 1720–1721.
12. *Op. cit.* 1, pp. 9–10.
13. *Op. cit.* 1, p. 11.
14. Robert J. Diaz and Rutger Rosenberg, "Marine Benthic Hypoxia: A Review of Its Ecological Effects and the Behavioral Responses of Benthic Macrofauna," *Oceanography and Marine Biology: An Annual Review*, Vol. 33 (1995), p. 245.
15. "'Dead Zone' Plagues Gulf Fishermen," *The Washington Post* (August 24, 1997), p. A-1.
16. Donald M. Anderson, "Red Tides," *Scientific American* (August 1994), pp. 62–68.
17. Tony Socci, "Ecological Consequences of Human-Induced Changes in the Global Nitrogen Cycle," briefing paper for lecture by William Schlesinger and David Tillman on global nitrogen cycle, U.S. Global Change Research Program (February 26, 1997), p. 2.
18. *Op. cit.* 1, pp. 6–7.
19. *Op. cit.* 2.
20. *Op. cit.* 17.
21. *Op. cit.* 1.

Acid Rain: Downpour in Asia?

1. R. Downing, R. Ramankutty, and J. Shah, *RAINS-ASIA: An Assessment Model for Acid Deposition in Asia* (The World Bank, Washington, D.C., 1997), pp. 11, 48, 54; Table 3, p. 27.
2. Food and Agriculture Organization of the United Nations (FAO), *State of the World's Forests 1997* (FAO, Rome, 1997), p. 157.
3. European Commission and United Nations Economic Commission for Europe (EC-UN/ECE), *Forest Conditions in Europe: Results of the 1995 Survey* (EC-UN/ECE, Brussels and Geneva, 1996), pp. 23, 42–43.
4. *Op. cit.* 1, p. 38.
5. World Resources Institute in collaboration with the United Nations Environment Programme, the United Nations Development Programme, and the World Bank, *World Resources 1996–97* (Oxford University Press, New York, 1996), p. 331.
6. Tara Pattel, "Rampant Urban Pollution Blights Asia's Crops," *New Scientist* (June 14, 1997), p. 11.
7. *Op. cit.* 1, p. 6.
8. *Op. cit.* 1, pp. 1–3;, Figure 11, p. 11.
9. *Op. cit.* 1, pp. 38–39, 54.
10. *Op. cit.* 1, pp. 3, 39.
11. *Op. cit.* 1, pp. 48, 50.
12. *Op. cit.* 1, pp. 38–51.
13. David Spurgeon, "Canada 'Still Has a Long Way to Go' in Effective Control of Acid Rain," *Nature*, Vol. 390 (1997), p. 6.
14. Commission of the European Communities (CEC), *Progress Report from the Commission on the Implementation of the European Community Programme of Policy and Action in Relation to the Environment and Sustainable Development* (CEC, Brussels, 1996), p. 56.
15. Jocelyn Kaiser, "Acid Rain's Dirty Business: Stealing Minerals from Soil," Science, Vol. 272 (April 12, 1996), p. 198.
16. D.W. Schindler *et al.*, "Consequences of Climate Warming and Lake Acidification for UV-B Penetration in North American Boreal Lakes," *Nature*, Vol. 379 (1996), pp. 705–708.
17. Norman D. Yan *et al.*, "Increased UV-B Penetration in a Lake Owing to Drought-Induced Acidification," *Nature*, Vol. 381 (1996), pp. 141–143.
18. *Op. cit.* 16.

Chapter 4: Critical Trends/Resources at Risk

Deforestation: The Global Assault Continues

1. Food and Agriculture Organization of the United Nations (FAO), *State of the World's Forests 1997* (FAO, Rome, 1997), p. 16.
2. *Ibid.*, p. 17.
3. The basis of some experts' objections to FAO's recent deforestation estimates is that these estimates derive primarily from mathematical models based mostly on human population trends, with few on-the-ground forest inventories for corroboration.
4. Brazilian National Institute for Space Research (INPE), *Average Annual Deforestation Rate in the Legal Amazon*. Available online at: http://www.inpe.br/amz-04.htm (January 29, 1998).
5. Stephan Schwartzman, *Fires In the Amazon: An Analysis of NOAA-12 Satellite Data, 1996-1997* (Environmental Defense Fund, Washington, D.C., 1997), pp. 1–2.
6. European Union GIS/Remote Sensing Expert Group, *Fires in Indonesia, September 1997*, a report to the European Union (European Union, Brussels, 1997), pp. 1–3.
7. Charles Barber, Asia/Pacific Representative, World Resources Institute, Manila, January 1998 (personal communication).
8. Robert Repetto, *The Forest for the Trees? Government Policies and the Misuse of Forest Resources* (World Resources Institute, Washington, D.C., 1988), pp. 43–51, 73–80.
9. Estimates are approximate due to the difficulty of separating plantations from natural forests in developed countries. *Op. cit.* 1, p. 140.
10. *Op. cit.* 1, p. 17.
11. United Nations Economic Commission for Europe/European Commission (EC-UN/ECE), *Forest Condition in Europe: Results of the 1995 Survey* (EC-UN/ECE, Brussels, 1996), p. 10, 121.
12. United Nations Environment Programme (UNEP), *Global Environment Outlook* (Oxford University Press, New York, 1997), pp. 240–241, Figures 4.16 and 4.17.

Fragmenting Forests: The Loss Of Large Frontier Forests

1. Dirk Bryant, Daniel Nielsen, and Laura Tangley, *The Last Frontier Forests: Ecosystems and Economies on the Edge* (World Resources Institute, Washington, D.C., 1997), p. 1.
2. Walt Reid and Kenton Miller, *Keeping Options Alive: The Scientific Basis for Conserving Biodiversity* (World Resources Institute, Washington, D.C., 1989), p. 15.
3. Calculated by multiplying regional frontier forest area by per hectare carbon estimates for forest areas, presented in R.K. Dixon *et al.*, "Carbon Pools and Flux of Global Forest Ecosystems," *Science*, Vol. 263; pp. 185–190. Dixon *et al.'s* estimates are for closed and open forests for both soil and aboveground vegetation. For this reason, and because these averages include degraded forest (which contains less carbon than intact forest), the text figure on total carbon stored in frontier forest is likely an underestimate. Soil carbon figures include peat. We used averaged per hectare carbon figures in estimating carbon stored in frontier forests that contain more than one dominant forest type (e.g., temperate and boreal forest).
4. *Op. cit.* 1, pp. 19, 21.
5. *Op. cit.* 1, p. 17.

6. *Op. cit.* 1, pp. 19, 25.
7. *Op. cit.* 1, p. 15.

Water: Critical Shortages Ahead?

1. World Meteorological Organization (WMO), *Comprehensive Assessment of the Freshwater Resources of the World* (WMO, Geneva, 1997), p. 9.
2. *Ibid.*, p. 10.
3. Raskin *et al.*, "Water Futures: Assessment of Long-Range Patterns and Problems," *Comprehensive Assessment of the Freshwater Resources of the World* (Stockholm Environment Institute, Stockholm, 1997), p. 23.
4. *Op. cit.* 1, pp. 1, 14.
5. *Op. cit.* 1, pp. 1, 20-21.
6. *Op. cit.* 1, pp. 1, 21.
7. European Environment Agency, *Environment in the European Union 1995: Report for the Review of the Fifth Environmental Action Programme* (Office for the Official Publications of the European Communities, Luxembourg, 1995), p. 81.
8. World Health Organization (WHO), *Health and Environment in Sustainable Development: Five Years After the Earth Summit* (WHO, Geneva, 1997), pp. 54–55.
9. United Nations Environment Programme (UNEP), Division of Environment Information and Assessment, *Characterization and Assessment of Groundwater Quality Concerns in Asia-Pacific Region* (UNEP, Nairobi, 1996), p. 3.
10. Sandra Postel, "Water and Agriculture," in *Water in Crisis: A Guide to the World's Freshwater Resources*, Peter H. Gleick, ed.(Oxford University Press, New York, 1993), p. 60.
11. John Langford, "An Australian Approach to the Sustainable Use of Water," paper presented at Workshop on Policy Measures for Changing Consumption Patterns, August 30–September 1, 1995 (Ministry of Environment, Kwacheon, Republic of Korea, 1995).
12. *Op. cit.* 10, p. 60.
13. Mark W. Rosegrant, *Water Resources in the Twenty-First Century: Challenges and Implications for Action*, Food, Agriculture, and the Environment Discussion Paper 20 (International Food Policy Research Institute, Washington, D.C., 1997), p. 4.
14. *Op. cit.* 10, p. 61.
15. Ismael Serageldin, *Towards Sustainable Management of Water Resources* (The World Bank, Washington, D.C., 1995), p. 14.

The Decline of Freshwater Ecosystems

1. The World Conservation Union (IUCN), *1996 IUCN Red List of Threatened Animals* (IUCN, Gland, Switzerland, 1996), pp. Intro-24.
2. Don E. McAllister, Andrew L. Hamilton, and Brian Harvey, "Global Freshwater Biodiversity: Striving for the Integrity of Freshwater Ecosystems," *Sea Wind*, Vol. 11, No. 3 (1997), p. 7.
3. Janet Abramovitz, "Imperiled Waters, Impoverished Future: The Decline of Freshwater Ecosystems," Worldwatch Paper No. 128 (Worldwatch Institute, Washington, D.C., 1996), p. 59.
4. *Ibid.*, p. 5.
5. Peter B. Moyle and Robert A. Leidy, "Loss of Biodiversity in Aquatic Ecosystems: Evidence from Fish Faunas," in *Conservation Biology, the Theory and Practice of Nature Conservation, Preservation, and*

Management, Peggy L. Fiedler and Subodh K. Jain, eds. (Chapman and Hall, New York, 1992), p. 130.
6. Peter H. Gleick, ed., *Water in Crisis: A Guide to the World's Freshwater Resources* (Oxford University Press, New York, 1993), p. 5.
7. *Op. cit.* 5, p. 130.
8. Food and Agriculture Organization of the United Nations (FAO), *The State of World Fisheries and Aquaculture, 1996* (FAO, Rome, 1997), p. 5.
9. Sandra Postel, "Dividing the Waters: Food Security, Ecosystem Health, and the New Politics of Scarcity," Worldwatch Paper No. 132 (Worldwatch Institute, Washington, D.C., 1996), p. 29.
10. *Op. cit.* 3, p. 15.
11. *Op. cit.* 3, p. 13.
12. *Op. cit.* 3, p. 13.
13. Maurice Kottelat and Tony Whitten, "Freshwater Biodiversity in Asia With Special Reference to Fish," World Bank Technical Paper No. 343 (The World Bank, Washington, D.C., 1996), pp. 7, 20.
14. Denis D. Gray, "Dam Builders Eye Mekong: Poverty, Energy, Thirst May Tame Mighty River," *Washington Times* (May 26, 1997), p. A14.
15. *Op. cit.* 3, pp. 29–30.
16. *Op. cit.* 3, p. 21.
17. Peter Muello, "South American Water Project Hits Ecological Snags," *Washington Times* (May 26, 1997), p. A14.
18. *Op. cit.* 5, pp. 155–156.
19. H. Reed, "Caviar Trade Threatens Caspian Sea Sturgeon," TRAFFIC USA. Available online at: http://www.wwf.org/new/traffic/dec96/trafcav.htm (December 1997).
20. *Op. cit.* 5, pp. 136–137.
21. *Op. cit.* 5, pp. 151–152.
22. *Op. cit.* 3, pp. 48–49.
23. Marco Ehrlich, Environmental Specialist, Inter-American Development Bank, Washington, D.C., February 9, 1998, (personal communication).
24. Marlise Simons, "Big, Bold Effort Brings Danube Back to Life," *New York Times* (October 1, 1997), p. 1, sec. 1.
25. *Op. cit.* 9, p. 34.

Valuing Ecosystem Services

1. Robert Costanza *et al.*, "The Value of the World's Ecosystem Services and Natural Capital," *Nature*, Vol. 387 (1997), p. 259.
2. Mark Sagoff, "Can We Put a Price on Nature's Services?," The Institute for Philosophy and Public Policy. Available online at: http//www.puaf.umd.edu/ippp/nature.htm (November 28, 1997).
3. *Op. cit.* 1, p. 255.
4. *Op. cit.* 1, p. 259.
5. Robert Goodland and Herman Daly, "Environmental Sustainability: Universal and Nonnegotiable," *Ecological Applications*, Vol. 6, No. 4 (1996), p. 1016.
6. *Op. cit.* 1, pp. 253–260.
7. *Op. cit.* 1, p. 256, Table 2.
8. *Op. cit.* 1, p. 259.
9. Stuart L. Pimm, "The Value of Everything," *Nature*, Vol. 387 (1997), p. 232.
10. Richard M. Stapleton, *Protecting the Source: Land Conservation and the Future of America's Drinking Water* (The Trust for Public Land, San Francisco, 1997), pp. 5–6.
11. E.B. Barbier *et al.*, "An Economic Valuation of Wetland Benefits," in *The Hadejia-Nguru Wetlands: Environment, Economy, and Sustainable Development*

Global Environmental Trends

of a Sahelian Flood Plain Wetland, G.E. Hollis *et al.*, eds. (World Conservation Union-IUCN, Gland, Switzerland, 1993).

Coral Reefs: Assessing the Threat

1. Stephen C. Jameson *et al.*, *State of the Reefs: Regional and Global Perspectives*, Background Paper, Executive Secretariat, International Coral Reef Initiative (U.S. National Oceanic and Atmospheric Administration, Washington, D.C., 1995), p. 24.
2. Clive Wilkinson, "Coral Reefs of the World Are Facing Widespread Devastation: Can We Prevent This Through Sustainable Management Practices?," in *Proceedings of the 7th International Coral Reef Symposium*, Vol. 1 (University of Guam, Guam, 1993), pp. 11–21.
3. Elizabeth Pennisi, "Brighter Prospects for the World's Coral Reefs?," *Science*, Vol. 277 (July 25, 1997), p. 492.
4. Lauretta Burke *et al.*, *Reefs at Risk: A Map-Based Indicator of Potential Threats to the World's Coral Reefs*, draft report (World Resources Institute, Washington, D.C., 1998), pp. 3–11.
5. *Ibid.*, p. 2.
6. *Op. cit.* 4, p. 9.
7. Terrence P. Hughes, "Catastrophes, Phase Shifts, and Large-Scale Degradation of a Caribbean Coral Reef," *Science*, Vol. 265 (September 9, 1994), p. 1547.
8. *Op. cit.* 3, pp. 491–493.
9. Robert H. Richmond, "Coral Reef Resources: Pollution's Impacts," *Forum for Applied Research and Public Policy* (Spring 1994), p. 55.
10. Global Environment Facility, "The Hashemite Kingdom of Jordan: Gulf of Aqaba Environmental Action Plan," Project Document No. 15290JO, Global Environment Division, Environment Department (The World Bank, Washington, D.C., 1996), p. 3.
11. Gustav Paualy, "Diversity and Distribution of Reef Organisms," in *Life and Death of Coral Reefs*, Charles Birkeland, ed. (Chapman and Hall, New York, 1997), pp. 302–304.
12. David Malakoff, "Extinction on the High Seas," *Science*, Vol. 277 (July 25, 1997), p. 487.
13. *Op. cit.* 1, p. 24.
14. Herman Cesar, *Economic Analysis of Indonesian Coral Reefs*, (The World Bank, Washington, D.C., 1996), p. 16.
15. *Op. cit.* 1, p. 24.
16. Charles Barber and Vaughan R. Pratt, *Sullied Seas: Strategies for Combating Cyanide Fishing in Southeast Asia and Beyond* (World Resources Institute and International Marine Life Alliance, Washington, D.C., and Manila, 1997), p. 4.
17. Clive Wilkinson, Coordinator, Global Coral Reef Monitoring Network, Townsville MC, Australia, December 1997 (personal communication).
18. *Op. cit.* 4, p. 23.
19. *Op. cit.* 4, p. 25.

Diminishing Returns: World Fisheries Under Pressure

1. Food and Agriculture Organization of the United Nations (FAO), *The State of World Fisheries and Aquaculture, 1996* (FAO, Rome, 1997), p. 13.
2. R. Grainger and S. Garcia, *Chronicles of Marine Fishery Landings (1950–1994): Trend Analysis and Fisheries Potential*, FAO Fisheries Technical Paper 359 (Food and Agriculture Organization of the United Nations, Rome, 1996), pp. 8–9, 42–43.
3. *Ibid.*, p. 31.
4. *Op. cit.* 2, pp. 10–11.

5. William Stevens, "Fierce Debate Erupts Over Degree of Peril Facing Ocean Species," *New York Times* (September 17, 1996), p. C-1.
6. Meryl Williams, *The Transition in the Contribution of Living Aquatic Resources to Food Security*, Food, Agriculture, and the Environment Discussion Paper 13 (International Food Policy Research Institute, Washington, D.C., 1996), pp. 3, 24.
7. *Op. cit.* 1, pp. 24–27.
8. *Op. cit.* 6, pp. 25–26.
9. *Op. cit.* 6, pp. 27–28.
10. S. Garcia and R. Grainger, "Fisheries Management and Sustainability: A New Perspective of an Old Problem," paper prepared for the Second World Fisheries Congress, Brisbane, Australia, July 1996 (Food and Agriculture Organization of the United Nations, Rome, 1996), p. 13.
11. Food and Agriculture Organization of the United Nations (FAO), "Review of the State of World Fishery Resources: Marine Fisheries," FAO Fisheries Circular No. 884 (FAO, Rome, 1995), p. 22.
12. *Op. cit.* 2, p. 48.
13. Edward Trippel, "Age at Maturity as a Stress Indicator in Fisheries," *Bioscience*, Vol. 45, No. 11 (1995), pp. 768–69.
14. David Spurgeon, "Canada's Cod Leaves Science in Hot Water," *Nature*, Vol. 386 (1997), p. 107.
15. Anthony DePalma, "Newfoundland to Ease Ban on Fishing; Some Say It's Too Soon," *New York Times* (April 18, 1997), p. A-7.
16. *Op. cit.* 1, p. 15.
17. "EU: Ministers Agree on Fishing Limits," *Greenwire*, Vol. 6, No. 234 (April 16, 1997), Item number 16.
18. Alison Maitland, "Unilever in Fight to Save Global Fisheries," *Financial Times* (February 22, 1996, London).
19. Michael Sutton and Caroline Whitfield, "The Marine Stewardship Council: New Hope for Marine Fisheries," background paper (World Wide Fund for Nature and Unilever, London, October 1996), p. 2.

Bioinvasions: Stemming The Tide of Exotic Species

1. Ian A.W. Macdonald *et al.*, "Wildlife Conservation and the Invasion of Nature Reserves by Introduced Species: A Global Perspective," in *Biological Invasions: A Global Perspective*, SCOPE 37, J.A. Drake *et al.*, eds. (John Wiley & Sons Ltd., Chichester, U.K., 1989), pp. 232–233.
2. Edward O. Wilson, *The Diversity of Life* (W.W. Norton & Co., New York, 1992), p. 253.
3. Andrew Cohen, "Stopping Ballast Water Invaders," *Native Species Network*, Vol. 1, Issue 2 (Spring 1996), p. 1.
4. Jeff Crooks and Michael E. Soulé, "Lag Times in Population Explosions of Invasive Species: Causes and Implications," in *Proceedings of the Norway/UN Conference on Alien Species, The Trondheim Conferences on Biodiversity, July 1–5, 1996*, O.T. Sandlund *et al.*, eds. (Directorate for Nature Management/Norwegian Institute for Nature Research, Trondheim, Norway, 1996), p. 39.
5. James T. Carlton, "Invasions in the World's Seas: Six Centuries of Reorganizing Earth's Marine Life," in *Proceedings of the Norway/UN Conference on Alien Species, The Trondheim Conferences on Biodiversity, July 1–5, 1996*, O.T. Sandlund *et al.*, eds. (Directorate for Nature Management/Norwegian Institute for Nature Research, Trondheim, Norway, 1996), p. 100.
6. O.T. Sandlund *et al.*, eds., *Proceedings of the Norway/UN Conference on Alien Species, The Trondheim Conferences on Biodiversity, July 1–5, 1996*

(Directorate for Nature Management/Norwegian Institute for Nature Research, Trondheim, Norway, 1996).
7. Jeffrey A. McNeely, "The Great Reshuffling: How Alien Species Help Feed the Global Economy," in *Proceedings of the Norway/UN Conference on Alien Species, The Trondheim Conferences on Biodiversity, July 1–5, 1996*, O.T. Sandlund *et al.*, eds. (Directorate for Nature Management/Norwegian Institute for Nature Research, Trondheim, Norway, 1996), p. 53.
8. *Op. cit.* 5, p. 100.
9. *Op. cit.* 7, p. 53.
10. Rosamond Naylor, "Invasions in Agriculture: Assessing the Cost of the Golden Apple Snail in Asia," *Ambio*, Vol. 25, No. 7 (1996), p. 443.
11. Peter Jenkins, "Free Trade and Exotic Species Introductions," in *Proceedings of the Norway/UN Conference on Alien Species, The Trondheim Conferences on Biodiversity, July 1–5, 1996*, O.T. Sandlund *et al.*, eds. (Directorate for Nature Management/Norwegian Institute for Nature Research, Trondheim, Norway, 1996), p. 145.
12. *Op. cit.* 10, p. 443.
13. H.A. Mooney and J.A. Drake, "Biological Invasions: A SCOPE Program Overview," in *Biological Invasions: A Global Perspective*, SCOPE 37, J.A. Drake *et al.*, eds. (John Wiley & Sons Ltd., Chichester, U.K., 1989), pp. 499–500.
14. Vernon H. Heywood, "Patterns, Extents, and Modes of Invasions by Terrestrial Plants," in *Biological Invasions: A Global Perspective*, SCOPE 37, J.A. Drake *et al.*, eds. (John Wiley & Sons Ltd., Chichester, U.K., 1989), p. 40.
15. Michael J. Bean, "Legal Authorities for Controlling Alien Species: A Survey of Tools and Their Effectiveness," in *Proceedings of the Norway/UN Conference on Alien Species, The Trondheim Conferences on Biodiversity, July 1–5, 1996*, O.T. Sandlund *et al.*, eds. (Directorate for Nature Management/Norwegian Institute for Nature Research, Trondheim, Norway, 1996), pp. 204–210.
16. Thorbjørn Berntsen, "Opening Speech," in *Proceedings of the Norway/UN Conference on Alien Species, The Trondheim Conferences on Biodiversity, July 1–5, 1996*, O.T. Sandlund *et al.*, eds. (Directorate for Nature Management/Norwegian Institute for Nature Research, Trondheim, Norway, 1996), p. 8.
17. *Op. cit.* 11, pp. 145–147.
18. *Op. cit.* 5, p. 101.
19. U.S. National Research Council Committee on Ship's Ballast Operations, *Stemming the Tide: Controlling Introductions of Nonindigenous Species by Ships' Ballast Water* (National Academy Press, Washington, D.C., 1996), pp. 59–60.
20. The White House Office of the Press Secretary, "Statement by the President," October 26, 1996.
21. National Academy of Sciences, *Stemming the Tide: Controlling Introductions of Nonindigenous Species by Ships' Ballast Water*, National Research Council Committee on Ship's Ballast Operations of the National Academy of Sciences (National Academy Press, Washington, D.C., 1996), p. 59.
22. Australian Quarantine and Inspection Service (AQIS), "Australian Ballast Water Management Strategy," AQIS. Available online at: http://www.dpie.gov.au/aqis/homepage/inadvice/bstrategy.html (June 6, 1997).
23. Harold A. Mooney, "The SCOPE Initiatives: The Background and Plans for a Global Strategy on Invasive Species," in *Proceedings of the Norway/UN Conference on Alien Species, The Trondheim Conferences on Biodiversity, July 1–5, 1996*, O.T. Sandlund *et al.*, eds. (Directorate for Nature Management/Norwegian Institute for Nature Research, Trondheim, Norway, 1996), pp. 30–33.

24. Michael N. Clout and Sarah J. Lowe, "Reducing the Impacts of Invasive Species on Global Biodiversity: The Role of the IUCN Invasive Species Specialist Group," in *Proceedings of the Norway/UN Conference on Alien Species, The Trondheim Conferences on Biodiversity, July 1–5, 1996*, O.T. Sandlund *et al.*, eds. (Directorate for Nature Management/Norwegian Institute for Nature Research, Trondheim, Norway, 1996), pp. 34–38.

PART III

Data Tables

OVERVIEW

This section presents some of the data required to build a basic picture of the state of the Earth in its human, economic, and environmental dimensions. Where possible, the data tables assembled here show how these dimensions have changed over time. In an increasingly interdependent world, a picture of the whole is needed to understand the interactions of human development, population growth, economic growth, and the environment. Managing communities, nations, or global resources for sustainable development requires this same information.

Our understanding of the state of the Earth, including its human and natural resources, their spatial extent, and their rate of change, remains fragmented in part because no single organization is charged with assembling such information. As a consequence, *World Resources 1998–99* depends on the work of a variety of people and organizations. Some of these organizations, especially the United Nations (U.N.)-affiliated organizations, are given specific mandates for information gathering from their member countries. The U.N. Food and Agricultural Organization (FAO), for example, is charged with assembling data on agricultural production.

Others, such as the Organisation for Economic Co-Operation and Development's (OECD's) International Energy Administration, expand their mandate to describe the energy balances of non-member as well as member countries. In some instances, several international organizations come together to create an institution to generate essential information. For example, the World Conservation Monitoring Centre (WCMC) in Cambridge, United Kingdom, provides essential information on the status of animal and plant species. Individual na-

tions provide the locus for some information. The United States funds the Carbon Dioxide Information Analysis Center (CDIAC), which houses much of the basic data related to atmospheric chemistry and greenhouse gases.

Yet, for many areas of information, there are no institutions with a viable mandate for assembling all the available national data. Data on urban air quality, for example, exist for many cities in many countries, but no single organization is charged with assembling that information. The World Resources Institute has assembled such data where possible. For many more areas, no data even exist. For instance, data on the health of the world's remaining wild grasslands are not collected at a national level, much less compiled internationally.

The sources of these data tables are varied but depend primarily on the cooperation of many international organizations. World economic data are maintained at the World Bank, which has supplied the basic economic indicators used in this edition, including data on national income, debt, investment, and the prices of commodities. The U.N. Population Division is the source of data on population and population parameters (rates of growth, fertility, and mortality). The World Health Organization (WHO) provides the bulk of information on public health issues and infectious disease. The FAO is the source for data in this book on agriculture, irrigation, land use, forestry, deforestation, water, and fisheries. The U.N. Statistical Division has provided data on energy production and consumption. Other important data sources include WCMC (biodiversity information), CDIAC (greenhouse gases),OECD (air pollution), the International Energy Agency (energy balances), and the U.N. Children's Fund (UNICEF) (children's health). Many other organizations and individuals have also helped prepare these tables.

Each data table in this section is accompanied by an extensive listing of sources and technical notes. These technical notes attempt to provide sufficient information to enable readers to understand the general method used to generate the data and to assess their relative quality. The data compiled here vary in quality (coverage, accuracy, and precision) from topic to topic and country to country. For example, estimates of sectoral energy use are far superior to estimates of sectoral water use, and in both instances, the data for developed countries are based on much more detailed monitoring than the data for most developing nations. Some data, such as greenhouse gas emissions, are modeled rather than measured directly. Where possible, WRI has included the Internet address from which to download data directly from the original data supplier. WRI has also provided information on data quality so that users can carefully assess the appropriateness of these data for any particular use or analysis. An additional source of data is the *World Resources* *1998–99 Database Diskette*, which contains all the vital economic, population, and environmental resource statistics found in the print edition of *World Resources 1998–99* plus an expanded 20-year time series for many variables.

In the following tables:
• "0" is either zero or less than one half the unit of measure;
• "X" is information not available or not applicable; and
• negative numbers are shown in parentheses.

Regional summaries include the countries as listed or, in the case of economic regions (such as developed and developing), as defined by the data source. These latter definitions may vary between tables. Regional time-series data are sometimes unavailable due to difficulties in aggregating or disaggregating information from the countries of the former Soviet Union.

*C*hapter 6

Economic Indicators

Data Table 6.1

Gross National and Domestic Product Estimates, 1995

Sources: The World Bank and United Nations Population Division

	Gross National Product (GNP) 1995 (Atlas method)		Gross Domestic Product (GDP) Exchange Rate Based (GDP) (1995 US$)		Purchasing Power Parity (PPP) (1995 Int$)		Average Annual Growth Rate (percent) GDP		Distribution of GDP, 1995 (percent)		
	Total (million US$)	Per Capita (US$)	Total (million US$)	Per Capita (US$)	Total (million Int$)	Per Capita (Int$)	1975-85	1985-95	Agriculture	Industry	Services
WORLD	27,687,323	4,880	27,846,241	4,896					5 a	33 b	63 b
AFRICA											
Algeria	44,609	1,600	41,435	1,474	157,410	5,600	6.1	0.3	13	47	41
Angola	4,422	410	3,722	344	12,655	1,170	X	0.4	12	59	28
Benin	2,034	370	1,522 a	289 a	8,730 a	1,660 a	3.7	X	34 a	12 a	53 a
Botswana	4,381	3,020	4,318	2,978	8,164	5,630	10.8	7.1	5	46	48
Burkina Faso	2,417	230	2,325	222	8,278	790	4.5	2.9	34 a	27 a	39 a
Burundi	984	160	1,062	175	3,881	640	4.6	0.9	56	18	26
Cameroon	8,615	650	7,931	601	30,342	2,300	8.0	(2.1)	39	23	38
Central African Rep	1,123	340	1,128	345	3,535	1,080	1.4	1.0	44 a	13 a	43 a
Chad	1,144	180	1,138	180	4,498	710	2.4	2.6	44 b	22 b	35 b
Congo, Dem Rep	5,313	120	8,770 c	243 c	17,056 c	473 c	X	X	30 c	33 c	36 c
Congo, Rep	1,784	680	2,163	834	6,431	2,480	8.4	(0.3)	10	38	51
Côte d'Ivoire	9,248	660	10,069	735	24,238	1,770	3.5	0.1	31	20	50
Egypt	45,507	790	47,349	763	241,553	3,890	9.5	2.2	20	21	59
Equatorial Guinea	152	380	169	421	X	X	X	X	50 a	33 a	17 a
Eritrea	X	X	X	X	X	X	X	X	11	20	69
Ethiopia	5,722	100	5,287	94	25,946	460	X	3.6	57 a	10 a	33 a
Gabon	3,759	3,490	4,691	4,360	3,943 d	3,983 d	1.9	(0.5)	8 a	52 a	40 a
Gambia, The	354	320	384	346	1,055	950	3.4	2.6	28 a	15 a	58 a
Ghana	6,719	390	6,315	364	35,196	2,030	(0.9)	4.4	46	16	38
Guinea	3,593	550	3,686	502	3,694 d	577 d	X	X	24	31	45
Guinea-Bissau	265	250	257	240	855	800	2.6	3.7	46	24	30
Kenya	7,583	280	9,095	335	38,825	1,430	4.5	3.5	29	17	54
Lesotho	1,519	770	1,029	508	2,513	1,240	4.0	7.0	11	40	49
Liberia	X	X	1,202 c	467 c	X	X	0.2	X	X	X	X
Libya	X	X	21,864 c	4,984 c	X	X	1.0	X	X	X	X
Madagascar	3,178	230	3,198	215	10,114	680	0.2	0.9	34	13	53
Malawi	1,623	170	1,465	151	7,448	770	4.0	2.1	42	27	31
Mali	2,410	250	2,431	225	6,045	560	2.6	4.3	46	17	37
Mauritania	1,049	460	1,068	470	3,684	1,620	1.1	3.1	27 b	30 b	43 b
Mauritius	3,815	3,380	3,919	3,508	14,823	13,270	X	5.9	9	33	58
Morocco	29,545	1,110	32,412	1,222	92,038	3,470	5.4	2.6	14	33	53
Mozambique	1,353	80	1,469	85	15,707	910	X	5.8	33 a	12 a	55 a
Namibia	3,098	2,000	3,033	1,974	6,298	4,100	X	3.2	14 a	29 a	56 a
Niger	1,961	220	1,860	203	6,863	750	0.8	1.4	39 b	18 b	44 b
Nigeria	28,411	260	40,477	362	146,355	1,310	0.4	3.8	28	53	18
Rwanda	1,128	180	1,128	218	2,799	540	6.1	(4.8)	37	17	46
Senegal	5,070	600	4,867	586	15,211	1,830	2.9	2.8	20	18	62
Sierra Leone	762	180	824	196	2,601	620	2.5	(1.5)	42	27	31
Somalia	X	X	917 e	106 e	7,923 c	933 c	6.2	X	X	X	X
South Africa	130,918	3,160	136,035	3,281	217,277	5,240	2.3	1.1	5	31	64
Sudan	X	X	5,989 d	239 d	17,852 f	726 f	3.6	X	X	X	X
Swaziland	1,051	1,170	1,073	1,252	2,528	2,950	3.8	3.5	X	X	X
Tanzania	3,703	120	3,602	120	20,117	670	X	3.6	58	17	24
Togo	1,266	310	1,263	309	4,739	1,160	2.5	0.9	38 a	21 a	41 a
Tunisia	16,369	1,820	18,035	2,007	47,272	5,260	5.9	3.3	12	29	59
Uganda	4,668	240	5,655	287	29,337	1,490	X	5.7	50	14	36
Zambia	3,605	400	4,073	504	8,000	990	0.1	0.5	22	40	37
Zimbabwe	5,933	540	6,522	583	23,947	2,140	2.6	2.1	15 b	36 b	48 b
EUROPE											
Albania	2,199	670	2,192	648	X	X	X	3.3	56	21	23
Austria	216,547	26,890	233,427	29,015	171,519	21,320	2.2	2.5	2 a	34 a	63 a
Belarus, Rep	21,356	2,070	20,561	1,986	43,996	4,250	X	X	13	35	52
Belgium	250,710	24,710	269,081	26,571	218,338	21,560	1.8	2.1	2 e	30 e	68 e
Bosnia and Herzegovina	X	X	X	X	X	X	X	X	X	X	X
Bulgaria	11,225	1,330	12,366	1,453	39,992	4,700	X	(1.6)	13	34	53
Croatia, Rep	15,508	3,250	18,081	4,014	X	X	X	X	12	25	62
Czech Rep	39,990	3,870	44,772	4,362	100,270	9,770	X	(0.8)	6 a	39 a	55 a
Denmark	156,027	29,890	172,220	32,973	114,854	21,990	2.5	1.7	4 a	29 a	67 a
Estonia, Rep	6,136	2,860	60,766	40,838	6,279	4,220	X	(4.2)	8	28	64
Finland	105,174	20,580	125,432	24,561	94,684	18,540	2.8	1.3	6 a	37 a	57 a
France	1,451,051	24,990	1,536,089	26,437	1,230,643	21,180	2.3	2.1	2 a	27 a	71 a
Germany	2,252,343	27,510	2,415,764	29,607	1,641,671	20,120	X	X	1 f	38	61
Greece	85,885	8,210	90,550	8,662	121,685	11,640	2.9	1.3	21 a	36 a	43 a
Hungary	42,129	4,120	43,712	4,325	67,508	6,680	3.1	(0.2)	8	33	59
Iceland	6,686	24,950	7,052	26,215	5,671	21,080	4.2	2.0	12 f	28	60
Ireland	52,765	14,710	60,780	17,141	63,119	17,800	4.0	4.5	8 f	10	82
Italy	1,088,085	19,020	1,086,932	19,001	1,154,377	20,180	2.8	2.1	3 a	31	66
Latvia, Rep	5,708	2,270	5,689	2,243	8,521	3,360	4.1	(5.1)	9	31	60
Lithuania, Rep	7,070	1,900	7,089	1,897	15,392	4,120	X	X	11	36	53
Macedonia, FYR	1,813	860	1,975	937	X	X	X	X	X	X	X
Moldova, Rep	3,996	920	3,518	793	17,434 f	3,976 f	X	X	50	28	22
Netherlands	371,039	24,000	395,900	25,572	307,782	19,880	1.9	2.5	3 a	27 a	70 a
Norway	136,077	31,250	145,954	33,692	97,253	22,450	4.3	2.5	3 f	35	62
Poland, Rep	107,829	2,790	117,663	3,052	209,365	5,430	X	0.8	6	39	54
Portugal	96,689	9,740	102,337	10,427	124,552	12,690	2.5	3.0	6 e	38 e	56 e
Romania	33,488	1,480	35,533	1,563	99,776	4,390	X	(2.4)	21	40	39
Russian Federation	331,948	2,240	346,383	2,333	715,577	4,820	4.4	(3.9)	7 a	38 a	55 a
Slovak Rep	15,848	2,950	17,414	3,262	19,217	3,600	X	(0.8)	6	33	61
Slovenia, Rep	16,328	8,200	18,550	9,636	X	X	X	X	5	39	57
Spain	532,347	13,580	558,617	14,097	585,687	14,780	1.7	2.9	3 d	33 d	64 d
Sweden	209,720	23,750	228,679	26,022	169,696	19,310	1.8	1.2	2 a	32 a	66 a
Switzerland	286,014	40,630	300,508	41,935	178,433	24,900	0.8	1.4	X	X	X
Ukraine	84,084	1,630	80,127	1,548	126,287	2,440	X	X	18	42	41
United Kingdom	1,094,734	18,700	1,105,822	19,040	1,120,925	19,300	1.8	2.2	2 a	32 a	66 a
Yugoslavia, Fed Rep	X	X	X	X	55,523 e	5,467 e	X	X	X	X	X

| | Gross National Product (GNP) 1995 (Atlas method) | | Gross Domestic Product (GDP) | | | | Average Annual Growth Rate (percent) | | Distribution of GDP, 1995 (percent) | | |
| | | | Exchange Rate Based (GDP) (1995 US$) | | Purchasing Power Parity (PPP) (1995 Int$) | | GDP | | | | |
	Total (million US$)	Per Capita (US$)	Total (million US$)	Per Capita (US$)	Total (million Int$)	Per Capita (Int$)	1975-85	1985-95	Agriculture	Industry	Services
NORTH AMERICA											
Canada	573,695	19,380	568,928	19,350	643,904	21,900	3.6	2.2	3 d	31 d	66 d
United States	7,100,007	26,980	6,952,020	26,026	7,206,763	26,980	2.7	2.5	2 b	26 b	72 b
CENTRAL AMERICA											
Belize	560	2,630	578	2,714	1,197	5,620	4.0	6.5	20 a	28 b	53 b
Costa Rica	8,884	2,610	9,233	2,696	20,270	5,920	2.9	4.5	17	24	58
Cuba	X	X	X	X	X	X	X	X	X	X	X
Dominican Rep	11,390	1,460	11,277	1,442	29,258	3,740	3.6	3.6	15	22	64
El Salvador	9,057	1,610	9,471	1,673	14,721	2,600	(1.1)	4.0	14	22	65
Guatemala	14,255	1,340	14,489	1,364	34,943	3,290	2.4	3.3	25 a	19 a	56 a
Haiti	1,777	250	2,043	287	6,554	920	2.0	(2.8)	44 a	12 a	44 a
Honduras	3,566	600	3,937	696	11,534	2,040	4.6	3.2	21	33	46
Jamaica	3,803	1,510	4,406	1,785	12,167	4,930	(1.4)	3.6	9	38	53
Mexico	304,596	3,320	250,038	2,743	615,229	6,750	4.7	1.0	8	26	67
Nicaragua	1,659	380	1,911	463	10,019	2,430	X	X	33 a	20 a	46 a
Panama	7,235	2,750	7,413	2,818	16,470	6,260	4.6	2.3	11	15	74
Trinidad and Tobago	4,851	3,770	5,327	4,139	12,368	9,610	3.2	(0.5)	3	42	54
SOUTH AMERICA											
Argentina	278,431	8,030	281,060	8,084	293,790	8,450	0.2	2.6	6	31	63
Bolivia	5,905	800	6,131	827	19,870	2,680	1.1	3.0	33 g	32 g	35 g
Brazil	579,787	3,640	688,085	4,327	874,583	5,500	X	X	14	37	49
Chile	59,151	4,160	67,297	4,736	138,263	9,730	2.7	6.7	8 g	41 g	50 g
Colombia	70,263	1,910	76,112	2,125	226,703	6,330	4.0	4.4	14 b	32 b	54 b
Ecuador	15,997	1,390	17,939	1,565	52,258	4,560	4.8	2.7	12	36	52
Guyana	493	590	595	717	2,141	2,580	(1.7)	2.4	36 a	37 a	27 a
Paraguay	8,158	1,690	7,743	1,604	17,526	3,630	6.6	3.5	24 a	22 a	54 a
Peru	55,019	2,310	57,424	2,440	89,422	3,800	1.4	2.0	7	38	55
Suriname	360	880	335	784	905	2,120	3.6	3.7	26 b	26 b	48 b
Uruguay	16,458	5,170	17,847	5,602	21,346	6,700	0.9	3.5	9	26	65
Venezuela	65,382	3,020	75,016	3,434	176,936	8,100	1.0	2.8	5	38	56
ASIA											
Afghanistan, Islamic State	X	X	X	X	X	X	0.0	0.0	X	X	X
Armenia, Rep	2,752	730	2,843	783	8,281	2,280	7.3	(10.3)	44	35	20
Azerbaijan	3,601	480	3,473	461	10,995	1,460	X	X	27 b	32 b	41 b
Bangladesh	28,599	240	29,110	246	163,156	1,380	4.4	4.0	31	18	52
Bhutan	295	420	304	172	2,283	1,290	X	6.3	40 a	32 a	28 a
Cambodia	2,718	270	2,771	276	X	X	X	X	51	14	34
China	744,890	620	697,647	572	3,624,065	2,970	8.7	9.6	21	48	31
Georgia	2,358	440	2,325	427	8,066	1,480	6.0	(16.7)	67	22	11
India	319,660	340	324,082	349	1,319,187	1,420	5.0	5.2	29	29	41
Indonesia	190,105	980	198,079	1,003	783,916	3,970	7.2	7.2	17	42	41
Iran, Islamic Rep	X	X	110,771 d	1,756 d	379,426	5,550	1.0	1.9	25	34	40
Iraq	X	X	48,422 c	2,755 c	X	X	0.6	X	X	X	X
Israel	87,875	15,920	91,965	16,645	92,268	16,700	3.7	5.3	X	X	X
Japan	4,963,587	39,640	5,108,540	40,846	2,742,741	21,930	4.1	2.9	2 a	38 a	60 a
Jordan	6,354	1,510	6,105 a	1,187 a	21,292 a	4,140 a	X	X	8 a	27 a	65 a
Kazakstan, Rep	22,143	1,330	21,413	1,273	51,124	3,040	X	X	12	30	57
Korea, Dem People's Rep	X	X	X	X	X	X	X	X	X	X	X
Korea, Rep	435,137	9,700	455,476	10,142	518,699	11,550	8.6	8.4	7 a	43 a	50 a
Kuwait	28,941	17,390	26,650	15,760	37,303	22,060	(3.2)	3.7	0	53	46
Kyrgyz Rep	3,158	700	3,054	685	8,028	1,800	X	X	44	24	32
Lao People's Dem Rep	1,694	350	1,760	361	7,404 f	1,709 f	X	5.2	52 b	18 b	30 b
Lebanon	10,673	2,660	11,143	3,703	X	X	X	X	7 a	24 a	69 a
Malaysia	78,321	3,890	85,311	4,236	191,733	9,520	6.7	7.4	13	43	44
Mongolia	767	310	861	349	4,951	2,010	X	0.3	17 f	26	57
Myanmar	X	X	X	X	28,277 c	696 c	5.8	X	63 a	9 a	28 a
Nepal	4,391	200	4,232	197	24,460	1,140	3.7	4.7	42	22	36
Oman	10,578	4,820	12,102	5,483	20,635	9,350	11.3	4.3	3 d	53 d	43 d
Pakistan	59,991	460	60,649	445	301,128	2,210	6.7	5.1	26	24	50
Philippines	71,865	1,050	74,180	1,093	187,236	2,760	2.8	3.4	22	32	46
Saudi Arabia	133,540	7,040	125,501	6,875	158,636	8,690	1.6	2.9	6 e	50 e	43 e
Singapore	79,831	26,730	83,695	25,156	75,223	22,610	7.4	7.9	0	36	64
Sri Lanka	12,616	700	12,915	720	58,983	3,290	5.9	3.8	23	25	52
Syrian Arab Rep	15,780	1,120	16,783	1,182	80,247	5,650	6.5	4.2	29 e	24 e	48 e
Tajikistan, Rep	1,976	340	1,999	343	5,653	970	X	X	27 e	34 e	39 e
Thailand	159,630	2,740	167,056	2,868	449,046	7,710	6.9	9.0	11	40	49
Turkey	169,452	2,780	164,789	2,709	335,217	5,510	4.4	4.3	16	31	53
Turkmenistan, Rep	4,125	920	3,917	961	15,469 e	4,217 e	X	X	32 e	30 e	38 e
United Arab Emirates	42,806	17,400	39,107	17,696	31,912	14,440	6.8	X	2 b	57 b	40 b
Uzbekistan, Rep	21,979	970	21,556	947	53,946	2,370	X	X	33 a	34 a	34 a
Vietnam	17,634	240	20,351	276	X	X	X	6.3	28	30	42
Yemen	4,044	260	4,790	319	X	X	X	X	22 a	27 a	51 a
OCEANIA											
Australia	337,909	18,720	348,782	19,522	350,710	19,630	3.2	3.0	3 a	28 a	70 a
Fiji	1,895	2,440	2,068	2,638	4,861	6,200	2.1	3.2	20 c	21 c	59 c
New Zealand	51,655	14,340	57,070	16,026	61,214	17,190	1.4	1.9	8 e	26 e	66 e
Papua New Guinea	4,976	1,160	4,901	1,139	11,183	2,600	1.1	4.5	26	38 a	34 a
Solomon Islands	341	910	357	944	843	2,230	6.9	6.1	X	X	X
LOW INCOME	1,381,813	430	1,352,256	421	X	X	X	X	25	38	35
MIDDLE INCOME	3,797,316	2,390	3,744,877 a	2,357 a	X	X	X	X	11 a	35 a	52 a
HIGH INCOME	22,508,193	24,930	20,487,539 a	22,692 a	X	X	X	X	2 b	32 b	66 b

Notes: a. 1994. b. 1993. c. 1989. d. 1992. e. 1990. f. 1991. g. 1988.

Data Table 6.2
Official Development Assistance and Other Financial Flows, 1983–95

Sources: Organisation for Economic Co-Operation and Development, the World Bank, and United Nations Population Division

	Average Annual Official Development Assistance (ODA) (million US$) {a}		ODA as a Percentage of GNP {a}	1995 ODA Per Capita (US$) {a}	Total External Debt (million US$)		Total Debt Service (million US$)	Debt Service as a Percentage of Total Exports	Direct Foreign Investment (million US$)	Central Government Expenditures (million US$)	
	1983-85	1993-95	1993-95	1993-95	1983-85	1993-95	1993-95	1993-95	1993-95	1993-95	
WORLD											
AFRICA											
Algeria	130	359	1	11	16,841	29,603	6,197	57	13	X	
Angola	87	390	11	39	1,707	11,087	286	9	351	X	
Benin	86	274	13	51	736	1,587	40	7	5	X	
Botswana	101	105	3	63	286	678	92	4	(77)	1,618	b
Burkina Faso	189	463	18	46	440	1,171	43	11	0	X	
Burundi	139	240	24	31	370	1,114	39	35	1	X	
Cameroon	155	573	6	34	2,995	8,352	426	21	71	1,769	b
Central African Rep	110	167	14	49	288	900	16	8	(1)	X	
Chad	130	227	19	37	211	835	17	8	10	X	
Congo, Dem Rep	91	203	10	48	2,387	5,512	289	26	0	X	
Congo, Rep	307	203	5	4	5,599	12,243	23	X	1	889	
Côte d'Ivoire	132	1,186	13	88	9,021	18,472	1,128	31	41	X	
Egypt	1,664	2,363	6	32	32,841	32,755	2,278	14	782	16,734	b
Equatorial Guinea	14	39	26	82	124	282	2	X	17	X	
Eritrea	X	124	X	46	X	X	X	X	X	X	
Ethiopia	470	1,015	16	16	1,696	4,961	120	13	7	1,210	c
Gabon	67	143	3	133	1,013	4,113	289	11	(89)	X	
Gambia, The	48	68	19	42	229	424	28	13	10	76	b
Ghana	173	603	9	37	1,962	5,407	349	25	196	1,254	b
Guinea	101	387	12	53	1,356	3,066	121	17	23	X	
Guinea-Bissau	59	131	52	111	290	852	10	43	1	X	
Kenya	412	765	11	26	3,770	7,220	755	28	13	1,764	c
Lesotho	100	124	9	56	147	597	34	6	19	358	b
Liberia	113	102	X	56	1,108	2,046	13	X	0	X	
Libya	(43)	7	X	1	X	X	X	X	110	X	
Madagascar	173	318	10	20	2,228	4,079	71	11	10	592	
Malawi	137	465	26	44	926	1,987	85	22	1	X	
Mali	303	451	18	51	1,235	2,839	83	15	9	X	
Mauritania	185	273	26	98	1,362	2,323	117	25	7	X	
Mauritius	34	21	1	21	580	1,414	163	8	16	799	
Morocco	501	614	2	19	14,063	21,474	3,391	34	444	X	
Mozambique	257	1,159	86	61	1,568	5,547	143	34	33	X	
Namibia	2	160	5	122	X	X	X	X	46	1,044	b
Niger	213	331	16	29	1,038	1,605	72	23	1	X	
Nigeria	38	226	1	2	17,991	33,074	1,645	14	1,318	X	
Rwanda	165	561	42	118	300	943	15	6 b	2	X	b
Senegal	325	604	11	80	2,281	3,757	213	15	22	X	
Sierra Leone	63	230	32	49	658	1,403	91	X	(3)	159	c
Somalia	349	540	X	20	1,516	2,598	0	X	1	X	
South Africa	X	318	X	9	X	X	X	X	(142)	42,464	c
Sudan	903	365	X	8	8,314	16,792	31	1 c	0	X	
Swaziland	29	54	5	64	227	238	24	X	66	X	
Tanzania	544	932	24	29	3,677	7,028	207	22	73	X	
Togo	110	137	11	46	889	1,412	27	6	0	X	
Tunisia	182	135	1	8	4,346	9,323	1,432	19	419	X	
Uganda	160	723	19	41	1,103	3,320	148	43	88	X	
Zambia	259	1,207	35	251	4,054	6,761	1,120	78	60	603	
Zimbabwe	248	517	9	44	2,262	4,502	626	19 c	34	X	
EUROPE											
Albania	X	203	13	53	X	821	7	1	60	752	d
Austria	(196)	(655)	(0)	(95)	X	X	X	X	X	77,710	
Belarus, Rep	X	176	1	21	X	1,296	104	3	15	X	
Belgium	(455)	(857)	(0)	(102)	X	X	X	X	X	111,006	c
Bosnia and Herzegovina	X	X	X	0	X	509	11	X	0	X	
Bulgaria	X	128	1	13	2,725	11,620	752	13	98	4,863	
Croatia, Rep	X	X	0	0	X	3,047	362	6	84	6,113	
Czech Rep	X	129	0	14	2,936	12,148	2,156	10	1,367	15,753	
Denmark	(428)	(1,470)	(1)	(311)	X	X	X	X	X	66,322	
Estonia, Rep	X	47	1	37	X	216	22	1	192	599	c
Finland	(181)	(345)	(0)	(76)	X	X	X	X	X	40,515	c
France	(3,023)	(8,275)	(1)	(145)	X	X	X	X	X	642,060	
Germany	(3,800)	7,099	0	92	X	X	X	X	X	715,899	
Greece	12	22 c	0	0	X	X	X	X	1,004	31,538	b
Hungary	X	36	0	(26)	11,895	27,860	5,694	42	2,671	X	
Iceland	X	X	X	0	X	X	X	X	X	2,028	c
Ireland	(36)	(114)	(0)	(43)	X	X	X	X	X	20,229	b
Italy	(1,022)	(2,457)	(0)	(28)	X	X	X	X	X	515,454	c
Latvia, Rep	X	48	1	23	X	357	23	1	146	1,220	e
Lithuania, Rep	X	103	2	47	X	542	40	2	39	1,056	
Macedonia, FYR	X	X	X	0	X	1,073	X	X	0	X	
Moldova, Rep	X	48	1	14	X	493	29	3 e	30	X	
Netherlands	(1,200)	(2,756)	(1)	(208)	X	X	X	X	X	180,935	
Norway	(566)	(1,132)	(1)	(287)	X	X	X	X	X	49,890	c
Poland, Rep	X	2,203	2	98	24,863	43,340	2,956	12	2,416	45,987	e
Portugal	(10)	(275)	(0)	(28)	X	X	X	X	X	37,027	c
Romania	X	193	1	12	7,965	5,473	646	8	285	8,954	c
Russian Federation	X	1,932	1	10	17,019	118,441	4,104	5	1,118	81,680	e
Slovak Rep	X	74	1	18	894	4,653	840	9	195	X	
Slovenia, Rep	X	X	X	0	X	2,677	529	6	139	X	
Spain	(124)	(1,319)	(0)	(34)	X	X	X	X	X	188,590	b
Sweden	(778)	(1,764)	(1)	(194)	X	X	X	X	X	98,345	
Switzerland	(303)	(953)	(0)	(151)	X	X	X	X	X	62,871	c
Ukraine	X	310	0	6	X	5,862	475	2 e	209	X	
United Kingdom	(1,523)	(3,091)	(0)	(54)	X	X	X	X	X	429,427	
Yugoslavia, Fed Rep	X	1,718 f	X	0	X	X	X	X	X	X	

	Average Annual Official Development Assistance (ODA) (million US$) {a}		ODA as a Percentage of GNP {a}	1995 ODA Per Capita	Total External Debt (million US$)		Total Debt Service (million US$)	Debt Service as a Percentage of Total Exports	Direct Foreign Investment (million US$)	Central Government Expenditures (million US$)	
	1983-85	1993-95	1993-95	(US$) {a}	1983-85	1993-95	1993-95	1993-95	1993-95	1993-95	
NORTH AMERICA											
Canada	(1,562)	(2,239)	(0)	(70)	X	X	X	X	X	X	
United States	(8,732)	(9,139)	(0)	(28)	X	X	X	X	X	1,536,667	
CENTRAL AMERICA											
Belize	17	25	X	70	106	220	29	X	15	181	
Costa Rica	250	67	1	7	4,193	3,859	567	16	314	2,381	
Cuba	14	52	X	6	X	X	X	X	5	X	
Dominican Rep	165	66	1	16	3,181	4,424	425	8	198	1,725	c
El Salvador	299	343	4	54	1,807	2,261	305	12	25	1,035	c
Guatemala	75	214	2	19	2,272	3,090	309	12	94	1,131	c
Haiti	138	486	27	103	652	776	34	17	4	X	
Honduras	249	350	10	73	2,381	4,359	449	29	37	X	
Jamaica	173	110	3	44	3,718	4,232	604	19	121	X	
Mexico	120	411	0	4	94,890	145,757	23,239	29	7,441	61,873	c
Nicaragua	112	530	36	160	4,911	10,249	198	36	50	603	
Panama	63	57	1	19	4,504	7,086	356	4	192	1,875	c
Trinidad and Tobago	6	17	0	20	1,369	2,302	531	24	398	X	
SOUTH AMERICA											
Argentina	45	244	0	6	48,574	79,252	7,660	34	1,801	X	
Bolivia	180	616	11	93	4,397	4,815	351	31	65	1,393	
Brazil	128	314	0	2	101,992	151,497	16,591	31	3,074	163,231	b
Chile	14	167	0	11	19,350	23,641	3,644	23	1,426	11,039	
Colombia	79	156	0	6	12,566	19,115	3,571	28	1,709	7,311	b
Ecuador	112	231	2	21	8,201	14,381	1,112	24	490	2,388	c
Guyana	27	92	22	106	1,333	2,032	100	X	2	X	
Paraguay	51	129	2	30	1,567	1,957	275	X	164	894	b
Peru	308	475	1	18	12,124	26,976	1,694	30	1,808	8,658	
Suriname	7	72	21	179	X	X	X	X	(21)	X	
Uruguay	4	96	1	25	3,494	5,074	662	19	127	5,280	
Venezuela	12	43	0	2	36,841	36,745	4,168	21	695	11,103	c
ASIA											
Afghanistan, Islamic State	12	217	X	10	X	X	X	X	0	X	
Armenia, Rep	X	171	8	58	X	241	5	2	3	X	
Azerbaijan	X	91	2	14	X	156	3	X	37	X	
Bangladesh	1,122	1,470	5	11	6,129	15,737	633	14	9	X	
Bhutan	18	72	26	41	4	87	7	X	0	108	
Cambodia	22	407	17	56	7	1,925	14	4	91	X	
China	803	3,344	1	3	12,796	101,491	12,123	10	32,384	44,877	c
Georgia	X	161	6	37	X	1,053	13	X	0	X	
India	1,701	1,841	1	2	35,589	96,412	10,580	27	731	49,327	
Indonesia	673	1,683	1	7	32,990	97,841	14,929	32	2,820	27,500	c
Iran, Islamic Rep	26	151	X	3	6,108	22,670	3,978	X	(10)	18,148	c
Iraq	40	255	X	16	X	X	X	X	0	X	
Israel	1,526	946	1	61	X	X	X	X	X	35,182	
Japan	(3,959)	(12,996)	(0)	(116)	X	X	X	X	X	1,016,205	b
Jordan	671	405	7	100	3,503	7,684	593	14	4	1,832	c
Kazakstan, Rep	X	40	0	3	X	2,702	106	2	206	X	
Korea, Dem People's Rep	2	11	X	1	X	X	X	X	0	X	
Korea, Rep	(13)	(32)	(0)	1	X	X	X	X	X	67,983	
Kuwait	5	5	0	4	X	X	X	X	X	14,042	
Kyrgyz Rep	X	183	5	63	X	451	26	2	c	8	X	
Lao People's Dem Rep	34	246	16	64	529	2,077	25	6	89	X	
Lebanon	96	188	2	61	882	2,010	188	12	16	2,483	c
Malaysia	244	92	0	6	18,851	30,012	5,751	9	5,051	17,882	
Mongolia	1	173	24	84	1	444	35	8	9	X	e
Myanmar	305	135	X	3	2,587	6,027	175	9	c	6	6,916	c
Nepal	210	414	10	20	504	2,241	83	8	7	644	
Oman	72	53	1	7	1,816	2,950	547	9	126	4,985	
Pakistan	742	1,139	2	6	12,484	27,337	3,004	20	c	391	12,653	
Philippines	422	1,143	2	13	25,069	38,456	4,957	20	1,436	10,030	b
Saudi Arabia	(3,081)	25	0	1	X	X	X	X	(52)	X	
Singapore	26	19	0	5	X	X	X	X	X	10,150	b
Sri Lanka	465	601	5	31	3,139	7,658	399	8	141	3,207	
Syrian Arab Rep	688	450	3	24	9,353	20,618	325	6	128	10,129	b
Tajikistan, Rep	X	52	2	11	X	547	1	0	8	X	
Thailand	449	684	0	15	15,489	49,194	7,416	12	1,746	23,298	
Turkey	259	292	0	5	22,643	69,594	10,145	29	710	37,530	
Turkmenistan, Rep	X	25	1	6	X	365	70	1	c	0	X	
United Arab Emirates	4	(2)	(0)	4	X	X	X	X	X	4,263	c
Uzbekistan, Rep	X	39	0	4	X	1,285	124	3	70	X	
Vietnam	110	660	4	11	56	25,640	426	9	783	X	
Yemen	417	219	6	11	3,046	6,085	109	4	307	5,429	b
OCEANIA											
Australia	(760)	(1,080)	(0)	(67)	X	X	X	X	X	89,089	
Fiji	32	48	3	55	432	290	79	X	54	532	
New Zealand	(57)	(110)	(0)	(35)	X	X	X	X	X	17,854	
Papua New Guinea	303	336	7	86	2,003	2,786	786	27	149	1,619	c
Solomon Islands	23	50	16	123	48	154	11	X	16	X	
LOW INCOME					174,327	505,848		15			
MIDDLE INCOME					767,232	1,419,580		18			

Notes: a. For Official Development Assistance (ODA), flows to recipients are shown as positive numbers; flows from donors are shown as negative numbers (in parentheses).
b. 1993. c. 1993-94. d. 1995. e. 1994-95. f. 1994.

Data Table 6.3
World Bank Commodity Indexes and Prices, 1960–96

Source: The World Bank

Commodity Indexes (based on constant prices with 1990 = 100)

	1960	1965	1970	1975	1980	1985	1990	1991	1992	1993	1994	1995	1996
PETROLEUM	34	29	21	101	224	173	100	83	78	69	63	63	78
NON-ENERGY COMMODITIES	189	187	174	165	174	133	100	93	86	86	101	103	101
Total Agriculture	209	193	181	177	191	145	100	96	88	93	112	110	110
Total Food	184	196	184	221	191	124	100	97	94	93	97	98	108
-Grains	195	211	186	258	187	130	100	99	95	88	93	101	123
-Fats and Oils	251	288	257	228	206	165	100	102	105	105	114	115	129
-Other Foods	124	113	123	195	181	88	100	91	84	85	85	83	83
Beverages	237	216	228	181	253	239	100	91	73	79	135	127	111
Raw Materials	220	173	143	119	145	103	100	97	92	104	114	113	111
-Timber	129	130	127	92	110	86	100	102	107	143	142	117	122
-Other	282	202	153	138	169	115	100	94	82	77	95	111	104
Metals and Minerals	139	173	162	118	132	102	100	87	81	70	77	85	78
Fertilizers	180	179	121	350	179	130	100	100	90	79	85	87	105

Commodity Prices (in constant 1990 US$ per unit measure)

		1960	1965	1970	1975	1980	1985	1990	1991	1992	1993	1994	1995
Cocoa	kg	2.85	1.69	2.69	2.76	3.62	3.29	1.27	1.17	1.03	1.05	1.27	1.20
Coffee (Other Milds)	kg	4.46	4.64	4.57	3.19	4.81	4.71	1.97	1.83	1.32	1.47	3.00	2.80
Tea (London Auction)	kg	6.92	5.92	4.36	3.06	3.10	2.89	2.03	1.80	1.88	1.75	1.66	1.38
Sugar (Free Market)	kg	0.33	0.22	0.33	1.00	0.88	0.13	0.28	0.19	0.19	0.21	0.24	0.25
Oranges	mt	927.54	754.63	669.32	504.42	542.50	580.76	531.10	509.78	458.95	406.86	373.07	445.86
Bananas	mt	692.27	734.72	658.96	545.80	526.39	554.37	540.90	547.46	443.81	416.77	398.81	373.41
Maize	mt	209.18	254.63	232.67	264.60	174.03	163.56	109.30	105.09	97.80	96.04	97.60	103.60
Rice (Indicative)	mt	518.59	549.95	503.22	755.31	570.48	287.07	270.85	286.97	251.61	221.46	242.82	269.15
Sorghum	mt	182.13	218.52	206.37	247.57	179.03	150.15	103.90	102.84	96.39	93.16	94.26	99.87
Soybeans	mt	444.44	541.67	466.14	486.50	411.39	326.53	246.80	234.44	220.92	239.98	228.52	217.28
Wheat (US)	mt	280.16	275.29	218.73	329.77	239.90	198.00	135.52	125.89	141.84	131.93	135.87	148.47
Oil, Coconut	mt	1,507.25	1,610.19	1,582.87	870.58	935.83	860.06	336.50	423.68	541.84	423.57	551.27	562.08
Oil, Groundnut	mt	1,576.33	1,499.07	1,508.37	1,898.23	1,193.06	1,319.24	963.70	875.54	572.14	695.28	928.09	831.38
Oil, Palm	mt	1,102.42	1,261.57	1,036.25	960.62	810.42	730.32	289.80	331.70	369.14	355.36	479.51	526.85
Oil, Soybean	mt	1,081.72	1,250.00	1,140.77	1,246.31	830.01	833.82	447.33	444.38	402.36	451.95	558.60	524.33
Copra	mt	974.40	1,048.61	896.02	567.04	628.75	562.68	230.70	280.23	356.87	277.89	378.70	368.29
Meal, Groundnut	mt	405.80	472.22	406.37	309.73	333.75	214.29	184.80	146.87	146.03	158.14	152.75	141.78
Meal, Soybean	mt	376.81	435.19	410.36	342.92	363.89	228.86	200.20	192.86	191.74	195.83	174.61	165.27
Palm Kernels	mt	777.78	828.70	665.34	457.96	479.17	414.72	188.00	215.26	215.76	216.37	X	X
Beef	kg	3.56	4.08	5.20	2.94	3.83	3.14	2.56	2.61	2.30	2.46	2.12	1.60
Meal, Fish	mt	560.39	879.63	784.86	542.04	700.00	408.16	412.20	467.51	451.69	343.18	341.50	415.27
Shrimp	kg	X	X	X	X	X	15.29	10.79	11.30	10.27	10.72	11.87	11.25
Cotton, Index	kg	3.14	2.90	2.52	2.57	2.84	1.92	1.82	1.64	1.20	1.20	1.60	1.79
Jute	mt	1,608.70	1,175.93	1,091.63	820.80	427.78	849.71	408.30	372.14	299.79	257.13	270.66	308.76
Rubber	kg	3.77	2.34	1.62	1.24	1.98	1.11	0.86	0.81	0.81	0.78	1.02	1.33
Tobacco (U.S.)	mt	8,390.70	5,858.39	4,286.76	4,075.20	3,160.91	3,807.31	3,392.19	3,424.73	3,226.59	2,535.60	2,399.01	2,214.26
Logs, Malaysian	m³	154.30	162.15	171.84	149.36	271.55	177.46	177.19	187.36	196.54	366.71	279.08	214.45
Plywood	sheet	X	X	4.11	2.69	3.80	3.07	3.55	3.64	3.57	6.22	5.46	4.90
Sawnwood	m³	720.65	725.69	698.83	494.33	550.28	447.71	533.08	540.63	569.62	713.31	745.04	620.76
Woodpulp	mt	X	X	706.77	976.55	745.14	606.85	814.50	583.95	528.10	398.79	501.32	715.98
Aluminum	mt	2,429.95	2,194.44	2,215.14	1,763.27	2,022.22	1,517.49	1,639.00	1,274.17	1,176.64	1,071.54	1,340.09	1,514.81
Bauxite	mt	36.23	34.72	47.81	49.12	44.44	52.04	35.50	36.50	34.05	32.93	31.76	X
Copper	mt	3,270.53	5,972.22	5,629.48	2,736.73	3,030.56	2,066.18	2,661.50	2,288.45	2,139.92	1,799.70	2,093.85	2,462.76
Gold	troy oz	171.98	162.04	143.19	356.26	844.31	463.43	383.47	354.38	322.45	338.45	348.47	322.28
Iron Ore	mt (Fe)	55.17	47.41	39.20	38.27	39.01	38.72	30.80	32.53	29.64	26.47	23.11	22.61
Lead	kg	0.96	1.47	1.21	0.92	1.26	0.57	0.81	0.55	0.51	0.38	0.50	0.53
Manganese Ore (1% Mn)	unit	4.21	3.48	2.17	3.05	2.18	2.06	3.36	3.77	3.45	2.76	1.90	1.70
Nickel	mt	7,881.16	8,032.41	11,339.44	10,111.06	9,053.75	7,141.55	8,864.10	7,980.04	6,567.76	4,979.70	5,753.01	6,902.72
Silver	troy oz	4.42	5.99	7.06	9.78	28.66	8.95	4.82	3.95	3.69	4.04	4.80	4.36
Tin	kg	10.61	18.01	14.64	15.21	23.30	16.82	6.09	5.47	5.72	4.86	4.96	5.21
Zinc	kg	1.19	1.44	1.18	1.64	1.06	1.14	1.51	1.09	1.16	0.90	0.91	0.87
Diammonium Phosphate	mt	X	X	215.14	537.61	308.61	246.36	171.40	169.18	136.17	121.46	156.80	181.69
Phosphate Rock	mt	65.22	60.19	43.82	148.23	64.86	49.42	40.50	41.59	39.17	31.04	29.95	29.36
Potassium Chloride	mt	X	X	125.50	179.87	160.97	122.45	98.10	106.51	105.13	101.05	95.93	98.79
Triple Super Phosphate	mt	256.04	250.00	169.32	448.01	250.35	176.93	131.82	130.26	113.26	105.31	119.88	125.53
Urea	mt	X	X	192.43	438.05	308.47	198.69	157.00	168.30	131.61	100.42	134.23	177.43
Coal	mt	X	X	X	X	59.86	67.93	41.67	40.61	38.09	35.75	33.10	32.86
Crude Petroleum	bbl	7.87	6.57	4.82	23.08	51.21	39.62	22.88	18.95	17.84	15.84	14.42	14.41
Gas, Europe	mmbtu	X	X	X	2.43	4.72	5.39	2.55	3.05	2.40	2.51	2.22	2.29

Notes: kg = kilogram; mt = metric ton; m³ = cubic meter; oz = ounce; Fe = iron; bbl = barrel; mmbtu = million British Thermal Units.

Sources and Technical Notes

Gross National and Domestic Product Estimates, 1995

Sources: 1995 Gross national product (GNP), gross domestic product (GDP), GDP based on purchasing power parity (PPP), annual growth rates of GDP, distribution of GDP, and per capita PPP, GDP, and average annual growth rates of same: derived from The World Bank, *World Development Indicators 1997* on CD-ROM (Development Data Group, The World Bank, Washington, D.C., 1997). Population figures for calculations: United Nations (U.N.) Population Division, *World Population Prospects, 1950–2050 (The 1996 Revision),* on diskette (U.N., New York, 1996).

Data for years prior to 1993 (1992 for PPP) have been converted to 1995 U.S. dollars (US$) (1992 International dollars [Int$] for PPP) using deflators derived from U.S. data.

Gross national product is the sum of two components: the GDP and net income from abroad. GDP measures the final output of goods and services produced by the domestic economy. Net income from abroad is income in the form of compensation of employees, interest on loans, profits, and other factor payments that residents receive from abroad, less payments made for labor and capital. Most countries estimate GDP by the production method. This method sums the final outputs of the various sectors of the economy (e.g., agriculture, manufacturing, and government services), from which the value of the inputs to production have been subtracted.

GNP estimates in U.S. dollars are calculated according to *The World Bank Atlas* methodology. GNP estimates in local currencies were converted to U.S. dollars using a three-year average exchange rate, adjusted for domestic and U.S. inflation. The *Atlas* method of averaging three years of exchange rates smoothes fluctuations due to the currency market and provides a more reliable measure, over time, of overall income than do estimates based on a single year's exchange rate.

The *gross domestic product* estimates at purchaser values (market prices) are in 1995 U.S. dollars (based on 1995 exchange rates), and are the sum of GDP at factor cost (value added in the agriculture, industry, and services sectors) and indirect taxes, less subsidies. World Bank GDP estimates are in accord with the United Nations System of National Accounts.

Per capita estimates of GNP and GDP for 1995 are calculated using mid-year population data.

GDP and *GDP per capita* using *purchasing power parity* (PPP) are GDP estimates based on the purchasing power of currencies rather than on current exchange rates. GDP in PPP terms is derived by applying the ratio of GDP to GNP in local currency to the World Bank's estimates of GNP in PPP terms. The estimates are a blend of extrapolated and regression-based numbers, using the results of the International Comparison Programme (ICP).

The ICP benchmark studies are (essentially) multilateral pricing exercises. The intercountry price comparisons have been reported in seven phases: 1970, 1973, 1975, 1980, 1985, 1990, and 1993. PPP studies recast traditional national accounts through special price collections and the disaggregation of GDP by expenditure components. ICP details are reported by national statistical offices.

The international dollar values, which are different from the U.S. dollar values of GNP or GDP, are obtained using special conversion factors designed to equalize the purchasing powers of different currencies. This conversion factor, the PPP, is defined as the number of units of a country's currency required to buy the same amounts of goods and services in the domestic market as $1 would buy in the United States. The computation involves deriving implicit quantities from national accounts expenditure data and specially collected price data and then revaluing the implicit quantities in each country at a single set of average prices. Because the same international price averages are used for every country, cross-country comparisons reflect differences in quantities of goods and services free of price-level differences. This procedure is designed to bring cross-country comparisons in line with cross-time real value comparisons that are based on constant price series. PPP estimates tend to lower per capita GDPs in industrialized countries and raise per capita GDPs in developing countries.

The *average annual growth rates* of GDP are least-squares estimates of the real growth of output. Growth rates are computed from constant price data to exclude the effects of inflation.

The *distribution of GDP* is calculated using current local currency units provided in the *World Development Indicators 1997*. *Agriculture* includes agricultural and livestock production and agricultural services, logging, forestry, fishing, and hunting. *Industry* comprises mining and quarrying; manufacturing; construction; and electricity, gas, and water. *Services* include wholesale and retail trade; transport, storage, and communications; banking, insurance, and real estate; public administration and defense; ownership of dwellings; and others. The distribution of GDP does not always add up to 100 percent due to rounding.

Although considerable effort has been made to standardize economic data according to the United Nations System of National Accounts, care should be taken when interpreting the indicators presented in Data Table 6.1. Intercountry and intertemporal comparisons using economic data involve complicated technical problems that are not easily resolved; therefore, readers are urged to read these data as characterizing major differences between economies rather than as precise, quantitative measurements.

Official Development Assistance and Other Financial Flows, 1983–95

Sources: Official development assistance (ODA): Organisation for Economic Co-Operation and Development (OECD), *Development Co-Operation* (OECD, Paris, 1984, 1986, 1987, 1988, 1989, 1990, 1991, 1992, 1993, 1994, 1995, and 1996), and *Geographical Distribution of Financial Flows to Developing Countries 1981/84, 1983/86, 1984/87, 1986/89,* and *1988/91* (OECD, Paris, 1986, 1988, 1989, 1991, and 1993); *Geographical Distribution of Financial Flows to Aid Recipients, 1989–93* (OECD, Paris, 1995) and *World Development Indicators 1997* on CD-ROM (Development Data Group, The World Bank, Washington, D.C., 1997). ODA as a percentage of Gross National Product (GNP) was calculated using *World Development Indicators 1997* on CD-ROM. Population figures for per capita estimates of ODA: United Nations (U.N.) Population Division, *World Population Prospects, 1950–2050 (The 1996 Revision),* on diskette (U.N., New York, 1996). External debt, debt service, debt service as a percentage of total exports, direct foreign investment, and central government expenditures: The World Bank, *World Development Indicators 1997* on CD-ROM.

Net *average annual official development assistance* (in current U.S. dollars) is the net amount of disbursed grants and concessional loans given or received by a country less repayments of concessional loans. Grants include gifts of money, goods, or services for which no repayment is required. A concessional loan has a grant element of 25 percent or more. The grant element is the amount by which the face value of the loan exceeds its present market value because of below-market interest rates, favorable maturity schedules, or repayment grace periods. Nonconcessional loans are not a component of ODA.

ODA contributions are shown as negative numbers (in parentheses); receipts are shown as positive numbers. Data for some developing countries (e.g., Republic of Korea) are shown as negative numbers because of net repayments of concessional loans. Data for donor countries include contributions made directly to developing countries and through multilateral institutions.

ODA sources include the development assistance agencies of OECD and Organization of Petroleum Exporting Countries members as well as other countries. Grants and concessional loans to and from multilateral development agencies are also included in contributions and receipts. OECD gathers ODA data through questionnaires and reports from countries and multilateral agencies. Only limited data are available on ODA flows among developing countries. These data are included when known.

The GNP data used to calculate *ODA as a percentage of GNP* were GNP estimates calculated according to *The World Bank Atlas* methodology (using exchange rates averaged over three-year periods). For full comparability of these ratios, the GNP figures should be at current prices and calculated using single-year exchange rates, like the ODA figures.

The *1995 ODA per capita* estimates are calculated using 1995 ODA estimates in current dollars and United Nations Population Division population data.

The World Bank operates the Debtor Reporting System (DRS), which compiles reports supplied by the Bank's member countries. Countries submit detailed reports on the annual status, transactions, and terms of the long-term external debt of public agencies and of publicly guaranteed private debt. Additional data are drawn from the World Bank, the International Monetary Fund (IMF), regional development banks, government lending agencies, and the Creditor Reporting System (CRS). The CRS is operated by OECD to compile reports from the members of its Development Assistance Committee. For further information on international debt, refer to *Global Development Finance 1997*, Vols. 1 and 2 (The World Bank, Washington, D.C., 1997).

Total external debt (current U.S. dollars) includes long-term debt outstanding, short-term debt, use of IMF credit, and private nonguaranteed debt outstanding. A long-term debt is an obligation with a maturity of at least one year that is owed to nonresidents and is repayable in foreign currency, goods, or services. Long-term debt is divided into long-term public debt and long-term publicly guaranteed private debt. A short-term debt is a public or publicly guaranteed private debt that has a maturity of one year or less. This class of debt is especially difficult for countries to monitor. Only a few countries supply these data through the DRS; the World Bank supplements these data with creditor-country reports, information from international clearinghouse banks, and other sources to derive rough estimates of short-term debt.

Use of IMF credit refers to all drawings on the Fund's General Resources Account. Use of IMF credit is converted to dollars by applying the average special drawing right exchange rate in effect for the year being calculated.

A private debt is an external obligation of a private debtor that is not guaranteed by a public entity. Data for this class of debt are less extensive than those for public debt; many countries do not report these data through the DRS. These data are included in the total when available.

Total debt service (in foreign currencies, goods, and services) comprises interest payments and principal repayments made on the disbursed long-term public debt and private, nonguaranteed debt, IMF debt repurchases, IMF charges, and interest payments on short-term debt.

Debt data are reported to the World Bank in the units of currency in which they are payable. The World Bank converts these data to U.S. dollars, using the IMF par values, central rates, or the current market rates, where appropriate. Debt service data are converted to U.S. dollars at the average exchange rate for the given year. Comparability of data among countries and years is limited by variations in methods, definitions, and comprehensiveness of data collection and reporting. Refer to the World Bank's *World Debt Tables 1994–95*, Vols. 1 and 2, for details.

ODA figures are derived from the annual questionnaire completed by each Development Assistance Committee member country; for nonmembers, values are based on information published by governments or provided directly to the OECD by them.

External debt data pertain to only those countries within the DRS, which focuses on low- and middle-income economies. Many economies are not represented within the system, and the estimates that are presented may not be comprehensive due to different reporting frameworks. These data do not account for the term structure and the concessionality mix of debt, which can lead to a misrepresentation of a country's underlying solvency.

Direct foreign investment is the net inflow of capital to acquire a lasting management interest (10 percent or more of the voting stock) in a country other than that of the investor. It includes (as shown in the balance of payments) equity capital, reinvestment of earnings, other long-term capital, and short-term capital.

Central government expenditures include the expenditures of all bodies that are agencies or instruments of a central government authority. In countries with strong subnational authorities, these figures can substantially understate total government expenditures, thus care should be taken in making national comparisons.

Data Table 6.3

World Bank Commodity Indexes and Prices, 1960–96

Source: The World Bank, unpublished data (The World Bank, Washington, D.C., June 1997).

Price data are compiled from major international marketplaces for standard grades of each commodity. For example, maize refers to No. 2, yellow, FOB (free-on-board) U.S. gulf ports. The 1990 U.S. constant dollar figures were derived by converting current average monthly prices in local currencies to U.S. dollars using average monthly exchange rates. These average monthly dollar figures were then averaged to produce an average annual dollar figure, which was adjusted to 1990 constant dollars using the manufacturing unit value index. This index is a composite price index of all manufactured goods exported by the G-5 countries (the United States, the United Kingdom, France, Germany, and Japan) to developing countries.

The aggregate price indexes have the following components:

1. *Petroleum*

2. *Non-energy commodities*: individual commodities listed under items 4–12, below.

3. *Total agriculture*: total food, beverages, and raw materials.

4. *Total food*: grains, fats and oils, and other foods.

5. *Grains*: maize, rice, wheat, and grain sorghum.

6. *Fats and oils*: palm, coconut, and groundnut oils; soybeans; soybean oil; and soybean meal.

7. *Other foods*: sugar, beef, bananas, and oranges.

8. *Beverages*: coffee, cocoa, and tea.

9. *Raw materials*: cotton, rubber, tobacco, and timber.

10. *Timber*: logs and sawnwood.

11. *Metals and minerals*: copper, tin, nickel, aluminum, iron ore, lead, and zinc.

12. *Fertilizers*: phosphate rock and triple superphosphate (TSP).

The commodity prices reported here are specific to the markets named. The commodities themselves are often defined more specifically than is suggested in the table (e.g., coffee (ICO), indicator price, other mild arabicas, average New York and Bremen/Hamburg markets, ex-dock). Further information is available at the World Bank's Web site on commodities at http://www.worldbank.org/html/ieccp/ieccp.html.

Chapter 7

Population and Human Development

Size and Growth of Population and Labor Force, 1950–2050

Source: United Nations Population Division and International Labour Organisation

	Population (thousands)				Average Annual Population Change (percent)			Average Annual Increment to the Population (thousands)			Average Annual Growth of the Labor Force (percent)	
	1950	1998	2025	2050	1985-90	1995-00	2005-10	1985-90	1995-00	2005-10	1980-95	1995-10
WORLD	**2,523,878**	**5,929,839**	**8,039,130**	**9,366,724**	**1.7**	**1.4**	**1.2**	**86,996**	**80,848**	**80,011**	**1.9**	**1.5**
AFRICA	**223,974**	**778,484**	**1,453,899**	**2,046,401**	**2.8**	**2.6**	**2.5**	**16,330**	**20,083**	**24,232**	**2.7**	**2.9**
Algeria	8,753	30,175	47,322	58,991	2.6	2.3	1.9	610	698	690	3.8	3.9
Angola	4,131	11,967	25,547	38,897	2.9	3.3	2.9	245	393	461	2.4	3.3
Benin	2,046	5,881	12,276	18,095	3.0	2.8	2.9	132	163	227	2.5	3.2
Botswana	389	1,551	2,576	3,320	3.3	2.2	2.0	39	34	39	3.2	2.4
Burkina Faso	3,654	11,402	23,451	35,419	2.8	2.8	2.8	240	316	414	2.2	2.4
Burundi	2,456	6,589	12,341	16,937	2.9	2.8	2.4	148	182	205	2.3	3.0
Cameroon	4,466	14,323	28,521	41,951	2.8	2.7	2.7	301	387	496	2.6	2.9
Central African Rep	1,314	3,489	6,006	8,215	2.4	2.1	2.1	66	73	89	1.8	2.1
Chad	2,658	6,892	12,648	18,004	2.0	2.8	2.3	106	187	200	2.1	2.6
Congo, Dem Rep	12,184	49,208	105,925	164,635	3.3	2.6	3.0	1,142	1,259	1,943	3.1	2.9
Congo, Rep	808	2,822	5,747	8,729	3.0	2.8	2.7	62	78	99	2.8	2.9
Côte d'Ivoire	2,776	14,567	24,397	31,706	3.3	2.0	2.2	359	290	395	3.3	2.6
Egypt	21,834	65,675	95,766	115,480	2.5	1.9	1.6	1,313	1,205	1,197	2.6	2.8
Equatorial Guinea	226	430	798	1,144	2.4	2.5	2.4	8	10	13	3.6	2.6
Eritrea	1,140	3,548	6,504	8,808	1.3	3.7	2.3	37	128	104	1.8	3.0
Ethiopia	18,434	62,111	136,288	212,732	3.1	3.2	3.0	1,401	1,954	2,480	2.7	3.0
Gabon	469	1,170	2,118	2,952	3.1	2.8	2.3	26	32	34	2.3	2.1
Gambia, The	294	1,194	1,984	2,604	4.2	2.3	2.0	35	27	29	3.6	2.2
Ghana	4,900	18,857	36,341	51,205	3.1	2.8	2.6	436	518	636	3.1	3.0
Guinea	2,550	7,673	15,286	22,914	2.9	1.4	2.8	154	102	272	2.9	2.3
Guinea-Bissau	505	1,134	1,921	2,674	2.0	2.0	2.0	18	22	28	1.6	2.0
Kenya	6,265	29,020	50,202	66,054	3.3	2.2	2.4	721	638	880	3.6	2.9
Lesotho	734	2,184	4,031	5,643	2.6	2.5	2.4	44	53	67	2.4	2.8
Liberia	824	2,748	6,573	9,955	3.2	8.6	3.0	75	227	123	0.8	4.4
Libya	1,029	5,980	12,885	19,109	3.7	3.3	3.0	152	196	246	3.3	3.4
Madagascar	4,229	16,348	34,476	50,807	3.4	3.1	3.0	395	504	643	3.0	3.3
Malawi	2,881	10,377	20,391	29,825	5.1	2.5	2.6	417	262	341	2.7	2.5
Mali	3,520	11,832	24,575	36,817	3.0	3.0	2.8	259	353	441	2.7	2.9
Mauritania	825	2,453	4,443	6,077	2.5	2.5	2.4	47	61	73	2.2	2.6
Mauritius	493	1,154	1,481	1,654	0.8	1.1	1.0	8	12	13	2.1	1.3
Morocco	8,953	28,012	39,925	47,276	2.1	1.8	1.4	479	492	437	2.6	2.5
Mozambique	6,198	18,691	35,444	51,774	0.9	2.5	2.5	128	461	582	2.0	2.5
Namibia	511	1,653	2,999	4,167	2.7	2.4	2.3	35	39	48	2.3	2.4
Niger	2,400	10,119	22,385	34,576	3.1	3.3	3.1	225	331	418	3.0	3.2
Nigeria	32,935	121,773	238,397	338,510	2.9	2.8	2.6	2,617	3,413	4,152	2.6	2.9
Rwanda	2,120	6,528	12,981	16,937	2.8	7.9	2.4	180	498	215	0.2	4.6
Senegal	2,500	9,001	16,896	23,442	2.8	2.7	2.5	190	237	286	2.5	2.7
Sierra Leone	1,944	4,577	8,200	11,368	2.2	3.0	2.2	82	134	125	1.5	2.7
Somalia	3,072	10,653	23,669	36,408	1.8	3.9	3.1	150	408	445	2.0	3.3
South Africa	13,683	44,295	71,621	91,466	2.3	2.2	2.0	805	958	1,050	2.6	2.4
Sudan	9,190	28,526	46,850	59,947	2.3	2.2	2.1	520	623	721	2.8	2.7
Swaziland	264	931	1,675	2,228	2.7	2.8	2.4	19	25	28	2.8	3.2
Tanzania	7,886	32,189	62,436	88,963	3.1	2.3	2.6	740	732	1,088	3.2	2.7
Togo	1,329	4,434	8,762	12,655	3.0	2.7	2.6	99	118	150	2.6	2.8
Tunisia	3,530	9,497	13,524	15,907	2.1	1.8	1.4	166	170	151	2.8	2.7
Uganda	4,762	21,318	44,983	66,305	2.4	2.6	2.9	377	554	821	2.5	2.8
Zambia	2,440	8,690	16,163	21,965	2.4	2.5	2.5	163	210	275	2.2	3.0
Zimbabwe	2,730	11,924	19,347	24,904	3.2	2.1	2.0	293	247	293	3.2	2.4
EUROPE	**547,318**	**729,406**	**701,077**	**637,585**	**0.4**	**0.0**	**(0.1)**	**3,128**	**217**	**(844)**	**0.4**	**0.1**
Albania	1,230	3,445	4,295	4,747	2.1	0.6	0.8	65	22	28	2.1	1.2
Austria	6,935	8,210	8,305	7,430	0.4	0.1	0.1	29	49	9	0.7	0.4
Belarus, Rep	7,745	10,323	9,641	8,726	0.5	(0.1)	(0.2)	52	(14)	(22)	0.3	0.3
Belgium	8,639	10,213	10,271	9,763	0.2	0.3	0.0	19	26	4	0.4	0.0
Bosnia and Herzegovina	2,661	3,994	4,303	3,789	0.9	3.9	0.0	37	154	1	0.4	1.5
Bulgaria	7,251	8,387	7,453	6,690	(0.6)	(0.5)	(0.4)	(48)	(41)	(31)	(0.4)	(0.5)
Croatia, Rep	3,850	4,494	4,243	3,991	0.2	(0.1)	(0.2)	9	(4)	(8)	0.1	(0.1)
Czech Rep	8,925	10,223	9,627	8,572	0.0	(0.1)	(0.2)	0	(14)	(16)	0.3	(0.1)
Denmark	4,271	5,258	5,324	5,234	0.1	0.2	0.0	5	10	1	0.5	(0.4)
Estonia, Rep	1,101	1,442	1,256	1,084	0.7	(1.0)	(0.4)	10	(14)	(6)	(0.0)	(0.3)
Finland	4,009	5,156	5,294	5,172	0.3	0.3	0.1	17	14	5	0.5	(0.4)
France	41,829	58,733	60,393	58,370	0.6	0.3	0.1	310	191	67	0.5	0.3
Germany	68,376	82,401	80,877	69,542	0.4	0.3	(0.1)	339	219	(57)	0.6	0.1
Greece	7,566	10,551	10,074	9,013	0.6	0.3	(0.2)	57	29	(17)	1.1	0.3
Hungary	9,338	9,930	8,667	7,715	(0.4)	(0.6)	(0.5)	(43)	(59)	(48)	(0.5)	(0.5)
Iceland	143	277	336	363	1.1	1.0	0.8	3	3	2	1.7	1.0
Ireland	2,969	3,564	3,723	3,809	(0.3)	0.2	0.3	(10)	6	11	0.8	1.0
Italy	47,104	57,244	51,744	42,092	0.1	0.0	(0.3)	50	(2)	(175)	0.8	(0.2)
Latvia, Rep	1,949	2,447	2,108	1,891	0.7	(1.1)	(0.5)	18	(28)	(12)	(0.2)	(0.5)
Lithuania, Rep	2,567	3,710	3,521	3,297	1.0	(0.3)	(0.2)	36	(9)	(6)	0.4	0.1
Macedonia, FYR	1,230	2,205	2,541	2,646	1.2	0.7	0.6	25	15	14	1.7	0.9
Moldova, Rep	2,341	4,451	4,869	5,138	0.7	0.1	0.4	30	4	18	0.2	0.7
Netherlands	10,114	15,739	16,141	14,956	0.6	0.5	0.1	92	78	20	1.6	0.1
Norway	3,265	4,379	4,662	4,694	0.4	0.4	0.2	18	15	10	0.9	0.3
Poland, Rep	24,824	38,664	39,973	39,725	0.5	0.1	0.2	183	34	77	0.3	0.4
Portugal	8,405	9,798	9,438	8,701	(0.1)	(0.1)	(0.1)	(7)	(5)	(8)	0.4	(0.0)
Romania	16,311	22,573	21,098	19,009	0.4	(0.2)	(0.2)	96	(45)	(47)	(0.2)	0.1
Russian Federation	102,192	147,231	131,395	114,318	0.7	(0.3)	(0.4)	993	(453)	(513)	0.1	0.1
Slovak Rep	3,463	5,360	5,469	5,260	0.5	0.1	0.2	23	7	8	0.9	0.5
Slovenia, Rep	1,473	1,919	1,738	1,471	0.4	(0.1)	(0.3)	7	(2)	(5)	0.3	(0.2)
Spain	28,009	39,754	37,500	31,755	0.4	0.1	(0.1)	160	35	(57)	1.3	0.3
Sweden	7,014	8,863	9,511	9,574	0.5	0.3	0.2	42	22	22	0.8	0.0
Switzerland	4,694	7,325	7,581	6,935	0.9	0.7	0.2	60	49	15	1.5	0.5
Ukraine	36,906	51,218	45,979	40,802	0.4	(0.4)	(0.4)	190	(191)	(175)	(0.2)	0.0
United Kingdom	50,616	58,249	59,535	58,733	0.3	0.1	0.1	189	51	37	0.5	0.1
Yugoslavia, Fed Rep	7,131	10,410	10,679	10,979	0.6	0.5	(0.0)	62	50	(1)	0.6	0.4

	Population (thousands)				Average Annual Population Change (percent)			Average Annual Increment to the Population (thousands)			Average Annual Growth of the Labor Force (percent)	
	1950	1998	2025	2050	1985-90	1995-00	2005-10	1985-90	1995-00	2005-10	1980-95	1995-10
NORTH AMERICA	**171,617**	**304,078**	**369,016**	**384,054**	**1.0**	**0.8**	**0.8**	**2,822**	**2,398**	**2,436**	**1.3**	**0.9**
Canada	13,737	30,194	36,385	36,352	1.4	0.9	0.7	370	255	231	1.7	0.8
United States	157,813	273,754	332,481	347,543	1.0	0.8	0.8	2,450	2,142	2,204	1.3	0.9
CENTRAL AMERICA	**36,925**	**130,710**	**189,143**	**230,425**	**2.1**	**1.9**	**1.5**	**2,210**	**2,405**	**2,253**	**2.9**	**2.3**
Belize	69	230	375	480	2.4	2.5	2.0	4	6	6	3.2	3.3
Costa Rica	862	3,650	5,608	6,902	2.8	2.1	1.7	79	75	74	3.5	2.4
Cuba	5,850	11,115	11,798	11,284	1.0	0.4	0.3	103	47	29	2.3	0.8
Dominican Rep	2,353	8,232	11,164	13,141	2.2	1.7	1.2	147	134	117	3.0	2.3
El Salvador	1,951	6,059	9,221	11,364	1.5	2.2	1.7	71	131	121	2.7	3.1
Guatemala	2,969	11,562	21,668	29,353	2.9	2.8	2.5	247	320	371	3.1	3.6
Haiti	3,261	7,534	12,513	17,524	2.0	1.9	1.9	122	139	169	1.5	1.8
Honduras	1,380	6,147	10,656	13,920	3.1	2.8	2.2	139	166	171	3.5	3.7
Jamaica	1,403	2,539	3,370	3,886	0.5	0.9	1.2	11	24	32	1.9	1.5
Mexico	27,737	95,831	130,196	154,120	2.0	1.6	1.2	1,552	1,547	1,349	3.2	2.3
Nicaragua	1,098	4,464	7,639	9,922	2.2	2.6	2.2	73	114	123	3.4	3.5
Panama	860	2,767	3,779	4,365	2.0	1.6	1.3	46	45	40	3.0	2.1
Trinidad and Tobago	636	1,318	1,692	1,899	1.0	0.8	1.1	12	11	15	1.6	2.0
SOUTH AMERICA	**112,372**	**331,889**	**452,265**	**523,778**	**1.9**	**1.5**	**1.3**	**5,246**	**4,791**	**4,724**	**2.8**	**1.9**
Argentina	17,150	36,123	47,160	54,522	1.4	1.3	1.1	444	453	434	1.6	2.2
Bolivia	2,714	7,957	13,131	16,966	2.2	2.3	2.0	136	183	191	2.6	2.6
Brazil	53,975	165,158	216,596	243,259	1.8	1.2	1.1	2,548	2,037	2,067	2.8	1.4
Chile	6,082	14,824	19,548	22,215	1.7	1.4	1.1	210	200	175	2.6	2.0
Colombia	11,946	37,685	52,668	62,284	2.1	1.7	1.3	636	618	579	3.5	2.3
Ecuador	3,387	12,175	17,796	21,190	2.4	2.0	1.5	233	237	220	3.4	2.8
Guyana	423	856	1,114	1,239	0.1	1.0	1.0	0	9	10	2.2	1.9
Paraguay	1,488	5,222	9,355	12,565	3.1	2.6	2.3	122	134	153	2.9	3.1
Peru	7,632	24,797	35,518	42,292	2.0	1.7	1.4	415	426	416	2.9	2.8
Suriname	215	442	605	711	1.2	1.2	1.3	5	5	6	2.6	2.5
Uruguay	2,239	3,239	3,692	4,027	0.6	0.6	0.5	17	18	18	1.4	0.9
Venezuela	5,094	23,242	34,775	42,152	2.6	2.0	1.6	473	465	450	3.3	2.8
ASIA	**1,402,021**	**3,588,877**	**4,784,833**	**5,442,567**	**1.9**	**1.4**	**1.2**	**56,418**	**50,150**	**46,369**	**2.1**	**1.6**
Afghanistan, Islamic State	8,958	23,364	45,262	61,373	0.3	5.3	2.4	47	1,186	737	1.3	3.2
Armenia, Rep	1,354	3,646	4,185	4,376	1.2	0.2	0.7	41	6	25	1.3	1.4
Azerbaijan	2,896	7,714	9,714	10,881	1.4	0.8	0.9	98	59	72	1.2	1.8
Bangladesh	41,783	124,043	179,980	218,188	2.0	1.6	1.6	2,091	2,016	2,396	2.3	2.4
Bhutan	734	1,917	3,646	5,184	2.5	2.8	2.5	39	52	60	1.8	2.5
Cambodia	4,346	10,751	16,990	21,394	3.2	2.2	1.8	255	237	226	2.6	2.5
China	554,760	1,255,091	1,480,430	1,516,664	1.5	0.9	0.7	17,026	11,215	8,676	1.9	0.8
Georgia	3,527	5,428	5,762	6,028	0.6	(0.1)	0.2	35	(6)	11	0.2	0.4
India	357,561	975,772	1,330,201	1,532,674	2.1	1.6	1.3	16,571	15,553	14,020	1.9	1.9
Indonesia	79,538	206,522	275,245	318,264	1.8	1.5	1.1	3,096	3,021	2,488	2.8	2.1
Iran, Islamic Rep	16,913	73,057	128,251	170,269	3.8	2.2	2.4	2,061	1,613	2,250	3.7	3.9
Iraq	5,158	21,795	41,600	56,129	3.3	2.8	2.6	552	603	751	2.8	3.5
Israel	1,258	5,883	7,977	9,144	1.9	1.9	1.2	85	110	83	3.1	2.3
Japan	83,625	125,920	121,348	109,546	0.4	0.2	(0.0)	540	272	(30)	1.0	(0.0)
Jordan	1,237	5,956	11,894	16,671	2.1	3.3	2.8	85	191	217	5.2	4.0
Kazakstan, Rep	6,703	16,854	20,047	22,260	1.1	0.1	0.7	183	22	121	0.9	1.0
Korea, Dem People's Rep	9,488	23,206	30,046	32,873	1.5	1.6	0.9	284	363	232	2.8	1.1
Korea, Rep	20,357	46,115	52,533	52,146	1.0	0.9	0.6	413	395	288	2.3	1.3
Kuwait	152	1,809	2,904	3,406	4.4	3.0	1.7	85	55	40	1.5	4.0
Kyrgyz Rep	1,740	4,497	5,950	7,182	1.8	0.4	1.1	76	17	51	1.2	1.6
Lao People's Dem Rep	1,755	5,358	10,202	13,889	3.1	3.1	2.6	122	162	181	2.4	2.9
Lebanon	1,443	3,194	4,424	5,189	(0.9)	1.8	1.1	(23)	56	41	1.9	2.7
Malaysia	6,110	21,450	31,577	38,089	2.6	2.0	1.5	443	432	382	2.8	2.7
Mongolia	761	2,624	4,052	4,986	3.0	2.1	1.8	61	55	58	2.9	2.8
Myanmar	17,832	47,625	67,643	80,896	1.9	1.8	1.4	762	847	796	2.1	2.0
Nepal	7,862	23,168	40,554	53,621	2.6	2.5	2.3	454	578	657	2.3	2.7
Oman	456	2,504	6,538	10,930	4.5	4.2	3.8	72	102	137	3.8	4.0
Pakistan	39,513	147,811	268,904	357,353	3.3	2.7	2.4	3,589	3,950	4,606	3.3	3.4
Philippines	20,988	72,164	105,194	130,511	2.1	2.0	1.6	1,222	1,440	1,342	2.6	2.4
Saudi Arabia	3,201	20,207	42,363	59,812	4.8	3.4	2.9	680	681	793	4.9	3.4
Singapore	1,022	3,491	4,212	4,190	2.2	1.5	0.7	61	52	27	2.7	0.6
Sri Lanka	7,678	18,450	23,934	26,995	1.2	1.0	1.1	199	179	224	2.1	1.7
Syrian Arab Rep	3,495	15,335	26,303	34,463	3.5	2.5	2.3	398	385	446	3.5	3.9
Tajikistan, Rep	1,532	6,161	9,747	12,366	3.0	1.9	1.9	147	114	141	2.3	3.2
Thailand	20,010	59,612	69,089	72,969	1.7	0.8	0.6	890	451	391	2.3	0.9
Turkey	20,809	63,763	85,791	97,911	2.2	1.6	1.2	1,151	979	834	2.7	2.0
Turkmenistan, Rep	1,211	4,316	6,470	7,916	2.6	1.9	1.7	88	81	85	2.4	2.7
United Arab Emirates	70	2,354	3,297	3,668	4.3	2.0	1.5	74	47	42	4.7	1.5
Uzbekistan, Rep	6,314	24,105	36,500	45,094	2.4	1.9	1.7	468	451	495	2.4	2.8
Vietnam	29,954	77,896	110,107	129,763	2.2	1.8	1.2	1,358	1,351	1,083	2.5	1.9
Yemen	4,316	16,891	39,589	61,129	3.6	3.7	3.3	379	618	775	4.6	3.8
OCEANIA	**12,612**	**29,460**	**40,687**	**45,684**	**1.6**	**1.3**	**1.3**	**395**	**390**	**420**	**2.1**	**1.4**
Australia	8,219	18,445	23,931	25,286	1.5	1.1	1.0	249	194	201	2.0	1.0
Fiji	289	822	1,170	1,393	0.8	1.6	1.5	5	13	14	2.4	2.9
New Zealand	1,908	3,680	4,878	5,271	0.7	1.1	1.1	23	40	43	1.9	1.2
Papua New Guinea	1,613	4,602	7,546	9,637	2.2	2.2	2.0	79	102	113	2.2	2.3
Solomon Islands	90	417	844	1,192	3.4	3.2	2.8	10	13	16	3.5	3.0
DEVELOPING	**1,711,191**	**4,748,310**	**6,818,880**	**8,204,983**	**2.0**	**1.7**	**1.4**	**80,235**	**77,726**	**78,204**	**2.3**	**1.8**
DEVELOPED	**812,687**	**1,181,530**	**1,220,250**	**1,161,741**	**0.6**	**0.3**	**0.2**	**6,761**	**3,121**	**1,806**	**0.7**	**0.3**

Note: World and regional totals include countries not listed here.

Trends in Births, Life Expectancy, Fertility, and Age Structure, 1975–2000

Source: United Nations Population Division

| | Crude Birth Rate (births per 1,000 population) | | Life Expectancy at Birth (years) | | Life Expectancy of Females as a Percentage of Males (years) | | Total Fertility Rate | | Percentage of Population in Specific Age Groups | | | | | |
| | | | | | | | | | 1980 | | | 2000 | | |
	1975-80	1995-00	1975-80	1995-00	1975-80	1995-00	1975-80	1995-00	<15	15-65	>65	<15	15-65	>65
WORLD	28.3	22.6	59.7	65.6	106.0	106.8	3.9	2.8	35.2	58.9	5.9	30.0	63.2	6.8
AFRICA	46.0	39.2	47.9	53.8	106.7	105.7	6.5	5.3	44.7	52.2	3.1	43.0	53.8	3.2
Algeria	45.0	29.2	57.5	68.9	103.5	104.1	7.2	3.8	46.5	49.6	3.9	36.6	59.6	3.8
Angola	50.2	47.7	40.0	46.5	108.1	107.1	6.8	6.7	44.7	52.4	2.9	47.4	49.8	2.8
Benin	51.4	42.0	47.0	54.8	108.2	109.2	7.1	5.8	45.1	50.8	4.1	46.5	50.7	2.8
Botswana	46.6	35.0	56.4	50.4	106.6	105.7	6.4	4.5	48.7	49.3	2.0	41.9	55.6	2.4
Burkina Faso	50.8	45.9	42.9	46.0	106.0	104.2	7.8	6.6	47.4	49.8	2.8	47.0	50.3	2.7
Burundi	44.7	42.5	46.0	47.2	107.2	107.3	6.8	6.3	44.7	51.8	3.4	45.0	52.3	2.7
Cameroon	45.5	39.3	48.5	55.9	106.4	105.0	6.5	5.3	44.4	52.0	3.6	43.5	52.9	3.6
Central African Rep	44.1	37.6	44.5	48.6	111.9	109.9	5.9	5.0	41.7	54.4	4.0	41.6	54.4	4.0
Chad	44.1	41.6	41.0	47.7	108.1	106.5	5.9	5.5	41.9	54.5	3.6	43.0	53.4	3.6
Congo, Dem Rep	47.8	44.9	48.0	52.9	107.1	106.2	6.5	6.2	46.0	51.1	2.8	48.0	49.1	2.9
Congo, Rep	45.8	42.5	48.7	50.9	111.3	109.9	6.3	5.9	45.1	51.5	3.4	45.7	51.1	3.3
Côte d'Ivoire	50.7	37.2	47.9	51.0	107.1	104.4	7.4	5.1	46.6	51.0	2.5	43.0	54.0	3.0
Egypt	38.9	26.1	54.1	66.0	104.5	104.0	5.3	3.4	39.5	56.5	4.0	35.0	60.5	4.5
Equatorial Guinea	42.7	40.8	42.0	50.0	107.9	106.6	5.7	5.5	41.0	54.8	4.1	43.1	52.9	4.0
Eritrea	45.1	39.8	45.3	50.6	106.8	106.1	6.1	5.3	44.2	53.1	2.6	43.6	53.3	3.1
Ethiopia	49.0	48.2	42.0	49.9	107.9	106.6	6.8	7.0	46.1	51.2	2.7	47.1	50.2	2.8
Gabon	32.9	37.6	47.0	55.5	107.3	106.3	4.4	5.4	34.4	59.5	6.1	39.8	54.6	5.7
Gambia, The	48.8	39.9	39.0	47.0	108.3	107.3	6.5	5.2	42.6	54.4	2.8	41.2	55.5	3.1
Ghana	45.1	38.2	51.0	58.0	106.9	106.6	6.5	5.3	44.9	52.3	2.8	43.4	53.6	3.0
Guinea	51.6	48.2	38.8	46.5	102.6	102.2	7.0	6.6	45.8	51.6	2.6	47.0	50.4	2.6
Guinea-Bissau	42.4	40.3	37.5	43.8	108.6	106.6	5.6	5.4	39.0	57.0	4.0	41.7	54.2	4.2
Kenya	53.6	36.9	53.4	54.5	107.8	106.5	8.1	4.9	50.1	46.5	3.4	43.4	53.7	2.9
Lesotho	41.9	35.4	51.8	58.6	107.0	104.5	5.7	4.9	41.9	53.9	4.2	41.0	55.0	4.1
Liberia	47.4	47.5	49.5	51.5	106.3	106.0	6.8	6.3	44.3	52.0	3.7	43.7	52.7	3.6
Libya	47.3	40.0	55.8	65.5	106.3	105.6	7.4	5.9	46.7	51.1	2.2	44.7	52.4	2.9
Madagascar	46.9	41.1	49.5	58.5	106.3	105.3	6.6	5.7	45.9	51.4	2.7	45.8	51.6	2.6
Malawi	57.2	47.7	43.1	40.7	103.3	102.0	7.6	6.7	47.5	50.3	2.3	46.4	50.9	2.7
Mali	50.7	47.4	40.0	48.0	108.1	107.1	7.1	6.6	46.8	50.7	2.5	47.2	50.2	2.5
Mauritania	44.7	38.3	45.5	53.0	107.3	106.2	6.5	5.0	43.7	53.3	3.0	41.5	55.2	3.3
Mauritius	26.7	19.3	64.9	71.6	108.3	109.8	3.1	2.3	35.6	60.8	3.6	26.6	67.3	6.0
Morocco	39.4	25.3	55.8	66.7	106.3	105.7	5.9	3.1	43.2	52.7	4.1	33.8	61.9	4.3
Mozambique	45.4	42.5	43.5	46.9	107.6	106.4	6.5	6.1	43.4	53.4	3.2	44.7	52.1	3.2
Namibia	41.9	35.9	51.3	55.5	105.0	103.5	6.0	4.9	43.1	53.4	3.5	41.6	54.6	3.8
Niger	59.7	50.2	40.5	48.5	108.2	107.0	8.1	7.1	46.8	50.8	2.5	48.6	49.0	2.4
Nigeria	46.6	42.3	45.0	52.4	107.4	106.3	6.5	6.0	44.3	53.1	2.6	45.0	52.1	2.9
Rwanda	52.8	42.8	45.0	42.1	107.4	106.4	8.5	6.0	48.8	48.8	2.4	44.7	53.0	2.4
Senegal	49.3	41.1	42.8	51.3	104.8	104.0	7.0	5.6	45.3	51.8	2.8	43.6	53.4	3.0
Sierra Leone	48.8	46.5	35.2	37.5	108.9	108.6	6.5	6.1	43.0	53.9	3.1	43.9	53.1	3.0
Somalia	50.4	50.0	42.0	49.0	107.9	106.8	7.0	7.0	46.0	51.0	3.0	48.0	49.5	2.6
South Africa	37.3	29.7	55.9	65.2	111.3	109.6	5.1	3.8	40.3	55.9	3.9	36.2	59.3	4.5
Sudan	47.1	33.7	46.7	55.0	106.2	105.2	6.7	4.6	44.9	52.4	2.7	38.7	58.1	3.2
Swaziland	46.2	36.8	49.9	60.0	109.9	108.0	6.5	4.5	45.9	51.3	2.9	41.7	55.6	2.7
Tanzania	47.5	41.2	49.0	51.4	107.2	105.6	6.8	5.5	47.6	50.1	2.3	45.1	52.3	2.6
Togo	45.2	41.9	48.0	50.1	107.1	105.5	6.6	6.1	44.6	52.3	3.2	45.6	51.3	3.1
Tunisia	36.4	23.9	60.0	69.6	101.7	103.4	5.7	2.9	41.6	54.6	3.8	32.2	62.9	4.9
Uganda	50.3	51.1	47.0	41.4	107.0	104.7	6.9	7.1	47.8	49.7	2.5	49.1	48.6	2.2
Zambia	51.6	42.4	49.3	43.0	106.9	103.6	7.2	5.5	49.4	48.2	2.4	46.3	51.4	2.3
Zimbabwe	44.2	37.1	53.8	48.5	106.9	103.8	6.6	4.7	47.9	49.5	2.6	43.6	53.7	2.7
EUROPE	14.8	10.5	71.3	72.6	111.4	112.7	2.0	1.5	22.2	65.5	12.3	17.5	67.9	14.6
Albania	30.3	21.4	68.9	70.9	106.6	108.8	4.2	2.6	35.9	58.9	5.2	29.7	64.4	6.0
Austria	11.5	10.3	72.0	77.0	110.4	108.7	1.7	1.4	20.4	64.2	15.4	17.1	68.5	14.4
Belarus, Rep	16.1	10.0	71.1	69.6	114.7	116.1	2.1	1.4	22.9	66.4	10.7	18.8	67.3	13.8
Belgium	12.4	11.2	72.3	77.3	109.6	109.1	1.7	1.6	20.2	65.5	14.3	17.4	66.2	16.4
Bosnia and Herzegovina	19.6	10.8	69.9	73.2	107.0	107.7	2.2	1.4	27.3	66.7	6.1	18.9	71.2	9.8
Bulgaria	15.8	10.3	71.3	71.3	107.9	110.5	2.2	1.5	22.1	66.0	11.9	16.9	67.2	15.8
Croatia, Rep	15.6	10.8	70.6	72.2	110.4	112.3	2.0	1.6	21.1	67.2	11.7	17.3	68.0	14.6
Czech Rep	17.4	10.7	70.6	72.9	110.4	108.9	2.3	1.4	23.5	63.2	13.4	17.6	69.8	12.6
Denmark	12.3	13.0	74.2	75.6	108.4	107.3	1.7	1.8	20.8	64.7	14.4	18.6	66.7	14.7
Estonia, Rep	15.0	9.0	69.7	69.4	115.3	117.4	2.1	1.3	21.7	65.8	12.5	17.6	68.5	13.9
Finland	13.6	12.0	72.2	76.6	112.6	109.7	1.6	1.8	20.3	67.7	12.0	18.4	67.1	14.6
France	14.0	11.6	73.7	78.8	111.6	111.1	1.9	1.6	22.3	63.8	14.0	18.3	65.4	16.2
Germany	10.4	9.3	72.5	76.7	109.4	108.9	1.5	1.3	18.5	65.9	15.6	15.4	68.8	15.9
Greece	15.6	10.0	73.7	78.1	105.7	106.8	2.3	1.4	22.8	64.0	13.1	15.3	66.9	17.8
Hungary	16.2	10.2	69.4	69.0	109.8	114.4	2.1	1.4	21.9	64.6	13.4	17.0	68.5	14.5
Iceland	19.2	16.5	76.3	79.3	108.0	104.9	2.3	2.2	27.6	62.7	10.1	23.8	64.9	11.3
Ireland	21.2	13.0	72.0	76.6	107.2	107.3	3.5	1.8	30.6	58.7	10.7	21.1	67.5	11.4
Italy	13.0	9.1	73.6	78.3	109.2	108.4	1.9	1.2	22.3	64.6	13.1	14.2	68.1	17.7
Latvia, Rep	14.0	9.8	69.2	68.4	115.6	118.9	2.0	1.4	20.4	66.5	13.0	18.2	67.5	14.4
Lithuania, Rep	15.4	10.8	70.8	70.4	114.2	117.1	2.1	1.5	23.6	65.1	11.3	19.5	67.0	13.5
Macedonia, FYR	22.6	14.5	69.6	72.5	105.2	106.3	2.7	1.9	28.6	64.5	6.9	22.3	68.3	9.4
Moldova, Rep	19.6	13.6	64.8	67.5	111.2	112.6	2.4	1.8	26.7	65.5	7.8	23.4	66.8	9.8
Netherlands	12.7	11.9	75.3	77.9	109.0	107.5	1.6	1.6	22.3	66.2	11.5	18.2	68.2	13.6
Norway	12.9	13.4	75.3	77.6	108.9	107.8	1.8	1.9	22.2	63.1	14.8	19.8	65.1	15.0
Poland, Rep	19.2	11.9	70.9	71.1	111.9	113.5	2.3	1.7	24.3	65.6	10.1	19.8	68.4	11.8
Portugal	18.2	11.2	70.2	75.4	110.6	109.9	2.4	1.5	25.9	63.6	10.5	16.7	67.5	15.7
Romania	19.1	11.0	69.6	69.5	107.0	110.9	2.6	1.4	26.7	63.1	10.3	18.5	68.4	13.2
Russian Federation	15.8	9.6	67.4	64.4	118.1	123.3	1.9	1.4	21.6	68.1	10.2	18.0	69.3	12.7
Slovak Rep	20.6	11.7	70.4	71.3	110.9	113.1	2.5	1.5	26.1	63.5	10.4	20.0	68.8	11.1
Slovenia, Rep	16.6	9.5	71.0	73.5	111.6	112.4	2.2	1.3	23.4	65.3	11.4	15.7	70.2	14.2
Spain	17.4	9.7	74.3	78.0	108.4	109.4	2.6	1.2	26.6	62.7	10.7	15.0	68.4	16.5
Sweden	11.7	11.9	75.2	78.5	108.3	106.0	1.7	1.8	19.6	64.1	16.3	19.1	64.3	16.7
Switzerland	11.6	10.9	75.2	78.6	109.2	108.6	1.5	1.5	19.7	66.4	13.8	17.2	68.1	14.7
Ukraine	14.9	9.7	69.3	68.8	114.8	116.4	2.0	1.4	21.4	66.7	11.9	17.8	67.9	14.3
United Kingdom	12.4	11.9	72.8	77.1	109.0	107.1	1.7	1.7	20.9	64.0	15.1	18.9	65.4	15.8
Yugoslavia, Fed Rep	18.4	12.6	70.3	72.5	106.5	107.9	2.4	1.8	24.1	66.1	9.8	19.8	66.9	13.3

| | Crude Birth Rate (births per 1,000 population) | | Life Expectancy at Birth (years) | | Life Expectancy of Females as a Percentage of Males (years) | | Total Fertility Rate | | Percentage of Population in Specific Age Groups | | | | | |
| | | | | | | | | | 1980 | | | 2000 | | |
	1975-80	1995-00	1975-80	1995-00	1975-80	1995-00	1975-80	1995-00	<15	15-65	>65	<15	15-65	>65
NORTH AMERICA	**15.1**	**13.6**	**73.3**	**76.9**	**111.2**	**109.1**	**1.8**	**1.9**	**22.5**	**66.4**	**11.0**	**21.2**	**66.4**	**12.4**
Canada	15.4	11.9	74.2	78.9	110.8	107.5	1.8	1.6	22.7	67.9	9.4	19.3	68.1	12.6
United States	15.1	13.8	73.2	76.7	111.2	109.1	1.8	2.0	22.5	66.3	11.2	21.4	66.2	12.4
CENTRAL AMERICA	**38.2**	**26.5**	**63.7**	**71.7**	**110.2**	**108.4**	**5.4**	**3.0**	**45.1**	**51.2**	**3.6**	**34.8**	**60.7**	**4.5**
Belize	40.9	31.3	69.7	74.7	102.5	103.7	6.2	3.7	47.3	48.6	4.8	39.7	55.8	4.1
Costa Rica	31.7	24.0	71.0	76.8	106.4	106.3	3.9	3.0	38.9	57.5	3.6	33.1	61.8	5.1
Cuba	17.2	13.1	73.0	76.0	104.8	105.1	2.1	1.6	31.9	60.5	7.6	21.2	69.2	9.6
Dominican Rep	34.9	24.1	62.0	70.9	106.1	106.1	4.7	2.8	42.3	54.6	3.1	33.1	62.5	4.5
El Salvador	41.5	27.9	57.2	69.5	119.5	109.0	5.7	3.1	46.1	50.8	3.1	35.6	59.7	4.7
Guatemala	44.3	36.3	56.4	67.2	107.2	107.9	6.4	4.9	45.9	51.3	2.8	42.9	53.3	3.7
Haiti	36.8	34.1	50.7	54.4	106.3	106.1	5.4	4.6	40.7	54.8	4.4	40.0	56.2	3.8
Honduras	44.9	33.5	57.7	69.8	107.7	107.1	6.6	4.3	47.2	50.1	2.7	41.6	54.9	3.4
Jamaica	28.8	21.7	70.1	74.6	106.3	106.1	4.0	2.4	40.2	53.0	6.8	30.2	63.4	6.4
Mexico	37.1	24.6	65.3	72.5	110.3	108.6	5.3	2.8	45.1	51.1	3.8	33.1	62.1	4.7
Nicaragua	45.7	33.5	57.6	68.2	108.5	107.3	6.4	3.9	47.7	49.8	2.5	40.8	56.0	3.2
Panama	31.0	22.5	69.0	73.9	105.8	106.4	4.1	2.6	40.5	55.0	4.5	31.3	63.2	5.5
Trinidad and Tobago	29.3	16.6	68.3	73.7	107.6	106.6	3.4	2.1	34.2	60.2	5.5	26.1	67.4	6.5
SOUTH AMERICA	**32.0**	**21.5**	**62.9**	**69.0**	**108.8**	**110.7**	**4.3**	**2.5**	**37.8**	**57.6**	**4.6**	**30.2**	**64.2**	**5.6**
Argentina	25.7	19.9	68.7	73.2	110.4	110.3	3.4	2.6	30.5	61.4	8.1	27.7	62.6	9.7
Bolivia	41.0	33.2	50.1	61.5	108.8	105.7	5.8	4.4	42.6	53.9	3.5	39.6	56.4	4.0
Brazil	32.6	19.6	61.8	67.1	108.1	112.3	4.3	2.2	38.1	57.8	4.2	28.4	66.4	5.2
Chile	24.0	19.9	67.2	75.3	110.5	108.3	3.0	2.4	33.5	60.9	5.6	28.5	64.4	7.2
Colombia	31.7	23.4	64.0	70.9	107.3	108.1	4.1	2.7	40.0	56.2	3.7	32.5	62.8	4.6
Ecuador	38.2	25.6	61.4	69.8	105.9	107.7	5.4	3.1	42.8	53.2	4.0	33.8	61.5	4.7
Guyana	31.5	21.9	60.7	64.4	108.4	111.1	3.9	2.3	40.8	55.2	4.0	29.9	65.9	4.2
Paraguay	35.9	31.3	66.6	69.7	106.7	106.7	5.2	4.2	42.2	53.3	4.5	39.5	57.0	3.5
Peru	38.0	24.9	58.5	68.3	106.7	107.6	5.4	3.0	41.9	54.5	3.6	33.4	61.8	4.8
Suriname	29.5	21.8	65.1	71.5	107.8	107.2	4.2	2.4	39.7	55.8	4.5	32.3	62.4	5.5
Uruguay	20.3	16.8	69.6	72.9	110.2	109.3	2.9	2.3	26.9	62.5	10.5	23.9	63.5	12.7
Venezuela	34.2	24.9	67.6	72.8	109.1	108.1	4.5	3.0	40.7	56.1	3.2	34.0	61.5	4.4
ASIA	**29.6**	**22.3**	**58.5**	**66.2**	**102.6**	**104.5**	**4.2**	**2.7**	**37.6**	**58.0**	**4.4**	**30.1**	**64.1**	**5.8**
Afghanistan, Islamic State	50.8	53.4	40.0	45.5	100.0	102.2	7.2	6.9	43.0	54.5	2.5	41.7	55.6	2.7
Armenia, Rep	20.9	13.3	72.3	70.6	109.0	110.1	2.5	1.7	30.4	63.6	6.0	24.5	66.8	8.7
Azerbaijan	24.7	19.2	68.5	70.6	112.1	112.0	3.6	2.3	34.5	60.0	5.4	29.5	63.6	6.9
Bangladesh	47.2	26.8	46.6	58.1	97.9	100.2	6.7	3.1	46.0	50.5	3.4	35.6	61.2	3.3
Bhutan	42.8	41.3	42.6	53.2	104.8	106.4	5.9	5.9	41.3	55.6	3.1	43.0	53.8	3.2
Cambodia	30.0	33.7	31.2	54.1	108.3	105.3	4.1	4.5	39.2	57.9	2.9	40.4	56.6	3.0
China	21.5	16.2	65.3	69.9	103.0	105.1	3.3	1.8	35.5	59.7	4.7	24.9	68.4	6.7
Georgia	18.1	13.8	70.7	72.7	111.9	112.0	2.4	1.9	25.7	65.1	9.1	22.0	65.4	12.6
India	34.7	25.2	52.9	62.4	98.3	101.0	4.8	3.1	38.5	57.4	4.0	32.7	62.3	5.0
Indonesia	35.4	23.1	52.8	65.1	104.9	105.8	4.7	2.6	41.0	55.6	3.3	30.8	64.6	4.7
Iran, Islamic Rep	44.7	34.0	58.6	69.2	101.4	102.2	6.5	4.8	44.9	51.8	3.3	43.1	52.8	4.1
Iraq	41.9	36.4	61.4	62.4	103.0	104.9	6.6	5.3	46.0	51.3	2.7	41.4	55.5	3.1
Israel	26.0	20.3	73.1	77.7	104.9	105.0	3.4	2.8	33.2	58.2	8.6	28.1	62.4	9.5
Japan	15.2	10.3	75.5	80.0	107.4	107.8	1.8	1.5	23.6	67.4	9.0	15.2	68.3	16.5
Jordan	45.0	37.5	61.2	69.7	106.1	106.1	7.4	5.1	49.4	47.5	3.1	43.3	53.8	2.9
Kazakstan, Rep	24.9	18.1	65.4	67.6	117.1	115.4	3.1	2.3	32.4	61.5	6.1	27.5	65.4	7.1
Korea, Dem People's Rep	22.2	21.3	65.8	72.2	110.3	109.0	3.3	2.1	39.5	57.0	3.5	27.3	67.4	5.3
Korea, Rep	23.9	15.0	64.8	72.4	111.6	110.5	2.9	1.7	34.0	62.2	3.8	21.4	72.0	6.7
Kuwait	40.1	21.3	69.6	76.0	106.2	105.5	5.9	2.8	40.2	58.3	1.4	33.2	64.8	2.0
Kyrgyz Rep	29.9	25.5	64.2	67.6	114.2	113.4	4.1	3.2	37.1	57.1	5.8	35.0	59.0	6.0
Lao People's Dem Rep	45.1	44.2	43.5	53.5	106.9	105.8	6.7	6.7	42.0	55.2	2.8	45.4	51.7	3.0
Lebanon	30.1	24.2	65.0	69.9	106.2	105.3	4.3	2.8	40.1	54.5	5.4	32.9	61.3	5.8
Malaysia	30.4	25.2	65.3	72.0	105.7	106.3	4.2	3.2	39.3	57.0	3.7	35.3	60.6	4.1
Mongolia	39.2	27.8	56.3	65.8	104.5	104.7	6.7	3.3	43.2	53.9	2.9	36.4	59.8	3.8
Myanmar	37.5	27.2	52.1	60.1	106.4	105.6	5.3	3.3	39.6	56.4	4.0	34.0	61.4	4.6
Nepal	43.4	36.3	46.2	57.3	96.6	99.1	6.2	5.0	42.9	54.1	3.0	42.0	54.5	3.5
Oman	46.1	44.1	54.9	70.8	104.3	106.4	7.2	7.2	44.6	52.8	2.6	47.7	49.9	2.3
Pakistan	47.3	36.1	53.4	63.9	101.3	103.5	7.0	5.0	44.4	52.7	2.9	41.8	55.0	3.2
Philippines	35.9	28.4	59.9	68.3	105.5	105.4	5.0	3.6	41.9	55.3	2.8	36.7	59.7	3.6
Saudi Arabia	45.9	34.3	58.8	71.4	104.0	105.0	7.3	5.9	44.3	52.9	2.8	40.7	56.4	2.9
Singapore	17.2	15.7	70.8	77.3	106.6	105.9	1.9	1.8	27.0	68.2	4.7	22.6	70.3	7.1
Sri Lanka	28.5	17.8	66.8	73.1	105.4	106.3	3.8	2.1	35.3	60.4	4.3	26.2	67.2	6.6
Syrian Arab Rep	46.0	30.4	60.1	68.9	106.2	106.7	7.4	4.0	48.5	48.3	3.2	40.8	56.1	3.1
Tajikistan, Rep	37.2	30.4	64.5	67.2	108.3	109.3	5.9	3.9	42.9	52.5	4.6	39.5	55.9	4.6
Thailand	31.6	16.7	61.2	69.3	106.6	109.0	4.3	1.7	40.0	56.5	3.5	25.2	69.1	5.8
Turkey	32.0	21.9	60.3	69.0	107.8	107.8	4.5	2.5	39.2	56.0	4.7	28.3	65.7	5.9
Turkmenistan, Rep	35.3	28.6	61.6	64.6	112.0	111.1	5.3	3.6	41.3	54.4	4.3	37.4	58.3	4.2
United Arab Emirates	30.5	18.7	66.8	74.8	106.5	103.5	5.7	3.5	28.6	70.1	1.3	28.1	69.4	2.5
Uzbekistan, Rep	34.4	28.2	65.1	67.5	111.0	110.0	5.1	3.5	40.9	54.0	5.1	37.5	57.9	4.6
Vietnam	38.3	25.1	55.8	67.4	108.2	107.2	5.6	3.0	42.5	52.7	4.8	34.3	60.5	5.2
Yemen	53.7	47.7	44.1	58.0	101.1	101.7	7.6	7.6	50.2	47.2	2.6	48.3	49.3	2.3
OCEANIA	**20.9**	**18.4**	**68.2**	**73.9**	**108.7**	**106.9**	**2.8**	**2.5**	**29.3**	**62.7**	**8.0**	**25.5**	**64.9**	**9.7**
Australia	16.0	14.3	73.4	78.3	109.8	107.7	2.1	1.9	25.3	65.1	9.6	21.0	67.1	11.9
Fiji	33.2	22.6	67.1	72.6	105.3	106.1	4.0	2.8	39.1	58.0	2.8	31.3	64.3	4.5
New Zealand	17.2	15.4	72.4	77.2	109.2	106.7	2.2	2.0	26.7	63.3	10.0	23.0	65.6	11.3
Papua New Guinea	39.6	32.3	49.7	57.9	101.0	102.6	5.9	4.7	43.0	55.5	1.6	38.7	58.3	3.0
Solomon Islands	45.0	36.1	65.3	71.6	106.2	106.2	7.1	5.0	47.6	49.3	3.1	43.0	54.1	2.9
DEVELOPING	**32.8**	**25.4**	**56.7**	**63.6**	**103.8**	**105.0**	**4.7**	**3.1**	**39.3**	**56.6**	**4.1**	**32.8**	**62.2**	**5.0**
DEVELOPED	**14.9**	**11.4**	**72.2**	**74.5**	**110.8**	**111.0**	**1.9**	**1.6**	**22.5**	**65.9**	**11.6**	**18.3**	**67.5**	**14.2**

Note: World and regional totals include countries not listed here.

Data Table 7.3
Distribution of Income, Land, and Poverty, 1977–96

Source: The World Bank and the Food and Agriculture Organization of the United Nations

| | Income Distribution | | Percentage of Income in Each Quintile of Population | | | | | Distribution of Agricultural Land Ownership | | | Population in Poverty | | | |
| | | | | | | | | | | | International Poverty Line (<1Int$/day) {b} | | National Poverty Line (national criteria) | |
	Survey Year	Gini Coefficient {a}	Poorest 0-20%	20-40%	40-60%	60-80%	Richest 80-100%	Survey Year	Gini Coefficient {a}	% Owning <10 ha	Year(s)	(percent)	Year(s)	(percent)
WORLD														
AFRICA														
Algeria	1988	39	6.8	11.0	14.9	20.7	46.6	X	X	X	1988	1.6	X	X
Angola	X	X	X	X	X	X	X	X	X	X	X	X	X	X
Benin	X	X	X	X	X	X	X	X	X	X	X	X	1995	33.0
Botswana	1986	54	3.6	6.9	11.4	19.2	58.9	X	X	X	1985-86	34.7	X	X
Burkina Faso	X	X	X	X	X	X	X	X	X	X	X	X	X	X
Burundi	X	X	X	X	X	X	X	X	X	X	X	X	1990	36.2
Cameroon	1983	49	X	X	X	X	X	X	X	X	X	X	1984	40.0
Central African Rep	1992	55	X	X	X	X	X	X	X	X	X	X	X	X
Chad	X	X	X	X	X	X	X	X	X	X	X	X	X	X
Congo, Dem Rep	X	X	X	X	X	X	X	1990	39.4	X	X	X	X	X
Congo, Rep	X	X	X	X	X	X	X	X	X	X	X	X	X	X
Côte d'Ivoire	1988	37	6.8	11.2	15.8	22.2	44.1	X	X	X	1988	17.7	X	X
Egypt	1991	32	8.7	12.5	16.3	21.4	41.1	X	X	X	1990-91	7.6	X	X
Equatorial Guinea	X	X	X	X	X	X	X	X	X	X	X	X	X	X
Eritrea	X	X	X	X	X	X	X	X	X	X	X	X	X	X
Ethiopia	X	X	X	X	X	X	X	1989-92	32.3	100.0	1981-82	33.8	X	X
Gabon	1977	63	2.9	4.6	9.6	16.6	66.3	X	X	X	X	X	X	X
Gambia, The	X	X	X	X	X	X	X	X	X	X	X	X	1992	64.0
Ghana	1992	34	7.9	12.0	16.1	21.8	42.2	X	X	X	X	X	1992	31.4
Guinea	X	X	X	X	X	X	X	1989	18.9	99.4	1991	26.3	X	X
Guinea-Bissau	1991	56	2.1	6.5	12.0	20.6	58.9	1988	NA	99.8	1991	87.0	1991	48.8
Kenya	1992	54	3.4	6.7	10.7	17.3	61.8	X	X	X	1992	50.2	1992	46.4
Lesotho	1987	56	2.9	6.4	11.3	19.5	60.0	X	X	X	1986-87	50.4	1993	49.2
Liberia	X	X	X	X	X	X	X	X	X	X	X	X	X	X
Libya	X	X	X	X	X	X	X	1987	NA	72.4	X	X	X	X
Madagascar	1993	43	5.9	9.8	14.1	20.4	49.8	X	X	X	1993	72.3	X	X
Malawi	X	X	X	X	X	X	X	X	X	X	X	X	X	X
Mali	X	X	X	X	X	X	X	X	X	X	X	X	X	X
Mauritania	1988	43	3.5	10.7	16.2	23.3	46.3	X	X	X	1988	31.4	1990	57.0
Mauritius	1991	37	6.7	11.6	15.7	22.6	43.4	X	X	X	X	X	1992	10.6
Morocco	1991	39	6.6	10.5	15.0	21.7	46.3	X	X	X	1990-91	1.1	1990-91	13.1
Mozambique	X	X	X	X	X	X	X	X	X	X	X	X	X	X
Namibia	X	X	X	X	X	X	X	X	X	X	X	X	X	X
Niger	1992	36	7.5	11.8	15.5	21.1	44.1	X	X	X	1992	61.5	X	X
Nigeria	1993	37	4.0	8.9	14.4	23.4	49.3	X	X	X	1992-93	28.9	1992-93	34.1
Rwanda	1983	29	9.7	13.1	16.7	21.6	38.9	X	X	X	1983-85	45.7	1993	51.2
Senegal	1991	54	3.5	7.0	11.6	19.3	58.6	X	X	X	1991-92	54.0	X	X
Sierra Leone	1968	61	2.8	2.6	11.1	21.6	62.0	X	X	X	X	X	X	X
Somalia	X	X	X	X	X	X	X	X	X	X	X	X	X	X
South Africa	1993	62	2.0	4.9	9.5	18.8	64.9	X	X	X	1993	23.7	X	X
Sudan	1968	39	8.2	8.3	20.9	16.7	46.0	X	X	X	X	X	X	X
Swaziland	X	X	X	X	X	X	X	X	X	X	X	X	X	X
Tanzania	1993	38	6.9	10.9	15.3	21.5	45.4	X	X	X	1993	16.4	1991	51.1
Togo	X	X	X	X	X	X	X	X	X	X	X	X	1987-89	32.3
Tunisia	1990	40	5.9	10.4	15.3	22.1	46.3	X	X	X	1990	3.9	1990	14.1
Uganda	1992	41	6.8	X	14.4	20.4	48.1	1991	62.2	96.5	1989-90	50.0	1992-93	55.0
Zambia	1991	50	X	X	X	X	X	X	X	X	1993	84.6	1993	86.0
Zimbabwe	1990	57	4.0	6.3	10.0	17.4	62.3	X	X	X	1990-91	41.0	1990-91	25.5
EUROPE														
Albania	X	X	X	X	X	X	X	X	X	X	X	X	1996	19.6
Austria	X	X	X	X	X	X	X	1990	44.6	53.2	X	X	X	X
Belarus, Rep	1995	29	8.7	13.7	17.7	22.7	37.3	X	X	X	X	X	X	X
Belgium	1992	27	8.1	14.2	18.8	23.8	35.0	1990	26.8	53.4	1992	0.9 c	1992	2.6 c
Bosnia and Herzegovina	X	X	X	X	X	X	X	X	X	X	X	X	X	X
Bulgaria	1993	34	7.1	12.2	16.6	22.4	41.7	X	X	X	1992	2.6	X	X
Croatia, Rep	X	X	X	X	X	X	X	X	X	X	X	X	X	X
Czech Rep	1994	28	9.7	13.5	17.0	21.7	38.1	X	X	X	1993	3.1	X	X
Denmark	1992	33	5.5	12.1	19.2	25.5	37.8	1989	27.3	18.1	1992	0.9 c	1992	4.1 c
Estonia, Rep	1995	40	5.1	11.1	15.8	22.1	45.8	X	X	X	1993	6.0	1994	8.9
Finland	1991	26	7.8	14.6	19.7	24.1	33.8	X	X	X	1991	0.1 c	1991	2.8 c
France	1984	35	6.6	12.4	16.7	22.3	42.0	1988	26.7	37.7	1984	0.8 c	1984	4.3 c
Germany	1984	32	6.6	12.8	18.0	23.8	38.9	X	X	X	1989	0.7 c	1989	5.2 c
Greece	1988	35	6.2	11.6	17.0	24.0	41.2	X	X	X	X	X	X	X
Hungary	1993	28	9.7	13.9	16.9	21.4	38.1	X	X	X	1993	0.7	1993	25.3
Iceland	X	X	X	X	X	X	X	X	X	X	X	X	X	X
Ireland	1987	35	4.9	9.7	15.8	24.9	44.6	1991	X	25.4	1987	1.4 c	1987	4.4 c
Italy	1991	32	8.4	13.2	17.7	23.3	37.4	1990	76.8	87.7	X	X	1991	2.7 c
Latvia, Rep	1993	27	9.6	13.6	17.5	22.6	36.7	X	X	X	X	X	X	X
Lithuania, Rep	1993	34	8.1	12.3	16.2	21.3	42.1	X	X	X	1993	2.1	X	X
Macedonia, FYR	X	X	X	X	X	X	X	X	X	X	X	X	X	X
Moldova, Rep	1992	34	6.9	11.9	16.7	23.1	41.5	X	X	X	1992	6.8	X	X
Netherlands	1991	29	6.9	14.2	18.9	23.7	36.4	1989	X	48.4	1991	1.9 c	1991	4.3 c
Norway	1991	33	5.4	11.2	17.0	24.9	41.6	X	X	X	1991	0.4 c	1991	2.4 c
Poland, Rep	1993	33	6.3	12.9	17.8	23.5	39.5	X	X	X	1993	6.8	1993	23.8
Portugal	1991	36	6.1	12.0	17.2	24.3	40.4	1989	71.6	91.5	X	X	X	X
Romania	1994	29	8.7	13.4	17.6	23.0	37.3	X	X	X	1992	17.7	1994	21.5
Russian Federation	X	X	X	X	X	X	X	X	X	X	1993	1.1	1994	30.9
Slovak Rep	1992	19	11.9	15.8	18.8	22.2	31.3	X	X	X	1992	12.8	X	X
Slovenia, Rep	1993	28	9.5	13.5	17.1	21.9	37.9	X	X	X	X	X	X	X
Spain	1989	26	8.4	14.3	18.7	23.3	35.3	1989	79.6	78.5	1990	0.5 c	1990	5.5 c
Sweden	1992	32	6.7	12.2	17.6	24.5	39.0	X	X	X	1992	0.3 c	1992	4.2 c
Switzerland	X	X	X	X	X	X	X	1990	23.2	52.3	X	X	1995	31.7
Ukraine	1992	26	9.5	14.1	18.0	22.9	35.4	X	X	X	X	X	X	X
United Kingdom	1991	32	7.6	12.6	16.0	23.0	40.8	X	X	X	1991	0.5 c	1991	6.7 c
Yugoslavia, Fed Rep	1990	32	7.3	12.5	17.4	23.7	39.0	X	X	X	X	X	X	X

	Income Distribution		Percentage of Income in Each Quintile of Population					Distribution of Agricultural Land Ownership			Population in Poverty			
											International Poverty Line (<1Int$/day) {b}		National Poverty Line (national criteria)	
	Survey Year	Gini Coefficient {a}	Poorest 0-20%	20-40%	40-60%	60-80%	Richest 80-100%	Survey Year	Gini Coefficient {a}	% Owning <10 ha	Year(s)	(percent)	Year(s)	(percent)
NORTH AMERICA														
Canada	1991	28	7.7	13.7	19.0	24.8	34.8	X	X	X	1991	0.3 c	1991	7.0 c
United States	1991	38	4.5	10.7	16.6	24.1	44.1	1987	70.8	X	1994	1.4 c	1994	13.2 c
CENTRAL AMERICA														
Belize	X	X	X	X	X	X	X	X	X	X	X	X	X	X
Costa Rica	1989	46	4.0	9.1	14.3	21.9	50.7	X	X	X	1989	18.9	X	X
Cuba	X	X	X	X	X	X	X	X	X	X	X	X	X	X
Dominican Rep	1992	49	X	X	X	X	X	X	X	X	1989	19.9	1992	20.6
El Salvador	1977	48	5.0	7.4	12.2	22.2	53.2	X	X	X	X	X	1992	48.3
Guatemala	1989	59	2.1	5.8	10.5	18.6	63.0	X	X	X	1989	53.3	X	X
Haiti	X	X	X	X	X	X	X	X	X	X	X	X	1987	65.0
Honduras	1993	54	X	X	X	X	X	1993	73.3	70.9	1992	46.5	1992	50.0
Jamaica	1993	38	6.8	11.1	15.4	21.5	45.2	X	X	X	1993	4.7	1992	34.2
Mexico	1992	57	X	X	X	X	X	X	X	X	1992	14.9	1988	10.1
Nicaragua	1993	50	4.2	8.0	12.6	20.1	55.1	X	X	X	1993	43.8	1993	50.3
Panama	1989	56	2.0	6.3	11.6	20.3	59.8	1990	87.8	79.1	X	X	X	X
Trinidad and Tobago	1981	42	3.4	10.1	16.1	25.5	44.9	X	X	X	X	X	1992	21.0
SOUTH AMERICA														
Argentina	X	X	X	X	X	X	X	1988	79.1	23.5	X	X	1991	25.5
Bolivia	1990	42	5.6	9.7	14.5	22.0	48.2	X	X	X	1990-91	7.1	X	X
Brazil	1989	60	2.5	4.9	9.2	18.3	65.2	X	X	X	1989	28.7	1990	17.4
Chile	1994	56	3.5	6.6	10.9	18.1	61.0	X	X	X	1992	15.0	X	X
Colombia	1991	51	3.6	8.8	12.9	20.4	54.4	X	X	X	1991	7.4	1992	18.8
Ecuador	1994	43	5.4	8.9	13.2	19.9	52.6	X	X	X	1994	30.4	1994	35.0
Guyana	1993	47	X	X	X	X	X	X	X	X	X	X	X	X
Paraguay	X	X	X	X	X	X	X	1991	91.3	61.6	X	X	1991	21.8
Peru	1994	45	4.9	9.2	14.1	21.4	50.4	X	X	X	1994	49.4	1991	54.0
Suriname	X	X	X	X	X	X	X	X	X	X	X	X	X	X
Uruguay	X	X	X	X	X	X	X	X	X	X	X	X	X	X
Venezuela	1990	54	3.6	7.1	11.7	19.3	58.4	X	X	X	1991	11.8	1989	31.3
ASIA														
Afghanistan, Islamic State	X	X	X	X	X	X	X	X	X	X	X	X	X	X
Armenia, Rep	1989	39	1.7	11.8	19.0	26.9	40.6	X	X	X	X	X	X	X
Azerbaijan	X	X	X	X	X	X	X	X	X	X	X	X	X	X
Bangladesh	1992	35	X	X	X	X	X	X	X	X	X	X	1991-92	47.5
Bhutan	X	X	X	X	X	X	X	X	X	X	X	X	X	X
Cambodia	X	X	X	X	X	X	X	X	X	X	X	X	X	X
China	1992	38	6.0	10.7	15.8	25.8	41.7	X	X	X	1993	29.4	1990	8.6
Georgia	X	X	X	X	X	X	X	X	X	X	X	X	X	X
India	1992	32	8.8	12.5	16.2	21.4	41.1	1986	42.8	98.0	1992	52.5	X	X
Indonesia	1993	32	8.7	12.3	16.3	22.1	40.7	X	X	X	1993	14.5	1990	15.1
Iran, Islamic Rep	1984	43	X	X	X	X	X	X	X	X	X	X	X	X
Iraq	X	X	X	X	X	X	X	X	X	X	X	X	X	X
Israel	X	X	X	X	X	X	X	X	X	X	X	X	X	X
Japan	1990	35	X	X	X	X	X	X	X	X	1992	0.2 c	1992	6.9 c
Jordan	1991	41	6.5	10.3	14.6	20.9	47.7	X	X	X	1992	2.5	1991	15.0
Kazakstan, Rep	1993	33	7.5	12.3	16.9	22.9	40.4	X	X	X	X	X	X	X
Korea, Dem People's Rep	X	X	X	X	X	X	X	X	X	X	X	X	X	X
Korea, Rep	1988	34	7.4	12.3	16.3	21.8	42.2	X	X	X	X	X	X	X
Kuwait	X	X	X	X	X	X	X	X	X	X	X	X	X	X
Kyrgyz Rep	1993	35	6.7	11.5	16.4	23.1	42.3	X	X	X	1993	18.9	1993	45.4
Lao People's Dem Rep	1992	30	9.6	12.9	16.3	21.0	40.2	X	X	X	X	X	1993	46.1
Lebanon	X	X	X	X	X	X	X	X	X	X	X	X	X	X
Malaysia	1989	48	4.6	8.3	13.0	20.4	53.7	X	X	X	1989	5.6	1989	15.5
Mongolia	X	X	X	X	X	X	X	X	X	X	X	X	1995	36.3
Myanmar	X	X	X	X	X	X	X	1993	25.0	X	X	X	X	X
Nepal	1984	30	9.1	12.9	16.7	21.8	39.5	1992	33.2	99.7	1995-96	53.1	1995-96	42.0
Oman	X	X	X	X	X	X	X	X	X	X	X	X	X	X
Pakistan	1991	31	8.4	12.9	16.9	22.2	39.7	1990	37.1	93.2	1991	11.6	1991	34.0
Philippines	1991	45	X	X	X	X	X	X	X	X	1988	27.5	1991	54.0
Saudi Arabia	X	X	X	X	X	X	X	X	X	X	X	X	X	X
Singapore	1989	39	X	X	X	X	X	X	X	X	X	X	X	X
Sri Lanka	1990	30	8.9	13.1	16.9	21.7	39.3	X	X	X	1990	4.0	1991	22.4
Syrian Arab Rep	X	X	X	X	X	X	X	X	X	X	X	X	X	X
Tajikistan, Rep	X	X	X	X	X	X	X	X	X	X	X	X	X	X
Thailand	1992	52	3.7	7.6	11.6	18.6	58.5	1988	12.9	X	1992	0.1	1992	13.1
Turkey	1987	44	5.2	9.6	14.1	21.2	49.9	1991	40.0	85.4	X	X	X	X
Turkmenistan, Rep	X	X	X	X	X	X	X	X	X	X	1993	4.9	X	X
United Arab Emirates	X	X	X	X	X	X	X	X	X	X	X	X	X	X
Uzbekistan, Rep	X	X	X	X	X	X	X	X	X	X	X	X	X	X
Vietnam	1992	36	7.8	11.4	15.4	22.4	43.0	X	X	X	X	X	1993	50.9
Yemen	X	X	X	X	X	X	X	X	X	X	X	X	1992	19.1
OCEANIA														
Australia	1990	42	4.6	9.7	15.5	23.8	46.4	1990	X	5.0	1989	0.8 c	1989	7.0 c
Fiji	1977	43	X	X	X	X	X	1991	74.3	88.0	X	X	X	X
New Zealand	1990	40	4.6	10.5	16.3	23.9	44.7	X	X	X	X	X	X	X
Papua New Guinea	X	X	X	X	X	X	X	X	X	X	X	X	X	X
Solomon Islands	X	X	X	X	X	X	X	X	X	X	X	X	X	X

Notes: a. Gini coefficients measure the equality of distribution (0 would be perfectly equal, 100 perfectly unequal). b. Adjusted for purchasing power parity. c. Luxembourg Income Study estimates (national poverty is here defined as 40% of the national median income).

Social Investment, 1990–96

Sources: United Nations Children's Fund; the World Bank; United Nations Educational, Scientific and Cultural Organization; and National Center for Education Statistics

| | Percentage of Population with Access to: {a} | | | | | | | | | Health Expenditure as a Percentage of GDP {a} | | Public Education Expenditure as a Percentage of: | | Number of Public Libraries |
| | Safe Drinking Water 1990-96 | | | Adequate Sanitation 1990-96 | | | Health Services 1990-96 | | | Total 1990-95 | Public 1990-95 | GNP 1995 | Total Gov't Expenditure 1995 | 1990-96 {a} |
	Urban	Rural	Total	Urban	Rural	Total	Urban	Rural	Total					
WORLD														
AFRICA														
Algeria	91	64	78	99	80	91	100	95	98	4.6	3.3	X	X	X
Angola	69	15	32	34	8	16	X	X	X	X	4.0	X	X	X
Benin	41	53	50	54	6	20	X	X	18 b	X	1.7	3.1	15.2	12
Botswana	100	91	93 b	91	41	55	X	X	X	X	1.9	9.6	20.5	X
Burkina Faso	X	X	78	42	11	18	100	89	90	5.5	2.3	3.6	11.1	21 c
Burundi	93	54	59	60	51	51	100	79	80	X	0.9	2.8	X	X
Cameroon	57	43	50	64	36	50	96	69	80	1.4	1.0	X	X	X
Central African Rep	59	23	38	83	36	52	89	30	52	X	1.7	X	X	X
Chad	48	17	24	73	7	21	64	X	30	X	1.8	2.2	X	X
Congo, Dem Rep	89	26	42	53	6	18	40	17	26 b	X	X	X	X	X
Congo, Rep	53	7	34	X	X	69	97	70	83 b	6.8	3.6	5.9	14.7	X
Côte d'Ivoire	X	X	75	X	X	43	X	X	X	3.4	1.4	X	X	X
Egypt	X	X	79	X	X	32	100	99	99	4.9	X	5.6	13.8	X
Equatorial Guinea	X	X	X	X	X	X	X	X	X	X	X	1.8	5.6	3
Eritrea	X	7	X	X	X	X	X	X	X	X	1.1	X	X	X
Ethiopia	91	19	25	97	7	19	X	X	46	X	1.1	4.7	13.0	X
Gabon	90	50	68 b	X	X	X	X	X	X	X	0.5	X	X	X
Gambia, The	67	X	48	51	50	37	X	X	93	X	1.8	5.5	16.0	2 c
Ghana	88	52	65	62	44	55	92	45	60 b	X	1.0	X	X	X
Guinea	50	56	55	84	10	21	100	70	80	X	0.9	X	X	X
Guinea-Bissau	32	67	59	24	32	30	X	X	40	X	1.1	X	X	X
Kenya	67	49	53	69	81	77	X	X	77	X	1.9	7.4	X	21
Lesotho	44	58	56	42	25	28	X	X	80 b	X	3.5	5.9	X	X
Liberia	79	13	46	56	4	30	50	30	39 b	X	X	X	X	X
Libya	97	97	97	99	94	98	100	85	95	X	X	X	X	X
Madagascar	83	10	29	12	3	3	81	19	38	X	1.0	X	X	X
Malawi	80	32	37	22	4	6	81	29	35	X	2.3	5.7	15.0	7
Mali	46	43	45	58	21	31	X	X	40	X	1.3	2.2	X	X
Mauritania	67	65	66 b	34	X	X b	X	X	63	X	1.5	5.0	16.1	X
Mauritius	95	100	99	99	99	99	100	100	100 b	X	2.2	4.3	17.3	X
Morocco	94	18	55	69	18	41	100	50	70 b	3.4	1.6	5.6	22.6	X
Mozambique	X	X	63	X	X	54	100	30	39 b	X	4.6	X	X	X
Namibia	87	42	57	77	12	34	87	42	59	7.6	3.9	9.4	21.3	X
Niger	46	55	54	71	4	15	99	30	32	X	2.2	X	X	X
Nigeria	84	40	51	84	48	58	X	X	51	X	X	X	X	76
Rwanda	X	79	X	X	85	X	X	X	80	X	1.9	X	X	X
Senegal	85	28	52	83	40	58	100	85	90	1.6	X	3.6	33.1	26 c
Sierra Leone	58	21	34	17	8	11	90	20	38	X	1.6	X	X	X
Somalia	X	28	31	6	2	12	X	X	X	X	X	X	X	X
South Africa	99	53	99	85	12	53	X	X	X	7.9	3.6	6.8	20.5	X
Sudan	84	41	60	79	4	22	X	X	70	0.3	X	X	X	X
Swaziland	X	X	X	X	X	X	X	X	X	X	X	8.1	21.7	X
Tanzania	73	29	38	96	84	86	X	X	42	X	2.8	X	X	X
Togo	74	58	63	56	10	23	80	X	X	X	1.7	5.6	18.7	23
Tunisia	100	95	98	96	52	80	X	X	X	5.9	3.0	6.8	17.4	250 c
Uganda	60	35	38	96	47	64	99	42	49	3.9	1.8	X	X	17
Zambia	50	17	27	89	43	64	X	X	X	3.3	2.6	1.8	X	X
Zimbabwe	99	64	77	99	48	66	96	80	85	X	2.1	8.5	X	X
EUROPE														
Albania	X	X	X	X	X	X	X	X	X	X	2.7	3.4	X	X
Austria	X	X	X	X	X	X	X	X	X	9.7	6.2	5.5	10.2	2,592
Belarus, Rep	X	X	X	X	X	X	X	X	X	6.4	5.3	5.6	17.1	9,121
Belgium	X	X	X	X	X	X	X	X	X	8.2	7.2	5.7	10.2	1,151
Bosnia and Herzegovina	X	X	X	X	X	X	X	X	X	X	X	X	X	X
Bulgaria	X	X	X	X	X	X	X	X	X	X	4.0	4.2	X	4,879 c
Croatia, Rep	X	X	X	X	X	X	X	X	X	10.1	8.5	5.3	X	250 c
Czech Rep	X	X	X	X	X	X	X	X	X	9.9	7.8	6.1	16.9	7,986
Denmark	X	X	X	X	X	X	X	X	X	6.6	5.5	8.3	12.6	904
Estonia, Rep	X	X	X	X	X	X	X	X	X	X	5.9	6.9	25.5	773
Finland	X	X	X	X	X	X	X	X	X	8.3	6.2	7.6	11.9	1,339
France	X	X	X	X	X	X	X	X	X	9.7	7.6	5.9	10.8	3,366
Germany	X	X	X	X	X	X	X	X	X	9.5	7.0	4.7	9.4	13,032
Greece	X	X	X	X	X	X	X	X	X	6.4	X	3.7	9.9	669
Hungary	X	X	X	X	X	X	X	X	X	7.3	6.8	6.6	6.9	4,468
Iceland	X	X	X	X	X	X	X	X	X	X	X	5.0	12.0	190
Ireland	X	X	X	X	X	X	X	X	X	7.9	6.0	6.3	13.2	516
Italy	X	X	X	X	X	X	X	X	X	8.3	5.9	4.9	8.8	2,366
Latvia, Rep	X	X	X	X	X	X	X	X	X	X	3.7	6.3	16.8	1,037 c
Lithuania, Rep	X	X	X	X	X	X	X	X	X	X	4.8	6.1	21.8	1,511
Macedonia, FYR	X	X	X	X	X	X	X	X	X	7.7	6.8	5.5	18.7	122
Moldova, Rep	98	18	55	90	8	50	X	X	X	X	5.1	6.1	22.9	X
Netherlands	X	X	X	X	X	X	X	X	X	8.8	6.9	5.3	9.5	1,265
Norway	X	X	X	X	X	X	X	X	X	7.3	6.9	8.3	15.0	1,157
Poland, Rep	X	X	X	X	X	X	X	X	X	X	4.6	4.6	X	9,505 c
Portugal	X	X	X	X	X	X	X	X	X	7.6	4.3	5.4	X	161 c
Romania	X	X	X	X	X	X	X	X	X	X	3.3	3.2	9.1	2,917 c
Russian Federation	X	X	X	X	X	X	X	X	X	4.8	4.1	4.1	9.6	96,177 c
Slovak Rep	X	X	X	X	X	X	X	X	X	X	6.3	5.1	X	3,005
Slovenia, Rep	X	X	X	X	X	X	X	X	X	X	7.9	5.8	12.6	954
Spain	X	X	X	X	X	X	X	X	X	7.4	5.8	5.0	12.6	4,880
Sweden	X	X	X	X	X	X	X	X	X	7.7	6.4	8.0	11.0	1,656
Switzerland	X	X	X	X	X	X	X	X	X	9.6	6.9	5.5	15.6	2,555
Ukraine	X	X	X	X	X	X	X	X	X	X	5.4	7.7	X	21,857 c
United Kingdom	X	X	X	X	X	X	X	X	X	6.9	5.8	5.5	11.4	24,869
Yugoslavia, Fed Rep	X	X	X	X	X	X	X	X	X	X	X	X	X	800

	Safe Drinking Water 1990-96			Adequate Sanitation 1990-96			Health Services 1990-96			Health Expenditure as a Percentage of GDP {a}		Public Education Expenditure as a Percentage of:		Number of Public Libraries 1990-96 {a}
	Urban	Rural	Total	Urban	Rural	Total	Urban	Rural	Total	Total 1990-95	Public 1990-95	GNP 1995	Total Gov't Expenditure 1995	
NORTH AMERICA														
Canada	X	X	X	X	X	X	X	X	X	9.8	7.0	7.3	13.7	3,672
United States	X	X	X	X	X	X	X	X	X	14.3	6.3	5.3	14.2	122,663 d
CENTRAL AMERICA														
Belize	X	X	X	X	X	X	X	X	X	X	X	6.1	21.3	X
Costa Rica	100	92	96	95	70	84	X	X	X	8.5	6.3	4.5	19.9	60 c
Cuba	96	69	89	95	82	92	X	X	100	X	7.9	X	10.2	354 c
Dominican Rep	80	X	65	76	83	78	84	67	78	5.3	2.0	1.9	13.2	X
El Salvador	85	46	69	91	65	81	X	X	40	5.0	1.2	2.2	X	X
Guatemala	87	49	64	72	52	59	X	X	57	2.7	0.9	1.7	18.2	X
Haiti	37	23	28	42	16	24	X	39	60	3.6	1.3	X	X	X
Honduras	96	79	87	97	78	87	86	55	69	5.6	2.8	3.9	16.5	X
Jamaica	X	X	86	100	80	89	X	X	90 b	5.4	3.0	8.2	7.7	X
Mexico	92	57	83	85	32	72	X	X	93	5.3	2.8	5.3	26.0	5,630
Nicaragua	84	29	53	77	34	60	100	60	83 b	7.8	4.3	X	X	X
Panama	X	X	93	X	X	83	X	X	70	7.5	5.4	5.2	20.9	X
Trinidad and Tobago	99	91	97	99	98	79	100	99	100	3.9	2.6	4.5	X	X
SOUTH AMERICA														
Argentina	77	29	71	73	37	68	80	21	71 b	10.6	4.3	4.5	15.0	1,545 c
Bolivia	87	36	66	72	32	55	77	52	67	5.0	2.7	6.6	8.2	250
Brazil	85	69	73	55	4	44	X	X	X	7.4	2.7	X	X	X
Chile	98	81	X	86	X	X	X	X	97 b	6.5	2.5	2.9	14.0	289
Colombia	97	56	85	97	56	85	86	72	81	7.4	3.0	3.5	12.9	X
Ecuador	80	49	68	95	49	76	70	20	X b	5.3	2.0	3.4	X	X
Guyana	X	X	X	X	X	X	X	X	X	X	X	4.1	8.1	X
Paraguay	70	10	42	65	14	41	90	38	63 b	4.3	1.0	2.9	16.9	X
Peru	75	18	72	58	25	57	X	X	44	4.9	2.6	3.8	X	X
Suriname	X	X	X	X	X	X	X	X	X	X	X	3.5	X	X
Uruguay	85	5	75 b	60	65	61 b	X	X	82 b	8.5	2.0	2.8	13.3	X
Venezuela	80	75	79	64	30	59	X	X	X	7.1	2.3	5.2	22.4	701
ASIA														
Afghanistan, Islamic State	39	5	12	13	X	X	80	17	29 b	X	X	X	X	X
Armenia, Rep	X	X	X	X	X	X	X	X	X	7.8	3.1	X	X	1,293 c
Azerbaijan	X	X	X	X	X	X	X	X	X	7.5	1.4	3.0	17.5	4,647 c
Bangladesh	99	96	97	79	44	48	X	X	45	2.4	1.2	2.3	8.7	X
Bhutan	75	54	58	90	66	70	X	X	65 b	X	X	X	X	X
Cambodia	65	33	36	81	8	14	80	50	53 b	7.2	0.7	X	X	X
China	97	56	67	74	7	24	100	83	88	3.8	1.8	2.3	X	2,579
Georgia	X	X	X	X	X	X	X	X	X	X	0.3	5.2	6.9	3,929
India	85	79	81	70	14	29	100	80	85	3.5	0.7	3.5	12.1	X
Indonesia	79	54	62	73	40	51	99	91	93	1.5	0.7	X	X	X
Iran, Islamic Rep	98	82	90	86	74	81	100	75	88	4.8	2.8	4.0	17.8	1,002
Iraq	92	44	78	85	37	70	97	78	93 b	X	X	X	X	X
Israel	X	X	X	X	X	X	X	X	X	X	4.1	6.6	12.3	1,180
Japan	100	85	97	85	X	X	X	X	X	7.0	5.5	3.8	10.8	1,950
Jordan	X	X	98	X	X	77	98	95	97 b	7.9	3.7	6.3	16.6	X
Kazakstan, Rep	X	X	X	X	X	X	X	X	X	X	2.2	4.5	17.6	15,055
Korea, Dem People's Rep	X	X	X	X	X	X	X	X	X	X	X	X	X	X
Korea, Rep	100	76	93	100	100	100	100	100	100	5.4	1.8	3.7	17.4	329
Kuwait	X	X	X	100	X	X b	X	X	100 b	7.0	X	5.6	X	18
Kyrgyz Rep	84	X	X	60	10	30	X	X	X	X	3.5	6.8	23.1	1,001 c
Lao People's Dem Rep	60	51	52	98	16	28	X	X	67 b	2.6	0.8	2.4	X	X
Lebanon	96	88	94	81	8	63	98	85	95	5.3	1.7	2.0	X	X
Malaysia	96	66	78	X	X	94	X	X	X	X	1.4	5.3	15.5	471
Mongolia	100	58	80	100	47	74	X	X	95 b	4.7	4.4	5.6	X	X
Myanmar	78	50	60	56	36	43	100	47	60	0.9	0.5	1.3	14.4	X
Nepal	88	60	63	58	12	18	X	X	X	5.0	1.2	2.9	13.2	X
Oman	X	X	82	X	X	78	100	94	96	X	2.5	4.6	15.2	20
Pakistan	82	69	74	77	22	47	99	35	55 b	X	0.8	X	X	10
Philippines	92	80	86	88	66	77	X	X	71	2.4	1.3	2.2	X	X
Saudi Arabia	100	74	95 b	100	30	86 b	100	88	97 b	2.2	X	5.5	X	X
Singapore	100	X	100 b	X	X	X	X	X	X	3.5	1.1	3.0	23.4	10
Sri Lanka	88	52	57	68	62	63	X	X	X	1.9	1.4	3.1	8.1	X
Syrian Arab Rep	92	78	85	84	82	83	96	84	90	X	X	X	X	X
Tajikistan, Rep	82	49	X	46	X	X	X	X	X	X	6.4	8.6	17.9	X
Thailand	94	88	89	98	95	96	90	90	90 b	5.3	1.4	4.2	20.1	X
Turkey	91	59	80	X	X	X	X	X	X	4.2	2.7	3.4	X	1,171
Turkmenistan, Rep	X	X	74	X	X	90	X	X	100	X	2.8	X	X	X
United Arab Emirates	X	X	95	93	22	77	X	X	99	2.2	1.9	1.8	16.3	X
Uzbekistan, Rep	82	49	62	46	X	22	X	X	X	X	3.5	9.5	24.4	X
Vietnam	X	X	X	X	X	X	X	X	X	5.2	1.1	X	X	X
Yemen	88	55	61	47	17	24	81	32	38	2.6	1.1	7.5	20.8	X
OCEANIA														
Australia	X	X	X	X	X	X	X	X	X	8.4	5.8	5.6	13.6	X
Fiji	X	X	X	X	X	X	X	X	X	X	X	5.4	18.6	X
New Zealand	100	82	97	X	X	X	X	X	X	7.5	5.7	6.7	17.2	X
Papua New Guinea	84	17	28	82	11	22	X	X	96 b	X	2.8	X	X	X
Solomon Islands	X	X	X	X	X	X	X	X	X	X	X	X	X	X

Notes: a. Data are for the most recent year available, within the range given. b. Data are for years other than noted, differ from the standard definition, or refer to only part of a country. c. Refers to number of administrative units; number of libraries, or service points, is likely the same or greater. d. Data are from 1990-95.

Sources and Technical Notes

the actual distribution of land ownership differs from a perfectly equal distribution. A coefficient of zero would reflect perfect sharing of land resources, a coefficient of 100 would represent perfect inequality. Graphically, the index is the area between a cumulative frequency distribution (the cumulative percentage of total land area against the cumulative percentage of owners—starting with the land poor) and a hypothetical line of absolute equality (expressed as a percentage of the area under the line).

The percentage of people *owning less than 10 hectares* was calculated directly from agricultural census data.

The percentage of people falling below the *international poverty line* was calculated by the World Bank from primary household survey data obtained from government statistical agencies and World Bank country departments. It is the percentage of people living on less than $1 a day (at 1985 international prices) adjusted for purchasing power parity (for more information, see the Technical Notes to Data Table 6.1).

The percentage of people falling below the *national poverty line* is calculated using World Bank poverty assessments based on household surveys. The line is defined by the appropriate authorities in each nation. Data for poverty in selected developed countries are the product of the Luxembourg Income Study (LIS). The definition of a national poverty line chosen here (40 percent of the median income) is just one of several alternative definitions offered by the LIS. Forty percent of the median income provides a close approximation to the percentage of poor reported by the United States (14.5 percent in 1994—using a more complex algorithm, U.S. Department of Commerce, *Statistical Abstract of the United States 1996* [U.S. Department of Commerce, Washington, D.C. 1996], p. 472.). With the exception of the United States and the United Kingdom, these developed countries do not commonly report poverty estimates. All poverty data are limited. In general, such estimates do not include allowances for goods and services—in-kind benefits such as housing, food, medical care, schooling, etc.—provided, for example, by a government.

Data Table 7.4

Social Investment, 1990–96

Sources: Access to safe drinking water, adequate sanitation services, and health care: United Nations Children's Fund (UNICEF), *The State of the World's Children 1997*, (UNICEF, New York, 1997), including input from Multiple Indicator Cluster Surveys, the World Health Organization (WHO), and

Demographic and Health Surveys (DHS). Total expenditure on health as a percentage of GDP and public expenditure on health as a percentage of gross domestic product (GDP): The World Bank, *World Development Indicators 1997* (The World Bank, Washington, D.C., 1997). Public expenditure on education as a percentage of gross national product (GNP) and number of public libraries (except for the United States): United Nations Educational, Scientific and Cultural Organization (UNESCO), *1996 UNESCO Statistical Yearbook* (UNESCO, Paris and Bernan Press, Lanham, Maryland, 1997). Number of public libraries for the United States: National Center for Education Statistics surveys, as reported by the American Library Association.

WHO collected data on drinking water and sanitation from national governments in 1980, 1983, 1988, and 1990 using questionnaires completed by public health officials, WHO experts, and resident representatives of the United Nations Development Programme (UNDP). In 1990, the Joint Monitoring Programme was established by WHO and UNICEF to build national capacity in measuring all aspects of water and sanitation services. The most recent round of data collection from the Programme yielded figures for access to clean water and sanitation for many countries as of 1994.

Definitions of safe drinking water and appropriate access to sanitation and health services vary depending upon location and condition of local resources, thus, comparisons can be misleading. In addition, urban and rural populations were defined by each national government and might not be strictly comparable. The official definitions of access to safe drinking water, adequate sanitation, and health services are listed below, but, countries are at liberty to adapt these definitions to reflect local conditions.

Percentage of population with access to safe drinking water is the portion of the population with reasonable access to an adequate amount of safe water (including treated surface water and untreated water from protected springs, boreholes, and sanitary wells). WHO defines "reasonable access" to safe drinking water in urban areas as access to piped water or a public standpipe within 200 meters of a dwelling or housing unit. In rural areas, reasonable access implies that a family member need not spend a "disproportionate" part of the day fetching water.

Percentage of population with access to adequate sanitation is the portion of the population with at least adequate excreta disposal facilities that can effectively prevent human, animal, and insect contact with excreta. Urban areas with access to sanitation services are defined as urban populations served by connections to public sewers or household systems

such as pit privies, pour-flush latrines, septic tanks, communal toilets, and other such facilities. Rural populations with access to sanitation are defined as those with adequate disposal, such as pit privies and pour-flush latrines.

Percentage of population with access to health services is the portion of the population that can reach appropriate local health services via local means of transport in no more than 1 hour. However, as noted by UNICEF, many of the data on access to health services are quite old (i.e., pre-1990). In addition, the quality of these data are questionable. Many countries may report distance to health services rather than the time it takes to get to them, and the definition of "appropriate services" varies.

Total health expenditure includes public and private outlays for the provision of health services (preventive and curative), population activities, nutrition activities, and emergency aid designated for health. It does not include expenditures for water and sanitation. *Public health expenditure* excludes private expenditures but includes recurrent and capital government expenditures on health care (including government and social security expenditures for medical care) and donor assistance for health services.

Public education expenditure is public expenditure on public education plus subsidies for private education. It is not possible to show private expenditure on education because of a lack of data for many countries. Public expenditure includes educational expenditure at every level of administration according to the constitution of the country (i.e., central or federal government, state government, provincial or regional authorities, and municipal and local authorities). For almost all countries, data on GNP are supplied by the World Bank.

For further information on World Bank data, visit the World Bank's Web site at: http://www.worldbank.org.

Public libraries are defined as those that serve the population of a community or region free of charge or for a nominal fee; they may service the general public or special categories of users such as children, members of the armed forces, hospital patients, prisoners, workers, and employees. UNESCO counts libraries in numbers of administrative units and service points. An administrative unit is any independent library or group of libraries under a single director or a single administration; a service point is any library that provides in separate quarters a service for users, whether it is an independent library or part of a larger administrative unit.

For further information on libraries in the United States, visit the American Library Association's Web site at: http://www.ala.org/library/factl.html.

Chapter 8

Health

Nutrition, 1971–96

Sources: United Nations Children's Fund, United Nations Statistical Division, and the World Health Organization

	Percentage of Low-Birthweight Infants 1990-94 {a}	Percentage of Children Under 5 Suffering from (1990-96) {a} Under-weight	Wasting	Stunting	Daily Per Capita Calorie Supply as a Percentage of Total Requirements 1988-90 {a}	Percentage of Pregnant Women Aged 15-49 With Anemia	Year of Anemia Data	Percentage of Children Aged 6-11 with Goiter 1971-91 {a}	Percentage of Households Consuming Iodized Salt 1992-96 {a}	Percentage of Children Under 5 with Vitamin A Deficiency 1971-95 {a}
WORLD										
AFRICA										
Algeria	9	13	9	18	123	X		9	92	X
Angola	19	X	X	X	80	X		7 g	0	3
Benin	X	X	X	X	104	X		24	35	8
Botswana	8	15 b	X	44 b	97	X		8	27	X
Burkina Faso	21	30	13	29	94	X		16	22	74
Burundi	X	37	9	43	84	X		42	80	X
Cameroon	13	14	3	24	95	X		26	86	20
Central African Rep	15	27	7	34	82	X		63	28	X
Chad	X	X	X	X	73	X		15 g	31	5
Congo, Dem Rep	15	34	10	45	96	X		9 g	12	X
Congo, Rep	16	24 b	4 b	21 b	103	X		8 g	X	26
Côte d'Ivoire	14	24	8	24	111	X		6 g	0	47
Egypt	10	9	3	24	132	X		5	90	X
Equatorial Guinea	X	X	X	X	X	X		10 g	X	X
Eritrea	13	41	10	66	X	X		X	80	X
Ethiopia	16	48	8	64	73	X		22	0	56
Gabon	X	X	X	X	104	X		5 g	X	X
Gambia, The	X	X	X	X	X	X		20 g	0	X
Ghana	7	27	11	26	93	X		10 g	0	X
Guinea	21	26	12	32	97	X		19	X	X
Guinea-Bissau	20	23 b	X	X	97	X		19 g	0	X
Kenya	16	23	8	34	89	X		7 g	100	1
Lesotho	11	21	2	33	93	X		16	X	78
Liberia	X	X	X	X	98	78	1982 c	6 g	X	X
Libya	X	5	3	15	140	X		6 g	90	X
Madagascar	17	34	7	50	95	X		24	1	X
Malawi	20	30	7	48	88	X		13	58	2
Mali	17	31 b	11 b	24 b	96	50	1987 d	29 g	20	80
Mauritania	11	23	7	44	106	X		X	3	44
Mauritius	13	16	15	10	128	X		X	0	X
Morocco	9	9	2	23	125	X		20 g	X	X
Mozambique	20	27	5	55	77	58	1986 d	20	62	1
Namibia	16	26	9	28	X	X		35	80	20
Niger	15	36	16	32	95	X		9 g	0	2
Nigeria	16	36	9	43	93	65	1987 d	10 g	83	1
Rwanda	17	29	4	48	82	X		50	90	1
Senegal	11	20	9	22	98	X		12 g	10	72
Sierra Leone	11	29	9	35	83	X		7 g	75	X
Somalia	16	X	X	X	81	X		7 g	X	2
South Africa	X	9	3	23	128	X		2 g	40	49
Sudan	15	34	13	34	87	X		20 g	X	2
Swaziland	X	X	X	X	X	X		10 g	X	X
Tanzania	14	29	6	47	95	X		37	74	47
Togo	20	24 b	5 b	30 b	99	X		22	0	10
Tunisia	8	9	4	22	131	X		4	X	X
Uganda	X	23 b	2 b	45 b	93	X		7 g	50	4
Zambia	13	28	6	53	87	X		51	90	18
Zimbabwe	14	16	6	21	94	X		42	80	1
EUROPE										
Albania	7	X	X	X	107	X		41	X	X
Austria	6	X	X	X	133	X		X	X	X
Belarus, Rep	X	X	X	X	X	X		22	37	X
Belgium	6	X	X	X	149	X		5 g	X	X
Bosnia and Herzegovina	X	X	X	X	X	X		10 g	X	X
Bulgaria	6	X	X	X	148	X		20 g	X	X
Croatia, Rep	X	X	X	X	X	X		25	100	X
Czech Rep	6	X	X	X	X	X		3 g	X	X
Denmark	6	X	X	X	135	X		5 g	X	X
Estonia, Rep	X	X	X	X	X	X		X	X	X
Finland	4	X	X	X	113	X		X	X	X
France	5	X	X	X	143	X		5 g	X	X
Germany	X	X	X	X	X	X		10 g	X	X
Greece	6	X	X	X	151	X		10 g	X	X
Hungary	9	X	X	X	137	X		X	X	X
Iceland	X	X	X	X	X	X		X	X	X
Ireland	4	X	X	X	157	X		X	X	X
Italy	5	X	X	X	139	X		20 g	X	X
Latvia, Rep	X	X	X	X	X	X		X	X	X
Lithuania, Rep	X	X	X	X	X	X		X	X	X
Macedonia, FYR	X	X	X	X	X	X		X	100	X
Moldova, Rep	4	X	X	X	X	X		X	X	X
Netherlands	X	X	X	X	114	X		3 g	X	X
Norway	4	X	X	X	120	X		X	X	X
Poland, Rep	X	X	X	X	131	X		10 g	X	X
Portugal	5	X	X	X	136	X		15 g	X	X
Romania	11	X	X	X	116	X		10 g	X	X
Russian Federation	X	X	X	X	X	X		10 g	30	X
Slovak Rep	X	X	X	X	X	X		X	X	X
Slovenia, Rep	X	X	X	X	X	X		15	X	X
Spain	4	X	X	X	141	9	1985 d,e	10 g	X	X
Sweden	5	X	X	X	111	X		X	X	X
Switzerland	5	X	X	X	130	X		X	4	X
Ukraine	X	X	X	X	X	X		10 g	4	X
United Kingdom	7	X	X	X	130	12	1990 d,f	X	X	X
Yugoslavia, Fed Rep	X	X	X	X	X	X		5 g	70	X

	Percentage of Low-Birthweight Infants 1990-94 {a}	Percentage of Children Under 5 Suffering from (1990-96) {a}			Daily Per Capita Calorie Supply as a Percentage of Total Requirements 1988-90 {a}	Percentage of Pregnant Women Aged 15-49 With Anemia	Year of Anemia Data	Percentage of Children Aged 6-11 with Goiter 1971-91 {a}	Percentage of Households Consuming Iodized Salt 1992-96 {a}	Percentage of Children Under 5 with Vitamin A Deficiency 1971-95 {a}
		Under-weight	Wasting	Stunting						
NORTH AMERICA										
Canada	6	X	X	X	122	X		X	X	X
United States	7	X	X	X	138	X		X	X	X
CENTRAL AMERICA										
Belize	X	X	X	X	X	65	1984	X	X	10
Costa Rica	6	2	2	8	121	X		3	91	X
Cuba	9	X	1 b	X	135	X		10 g	0	X
Dominican Rep	11	10	1	19	102	X		X	40	22
El Salvador	11	11	1	23	102	X		25	91	36
Guatemala	14	27	3	50	103	X		20	93	26
Haiti	15	28	8	32	89	X		4	10	8
Honduras	9	18	2	40	98	X		9	85	20
Jamaica	10	10	4	6	114	62	1982	X	100	X
Mexico	8	14 b	6 b	22 b	131	X		15 g	87	32
Nicaragua	15	12	2	24	99	X		4	79	31
Panama	9	7	1	9	98	X		13	92	X
Trinidad and Tobago	10	7 b	4 b	5 b	114	X		X	X	X
SOUTH AMERICA										
Argentina	7	X	X	X	131	X		8	90	X
Bolivia	12	16	4	28	84	X		21	92	11
Brazil	11	7 b	2 b	16 b	114	X		14	79	55
Chile	5	1	0	3	102	X		9	90	X
Colombia	10	8	1	15	106	X		10 g	90	24
Ecuador	13	17 b	2 b	34 b	105	X		10 g	90	16
Guyana	X	X	X	X	X	58	1986	X	X	X
Paraguay	5	4	0	17	116	X		49	64	X
Peru	11	11	1	37	87	X		36	90	22
Suriname	X	X	X	X	X	X		X	X	X
Uruguay	8	7 b	X	16 b	101	X		X	X	X
Venezuela	9	6 b	2 b	6 b	99	52	1987 d	11	65	X
ASIA										
Afghanistan, Islamic State	20	X	X	X	72	X		20 g	X	X
Armenia, Rep	X	X	X	X	X	X		10 g	X	X
Azerbaijan	X	X	X	X	X	X		20 g	X	X
Bangladesh	50	67	17	63	88	X		11	44	5
Bhutan	X	38 b	4 b	56 b	128	X		25	96	1
Cambodia	X	40	8	38	96	X		15 g	0	7
China	9	16	4	32	112	X		9	51	19
Georgia	X	X	X	X	X	X		20 g	X	X
India	33	53	18	52	101	88	1985-86	9 g	67	1
Indonesia	14	35	X	X	121	74	1986	28	50	65
Iran, Islamic Rep	9	16	7	19	125	X		30 g	82	X
Iraq	15	12	3	22	128	X		7 g	50	2
Israel	7	X	X	X	125	X		X	X	X
Japan	7	X	X	X	125	X		X	X	X
Jordan	7	9	2	16	110	X		X	75	X
Kazakstan, Rep	X	X	X	X	X	X		20 g	14	X
Korea, Dem People's Rep	X	X	X	X	121	X		15	5	X
Korea, Rep	9	X	X	X	120	X		X	X	X
Kuwait	7	6 b	3 b	12 b	X	X		X	X	X
Kyrgyz Rep	X	X	X	X	X	X		20 g	X	X
Lao People's Dem Rep	18	44	10	48	111	X		25 g	X	X
Lebanon	10	X	X	X	127	X		15 g	92	X
Malaysia	8	23	X	X	120	X		20 g	X	12
Mongolia	6	12	2	26	97	X		7 g	X	X
Myanmar	16	43	8	45	114	60	1980	18	14	34
Nepal	X	49	6	63	100	X		44	68	3
Oman	8	12	X	12	X	X		X	X	21
Pakistan	25	38	9	50	99	X		32 g	19	70
Philippines	15	30	8	33	104	48	1987	15	40	X
Saudi Arabia	7	X	X	X	121	23	1978-82	X	X	X
Singapore	7	X	X	X	136	X		X	X	X
Sri Lanka	25	38	16	24	101	X		14	7	1
Syrian Arab Rep	11	12	8	27	126	X		73	21	X
Tajikistan, Rep	X	X	X	X	X	X		20 g	20	X
Thailand	13	26 b	6 b	22 b	103	X		12	50	20
Turkey	8	10	3	21	127	X		36	31	X
Turkmenistan, Rep	5	X	X	X	X	X		20 g	0	X
United Arab Emirates	6	X	X	X	X	X		X	X	X
Uzbekistan, Rep	X	X	X	X	X	X		18	0	X
Vietnam	X	X	X	X	X	X		20 g	X	1
Yemen	19	39	13	39	X	X		32 g	21	65
OCEANIA										
Australia	6	X	X	X	124	X		X	X	X
Fiji	X	X	X	X	X	40	1975-82	47 g	X	X
New Zealand	6	X	X	X	131	X		X	X	X
Papua New Guinea	23	35 b	X	X	114	X		30 g	X	92
Solomon Islands	X	X	X	X	X	30	1989	X	X	2

Notes: a. Data are for most recent year available, within the range given. b. Data are for years other than noted, differ from the standard definition, or refer to only part of a country. c. Data for Monrovia only. d. Reference year not known; publication year given instead. e. Data for Madrid only. f. Data are for all women.
g. Data are estimated from subnational data and total goiter rate prevalence of border regions in neighboring countries.

Mortality, 1975–2020

Sources: United Nations Population Division and United Nations Children's Fund

	Crude Death Rate (per 1,000)			Infant Mortality Rate {a} (per 1,000 live births)			Under-5 Mortality Rate (per 1,000 live births)			Average Annual Change in Under-5 Mortality (percent)		Maternal Mortality Rate (per 100,000 live births)
	1975-80	1995-00	2015-20	1975-80	1995-00	2015-20	1960	1980	1995	1960-80	1980-95	1990
WORLD	**11.0**	**8.9**	**8.0**	**87**	**57**	**35**	**X**	**X**	**X**	**X**	**X**	**X**
AFRICA	**17.7**	**12.9**	**8.4**	**120**	**86**	**55**	**X**	**X**	**X**	**X**	**X**	**X**
Algeria	13.4	5.6	4.6	112	44	21	243	145	61	(2.6)	(5.7)	160
Angola	24.4	18.7	11.1	160	124	79	345	261	292	(1.4)	0.7	X
Benin	21.1	12.4	6.9	122	84	46	310	176	142	(2.8)	(1.4)	990
Botswana	11.3	13.0	7.5	76	56	33	170	94	52	(3.0)	(3.9)	250
Burkina Faso	21.9	17.7	10.7	127	97	63	318	218	164	(1.3)	(2.7)	930
Burundi	18.8	17.0	10.8	127	114	78	255	193	176	(1.4)	(0.6)	1,300
Cameroon	17.6	11.9	6.5	102	58	34	264	173	106	(2.1)	(3.3)	550
Central African Rep	20.6	16.4	10.3	122	96	60	294	202	165	(1.9)	(1.4)	700
Chad	23.1	17.3	11.3	154	115	79	325	254	152	(2.3)	(2.0)	1,500
Congo, Dem Rep	17.5	13.5	8.0	117	89	53	286	204	185	(1.7)	(0.6)	870
Congo, Rep	17.4	14.6	8.5	91	90	55	220	125	108	(2.8)	(1.0)	890
Côte d'Ivoire	17.5	13.8	8.7	117	86	54	300	180	150	(2.8)	(0.8)	810
Egypt	14.2	7.1	6.0	131	54	25	258	180	51	(1.8)	(8.4)	170
Equatorial Guinea	22.7	16.2	10.7	149	107	73	316	243	X	X	X	X
Eritrea	18.9	14.7	9.0	130	98	57	X	X	195	(0.6)	(1.9)	1,400
Ethiopia	22.1	16.2	9.4	149	107	65	294	260	195	(0.6)	(1.9)	1,400
Gabon	19.2	14.3	9.3	122	85	47	287	194	148	(2.0)	(1.8)	500
Gambia, The	24.9	17.4	12.3	167	122	85	375	278	110	(2.0)	(5.5)	1,100
Ghana	15.3	10.4	6.9	103	73	43	215	157	130	(1.6)	(1.2)	740
Guinea	25.4	18.4	12.1	167	124	87	337	276	219	(1.0)	(1.5)	1,600
Guinea-Bissau	26.2	20.6	14.0	176	132	94	336	290	227	(0.7)	(1.6)	910
Kenya	15.5	11.3	6.2	88	65	37	202	112	90	(2.9)	(1.5)	650
Lesotho	16.5	10.6	6.6	121	72	37	204	173	154	(0.8)	(0.8)	610
Liberia	18.1	15.3	8.0	167	153	67	288	235	216	(1.0)	(0.6)	560
Libya	12.7	6.9	4.5	107	56	25	269	150	63	(4.1)	(4.2)	220
Madagascar	16.1	9.9	6.0	150	77	42	364	216	164	(2.6)	(1.8)	490
Malawi	24.0	22.4	12.6	177	142	93	365	290	219	(1.1)	(1.9)	560
Mali	24.1	17.1	11.1	191	149	107	400	310	210	(1.3)	(2.6)	1,200
Mauritania	20.0	13.1	8.8	125	92	59	321	249	195	(1.3)	(1.6)	930
Mauritius	6.3	6.5	6.9	38	15	8	84	42	23	(3.4)	(4.1)	120
Morocco	13.0	6.7	5.8	110	51	24	215	145	75	(2.0)	(4.4)	610
Mozambique	20.8	17.5	11.1	160	110	74	331	269	275	(1.0)	0.1	1,500
Namibia	15.1	11.8	7.4	98	60	36	206	114	78	(3.0)	(2.5)	370
Niger	23.8	17.1	10.9	157	114	79	320	320	320	0.0	0.0	X
Nigeria	19.2	13.9	9.2	105	77	51	204	196	191	(0.2)	(0.2)	1,000
Rwanda	20.2	19.7	11.7	133	125	84	191	222	139	0.8	(3.1)	1,300
Senegal	21.7	14.5	9.6	97	62	39	303	221	110	(1.6)	(4.6)	1,200
Sierra Leone	29.0	25.7	16.1	192	169	114	385	301	284	(1.2)	(0.4)	1,800
Somalia	22.7	16.9	10.7	149	112	77	294	246	211	(0.9)	(1.0)	1,600
South Africa	12.4	7.9	6.0	72	48	27	126	91	67	(1.6)	(2.1)	230
Sudan	17.8	11.7	8.4	97	71	45	292	210	115	(1.9)	(3.7)	660
Swaziland	16.0	9.2	5.7	108	65	34	233	151	X	X	X	X
Tanzania	16.4	13.5	8.0	113	80	51	249	202	160	(1.6)	(0.8)	770
Togo	17.4	14.9	8.5	117	86	52	264	175	128	(2.0)	(2.1)	640
Tunisia	10.0	5.9	5.5	88	37	18	244	102	37	(4.4)	(6.7)	170
Uganda	17.6	21.0	10.7	114	113	72	218	181	185	(0.9)	0.2	1,200
Zambia	16.5	18.0	9.3	94	103	55	220	160	203	(1.6)	1.6	940
Zimbabwe	13.1	14.6	8.0	86	68	39	181	125	74	(1.8)	(3.5)	570
EUROPE	**10.5**	**11.5**	**12.4**	**22**	**12**	**8**	**X**	**X**	**X**	**X**	**X**	**X**
Albania	6.4	6.2	7.1	50	32	20	151	57	40	(4.9)	(2.4)	65
Austria	12.4	10.0	10.7	17	6	5	43	17	7	(4.6)	(5.6)	10
Belarus, Rep	9.4	12.1	13.3	22	15	10	X	X	20	X	(3.1)	37
Belgium	11.7	10.5	11.3	14	7	5	35	15	10	(4.3)	(3.0)	10
Bosnia and Herzegovina	6.5	7.3	10.9	36	13	9	X	X	17	(7.0)	(5.4)	X
Bulgaria	10.5	13.3	13.9	22	16	10	70	25	19	(5.1)	(1.8)	27
Croatia, Rep	10.8	11.7	13.4	21	10	7	X	X	14	(7.2)	(3.1)	X
Czech Rep	13.2	12.0	12.3	18	9	6	X	X	10	X	(4.8)	15
Denmark	10.4	11.8	11.8	9	7	5	25	10	7	(4.4)	(2.8)	9
Estonia, Rep	12.1	13.1	13.9	22	12	6	X	X	22	X	(2.1)	41
Finland	9.3	10.2	11.3	9	5	5	28	9	5	(5.9)	(3.6)	11
France	10.3	9.1	10.5	11	7	6	X	X	9	(4.9)	(2.3)	15
Germany	12.2	10.9	12.6	15	6	5	40	16	7	(4.7)	(5.5)	22
Greece	8.8	9.9	12.3	25	8	7	64	23	10	(5.2)	(5.8)	10
Hungary	12.8	14.6	14.5	27	14	9	57	26	14	(3.9)	(4.2)	30
Iceland	6.4	6.8	7.4	9	5	5	22	9	X	X	X	X
Ireland	10.2	8.6	8.9	15	6	5	36	14	7	(4.6)	(4.6)	10
Italy	9.8	9.9	12.4	18	7	6	X	X	8	(5.3)	(5.3)	12
Latvia, Rep	12.4	13.8	14.6	23	16	11	X	X	26	X	(2.2)	40
Lithuania, Rep	9.9	11.6	12.9	22	13	7	X	X	19	X	(2.6)	36
Macedonia, FYR	7.1	7.4	9.3	57	23	13	X	X	31	(4.7)	(5.3)	X
Moldova, Rep	10.6	10.8	10.6	46	26	19	X	X	34	X	(2.4)	60
Netherlands	8.1	8.8	10.3	10	6	5	22	11	8	(3.4)	(2.4)	12
Norway	10.0	10.7	10.3	9	5	5	X	X	8	(3.8)	(2.2)	6
Poland, Rep	9.2	10.7	11.1	23	13	8	70	24	16	(5.3)	(2.7)	19
Portugal	10.3	10.9	11.7	30	8	5	112	31	11	(6.4)	(6.9)	15
Romania	9.7	11.6	12.8	31	24	14	82	36	29	(4.1)	(1.4)	130
Russian Federation	10.3	14.5	14.8	30	19	12	X	X	30	X	(2.4)	75
Slovak Rep	10.4	10.5	10.8	22	12	8	X	X	15	X	(2.7)	X
Slovenia, Rep	10.4	10.7	13.3	17	7	5	X	X	8	(4.6)	(5.2)	13
Spain	8.1	9.4	11.3	16	7	6	57	16	9	(6.2)	(3.7)	7
Sweden	10.9	11.2	10.4	8	5	5	20	9	5	(4.1)	(3.9)	7
Switzerland	9.0	9.1	10.4	10	5	5	27	11	7	(4.5)	(2.7)	6
Ukraine	11.0	13.8	14.4	23	18	10	X	X	24	X	(1.7)	50
United Kingdom	11.9	11.1	11.0	14	6	5	27	14	7	(3.1)	(4.3)	9
Yugoslavia, Fed Rep	9.2	9.7	11.6	38	19	12	X	X	23	(5.0)	(4.3)	X

	Crude Death Rate (per 1,000)			Infant Mortality Rate {a} (per 1,000 live births)			Under-5 Mortality Rate (per 1,000 live births)			Average Annual Change in Under-5 Mortality (percent)		Maternal Mortality Rate (per 100,000 live births)
	1975-80	1995-00	2015-20	1975-80	1995-00	2015-20	1960	1980	1995	1960-80	1980-95	1990
NORTH AMERICA	**8.5**	**8.6**	**8.8**	**14**	**7**	**5**	**X**	**X**	**X**	**X**	**X**	**X**
Canada	7.2	7.4	8.7	12	6	5	33	13	8	(4.8)	(3.6)	6
United States	8.6	8.7	8.8	14	7	5	30	15	10	(3.3)	(2.8)	12
CENTRAL AMERICA	**8.3**	**5.3**	**5.5**	**62**	**33**	**22**	**X**	**X**	**X**	**X**	**X**	**X**
Belize	6.5	4.3	3.6	45	30	21	X	X	X	X	X	X
Costa Rica	4.8	3.8	4.7	30	12	8	112	29	16	(6.8)	(3.8)	60
Cuba	6.0	7.0	8.9	22	9	6	50	26	10	(3.3)	(6.0)	95
Dominican Rep	8.4	5.3	5.6	84	34	19	152	94	44	(2.4)	(5.0)	110
El Salvador	11.2	6.0	5.6	87	39	25	210	120	40	(2.8)	(7.3)	300
Guatemala	12.0	6.7	5.2	82	40	25	205	136	67	(2.0)	(4.7)	200
Haiti	16.0	12.8	8.8	121	82	51	270	195	124	(1.4)	(3.0)	1,000
Honduras	11.0	5.4	4.8	81	35	21	203	100	38	(3.6)	(6.4)	220
Jamaica	7.4	5.8	5.3	26	12	7	76	39	13	(3.4)	(7.2)	120
Mexico	7.7	5.1	5.6	57	31	21	141	81	32	(2.7)	(6.7)	110
Nicaragua	11.3	5.8	4.8	90	44	28	209	143	60	(1.9)	(5.8)	160
Panama	6.3	5.1	5.8	35	21	13	104	31	20	(6.0)	(2.9)	55
Trinidad and Tobago	7.1	6.0	6.4	32	14	7	73	40	18	(3.0)	(5.3)	90
SOUTH AMERICA	**8.9**	**6.8**	**6.8**	**72**	**36**	**23**	**X**	**X**	**X**	**X**	**X**	**X**
Argentina	8.9	7.9	7.5	39	22	14	68	41	27	(2.5)	(2.8)	100
Bolivia	16.0	9.1	6.4	131	66	33	252	170	105	(2.0)	(3.2)	650
Brazil	9.1	7.1	7.4	79	42	26	181	93	60	(3.3)	(2.9)	220
Chile	7.5	5.6	6.6	45	13	9	138	35	15	(6.9)	(5.6)	65
Colombia	7.6	5.6	5.9	59	24	21	132	59	36	(4.1)	(3.2)	100
Ecuador	9.8	6.0	6.0	82	46	29	180	101	40	(2.9)	(6.2)	150
Guyana	9.2	7.4	7.0	67	58	37	126	88	X	X	X	X
Paraguay	7.8	5.4	4.7	51	39	27	90	61	34	(1.9)	(3.9)	160
Peru	10.9	6.4	6.1	99	45	24	236	130	55	(3.0)	(5.7)	280
Suriname	7.3	5.5	5.4	44	24	12	96	52	X	X	X	X
Uruguay	10.1	10.4	10.3	42	17	14	47	42	21	(0.6)	(4.6)	85
Venezuela	5.8	4.7	5.2	39	21	14	70	42	24	(2.6)	(3.8)	120
ASIA	**10.5**	**7.9**	**7.4**	**94**	**56**	**32**	**X**	**X**	**X**	**X**	**X**	**X**
Afghanistan, Islamic State	24.0	20.8	12.8	183	154	118	360	280	257	(1.3)	(0.6)	1,700
Armenia, Rep	5.9	7.5	9.0	22	25	19	X	X	31	X	(0.6)	50
Azerbaijan	7.0	6.6	7.3	41	33	24	X	X	50	X	(1.1)	22
Bangladesh	18.9	9.7	6.7	137	78	38	247	211	115	(0.8)	(4.0)	850
Bhutan	21.2	13.7	8.0	165	104	56	324	249	189	(1.3)	(1.8)	1,600
Cambodia	40.0	12.2	8.1	263	102	55	217	330	174	2.1	(4.3)	900
China	6.7	7.1	8.2	52	38	20	209	65	47	(5.9)	(2.1)	95
Georgia	8.7	9.5	10.7	36	23	18	X	X	26	X	(2.9)	33
India	13.9	9.0	7.6	129	72	45	236	177	115	(1.4)	(2.9)	570
Indonesia	15.1	7.6	7.0	105	48	23	216	128	75	(2.6)	(3.5)	650
Iran, Islamic Rep	11.8	6.0	4.4	100	39	20	233	126	40	(3.1)	(7.6)	120
Iraq	8.8	8.5	4.5	84	95	23	171	83	71	(3.6)	(1.0)	310
Israel	6.8	6.4	6.5	18	7	5	39	19	9	(3.6)	(5.3)	7
Japan	6.1	8.2	12.1	9	4	4	40	11	6	(6.6)	(3.5)	18
Jordan	9.6	4.8	3.7	65	30	15	149	66	25	(4.1)	(6.4)	150
Kazakstan, Rep	8.8	8.5	8.7	45	34	24	X	X	47	X	(2.8)	80
Korea, Dem People's Rep	6.2	5.5	6.7	38	22	13	120	43	30	(5.1)	(2.5)	70
Korea, Rep	7.1	6.4	8.4	30	9	6	124	18	9	(9.8)	(4.4)	130
Kuwait	4.2	2.2	4.0	34	14	7	X	X	14	(6.6)	(6.2)	29
Kyrgyz Rep	9.6	7.4	6.5	55	39	27	X	X	54	X	(3.4)	110
Lao People's Dem Rep	20.7	13.5	7.5	135	86	49	233	190	134	(1.0)	(2.3)	650
Lebanon	8.7	6.4	6.0	48	29	17	91	62	40	(3.8)	0.0	300
Malaysia	7.2	4.8	5.1	34	11	7	105	42	13	(4.6)	(7.8)	80
Mongolia	11.4	6.8	5.2	88	52	33	185	112	74	(2.5)	(2.8)	65
Myanmar	14.9	9.8	7.1	114	78	33	237	146	150	(2.4)	0.2	580
Nepal	18.4	11.0	6.6	142	82	40	279	177	114	(2.4)	(3.0)	1,500
Oman	12.4	4.3	3.2	95	25	12	300	95	25	(5.7)	(8.9)	190
Pakistan	15.4	7.8	5.2	130	74	45	221	151	137	(1.9)	(0.6)	340
Philippines	9.0	5.7	5.3	62	35	18	102	70	53	(1.9)	(1.8)	280
Saudi Arabia	10.7	4.2	3.7	75	23	10	X	X	34	(5.9)	(6.5)	130
Singapore	5.1	5.0	7.1	13	5	5	40	13	6	(5.6)	(5.7)	10
Sri Lanka	7.1	5.9	6.6	44	15	8	130	52	19	(4.6)	(6.7)	140
Syrian Arab Rep	8.9	4.9	4.0	67	33	17	201	73	36	(5.1)	(4.7)	180
Tajikistan, Rep	8.9	6.9	5.5	69	56	38	X	X	79	X	(3.1)	130
Thailand	8.3	6.6	7.4	56	30	13	146	61	32	(4.4)	(4.2)	200
Turkey	10.2	6.5	6.7	120	44	22	217	141	50	(2.2)	(6.9)	180
Turkmenistan, Rep	9.6	7.6	6.0	73	57	38	X	X	85	X	(2.6)	55
United Arab Emirates	7.4	2.9	6.0	38	15	6	240	64	19	(6.6)	(8.1)	26
Uzbekistan, Rep	8.5	6.6	5.7	58	43	30	X	X	62	X	(3.1)	55
Vietnam	11.4	7.0	5.8	82	37	21	219	105	X	X	X	X
Yemen	20.7	10.4	5.2	158	80	38	X	X	110	(2.4)	(4.3)	1,400
OCEANIA	**8.7**	**7.7**	**7.6**	**35**	**24**	**15**	**X**	**X**	**X**	**X**	**X**	**X**
Australia	7.7	7.5	8.1	13	6	5	24	13	8	(3.0)	(3.5)	9
Fiji	5.8	4.6	5.5	37	20	10	97	42	X	X	X	X
New Zealand	8.2	7.9	8.0	14	7	5	26	16	9	(2.5)	(4.0)	25
Papua New Guinea	15.0	9.9	7.0	77	61	37	248	95	95	(4.8)	0.0	930
Solomon Islands	7.4	4.1	3.4	47	23	12	X	X	X	X	X	X
DEVELOPING	**11.5**	**8.5**	**7.4**	**98**	**62**	**38**	**X**	**X**	**X**	**X**	**X**	**X**
DEVELOPED	**9.5**	**10.3**	**11.2**	**18**	**9**	**7**	**X**	**X**	**X**	**X**	**X**	**X**

Note: a. Under 1 year of age.

Data Table 8.3
Reported Cases of Infectious Diseases per 100,000 Population, 1985–95

Source: World Health Organization

Cases per 100,000 Population

	Tuberculosis			Measles			Malaria			Polio			Cholera		
	1985	1990	1995	1985	1990	1995	1988	1991	1994	1980	1988	1995	1987	1991	1995
WORLD	X	X	X	58	25	11	101	104	620	1.17	0.68	0.11	0.97	11.08	3.71
AFRICA	70	87	83	224	79	47	X	X	3,945	2.34	0.87	0.22	5.41	23.72	9.88
Algeria	63	47	49 a	92	7	29	X	X	1	0.62	0.04	0.01	6.52	X	X
Angola	108	112	72	285	315	6	X	X	6,377	0.46	0.23	1.41	191.82	90.28	30.46
Benin	51	45	44	328	72 e	194	X	X	10,398	4.48	0.70	0.13	X	154.93	3.75
Botswana	251	230	380	156	96	16	X	X	2,089	0.11	0.00	0.00	X	X	X
Burkina Faso	58	17	14	222	108	54	X	X	4,637	2.10	0.24	0.11	X	5.75	13.85
Burundi	49	83	62 a	774	242	244	X	X	14,022	1.04	0.23	0.16	10.36	0.05	37.88
Cameroon	34	51	57 a	473	184	19	X	X	1,065	2.95	1.13	0.06	0.89	34.10	4.66
Central African Rep	20	73	101	94	44	28	X	X	2,562	0.91	1.93	0.12	X	244.68	X
Chad	30	47	50	128	132	10	X	X	X	0.00	0.00	3.03	X	X	X
Congo, Dem Rep	15 b	55 c	91	62	12	12	X	X	X	X	X	X	3.41	10.45	1.22
Congo, Rep	138	26	140	395	162	84	X	X	1,428	8.15	0.05	0.00	X	X	X
Côte d'Ivoire	58	65	84	90	152	219	X	X	X	0.57	0.30	0.85	X	5.00	36.46
Egypt	3	4	37	11	2	3	X	X	X	4.59	1.02	0.11	X	X	X
Equatorial Guinea	5	74	77	149	9	11	X	X	1,241	0.00	0.00	0.00	X	X	X
Eritrea	X	120	608	X	X	6	X	X	X	0.00	0.00	0.32	X	X	X
Ethiopia	174	187	26	162	4	1	X	X	X	0.64	0.29	0.35	X	X	X
Gabon	87	80	84	650	79	X	X	X	X	10.13	0.34	0.84	X	X	X
Gambia, The	X	X	92	219	0	12	X	X	X	0.16	0.59	0.00	X	X	1.35
Ghana	25	43	24	503	215	232	X	X	X	1.34	0.42	0.20	X	85.16	27.10
Guinea	26	35	52	60	222	15	X	X	8,567	0.72	4.76	0.37	X	X	88.53
Guinea-Bissau	61	121	163	152	27	49	X	X	X	0.38	0.54	0.00	269.65	X	11.13
Kenya	53	50	100	561	328	12	X	X	23,068	2.74	7.67	0.04	1.20	X	5.68
Lesotho	187	141	236	471	123	15	X	X	X	2.63	0.00	0.00	X	X	X
Liberia	19	37 d	46	122	72 e	3	X	X	X	5.22	0.24	0.00	1.37	5.28	161.09
Libya	9	10	27	111	20	22 a	X	X	1	0.99	0.24	0.00	X	X	0.41
Madagascar	30	50	80	655	114	79	X	X	X	0.75	0.36	0.00	X	X	X
Malawi	74	132	172	1,747	0	44	X	X	49,410	1.13	0.13	0.00	X	85.09	0.01
Mali	20	32	29	376	15	31	X	X	X	3.41	1.40	0.24	4.19	X	18.97
Mauritania	249	264	169	856	69	9	X	X	X	10.25	0.89	0.22	84.93	X	X
Mauritius	11	11	14	0	0	1	X	X	3	0.00	0.00	0.00	X	X	X
Morocco	123	114	110	19	7	9	X	X	1	0.27	0.00	0.00	X	X	X
Mozambique	42	112	112	122	127	24	X	X	X	0.54	0.05	0.00	X	53.60	X
Namibia	411	198	100	X	350 d	112	X	X	27,209	0.00	0.00	0.98	X	X	X
Niger	11	67	22	979	265	743	X	X	9,238	5.57	0.45	0.44	X	40.52	2.88
Nigeria	18	21	12	195	120	11	X	X	X	1.13	1.61	0.39	1.47	60.03	0.95
Rwanda	22	91	38	277	129	541	X	X	X	0.46	0.13	0.02	1.53	10.18	0.06
Senegal	17	68	91	104 c	68	73 a	X	X	X	2.49	0.26	0.01	46.69	X	38.76
Sierra Leone	24	16	43	93	21	8	X	X	X	0.34	0.10	0.00	14.81	X	245.17
Somalia	35	15 e	31	2	12 e	X	X	X	X	0.00	0.65	0.00	X	X	97.51
South Africa	180	217	210	54	29	3	X	X	25	0.38	0.49	0.00	0.11	0.03	X
Sudan	7	1	39	315	58	3	X	X	X	22.22	0.40	0.08	X	X	X
Swaziland	319 f	193 e	240	501	197	20	X	X	X	34.29	0.28	0.00	X	X	X
Tanzania	63	87	134	211	59	11	X	X	27,343	0.49	0.02	0.07	8.17	21.53	5.66
Togo	25	37	37	850	129	150	X	X	8,274	6.81	0.75	0.12	X	65.97	1.59
Tunisia	35	25	27	65	7	8	X	X	X	0.23	0.03	0.00	X	X	X
Uganda	9 b	82	120	X	16	217	X	X	X	0.28	0.10	0.51	0.91	1.62	2.73
Zambia	98	281	135	796	93	106	X	X	44,498	4.81	1.23	0.07	X	178.02	X
Zimbabwe	57	92	274	266	139	50	X	X	2,964	0.45	0.04	0.01	X	X	X
EUROPE	X	X	X	50	18	10	X	X	1	0.03	0.00	0.02	X	0.04	0.13
Albania	31	20	19	0	13	0	X	X	X	0.04	0.00	0.00	X	X	X
Austria	19	20	18	X	X	X	X	X	X	0.01	0.00	0.00	X	X	X
Belarus, Rep	49	30	48	X	13 c	15	X	X	X	0.00	0.00	0.00	X	X	0.03
Belgium	20	16	14	X	817 e	0	X	X	X	0.01	0.00	0.00	X	X	X
Bosnia and Herzegovina	X	14	62	X	4 c	4	X	X	X	0.00	0.00	0.00	X	X	X
Bulgaria	29	25	37	11	2	2	X	X	X	0.17	0.00	0.00	X	X	X
Croatia, Rep	81	57	47	X	3 c	15	X	X	X	0.00	0.00	0.00	X	X	X
Czech Rep	30	19	18	X	8 c	0	X	X	X	0.00	0.00	0.00	X	X	X
Denmark	6	7	9	258	4	0	X	X	X	0.00	0.00	0.00	X	X	0.06
Estonia, Rep	35	21	41	X	8 c	1	X	X	X	0.00	0.00	0.00	X	X	X
Finland	37	15	13	13	0	0	X	X	X	0.00	0.00	0.00	X	X	0.02
France	20	16	15	1	254 c	X	X	X	X	0.02	0.00	0.00	0.01	0.01	0.01
Germany	26	18	15	X	88 c	X	X	X	X	0.01	0.00	0.00	X	X	X
Greece	16	9	X	15	2	1	X	X	X	0.00	0.00	0.00	X	X	X
Hungary	46	35	43	0	0	0	X	X	X	0.01	0.00	0.00	X	X	X
Iceland	5	7	4	155	5	0	X	X	X	0.00	0.00	0.00	X	X	X
Ireland	23	18	X	279	16	7	X	X	X	0.03	0.00	0.00	X	X	X
Italy	7	7	10	132	9	65	X	X	1	0.00	0.00	0.00	X	X	X
Latvia, Rep	47	34	60	X	0 c	0	X	X	X	0.00	0.00	0.00	X	X	X
Lithuania, Rep	41	40	64	X	4 c	5	X	X	X	0.00	0.00	0.00	X	X	X
Macedonia, FYR	X	X	36	X	9 c	10	X	X	112	0.00	0.00	0.00	X	X	X
Moldova, Rep	65	40	66	X	14 c	26	X	X	X	X	X	X	X	X	5.41
Netherlands	9	9	10	0	0	1	X	X	2	0.00	0.00	0.00	X	X	0.06
Norway	9	7	5	32	2	0	X	X	X	0.00	0.00	0.00	0.02	X	0.02
Poland, Rep	58	42	42	96	148	2	X	X	X	0.01	0.00	0.00	X	X	X
Portugal	70	63	57	X	4	2	X	X	X	0.00	0.00	0.00	X	X	0.01
Romania	56	70	102	22	20	10	X	X	X	0.56	0.00	0.00	X	0.98	0.52
Russian Federation	45	34	58	X	14 c	4	X	X	0	0.00	0.00	0.10	X	X	0.01
Slovak Rep	39	27	0	X	4 c	0	X	X	X	0.00	0.00	0.00	X	X	X
Slovenia, Rep	49	38	27	X	2 c	21	X	X	X	0.00	0.00	0.00	X	X	X
Spain	28	19	22	210	55	22	X	X	X	0.05	0.00	0.00	0.01	X	0.02
Sweden	8	7	6	4	0	0	X	X	X	0.00	0.00	0.00	0.01	X	0.02
Switzerland	15	19	12	X	34	0	X	X	X	0.02	0.00	0.00	X	X	0.03
Ukraine	47	32	42	X	10 c	4	X	X	X	0.00	0.00	0.00	X	0.14	1.01
United Kingdom	12	10	11	185	185	13	X	X	3	0.01	0.00	0.00	X	0.01	0.02
Yugoslavia, Fed Rep	63	41	26	257	69	4	X	X	X	0.04	0.00	0.03	X	X	X

	Tuberculosis			Measles			Malaria			Polio			Cholera		
Cases per 100,000 Population	1985	1990	1995	1985	1990	1995	1988	1991	1994	1980	1988	1995	1987	1991	1995
NORTH AMERICA	X	X	X	2	10	1	X	X	1	0.00	0.00	0.00	X	0.01	0.01
Canada	8	7	7 a	11	3	8	X	X	1	0.00	0.00	0.00	X	0.01	0.02
United States	9	10	9	1	11	0	X	X	0	0.00	0.00	0.00	X	0.01	0.01
CENTRAL AMERICA	X	X	X	53	107	0	253	198	138	1.12	0.08	0.00	X	7.47	33.13
Belize	15	30	28	4	33	2	1,531	1,728	4,787	2.05	0.00	0.00	X	X	8.92
Costa Rica	14	8	9	0	3	1	35	105	1	0.00	0.00	0.00	X	X	0.70
Cuba	7	5	15	38	0	0	X	X	0	0.00	0.00	0.00	X	X	X
Dominican Rep	37	37	52	69	49	0	16	5	22	2.58	0.01	0.00	X	X	X
El Salvador	31	46	42	30	22	0	188	115	51	1.21	0.16	0.00	X	18.42	51.62
Guatemala	83	41	32	29	96	0	605	611	214	1.10	0.44	0.00	X	38.81	75.04
Haiti	85	155 c	X	36	22	X	198	387	331	0.37	0.14	0.00	X	X	X
Honduras	81	75	88	155	171	0	648	1,459	949	0.08	0.13	0.00	X	0.22	83.43
Jamaica	6	5	4	3	154	1	X	X	0	0.00	0.00	0.00	X	X	X
Mexico	20	17	12	31	83	0	145	31	14	1.01	0.03	0.00	X	3.17	18.03
Nicaragua	81	80	64	30	537	0	1,348	755	1,035	0.75	0.00	0.00	X	0.03	214.04
Panama	28	35	50	198	79	1	19	46	26	0.00	0.00	0.00	X	48.20	X
Trinidad and Tobago	10	10	14	301	41	0	X	X	2	0.00	0.00	0.00	X	X	X
SOUTH AMERICA	X	X	X	52	34	1	304	337	300	0.71	0.08	0.00	X	128.49	14.13
Argentina	53	38	39	30	6	2	2	2	3	0.09	0.00	0.00	X	X	0.54
Bolivia	130	170	130	4	15	1	354	283	480	0.75	0.02	0.00	X	3.06	30.93
Brazil	62	50	54	56	42	0	391	409	360	1.06	0.07	0.00	X	1.04	10.01
Chile	55	47	29 a	139	15	0	X	X	X	0.00	0.00	0.00	X	0.31	X
Colombia	41	39	28	19	54	1	322	554	362	0.49	0.11	0.00	X	36.03	5.37
Ecuador	53	80	69	13	16	8	547	566	267	0.14	0.10	0.00	X	441.06	18.85
Guyana	27	21	35	11	0	0	4,467	5,282	4,819	0.00	0.00	0.00	X	X	X
Paraguay	52	50	36	18	33	2	73	69	12	0.22	0.03	0.00	X	X	X
Peru	125	176	191	40	7	2	156	153	528	1.05	0.26	0.00	X	1,468.59	95.18
Suriname	13	21	13 a	29	7	0	688	367	1,115	0.00	0.00	0.00	X	X	X
Uruguay	40	29	20	5	4	0	X	X	X	0.00	0.00	0.00	X	X	X
Venezuela	28	28	25	125	51	1	247	214	64	0.07	0.09	0.00	X	0.08	X
ASIA	X	X	X	35	13	5	125	127	155	1.44	0.96	0.13	0.58	1.54	1.55
Afghanistan, Islamic State	74	29	X	100	11 c	X	2,675	1,934	X	5.48	2.17	0.00	X	X	101.23
Armenia, Rep	24	18	28	X	5 c	5	X	X	X	0.00	0.00	0.08	X	X	X
Azerbaijan	57	37	19	X	85 c	6	X	X	9	0.00	0.00	0.07	X	X	X
Bangladesh	42	45	35	12	2	4	32	57	143	0.07	0.51	0.04	X	X	X
Bhutan	78	75	79	56	11	7	719	1,353	2,238	0.46	2.29	0.00	X	25.24	1.41
Cambodia	134	74	142	600	28	20	X	1,291	870	9.10	1.27	1.30	X	8.59	41.80
China	21	33	29	39	7	4	8	7	3	0.75	0.06	0.01	X	0.02	0.85
Georgia	35	28	30	0	0	2	X	X	X	0.00	0.00	0.00	X	X	X
India	152	179	130	21	11	4	227	244	243	2.75	2.97	0.35	1.17	0.81	0.36
Indonesia	11	41	16	6	50	11	18	8	X	0.12	0.44	0.01	0.38	3.34	X
Iran, Islamic Rep	18	16	30	42	9	0	97	13	77	0.20	0.07	0.15	0.56	3.07	3.18
Iraq	42	81	132	145	17	38	40	X	500	7.67	0.41	0.17	X	4.74	4.08
Israel	9	5	7 a	71	5	0	X	X	X	0.28	0.00	0.00	0.05	X	X
Japan	48	42	34	2	3	X	X	X	X	0.00	0.00	0.00	0.03	0.07	0.26
Jordan	20	10	9	15	7	6	X	X	X	0.51	0.05	0.00	X	X	X
Kazakstan, Rep	79	66	66	X	20 c	2	X	X	X	0.00	0.00	0.01	X	X	0.05
Korea, Dem People's Rep	X	X	X	0	0	0	X	X	X	0.00	0.04	0.03	X	X	X
Korea, Rep	214	149	74	3	8	0	X	X	0	0.04	0.00	0.00	X	0.26	0.16
Kuwait	42	13	22	120	3	1	X	X	50	2.33	0.00	0.00	X	X	X
Kyrgyz Rep	52	53	0	X	20 c	0	X	X	X	0.00	0.00	0.00	X	X	X
Lao People's Dem Rep	118	43	25	42	52	65	957	918	1,111	36.38	3.91	0.16	X	X	27.96
Lebanon	73	34 c	33	X	X	0	X	X	X	0.00	0.00	0.00	X	X	X
Malaysia	67	65	60	33	3	3	299	237	299	0.04	0.00	0.00	3.53	2.76	10.97
Mongolia	157	72	125	28	13	23	X	X	X	0.00	0.05	0.00	X	X	X
Myanmar	28	30	39	44	19	3	238	302	1,582	0.72	0.15	0.04	X	2.19	2.87
Nepal	0	53	90	6	1	22	133	151	45	0.36	0.05	0.04	X	158.97	0.73
Oman	62	28	10	292	71	3	1,507	1,034	341	3.27	7.22	0.00	X	X	X
Pakistan	109	129	7	26	18	1	52	54	82	3.49	0.83	0.37	X	X	X
Philippines	276	522	348	115	71	6	266	139	345	0.89	0.59	0.06	X	X	1.25
Saudi Arabia	31	15	14 a	145	34	14	66	60	56	2.68	0.02	0.02	X	X	X
Singapore	76	59	66	5	5	6	X	X	8	0.04	0.00	0.00	2.22	1.10	0.42
Sri Lanka	37	39	32	55	23	1	2,297	2,322	1,540	1.78	0.00	0.00	X	0.41	X
Syrian Arab Rep	21	49	30	4	4	10	1	0	4	3.58	0.29	0.03	X	X	X
Tajikistan, Rep	55	47	33	X	23 c	3	X	X	X	0.00	0.00	0.00	X	X	X
Thailand	152	84	77	63	53	19	648	353	177	0.64	0.02	0.00	11.99	X	X
Turkey	61	44	37	29	20	22	30	21	141	0.41	0.00	0.05	X	X	X
Turkmenistan, Rep	50	64	47	X	36 c	10	X	X	X	0.00	0.00	0.20	X	X	X
United Arab Emirates	41	17	23 a	155	62	30	171	174	X	4.73	0.50	0.00	X	X	X
Uzbekistan, Rep	48	46	43	X	18 c	1	X	X	X	0.00	0.00	0.00	X	X	X
Vietnam	78	75	47	137	12	8	237	489	1,189	3.24	1.31	0.19	0.30	0.08	8.25
Yemen	75	39	99	289	240 e	1	106	104	260	0.00	0.00	0.30	X	X	X
OCEANIA	X	X	X	32	22	19	682	914	2,742	0.11	0.07	0.00	X	X	0.02
Australia	7	6	6	0	5	7	X	X	4	0.00	0.00	0.00	0.01	X	0.03
Fiji	33	31	26	22	4	53	X	X	X	0.00	0.00	0.00	X	X	X
New Zealand	11	10	9	0	0	0	X	X	X	0.00	0.00	0.00	X	X	0.06
Papua New Guinea	100	65	187	165	119	87	2,285	2,204	14,974	0.71	0.49	0.02	X	X	X
Solomon Islands	140	119	93	1	107	0	21,369	42,731	35,980	0.00	0.00	0.00	X	X	X

Notes: a. Data are for 1994. b. Data are for 1986. c. Data are for 1991. d. Data are for 1988. e. Data are for 1989. f. Data are for 1983.

Data Table 8.4
Health Care, 1971–96

Sources: United Nations Children's Fund, the World Health Organization, and the World Bank

| | Percentage of Births Attended by Trained Personnel 1990-96 {a} | Percentage of 1-Year-Olds Immunized Against | | | | | Percentage of Pregnant Women Immunized for Tetanus 1992-95 {a} | ORT {a,d} Use (percent) 1990-96 | Contraceptive Prevalence (percent) Any Method/ Modern Method 1971-96 {a} | Population per {a} | | | |
		TB {b} 1992-95 {a}	DPT {c} 1992-95 {a}	Polio 1992-95 {a}	Measles 1980	Measles 1995				Doctor 1980-83	Doctor 1990-93	Nurse 1980-83	Nurse 1990-93
WORLD	X	X	X	X	X	X	X	X	57/49	3,770	X	X	X
AFRICA	X	X	X	X	X	X	X	X	X	X	X	X	X
Algeria	77	93	83	83	X	X	52	98	52/49	X	1,062	X	X
Angola	X	40	21	23	X	32	14	X	X	X	23,725	X	X
Benin	45	91	79	79	X	81	77	60	9/0.5	13,408	X	1,755	4,182
Botswana	78	81	78	78	63	68	56	X	33/32	6,906	X	703	X
Burkina Faso	42	78	47	47	X	55	39	100	8/4	57,181	X	1,683	X
Burundi	19	77	63	62	X	44	30	X	9/1	X	17,153	X	4,778
Cameroon	64	54	46	46	X	51	12	X	16/4	X	11,996	X	1,999
Central African Rep	46	73	38	37	12	70	50	34	24/4	23,302	25,920	2,193	11,309
Chad	15	36	17	16	X	X	50	X	1 e	X	30,030	X	X
Congo, Dem Rep	X	46	26	27	18	41	33	90	8/2	X	15,150	X	1,355
Congo, Rep	X	94	79	79	X	39	75	41	X	8,425	3,713	595	1,401
Côte d'Ivoire	45	48	40	40	X	57	22	18	11/4	X	11,739	X	3,244
Egypt	46	95	90	91	78	89	64	43	47/46	732	1,316	782	489
Equatorial Guinea	X	X	X	X	X	X	X	X	X	X	3,556	X	2,286
Eritrea	21	57	45	45	X	29	19	38	5/4	X	X	X	X
Ethiopia	14	63	51	48	4	38	22	95	4/3	88,119	X	4,998	X
Gabon	80	73	56	57	X	X	29	X	X	2,305	X	225	X
Gambia, The	44	98	90	92	X	X	93	X	12/7	X	X	X	X
Ghana	44	70	55	55	16	54	64	93	20/10	X	X	640	X
Guinea	31	86	73	73	X	X	56	38	2/1	46,401	7,445	5,161	5,166
Guinea-Bissau	27	100	100	98	X	X	53	X	1 e	7,491	X	1,130	X
Kenya	45	92	84	84	X	35	72	76	33/27	8,319	21,970	942	8,675
Lesotho	40	59	58	59	X	X	12	42	23/19	X	24,095	X	2,040
Liberia	58	92	62	62	X	X	77	94	6/5	9,396	X	1,382	X
Libya	76	99	96	96	65	92	45	49	X	693	957	350	340
Madagascar	57	77	64	63	X	59	33	85	17/5	9,891	8,385	1,721	3,736
Malawi	55	91	76	80	49	X	77	78	13/7	53,605	X	3,024	X
Mali	24	75	46	46	X	49	19	X	7/5	25,997	X	1,348	X
Mauritania	40	93	50	50	X	X	28	31	3/1	X	15,772	X	2,261
Mauritius	97	87	89	89	X	X	78	X	75/49	1,817	X	583	X
Morocco	40	93	90	90	X	88	37	29	50/42	15,493	X	915	X
Mozambique	25	58	46	46	X	71	61	83	4 e	37,948	X	5,759	X
Namibia	68	94	76	74	X	57	72	66	29/26	X	4,328	X	317
Niger	X	32	18	18	X	38	57	20	4/2	X	53,986	X	3,765
Nigeria	31	57	27	27	X	X	21	X	6/4	6,709	X	856	X
Rwanda	26	86	57	57	X	X	88	47	21/13	34,797	X	3,659	X
Senegal	46	90	80	80	X	80	39	18	7/5	13,039	18,192	1,931	13,174
Sierra Leone	25	60	43	43	36	X	61	X	4 e	18,973	X	2,078	X
Somalia	2	37	28	28	9	X	11	97	1 e	25,334	X	2,809	X
South Africa	82	95	73	72	X	X	26	X	50/48	X	X	X	X
Sudan	69	88	76	77	X	77	65	X	8/7	9,582	X	1,408	X
Swaziland	X	X	X	X	X	94	X	X	20/17	18,698	9,566	1,046	628
Tanzania	53	92	88	86	45	75	71	76	20/13	X	X	X	X
Togo	54	81	73	71	X	65	43	X	12/3	21,357	11,385	1,657	3,060
Tunisia	69	89	92	92	65	91	49	X	60/51	3,642	1,549	956	411
Uganda	38	98	79	78	X	X	76	46	15/8	21,832	X	2,049	X
Zambia	51	63	72	72	X	78	44	99	15/9	7,327	10,917	765	X
Zimbabwe	69	95	80	80	X	X	46	60	48/42	7,074	7,384	997	1,594
EUROPE	X	X	X	X	X	X	X	X	72/45	X	X	X	X
Albania	99	97	97	98	X	91	X	X	X	1,075	735	X	X
Austria	100	X	90	90	X	X	X	X	71/56	436	231	170	X
Belarus, Rep	100	93	90	93	X	X	X	X	50/42	283	236	98	89
Belgium	100	X	97	94	X	X	X	X	79/75	370	274	108	X
Bosnia and Herzegovina	X	85	67	69	X	X	X	X	X	X	X	X	X
Bulgaria	100	98	100	94	X	X	X	X	76/8	385	306	188	162
Croatia, Rep	X	98	90	90	X	X	93	X	X	X	X	X	X
Czech Rep	X	X	96	98	X	96	X	X	69/45	X	273	X	X
Denmark	100	X	89	100	X	X	X	X	78/72	420	360	140	153
Estonia, Rep	X	99	84	89	74	81	X	X	70/56	228	253	89	127
Finland	100	100	100	100	X	98	X	X	80/78	460	406	93	X
France	99	78	89	92	X	X	X	X	77/70	462	X	111	X
Germany	99	X	45	80	X	X	X	X	75/72	433	X	X	X
Greece	97	50	78	95	X	X	X	X	X	394	X	370	X
Hungary	99	100	100	100	99	100	X	X	73/64	381	306	157	X
Iceland	X	X	X	X	X	X	X	X	X	435	X	87	X
Ireland	X	X	X	X	X	X	X	X	60 f	775	X	141	X
Italy	X	X	50	98	X	50	X	X	78/32	750	X	250	X
Latvia, Rep	X	100	65	70	X	85	X	X	X	242	278	102	118
Lithuania, Rep	X	97	96	89	X	94	X	X	X	243	235	87	92
Macedonia, FYR	X	96	88	91	X	X	91	X	X	X	427	X	X
Moldova, Rep	X	98	96	99	X	98	X	X	X	295	250	100	90
Netherlands	100	X	97	97	91	X	X	X	78/76	480	399	168	X
Norway	100	X	92	92	X	X	X	X	76/72	460	308	70	73
Poland, Rep	99	94	95	95	92	X	X	X	75/26	541	451	227	189
Portugal	90	94	93	95	54	94	X	X	66/33	494	353	X	X
Romania	100	100	98	94	X	93	X	X	57/15	612	538	277	X
Russian Federation	X	96	93	92	X	X	X	X	X	235	222	85	90
Slovak Rep	X	98	99	98	X	99	X	X	74/41	X	287	X	105
Slovenia, Rep	X	99	98	98	X	X	X	X	X	X	X	X	X
Spain	96	X	88	88	X	X	X	X	59/38	362	261	277	X
Sweden	100	X	99	99	X	X	X	X	78/71	410	394	95	X
Switzerland	99	X	X	X	X	X	X	X	71/65	X	X	129	X
Ukraine	100	92	94	95	X	X	X	X	X	84	227	94	87
United Kingdom	100	X	92	94	X	X	X	X	82/X	612	X	120	X
Yugoslavia, Fed Rep	X	68	92	93	X	X	X	X	X	290	232	X	X

| | Percentage of Births Attended by Trained Personnel 1990-96 {a} | Percentage of 1-Year-Olds Immunized Against | | | | | Percentage of Pregnant Women Immunized for Tetanus 1992-95 {a} | ORT {a,d} Use (percent) 1990-96 | Contraceptive Prevalence (percent) Any Method/ Modern Method 1971-96 {a} | Population per {a} | | | |
		TB {b} 1992-95 {a}	DPT {c} 1992-95 {a}	Polio 1992-95 {a}	Measles 1980	Measles 1995				Doctor 1980-83	Doctor 1990-93	Nurse 1980-83	Nurse 1990-93
NORTH AMERICA	X	X	X	X	X	X	X	X	71/67	X	X	X	X
Canada	99	X	93	89	X	X	X	X	73/70	560	464	123	107
United States	99	X	94	84	86	X	X	X	71/67	500	X	180	X
CENTRAL AMERICA	X	X	X	X	X	X	X	X	X	X	X	X	X
Belize	X	X	X	X	21	87	X	X	47/42	X	2,028	X	490
Costa Rica	93	99	85	86	60	94	90	31	75/65	X	X	X	X
Cuba	90	99	100	93	48	100	61	X	70/67	721	275	X	X
Dominican Rep	92	74	83	80	29	85	52	X	56/52	X	949	1,239	X
El Salvador	87	100	100	94	45	93	80	69	53/48	2,560	X	X	X
Guatemala	35	78	59	56	23	83	55	22	32/27	X	X	1,360	X
Haiti	21	68	34	34	X	X	49	31	18/14	9,079	10,855	X	8,945
Honduras	88	99	96	96	35	90	48	32	47/35	3,100	X	X	X
Jamaica	82	100	92	92	X	89	82	X	62/58	2,786	6,420	X	489
Mexico	77	98	92	92	35	90	42	81	53/45	1,176	X	X	X
Nicaragua	61	100	85	96	15	81	49	54	49/45	2,243	X	594	X
Panama	86	100	86	86	47	84	24	94	64/58	1,010	X	X	X
Trinidad and Tobago	98	X	89	90	X	90	19	X	53/44	1,485	1,520	386	247
SOUTH AMERICA	X	X	X	X	X	X	X	X	X	X	X	X	X
Argentina	97	96	66	70	58	95	X	X	74 e	X	X	X	X
Bolivia	47	85	85	86	13	83	65	43	45/18	1,911	2,348	X	X
Brazil	81	100	83	83	56	88	70	X	66/57	1,301	X	1,140	X
Chile	98	96	92	92	87	95	X	X	43 e	X	942	X	X
Colombia	85	99	93	95	14	80	57	45	72/59	X	X	X	X
Ecuador	64	91	72	70	24	73	21	64	57/46	X	652	X	1,853
Guyana	X	X	X	X	X	77	X	X	31/28	X	8,948	X	893
Paraguay	66	92	79	79	19	75	66	33	56/41	1,746	1,231	X	X
Peru	52	96	95	93	21	97	21	92	59/33	1,104	939	X	X
Suriname	X	X	X	X	X	79	X	X	X	X	1,274	X	270
Uruguay	96	99	86	86	50	84	13	X	X	501	X	X	X
Venezuela	69	91	68	85	50	67	18	X	49/38	1,185	633	X	329
ASIA	X	X	X	X	X	X	X	X	59/55	X	X	X	X
Afghanistan, Islamic State	9	31	41	56	11	X	3	X	2/2	13,237	7,001	8,955	X
Armenia, Rep	X	83	83	92	X	X	X	X	X	275	261	114	101
Azerbaijan	X	93	93	98	X	X	X	X	X	284	257	113	106
Bangladesh	14	94	69	69	X	96	78	96	47/39	8,424	12,884	14,750	11,549
Bhutan	15	98	87	86	21	85	70	85	19 e	9,761	4,256	1,250	2,576
Cambodia	47	95	79	80	X	75	36	X	X	16,286	9,374	X	1,231
China	84	92	92	94	X	93	11	85	83/80	1,003	1,063	1,705	1,490
Georgia	X	30	58	82	X	X	X	X	X	198	182	88	85
India	34	96	89	98	X	79	79	31	41/37	3,703	X	4,674	X
Indonesia	36	86	78	79	X	92	74	99	55/52	9,412	X	X	X
Iran, Islamic Rep	77	99	97	97	39	96	82	37	65/45	2,949	X	1,179	X
Iraq	54	99	91	91	35	95	72	X	14/10	1,760	1,659	2,195	1,398
Israel	99	X	92	93	69	X	X	X	X	345	X	107	X
Japan	100	91	85	91	69	X	X	X	59/53	735	X	210	X
Jordan	87	X	100	99	29	92	59	41	35/27	887	554	862	548
Kazakstan, Rep	99	89	93	94	X	X	X	X	59/47	294	254	95	91
Korea, Dem People's Rep	100	99	96	99	29	98	95	X	62/53	426	X	X	X
Korea, Rep	98	93	93	93	4	93	X	X	79/70	1,386	951	X	454
Kuwait	99	X	100	100	48	98	21	X	35/32	617	X	178	X
Kyrgyz Rep	X	90	82	81	X	X	X	98	X	322	303	110	105
Lao People's Dem Rep	X	59	53	64	X	68	35	X	19/15	X	4,446	X	493
Lebanon	45	X	92	92	X	85	X	82	53/23	752	X	X	2,971
Malaysia	94	97	90	90	X	X	79	X	48/31	3,921	2,441	570	480
Mongolia	99	94	88	86	17	85	X	X	61/25	104	371	217	219
Myanmar	57	82	72	72	X	82	83	96	17/14	4,952	X	4,943	1,227
Nepal	7	61	63	62	X	71	11	27	29/26	30,062	13,634	7,783	2,257
Oman	87	96	99	99	22	100	95	85	9/8	1,822	X	863	X
Pakistan	19	75	35	37	1	56	36	97	12/9	2,931	1,923	5,870	3,330
Philippines	53	91	85	86	X	86	48	63	40/25	6,713	8,273	2,591	X
Saudi Arabia	82	93	97	97	8	94	62	58	X	1,819	749	738	329
Singapore	100	97	95	93	47	88	X	X	74/73	1,046	714	321	X
Sri Lanka	94	90	93	92	X	88	81	34	66/44	7,464	X	1,262	X
Syrian Arab Rep	67	100	100	100	13	90	76	36	36/28	2,160	X	1,421	1,047
Tajikistan, Rep	X	96	93	96	X	X	X	X	X	396	424	148	139
Thailand	71	98	94	94	X	89	93	95	74/72	6,268	4,416	1,873	X
Turkey	76	42	51	51	27	65	38	16	63/35	1,539	976	1,156	1,098
Turkmenistan, Rep	X	88	80	83	X	X	X	98	X	338	306	121	100
United Arab Emirates	96	98	90	90	34	90	X	X	X	936	1,208	410	718
Uzbekistan, Rep	X	95	89	99	X	X	X	X	X	321	282	114	86
Vietnam	X	X	X	X	X	X	X	X	65/44	4,048	2,279	1,241	1,149
Yemen	16	87	37	36	2	53	3	92	7/6	6,912	4,498	2,014	1,833
OCEANIA	X	X	X	X	X	X	X	X	X	X	X	X	X
Australia	100	X	X	X	X	87	X	X	76/72	524	X	140	X
Fiji	X	X	X	X	32	178	X	X	41/35	2,025	X	490	X
New Zealand	99	20	84	84	80	84	X	X	70/62	611	518	145	X
Papua New Guinea	20	78	50	55	X	63	31	X	4 e	16,018	12,754	957	1,569
Solomon Islands	X	X	X	X	X	68	X	X	X	X	6,154	X	716

Notes: a. Data are for most recent year available. b. TB: tuberculosis c. DPT: diphtheria, pertussis (whooping cough), and tetanus. d. ORT: Oral rehydration therapy. e. Data are from UNICEF for the most recent year available from 1990 to 1996 and refer to any method. f. Data are from the World Bank for the most recent year available from 1990 to 1995 and refer to any method.

Data Table 8.5
City Air Pollution, 1990–95

Source: Compiled by World Resources Institute

	City Name	City Population 1995 (000)	Mean Annual TSP {a} (ug/m3)	Year of Data	Mean Annual Black Smoke {b} (ug/m3)	Year of Data	Mean Annual PM-10 {c} (ug/m3)	Year of Data	Mean Annual SO2 {d} (ug/m3)	Year of Data	Mean Annual NO2 {e} (ug/m3)	Year of Data
AFRICA												
Egypt	Cairo	9,690	X	X	82 f	1993	X	X	69 f	1993	X	X
Ghana	Accra	1,673	137 f	1990	X	X	X	X	X	X	X	X
Kenya	Nairobi	1,810	69	1995	X	X	X	X	X	X	X	X
South Africa	Capetown	2,671	X	X	X	X	27	1995	21	1994	72 f	1995
	Durban	1,149	X	X	X	X	X	X	31	1995	X	X
	Johannesburg	1,849	X	X	61 f	1995	X	X	19	1995	31	1995
EUROPE												
Austria	Graz	259	45	1995	X	X	X	X	12	1995	34	1995
	Linz	213	34	1995	X	X	X	X	7	1995	25	1995
	Vienna	2,060	47	1995	X	X	X	X	14	1995	42	1995
Belgium	Antwerp	499	76	1995	X	X	X	X	25	1995	49	1995
	Brussels	1,122	78	1995	X	X	X	X	20	1995	48	1995
	Liege	209	82	1995	X	X	X	X	17	1995	35	1995
Bulgaria	Plovdiv	367	213 g	1995	X	X	X	X	96 f	1995	76 f	1995
	Sofia	1,188	195 g	1995	X	X	X	X	39	1995	122 g	1995
Croatia, Rep	Zagreb	981	71	1995	21	1995	X	X	31	1995	X	X
Czech Rep	Brno	390	50	1995	X	X	X	X	13	1995	28	1995
	Ostrava	331	66	1995	X	X	X	X	27	1995	50	1995
	Prague	1,225	59	1995	X	X	X	X	32	1995	23	1995
Denmark	Copenhagen	1,326	61	1995	X	X	X	X	7	1995	54 f	1995
Finland	Helsinki	1,059	40	1995	X	X	X	X	4	1995	35	1995
	Tempere	185	96 f	1995	X	X	X	X	5	1995	X	X
	Turku	176	61	1995	X	X	X	X	6	1995	37	1995
France	Nantes	257	20	1994	X	X	X	X	10	1994	42	1993
	Paris	9,523	14	1994	21	1993	X	X	14	1994	57 f	1993
Germany	Berlin	3,317	50	1995	X	X	X	X	18	1995	26	1995
	Frankfurt	3,606	36	1995	X	X	X	X	11	1995	45	1995
	Munich	2,238	45	1995	X	X	X	X	8	1995	53 f	1995
Greece	Athens	3,093	178 f	1990	61 f	1995	X	X	34	1995	64 f	1995
Hungary	Budapest	2,017	63	1995	X	X	X	X	39	1995	51 f	1995
	Debrecen	221	X	X	X	X	X	X	45	1993	30	1994
	Miskolc	219	42	1995	X	X	X	X	34	1995	30	1995
	Szekesfehervar	116	239 g	1993	X	X	X	X	X	X	X	X
Iceland	Reykjavik	100	24	1995	X	X	X	X	5	1995	42	1995
Ireland	Cork	146	X	X	41	1990	X	X	12	1993	X	X
	Dublin	911	X	X	41	1990	X	X	20	1993	X	X
Italy	Milan	4,251	77	1993	X	X	X	X	31	1993	248 g	1992
	Rome	2,931	73	1994	X	X	X	X	X	X	X	X
	Turin	1,294	151 f	1993	X	X	X	X	X	X	X	X
Netherlands	Amsterdam	1,108	40	1990	X	X	X	X	10	1990	58 f	1990
Norway	Bergen	221	X	X	X	X	X	X	X	X	64 f	1993
	Oslo	477	15	1993	X	X	X	X	8	1993	43	1995
Poland, Rep	Katowice	3,552	X	X	X	X	147 f	1990	89 f	1990	79 f	1990
	Lodz	1,063	X	X	28	1995	X	X	21	1995	43	1995
	Warsaw	2,219	X	X	44	1995	X	X	16	1995	32	1995
Portugal	Lisbon	1,863	61	1995	91	1991	X	X	8	1995	52 f	1995
	Porto	392	X	X	15	1992	X	X	15	1995	38	1995
Romania	Bucharest	2,100	82	1995	X	X	X	X	10	1995	71 f	1995
Russian Federation	Moscow	9,269	100 f	1992	X	X	X	X	109 g	1992	X	X
	Omsk	1,199	100 f	1993	X	X	X	X	9	1993	30	1993
Slovak Rep	Bratislava	651	62	1995	X	X	X	X	21	1991	27	1991
	Kosice	249	71	1995	X	X	X	X	27	1991	22	1991
Spain	Barcelona	2,819	117 f	1991	X	X	X	X	11	1991	43	1991
	Madrid	4,072	42	1992	44	1995	X	X	11	1995	25	1995
Sweden	Goteborg	449	9	1995	X	X	X	X	6	1995	32	1995
	Stockholm	1,545	9	1995	X	X	X	X	5	1995	29	1995
Switzerland	Geneva	182	29	1995	X	X	X	X	13	1995	58 f	1995
	Zurich	897	31	1995	X	X	X	X	11	1995	39	1995
United Kingdom	Birmingham	2,271	X	X	0	1995	23	1995	9	1995	45	1995
	Glasgow	900	X	X	X	X	X	X	18	1995	49	1995
	London	7,640	X	X	14	1992	28	1995	25	1995	77 f	1995
	Manchester	2,434	X	X	18	1995	X	X	26	1995	49	1995
NORTH AMERICA												
Canada	Hamilton	322	55	1993	X	X	X	X	23	1993	38	1993
	Montreal	3,320	34	1993	X	X	X	X	10	1993	42	1993
	Ottawa	1,057	X	X	X	X	X	X	X	X	40	1993
	Toronto	4,319	36	1993	X	X	X	X	17	1993	43	1993
	Vancouver	1,823	29	1993	X	X	X	X	14	1993	37	1993
United States	Atlanta	2,462	X	X	X	X	31	1995	11	1995	32	1995
	Chicago	6,844	X	X	X	X	34	1995	14	1995	56 f	1995
	Dallas	3,609	X	X	X	X	30	1995	X	X	26	1995
	Denver	1,609	X	X	X	X	24	1995	11	1995	55 f	1995
	Detroit	3,723	X	X	X	X	35	1995	17	1995	41	1995
	Los Angeles	12,410	X	X	X	X	39	1995	9	1995	73 f	1995
	Miami	2,080	X	X	X	X	24	1995	X	X	21	1995
	New York	16,332	X	X	X	X	26	1995	26	1995	79 f	1995
	Washington, D.C.	3,685	X	X	X	X	23	1995	20	1995	43	1995

*D*ata *Tables*
HEALTH

City Name	City Population 1995 (000)	Mean Annual TSP {a} (ug/m3)		Year of Data	Mean Annual Black Smoke {b} (ug/m3)		Year of Data	Mean Annual PM-10 {c} (ug/m3)		Year of Data	Mean Annual SO2 {d} (ug/m3)		Year of Data	Mean Annual NO2 {e} (ug/m3)		Year of Data
CENTRAL AMERICA																
Cuba — Havana	2,241	X		X	X		X	X		X	1		1995	5		1995
Mexico — Mexico City	16,562	279	g	1994	X		X	X		X	74	f	1994	130	g	1994
SOUTH AMERICA																
Argentina — Cordoba City	1,294	97	f	1992	X		X	X		X	X		X	97	f	1991
Mendoza	851	X		X	51	f	1995	X		X	3		1995	20		1995
Santa Fe	365	X		X	54	f	1994	X		X	X		X	X		X
Brazil — Rio de Janeiro	10,181	139	f	1995	X		X	X		X	129	g	1987	X		X
Sao Paulo	16,533	86		1995	66	f	1995	X		X	43		1995	83	f	1988
Chile — Santiago	4,891	X		X	X		X	86	f	1995	29		1995	81	f	1995
Colombia — Bogota	6,079	120	f	1986	X		X	X		X	X		X	X		X
Ecuador — Ambato	147	X		X	60	f	1995	X		X	45		1995	X		X
Cuenca	223	X		X	89	f	1995	X		X	16		1995	X		X
Esmeraldas	157	X		X	71	f	1995	X		X	5		1988	X		X
Guayaquil	1,831	127	f	1995	55	f	1990	X		X	15		1990	X		X
Quito	1,298	175	f	1995	270	g	1995	56		1995	31		1995	X		X
Venezuela — Caracas	3,007	53		1995	25		1991	X		X	33		1994	57	f	1995
ASIA																
China — Beijing	11,299	377	g	1995	X		X	X		X	90	f	1995	122	g	1995
Chengdu	4,323	366	g	1995	X		X	X		X	77	f	1995	74	f	1995
Chongqing	3,525	320	g	1995	X		X	X		X	340	g	1995	70	f	1995
Guangzhou	4,056	295	g	1995	X		X	X		X	57	f	1995	136	g	1995
Harbin	3,303	359	g	1995	X		X	X		X	23		1995	30		1995
Liupanshui	3,615	408	g	1995	X		X	X		X	102	g	1995	X		X
Quingdao	3,138	X		X	X		X	X		X	190	g	1995	64		1995
Shanghai	13,584	246	g	1995	X		X	X		X	53	f	1995	73	f	1995
Shenyang	5,116	374	g	1995	X		X	X		X	99	f	1995	73	f	1995
Tianjin	9,415	306	g	1995	X		X	X		X	82	f	1995	50		1995
Wuhan	4,247	211	g	1995	X		X	X		X	40		1995	43		1995
Zibo	3,779	453	g	1995	X		X	X		X	198	g	1995	43		1995
India — Ahmedabad	3,711	299	g	1994	X		X	X		X	30		1994	21		1994
Bangalore	4,799	123	f	1991	X		X	X		X	23		1991	13		1991
Bombay	15,138	240	g	1994	X		X	X		X	33		1994	39		1994
Calcutta	11,923	375	g	1994	X		X	X		X	49		1994	34		1994
Delhi	9,948	415	g	1994	X		X	X		X	24		1994	41		1994
Hyderabad	5,477	123	f	1994	X		X	X		X	12		1994	17		1994
Jaipur	1,483	283	g	1994	X		X	X		X	9		1994	28		1994
Kanpur	2,227	459	g	1994	X		X	X		X	15		1994	14		1994
Lucknow	2,078	463	g	1994	X		X	X		X	26		1994	25		1994
Madras	6,002	131	f	1994	X		X	X		X	15		1994	17		1994
Nagpur	1,851	185	g	1994	X		X	X		X	6		1994	13		1994
Pune	2,955	208	g	1991	X		X	X		X	17		1991	40		1991
Indonesia — Jakarta	8,621	271	g	1990	X		X	X		X	X		X	X		X
Iran, Islamic Rep — Tehran	6,830	248	g	1993	119	g	1993	X		X	209	g	1993	X		X
Japan — Kanazawa	440	23		1994	X		X	X		X	11		1994	25		1994
Kawasaki	1,153	52		1994	X		X	X		X	18		1994	62	f	1994
Osaka	10,609	43		1993	X		X	44		1994	19		1994	63	f	1994
Tokyo	26,959	49		1993	X		X	47		1994	18		1995	68	f	1995
Yokohama	3,178	X		X	X		X	41		1995	100	f	1995	13		1995
Korea, Rep — Incheon	2,340	93	f	1995	X		X	X		X	60	f	1995	45		1995
Kwanjin	1,424	64		1995	X		X	X		X	26		1995	38		1995
Pusan	4,082	94	f	1994	X		X	X		X	60	f	1995	51	f	1995
Seoul	11,609	84		1995	X		X	X		X	44		1995	60	f	1995
Taegu	2,432	72		1995	X		X	X		X	81	f	1995	62	f	1995
Taejeon	1,285	68		1995	X		X	X		X	44		1995	39		1995
Ulsan	758	99	f	1994	X		X	X		X	89	f	1994	X		X
Malaysia — Georgetown	212	130	f	1993	X		X	X		X	X		X	X		X
Kuala Lumpur	1,238	85		1993	X		X	X		X	24		1990	X		X
Philippines — Manila	9,286	200	g	1995	X		X	X		X	33		1993	X		X
Singapore — Singapore	2,848	X		X	X		X	34		1995	20		1995	30		1995
Thailand — Bangkok	6,547	223	g	1995	X		X	X		X	11		1993	23		1993
Turkey — Ankara	2,826	57		1995	X		X	X		X	55	f	1995	46		1995
Eskisehir	585	X		X	59	f	1995	X		X	124	g	1995	7		1995
Istanbul	7,911	X		X	66	f	1995	X		X	120	g	1995	X		X
Izmir	2,031	X		X	81	f	1994	X		X	X		X	X		X
Kocaeli	453	X		X	62	f	1995	X		X	88	f	1995	X		X
Samsun	384	X		X	27		1995	X		X	46		1995	X		X
OCEANIA																
Australia — Canberra	313	27		1993	X		X	X		X	X		X	76	f	1991
Melbourne	3,094	35		1995	X		X	19		1995	0		1995	30		1995
Perth	1,220	45		1995	X		X	22		1995	5		1995	19		1995
Sydney	3,590	54		1995	X		X	24		1995	28		1990	X		X
Wollongong	271	5		1990	X		X	X		X	19		1992	X		X
New Zealand — Auckland	945	26		1995	6		1995	25		1995	3		1995	20		1995
Christchurch	186	34		1995	X		X	22		1995	6		1995	17		1995

Notes: a. Total suspended particulates (TSP) in the air in micrograms per cubic meter. b. Black smoke (particles large or dark enough to be seen as soot or smoke) measured in micrograms per cubic meter. c. Particulate matter includes particles with aerodynamic size less than or equal to a standard particle with a diameter of 10 micrometers; measured in micrograms per cubic meter. d. Sulfur dioxide measured in micrograms per cubic meter. e. Nitrogen dioxide measured in micrograms per cubic meter. f. Level exceeds World Health Organization (WHO) guidelines. g. Level is more than double WHO guidelines.

Lead in Gasoline and Lead Production, 1986–96

Source: United Nations Department for Economic and Social Information and Policy Analysis, Statistics Division; The World Bank; United States Geological Survey

	Lead in Gasoline				Lead Production					
	Consumption of Motor Gasoline (million liters) 1995	Gasoline Cost per Liter (US$) 1996	Market Share of Leaded Gasoline (percent) 1992-1996 {a}	Maximum Concentration of Lead in Gasoline (grams/liter) 1992-1996 {a}	Mines in Concentrates (000 metric tons)		Refineries (000 metric tons)			
							Primary		Secondary	
					1986	1996	1986	1996	1986	1996
WORLD	1,064,280	X	X	X	3,335	2,920	3,193	2,830	2,359	2,650
AFRICA	28,407	X	X	X	X	X	X	X	X	X
Algeria	2,837	0.40	100	0.63	4	1	0	1	0	8
Angola	99	X	100	0.77	0	0	0	0	0	0
Benin	88	0.36	100	0.84	0	0	0	0	0	0
Botswana	X	0.38	100	0.44	0	0	0	0	0	0
Burkina Faso	91	0.81	100	0.84	0	0	0	0	0	0
Burundi	34	0.52	100	0.84	0	0	0	0	0	0
Cameroon	478	0.68	100	0.84	0	0	0	0	0	0
Central African Rep	22	0.82	X	X	0	0	0	0	0	0
Chad	9	0.80	100	0.84	0	0	0	0	0	0
Congo, Dem Rep	200	X	X	X	0	0	0	0	0	0
Congo, Rep	70	X	X	X	1	0	0	0	0	0
Côte d'Ivoire	769	0.83	100	0.26	0	0	0	0	0	0
Egypt	2,607	0.29	X b	0.80	0	0	0	0	0	0
Equatorial Guinea	7	X	X	X	0	0	0	0	0	0
Eritrea	X	X	X	X	0	0	0	0	0	0
Ethiopia	172	0.32	100	0.76	0	0	0	0	0	0
Gabon	38	X	100	0.80	0	0	0	0	0	0
Gambia, The	38	X	X	X	0	0	0	0	0	0
Ghana	455	0.38	100	0.63	0	0	0	0	0	0
Guinea	99	X	X	X	0	0	0	0	0	0
Guinea-Bissau	20	X	X	X	0	0	0	0	0	0
Kenya	458	0.56	100	0.40	1	0	0	0	2	0
Lesotho	X	X	X	X	0	0	0	0	0	0
Liberia	36	X	100	0.77	0	0	0	0	0	0
Libya	2,162	X	100	0.80	0	0	0	0	0	0
Madagascar	105	0.47	100	0.80	0	0	0	0	0	0
Malawi	92	X	100	0.53	0	0	0	0	0	0
Mali	82	0.82	100	0.80	0	0	0	0	0	0
Mauritania	359	0.94	100	0.25	0	0	0	0	0	0
Mauritius	113	0.53	100	0.40	0	0	0	0	0	0
Morocco	499	X	100	0.50	76	72	60	60	2	2
Mozambique	53	X	100	0.65	0	0	0	0	0	0
Namibia	X	X	100	0.40	38	15	40	19	0	0
Niger	63	0.79	100	0.65	0	0	0	0	0	0
Nigeria	4,199	0.13	100	0.66	0	4	0	0	1	0
Rwanda	45	X	X	X	0	0	0	0	0	0
Senegal	242	0.94	100	0.60	0	0	0	0	0	0
Sierra Leone	41	X	X	X	0	0	0	0	0	0
Somalia	X	X	X	X	0	0	0	0	0	0
South Africa	10,133	0.48	88	0.40	98	89	0	0	41	36
Sudan	262	0.50	X	X	0	0	0	0	0	0
Swaziland	X	X	X	X	0	0	0	0	0	0
Tanzania	149	0.56	X	X	0	0	0	0	0	0
Togo	86	0.47	X	X	0	0	0	0	0	0
Tunisia	420	X	100	0.50	2	5	2	3	1	5
Uganda	127	0.98	100	0.84	0	0	0	0	0	0
Zambia	145	0.60	X	X	15	0	7	0	0	0
Zimbabwe	405	X	100	0.84	0	0	0	0	0	0
EUROPE	239,823	X	X	X	X	X	X	X	X	X
Albania	74	X	X	X	0	0	0	0	0	0
Austria	3,286	1.15	0	0.00	5	0	6	0	19	22
Belarus, Rep	1,714	X	3	0.82	0	0	0	0	0	0
Belgium	3,846	1.19	26	0.15	0	0	65	94	34	26
Bosnia and Herzegovina	84	X	X	X	0	0	0	0	0	0
Bulgaria	1,551	0.46	95	0.15	95	21	97	60	17	10
Croatia, Rep	767	0.75	70	0.60	0	0	0	0	0	0
Czech Rep	2,413	0.85	45	0.15	0	0	0	0	0	0
Denmark	2,607	1.13	0	0.00	0	0	0	0	1	0
Estonia, Rep	611	0.33	20	0.15	0	0	0	0	0	0
Finland	2,940	1.20	0	0.00	2	0	0	0	1	0
France	21,808	1.18	38	0.15	3	0	132	135	98	160
Germany	42,996	1.11	5	0.15	17	0	0	190	0	150
Greece	3,938	0.93	67	0.40 c	21	20	19	0	0	0
Hungary	2,093	0.74	36	0.15	0	0	0	0	0	0
Iceland	184	1.05	15	0.15	0	0	0	0	0	0
Ireland	1,402	1.04	35	0.15	36	45	0	0	10	10
Italy	25,295	1.22	56	0.15	11	14	29	47	102	96
Latvia, Rep	557	0.41	X	X	0	0	0	0	0	0
Lithuania, Rep	820	0.62	2	0.15	0	0	0	0	0	0
Macedonia, FYR	280	0.93	X	X	0	15	0	8	0	2
Moldova, Rep	304	X	100	0.40	0	0	0	0	0	0
Netherlands	11,250	1.16	14	0.15	0	0	0	0	33	25
Norway	3,010	1.34	2	0.15	3	1	0	0	0	0
Poland, Rep	6,725	0.55	30	0.15	43	58	63	51	25	15
Portugal	2,566	1.03	61	0.40	0	0	0	0	6	12
Romania	1,948	0.29	94	0.60	34	19	36	20	16	5
Russian Federation	35,231	0.40	50	0.60	0	16	0	15	0	12
Slovak Rep	676	0.66	0	0.00	0	1	0	0	0	0
Slovenia, Rep	1,111	0.59	46	0.15	0	0	0	0	0	7
Spain	11,960	0.91	77	0.40	80	30	88	75	42	80
Sweden	5,892	1.17	0	0.00	89	100	49	45	28	35
Switzerland	4,999	1.02	13	0.15	0	0	0	0	3	6
Ukraine	5,382	X	16	0.37	0	0	0	12	0	0
United Kingdom	29,332	0.92	33	0.15	1	2	156	168	173	178
Yugoslavia, Fed Rep	173	0.76	X	X	0	17	0	12	0	0

	Lead in Gasoline				Lead Production					
	Consumption of Motor Gasoline (million liters) 1995	Gasoline Cost per Liter (US$) 1996	Market Share of Leaded Gasoline (percent) 1992-1996 {a}	Maximum Concentration of Lead in Gasoline (grams/liter) 1992-1996 {a}	Mines in Concentrates (000 metric tons)		Refineries (000 metric tons)			
							Primary		Secondary	
					1986	1996	1986	1996	1986	1996
NORTH AMERICA	**487,037**	X	X	X	X	X	X	X	X	X
Canada	35,184	0.51	0	0.00	349	241	170	194	88	115
United States	451,853	0.39	0	0.00	353	436	370	326	625	1,100
CENTRAL AMERICA	**40,579**	X	X	X	X	X	X	X	X	X
Belize	35	X	X	X	0	0	0	0	0	0
Costa Rica	547	0.41	20	0.20	0	0	0	0	0	0
Cuba	1,293	X	100	0.84	0	0	0	0	0	0
Dominican Rep	811	X	69	0.40	0	0	0	0	0	0
El Salvador	380	0.47	47	0.20	0	0	0	0	0	0
Guatemala	576	0.45	0	0.00	0	0	0	0	0	0
Haiti	73	X	X	X	0	0	0	0	0	0
Honduras	309	0.40	35	X	13	3	0	0	0	0
Jamaica	467	0.27	70	0.77	0	0	0	0	1	1
Mexico	35,261	0.39	44	0.26	183	174	182	144	33	10
Nicaragua	151	0.89	100	X	0	0	0	0	0	0
Panama	403	0.49	7	0.63	0	0	0	0	0	0
Trinidad and Tobago	273	0.48	99	X	0	0	0	0	2	16
SOUTH AMERICA	**56,180**	X	X	X	X	X	X	X	X	X
Argentina	8,407	0.84	0	0.00	27	10	16	2	15	26
Bolivia	546	0.60	0	0.00	3	16	0	0	0	0
Brazil	18,471	0.65	0	0.00	14	0	33	15	52	3
Chile	2,814	0.55	72	0.31	2	1	0	0	0	0
Colombia	7,533	0.34	0	0.00	0	0	0	0	4	4
Ecuador	1,670	0.33	76	0.80	0	0	0	0	0	0
Guyana	97	X	X	X	0	0	0	0	0	0
Paraguay	326	0.44	99	0.20	0	0	0	0	0	0
Peru	1,046	0.77	75	0.40	194	249	66	95	5	0
Suriname	85	X	100	X	0	0	0	0	0	0
Uruguay	401	0.95	94	0.79	0	0	0	0	0	0
Venezuela	14,784	0.12	100	1.46	0	0	0	0	16	16
ASIA	**191,643**	X	X	X	X	X	X	X	X	X
Afghanistan, Islamic State	101	X	X	X	0	0	0	0	0	0
Armenia, Rep	74	X	X	X	0	0	0	0	0	0
Azerbaijan	1,216	X	94	0.37	0	0	0	0	0	0
Bangladesh	177	0.36	100	0.80	0	0	0	0	0	0
Bhutan	7	X	X	X	0	0	0	0	0	0
Cambodia	49	X	X	X	0	0	0	0	0	0
China	38,593	0.28	40	0.33	227	500	200	430	40	100
Georgia	69 d	X	X	X	0	0	0	0	0	0
India	5,893	0.54	X e	0.42	38	31	20	33	11	27
Indonesia	7,890	X	100 f	0.45	0	0	0	0	0	0
Iran, Islamic Rep	10,046	X	100	0.19	22	16	0	6	8	41
Iraq	4,039	X	100	0.60	0	0	0	0	0	0
Israel	2,706	0.62	90	0.15	0	0	0	0	0	0
Japan	50,723	1.08	0	0.00	40	8	233	141	129	147
Jordan	657	X	100	0.30	0	40	0	0	0	0
Kazakstan, Rep	3,017	X	40	0.37	0	0	0	69	0	10
Korea, Dem People's Rep	2,432	X	X	X	110	80	95	75	0	5
Korea, Rep	9,438	0.79	17	X	12	5	32	89	28	10
Kuwait	1,990	0.15	100	0.53	0	0	0	0	0	0
Kyrgyz Rep	285	X	X	X	0	0	0	0	0	0
Lao People's Dem Rep	26	X	100	0.40	0	0	0	0	0	0
Lebanon	1,728	X	100	0.84	0	0	0	0	0	0
Malaysia	5,531	X	45	0.15	0	0	0	0	14	34
Mongolia	250	X	X	X	0	0	0	0	0	0
Myanmar	282	X	X	X	18	3	0	0	0	0
Nepal	30	0.52	X	X	0	0	0	0	0	0
Oman	852	X	100	0.62	0	0	0	0	0	0
Pakistan	1,459	0.45	100	0.42	0	0	0	0	1	2
Philippines	2,276	X	90	0.15	0	0	0	0	7	17
Saudi Arabia	13,247	0.16	100	0.40	0	0	0	0	0	0
Singapore	1,785	X	40	0.15	0	0	0	0	0	0
Sri Lanka	245	0.74	100	0.20	0	0	0	0	0	0
Syrian Arab Rep	1,382	X	100	0.40	0	0	0	0	0	0
Tajikistan, Rep	4,037 d	X	X	X	0	1	0	0	0	0
Thailand	5,919	0.31	0	0.15	26	20	0	0	9	19
Turkey	5,844	0.63	96	0.40	10	10	7	5	3	5
Turkmenistan, Rep	676	X	X	X	0	0	0	0	0	0
United Arab Emirates	1,564	X	100	0.40	0	0	0	0	0	0
Uzbekistan, Rep	2,209	X	X	X	0	10	0	0	0	0
Vietnam	1,360	0.34	100	0.40	0	0	0	0	0	0
Yemen	1,540	X	100	0.45	0	0	0	0	0	0
OCEANIA	**20,611**	X	X	X	X	X	X	X	X	X
Australia	17,636	0.54	55	0.45 g	448	522	156	204	15	20
Fiji	61	X	X	X	0	0	0	0	0	0
New Zealand	2,795	0.63	56	X	0	0	0	0	4	6
Papua New Guinea	108	X	X	X	0	0	0	0	0	0
Solomon Islands	11	X	X	X	0	0	0	0	0	0

Notes: a. Data are for most recent year available. b. Unleaded gasoline has been introduced recently. c. 0.15 in Athens. d. Data are for 1993. e. Unleaded gasoline in four largest cities only. f. Less than 1% unleaded gasoline, in Jakarta only (1995). g. Varies by state.

Demographic and Health Surveys, 1990–95

Source: Demographic and Health Surveys

| | | Percentage of Households Without | | | | | | | | | | Maximum Number of Households Surveyed | Percentage of Children Under 5 With | | | | Maximum Number of Households Surveyed |
| | Year of DHS Survey | Piped Water | | Own Flush Toilet | | Finished Floor | | Refrigerator | | Radio or Television | | | Diarrhea | | a Cough | | |
		Urban	Rural	Urban	Rural	Urban	Rural	Urban	Rural	Urban	Rural		Urban	Rural	Urban	Rural	
AFRICA																	
Burkina Faso	1992-93	74	99	97	100	14	83	87	100	25	59	4,877	19	21	29	32	5,522
Cameroon	1991	85	99	86	99	25	78	75	98	29	55	3,407	17	18	30	27	3,188
Central African Rep	1994-95	96	100	98	100	74	97	96	100	39	64	5,387	20	25	65	59	2,577
Côte d'Ivoire	1994	49	96	80	99	2	43	79	96	33	55	5,815	25	20	37	33	3,645
Egypt	1992	9	55	54	94	6	60	22	71	8	28	10,628	13	13	30	22	8,089
Ghana	1993	63	98	90	100	2	23	77	99	43	66	5,637	17	21	21	24	2,053
Kenya	1993	43	89	77	99	21	80	88	99	31	52	7,532	12	14	37	43	5,620
Madagascar	1992	70	99	91	100	63	93	92	100	34	69	5,961	11	13	41	37	5,007
Morocco	1992	24	91	22	82	4	54	43	95	6	18	6,364	10	14	30	33	4,848
Namibia	1992	18	87	17	94	12	80	44	95	19	41	3,927	14	24	37	45	3,573
Niger	1992	77	100	97	100	36	97	87	100	38	72	5,173	20	29	17	23	5,702
Nigeria	1990	X	X	X	X	X	X	X	X	X	X	X	12	20	17	20	7,069
Rwanda	1992	93	100	100	100	43	92	90	100	X	X	5,976	21	22	37	46	5,020
Senegal	1992-93	46	93	86	99	8	67	79	99	19	35	3,362	16	23	26	30	5,108
Tanzania	1991-92	59	98	97	100	47	92	96	100	43	74	8,026	15	13	34	27	7,230
Uganda	1995	87	100	93	100	33	93	95	100	32	67	7,368	20	24	42	50	5,431
Zambia	1992	45	97	57	99	15	84	85	99	39	77	5,872	20	25	X	X	5,387
Zimbabwe	1994	8	96	34	98	5	59	76	98	33	68	5,786	18	26	42	51	2,221
CENTRAL AMERICA																	
Dominican Rep	1991	72	92	50	93	3	24	42	82	17	41	6,228	17	16	34	38	3,645
Guatemala	1995	39	59	46	91	68	76	53	89	8	27	10,385	20	21	37	33	8,616
SOUTH AMERICA																	
Bolivia	1994	22	77	59	98	22	77	58	93	5	30	8,560	31	28	34	30	3,333
Brazil	1991	23	87	28	83	8	39	39	86	16	37	5,739	17	13	40	39	3,158
Colombia	1995	5	88	10	87	6	41	28	71	4	14	9,417	16	17	43	40	4,891
Paraguay	1990	X	X	X	X	X	X	X	X	X	X	X	8	8	X	X	3,809
Peru	1991-92	25	82	42	97	29	86	45	96	5	30	12,314	16	22	36	35	7,991
ASIA																	
Bangladesh	1993-94	74	100	51	96	48	96	X	X	47	77	8,936	11	13	40	35	3,595
Indonesia	1994	77	98	X	X	16	58	79	99	16	40	33,626	12	12	33	27	15,870
Jordan	1990	X	X	X	X	X	X	X	X	X	X	X	9	8	16	15	7,955
Kazakstan, Rep	1995	9	68	26	98	60	96	7	29	4	12	4,180	15	16	20	11	779
Pakistan	1990-91	53	95	100	100	X	X	66	96	28	70	7,285	15	14	37	32	5,833
Philippines	1993	56	88	37	57	42	66	58	87	X	X	12,432	10	10	32	34	8,493
Turkey	1993	25	58	16	89	23	58	5	26	3	10	8,271	23	28	25	32	3,531

Sources and Technical Notes

Data Table 8.1

Nutrition, 1971–96

Sources: Low-birthweight infants, under-5 children suffering from underweight, wasting and stunting, daily per capita calorie supply as a percentage of total requirements, and households consuming iodized salt: United Nations Children's Fund (UNICEF), *State of the World's Children 1997* (UNICEF, New York, 1997), including information from World Health Organization (WHO), Demographic and Health Surveys, and Multiple Indicator Cluster Surveys. Pregnant women aged 15–49 with anemia: United Nations (U.N.) Statistical Division, Department for Economic and Social Information and Policy Analysis, *Women's Indicators and Statistics* (Wistat Version 3.0, New York; 11 disks). Total goiter rate in children aged 6–11: WHO, *Global Prevalence of Iodine Deficiency Disorders* (WHO, Geneva, 1993). Children under 5 with vitamin A deficiency: WHO, *Global Prevalence of Vitamin A Deficiency* (WHO, Geneva, 1995).

The *percentage of low-birthweight infants* refers to all babies weighing less than 2,500 grams at birth. WHO has adopted the standard that healthy babies, regardless of race, should weigh more than 2,500 grams at birth. These data are provided by UNICEF and WHO, and refer to a single year between 1990 and 1994.

Underweight refers to children under 5 whose weight-for-age is below minus 2 standard deviations (for moderate underweight) or below minus 3 standard deviations (for severe underweight) from the median weight-for-age of the reference population. *Wasting* indicates current acute malnutrition and refers to the percentage of children under 5 whose weight-for-height is below minus 2 standard deviations from the median of the reference population, as defined by the U.S. National Center for Health Statistics (NCHS). *Stunting*, an indicator of chronic undernutrition, refers to the percentage of children under 5 whose height-for-age is below minus 2 standard deviations from the median of the reference population. NCHS, among others, has found that healthy children in one country differ little, as a group, in terms of weight and height from healthy children in other countries. WHO has accepted the NCHS weight-for-age and weight-for-height standards; however, several countries still use local reference populations, and the estimates provided may use several sources, rather than solely or primarily the WHO database. Children with low weight-for-age are at a high risk of mortality. Data on wasting and stunting, provided to UNICEF by WHO, refer to a single year between 1990 and 1996. Data for wasting and stunting are generally good if derived from recent national household surveys, such as the Demographic and Health Surveys, but are not good if they are old or from local subnational studies.

Daily per capita calorie supply as a percentage of total requirements are calories from all food sources: domestic production, international trade, stock draw-downs, and foreign aid. The quantity of food available for human consumption, as estimated by the Food and Agriculture Organization of the United Nations (FAO), is the amount that reaches the consumer. Per capita supplies by weight are derived from the total supplies available for human consumption by dividing the quantities of food by the total population actually partaking of the food supplies during the reference period. In almost all cases, the population figures used are the midyear estimates published by the U.N. Population Division. The calories actually consumed may be lower than the figures shown, depending on how much food is lost during home storage, preparation, and cooking, and on how much is fed to pets and domestic animals or discarded. Estimates of daily caloric requirements vary for individual countries according to the population's age distribution and estimated level of activity. For further information on FAO data, visit the FAO web site at: http://www.fao.org.

The *percentage of pregnant women aged 15–49 with anemia* is an indicator of nutritional status, dietary practices, and prenatal care. A woman becomes especially susceptible to iron-deficiency while pregnant and where malnutrition is widespread. Anemia can be easily treated with iron supplements.

The *percentage of children aged 6–11 with goiter* is the percentage with a visible goiter. Iodine deficiency is at least partially due to environmental causes and is found in areas with iodine-depleted soils due to leaching and floods, in mountainous areas, and in high-elevation areas subject to high rainfall. Iodine deficiency is the world's greatest single cause of preventable brain damage and mental retardation. *Percentage of households consuming iodized salt* is derived from surveys at the household level conducted by UNICEF, called Multiple Indicator Cluster Surveys.

The *percentage of children under 5 with vitamin A deficiency* is the percentage of the under-5 population affected by vitamin A deficiency, including those affected clinically and subclinically. Vitamin A deficiency is at least partially due to environmental causes and is found in areas with water shortages and high, constant temperatures. Vitamin A deficiency is the most important cause of childhood blindness. Criteria used to define the severity of vitamin A deficiency include prevalence of clinical eye signs (e.g., corneal scars) or symptoms (e.g., nightblindness) and low blood values (or plasma retinol levels). For more detailed information, see the WHO publication on vitamin A deficiency cited previously.

Data Table 8.2

Mortality, 1975–2020

Sources: Crude death rate and infant mortality rate data: United Nations (U.N.) Population Division, *World Population Prospects 1950–2050 (The 1996 Revision)*, on diskette (U.N., New York, 1996). Under-5 mortality rate, average annual change in under-5 mortality, and maternal mortality rate: United Nations Children's Fund (UNICEF), *State of the World's Children 1997* (UNICEF, New York, 1997), including information from the U.N. Population Division, U.N. Statistical Division, the World Bank, the U.S. Bureau of Census, and the World Health Organization (WHO).

The *crude death rate* is derived by dividing the number of deaths in a given year by the midyear population and multiplying by 1,000. The *infant mortality rate* is the probability of dying by exact age 1, multiplied by 1,000.

The *under-5 mortality rate* is the probability of dying by exact age 5, multiplied by 1,000. UNICEF provides this cohort measure, which is derived from *Child Mortality Since the 1960s: A Database for Developing Countries* (U.N., New York, 1992) and from infant mortality estimates provided by the U.N. Population Division. The mix is the result of a move from modeled estimates to estimates based on a periodically updated child mortality database. Nonetheless, this variable should not be compared to the U.N. Population Division's infant mortality rate, which is derived from population models where otherwise not available.

The *average annual change in under-5 mortality* is UNICEF's separate estimate of the average annual reduction in the rate of children dying between birth and exact age 5 for the range of years specified (either 1960–80 or 1980–95).

The *maternal mortality rate* is the annual number of deaths from pregnancy- or childbirth-related causes per 100,000 live births. A maternal death is defined by WHO as the death of a woman while pregnant or within 42 days of the termination of pregnancy from any cause related to or aggravated by the pregnancy, including abortion. Most official maternal mortality rates are underestimated because of underreporting, incorrect classification, and unavailable cause of death information. In some countries, over 60 percent of women's deaths are registered without a specified cause. Maternal deaths are highest among women aged 10–15 years, over 40 years, and in women with five or more children. Data are provided to UNICEF by WHO and refer to a single year between 1980 and 1990. Data for a few countries are outside the range of years indicated. The models used for deriving estimates of maternal mortality are relatively new. In addition, in many cases it is difficult to estimate the number of maternal deaths outside a hospital setting. For the data presented in this table, UNICEF states that: "Several of the maternal mortality rates ... are substantially different from official government estimates. These and other rates are being reviewed by WHO and UNICEF and will be revised where necessary, as part of the ongoing process of improving maternal mortality estimates."

Data Table 8.3

Reported Cases of Infectious Diseases per 100,000 Population, 1985–95

Source: World Health Organization (WHO). Tuberculosis, measles, polio, and cholera data: published in various issues of the *Weekly Epidemiological Record* and in the *World Health Report* (WHO, Geneva). WRI obtained electronic data for the years included in this table. Malaria data (number of reported cases): published in various *World Malaria Situation* reports. Data for 1994 and 1995 are published in the corresponding *World Health Report*.

Data presented in this table are reported cases of *tuberculosis*. In 1995, the Global Tuberculosis Programme developed a global monitoring and surveillance project to describe the magnitude of the worldwide tuberculosis epidemic and assess the status of control measures. The project's first year results, reported in 1997 by WHO, show discrepancies between reported case rates and incidence estimates for tuberculosis for 1995, with incidence estimates generally higher than case notification rates. See the above sources for further information.

Measles data are the number of measles cases reported by WHO member states to WHO, published biannually. WHO is currently trying to improve the completeness of 1995 and 1996 data. A large percentage of measles cases are not treated at a health facility and therefore remain unreported. Thus, these case data are an underestimate of the actual number of cases.

Malaria data are the officially reported malaria cases from WHO member states to WHO, published annually. The majority of malaria cases are not treated at a health facility and remain unreported, particularly in areas known to be highly endemic. In line with the Global Malaria Control Strategy that was adopted in 1992, malaria reporting must focus primarily on clinical disease. The data for 1994 still mark the transition in reporting: some countries report clinically diagnosed cases, others report microscopically confirmed infections, or a combination of both.

Polio is rapidly disappearing from significant areas of the world. When the global polio eradication goal was set in 1988, approximately 35,000 cases were reported worldwide. In 1995, that number had fallen to 7,000, an 80 percent decline. Although reporting for 1996 is incomplete, significant declines are anticipated. It should be noted, though, that many cases of polio are not reported. It is estimated that the reported total represents only 10 percent of the cases that actually occur.

Cholera data are based on official reports from countries to the WHO regional offices, as well as on reports from scientific literature and qualified laboratories, summarized by the Global Task Force on Cholera Control at WHO headquarters.

For more extensive information see WHO's Web site at: http://www.who.ch.

Data Table 8.4

Health Care, 1971–96

Sources: Percentage of births attended by trained personnel; percentage of 1-year-olds immunized against tuberculosis (TB), against diphtheria, pertussis (whooping cough), and tetanus (DPT), and against polio; percentage of pregnant women immunized for tetanus; oral rehydration therapy (ORT) use: United Nations Children's Fund (UNICEF), *State of the World's Children 1997* (UNICEF, New York, 1997). Contraceptive prevalence: United Nations (U.N.) Population Division, World Population Prospects, 1950–2050 (The 1996 Revision), on diskette (U.N., New York, 1996). Percentage of 1-year-olds immunized against measles: WHO and personal communication with Rachel Horner, WHO, March 1997. Population per doctor and nurse: the World Bank, *World Development Indicators* (The World Bank, Washington, D.C., 1997), including information from government statistical yearbooks, the Organisation for Economic Co-Operation and Development, and the World Health Organization (WHO).

Percentage of births attended by trained personnel is the percentage of births attended by physicians, nurses, midwives, or primary health care workers trained in midwifery skills. *Immunization* data show the percentage of 1-year-olds immunized against: TB, DPT, polio, and measles, as well as the *percentage of pregnant women immunized for tetanus. ORT use* refers to the percentage of all cases of diarrhea in children under 5 years of age treated with oral rehydration salts or recommended home fluids to combat diarrheal diseases leading to dehydration or malnutrition.

Contraceptive prevalence is the percentage of contraceptive use of either any method or modern methods among couples in which the woman is of childbearing age (15–49). Among the contraceptive methods used are sterilization, oral and injectable contraceptives, condoms, intrauterine devices, vaginal barriers (including diaphragms, cervical caps, and spermicides), and traditional methods (including rhythm, withdrawal, abstinence, douching, and folk remedies). Data are collected by the U.N. Population Division and by Demographic and Health Surveys.

Population per doctor and *per nurse* refers to data mainly from WHO's second evaluation of progress in implementing national health-for-all strategies. These data for developing countries are supplemented by country statistical yearbooks and by World Bank sector studies. The comparability of WHO's physician ratios are influenced by treatments received from practitioners of indigenous medicine not included in WHO's definition of a physician and by the variation in data included on the use of homeopaths and osteopaths across countries. Thus, the data presented in the table indicate availability rather than quality or use; they do not show training of physicians or whether hospitals or medical centers are well equipped. Physicians are defined as graduates of any faculty or school of medicine who are working in the country in any medical field (practice, teaching, or research). Nurses are defined as persons who have completed a program of basic nursing education; are qualified and registered or authorized to provide service for the promotion of health, prevention of illness, care of the sick, and rehabilitation; and are working in the country. These data do not cover auxiliary and paraprofessional personnel.

Data Table 8.5

City Air Pollution, 1990–95

Sources: City population: United Nations (U.N.) Population Division, *Urban and Rural Agglomerations 1950–2015 (The 1996 Revision)*, on CD-Rom (U.N., New York, 1997); *World Cities Population Database* (WCPD), Birkbeck College, University of London, 1995; *Information Malaysia: 1996 Yearbook* (personal communication with Malaysian Embassy, January 1998); National Institute of Public Health and the Environment (RIVM) and Norwegian Institute for Air Research (NILU), *Air Quality In Major European Cities*, R.J.C.F. Sluyter, ed. (RIVM, Biltoven, Netherlands and NILU, Kjeller, Norway, 1995); and City Net home page at: http://www.city.net. Primary sources for levels of total suspended particulates (TSP), black smoke (BS), particulate matter (PM-10), sulfur dioxide (SO_2), and nitrogen dioxide (NO_2) include: World Health Organization (WHO), *Healthy Cities Air Management*, Information System, AMIS 1.0, on diskette (WHO, Geneva, 1997); U.S. Environmental Protection Agency (EPA), *AIRS Executive International* (U.S. EPA, Research Triangle Park, North Carolina). Available online at: www.epa.gov/airs/aexec.html; U.S. EPA, *Air Quality and Emissions Trends Report 1995* (U.S. EPA, Research Triangle Park, North Carolina, 1996); and Organisation for Economic Co-Operation and Development (OECD), *Environmental Data*, Compendiums (OECD, Paris, 1992, 1993, 1995, and 1997); National Environmental Protection Agency, China, *China Environment Yearbook* (China Environmental Yearbook Press, Beijing, 1996); India Central Pollution Control Board, *Ambient Air Quality—Status and Statistics* (Central Pollution Control Board, Delhi, India, 1993 and 1994).

Additional sources of air pollution data for one city or several include: United Nations Environment Program (UNEP) and WHO, *Urban Air Pollution in Megacities of the World* (Blackwell Publishers, Oxford, U.K., 1992); The World Bank, *World Development Indicators 1997* (The World Bank, Washington, D.C., 1997); National Statistical Office, Republic of Korea, *Korea Statistical Yearbook 1995*, 42nd edition (National Statistical Office, Seoul, Korea, 1995); City of Yokohama Environmental Affairs Bureau, 1995; Department of the Environment, Malaysia, *Environmental Quality Report 1993* (Department of the Environment, Kuala Lumpur, Malaysia, 1994); Ministry of the Environment, Singapore, *1995 Pollution Control Report and Annual Report* (Ministry of the Environment, Singapore, 1995); Isabelle Romieu, Henyk Weitzenfeld, and Jacob Finkelman, "Urban Air Pollution in Latin America and the Caribbean: Health Perspectives," *World Health Statistics Quarterly*, Vol. 43 (1990); and National Institute of Public Health and the Environment (RIVM) and Norwegian Institute for Air Research (NILU), *Air Quality in Major European Cities,* Part I: Scientific Background Document to Europe's Environment, R.J.C.F. Sluyter, ed. (RIVM, Biltoven, Netherlands and NILU, Kjeller, Norway, 1995)

Cities are included in this table based on the availability of air pollution data, population size, and regional representation.

The U.N. provides estimated and projected populations for major urban agglomerations of the world. Estimates and projections are based, to the extent possible, on actual recorded data. For a complete description of the sources of data for urban populations, see U.N. Population Division, *World Urbanization Prospects: The 1996 Revision* (U.N., New York, 1997). The *World Cities Population Database* provides close approximations of a global georeferenced data set of cities and their populations.

Particulate matter is the general term for solid or liquid particles found in the atmosphere. Data for *total suspended particulates (TSP)* are presented in micrograms per cubic meter ($\mu g/m_3$). WHO's 1987 mean annual guideline for TSP is 90 $\mu g/m_3$. *Black smoke and particulate matter (PM-10)* are additional measures of suspended particulates. Black smoke includes particles large or dark enough to be seen as soot or smoke. PM-10 includes smaller particles that are likely to be responsible for adverse health effects because they can reach the lower respiratory tract. PM-10 includes particles with an aerodynamic size less than or equal to a standard particle with a diameter of 10 micrometers (0.0004 inches). WHO's 1987 *mean annual* guideline for black smoke is 50 $\mu g/m_3$; for PM-10, it is 70 $\mu g/m_3$. The 1997 WHO air quality guidelines do not include guideline values for suspended particulate matter. For further information, see the WHO Web site at: http://www.who.ch.

Sulfur dioxide (SO_2) belongs to the family of sulfur oxide gases. The major health concerns associated with exposure to high concentrations of SO_2 include effects on breathing, respiratory illness, alterations in the lungs' defenses, and aggravation of existing cardiovascular disease. Levels of SO_2 in the air are presented in micrograms per cubic meter ($\mu g/m_3$). WHO's *mean annual* 1997 guideline for SO_2 is 50 $\mu g/m_3$.

Nitrogen dioxide (NO_2) belongs to a family of poisonous, highly reactive gases called oxides of nitrogen. NO_2 can irritate the lungs and lower resistance to respiratory infections such as influenza. NO_2 levels in the air are presented in micrograms

per cubic meter ($\mu g/m_3$). WHO's *mean annual* 1997 guideline for NO_2 is 50$\mu g/m_3$.

Data Table 8.6

Lead in Gasoline and Lead Production, 1986–96

Sources: Consumption of motor gasoline: United Nations (U.N.) Department for Economic and Social Information and Policy Analysis, Statistics Division, *1995 Energy Statistics Yearbook* (U.N., New York, 1997). Cost of gasoline per liter: The World Bank, *Air Pollution from Motor Vehicles, Standards and Technologies for Controlling Emissions* (The World Bank, Washington, D.C., 1996). Market share of leaded gasoline and maximum concentration of lead in gasoline: The World Bank, *Phasing-out Lead From Gasoline: World-Wide Experience and Policy Implications*, Annex A update (The World Bank, Washington, D.C., 1996, 1997); and The World Bank, *Elimination of Lead in Gasoline in Latin America and the Caribbean*, Report No. 194/97EN, Energy Sector Management Assistance Programme (The World Bank, Washington, D.C., 1996). Lead production from mines and refineries: U.S. Geological Survey.

One of the oldest metals used by humans, *lead* is a cumulative neurotoxin that impairs brain development among children and has been connected to elevated blood pressure and resulting hypertension, heart attacks, and premature death in adults. Emissions from vehicles is the largest source of lead exposure in many urban areas.

Consumption of motor gasoline is the amount of motor gasoline consumed per country in 1995, reported by the U.N. in thousand metric tons, converted to million liters (1 metric ton = 1,351 liters). *Gasoline cost per liter* is reported by the World Bank for 1996 in U.S. dollars per liter. *Market share of leaded gasoline* is the percentage of gasoline containing lead sold in each country. *Maximum concentration of lead in gasoline* is the maximum content of lead in gasoline sold in the country reported in grams per liter, although actual lead content may vary.

Lead toxicity also presents health problems for those involved in its production, causing concern about emissions from lead smelters and refineries, workers' blood-lead levels, and in-plant permissible exposure limits. *Lead production* from *mines* and from *refineries* is the amount of lead produced in thousand metric tons. Lead production from mines is reported as the quantity contained in concentrates. In mining, a concentrate is the fraction of valuable mineral that has been separated from the valueless or unneeded rock and earth. The concentrate (enriched ore) provides the appropriate material for subsequent smelting and refining. Lead production from refineries is reported according to *primary* production (derived from the mining of ores) and *secondary* production (derived from recycled materials).

For further information on lead, please visit the U.S. Geological Survey Minerals Information Web

site at: http://minerals.er.usgs.gov/ minerals/pubs/commodity/lead.

Data Table 8.7

Demographic and Health Surveys (DHS), 1990–95

Source: Demographic and Health Surveys (DHS), Macro International, Inc., Calverton, Maryland.

Since 1984, the DHS program has assisted countries in conducting national surveys on fertility, family planning, and maternal and child health. Macro International, Inc., provides technical assistance and administrative support for the DHS program, which is funded by the U.S. Agency for International Development. Surveys are implemented in collaboration with agencies in participating countries, usually the Bureau of Statistics, Ministry of Planning, or Ministry of Health.

The main objectives of the DHS program are to improve the information base for policy development, economic and social planning, and population and health program management; to promote the widespread dissemination and use of DHS data by policymakers and planners; to expand the institutional capabilities in participating countries for collecting and analyzing survey data; and to advance the methodologies and procedures for conducting and analyzing demographic and health surveys.

The first two phases of the DHS project included assistance for more than 50 surveys (Phase I surveys were conducted between 1986 and 1990; Phase II surveys were conducted between 1990 and 1993). In its third phase, the DHS program will provide technical assistance for at least 30 surveys conducted between 1993 and 1997. The present table includes data from surveys conducted in the second and third phases of the DHS program. Data collected in Phase II include: Brazil, Burkina Faso, Cameroon, Dominican Republic, Egypt, Jordan, Madagascar, Morocco, Namibia, Niger, Nigeria, Pakistan, Paraguay, Peru, Rwanda, Senegal, Tanzania, and Zambia. All other countries included in the table represent data collected from Phase III surveys.

On average, 4,000 to 8,000 women of childbearing age are interviewed in a standard survey. The DHS questionnaires are designed to elicit information on family planning knowledge, attitudes, and practices; maternal and child health; nutritional status of women and their children; and social and economic background indicators.

Percentage of households without piped water presents the percentage of urban and rural households included in the surveys (maximum 33,626 from Indonesia, minimum 3,362 from Senegal) without piped water into their residences; these households rely instead on other water sources such as a public tap, well water, surface water, rainwater, or bottled water.

Percentage of households without own flush toilet presents the percentage of urban and rural households included in the surveys (maximum 12,432 from the Phillippines, mininimum 3,358 from Senegal) without their own flush toilet; these households rely instead on other sanitation facilities, such as a pit toilet or no facility.

Percentage of households without a finished floor presents the percentage of urban and rural households included in the surveys (maximum 33,600 from Indonesia, minimum 3,357 from Senegal) without a finished floor. A finished floor could include polished wood, vinyl, tiles, cement, or carpeting. Unfinished floors include natural floors of dirt or dung, as well as wood planks, palm, or bamboo.

Percentage of households without a refrigerator presents the percentage of urban and rural households included in the surveys (maximum 33,615 from Indonesia, minimum 3,352 from Senegal) without a refrigerator.

Percentage of households without a radio or television presents the percentage of urban and rural households included in the surveys (maximum 33,616 from Indonesia, minimum 3,352 from Senegal) without a radio or television.

Children under 5 with diarrhea presents the percentage of children under age 5 in urban and rural households included in the surveys (maximum 15,870 from Indonesia, minimum 779 from the Republic of Kazakstan) with diarrhea in the 2 weeks preceding the survey.

Children under 5 with a cough presents the percentage of children under age 5 in urban and rural households included in the surveys (maximum 15,864 from Indonesia, minimum 779 from Republic of Kazakstan) with a cough in the 2 weeks preceding the survey.

Additional information about the DHS program and data sets may be obtained from Demographic and Health Surveys, Macro International, Inc., Suite 300, 11785 Beltsville Drive, Calverton, Maryland 20705-3119; telephone: 301-572-0200, fax: 301-572-0993, and Web site: http://www.macroint.com/dhs/.

*C*hapter 9

Urban Data

Data Table 9.1
Urban Indicators, 1980–2025

Source: United Nations Population Division

	Urban Population (000)			Percentage Urban			Population Growth Rate (percent) Urban			Rural			Population in Urban Agglomerations > 750,000 (percent)	
	1980	2000	2020	1980	2000	2020	1980-85	2000-05	2020-25	1980-85	2000-05	2020-25	1995	2015
WORLD	**1,754,308**	**2,889,855**	**4,346,897**	**39**	**47**	**57**	**2.6**	**2.2**	**1.7**	**1.1**	**0.4**	**(0.1)**	**X**	**X**
AFRICA	**129,842**	**309,651**	**646,106**	**27**	**38**	**49**	**4.4**	**4.0**	**3.0**	**2.2**	**1.6**	**0.9**	**X**	**X**
Algeria	8,127	18,727	30,949	43	59	70	4.9	3.2	1.8	1.6	0.5	(0.1)	13	15
Angola	1,467	4,371	10,697	21	34	47	5.6	4.9	3.8	1.8	2.0	1.2	19	25
Benin	946	2,630	6,109	27	42	56	5.4	4.6	3.3	2.1	1.5	1.0	0	0
Botswana	137	1,191	2,142	15	74	89	13.7	4.2	1.6	0.9	(5.5)	0.2	0	0
Burkina Faso	585	2,226	6,343	8	18	31	8.6	5.6	4.4	2.0	2.1	1.5	8	14
Burundi	179	625	1,875	4	9	17	6.5	5.9	4.7	2.6	2.1	1.4	0	0
Cameroon	2,719	7,401	15,671	31	49	62	5.4	4.2	3.1	1.5	1.2	0.9	18	24
Central African Rep	811	1,499	2,897	35	41	53	3.0	3.3	2.9	1.9	1.3	0.5	0	0
Chad	843	1,729	3,909	19	24	34	3.4	4.0	3.9	2.0	1.9	1.0	13	18
Congo, Dem Rep	7,756	15,670	39,648	29	30	43	2.7	4.5	4.1	3.4	2.3	1.4	11	14
Congo, Rep	685	1,865	3,671	41	63	72	5.8	3.7	2.9	0.5	1.0	1.1	39	46
Côte d'Ivoire	2,849	7,046	13,351	35	47	59	5.3	3.6	2.2	2.9	1.1	0.0	20	25
Egypt	19,178	31,297	51,098	44	46	56	2.6	2.6	2.1	2.6	1.0	(0.2)	23	26
Equatorial Guinea	59	218	461	27	48	64	8.9	4.5	2.8	6.6	0.3	0.7	0	0
Eritrea	322	714	1,738	14	19	29	4.3	4.4	3.9	2.2	1.9	0.9	0	0
Ethiopia	3,812	11,679	34,429	10	18	29	4.6	5.7	4.7	2.2	2.5	1.7	4	6
Gabon	235	682	1,319	34	55	68	5.8	4.0	2.5	1.4	0.4	0.5	0	0
Gambia, The	126	404	838	20	32	46	5.8	4.1	3.0	2.3	1.0	0.4	0	0
Ghana	3,368	7,644	16,742	31	38	53	4.2	4.2	3.2	3.1	1.7	0.7	10	12
Guinea	852	2,577	6,269	19	33	46	5.3	4.9	3.7	1.4	1.8	1.1	21	30
Guinea-Bissau	135	280	613	17	24	35	3.6	3.9	3.6	1.5	1.4	0.8	0	0
Kenya	2,673	10,043	22,468	16	33	48	7.7	5.0	2.6	2.7	1.2	0.1	7	10
Lesotho	183	641	1,544	13	28	42	6.8	5.1	3.4	2.0	1.3	0.8	0	0
Liberia	656	1,560	3,457	35	48	60	5.5	4.5	3.4	1.8	2.1	1.1	45	51
Libya	2,109	5,597	10,410	69	88	91	6.4	3.5	2.5	(1.1)	0.8	1.1	46	46
Madagascar	1,660	5,133	13,088	18	30	43	5.8	5.1	3.8	2.6	2.1	1.1	6	8
Malawi	565	1,686	4,657	9	15	26	5.8	5.2	4.5	2.9	2.0	1.4	0	0
Mali	1,267	3,773	9,462	18	30	43	5.4	5.0	3.8	2.2	1.9	1.2	9	12
Mauritania	424	1,489	2,865	27	58	71	7.5	4.1	2.4	0.4	(0.1)	0.5	0	0
Mauritius	409	487	737	42	41	52	0.5	1.8	1.9	1.4	0.5	(0.5)	0	0
Morocco	7,969	16,035	25,188	41	55	67	3.9	2.7	1.8	1.0	0.0	(0.3)	17	19
Mozambique	1,586	7,869	17,344	13	40	55	10.1	4.8	3.2	0.8	0.7	0.9	13	19
Namibia	235	708	1,528	23	41	56	5.7	4.5	2.9	1.7	0.7	0.6	0	0
Niger	704	2,222	6,362	13	21	32	5.8	5.6	4.5	3.0	2.5	1.6	0	0
Nigeria	19,353	56,651	124,888	27	44	58	5.5	4.6	3.0	1.8	1.2	0.8	11	14
Rwanda	243	472	1,248	5	6	10	4.4	4.5	4.8	3.1	2.2	1.3	0	0
Senegal	1,988	4,463	9,090	36	47	59	3.9	4.0	2.8	2.2	1.3	0.6	21	25
Sierra Leone	779	1,783	3,719	24	37	50	4.3	4.0	3.1	1.3	1.1	0.6	0	0
Somalia	1,492	3,170	8,183	22	27	39	4.1	4.8	4.1	2.9	2.5	1.4	11	14
South Africa	14,043	23,291	39,548	48	50	59	2.6	2.7	2.2	2.4	1.5	0.0	30	34
Sudan	3,728	10,772	22,667	20	36	52	5.1	4.6	2.5	2.2	0.7	0.1	8	12
Swaziland	100	351	777	18	36	50	7.0	4.9	2.8	2.0	1.2	0.4	0	0
Tanzania	2,741	9,376	23,354	15	28	42	6.7	5.2	3.7	2.5	1.7	1.0	9	14
Togo	599	1,556	3,589	23	33	46	5.9	4.3	3.6	2.0	1.8	1.0	0	0
Tunisia	3,323	6,445	9,654	52	66	75	3.5	2.5	1.5	1.6	(0.3)	(0.3)	19	21
Uganda	1,154	3,180	9,333	9	14	23	4.8	5.5	4.8	2.1	2.5	1.7	5	7
Zambia	2,285	4,067	8,019	40	45	55	2.8	3.3	2.9	1.8	1.8	0.6	16	22
Zimbabwe	1,587	4,387	8,928	22	35	49	5.8	4.1	2.5	2.5	1.0	(0.0)	13	19
EUROPE	**480,186**	**546,162**	**570,353**	**69**	**75**	**80**	**0.8**	**0.3**	**0.1**	**(0.6)**	**(1.2)**	**(1.6)**	**X**	**X**
Albania	903	1,367	2,096	34	39	51	2.6	1.9	2.0	1.8	(0.1)	(0.5)	0	0
Austria	4,903	5,361	5,925	65	65	71	(0.0)	0.6	0.3	0.1	(0.2)	(1.6)	26	25
Belarus, Rep	5,456	7,654	8,004	56	74	82	2.5	0.5	(0.0)	(1.9)	(2.4)	(1.7)	17	19
Belgium	9,402	9,985	10,109	95	97	98	0.1	0.2	(0.0)	(2.7)	(2.1)	(1.3)	11	11
Bosnia and Herzegovina	1,391	1,872	2,352	36	43	54	2.2	1.2	0.8	0.4	(0.8)	(1.5)	0	0
Bulgaria	5,420	5,820	5,867	61	70	77	1.3	0.0	(0.1)	(1.6)	(1.7)	(1.8)	14	15
Croatia, Rep	2,191	2,589	2,871	50	58	67	1.3	0.6	0.4	(0.5)	(1.2)	(1.7)	22	26
Czech Rep	6,542	6,755	7,127	64	66	73	0.3	0.2	0.1	(0.4)	(0.9)	(1.8)	12	12
Denmark	4,289	4,522	4,711	84	86	89	0.1	0.3	0.2	(0.8)	(0.8)	(1.3)	25	25
Estonia, Rep	1,027	1,053	1,033	70	74	80	0.9	(0.3)	(0.2)	(0.1)	(1.8)	(1.9)	0	0
Finland	2,859	3,366	3,850	60	65	73	0.5	0.7	0.5	0.5	(1.0)	(1.4)	21	24
France	39,497	44,630	48,740	73	76	81	0.6	0.5	0.3	0.2	(0.8)	(1.3)	22	22
Germany	64,696	72,386	73,807	83	88	91	0.2	0.2	(0.0)	(1.8)	(1.5)	(1.4)	44	45
Greece	5,567	6,368	6,908	58	60	67	0.8	0.5	0.3	0.3	(0.6)	(1.7)	39	41
Hungary	6,089	6,568	6,661	57	67	75	0.7	0.1	(0.1)	(1.5)	(2.0)	(1.9)	20	22
Iceland	201	260	308	88	92	94	1.4	1.0	0.6	(1.1)	(0.8)	(0.7)	0	0
Ireland	1,882	2,092	2,475	55	59	66	1.2	0.7	0.6	0.4	(0.5)	(1.4)	26	26
Italy	37,608	38,317	38,681	67	67	73	0.2	0.1	(0.1)	0.0	(0.7)	(1.9)	23	24
Latvia, Rep	1,726	1,781	1,732	68	74	80	1.0	(0.4)	(0.2)	(0.5)	(2.1)	(1.8)	36	42
Lithuania, Rep	2,092	2,755	2,901	61	75	81	2.0	0.3	0.1	(1.3)	(2.1)	(1.6)	0	0
Macedonia, FYR	960	1,385	1,765	53	62	71	2.2	1.3	0.9	0.4	(0.6)	(1.0)	0	0
Moldova, Rep	1,601	2,460	3,178	40	55	66	2.9	1.4	1.0	(0.3)	(1.3)	(1.1)	17	21
Netherlands	12,503	14,181	14,808	88	89	92	0.5	0.4	0.1	0.3	(0.6)	(1.3)	14	14
Norway	2,882	3,269	3,672	71	74	79	0.6	0.6	0.5	(0.3)	(0.7)	(1.2)	0	0
Poland, Rep	20,667	25,389	29,268	58	66	73	1.5	0.7	0.5	(0.0)	(1.0)	(1.3)	22	23
Portugal	2,876	3,719	4,752	29	38	50	1.6	1.3	1.0	(0.3)	(1.0)	(1.5)	19	24
Romania	10,897	13,100	14,508	49	58	68	1.4	0.6	0.3	(0.5)	(1.4)	(1.7)	9	10
Russian Federation	96,717	113,567	112,020	70	78	83	1.3	0.1	(0.2)	(0.8)	(1.8)	(1.8)	21	22
Slovak Rep	2,570	3,283	3,846	52	61	70	1.6	0.9	0.5	(0.4)	(1.1)	(1.4)	0	0
Slovenia, Rep	880	1,007	1,098	48	53	61	1.2	0.4	0.3	(0.1)	(0.9)	(1.9)	0	0
Spain	27,326	30,895	31,587	73	78	83	0.9	0.3	(0.1)	(0.6)	(1.1)	(1.8)	19	20
Sweden	6,905	7,414	8,084	83	83	86	0.1	0.3	0.5	0.1	(0.3)	(1.1)	26	26
Switzerland	3,602	4,638	5,370	57	63	70	1.1	1.0	0.4	0.0	(0.5)	(1.5)	0	0
Ukraine	30,870	36,838	37,364	62	73	79	1.3	0.2	(0.1)	(1.3)	(1.9)	(1.8)	19	21
United Kingdom	50,017	52,198	54,165	89	89	91	0.1	0.2	0.2	(0.1)	(0.6)	(1.2)	27	26
Yugoslavia, Fed Rep	4,409	6,286	7,461	46	60	70	2.1	1.0	0.6	(0.7)	(1.5)	(1.3)	12	12

	Urban Population (000)			Percentage Urban			Population Growth Rate (percent) Urban			Rural			Population in Urban Agglomerations >750,000 (percent)	
	1980	2000	2020	1980	2000	2020	1980-85	2000-05	2020-25	1980-85	2000-05	2020-25	1995	2015
NORTH AMERICA	**188,603**	**238,271**	**293,832**	**74**	**77**	**82**	**1.2**	**1.0**	**0.9**	**0.4**	**(0.3)**	**(0.7)**	**X**	**X**
Canada	18,608	23,645	28,674	76	77	81	1.3	0.9	0.9	0.5	0.2	(0.8)	41	42
United States	169,898	214,504	265,021	74	77	82	1.2	1.0	0.9	0.4	(0.4)	(0.7)	42	42
CENTRAL AMERICA	**54,083**	**91,244**	**131,046**	**60**	**67**	**73**	**3.1**	**2.0**	**1.5**	**0.8**	**0.9**	**(0.2)**	**X**	**X**
Belize	72	112	188	49	47	54	2.2	2.6	2.5	2.9	2.0	0.2	0	0
Costa Rica	985	1,970	3,308	43	52	63	3.7	2.9	2.0	2.3	0.7	(0.1)	27	31
Cuba	6,613	8,727	9,838	68	78	84	1.7	0.8	0.3	(1.1)	(1.4)	(1.2)	20	21
Dominican Rep	2,877	5,537	8,013	51	65	75	3.8	2.3	1.2	0.5	(0.3)	(0.6)	57	66
El Salvador	1,890	2,947	4,914	42	47	57	1.1	2.8	2.2	0.2	1.2	(0.1)	21	25
Guatemala	2,587	4,932	10,140	37	40	51	3.0	3.7	3.0	2.7	2.0	0.6	21	25
Haiti	1,269	2,727	5,471	24	35	48	3.7	3.6	3.1	1.2	0.8	0.6	21	29
Honduras	1,244	3,042	5,809	35	47	59	4.8	3.8	2.4	2.3	1.3	0.2	18	22
Jamaica	998	1,451	2,116	47	56	66	2.6	1.8	1.7	0.7	(0.2)	(0.4)	0	0
Mexico	44,832	73,553	99,069	66	74	79	3.2	1.7	1.2	0.2	0.6	(0.5)	33	32
Nicaragua	1,490	3,038	5,182	53	65	73	3.9	3.1	2.0	1.4	1.0	0.1	27	29
Panama	984	1,649	2,435	50	58	67	2.8	2.2	1.5	1.4	0.3	(0.5)	37	41
Trinidad and Tobago	682	993	1,316	63	74	81	2.7	1.5	1.0	(0.0)	(0.6)	(0.6)	0	0
SOUTH AMERICA	**163,450**	**272,495**	**369,853**	**68**	**80**	**85**	**3.1**	**1.8**	**1.1**	**(0.2)**	**(0.7)**	**(0.4)**	**X**	**X**
Argentina	23,282	33,089	41,880	83	89	92	2.0	1.4	0.9	(0.9)	(0.9)	(0.5)	43	42
Bolivia	2,434	5,400	9,204	45	65	75	4.0	3.2	1.9	(0.0)	(0.0)	0.1	28	35
Brazil	80,589	137,527	182,139	66	81	87	3.4	1.7	0.9	(0.7)	(1.4)	(0.6)	34	35
Chile	9,056	12,868	16,478	81	85	88	1.9	1.4	1.0	0.0	0.2	(0.5)	34	34
Colombia	16,957	29,154	40,867	64	75	81	3.0	2.0	1.2	0.3	(0.2)	(0.4)	37	39
Ecuador	3,739	7,892	12,269	47	62	73	4.4	2.7	1.5	1.0	0.0	(0.4)	27	32
Guyana	232	334	547	31	38	51	1.6	2.7	2.0	0.6	(0.1)	(0.5)	0	0
Paraguay	1,298	3,077	5,766	42	56	67	4.5	3.6	2.4	1.8	0.9	0.4	22	25
Peru	11,187	18,674	26,778	65	73	79	3.1	2.1	1.4	1.0	0.2	(0.3)	28	29
Suriname	159	236	364	45	52	63	1.5	2.1	1.8	1.0	(0.3)	(0.3)	0	0
Uruguay	2,484	2,990	3,384	85	91	94	1.1	0.7	0.5	(2.2)	(1.4)	(0.8)	42	41
Venezuela	11,985	21,113	29,932	79	87	91	3.2	2.1	1.2	(0.1)	(0.2)	(0.2)	36	37
ASIA	**706,203**	**1,386,721**	**2,275,015**	**27**	**38**	**50**	**3.6**	**2.8**	**2.0**	**1.2**	**0.3**	**(0.3)**	**X**	**X**
Afghanistan, Islamic State	2,514	5,600	13,642	16	22	33	(0.5)	4.9	3.9	(2.3)	2.2	1.0	10	14
Armenia, Rep	2,033	2,562	3,150	66	70	77	1.8	1.0	0.8	1.0	(0.5)	(1.0)	35	37
Azerbaijan	3,255	4,483	6,200	53	57	66	1.9	1.4	1.5	1.3	(0.2)	(0.6)	25	26
Bangladesh	9,968	27,172	58,317	11	21	34	5.7	4.5	2.8	1.9	0.9	(0.1)	10	16
Bhutan	50	145	442	4	7	13	5.0	5.9	5.0	2.2	2.3	1.6	0	0
Cambodia	804	2,631	5,751	12	23	36	6.2	4.4	3.1	2.1	1.0	0.3	0	0
China	195,908	438,236	711,698	20	34	49	4.2	2.9	1.7	0.6	(0.6)	(0.8)	12	17
Georgia	2,620	3,289	3,966	52	61	70	1.7	0.8	0.9	(0.1)	(1.2)	(1.1)	25	27
India	158,851	286,323	498,777	23	28	39	3.2	2.9	2.5	1.8	0.9	(0.2)	11	14
Indonesia	33,514	85,458	146,176	22	40	55	5.3	3.4	1.9	1.0	(0.3)	(0.5)	9	12
Iran, Islamic Rep	19,482	47,085	84,924	50	62	71	5.9	3.4	1.9	2.9	1.2	(0.0)	22	24
Iraq	8,523	17,752	31,483	66	77	83	4.2	3.4	2.1	1.3	1.1	0.5	35	36
Israel	3,436	5,541	7,113	89	91	93	2.0	1.7	0.9	(0.5)	0.5	(0.4)	36	35
Japan	88,990	99,724	102,966	76	79	83	0.8	0.4	(0.1)	0.3	(0.8)	(1.7)	39	41
Jordan	1,752	4,697	8,707	60	74	81	6.8	3.7	2.4	3.3	1.2	0.7	22	24
Kazakstan, Rep	8,061	10,442	13,682	54	62	70	1.8	1.2	1.2	0.4	(0.7)	(0.7)	7	8
Korea, Dem People's Rep	10,052	15,021	20,465	57	63	71	2.1	1.8	1.4	0.4	0.2	(0.6)	11	12
Korea, Rep	21,678	40,395	48,105	57	86	93	4.0	1.4	0.3	(2.8)	(4.4)	(1.0)	58	63
Kuwait	1,240	1,919	2,704	90	98	98	5.3	2.2	1.1	(4.8)	(0.8)	(0.1)	64	58
Kyrgyz Rep	1,389	1,821	2,870	38	40	51	2.0	1.8	2.3	2.0	0.2	(0.2)	0	0
Lao People's Dem Rep	429	1,336	3,361	13	23	36	5.4	5.2	3.5	1.8	2.0	0.7	0	0
Lebanon	1,967	2,951	3,902	74	90	93	1.5	1.8	1.2	(4.9)	(1.7)	(0.2)	61	63
Malaysia	5,787	12,767	20,395	42	57	68	4.3	2.9	1.8	1.2	0.1	(0.2)	6	7
Mongolia	866	1,738	2,765	52	64	72	3.9	2.8	1.7	1.5	0.6	(0.2)	0	0
Myanmar	8,108	13,661	25,748	24	28	40	2.1	3.4	2.6	2.1	0.9	(0.1)	9	11
Nepal	949	2,893	7,740	7	12	21	6.0	5.2	4.1	2.3	2.0	0.9	0	0
Oman	356	2,282	5,228	32	84	93	12.4	5.0	3.2	(0.3)	(3.2)	1.8	0	0
Pakistan	23,946	57,792	123,489	28	37	50	4.6	4.2	2.8	2.9	1.6	0.4	18	22
Philippines	18,110	43,985	69,862	37	59	70	5.2	3.1	1.6	0.6	(0.1)	(0.4)	15	17
Saudi Arabia	6,325	18,572	34,252	66	86	90	7.5	3.5	2.4	1.1	0.1	0.9	27	28
Singapore	2,414	3,587	4,111	100	100	100	2.3	1.0	0.5	0.0	0.0	0.0	100	100
Sri Lanka	3,196	4,434	8,148	22	24	35	1.2	2.9	2.5	1.7	0.5	(0.3)	0	0
Syrian Arab Rep	4,066	8,784	15,865	47	54	65	4.3	3.3	2.1	2.9	1.4	0.0	27	30
Tajikistan, Rep	1,355	2,102	3,981	34	33	43	2.3	2.8	2.7	3.2	1.4	0.0	0	0
Thailand	7,961	13,057	22,049	17	22	33	2.8	2.5	2.3	1.6	0.2	(0.6)	11	15
Turkey	19,455	49,517	70,311	44	75	85	6.1	2.5	1.1	(0.9)	(2.5)	(0.5)	25	31
Turkmenistan, Rep	1,347	2,038	3,381	47	46	55	2.0	2.5	2.2	2.8	1.3	(0.2)	0	0
United Arab Emirates	726	2,099	2,851	71	86	90	9.9	2.0	0.8	4.3	(0.3)	(0.6)	36	38
Uzbekistan, Rep	6,504	10,606	18,261	41	42	53	2.6	2.7	2.3	2.6	1.1	(0.1)	10	11
Vietnam	10,338	15,891	28,439	19	20	27	2.5	2.4	3.3	2.1	1.3	0.2	6	7
Yemen	1,660	6,886	18,055	20	38	52	7.1	5.6	3.8	2.2	2.1	1.4	0	0
OCEANIA	**16,152**	**21,180**	**27,966**	**71**	**70**	**72**	**1.4**	**1.3**	**1.3**	**1.8**	**1.3**	**0.2**	**X**	**X**
Australia	12,495	15,954	19,920	86	85	87	1.4	1.1	1.0	1.8	0.8	(0.5)	58	55
Fiji	239	359	596	38	42	54	2.4	2.6	2.1	1.7	0.8	(0.3)	0	0
New Zealand	2,597	3,268	4,186	83	87	90	0.9	1.3	1.1	0.6	(0.4)	(0.3)	27	27
Papua New Guinea	403	838	1,880	13	17	27	3.6	4.0	3.6	2.0	1.7	0.5	0	0
Solomon Islands	24	87	242	11	20	32	6.8	5.8	4.0	3.1	2.3	1.1	0	0
DEVELOPING	**981,438**	**1,986,476**	**3,355,639**	**29**	**41**	**52**	**3.8**	**2.9**	**2.1**	**1.3**	**0.5**	**(0.1)**	**X**	**X**
DEVELOPED	**772,870**	**903,379**	**991,257**	**71**	**76**	**81**	**0.9**	**0.5**	**0.3**	**(0.3)**	**(0.9)**	**(1.3)**	**X**	**X**

Data Table 9.2
Urban Characteristics, City Level, 1993

Source: United Nations Centre for Human Settlements and United Nations Population Division

		Population (000)			Average Annual Growth Rate {a} (percent)		Urban Residential Density (persons/ha)	Gross City Product Per Capita	Socioeconomic Indicators, 1993			
	City Name	1950 {a}	1995 {a}	2015 {b}	1970-75	1990-95	1993	(1993 US$)	Informal Employment (percent)	Percent of Poor Households	Percent of Female-Headed Households	Percent of Female-Headed Households that Are Poor
WORLD												
AFRICA												
Angola	Luanda	138	2,081	4,969	7.5	5.2	X	X	36	36	17	41
Benin	Porto Novo	X	183 c	X	X	X	X	491	90	32	32	X
Botswana	Gaborone	X	473 c	X	X	X	X	594 d	45	55	9	40
Burkina Faso	Ouagadougou	30	824	2,546	6.9	6.5	71	323	60	11	12	X
Burundi	Bujumbura	X	278 c	X	X	X	91	216	31	42	19	X
Cameroon	Douala	101	1,320	2,894	5.3	5.5	128	1,694	66	31	19	49
	Yaounde	50	1,119	2,533	6.8	6.2	X	1,167	57	27	25	25
Central African Rep	Bangui	X	471 c	X	X	X	X	X	83	40	22	27
Congo, Dem Rep	Kinshasa	173	4,241	9,430	4.7	4.2	208	X	80	70	14	80
Congo, Rep	Brazzaville	216	1,004	2,064	2.8	4.8	X	328 d	50	48	34	X
Côte d'Ivoire	Abidjan	59	2,793	5,259	11.0	4.9	424	863	65	37	14	X
Egypt	Cairo	2,410	9,690	14,418	2.6	2.3	X	X	X	43	X	X
Ethiopia	Addis Ababa	392	2,431	6,578	4.8	4.8	314	X	61	X	X	X
Gabon	Libreville	X	362 c	X	X	X	X	X	58	X	23	X
Gambia, The	Banjul	X	479 c	X	X	X	129	389	67	17	19	X
Ghana	Accra	250	1,673	3,469	3.3	3.5	65	X	70	25	42	X
Guinea	Conakry	39	1,558	3,527	8.0	6.6	164	487	73	41	7	65
Kenya	Nairobi	87	1,810	4,228	4.9	5.1	93	744 d	52	27	16	25
Lesotho	Maseru	X	112 e	X	X	X	X	X	31	49	23	59
Liberia	Monrovia	49	962	2,609	6.4	7.2	X	277	35	X	6	X
Madagascar	Antananarivo	180	876	2,218	2.6	4.9	X	229	57	32	21	47
Malawi	Lilongwe	X	220 c	X	X	X	X	X	51	66	X	X
Mali	Bamako	62	919	2,249	7.2	4.4	X	357	36	36	16	X
Mauritania	Nouakchott	X	576 c	X	X	X	132	451	41	25	55	X
Morocco	Rabat	145	1,293	2,093	5.2	2.9	X	1,550	X	7	21	X
Mozambique	Maputo	91	2,212	5,306	7.1	7.6	191	X	X	X	19	95
Namibia	Windhoek	X	142 c	X	X	X	37	5,705 d	X	30	29	X
Niger	Niamey	X	506 c	X	X	X	45	525	51	42	11	60
Nigeria	Ibadan	427	1,484	2,968	2.6	2.8	31	X	77	62	19	X
	Lagos	288	10,287	24,640	9.8	5.7	194	X	69	66	17	67
Rwanda	Kigali	X	275 c	X	X	X	79	586	75	50	X	X
Senegal	Dakar	223	1,708	3,489	5.0	4.0	X	1,002	47	13	23	X
Sudan	Khartoum	182	2,249	4,667	6.0	4.2	67	56	15	70	17	24
Tanzania	Dar es Salaam	X	2,323 e	X	X	X	191	X	X	23	17	X
Togo	Lome	X	802 c	X	X	X	X	X	27	12	X	X
Tunisia	Tunis	472	1,722	2,500	3.2	1.9	90	1,750	28	6	X	12
Uganda	Kampala	53	954	2,548	3.2	4.7	X	430	46	77	27	36
Zambia	Lusaka	26	1,317	2,923	6.5	6.0	X	X	X	17	2	69
Zimbabwe	Harare	84	1,410	3,164	5.5	6.0	X	2,370 d	17	X	X	X
EUROPE												
Albania	Tirana	X	310 c	X	X	X	198	X	X	X	X	X
Belarus, Rep	Minsk	323	1,784	1,903	3.7	1.6	X	X	X	X	X	X
Bulgaria	Sofia	547	1,188	1,188	1.7	(0.0)	163	1,064	12	X	27	X
Croatia, Rep	Zagreb	334	981	1,148	1.5	2.9	X	4,195	20	6	9	2
Czech Rep	Prague	1,002	1,225	1,240	0.9	0.2	111	4,155	X	3	24	X
Denmark	Copenhagen	1,212	1,326	1,326	0.0	(0.3)	X	34,303	X	X	35	X
Estonia, Rep	Tallinn	X	468 c	X	X	X	73	2,429	X	7	31	X
France	Lyon	572	1,319	1,400	1.3	0.8	X	X	X	X	29	X
	Marseille	X	800 c	X	X	X	98	21,176	10	15	26	24
	Paris	5,441	9,523	9,694	0.9	0.4	109	35,060	X	X	29	X
Germany	Essen	5,296	6,482	6,596	(0.4)	0.4	X	X	X	X	X	X
	Leipzig	X	481 c	X	X	X	X	X	X	X	36	X
Greece	Athens	1,783	3,093	3,118	1.7	0.2	95	6,027	X	X	23	X
Hungary	Budapest	1,618	2,017	2,017	0.6	0.0	123	4,750	X	37	X	51
Italy	Milan	3,633	4,251	4,251	0.0	(1.6)	X	X	X	X	X	X
Latvia, Rep	Riga	490	921	921	1.6	0.0	X	X	X	20	25	X
Lithuania, Rep	Vilnius	X	670 c	X	X	X	X	770 d	X	15	X	X
Moldova, Rep	Chisinau	X	662 c	X	X	X	105	233 d	X	92	X	X
Netherlands	Amsterdam	855	1,108	1,171	(1.0)	1.0	152	28,251	2	X	39	29
Poland, Rep	Warsaw	1,014	2,219	2,400	2.0	0.5	111	3,282	X	5	17	10
Romania	Bucharest	1,111	2,100	2,192	2.3	0.4	271	3,850	6	6	X	X
Russian Federation	Moscow	5,356	9,269	9,299	1.4	0.5	X	5,100	16	15	29	63
	Nizhny Novgorod	796	1,461	1,461	1.5	0.2	X	2,164	17	24	26	64
Slovak Rep	Bratislava	X	651 c	X	X	X	71	4,350	X	X	X	X
Slovenia, Rep	Ljubljana	X	316 c	X	X	X	102	12,102 d	3	4	X	X
Sweden	Stockholm	741	1,545	1,626	2.2	0.7	24	25,030	X	X	X	X
Ukraine	Donetsk	585	1,150	1,162	1.7	0.5	X	X	X	X	X	X
United Kingdom	Cardiff	X	306 c	X	X	X	54	20,280	X	X	31	X
	London	8,733	7,640	7,640	(1.0)	(0.0)	X	X	X	X	X	X
Yugoslavia, Fed Rep	Belgrade	432	1,204	1,300	2.1	0.7	96	6,791	X	2	X	X
NORTH AMERICA												
Canada	Toronto	1,068	4,319	5,220	1.8	2.6	92	19,415	X	23	26	18
United States	Atlanta	513	2,462	3,041	3.2	2.5	9	26,444	X	25	3	45
	Los Angeles	4,046	12,410	14,217	1.3	1.6	X	X	X	X	X	X
	Seattle	627	1,937	2,351	1.2	2.0	19	29,633	X	7	2	24
	New York	12,339	16,332	17,602	(0.4)	0.3	72	30,952	X	16	16	35
CENTRAL AMERICA												
Belize	Belize City	X	49 e	X	X	X	X	X	X	21	36	58
Cuba	Havana	1,147	2,221	2,422	0.9	1.0	X	X	X	X	X	X
El Salvador	San Salvador	162	1,214	2,056	4.1	3.2	24	2,249	38	40	7	14
Guatemala	Guatemala City	428	2,205	4,467	1.6	5.5	147	4,830	X	80	24	73
Jamaica	Kingston	X	538 c	X	X	X	X	X	X	X	X	X
Mexico	Mexico City	2,885	16,562	19,180	4.3	1.8	X	X	X	X	X	X

Country	City Name	Population (000) 1950 {a}	1995 {a}	2015 {b}	Average Annual Growth Rate {a} (percent) 1970-75	1990-95	Urban Residential Density (persons/ha) 1993	Gross City Product Per Capita (1993 US$)	Informal Employment (percent)	Percent of Poor Households	Percent of Female-Headed Households	Percent of Female-Headed Households that Are Poor
SOUTH AMERICA												
Argentina	Buenos Aires	5,042	11,802	13,856	1.7	1.2	X	X	X	X	X	X
Bolivia	El Alto	X	726 c	X	X	X	173	896	17	87	26	86
	La Paz	265	1,250	2,125	3.3	3.6	X	1,384	17	62	26	61
Brazil	Brasilia	36	1,778	2,440	8.0	2.8	29	3,366	36	19	X	21
	Curitiba	137	2,240	3,106	5.6	3.0	217	5,149	33	6	21	6
	Recife	643	3,080	3,899	2.7	1.8	210	2,710	41	35	X	43
	Rio de Janeiro	2,864	10,181	11,860	2.2	1.0	136	5,850	34	19	26	22
	Sao Paulo	2,423	16,533	20,320	4.4	1.8	X	X	X	X	X	X
Chile	Santiago	1,332	4,891	6,066	2.7	1.7	X	4,150	23	22	28	20
Colombia	Bogota	676	6,079	8,394	4.9	3.0	194	1,790	54	23	25	23
Ecuador	Guayaquil	254	1,831	2,959	4.4	3.1	177	1,425	44	31	19	46
	Quito	206	1,298	2,101	4.6	3.0	282	X	34	25	X	X
Guyana	Georgetown	X	150 c	X	X	X	214	X	14	41	46	44
Paraguay	Asuncion	223	1,081	1,959	4.0	3.1	158	2,545	41	34	28	24
Peru	Lima	973	6,667	9,388	4.4	2.7	264	673 d	49	29	24	7
Venezuela	Caracas	676	3,007	3,777	2.6	1.0	X	X	X	X	X	X
	Valencia	108	1,462	2,548	5.7	5.2	X	X	X	33	X	X
ASIA												
Armenia, Rep	Yerevan	371	1,278	1,478	3.2	1.1	X	217	27	X	X	X
Azerbaijan	Baku	793	1,848	2,335	2.3	1.1	68	293 d	X	X	29	58
Bangladesh	Chittagong	629	2,477	4,857	2.5	4.0	61	218	X	51	7	X
	Dhaka	420	8,545	19,486	7.9	6.4	X	219	X	54	7	X
	Tangail	X	155 e	X	X	X	237	172	X	51	6	X
China	Beijing	3,913	11,299	15,572	1.1	0.9	X	X	X	X	X	X
	Chengdu	725	4,323	7,840	2.5	4.3	X	465	X	X	X	X
	Foshan	X	385 c	X	X	X	X	1,717 d	3	1	15	X
	Heifei	256	1,319	2,323	3.6	3.6	X	2,564 d	2	X	X	X
	Qingdao	894	3,138	7,292	0.9	7.6	102	X	21	1	X	X
	Shanghai	5,333	13,584	17,969	0.5	0.4	X	1,832	X	X	X	X
	Shenyang	2,091	5,116	7,715	1.1	1.9	X	X	X	X	X	X
	Tianjin	2,374	9,415	13,530	3.3	1.4	X	X	X	X	X	X
	Wuhan	1,228	4,247	6,509	1.5	2.1	X	X	X	X	X	X
	Zhangjiagang	X	178 c	X	X	X	X	2,111	X	X	X	X
Georgia	Tbilisi	X	5,429 c	X	X	X	X	84	5	80	11	X
India	Bangalore	764	4,799	8,005	5.4	3.5	246	264	32	12	17	X
	Bombay	2,901	15,138	26,218	3.3	4.2	603	275	68	17	11	7
	Calcutta	4,446	11,923	17,305	2.6	1.8	X	X	X	X	X	X
	Delhi	1,391	9,948	16,860	4.5	3.9	X	209	67	17	16	14
	Gulbarga	X	330 c	X	X	X	X	184	27	17	8	X
	Lucknow	488	2,078	3,959	2.2	5.1	375	165	48	22	6	X
	Madras	1,397	6,002	9,173	3.5	2.3	296	204	61	19	13	X
	Tumkur	X	194 c	X	X	X	199	97	63	25	15	X
	Varanasi	348	1,152	1,845	2.7	2.6	242	167	49	28	6	23
Indonesia	Bandung	511	2,896	5,089	3.3	3.3	X	739	32	11	18	6
	Jakarta	1,452	8,621	13,923	4.1	2.4	X	2,843 d	33	9	7	8
	Medan	284	1,699	2,746	4.4	2.0	189	925	41	9	X	4
	Semarang	371	795	1,121	3.4	(0.2)	165	576	35	7	17	5
	Surabaja	679	2,253	3,558	3.0	1.8	206	1,085	35	5	19	3
Iran, Islamic Rep	Mashhad	173	2,016	3,656	6.0	3.6	X	X	X	X	7	X
	Tehran	3,290	6,830	10,211	5.2	1.5	X	X	X	X	7	X
Israel	Tel Aviv	418	1,976	2,580	3.2	2.0	X	X	X	X	X	X
Japan	Osaka	4,147	10,609	10,609	1.0	0.2	X	X	X	X	X	X
	Tokyo	6,920	26,959	28,887	3.7	1.5	X	X	X	X	X	X
Jordan	Amman	90	1,183	2,284	5.1	4.3	76	1,494	X	16	8	7
Kazakstan, Rep	Almaty	X	1,173 c	X	X	X	120	665 d	12	37	9	74
Korea, Rep	Seoul	1,021	11,609	12,980	5.0	1.9	X	X	X	X	X	X
Kyrgyz Rep	Bishkek	X	703 c	X	X	X	85	810	32	X	X	X
Lao People's Dem Rep	Vientiane	X	156 e	X	X	X	139	X	X	24	9	X
Mongolia	Ulan Bator	X	588 e	X	X	X	127	154	12	12	9	48
Nepal	Bharatpur	X	63 e	X	X	X	161	X	90	X	X	X
	Kathmandu	X	472 e	X	X	X	213	X	X	X	10	X
Pakistan	Karachi	1,028	9,733	19,377	4.9	4.1	X	X	X	X	X	X
	Lahore	826	5,012	10,047	4.0	3.6	37	428	60	30	5	2
Philippines	Davao	124	1,010	1,700	4.2	3.4	276	X	X	77	7	X
	Metro Manila	1,544	9,286	14,657	6.9	3.1	148	2,134	20	13	1	9
Sri Lanka	Colombo	X	2,190 c	X	X	X	86	1,036	19	14	X	40
Thailand	Bangkok	1,360	6,547	9,844	4.2	2.1	X	X	X	X	X	X
Turkey	Istanbul	1,077	7,911	12,328	5.1	3.8	X	X	X	X	X	X
United Arab Emirates	Dubai	X	594 c	X	X	X	161	14,957	X	X	1	X
Vietnam	Hanoi	280	1,236	1,762	2.2	2.0	X	695 d	X	51	39	X
Yemen	Sana	X	886 e	X	X	X	99	247 d	65	X	X	X
OCEANIA												
Australia	Melbourne	1,331	3,094	3,506	1.9	0.6	67	X	X	X	8	X
Fiji	Suva	X	141 e	X	X	X	X	2,960	51	25	X	X
New Zealand	Auckland	319	945	1,194	2.8	1.5	X	15,684	X	X	40	X

Notes: a. United Nations estimates of population of urban agglomeration. b. United Nations projections. c. 1993 data from United Nations Centre for Human Settlements (Habitat). d. According to Habitat, reported gross city product seems either too high or too low to be accurate (differs from country GNP by 60 percent or more). e. 1993 data from Habitat; also refers to population of metropolitan area.

Data Table 9.3
The Urban Environment, City Level, 1993

Source: United Nations Centre for Human Settlements

City Name	Crowding (floor area/ person) (m²)	Percentage of Urban Households Connected to — Water	Sewerage	Electricity	Per Capita Water Use (l/day)	Waste- water Treated (percent)	Per capita Solid Waste Generation (kg/day)	Households with Garbage Collection (percent)	Cars per 1,000 Population	Percentage of Work Trips by Public Transport	Murders per 100,000 Population
WORLD											
AFRICA											
Angola — Luanda	X	41	13	10	50	0	X	50	16	3	X
Benin — Porto Novo	5	16	1	43	22	X	0.5	25	60	0	X
Botswana — Gaborone	13	40	33	24	125	95	X	98	33	42	1
Burkina Faso — Ouagadougou	12	32	0	35	26	0	0.7	40	37	X	X
Burundi — Bujumbura	6	35	29	30	75	4	1.4	41	11	X	5
Cameroon — Douala	10	19	3	42	33	5	0.7	60	29	11	2
Yaounde	13	22	3	47	61	20	0.8	44	17	6	8
Central African Rep — Bangui	11	13	1	12	30	0	X	25	X	7	7
Congo, Dem Rep — Kinshasa	X	50	3	40	45	3	1.2	0	25	61	X
Congo, Rep — Brazzaville	14	63	0	45	50	0	0.6	72	16	22	1
Côte d'Ivoire — Abidjan	7	62	45	64	111	58	1.0	70	38	49	10
Egypt — Cairo	12	89	91	99	X	98	0.5	65	59	58	1
Ethiopia — Addis Ababa	X	58	0	96	27	X	X	2	21	X	250
Gabon — Libreville	12	40	0	66	100	0	X	40	34	38	5
Gambia, The — Banjul	12	36	13	56	106	0	0.3	35	10	60	X
Ghana — Accra	6	46	12	17	4	0	0.4	60	X	47	X
Guinea — Conakry	7	48	17	51	50	0	0.7	50	24	26	X
Kenya — Nairobi	11	78	35	40	116	90	X	47	134	68	6
Lesotho — Maseru	X	30	5	3	X	0	X	7	18	X	X
Liberia — Monrovia	14	1	1	22	23	0	X	X	8	75	X
Madagascar — Antananarivo	6	31	17	60	40	0	0.3	X	127	30	16
Malawi — Lilongwe	7	17	12	10	105	30	X	X	11	5	X
Mali — Bamako	3	26	2	30	50	0	X	95	70	12	X
Mauritania — Nouakchott	10	18	4	22	35	10	0.9	15	81	45	7
Morocco — Rabat	10	87	95	93	48	0	0.6	90	78	X	X
Mozambique — Maputo	12	28	23	46	80	X	X	37	X	13	X
Namibia — Windhoek	X	90	75	84	150	99	0.7	93	X	9	25
Niger — Niamey	8	30	0	42	75	0	1.0	25	40	17	7
Nigeria — Ibadan	9	68	0	73	80	X	1.1	40	4	40	1
Lagos	6	65	2	100	70	2	0.3	8	4	54	2
Rwanda — Kigali	X	36	X	57	130	20	0.6	X	27	32	X
Senegal — Dakar	8	41	25	64	69	4	0.7	75	36	53	X
Sudan — Khartoum	22	52	3	45	50	45	X	12	40	63	6
Tanzania — Dar es Salaam	5	22	6	37	50	2	1.0	25	20	48	10
Togo — Lome	12	43	0	28	35	X	1.9	37	X	30	13
Tunisia — Tunis	12	92	73	94	70	82	0.5	61	38	X	X
Uganda — Kampala	4	30	9	42	25	27	6.0	20	53	45	28
Zambia — Lusaka	7	36	36	27	175	36	X	X	X	65	X
Zimbabwe — Harare	8	89	93	64	80	93	0.7	100	X	48	1
EUROPE											
Albania — Tirana	8	95	91	100	150	0	0.7	90	37	X	X
Belarus, Rep — Minsk	17	X	X	X	471	87	3.0	100	98	X	5
Bulgaria — Sofia	17	99	98	100	309	71	X	95	310	75	3
Croatia, Rep — Zagreb	22	86	80	100	116	4	2.2	100	215	52	3
Czech Rep — Prague	26	100	94	100	168	89	0.5	100	500	67	4
Denmark — Copenhagen	44	100	100	100	220	100	1.4	100	223	27	10
Estonia, Rep — Tallinn	21	99	95	100	403	95	1.1	99	233	X	23
France — Lyon	X	100	90	100	275	100	1.1	100	542	X	X
Marseille	X	99	99	100	315	100	1.3	99	X	X	X
Paris	30	100	98	100	212	45	1.3	100	426	40	6
Germany — Essen	X	X	X	X	X	X	X	X	X	X	X
Leipzig	33	100	95	100	86	80	1.2	100	396	33	2
Greece — Athens	26	100	95	100	130	90	1.1	90	354	34	3
Hungary — Budapest	29	98	90	100	222	92	0.5	100	288	66	5
Italy — Milan	X	X	X	X	X	X	X	X	X	X	X
Latvia, Rep — Riga	19	99	97	100	270	96	X	85	104	57	33
Lithuania, Rep — Vilnius	16	95	94	100	220	80	0.5	95	215	49	14
Moldova, Rep — Chisinau	15	93	86	100	527	100	X	83	60	48	15
Netherlands — Amsterdam	38	100	100	100	159	90	1.1	100	351	X	7
Poland, Rep — Warsaw	18	95	91	99	240	36	0.5	97	359	X	4
Romania — Bucharest	13	96	90	99	430	0	1.1	86	X	65	4
Russian Federation — Moscow	20	100	100	100	555	100	0.8	100	138	85	30
Nizhny Novgorod	17	96	95	100	325	85	2.7	100	69	78	30
Slovak Rep — Bratislava	22	99	96	100	265	98	0.8	100	282	72	3
Slovenia, Rep — Ljubljana	X	100	99	99	160	98	1.6	99	416	X	5
Sweden — Stockholm	40	100	100	100	228	99	1.2	100	390	37	2
Ukraine — Donetsk	X	100	75	100	196	76	X	X	76	X	14
United Kingdom — Cardiff	18	100	100	100	420	X	0.8	100	350	13	1
London	X	X	X	X	X	X	X	X	X	X	X
Yugoslavia, Fed Rep — Belgrade	19	99	71	97	X	12	X	86	30	64	X
NORTH AMERICA											
Canada — Toronto	X	100	100	100	517	100	1.4	100	430	30	3
United States — Atlanta	X	100	98	X	358	100	X	X	473	20	12
Los Angeles	X	X	X	X	X	X	X	X	X	X	X
Seattle	X	100	100	X	297	100	X	X	654	16	5
New York	X	100	99	X	466	100	1.7	X	232	51	23
CENTRAL AMERICA											
Belize — Belize City	10	X	X	X	X	X	X	100	83	X	X
Cuba — Havana	16	85	85	85	100	100	1.6	100	32	58	X
El Salvador — San Salvador	7	86	80	98	186	2	0.9	46	113	X	12
Guatemala — Guatemala city	8	52	X	X	240	3	X	53	109	53	33
Jamaica — Kingston	15	X	X	X	X	X	X	X	X	X	100
Mexico — Mexico City	X	X	X	X	X	X	X	X	X	X	X

Country	City Name	Crowding (floor area/person) (m²)	Percentage of Urban Households Connected to — Water	Sewerage	Electricity	Per Capita Water Use (l/day)	Waste-water Treated (percent)	Per capita Solid Waste Generation (kg/day)	Households with Garbage Collection (percent)	Cars per 1,000 Population	Percentage of Work Trips by Public Transport	Murders per 100,000 Population
SOUTH AMERICA												
Argentina	Buenos Aires	X	X	X	X	X	X	X	X	X	X	X
Bolivia	El Alto	X	33	20	83	43	0	0.4	95	X	X	X
	La Paz	X	55	58	94	73	0	0.5	92	71	51	6
Brazil	Brasilia	17	90	74	98	213	54	0.5	95	301	X	20
	Curitiba	21	96	75	99	150	56	0.8	95	286	72	12
	Recife	16	79	38	99	100	52	1.3	95	185	70	34
	Rio de Janeiro	19	95	87	100	299	23	1.1	88	177	67	75
	Sao Paulo	X	X	X	X	X	X	X	X	X	X	X
Chile	Santiago	14	98	92	94	286	2	X	95	90	54	3
Colombia	Bogota	9	99	99	99	176	X	0.6	94	52	75	82
Ecuador	Guayaquil	16	80	55	95	261	10	0.6	70	27	50	40
	Quito	9	94	93	100	X	X	0.8	89	82	X	4
Guyana	Georgetown	11	64	77	85	427	23	X	26	24	X	X
Paraguay	Asuncion	5	58	10	59	236	4	0.8	79	87	31	15
Peru	Lima	26	70	69	76	211	5	0.5	57	49	65	X
Venezuela	Caracas	X	X	X	X	X	X	X	X	X	X	X
	Valencia	X	90	86	90	X	X	X	X	X	X	X
ASIA												
Armenia, Rep	Yerevan	13	96	93	100	280	71	0.8	81	86	98	X
Azerbaijan	Baku	13	95	79	100	246	61	1.5	X	46	80	10
Bangladesh	Chittagong	5	86	53	75	115	82	X	50	X	X	X
	Dhaka	3	80	44	74	119	55	0.1	50	7	X	3
	Tangail	X	24	0	67	233	64	X	50	3	X	X
China	Beijing	X	X	X	X	X	X	X	X	X	X	X
	Chengdu	13	99	37	100	273	37	0.9	X	39	X	X
	Foshan	16	100	100	100	X	X	1.5	X	X	X	X
	Hefei	11	100	57	100	221	57	0.5	X	69	X	X
	Qingdao	11	100	11	100	118	11	0.7	X	47	X	X
	Shanghai	10	100	58	100	271	58	0.8	X	32	X	X
	Shenyang	X	X	X	X	X	X	X	X	X	X	X
	Tianjin	X	X	X	X	X	X	X	X	X	X	X
	Wuhan	X	X	X	X	X	X	X	X	X	X	X
	Zhangjiagang	14	100	91	100	226	X	0.9	X	11	X	X
Georgia	Tbilisi	16	100	100	100	X	60	0.7	52	71	98	7
India	Bangalore	9	47	35	82	93	68	0.4	96	130	46	4
	Bombay	3	55	51	90	127	10	0.5	90	51	79	14
	Calcutta	X	X	X	X	X	X	X	X	X	X	X
	Delhi	7	57	40	70	133	69	1.2	77	205	53	4
	Gulbarga	6	27	14	78	69	0	0.4	74	60	8	10
	Lucknow	6	33	30	76	155	0	0.8	74	130	1	4
	Madras	6	34	37	82	70	0	0.8	90	102	42	2
	Tumkur	7	31	0	87	75	0	0.4	50	85	21	2
	Varanasi	5	40	41	86	220	71	0.4	88	85	21	4
Indonesia	Bandung	13	28	27	98	136	6	2.5	97	42	X	X
	Jakarta	15	15	0	99	188	16	2.6	84	68	38	1
	Medan	14	51	19	93	166	16	0.3	19	39	44	2
	Semarang	12	43	0	95	162	15	2.0	69	37	14	1
	Surabaja	11	29	0	97	151	9	0.5	87	47	23	2
Iran, Islamic Rep	Mashhad	X	99	X	100	X	X	X	X	28	X	35
	Tehran	23	99	X	100	X	X	X	100	66	36	22
Israel	Tel Aviv	28	X	75	X	X	X	X	X	280	40	2
Japan	Osaka	X	X	X	X	X	X	X	X	X	X	X
	Tokyo	X	X	X	X	X	X	X	X	X	X	X
Jordan	Amman	15	X	79	98	110	51	0.6	100	112	14	6
Kazakstan, Rep	Almaty	15	93	88	100	372	79	X	83	106	43	20
Korea, Rep	Seoul	X	X	X	X	X	X	X	X	X	X	X
Kyrgyz Rep	Bishkek	X	92	65	100	161	100	1.4	89	35	X	17
Lao People's Dem Rep	Vientiane	X	95	0	99	150	0	0.9	5	47	3	2
Mongolia	Ulan Bator	9	51	51	100	X	60	X	X	22	85	32
Nepal	Bharatpur	X	10	X	45	120	0	0.1	70	X	10	5
	Kathmandu	X	71	25	83	80	0	0.5	50	3	26	7
Pakistan	Karachi	X	X	X	X	X	X	X	X	X	X	X
	Lahore	X	84	74	97	194	0	1.2	50	45	16	6
Philippines	Davao	6	X	X	X	X	X	X	X	11	X	11
	Metro Manila	34	95	80	86	X	X	0.7	85	94	40	9
Sri Lanka	Colombo	19	64	60	61	X	0	0.5	94	47	74	8
Thailand	Bangkok	X	X	X	X	X	X	X	X	X	X	X
Turkey	Istanbul	X	X	X	X	X	X	X	X	X	X	X
United Arab Emirates	Dubai	X	100	60	100	X	100	2.3	100	162	X	1
Vietnam	Hanoi	6	80	40	100	110	X	1.2	45	X	X	2
Yemen	Sana	4	27	12	95	70	10	0.8	51	104	X	4
OCEANIA												
Australia	Melbourne	55	99	99	99	380	100	X	100	500	16	4
Fiji	Suva	X	99	87	88	203	87	1.1	X	668	X	2
New Zealand	Auckland	40	98	98	98	800	X	X	X	500	6	2

Sources and Technical Notes

Data Table 9.1

Urban Indicators, 1980–2025

Sources: Urban population, percentage urban, urban growth rates, and rural growth rates: United Nations (U.N.) Population Division, *Urban and Rural Areas, 1950–2030 (The 1996 Revision)*, on diskette (U.N., New York, 1997). Population in urban agglomerations greater than 750,000: U.N. Population Division, *Urban Agglomerations, 1950–2015 (The 1996 Revision)* on diskette (U.N., New York, 1997).

Urban population and *percentage urban* refer to the census population of areas defined as urban in each of the countries of the world. Because each country sets its own definition of "urban," there is a wide range of definitions around the world. Governments of small or relatively rural countries may declare one or more settlements urban, regardless of size or function. In many countries, the definition is based on a threshold number of inhabitants; when the population of a region exceeds a certain threshold, that region is considered urban. This threshold ranges from a few hundred, as in Peru and Uganda, to more than 10,000, as in Italy and Senegal. These definitional differences can skew international comparisons. For more information on country definitions of urban, see the text version of United Nations (U.N.) Population Division, *World Urbanization Prospects: The 1996 Revision* (U.N., New York, forthcoming).

Rural is defined as not urban. *Urban* and *rural population growth rates* include the effects of urban–rural migration. *Population in urban agglomerations greater than 750,000* is the percent of the population in each country in cities of population of 750,000 or more.

Data Table 9.2

Urban Characteristics, City Level, 1993

Sources: Urban population and urban agglomeration growth rates: United Nations (U.N.) Population Division, *Urban Agglomerations 1950–2015 (The 1996 Revision)*, on diskette (U.N., New York, 1997); urban residential density, gross city product per capita, informal employment, percent of poor households, percent of households headed by females, and percent of female-headed households that are poor: United Nations Centre for Human Settlements (Habitat), The Global Urban Observatory, *Global Urban Indicators Database,* Urban Indicators Programme (Habitat, Nairobi, 1997).

The U.N. provides estimated and projected populations for major urban agglomerations of the world. Estimates and projections are based, to the extent possible, on actual recorded data. For a complete description of the sources of data for urban populations and definitions of "urban," see U.N. Population Division, *World Urbanization Prospects: The 1996 Revision* (U.N., New York, 1997).

For a complete description of the Habitat Urban Indicators Programme, see United Nations Centre for Human Settlements (Habitat), The Global Urban Observatory, *Programme Activities: Analysis of Data and Global Urban Indicators Database (Urban Indicators Programme: Phase One: 1994–96)* [Habitat, Nairobi, 1997]). The data in this table were selected from the Habitat programme database for 237 cities covering 43 indicators. These data were originally collected from questionnaires filled out by city officials. Assembling these indicators and adjusting them to 1993 was a substantial accomplishment. The resulting indicator set provides information for a broad range of social, economic, and environmental variables and reflects the diversity of the world's cities in terms of size and regional representation. For more information and data, please see the above publication or access it online at: http://www.unon.org/unon/unchs/indicat/indihome.htm.

However, these data should be used with care. Because different data collection methods and definitions may have been used in each city, comparisons can be misleading. There is evidence of consistent misreporting of certain indicators in some cities, possibly because informal settlements have been left out of calculations. Furthermore, because data are only provided for 1993, it is impossible to determine whether an indicator is improving or declining.

Population refers to the population of the urban agglomeration (i.e., the population contained within the contours of a contiguous territory inhabited at urban levels without regard to administrative boundaries). It incorporates population in a city or town plus the suburban fringe lying outside of, but adjacent to, city boundaries. It should be noted that these population numbers are estimates and projections and not actual census data. Therefore, they incorporate assumptions (which may be false) and are sometimes based on old data. Because the U.N. does not report data for cities with populations less than 750,000 in 1990, WRI used 1993 data from Habitat for smaller cities.

Average annual growth rate is defined as the average annual growth rate of the urban agglomeration during a five-year period. These rates include estimates of the effects of urban–rural migration, changes in administrative boundaries, and natural increase.

Urban residential density is defined as the number of persons per hectare in residential areas. City densities should be regarded as rough estimates because the reported area of residential land may not refer to the same jurisdiction as population figures. In addition, densities vary greatly within a city depending on the neighborhood and do not include "commuter" populations.

Gross city product per capita is an indicator constructed to reflect urban productivity—the value of the goods and services produced within the urban area—consisting of essentially the gross domestic product of the city. It is seldom available from direct data sources. Habitat requested that cities attempt to calculate their productivity using various formulas that include national accounts figures, household income, and employment data. The gross city product was divided by the population to get a per capita figure and was then adjusted to 1993 U.S. dollars.

Informal employment is defined as the percentage of the employed population whose activity is part of the "informal sector." The informal sector can encompass many different types of revenue-generating activities, but generally consists of labor-intensive, small-scale, or family-based enterprises. The informal sector includes all unregistered commercial enterprises and all noncommercial enterprises that have no formal structure in terms of organization and operation. In developing countries, the informal sector often comprises a major part of labor market activities and has played an increasing role in the expansion of production. However, workers in the informal economy often have no legally defined rights, no access to government welfare in the event of illness or old age, and may work under unsafe conditions.

Female-headed households are defined as the percentage of households headed by women. This indicator may vary due to a range of definitions of "head of household." In some cities, data include only single parents, whereas in others, they do not.

Poor households and *female-headed households that are poor* are defined as the percentage of households situated below a locally defined poverty line. Countries were asked to submit an absolute poverty line at the city level, taken as the income necessary to afford a minimum nutritionally adequate diet plus essential nonfood requirements for a household of a given size. If the poverty line was not defined at the city level, a national poverty line was used. Poverty lines differ among countries and cities, so comparisons should be made with caution.

Data Table 9.3

The Urban Environment, City Level, 1993

Source: United Nations Centre for Human Settlements (Habitat), The Global Urban Observatory, *Global Urban Indicators Database*, Urban Indicators Programme (Habitat, Nairobi, 1997).

For a complete description of the Habitat Urban Indicators Programme, see United Nations Centre for Human Settlements (Habitat), The Global Urban Observatory, *Programme Activities: Analysis of*

Data and Global Urban Indicators Database (Urban Indicators Programme: Phase One: 1994–96) [Habitat, Nairobi, 1997]). The data in this table were selected from the Habitat programme database of 237 cities covering 43 indicators. These data were originally collected by questionnaires filled out by city officials. Assembling these indicators and adjusting them to 1993 was a substantial accomplishment. The resulting indicator set provides information for a broad range of social, economic, and environmental variables and reflects the diversity of the world's cities in terms of size and regional representation. For more information and data, please see the above publication or access it online at: http://www.unon.org/unon/unchs/indicat/indi-home.htm.

However, these data should be used with care. Because different data collection methods and definitions may have been used in each city, comparisons can be misleading. There is evidence of consistent misreporting of certain indicators in some cities, possibly because informal settlements have been left out of calculations. Some indicators such as the murder rate have been significantly underreported in cities that are known to have a high crime rate. Furthermore, because data are only provided for 1993, it is impossible to determine whether an indicator is improving or declining.

Crowding is defined as the floor area per person, the median usable living space per person in meters squared. *Percentage of urban households connected to* services is defined as the percentage of households with connections to water, sewerage, and electricity networks.

Per capita water use is defined as average consumption of water in liters per person per day, for all uses. Consumption of water per person depends on the availability and price of water, the climate, and the uses to which water is customarily put by individuals (e.g., drinking, bathing, washing, and gardening).

Wastewater treated is defined as the percentage of all wastewater undergoing any form of treatment, including primary (physical and mechanical processes that remove 20 to 30 percent of the biological oxygen demand [BOD]), secondary (additional use of biological treatments that remove 80 to 90 percent of BOD), and tertiary (advanced added chemical treatments that remove 95 percent or more of BOD). The form of treatment varies dramatically among cities and countries.

Per capita solid waste generation is defined as solid waste generated per person, in kilograms per day. This indicator should be regarded as a rough estimate because it is difficult to account for waste that is informally disposed of, incinerated, or composted.

Households with garbage collection are defined as the percentage of households enjoying regular waste collection. Regular waste collection can include household collection, regular "dumpmaster" group collection, but not local dumps to which the household must carry garbage.

Cars are measured as a ratio of the number of automobiles per 1,000 population. Automobiles in this case are taken to include all vehicles used for personal transport. *Percentage of work trips by public transport* is defined as the percentage of trips to work made by bus, tram, or train. Bus or minibus includes road vehicles other than cars taking passengers on a fare-paying basis. It does not include other means of transport commonly used in developing countries such as ferry, taxi, animal, or rickshaw.

Murders are defined as the number of murders reported annually per 100,000 population. Reported figures on crime may be misleading or underreported.

Chapter 10

Food and Agriculture

Food and Agricultural Production, 1984–96

Source: Food and Agriculture Organization of the United Nations

	Index of Agricultural Production (1989-91 = 100)				Index of Food Production (1989-91 = 100)				Average Production of Cereals (000 metric tons)	% Change Since 1984-86	Average Production of Roots and Tubers (000 metric tons)	% Change Since 1984-86	Average Production of Pulses (000 metric tons)	% Change Since 1984-86
	Total		Per Capita		Total		Per Capita		1994-96	1984-86	1994-96	1984-86	1994-96	1984-86
	1984-86	1994-96	1984-86	1994-96	1984-86	1994-96	1984-86	1994-96						
WORLD	**91**	**110**	**99**	**102**	**99**	**103**	**91**	**111**	**1,970,331**	**8**	**622,036**	**9**	**56,798**	**12**
AFRICA	**84**	**112**	**97**	**98**	**96**	**98**	**84**	**112**	**113,585**	**30**	**135,876**	**38**	**7,268**	**27**
Algeria	84	115	96	102	95	102	84	115	2,569	12	1,022	30	42	(34)
Angola	98	125	113	106	112	108	97	126	372	13	2,641	41	169	76
Benin	79	140	92	122	94	108	81	125	687	26	2,595	40	72	37
Botswana	97	95	115	83	115	83	97	95	60	73	9	22	14	2
Burkina Faso	82	119	94	103	96	105	83	121	2,420	37	66	(109)	65	10
Burundi	88	94	102	85	102	85	88	94	255	3	1,318	6	314	(0)
Cameroon	94	112	108	97	107	99	93	114	1,162	26	2,183	6	91	31
Central African Rep	87	108	98	97	96	99	85	110	107	(21)	827	(2)	25	54
Chad	77	121	85	106	88	109	80	124	966	41	535	(7)	34	(16)
Congo, Dem Rep	85	101	101	83	100	84	84	102	1,680	33	4,761	17	8	0
Congo, Rep	94	112	109	96	108	96	93	112	27	35	770	3	10	27
Côte d'Ivoire	83	114	98	98	100	105	85	123	1,768	39	1,953	19	463	20
Egypt	84	117	95	106	92	107	81	118	16,146	47	83	17	X	X
Equatorial Guinea	96	95	109	84	107	82	94	93	X	X	109	X	42	X
Eritrea	X	113	X	103	X	103	X	114	211	X	2,127	X	1,057	X
Ethiopia	89	117	103	X	103	X	89	117	9,401	X	407	21	0	16
Gabon	88	105	102	92	102	92	88	106	27	40	6	0	4	(1)
Gambia, The	99	85	122	70	122	69	99	83	100	(2)	9,953	55	20	26
Ghana	87	144	102	125	102	123	87	142	1,740	45	781	19	60	21
Guinea	91	124	106	98	110	99	95	125	817	17	61	13	2	9
Guinea-Bissau	89	111	98	100	97	100	88	111	188	15	1,676	24	265	20
Kenya	80	103	94	89	94	88	80	102	3,278	19	62	55	5	(5)
Lesotho	93	113	106	99	104	93	91	106	197	27	523	39	3	(5)
Liberia	X	X	X	X	X	X	X	X	54	(443)	129	19	12	9
Libya	92	91	110	76	110	76	91	91	315	16	3,333	9	77	29
Madagascar	94	104	111	88	110	89	93	105	2,673	13	569	7	271	14
Malawi	91	106	116	101	122	97	96	102	1,610	12	26	7	36	(27)
Mali	78	116	91	99	94	97	81	114	2,319	41	5	(7)	17	(29)
Mauritania	84	100	96	88	96	88	84	100	218	56	20	(7)	2	16
Mauritius	98	101	102	96	99	98	96	103	2	(209)	989	26	212	(77)
Morocco	70	101	78	91	77	91	70	101	7,178	22	4,030	7	123	32
Mozambique	93	105	98	87	98	86	93	105	1,067	30	225	11	8	19
Namibia	83	107	95	94	94	94	82	107	88	12	263	7	435	54
Niger	79	121	92	102	92	102	79	121	2,300	31	55,829	69	1,663	63
Nigeria	71	132	82	114	83	114	71	133	21,077	41	1,347	(31)	126	(133)
Rwanda	100	71	114	92	114	94	100	72	158	(96)	75	21	36	(29)
Senegal	83	112	95	98	95	98	83	111	1,017	7	294	56	41	21
Sierra Leone	92	94	102	89	103	88	93	93	415	(31)	42	(4)	13	(38)
Somalia	X	X	X	X	X	X	X	X	361	(47)	1,473	27	76	(33)
South Africa	88	95	99	85	98	87	87	97	12,408	19	159	(51)	111	(6)
Sudan	104	126	116	113	113	116	101	129	4,565	32	8	(25)	5	24
Swaziland	93	92	107	80	110	84	96	97	107	(55)	7,003	(21)	355	(12)
Tanzania	90	99	106	84	106	84	91	98	4,160	15	846	2	29	(17)
Togo	78	106	91	91	98	90	84	104	534	27	250	39	72	(3)
Tunisia	79	96	88	87	88	88	79	96	1,392	10	5,038	7	506	30
Uganda	82	116	92	98	91	96	80	113	2,047	48	18,702	12	200	10
Zambia	81	96	91	86	91	86	81	97	1,208	5	588	37	24	70
Zimbabwe	93	96	109	85	109	80	93	91	2,292	(15)	176	37	46	(7)
EUROPE	**X**	**X**	**X**	**X**	**X**	**X**	**X**	**X**	**383,382**	**X**	**147,785**	**X**	**10,461**	**X**
Albania	X	X	X	X	X	X	X	X	622	(65)	119	20	23	1
Austria	98	101	100	97	100	97	98	101	4,416	(21)	704	(50)	114	50
Belarus, Rep	X	92	X	X	X	X	X	93	5,464	X	9,474	X	439	X
Belgium {a}	93	114	94	112	94	112	93	114	2,468	3	2,311	25	25	72
Bosnia and Herzegovina	X	X	X	X	X	X	X	X	881	X	301	X	16	X
Bulgaria	110	67	107	68	104	70	107	68	5,465	(41)	483	7	46	(67)
Croatia, Rep	X	59	X	59	X	59	X	58	2,705	X	640	X	25	X
Czech Rep	X	87	X	88	X	88	X	88	6,690	X	1,440	X	148	X
Denmark	94	102	95	101	95	101	94	102	8,796	4	1,491	25	316	(45)
Estonia, Rep	X	67	X	X	X	X	X	67	530	X	553	X	7	X
Finland	101	92	103	90	103	90	101	92	3,473	(4)	763	3	13	19
France	100	101	103	99	103	99	100	101	56,530	3	5,932	(23)	3,092	63
Germany	101	90	104	88	103	88	101	90	39,527	5	11,539	(71)	206	(17)
Greece	97	106	100	104	101	100	98	102	4,764	(7)	1,105	6	42	(47)
Hungary	100	71	98	73	98	73	100	71	11,025	(36)	1,015	(38)	151	(52)
Iceland	119	96	126	91	125	92	119	97	X	X	9	(89)	X	X
Ireland	97	105	96	104	96	104	97	106	1,850	(18)	664	(9)	19	93
Italy	100	100	101	100	101	101	100	101	19,793	5	2,089	(19)	162	(68)
Latvia, Rep	X	67	X	71	X	71	X	67	830	X	997	X	5	X
Lithuania, Rep	X	74	X	74	X	75	X	75	2,161	X	1,571	X	34	X
Macedonia, FYR	X	95	X	90	X	91	X	96	640	X	149	X	26	X
Moldova, Rep	X	63	X	62	X	63	X	64	1,926	X	402	X	65	X
Netherlands	98	104	101	100	101	100	98	104	1,506	16	7,503	8	22	(401)
Norway	97	100	99	98	99	97	97	99	1,293	2	424	(4)	X	X
Poland, Rep	98	82	100	81	99	82	97	83	24,484	0	23,483	(60)	253	(77)
Portugal	78	94	77	94	77	94	77	93	1,566	4	1,382	14	40	(97)
Romania	120	97	122	99	122	100	120	98	17,437	(13)	3,056	(99)	90	(207)
Russian Federation	X	64	X	64	X	64	X	64	69,524	X	37,419	X	1,824	X
Slovak Rep	X	75	X	74	X	74	X	75	3,733	X	469	X	171	X
Slovenia, Rep	X	95	X	95	X	95	X	95	552	X	419	X	11	X
Spain	91	92	93	91	93	91	91	92	16,412	(19)	4,052	(41)	212	(55)
Sweden	108	96	111	93	111	93	108	96	4,972	(23)	1,216	(4)	74	(61)
Switzerland	101	97	105	93	105	93	101	97	1,312	20	635	(30)	10	67
Ukraine	X	74	X	74	X	75	X	75	29,535	X	16,410	X	2,000	X
United Kingdom	100	101	102	100	102	100	100	101	22,102	(11)	6,682	(3)	662	38
Yugoslavia, Fed Rep	X	93	X	93	X	92	X	93	8,391	X	850	X	116	X

Data Table 10.1 continued

	Index of Agricultural Production (1989-91 = 100)				Index of Food Production (1989-91 = 100)				Average Production of Cereals		Average Production of Roots and Tubers		Average Production of Pulses	
	Total		Per Capita		Total		Per Capita		(000 metric tons)	% Change Since	(000 metric tons)	% Change Since	(000 metric tons)	% Change Since
	1984-86	1994-96	1984-86	1994-96	1984-86	1994-96	1984-86	1994-96	1994-96	1984-86	1994-96	1984-86	1994-96	1984-86
NORTH AMERICA	**94**	**91**	**100**	**88**	**100**	**88**	**94**	**91**	**375,707**	**0**	**25,643**	**20**	**3,584**	**57**
Canada	93	111	100	105	99	104	93	110	51,760	5	3,751	24	2,006	83
United States	98	114	103	108	104	108	99	113	323,947	(1)	21,892	19	1,578	22
CENTRAL AMERICA	**X**	**X**	**X**	**X**	**X**	**X**	**X**	**X**	**31,357**	**3**	**4,154**	**8**	**2,086**	**18**
Belize	78	134	88	117	88	117	78	134	35	34	4	14	3	56
Costa Rica	81	119	93	106	92	109	80	123	208	(74)	209	69	29	18
Cuba	99	62	104	60	104	59	99	61	312	(107)	758	(22)	18	0
Dominican Rep	95	103	106	94	103	96	93	105	555	(8)	258	13	84	(1)
El Salvador	99	104	107	93	99	95	92	107	834	18	110	72	54	18
Guatemala	85	106	98	92	91	95	79	110	1,232	(4)	72	3	0	(9)
Haiti	110	91	121	83	122	84	110	92	391	(15)	771	(0)	78	(18)
Honduras	82	107	96	92	97	90	83	105	693	20	31	31	55	33
Jamaica	92	115	94	110	94	110	92	115	4	(101)	341	27	8	5
Mexico	96	118	106	108	106	108	96	119	26,125	5	1,330	18	1,532	21
Nicaragua	112	113	125	98	110	104	99	120	601	20	81	0	88	38
Panama	94	103	104	94	105	94	95	103	346	17	67	(26)	12	42
Trinidad and Tobago	93	105	98	101	98	102	93	106	18	59	12	22	2	(14)
SOUTH AMERICA	**88**	**115**	**97**	**106**	**96**	**108**	**88**	**118**	**91,056**	**15**	**45,148**	**8**	**3,964**	**17**
Argentina	101	115	109	108	110	109	102	117	26,258	(9)	2,599	(2)	286	18
Bolivia	78	119	87	105	86	105	77	119	1,090	18	1,064	(10)	27	0
Brazil	86	115	94	107	92	109	84	118	47,164	25	28,278	7	3,073	18
Chile	77	125	84	115	83	116	76	125	2,654	10	873	(5)	94	(56)
Colombia	81	107	89	97	88	99	80	109	3,523	10	4,801	24	186	21
Ecuador	80	128	90	115	90	116	80	130	2,095	56	575	(8)	59	43
Guyana	124	170	125	163	124	163	124	170	475	41	47	37	1	5
Paraguay	75	104	87	91	87	99	74	113	1,166	58	2,846	(3)	64	19
Peru	91	120	100	109	99	112	89	122	2,378	18	3,118	21	126	11
Suriname	112	93	119	88	119	88	112	93	221	(36)	7	46	0	100
Uruguay	89	115	91	111	91	115	89	119	1,790	44	181	(10)	6	4
Venezuela	88	117	100	104	100	105	88	118	2,217	17	732	13	43	8
ASIA	**X**	**X**	**X**	**X**	**X**	**X**	**X**	**X**	**948,317**	**X**	**260,294**	**X**	**27,384**	**X**
Afghanistan, Islamic State	X	X	X	X	X	X	X	X	3,019	(8)	260	4	40	3
Armenia, Rep	X	83	X	81	X	82	X	84	256	X	425	X	4	X
Azerbaijan	X	58	X	55	X	51	X	54	981	X	186	X	X	X
Bangladesh	89	104	98	96	96	96	87	104	27,887	14	1,882	4	531	(1)
Bhutan	101	109	114	101	114	101	101	109	111	(54)	56	15	2	(69)
Cambodia	73	119	85	103	85	102	73	118	3,024	42	133	52	19	6
China	82	140	88	132	88	136	81	144	416,954	15	163,572	15	4,777	(21)
Georgia	X	62	X	62	X	67	0	67	543	X	337	X	X	X
India	83	114	92	105	92	104	83	114	213,326	23	24,846	25	15,143	16
Indonesia	84	115	91	107	91	107	83	115	57,197	23	18,792	14	826	27
Iran, Islamic Rep	85	135	102	117	102	117	84	135	16,944	36	3,120	37	648	47
Iraq	101	97	119	87	119	87	101	97	2,312	9	406	68	37	21
Israel	101	107	112	90	106	91	96	107	153	(17)	284	27	8	7
Japan	102	98	105	97	104	97	101	98	14,566	(9)	5,081	(17)	128	(17)
Jordan	85	147	107	116	108	117	86	148	93	34	98	78	4	(33)
Kazakstan, Rep	X	62	X	61	X	61	X	62	12,340	X	1,805	X	43	X
Korea, Dem People's Rep	X	X	X	X	X	X	X	X	5,022	(33)	2,050	(11)	300	3
Korea, Rep	91	113	96	108	95	108	90	113	6,877	(29)	706	(86)	24	(96)
Kuwait	144	125	177	156	175	157	142	126	2	(27)	1	49	X	X
Kyrgyz Rep	X	76	X	75	X	73	X	74	1,132	X	434	X	X	X
Lao People's Dem Rep	91	114	106	98	107	98	92	114	1,485	4	211	10	43	42
Lebanon	69	118	67	101	66	100	68	117	76	53	324	41	39	67
Malaysia	78	115	88	102	79	109	70	122	2,158	19	530	8	X	X
Mongolia	94	78	109	70	109	68	94	76	264	(197)	51	(144)	1	(57)
Myanmar	111	139	123	127	121	127	110	139	20,040	25	261	(14)	1,063	44
Nepal	82	107	93	94	92	94	81	107	5,686	19	984	41	186	26
Oman	92	90	115	72	114	71	91	88	5	59	6	64	X	X
Pakistan	79	119	92	104	94	109	80	125	23,818	21	1,457	45	766	2
Philippines	90	117	100	105	100	106	90	119	15,119	18	2,761	8	39	1
Saudi Arabia	62	98	79	86	78	86	61	98	3,871	48	360	94	7	7
Singapore	147	42	163	38	163	38	147	42	X	X	X	X	X	X
Sri Lanka	105	108	112	103	113	103	107	108	2,313	(13)	436	(79)	39	(17)
Syrian Arab Rep	101	130	120	113	122	115	102	132	5,816	59	443	24	224	37
Tajikistan, Rep	X	59	X	54	X	58	X	64	288	X	121	100	6	X
Thailand	91	110	99	105	100	101	92	106	25,759	5	17,960	(3)	370	(24)
Turkey	89	105	99	97	100	97	89	105	28,179	3	4,684	20	1,778	12
Turkmenistan, Rep	X	89	X	80	X	95	X	105	988	X	25	X	X	X
United Arab Emirates	71	165	88	144	88	145	70	166	7	19	4	(6)	X	X
Uzbekistan, Rep	X	83	X	75	X	78	X	87	2,718	X	499	X	X	X
Vietnam	82	126	92	114	92	113	83	125	26,040	37	4,260	(18)	217	21
Yemen	83	113	98	87	97	86	82	112	759	29	183	(15)	68	37
OCEANIA	**97**	**111**	**105**	**104**	**105**	**107**	**97**	**115**	**26,928**	**(0)**	**3,137**	**8**	**2,050**	**45**
Australia	94	110	102	104	102	107	95	113	26,084	1	1,151	14	1,973	47
Fiji	95	107	98	99	99	99	95	107	20	(32)	48	(40)	1	56
New Zealand	104	114	108	108	106	113	102	119	819	(42)	296	3	72	(3)
Papua New Guinea	98	108	109	96	110	96	99	107	3	29	1,267	6	2	22
Solomon Islands	121	106	144	90	144	90	121	106	9	X	111	14	2	X
DEVELOPING	**85**	**122**	**94**	**111**	**94**	**113**	**85**	**123**	**1,137,967**	**19**	**436,491**	**21**	**40,442**	**15**
DEVELOPED	**98**	**96**	**101**	**94**	**101**	**94**	**98**	**97**	**832,364**	**(7)**	**185,545**	**(20)**	**16,357**	**4**

Notes: a. Data for Belgium and Luxembourg are combined under Belgium.

World and regional totals include some countries not listed here.

Agricultural Land and Inputs, 1982–94

Sources: Food and Agriculture Organization of the United Nations and United Nations Population Division

	Cropland Total Hectares (000) 1984	Cropland Hectares Per Capita 1984	Cropland Total Hectares (000) 1994	Cropland Hectares Per Capita 1994	Irrigated Land as a Percentage of Cropland 1982-84	Irrigated Land as a Percentage of Cropland 1992-94	Annual Fertilizer Use (kilograms per hectare of cropland) 1984	Annual Fertilizer Use 1994	Tractors Average Number 1992-94	Tractors Percent Change Since 1982-84	Harvesters Average Number 1992-94	Harvesters Percent Change Since 1982-84
WORLD	1,208,584	0.25	1,238,812	0.22	17	19	107	113	25,951,850	11	4,134,798	8
AFRICA	179,281	0.34	190,022	0.27	6	6	19	18	539,098	15	40,332	(26)
Algeria	7,510	0.35	8,043	0.29	4	7	27	15	95,562	78	9,786	92
Angola	3,400	0.44	3,500	0.33	2	2	2	3	10,300	0	X	X
Benin	1,818	0.47	1,880	0.36	0	0	4	11	140	25	X	X
Botswana	400	0.38	420	0.30	1	0	3	2	6,000	133	95	16
Burkina Faso	2,985	0.39	3,431	0.34	0	1	4	7	1,380	1,050	X	X
Burundi	1,180	0.26	1,110	0.19	1	1	2	3	170	55	2	100
Cameroon	6,965	0.72	7,040	0.55	0	0	6	4	500	(21)	X	X
Central African Rep	1,982	0.78	2,020	0.63	0	0	1	1	210	24	20	76
Chad	3,150	0.64	3,256	0.53	0	0	2	2	170	6	17	0
Congo, Dem Rep	7,750	0.25	7,900	0.18	0	0	1	1	2,430	14	X	X
Congo, Rep	158	0.08	170	0.07	1	1	18	11	707	4	73	88
Côte d'Ivoire	3,486	0.37	4,190	0.31	2	2	12	16	3,700	16	65	44
Egypt	2,493	0.05	3,265	0.05	100	100	341	264	72,648	61	2,370	11
Equatorial Guinea	230	0.78	230	0.59	0	0	0	0	100	2	X	X
Eritrea	X	X	519	0.17	X	5	X	0	567	2	27	X
Ethiopia	13,930	0.35	11,012	0.20	1	1	2	14	3,283	(16)	113	(24)
Gabon	452	0.58	460	0.44	1	1	6	1	1,500	15	X	X
Gambia, The	169	0.24	172	0.16	1	1	12	5	45	4	5	25
Ghana	3,900	0.31	4,500	0.27	0	0	2	3	4,100	12	540	50
Guinea	715	0.15	820	0.12	13	12	0	1	437	118	X	X
Guinea-Bissau	315	0.37	340	0.32	6	5	0	2	19	12	X	X
Kenya	4,285	0.22	4,520	0.17	1	1	18	31	14,000	73	650	50
Lesotho	297	0.20	320	0.16	1	1	15	19	1,850	22	35	17
Liberia	371	0.18	370	0.17	1	1	3	0	327	6	X	X
Libya	2,115	0.58	2,170	0.42	13	22	48	32	34,000	28	3,410	18
Madagascar	3,020	0.29	3,105	0.22	25	35	2	4	3,200	17	150	15
Malawi	1,445	0.21	1,700	0.18	1	2	31	16	1,420	11	X	X
Mali	2,053	0.27	3,000	0.29	3	3	24	8	2,383	99	50	9
Mauritania	195	0.11	208	0.09	25	24	3	19	333	7	X	X
Mauritius	107	0.11	106	0.10	15	17	253	275	370	10	X	X
Morocco	8,352	0.39	9,291	0.36	15	13	32	32	42,000	34	4,500	13
Mozambique	3,080	0.23	3,180	0.19	3	3	1	2	5,750	0	X	X
Namibia	662	0.58	750	0.50	1	1	0	0	3,150	17	X	X
Niger	3,535	0.55	4,500	0.51	1	2	1	1	180	39	X	X
Nigeria	30,873	0.38	32,700	0.30	1	1	9	9	11,900	25	X	X
Rwanda	1,108	0.19	1,150	0.22	0	0	1	1	90	7	X	X
Senegal	2,350	0.38	2,365	0.29	3	3	8	8	550	20	155	7
Sierra Leone	523	0.15	540	0.13	5	5	2	6	550	34	6	38
Somalia	1,020	0.13	1,020	0.11	16	19	4	0	1,980	7	X	X
South Africa	13,169	0.41	15,500	0.38	9	8	73	49	125,962	(26)	12,562	(64)
Sudan	12,608	0.60	12,975	0.50	15	15	3	4	10,500	6	1,600	70
Swaziland	179	0.28	191	0.23	39	35	47	70	4,060	17	X	X
Tanzania	2,895	0.14	3,675	0.13	4	4	12	10	6,600	(25)	X	X
Togo	2,360	0.80	2,400	0.60	0	0	3	5	370	42	X	X
Tunisia	4,990	0.70	4,813	0.55	6	8	17	18	30,158	15	3,070	19
Uganda	6,500	0.45	6,800	0.36	0	0	0	0	4,700	44	15	36
Zambia	5,158	0.82	5,273	0.67	0	1	11	11	6,000	19	293	8
Zimbabwe	2,808	0.35	2,878	0.26	3	4	52	59	20,833	31	720	11
EUROPE	X	X	316,378	0.43	X	X	X	X	11,505,372	X	1,320,468	X
Albania	713	0.25	702	0.21	55	49	132	21	9,050	(12)	902	(35)
Austria	1,522	0.20	1,513	0.19	0	0	257	168	345,753	6	24,992	(17)
Belarus, Rep	X	X	6,225	0.60	X	2	X	87	124,997	X	35,242	X
Belgium {a}	775	0.08	794	0.08	0	0	538	402	112,047	(4)	9,190	(1)
Bosnia and Herzegovina	X	X	800	0.22	X	0	X	6	24,667	X	1,083	X
Bulgaria	4,135	0.46	4,219	0.49	29	24	227	52	37,145	(36)	6,802	(24)
Croatia, Rep	X	X	1,221	0.27	X	0	X	152	4,173	X	1,025	X
Czech Rep	X	X	3,386	0.33	X	1	X	100	43,151	X	6,823	X
Denmark	2,627	0.51	2,374	0.46	15	18	251	196	152,084	(14)	30,912	(17)
Estonia, Rep	X	X	1,144	0.76	X	0	X	36	47,742	X	2,300	X
Finland	2,439	0.50	2,593	0.51	2	2	208	148	232,000	(0)	38,000	(17)
France	19,145	0.35	19,488	0.34	5	8	302	242	1,366,667	(8)	154,000	4
Germany	12,428	0.16	12,037	0.15	4	4	381	241	1,307,300	(20)	136,927	(23)
Greece	3,952	0.40	3,502	0.34	25	37	167	152	230,409	36	6,173	(4)
Hungary	5,289	0.50	4,974	0.49	4	4	288	63	38,500	(31)	8,367	(32)
Iceland	7	0.03	6	0.02	0	0	3,806	3,433	10,595	(24)	2	(65)
Ireland	1,044	0.30	1,317	0.37	0	0	649	569	167,500	10	5,100	(2)
Italy	12,232	0.22	11,143	0.19	20	23	171	170	1,455,192	24	49,643	27
Latvia, Rep	X	X	1,740	0.68	X	0	X	55	58,200	X	35,233	X
Lithuania, Rep	X	X	3,017	0.81	X	0	X	26	58,853	X	8,000	X
Macedonia, FYR	X	X	661	0.31	X	11	X	88	47,976	X	1,251	X
Moldova, Rep	X	X	2,190	0.49	X	14	X	53	51,911	X	6,400	X
Netherlands	846	0.06	920	0.06	61	61	851	592	182,000	(0)	5,587	(4)
Norway	855	0.21	901	0.21	10	11	295	227	149,033	4	16,000	(8)
Poland, Rep	14,863	0.40	14,652	0.38	1	1	221	98	1,212,810	60	89,156	83
Portugal	3,153	0.32	3,000	0.31	20	21	69	83	142,530	41	4,362	(13)
Romania	10,574	0.47	9,926	0.43	24	31	142	48	155,380	(9)	42,533	(2)
Russian Federation	X	X	132,302	0.89	X	4	X	11	1,227,187	X	344,923	X
Slovak Rep	X	X	1,611	0.30	X	19	X	59	21,220	X	3,919	X
Slovenia, Rep	X	X	286	0.15	X	1	X	286	84,000	X	1,300	X
Spain	20,512	0.54	20,129	0.51	15	18	80	95	777,104	31	48,946	12
Sweden	2,933	0.35	2,780	0.32	3	4	156	116	165,000	(12)	40,000	(17)
Switzerland	412	0.06	434	0.06	6	6	437	336	114,000	10	4,000	(18)
Ukraine	X	X	34,357	0.66	X	8	X	33	445,282	X	99,218	X
United Kingdom	6,990	0.12	5,949	0.10	2	2	371	381	500,000	(5)	47,000	(16)
Yugoslavia, Fed Rep	X	X	4,085	0.40	X	2	X	21	403,916	X	5,157	X

	Cropland Total Hectares (000) 1984	Cropland Hectares Per Capita 1984	Cropland Total Hectares (000) 1994	Cropland Hectares Per Capita 1994	Irrigated Land as a Percentage of Cropland 1982-84	Irrigated Land as a Percentage of Cropland 1992-94	Annual Fertilizer Use (kilograms per hectare of cropland) 1984	Annual Fertilizer Use (kilograms per hectare of cropland) 1994	Tractors Average Number 1992-94	Tractors Percent Change Since 1982-84	Harvesters Average Number 1992-94	Harvesters Percent Change Since 1982-84
NORTH AMERICA	**235,854**	**0.89**	**233,276**	**0.79**	**9**	**9**	**94**	**92**	**5,540,000**	**3**	**817,000**	**(2)**
Canada	46,055	1.80	45,500	1.56	1	2	52	50	740,000	8	155,000	(3)
United States	189,799	0.79	187,776	0.71	11	11	104	103	4,800,000	3	662,000	(1)
CENTRAL AMERICA	**38,107**	**0.39**	**41,112**	**0.34**	**17**	**20**	**65**	**58**	**293,727**	**14**	**32,612**	**13**
Belize	53	0.33	83	0.40	4	4	37	75	1,150	32	45	32
Costa Rica	518	0.20	530	0.16	17	23	186	243	7,000	15	1,190	12
Cuba	3,337	0.33	4,512	0.41	25	24	174	27	78,000	18	7,400	8
Dominican Rep	1,430	0.23	1,820	0.24	13	14	42	51	2,350	6	X	X
El Salvador	725	0.16	755	0.14	15	16	76	101	3,430	2	420	24
Guatemala	1,785	0.23	1,910	0.19	5	7	5	4	4,300	6	3,050	11
Haiti	902	0.16	910	0.13	8	9	4	6	230	21	X	X
Honduras	1,777	0.44	2,030	0.37	4	4	21	28	4,391	33	X	X
Jamaica	220	0.10	219	0.09	15	15	105	119	3,080	5	X	X
Mexico	24,688	0.33	24,730	0.28	20	25	67	62	172,000	14	19,500	18
Nicaragua	1,683	0.54	2,569	0.64	5	4	29	12	2,700	15	X	X
Panama	586	0.28	665	0.26	5	5	48	48	5,000	(6)	1,000	(26)
Trinidad and Tobago	118	0.10	122	0.10	18	18	52	49	2,650	6	X	X
SOUTH AMERICA	**104,544**	**0.40**	**114,901**	**0.37**	**7**	**8**	**44**	**60**	**1,214,093**	**21**	**121,732**	**16**
Argentina	27,200	0.91	27,200	0.79	6	6	5	17	280,000	38	50,000	10
Bolivia	2,217	0.38	2,370	0.33	6	4	2	4	5,350	19	123	1
Brazil	51,680	0.39	60,000	0.38	4	5	65	79	735,000	19	48,000	23
Chile	4,325	0.36	4,154	0.30	29	30	42	95	40,974	19	8,767	5
Colombia	5,264	0.18	6,220	0.18	8	14	69	92	27,000	(16)	2,850	27
Ecuador	2,505	0.28	3,036	0.27	16	9	29	51	8,900	20	780	24
Guyana	495	0.63	496	0.60	26	26	30	30	3,630	3	440	6
Paraguay	1,967	0.56	2,270	0.48	3	3	5	10	16,500	72	X	X
Peru	3,691	0.19	4,140	0.18	33	43	21	41	12,933	8	X	X
Suriname	59	0.16	68	0.16	79	88	196	63	1,330	15	275	25
Uruguay	1,346	0.45	1,304	0.41	7	11	39	77	33,000	(2)	4,687	2
Venezuela	3,790	0.23	3,630	0.17	4	5	71	68	49,000	19	5,800	45
ASIA	**X**	**X**	**621,590**	**0.18**	**X**	**X**	**X**	**X**	**7,197,097**	**X**	**1,856,053**	**X**
Afghanistan, Islamic State	8,054	0.54	8,054	0.44	32	36	9	6	840	6	X	X
Armenia, Rep	X	X	600	0.17	X	49	X	12	15,852	X	2,085	X
Azerbaijan	X	X	2,000	0.27	X	54	X	20	31,000	X	4,233	X
Bangladesh	9,132	0.09	8,700	0.07	20	37	65	120	5,300	13	X	X
Bhutan	127	0.09	140	0.08	24	29	1	1	X	X	X	X
Cambodia	2,110	0.29	3,838	0.39	5	4	1	3	1,190	(3)	20	0
China	98,746	0.09	95,782	0.08	45	52	200	309	740,425	(12)	56,781	61
Georgia	X	X	1,127	0.21	X	44	X	28	20,567	X	1,271	X
India	169,078	0.22	169,700	0.19	24	29	49	80	1,196,268	136	3,167	21
Indonesia	25,934	0.16	30,171	0.16	17	15	72	80	46,976	353	237,148	1,460
Iran, Islamic Rep	15,540	0.33	18,500	0.28	40	39	60	54	229,335	107	5,488	79
Iraq	5,450	0.37	5,750	0.29	32	64	22	65	32,000	(5)	1,900	(24)
Israel	419	0.10	434	0.08	54	44	229	240	25,707	(5)	260	(25)
Japan	4,780	0.04	4,422	0.04	62	62	440	398	2,031,333	28	1,168,667	16
Jordan	351	0.10	405	0.08	12	17	43	35	7,378	55	75	17
Kazakhstan, Rep	X	X	34,978	2.08	X	6	X	3	208,586	X	79,628	X
Korea, Dem People's Rep	1,945	0.10	2,000	0.09	63	73	398	377	75,000	22	X	X
Korea, Rep	2,153	0.05	2,033	0.05	61	65	361	472	76,555	903	66,373	1,030
Kuwait	3	X	5	0.00	57	73	150	200	100	329	X	X
Kyrgyz Rep	X	X	1,420	0.32	X	74	X	20	26,059	X	3,698	X
Lao People's Dem Rep	810	0.23	900	0.19	16	16	0	2	890	24	X	X
Lebanon	298	0.11	306	0.10	29	29	170	114	3,800	27	97	7
Malaysia	5,300	0.35	7,604	0.39	6	5	105	159	34,617	283	X	X
Mongolia	1,336	0.72	1,320	0.55	4	6	13	1	8,107	(24)	2,001	(21)
Myanmar	10,061	0.27	10,076	0.23	10	11	19	12	11,000	22	3,910	56
Nepal	2,329	0.14	2,743	0.13	29	35	18	33	4,600	71	X	X
Oman	47	0.03	63	0.03	92	95	20	159	150	44	45	246
Pakistan	20,330	0.21	21,510	0.16	76	80	62	98	289,433	119	1,633	173
Philippines	8,920	0.17	9,370	0.14	16	17	29	64	11,500	24	700	35
Saudi Arabia	2,423	0.20	3,800	0.21	34	34	108	95	8,633	220	2,233	244
Singapore	6	X	1	0.00	0	0	833	4,800	65	30	X	X
Sri Lanka	1,872	0.12	1,883	0.11	29	29	102	113	31,500	21	6	64
Syrian Arab Rep	5,654	0.56	5,971	0.43	10	17	39	59	73,428	99	4,428	56
Tajikistan, Rep	X	X	860	0.15	X	85	X	81	31,909	X	1,100	X
Thailand	19,331	0.38	20,445	0.35	18	22	23	64	99,549	288	55,462	85
Turkey	27,413	0.56	27,771	0.46	11	15	56	54	745,248	44	11,408	(16)
Turkmenistan, Rep	X	X	1,480	0.37	X	90	X	84	55,015	X	14,672	X
United Arab Emirates	32	0.02	82	0.04	185	89	118	432	175	5	5	67
Uzbekistan, Rep	X	X	4,500	0.20	X	88	X	105	173,333	X	7,333	X
Vietnam	6,590	0.11	6,758	0.09	26	28	57	192	37,209	31	X	X
Yemen	1,465	0.16	1,540	0.11	20	29	13	7	5,943	12	55	22
OCEANIA	**51,849**	**2.15**	**51,515**	**1.84**	**4**	**5**	**34**	**46**	**401,364**	**(5)**	**60,095**	**(3)**
Australia	47,239	3.07	47,205	2.67	4	5	26	35	315,000	(3)	56,500	(2)
Fiji	190	0.28	260	0.34	1	1	83	69	7,017	43	X	X
New Zealand	3,500	1.09	3,071	0.87	7	9	147	212	76,000	(16)	3,100	(19)
Papua New Guinea	376	0.11	440	0.10	0	0	18	30	1,140	(8)	475	14
Solomon Islands	54	0.21	57	0.16	0	0	0	0	X	X	X	X
DEVELOPING	**763,202**	**0.21**	**799,479**	**0.18**	**21**	**23**	**63**	**89**	**5,730,613**	**44**	**636,207**	**133**
DEVELOPED	**677,068**	**0.61**	**667,273**	**0.57**	**9**	**10**	**121**	**78**	**20,221,237**	**4**	**3,498,591**	**(2)**

Notes: a. Data for Belgium and Luxembourg are combined under Belgium.
World and regional totals include some countries not listed here.

Data Table 10.3
Food Security, 1982–97

Sources: Food and Agriculture Organization of the United Nations, United Nations Population Division, and U.S. Department of Agriculture

| | Average Annual Net Trade in Cereals (000 metric tons) | | Average Annual Donations or Receipts of Cereals (000 metric tons) | | Grain Consumption as a Percent of Domestic Production | | Grains Fed to Livestock as a Percent of Total Grain Consumption | | Average Daily Per Capita Calorie Supply (kilocalories) | | Average Daily Per Capita Protein Supply (grams) | | Average Yield of Cereals | | Average Yield of Roots and Tubers | |
| | | | | | | | | | | | | | Kilograms Per Hectare | Percent Change Since | Kilograms Per Hectare | Percent Change Since |
	1983-85	1993-95	1983-85	1993-95	1983-85	1993-95	1985-87	1995-97	1982-84	1992-94	1982-84	1992-94	1994-96	1984-86	1994-96	1984-86
WORLD							40	40	2,624	2,709	62	72	2,817	10.1	12,752	2
AFRICA	27,997	31,242	6,940	3,192	150	133	16	14	X	X	X	X	1,220	9.5	8,161	17
Algeria	4,332	6,430	4	20	329	524	31	22	2,626	2,959	69	82	953	19.6	12,216	35
Angola	339	443	89	225	233	321	0	0	1,986	1,756	50	39	405	(6.7)	6,041	38
Benin	112	132	13	16	128	122	0	0	1,983	2,325	46	56	1,008	17.6	9,275	10
Botswana	215	172	43	5	1,934	472	0	0	2,215	2,268	70	69	300	43.6	6,000	10
Burkina Faso	191	147	119	28	125	107	2	3	1,698	2,471	50	72	808	17.6	5,219	(55)
Burundi	32	70	14	37	120	140	0	0	1,904	1,802	61	57	1,298	10.7	6,471	(7)
Cameroon	251	336	9	3	133	132	0	0	2,247	2,167	55	51	1,313	8.3	6,076	(0)
Central African Rep	22	47	16	2	136	148	0	0	2,154	1,959	36	41	790	(28.2)	3,280	(23)
Chad	79	52	130	14	142	107	0	0	1,441	1,840	41	53	639	14.0	4,163	(17)
Congo, Dem Rep	378	323	102	51	145	122	4	0	2,080	2,032	34	32	793	(2.5)	8,174	6
Congo, Rep	117	129	1	8	930	605	0	0	2,312	2,188	47	49	936	19.7	6,894	(3)
Côte d'Ivoire	658	665	0	44	166	143	3	4	2,740	2,358	56	50	1,111	14.9	5,792	(1)
Egypt	8,208	7,846	1,885	208	218	152	35	31	3,054	3,227	78	87	6,082	25.6	21,484	5
Equatorial Guinea	X	X	8	3	X	X	X	X	X	X	X	X	X	X	2,632	(19)
Eritrea	X	127 a	X	154	X	261	X	X	X	1,608 b	X	X	699	X	2,812	X
Ethiopia	478	426	738	657	125	114	0	0	1,681	1,661	X	X	1,354	24.4	3,679	2
Gabon	79	98	0	0	689	476	0	0	2,523	2,472	75	73	1,779	10.0	5,449	3
Gambia, The	70	94	25	6	206	203	0	0	2,226	2,295	49	47	1,106	(19.7)	3,000	0
Ghana	210	383	101	88	138	128	4	3	1,862	2,360	40	50	1,399	35.3	10,995	50
Guinea	151	404	58	27	131	156	0	0	2,251	2,346	51	46	1,219	26.1	7,091	4
Guinea-Bissau	35	74	27	4	141	141	0	0	2,191	2,571	46	50	1,389	15.9	7,038	4
Kenya	262	270	225	135	120	113	3	1	2,042	1,914	55	50	1,822	11.2	8,031	9
Lesotho	196	220	59	32	281	253	27	21	2,267	2,164	67	60	1,560	56.2	14,804	(4)
Liberia	144	153 a	48	155	165	640	0	0	2,496	1,728	X	X	1,110	(13.3)	7,356	15
Libya	992	1,987	0	0	421	726	33	30	3,386	3,288	88	74	679	9.3	7,261	8
Madagascar	239	126	86	25	114	106	0	0	2,419	2,056	57	48	2,010	12.5	6,707	9
Malawi	(80)	459	5	152	95	136	2	3	2,188	1,911	64	54	1,194	4.4	4,632	5
Mali	229	72	202	18	133	104	1	1	1,954	2,040	56	56	809	(6.5)	5,007	17
Mauritania	302	241	176	37	792	238	1	0	2,317	2,578	78	78	750	18.2	2,000	5
Mauritius	195	250	13	0	6,414	14,073	0	0	2,669	2,942	61	78	4,339	(4.4)	17,489	(35)
Morocco	2,310	2,962	373	45	164	163	24	21	2,833	3,114	76	84	1,236	6.8	16,203	(1)
Mozambique	460	537	404	303	227	197	0	0	1,809	1,685	32	31	647	18.3	4,099	0
Namibia	75	108	0	4	196	233	X	X	2,179	2,174	62	60	264	(43.5)	8,438	(3)
Niger	184	145	148	32	121	108	0	0	2,139	2,154	61	62	338	(8.4)	7,450	(8)
Nigeria	1,928	1,345	0	0	118	107	5	2	1,973	2,589	42	54	1,172	(13.5)	10,573	22
Rwanda	64	102 a	32	202	130	281	11	9	2,238	1,861	X	X	1,491	21.0	6,278	(22)
Senegal	660	658	159	22	199	166	0	0	2,368	2,288	68	66	824	11.3	3,394	(28)
Sierra Leone	88	211	33	35	123	155	0	3	1,974	1,888	42	43	1,192	(19.4)	4,968	19
Somalia	173	234 a	226	34	187	194	2	4	1,969	1,533	X	X	426	(81.1)	10,000	(7)
South Africa	1,220	195	0	5	115	102	35	36	2,867	2,776	75	72	1,918	23.7	21,062	34
Sudan	726	368	832	164	160	114	0	0	2,138	2,274	62	70	527	9.4	2,964	(1)
Swaziland	86	107	4	8	174	233	0	0	2,529	2,653	64	63	1,735	(12.0)	1,930	(29)
Tanzania	318	219	137	60	114	107	2	3	2,286	2,054	56	49	1,310	3.6	7,713	(15)
Togo	87	69	14	8	127	115	12	19	2,108	2,052	48	49	762	(10.3)	5,716	(37)
Tunisia	987	1,686	182	29	185	260	28	26	2,835	3,168	77	84	1,164	31.0	13,544	17
Uganda	4	(49)	19	49	102	100	0	0	2,246	2,160	50	52	1,552	20.7	5,727	(9)
Zambia	233	192	98	32	132	118	2	3	2,114	1,954	55	51	1,538	(17.4)	5,370	(2)
Zimbabwe	(41)	(19)	83	9	102	100	14	9	2,162	1,999	55	49	1,163	(24.6)	4,508	(12)
EUROPE	X	(20,823)	X	679	X	95	63	59	X	X	X	X	2,884	X	15,134	X
Albania	59	341	0	94	106	165	0	0	2,781	2,349	82	77	2,537	(16.4)	9,971	34
Austria	(684)	(364)	(18)	(12)	87	91	73	68	3,365	3,474	96	101	5,384	6.0	25,649	(8)
Belarus, Rep	X	510	X	62	X	109	76	67	X	3,235	X	101	2,161	X	13,261	X
Belgium {b}	1,993	2,287	(52)	(38)	187	196	38	44	3,361	3,700	102	106	7,369	17.1	41,038	(5)
Bosnia and Herzegovina	X	0	X	7	X	101	X	X	X	1,734	X	X	2,957	X	6,400	X
Bulgaria	167	(304)	0	52	102	96	63	52	3,640	2,915	106	85	2,615	(46.1)	9,906	(15)
Croatia, Rep	X	(117)	X	12	X	96	X	X	X	2,358	X	60	4,340	X	9,681	X
Czech Rep	X	(409)	X	0	X	94	X	58	X	3,012 b	X	92 b	4,167	X	17,817	X
Denmark	(897)	(1,524)	(15)	(43)	88	81	84	81	3,390	3,722	87	102	5,934	12.5	35,352	(3)
Estonia, Rep	X	96	X	0	X	116	80	63	X	2,447	X	110	1,756	X	14,775	X
Finland	(458)	(657)	(22)	(11)	87	80	69	63	3,027	3,050	94	94	3,478	14.7	21,329	13
France	(25,154)	(29,943)	(216)	(190)	52	44	64	67	3,453	3,544	114	115	6,698	15.3	34,527	9
Germany	5,565	(5,600)	0	0	115	85	X	64	3,367	3,382	98	96	6,049	16.3	33,407	17
Greece	(924)	(65)	(10)	(12)	81	98	57	49	3,606	3,689	109	113	3,590	5.2	22,025	17
Hungary	(1,663)	(1,674)	0	0	89	84	73	72	3,480	3,400	98	93	3,910	(32.3)	14,276	(37)
Iceland	60	70	0	0	X	X	X	X	3,137	3,088	126	121	X	X	10,747	(52)
Ireland	280	275	(4)	(5)	113	116	73	60	3,598	3,630	110	114	6,687	17.5	29,377	26
Italy	3,935	2,443	(118)	(116)	120	112	50	51	3,382	3,464	104	108	4,716	18.6	23,411	23
Latvia, Rep	X	19	X	0	X	102	74	60	X	2,958	X	93	1,854	X	12,564	X
Lithuania, Rep	X	85	X	26	X	105	81	64	X	2,916	X	96	2,024	X	12,780	X
Macedonia, FYR	X	114	X	15	X	121	X	0	X	2,392	X	68	2,719	X	10,420	X
Moldova, Rep	X	157	X	130	X	111	62	53	X	2,892	X	81	2,711	X	6,611	X
Netherlands	3,519	3,866	(136)	(137)	364	359	48	43	3,046	3,343	94	100	7,752	10.6	42,046	1
Norway	387	577	(31)	(35)	128	141	67	65	3,155	3,244	99	101	3,807	(0.0)	23,320	(5)
Poland, Rep	2,552	1,951	38	0	111	108	63	61	3,347	3,347	99	99	2,854	(4.2)	15,049	(20)
Portugal	2,821	2,244	0	0	312	248	52	60	2,944	3,608	81	109	2,310	32.0	15,117	41
Romania	(44)	897	0	25	100	105	69	66	3,335	3,191	99	92	2,812	(12.4)	12,218	(55)
Russian Federation	X	536	X	856	X	102	64	50	X	2,927	X	93	1,313	X	11,214	X
Slovak Rep	X	(382)	X	0	X	89	X	64	X	2,774 b	X	86 b	4,298	X	11,397	X
Slovenia, Rep	X	846	X	1	X	262	X	X	X	3,007	X	91	5,026	X	18,282	X
Spain	4,253	3,782	(30)	(9)	123	126	67	70	3,335	3,673	98	107	2,478	(3.3)	19,552	11
Sweden	(1,165)	(221)	(80)	(92)	79	94	75	76	3,006	2,914	97	100	4,399	7.7	34,735	8
Switzerland	1,268	634	(31)	(52)	221	146	65	53	3,418	3,252	95	93	6,362	11.1	36,737	(5)
Ukraine	X	783	X	51	X	102	65	48	X	3,212	X	89	2,410	X	10,683	X
United Kingdom	(2,046)	(2,090)	(129)	(177)	91	89	53	54	3,123	3,216	88	94	6,909	11.9	39,179	7
Yugoslavia, Fed Rep	X	11	X	277	X	103	X	X	X	2,984	X	88	3,471	X	8,171	X

Data Table 10.3 continued

	Average Annual Net Trade in Cereals (000 metric tons)		Average Annual Donations or Receipts of Cereals (000 metric tons)		Grain Consumption as a Percent of Domestic Production		Grains Fed to Livestock as a Percent of Total Grain Consumption		Average Daily Per Capita Calorie Supply (kilocalories)		Average Daily Per Capita Protein Supply (grams)		Average Yield of Cereals		Average Yield of Roots and Tubers	
													Kilograms Per Hectare	Percent Change Since	Kilograms Per Hectare	Percent Change Since
	1983-85	1993-95	1983-85	1993-95	1983-85	1993-95	1985-87	1995-97	1982-84	1992-94	1982-84	1992-94	1994-96	1984-86	1994-96	1984-86
NORTH AMERICA	(118,959)	(108,419)	(7,614)	(5,723)	62	67	68	65	X	X	X	X	X	X	22,863	38
Canada	(25,074)	(23,168)	(992)	(594)	44	52	76	78	2,984	3,058	93	96	2,702	15.9	26,706	6
United States	(93,886)	(85,251)	(6,622)	(5,128)	65	70	71	67	3,279	3,609	99	110	5,136	10.1	36,616	15
CENTRAL AMERICA	10,631	12,216	976	525	139	141	17	31	X	X	X	X	X	X	X	X
Belize	9	19	0	0	140	155	0	0	2,585	2,683	67	67	1,888	15.3	21,765	5
Costa Rica	137	521	107	3	165	354	30	51	2,595	2,776	62	66	3,426	32.9	22,392	61
Cuba	2,249	1,536	0	6	458	677	0	0	3,133	2,504	74	56	1,877	(42.5)	5,426	(12)
Dominican Rep	408	995	128	4	188	297	40	63	2,304	2,275	50	51	4,034	11.5	6,845	8
El Salvador	243	372	248	33	172	148	24	26	2,366	2,483	56	62	1,887	5.0	18,718	25
Guatemala	64	62	32	109	108	113	23	29	2,553	2,670	83	85	1,915	12.1	5,596	6
Haiti	82	393 a	108	104	144	225	3	3	2,026	1,721	X	X	929	(9.2)	3,815	0
Honduras	100	275	119	88	140	152	23	54	2,133	2,352	51	55	1,436	3.9	8,536	(0)
Jamaica	421	436	162	86	7,317	13,675	28	39	2,576	2,662	63	67	1,374	(27.6)	15,291	20
Mexico	6,396	6,948	6	49	126	127	29	44	3,194	3,053	83	83	2,506	4.6	19,888	28
Nicaragua	163	170	64	44	149	137	0	6	2,395	2,267	61	55	1,687	(2.5)	11,563	(0)
Panama	113	263	1	2	140	178	29	43	2,395	2,420	61	65	2,078	23.4	5,739	(29)
Trinidad and Tobago	246	227	0	0	3,765	1,259	36	38	3,056	2,499	81	59	3,649	33.9	10,222	6
SOUTH AMERICA	(8,899)	4,361	452	539	89	106	49	54	X	X	X	X	2,547	19.9	12,320	7
Argentina	(20,160)	(12,376)	(42)	(4)	34	50	56	49	3,103	3,076	99	98	2,811	9.9	19,722	14
Bolivia	353	267	237	149	176	139	40	33	2,058	2,190	53	58	1,561	16.1	5,605	4
Brazil	4,892	9,129	7	19	115	120	55	64	2,630	2,797	62	69	2,383	27.7	13,020	7
Chile	928	1,038	14	1	148	139	30	39	2,574	2,735	69	78	4,409	31.9	14,698	5
Colombia	941	2,222	5	15	129	163	19	32	2,466	2,662	53	62	2,623	1.7	12,778	11
Ecuador	353	305	14	15	150	116	29	37	2,306	2,378	46	49	2,066	16.8	6,351	(47)
Guyana	(47)	(139)	0	35	82	75	5	6	2,512	2,410	54	64	3,807	16.1	10,523	32
Paraguay	52	(49)	5	1	112	95	1	2	2,534	2,372	73	74	2,137	25.6	14,044	(3)
Peru	1,346	2,325	212	289	183	220	23	42	2,143	2,121	55	54	2,915	18.2	9,165	10
Suriname	(99)	(30)	0	19	66	95	0	0	2,507	2,580	66	65	3,778	(5.9)	11,827	51
Uruguay	(383)	(582)	0	0	64	63	27	14	2,711	2,738	82	87	3,016	37.4	10,232	43
Venezuela	2,925	2,249	0	0	293	205	51	42	2,673	2,494	70	65	2,719	26.4	9,446	10
ASIA	X	77,933	X	3,435	X	109	15	24	X	X	X	X	2,895	X	15,195	X
Afghanistan, Islamic State	78	190 a	213	116	109	110	0	0	2,139	1,696	X	X	1,292	(2.7)	16,742	12
Armenia, Rep	X	452	X	307	X	377	50	21	X	1,864	X	57	1,431	X	13,043	X
Azerbaijan	X	626	X	221	X	185	46	30	X	2,293	X	70	1,599	X	11,589	X
Bangladesh	2,218	1,539	1,365	809	115	109	0	0	1,954	2,023	42	44	2,602	17.6	10,635	1
Bhutan	X	X	6	4	X	X	0	0	X	X	X	X	1,091	(28.4)	10,750	33
Cambodia	94	98	51	68	108	106	0	0	1,777	1,805	43	43	1,638	23.1	6,076	(0)
China	10,648	10,887	200	166	103	103	18	31	2,681	3,082	59	68	4,673	16.6	16,583	8
Georgia	X	732	X	478	X	362	51	26	X	2,248	0	65	1,881	X	13,624	X
India	1,452	(2,690)	278	304	101	99	2	4	2,157	2,397	54	58	2,136	26.0	16,936	16
Indonesia	2,096	5,406	270	26	106	110	4	20	2,331	2,609	49	62	3,895	11.3	11,647	15
Iran, Islamic Rep	4,457	5,308	11	22	145	132	21	19	2,787	2,899	74	77	1,826	31.0	20,930	25
Iraq	4,077	1,296	0	83	309	150	28	16	3,172	2,264	84	53	717	(31.2)	16,102	(3)
Israel	1,637	2,512	6	0	748	1,524	56	49	3,100	3,116	104	105	1,424	(14.3)	37,005	(3)
Japan	26,567	29,275	(397)	(522)	271	312	48	54	2,803	2,890	89	95	6,119	3.6	26,890	7
Jordan	675	1,412	34	153	877	1,800	40	57	2,713	2,727	74	75	1,209	51.2	25,256	33
Kazakstan, Rep	X	(4,070)	X	20	X	74	60	39	X	2,809	X	95	650	X	8,815	X
Korea, Dem People's Rep	131	804	0	270	102	122	0	0	2,691	2,310	84	81	3,472	(18.4)	12,059	(8)
Korea, Rep	6,445	11,907	0	0	171	270	35	54	3,083	3,229	81	84	5,813	0.3	20,090	(8)
Kuwait	481	478	0	0	29,710	25,969	46	42	3,070	2,915	93	88	4,937	2.3	18,434	(7)
Kyrgyz Rep	X	426	X	120	X	147	68	33	X	2,505	X	81	1,923	X	13,713	X
Lao People's Dem Rep	41	29	4	19	103	103	0	0	2,148	2,106	55	55	2,561	18.6	9,005	(4)
Lebanon	508	724	25	8	1,929	1,057	27	43	2,909	3,275	79	83	1,969	31.7	23,041	15
Malaysia	2,192	3,612	0	0	226	267	39	56	2,706	2,782	58	65	3,052	12.6	9,701	4
Mongolia	19	91	0	12	102	129	0	0	2,398	1,917	79	67	734	(70.1)	7,505	(60)
Myanmar	(839)	(481)	2	3	94	97	0	0	2,563	2,619	65	66	3,015	4.3	8,995	(10)
Nepal	(3)	61	20	38	100	102	0	0	1,951	2,126	53	59	1,819	12.9	7,704	19
Oman	X	X	X	X	100	100	0	0	X	X	X	X	2,180	27.9	22,917	4
Pakistan	(718)	1,101	455	63	99	105	3	4	2,177	2,399	53	61	1,943	14.6	14,233	22
Philippines	1,524	2,560	101	38	114	118	18	31	2,161	2,370	51	56	2,283	19.7	6,880	9
Saudi Arabia	6,404	4,244	(66)	(0)	522	186	77	74	2,855	2,395	79	72	4,143	15.1	19,496	11
Singapore	X	X	X	X	X	X	42	23	X	X	X	X	X	X	10,000	(11)
Sri Lanka	810	1,062	344	268	145	155	0	0	2,295	2,242	47	48	2,568	(11.4)	8,903	(17)
Syrian Arab Rep	1,581	478	33	35	172	109	29	21	3,245	3,245	88	85	1,660	45.9	18,710	9
Tajikistan, Rep	X	536	X	131	X	369	36	19	X	2,190	X	69	1,109	100.0	22,389	100
Thailand	(7,767)	(5,420)	37	4	68	78	16	50	2,215	2,365	49	53	2,434	13.5	13,671	(1)
Turkey	(204)	(303)	2	1	99	99	32	33	3,319	3,527	97	102	2,019	0.3	23,402	19
Turkmenistan, Rep	X	588	X	63	X	155	45	37	X	2,681	X	80	2,570	100.0	4,603	100
United Arab Emirates	295	696	0	0	5,244	10,362	29	15	3,308	3,323	104	102	7,528	36.8	19,741	42
Uzbekistan, Rep	X	1,793	X	0	X	169	40	19	X	2,598	X	79	1,762	X	10,168	X
Vietnam	288	(1,729)	18	57	102	93	0	0	2,246	2,302	50	55	3,504	23.3	6,833	(7)
Yemen	932	1,705	55	52	312	315	0	0	2,023	2,130	58	56	1,046	40.9	13,363	(71)
OCEANIA	(16,424)	(13,382)	(423)	(242)	42	44	56	57	X	X	X	X	1,779	11.5	11,198	2
Australia	(16,599)	(14,126)	(424)	(242)	40	39	60	59	3,040	3,080	103	103	1,740	12.2	27,723	5
Fiji	89	148	1	0	475	805	0	0	2,571	3,023	64	73	2,533	11.4	5,502	(60)
New Zealand	(131)	277	0	0	88	135	45	47	3,153	3,314	97	103	5,356	13.7	26,212	(12)
Papua New Guinea	204	293	0	0	7,344	9,326	0	0	2,167	2,237	44	48	1,698	(30.0)	7,073	(1)
Solomon Islands	13	26	0	0	270	X	X	X	2,229	2,046	57	44	X	X	17,251	6
DEVELOPING	72,135	85,968	X	X	X	X	X	X	2,406	2,555	58	64	2,598	14.5	11,617	8
DEVELOPED	(76,402)	X	X	X	X	X	65	64	3,260	3,223	72	98	3,183	6.9	16,570	(5)

Notes: a. Data for 1992-94. b. Data for 1993-94. c. Data for Belgium and Luxembourg are combined under Belgium.

Imports and food aid receipts are shown as positive numbers; exports and food aid donations are shown as negative numbers in parentheses.

World and regional totals include some countries not listed here.

Sources and Technical Notes

Data Table 10.1

Food and Agricultural Production, 1984–96

Source: Food and Agriculture Organization of the United Nations (FAO), *FAOSTAT Statistical Database* (FAO, Rome, 1997).

Indexes of agricultural production and *food production* portray the disposable output (after deduction for feed and seed) of a country's agriculture sector relative to the base period 1989–91. For a given year and country, the index is calculated as the disposable average output of a commodity in terms of weight or volume during the period of interest multiplied by the 1989–91 average national producer price per unit. The index represents the total value of the commodity for that period in terms of the 1989–91 price. The values of all crop and livestock products are totaled to yield an aggregated value of agricultural production in 1989–91 prices. The ratio of this aggregate for a given year to that for 1989–91 is multiplied by 100 to obtain the index number.

The multiplication of disposable outputs with the 1989–91 unit value eliminates inflationary or deflationary distortions. However, the base period's relative prices among the individual commodities are also preserved. Especially in economies with high inflation, price patterns among agricultural commodities can change dramatically over time.

The continental and world index values for a given year are calculated by totaling the disposable outputs of all relevant countries for each agricultural commodity. Each of these aggregates is multiplied by a respective 1989–91 average "international" producer price and then summed to give a total agricultural output value for that region or for the world in terms of 1989–91 prices. This method avoids distortion caused by the use of international exchange rates. The agricultural production index includes all crop and livestock products originating in each country. The food production index covers all edible agricultural products that contain nutrients. Coffee and tea are excluded.

Average production of cereals includes cereal production for feed and seed. Cereals comprise all cereals harvested for dry grain, exclusive of crops cut for hay or harvested green. *Average production of roots and tubers* covers all root crops grown principally for human consumption, such as cassava, yucca, taro, and yams; root crops grown principally for feed are excluded. *Average production of pulses* includes those harvested for dry harvest only, such as lentils, pigeon peas, cowpeas, and vetches, and does not exclude those used for feed.

For more information, please refer to *FAOSTAT Statistical Database* at: http://www.fao.org.

Data Table 10.2

Agricultural Land and Inputs, 1982–94

Sources: Food and Agriculture Organization of the United Nations (FAO), *FAOSTAT Statistical Database* (FAO, Rome, 1997). Per capita figures: United Nations (U.N.) Population Division, *World Population Prospects, 1950–2050 (The 1996 Revision)*, on diskette (U.N., New York, 1996).

Cropland refers to land under temporary and permanent crops, temporary meadows, market and kitchen gardens, and temporarily fallow land. Permanent cropland is land under crops that do not need to be replanted after each harvest, such as cocoa, coffee, fruit trees, rubber, and vines. Human population data used to calculate hectares per capita are for 1994. For trends in cropland area, see Data Table **11.4**. *Irrigated land as a percentage of cropland* refers to areas purposely provided with water, including land flooded by river water for crop production or pasture improvement, whether or not this area is irrigated several times or only once during the year.

Annual fertilizer use refers to the application of nutrients in terms of nitrogen (N), phosphate (P_2O_5), and potash (K_2O). The fertilizer year is July 1–June 30.

Tractors generally refer to wheeled and crawler tractors used in agriculture. Garden tractors are excluded. *Harvesters* refer to harvesters and threshers.

For more information, please refer to the FAOSTAT Statistics Database at: http://www.fao.org.

Data Table 10.3

Food Security, 1982–97

Sources: Trade, food aid, calorie-supply, protein-supply, and yield data: Food and Agriculture Organization of the United Nations (FAO), *FAOSTAT Statistical Database* (FAO, Rome, 1997). Population data: United Nations (U.N.) Population Division, *World Population Prospects, 1950–2050 (The 1996 Revision)*, on diskette (U.N., New York, 1996). Feed data: Economic Research Service, U.S. Department of Agriculture (USDA), *PS&D View,* online data (USDA, Washington, D.C., 1997).

Figures shown for food trade are *net* imports or exports. Exports were subtracted from imports. Trade in cereals includes wheat and wheat flour, rice, barley, maize, rye, and oats.

Two definitions of trade are used by countries reporting trade data. "Special trade" refers only to imports for domestic consumption and exports of domestic goods. "General trade" encompasses total imports and total exports, including reexports. In some cases, trade figures include goods purchased by a country that are reexported to a third country without ever entering the purchasing country. For information on the definition used by a particular country, see the *FAO Trade Yearbook 1996* (FAO, Rome, 1997).

Average annual donations or receipts of cereals refers to the donation or concessional sale of food commodities. Cereals include wheat, rice, coarse grains, bulgur wheat, wheat flour, and the cereal component of blended foods. Food aid data are reported by donor countries and international organizations and are shown as either positive or negative numbers: receipts are shown as positive numbers and donations as negative numbers in parentheses. For countries that are both recipients and donors of food aid, donations were subtracted from receipts.

Grains fed to livestock as a percent of total grain consumption was calculated using USDA grain consumption and feed numbers. Grains include wheat, rice (milled weight), corn, barley, sorghum, millet, rye, oats, and mixed grains. Grain consumption is the total domestic use during the local marketing year of the individual country. It is the sum of feed, food, seed, and industrial uses.

Average daily per capita calorie supply and *average daily per capita protein supply* are from FAO food balance sheets. Figures are arrived at by adding values from all food sources: domestic production, international trade, stock draw-downs, and foreign aid. The quantity of food available for human consumption, as estimated by the FAO, is the amount that reaches the consumer. The calories and protein actually consumed may be lower than the figures shown, depending on how much is lost during home storage, preparation, and cooking, and how much is fed to pets and domestic animals or discarded.

Crop yields *(average yield of cereals* and *average yield of roots and tubers* per unit area*)* are calculated from production and area data. Area refers to the area harvested. Cereals include wheat, rice, corn, barley, sorghum, millet, rye, oats, and other grains such as mixed grains and buckwheat. Roots and tubers include all root crops grown principally for human consumption, including yautia and arrowroot. Root crops grown principally for feed—such as turnips, mangels, and swedes—are excluded.

For more information, please refer to the *FAOSTAT Statistical Database* at: http://www.fao. org. A PS&D (Production, Supply, and Distribution) view of USDA can be found at http://www.mannlib.cornell.edu/data-sets/international/93002/.

C hapter 11

Forests and Land Cover

Forest Cover and Change, and Forest Industry Structure, 1980–95

Sources: Food and Agriculture Organization of the United Nations and International Tropical Timber Organization

	Total Forest					Natural Forest				Plantations {a}		Forest Industry Structure {b}	
	Extent 1980 (000 ha)	Extent 1990 (000 ha)	Extent 1995 (000 ha)	Average Annual Percent Change 1980-90	1990-95	Extent 1990 (000 ha)	Extent 1995 (000 ha)	Average Annual Percent Change 1980-90	1990-95	Extent 1990 (000 ha)	Average Annual % Change 1980-90	No. of Enterprises 1995	No. of Employees 1995
WORLD {c}	X	3,510,728	3,454,382	X	(0.3)	X	X	X	X	X	X	X	X
AFRICA	585,858	538,978	520,237	(0.8)	(0.7)	534,226	515,455	(0.9)	(0.7)	4,416	4	1,438	175,718
Algeria	2,236	1,978	1,861	(1.2)	(1.2)	1,493	1,376	(2.6)	(1.6)	485	5	X	X
Angola	24,922	23,385	22,200	(0.6)	(1.0)	23,265	22,080	(0.6)	(1.0)	120	1	X	X
Benin	5,652	4,923	4,625	(1.4)	(1.2)	4,909	4,611	(1.4)	(1.3)	14	5	X	X
Botswana	15,030	14,271	13,917	(0.5)	(0.5)	14,270	13,916	(0.5)	(0.5)	1	0	X	X
Burkina Faso	4,744	4,431	4,271	(0.7)	(0.7)	4,411	4,251	(0.7)	(0.7)	20	8	X	X
Burundi	260	324	317	2.2	(0.4)	232	225	(0.6)	(0.6)	92	19	X	X
Cameroon	21,573	20,244	19,598	(0.6)	(0.6)	20,228	19,582	(0.6)	(0.6)	16	14	414	19,235
Central African Rep	31,854	30,571	29,930	(0.4)	(0.4)	30,565	29,924	(0.4)	(0.4)	6	48	X	X
Chad	12,322	11,496	11,025	(0.7)	(0.8)	11,492	11,021	(0.7)	(0.8)	4	6	X	X
Congo, Dem Rep	120,613	112,946	109,245	(0.7)	(0.7)	112,904	109,203	(0.7)	(0.7)	42	10	X	25,000 d
Congo, Rep	20,200	19,745	19,537	(0.2)	(0.2)	19,708	19,500	(0.2)	(0.2)	37	12	X	6,000 d
Côte d'Ivoire	12,128	5,623	5,469	(7.7)	(0.6)	5,560	5,403	(7.8)	(0.6)	63	7	276	14,000
Egypt	28	34	34	1.8	0.0	0	0	0.0	0.0	34	2	X	X
Equatorial Guinea	1,899	1,829	1,781	(0.4)	(0.5)	1,826	1,778	(0.4)	(0.5)	3	0	X	X
Eritrea	X	282	282	X	0.0	233	233	X	0.0	X	X	X	X
Ethiopia {e}	14,621	13,891	13,579	X	(0.5)	13,751	13,439	X	(0.5)	189	10	X	X
Gabon	19,411	18,314	17,859	(0.6)	(0.5)	18,293	17,838	(0.6)	(0.5)	21	5	330	29,938
Gambia, The	106	95	91	(1.1)	(0.9)	94	90	(1.1)	(0.9)	1	0	X	X
Ghana	10,973	9,608	9,022	(1.3)	(1.3)	9,555	8,969	(1.3)	(1.3)	53	2	411	79,500
Guinea	7,561	6,741	6,367	(1.1)	(1.1)	6,737	6,363	(1.2)	(1.1)	4	5	X	X
Guinea-Bissau	2,181	2,361	2,309	0.8	(0.4)	2,360	2,308	0.8	(0.4)	1	0	X	X
Kenya	1,358	1,309	1,292	(0.4)	(0.3)	1,191	1,174	(0.5)	(0.3)	118	1	X	X
Lesotho	1	6	6	14.6	0.0	0	0	0.0	0.0	7	16	X	X
Liberia	4,892	4,641	4,507	(0.5)	(0.6)	4,635	4,501	(0.5)	(0.6)	6	1	5	2,000 d
Libya	290	400	400	3.2	0.0	190	190	0.0	0.0	210	7	X	X
Madagascar	17,314	15,756	15,106	(0.9)	(0.8)	15,539	14,889	(1.0)	(0.9)	217	2	X	X
Malawi	4,067	3,612	3,339	(1.2)	(1.6)	3,486	3,213	(1.4)	(1.6)	126	8	X	X
Mali	13,208	12,154	11,585	(0.8)	(1.0)	12,140	11,571	(0.8)	(1.0)	14	27	X	X
Mauritania	554	556	556	0.0	0.0	554	554	0.0	0.0	2	24	X	X
Mauritius	11	12	12	1.2	0.0	3	3	(0.7)	1.4	9	2	X	X
Morocco	4,032	3,894	3,835	(0.3)	(0.3)	3,573	3,514	(0.6)	(0.3)	321	4	X	X
Mozambique	18,701	17,443	16,862	(0.7)	(0.7)	17,415	16,834	(0.7)	(0.7)	28	4	X	X
Namibia	13,000	12,584	12,374	(0.3)	(0.3)	12,584	12,374	(0.3)	(0.3)	0	0	X	X
Niger	2,554	2,562	2,562	0.0	0.0	2,550	2,550	0.0	0.0	12	10	X	X
Nigeria	16,935	14,387	13,780	(1.6)	(0.9)	14,236	13,629	(1.7)	(0.9)	151	3	X	X
Rwanda	213	252	250	1.7	(0.2)	164	162	(0.2)	(0.2)	88	7	X	X
Senegal	8,072	7,629	7,381	(0.6)	(0.7)	7,517	7,269	(0.7)	(0.7)	112	25	X	X
Sierra Leone	2,015	1,522	1,309	(2.8)	(3.0)	1,516	1,303	(2.8)	(3.0)	6	3	X	X
Somalia	786	760	754	(0.3)	(0.2)	756	750	(0.3)	(0.2)	4	0	X	X
South Africa	8,682	8,574	8,499	(0.1)	(0.2)	7,279	7,204	(0.8)	(0.2)	965	2	X	X
Sudan	47,909	43,376	41,613	(1.0)	(0.8)	43,301	41,410	(1.0)	(0.8)	203	6	X	X
Swaziland	145	146	146	0.0	0.0	74	74	0.0	0.0	72	0	X	X
Tanzania	38,004	34,123	32,510	(1.1)	(1.0)	33,969	32,356	(1.1)	(1.0)	154	8	X	X
Togo	1,576	1,338	1,245	(1.6)	(1.4)	1,317	1,224	(1.8)	(1.5)	17	12	2	45
Tunisia	521	570	555	0.9	(0.5)	369	354	(1.6)	(0.8)	201	8	X	X
Uganda	7,011	6,400	6,104	(0.9)	(0.9)	6,380	6,084	(0.9)	(1.0)	20	0	X	X
Zambia	35,958	32,720	31,398	(0.9)	(0.8)	32,677	31,355	(0.9)	(0.8)	48	6	X	X
Zimbabwe	9,576	8,960	8,710	(0.7)	(0.6)	8,876	8,626	(0.7)	(0.6)	84	2	X	X
EUROPE	X	144,044	145,988	X	0.3	X	X	X	X	X	X	X	X
Albania	X	1,046	1,046	X	0.0	X	X	X	X	X	X	X	X
Austria	X	3,877	3,877	X	0.0	X	X	X	X	X	X	X	X
Belarus, Rep	X	7,028	7,372	X	1.0	X	X	X	X	X	X	X	X
Belgium {f}	X	709	709	X	0.0	X	X	X	X	X	X	X	X
Bosnia and Herzegovina	X	2,710	2,710	X	0.0	X	X	X	X	X	X	X	X
Bulgaria	X	3,237	3,240	X	0.0	X	X	X	X	X	X	X	X
Croatia, Rep	X	1,825	1,825	X	0.0	X	X	X	X	X	X	X	X
Czech Rep	X	2,629	2,630	X	0.0	X	X	X	X	X	X	X	X
Denmark	X	417	417	X	0.0	X	X	X	X	X	X	X	X
Estonia, Rep	X	1,913	2,011	X	1.0	X	X	X	X	X	X	X	X
Finland	X	20,112	20,029	X	(0.1)	X	X	X	X	X	X	X	X
France	X	14,230	15,034	X	1.1	X	X	X	X	X	X	X	X
Germany	X	10,740	10,740	X	0.0	X	X	X	X	X	X	X	X
Greece	X	5,809	6,513	X	2.3	X	X	X	X	X	X	X	X
Hungary	X	1,675	1,719	X	0.5	X	X	X	X	X	X	X	X
Iceland	X	11	11	X	0.0	X	X	X	X	X	X	X	X
Ireland	X	500	570	X	2.6	X	X	X	X	X	X	X	X
Italy	X	6,467	6,496	X	0.1	X	X	X	X	X	X	X	X
Latvia, Rep	X	2,757	2,882	X	0.9	X	X	X	X	X	X	X	X
Lithuania, Rep	X	1,920	1,976	X	0.6	X	X	X	X	X	X	X	X
Macedonia, FYR	X	989	988	X	(0.0)	X	X	X	X	X	X	X	X
Moldova, Rep	X	357	357	X	0.0	X	X	X	X	X	X	X	X
Netherlands	X	334	334	X	0.0	X	X	X	X	X	X	X	X
Norway	X	7,938	8,073	X	0.3	X	X	X	X	X	X	X	X
Poland, Rep	X	8,672	8,732	X	0.1	X	X	X	X	X	X	X	X
Portugal	X	2,755	2,875	X	0.9	X	X	X	X	X	X	X	X
Romania	X	6,252	6,246	X	(0.0)	X	X	X	X	X	X	X	X
Russian Federation	X	763,500	763,500	X	0.0	X	X	X	X	X	X	X	X
Slovak Rep	X	1,977	1,989	X	0.1	X	X	X	X	X	X	X	X
Slovenia, Rep	X	1,077	1,077	X	0.0	X	X	X	X	X	X	X	X
Spain	X	8,388	8,388	X	0.0	X	X	X	X	X	X	X	X
Sweden	X	24,437	24,425	X	(0.0)	X	X	X	X	X	X	X	X
Switzerland	X	1,130	1,130	X	0.0	X	X	X	X	X	X	X	X
Ukraine	X	9,213	9,240	X	0.1	X	X	X	X	X	X	X	X
United Kingdom	X	2,326	2,390	X	0.5	X	X	X	X	X	X	X	X
Yugoslavia, Fed Rep	X	1,769	1,769	X	0.0	X	X	X	X	X	X	X	X

Data Table 11.1 continued

	Forest Area											Forest Industry Structure {b}	
	Total Forest					Natural Forest				Plantations {a}			
	Extent 1980 (000 ha)	Extent 1990 (000 ha)	Extent 1995 (000 ha)	Average Annual Percent Change 1980-90	1990-95	Extent 1990 (000 ha)	Extent 1995 (000 ha)	Average Annual Percent Change 1980-90	1990-95	Extent 1990 (000 ha)	Average Annual % Change 1980-90	No. of Enterprises 1995	No. of Employees 1995
NORTH AMERICA	X	**453,270**	**457,086**	X	**0.2**	X	X	X	X	X	X	X	X
Canada	X	243,698	244,571	X	0.1	X	X	X	X	X	X	X	X
United States	X	209,572	212,515	X	0.3	X	X	X	X	X	X	X	X
CENTRAL AMERICA	**88,344**	**84,628**	**79,443**	**(0.4)**	**(1.3)**	**84,142**	**78,958**	**(0.2)**	**(1.3)**	**501**	**8**	**136**	**11,313**
Belize	2,048	1,995	1,962	(0.3)	(0.3)	1,993	1,960	(0.3)	(0.3)	2	0	X	X
Costa Rica	1,925	1,455	1,248	(2.8)	(3.1)	1,427	1,220	(3.0)	(3.1)	28	27	X	X
Cuba	1,998	1,960	1,842	(0.2)	(1.2)	1,715	1,597	(1.0)	(1.4)	245	8	X	X
Dominican Rep	1,432	1,714	1,582	1.8	(1.6)	1,707	1,575	1.8	(1.6)	7	6	X	X
El Salvador	156	124	105	(2.3)	(3.3)	120	101	(2.5)	(3.5)	4	15	X	X
Guatemala	5,049	4,253	3,841	(1.7)	(2.0)	4,225	3,813	(1.8)	(2.1)	28	10	X	X
Haiti	38	25	21	(4.3)	(3.5)	17	13	(8.1)	(5.2)	8	33	X	X
Honduras	5,720	4,626	4,115	(2.1)	(2.3)	4,623	4,112	(2.1)	(2.3)	3	24	X	10,000 d
Jamaica	516	254	175	(7.1)	(7.5)	239	160	(7.5)	(8.0)	15	5	X	X
Mexico	55,423	57,927	55,387	0.4	(0.9)	57,818	55,278	0.4	(0.9)	109	7	X	X
Nicaragua	7,255	6,314	5,560	(1.4)	(2.5)	6,300	5,546	(1.4)	(2.6)	14	27	X	X
Panama	3,764	3,118	2,800	(1.9)	(2.2)	3,112	2,794	(1.9)	(2.2)	6	9	4	363
Trinidad and Tobago	204	174	161	(1.6)	(1.6)	161	148	(1.8)	(1.6)	13	1	132	950
SOUTH AMERICA	**954,771**	**894,466**	**870,594**	**(0.7)**	**(0.5)**	**887,187**	**863,315**	**(0.7)**	**(0.5)**	**7,264**	**5**	**6,426**	**806,102**
Argentina	36,527	34,389	33,942	(0.6)	(0.3)	33,842	33,395	(0.6)	(0.3)	547	1	X	X
Bolivia	55,582	51,217	48,310	(0.8)	(1.2)	51,189	48,282	(0.8)	(1.2)	28	4	X	100,000 d
Brazil	600,762	563,911	551,139	(0.6)	(0.5)	559,011	546,229	(0.7)	(0.5)	4,900	5	X	400,000 d
Chile	8,087	8,038	7,892	(0.1)	(0.4)	7,023	6,877	(0.8)	(0.4)	1,015	8	X	X
Colombia	57,771	54,299	52,988	(0.6)	(0.5)	54,173	52,862	(0.6)	(0.5)	126	12	5,114	18,482
Ecuador	14,372	12,082	11,137	(1.7)	(1.6)	12,037	11,092	(1.8)	(1.6)	45	4	X	40,000 d
Guyana	18,597	18,620	18,577	0.0	(0.0)	18,612	18,569	0.0	(0.0)	8	29	529	13,320
Paraguay	16,886	13,160	11,527	(2.5)	(2.6)	13,151	11,518	(2.5)	(2.7)	9	15	X	X
Peru	70,714	68,646	67,562	(0.3)	(0.3)	68,462	67,378	(0.3)	(0.3)	184	7	367	219,250
Suriname	14,901	14,782	14,721	(0.1)	(0.1)	14,774	14,713	(0.1)	(0.1)	8	4	X	X
Uruguay	803	816	814	0.2	(0.0)	660	658	(0.1)	(0.1)	156	1	X	X
Venezuela	51,768	46,512	43,995	(1.1)	(1.1)	46,259	43,742	(1.1)	(1.1)	253	11	416	15,050
ASIA	X	**490,812**	**474,172**	X	**(0.7)**	**398,985**	**255,751**	X	**(8.9)**	**56,115**	**7**	**4,556**	**2,582,037**
Afghanistan, Islamic State	1,203	1,990	1,398	5.0	(7.1)	1,982	1,390	5.1	(7.1)	8	0	X	X
Armenia, Rep	X	292	334	X	2.7	X	X	X	X	X	X	X	X
Azerbaijan	X	990	990	X	0.0	X	X	X	X	X	X	X	X
Bangladesh	1,258	1,054	1,010	(1.8)	(0.9)	819	700	(3.3)	(3.1)	235	7	X	X
Bhutan	2,975	2,803	2,756	(0.6)	(0.3)	2,799	2,748	(0.6)	(0.4)	4	7	X	X
Cambodia	13,484	10,649	9,830	(2.4)	(1.6)	10,642	9,823	(2.4)	(1.6)	7	0	X	X
China	126,398	133,756	133,323	0.6	(0.1)	101,925	99,523	(0.4)	(0.5)	31,831	4	X	X
Georgia	X	2,988	2,988	X	0.0	X	X	X	X	X	X	X	X
India	58,259	64,969	65,005	1.1	0.0	51,739	50,385	(0.6)	(0.5)	13,230	14	X	500,000 d
Indonesia	124,476	115,213	109,791	(0.8)	(1.0)	109,088	103,666	(1.1)	(1.0)	6,125	8	X	1,600,000 d
Iran, Islamic Rep	2,016	1,686	1,544	(1.8)	(1.8)	1,607	1,465	(2.1)	(1.9)	79	10	X	X
Iraq	83	83	83	0.0	0.0	69	69	0.0	0.0	14	0	X	X
Israel	X	102	102	X	0.0	X	X	X	X	X	X	X	X
Japan	X	25,212	25,146	X	(0.1)	X	X	X	X	X	X	X	X
Jordan	50	51	45	0.3	(2.5)	28	22	(2.2)	(4.8)	23	5	X	X
Kazakstan, Rep	X	9,540	10,504	X	1.9	X	X	X	X	X	X	X	X
Korea, Dem People's Rep	5,400	6,170	6,170	1.3	0.0	4,700	4,700	0.0	0.0	1,470	7	X	X
Korea, Rep	6,304	7,691	7,626	2.0	(0.2)	6,291	6,226	(0.0)	(0.2)	0	0	X	X
Kuwait	0	5	5	33.8	0.0	0	0	0.0	0.0	5	34	X	X
Kyrgyz Rep	X	730	730	X	0.0	X	X	X	X	X	X	X	X
Lao People's Dem Rep	14,470	13,177	12,435	(0.9)	(1.2)	13,173	12,431	(0.9)	(1.2)	4	4	X	X
Lebanon	84	78	52	(0.7)	(8.1)	65	39	(0.8)	(10.3)	13	0	X	X
Malaysia	21,564	17,472	15,471	(2.1)	(2.4)	17,391	15,371	(2.1)	(2.5)	81	15	3,499	204,163
Mongolia	9,406	9,406	9,406	0.0	0.0	9,406	9,406	0.0	0.0	0	0	X	X
Myanmar	32,901	29,088	27,151	(1.2)	(1.4)	28,853	26,875	(1.3)	(1.4)	235	18	109	13,224
Nepal	5,580	5,096	4,822	(0.9)	(1.1)	5,040	4,766	(1.0)	(1.1)	56	14	X	X
Oman	X	0	0	X	0.0	0	0	0.0	0.0	0	0	X	X
Pakistan	2,749	2,023	1,748	(3.1)	(2.9)	1,855	1,580	(3.5)	(3.2)	168	3	X	X
Philippines	11,194	8,078	6,766	(3.3)	(3.5)	7,875	6,563	(3.3)	(3.6)	203	0	203	204,650
Saudi Arabia	248	231	222	(0.7)	(0.8)	230	221	(0.7)	(0.8)	1	0	X	X
Singapore	4	4	4	0.0	0.0	4	4	0.7	(1.4)	0	0	X	X
Sri Lanka	2,094	1,897	1,796	(1.0)	(1.1)	1,758	1,657	(1.4)	(1.2)	139	6	X	X
Syrian Arab Rep	191	245	219	2.5	(2.2)	118	92	(3.2)	(5.0)	127	15	X	X
Tajikistan, Rep	X	410	410	X	0.0	X	X	X	X	X	X	X	X
Thailand	18,123	13,277	11,630	(3.1)	(2.6)	12,748	11,101	(3.4)	(2.8)	529	8	745	60,000 d
Turkey	X	8,856	8,856	X	0.0	X	X	X	X	X	X	X	X
Turkmenistan, Rep	X	3,754	3,754	X	0.0	X	X	X	X	X	X	X	X
United Arab Emirates	1	60	60	46.6	0.0	0	0	0.0	0.0	60	47	X	X
Uzbekistan, Rep	X	7,989	9,119	X	2.6	X	X	X	X	X	X	X	X
Vietnam	10,663	9,793	9,117	(0.9)	(1.4)	8,323	7,647	(1.5)	(1.7)	1,470	4	X	X
Yemen	9	9	9	0.0	0.0	9	9	0.0	0.0	0	0	X	X
OCEANIA	X	**91,149**	**90,695**	X	**(0.1)**	**42,507**	**41,752**	**0.3**	**(0.4)**	**149**	**8**	**760**	**19,850**
Australia	X	40,823	40,908	X	0.0	X	X	X	X	X	X	X	X
Fiji	839	853	835	0.2	(0.4)	775	757	(0.5)	(0.5)	78	10	48	3,800
New Zealand	X	7,667	7,884	X	0.6	X	X	X	X	X	X	X	X
Papua New Guinea	37,145	37,605	36,939	0.1	(0.4)	37,575	36,909	0.1	(0.4)	30	7	712	16,050
Solomon Islands	2,453	2,412	2,389	(0.2)	(0.2)	2,394	2,371	(0.2)	(0.2)	16	2	X	X
TROPICAL REGIONS	**1,930,061**	**1,796,927**	**1,733,959**	**(0.7)**	**(0.7)**	**1,766,116**	**1,701,589**	**(0.8)**	**(0.7)**	**30,801**	**9**	**X**	**X**
NONTROPICAL REGIONS	X	**1,713,801**	**1,720,423**	X	**0.1**	X	X	X	X	X	X	X	X

Notes: a. Plantation figures for 1995 are approximately the difference between total and natural forest. They are not included in this table because FAO considers them to be unreliable. b. Only includes International Tropical Timber Organization (ITTO) producer countries. c. World and regional totals include countries not listed. d. ITTO estimate. e. 1980 figures include Eritrea. f. Includes Luxembourg.

Forest Ecosystems, 1996

Sources: World Conservation Monitoring Centre, Centre for International Forestry Research, World Resources Institute, and Food and Agriculture Organization of the United Nations

	Land Area (000 hectares)	Original Forest as a % of Land Area {a}	Closed Forests — Forests as a % of Original Forest — Current Forests {b} 1996	Frontier Forests {c} 1996	Percent Frontier Forests {c} Threatened 1996	Mangroves Area (000 ha)	Mangroves Percent Protected	Tropical Forests Area (000 ha)	Tropical Forests Percent Protected	Nontropical Forests Area (000 ha)	Nontropical Forests Percent Protected	Sparse Trees and Parkland Area (000 ha)	Sparse Trees and Parkland Percent Protected
WORLD {d}	13,048,300	47.7	53.4	21.7	39.5	16,945	13.3	1,407,649	11.7	1,823,787	6.0	541,616	5.5
AFRICA	2,963,468	22.9	33.9	7.8	76.8	3,801	1.4	448,197	9.1	8,249	2.0	69,710	11.3
Algeria	238,174	4.6	12.0	0.0	0.0	0	0.0	0	0.0	2,694	3.7	1	83.3
Angola	124,670	19.8	15.3	0.0	0.0	0	0.0	37,564	2.6	0	0.0	0	0.0
Benin	11,062	15.5	3.5	0.0	0.0	0	0.0	1,516	18.2	0	0.0	585	2.3
Botswana	56,673	2.1	100.0	0.0	0.0	0	0.0	12,123	2.2	0	0.0	0	0.0
Burkina Faso	27,360	0.0	0.0	0.0	0.0	0	0.0	0	0.0	0	0.0	5,667	15.9
Burundi	2,568	46.3	3.5	0.0	0.0	0	0.0	219	18.2	0	0.0	139	2.6
Cameroon	46,540	80.4	42.4	7.9	97.4	227	1.9	20,009	6.0	0	0.0	2,416	21.8
Central African Rep	62,298	51.8	15.9	4.4	100.0	0	0.0	17,101	20.1	0	0.0	1,451	47.7
Chad	125,920	0.0	0.0	0.0	0.0	0	0.0	3,516	3.6	0	0.0	2,857	0.7
Congo, Dem Rep	226,705	82.5	60.4	15.6	70.4	22	0.0	135,071	6.6	0	0.0	172	40.0
Congo, Rep	34,150	100.0	67.8	28.7	64.6	19	75.8	24,321	4.4	0	0.0	0	0.0
Côte d'Ivoire	31,800	74.9	9.9	2.2	100.0	0	0.0	2,702	22.8	0	0.0	625	18.4
Egypt	99,545	0.6	0.0	0.0	0.0	0	0.0	134	0.0	4	0.0	0	0.0
Equatorial Guinea	2,805	95.6	38.4	0.0	0.0	25	0.0	1,749	0.0	0	0.0	0	0.0
Eritrea	X	X	X	X	X	0	0.0	1	0.0	0	0.0	0	0.0
Ethiopia {e}	110,000	24.5	17.3	0.0	0.0	0	0.0	11,937	18.8	0	0.0	4,804	21.4
Gabon	25,767	100.0	90.4	32.4	100.0	147	3.0	21,481	3.6	0	0.0	0	0.0
Gambia, The	1,000	39.1	61.9	0.0	0.0	51	4.8	188	5.1	0	0.0	244	2.5
Ghana	22,754	65.9	8.6	0.0	0.0	0	0.0	1,694	7.1	0	0.0	336	16.7
Guinea	24,572	75.6	5.0	0.0	0.0	316	0.0	3,073	1.1	0	0.0	2,723	1.2
Guinea-Bissau	2,812	100.0	33.7	0.0	0.0	317	0.0	1,141	0.0	0	0.0	550	0.0
Kenya	56,914	16.8	18.5	0.0	0.0	0	0.0	3,423	8.3	0	0.0	2,754	2.8
Lesotho	3,035	2.4	0.0	0.0	0.0	0	0.0	89	8.7	0	0.0	0	0.0
Liberia	9,632	99.6	44.2	0.0	0.0	0	0.0	3,149	2.9	0	0.0	1	0.0
Libya	175,954	0.8	0.0	0.0	0.0	0	0.0	0	0.0	53	0.0	0	0.0
Madagascar	58,154	92.6	13.1	0.0	0.0	310	0.2	6,940	5.5	0	0.0	0	0.0
Malawi	9,408	12.2	0.0	0.0	0.0	0	0.0	3,830	8.5	0	0.0	0	0.0
Mali	122,019	0.0	0.0	0.0	0.0	0	0.0	6,132	2.3	0	0.0	336	0.4
Mauritania	102,522	0.0	0.0	0.0	0.0	X	X	X	X	X	X	X	X
Mauritius	203	X	X	X	X	X	X	X	X	X	X	X	X
Morocco	44,630	21.6	7.3	0.0	0.0	0	0.0	0	0.0	1,862	2.6	0	0.0
Mozambique	78,409	33.2	13.6	0.0	0.0	565	3.7	20,863	7.5	0	0.0	14,414	6.6
Namibia	82,329	0.0	95.3	0.0	0.0	0	0.0	3,436	10.6	0	0.0	0	0.0
Niger	126,670	0.0	0.0	0.0	0.0	0	0.0	27	15.6	0	0.0	0	0.0
Nigeria	91,077	45.1	10.7	0.6	100.0	1,145	0.0	11,634	7.4	0	0.0	10,588	4.0
Rwanda	2,467	36.1	16.1	0.0	0.0	0	0.0	291	77.0	0	0.0	162	1.8
Senegal	19,253	14.2	16.0	0.0	0.0	158	2.9	2,076	7.0	0	0.0	8,816	13.1
Sierra Leone	7,162	100.0	9.7	0.0	0.0	176	0.8	260	20.3	0	0.0	104	0.0
Somalia	62,734	4.2	0.0	0.0	0.0	0	0.0	11,800	1.1	0	0.0	1,530	0.9
South Africa	122,104	12.8	0.2	0.0	0.0	0	0.0	10,333	5.2	52	26.4	0	0.0
Sudan	237,600	1.2	0.0	0.0	0.0	0	0.0	12,288	12.3	0	0.0	5,870	8.9
Swaziland	1,720	21.5	0.0	0.0	0.0	0	0.0	286	3.2	0	0.0	0	0.0
Tanzania	88,359	22.4	9.1	0.0	0.0	323	0.4	14,356	15.8	0	0.0	583	3.3
Togo	5,439	32.9	7.0	0.0	0.0	0	0.0	224	2.6	0	0.0	91	9.1
Tunisia	15,536	18.1	4.7	0.0	0.0	0	0.0	0	0.0	300	2.2	0	0.0
Uganda	19,965	70.0	4.4	0.0	0.0	0	0.0	3,772	17.0	0	0.0	1,850	65.2
Zambia	74,339	7.1	70.1	0.0	0.0	0	0.0	21,989	31.9	0	0.0	39	14.1
Zimbabwe	38,685	7.0	67.3	0.0	0.0	0	0.0	15,397	12.2	0	0.0	0	0.0
EUROPE	2,260,320	72.7	58.4	21.3	18.7	0	0.0	0	0.0	1,019,178	2.9	10,350	1.0
Albania	2,740	92.5	37.3	0.0	0.0	0	0.0	0	0.0	1,066	1.2	0	0.0
Austria	8,273	95.1	52.8	0.0	0.0	0	0.0	0	0.0	3,593	20.9	0	0.0
Belarus, Rep	20,748	91.1	27.2	0.0	0.0	0	0.0	0	0.0	6,280	6.5	0	0.0
Belgium	30,230	9.5	21.0	0.0	0.0	0	0.0	0	0.0	687	7.8	0	0.0
Bosnia and Herzegovina	5,100	X	X	X	X	0	0.0	0	0.0	2,303	1.0	0	0.0
Bulgaria	11,055	92.3	31.7	0.0	0.0	0	0.0	0	0.0	3,787	5.9	0	0.0
Croatia, Rep	5,592	X	X	X	X	0	0.0	0	0.0	1,391	9.9	0	0.0
Czech Rep	7,728	X	X	X	X	0	0.0	0	0.0	2,481	27.5	0	0.0
Denmark	4,243	88.5	0.8	0.0	0.0	0	0.0	0	0.0	459	4.2	0	0.0
Estonia, Rep	4,227	96.0	29.4	0.0	0.0	0	0.0	0	0.0	1,524	6.7	0	0.0
Finland	30,459	100.0	82.3	1.1	100.0	0	0.0	0	0.0	25,309	5.8	0	0.0
France	55,010	95.3	16.5	0.0	0.0	0	0.0	0	0.0	10,831	13.7	0	0.0
Germany	34,927	92.6	26.3	0.0	0.0	0	0.0	0	0.0	10,401	24.8	0	0.0
Greece	12,890	84.3	17.0	0.0	0.0	0	0.0	0	0.0	4,423	1.7	0	0.0
Hungary	9,234	50.4	8.2	0.0	0.0	0	0.0	0	0.0	777	26.1	0	0.0
Iceland	10,025	43.7	0.0	0.0	0.0	X	X	X	X	X	X	X	X
Ireland	6,889	64.4	3.6	0.0	0.0	0	0.0	0	0.0	457	2.1	0	0.0
Italy	29,406	94.5	20.4	0.0	0.0	0	0.3	0	0.0	6,757	6.1	0	0.0
Latvia, Rep	6,205	100.0	19.8	0.0	0.0	0	0.0	0	0.0	1,624	10.1	0	0.0
Lithuania, Rep	6,480	99.3	16.0	0.0	0.0	0	0.0	0	0.0	1,509	10.3	0	0.0
Macedonia, FYR	2,543	X	X	X	X	0	0.0	0	0.0	1,091	9.9	0	0.0
Moldova, Rep	3,297	48.3	3.7	0.0	0.0	0	0.0	0	0.0	143	5.4	0	0.0
Netherlands	3,392	46.2	4.8	0.0	0.0	0	0.0	0	0.0	235	7.4	0	0.0
Norway	30,683	33.8	90.4	0.0	0.0	0	0.0	0	0.0	8,139	2.0	0	0.0
Poland, Rep	30,442	95.6	22.2	0.0	0.0	0	0.0	0	0.0	8,939	12.9	0	0.0
Portugal	9,150	91.2	9.4	0.0	0.0	0	0.0	0	0.0	2,661	5.6	0	0.0
Romania	23,034	75.2	41.5	0.0	0.0	0	0.0	0	0.0	8,137	2.5	0	0.0
Russian Federation	1,688,850	69.6	68.7	29.3	18.6	0	0.0	0	0.0	815,551	1.8	10,350	1.0
Slovak Rep	4,808	X	X	X	X	0	0.0	0	0.0	2,308	29.6	0	0.0
Slovenia, Rep	2,012	X	X	X	X	0	0.0	0	0.0	696	8.9	0	0.0
Spain	49,944	94.2	15.1	0.0	0.0	0	0.0	0	0.0	14,024	10.8	0	0.0
Sweden	41,162	93.3	86.0	2.9	100.0	0	0.0	0	0.0	29,364	1.6	0	0.0
Switzerland	3,955	85.5	44.8	0.0	0.0	0	0.0	0	0.0	1,309	12.6	0	0.0
Ukraine	57,935	45.7	20.4	0.0	0.0	0	0.0	0	0.0	7,046	1.6	0	0.0
United Kingdom	24,160	77.5	6.0	0.0	0.0	0	0.0	0	0.0	2,303	20.7	0	0.0
Yugoslavia, Fed Rep	10,200	X	X	X	X	0	0.0	0	0.0	3,664	3.4	0	0.0

	Land Area (000 hectares)	Original Forest as a % of Land Area {a}	Closed Forests — Forests as a % of Original Forest — Current Forests {b} 1996	Closed Forests — Frontier Forests {c} 1996	Percent Frontier Forests {c} Threatened 1996	Mangroves Area (000 ha)	Mangroves Percent Protected	Tropical Forests Area (000 ha)	Tropical Forests Percent Protected	Nontropical Forests Area (000 ha)	Nontropical Forests Percent Protected	Sparse Trees and Parkland Area (000 ha)	Sparse Trees and Parkland Percent Protected
NORTH AMERICA	**1,838,009**	**59.7**	**77.3**	**34.1**	**26.2**	**199**	**60.0**	**443**	**6.7**	**683,700**	**8.9**	**148,827**	**5.7**
Canada	922,097	65.8	91.2	56.5	20.9	0	0.0	0	0.0	404,313	7.9	143,573	5.6
United States	915,912	53.5	60.2	6.3	84.7	199	60.0	443	6.7	279,386	10.4	5,254	9.0
CENTRAL AMERICA	**264,835**	**67.2**	**54.5**	**9.7**	**87.0**	**1,679**	**14.9**	**71,893**	**12.3**	**21,293**	**3.1**	**26**	**0.0**
Belize	2,280	91.8	95.7	35.5	66.1	30	9.6	1,440	43.6	0	0.0	0	0.0
Costa Rica	5,106	98.4	34.9	9.5	100.0	53	1.9	1,464	44.8	0	0.0	0	0.0
Cuba	10,982	90.4	28.8	0.0	0.0	767	7.0	1,761	15.3	0	0.0	0	0.0
Dominican Rep	4,838	97.7	25.1	0.0	0.0	70	52.1	1,171	16.9	0	0.0	0	0.0
El Salvador	2,072	99.4	9.9	0.0	0.0	45	0.0	111	4.5	0	0.0	0	0.0
Guatemala	10,843	98.7	46.2	2.2	100.0	16	16.7	3,862	31.9	0	0.0	0	0.0
Haiti	2,756	93.2	0.8	0.0	0.0	0	0.0	64	2.0	0	0.0	0	0.0
Honduras	11,189	99.5	51.6	16.4	100.0	231	42.2	5,273	18.3	0	0.0	0	0.0
Jamaica	1,083	96.7	35.6	0.0	0.0	9	10.8	399	20.5	0	0.0	0	0.0
Mexico	190,869	55.7	63.4	8.1	77.0	0	0.0	45,765	4.3	21,293	3.1	0	0.0
Nicaragua	12,140	100.0	44.3	21.6	100.0	94	14.8	5,322	24.7	0	0.0	0	0.0
Panama	7,443	97.2	62.0	34.8	100.0	180	2.1	3,744	30.9	0	0.0	0	0.0
Trinidad and Tobago	513	93.5	35.5	0.0	0.0	5	5.9	124	7.0	0	0.0	0	0.0
SOUTH AMERICA	**1,752,925**	**55.6**	**69.1**	**45.6**	**54.0**	**2,929**	**32.1**	**620,514**	**12.2**	**39,291**	**15.7**	**168,216**	**2.4**
Argentina	273,669	5.5	59.5	6.3	99.9	0	0.0	4,360	5.5	19,094	10.1	6,392	9.4
Bolivia	108,438	53.9	77.2	43.6	96.9	0	0.0	68,638	12.1	0	0.0	0	0.0
Brazil	845,651	64.0	66.4	42.2	47.8	1,340	28.4	301,273	6.9	2,613	6.9	137,494	1.3
Chile	74,880	39.7	40.6	54.5	76.0	0	0.0	0	0.0	14,526	27.1	263	0.6
Colombia	103,870	92.2	53.5	36.4	18.7	368	22.2	53,186	10.8	0	0.0	0	0.0
Ecuador	27,684	78.8	66.4	36.9	99.5	238	14.2	13,508	23.9	0	0.0	755	46.9
Guyana	19,685	98.9	97.4	81.8	41.1	159	0.0	17,844	1.3	0	0.0	0	0.0
Paraguay	39,730	21.9	44.5	0.0	0.0	0	0.0	9,290	2.6	2,848	4.9	16,253	2.7
Peru	128,000	74.4	86.6	56.7	99.6	0	0.0	75,636	5.1	0	0.0	2,660	3.0
Suriname	15,600	91.7	95.6	92.2	21.7	109	35.9	13,219	4.0	0	0.0	0	0.0
Uruguay	17,481	1.6	0.0	0.0	0.0	0	0.0	2	0.0	97	1.0	325	1.6
Venezuela	88,205	74.7	83.6	59.3	37.3	621	65.1	55,615	59.0	0	0.0	3,997	18.6
ASIA	**3,085,414**	**49.1**	**28.2**	**5.3**	**63.1**	**4,033**	**26.5**	**210,720**	**16.4**	**145,101**	**5.1**	**42,384**	**7.0**
Afghanistan, Islamic State	65,209	48.1	6.5	0.0	0.0	0	0.0	0	0.0	2,076	0.0	0	0.0
Armenia, Rep	2,820	45.6	21.1	0.0	0.0	0	0.0	0	0.0	355	10.1	0	0.0
Azerbaijan	8,660	32.0	32.0	0.0	0.0	0	0.0	0	0.0	1,133	0.0	0	0.0
Bangladesh	13,017	100.0	7.9	3.8	100.0	440	8.3	862	3.7	0	0.0	0	0.0
Bhutan	4,700	67.3	61.8	24.0	100.0	0	0.0	966	22.9	1,129	37.6	0	0.0
Cambodia	17,652	100.0	65.1	10.3	100.0	47	66.5	11,516	25.6	0	0.0	0	0.0
China {f}	929,100	51.8	21.6	1.8	92.8	0	0.0	109	13.0	82,710	3.9	26,715	4.7
Georgia	6,970	76.6	57.3	0.0	0.0	0	0.0	0	0.0	3,158	0.0	0	0.0
India	297,319	79.0	20.5	1.3	57.2	304	49.6	44,450	8.9	9,260	8.3	0	0.0
Indonesia	181,157	100.0	64.6	28.5	53.8	2,390	32.8	88,744	20.9	0	0.0	0	0.0
Iran, Islamic Rep	162,200	43.1	3.3	0.0	0.0	0	0.0	0	0.0	2,348	12.0	0	0.0
Iraq	43,737	13.4	0.0	0.0	0.0	X	X	X	X	X	X	X	X
Israel	2,062	86.6	0.0	0.0	0.0	X	X	X	X	X	0.0	X	X
Japan	37,652	91.4	58.2	0.0	0.0	0	0.0	0	0.0	5,677	9.7	0	0.0
Jordan	8,893	13.1	0.0	0.0	0.0	X	X	X	0.0	X	0.0	X	0.0
Kazakstan, Rep	267,073	2.6	22.9	2.9	100.0	0	0.0	0	0.0	2,638	9.6	0	0.0
Korea, Dem People's Rep	12,041	97.3	38.7	0.0	0.0	0	0.0	0	0.0	3,967	1.1	506	0.0
Korea, Rep	9,873	88.5	16.5	0.0	0.0	0	0.0	0	0.0	1,426	3.4	0	0.0
Kuwait	1,782	0.0	0.0	0.0	0.0	X	X	X	0.0	X	0.0	X	X
Kyrgyz Rep	19,180	8.4	14.0	0.0	0.0	0	0.0	0	0.0	785	0.2	0	0.0
Lao People's Dem Rep	23,080	99.9	30.0	2.1	100.0	0	0.0	3,639	23.0	849	5.0	0	0.0
Lebanon	1,023	73.7	0.7	0.0	0.0	0	0.0	0	0.0	36	0.0	0	0.0
Malaysia	32,855	99.5	63.8	14.5	48.5	166	6.6	13,007	11.7	0	0.0	0	0.0
Mongolia	156,650	22.5	49.6	8.2	0.0	0	0.0	0	0.0	2,636	25.2	14,697	11.2
Myanmar	65,755	100.0	40.6	0.0	0.0	0	0.0	20,661	0.8	9,574	2.0	0	0.0
Nepal	14,300	83.6	22.4	0.0	0.0	0	0.0	1,162	18.8	2,660	20.7	0	0.0
Oman	21,246	0.0	0.0	0.0	0.0	X	X	X	X	X	X	X	X
Pakistan	77,088	44.8	5.8	0.0	0.0	73	39.9	807	0.6	2,083	4.7	0	0.0
Philippines	29,817	95.3	6.0	0.0	0.0	2	0.0	2,402	5.2	0	0.0	0	0.0
Saudi Arabia	214,969	0.0	0.0	0.0	0.0	X	X	X	X	X	X	X	X
Singapore	61	78.8	3.1	0.0	0.0	X	X	X	X	X	X	X	X
Sri Lanka	6,463	94.7	18.1	11.9	76.2	9	9.2	1,581	27.6	0	0.0	466	19.4
Syrian Arab Rep	18,378	19.2	0.0	0.0	0.0	0	0.0	0	0.0	47	0.0	0	0.0
Tajikistan, Rep	14,060	50.7	4.2	0.0	0.0	X	X	X	X	X	X	X	X
Thailand	51,089	100.0	22.2	4.9	100.0	509	5.0	16,237	31.2	361	11.3	0	0.0
Turkey	76,963	66.4	11.3	0.0	0.0	0	0.0	0	0.0	8,390	1.2	0	0.0
Turkmenistan, Rep	46,993	7.9	4.1	0.0	0.0	0	0.0	0	0.0	216	0.7	0	0.0
United Arab Emirates	8,360	0.0	0.0	0.0	0.0	X	X	X	X	X	X	X	X
Uzbekistan, Rep	41,424	2.8	10.2	0.0	0.0	0	0.0	0	0.0	231	0.0	0	0.0
Vietnam	32,549	99.7	17.2	1.9	100.0	73	2.2	4,218	10.3	723	8.8	0	0.0
Yemen	52,797	0.0	0.0	0.0	0.0	X	X	X	X	X	X	X	X
OCEANIA	**849,135**	**16.9**	**64.9**	**22.3**	**76.3**	**5,466**	**6.6**	**53,560**	**9.1**	**27,088**	**18.7**	**102,126**	**6.1**
Australia	768,230	9.3	64.3	17.8	62.8	4,902	5.2	14,088	7.3	22,877	14.1	101,485	6.1
Fiji	1,827	84.1	49.9	0.0	0.0	52	0.0	641	1.0	0	0.0	0	0.0
New Zealand	26,799	84.7	29.2	8.9	100.0	0	0.0	0	0.0	4,212	43.8	0	0.0
Papua New Guinea	45,286	96.0	85.4	39.6	83.5	459	23.2	35,791	10.7	0	0.0	0	0.0
Solomon Islands	2,799	82.1	93.9	0.0	0.0	0	0.0	2,669	0.0	0	0.0	0	0.0

Notes: a. Original forest is that estimated to have covered the planet 8,000 years ago given current climate conditions. b. Includes frontier and nonfrontier forests. c. Frontier forests are large, relatively undisturbed forest ecosystems. d. World and regional totals include countries not listed here. Antarctica is excluded from world total. e. Land area and closed forest data include Eritrea. f. Land area and closed forest data include Taiwan.

Wood Production and Trade, 1983–95

Source: Food and Agriculture Organization of the United Nations

	Total Cubic Meters (000) 1993-95	Total Percent Change Since 1983-85	Fuel and Charcoal Cubic Meters (000) 1993-95	Fuel and Charcoal Percent Change Since 1983-85	Industrial Roundwood Cubic Meters (000) 1993-95	Industrial Roundwood Percent Change Since 1983-85	Sawnwood Cubic Meters (000) 1993-95	Sawnwood Percent Change Since 1983-85	Paper Metric Tons (000) 1993-95	Paper Percent Change Since 1983-85	Quantity {a} Cubic Meters (000) 1993-95	Quantity {a} Percent Change Since 1983-85	Balance of Trade {b} Value (million US$) 1993-95	Balance of Trade {b} Percent Change Since 1983-85
WORLD {c}	3,374,100	8	1,891,608	17	1,482,492	(1)	430,894	(6)	272,082	46				
AFRICA	567,133	33	502,378	34	64,754	23	8,761	18	2,580	24	(5,717)	42	938,740	221
Algeria	2,489	35	2,081	29	408	81	13	0	86	(27)	51	(79)	(14,133)	(57)
Angola	6,794	32	5,830	33	964	28	5	15	0	0	(1)	3,926	612	9,563
Benin	5,725	36	5,413	36	312	44	24	227	X	X	(1)	X	30	X
Botswana	1,538	39	1,443	39	95	39	X	X	X	X	X	X	X	X
Burkina Faso	9,770	31	9,328	31	442	30	2	(10)	X	X	X	X	X	X
Burundi	4,828	36	4,725	35	104	145	21	681	X	X	X	X	X	X
Cameroon	15,263	30	12,065	32	3,197	24	1,088	136	5	0	(991)	82	159,354	262
Central African Rep	3,795	15	3,250	15	545	13	68	16	X	X	(62)	(24)	16,676	33
Chad	4,407	26	3,773	26	633	28	2	135	X	X	X	X	X	X
Congo, Dem Rep	3,668	46	2,288	34	1,380	73	57	(3)	X	X	(286)	20	78,364	216
Congo, Rep	45,830	43	42,599	44	3,231	28	95	(19)	3	29	(93)	(2)	30,670	261
Côte d'Ivoire	14,298	18	11,204	44	3,094	(29)	667	(7)	X	X	(371)	(81)	53,180	(69)
Egypt	2,643	27	2,520	27	123	27	X	X	220	65	262	(11)	(18,478)	(62)
Equatorial Guinea	721	26	447	0	274	122	5	(83)	X	X	(213)	190	23,071	229
Eritrea	X	X	X	X	X	X	X	X	X	X	X	X	X	X
Ethiopia {d}	46,002	24	44,279	25	1,724	(4)	35	(21)	8	(21)	(2)	X	122	X
Gabon	4,717	36	2,813	35	1,905	37	165	59	X	X	(1,255)	0	349,682	241
Gambia, The	1,206	41	1,094	31	112	442	1	0	X	X	0	X	(38)	X
Ghana	25,990	59	24,331	58	1,660	67	727	141	X	X	(447)	413	86,131	1,260
Guinea	4,794	39	4,191	44	603	16	74	(18)	X	X	(17)	38	4,012	234
Guinea-Bissau	577	4	422	0	155	16	16	0	X	X	(7)	X	1,534	X
Kenya	40,353	42	38,462	42	1,891	28	185	7	132	81	(0)	(99)	35	(95)
Lesotho	690	32	690	32	X	X	X	X	X	X	X	X	X	X
Liberia	6,181	45	5,200	38	981	101	90	(44)	X	X	(600)	171	69,620	149
Libya	650	2	536	0	114	16	31	0	6	15	(0)	X	(19)	(100)
Madagascar	10,455	48	9,950	59	506	(37)	94	(60)	5	(49)	(1)	56	121	53
Malawi	10,196	56	9,669	55	527	70	45	133	X	X	(0)	X	21	X
Mali	6,341	36	5,937	36	404	38	13	151	X	X	0	X	(143)	X
Mauritania	13	33	8	33	5	33	X	X	X	X	(0)	X	96	X
Mauritius	18	(10)	8	(45)	10	98	4	167	X	X	9	841	(2,148)	750
Morocco	2,263	14	1,432	14	831	13	83	(29)	103	1	424	103	(57,087)	152
Mozambique	17,852	19	16,844	20	1,008	8	34	(6)	1	(42)	(10)	630	1,232	82
Namibia	X	X	X	X	X	X	X	X	X	X	X	X	X	X
Niger	5,672	38	5,322	38	350	39	4	X	X	X	0	X	X	X
Nigeria	108,074	32	99,811	34	8,263	9	2,723	7	56	129	(54)	(4)	3,303	(40)
Rwanda	5,660	1	5,392	1	268	17	36	209	X	X	(4)	X	207	X
Senegal	5,107	25	4,405	23	702	38	23	54	X	X	33	14	(3,947)	9
Sierra Leone	3,249	23	3,126	25	124	(12)	5	(69)	X	X	(0)	X	6	X
Somalia	8,648	19	8,543	19	105	13	14	0	X	X	0	(100)	0	(100)
South Africa {e}	23,978	23	7,162	1	16,816	35	1,485	(6)	1,755	19	(2,065)	X	161,545	X
Sudan	24,747	31	22,456	31	2,291	30	3	(75)	3	(67)	1	X	(8)	X
Swaziland	1,469	(34)	560	0	909	(45)	75	(27)	X	X	0	X	X	X
Tanzania	35,680	36	33,533	35	2,147	67	29	(71)	25	X	(9)	1,429	1,718	3,203
Togo	2,053	175	1,836	207	217	47	8	381	X	X	(0)	(318)	26	(126)
Tunisia	3,502	26	3,293	23	209	80	20	363	87	147	37	42	(8,503)	142
Uganda	16,684	41	14,466	41	2,218	43	83	262	3	275	0	X	X	X
Zambia	14,422	39	13,341	35	1,081	111	351	601	3	(20)	(30)	(443)	1,286	(223)
Zimbabwe	8,075	15	6,269	10	1,806	41	250	79	79	16	(19)	256	1,511	395
EUROPE	484,169	X	86,986	X	397,184	X	118,338	X	79,251	X	4,096	X	(817,505)	X
Albania	471	(80)	410	(75)	61	(92)	4	(98)	44	444	(1)	X	132	X
Austria	14,074	0	3,156	80	10,918	(11)	7,387	19	3,501	80	5,727	76	(255,824)	200
Belarus, Rep	10,020	X	814	X	9,206	X	1,545	X	146	X	(173)	X	(6,745)	X
Belgium {f}	4,255	36	550	2	3,705	43	1,201	57	1,108	31	2,626	0	(77,994)	28
Bosnia and Herzegovina	X	X	X	X	X	X	X	X	X	X	(0)	X	(62)	X
Bulgaria	3,041	(36)	1,173	(33)	1,868	(39)	253	(83)	141	(68)	(155)	(147)	10,391	(152)
Croatia, Rep	2,674	X	903	X	1,772	X	630	X	192	X	(232)	X	(17,961)	X
Czech Rep	11,758	X	779	X	10,979	X	3,200	X	694	X	(2,080)	X	(93,823)	X
Denmark	2,288	(13)	484	30	1,804	(20)	583	(31)	343	8	204	(120)	(11,858)	(198)
Estonia, Rep	3,240	X	722	X	2,518	X	330	X	42	X	(1,945)	X	(60,710)	X
Finland	47,069	17	4,118	31	42,950	16	9,190	17	10,614	51	6,633	15	(215,949)	79
France	43,086	11	10,456	0	32,630	15	9,894	9	8,432	58	(662)	(68)	(50,674)	70
Germany	37,312	X	3,795	X	33,517	X	13,038	X	14,106	X	(3,922)	X	(60,839)	X
Greece	2,467	(14)	1,393	(33)	1,074	34	337	6	750	164	36	(81)	(90)	(100)
Hungary	4,535	(30)	2,165	(23)	2,370	(36)	426	(66)	314	(36)	(504)	(446)	29,767	751
Iceland	X	X	X	X	X	X	X	X	X	X	10	166	(746)	1
Ireland	2,014	70	60	31	1,954	71	685	142	0	(100)	(400)	28	8,982	169
Italy	9,406	4	5,213	12	4,192	(4)	1,786	(22)	6,509	44	6,593	24	(635,360)	73
Latvia, Rep	5,850	X	1,146	X	4,704	X	899	X	7	X	(2,538)	X	(66,265)	X
Lithuania, Rep	3,940	X	1,507	X	2,433	X	800	X	27	X	(983)	X	(28,363)	X
Macedonia, FYR	160	X	X	X	160	X	54	X	23	X	36	X	380	X
Moldova, Rep	X	X	X	X	X	X	X	X	X	X	18	X	659	X
Netherlands	1,078	12	179	94	899	3	399	13	2,944	58	86	(59)	(36,665)	38
Norway	9,163	(5)	466	(44)	8,697	(2)	2,383	4	2,126	41	2,655	152	(146,158)	266
Poland, Rep	19,004	(21)	2,576	(19)	16,428	(21)	5,070	(25)	1,412	12	(1,208)	(30)	91,041	141
Portugal	9,890	12	598	0	9,292	13	1,632	(28)	935	42	448	(201)	(132,595)	477
Romania	11,659	(50)	2,527	(45)	9,132	(51)	1,988	(58)	337	(58)	5	(108)	(1,038)	(193)
Russian Federation	133,556	X	33,413	X	100,143	X	32,770	X	3,980	X	(12,955)	X	(722,174)	X
Slovak Rep	5,297	X	518	X	4,779	X	632	X	310	X	(714)	X	(28,406)	X
Slovenia, Rep	1,651	X	192	X	1,459	X	513	X	440	X	72	X	3,890	X
Spain	15,007	3	2,714	14	12,293	1	2,907	29	3,512	22	1,535	196	(166,960)	155
Sweden	56,757	8	3,824	(14)	52,933	10	13,771	16	9,078	35	5,452	90	(253,366)	167
Switzerland	4,611	5	842	(2)	3,769	7	1,403	(15)	1,411	45	(148)	(188)	47,567	1,608
Ukraine	X	X	X	X	X	X	X	X	X	X	(7)	X	(982)	X
United Kingdom	7,956	88	260	77	7,697	89	2,197	36	5,777	65	607	(1,319)	(101,413)	608
Yugoslavia, Fed Rep	880	X	33	X	847	X	430	X	X	X	(32)	X	(1,909)	X

Data Table 11.3 continued

	Average Annual Roundwood Production						Average Annual Production				Average Annual Net Trade in Roundwood			
	Total		Fuel and Charcoal		Industrial Roundwood		Sawnwood		Paper		Quantity {a}		Balance of Trade {b}	
	Cubic Meters (000) 1993-95	Percent Change Since 1983-85	Cubic Meters (000) 1993-95	Percent Change Since 1983-85	Cubic Meters (000) 1993-95	Percent Change Since 1983-85	Cubic Meters (000) 1993-95	Percent Change Since 1983-85	Metric Tons (000) 1993-95	Percent Change Since 1983-85	Cubic Meters (000) 1993-95	Percent Change Since 1983-85	Value (million US$) 1993-95	Percent Change Since 1983-85
NORTH AMERICA	**684,296**	**11**	**99,209**	**(7)**	**585,087**	**15**	**167,236**	**24**	**103,460**	**38**	**(14,397)**	**(25)**	**2,623,671**	**85**
Canada	184,423	12	6,293	(3)	178,130	13	60,620	24	18,199	30	3,655	(411)	(63,975)	(158)
United States	499,873	11	92,916	(7)	406,957	16	106,616	24	85,261	40	(18,059)	1	2,687,559	105
CENTRAL AMERICA	**69,766**	**20**	**59,594**	**26**	**10,173**	**(4)**	**4,409**	**28**	**2,825**	**16**	**(251)**	**(472)**	**14,084**	**(216)**
Belize	188	19	126	4	62	64	14	(25)	X	X	(3)	743	342	326
Costa Rica	4,550	34	3,287	30	1,263	46	775	105	20	51	8	1,417	(543)	266
Cuba	3,148	(4)	2,537	(8)	611	17	130	23	57	(53)	0	(99)	(7)	(100)
Dominican Rep	982	1	976	1	6	0	X	X	7	(26)	8	(75)	(598)	(88)
El Salvador	6,657	21	6,511	20	146	72	70	64	17	9	5	X	(372)	X
Guatemala	13,857	42	13,111	36	746	340	390	245	23	46	1	55	(193)	(737)
Haiti	6,294	21	6,055	22	239	0	14	0	X	X	1	X	(75)	X
Honduras	6,306	28	5,703	35	603	(14)	324	(27)	X	X	(68)	2,061	13,140	2,298
Jamaica	742	19	679	27	63	(30)	19	(34)	2	(88)	16	1,611	(4,169)	1,290
Mexico	22,116	11	16,097	24	6,019	(15)	2,527	26	2,670	21	(286)	(2,389)	14,505	(606)
Nicaragua	3,662	19	3,530	36	132	(73)	55	(75)	X	X	1	1,081	(118)	292
Panama	1,053	11	935	22	118	(34)	37	(23)	28	(24)	10	(234)	(970)	373
Trinidad and Tobago	61	(2)	22	0	39	(3)	50	148	X	X	4	(41)	(543)	(60)
SOUTH AMERICA	**382,557**	**27**	**256,063**	**21**	**126,494**	**39**	**26,785**	**11**	**8,793**	**42**	**(9,110)**	**775**	**451,115**	**1,731**
Argentina	11,756	4	5,519	(4)	6,236	13	1,053	7	943	5	(762)	(10,176)	49,615	(3,622)
Bolivia	2,430	92	1,296	23	1,134	434	205	346	0	(100)	(12)	X	5,393	X
Brazil	280,572	22	197,395	20	83,177	26	18,803	7	5,646	51	(1,225)	(13,816)	64,852	(1,278)
Chile	30,962	103	9,859	54	21,103	139	3,280	70	551	50	(6,848)	541	308,097	782
Colombia	20,240	15	17,504	20	2,736	(7)	661	0	652	60	(7)	X	793	X
Ecuador	8,470	27	4,735	9	3,735	59	1,165	(2)	88	159	(37)	X	3,211	X
Guyana	417	109	34	113	383	109	76	17	X	X	(16)	(5)	1,979	(1)
Paraguay	10,061	37	6,219	32	3,843	46	357	(52)	13	15	(3)	X	65	X
Peru	11,099	45	9,423	45	1,676	47	630	34	158	9	1	70	(97)	(37)
Suriname	118	(44)	19	41	99	(50)	30	(52)	X	X	(7)	(63)	1,056	(40)
Uruguay	4,089	32	3,046	7	1,043	309	269	526	84	89	(202)	X	16,296	(24,065)
Venezuela	2,212	74	943	47	1,269	103	239	(1)	657	24	10	(79)	(607)	(92)
ASIA	**1,137,710**	**X**	**878,628**	**X**	**259,083**	**X**	**98,720**	**X**	**72,153**	**X**	**52,720**	**X**	**(8,492,747)**	**X**
Afghanistan, Islamic State	7,260	24	5,625	28	1,636	11	400	0	X	X	(5)	X	178	X
Armenia, Rep	X	X	X	X	X	X	X	X	X	X	0	X	(1)	X
Azerbaijan	X	X	X	X	X	X	X	X	X	X	(1)	X	82	X
Bangladesh	31,353	20	30,627	22	726	(29)	79	(43)	157	17	4	(88)	(483)	(84)
Bhutan	1,393	2	1,336	20	57	(77)	18	200	X	X	38	(614)	(782)	(460)
Cambodia	7,429	40	6,531	38	898	58	175	307	0	X	(463)	X	102,495	X
China {g}	300,863	17	202,726	21	98,137	10	25,197	(2)	25,468	162	4,262	(68)	(733,136)	(25)
Georgia	X	X	X	X	X	X	X	X	X	X	(1)	X	(39)	X
India	294,016	21	269,223	22	24,793	8	17,460	9	2,837	85	272	3,520	(37,277)	3,502
Indonesia	185,206	20	148,949	19	36,257	27	7,271	9	3,178	647	(1,375)	(38)	21,238	(88)
Iran, Islamic Rep	7,489	12	2,547	7	4,942	15	169	(3)	223	186	(2)	(102)	(59)	(100)
Iraq	157	18	107	29	50	0	8	0	16	(42)	X	X	X	X
Israel	113	(4)	13	18	100	(7)	X	X	239	64	203	35	(41,320)	88
Japan	24,668	(25)	360	(35)	24,308	(24)	25,553	(12)	28,652	48	46,670	13	(7,092,729)	93
Jordan	10	30	6	64	4	0	X	X	30	264	10	(69)	(1,830)	(60)
Kazakstan, Rep	X	X	X	X	X	X	X	X	X	X	(15)	X	(1,262)	X
Korea, Dem People's Rep	4,876	9	4,276	11	600	0	280	0	80	0	(76)	(262)	3,728	(167)
Korea, Rep	6,485	(15)	4,491	(17)	1,994	(10)	3,500	10	6,372	194	9,042	47	(1,167,199)	110
Kuwait	X	X	X	X	X	X	X	X	X	X	50	23	(2,827)	62
Kyrgyz Rep	X	X	X	X	X	X	X	X	X	X	1	X	81	X
Lao People's Dem Rep	5,148	47	4,382	35	765	181	380	1,600	X	X	(195)	1,910	40,709	965
Lebanon	497	6	490	9	7	(64)	9	(58)	42	(7)	46	196	(1,524)	361
Malaysia	46,333	17	9,601	29	36,731	15	8,850	42	634	1,185	(8,445)	(54)	1,012,700	(11)
Mongolia	541	(77)	376	(72)	165	(84)	157	(67)	X	X	(24)	X	1,472	X
Myanmar	23,053	22	20,078	28	2,975	(7)	344	(47)	15	26	(1,171)	345	192,114	142
Nepal	20,317	28	19,697	29	620	11	620	182	13	926	0	(100)	(2)	(100)
Oman	X	X	X	X	X	X	X	X	X	X	(0)	(101)	(327)	(89)
Pakistan	29,229	43	27,329	42	1,900	65	1,299	119	395	413	116	541	(8,653)	373
Philippines	39,277	11	35,793	25	3,483	(48)	375	(68)	550	97	274	(122)	(192,636)	(281)
Saudi Arabia	X	X	X	X	X	X	X	X	X	X	113	(39)	(9,641)	(73)
Singapore	120	X	120	X	0	X	25	X	93	833	(45)	(115)	(5,035)	(87)
Sri Lanka	9,498	11	8,815	13	683	(2)	5	(80)	30	35	1	(101)	(539)	(121)
Syrian Arab Rep	55	8	20	17	35	3	9	0	1	(73)	11	(68)	(1,078)	(91)
Tajikistan, Rep	X	X	X	X	X	X	X	X	X	X	X	X	X	X
Thailand	38,908	10	36,132	16	2,776	(35)	733	(25)	1,643	310	1,326	(1,690)	(297,842)	797
Turkey	18,334	(3)	8,546	(34)	9,788	63	4,536	(4)	1,123	121	1,575	(2,076)	(181,528)	(1,742)
Turkmenistan, Rep	X	X	X	X	X	X	X	X	X	X	X	X	(2,504)	X
United Arab Emirates	X	X	X	X	X	X	X	X	X	X	56	X	31	X
Uzbekistan, Rep	X	X	X	X	X	X	X	X	X	X	0	X	31	X
Vietnam	34,213	21	29,813	24	4,399	3	721	85	120	121	(248)	(2,479)	20,765	(2,083)
Yemen	324	17	324	17	X	X	X	X	X	X	X	(94)	(21)	(99)
OCEANIA	**48,468**	**35**	**8,750**	**2**	**39,718**	**45**	**6,645**	**20**	**3,021**	**37**	**(16,105)**	**78**	**1,509,533**	**434**
Australia	21,558	20	2,898	6	18,660	23	3,436	12	2,153	44	(7,524)	20	367,438	139
Fiji	562	147	37	9	525	172	108	28	X	X	(394)	5,472	16,626	3,815
New Zealand	16,482	75	50	0	16,432	75	2,870	31	868	22	(5,440)	384	476,986	1,133
Papua New Guinea	8,955	18	5,533	0	3,422	64	185	52	X	X	(2,250)	72	545,137	683
Solomon Islands	702	29	138	18	564	32	13	(18)	X	X	X	X	X	X
DEVELOPING	**2,060,995**	**20**	**1,638,028**	**20**	**422,966**	**19**	**111,975**	**10**	**58,723**	**136**	**(10,284)**	**25**	**547,616**	**253**
DEVELOPED	**1,254,267**	**(11)**	**196,902**	**(24)**	**1,057,365**	**(8)**	**319,119**	**(10)**	**215,140**	**33**	**21,932**	**47**	**(4,343,572)**	**82**

Notes: a. Quantity of net trade is defined as the balance of imports minus exports. b. Balance of trade is defined as exports minus imports. c. World and regional totals include countries not listed here. d. Includes Eritrea. e. Includes Namibia. f. Includes Luxembourg. g. Includes Taiwan.

Land Area and Use, 1982–94

Sources: Food and Agriculture Organization of the United Nations and United Nations Population Division

	Land Area (000 hectares)	Population Density (per 1,000 hectares) 1996	Domesticated Land as a % of Land Area {a} 1994	Cropland 1992-94	Cropland Percent Change Since 1982-84	Permanent Pasture 1992-94	Permanent Pasture Percent Change Since 1982-84	Forest & Woodland 1992-94	Forest & Woodland Percent Change Since 1982-84	Other Land 1992-94	Other Land Percent Change Since 1982-84
WORLD {b}	13,048,300	442	37	1,465,814	2.0	3,410,203	3.2	4,177,088	(2.2)	3,992,533	(1.0)
AFRICA	2,963,468	249	36	189,803	6.5	889,350	0.0	713,405	(0.3)	1,171,024	(0.8)
Algeria	238,174	121	17	8,088	9.1	31,024	(2.8)	3,949	(10.0)	195,197	0.4
Angola	124,670	90	46	3,500	2.9	54,000	0.0	23,000	(0.9)	44,170	0.2
Benin	11,062	503	21	1,880	3.9	442	0.0	3,400	(11.0)	5,340	7.0
Botswana	56,673	26	46	420	5.0	25,600	0.0	26,500	0.0	4,153	(0.5)
Burkina Faso	27,360	394	34	3,465	18.0	6,000	0.0	13,800	0.0	4,082	(11.7)
Burundi	2,568	2,423	86	1,120	(5.1)	1,080	9.1	325	0.0	43	(41.1)
Cameroon	46,540	291	19	7,040	1.2	2,000	0.0	35,900	0.0	1,600	(4.9)
Central African Rep	62,298	54	8	2,020	2.5	3,000	0.0	46,700	0.0	10,578	(0.5)
Chad	125,920	52	38	3,256	3.4	45,000	0.0	32,400	0.0	45,264	(0.2)
Congo, Dem Rep	34,150	78	30	170	9.9	10,000	0.0	19,900	0.0	4,080	(0.4)
Congo, Rep	226,705	206	10	7,900	2.5	15,000	0.0	166,000	0.0	37,805	(0.5)
Côte d'Ivoire	31,800	441	54	4,031	22.5	13,000	0.0	9,600	(5.9)	5,149	(3.0)
Egypt	99,545	636	3	3,137	26.5	X	X	34	9.7	96,374	(0.7)
Equatorial Guinea	2,805	146	12	230	0.0	104	0.0	1,830	0.0	641	0.0
Eritrea	10,000	328	75	366	X	4,622	X	523	X	1,155	X
Ethiopia	100,000	582	31	12,197	X	28,267	X	13,633	X	49,269	X
Gabon	25,767	43	20	460	1.8	4,700	0.0	19,900	(0.4)	707	11.3
Gambia, The	1,000	1,141	37	165	(10.6)	194	2.1	94	(6.0)	547	4.1
Ghana	22,754	784	57	4,407	15.0	8,400	0.0	9,300	(3.1)	647	(29.7)
Guinea	24,572	306	47	787	10.2	10,700	0.0	6,700	0.0	6,385	(1.1)
Guinea-Bissau	2,812	388	50	340	10.3	1,080	0.0	1,070	0.0	322	(9.0)
Kenya	56,914	488	45	4,520	5.6	21,300	0.0	16,800	0.0	14,294	(1.6)
Lesotho	3,035	685	76	320	10.6	2,000	0.0	X	X	715	(4.1)
Liberia	9,632	233	25	371	(0.1)	2,000	0.0	4,600	0.0	2,661	0.0
Libya	175,954	32	9	2,170	3.1	13,300	0.3	840	33.0	159,644	(0.2)
Madagascar	58,154	264	47	3,105	3.1	24,000	0.0	23,200	0.0	7,849	(1.2)
Malawi	9,408	1,046	38	1,700	19.9	1,840	0.0	3,700	(1.1)	2,168	(10.0)
Mali	122,019	91	27	2,569	25.1	30,000	0.0	11,800	(1.7)	77,650	(0.4)
Mauritania	102,522	23	38	208	6.7	39,250	0.0	4,410	(2.0)	58,654	0.1
Mauritius	203	5,562	56	106	(0.9)	7	0.0	44	(24.1)	46	48.4
Morocco	44,630	605	68	9,686	13.9	20,933	0.2	8,613	9.9	5,397	(28.8)
Mozambique	78,409	227	60	3,180	3.2	44,000	0.0	17,300	0.0	13,929	(0.7)
Namibia	82,329	19	47	704	6.6	38,000	0.0	12,500	0.0	31,125	(0.1)
Niger	126,670	75	12	4,035	13.9	10,440	13.1	2,500	0.0	109,695	(1.5)
Nigeria	91,077	1,263	80	32,579	6.1	40,000	0.0	14,300	(10.6)	4,198	(3.9)
Rwanda	2,467	2,188	75	1,150	5.4	695	(0.7)	250	0.0	372	(12.7)
Senegal	19,253	443	42	2,355	0.2	5,700	0.0	7,467	(1.8)	3,731	3.6
Sierra Leone	7,162	600	38	540	4.4	2,201	(0.1)	1,947	2.5	2,474	(2.6)
Somalia	62,734	157	70	1,026	1.1	43,000	0.0	16,000	6.7	2,708	(27.2)
South Africa	122,104	347	79	15,200	15.4	81,433	0.1	8,200	0.0	17,271	(10.8)
Sudan	237,600	115	52	12,975	3.3	110,000	12.2	42,367	(1.5)	72,258	(14.0)
Swaziland	1,720	512	73	191	24.3	1,070	(5.1)	119	16.6	340	0.9
Tanzania	88,359	349	44	3,660	23.7	35,000	0.0	33,067	(1.9)	16,632	(0.4)
Togo	5,439	772	48	2,420	2.5	200	0.0	900	(11.8)	1,919	3.2
Tunisia	15,536	589	51	4,882	(0.1)	3,416	1.8	666	17.1	6,602	(1.8)
Uganda	19,965	1,015	43	6,780	9.1	1,800	0.0	6,300	5.0	5,085	(14.6)
Zambia	74,339	111	47	5,273	2.2	30,000	0.0	32,000	6.7	7,066	(23.0)
Zimbabwe	38,685	296	52	2,876	2.5	17,190	0.5	8,800	(7.4)	9,819	5.8
EUROPE	2,260,320	322	22	317,837	X	178,549	X	947,761	X	816,036	X
Albania	2,740	1,241	41	702	(1.2)	424	5.6	1,049	1.7	565	(5.2)
Austria	8,273	980	43	1,506	(3.3)	1,985	(1.0)	3,233	(0.3)	1,550	5.4
Belarus, Rep	20,748	499	44	6,245	X	3,070	X	7,109	X	4,324	X
Belgium {c}	3,282	3,221	45	790	2.4	687	(9.0)	709	2.0	1,095	3.4
Bosnia and Herzegovina	5,100	711	39	893	X	1,200	X	2,033	X	973	X
Bulgaria	11,055	766	54	4,286	3.5	1,811	(11.0)	3,348	0.1	1,609	5.0
Croatia, Rep	5,592	805	41	1,242	X	1,088	X	2,075	X	1,187	X
Czech Rep	7,728	1,326	55	2,265	X	588	X	1,753	X	547	X
Denmark	4,243	1,234	63	2,488	(5.3)	241	2.1	417	(13.8)	1,097	23.1
Estonia, Rep	4,227	348	34	1,145	X	311	X	2,018	X	753	X
Finland	30,459	168	9	2,585	4.5	112	(21.7)	23,186	(0.6)	4,575	1.2
France	55,010	1,060	55	19,387	1.7	10,830	(13.4)	14,938	2.3	9,854	11.5
Germany	34,927	2,346	50	11,885	(4.5)	5,255	(10.8)	10,700	4.0	7,087	12.5
Greece	12,890	814	68	3,502	(11.3)	5,252	(0.1)	2,620	0.0	1,516	42.2
Hungary	9,234	1,088	66	4,973	(6.1)	1,156	(9.4)	1,717	5.1	1,388	34.5
Iceland	10,025	27	23	6	(21.7)	2,274	0.0	120	0.0	7,625	0.0
Ireland	6,889	516	64	1,266	21.6	3,137	(32.8)	570	14.0	1,916	181.8
Italy	29,406	1,946	53	11,594	(5.8)	4,479	(11.2)	6,794	6.4	6,519	14.9
Latvia, Rep	6,205	404	41	1,720	X	808	X	2,841	X	836	X
Lithuania, Rep	6,480	575	54	3,041	X	472	X	1,983	X	984	X
Macedonia, FYR	2,543	855	51	662	X	638	X	1,035	X	227	X
Moldova, Rep	3,297	1,348	78	2,195	X	363	X	358	X	381	X
Netherlands	3,392	4,592	58	922	10.8	1,060	(10.0)	334	12.6	1,076	(0.9)
Norway	30,683	142	3	891	5.1	124	25.7	8,330	0.0	21,338	(0.3)
Poland, Rep	30,442	1,268	61	14,673	(1.0)	4,049	(0.7)	8,732	0.7	2,988	3.9
Portugal	9,150	1,072	43	3,057	(3.0)	900	7.4	3,102	4.6	2,091	(4.7)
Romania	23,034	984	64	9,942	(5.8)	4,851	9.6	6,681	1.8	1,559	4.6
Russian Federation	1,688,850	88	13	133,072	X	86,858	X	767,347	X	701,573	X
Slovak Rep	4,808	1,112	51	1,074	X	557	X	1,326	X	249	X
Slovenia, Rep	2,012	956	39	296	X	540	X	1,077	X	98	X
Spain	49,944	794	62	19,910	(2.9)	10,416	0.5	16,063	3.1	3,555	1.7
Sweden	41,162	214	8	2,776	(4.5)	576	(17.0)	28,025	0.1	9,652	1.3
Switzerland	3,955	1,827	40	433	5.1	1,148	(28.6)	1,186	12.7	1,187	34.6
Ukraine	57,935	891	72	34,410	X	7,483	X	9,239	X	6,803	X
United Kingdom	24,160	2,407	71	6,224	(10.9)	11,090	(1.4)	2,390	8.2	4,456	19.7
Yugoslavia, Fed Rep	10,200	1,009	61	4,080	X	2,119	X	1,769	X	2,233	X

	Land Area (000 hectares)	Population Density (per 1,000 hectares) 1996	Domesticated Land as a % of Land Area {a} 1994	Cropland 1992-94	Cropland Percent Change Since 1982-84	Permanent Pasture 1992-94	Permanent Pasture Percent Change Since 1982-84	Forest & Woodland 1992-94	Forest & Woodland Percent Change Since 1982-84	Other Land 1992-94	Other Land Percent Change Since 1982-84
NORTH AMERICA	**1,838,009**	**163**	**27**	**233,276**	**(1.1)**	**267,072**	**(1.2)**	**749,290**	**2.9**	**588,371**	**(2.6)**
Canada	922,097	32	8	45,500	(1.3)	27,900	(3.1)	453,300	3.9	395,397	(3.8)
United States	915,912	294	47	187,776	(1.1)	239,172	(1.0)	295,990	1.5	192,974	(0.0)
CENTRAL AMERICA	**264,835**	**475**	**53**	**40,053**	**5.4**	**98,503**	**6.2**	**74,524**	**1.2**	**85,910**	**(9.2)**
Belize	2,280	96	6	81	52.2	49	11.4	2,100	0.0	50	(39.4)
Costa Rica	5,106	685	56	530	2.9	2,340	6.9	1,570	(3.4)	666	(14.4)
Cuba	10,982	1,003	61	3,745	12.4	2,705	0.8	2,505	(6.2)	2,027	(11.8)
Dominican Rep	4,838	1,646	81	1,743	21.9	2,090	(0.1)	603	(4.1)	401	(41.6)
El Salvador	2,072	2,797	65	742	2.3	600	(1.6)	105	(13.9)	625	1.7
Guatemala	10,843	1,008	42	1,858	4.1	2,568	65.5	5,212	15.8	1,171	(60.9)
Haiti	2,756	2,634	51	910	1.2	495	(2.2)	140	0.0	1,211	0.0
Honduras	11,189	520	32	1,967	11.0	1,524	1.6	6,000	0.0	1,698	(11.4)
Jamaica	1,083	2,300	44	219	(1.9)	257	0.0	185	(3.8)	422	2.8
Mexico	190,869	486	55	24,730	0.2	79,000	6.0	48,700	4.3	38,439	(14.6)
Nicaragua	12,140	349	61	2,480	55.6	4,815	0.0	3,200	(22.9)	1,645	4.0
Panama	7,443	360	29	662	14.0	1,483	9.1	3,260	(16.0)	2,038	25.6
Trinidad and Tobago	513	2,528	26	122	3.4	11	0.0	235	3.5	145	(7.6)
SOUTH AMERICA	**1,752,925**	**184**	**35**	**113,116**	**9.0**	**495,341**	**3.0**	**934,860**	**0.6**	**209,471**	**(12.3)**
Argentina	273,669	129	62	27,200	0.0	142,000	(0.6)	50,900	0.0	53,569	1.7
Bolivia	108,438	70	27	2,370	8.9	26,500	(1.7)	58,000	0.0	21,565	1.2
Brazil	845,651	190	29	58,667	15.0	185,600	5.9	557,667	0.8	43,718	(34.1)
Chile	74,880	193	23	4,216	(2.0)	13,100	(0.4)	16,500	0.3	41,030	0.3
Colombia	103,870	351	45	6,073	15.7	40,083	(0.0)	53,167	(3.3)	4,547	29.1
Ecuador	27,684	423	29	3,010	20.8	5,009	11.1	15,600	0.6	4,065	(21.6)
Guyana	19,685	43	9	496	0.2	1,230	0.3	16,456	0.5	1,503	(5.7)
Paraguay	39,730	125	60	2,270	17.6	21,700	27.6	12,850	(31.6)	2,910	43.6
Peru	128,000	187	24	3,767	3.3	27,120	0.0	84,800	(0.1)	12,213	(1.4)
Suriname	15,600	28	1	68	19.3	21	12.5	15,000	0.8	511	(21.3)
Uruguay	17,481	183	85	1,304	(5.0)	13,520	(0.5)	930	(2.3)	1,727	8.8
Venezuela	88,205	253	25	3,663	(3.0)	18,242	2.7	45,000	22.3	21,300	(28.7)
ASIA	**3,085,414**	**1,130**	**51**	**520,175**	**X**	**1,051,311**	**X**	**556,996**	**X**	**956,913**	**X**
Afghanistan, Islamic State	65,209	320	58	8,054	0.0	30,000	0.0	1,700	(10.5)	25,455	0.8
Armenia, Rep	2,820	1,290	46	582	X	688	X	413	X	1,137	X
Azerbaijan	8,660	877	48	1,967	X	2,200	X	950	X	3,543	X
Bangladesh	13,017	9,224	71	8,849	(3.1)	600	0.0	1,891	(11.3)	1,677	45.2
Bhutan	4,700	386	9	136	7.7	273	2.5	3,100	14.2	1,191	(25.2)
Cambodia	17,652	582	30	3,832	81.9	1,500	158.5	12,200	(7.3)	120	(93.4)
China	929,100	1,321 d	53	95,145	(3.6)	400,000	12.5	128,630	(1.1)	305,324	(11.4)
Georgia	6,970	781	43	1,036	X	1,962	X	2,988	X	984	X
India	297,319	3,177	61	169,569	0.5	11,424	(4.8)	68,173	1.2	48,136	(2.1)
Indonesia	181,157	1,107	23	31,146	19.9	11,800	1.2	111,516	(2.6)	26,695	(8.1)
Iran, Islamic Rep	162,200	431	39	18,500	21.7	44,000	0.0	11,400	0.0	88,300	(3.6)
Iraq	43,737	471	22	5,550	1.9	4,000	0.0	192	0.0	33,995	(0.3)
Israel	2,062	2,747	28	434	4.6	145	5.8	126	16.7	1,357	(3.2)
Japan	37,652	3,329	13	4,467	(7.0)	660	8.9	25,110	(0.2)	7,416	4.8
Jordan	8,893	628	13	405	17.1	791	0.0	70	5.5	7,627	(0.8)
Kazakstan, Rep	267,073	63	83	35,239	X	186,549	X	9,600	X	35,685	X
Korea, Dem People's Rep	12,041	1,866	17	2,007	3.7	50	0.0	7,370	0.0	2,614	(2.7)
Korea, Rep	9,873	4,590	22	2,053	(5.3)	91	30.8	6,460	(1.3)	1,270	16.5
Kuwait	1,782	947	8	5	114.3	137	2.2	2	0.0	1,638	(0.3)
Kyrgyz Rep	19,180	233	54	1,387	X	8,900	X	730	X	8,163	X
Lao People's Dem Rep	23,080	218	7	900	18.5	800	0.0	12,560	(4.1)	8,820	4.7
Lebanon	1,023	3,015	31	306	2.7	14	40.0	80	(3.6)	623	(1.5)
Malaysia	32,855	626	24	7,536	46.6	281	8.9	22,248	0.0	2,790	(46.4)
Mongolia	156,650	16	76	1,357	4.4	117,983	(4.4)	13,750	(9.4)	23,560	40.5
Myanmar	65,755	698	16	10,067	(0.1)	354	(1.8)	32,398	0.8	22,935	(1.0)
Nepal	14,300	1,540	31	2,556	10.0	1,757	(9.4)	5,750	4.7	4,237	(6.8)
Oman	21,246	108	5	63	44.3	1,000	0.0	X	X	20,183	(0.1)
Pakistan	77,088	1,816	34	21,323	4.7	5,000	0.0	3,477	15.1	47,288	(2.9)
Philippines	29,817	2,324	36	9,320	5.0	1,280	14.3	13,600	15.6	5,617	(30.3)
Saudi Arabia	214,969	88	58	3,777	67.6	120,000	38.5	1,800	33.3	89,392	(28.3)
Singapore	61	55,459	2	1	(83.3)	X	X	3	0.0	57	9.6
Sri Lanka	6,463	2,801	36	1,889	1.3	440	0.2	2,100	20.2	2,034	(15.6)
Syrian Arab Rep	18,378	793	78	5,985	5.2	8,191	(1.8)	484	(2.4)	3,718	(3.6)
Tajikistan, Rep	14,060	422	31	846	X	3,533	X	537	X	9,144	X
Thailand	51,089	1,149	42	20,488	6.7	800	14.3	14,833	(3.7)	14,968	(5.1)
Turkey	76,963	803	52	27,611	2.1	12,378	22.2	20,199	0.0	16,775	(14.4)
Turkmenistan, Rep	46,993	88	67	1,471	X	33,202	X	4,000	X	8,320	X
United Arab Emirates	8,360	270	4	75	148.4	280	40.0	3	0.0	8,002	(1.5)
Uzbekistan, Rep	41,424	560	61	4,618	X	21,490	X	1,311	X	14,005	X
Vietnam	32,549	2,310	22	6,738	2.3	328	5.1	9,650	(3.9)	15,833	1.4
Yemen	52,797	297	33	1,520	3.8	16,065	0.0	2,000	(25.0)	33,212	1.9
OCEANIA	**849,135**	**34**	**57**	**51,553**	**1.4**	**430,077**	**(2.8)**	**200,252**	**(0.2)**	**164,807**	**6.3**
Australia	768,230	24	60	47,023	1.7	415,700	(2.8)	145,000	(0.4)	158,057	6.4
Fiji	1,827	436	24	260	40.5	174	29.1	1,185	0.0	208	(35.5)
New Zealand	26,799	134	62	3,307	(5.5)	13,774	(2.2)	7,667	2.6	2,051	17.2
Papua New Guinea	45,286	97	1	423	13.4	90	(4.6)	42,000	0.0	2,776	(1.5)
Solomon Islands	2,799	140	3	57	6.9	39	0.0	2,450	(2.8)	253	35.5
DEVELOPING	**7,585,948**	**605**	**39**	**797,124**	**4.8**	**2,194,347**	**4.6**	**2,273,406**	**(0.0)**	**2,320,992**	**(5.4)**
DEVELOPED	**5,462,356**	**215**	**34**	**668,690**	**(1.1)**	**1,215,856**	**1.0**	**1,903,683**	**(4.8)**	**1,671,541**	**5.9**

Notes: a. Domesticated land is the sum of cropland and permanent pasture. b. Does not include Antarctica. World and regional totals include countries not listed here.
c. Includes Luxembourg. d. Includes Taiwan.

Sources and Technical Notes

Forest Cover and Change, and Forest Industry Structure, 1980–95

Sources: Forest cover and change: Food and Agriculture Organization of the United Nations (FAO), Forest Resources Division, *State of the World's Forests 1997* (FAO, Rome, 1997) and *Forest Resources Assessment 1990: Global Synthesis (FRA 1990)* (FAO, Rome, 1995). Forest industry data: International Tropical Timber Organization (ITTO), *Annual Review and Assessment of the World Tropical Timber Situation 1996* (ITTO, Yokohama, Japan, 1997).

Total forest consists of all forest area for temperate developed countries, and the sum of natural forest and plantation area categories for tropical and temperate developing countries. For developed countries, forest cover data were obtained from official sources in response to a questionnaire from the United Nations Economic Commission for Europe and the FAO liaison office in Geneva (UN–ECE/FAO). The countries surveyed include countries in Europe, North America, and the former Soviet Union, as well as Japan, Australia, and New Zealand. Forest areas in developed countries are defined as land where tree crowns cover 20 percent of the area, including open forests; forest roads and fire breaks; temporarily cleared areas; young stands expected to achieve at least 20 percent crown cover upon maturity, etc. Forest areas in developed countries are not broken down into the subcategories of natural forests and plantations due to the difficulty in distinguishing the two in many countries. Comparable forest area data for 1980 are only available for developing countries due to methodological constraints.

FAO defines a *natural forest* in tropical and temperate developing countries as a forest composed primarily of indigenous (native) tree species. Natural forests include closed forest, where trees cover a high proportion of the ground and where grass does not form a continuous layer on the forest floor (e.g., broadleaved forests, coniferous forests, and bamboo forests), and open forest, which FAO defines as mixed forest/grasslands with at least 10 percent tree cover and a continuous grass layer on the forest floor. Natural forests in tropical and temperate developing countries encompass all stands except plantations and include stands that have been degraded to some degree by agriculture, fire, logging, and other factors. For all regions, trees are distinguished from shrubs on the basis of height. A mature tree has a single well-defined stem and is taller than 7 meters. A mature shrub is usually less than 7 meters tall.

Plantations refer to forest stands established artificially by afforestation and reforestation for industrial and nonindustrial usage. Reforestation does not include regeneration of old tree crops (through either natural regeneration or forest management), although some countries may report regeneration as reforestation. Many trees are also planted for nonindustrial uses, such as village wood lots. Reforestation data often exclude this component. The data presented here reflect plantation survival rates as estimated by FAO.

Average annual percent change is shown as a percentage of the exponential growth rate. If negative (in parentheses), these figures reflect net deforestation, which is defined as the clearing of forest lands for all forms of agricultural uses (shifting cultivation, permanent agriculture, and ranching) and for other land uses such as settlements, other infrastructure, and mining. In tropical countries, this entails clearing that reduces tree crown cover to less than 10 percent. It should be noted that deforestation, as defined here, does not reflect changes within the forest stand or site, such as selective logging (unless the forest cover is permanently reduced to less than 10 percent). Such changes are termed forest degradation, and they can substantially affect forests, forest soil, wildlife and its habitat, and the global carbon cycle. Thus, the effects from the reported deforestation figures may be less than the effects from the total deforestation that includes all types of forest alterations. Positive change figures reflect net afforestation within a country or region.

Forest area information for tropical and temperate developing countries is based on FAO's forest assessments. It is extracted mainly from the publication *State of the World's Forests 1997*. Only forest cover data for 1980 and plantation figures for 1990 are based on FAO's *Forest Resources Assessment 1990: Global Synthesis* (FRA 1990). Comparable plantation figures for 1995 were not sufficiently reliable for publication. Please note that forest cover data for 1980 were estimated by the World Resources Institute based on the *FRA 1990* natural forest and plantation figures. FAO's forest assessments produce consistent estimates on forest status for common reference years (1980, 1990, and 1995) and forest area change for the periods between these years. The estimates are made using a model to adjust baseline forest inventory data from each country to the common reference years. This model correlates the share of forest cover for each subnational unit to population density and growth, initial forest extent, and ecological zone. Existing forest inventory data at national and subnational scales are reviewed, adjusted to a common set of classifications and concepts, and combined in a database. To accomplish this, FAO uses a geographic information system to integrate statistical and map data. For the latest update (1995), forest inventory data additional to that available for the 1990 assessment was used for Brazil, Bolivia, Mexico, Cambodia,

Papua New Guinea, the Philippines, Côte d'Ivoire, Guinea-Bissau, and Sierra Leone.

The reliability of these modeled estimates hinges partly on the quality of the primary data sources feeding into the model. For the *FRA 1990*, FAO assessed the quality and appropriateness of the national forestry inventories and their contribution to the reliability of the reported state and change assessments. The variation in quality, comprehensiveness, and timeliness of the forest information is tremendous, and acute information deficits in regard to forest resources can easily be observed.

Although the deforestation model allowed standardization of country data to a common baseline, a number of additional factors may have contributed to discrepancies in forest area and change estimates for specific countries. Potential forest cover estimates for dry forests and the related adjustment function are of unknown reliability; in addition, for some countries, socioeconomic factors such as livestock projects in Central America and resettlement schemes in Indonesia may have played a larger role in deforestation. FAO acknowledged these shortcomings implicitly and noted that country estimates are "not intended to replace the original country information, which remain a unique source of reference."

Because of these shortcomings, readers are encouraged to refer to the original sources and the latest country inventories that use satellite data or extensive ground data for estimates of forest cover and deforestation.

Figures for the *number of enterprises* and *number of employees* in the *forest industry* are obtained for ITTO producer countries through responses to the ITTO Forecasting and Statistics Enquiry. In 1995 there were 25 ITTO producer countries. For those countries that did not respond to the 1995 Enquiry, estimates are provided by ITTO based on FAO statistical reports, Year 2000 progress reports, ITTO project reports, trade association statistics, etc. Figures are for enterprises and employees participating in forestry activities including logging and processing mills (sawmills, veneer mills, plywood mills, etc.).

Forest Ecosystems, 1996

Sources: Land area: Food and Agriculture Organization of the United Nations (FAO), *FAOSTAT Statistics Database.* Available online at http://www.fao.org (FAO, Rome, 1997). Closed forest data: D. Bryant, D. Nielsen, and L. Tangley, *The Last Frontier Forests: Ecosystems and Economies on the Edge* (World Resources Institute, Washington, D.C., 1997). Forest ecosystems: S. Iremonger, C. Ravilious, and T. Quinton, "A Statistical Analysis of Global Forest Conservation," in S. Iremonger, C. Ravilious, and T. Quinton, eds., *A Global Overview* of *Forest Conservation CD-ROM* (World Conservation Monitoring Centre [WCMC] and Centre for International Forestry Research, Cambridge, U.K., 1997).

Closed forests exclude some woodlands and wooded savannah.

Original forest as a percentage of land area refers to the estimate of the percentage of land that would have been covered by closed forest about 8,000 years ago assuming current climatic conditions, before large-scale disturbance by human society began. These data of estimated forest cover were developed by WCMC based on numerous global and regional biogeographic maps. These data overestimate where forests were in the northern boreal regions, particularly in Russia, because tundraforest transition zones were considered forest.

Current forests refer to estimated closed forest cover within the last 10 years or so (this varies by country). Only closed moist forests are depicted for Africa and Asia.

Frontier forests are large, relatively intact forest ecosystems. They represent undisturbed forest areas that are large enough to maintain all of their biodiversity, including viable populations of wideranging species associated with each forest type. A frontier forest must meet the following criteria:

- It is primarily forested.
- It is large enough to support viable populations of all species associated with that forest type, even in the face of natural disasters (such as hurricanes, etc.) of a magnitude to occur once in a century.
- Its structure and composition are determined mainly by natural events (such as fires, etc.), and it remains relatively unmanaged by humans, although limited human disturbance by traditional activities is acceptable.
- In forests where patches of trees of different ages occur naturally, the landscape shows this type of heterogeneity.
- It is dominated by indigenous tree species.
- It is home to most, if not all, other plants and animals that typically live in this type of forest.

Percent of *frontier forests threatened* refers to those frontier forests where ongoing or planned human activities such as logging, mining, and other large-scale disturbances will eventually degrade the ecosystem through species decline or extinction, drastic changes in the forest's age structure, etc., and would result, if continued, in the violation of one of the abovementioned criteria.

Forest ecosystems data for forest cover are for 1996. The WCMC analysis was carried out by overlaying forest maps with maps of protected areas using a Geographic Information System. The forest maps were created by WCMC from many national and regional maps showing forest extent. The legends of these maps were harmonized into 15 different tropical and 11 nontropical forest types for the globe, defined specifically for this study. The classification was designed to be of relevance for forest

conservation information. In general, WCMC assumed that the land cover categories shown in the source maps were correct and translated the legends directly to the 25 type classes for the world without attempting to assess the accuracy of the source data. Documentation for the source data is given in full by Iremonger *et al.* (1997).

Shrub-dominated lands were not included in the WCMC publication, but areas with sparse tree cover were. Although the aim was to exclude areas significantly affected by people from the *sparse trees and parkland* category, the source data for these areas generally gave vegetation structure and did not specify degree of anthropogenic disturbance. Some patchworks of disturbed forests and grasslands may have been included. The forest type categories were split between "tropical" and "nontropical." *Tropical* forests included all forests located between the Tropics of Cancer and Capricorn. All other forests were put into the *nontropical* category. Montane forests within the tropics that were classified in the source maps as "temperate" were registered in the "tropical" forests category in this study. The WCMC categories that included plantation forests and disturbed forests were excluded from this table. However, as the source data for plantation forests were scant, most of the plantation forests in the world were not recorded as such in the WCMC study and are therefore included in the categories describing natural forests. For example, all forests in Europe are classified as "natural" forests.

Percent protected includes forest areas that fall within the protected areas in the world that are listed as the World Conservation Union's (IUCN) management categories I–V. Please refer to Iremonger *et al.* (1997) or to the Sources and Technical Notes of Data Table 14.1 for a description of these management categories.

Data Table 11.3

Wood Production and Trade, 1983–95

Source: Food and Agriculture Organization of the United Nations (FAO), *FAOSTAT Statistics Database.* Available online at: http://www.fao.org (FAO, Rome, 1997).

Total roundwood production refers to all wood in the rough, whether destined for industrial or fuelwood uses. All wood felled or harvested from forests and trees outside the forest, with or without bark, round, split, roughly squared, or in other forms such as roots and stumps, is included.

Fuel and charcoal production covers all rough wood used for cooking, heating, and power production. Wood intended for charcoal production, pit kilns, and portable ovens is also included.

Industrial roundwood production comprises all roundwood products other than fuelwood and charcoal: sawlogs or veneer logs, posts, pitprops, pulpwood, and other roundwood industrial products.

Sawnwood production includes wood that has been sawn, planed, or shaped into products such as planks, beams, boards, rafters, "lumber," sleepers, etc. Wood flooring and wood-based panels are excluded. Sawnwood generally is thicker than 5 millimeters.

Paper production includes newsprint, printing and writing paper, packaging paper, household and sanitary paper, and other paper and paperboard.

The *quantity of net trade in roundwood* is the balance of imports minus exports. Exports are shown as a negative balance (in parentheses). Trade in roundwood includes sawlogs and veneer logs, fuelwood, pulpwood, other industrial roundwood, and the roundwood equivalent of trade in charcoal, wood residues, and chips and particles. Figures are the national totals averaged over a 3-year period in thousands of cubic meters. Imports are usually on a cost, insurance, and freight basis (c.i.f.) (i.e., insurance and freight costs added in). Exports are generally on a free-on-board basis (FOB) (i.e., not including insurance or freight costs).

Balance of trade is defined as exports minus imports. Figures are the national totals averaged over a 3-year period in millions of U.S. dollars. Imports are usually on a c.i.f. basis. Exports are generally on an FOB basis. Imports are shown as surplus over exports (in parentheses).

All data refer to both coniferous and nonconiferous wood. FAO compiles forest products data from responses to annual questionnaires sent to national governments. Data from other sources, such as national statistical yearbooks, are also used. In some cases, FAO prepares its own estimates. FAO continually revises its data using new information; the latest figures are subject to revision.

Statistics on the production of fuelwood and charcoal are lacking for many countries. FAO uses survey data when available to estimate fuelwood. Annual change is estimated based on population change.

For more information, please refer to the *FAOSTAT Statistics Database* online at: http://www.fao.org.

Data Table 11.4

Land Area and Use, 1982–94

Sources: Land area and use: Food and Agriculture Organization of the United Nations (FAO), *FAOSTAT Statistics Database.* Available online at: **http://www.fao.org** (FAO, Rome, 1997); population density: calculated from FAO land area data and population figures provided by United Nations (U.N.) Population Division, *World Population Prospects, 1950–2050 (The 1996 Revision),* on diskette (U.N., New York, 1996).

Land area and *land use* data are provided to FAO by national governments in response to annual questionnaires. FAO also compiles data from national agricultural censuses. When official information is lacking, FAO prepares its own estimates or relies on unofficial data. Several countries use definitions of total area and land use that differ from those used in this chapter. Please refer to the original sources for details.

FAO often adjusts the definitions of land use categories and sometimes substantially revises earlier data. For example, in 1985, FAO began to exclude from the cropland category land used for shifting cultivation but currently lying fallow. Because land use changes can reflect changes in data-reporting procedures along with actual land use changes, apparent trends should be interpreted with caution.

Land use data are periodically revised and may change significantly from year to year. For the most recent land use statistics, see the *FAOSTAT Statistics Database* online at: http://www.fao.org.

Land area data are for 1994. They exclude major inland water bodies, national claims to the continental shelf, and Exclusive Economic Zones.

The *population density* and *land use* figures for the world refer to the six inhabited continents. Population density was derived by using the population figures for 1996 published by the United Nations Population Division and land area data for 1994 from FAO. For more details on population data, please refer to the Sources and Technical Notes to Data Table 7.1.

Domesticated land as a percentage of land area provides a crude indicator of the degree to which national landscapes have been heavily modified through agricultural use. Domesticated land, as defined here, is a sum of FAO's "cropland" and "permanent pasture" land use categories. This indicator may overestimate or underestimate the actual degree to which a country's land area has been modified. Permanent pasture, for example, may include a significant proportion of rangeland in some countries, while consisting largely of heavily modified pasturelands in others. Domesticated land area does not include built-up lands or plantation forests, the latter constituting a major portion of heavily modified land area in many countries of the world.

Cropland includes land under temporary and permanent crops, temporary meadows, market and kitchen gardens, and temporary fallow. Permanent crops are those that do not need to be replanted after each harvest, such as cocoa, coffee, fruit, rubber, and vines. It excludes land used to grow trees for wood or timber.

Permanent pasture is land used for 5 or more years for forage, including natural crops and cultivated crops. This category is difficult for countries to assess because it includes wildland used for pasture. This means that shrub land and savannah areas can be reported either under this category or under *forest and woodland*. In addition, few countries regularly report data on permanent pasture. As a result, the absence of a change in permanent pasture area (e.g., 0 percent change for many African and Asian countries) may indicate differences in land classification and data reporting rather than actual conditions. Grassland not used for forage is included under *other land*.

Forest and woodland includes land under natural or planted stands of trees, as well as logged-over areas that will be reforested in the near future. Forest and woodland areas used exclusively for recreational purposes are excluded (these areas are reported under *other land*). These data are not comparable with data for total forest area presented in Data Table 11.2.

Other land includes uncultivated land, grassland not used for pasture, built-on areas, wetlands, wastelands, barren land, and roads.

C hapter 12

Fresh Water

Freshwater Resources and Withdrawals, 1970–98

Sources: Various

	Annual Internal Renewable Water Resources		Annual River Flows		Annual Withdrawals				Sectoral Withdrawals (percent)		
	Total (cubic km)	1998 Per Capita (cubic meters)	From Other Countries (cubic km)	To Other Countries (cubic km)	Year of Data	Total (cubic km)	Percentage of Water Resources	Per Capita (cubic meters)	Domestic	Industrial	Agricultural
WORLD	**41,022.00**	**6,918**			**1987**	**3,240.00**	**8**	**645**	**8**	**23**	**69**
AFRICA	**3,996.00**	**5,133**			**1995**	**145.14**	**4**	**202**	**7**	**5**	**88**
Algeria	13.87	460	0.4	0.7	1990	4.50	32	180	25	15	60
Angola	184.00	15,376	X	X	1987	0.48	0	57	14	10	76
Benin	10.30	1,751	15.5	X	1994	0.15	1	28	23	10	67
Botswana	2.90	1,870	11.8	X	1992	0.11	4	84	32	20	48
Burkina Faso	17.50	1,535	X	X	1992	0.38	2	39	19	0	81
Burundi	3.60	546	X	X	1987	0.10	3	20	36	0	64
Cameroon	268.00	18,711	0.0	0.0	1987	0.40	0	38	46	19	35
Central African Rep	141.00	40,413	X	X	1987	0.07	0	26	21	5	74
Chad	15.00	2,176	28.0	X	1987	0.18	1	34	16	2	82
Congo, Dem Rep	935.00	19,001	84.0	X	1990	0.36	0	10	61	16	23
Congo, Rep	222.00	78,668	610.0	X	1987	0.04	0	20	62	27	11
Côte d'Ivoire	76.70	5,265	1.0	X	1987	0.71	1	67	22	11	67
Egypt	2.80	43	55.5	0.0	1993	55.10	1,968	921	6	8	86
Equatorial Guinea	30.00	69,767	0.0	X	1987	0.01	0	15	81	13	6
Eritrea	2.80	789	6.0	X	X	X	X	X	X	X	X
Ethiopia	110.00	1,771	0.0	X	1987	2.21	2	51	11	3	86
Gabon	164.00	140,171	0.0	X	1987	0.06	0	70	72	22	6
Gambia, The	3.00	2,513	5.0	X	1982	0.02	1	29	7	2	91
Ghana	30.30	1,607	22.9	X	1970	0.30	1	35	35	13	52
Guinea	226.00	29,454	0.0	X	1987	0.74	0	142	10	3	87
Guinea-Bissau	16.00	14,109	11.0	X	1991	0.02	0	17	60	4	36
Kenya	20.20	696	10.0	X	1990	2.05	10	87	20	4	76
Lesotho	5.23	2,395	0.0	X	1987	0.05	1	30	22	22	56
Liberia	200.00	72,780	32.0	X	1987	0.13	0	54	27	13	60
Libya	0.60	100	0.0	0.0	1994	4.60	767	880	11	2	87
Madagascar	337.00	20,614	0.0	0.0	1984	16.30	5	1,579	1	0	99
Malawi	17.54	1,690	1.1	X	1994	0.94	5	98	10	3	86
Mali	60.00	5,071	40.0	X	1987	1.36	2	162	2	1	97
Mauritania	0.40	163	11.0	X	1985	1.63	407	923	6	2	92
Mauritius	2.21	1,915	0.0	0.0	1974	0.36	16	410	16	7	77
Morocco	30.00	1,071	0.0	0.3	1992	10.85	36	433	5	3	92
Mozambique	100.00	5,350	116.0	0.0	1992	0.61	1	40	9	2	89
Namibia	6.20	3,751	39.3	X	1991	0.25	4	179	29	3	68
Niger	3.50	346	29.0	X	1988	0.50	14	69	16	2	82
Nigeria	221.00	1,815	59.0	X	1987	3.63	2	41	31	15	54
Rwanda	6.30	965	X	X	1993	0.77	12	135	5	2	94
Senegal	26.40	2,933	13.0	X	1987	1.36	5	202	5	3	92
Sierra Leone	160.00	34,957	0.0	X	1987	0.37	0	98	7	4	89
Somalia	6.00	563	7.5	X	1987	0.81	14	99	3	0	97
South Africa	44.80	1,011	5.2	X	1990	13.31	30	359	17	11	72
Sudan	35.00	1,227	119.0	65.5	1995	17.80	51	666	4	1	94
Swaziland	2.64	2,836	1.9	X	1980	0.66	25	1,171	2	2	96
Tanzania	80.00	2,485	9.0	X	1994	1.16	1	40	9	2	89
Togo	11.50	2,594	0.5	X	1987	0.09	1	28	62	13	25
Tunisia	3.52	371	0.6	0.0	1990	3.07	87	376	9	3	89
Uganda	39.00	1,829	27.0	X	1970	0.20	1	20	32	8	60
Zambia	80.20	9,229	35.8	X	1994	1.71	2	216	16	7	77
Zimbabwe	14.10	1,182	5.9	X	1987	1.22	9	136	14	7	79
EUROPE	**6,234.56**	**8,547**			**1995**	**455.29**	**7**	**625**	**14**	**55**	**31**
Albania	44.50	2,903	11.3	X	1970	0.20	2	94	6	18	76 a
Austria	56.30	6,857	34.0	X	1991	2.36	4	304	33	58	9
Belarus, Rep	37.20	3,595	20.8	54.9	1990	2.73	7	264	22	43	35
Belgium	8.40	822	4.1	X	1980	9.03	108	917	11	85	4 a
Bosnia and Herzegovina	X	X	X	X	X	X	X	X	X	X	X
Bulgaria	18.00	2,146	187.0	X	1988	13.90	77	1,574	3	76	22 a
Croatia, Rep	61.40	13,663	X	X	X	X	X	X	X	X	X
Czech Rep	58.21	5,694	X	X	1991	2.74	5	266	41	57	2
Denmark	11.00	2,092	2.0	X	1990	1.20	11	233	30	27	43 a
Estonia, Rep	12.72	8,642	0.1	X	1995	0.16	1	107	56	39	5
Finland	110.00	21,334	3.0	X	1991	2.20	2	440	12	85	3 a
France	180.00	3,065	18.0	20.5	1990	37.73	21	665	16	69	15 a
Germany	96.00	1,165	75.0	X	1991	46.27	48	580	11	70	20
Greece	45.15	4,279	13.5	3.0	1980	5.04	11	523	8	29	63 a
Hungary	6.00	604	114.0	X	1991	6.81	114	660	9	55	36 a
Iceland	168.00	606,498	0.0	0.0	1991	0.16	0	636	31	63	6 a
Ireland	47.00	13,187	3.0	X	1980	0.79	2	233	16	74	10 a
Italy	159.40	2,785	7.6	0.0	1990	56.20	35	986	14	27	59 a
Latvia, Rep	16.74	6,685	18.7	X	1994	0.29	2	114	55	32	13
Lithuania, Rep	15.56	4,174	9.3	X	1993	0.25	2	68	81	16	3
Macedonia, FYR	X	X	X	X	X	X	X	X	X	X	X
Moldova, Rep	1.00	225	11.7	12.0	1992	2.96	296	667	9	65	26
Netherlands	10.00	635	80.0	X	1991	7.81	78	518	5	61	34 a
Norway	384.00	87,691	8.0	X	1985	2.03	1	488	20	72	8 a
Poland, Rep	49.40	1,278	6.8	X	1991	12.28	25	321	13	76	11 a
Portugal	38.00	3,878	31.6	X	1990	7.29	19	738	15	37	48 a
Romania	37.00	1,639	171.0	X	1994	26.00	70	1,139	8	33	59 a
Russian Federation	4,312.70	29,115	185.5	54.0	1994	77.10	2	521	19	62	20
Slovak Rep	30.79	5,745	X	X	1991	1.78	6	337	X	X	X
Slovenia, Rep	X	X	X	X	X	X	X	X	X	X	X
Spain	110.30	2,775	1.0	17.0	1991	30.75	28	781	12	26	62 a
Sweden	176.00	19,858	4.0	X	1991	2.93	2	340	36	55	9 a
Switzerland	42.50	5,802	7.5	X	1991	1.19	3	173	23	73	4 a
Ukraine	53.10	1,029	86.5	X	1992	25.99	49	504	18	52	30
United Kingdom	71.00	1,219	0.0	X	1991	11.79	17	204	20	77	3 a
Yugoslavia, Fed Rep	X	X	X	X	X	X	X	X	X	X	X

	Annual Internal Renewable Water Resources		Annual River Flows			Annual Withdrawals			Sectoral Withdrawals (percent)		
	Total (cubic km)	1998 Per Capita (cubic meters)	From Other Countries (cubic km)	To Other Countries (cubic km)	Year of Data	Total (cubic km)	Percentage of Water Resources	Per Capita (cubic meters)	Domestic	Industrial	Agricultural
NORTH AMERICA	**5,308.60**	**17,458**			**1991**	**512.43**	**10**	**1,798**	**13**	**47**	**39**
Canada	2,849.50	94,373	51.5	X	1991	45.10	2	1,602	18	70	12 a
United States	2,459.10	8,983	18.9	X	1990	467.34	19	1,839	13	45	42
CENTRAL AMERICA	**1,056.67**	**8,084**			**1987**	**96.01**	**9**	**916**	**6**	**8**	**86**
Belize	16.00	69,565	X	X	1987	0.02	0	109	10	0	90 a
Costa Rica	95.00	26,027	X	X	1970	1.35	1	780	4	7	89 a
Cuba	34.50	3,104	0.0	X	1975	8.10	23	870	9	2	89 a
Dominican Rep	20.00	2,430	X	X	1987	2.97	15	446	5	6	89 a
El Salvador	18.95	3,128	X	X	1975	1.00	5	244	7	4	89 a
Guatemala	116.00	10,033	X	X	1970	0.73	1	139	9	17	74 a
Haiti	11.00	1,460	X	X	1987	0.04	0	7	24	8	68 a
Honduras	55.42	9,015	8.0	8.0	1992	1.52	3	294	4	5	91 a
Jamaica	8.30	3,269	0.0	X	1975	0.32	4	159	7	7	86 a
Mexico	357.40	3,729	X	X	1991	77.62	22	915	6	8	86 a
Nicaragua	175.00	39,203	X	X	1975	0.89	1	368	25	21	54 a
Panama	144.00	52,042	X	X	1975	1.30	1	754	12	11	77 a
Trinidad and Tobago	5.10	3,869	0.0	X	1975	0.15	3	148	27	38	35 a
SOUTH AMERICA	**9,526.00**	**28,702**			**1995**	**106.21**	**1**	**335**	**18**	**23**	**59**
Argentina	694.00	19,212	300.0	X	1976	27.60	4	1,043	9	18	73 a
Bolivia	300.00	37,703	X	X	1987	1.24	0	201	10	5	85 a
Brazil	5,190.00	31,424	1,760.0	X	1990	36.47	1	246	22	19	59 a
Chile	468.00	31,570	X	X	1975	16.80	4	1,625	6	5	89 a
Colombia	1,070.00	28,393	X	X	1987	5.34	0	174	41	16	43 a
Ecuador	314.00	25,791	X	X	1987	5.56	2	581	7	3	90 a
Guyana	241.00	281,542	X	X	1992	1.46	1	1,819	1	0	99 a
Paraguay	94.00	18,001	220.0	X	1987	0.43	0	112	15	7	78 a
Peru	40.00	1,613	X	X	1987	6.10	15	300	19	9	72 a
Suriname	200.00	452,489	X	X	1987	0.46	0	1,192	6	5	89 a
Uruguay	59.00	18,215	65.0	X	1965	0.65	1	241	6	3	91 a
Venezuela	856.00	36,830	461.0	X	1970	4.10	0	382	43	11	46 a
ASIA	**13,206.74**	**3,680**			**1987**	**1,633.85**	**12**	**542**	**6**	**9**	**85**
Afghanistan, Islamic State	55.00	2,354	10.0	X	1987	25.85	47	1,825	1	0	99 a
Armenia, Rep	9.07	2,493	1.5	5.2	1994	2.93	32	804	30	4	66
Azerbaijan	8.12	1,069	22.2	X	1995	16.53	204	2,177	5	25	70
Bangladesh	1,357.00	10,940	1,000.0	X	1987	22.50	2	217	3	1	96 a
Bhutan	95.00	49,557	X	X	1987	0.02	0	13	36	10	54 a
Cambodia	88.10	8,195	410.0	X	1987	0.52	1	66	5	1	94 a
China	2,800.00	2,231	0.0	X	1980	460.00	16	461	6	7	87 a
Georgia	58.13	10,682	5.2	20.2	1990	3.47	6	637	21	20	59
India	1,850.00	1,896	235.0	X	1975	380.00	21	612	3	4	93 a
Indonesia	2,530.00	12,251	X	X	1987	16.59	1	96	13	11	76 a
Iran, Islamic Rep	128.20	1,755	9.3	55.9	1993	70.03	55	1,079	6	2	92
Iraq	35.20	1,615	40.2	X	1990	42.80	122	2,368	3	5	92
Israel	1.70	289	0.5	0.0	1989	1.85	109	407	16	5	79
Japan	547.00	4,344	0.0	X	1990	90.80	17	735	17	33	50 a
Jordan	0.68	114	0.2	X	1993	0.98	145	201	22	3	75
Kazakstan, Rep	75.42	4,484	34.2	32.0	1993	33.67	45	2,002	2	17	81
Korea, Dem People's Rep	67.00	2,887	X	X	1987	14.16	21	727	11	16	73 a
Korea, Rep	66.12	1,434	X	X	1992	27.60	42	632	19	35	46 a
Kuwait	0.02	11	0.0	X	1994	0.54	2,690	307	37	2	60
Kyrgyz Rep	46.45	10,394	25.9	35.6	1994	10.08	22	2,257	3	3	94
Lao People's Dem Rep	270.00	50,392	X	X	1987	0.99	0	259	8	10	82 a
Lebanon	4.20	1,315	0.6	0.9	1994	1.29	31	444	28	4	68
Malaysia	456.00	21,259	X	X	1975	9.42	2	768	23	30	47 a
Mongolia	24.60	9,375	X	X	1987	0.55	2	271	11	27	62 a
Myanmar	1,082.00	22,719	X	X	1987	3.96	0	101	7	3	90 a
Nepal	170.00	7,338	X	X	1987	2.68	2	154	4	1	95 a
Oman	0.99	393	0.0	X	1991	1.22	124	656	5	2	94
Pakistan	248.00	1,678	170.3	X	1991	155.60	63	1,269	2	2	97
Philippines	323.00	4,476	0.0	X	1975	29.50	9	686	18	21	61 a
Saudi Arabia	2.40	119	0.0	X	1992	17.02	709	1,003	9	1	90
Singapore	0.60	172	0.0	X	1975	0.19	32	84	45	51	4 a
Sri Lanka	43.20	2,341	0.0	X	1970	6.30	15	503	2	2	96 a
Syrian Arab Rep	7.00	456	37.7	32.0	1993	14.41	206	1,069	4	2	94
Tajikistan, Rep	66.30	11,171	50.3	86.9	1994	11.87	18	2,001	3	4	92
Thailand	110.00	1,845	69.0	X	1987	31.90	29	602	4	6	90 a
Turkey	196.00	3,074	7.6	60.4	1992	31.60	16	544	16	11	72
Turkmenistan, Rep	1.00	232	70.0	52.6	1994	23.78	2,378	5,723	1	1	98
United Arab Emirates	0.15	64	0.0	X	1995	2.11	1,405	954	7	1	92
Uzbekistan, Rep	16.34	704	34.1	X	1994	58.05	355	2,501	4	2	94
Vietnam	376.00	4,827	X	X	1992	28.90	8	416	13	9	78 a
Yemen	4.10	243	X	X	1990	2.93	72	253	7	1	92
OCEANIA	**1,614.25**	**54,795**			**1995**	**16.73**	**1**	**591**	**64**	**2**	**34**
Australia	343.00	18,596	0.0	X	1985	14.60	4	933	65	2	33 a
Fiji	28.55	34,732	0.0	X	1987	0.03	0	42	20	20	60 a
New Zealand	327.00	88,859	0.0	325.0	1991	2.00	1	589	46	10	44 a
Papua New Guinea	801.00	174,055	X	X	1987	0.10	0	28	29	22	49 a
Solomon Islands	44.70	107,194	0.0	X	1987	0.00	0	0	40	20	40 a

Notes: a. Sectoral withdrawal estimates are for 1987.
Regional and world totals include countries not listed.
Total withdrawals may exceed 100 percent due to groundwater drawdowns, withdrawals from river inflows, and the operation of desalinization plants.

Groundwater and Desalinization, 1998

Sources: Economic Commission for Europe, Organisation for Economic Co-Operation and Development, and Food and Agriculture Organization of the United Nations

	Average Annual Groundwater Recharge			Annual Groundwater Withdrawals							1990 Desalinated Water Production (million cubic meters)
	Total (cubic km)		1998 Per Capita (cubic meters)	Year	Total (cubic km)	Percent of Annual Recharge	Per Capita (cubic meters)	Sectoral Share (percentage)			
								Domestic	Industry	Agriculture	
WORLD											
AFRICA											
Algeria	1.70		56	1985	2	117.6	91	X	X	X	30.00
Angola	72.00		6,017	X	X	X	X	X	X	X	0.14
Benin	1.80	a	306	X	X	X	X	X	X	X	X
Botswana	1.70	a	1,096	X	X	X	X	X	X	X	X
Burkina Faso	9.50	a	833	X	X	X	X	X	X	X	X
Burundi	2.10	b	319	X	X	X	X	X	X	X	X
Cameroon	100.00	b	6,982	X	X	X	X	X	X	X	X
Central African Rep	56.00	b	16,050	X	X	X	X	X	X	X	X
Chad	11.50	b	1,669	1990	0	0.7	15.3	29.4	0.0	70.6	X
Congo, Dem Rep	421.00	b	149,185	X	X	X	X	X	X	X	0.20
Congo, Rep	198.00	b	70,163	X	X	X	X	X	X	X	X
Côte d'Ivoire	37.70	a	2,588	X	X	X	X	X	X	X	X
Egypt	1.30	a	20	1985	3	261.5	68.3	X	X	X	10.00
Equatorial Guinea	10.00	b	23,256	X	X	X	X	X	X	X	X
Eritrea	X		X	X	X	X	X	X	X	X	X
Ethiopia	44.00	b,c	708	X	X	X	X	X	X	X	X
Gabon	62.00	b	52,991	1989	0	0.0	0.6	100.0	0.0	0.0	X
Gambia, The	0.50	b	419	X	X	X	X	X	X	X	X
Ghana	26.30	a	1,326	X	X	X	X	X	X	X	X
Guinea	38.00	b	4,952	X	X	X	X	X	X	X	X
Guinea-Bissau	14.00	b	12,346	X	X	X	X	X	X	X	X
Kenya	3.00	a	103	X	X	X	X	X	X	X	X
Lesotho	0.50	b	229	X	X	X	X	X	X	X	X
Liberia	60.00	b	21,834	X	X	X	X	X	X	X	X
Libya	0.50	a	84	1985	2	420.0	554.7	13.3	4.3	82.5	3.00
Madagascar	55.00	b	3,364	1984	5	8.7	461.2	100.0	0.0	0.0	X
Malawi	1.40	b	135	X	X	X	X	X	X	X	X
Mali	20.00	a	1,690	1989	0	0.5	11.2	7.1	0.0	92.9	X
Mauritania	0.30	a	122	1985	1	293.3	498.3	X	X	X	1.70
Mauritius	0.68	a	589	X	X	X	X	X	X	X	X
Morocco	7.50	a	268	1985	3	40.0	138.6	X	X	X	4.00
Mozambique	17.00	b	910	X	X	X	X	X	X	X	0.10
Namibia	2.10	b	1,270	X	X	X	X	X	X	X	3.00
Niger	2.50	a	247	1988	0		17.9	57.7	3.8	38.5	X
Nigeria	87.00	b	714	X	X	X	X	X	X	X	3.00
Rwanda	3.60	b	551	X	X	X	X	X	X	X	X
Senegal	7.60	b	844	1985	0	3.3	39.2	25.0	0.0	75.0	0.05
Sierra Leone	50.00	b	10,924	X	X	X	X	X	X	X	X
Somalia	3.30	b	310	1985	0	9.1	38.1	X	X	X	0.10
South Africa	4.80		108	1980	2	37.3	61.4	10.6	5.6	83.8	17.50
Sudan	7.00		245	1985	0	4.0	13.0	X	X	X	0.40
Swaziland	X		X	X	X	X	X	X	X	X	X
Tanzania	30.00	b	932	X	X	X	X	X	X	X	X
Togo	5.70	a	1,286	X	X	X	X	X	X	X	X
Tunisia	1.21	a	127	1985	1	101.7	167.7	13.6	0.0	86.4	9.00
Uganda	29.00	b	1,360	X	X	X	X	X	X	X	X
Zambia	47.10		5,420	X	X	X	X	X	X	X	X
Zimbabwe	5.00	b	419	X	X	X	X	X	X	X	X
EUROPE											
Albania	7.00	b	2,032	X	X	X	X	X	X	X	X
Austria	22.30	b	2,716	1990	1	5.0	144.7	52.1	42.7	5.1 f	X
Belarus, Rep	18.00		1,740	1985	1	5.9	106.0	55.6	14.1	30.3	X
Belgium	0.86	a	84	1980	1	90.7	79.2	68.3	27.0	4.8	X
Bosnia and Herzegovina	X		X	X	X	X	X	X	X	X	X
Bulgaria	13.40	a	1,598	1988	5	37.3	566.1	X	X	X	X
Croatia, Rep	X		X	X	X	X	X	X	X	X	X
Czech Rep	X		X	1990	1	X	77.9	X	X	X	X
Denmark	30.00		5,706	1985	1	3.7	215.1	40.2	22.0	37.9 f	X
Estonia, Rep	4.00		2,718	X	X	X	X	X	X	X	X
Finland	1.90		369	1990	0	12.4	47.3	64.9	10.8	24.3 f	X
France	100.00	b	1,703	1990	6	6.2	109.5	52.5	30.2	17.3 f	X
Germany	45.70	b	555	1990	8 g	16.9	97.4	48.6	47.5	3.9 f	X
Greece	2.50	h	237	1980	2	74.8	193.9	12.8	2.7	84.5	X
Hungary	6.80	b	685	1990	1	15.1	99.1	35.0	47.5	17.5 f	X
Iceland	24.00	b	86,643	1985	0	0.4	394.2	X	X	X	X
Ireland	3.46	a	971	1980	0	4.9	50.0	34.5	36.8	28.7	X
Italy	30.00	b	524	1985	12	40.0	211.4	53.1	13.3	33.7	X
Latvia, Rep	2.20		879	X	X	X	X	X	X	X	X
Lithuania, Rep	1.20		322	X	X	X	X	X	X	X	X
Macedonia, FYR	X		X	X	X	X	X	X	X	X	X
Moldova, Rep	0.40		90	X	X	X	X	X	X	X	X
Netherlands	4.50	h	286	1985	1	25.3	78.7	32.0	44.5	23.4 f	X
Norway	96.00	b	21,923	1985	0	0.1	26.5	27.3	72.7	0.0	X
Poland, Rep	36.00		931	1990	2	6.7	63.2	70.0	30.0	0.0 f	X
Portugal	5.10	a	521	1990	3	60.1	310.6	38.6	22.8	38.6 f	X
Romania	8.30	h	368	1975	1	14.2	55.5	61.0	38.1	0.8	X
Russian Federation	788.00		5,320	X	X	0.0	X	X	X	X	X
Slovak Rep	X		X	1990	1	X	142.5	X	X	X	X
Slovenia, Rep	X		X	X	X	X	X	X	X	X	X
Spain	20.70	i	521	1990	6	26.6	140.0	X	22.2 j	77.8 f	X
Sweden	20.00	a	2,257	1990	1	3.0	69.8	91.7	8.3	0.0	X
Switzerland	2.70		369	1990	1	35.1	138.6	94.7	5.3	0.0 f	X
Ukraine	20.00		388	1985	4	21.1	82.8	30.3	17.5	52.1	X
United Kingdom	9.80		168	1990	3	27.6	47.1	51.3	46.6	2.1 f	X
Yugoslavia, Fed Rep	X		X	X	X	X	X	X	X	X	X

Data Table 12.2 continued

	Average Annual Groundwater Recharge		Annual Groundwater Withdrawals							1990 Desalinated Water Production (million cubic meters)
	Total (cubic km)	1998 Per Capita (cubic meters)	Year	Total (cubic km)	Percent of Annual Recharge	Per Capita (cubic meters)	Domestic	Industry	Agriculture	
NORTH AMERICA										
Canada	369.60	12,241	1990	1	0.3	38.8	43.3	14.2	42.5	X
United States	1,514.00	5,531	1990	110	7.3	432.9	22.7	6.1	71.1	X
CENTRAL AMERICA										
Belize	X	X	X	X	X	X	X	X	X	X
Costa Rica	21.00 b	5,753	X	X	X	X	X	X	X	X
Cuba	8.00 b	720	1975	4	47.5	408.3	X	X	X	X
Dominican Rep	3.00 b	364	X	X	X	X	X	X	X	X
El Salvador	X	X	X	X	X	X	X	X	X	X
Guatemala	31.00 b	2,681	X	X	X	X	X	X	X	X
Haiti	2.50 b	332	X	X	X	X	X	X	X	X
Honduras	39.00 b	6,345	X	X	X	X	X	X	X	X
Jamaica	X	X	X	X	X	X	X	X	X	X
Mexico	139.00 b	1,450	1985	24	16.9	311.4	13.2	23.0	63.8	X
Nicaragua	59.00	13,217	X	X	X	X	X	X	X	X
Panama	42.00 b	15,179	X	X	X	X	X	X	X	X
Trinidad and Tobago	X	X	X	X	X	X	X	X	X	X
SOUTH AMERICA										
Argentina	128.00 b	3,543	1975	5	3.7	180.4	10.6	19.1	70.2	X
Bolivia	130.00 b	16,338	X	X	X	X	X	X	X	X
Brazil	1,874.00 b	11,347	X	X	X	X	X	X	X	X
Chile	140.00 b	9,444	X	X	X	X	X	X	X	X
Colombia	510.00 b	13,533	X	X	X	X	X	X	X	X
Ecuador	134.00 b	11,006	X	X	X	X	X	X	X	X
Guyana	103.00 b	120,327	X	X	X	X	X	X	X	X
Paraguay	41.00 b	7,851	X	X	X	X	X	X	X	X
Peru	303.00 b	12,219	1973	2	0.7	139.4	25.0	15.0	60.0	X
Suriname	80.00 b	180,995	X	X	X	X	X	X	X	X
Uruguay	23.00 b	7,101	X	X	X	X	X	X	X	X
Venezuela	227.00 b	9,767	X	X	X	X	X	X	X	X
ASIA										
Afghanistan, Islamic State	29.00 b	1,241	X	X	X	X	X	X	X	X
Armenia, Rep	4.20	1,154	X	X	X	X	X	X	X	X
Azerbaijan	6.50	856	X	X	X	X	X	X	X	X
Bangladesh	34.00 b	274	1979	3	10.0	39.6	12.9	0.9	86.2	X
Bhutan	X	X	X	X	X	X	X	X	X	X
Cambodia	30.00 b	2,790	X	X	X	X	X	X	X	X
China	870.00 b	693	1985	75	8.6	69.7	X	46.4 j	53.6	X
Georgia	17.23	3,166	X	X	X	X	X	X	X	X
India	350.00 b	359	1979	150	42.9	222.4	3.1	1.3	95.7	X
Indonesia	226.00 b	1,094	X	X	X	X	X	X	X	X
Iran, Islamic Rep	49.00	671	1980	29	59.2	738.8	X	X	X	2.90 k
Iraq	1.20	55	1985	0	16.7	13.1	55.6	44.4	0.0	X
Israel	1.10 a	187	1986	1	109.1	279.1	X	X	X	X
Japan	185.00 b	1,469	1990	13	7.0	104.3	29.3	40.7	30.1	X
Jordan	0.58 a	97	1985	0	70.7	107.0	X	X	X	2.00 l
Kazakstan, Rep	35.87	2,133	X	X	X	X	X	X	X	X
Korea, Dem People's Rep	X	X	X	X	X	X	X	X	X	X
Korea, Rep	X	X	1985	1	X	29.4	0.0	83.3 j	16.7	X
Kuwait	X	X	X	X	X	X	X	X	X	231.00 l
Kyrgyz Rep	13.60	3,043	X	X	X	X	X	X	X	X
Lao People's Dem Rep	50.00 b	9,332	X	X	X	X	X	X	X	X
Lebanon	3.20 b	1,002	1985	1	18.8	224.9	X	X	X	X
Malaysia	71.00 b	3,310	X	X	X	X	X	X	X	X
Mongolia	23.00 b	8,765	X	X	X	X	X	X	X	X
Myanmar	156.00 b	3,276	X	X	X	X	X	X	X	X
Nepal	X	X	X	X	X	X	X	X	X	X
Oman	0.96	381	1985	0	41.9	280.7	X	X	X	34.00 m
Pakistan	55.00	372	1980	45	81.8	527.6	X	11.1 j	88.9	X
Philippines	180.00 b	2,494	1980	4	2.2	82.8	0.0	50.0	50.0	X
Saudi Arabia	2.20	109	1985	7	337.7	587.4	5.4	8.1	86.5	714.00 m
Singapore	X	X	X	X	X	X	X	X	X	X
Sri Lanka	17.00 b	921	X	X	X	X	X	X	X	X
Syrian Arab Rep	4.29	280	1985	4	85.5	353.0	X	X	X	X
Tajikistan, Rep	6.00	1,011	X	X	X	X	X	X	X	X
Thailand	43.00 b	721	1980	1	1.6	15.0	60.0	25.7	14.3	X
Turkey	20.00 h	314	1990	6	31.5	112.3	42.9	0.0	57.1	0.50
Turkmenistan, Rep	3.36	778	X	X	X	X	X	X	X	X
United Arab Emirates	0.12	51	1985	0	X	251.3	X	X	X	385.00 m
Uzbekistan, Rep	19.68	848	X	X	X	X	X	X	X	X
Vietnam	84.00 b	1,078	X	X	X	X	X	X	X	X
Yemen	1.50	89	1985	1	90.0	139.2	X	X	X	10.00 n
OCEANIA										
Australia	X	X	1983	2	X	162.2	X	22.6 j	77.4	X
Fiji	72.00 a	87,591	X	X	X	X	X	X	X	X
New Zealand	198.00 b	53,804	X	X	X	X	X	X	X	X
Papua New Guinea	X	X	X	X	X	X	X	X	X	X
Solomon Islands	X	X	X	X	X	X	X	X	X	X

Notes: a. Sum of all aquifer recharge flows. b. Sum of all groundwater flows (as a constituent of surface water flows). c. Ethiopia includes Eritrea. d. 1988. e. 1992. f. Sectoral data predate other withdrawal data. g. Sum of the total groundwater flow that is exploitable. h. Combined with 1975 withdrawal data from the former German Democratic Republic. i. Sum of groundwater flows collected by water courses and those that discharge directly to the sea. j. Domestic and industrial withdrawals combined. k. 1991. l. 1993. m. 1995. n. 1989.

Water Quality in European Lakes, 1994

Source: European Environment Agency

Lake	Countries	Surface Area (km²)	Volume (km³)	Maximum Depth (m)	Mean Depth (m)	Catchment Area (km²)	Years of Data	Secchi Depth (m) {a}	pH	Chlorophyll (µg/l)	Phosphorous (µg/l)	Nitrogen (mg/l)	Chloride (mg/l)
Ammersee	DE	47	1.8	81	38	993	1975	4.0	X	X	55	X	X
Arresø	DK	42	0.1	6	3	258	1990	0.4	9.5	345	514	3.5	X
Attersee	AT	46	3.9	171	84	464	1975-79	8.0-9.0	8.0	X	7	X	X
Balaton	HU	593	1.9	12	3	5,181	1979-83	0.6	8.4	8-36	30-86	0.7-1.4	X
Bodensee	AT, DE, CH	539	49.0	252	90	10,900	1991	X	X	X	32	1.0	X
Bolsena	IT	114	9.2	151	81	273	X	7.0	X	X	25	X	X
Bracciano	IT	57	5.1	165	89	147	X	6.0	X	X	10	X	X
Chiemsee	DE	80	2.0	73	26	1,399	1983	X	X	6	30	X	X
Como	IT	146	22.5	410	153	4,570	X	1.0	X	X	48	X	X
Corrib	IR	170	X	X	X	X	1991	4.7	X	3	11	X	X
Derg	IR	116	0.9	36	8	10,280	1991-92	1.7	X	17	43	X	X
Dospat reservoir	BG	22	0.4	46	20	432	1984-86	X	6.5	45	60	0.8	X
Dubasari	MD	68	0.3	20	4	53,590	1991	X	8.0	X	111	1.9	49.0
Eemmeer & Gooimeer	NL	54	X	10	2	X	1990	X	8.8	130	680	0.4	X
Femunden	NO	204	6.0	150	30	1,723	1991	11.0	6.7	1	4	0.2	X
Garda	IT	368	49.0	350	133	2,290	X	5.0	X	X	10	X	X
Haringvliet	NL	86	X	38	10	X	1990	1.0	8.1	9	195	0.3	X
Hjälmaren	SE	478	3.0	20	6	3,569	1990	2.0	7.6	12	46	0.7	12.0
Ijsselmeer	NL	2,000	X	6	5	X	1990	1.0	8.5	81	170	0.1	X
Ilmen	RS	1,124	2.9	10	3	66,400	X	X	X	3	70	0.9	28.0
Inari	FI	1,102	15.1	96	14	13,400	1991	8.0	7.2	1	4	0.2	X
Iseo	IT	61	7.6	251	123	1,736	X	4.0	X	X	32	X	X
Lac Léman	FR, CH	584	89.0	310	153	7,975	1991	8.0	X	6	52	0.7	6.0
Lac Lucerne	CH	114	11.8	214	104	1,831	1991	X	X	X	5	0.6	X
Lac Neuchâtel	CH	218	14.0	152	64	2,670	1991	12.0	8.4	1	20	1.3	X
Ladoga	RS	17,670	908.0	258	51	258,600	1976-85	3.0	X	3	27	0.6	X
Lago Maggiore	IT, CH	213	37.5	372	177	6,598	X	2.0	8.8	3	14-25	0.9	X
Lago Trasimeno	IT	124	0.6	6	5	396	X	1.0	X	X	55	X	X
Lebsko	PL	71	0.1	6	2	1,536	1990	1.0	X	100	137	1.6	X
Loch Awe	UK	39	1.2	94	32	780	1977-78	3.0	6.9	2	X	X	X
Loch Lomond	UK	71	2.6	190	37	781	1991-92	X	8.9	137	120	2.2	X
Loch Morar	UK	27	2.3	310	87	142	1977-78	6-10	6.6	1	X	X	X
Loch Ness	UK	56	7.5	230	132	1,775	1977-78	4.0	6.7	1	X	X	X
Lough Neigh	UK	396	4.8	34	12	4,453	1975-87	1.1	8.3	49	108	2.2	X
Mälaren	SE	1,140	14.0	61	13	21,463	1990	1.0	7.6	10	32	0.9	8.0
Mamry Pólnocne	PL	26	0.3	44	12	596	1990	4.0	X	3	60	1.0	X
Markemeer	NL	670	X	5	4	X	1990	X	8.3	10	45	0.1	X
Mask	IR	80	X	X	X	X	1991	4.5	X	3	11	X	X
Mjøsa	NO	362	56.2	449	153	16,420	1991	9.0	7.1	3	7	0.4	X
Müritz	DE	114	0.9	31	8	X	X	2.0	X	X	80	X	X
Neusiedlersee	AT, HU	300	0.3	2	1	1,000	1977	X	8.7	12	102	X	X
Niegocin	PL	26	0.3	40	10	378	1990	1.0	X	34	300	1.3	X
Ohri	AL	363	52.6	287	145	599	X	X	X	X	X	X	X
Onega	RS	9,670	292.0	120	30	52,970	1967-89	4.0	X	4	12	0.6	2.0
Oulujärvi	FI	893	6.8	35	8	19,000	1991	2.0	6.7	7	14	0.4	X
Øyeren	NO	85	1.1	70	13	40,000	1991	3.0	7.2	4	9	0.4	X
Päijänne	FI	1,054	17.8	98	17	25,400	1991	X	7.1	X	7	0.5	X
Peipus	EE, RS	3,570	27.0	47	7	44,350	1980-86	1.8-3.6	7.8-8.1	14	X	0.8	5.3-11.8
Pielinen	FI	867	8.5	60	10	12,823	1991	4.0	6.4	3	10	0.5	X
Prespa	AL, GR	329	5.9	35	18	599	X	X	X	X	X	X	X
Randsfjorden	NO	137	6.1	121	44	3,663	1991	8.0	7.3	1	5	0.5	X
Ree	IR	105	0.7	35	6	4,530	1993-94	1.5	X	15	40	X	X
Saimaa	FI	1,147	13.9	82	12	60,100	1991	4.0	6.9	3	6	0.5	X
Shkrodra	AL, FYROM	368	2.9	10	8	1,026	1972-73	4.0	7.8	X	X	X	X
Sniardwy	PL	114	0.7	23	6	2,425	1990	2.0	X	17	115	1.1	X
Snåsavatnet	NO	121	5.5	121	46	1,433	1988	4.0	7.1	2	5	0.2	X
Starnberger See	DE	56	3.0	128	53	258	1978-79	8.0	X	6	26	X	X
Storsjøen	NO	51	7.1	309	145	1,912	1990	X	7.0	2	8	0.2	X
Thingvalla	IS	84	2.9	114	34	X	1975	X	7.3	X	X	0.1	7.0
Thrichonis	GR	97	X	58	X	215	1978	6.0	8.3	1	24	0.2	X
Tyrifjorden	NO	121	13.8	295	114	9,808	1991	7.0	X	2	5	0.4	X
Volvi	GR	67	0.9	23	14	1,247	1985-86	1.6	8.5	X	X	0.0	X
Vänern	SE	5,670	152.0	106	27	41,180	1990	5.0	7.4	2	9	0.8	6.0
Vättern	SE	1,912	74.0	128	39	4,447	1990	12.0	7.5	1	6	0.7	9.0
Vörtjärv	EE	270	0.8	6	3	3,100	1991	X	7.8	22	43	2.4	17.0
Windermere	UK	15	0.3	64	24	231	1991-92	X	7.0	23	20	1.0	X
Zürich See	CH	90	3.9	143	51	1,740	1991	X	X	X	45	0.8	X

Notes: a. Indicates water transparency. AL: Albania; AT: Austria; BG: Bulgaria; CH: Switzerland; DE: Germany; DK: Denmark; EE: Estonia; FI: Finland; FR: France; FYROM: Former Yugoslav Rep of Macedonia; GR: Greece; HU: Hungary; IR: Ireland; IS: Iceland; IT: Italy; MD: Moldova; NL: the Netherlands; NO: Norway; PL: Poland; RS: Russian Federation; SE: Sweden; UK: United Kingdom.

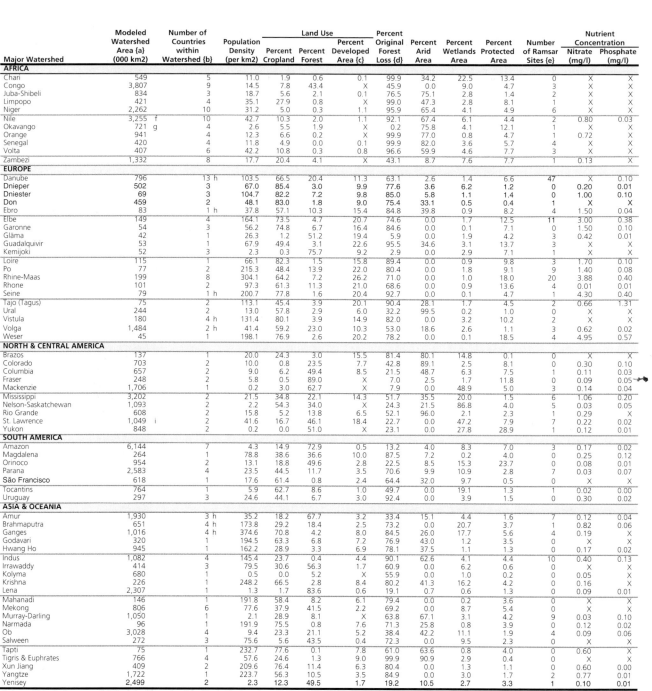

Major Watershed	Modeled Watershed Area {a} (000 km2)	Number of Countries within Watershed {b}	Population Density (per km2)	Land Use Percent Cropland	Land Use Percent Forest	Percent Developed Area {c}	Percent Original Forest Loss {d}	Percent Arid Area	Percent Wetlands Area	Percent Protected Area	Number of Ramsar Sites {e}	Nutrient Concentration Nitrate (mg/l)	Nutrient Concentration Phosphate (mg/l)
AFRICA													
Chari	549	5	11.0	1.9	0.6	0.1	99.9	34.2	22.5	13.4	0	X	X
Congo	3,807	9	14.5	7.8	43.4	X	45.9	0.0	9.0	4.7	3	X	X
Juba-Shibeli	834	3	18.7	5.6	2.1	0.1	76.5	75.1	2.8	1.4	2	X	X
Limpopo	421	4	35.1	27.9	0.8	X	99.0	47.3	2.8	8.1	1	X	X
Niger	2,262	10	31.2	5.0	0.3	1.1	95.9	65.4	4.1	4.9	6	X	X
Nile	3,255 f	10	42.7	10.3	2.0	1.1	92.1	67.4	6.1	4.4	2	0.80	0.03
Okavango	721 g	4	2.6	5.5	1.9	X	0.2	75.8	4.1	12.1	1	X	X
Orange	941	4	12.3	6.6	0.2	X	99.9	77.0	0.8	4.7	1	0.72	X
Senegal	420	4	11.8	4.9	0.0	0.1	99.9	82.0	3.6	5.7	4	X	X
Volta	407	6	42.2	10.8	0.3	0.8	96.6	59.9	4.6	7.7	3	X	X
Zambezi	1,332	8	17.7	20.4	4.1	X	43.1	8.7	7.6	7.7	1	0.13	X
EUROPE													
Danube	796	13 h	103.5	66.5	20.4	11.3	63.1	2.6	1.4	6.6	47	X	0.10
Dnieper	502	3	67.0	85.4	3.0	9.9	77.6	3.6	6.2	1.2	0	0.20	0.01
Dniester	69	3	104.7	82.2	7.2	9.8	85.0	5.8	1.1	1.4	0	1.00	0.10
Don	459	2	48.1	83.0	1.8	9.0	75.4	33.1	0.5	0.4	1	X	X
Ebro	83	1 h	37.8	57.1	10.3	15.4	84.8	39.8	0.9	8.2	4	1.50	0.04
Elbe	149	4	164.1	73.5	4.7	20.7	74.6	0.0	1.7	12.5	11	3.00	0.38
Garonne	54	3	56.2	74.8	6.7	16.4	84.6	0.0	0.1	7.1	0	1.50	0.10
Gläma	42	1	26.3	1.2	51.2	19.4	5.9	0.0	1.9	4.2	3	0.42	0.01
Guadalquivir	53	1	67.9	49.4	3.1	22.6	95.5	34.6	3.1	13.7	3	X	X
Kemijoki	52	3	2.3	0.3	75.7	9.2	2.9	0.0	2.9	7.1	1	X	X
Loire	115	1	66.1	82.3	1.5	15.8	89.4	0.0	0.9	9.8	3	1.70	0.10
Po	77	2	215.3	48.4	13.9	22.0	80.4	0.0	1.8	9.1	9	1.40	0.08
Rhine-Maas	199	8	304.1	64.2	7.2	26.2	71.0	0.0	1.0	18.0	20	3.88	0.40
Rhone	101	2	97.3	61.3	11.3	21.0	68.6	0.0	0.9	13.6	4	0.01	0.01
Seine	79	1 h	200.7	77.8	1.6	20.4	92.7	0.0	0.1	4.7	1	4.30	0.40
Tajo (Tagus)	75	2	113.1	45.4	3.9	20.1	90.4	28.1	1.7	4.5	2	0.66	1.31
Ural	244	2	13.0	57.8	2.9	6.0	32.2	99.5	0.2	1.0	0	X	X
Vistula	180	4 h	131.4	80.1	3.9	14.9	82.0	0.0	3.2	10.2	2	X	X
Volga	1,484	2 h	41.4	59.2	23.0	10.3	53.0	18.6	2.6	1.1	3	0.62	0.02
Weser	45	1	198.1	76.9	2.6	20.2	78.2	0.0	0.1	18.5	4	4.95	0.57
NORTH & CENTRAL AMERICA													
Brazos	137	1	20.0	24.3	3.0	15.5	81.4	80.1	14.8	0.1	0	X	X
Colorado	703	2	10.0	8.0	23.5	7.7	42.8	89.1	2.5	8.1	0	0.30	0.10
Columbia	657	2	9.0	6.2	49.4	8.5	21.5	48.7	6.3	7.5	1	0.11	0.03
Fraser	248	2	5.8	0.5	89.0	X	7.0	2.5	1.7	11.8	0	0.09	0.05
Mackenzie	1,706	1	0.2	3.0	62.7	X	7.9	0.0	48.9	5.0	3	0.14	0.04
Mississippi	3,202	2	21.5	34.8	22.1	14.3	51.7	35.5	20.0	1.5	6	1.06	0.20
Nelson-Saskatchewan	1,093	2	2.2	54.3	34.0	X	24.3	21.5	86.8	4.0	5	0.03	0.05
Rio Grande	608	2	15.8	5.2	13.8	6.5	52.1	96.0	2.1	2.3	1	0.29	X
St. Lawrence	1,049 i	2	41.6	16.7	46.1	18.4	22.7	0.0	47.2	7.9	7	0.22	0.02
Yukon	848	2	0.2	0.0	51.0	X	23.1	0.0	27.8	28.9	1	0.12	0.01
SOUTH AMERICA													
Amazon	6,144	7	4.3	14.9	72.9	0.5	13.2	4.0	8.3	7.0	3	0.17	0.02
Magdalena	264	1	78.8	38.6	36.6	10.0	87.5	7.2	0.2	4.0	0	0.25	0.12
Orinoco	954	2	13.1	18.8	49.6	2.8	22.5	8.5	15.3	23.7	0	0.08	0.01
Parana	2,583	4	23.5	44.5	11.7	3.5	70.6	9.9	10.9	2.8	7	0.03	0.07
São Francisco	618	1	17.6	61.4	0.8	2.4	64.4	32.0	9.7	0.5	0	X	X
Tocantins	764	1	5.9	62.7	8.6	1.0	49.7	0.0	19.1	1.3	1	0.02	0.00
Uruguay	297	3	24.6	44.1	6.7	3.0	92.4	0.0	3.9	1.5	0	0.30	0.02
ASIA & OCEANIA													
Amur	1,930	3 h	35.2	18.2	67.7	3.2	33.4	15.1	4.4	1.6	7	0.12	0.04
Brahmaputra	651	4 h	173.8	29.2	18.4	2.5	73.2	0.0	20.7	3.7	1	0.82	0.06
Ganges	1,016	4 h	374.6	70.8	4.2	8.0	84.5	26.0	17.7	5.6	4	0.19	X
Godavari	320	1	194.5	63.3	6.8	7.2	76.9	43.0	1.2	3.5	0	X	X
Hwang Ho	945	1	162.2	28.9	3.3	6.9	78.1	37.5	1.1	1.3	0	0.17	0.02
Indus	1,082	4	145.4	23.7	0.4	4.4	90.1	62.6	4.1	4.4	10	0.40	0.13
Irrawaddy	414	3	79.5	30.6	56.3	1.7	60.9	0.0	6.2	0.6	0	X	X
Kolyma	680	1	0.5	0.0	5.2	X	55.9	0.0	1.0	0.2	0	0.05	X
Krishna	226	1	248.2	66.5	2.8	8.4	80.2	41.3	16.2	4.2	0	0.16	X
Lena	2,307	1	1.3	1.7	83.6	0.6	19.1	0.7	0.6	1.3	0	0.09	0.01
Mahanadi	146	1	191.8	58.4	8.2	6.1	79.4	0.0	0.2	3.6	0	X	X
Mekong	806	6	77.6	37.9	41.5	2.2	69.2	0.0	8.7	5.4	0	X	X
Murray-Darling	1,050	1	2.1	28.9	8.1	X	63.8	67.1	3.1	4.2	9	0.03	0.10
Narmada	96	1	191.9	75.5	0.8	7.6	71.3	25.8	0.8	3.9	0	0.12	0.02
Ob	3,028	4	9.4	23.3	21.1	5.2	38.4	42.2	11.1	1.9	4	0.09	0.06
Salween	272	3	75.6	5.6	43.5	0.4	72.3	0.0	9.5	2.3	0	X	X
Tapti	75	1	232.7	77.6	0.1	7.8	61.0	63.6	0.8	4.0	0	0.60	X
Tigris & Euphrates	766	4	57.6	24.6	1.3	9.0	99.9	90.9	2.9	0.4	0	X	X
Xun Jiang	409	2	209.6	76.4	11.4	6.3	80.4	0.0	1.3	1.1	0	0.60	0.00
Yangtze	1,722	1	223.7	56.3	10.5	3.5	84.9	0.0	3.0	1.7	2	0.77	0.01
Yenisey	2,499	2	2.3	12.3	49.5	1.7	19.2	10.5	2.7	3.3	1	0.10	0.01

Notes: a. Watershed area was digitally derived from elevation data. b. Number of countries may differ from the U.N. listing under the Registry of International Rivers due to recent changes in political boundaries of many countries. c. Based on stable nighttime lights data. These figures overestimate the actual area lit. Data were not available for all regions of the world. d. Closed forest cover estimated to exist 8,000 years ago assuming current climate conditions. e. Wetlands of international importance. f. The number of countries sharing the Nile basin has increased to 10 with the independence of Eritrea. g. Watershed includes intermittent tributaries in Botswana (Northern Kalahari desert). h. Excludes countries that have <1% area in the watershed. i. Basin excludes the tidal area of the St. Lawrence River.

Sources and Technical Notes

Data Table 12.1

Freshwater Resources and Withdrawals, 1970–98

Sources: Water resources and withdrawal data come from a variety of sources: J. Forkasiewicz and J. Margat, *Tableau Mondial de Données Nationales d'Economie de l'Eau, Ressources et Utilisation* (Departement Hydrogéologie, Orléans, France, 1980); J. Margat, Bureau de Recherches Géologiques et Minières, Orléans, France, April 1988 (personal communication); and Alexander V. Belyaev, Institute of Geography, U.S.S.R. National Academy of Sciences, Moscow, September 1989 and January 1990 (personal communication). Withdrawal and sectoral use data for the United States: Wayne B. Solley, Robert R. Pierce, and Howard A. Perlman, "Estimated Use of Water in the United States, in 1990," *U.S. Geological Survey Circular,* No. 1081 (U.S. Geological Survey, Reston, Virginia, 1993); European Communities–Commission, *Environment Statistics 1989* (Office des Publications Officielles des Communautés Européennes, Luxembourg, 1990); United Nations Economic Commission for Europe (ECE), *The Environment in Europe and North America* (U.N., New York, 1992); ECE, *ECE Environmental Statistical Database,* on diskette (Statistical Division, U.N./ECE, 1995); Organisation for Economic Co-Operation and Development (OECD), *OECD Environmental Data Compendium* (OECD, Paris, 1995); Food and Agriculture Organization of United Nations (FAO), *Water Resources of African Countries, A Review* (FAO, Rome, 1995); FAO, *Irrigation in Africa in Figures, Water Reports No. 9* (FAO, Rome, 1997); FAO, *Water Resources of the Near East Region,* Water Report (FAO, Rome, 1997); FAO, *Irrigation in the Near East Region in Figures,* Water Reports No. 7 (FAO, Rome, 1995); FAO, *Irrigation in the Former Soviet Union in Figures,* Water Report (FAO, Rome, forthcoming); and FAO, *Water Resources of the Former Soviet Union,* Water Report (FAO, Rome, in preparation).

Population: United Nations (U.N.) Population Division, *World Population Prospects, 1950–2050 (The 1996 Revision),* on diskette (U.N., New York, 1996). Withdrawal data in this table were updated or confirmed from individual country reports when possible. For example, this was accomplished for Egypt, Morocco, South Africa, the Republic of Korea, Vietnam, Honduras, Brazil, Guyana, and Japan, based on reports prepared by each country for the United Nations Conference on Environment and Development in Rio de Janeiro, Brazil, in 1992. In general, data are compiled from published documents (including national, United Nations, and professional literature) and from estimates, when necessary, of resources and consumption from models using other data, such as area under irrigated agriculture, livestock populations, and precipitation.

Annual internal renewable water resources refers to the average annual flow of rivers and recharge of groundwater generated from endogenous precipitation. Caution should be used when comparing different countries because these estimates are based on differing sources and dates. These annual averages also disguise large seasonal, interannual, and long-term variations. When data for *annual river flows from* and *to other countries* are not shown, the internal renewable water resources figure *may* include these flows. When such data are shown, they are not included in a country's total internal renewable water resources. *Per capita* annual internal renewable water resources data were calculated using 1998 population estimates. Actual annual renewable water resources available for use is usually less than the sum of internal renewable resources and river flows. This is due to the fact that not all resources can be mobilized for use and that part of the flow coming from upstream countries or leaving for downstream countries might be reserved to those countries by treaty or other agreement. For example, Sudan's actual water resources include the flow of the Nile, less the amount that it is committed by treaty to deliver to Egypt at Aswan.

Annual withdrawals as a *percentage of water resources* refer to *total* water withdrawals, not counting evaporative losses from storage basins, as a percentage of internal renewable water resources. Water withdrawals also include water from nonrenewable groundwater sources, river flows from other countries, and desalination plants in countries where that source is a significant part of all water withdrawals. *Per capita* annual withdrawals were calculated using national population data for the year of data shown.

Sectoral withdrawals are classified as *domestic* (drinking water, homes, commercial establishments, public services [e.g., hospitals], and municipal use); *industrial* (some countries include water withdrawn to cool thermoelectric plants, while others do not; these can be significant amounts of total water withdrawals); and *agricultural* (irrigation and livestock).

Totals may not add because of rounding.

Data Table 12.2

Groundwater and Desalinization, 1998

Sources: Groundwater resources and withdrawal data come from several sources: J. Margat, *Les Eaux Souterraines Dans Le Monde* (BRGM—Services Sol et Sous-Sol, Departement Eau, Orléans, France, December 1990); Organisation for Economic Co-Operation and Development (OECD), *OECD Environmental Data Compendium 1993,* (OECD, Paris, 1993); and Economic Commission for Europe (ECE), *The Environment in Europe and North America* (U.N., New York, 1992). Groundwa-

ter resources and desalinization activities: Food and Agriculture Organization of the United Nations (FAO), *Irrigation in Africa in Figures,* Water Reports 7 (FAO, Rome, 1995); FAO, *Water Resources of African Countries: A Review* (FAO, Rome, 1995); FAO, *Water Resources of the Near East Region,* Water Report (FAO, Rome, 1997); FAO, *Irrigation in the Near East Region in Figures,* Water Reports No. 7 (FAO, Rome, 1995); FAO, *Irrigation in the Former Soviet Union in Figures,* Water Report (FAO, Rome, forthcoming); and FAO, *Water Resources of the Former Soviet Union,* Water Report (FAO, Rome, in preparation).

Average annual groundwater recharge is the amount of water that is estimated to annually infiltrate soils, including water from rivers and streams that lose it to underlying strata. In general, this figure would represent the maximum amount of water that could be withdrawn annually without ultimately depleting the groundwater resource. These data are estimated in a variety of ways (see footnotes and J. Margat), and caution should be used in comparing values for different countries.

Per capita recharge is the amount of water that annually infiltrates soils on a per-person basis, using 1998 population estimates.

Annual total groundwater withdrawals refer to abstractions from all groundwater sources—even nonrenewable sources. The *percent of annual recharge* refers to *total* groundwater withdrawals.

Per capita annual withdrawals were calculated using national population data for the year of data shown for withdrawals.

Sectoral share of withdrawals of groundwater is classified as *domestic* (drinking water, homes, commercial establishments, public services [e.g., hospitals], and municipal use or provision); *industry* (including water withdrawn to cool thermoelectric plants); and *agriculture* (irrigation and livestock).

Desalinated water production refers to the removal of salt from saline waters—usually seawater—using a variety of techniques including reverse osmosis. Most desalinated water is used for domestic purposes.

Totals may not add because of rounding.

Data Table 12.3

Water Quality in European Lakes, 1994

Source: Physical lake characteristics and water quality data: P. Kristensen and H.O. Hansen, *European Rivers and Lakes—Assessment of Their Environmental State,* European Environment Agency Environmental Monographs No. 1 (European Environment Agency, Copenhagen, 1994).

These data were compiled from questionnaires distributed to the European countries, scientific literature, National State of the Environment reports, and from the International Lake Environment Committee Foundation database. Because these data are from very different primary sources, lake data are not strictly comparable. The table, however, provides a good indication of the lake water quality in various European regions.

The majority of European lakes have a small surface area between 0.01–1.0 square kilometers. There are 16,000 lakes with a surface area larger than 1 square kilometer. Of these, 14,525 are located in the Nordic countries and the Russian Federation. For the purpose of this table, a subset of the most well-known lakes in Europe was selected. These were data-rich lakes representing different regions in Europe. Lakes are identified by the name most commonly used in the country or region where they are located.

Measurements of *surface area* are generally reported as the largest area for lakes subject to normal size variations and usually include the area of any islands within the lakes.

Calculation of *volume* and *mean depth* requires detailed knowledge of the lake bottom and is usually estimated. *Maximum depth* can be measured directly. Mean and maximum depths and water volume are important factors in understanding potential productivity.

Catchment area is the area of the drainage basin (excluding the area of the lake) that provides water to the lake.

Years of data shows the years for which water quality data were available. Some countries specified annual averages, while others provided only summer averages. For countries showing more than one year, water quality data represent an average for the period shown. Therefore, care should be taken when making comparisons. For some countries, the year or period of the data is unknown and has been marked as missing data.

Secchi depth is a measure of transparency of water obtained by lowering a white disk into the water until it is no longer visible.

The *pH* of the water can range from pH 4 for acidic waters to a pH 11 for alkaline waters. A pH 7 is neutral.

Concentrations of *chlorophyll, phosphorous, nitrogen,* and *chloride* provide information on the nutrient and pollution levels of a lake. Lakes located in pristine areas usually have low nutrient levels (total phosphorous concentrations are less than 10 to 20 micrograms per liter and total nitrogen concentrations are less than 0.5 milligrams per liter). The nutrient levels in a lake depend on the external loading and on the characteristics of the catchment area. Lakes in catchment areas with intensive agriculture have more nutrient loadings from fertilizer runoff, etc. High nutrient levels produce an increase in phytoplankton (chlorophyll levels), which in turn increases the turbidity of the water (low water transparency) and can alter the biological composition of the aquatic community.

Data Table 12.4

Major Watersheds of the World, 1998

Sources: Watershed selection and nutrient concentration: United Nations Environment Programme (UNEP)/Global Environment Monitoring System (GEMS), *Water Quality of World River Basins*, UNEP Environmental Library No. 14 (UNEP, Nairobi, 1995), and Oxford University Press, *Atlas of the World,* Second Edition (Oxford University Press, Inc., New York, 1993). Modeled watershed area: Center for Remote Sensing and Spatial Analysis (CRSSA), Cook College, Rutgers University, and U.S. Army Corps of Engineers Construction Engineering Research Laboratories (CERL), *Major Watershed Basins of the World* in Global ARC GIS Database CD-ROM (CRSSA, New Brunswick, New Jersey, 1996) and edited by the World Resources Institute. Number of countries within watershed: Environmental Systems Research Institute (ESRI) software (ESRI, Redlands, California, 1995). Mean population density: National Consortium for Geographic Information and Analysis (NCGIA), Global Demography Project, *Gridded Population of the World*, data set for 1995 distributed by the Consortium for International Earth Science Information Network (CIESIN), available online at: http://www.ciesin.org/datasets/gpw/globldem. doc.html (CIESIN, 1995). Cropland and forest: U.S. Geological Survey (USGS), University of Nebraska–Joint Research Center for the European Commission, *Global Land Cover Characterization* database, distributed by USGS Earth Resources Observation System (EROS) Data Center, available online at: http://edcwww.cr.usgs.gov/landdaac/ glcc/glcc.html (USGS, 1992–93). Developed area: National Oceanic and Atmospheric Administration National Geophysical Data Center (NOAA-NGDC), *Nighttime Lights of the World* database, available online at: http://www.ngdc.noaa. Gov:8080/production/html/BIOMASS/night. html (NOAA-NGDC, 1994–95). Original forest data: D. Bryant, D. Nielsen, and L. Tangley, *The Last Frontier Forests: Ecosystems and Economies on the Edge* (World Resources Institute, Washington, D.C., 1997). Arid area: UNEP, *World Atlas of Desertification Global Aridity Zone Map* (UNEP, Nairobi, 1992). Wetlands areas and protected areas: World Conservation Monitoring Centre (WCMC), *Biodiversity Map Library* software (WCMC, Cambridge, U.K., 1996). Ramsar sites: Ramsar Convention Bureau, *List of Wetlands of International Importance* (Ramsar Convention Bureau, Gland, Switzerland, 1997).

The *major watersheds* included in the table are from the 82 major watersheds of the world identified by UNEP/GEMS. This list includes major river systems and smaller river systems of regional significance. Sixteen watersheds were excluded for their small size or because our derived basin area differed considerably from the United Nations estimate of river basins in the *Register of International Rivers* (Center for Natural Resources, Energy, and Transport of the Department of Economic and So-

cial Affairs of the United Nations, Pergamon Press, Oxford, U.K., 1978). Several additional river basins were added to this table from the *Atlas of the World* list of major river basins to gain more complete geographic coverage. The basins in this table represent approximately 42 percent of the world's land area.

Most of the data in this table were obtained through geographic information system (GIS) analysis of multiple data sets. The base data layer used for geographic definition of the watersheds was a 5-minute resolution data set (one-twentieth of a degree latitude longitude) of major watershed basins. There are some limitations associated with the scale of this base data: watershed boundaries are coarse, and some smaller basins and small tributaries are not identified. Subbasins were then aggregated to include all tributaries of the major river systems. Summary statistics for each watershed were digitally extracted by overlaying the basin map onto other existing digital data sets.

Modeled watershed area was estimated using an equal area projection and summing the number of 1 km² cells within each basin. The derived basin area was compared to the U.N. data from the *Register of International Rivers* and only those whose area did not vary more than 10–15 percent from the U.N. data were included in the table. There are two exceptions to this: the Okavango and the St. Lawrence River basins. Intermittent tributaries are included in the northern part of the Kalahari desert in Botswana within the Okavango basin. The tidal area of the St. Lawrence River is excluded. Water surface of rivers and lakes (e.g., the Great Lakes in the St. Lawrence River watershed) are included in the drainage area.

Number of countries within watershed were identified using updated 1995 country boundaries from the Environmental Systems Research Institute (ESRI). Countries included in each basin are listed below. Countries are listed in descending order as to their share of the basin (i.e., countries with more land within a basin are listed first). The countries listed may differ with the U.N. due to the recent independence of many countries (i.e., the Nile basin now includes both Ethiopia and Eritrea). *Chari:* Chad, Central African Republic, Cameroon, Sudan, and Nigeria. *Congo:* Dem. Rep. Congo, Central African Republic, Angola, Rep. Congo, Tanzania, Zambia, Cameroon, Burundi, and Rwanda. *Juba-Shibeli:* Ethiopia, Somalia, and Kenya. *Limpopo:* South Africa, Botswana, Mozambique, and Zimbabwe. *Niger:* Mali, Nigeria, Niger, Algeria, Guinea, Cameroon, Burkina Faso, Benin, Côte d'Ivoire, and Chad. *Nile:* Sudan, Ethiopia, Egypt, Uganda, Tanzania, Kenya, Dem. Rep. Congo, Rwanda, Burundi, and Eritrea. *Okavango:* Botswana, Namibia, Angola, and Zimbabwe. *Orange:* South Africa, Namibia, Botswana, and Lesotho. *Senegal:* Mali, Mauritania, Senegal, and Guinea. *Volta:* Burkina Faso, Ghana, Mali, Togo, Côte d'Ivoire, and Benin. *Zambezi:* Zambia, Angola, Zimbabwe, Mozambique, Malawi, Botswana, Tanzania, and Namibia. *Danube:* Romania, Hungary, Serbia, Austria, Germany, Slovakia, Bosnia and Herzegovina, Bulgaria, Croatia, Ukraine, Czech Republic, Slovenia, and

Moldova, and with less than 1 percent of the basin area: Switzerland, Italy, Poland, and Albania. *Dnieper:* Ukraine, Belarus, and Russia. *Dniester:* Ukraine, Moldova, and Poland. *Don:* Russia and Ukraine. *Ebro:* Spain, and with less than 1 percent of the basin area: France and Andorra. *Elbe:* Germany, Czech Republic, Austria, and Poland. *Garonne:* France, Spain, and Andorra. *Gläma:* Norway. *Guadalquivir:* Spain. *Kemijoki:* Finland, Norway, and Russia. *Loire:* France. *Po:* Italy and Switzerland. *Rhine-Maas:* Germany, France, Switzerland, Austria, Belgium, Netherlands, Luxembourg, and Liechtenstein. *Rhone:* France and Switzerland. *Seine:* France. *Tajo (Tagus):* Spain and Portugal. *Ural:* Kazakhstan and Russia. *Vistula:* Poland, Ukraine, Belarus, and Slovakia. *Volga:* Russia and Kazakhstan. *Weser:* Germany. *Brazos:* United States. *Colorado:* United States and Mexico. *Columbia:* United States and Canada. *Fraser:* Canada and United States. *Mackenzie:* Canada. *Mississippi:* United States and Canada. *Nelson-Saskatchewan:* Canada and United States. *Rio Grande:* United States and Mexico. *St. Lawrence:* Canada and United States. *Yukon:* United States and Canada. *Amazon:* Brazil, Peru, Bolivia, Colombia, Ecuador, Venezuela, and Guyana. *Magdalena:* Colombia. *Orinoco:* Venezuela and Colombia. *Parana:* Brazil, Argentina, Paraguay, and Bolivia. *São Francisco:* Brazil. *Tocantins:* Brazil. *Uruguay:* Brazil, Uruguay, and Argentina. *Amur:* Russia, China, and Mongolia. *Brahmaputra:* China, India, Bangladesh, and Bhutan. *Ganges:* India, Nepal, China, and Bangladesh. *Godavari:* India. *Hwang Ho:* China. *Indus:* Pakistan, India, Afghanistan, and China. *Irrawaddy:* Myanmar, China, and India. *Kolyma:* Russia. *Krishna:* India. *Lena:* Russia. *Mahanadi:* India. *Mekong:* Laos, Thailand, China, Cambodia, Vietnam, and Myanmar. *Murray-Darling:* Australia. *Narmada:* India. *Ob:* Russia, Kazakhstan, China, and Mongolia. *Salween:* China, Myanmar, and Thailand. *Tapti:* India. *Tigris and Euphrates:* Iraq, Turkey, Iran, and Syria. *Xun Jiang:* China and Vietnam. *Yangtze:* China. *Yenisey:* Russia and Mongolia.

Population density was extracted from a global 5-minute resolution population map. Basins were overlaid on population data, and the population density was calculated for each basin. Data are presented as the number of people per square kilometer.

Land use: The USGS Global Land Cover Characterization database with the International Geosphere Biosphere Programme (IGBP) classification was used to identify the extent of different land cover types within each basin. The land cover database is derived from 1-km resolution satellite data spanning April 1992 through March 1993. *Percent cropland* indicates the percentage of the basin defined as cropland or a crop/natural vegetation mosaic. *Percent forest* indicates the percentage of the basin defined as evergreen needleleaf forest, evergreen broadleaf forest, deciduous needleleaf forest, deciduous broadleaf forest, or mixed forest. The *Nighttime Lights of the World* database used for the *percent developed area* is a 1-km by 1-km resolution map derived from nighttime imagery from the Defense Meteorological Satellite Program (DMSP) Operational Linescan System (OLS) of the United States. The data set contains the locations of stable lights, including frequently observed light sources such as gas flares at oil drilling sites. Time series analysis is used to exclude transient light sources such as fires and lightning. The extent of "lit" area may be slightly overestimated due to the sensor's resolution and factors such as reflection from water and other surface features. It is a good indicator of the spatial distribution of settlements and infrastructure but should not be interpreted as a measure of population density. (The mean settlement size required to produce enough light to be detected is much greater in developing countries than in industrialized countries because of differences in energy consumption.) The *Nighttime Lights of the World* data are more highly correlated with measures of economic activity and energy consumption and are therefore considered a measure of relative development within the watershed. The percentage of developed area was calculated by dividing the area within a watershed indicated as "lit" by the total area of the watershed. Data were not available for regions below the equator in Africa and Asia or for regions above 50°N in North America and above 80°N in Asia.

Percent original forest loss was calculated by dividing the difference between original and current forest cover by the extent of original forest cover within each basin. For definitions of original and current forests, please refer to the Sources and Technical Notes of Data Table 11.2.

Percent arid area indicates the percentage of the basin that falls in an area defined as semiarid, arid, or hyperarid on the *World Atlas of Desertification Global Aridity Zone Map.* This map is based on an aridity index derived from the ratio of mean annual precipitation to the mean annual potential evapotranspiration.

Percent wetlands area was calculated by dividing the sum of the areas of wetlands within the basin by the total watershed area. It includes all areas designated as wetland in the *Biodiversity Map Library* software.

Percent protected area was calculated by dividing the sum of the protected areas that fall within the World Conservation Union (IUCN) I–V management categories in the watershed by the total watershed area. For a description of the IUCN categories, please refer to the Sources and Technical Notes of Data Table 14.1.

Ramsar sites are sites designated as "wetlands of international importance" according to the terms of the Convention on Wetlands (Ramsar, Iran, 1971). Spatial accuracy of the coordinates varies. For more information, please refer to the Sources and Technical Notes of Data Table 14.1.

The *concentration of nitrates* and *phosphates* provide information on the nutrient and pollution levels of rivers and lakes. Nutrient levels will depend in part on the runoff from agricultural lands and water discharge from urban centers that carry high loads of phosphorous and nitrogen from fertilizers, animal waste, and municipal sewage. High nutrient levels produce eutrophication of rivers and lakes (i.e., an increase in biomass such as algae that can alter the chemical makeup of the water and therefore the biological composition of the aquatic community). For more detailed information on nutrient concentration, please refer to the original source.

*C*hapter 13

Oceans and Fisheries

Marine and Freshwater Catches, Aquaculture, Balance of Trade, and Fish Consumption

Sources: Food and Agriculture Organization of the United Nations and United Nations Population Division

	Average Annual Marine Catch {a} (000 metric tons) 1993-95	Average Annual Marine Catch {a} Percent Change Since 1983-85	Average Annual Freshwater Catch {a} (000 metric tons) 1993-95	Average Annual Freshwater Catch {a} Percent Change Since 1983-85	Average Annual Aquaculture Production 1993-95 (metric tons) Marine Fish	Dia-dromous Fish	Fresh-water Fish	Molluscs & Crus-taceans	Average Annual Balance of Trade {b} 1993-95 (million US$) Fish	Molluscs & Crustaceans	Fish Meal	Per Capita Annual Food Supply from Fish and Seafood Total 1993-95 (kg)	% Change Since 1983-85
WORLD {c}	91,219.2	23	17,152.7	102	472,243	1,287,589	11,204,330	5,590,184				13.4	9.2
AFRICA	3,916.9	31	1,373.1	19	14,597	1,788	54,785	4,511	299.6	868.2	(62.4)	6.8	(13.6)
Algeria	114.2	74	0.3	862	53	14	254	31	(6.7)	2.3	(0.3)	3.5	1.8
Angola	77.5	(1)	6.7	(11)	X	X	X	X	(6.6)	(2.7)	0.0	12.4	(51.1)
Benin	13.5	192	25.2	(18)	X	X	98	X	(9.0)	0.6	(0.0)	10.2	(5.8)
Botswana	X	X	2.0	41	X	X	X	X	(4.6)	(0.6)	(0.1)	7.1	98.4
Burkina Faso	X	X	7.7	5	0	0	0	0	(3.6)	(0.0)	(0.0)	1.3	(22.3)
Burundi	20.9	246	0.4	(92)	0	0	53	0	(0.6)	(0.0)	0.0	3.8	39.3
Cameroon	41.9	(25)	23.2	15	0	0	51	0	(22.2)	1.7	(0.3)	8.5	(41.2)
Central African Rep	X	X	13.3	1	0	0	367	0	(0.7)	(0.0)	0.0	4.5	(19.7)
Chad	X	X	75.8	57	X	X	X	X	(0.3)	(0.0)	0.0	5.9	102.1
Congo, Dem Rep	4.0	140	166.7	27	0	0	733	0	(40.1)	(0.1)	0.0	5.1	(44.1)
Congo, Rep	17.5	(8)	18.8	38	0	0	5	0	(18.5)	0.0	0.0	31.4	(23.9)
Côte d'Ivoire	57.5	(22)	14.1	(41)	0	0	255	0	12.1	4.4	0.8	12.5	(22.6)
Egypt	116.1	225	190.0	33	11,732	0	26,859	0	(64.4)	0.4	(5.4)	6.9	4.0
Equatorial Guinea	3.3	15	0.4	48	X	X	X	X	(1.6)	(0.0)	0.0	X	X
Eritrea	2.4	X	0.0	X	X	X	X	X	0.0	X	0.0	X	X
Ethiopia {d}	0.3	X	5.0	X	0	0	39	0	(0.3)	(0.0)	0.0	X	X
Gabon	24.0	28	2.5	39	0	0	6	0	(10.3)	3.2	(0.0)	44.0	(18.8)
Gambia, The	19.5	124	2.5	(9)	0	0	0	0	0.8	3.1	(0.0)	17.5	8.2
Ghana	299.6	34	52.7	24	0	0	505	0	17.7	5.9	(0.9)	22.8	5.5
Guinea	60.3	130	4.1	130	0	0	5	0	2.0	4.8	0.0	6.7	(18.0)
Guinea-Bissau	5.3	75	0.3	317	X	X	X	X	0.6	0.1	0.0	5.6	149.4
Kenya	107.6	86	86.0	112	0	314	823	68	20.1	0.9	(0.3)	5.7	12.4
Lesotho	0.0	367	0.0	66	0	5	12	0	0.0	0.0	0.0	4.0	13.7
Liberia	3.8	(61)	3.9	(3)	0	0	0	0	(0.9)	0.3	0.0	X	X
Libya	33.2	162	0.1	X	0	0	90	0	16.2	(0.5)	(0.0)	3.9	19.1
Madagascar	85.1	180	32.0	(12)	0	0	2,521	911	17.6	60.5	0.5	7.3	21.4
Malawi	X	X	57.5	(11)	0	0	231	5	0.1	(0.0)	(0.6)	6.8	(25.9)
Mali	5.2	53	81.6	53	0	0	84	0	(1.5)	(0.0)	0.0	6.4	(12.4)
Mauritania	86.6	(0)	5.2	(14)	X	X	X	X	19.7	127.0	(0.0)	16.2	23.4
Mauritius	19.0	74	0.1	270	29	0	42	72	6.9	(3.7)	(2.2)	27.7	56.4
Morocco	738.6	59	1.7	40	1,030	198	200	148	241.0	399.2	(0.4)	7.6	8.7
Mozambique	24.8	(27)	3.4	(15)	0	0	54	0	(10.7)	69.8	(0.1)	2.1	(40.6)
Namibia	304.5	2,336	1.1	183	0	0	4	42	58.7	0.0	6.7	10.8	5.0
Niger	X	X	2.8	0	0	0	29	0	(1.6)	0.4	(0.0)	0.4	(28.1)
Nigeria	187.0	14	114.2	19	1,053	14	15,179	0	(138.6)	35.4	(1.3)	6.9	(27.1)
Rwanda	X	X	3.5	247	0	0	51	0	(0.2)	(0.0)	0.0	X	X
Senegal	329.7	43	30.7	45	0	0	29	14	88.7	32.2	0.6	26.8	22.1
Sierra Leone	47.1	34	14.7	(10)	0	0	22	0	3.4	10.6	0.0	15.0	(16.8)
Somalia	15.4	(3)	0.3	(6)	X	X	X	X	5.0	2.5	0.0	X	X
South Africa	552.2	(32)	0.9	16	23	937	117	2,942	119.5	50.2	(56.1)	7.6	(14.7)
Sudan	3.5	70	39.6	50	0	0	467	0	(2.4)	0.0	(0.0)	1.7	23.9
Swaziland	X	X	0.1	29	0	0	23	0	X	X	X	0.0	X
Tanzania	243.4	68	100.1	(21)	0	0	183	0	9.8	6.9	0.0	11.8	(8.5)
Togo	8.7	(23)	5.9	69	0	0	607	0	(12.4)	1.5	(0.0)	10.7	(12.0)
Tunisia	84.0	7	0.4	X	676	206	174	108	17.7	56.3	(0.0)	7.9	(18.6)
Uganda	96.3	6	117.6	29	0	0	153	0	18.9	0.0	0.0	10.4	(17.6)
Zambia	11.0	(1)	57.1	3	0	0	4,422	0	(1.0)	(0.0)	0.4	9.2	(17.1)
Zimbabwe	19.6	72	1.1	(74)	0	100	37	13	(8.4)	(0.7)	(0.5)	2.2	7.1
EUROPE {e}	17,507.2	X	544.1	X	34,235	557,258	258,074	623,426	(504.4)	(2,194.5)	(200.4)	17.8	X
Albania	2.3	(65)	0.8	(73)	1	20	92	284	1.4	(0.2)	(0.0)	1.3	(58.3)
Austria	3.0	(0)	1.5	(11)	0	2,997	1,137	4	(137.8)	(21.3)	(10.5)	12.4	62.7
Belarus, Rep	0.0	X	14.4	X	0	9	13,727	0	(1.2)	(1.5)	(0.6)	0.0	X
Belgium	35.5	(25)	0.7	307	0	546	300	0	(327.3)	(224.8)	(23.7)	19.8 †	5.8 †
Bosnia and Herzegovina	0.0	X	2.5	X	X	X	X	X	(4.7)	(0.0)	(0.0)	X	X
Bulgaria	13.3	(87)	9.0	(28)	0	744	7,355	0	(0.4)	0.8	(1.2)	2.4	(73.6)
Croatia, Rep	19.6	X	4.0	X	264	301	3,706	252	29.8	0.0	(8.6)	0.0	X
Czech Rep	0.9	X	21.7	X	0	609	20,888	0	(32.9)	(1.1)	(8.8)	5.0	X
Denmark	1,870.8	2	0.3	(12)	0	42,397	0	0	702.9	93.9	140.7	23.2	(9.0)
Estonia, Rep	131.2	X	3.2	X	0	288	66	0	74.4	(0.4)	0.4	0.0	X
Finland	129.0	2	50.9	(18)	0	17,160	24	0	(61.3)	(16.7)	(19.1)	35.0	9.4
France	822.1	2	13.1	175	3,504	50,702	8,653	216,671	(1,155.7)	(743.0)	(35.3)	28.5	13.9
Germany	267.4	(44)	28.3	(2)	0	25,300	13,233	16,249	(1,220.8)	(290.2)	(0.6)	16.1	24.9
Greece	192.8	93	14.1	77	15,471	2,309	223	14,799	7.0	(24.1)	(17.3)	26.2	56.9
Hungary	0.4	180	23.0	(42)	0	38	9,579	0	(11.6)	(0.3)	(19.8)	4.2	(23.1)
Iceland	1,630.6	21	0.0	X	32	3,176	0	0	893.1	207.1	81.8	99.3	8.2
Ireland	344.7	61	1.9	X	6	13,439	0	17,931	179.2	53.7	(4.5)	19.8	26.4
Italy	571.6	1	11.5	21	8,117	41,294	5,441	134,892	(1,241.4)	(641.4)	(40.3)	22.7	15.6
Latvia, Rep	142.4	X	1.2	X	0	7	468	0	35.3	(0.2)	0.6	36.4	X
Lithuania, Rep	70.3	X	3.2	X	0	0	2,165	0	3.1	0.4	(1.9)	33.2	X
Macedonia, FYR	0.6	X	0.7	X	0	617	579	0	(5.2)	(0.1)	(2.1)	3.3	X
Moldova, Rep	0.0	X	4.8	X	0	0	4,754	0	(2.5)	0.0	(0.4)	1.1	X
Netherlands	526.3	(2)	1.6	(6)	0	1,545	973	85,479	295.6	118.6	(54.4)	15.8	18.7
Norway	2,640.1	7	X	X	527	223,887	0	20	2,266.5	92.7	(1.0)	45.3	5.6
Poland, Rep	397.1	(42)	47.8	53	0	4,500	18,240	0	(43.2)	2.2	(1.1)	10.1	(26.8)
Portugal	276.3	(5)	0.0	636	580	1,513	3	3,754	(352.4)	(107.8)	(3.1)	59.2	27.3
Romania	19.9	(89)	29.0	(46)	0	387	20,057	0	(8.3)	(0.1)	(9.3)	1.9	(79.6)
Russian Federation	4,032.5	X	170.4	X	60	2,442	72,504	1,273	936.8	355.3	(4.8)	15.4	X
Slovak Rep	0.9	X	2.4	X	0	841	847	0	(16.7)	0.1	(3.9)	X	X
Slovenia, Rep	2.6	X	0.4	X	47	497	179	29	(9.5)	(5.5)	(2.6)	5.9	X
Spain	1,304.3	(9)	11.3	68	4,660	21,462	318	123,117	(855.2)	(905.6)	(23.1)	41.0	21.1
Sweden	383.1	49	1.6	(17)	0	5,515	0	1,462	(131.5)	(130.0)	(3.0)	32.4	11.7
Switzerland	1.9	(8)	0.9	(56)	X	1,142	35	0	(280.4)	(84.8)	(13.8)	16.3	36.9
Ukraine	307.6	X	61.4	X	148	415	51,039	396	99.1	1.5	(0.3)	9.6	X
United Kingdom	965.4	13	0.1	(16)	X	76,918	55	5,798	(404.4)	(114.4)	(109.9)	20.3	13.4
Yugoslavia, Fed Rep	0.3	X	6.3	X	X	6	1,433	1	(0.3)	(0.0)	(0.3)	2.0	X

OCEANS AND FISHERIES
Data Tables

	Average Annual Marine Catch {a}		Average Annual Freshwater Catch {a}		Average Annual Aquaculture Production 1993-95 (metric tons)				Average Annual Balance of Trade {b} 1993-95 (million US$)			Per Capita Annual Food Supply from Fish and Seafood	
	(000 metric tons) 1993-95	Percent Change Since 1983-85	(000 metric tons) 1993-95	Percent Change Since 1983-85	Marine Fish	Diadromous Fish	Freshwater Fish	Molluscs & Crustaceans	Fish	Molluscs & Crustaceans	Fish Meal	Total 1993-95 (kg)	% Change Since 1983-85
NORTH AMERICA	**6,574.6**	**11**	**289.3**	**45**	**3,310**	**79,087**	**219,207**	**162,664**	**10.7**	**(2,275.6)**	**(50.2)**	**22.2**	**16.0**
Canada	1,046.9	(22)	18.4	(23)	0	42,254	0	14,788	680.6	600.6	(17.4)	23.9	17.5
United States	5,527.7	21	270.9	54	3,310	36,833	219,207	147,876	(669.9)	(2,876.2)	(35.3)	22.0	15.9
CENTRAL AMERICA	**1,512.1**	**(1)**	**205.0**	**59**	**944**	**1,632**	**47,735**	**65,507**	**(39.0)**	**846.5**	**(21.9)**	**12.6**	**0.9**
Belize	2.1	48	0.0	260	0	0	0	731	(0.1)	13.1	0.0	7.7	26.5
Costa Rica	18.3	19	4.2	921	0	68	2,996	1,588	56.1	31.5	(0.4)	5.3	15.6
Cuba	71.2	(62)	20.5	34	15	0	18,701	442	(18.9)	98.4	0.0	11.4	(42.7)
Dominican Rep	15.8	21	4.7	59	469	29	1,320	694	(34.4)	0.1	0.0	12.3	22.5
El Salvador	9.4	(8)	4.6	160	403	0	116	246	(0.3)	26.9	(0.6)	2.3	21.7
Guatemala	6.7	142	4.7	5,575	0	0	430	3,126	(1.8)	25.6	(3.8)	0.9	111.6
Haiti	4.9	(22)	0.5	78	X	X	X	X	(3.7)	1.9	0.1	X	X
Honduras	24.2	149	0.3	119	0	0	190	7,377	5.7	60.1	(0.7)	0.9	(47.3)
Jamaica	9.7	8	3.6	525	0	0	2,900	72	(28.3)	9.2	0.0	22.1	(14.3)
Mexico	1,113.0	9	160.4	49	47	1,535	20,698	43,746	34.4	419.5	(21.0)	11.9	18.9
Nicaragua	10.9	161	0.6	229	0	0	4	1,801	7.7	45.0	(0.1)	1.6	56.9
Panama	171.9	(14)	0.4	169	0	0	228	5,409	11.1	78.8	4.9	14.4	1.0
Trinidad and Tobago	12.5	182	0.0	X	0	0	4	7	0.6	2.8	0.0	9.4	(60.5)
SOUTH AMERICA	**19,750.8**	**104**	**388.2**	**13**	**31**	**114,991**	**46,402**	**120,376**	**1,211.9**	**1,422.4**	**1,128.7**	**8.8**	**15.4**
Argentina	998.3	171	11.8	6	0	921	0	11	417.0	304.5	2.5	8.1	33.5
Bolivia	1.4	338	4.7	25	0	521	106	0	(1.4)	(0.2)	(0.0)	1.7	7.8
Brazil	585.9	(19)	214.1	2	0	867	26,500	3,033	(225.1)	115.9	(0.0)	5.9	(8.7)
Chile	7,109.4	61	0.0	1,100	30	106,922	0	13,543	643.2	182.6	484.8	31.1	76.1
Colombia	100.2	389	46.0	(6)	0	4,273	16,350	8,127	51.7	103.4	(25.2)	3.8	22.2
Ecuador	418.6	(46)	2.4	164	0	443	1,253	88,868	158.0	551.1	6.2	8.0	(30.0)
Guyana	44.8	25	0.8	(4)	0	0	140	63	4.2	13.1	0.0	42.1	(4.0)
Paraguay	X	X	14.8	178	0	0	98	0	(1.5)	(0.2)	0.0	4.0	139.5
Peru	9,939.5	234	43.7	45	1	841	276	4,394	56.8	64.1	666.7	20.0	28.7
Suriname	12.2	225	0.2	21	0	0	2	0	4.9	0.1	0.0	19.2	60.7
Uruguay	121.2	(12)	0.8	111	0	0	4	4	73.6	3.4	0.6	7.9	141.8
Venezuela	398.6	82	48.8	51	0	203	1,673	2,332	27.8	46.5	(6.7)	15.5	31.9
ASIA {e}	**40,904.7**	**X**	**14,336.7**	**X**	**417,825**	**521,450**	**10,577,856**	**4,546,936**	**(3,635.0)**	**(667.2)**	**(1,078.3)**	**13.4**	**X**
Afghanistan, Islamic State	X	X	1.3	58	X	X	X	X	X	X	X	X	X
Armenia, Rep	2.0	X	2.5	X	0	1,810	1,870	0	(0.3)	X	X	1.2	X
Azerbaijan	33.3	X	2.7	X	10	0	1,946	0	(0.1)	(0.0)	X	4.8	X
Bangladesh	388.5	72	713.5	36	0	0	250,988	30,439	29.7	195.1	0.0	8.7	15.3
Bhutan	X	X	0.3	32	0	0	30	0	X	X	X	X	X
Cambodia	31.8	237	76.4	31	0	0	7,940	597	15.9	0.1	0.0	8.5	(9.9)
China	11,699.6	223	9,060.5	291	118,394	0	7,875,707	2,756,841	854.9	865.2	(269.1)	14.5	147.2
Georgia	28.1	X	2.7	X	0	10	2,661	0	(0.5)	(0.0)	(0.0)	6.8	X
India	2,731.1	62	1,998.0	90	0	0	1,434,302	86,910	191.2	874.4	(4.3)	4.0	23.5
Indonesia	3,277.5	79	611.5	45	9,273	161,268	292,635	139,936	510.2	1,027.9	(87.2)	15.7	18.6
Iran, Islamic Rep	288.6	195	51.0	188	0	1,188	24,215	0	23.5	6.8	(25.5)	5.1	100.1
Iraq	4.2	(24)	18.5	15	0	0	13,967	0	0.0	0.0	0.0	1.2	(18.4)
Israel	4.9	(60)	15.1	19	1,481	497	12,803	2	(81.4)	(0.8)	(21.4)	20.3	23.5
Japan	7,221.4	(36)	70.0	(32)	250,770	79,903	17,270	454,891	(7,989.3)	(7,080.1)	(225.1)	67.6	(1.2)
Jordan	X	(71)	0.1	251	0	0	105	0	(19.7)	(0.5)	(0.3)	3.4	(16.5)
Kazakstan, Rep	13.3	X	39.0	X	0	0	1,763	X	3.6	(0.1)	(0.0)	3.5	X
Korea, Dem People's Rep	1,697.7	10	113.6	14	0	2,267	11,500	69,317	26.7	40.1	(0.1)	46.3	12.7
Korea, Rep	2,610.6	7	25.5	(47)	6,825	4,957	14,841	307,853	470.4	297.2	(11.4)	51.2	11.9
Kuwait	8.3	(12)	0.0	X	33	0	0	0	(9.8)	(2.6)	0.0	10.4	(24.6)
Kyrgyz Rep	0.1	X	0.3	X	0	17	171	0	(0.3)	X	X	0.1	X
Lao People's Dem Rep	X	X	35.3	36	0	0	13,067	0	(0.2)	0.0	(0.0)	6.6	(11.4)
Lebanon	3.0	95	0.0	X	0	227	0	0	0.0	0.0	0.0	0.7	30.5
Malaysia	1,164.6	50	16.1	52	3,111	5,970	14,468	93,812	(74.8)	111.1	(10.3)	28.3	(23.6)
Mongolia	X	X	0.1	(65)	X	X	X	X	(1.8)	0.0	0.0	0.9	(34.0)
Myanmar	610.6	30	220.7	50	0	0	70,987	7	6.8	69.5	0.0	16.1	12.0
Nepal	X	X	18.3	195	0	0	9,672	0	0.0	0.0	0.0	X	X
Oman	125.0	19	0.0	X	0	0	0	0	46.4	3.5	0.0	X	X
Pakistan	441.1	44	130.3	90	0	20	14,365	43	73.9	88.9	(0.0)	2.4	40.5
Philippines	1,961.9	24	305.3	(10)	1,283	147,934	95,931	127,670	142.0	298.8	(49.0)	33.5	(3.8)
Saudi Arabia	51.6	32	2.3	X	0	0	2,343	135	(51.5)	(5.7)	(6.0)	6.7	(38.2)
Singapore	13.0	(43)	0.0	(90)	315	239	22	2,203	(15.7)	(52.7)	(2.8)	X	X
Sri Lanka	213.6	37	15.0	(55)	0	0	2,833	2,876	(25.9)	26.8	(2.7)	15.7	(0.5)
Syrian Arab Rep	2.0	67	8.0	96	0	0	4,732	0	(1.1)	(0.1)	(1.4)	0.6	(75.2)
Tajikistan, Rep	0.0	X	3.8	X	0	0	3,550	0	(0.1)	0.0	X	0.6	X
Thailand	3,081.8	56	332.5	103	1,080	3,128	138,224	335,820	628.7	2,676.7	(110.3)	26.3	28.8
Turkey	573.3	7	30.1	(3)	6,713	9,464	419	85	15.0	22.1	(11.2)	7.9	6.0
Turkmenistan, Rep	16.5	X	2.5	X	0	0	1,142	0	0.0	(0.0)	X	8.4	X
United Arab Emirates	102.9	42	0.0	X	0	0	0	0	(6.0)	(2.6)	(0.1)	21.5	(2.0)
Uzbekistan, Rep	0.0	X	21.7	X	0	18	14,582	0	0.3	X	X	1.0	X
Vietnam	862.4	55	287.6	29	0	0	141,667	58,300	44.1	399.9	(0.4)	13.1	4.7
Yemen	90.4	35	0.9	X	X	X	X	X	(5.4)	72.4	0.0	6.2	(7.9)
OCEANIA	**910.0**	**83**	**16.3**	**4**	**1,301**	**11,384**	**273**	**66,763**	**294.0**	**741.2**	**(13.0)**	**21.6**	**5.7**
Australia	228.0	39	1.4	(35)	1,298	8,684	25	11,751	(129.9)	503.7	(16.5)	21.1	20.6
Fiji	28.8	14	3.3	44	0	X	71	100	6.7	1.8	0.0	33.4	(15.0)
New Zealand	523.3	146	0.5	158	X	2,618	X	54,006	444.1	224.6	3.9	16.0	(15.6)
Papua New Guinea	14.7	71	11.0	(1)	X	7	9	2	(43.6)	9.9	(0.4)	27.4	(5.5)
Solomon Islands	46.4	(1)	X	X	X	X	3	9	28.0	0.0	0.0	21.3	(64.7)
DEVELOPING	**58,676.4**	**78**	**16,159.1**	**120**	**181,116**	**556,751**	**10,669,150**	**4,280,501**	**5,852.0**	**9,697.6**	**276.0**	**10.1**	**36.3**
DEVELOPED	**32,542.6**	**(21)**	**993.7**	**(13)**	**291,126**	**730,838**	**535,180**	**1,309,683**	**(7,895.8)**	**(10,912.1)**	**(557.6)**	**25.0**	**22.5**

Notes: a. Aquaculture production is included in country totals. b. Exports minus imports. Surpluses of imports over exports are shown in parentheses. c. World and regional totals include countries not listed here. d. Prior to 1992, Ethiopia included Eritrea, therefore percent change since 1983-85 is not meaningful and has been omitted. e. Due to recent independence of Soviet republics, percent change since 1983-85 is not meaningful and therefore has been omitted. f. Data are for Belgium and Luxembourg.

Marine Fisheries, Yield and State of Exploitation, 1950s–1990s

Source: Food and Agriculture Organization of the United Nations

| | Average Marine Fish Catch (000 metric tons) | | | | | | | | Total Average Marine Catch {c} (000 metric tons) | | | | Status {d} in 1995 | Fully Fished by | Discards (as a % of overall catch {e}) 1988-92 |
| | Demersal Fishes {a} | | | | Pelagic Fishes {b} | | | | | | | | | | |
	1953-55	1973-75	1983-85	1993-95	1953-55	1973-75	1983-85	1993-95	1953-55	1973-75	1983-85	1993-95			
WORLD	7,018	18,836	18,998	18,219	9,505	24,966	34,818	42,753	21,978	56,910	71,378	87,380	X	1999	24
ATLANTIC OCEAN	4,870	9,510	8,429	7,177	5,145	11,467	10,308	9,909	11,693	24,046	23,091	21,669	I-F	1983	25
Northeast	3,179	5,698	5,200	4,832	3,252	4,973	4,782	4,963	6,937	11,557	11,266	10,938	O	1983	19
Northwest	1,388	1,856	1,275	457	693	1,408	625	628	2,645	4,013	2,756	2,114	O	1971	27
Eastern Central	46	504	403	322	190	2,190	1,892	2,165	340	3,288	2,836	2,999	O	1984	47
Western Central	61	182	145	183	356	762	1,192	927	670	1,488	2,355	2,012	O	1987	14
Southeast	102	871	583	299	586	1,824	1,499	1,011	887	2,817	2,198	1,352	O	1978	27
Southwest	95	399	823	1,083	68	310	318	215	213	883	1,681	2,256	I	X	14
PACIFIC OCEAN	1,755	8,409	9,370	9,290	3,592	11,703	21,456	29,014	8,486	28,458	41,313	56,147	I-F	1999	24
Northeast	181	1,658	2,003	2,320	173	132	88	92	416	2,003	2,273	2,714	O	1990	26
Northwest	1,175	5,712	6,185	4,930	2,612	5,012	8,931	6,910	6,334	16,367	22,364	24,768	I	1998	22
Eastern Central	25	120	70	76	249	682	1,073	885	349	983	1,373	1,389	O	1988	27
Western Central	250	550	659	1,031	380	1,844	2,878	4,356	1,021	4,380	5,861	8,911	I	2003	33
Southeast	96	251	204	477	172	3,926	8,386	16,635	311	4,430	8,936	17,558	I	2001	21
Southwest	28	118	249	456	6	107	100	136	54	296	506	807	O	1991	15
INDIAN OCEAN	290	698	811	1,402	430	1,115	1,829	2,856	1,140	3,207	4,785	7,643	I	X	26
Eastern	67	181	268	485	140	312	703	1,109	434	1,273	2,330	3,742	I	X	30
Western	223	518	543	917	289	803	1,126	1,748	706	1,934	2,455	3,901	I	X	22
MEDITERRANEAN AND BLACK SEA	103	167	266	343	339	680	1,224	974	659	1,123	1,871	1,818	F	X	25
ANTARCTIC	0	51	122	7	0	0	1	0	0	75	317	103	O	1980	10
ARCTIC	0	0	0	0	X	X	X	X	X	X	X	X	X	X	X

Notes: a. Demersal fish species include: flounders, halibuts, soles, cods, hakes, haddocks, redfishes, basses, congers, sharks, rays, and chimeras. b. Pelagic fish species include: jacks, mullets, sauries, herrings, sardines, anchovies, tunas, bonitos, billfishes, mackerels, snooks, and cutlassfishes. c. Marine catch includes marine fish (except diadromous fish), marine crustaceans, cephalopods, and molluscs. Marine catch includes aquaculture production. d. Status assessed by FAO. O = overfished; I = catch is increasing; F = fully fished. e. Overall catch refers to total catch plus discards.

Marine Biodiversity of Regional Seas, 1990s

Source: World Conservation Monitoring Centre

| | Seagrasses No. of Species | | Corals No. of Genera | | Molluscs No. of Species | | Shrimps & Lobsters No. of Species | | Sharks No. of Species | | Seabirds No. of Species | | Marine Mammals {a} | | |
Regional Seas	Endemic	Total	Endemic	Total	Endemic	Total	Endemic	Total	Endemic	Total	Endemic	Total	No. of Species Endemic	Total	% Endemic Threatened
Africa, East	0	11	0	63	0	80	2	91	3	73	2	44	0	28	0
Africa, South {b}	0	7	0	46	0	145	2	42	7	93	X	39	0	36	0
Africa, West & Central	0	1	1	10	1	238	3	47	1	89	2	51	2	44	100
Antarctica {b}	X	0	X	0	0	7	2	3 c	X	0	14	51	6	20	0
Arctic {b}	0	1	X	0	0	44	0	9	0	5	0	27	0	23	0
Asia, South	0	9	1	63	0	246	0	117	6	58	0	26	0	29	0
Atlantic, North {b}	0	5	0	13	0	432	1	77	4	87	4	56	3	48	0
Atlantic, Southwest	0	1	1	10	0	299	2	46	6	68	1	33	2	49	0
Australia, Southwest {b}	5	17	0	62	0	197	1	25	7	64	0	22	1	43	0
Black Sea	X	4	X	0	0	6	0	7	X	1	1	17	0	4	0
Caribbean	2	7	9	25	0	633	8	68	14	76	1	23	0	31	0
East Asian Seas	1	17	4	82	0	1,114	6	210	23	140	2	39	0	29	0
Kuwait Marine Area {b}	0	5	1	37	0	66	0	26	1	34	0	21	0	27	0
Mediterranean Sea	1	5	X	0	0	138	0	42	0	43	1	22	0	17	0
Pacific, Northeast {b}	3	7	0	7	0	517	6	45	5	57	14	66	3	50	100
Pacific, Northwest	5	13	0	69	4	404	7	128	9	93	6	69	1	45	0
Pacific, South	2	19	0	76	7	984	13	105	35	128	39	115	4	52	100
Pacific, Southeast	0	5	0	8	2	393	2	33	9	67	21	68	4	47	100
Red Sea & Gulf of Aden	0	11	1	53	0	57	0	38	0	39	0	22	0	26	0

Notes: a. Marine mammals include: cetaceans, sirenians, and pinnipeds. b. Indicates marine areas (regional seas) defined for the WCMC report "The Diversity of the Seas: A Regional Approach." These areas do not coincide with UNEP Regional Seas areas. For a description of each area, please refer to the Sources and Technical Notes. c. Krill are not included in this category.

Sources and Technical Notes

Marine and Freshwater Catches, Aquaculture, Balance of Trade, and Fish Consumption

Sources: Marine, freshwater, and aquaculture catches: Food and Agriculture Organization of the United Nations (FAO), *Fishstat-PC* and *Aquacult-PC* (FAO, Rome, 1997). Balance of trade in fish and seafood: *Fishcomm-PC* (FAO, Rome, 1997). Food supply from fish and seafood: FAO, *FAOSTAT Statistics Database*, available online at http://www.fao.org *(FAO, Rome, 1997), and United Nations (U.N.) Population Division, World Population Prospects, 1950–2050 (The 1996 Revision),* on diskette (U.N., New York, 1996).

Marine and *freshwater catch* data refer to marine and freshwater fish killed, caught, trapped, collected, bred, or cultivated for commercial, industrial, and subsistence use (catches from recreational activities are included where available). Crustaceans and molluscs are included. Statistics for mariculture, aquaculture, and other kinds of fish farming are included in the country totals. Figures are the national totals averaged over a 3-year period; they include fish caught by a country's fleet anywhere in the world. Catches of freshwater species caught in low-salinity seas are included in the statistics of the appropriate marine area. Marine catch includes catches of diadromous (migratory between saltwater and freshwater) species (please refer to the Sources and Technical Notes to Data Table 13.2 for a listing of the species groupings in this category).

Data are represented as nominal catches, which are the landings converted to a live-weight basis, that is, the weight when caught.

Landings for some countries are identical to catches. Catch data are provided annually to the FAO Fisheries Department by national fishery offices and regional fishery commissions. Some countries' data are provisional for the latest year. If no data are submitted, FAO uses the previous year's figures or makes estimates based on other information. For details on data quality, please refer to the Sources and Technical Notes to Data Table 13.2.

Years are calendar years except for Antarctic fisheries data, which are for split years (July 1–June 30). Data for Antarctic fisheries are given for the calendar year in which the split year ends.

Aquaculture is defined by FAO as "the farming of aquatic organisms, including fish, molluscs, crustaceans, and aquatic plants. Farming implies some form of intervention in the rearing process to enhance production, such as regular stocking, feeding, and protection from predators, etc. [It] also implies ownership of the stock being cultivated. . . ." Aquatic organisms that are exploitable by the public as a common property resource are included in the harvest of fisheries.

FAO's global collection of aquaculture statistics by questionnaire was begun in 1984; today, these data are a regular feature of the annual FAO survey of world fishery statistics.

FAO's *Aquacult-PC* has 301 "species items" that are grouped into six categories. *Marine fish* include a variety of species groups such as mullets, seabasses, groupers, snappers, tunas, mackerels, etc. *Diadromous fish* include sturgeons, river eels, salmons, trouts, etc. *Freshwater fish* include carps, perches, catfish, and tilapias, among others. *Molluscs* include freshwater molluscs, oysters, mussels, scallops, clams, abalones, and cephalopods. *Crustaceans* include, among others, freshwater crustaceans, crabs, lobsters, shrimps, and prawns. Data on whales and other marine mammals are excluded from this table. For a detailed listing of species, please refer to *Aquacult-PC* or the most recent *FAO Yearbook of Fishery Statistics* (FAO, Rome).

Balance of trade is defined as exports minus imports. Figures are the national totals averaged over a 3-year period in millions of U.S. dollars. Imports are usually on a cost, insurance, and freight basis (c.i.f.) (i.e., insurance and freight costs added in). Exports are generally on a free-on-board basis (FOB) (i.e., not including insurance or freight costs). A surplus of imports over exports is shown in parentheses. Trade in *fish* includes fish that is fresh, frozen, chilled, salted, or smoked as well as fish products and preparations. Trade in *molluscs and crustaceans* includes molluscs and crustaceans that are fresh, chilled, smoked, derived products, etc. Trade in *fish meal* includes meals, solubles, etc.

Per capita annual food supply from fish and seafood is the quantity of both freshwater and marine fish, seafood, and derived products available for human consumption. It was calculated based on the FAO country data on food supply from fish and seafood in metric tons and the country population data from the U.N. Population Division. Data on aquatic plants and whale meat are excluded from the totals. The amount of fish and seafood actually consumed may be lower than the figures provided, depending on how much is lost during storage, preparation, and cooking, and on how much is discarded. Data are presented in kilograms per capita. Years shown are 3-year averages. For more information, please refer to the *FAOSTAT Statistics Database* at: http://www.fao.org.

Marine Fisheries, Yield, and State of Exploitation, 1950–1990s

Source: Marine fishery production: Food and Agriculture Organization of the United Nations (FAO), *Fishstat-PC* (FAO, Rome, 1997); fisheries status: R.J.R. Grainger and S.M. Garcia, *Chronicles of Marine Fishery Landings (1950–1994): Trends*

Analysis and Fisheries Potential, FAO Fisheries Technical Paper No. 359 (FAO, Fisheries Department, Rome, 1996); discards: FAO, *The State of World Fisheries and Aquaculture* (FAO, Fisheries Department, Rome, 1995).

FAO divides the world into 27 statistical fishing areas (19 marine and 8 inland) and organizes annual *catch* data by 1,477 "species items"—species groups separated at the family, genus, or species level. "Catch" refers to average landings and does not include discards (see below). Data Table 13.2 only shows data for the marine fishing areas.

FAO species groupings for each category are as follows: *demersal fish:* flounders, halibuts, soles, etc.; cods, hakes, haddocks, etc.; redfishes, basses, congers, etc.; and sharks, rays, chimeras, etc.; *pelagic fish:* jacks, mullets, sauries, etc.; herrings, sardines, anchovies, etc.; tunas, bonitos, billfishes, etc.; and mackerels, snooks, cutlassfishes, etc. *Marine catch* includes demersal, pelagic, and miscellaneous marine fishes; cephalopods (squids, cuttlefishes, octopuses, etc.); marine crustaceans (sea-spiders, crabs, etc.); lobsters, spiny-rock lobsters, etc.; squat lobsters; shrimps, prawns, etc.; krill, planktonic crustaceans, etc.; and miscellaneous marine crustaceans); and marine molluscs (abalones, winkles, conchs, etc.; oysters; mussels; scallops, pectens, etc.; clams, cockels, arkshells, etc.; and miscellaneous marine molluscs). Years shown are 3-year averages. *Average marine catch* differs from marine catch in Data Table 13.1 because the following diadromous fish categories are not included: sturgeons, paddlefishes, etc.; river eels; salmons, trouts, smelts, etc.; shads; and miscellaneous diadromous fishes. Please refer to the Technical Notes for Data Table 13.1 for the definition of nominal fish catch and additional information on FAO's fishery database. Fish catch data presented in this table include harvests from marine aquaculture production.

Status of fish resources: *fully fished (F), overfished (O),* or *catch is increasing (I)* provides a measure of the degree to which fish stocks within FAO's marine statistical areas were exploited as of 1994. FAO used landings data collected between 1950 and 1994 for the top 200 species/fishing-area combinations to estimate status. These 200 species-area combinations represent 77 percent of the world's marine production. Exploitation levels were determined by comparing the average landings from 1990 to 1994 to the estimated maximum potential landings for each fishing area. FAO estimated the potential landings for each area based on a generalized fishery development model. This model shows that a fishery has four phases: undeveloped (the fishery is being exploited at a very low level), developing (the fishery starts to develop rapidly), mature (fishery yields are at their peak and their annual rate of increase is zero), and senescent (yields are decreasing). Based on this model, FAO estimated the year in which the fishery would be fully fished, that is the mature phase of the development had been or would be reached (i.e., the rate of increase is zero). For more detailed information on the analysis, please refer to R.J.R. Grainger and S.M. Garcia Technical Paper No. 359, *Chronicles of Marine Fishery Landings (1950–1994): Trends Analysis and Fisheries Potential* (FAO, Rome, 1996).

Discards as a percentage of overall catch refers to the percentage of overall catch (discards plus landings) during the 1988–92 period that consisted of nontarget or low-value species and undersized fish of targeted species.

Individual countries are charged with collecting catch data and reporting them to FAO. The quality of these estimates varies because many countries lack the resources to adequately monitor catch landings within their borders. In addition, fishers sometimes underreport their catches because they have not kept within harvest limits established to manage the fishery. In some cases, catch statistics are inflated to increase the importance of the fishing industry to the national economy.

Data Table 13.3

Marine Biodiversity of Regional Seas, 1990s

Source: World Conservation Monitoring Centre (WCMC), *The Diversity of the Seas: A Regional Approach; Biodiversity Series No. 4* (WCMC, Cambridge, U.K., 1996).

In WCMC's *The Diversity of the Seas* report, the world's oceans were divided into 19 regional seas. Some of these regional seas coincide with FAO's statistical fishing areas and/or with the United Nations Environment Programme's Regional Seas. Other areas were defined for the purpose of the report. Regional areas defined by WCMC are: *East Africa* (Somali Coastal Current and much of the Agulhas Current); *South Africa* (Benguela Current and the Agulhas Current of the coast of South Africa); *West and Central Africa* (West African coast from Mauritania to Namibia); *Antarctica* (marine area south of the Antarctic Convergence); *Arctic* (Barents Sea and the Arctic Ocean); *South Asia* (Arabian Sea, Bay of Bengal, and central Indian Ocean); *North Atlantic* (Southeast U.S. Continental Shelf, Northeast U.S. Continental Shelf, Scotian Shelf, Newfoundland Shelf, East and West Greenland Shelves, Iceland Shelf, Norwegian Shelf, North Sea, Baltic Sea, Celtic-Biscay Shelf, Iberian Coastal, Canary Current, and Faroe Plateau); *Southwest Atlantic* (Patagonian Shelf, Brazil Current, and the southern part of the Northeast Brazil Shelf); *Southwest Australia* (Australian coastline that extends from Shark Bay to the border of Southern Australia and New South Wales); *Black Sea; Caribbean* (Gulf of Mexico, Caribbean Sea, and northern part of the Northeast Brazil Shelf); *East Asian Seas* (eastern part of the Bay of Bengal, China Sea, Sulu-Celebes Sea, Indonesian Seas, and Northern Australian Shelf); *Kuwait marine area* (Persian [Arabian] Gulf and Gulf of Oman); *Mediterranean Sea; Northeast Pacific* (Eastern Bering Sea, Gulf of Alaska, California Current, and Gulf of California); *Northwest Pacific* (East China Sea, Yellow Sea, Kuroshio Current, Sea of Japan, Oyashio Current, Sea of Okhotsk, and West Bering Sea); *South Pacific* (Insular Pacific-Hawaiian complex, Great Barrier Reef, and New Zealand Shelf); *Southeast Pacific* (Humbolt Current and Easter Island and Sala-y-Gomez areas); *Red Sea and Gulf of Aden.*

These data represent the numbers of *endemic* and *total* species except for corals, which represent endemic and total *genera*. Endemic species are those that are known to be found only in a particular country or region. Marine mammals include cetaceans (whales, etc.), sirenians (sea cows), and pinnipeds (seals, etc.). The *percentage of endemic species threatened* represents endemic marine mammals that fall within The World Conservation Union (IUCN) categories of critically endangered, endangered, or vulnerable. For a description of these IUCN categories, please refer to the Sources and Technical Notes for Data Table 14.2.

As noted in *The Diversity of the Seas: A Regional Approach,* "with some exceptions, the flora and fauna of the coastal and marine regions discussed in this document remain very incompletely known" and, therefore, "the values given for species richness and endemism in the regional accounts must be taken as approximations" (p. 33). The following list of sources for the different species categories is taken from the original source. *Seagrasses:* Phillips and Meñez (1988). *Corals:* data from maps in Veron (1993). *Molluscs:* includes marine molluscs from the classes Gastropoda and Bivalvia found in coastal and shallow waters. *Shrimps and lobsters:* includes shrimps and prawns from the suborder Natantia and lobsters from the suborder Reptantia that have or may have commercial value. Data were derived from Holthius (1980 and 1991). *Sharks:* data were derived from Conpagno (1984). Endemic species information for Australian waters was obtained from Last and Stevens (1994). *Seabirds:* includes species that breed in the region listed in Croxall *et al.* (1984) and Croxall (1991). *Marine mammals:* Reijnders *et al.* (1993) and Jefferson *et al.* (1993).

*hapter 14*

Biodiversity

National and International Protection of Natural Areas, 1997

Sources: World Conservation Monitoring Centre, United Nations Educational, Scientific and Cultural Organization, and Ramsar Convention Bureau

	National Protection Systems								International Protection Systems {a}					
	All Protected Areas (IUCN Categories I-V)			Totally Protected Areas (IUCN Cat. I-III)		Partially Protected Areas (IUCN Cat. IV-V)		% of Protected Areas (IUCN Cat. I-V) at Least		Biosphere Reserves		World Heritage Sites		Wetlands of International Importance {b}
	Number	Area (000 ha)	Percent of Land Area	Number	Area (000 ha)	Number	Area (000 ha)	100,000 ha in Size	1 million ha in Size	Number	Area (000 ha)	Number	Area (000 ha)	Number	Area (000 ha)
WORLD {c}	10,401	841,041	6.4	4,502	499,446	5,899	348,433	12.1	1.5	337	219,891	126	127,001	895	66,840
AFRICA	746	154,043	5.2	300	90,091	446	63,952	28.0	4.8	46	24,033	30	29,910	72	13,522
Algeria	18	5,891	2.5	13	5,762	5	129	11.1	11.1	2	7,276	1	X	2	5
Angola	12	8,181	6.6	6	5,423	6	2,758	50.0	X	0	X	0	0	0	X
Benin	2	778	7.0	2	778	0	0	100.0	X	1	880	0	0	0	X
Botswana	8	10,497	18.5	4	4,551	4	5,945	87.5	37.5	0	X	0	0	1	6,864
Burkina Faso	12	2,855	10.4	3	534	9	2,321	50.0	8.3	1	16	0	0	3	299
Burundi	9	144	5.6	0	0	9	144	X	X	0	X	0	0	0	X
Cameroon	16	2,097	4.5	7	1,032	9	1,066	50.0	X	3	850	1	526	0	X
Central African Rep	13	5,110	8.2	5	3,188	8	1,922	84.6	15.4	2	1,640	1	1,740	0	X
Chad	9	11,494	9.1	2	414	7	11,080	100.0	22.2	0	X	0	0	1	195
Congo, Dem Rep	11	10,191	4.5	10	10,187	1	4	81.8	36.4	3	298	5	6,855	2	866
Congo, Rep	9	1,545	4.5	2	513	7	1,032	55.6	X	2	172	0	0	0	X
Côte d'Ivoire	11	1,986	6.2	10	1,891	1	95	36.4	9.1	2	1,480	3	1,484	1	19
Egypt	12	793	0.8	4	99	8	695	8.3	X	2	2,577	0	0	2	106
Equatorial Guinea	X	X	X	X	X	X	X	X	X	0	X	0	0	0	X
Eritrea	3	501	5.0	0	0	3	501	66.7	X	0	X	0	0	0	X
Ethiopia	20	5,518	5.5	12	3,036	8	2,482	70.0	X	0	X	1	22	0	X
Gabon	5	723	2.8	1	15	4	708	20.0	X	1	15	0	0	3	1,080
Gambia, The	4	22	2.2	3	18	1	4	X	X	0	X	0	0	1	20
Ghana	9	1,104	4.8	7	1,097	2	7	33.3	X	1	8	0	0	6	178
Guinea	3	164	0.7	3	164	0	0	33.3	X	2	133	1	13	6	225
Guinea-Bissau	X	X	X	X	X	X	X	X	X	1	110	0	0	1	39
Kenya	36	3,504	6.2	32	3,451	4	52	19.4	2.8	5	1,335	0	0	2	49
Lesotho	1	7	0.2	0	0	1	7	X	X	0	X	0	0	0	X
Liberia	1	129	1.3	1	129	0	0	100.0	X	0	X	0	0	0	X
Libya	6	173	0.1	3	51	3	122	16.7	X	0	X	0	0	0	X
Madagascar	36	1,119	1.9	16	744	20	375	2.8	X	1	140	1	152	0	X
Malawi	9	1,059	11.3	5	696	4	362	33.3	X	0	X	1	9	1	225
Mali	13	4,532	3.7	2	750	11	3,782	61.5	15.4	1	771	1	400	3	162
Mauritania	4	1,746	1.7	3	1,496	1	250	75.0	25.0	0	X	1	1,200	2	1,189
Mauritius	3	12	6.0	1	7	2	6	X	X	1	4	0	0	0	X
Morocco	7	316	0.7	2	9	5	307	14.3	X	0	X	0	0	4	11
Mozambique	11	4,779	6.1	5	1,967	6	2,812	63.6	18.2	0	X	0	0	0	X
Namibia	16	10,616	12.9	10	9,775	6	841	43.8	18.8	0	X	0	0	4	630
Niger	6	9,694	7.7	2	1,500	4	8,194	66.7	33.3	1	728	2	7,956	1	220
Nigeria	20	3,020	3.3	7	2,276	13	745	45.0	X	1	0	0	0	0	X
Rwanda	5	362	14.7	2	264	3	98	20.0	X	1	15	0	0	0	X
Senegal	9	2,180	11.3	5	1,012	4	1,168	33.3	X	3	1,094	2	929	4	100
Sierra Leone	2	82	1.1	0	0	2	82	X	X	0	X	0	0	0	X
Somalia	1	180	0.3	0	0	1	180	100.0	X	0	X	0	0	0	X
South Africa	232	6,578	5.4	35	4,262	197	2,316	3.9	0.4	0	X	0	0	15	486
Sudan	11	8,642	3.6	8	8,499	3	143	63.6	36.4	2	1,901	0	0	0	X
Swaziland	2	35	2.0	0	0	2	35	X	X	0	X	0	0	0	X
Tanzania	30	13,816	15.6	12	4,100	18	9,716	66.7	10.0	2	2,338	4	7,380	0	X
Togo	8	428	7.9	3	357	5	71	25.0	X	0	X	0	0	2	194
Tunisia	6	44	0.3	6	44	0	0	X	X	4	32	1	13	1	13
Uganda	32	1,910	9.6	7	876	25	1,034	18.8	X	1	220	2	132	1	15
Zambia	21	6,364	8.6	21	6,364	0	0	52.4	4.8	0	X	1	4	2	333
Zimbabwe	25	3,068	7.9	11	2,704	14	364	24.0	4.0	0	X	2	1,095	0	X
EUROPE	3,153	105,209	4.7	615	47,665	2,538	57,544	6.6	0.3	130	94,031	24	16,621	566	13,045
Albania	25	76	2.8	16	38	9	37	X	X	0	X	0	0	1	20
Austria	176	2,344	28.3	2	18	174	2,326	1.1	X	4	28	0	0	9	103
Belarus, Rep	57	864	4.2	4	303	53	561	X	X	2	253	1	88	0	X
Belgium	4	78	2.6	0	0	4	78	X	X	0	X	0	0	6	8
Bosnia and Herzegovina	5	25	0.5	1	17	4	8	X	X	0	X	0	0	0	X
Bulgaria	49	491	4.4	33	291	16	200	4.1	X	17	25	2	41	5	3
Croatia, Rep	26	375	6.7	13	92	13	283	3.8	X	1	150	1	19	4	80
Czech Rep	44	1,223	15.8	6	88	38	1,135	2.3	X	6	434	0	0	9	39
Denmark	112	1,368	32.2	8	28	104	1,340	1.8	X	1	70,000	0	0	38	1,833
Estonia, Rep	53	507	12.0	4	178	49	330	1.9	X	1	1,560	0	0	10	216
Finland	126	1,823	6.0	42	1,087	84	736	3.2	X	2	770	0	0	11	101
France	132	6,416	11.7	11	394	121	6,021	17.4	X	8	647	1	12	15	582
Germany	518	9,414	27.0	3	37	515	9,377	5.0	X	13	1,185	1	0	31	673
Greece	24	288	2.2	11	147	13	141	4.2	X	2	9	2	0	10	164
Hungary	54	629	6.8	5	159	49	470	X	X	5	129	1	0	19	150
Iceland	24	972	9.7	7	204	17	768	8.3	X	0	X	0	0	3	59
Ireland	13	59	0.9	5	47	8	12	X	X	2	9	0	0	45	67
Italy	169	2,146	7.3	11	372	158	1,774	1.2	X	3	4	0	0	46	57
Latvia, Rep	45	775	12.5	6	51	39	723	2.2	X	0	X	0	0	3	43
Lithuania, Rep	79	646	10.0	9	172	70	473	X	X	0	X	0	0	5	50
Macedonia, FYR	16	180	7.1	10	163	6	17	X	X	0	X	1	38	1	40
Moldova, Rep	13	39	1.2	4	19	9	21	X	X	0	X	0	0	0	X
Netherlands	75	228	6.7	22	74	53	153	X	X	1	260	0	0	18	325
Norway	118	2,075	6.8	80	1,585	38	490	5.9	X	1	1,555	0	0	23	70
Poland, Rep	106	2,911	9.6	16	165	90	2,746	3.8	X	7	164	1	5	8	90
Portugal	24	595	6.5	3	34	21	561	4.2	X	1	0	0	0	10	66
Romania	39	1,074	4.7	26	1,038	13	35	2.6	X	3	614	0	0	1	647
Russian Federation	210	51,670	3.1	118	37,406	92	14,264	43.8	5.2	16	14,561	3	15,380	35	6,338
Slovak Rep	41	1,046	21.8	7	202	34	844	2.4	X	4	203	1	0	7	26
Slovenia, Rep	14	115	5.7	1	84	13	31	X	X	0	X	1	0	1	1
Spain	217	4,216	8.4	13	224	204	3,992	3.2	X	14	954	2	55	38	158
Sweden	241	3,709	9.0	89	2,061	152	1,648	3.3	X	1	97	1	940	30	383
Switzerland	107	713	18.0	1	17	106	696	X	X	1	17	0	0	8	7
Ukraine	25	898	1.6	21	725	4	173	4.0	X	3	160	0	0	4	211
United Kingdom	148	4,942	20.5	0	0	148	4,942	10.1	X	13	44	4	11	107	453
Yugoslavia, Fed Rep	27	327	3.2	8	145	19	183	X	X	1	200	1	32	4	74

	National Protection Systems								International Protection Systems {a}					
	All Protected Areas (IUCN Categories I-V)			Totally Protected Areas (IUCN Cat. I-III)		Partially Protected Areas (IUCN Cat. IV-V)		% of Protected Areas (IUCN Cat. I-V) at Least		Biosphere Reserves		World Heritage Sites		Wetlands of International Importance {b}
	Number	Area (000 ha)	Percent of Land Area	Number	Area (000 ha)	Number	Area (000 ha)	100,000 ha in Size	1 million ha in Size	Number	Area (000 ha)	Number	Area (000 ha)	Number	Area (000 ha)
NORTH AMERICA	**2,333**	**214,714**	**11.7**	**1,243**	**113,370**	**1,090**	**101,344**	**11.2**	**2.0**	**53**	**22,194**	**18**	**20,797**	**50**	**14,202**
Canada	718	92,110	10.0	431	43,126	287	48,984	15.2	2.9	6	1,050	7	10,664	35	13,038
United States	1,615	122,604	13.4	812	70,244	803	52,360	9.5	1.6	47	21,144	12	10,134	15	1,164
CENTRAL AMERICA	**414**	**14,793**	**5.6**	**200**	**8,346**	**214**	**6,446**	**8.2**	**0.7**	**21**	**10,074**	**8**	**2,940**	**33**	**1,288**
Belize	18	478	20.9	10	197	8	281	11.1	X	0	X	1	96	0	X
Costa Rica	35	702	13.7	27	580	8	122	2.9	X	2	729	1	585	6	146
Cuba	65	1,907	17.4	18	157	47	1,750	6.2	X	4	324	0	0	0	X
Dominican Rep	26	1,523	31.5	15	950	11	573	23.1	3.8	0	X	0	0	0	X
El Salvador	2	5	0.3	1	3	1	2	X	X	0	X	0	0	0	X
Guatemala	30	1,825	16.8	28	1,821	2	4	13.3	X	2	1,236	1	58	3	83
Haiti	3	10	0.4	2	8	1	2	X	X	0	X	0	0	0	X
Honduras	49	1,112	9.9	16	681	33	431	6.1	X	1	500	1	500	3	103
Jamaica	1	2	0.1	1	2	0	0	X	X	0	X	0	0	1	6
Mexico	69	4,553	2.4	46	1,996	23	2,556	13.0	2.9	11	6,688	2	898	6	701
Nicaragua	59	903	7.4	6	389	53	514	1.7	X	0	X	0	0	1	44
Panama	21	1,421	19.1	15	1,365	6	56	19.0	X	1	597	2	804	3	111
Trinidad and Tobago	5	16	3.0	1	2	4	14	X	X	0	X	0	0	1	6
SOUTH AMERICA	**810**	**129,014**	**7.4**	**487**	**81,080**	**323**	**47,933**	**24.4**	**3.0**	**29**	**50,839**	**10**	**6,960**	**41**	**9,766**
Argentina	100	4,658	1.7	76	3,172	24	1,486	12.0	X	7	2,690	2	500	6	420
Bolivia	31	15,602	14.4	13	10,145	18	5,456	48.4	12.9	3	435	0	0	1	5
Brazil	321	35,548	4.2	208	22,316	113	13,232	19.3	1.6	2	29,940	1	170	5	4,537
Chile	72	14,134	18.9	34	8,728	38	5,406	25.0	6.9	7	2,407	0	0	7	100
Colombia	79	9,358	9.0	40	9,013	39	345	22.8	2.5	3	2,514	1	72	0	X
Ecuador	20	11,927	43.1	16	3,903	4	8,024	50.0	5.0	2	1,446	2	1,038	2	90
Guyana	1	59	0.3	1	59	0	0	X	X	0	X	0	0	0	X
Paraguay	18	1,401	3.5	13	1,366	5	35	16.7	X	0	X	0	0	4	775
Peru	19	3,462	2.7	14	3,000	5	462	31.6	5.3	3	2,507	4	2,180	7	2,932
Suriname	13	736	4.7	1	8	12	728	23.1	X	0	X	0	0	1	12
Uruguay	9	46	0.3	2	15	7	31	X	X	1	200	0	0	1	435
Venezuela	124	31,976	36.3	68	19,255	56	12,721	40.3	4.8	1	8,700	1	3,000	5	264
ASIA	**1,733**	**162,877**	**5.3**	**629**	**105,553**	**1,104**	**57,324**	**13.1**	**1.4**	**46**	**13,633**	**23**	**4,612**	**78**	**5,364**
Afghanistan, Islamic State	6	218	0.3	1	41	5	177	X	X	0	X	0	0	0	X
Armenia, Rep	4	214	7.6	4	214	0	0	25.0	X	0	X	0	0	2	492
Azerbaijan	29	476	5.5	12	192	17	284	X	X	0	X	0	0	1	133
Bangladesh	9	98	0.8	0	0	9	98	X	X	0	X	0	0	1	60
Bhutan	9	998	21.2	5	757	4	241	33.3	X	0	X	0	0	0	X
Cambodia	20	2,863	16.2	7	736	13	2,127	50.0	X	0	X	0	0	0	X
China	265	59,807	6.4	66	49,564	199	10,243	15.1	4.2	12	2,514	6	224	7	588
Georgia	16	195	2.8	16	195	0	0	X	X	0	X	0	0	2	34
India	344	14,273	4.8	65	3,447	279	10,826	5.8	X	0	X	5	281	6	193
Indonesia	170	17,509	9.7	100	13,550	70	3,958	20.6	2.9	6	1,482	2	298	2	243
Iran, Islamic Rep	67	8,299	5.1	9	1,081	58	7,218	26.9	1.5	9	2,610	0	0	18	1,358
Iraq	0	0	0.0	0	0	0	0	X	X	0	X	0	0	0	X
Israel	15	308	14.9	1	3	14	305	6.7	X	1	27	0	0	2	0
Japan	65	2,550	6.8	23	1,320	42	1,230	12.3	X	4	116	2	28	10	84
Jordan	9	298	3.4	1	1	8	297	11.1	X	0	X	0	0	1	7
Kazakstan, Rep	70	7,337	2.7	11	1,268	59	6,069	28.6	1.4	0	X	0	0	2	609
Korea, Dem People's Rep	19	315	2.6	13	161	6	154	5.3	X	1	132	0	0	0	X
Korea, Rep	25	682	6.9	0	0	25	682	4.0	X	1	37	0	0	1	0
Kuwait	2	27	1.5	1	2	1	25	X	X	0	X	0	0	0	X
Kyrgyz Rep	31	688	3.6	11	300	20	389	3.2	X	1	71	0	0	1	630
Lao People's Dem Rep	X	X	X	X	X	X	X	X	X	0	X	0	0	0	X
Lebanon	1	4	0.3	1	4	0	0	X	X	0	X	0	0	0	X
Malaysia	50	1,483	4.5	40	903	10	581	10.0	X	0	X	0	0	1	38
Mongolia	35	16,129	10.3	34	16,079	1	50	40.0	11.4	2	5,367	0	0	0	X
Myanmar	2	173	0.3	1	161	1	13	50.0	X	0	X	0	0	0	X
Nepal	12	1,112	7.8	8	1,017	4	94	33.3	X	0	X	2	208	1	18
Oman	3	3,428	16.1	1	3,400	2	28	33.3	33.3	0	X	1	2,750	0	X
Pakistan	55	3,721	4.8	6	882	49	2,839	20.0	X	1	31	0	0	8	62
Philippines	17	1,453	4.9	7	463	10	990	11.8	X	2	1,174	1	33	1	6
Saudi Arabia	18	4,961	2.3	6	2,837	12	2,124	X	11.1	0	X	0	0	0	X
Singapore	1	3	4.4	0	0	1	3	X	X	0	X	0	0	0	X
Sri Lanka	69	859	13.3	37	530	32	329	X	X	2	9	0	0	1	6
Syrian Arab Rep	X	X	X	X	X	X	X	X	X	0	X	0	0	0	X
Tajikistan, Rep	18	587	4.2	4	87	14	500	5.6	X	0	X	0	0	0	X
Thailand	112	6,688	13.1	74	3,947	38	2,741	17.0	X	3	26	1	622	0	X
Turkey	49	1,071	1.4	23	417	26	655	2.0	X	0	X	1	10	5	66
Turkmenistan, Rep	22	1,977	4.2	9	821	13	1,156	22.7	X	1	35	0	0	1	189
United Arab Emirates	0	0	0.0	0	0	0	0	X	X	0	X	0	0	0	X
Uzbekistan, Rep	12	850	2.1	12	850	0	0	8.3	X	0	X	0	0	0	X
Vietnam	52	994	3.1	9	202	43	792	1.9	X	0	X	1	150	1	12
Yemen	0	0	0.0	0	0	0	0	X	X	0	X	0	0	0	X
OCEANIA	**1,212**	**60,382**	**7.1**	**1,028**	**53,341**	**184**	**7,041**	**10.2**	**1.1**	**12**	**5,093**	**13**	**45,159**	**55**	**5,668**
Australia	966	53,708	7.0	879	48,455	87	5,253	11.4	1.2	12	5,093	11	42,479	49	5,067
Fiji	5	19	1.0	5	19	0	0	X	X	0	X	0	0	0	X
New Zealand	201	6,322	23.6	124	4,732	77	1,590	7.0	0.5	0	X	2	2,680	5	39
Papua New Guinea	3	7	0.0	3	7	0	0	X	X	0	X	0	0	1	590
Solomon Islands	X	X	X	X	X	X	X	X	X	0	X	0	0	0	X

Notes: a. Areas listed often include nationally protected systems. b.Total area of wetlands of international importance for the world is for 891 Ramsar sites; total area for the remaining sites is not available. c. World and regional totals for national protected areas exclude Greenland. World totals exclude Antarctica. World and regional totals include countries not listed here.

Data Table 14.2
Globally Threatened Species: Mammals, Birds, and Higher Plants, 1990s

Source: World Conservation Monitoring Centre and World Conservation Union

	Mammals				Birds				Higher Plants			
	Total Number of Known Species			No. of Species per 10,000 km² {a}	Total Number of Known Species			No. of Species per 10,000 km² {a}	Total Number of Known Species			No. of Species per 10,000 km² {a}
	All Species	Endemic Species	Threatened Species		Breeding Species	Endemic Species	Threatened Species		All Species {b}	Endemic Species	Threatened Species	
WORLD {c}	4,629 d	X	X	X	9,672	X	X	X	270,000 e	X	X	X
AFRICA	X	X	X	X	X	X	X	X	X	X	X	X
Algeria	92	2	15	15	192	1	8	32	3,100	250	145	509
Angola	276	7	17	56	765	13	13	156	5,000	1,260	25	1,017
Benin	188	0	9	85	307	0	1	138	2,000	X	3	899
Botswana	164	0	5	43	386	0	7	101	X	17	4	X
Burkina Faso	147	0	6	49	335	0	1	112	1,100	X	0	369
Burundi	107	0	5	76	451	0	6	322	2,500	X	1	1,783
Cameroon	297	13	32	83	690	8	14	193	8,000	156	74	2,237
Central African Rep	209	2	11	53	537	0	2	137	3,600	100	0	921
Chad	134	1	14	27	370	0	3	75	1,600	X	12	322
Congo, Dem Rep	415	28	38	69	929	22	26	153	11,000	1,100	7	1,817
Congo, Rep	200	1	10	62	449	0	3	140	4,350	1,200	3	1,356
Côte d'Ivoire	230	1	16	73	535	0	12	170	3,517	62	66	1,118
Egypt	98	7	15	21	153	0	11	33	2,066	70	84	452
Equatorial Guinea	184	3	12	131	273	3	4	194	3,000	66	9	2,135
Eritrea	112	X	6	49	319	0	3	140	X	X	X	X
Ethiopia	255	31	35	54	626	28	20	133	6,500	1,000	153	1,378
Gabon	190	2	12	64	466	0	4	157	6,500	X	78	2,197
Gambia, The	108	0	4	104	280	0	1	269	966	X	0	928
Ghana	222	1	13	78	529	1	10	186	3,600	43	32	1,264
Guinea	190	1	11	66	409	0	12	142	3,000	88	35	1,043
Guinea-Bissau	108	0	4	71	243	0	1	159	1,000	12	0	655
Kenya	359	21	43	94	844	6	24	221	6,000	265	158	1,571
Lesotho	33	0	2	23	58	0	5	40	1,576	2	7	1,093
Liberia	193	0	11	87	372	1	13	168	2,200	103	1	1,037
Libya	76	5	11	14	91	0	2	17	1,800	134	57	327
Madagascar	105	84	46	27	202	104	28	53	9,000	6,500	189	2,347
Malawi	195	0	7	86	521	0	9	230	3,600	49	61	1,592
Mali	137	0	13	28	397	0	6	81	1,741	11	14	355
Mauritania	61	1	14	13	273	0	3	59	1,100	X	3	239
Mauritius	4	2	4	7	27	9	10	46	700	325	222	1,183
Morocco	105	4	18	30	210	0	11	60	3,600	625	195	1,028
Mozambique	179	1	13	42	498	0	14	117	5,500	219	92	1,294
Namibia	154	3	11	36	469	1	8	109	3,128	X	23	729
Niger	131	0	11	27	299	0	2	60	1,170	X	0	237
Nigeria	274	6	26	62	681	2	9	153	4,614	205	9	1,036
Rwanda	151	0	9	110	513	0	6	373	2,288	26	0	1,662
Senegal	155	0	13	58	384	0	6	144	2,062	26	32	771
Sierra Leone	147	0	9	77	466	0	12	243	2,090	74	12	1,091
Somalia	171	11	18	43	422	10	8	107	3,000	500	57	761
South Africa	247	27	33	51	596	8	16	122	23,000	X	953	4,711
Sudan	267	11	21	43	680	0	9	110	3,132	50	8	506
Swaziland	47	0	5	39	364	0	6	303	2,636	4	41	2,197
Tanzania	316	12	33	70	822	24	30	183	10,000	1,122	406	2,229
Togo	196	1	8	110	391	0	1	220	2,000	X	0	1,128
Tunisia	78	1	11	31	173	0	6	69	2,150	X	24	855
Uganda	338	6	18	118	830	3	10	290	5,000	X	6	1,762
Zambia	229	3	11	55	605	1	10	145	4,600	211	9	1,105
Zimbabwe	270	1	9	81	532	0	9	159	4,200	95	94	1,253
EUROPE	X	X	X	X	X	X	X	X	7,777	X	X	X
Albania	68	0	2	48	230	0	7	162	2,965	24	50	2,093
Austria	83	0	7	41	213	0	5	106	2,950	35	22	1,462
Belarus, Rep	X	X	4	X	221	0	4	81	X	X	0	X
Belgium	58	0	6	40	180	0	3	125	1,400	1	3	969
Bosnia and Herzegovina	X	X	10	X	X	0	2	X	X	X	0	X
Bulgaria	81	0	13	37	240	0	12	108	3,505	320	94	1,584
Croatia, Rep	X	X	10	X	224	0	4	126	X	X	0	X
Czech Rep	X	X	7	X	199	0	6	101	X	X	X	X
Denmark	43	0	3	27	196	0	2	121	1,200	1	6	741
Estonia, Rep	65	0	4	40	213	0	2	130	1,630	X	2	992
Finland	60	0	4	19	248	0	3	78	1,040	X	11	325
France	93	0	13	25	269	1	7	72	4,500	133	117	1,198
Germany	76	0	8	23	239	0	5	73	X	X	X	X
Greece	95	2	13	41	251	0	10	107	4,900	742	539	2,091
Hungary	72	0	8	34	205	0	10	98	2,148	38	24	1,029
Iceland	11	0	1	5	88	0	0	41	340	1	1	157
Ireland	25	0	2	13	142	0	1	75	892	X	9	469
Italy	90	3	10	29	234	0	7	76	5,463	712	273	1,776
Latvia, Rep	83	0	4	45	217	0	6	117	1,153	X	0	623
Lithuania, Rep	68	0	5	37	202	0	4	109	1,200	X	0	646
Macedonia, FYR	X	X	10	X	X	X	3	X	X	X	X	X
Moldova, Rep	68	X	2	46	177	X	7	119	X	X	1	X
Netherlands	55	0	6	35	191	0	3	120	1,170	X	1	758
Norway	54	0	4	17	243	0	3	77	1,650	1	20	524
Poland, Rep	84	0	10	27	227	0	6	72	2,300	3	27	738
Portugal	63	1	13	30	207	2	7	99	2,500	150	240	1,200
Romania	84	0	16	29	247	0	11	87	3,175	41	122	1,116
Russian Federation	269	19	31	23	628	13	38	54	X	X	127	X
Slovak Rep	X	0	8	X	209	X	4	124	X	X	X	X
Slovenia, Rep	69	0	10	55	207	0	3	164	X	X	11	X
Spain	82	4	19	22	278	5	10	76	X	X	896	X
Sweden	60	0	5	17	249	0	4	71	4,916	941	19	1,400
Switzerland	75	0	6	47	193	0	4	121	1,650	1	9	1,033
Ukraine	X	1	15	X	263	0	10	85	2,927	1	16	756
United Kingdom	50	0	4	17	230	0	2	80	1,550	16	28	539
Yugoslavia, Fed Rep	X	X	12	X	X	X	8	X	X	X	X	X

	Mammals				Birds				Higher Plants			
	Total Number of Known Species			No. of Species per 10,000 km² {a}	Total Number of Known Species			No. of Species per 10,000 km² {a}	Total Number of Known Species			No. of Species per 10,000 km² {a}
	All Species	Endemic Species	Threatened Species		Breeding Species	Endemic Species	Threatened Species		All Species {b}	Endemic Species	Threatened Species	
NORTH AMERICA	X	X	X	X	X	X	X	X	X	X	X	X
Canada	193	7	7	20	426	3	5	44	2,920	147	649	299
United States	428	101	35	45	650	69	50	68	16,302	4,036	1,845	1,679
CENTRAL AMERICA	X	X	X	X	X	X	X	X	X	X	X	X
Belize	125	0	5	95	356	0	1	271	2,750	150	41	2,090
Costa Rica	205	6	14	120	600	7	13	350	11,000	950	456	6,421
Cuba	31	12	9	14	137	22	13	62	6,004	3,229	811	2,714
Dominican Rep	20	0	4	12	136	0	11	81	5,000	1,800	73	2,965
El Salvador	135	0	2	106	251	0	0	196	2,500	17	35	1,956
Guatemala	250	3	8	114	458	1	4	208	8,000	1,171	315	3,638
Haiti	3	0	4	2	75	0	11	54	4,685	1,623	28	3,345
Honduras	173	1	7	78	422	1	4	190	5,000	148	55	2,252
Jamaica	24	3	4	23	113	25	7	110	2,746	923	371	2,662
Mexico	450	140	64	79	769	89	36	135	25,000	12,500	1,048	4,382
Nicaragua	200	2	4	86	482	0	3	207	7,000	40	78	3,003
Panama	218	14	17	112	732	8	10	376	9,000	1,222	561	4,618
Trinidad and Tobago	100	1	1	125	260	1	3	324	1,982	236	16	2,470
SOUTH AMERICA	X	X	X	X	X	X	X	X	4,958	X	X	X
Argentina	320	49	27	50	897	19	41	140	9,000	1,100	170	1,407
Bolivia	316	20	24	67	X	16	27	X	16,500	4,000	49	3,500
Brazil	394	101	71	43	1,492	180	103	161	55,000	X	463	5,935
Chile	91	17	16	22	296	14	18	71	5,125	2,698	292	1,229
Colombia	359	29	35	75	1,695	63	64	355	50,000	1,500	376	10,479
Ecuador	302	24	28	100	1,388	38	53	460	18,250	4,000	375	6,052
Guyana	193	1	10	70	678	0	3	246	6,000	X	47	2,180
Paraguay	305	2	10	90	556	0	26	164	7,500	X	12	2,208
Peru	344	48	46	69	1,538	109	64	310	17,121	5,356	377	3,448
Suriname	180	0	10	72	603	0	2	240	4,700	X	48	1,870
Uruguay	81	1	5	31	237	0	11	92	2,184	40	11	845
Venezuela	305	17	24	69	1,181	42	22	266	20,000	8,000	107	4,510
ASIA	X	X	X	X	X	X	X	X	5,990	X	X	X
Afghanistan, Islamic State	123	1	11	31	235	0	13	59	3,500	800	6	882
Armenia, Rep	X	3	4	X	X	0	5	X	X	X	0	X
Azerbaijan	X	0	11	X	X	0	8	X	X	X	1	X
Bangladesh	109	0	18	45	295	0	30	122	5,000	X	24	2,074
Bhutan	99	0	20	59	448	0	14	269	5,446	75	20	3,268
Cambodia	123	X	23	47	307	0	18	118	X	X	7	X
China	394	77	75	41	1,100	68	90	114	30,000	18,000	343	3,112
Georgia	X	2	10	X	X	0	5	X	X	X	1	X
India	316	45	75	47	923	55	73	136	15,000	5,000	1,256	2,216
Indonesia	436	206	128	77	1,519	393	104	269	27,500	17,500	281	4,864
Iran, Islamic Rep	140	5	20	26	323	1	14	60	X	X	1	X
Iraq	81	1	7	23	172	1	12	49	X	X	2	X
Israel	92	4	13	72	180	0	8	141	X	X	38	X
Japan	132	38	29	40	>250	21	33	X	4,700	2,000	704	1,418
Jordan	71	0	7	34	141	0	4	68	2,200	X	10	1,069
Kazakstan, Rep	X	4	15	X	X	0	15	X	X	X	0	X
Korea, Dem People's Rep	X	X	7	X	115	0	19	51	2,898	107	7	1,274
Korea, Rep	49	0	6	23	112	0	19	53	2,898	224	69	1,360
Kuwait	21	0	1	17	20	0	3	17	234	X	0	193
Kyrgyz Rep	X	1	6	X	X	0	5	X	X	X	1	X
Lao People's Dem Rep	172	0	30	61	487	1	27	171	X	X	5	X
Lebanon	54	0	5	53	154	0	5	152	X	X	4	X
Malaysia	286	28	42	90	501	9	34	158	15,000	3,600	510	4,732
Mongolia	134	X	12	25	X	0	14	X	2,272	229	1	429
Myanmar	251	6	31	62	867	4	44	216	7,000	1,071	29	1,742
Nepal	167	1	28	70	611	2	27	255	6,500	315	21	2,716
Oman	56	2	9	20	107	0	5	39	1,018	73	4	371
Pakistan	151	4	13	36	375	0	25	88	4,929	372	12	1,163
Philippines	153	98	49	50	395	184	86	129	8,000	3,500	371	2,604
Saudi Arabia	77	0	9	13	155	0	11	26	1,729	X	6	294
Singapore	45	1	6	113	118	0	9	295	2,000	2	14	5,007
Sri Lanka	88	13	14	47	250	23	11	134	3,000	890	436	1,613
Syrian Arab Rep	63	2	4	24	204	0	7	78	X	X	10	X
Tajikistan, Rep	X	2	5	X	X	0	9	X	X	X	0	X
Thailand	265	7	34	72	616	3	45	168	11,000	X	382	2,999
Turkey	116	1	15	28	302	0	14	72	8,472	2,675	1,827	2,012
Turkmenistan, Rep	X	0	11	X	X	0	12	X	X	X	1	X
United Arab Emirates	25	0	3	12	67	0	4	33	X	X	0	X
Uzbekistan, Rep	X	X	7	X	X	0	11	X	X	X	5	X
Vietnam	213	6	38	67	535	10	47	168	>7,000	1,260	350	X
Yemen	66	2	5	18	143	8	13	39	X	X	X	X
OCEANIA	X	X	X	X	X	X	X	X	5,825	X	X	X
Australia	252	201	58	28	649	353	45	72	15,000	14,074	1,597	1,672
Fiji	4	1	4	3	74	26	9	61	1,307	760	72	1,071
New Zealand	10	4	3	3	150	76	44	51	2,160	1,942	236	727
Papua New Guinea	214	59	57	60	644	80	31	182	10,000	X	95	2,821
Solomon Islands	53	19	20	37	163	44	18	115	2,780	30	43	1,959

Notes: a. Values are standardized using a species-area curve. b. Includes flowering plants only. c. World and regional totals include countries not listed.
d. Includes cetaceans. e. World total includes vascular plants.
Threatened species data are as of 1996, except for higher plants, which are as of June 1993.

Data Table 14.3
Globally Threatened Species: Reptiles, Amphibians, and Fish, 1990s

Sources: World Conservation Monitoring Centre and World Conservation Union

	Reptiles				Amphibians				Freshwater Fish	
	Total Number of Known Species			No. of Species	Total Number of Known Species			No. of Species	Total Number of Known Species	
	All Species	Endemic Species	Threatened Species	per 10,000 km² {a}	All Species	Endemic Species	Threatened Species	per 10,000 km² {a}	All Species	Threatened Species {b}
WORLD {c}	6,900	X	X	X	4,522	X	X	X	25,000 d	X
AFRICA	X	X	X	X	X	X	X	X	X	X
Algeria	X	4	1	X	X	0	0	X	X	1
Angola	X	18	5	X	X	22	0	X	X	0
Benin	X	1	2	X	X	0	0	X	X	0
Botswana	157	2	0	41	38	0	0	10	92	0
Burkina Faso	X	3	1	X	X	0	0	X	X	0
Burundi	X	0	0	X	X	2	0	X	X	0
Cameroon	X	20	3	X	X	66	1	X	X	26
Central African Rep	X	0	1	X	X	0	0	X	X	0
Chad	X	1	1	X	X	0	0	X	X	0
Congo, Dem Rep	X	33	3	X	X	53	0	X	X	1
Congo, Rep	X	1	2	X	X	1	0	X	X	0
Côte d'Ivoire	X	3	4	X	X	3	1	X	X	0
Egypt	83	0	6	18	6	0	0	1	70	0
Equatorial Guinea	X	3	2	X	X	2	1	X	X	0
Eritrea	X	X	3	X	X	0	0	X	X	0
Ethiopia	X	8	1	X	X	34	0	X	X	0
Gabon	X	3	3	X	X	4	0	X	X	0
Gambia, The	X	1	1	X	X	0	0	X	79	0
Ghana	X	1	4	X	X	4	0	X	X	0
Guinea	X	3	3	X	X	3	1	X	X	0
Guinea-Bissau	X	2	3	X	X	1	0	X	X	0
Kenya	187	17	5	49	88	11	0	23	X	20
Lesotho	X	2	0	X	X	1	0	X	8	1
Liberia	62	2	3	28	38	4	1	17	X	0
Libya	X	1	3	X	X	0	0	X	X	0
Madagascar	252	227	17	66	144	149	2	38	40	13
Malawi	124	6	0	55	69	3	0	31	X	0
Mali	16	3	1	3	X	1	0	X	X	0
Mauritania	X	1	3	X	X	0	0	X	X	0
Mauritius	11	8	6	19	0	0	0	0	X	0
Morocco	X	11	2	X	X	1	0	X	X	1
Mozambique	X	5	5	X	62	1	0	15	X	2
Namibia	X	26	3	X	32	2	1	7	102	3
Niger	X	X	1	X	X	X	0	X	X	0
Nigeria	>135	7	4	X	>109	1	0	X	260	0
Rwanda	X	1	0	X	X	1	0	X	X	0
Senegal	X	1	7	X	X	1	0	X	83	0
Sierra Leone	X	1	3	X	X	2	0	X	X	0
Somalia	193	49	2	49	27	3	0	7	X	3
South Africa	299	91	19	61	95	48	9	19	94	27
Sudan	X	7	3	X	X	1	0	X	X	0
Swaziland	102	1	0	85	40	0	0	33	40	0
Tanzania	284	64	4	63	124	48	0	28	X	19
Togo	X	1	3	X	X	3	0	X	X	0
Tunisia	X	1	2	X	X	0	0	X	X	0
Uganda	149	2	1	52	50	1	0	17	291	28
Zambia	X	2	0	X	83	1	0	20	X	0
Zimbabwe	153	2	0	46	120	3	0	36	112	0
EUROPE	X	X	X	X	X	X	X	X	X	X
Albania	31	0	1	22	13	0	0	9	39	7
Austria	14	0	1	7	20	0	0	10	60	7
Belarus, Rep	8	X	0	3	10	0	0	4	X	0
Belgium	8	0	0	6	17	0	0	12	X	1
Bosnia and Herzegovina	X	X	X	X	X	X	1	X	X	6
Bulgaria	33	0	1	15	17	0	0	8	X	8
Croatia, Rep	X	X	X	X	X	X	1	X	X	20
Czech Rep	X	X	X	X	X	X	X	X	X	6 .
Denmark	5	0	0	3	14	0	0	9	41	0
Estonia, Rep	5	0	0	3	11	0	0	7	30	1
Finland	5	0	0	2	5	0	0	2	66	1
France	32	0	3	9	32	3	2	9	53	3
Germany	12	0	0	4	20	0	0	6	71	7
Greece	51	3	6	22	15	2	1	6	98	16
Hungary	15	0	1	7	17	0	0	8	X	11
Iceland	0	0	0	0	0	0	0	0	7	0
Ireland	1	0	0	1	3	0	0	2	25	1
Italy	40	0	4	13	34	8	4	11	45	9
Latvia, Rep	7	0	0	4	13	0	0	7	109	1
Lithuania, Rep	7	0	0	4	13	0	0	7	X	1
Macedonia, FYR	X	X	1	X	X	X	X	X	X	4
Moldova, Rep	9	0	1	6	13	X	0	9	82	9
Netherlands	7	38	0	4	16	0	0	10	X	1
Norway	5	0	0	2	5	0	0	2	X	0
Poland, Rep	9	0	0	3	18	0	0	6	104	2
Portugal	29	2	0	14	17	0	1	8	28	9
Romania	25	0	2	9	19	0	0	7	87	11
Russian Federation	58	0	5	5	23	0	0	2	290	13
Slovak Rep	X	0	0	X	X	0	0	X	X	7
Slovenia, Rep	21	0	0	17	X	0	1	X	98	5
Spain	53	9	6	15	25	3	3	7	50	10
Sweden	6	0	0	2	13	0	0	4	X	1
Switzerland	14	0	0	9	18	0	0	11	48	4
Ukraine	19	1	2	6	16	0	0	5	X	12
United Kingdom	8	0	0	3	7	0	0	2	36	1
Yugoslavia, Fed Rep	X	X	1	X	X	X	X	X	X	13

Data Table 14.3 continued

	Reptiles Total Number of Known Species			No. of Species per 10,000 km² {a}	Amphibians Total Number of Known Species			No. of Species per 10,000 km² {a}	Freshwater Fish Total Number of Known Species	
	All Species	Endemic Species	Threatened Species		All Species	Endemic Species	Threatened Species		All Species	Threatened Species{b}
NORTH AMERICA	X	X	X	X	X	X	X	X	X	X
Canada	41	0	3	4	41	0	1	4	177	13
United States	280	75	28	29	233	149	24	24	822	123
CENTRAL AMERICA	X	X	X	X	X	X	X	X	X	X
Belize	107	2	5	81	32	1	0	24	63	0
Costa Rica	214	38	7	125	162	38	1	95	130	0
Cuba	102	82	7	46	41	44	0	19	28	4
Dominican Rep	105	22	10	62	35	15	1	21	16	0
El Salvador	73	4	6	57	23	0	0	18	16	0
Guatemala	231	19	9	105	99	31	0	45	220	0
Haiti	102	29	6	73	46	23	1	33	16	0
Honduras	152	19	7	68	56	30	0	25	46	0
Jamaica	36	26	8	35	21	21	4	20	6	0
Mexico	687	394	18	120	285	195	3	50	384	86
Nicaragua	161	5	7	69	59	2	0	25	50	0
Panama	226	25	7	116	164	22	0	84	101	1
Trinidad and Tobago	70	3	5	87	26	3	0	32	76	0
SOUTH AMERICA	X	X	X	X	X	X	X	X	X	X
Argentina	220	72	5	34	145	46	5	23	410	1
Bolivia	208	19	3	44	112	33	0	24	389	0
Brazil	468	184	15	51	502	366	5	54	X	12
Chile	72	36	1	17	41	31	3	10	44	4
Colombia	584	111	15	122	585	225	0	123	X	5
Ecuador	374	121	12	124	402	163	0	133	706	1
Guyana	X	2	8	X	X	14	0	X	X	0
Paraguay	120	3	3	35	85	3	0	25	X	0
Peru	298	93	9	60	315	153	1	63	X	0
Suriname	151	0	6	60	95	8	0	38	300	0
Uruguay	X	1	0	X	X	4	0	X	X	0
Venezuela	259	61	14	58	199	121	0	45	X	5
ASIA	X	X	X	X	X	X	X	X	X	X
Afghanistan, Islamic State	103	4	1	26	6	1	1	2	84	0
Armenia, Rep	46	0	3	32	6	0	0	4	X	0
Azerbaijan	52	0	3	26	8	0	0	4	X	5
Bangladesh	119	1	13	49	19	0	0	8	X	0
Bhutan	19	2	1	11	24	0	0	14	X	0
Cambodia	82	1	9	32	28	0	0	11	>215	5
China	340	79	15	35	263	156	1	27	686	28
Georgia	46	0	7	24	11	0	0	6	X	3
India	389	187	16	57	197	120	3	29	X	4
Indonesia	511	305	19	90	270	111	0	48	X	60
Iran, Islamic Rep	164	27	8	30	11	5	2	2	269	7
Iraq	81	1	2	23	6	0	0	2	X	2
Israel	X	1	5	X	X	0	0	X	26	0
Japan	66	27	8	20	52	44	10	16	186	7
Jordan	X	0	1	X	X	0	0	X	26	0
Kazakstan, Rep	37	0	1	6	10	0	1	2	X	5
Korea, Dem People's Rep	19	1	0	8	14	X	0	6	X	0
Korea, Rep	25	2	0	12	14	2	0	7	130	0
Kuwait	29	0	2	24	2	0	0	2	X	0
Kyrgyz Rep	23	0	1	9	3	0	0	1	X	0
Lao People's Dem Rep	66	1	7	23	37	1	0	13	244	4
Lebanon	X	2	2	X	X	0	0	X	X	0
Malaysia	268	73	14	85	158	61	0	50	449	14
Mongolia	21	0	0	4	8	0	0	2	70	0
Myanmar	203	38	20	51	75	10	0	19	X	1
Nepal	80	1	5	33	36	10	0	15	120	0
Oman	64	10	4	23	X	0	0	X	3	3
Pakistan	172	23	6	41	17	4	0	4	156	1
Philippines	190	158	7	62	63	55	2	21	X	26
Saudi Arabia	84	4	2	14	X	0	0	X	8	0
Singapore	X	X	1	X	X	0	0	X	73	1
Sri Lanka	144	75	8	77	39	20	0	21	65	8
Syrian Arab Rep	X	2	3	X	X	0	0	X	X	0
Tajikistan, Rep	38	0	1	16	2	1	0	1	X	1
Thailand	298	36	16	81	107	17	0	29	>600	14
Turkey	102	8	12	24	18	2	2	4	>152	18
Turkmenistan, Rep	80	X	2	22	2	0	0	1	X	5
United Arab Emirates	37	1	2	18	X	0	0	X	5	1
Uzbekistan, Rep	51	0	0	15	2	0	0	1	X	3
Vietnam	180	43	12	57	80	27	1	25	X	3
Yemen	77	31	2	21	X	1	0	X	5	0
OCEANIA	X	X	X	X	X	X	X	X	X	X
Australia	748	628	37	83	205	178	25	23	216	37
Fiji	25	11	6	20	2	2	1	2	X	0
New Zealand	40	36	11	13	3	3	1	1	29	8
Papua New Guinea	280	77	10	79	197	117	0	56	282	13
Solomon Islands	61	12	4	43	17	9	0	12	X	0

Notes: a. Values are standardized using a species-area curve. b. Threatened species include a few marine species. c. World totals include countries not listed. d. World total includes both marine and freshwater fish species; freshwater species make up around 40-50 percent of this estimate.
Threatened species data are as of 1996.

Data Table 14.4
Endangered Species Management Programs, 1996

Sources: World Conservation Union, International Species Information System, and other multiple sources

Species, Common Name	Species, Scientific Name {a}	Distribution {b}	IUCN Status {c}	Species Management Programs {d}	Estimated Wild Population	Number of Zoos Housing Species	Number of Captive Animals	Number of Captive Births	Crude Rate of Change {e}
AMPHIBIANS									
Salamander, Japanese Giant	Andrias japonicus	Japan	VU	J	X	5	7	0	0.90
Toad, Puerto Rican Crested	Peltophryne lemur	Puerto Rico, British Virgin Islands	VU	S	<300	17	126	0	1.24
REPTILES									
Alligator, Chinese	Alligator sinensis	China	CR	S, UK	800-1,000	20	181	22	1.09
Boa, Dumeril's Ground	Acrantophis dumerili	Madagascar	VU	S	X	43	188	13	0.99
Boa, Madagascan Tree	Sanzinia madagascariensis	Madagascar	VU	UK	X	32	193	21	1.13
Boa, Madagascar	Acrantophis madagascariensis	Madagascar	VU	A	X	10	57	7	1.09
Boa, Mona Island	Epicrates monensis monensis	Puerto Rico	EN	S	X	1	11	3	0.58
Boa, Virgin Island	Epicrates monensis granti	Puerto Rico, Virgin Islands	EN	S	X	13	56	0	0.86
Crocodile, Cuban	Crocodylus rhombifer	Cuba	EN	S	3,000-6,000	15	52	0	1.00
Crocodile, W. African Dwarf	Osteolaemus tetraspis	Central and West Africa	VU	A, UK	X	45	141	2	1.03
Gecko, Standing's Day	Phelsuma standingi	Madagascar	VU	UK	X	37	315	68	1.21
Gila Monster	Heloderma suspectum {f}	Mexico, Puerto Rico	VU	E, UK	X	81	318	3	1.00
Iguana, Cayman Is. Ground	Cyclura nubila lewisi	Cayman Islands	CR	S	X	5	22	12	1.04
Iguana, Fiji Banded	Brachylophus fasciatus	Fiji, Tonga, Vanuatu [int.]	EN	Au	>10,000	13	46	0	1.02
Iguana, Jamaican	Cyclura collei	Jamaica	CR	S	X	6	104	0	1.27
Iguana, Rhinoceros	Cyclura cornuta {f}	Dominican Rep., Haiti, Puerto Rico	VU	UK	X	37	147	22	1.00
Lizard, Beaded	Heloderma horridum {f}	Guatemala, Mexico	VU	E, UK	X	40	167	29	1.09
Lizard, Giant Girdled	Cordylus giganteus	South Africa	VU	A	>150,000	16	55	6	1.02
Lizard, Striped Legless	Delma impar	Australia	VU	Au	X	2	51	0	2.29
Skink, Chevron	Oligosoma homolanotum	New Zealand	VU	Au	X	1	3	0	X
Skink, Robust	Cyclodina alani	New Zealand	VU	Au	<20,000	1	7	0	1.00
Tortoise, African Pancake	Malacochersus tornieri	Kenya, Tanzania	VU	UK	>20,000	47	228	11	1.05
Tortoise, Aldabra Giant	Geochelone gigantea	Seychelles	VU	Au	155,000	85	278	0	X
Tortoise, Geometric	Psammobates geometricus	South Africa	EN	A	2,000-4,000	1	10	0	1.03
Tortoise, Radiated	Geochelone radiata	Madagascar, Mauritius, Reunion	VU	A, S	2-2.5 million	54	412	25	1.00
Turtle, Western Swamp	Pseudemydura umbrina	Australia	CR	Au	55	1	135	38	1.24
BIRDS									
Amazon, Green-cheeked	Amazona viridigenalis	Mexico, Puerto Rico [int.], U.S. [int.]	EN	E, UK	3,000-6,500	37	118	3	0.99
Amazon, Red-browed	Amazona rhodocorytha	Brazil	EN	E	X	7	35	2	1.11
Amazon, Red-tailed	Amazona brasiliensis	Brazil	EN	E	X	4	18	0	1.02
Amazon, St. Vincent	Amazona guildingii	St. Vincent	VU	S	700-800	4	14	0	0.98
Cassowary, Southern	Casuarius casuarius	Australia, Indonesia, PNG	VU	UK	1,500-3,000	52	125	12	1.04
Cockatoo, Philippine	Cacatua haematuropygia	Philippines	CR	E	1,000-4,000	6	24	0	1.14
Cockatoo, Salmon-crested	Cacatua moluccensis	Indonesia, Singapore [int.]	VU	E, J	X	100	330	14	1.01
Cockatoo, Yellow-crested	Cacatua sulphurea citrinocristata {g}	Hong Kong [int.], Indonesia, Singapore	EN	E	2,376	28	62	3	1.06
Condor, California	Gymnogyps californianus	United States [re-int.]	CR	S	27	2	104	17	1.08
Crane, Red-crowned	Grus japonensis	East Asia, Mongolia	VU	E, J, S, UK	1,700	49	152	12	1.01
Crane, Wattled	Grus carunculatus	Africa	VU	J, S, UK	13,000-15,000	37	109	8	1.00
Crane, White-napped	Grus vipio	East Asia, Mongolia	VU	E, J, S, UK	4,500	59	197	29	1.02
Crowned-pigeon, Southern	Goura scheepmakeri	Indonesia, Papua New Guinea	VU	E, S	X	11	25	6	1.04
Crowned-pigeon, Victoria	Goura victoria	Indonesia, Papua New Guinea	VU	E, S	X	51	127	15	1.06
Crowned-pigeon, Western	Goura cristata	Indonesia	VU	E, S	X	37	84	15	0.94
Duck, Freckled	Stictonetta naevosa	Australia	VU	Au	X	5	81	0	1.06
Eagle, Stellar's Sea	Haliaeetus pelagicus	Japan, North and South Korea, Russia	VU	J	6,000-7,000	5	20	0	1.01
Griffon, Cape	Gyps coprotheres	Southern Africa	VU	A	X	5	36	2	1.05
Honeyeater, Regent	Xanthomyza phrygia	Australia	EN	Au	<1,000	1	14	7	0.40
Ibis, Northern Bald	Geronticus eremita	North Africa and Middle East	CR	E, J	X	55	708	94	1.04
Ibis, Southern Bald	Geronticus calvus	Lesotho, South Africa, Swaziland	VU	A	10,000	5	47	4	1.34
Kiwi, Brown	Apteryx australis mantelli {g}	New Zealand	VU	Au	X	11	50	14	1.01
Macaw, Blue-throated	Ara glaucogularis	Argentina (?), Bolivia, Paraguay (?)	EN	E	<1,000	9	36	4	1.11
Macaw, Hyacinthine	Anodorhynchus hyacinthinus	Bolivia, Brazil, Paraguay	VU	E, UK	3,000	86	320	11	1.05
Macaw, Red-fronted	Ara rubrogenys	Bolivia	EN	E, UK	1,000	38	154	12	0.97
Malleefowl	Leipoa ocellata	Australia	VU	Au	>4,000 (?)	5	66	29	1.18
Owl, Blackiston's Fish	Ketupa blakistoni	China, Japan, Russia	EN	J	680-900	1	1	0	X
Parakeet, Antipodes	Cyanoramphus unicolor	New Zealand	VU	Au	2,000-3,000	5	12	2	0.82
Parakeet, Blue-throated	Pyrrhura cruentata	Brazil	VU	UK	X	6	52	4	1.11
Parakeet, Golden	Aratinga quarouba	Brazil	EN	E	X	31	166	17	1.01
Parrot, Orange-bellied	Neophema chrysogaster	Australia	EN	Au	150	1	24	7	2.11
Parrot, Thick-billed	Rhynchopsita pachyrhyncha	Mexico, United States [re-int.]	EN	S, UK	X	26	108	8	1.08
Peafowl, Congo	Afropavo congensis	Democratic Republic of Congo	VU	E, S	X	18	96	41	0.99
Pelican, Dalmatian	Pelecanus crispus	Asia, Middle East, Southeast Europe	VU	E	6,400-8,600	18	100	16	1.01
Pheasant, Edwards	Lophura edwardsi	Vietnam	CR	E	Extinct (?)	31	146	38	1.22
Pigeon, Mauritius Pink	Columba mayeri	Mauritius	CR	E, S	77	32	233	51	1.14
Rail, Guam	Rallus owstoni	Guam	EW	S	0	13	53	7	0.91
Starling, Bali (Bali Mynah)	Leucopsar rosthschildi	Indonesia	CR	E, J, S, UK	30-35	106	572	155	1.03
Stork, Oriental	Ciconia boyciana	Japan, Northeast Asia	EN	J	2,500	8	52	13	1.09
Teal, Brown	Anas aucklandica {f}	New Zealand	VU	Au	X	7	61	8	1.00
MAMMALS									
Addax	Addax nasomaculatus	North Africa and the Sahel	EN	Au, E, S, UK	<250	62	514	93	1.02
Anoa, Lowland	Bubalus depressicornis	Indonesia	EN	E	<4,000	24	76	11	1.05
Anteater , Giant	Myrmecophaga tridactyla {f}	Central and South America	VU	E	X	29	64	12	0.59
Ass, Asiatic Wild	Equus hemionus {f}	Central and Western Asia	VU	E	X	37	194	14	0.97
Ass, Somali Wild	Equus africanus somaliensis {g}	Ethiopia, Somalia	CR	E	100-250	8	29	2	0.96
Babirusa	Babyrousa babyrussa {f}	Indonesia	VU	E, S	<8,500	37	135	24	1.05
Bandicoot, Eastern Barred	Perameles gunnii	Australia	VU	Au	X	7	60	39	1.16
Banteng	Bos javanicus {f}	Southeast Asia	EN	E	X	28	313	28	1.04
Bear, Sloth	Melursus ursinus {f}	Bangladesh, India, Nepal, Sri Lanka	VU	E, S	5,000-15,000	23	59	6	1.08
Bear, Spectacled	Tremarctos ornatus	South America	VU	E, S	>20,000	55	133	9	0.90
Bilby, Greater	Macrotis lagotis sagitta {g}	Australia	VU	Au	X	1	3	0	1.44
Bison, European	Bison bonasus {f}	Eastern Europe [re-int.], Russia [re-int]	EN	E	1,870	40	249	40	0.80
Cheetah	Acinonyx jubatus {f}	Africa	VU	A, Au, E, J, S,	9,000-12,000	117	666	70	0.82
Chimpanzee	Pan troglodytes {f}	Africa	EN	J, S, UK	105,000	146	2,697	76	1.01
Chimpanzee, Pygmy (Bonobo)	Pan paniscus	Democratic Republic of Congo	EN	E, S	10,000-20,000	17	98	5	1.04

Species, Common Name	Species, Scientific Name {a}	Distribution {b}	IUCN Status {c}	Species Management Programs {d}	Estimated Wild Population	Number of Zoos Housing Species	Number of Captive Animals	Number of Captive Births	Crude Rate of Change {e}
Chuditch	*Dasyurus geoffroii*	Australia	VU	Au	2,500-4,400	2	65	49	1.24
Deer, Swamp	*Cervus duvauceli {f}*	India, Nepal	VU	S	>5,000	23	222	46	0.98
Dog, African Wild	*Lycaon pictus {f}*	Africa	EN	A, E, S	3,000-5,000	43	241	60	1.03
Dog, Bush	*Speothos venaticus*	Panama, South America	VU	B, E	X	24	84	19	1.05
Drill	*Mandrillus leucophaeus {f}*	Cameroon, Equatorial Guinea, Nigeria	EN	E, J, S	<10,000	8	46	5	1.02
Elephant, African	*Loxodonta africana {f}*	Africa	EN	E, S	581,175	101	282	1	0.81
Elephant, Asian	*Elephas maximus {f}*	South and Southeast Asia	EN	E, J, S	38,000-51,000	131	460	14	0.90
Ferret, Black-footed	*Mustela nigripes*	United States	EW	S	60	14	198	161	X
Fossa	*Cryptoprocta ferox*	Madagascar	VU	E	X	7	29	2	1.03
Fox, Rodrigues Flying	*Pteropus rodricensis*	Mauritius (Rodrigues)	CR	S	350	17	557	156	1.16
Gazelle, Dama	*Gazella dama*	North Africa and the Sahel	EN	E	X	15	62	5	0.84
Gibbon, Black	*Hylobates concolor {f}*	Cambodia, China, Vietnam	EN	E, J	10,000	46	183	16	1.04
Gibbon, Pileated	*Hylobates pileatus*	Cambodia, Laos, Thailand	VU	E	30,000	15	55	1	1.01
Gibbon, Silvery	*Hylobates moloch {f}*	Indonesia	CR	E	1,000	18	67	5	1.02
Gorilla, Western Lowland	*Gorilla gorilla gorilla*	West Central Africa	EN	E, S	>110,000	95	643	38	X
Hippopotamus, Pygmy	*Hexaprotodon liberiensis {f}*	West Africa	VU	E, S, UK	X	61	164	11	0.98
Horse, Przewalski Wild	*Equus przewalskii*	China, Mongolia	EW	Au, E, S	X	69	548	35	0.98
Kowari	*Dasycercus byrnei*	Australia	VU	E	X	26	136	24	1.15
Lechwe, Kafue	*Kobus leche kafuensis*	Zambia	VU	UK	X	13	133	24	0.95
Lemur, Black	*Eulemur macaco macaco*	Madagascar	VU	E, J, S, UK	X	42	171	14	0.95
Lemur, Mongoose	*Eulemur mongoz {f}*	Comoros, Madagascar	VU	E, S	X	23	173	28	1.03
Lemur, Ring-tailed	*Lemur catta*	Madagascar	VU	S	X	167	1,087	128	1.00
Lemur, Ruffed	*Varecia variegata {f}*	Madagascar	EN	Au, E, J, S	X	158	895	135	1.05
Leopard, Amur	*Panthera pardus orientalis*	China, North and South Korea, Russia	CR	E	28-31	44	144	16	1.03
Leopard, Clouded	*Neofelis nebulosa {f}*	China, South and Southeast Asia	VU	E, S	X	57	185	11	1.02
Leopard, North Persian	*Panthera pardus saxicolor*	Afghanistan, Iran, Turkmenistan	EN	E	X	60	142	14	1.01
Leopard, Snow	*Uncia uncia*	Himalayan region	EN	E, J, S	4,500-7,350	142	467	36	1.00
Lion, African	*Panthera leo {e}*	Africa	VU	S	30,000-100,000	192	825	97	1.04
Lion, Asiatic	*Panthera leo persica*	India	EN	E	300	29	73	7	0.99
Loris, Pygmy	*Nycticebus pygmaeus*	Cambodia (?), China, Laos, Vietnam	VU	E, S, UK	300-500	28	160	27	1.08
Macaque, Celebes Black	*Macaca nigra {f}*	Indonesia	EN	UK	X	35	247	22	1.01
Macaque, Lion-tailed	*Macaca Silenus*	India	EN	E, J, S, UK	3,600-5,000	53	356	21	1.02
Mala	*Lagorchestes h. hirsutus {g}*	Australia	CR	Au	0	1	10	1	1.06
Marmoset, Geoffroy's Tufted-ear	*Callithrix geoffroyi*	Brazil	VU	E, UK	X	35	223	78	1.08
Marmoset, Goeldi's	*Callimico goeldii*	Bolivia, Brazil, Colombia, Peru	VU	E, S	X	64	309	28	0.97
Mink, European	*Mustela lutreola {f}*	Europe	EN	E	X	7	40	15	1.03
Monkey, Colombian Spider	*Ateles fusciceps robustus*	Colombia, Panama	VU	E	X	31	145	14	1.03
Monkey, Diana	*Cercopithecus diana {f}*	West Africa	VU	E, UK	X	47	144	12	0.97
Monkey, Douc	*Pygathrix nemaeus {f}*	Cambodia, China, Laos, Vietnam	EN	E	X	7	42	3	0.72
Numbat	*Myrmecobius fasciatus*	Australia	VU	Au	<2,000	1	21	0	1.56
Orangutan	*Pongo pygmaeus {f}*	Brunei, Indonesia, Malaysia	VU	Au, E, J, S, UK	21,500-29,771	118	616	27	0.99
Oryx, Arabian	*Oryx leucoryx*	Middle East	EN	E, S	X	61	625	54	1.00
Oryx, Scimitar-horned	*Oryx dammah*	Israel [int.], North Africa	CR	Au, E, S	X	80	897	165	0.81
Panda, Giant	*Ailuropoda melanoleuca*	China	EN	S	1,100	5	9	0	0.84
Panda, Lesser (Red)	*Ailurus fulgens {f}*	China, Laos, Myanmar, South Asia	EN	Au, E, J, S, UK	X	112	350	64	1.02
Peccary, Chacoan	*Catagonus wagneri*	Argentina, Bolivia, Paraguay	EN	S	X	1	11	10	1.82
Pudu, Southern	*Pudu puda*	Argentina, Chile	VU	E	X	31	151	42	1.09
Rat, Greater Stick-nest	*Leporillus conditor*	Australia	EN	Au	<2,500	4	19	8	0.82
Rhinoceros, Black	*Diceros bicornis {f}*	Africa	CR	Au, E, J, S, UK	2,400	57	170	5	1.07
Rhinoceros, Great Indian	*Rhinoceros unicornis*	Bhutan, India, Nepal	EN	E, J, S, UK	2,000	27	66	3	1.00
Rhinoceros, Sumatran	*Dicerorhinus sumatrensis {f}*	Southeast Asia	CR	S	250-400	2	4	0	0.88
Sika, Tonkin	*Cervus nippon pseudaxis*	Vietnam	EN	E	X	14	140	39	1.08
Tamarin, Cotton-top	*Saguinus oedipus {f}*	Colombia	EN	Au, E, J, S	2,000-3,000	138	705	152	1.00
Tamarin, Golden Lion	*Leontopithecus r. rosalia*	Brazil	CR	Au, E, S	<650	98	338	69	0.99
Tamarin, Golden-headed Lion	*Leontopithecus chrysomelas*	Brazil	EN	E	6,000-15,500	55	285	42	1.03
Tapir, Malayan	*Tapirus indicus*	Southeast Asia	VU	E, J	<1,500	50	126	8	1.02
Tiger, Amur	*Panthera tigris altaica*	China [ex?], North Korea [ex?], Russia	EN	E, J, S	330-371	120	348	47	1.00
Tiger, Sumatran	*Panthera tigris sumarae*	Indonesia	CR	Au, E, J, S, UK	400-500	56	133	10	1.01
Tree-kangaroo, Goodfellow's	*Dendrolagus goodfellowi*	Papua New Guinea	EN	E, S	X	10	49	3	1.00
Tree-kangaroo, Huon	*Dendrolagus matschiei*	Papua New Guinea	EN	E, S	X	31	99	8	1.03
Wildcat, Scottish	*Felis silvestris grampia*	United Kingdom	VU	UK	X	3	9	4	1.05
Wolf, Red	*Canis rufus {f}*	United States	CR	S	92	31	134	7	1.02
Wolverine	*Gulo gulo {f}*	North America, North Europe, Mongolia	VU	E	X	18	33	5	1.05
Zebra, Grevy's	*Equus grevyi*	Ethiopia, Kenya	EN	E, J, S	X	70	332	25	0.99
Zebra, Hartman's Mountain	*Equus zebra hartmannae {g}*	Angola, Namibia, South Africa	EN	E, S	7,350	21	77	7	0.92

Notes: a. Scientific names follow the "1996 IUCN Red List of Threatened Animals" nomenclature. b. From the "1996 IUCN Red List": [int] = introduced; [re-int] = reintroduced; [ex?] = believed to be extinct; [?] = unknown if the species is currently found in the area. c. IUCN threatened status: CR = critically endangered; EN = endangered; EW = extinct in the wild; VU = vulnerable. d. A = African Propagation Program (APP); Au = Australasian Species Management Program (ASMP); B = Zoological Society of Brazil Species Program (SZB); E = European Endangered Species Programs (EEP); J = Species Survival Committees Japan (SSCJ); S = North America Species Survival Plan (SSP); UK = United Kingdom Joint Management of Species Committee (JMSC). e. A rate > 1 indicates a net population increase; a rate < 1, a net population decrease; and a rate = 1 indicates that the captive population is stable. f. Zoo census data include all subspecies being held in captivity. g. IUCN status listed applies to the species; the subspecies is not listed separately under the "1996 IUCN Red List."

Sources and Technical Notes

National and International Protection of Natural Areas, 1997

Sources: National protected areas: Protected Areas Data Unit of the World Conservation Monitoring Centre (WCMC), unpublished data (WCMC, Cambridge, U.K., May 1997). Biosphere reserves: United Nations Educational, Scientific, and Cultural Organization (UNESCO), Man and the Biosphere Programme, *List of Biosphere Reserves* (UNESCO, Paris, April 1996). World heritage sites: UNESCO World Heritage Centre, *World Heritage List* (UNESCO, Paris, December 1996). Wetlands of international importance: Ramsar Convention Bureau, *List of Wetlands of International Importance* (Ramsar Convention Bureau, Gland, Switzerland, December 1997).

All protected areas combine natural areas of at least 1,000 hectares in five World Conservation Union (IUCN) management categories. *Totally protected areas* are maintained in a natural state, are closed to extractive uses, and encompass three management categories:

Category I. Scientific reserves and strict nature reserves possess outstanding, representative ecosystems. Public access is generally limited, with only scientific research and educational use permitted.

Category II. National parks and provincial parks are relatively large areas of national or international significance not materially altered by humans. Visitors may use them for recreation and study.

Category III. Natural monuments and natural landmarks contain unique geological formations, special animals or plants, or unusual habitats.

Partially protected areas are areas that may be managed for specific uses, such as recreation or tourism, or areas that provide optimum conditions for certain species or communities of wildlife. Some extractive use within these areas is allowed. They encompass two management categories:

Category IV. Managed nature reserves and wildlife sanctuaries are protected for specific purposes, such as conservation of a significant plant or animal species.

Category V. Protected landscapes and seascapes may be entirely natural or may include cultural landscapes (e.g., scenically attractive agricultural areas).

Nationally protected areas listed in this table do not include locally or provincially protected sites, or privately owned areas.

Protected areas at least 100,000 hectares and 1 million hectares in size refer to all IUCN category I–V protected areas that fall within these two classifications. The totals consist of an aggregation of single sites, and it is likely that some sites are not contiguous blocks. These data do not account for agglomerations of protected areas that together might exceed 100,000 or 1 million hectares.

International protection systems usually include sites that are listed under national protection systems. *Biosphere reserves* are representative of terrestrial and coastal environments that have been internationally recognized under UNESCO's Man and the Biosphere Programme. They have been selected for their value to conservation and are intended to foster the scientific knowledge, skills, and human values necessary to support sustainable development. Each reserve must contain a diverse, natural ecosystem of a specific biogeographical province, large enough to be an effective conservation unit. For further details, refer to M. Udvardy, *A Classification of the Biogeographical Provinces of the World* (IUCN, Morges, Switzerland, 1975), and to *World Resources 1986*, Chapter 6. Each reserve also must include a minimally disturbed core area for conservation and research and may be surrounded by buffer zones where traditional land uses, experimental ecosystem research, and ecosystem rehabilitation may be permitted. Several countries share biosphere reserves. These sites are counted only once in continental and world totals.

World heritage sites represent areas of "outstanding universal value" for their natural features, their cultural value, or for both natural and cultural values. The table includes only natural and mixed natural and cultural sites. Any party to the World Heritage Convention may nominate natural sites that contain examples of a major stage of Earth's evolutionary history; a significant ongoing geological process; a unique or superlative natural phenomenon, formation, or feature; or a habitat for a threatened species. Several countries share world heritage sites. These sites, referred to as international heritage sites, are counted only once in continental and world totals.

Any party to the Convention on Wetlands of International Importance Especially as Waterfowl Habitat (Ramsar, Iran, 1971) that agrees to respect a site's integrity and to establish wetland reserves can designate *wetlands of international importance*. There are 14 sites that are inscribed on both the Ramsar and the World Heritage lists.

Globally Threatened Species: Mammals, Birds, and Higher Plants, 1990s

Sources: Total and endemic species of mammals and birds: World Conservation Monitoring Centre (WCMC), unpublished data (WCMC, Cambridge, U.K., April 1997). Threatened species of mammals and birds: WCMC and World Conservation Union (IUCN), *1996 IUCN Red List of Threatened Animals* (IUCN, Gland, Switzerland, 1996). Higher plants data: WCMC, *Biodiversity Data Sourcebook* (World Conservation Press, Cambridge, U.K., 1994).

The *total number of known species* may include introductions in some instances. Data on *mammals*, in most cases, exclude cetaceans (whales and porpoises), except where otherwise indicated. Total *bird* species listed includes only birds that breed in that country, not those that migrate or winter there. Only flowering plants are listed under total *higher plants* species numbers.

The number of *endemic species* refers to those species known to be found only within the country listed. The number of total endemic plant species listed for each country includes flowering plants, ferns, and conifers and cycads.

Figures are not necessarily comparable among countries because taxonomic concepts and the extent of knowledge vary (for the latter reason, country totals of species and endemics may be underestimates). In general, numbers of mammals and birds are fairly well known, whereas plants have not been as well inventoried.

The number of *threatened species* listed for all countries includes full species that are critically endangered, endangered, or vulnerable, but excludes introduced species, species whose status is insufficiently known (categorized by IUCN as "data deficient" [DD]), those known to be extinct, and those for which a status has not been assessed (categorized by IUCN as "not evaluated" [NE]). If a species is listed under the DD or NE categories, it should not be treated as a nonthreatened species, but as one that has not been assessed. Threatened species data for animals presented in Data Tables 14.2 and 14.3 reflect estimates presented in the IUCN *Red List*. Bird Life International compiles and provides bird status assessments for the IUCN *Red List*. Threatened species data for birds are from *Birds to Watch 2: The World List of Threatened Birds* (Collar *et al.*, BirdLife International, Cambridge, U.K., 1994). The number of threatened species of birds is listed for countries included within their breeding or wintering ranges.

This is the first time that all *known* mammal and bird species have been assessed. This is also the first time that the new IUCN categories and criteria are being applied to assess the risk of extinction of species. A brief description of the new system is presented below. For more detailed information, please refer to the *1996 IUCN Red List*.

The IUCN classifies threatened species as "all full species categorized at the global level as Critically Endangered, Endangered, or Vulnerable." The definitions for these categories follow:

Critically Endangered: "When a taxon is facing an extremely high risk of extinction in the wild in the immediate future as defined by any of the criteria A–E." (See below.)

Endangered: "When a taxon is not Critically Endangered but is facing a very high risk of extinction in the wild in the near future as defined by any of the criteria A–E."

Vulnerable: "When a taxon is not Critically Endangered or Endangered but is facing a high risk of extinction in the wild in the medium-term future as defined by any of the criteria A–E."

For each threat category there are five criteria (A–E, see below) used to assess species status. This process provides a more rigorous approach from that used prior to revisions of the IUCN criteria. Species need to meet only one of the five criteria to be listed under that particular threat category. The five criteria are:

A—Declining population rate;

B—Small population and decline or fluctuation;

C—Small population size and decline rate;

D—Very small population/very restricted distribution; and

E—Quantitative analysis indicating the probability of extinction in the wild (e.g., Population Viability Analysis).

In addition, there are subcriteria that provide further information on the reasons to list a species, potential causes of threat, etc.

Number of species per 10,000 square kilometers provides a relative estimate for comparing numbers of species among countries of differing size. Because the relationship between area and species number is nonlinear (i.e., as the area sampled increases, the number of new species located decreases), a species-area curve has been used to standardize these species numbers. The curve predicts how many species a country would have, given its current number of species, if it was a uniform 10,000 square kilometers in size. This number is calculated using the formula: $S = cA^z$, where S = the number of species, A = area, and c and z are constants. The slope of the species-area curve is determined by the constant z, which is approximately 0.33 for large areas containing many habitats. This constant is based on data from previous studies of species-area relationships. In reality, the constant z would differ among regions and countries because of differences in species' range size (which tend to be smaller in the tropics) and differences in varieties of habitats present. For example, a tropical country with a broad variety of habitats would be expected to have a steeper species-area curve than a temperate, homogenous country because one would predict a greater number of species per unit area. Species-area curves also are steeper for islands than for mainland countries. At present, there are insufficient regional data to estimate separate slopes (z) for each country; therefore, these species estimates should be interpreted with caution.

Data Table 14.3

Globally Threatened Species: Reptiles, Amphibians, and Fish, 1990s

Sources: Total and endemic species data: World Conservation Monitoring Centre (WCMC), unpublished data (WCMC, Cambridge, U.K., April 1997). Threatened species data: WCMC and World Conservation Union (IUCN), *1996 IUCN Red List of Threatened Animals* (IUCN, Gland, Switzerland, 1996).

For definitions of *all species, endemic species,* and *threatened species,* refer to the Technical Notes for Data Table 14.2. The world total for the number of known freshwater fish species also includes marine species. Of this total, around 40 to 45 percent are estimated to be freshwater species. Threatened marine turtles and most threatened marine fish are excluded from country totals. However, a few marine fish species are included in the threatened category. This is the first time that the IUCN *Red List* criteria are applied to marine fish; the categories for marine fish should therefore be taken as a preliminary assessment that needs further evaluation.

The number of species per 10,000 square kilometers provides a relative estimate for comparing numbers of species among countries of differing size. For details, refer to the Technical Notes for Data Table 14.2.

Data Table 14.4

Endangered Species Management Programs, 1996

Sources: Species, distribution, and IUCN status: World Conservation Monitoring Centre (WCMC) and World Conservation Union (IUCN), *1996 IUCN Red List of Threatened Animals* (IUCN, Gland, Switzerland, 1996). Species management programs: IUCN/Species Survival Commission (SSC), Conservation Breeding Specialist Group (CBSG), F. Swengel, T. Hill, and E. Sullivan (eds.), *Global Zoo Directory 1996* (IUCN/SSC CBSG, Apple Valley, Minnesota, 1996); Christine Hopkins, Australasian Regional Association of Zoological Parks and Aquaria (personal communication), and Kevin Willis, American Zoo and Aquarium Association (AZA) (personal communication).

Estimated wild population data come from a variety of sources. The following list includes published and on-line sources: N.J. Collar, M.J. Crosby, and A.J. Stattersfield, *Birds to Watch 2: The World List of Threatened Birds* (BirdLife International, Cambridge, U.K., 1994); National Council for Nature Conservation and Bialowieza National Park, *1995 European Bison Pedigree Book* (Bialowieza National Park, Poland, 1995); IUCN/SSC Asian Rhino Specialist Group, *Asian Rhinos: Status, Survey and Conservation Action Plan* (IUCN, Gland, Switzerland, 1997); IUCN/SSC Pigs and Peccaries Specialist Group and Hippo Specialist Group, *Pigs, Peccaries and Hippos: Status, Survey and Conserva-*

tion Action Plan (IUCN, Gland, 1993); IUCN/SSC Primate Specialist Group, *African Primates: Status, Survey and Conservation Action Plan* (IUCN, Gland, 1996); J. Ballou, R. Lacy, and S. Ellis, *Leontopithecus II: The Second Population and Habitat Viability Assessment for the Lion Tamarins (Leontopithecus): Review Draft Report* (CBSG, Apple Valley, Minnesota, 1997); Mary Emanoil (ed.) and IUCN/SSC, *Encyclopedia of Endangered Species* (Gale Research Inc., Detroit, Michigan, 1994); B. Peyton *et al.,* "Status of Wild Andean Bears and Policies for their Management", in Proceedings from 10th International Conference on Bear Research and Management, Fairbanks, Alaska, July 1995; IUCN, *Species,* No. 28 (IUCN, Gland, June 1997), p. 47; IUCN/SSC Crocodile Specialist Group, *Status Survey and Conservation Action Plan: Revised Action Plan for Crocodiles* (IUCN, Gland, 1996). Available online at: http://www.flmnh.ufl.edu/natsci/herpetology/act-plan/a-plan01.htm; AZA, *Species Survival Plan 1995–96 Reports.* Available online at: http://www.aza.org/aza/ssp.html; IUCN/SSC African Rhino Specialist Group, "Rhino Information," International Rhino Foundation. Available online at: http://www.rhinos-irf.org/rhinos/black.html. IUCN/SSC African Elephant Specialist Group, "African Elephant Database." Available online at: http://www.iucn.org/themes/ssc/aed/home.htm; E. Kemf and P. Jackson, *Asian Elephants in the Wild: A WWF Species Status Report,* "The Status of the Asian Elephant." Available online at: http://www.wwf.org/species/elephants/page5.htm.

Estimated wild populations data were also provided by the following personal communications: Chris Banks, Melbourne Zoo, Australia; John Behler, Chair, IUCN/SSC Tortoise and Freshwater Turtle Specialist Group, Wildlife Conservation Society, New York; William Branch, Chair, IUCN/SSC African Reptile and Amphibian Specialist Group, Port Elizabeth Museum, South Africa; Kelly Cosgrave, Robust Skink Captive Coordinator, Auckland Zoo, New Zealand; Ardith Eudey, Vice-Chair for Asia, IUCN/SSC Primate Specialist Group California State University–Fullerton, Upland, California; Richard Gibson, Herpetology Department Head and Jersey Wildlife Preservation Trust, U.K.; Peter Gober, U.S. Fish and Wildlife Service (USFWS) Black-Footed Ferret Recovery Program Coordinator, Pierre, South Dakota; Jane Hendron, Information and Education Specialist, USFWS California Condor Recovery Program, Ventura, California; International Crane Foundation, Baraboo, Wisconsin; Peter Jackson, Chair, IUCN/SSC Cat Specialist Group, Switzerland; B. Kelly, USFWS Red Wolf Project, Manteo, North Carolina; Sharon Matola, Chair, IUCN/SSC Tapir Specialist Group, Belize Zoo, Belize; Alan Mootnick, International Center for Gibbon Studies, Santa Clarita, California; Luiz Paulo Pinto, Brazil Projects Coordinator, Conservation International, Belo Horizonte, Brazil; Christopher Servine, Co-Chair, IUCN/SSC Bear Specialist Group, University of Montana; USFWS Caribbean Field Office; Chris Wemmer, Chair, IUCN/SSC Deer Specialist Group Conservation and Research Center, Front Royal, Virginia; and Shuyi Zhang, Institute of Zoology, Chinese Academy of Sciences, Beijing. Zoo census data: International Species Information System (ISIS) species abstracts, available online at: http://www.world-zoo.org/abstract/abstract.htm and unpublished data (ISIS, Apple Valley, Minnesota, 1996).

Species: the list of species presents a selection of those being managed in zoos around the world. Zoos captive breed far more taxa than those species managed in organized programs. Species in this table are those mammals, birds, amphibians, and reptiles that: (a) have an ongoing management plan recognized and approved by regional zoo associations (e.g., the American Zoo and Aquarium Association [AZA], the European Association of Zoos and Aquaria [EAZA], etc.); (b) are listed as threatened or extinct in the wild under the *1996 IUCN Red List of Threatened Animals*; and (c) are housed in zoos that are members of the International Species Information System (ISIS). Although there are other threatened species being bred in captivity, the institutions breeding them are not members of ISIS and therefore their data are not readily available. The species' common and scientific names follow the IUCN *Red List* nomenclature, and thus species may have been given different names by ISIS and the Conservation Breeding Specialist Group (CBSG).

Distribution: the countries or regions where species are found in the wild follow the IUCN *Red List*. For birds, regions include migratory ranges. Where possible, the table indicates if a species has been reintroduced ("re-int.," i.e., the species has been reestablished after disappearing from that particular area), introduced ("int.," i.e., the species was not found in that area before its introduction), is believed to be extinct ("ex?"), or whether it is unknown if the species is currently found in the area ("?"). For more detailed information on distribution, please refer to the original source.

IUCN status refers to species that fall within the IUCN categories of Critically Endangered (CR), Endangered (EN), Vulnerable (VU), or Extinct in the Wild (EW). For a description of the categories CR, EN, or VU, please refer to the Sources and Technical Notes for Data Table 14.2. The category EW is described by IUCN as species "known only to survive in captivity or as a naturalized population well outside the past range." The status of several subspecies being managed in captivity was not listed separately under the IUCN *Red List*; therefore, the status for the whole species was listed in this table. For example, IUCN does not list a separate status for the subspecies of yellow-crested cockatoo (*Cacatua sulphurea citrinocristata*), but lists the species (*Cacatua sulphurea*) as endangered; therefore, the subspecies is also listed as endangered in this table.

Species management programs are active, regionally organized efforts of managed cooperation among zoos, usually for species at risk in the wild, although a few programs were initiated as a result of a need to maintain the species in captivity and not because of the species' threatened status. According to the AZA, species management programs breed species in captivity to "maintain a healthy and self-sustaining captive population that is both genetically diverse and demographically stable." There are species management programs in North America, Europe, Australasia, Japan, South Africa, Central and South America, India, and China. It is important to note, however, that for many taxa, zoos are past the first stage of trying to breed the species and are into the second stage of trying not to breed them too fast, because the available space in many zoos is full or because space needs to be made for more threatened taxa. Several species management programs include reintroduction of the species into the wild, and in some cases, these programs have been responsible for returning a species to its former habitat. However, species reintroduction is not the goal of all species management programs.

Estimated wild population: accurate numbers for wild populations are known for only a few well-studied species. Most figures presented here are estimates based on a number of different methodologies from extrapolating population estimates using remaining habitat to actual population counts; therefore, caution is recommended when using these figures. Figures for the California condor, the black-footed ferret, and the red wolf are all as of November 1, 1997. At that time, 13 more condors were scheduled to be released into the wild by the end of 1997.

Zoo census data include data from ISIS-member zoos exclusively. As of 1996, 495 institutions (about half of the world's recognized zoos) were ISIS members. This table underestimates the number of institutions, animals, and births in the world because other institutions that are breeding species in captivity are not members of ISIS. ISIS receives, archives, and analyzes standardized information from its member institutions on 255,000 living specimens and on 850,000 of their ancestors for 6,500 species using the within-zoo Animal Records Keeping System software and a pooled central database at ISIS. Of the non-ISIS-member institutions, some collaborate with species management programs while others do not. Ones that do not cooperate may breed species but with little consideration for maintaining a genetically diverse population. Special breeding facilities that may collaborate in species management programs also exist in the country of origin of some species.

Number of zoos housing species: this is number of ISIS-member zoos housing the species.

Number of captive animals includes all living individuals of a species housed in ISIS-member zoos as of December 1996. Not all individual animals participate in the species management programs. For many species, the figures include all subspecies being held in zoos, and this is indicated as such in the table.

Number of captive births refer to the total births minus deaths within the first 30 days of life that occurred during the last 6 months of 1996.

Crude rate of change is an indicator of captive population stability or the annual population increase or decrease per 100. A figure of 1.00 means the captive population is stable, whereas 0.90 indicates a 10 percent decrease in the captive population. This indicator is the net result of all processes including births, deaths, imports, exports, capture, escapes, etc. With the increasing number of species being managed in captivity, many zoos are scaling down their breeding programs for certain species to make space for more important taxa or because they lack the resources to continue expanding. However, the reason for the population's increase or decrease is not taken into account when calculating the crude rate of change. A declining population that is significantly bred in captivity often means intentional shrinkage to make room for other taxa in zoos, rather than failure of captive propagation. Therefore, this variable should not be taken as a measure of the ability to breed any particular species in captivity but should instead be used in combination with other information.

Chapter 15

Chapter 15

Energy and Materials

World Resources 1998–99 **331**

Data Table 15.1

Energy Production and Consumption, 1985–95

Source: United Nations Statistical Division

	Commercial Energy Production										Total Energy Consumption			
	Total		Solid Fuels		Liquid Fuels		Gaseous Fuels		Primary Electricity		Commercial Energy		Traditional Fuels	
	(peta-joules) 1995	Percent Change Since 1985	(peta-joules) 1995	Percent Change Since 1985	(peta-joules) 1995	Percent Change Since 1985	(peta-joules) 1995	Percent Change Since 1985	(peta joules) 1995	Percent Change Since 1985	(peta-joules) 1995	Percent Change Since 1985	(peta-joules) 1995	Percent Change Since 1985
WORLD	**364,891**	**25**	**102,356**	**15**	**138,531**	**18**	**88,699**	**46**	**35,305**	**47**	**347,262**	**19**	**24,941**	**41**
AFRICA	**22,667**	**35**	**4,480**	**12**	**14,364**	**31**	**3,499**	**117**	**324**	**46**	**8,976**	**15**	**5,227**	**26**
Algeria	4,997	55	1	326	2,565	24	2,431	109	1	(57)	1,352	134	21	30
Angola	1,121	129	0	0	1,109	131	7	56	5	4	26	(15)	59	50
Benin	4	(68)	0	0	4	(68)	0	0	0	0	7	3	55	34
Botswana	X	X	X	X	X	X	X	X	X	X	X	X	X	X
Burkina Faso	0	0	0	0	0	0	0	0	0	0	14	123	94	31
Burundi	1	220	0	(100)	0	0	0	0	0	(100)	3	38	48	9
Cameroon	222	(43)	0	(100)	213	(45)	0	0	10	20	56	15	222	136
Central African Rep	0	(100)	0	0	0	0	0	0	0	(100)	4	63	32	12
Chad	0	X	0	0	0	0	0	0	0	0	1	(67)	39	30
Congo, Dem Rep	72	(21)	3	(15)	48	(31)	0	0	21	19	44	(28)	448	59
Congo, Rep	385	57	0	0	383	57	0	(100)	2	141	23	92	24	34
Côte d'Ivoire	19	(60)	0	0	15	(65)			4	(18)	98	34	117	38
Egypt	2,530	23	0	0	1,961	4	530	279	39	34	1,348	57	50	27
Equatorial Guinea	10	138,789	0	0	10	0	0	0	0	(100)	2	121	4	(8)
Eritrea	X	X	X	X	X	X	X	X	X	X	X	X	X	X
Ethiopia	7	56	0	0	0	0	0	0	7	204	43	64	449	29
Gabon	799	119	0	0	764	112	32	38,642	3	25	61	167	29	36
Gambia, The	0	0	0	0	0	0	0	0	0	0	3	24	11	30
Ghana	22	93	0	0	0	(100)	0	0	22	104	67	51	246	63
Guinea	1	70	0	0	0	0	0	0	1	70	16	15	41	15
Guinea-Bissau	0	0	0	0	0	0	0	0	0	0	3	50	4	(3)
Kenya	22	21	0	0	0	0	0	0	22	21	111	82	388	17
Lesotho	X	X	X	X	X	X	X	X	X	X	X	X	X	X
Liberia	1	(23)	0	0	0	0	0	0	1	6	5	(53)	52	36
Libya	3,130	38	0	0	2,884	37	246	43	0	0	519	54	5	(4)
Madagascar	1	8	0	0	0	0	0	0	1	8	17	13	105	66
Malawi	3	74	0	0	0	0	0	0	3	75	12	38	103	(22)
Mali	1	88	0	0	0	0	0	0	1	107	7	15	60	32
Mauritania	0	(100)	0	0	0	0	0	0	0	(100)	40	347	0	(100)
Mauritius	0	(100)	0	0	0	0	0	0	0	(100)	21	134	13	(26)
Morocco	22	(23)	19	(16)	0	(100)	1	(70)	2	16	339	63	17	36
Mozambique	1	(36)	1	(3)	0	0	0	0	0	(100)	16	8	170	21
Namibia	X	X	X	X	X	X	X	X	X	X	X	X	X	X
Niger	5	14	5	14	0	0	0	0	0	0	15	16	54	50
Nigeria	4,054	26	1	(75)	3,857	24	174	59	22	180	465	8	1,005	17
Rwanda	1	65	0	0	0	0	0	(100)	1	69	7	22	53	(3)
Senegal	0	0	0	0	0	0	0	0	0	0	38	21	46	9
Sierra Leone	0	0	0	0	0	0	0	0	0	0	5	(40)	31	21
Somalia	X	X	X	X	X	X	X	X	0	0	X	X	X	X
South Africa {a}	4,931	27	4,379	14	373	0	72	0	108	137	3,659	(16)	151	13
Sudan	3	(10)	0	0	0	0	0	0	3	62	49	4	237	27
Swaziland	X	X	X	X	X	X	X	X	X	X	X	X	X	X
Tanzania	6	157	0	(100)	0	0	0	0	5	125	34	24	341	29
Togo	0	(100)	0	0	0	0	0	0	0	(100)	9	191	21	257
Tunisia	185	(24)	0	0	179	(21)	6	(65)	0	(100)	205	35	33	23
Uganda	3	31	0	0	0	0	0	0	3	29	16	65	149	38
Zambia	37	(24)	9	(29)	0	0	0	0	28	(22)	50	(10)	135	29
Zimbabwe	71	(31)	62	(32)	0	0	0	0	9	(19)	128	(7)	74	7
EUROPE	**94,496**	**X**	**20,963**	**X**	**25,902**	**X**	**33,329**	**X**	**14,302**	**X**	**105,553**	**X**	**1,725**	**X**
Albania	39	(66)	2	(94)	22	(56)	0	(100)	15	24	31	(68)	4	(75)
Austria	255	4	14	(64)	45	(8)	57	22	139	25	1,010	18	32	108
Belarus, Rep	120	X	30	X	81	X	9	X	0	X	946	X	8	X
Belgium	462	(16)	7	(96)	0	0	0	(100)	455	20	2,035	10	20	232
Bosnia and Herzegovina	15	X	10	X	0	X	0	X	5	X	31	X	X	X
Bulgaria	423	10	224	(2)	2	(55)	2	192	196	30	909	(20)	8	(54)
Croatia, Rep	113	X	3	X	16	X	75	X	19	X	276	X	9	X
Czech Rep	1,208	X	1,040	X	5	X	8	X	155	X	1,492	X	8	X
Denmark	598	260	0	0	384	217	210	368	4	68	738	(7)	29	635
Estonia, Rep	109	X	109	X	0	X	0	X	0	X	205	X	5	X
Finland	341	21	85	198	0	0	0	0	256	1	1,078	25	64	111
France {b}	4,866	42	230	(57)	123	(11)	130	(40)	4,383	72	9,045	16	98	(4)
Germany	5,860	X	3,303	X	122	X	669	X	1,766	X	13,511	X	100	X
Greece	349	29	314	56	19	(66)	2	(40)	14	39	1,008	50	15	(32)
Hungary	537	(23)	132	(50)	93	(22)	159	(35)	153	115	988	(16)	19	(35)
Iceland	27	30	0	0	0	0	0	0	27	30	51	22	0	0
Ireland	156	24	47	47	0	0	105	16	4	34	442	52	1	123
Italy	1,258	29	4	(70)	219	117	760	41	274	(15)	6,906	20	128	135
Latvia, Rep	14	X	3	X	0	X	0	X	11	X	156	X	34	X
Lithuania, Rep	137	X	1	X	5	X	0	X	131	X	358	X	21	X
Macedonia, FYR	85	X	82	X	0	X	0	X	3	X	122	X	8	X
Moldova, Rep	1	X	0	X	0	X	0	X	1	X	176	X	X	X
Netherlands	3,006	(2)	0	(100)	148	(14)	2,812	(1)	45	11	3,367	17	14	1,054
Norway	7,569	145	8	(45)	5,911	266	1,309	20	441	20	905	17	11	32
Poland, Rep	3,971	(23)	3,799	(23)	12	20	146	(10)	14	(0)	4,005	(18)	42	25
Portugal	35	(24)	3	(57)	0	0	0	0	32	(18)	716	100	6	1
Romania	1,270	(46)	313	(42)	292	(35)	605	(55)	60	40	1,776	(36)	506	865
Russian Federation	44,314	X	7,120	X	12,772	X	22,699	X	1,723	X	29,444	X	281	X
Slovak Rep	194	X	29	X	3	X	10	X	153	X	667	X	4	X
Slovenia, Rep	94	X	30	X	0	X	1	X	64	X	222	X	2	X
Spain	1,142	(0)	399	(35)	33	(67)	18	68	692	65	3,667	39	28	31
Sweden	1,013	13	10	2,962	0	(100)	0	0	1,003	12	1,717	10	54	(51)
Switzerland	401	16	0	0	0	0	0	(100)	401	16	928	10	23	194
Ukraine	3,485	X	2,038	X	172	X	650	X	625	X	6,955	X	26	X
United Kingdom	10,671	8	1,328	(41)	5,181	(3)	2,866	72	993	48	9,080	16	105	3,981
Yugoslavia, Fed Rep	352	X	245	X	38	X	29	X	40	X	410	X	9	X

| | Commercial Energy Production | | | | | | | | | | Total Energy Consumption | | | |
| | Total | | Solid Fuels | | Liquid Fuels | | Gaseous Fuels | | Primary Electricity | | Commercial Energy | | Traditional Fuels | |
	(peta-joules) 1995	Percent Change Since 1985	(peta-joules) 1995	Percent Change Since 1985	(peta-joules) 1995	Percent Change Since 1985	(peta-joules) 1995	Percent Change Since 1985	(peta joules) 1995	Percent Change Since 1985	(peta-joules) 1995	Percent Change Since 1985	(peta-joules) 1995	Percent Change Since 1985
NORTH AMERICA	**89,924**	**24**	**27,632**	**31**	**20,969**	**(14)**	**30,174**	**54**	**11,147**	**51**	**9,749**	**(87)**	**3,910**	**249**
Canada	14,537	46	1,656	11	4,547	29	6,137	92	2,196	25	9,404	25	57	(13)
United States	75,387	21	25,976	33	16,422	(21)	24,037	47	8,951	59	92,275	35	3,853	265
CENTRAL AMERICA	**8,992**	**10**	**182**	**(11)**	**6,807**	**4**	**1,450**	**15**	**554**	**148**	**99,404**	**1,746**	**765**	**(1)**
Belize	0	0	0	0	0	0	0	0	0	0	6	124	4	0
Costa Rica	30	201	0	0	0	0	0	0	30	201	96	180	12	(66)
Cuba	46	25	0	0	44	21	2	684	0	(100)	378	(7)	107	(35)
Dominican Rep	7	88	0	0	0	0	0	0	7	88	162	107	22	(31)
El Salvador	27	38	0	0	0	0	0	0	27	(9)	93	114	73	5
Guatemala	25	146	0	0	17	121	0	0	8	228	86	79	137	72
Haiti	1	(6)	0	0	0	0	0	0	1	7	9	(11)	61	20
Honduras	9	186	0	0	0	0	0	0	9	186	58	106	57	13
Jamaica	0	(100)	0	0	0	0	0	0	0	(100)	124	81	11	104
Mexico	8,288	10	182	(11)	6,470	6	1,206	13	430	180	5,473	35	257	15
Nicaragua	20	70	0	0	0	0	0	0	20	70	54	38	41	23
Panama	9	30	0	0	0	0	0	0	9	30	80	68	18	6
Trinidad and Tobago	514	(10)	0	0	273	(28)	240	25	0	0	283	22	3	30
SOUTH AMERICA	**17,937**	**68**	**988**	**112**	**11,890**	**58**	**3,275**	**100**	**1,784**	**65**	**11,923**	**61**	**2,730**	**(4)**
Argentina	2,797	66	8	(19)	1,535	49	1,062	109	192	40	2,256	55	93	(19)
Bolivia	216	59	0	0	69	48	142	66	6	942	126	118	18	14
Brazil	2,742	30	96	(39)	1,511	29	193	90	941	39	4,249	55	1,952	(12)
Chile	200	2	36	(5)	28	(67)	70	87	66	77	644	114	97	56
Colombia	2,242	163	708	178	1,247	227	164	10	123	57	941	49	270	41
Ecuador	882	43	0	0	847	41	10	165	24	79	262	49	46	(29)
Guyana	0	(100)	0	0	0	0	0	0	0	(100)	13	(33)	7	5
Paraguay	150	925	0	0	0	0	0	0	150	3,217	63	168	66	32
Peru	326	(28)	4	12	265	(33)	7	(71)	50	49	379	31	125	49
Suriname	16	159	0	0	12	348	0	0	5	51	25	8	0	(100)
Uruguay	27	16	0	0	0	0	0	0	27	104	92	99	31	10
Venezuela	8,338	81	136	11,225	136	(96)	1,626	124	200	160	2,861	72	23	21
ASIA	**122,438**	**X**	**42,385**	**X**	**57,248**	**X**	**15,848**	**X**	**6,957**	**X**	**106,770**	**X**	**10,308**	**X**
Afghanistan, Islamic State	8	(93)	0	(100)	X	(100)	7	(94)	1	(64)	20	(61)	59	40
Armenia, Rep	10	X	0	X	0	X	0	X	10	X	68	X	0	X
Azerbaijan	619	X	0	X	392	X	392	X	6	X	510	X	0	X
Bangladesh	272	148	0	0	0	(100)	270	161	1	(62)	349	109	336	29
Bhutan	6	20,733	0	0	0	0	0	0	6	20,733	3	201	13	44
Cambodia	0	(100)	0	0	0	0	0	0	0	(100)	7	18	66	43
China	36,263	49	28,457	56	6,281	20	699	39	826	148	34,310	62	2,112	20
Georgia	27	X	1	X	8	X	0	X	17	X	146	X	1	X
India	9,113	70	6,663	80	1,398	12	718	391	334	40	10,513	88	3,065	29
Indonesia	7,817	103	1,058	1,759	4,213	49	2,444	161	103	247	3,214	196	1,532	19
Iran, Islamic Rep	9,470	82	29	(21)	7,734	68	1,680	202	27	17	3,811	103	30	(0)
Iraq	1,706	(42)	0	0	1,581	(45)	123	293	2	(9)	1,078	247	1	18
Israel	1	(56)	0	0	0	(100)	1	(47)	0	0	538	62	0	(100)
Japan	3,887	47	152	(64)	30	30	91	(4)	3,614	71	18,711	30	105	1,123
Jordan	0	0	0	0	0	0	0	0	0	0	158	55	0	(100)
Kazakstan, Rep	3,190	X	2,095	X	864	X	201	X	30	X	2,767	X	3	X
Korea, Dem People's Rep	2,621	62	2,538	67	0	0	0	0	83	(18)	2,868	58	42	9
Korea, Rep	857	36	108	(75)	0	0	0	0	750	283	5,451	158	44	(48)
Kuwait	4,766	86	0	0	4,412	88	354	68	0	0	639	72	0	0
Kyrgyz Rep	59	X	15	X	4	X	1	X	40	X	110	X	0	X
Lao People's Dem Rep	3	(4)	0	0	0	0	0	0	3	(17)	5	46	44	36
Lebanon	3	42	0	0	0	0	0	0	3	42	167	56	5	12
Malaysia	2,613	111	3	0	1,450	58	1,132	270	27	99	1,448	209	98	28
Mongolia	72	(1)	72	(1)	X	0	0	0	0	0	98	(4)	4	(70)
Myanmar	84	(18)	2	15	2	(97)	57	57	6	66	115	43	212	24
Nepal	4	232	0	0	0	0	0	0	4	232	23	127	234	64
Oman	1,876	68	0	0	1,784	71	92	23	0	0	168	44	0	0
Pakistan	850	85	60	36	116	116	586	86	88	84	1,357	91	335	44
Philippines	269	12	26	4	6	(64)	0	0	237	20	860	72	396	23
Saudi Arabia	19,363	151	0	0	17,789	151	1,574	147	0	0	3,331	56	0	0
Singapore	0	0	0	0	0	0	0	0	0	0	840	175	0	0
Sri Lanka	16	86	0	0	0	0	0	0	16	86	93	89	97	19
Syrian Arab Rep	1,295	224	0	0	1,196	209	90	1,400	9	22	532	70	0	(100)
Tajikistan, Rep	56	X	1	X	3	X	1	X	51	X	114	X	0	X
Thailand	869	212	339	498	154	65	352	205	24	81	2,145	237	1,061	92
Turkey	788	15	503	(8)	147	66	6	135	131	201	2,131	63	83	(58)
Turkmenistan, Rep	1,296	X	0	X	209	X	1,086	X	0	X	416	X	0	X
United Arab Emirates	5,755	91	0	0	4,642	77	1,113	185	0	0	1,212	156	0	0
Uzbekistan, Rep	2,184	X	37	X	419	X	1,703	X	26	X	1,768	X	X	X
Vietnam	607	263	218	40	322	0	0	0	66	865	382	89	311	43
Yemen	712	0	0	0	712	0	0	0	0	0	183	0	3	0
OCEANIA	**8,436**	**60**	**5,725**	**79**	**1,351**	**16**	**1,124**	**49**	**237**	**22**	**4,888**	**46**	**234**	**26**
Australia	7,650	55	5,642	80	1,008	(10)	942	54	58	(25)	4,126	44	157	37
Fiji	2	90	0	0	0	0	0	0	2	90	11	32	12	25
New Zealand	506	43	83	47	70	54	179	28	173	55	610	41	0	(100)
Papua New Guinea	277	18,220	0	0	272	0	3	0	2	32	36	17	60	6
Solomon Islands	0	0	0	0	0	0	0	0	0	0	2	(5)	3	(0)

Notes: a. Data are for the South Africa Customs Union (Botswana, Lesotho, Namibia, South Africa, and Swaziland). b. Includes Monaco.

Electricity Production and Trade, 1985–95

Source: United Nations Statistical Division

	Electricity Production (million kilowatt-hours)										Trade (million kilowatt-hours)			
	Total		Thermal		Hydroelectric		Geothermal		Nuclear		Import		Export	
	1995	Percent Change Since 1985	1995	Percent Change Since 1985	1995	Percent Change Since 1985	1995	Percent Change Since 1985	1995	Percent Change Since 1985	1995	Percent Change Since 1985	1995	Percent Change Since 1985
WORLD	**13,097,664**	**34**	**8,249,317**	**32**	**2,532,516**	**27**	**48,040**	**69**	**2,267,791**	**56**	**422,117**	**95**	**427,947**	**99**
AFRICA	**364,764**	**51**	**297,459**	**56**	**57,345**	**24**	**360**	**7**	**9,600**	**145**	**5,307**	**19**	**5,157**	**22**
Algeria	19,714	61	19,521	68	193	(70)	0	0	0	0	218	80	491	211
Angola	1,870	4	485	7	1,385	4	0	0	0	0	0	0	0	0
Benin	6	20	6	20	0	0	0	0	0	0	263	53	0	0
Botswana	X	X	X	X	X	X	X	X	X	X	X	X	X	X
Burkina Faso	220	79	145	18	75	X	0	0	0	0	0	0	0	0
Burundi	120	1,900	2	0	118	2,850	0	0	0	0	29	(55)	0	0
Cameroon	2,746	14	84	(11)	2,662	15	0	0	0	0	0	0	0	0
Central African Rep	102	31	21	24	81	33	0	0	0	0	0	0	0	0
Chad	89	75	89	75	0	0	0	0	0	0	0	0	0	0
Congo, Dem Rep	5,920	17	18	(87)	5,902	20	0	0	0	0	58	729	1,080	764
Congo, Rep	435	87	3	50	432	87	0	0	0	0	112	104	0	0
Côte d'Ivoire	1,913	(5)	808	22	1,105	(19)	0	0	0	0	0	0	0	0
Egypt	48,864	61	38,054	71	10,810	33	0	0	0	0	0	0	0	0
Equatorial Guinea	20	(9)	18	(10)	2	0	0	0	0	0	0	0	0	0
Eritrea	X	X	X	X	X	X	X	X	X	X	X	X	X	X
Ethiopia	1,328	67	103	(34)	1,155	80	70	X	0	0	0	0	0	0
Gabon	940	9	215	11	725	9	0	0	0	0	0	0	0	0
Gambia, The	74	72	74	72	0	0	0	0	0	0	0	0	0	0
Ghana	6,159	100	42	(48)	6,117	104	0	0	0	0	4	X	228	(16)
Guinea	543	11	352	8	191	17	0	0	0	0	0	0	0	0
Guinea-Bissau	43	207	43	207	0	0	0	0	0	0	0	0	0	0
Kenya	3,747	50	334	(30)	3,123	86	290	(14)	0	0	172	(20)	0	0
Lesotho	X	X	X	X	X	X	X	X	X	X	X	X	X	X
Liberia	486	(36)	308	(39)	178	(32)	0	0	0	0	0	0	0	0
Libya	18,000	52	18,000	52	0	0	0	0	0	0	0	0	0	0
Madagascar	611	22	258	6	353	37	0	0	0	0	0	0	0	0
Malawi	803	64	19	19	784	65	0	0	0	0	0	0	0	0
Mali	290	73	65	91	225	68	0	0	0	0	0	0	0	0
Mauritania	152	41	124	61	28	(10)	0	0	0	0	0	0	0	0
Mauritius	1,120	115	985	143	135	17	0	0	0	0	0	0	0	0
Morocco	11,724	67	11,119	70	605	26	0	0	0	0	1,000	X	0	0
Mozambique	563	(60)	513	25	50	(95)	0	0	0	0	601	162	X	(100)
Namibia	X	X	X	X	X	X	X	X	X	X	X	X	X	X
Niger	175	14	175	14	0	0	0	0	0	0	195	51	0	0
Nigeria	14,810	50	8,810	14	6,000	175	0	0	0	0	0	0	0	(100)
Rwanda	164	(2)	4	33	160	(2)	0	0	0	0	14	(30)	3	0
Senegal	774	2	774	2	0	0	0	0	0	0	0	0	0	0
Sierra Leone	241	37	241	37	0	0	0	0	0	0	0	0	0	0
Somalia	272	23	272	23	0	0	0	0	0	0	0	0	0	0
South Africa {a}	190,515	56	180,085	53	830	8	0	0	9,600	145	60	(40)	1,600	617
Sudan	1,331	28	386	(26)	945	83	0	0	0	0	0	0	0	0
Swaziland	X	X	X	X	X	X	X	X	X	X	X	X	X	X
Tanzania	1,738	100	228	(10)	1,510	145	0	0	0	0	0	0	0	0
Togo	93	174	87	190	6	50	0	0	0	0	315	48	0	0
Tunisia	7,589	89	7,550	93	39	(64)	0	0	0	0	171	389	140	2,233
Uganda	792	21	7	(22)	785	22	0	0	0	0	0	0	115	(13)
Zambia	7,790	(22)	40	8	7,750	(22)	0	0	0	0	20	0	1,500	(52)
Zimbabwe	8,275	65	5,900	206	2,375	(23)	0	0	0	0	2,075	(32)	0	0
EUROPE	**4,060,888**	**X**	**2,272,438**	**X**	**719,627**	**X**	**6,815**	**X**	**1,062,008**	**X**	**263,292**	**X**	**276,239**	**X**
Albania	4,414	16	210	(54)	4,204	25	0	0	0	0	139	X	74	(88)
Austria	56,587	29	18,110	40	38,477	24	0	0	0	0	7,287	20	9,757	26
Belarus, Rep	24,918	X	24,898	X	20	X	0	X	0	X	10,066	X	2,907	X
Belgium	74,428	32	31,834	49	1,230	220	8	0 b	41,356	20	9,398	71	5,326	(4)
Bosnia and Herzegovina	2,203	X	783	X	1,420	X	0	X	0	X	387	X	182	X
Bulgaria	41,789	0	19,263	(27)	5,265	135	0	0	17,261	31	1,961	(67)	2,121	28
Croatia, Rep	8,863	X	7,137	X	1,726	X	0	X	0	X	5,382	X	886	X
Czech Rep	60,847	X	45,494	X	1,726	X	0	X b	13,627	X	3,100	X	5,900	X
Denmark	36,790	27	35,583	23	33	0	1,174	1,763	0	0	4,012	27	4,806	78
Estonia, Rep	7,607	X	7,604	X	3	X	0	X	0	X	245	X	1,005	X
Finland	63,885	28	31,744	73	12,925	5	0	0	19,216	1	7,253	29	279	(70)
France {c}	493,177	51	39,456	(24)	75,922	25	568	X	377,231	77	2,860	(48)	72,701	152
Germany	534,902	X	356,224	X	24,217	X	370	X	154,091	X	39,735	X	34,911	X
Greece	41,551	50	37,735	51	3,782	35	34	X	0	0	1,390	47	593	184
Hungary	34,017	27	19,827	(2)	164	6	0	X	14,026	116	3,181	(75)	776	(60)
Iceland	4,981	23	9	125	4,682	22	290	53	0	0	0	0	0	0
Ireland	17,878	52	16,875	55	968	17	35	X	0	0	20	X	35	X
Italy	241,111	32	195,754	49	41,907	2	3,450	29	0	(100)	38,662	54	1,235	(14)
Latvia, Rep	3,979	X	1,042	X	2,937	X	0	X	0	X	2,647	X	391	X
Lithuania, Rep	13,898	X	1,325	X	751	X	0	X	11,822	X	5,270	X	7,948	X
Macedonia, FYR	6,114	X	5,313	X	801	X	0	X	0	X	221 d	X	54 d	X
Moldova, Rep	8,392	X	8,112	X	280	X	0	X	0	X	5,600	X	5,100	X
Netherlands	80,832	28	76,408	29	88	X	318	X b	4,018	8	11,979	159	586	(36)
Norway	123,136	20	692	100	122,436	20	8	X	0	0	2,201	(46)	8,563	85
Poland, Rep	139,006	1	135,141	1	3,851	(1)	14	X	0	0	4,356	(20)	7,157	(5)
Portugal	33,263	75	24,751	200	8,454	(21)	58	1,350	0	0	2,655	(25)	1,741	36
Romania	59,266	(17)	42,573	(29)	16,693	40	0	0	0	0	755	(77)	456	X
Russian Federation	860,026	X	583,208	X	177,256	X	30	X	99,532	X	18,377	X	37,982	X
Slovak Rep	25,240	X	8,100	X	4,640	X	0	X	12,500	X	1,280	X	2,105	X
Slovenia, Rep	12,648	X	4,629	X	3,240	X	0	X	4,779	X	740	X	2,392	X
Spain	166,380	32	86,356	30	24,569	(21)	0	0	55,455	98	7,633	94	3,147	(37)
Sweden	147,035	8	9,972	43	67,029	(6)	99	X b	69,935	19	7,720	49	9,421	41
Switzerland	63,080	17	2,225	156	35,954	13	6	X	24,895	17	19,419	34	26,690	15
Ukraine	194,000	X	128,270	X	12,430	X	0	X	53,300	X	15,500	X	18,300	X
United Kingdom	334,454	(63)	238,302	(71)	6,836	67	352	X e	88,964	48	16,336	X	23	X
Yugoslavia, Fed Rep	37,176	X	7,550	X	11,220	X	0	X	0	X	0	X	0	X

| | Electricity Production (million kilowatt-hours) | | | | | | | | | | Trade (million kilowatt-hours) | | | |
| | Total | | Thermal | | Hydroelectric | | Geothermal | | Nuclear | | Import | | Export | |
	1995	Percent Change Since 1985	1995	Percent Change Since 1985	1995	Percent Change Since 1985	1995	Percent Change Since 1985	1995	Percent Change Since 1985	1995	Percent Change Since 1985	1995	Percent Change Since 1985
NORTH AMERICA	**3,882,428**	**28**	**2,459,494**	**24**	**639,115**	**8**	**18,111**	**58**	**765,708**	**72**	**52,751**	**9**	**51,596**	**8**
Canada	537,114	17	113,939	20	330,834	9	35	X f	92,306	53	7,428	176	43,321	1
United States	3,345,314	30	2,345,555	24	308,281	8	18,076	58 g	673,402	76	45,323	(1)	8,275	67
CENTRAL AMERICA	**225,827**	**57**	**166,488**	**57**	**44,987**	**27**	**8,943**	**(93)**	**5,409**	**X**	**1,576**	**259**	**2,287**	**1,199**
Belize	148	108	148	108	0	0	0	0	0	0	0	0	0	0
Costa Rica	4,840	71	752	1,175	3,620	31	468	X	0	0	179	X	151	202
Cuba	11,189	(8)	11,081	(9)	108	100	0	0	0	0	0	0	0	0
Dominican Rep	6,506	54	4,513	41	1,993	92	0	0	0	0	0	0	0	0
El Salvador	3,405	91	810	575	2,045	119	550	(25)	0	0	30	X	65	X
Guatemala	3,229	84	1,060	(2)	2,169	220	0	0	0	0	0	0	0	0
Haiti	407	9	242	110	165	(37)	0	0	0	0	0	0	0	0
Honduras	2,742	157	340	79	2,402	175	0	0	0	0	4	(98)	0 h	(100)
Jamaica	5,829	155	5,709	158	120	56	0	0	0	0	0	0	0	0
Mexico	150,820	61	108,750	66	29,255	11	7,406	351	5,409	X	1,081	1,401	1,862	1,533
Nicaragua	1,713	62	864	75	330	25	519	72	0	0	73	(63)	87	770
Panama	3,519	44	1,101	111	2,418	25	0	0	0	0	209	X	122	X
Trinidad and Tobago	4,229	40	4,229	40	0	0	0	0	0	0	0	0	0	0
SOUTH AMERICA	**572,465**	**61**	**98,772**	**34**	**462,874**	**70**	**0**	**0**	**10,819**	**18**	**38,228**	**1,270**	**38,598**	**296,808**
Argentina	67,169	48	30,769	63	28,100	36	0	0	8,300	44	2,342	X	220	3,567
Bolivia	3,020	100	1,298	(4)	1,722	976	0	0	0	0	13	550	3	X
Brazil	275,399	43	19,018	73	253,862	42	0	0	2,519	(25)	35,352	1,171	0	(100)
Chile	29,906	113	11,498	212	18,408	78	0	0	0	0	0 h	0	0	0
Colombia	45,303	50	11,043	30	34,260	57	0	0	0	0	316	6,220	0	0
Ecuador	8,349	76	4,601	351	3,748	0	0	0	0	0	0	0	0	0
Guyana	318	(18)	313	(19)	5	0	0	0	0	0	16	X	0	0
Paraguay	41,630	3,204	27	575	41,603	3,212	0	0	0	0	1	(50)	37,939	X
Peru	16,759	38	2,977	6	13,782	48	0	0	0	0	0	0	0	0
Suriname	1,614	24	335	(12)	1,279	39	0	0	0	0	0	0	0	0
Uruguay	7,650	99	150	(1)	7,500	104	0	0	0	0	188	X	302	X
Venezuela	74,886	56	19,281	(28)	55,605	160	0	0	0	0	0 d	X	0	(100)
ASIA	**3,778,298**	**X**	**2,788,739**	**X**	**563,596**	**X**	**11,716**	**X**	**414,247**	**X**	**60,963**	**X**	**54,070**	**X**
Afghanistan, Islamic State	625	(41)	209	(26)	416	(47)	0	0	0	0	120	X	0	0
Armenia, Rep	5,561	X	3,338	X	1,919	X	0	X	304	X	13	X	3 h	X
Azerbaijan	17,000	X	15,400	X	1,600	X	0	X	0	X	450	X	250	X
Bangladesh	11,689	140	11,317	174	372	(50)	0	0	0	0	0	0	0	0
Bhutan	1,717	8,076	7	(46)	1,710	21,275	0	0	0	0	4	(56)	1,717	X
Cambodia	194	177	120	200	74	147	0	0	0	0	0	0	0	0
China	1,007,726	(75)	804,316	(80)	190,577	106	0	0	12,833	X	2,000	80	4,200	10,400
Georgia	6,800	X	2,090	X	4,710	X	0	X b	0	X	950	X	180	X
India	414,622	114	335,900	145	71,665	40	57	X	7,000	41	1,675	10,369	130	21
Indonesia	68,804	130	56,572	140	10,418	69	1,814	764	0	0	0	0	0	0
Iran, Islamic Rep	81,330	118	73,800	139	7,530	18	0	0	0	0	0	0	0	0
Iraq	29,000	38	28,430	39	570	(7)	0	0	0	0	0	0	0	0
Israel	29,100	85	29,068	85	32	X	0	0	0	0	0	0	310	4
Japan	989,965	47	604,207	43	91,301	4	3,203	119 i	291,254	83	0	0	0	0
Jordan	5,616	125	5,598	124	18	X	0	0	0	0	0	0	0 d	(100)
Kazakstan, Rep	66,659	X	58,328	X	8,331	X	0	X	0	X	19,539	X	12,702	X
Korea, Dem People's Rep	36,000	(25)	13,000	(35)	23,000	(18)	0	0	0	0	0	0	0	0
Korea, Rep	205,102	227	132,595	213	5,478	50	0	0	67,029	300	0	0	0	0
Kuwait	24,126	54	24,126	54	0	0	0	0	0	0	0	0	0	0
Kyrgyz Rep	12,349	X	1,231	X	11,118	X	0	X	0	X	6,987	X	8,355	X
Lao People's Dem Rep	908	(14)	43	(14)	865	(14)	0	0	0	0	27	35	640	(11)
Lebanon	5,573	44	4,841	48	732	25	0	0	0	0	50 h	(100)	0	0
Malaysia	46,632	211	39,132	249	7,500	99	0	0	0	0	2	(96)	25	X
Mongolia	2,629	(2)	2,629	(2)	0	0	0	0	0	0	381	149	0	0
Myanmar	3,780	78	2,252	102	1,528	52	0	0	0	0	0	0	0	0
Nepal	1,007	177	33	14	974	191	0	0	0	0	110	34	42	282
Oman	8,258	185	8,258	185	0	0	0	0	0	0	0	0	0	0
Pakistan	60,155	118	36,786	146	22,858	87	0	0	511	48	0	0	0	0
Philippines	33,426	46	20,961	69	6,515	17	5,950	20	0	0	0	0	0	0
Saudi Arabia	99,833	208	99,833	208	0	0	0	0	0	0	0	0	0	0
Singapore	22,057	123	22,057	123	0	0	0	0	0	0	0	0	0	(100)
Sri Lanka	4,800	95	286	314	4,514	88	0	0	0	0	0	0	0	0
Syrian Arab Rep	15,300	90	12,790	114	2,510	22	0	0	0	0	0 j	X	0 h	(100)
Tajikistan, Rep	14,760	X	580	X	14,180	X	0	X	0	X	4,800	X	5,600	X
Thailand	83,660	246	76,946	276	6,713	82	1	X	0	X	699	(3)	79	295
Turkey	81,734	145	46,107	117	35,541	195	86	1,333	0	0	0	(100)	696	X
Turkmenistan, Rep	9,800	X	9,796	X	4	X	0	X	0	X	980	X	3,000	X
United Arab Emirates	19,070	64	19,070	64	0	0	0	0	0	0	0	0	0	0
Uzbekistan, Rep	47,200	X	5,085	X	7,100	X	0	X	0	X	14,500	X	14,900	X
Vietnam	14,867	197	1,920	(38)	12,342	550	605	X	0	X	0	X	0	X
Yemen	1,980	X	234	X	0	X	0	X	0	X	0	X	0	X
OCEANIA	**212,994**	**39**	**165,946**	**43**	**44,953**	**28**	**2,095**	**13**	**0**	**0**	**0**	**0**	**0**	**0**
Australia	173,404	43	157,164	48	16,240	14	X	(100)	0	0	0	0	0	0
Fiji	544	38	115	13	429	46	0	0	0	0	0	0	0	0
New Zealand	34,375	26	5,017	(23)	27,263	38	2,095	84	0	0	0	0	0	0
Papua New Guinea	1,790	16	1,295	15	495	18	0	0	0	0	0	0	0	0
Solomon Islands	29	X	29	X	0	X	0	X	0	0	0	0	0	0

Notes: a. Data are for the South Africa Customs Union (Botswana, Lesotho, Namibia, South Africa, and Swaziland). b. Refers to wind generation. c. Includes Monaco. d. Data are for 1994. e. Refers to wind and nonspecified combustibles generation. f. Refers to solar, tide, and wave generation. g. Includes solar and wind generation. h. Data are for 1993. i. Refers to solar, tide, wave, and fuel cell generation. j. Data are for 1991.

Data Table 15.3
Energy Balances, 1985–95

Source: International Energy Agency

| | Industry Sector | | | | Transportation Sector | | | | | | Agriculture | | Commercial and Public Services | | Residential | |
| | Total (% of Total Final Consumption) | | Iron and Steel (% of Total Final Consumption) | | Total (% of Total Final Consumption) | | Air (% of Total Final Consumption) | | Road (% of Total Final Consumption) | | (% of Total Final Consumption) | | (% of Total Final Consumption) | | (% of Total Final Consumption) | |
	1995	1985	1995	1985	1995	1985	1995	1985	1995	1985	1995	1985	1995	1985	1995	1985
WORLD	**37.5**	**40.7**	**4.0**	**4.5**	**26.5**	**24.2**	**3.3**	**3.0**	**20.9**	**18.2**	**3.2**	**3.7**	**18.7**	**16.5**	**7.6**	**8.4**
AFRICA	**37.5**	**43.3**	**6.1**	**11.6**	**29.3**	**32.2**	**3.9**	**4.0**	**24.1**	**26.2**	**2.4**	**2.8**	**13.2**	**12.3**	**2.3**	**3.2**
Algeria	23.1	24.9	4.2	8.6	22.2	39.4	2.3	4.2	16.1	34.3	0.0	0.3	29.2	21.5	0.0	2.3
Angola	26.5	23.9	0.0	0.0	50.6	58.6	27.1	26.2	23.6	32.4	0.0	0.0	18.0	14.0	0.0	0.0
Benin	14.7	7.2	0.0	0.0	58.2	74.8	21.0	10.8	37.2	64.0	0.0	0.0	25.4	14.4	0.7	0.4
Botswana	X	X	X	X	X	X	X	X	X	X	X	X	X	X	X	X
Burkina Faso	X	X	X	X	X	X	X	X	X	X	X	X	X	X	X	X
Burundi	X	X	X	X	X	X	X	X	X	X	X	X	X	X	X	X
Cameroon	17.5	14.5	0.0	0.0	43.7	53.9	4.8	5.0	38.9	48.9	0.0	0.1	16.3	9.0	0.0	0.5
Central African Rep	X	X	X	X	X	X	X	X	X	X	X	X	X	X	X	X
Chad	X	X	X	X	X	X	X	X	X	X	X	X	X	X	X	X
Congo, Dem Rep	8.7	10.5	0.0	0.0	66.1	70.5	22.6	11.9	43.5	58.6	0.0	0.0	18.6	7.7	0.0	0.0
Congo, Rep	29.1	24.7	0.0	0.0	38.6	43.5	8.8	8.8	29.8	34.6	0.0	0.0	16.7	17.7	0.0	0.0
Côte d'Ivoire	21.6	17.8	0.0	0.0	49.5	49.1	9.0	9.6	38.7	34.8	3.0	4.1	14.2	13.2	6.3	7.3
Egypt	49.7	46.0	2.9	4.0	19.9	24.2	2.8	2.6	17.1	20.0	0.7	3.3	20.6	18.7	0.0	1.0
Equatorial Guinea	X	X	X	X	X	X	X	X	X	X	X	X	X	X	X	X
Eritrea	X	X	X	X	X	X	X	X	X	X	X	X	X	X	X	X
Ethiopia	24.8	19.3	0.0	0.0	51.9	59.1	20.8	20.6	31.1	36.1	2.3	3.8	6.5	17.8	2.6	3.7
Gabon	29.0	46.3	0.0	0.0	42.5	19.8	13.9	4.2	24.5	15.6	0.0	0.0	12.9	19.2	2.6	0.3
Gambia, The	X	X	X	X	X	X	X	X	X	X	X	X	X	X	X	X
Ghana	34.5	29.7	0.0	0.0	44.4	47.2	4.4	3.9	38.4	39.8	1.7	3.8	13.0	10.8	2.0	2.3
Guinea	X	X	X	X	X	X	X	X	X	X	X	X	X	X	X	X
Guinea-Bissau	X	X	X	X	X	X	X	X	X	X	X	X	X	X	X	X
Kenya	26.4	24.3	0.0	0.0	51.6	54.9	16.7	14.8	33.0	37.7	3.1	2.8	11.8	8.9	1.1	4.9
Lesotho	X	X	X	X	X	X	X	X	X	X	X	X	X	X	X	X
Liberia	X	X	X	X	X	X	X	X	X	X	X	X	X	X	X	X
Libya	31.9	36.2	0.0	0.0	40.2	39.0	3.6	6.0	36.7	33.0	0.0	0.0	7.5	3.2	0.0	0.0
Madagascar	X	X	X	X	X	X	X	X	X	X	X	X	X	X	X	X
Malawi	X	X	X	X	X	X	X	X	X	X	X	X	X	X	X	X
Mali	X	X	X	X	X	X	X	X	X	X	X	X	X	X	X	X
Mauritania	X	X	X	X	X	X	X	X	X	X	X	X	X	X	X	X
Mauritius	X	X	X	X	X	X	X	X	X	X	X	X	X	X	X	X
Morocco	22.9	40.3	0.0	0.0	12.9	27.7	3.9	5.9	6.4	19.4	0.7	5.0	18.7	16.0	2.4	6.5
Mozambique	12.0	15.0	0.0	0.0	16.4	17.2	7.6	7.4	8.8	9.9	3.5	0.0	6.7	5.5	0.1	0.0
Namibia	X	X	X	X	X	X	X	X	X	X	X	X	X	X	X	X
Niger	X	X	X	X	X	X	X	X	X	X	X	X	X	X	X	X
Nigeria	16.0	17.9	0.6	0.6	51.6	56.5	4.9	5.0	46.2	50.1	0.0	0.6	13.5	18.2	2.3	0.7
Rwanda	X	X	X	X	X	X	X	X	X	X	X	X	X	X	X	X
Senegal	29.4	26.0	0.0	0.0	55.0	61.2	20.5	22.5	31.1	31.1	0.2	3.2	11.0	5.6	2.6	1.5
Sierra Leone	X	X	X	X	X	X	X	X	X	X	X	X	X	X	X	X
Somalia	X	X	X	X	X	X	X	X	X	X	X	X	X	X	X	X
South Africa	45.8	59.9	13.3	25.7	27.6	24.0	2.0	1.7	23.9	19.9	4.2	3.1	5.5	7.0	3.6	4.8
Sudan	29.6	28.6	0.0	0.0	43.4	45.1	11.5	6.6	30.4	34.4	8.9	12.0	7.0	3.2	2.2	2.6
Swaziland	X	X	X	X	X	X	X	X	X	X	X	X	X	X	X	X
Tanzania	15.2	30.6	0.0	0.1	44.4	32.5	6.3	6.1	34.0	19.7	4.6	3.7	28.0	25.3	4.3	3.9
Togo	X	X	X	X	X	X	X	X	X	X	X	X	X	X	X	X
Tunisia	33.5	34.1	2.0	3.2	31.3	31.1	5.9	3.9	24.8	21.5	7.3	5.7	15.0	18.4	8.6	7.5
Uganda	X	X	X	X	X	X	X	X	X	X	X	X	X	X	X	X
Zambia	57.5	63.4	0.0	0.0	20.1	18.7	3.8	4.1	16.3	13.3	2.9	2.3	4.3	5.4	7.9	6.6
Zimbabwe	52.2	48.9	14.1	17.6	20.3	25.3	2.3	3.1	13.8	15.9	10.2	12.0	5.8	5.1	8.3	6.8
EUROPE	**35.6**	**39.3**	**7.2**	**8.4**	**20.8**	**20.3**	**2.7**	**1.6**	**15.5**	**15.8**	**4.4**	**3.9**	**26.9**	**17.4**	**6.8**	**7.4**
Albania	16.6	35.6	0.0	5.8	40.5	17.7	0.0	0.0	40.5	17.7	0.5	0.0	23.0	4.1	0.4	0.0
Austria	25.6	31.2	8.2	10.4	28.5	23.1	2.1	1.1	24.6	20.4	4.9	0.5	29.1	33.4	2.0	3.4
Belarus, Rep	35.3	34.4	0.6	0.2	14.5	14.7	2.5	0.0	8.5	9.0	6.5	7.0	31.0	0.0	1.6	0.5
Belgium	37.9	41.3	11.2	14.6	22.7	19.1	2.6	1.8	19.0	16.0	2.9	1.1	24.6	28.0	9.1	8.0
Bosnia and Herzegovina	9.8	0.0	3.9	0.0	61.0	0.0	6.5	0.0	38.5	0.0	0.0	0.0	0.0	0.0	0.0	0.0
Bulgaria	58.8	51.2	10.9	2.3	5.3	9.7	2.9	2.1	1.8	7.0	3.4	1.3	25.5	11.5	1.7	2.1
Croatia, Rep	39.4	0.0	1.8	0.0	24.0	2.5	1.8	0.0	19.9	0.0	4.0	0.4	19.6	0.0	8.5	0.0
Czech Rep	48.1	56.4	14.9	12.2	13.5	7.9	0.9	0.9	11.5	6.5	4.9	3.5	20.0	17.4	6.0	3.7
Denmark	18.5	18.1	0.7	0.8	30.5	30.7	5.1	5.0	23.2	21.0	6.4	4.6	29.4	31.7	12.4	10.4
Estonia, Rep	33.9	48.2	0.3	0.0	17.5	2.8	0.8	0.0	14.7	0.0	3.6	26.0	35.1	0.0	6.6	0.0
Finland	45.9	44.9	6.2	6.1	18.1	17.5	1.8	1.4	15.4	15.1	3.3	4.2	22.7	24.1	4.2	3.5
France	29.1	33.0	4.9	6.2	29.3	25.3	3.1	2.0	25.0	21.9	1.9	2.2	16.9	15.8	18.7	20.7
Germany	32.0	37.0	5.9	7.8	26.0	19.0	2.5	1.7	22.4	16.1	1.1	1.3	25.5	25.9	10.4	11.9
Greece	24.9	28.8	0.9	1.6	40.8	37.2	8.0	9.6	29.0	24.2	6.3	7.4	19.4	18.1	5.8	2.8
Hungary	23.9	39.1	5.5	9.0	15.8	11.2	1.1	0.7	13.5	8.2	3.6	7.1	36.7	28.1	15.0	9.0
Iceland	24.6	27.5	5.9	6.7	15.7	15.7	4.4	4.9	10.6	9.5	17.8	13.2	31.8	37.5	4.7	3.0
Ireland	26.2	31.7	0.6	0.8	30.3	25.9	6.8	3.2	22.4	21.9	3.1	0.2	23.8	29.3	14.8	8.9
Italy	34.0	35.7	6.0	7.3	31.1	27.0	2.3	1.9	27.8	23.9	2.7	2.3	25.6	28.6	4.0	3.5
Latvia, Rep	18.4	44.1	2.2	0.0	24.4	2.5	0.9	0.0	15.6	0.0	2.8	12.4	46.2	0.0	14.4	0.7
Lithuania, Rep	32.2	38.8	0.1	0.0	24.8	13.4	0.8	3.3	18.0	9.5	4.0	3.4	32.4	0.0	9.9	0.3
Macedonia, FYR	37.1	X	13.5	X	24.9	X	2.5	X	22.1	X	10.4	X	21.8	X	4.9	X
Moldova, Rep	21.8	15.1	0.0	0.0	13.0	15.0	0.4	1.2	9.5	13.8	12.7	5.3	29.6	0.0	19.9	0.2
Netherlands	35.4	37.6	4.9	4.3	21.9	17.8	4.6	2.5	15.8	13.7	7.2	5.0	19.1	23.8	3.9	2.6
Norway	38.0	44.7	6.2	8.9	22.5	19.8	3.0	2.8	15.1	12.8	3.8	1.5	21.1	19.6	10.1	9.9
Poland, Rep	39.1	42.9	9.2	11.7	14.1	9.1	0.9	0.0	12.1	8.4	6.9	3.0	34.3	35.8	0.0	1.8
Portugal	39.3	46.2	1.8	2.6	34.4	28.6	4.5	5.1	28.9	22.1	3.3	4.3	12.7	13.2	6.1	4.8
Romania	57.0	58.4	14.5	13.6	13.0	3.5	0.8	0.0	9.9	3.1	3.9	2.3	21.6	13.1	0.0	0.7
Russian Federation	39.1	36.2	9.6	0.0	9.2	32.9	2.0	0.0	1.9	27.4	8.4	12.3	35.5	0.0	0.9	9.0
Slovak Rep	52.7	61.0	15.5	0.0	10.7	6.8	0.2	0.0	9.6	6.2	3.2	5.1	14.8	8.1	14.0	9.4
Slovenia, Rep	30.6	48.3	4.6	13.5	36.7	22.7	0.6	0.8	35.3	21.3	0.0	0.0	25.9	25.8	5.3	3.7
Spain	33.6	41.7	5.1	9.3	37.3	32.1	4.5	4.1	29.2	24.2	3.1	5.2	13.8	11.7	6.1	5.3
Sweden	38.3	38.3	4.9	5.0	22.2	19.9	2.5	1.7	18.6	16.4	1.4	1.7	22.7	29.9	13.3	7.7
Switzerland	18.5	22.6	0.0	0.0	32.0	27.0	6.8	5.0	24.1	20.9	1.3	0.9	29.4	28.4	16.1	17.0
Ukraine	48.0	50.1	11.1	23.7	8.2	9.1	0.9	0.0	4.0	0.0	4.7	5.2	27.6	0.0	8.5	0.3
United Kingdom	27.3	29.7	4.9	5.0	30.8	26.5	5.3	3.9	24.0	21.0	0.8	1.0	25.3	27.4	9.2	9.9
Yugoslavia, Fed Rep	35.2	24.2	0.4	0.0	6.5	0.5	0.7	0.0	5.6	0.0	0.2	0.3	21.3	0.0	0.4	0.9

	Industry Sector Total (% of Total Final Consumption) 1995	1985	Iron and Steel (% of Total Final Consumption) 1995	1985	Transportation Sector Total (% of Total Final Consumption) 1995	1985	Air (% of Total Final Consumption) 1995	1985	Road (% of Total Final Consumption) 1995	1985	Agriculture (% of Total Final Consumption) 1995	1985	Commercial and Public Services (% of Total Final Consumption) 1995	1985	Residential (% of Total Final Consumption) 1995	1985
NORTH AMERICA	**27.1**	**30.9**	**1.6**	**2.4**	**37.5**	**34.0**	**5.1**	**4.7**	**29.9**	**27.1**	**1.2**	**1.4**	**17.6**	**16.3**	**12.5**	**11.7**
Canada	36.5	37.6	3.0	4.1	27.7	26.1	2.5	2.5	20.2	20.0	2.1	1.8	17.0	17.8	13.7	13.6
United States	25.9	30.2	1.4	2.1	38.8	35.0	5.4	4.9	31.1	27.9	1.1	1.3	17.7	16.1	12.3	11.4
CENTRAL AMERICA	**39.6**	**42.4**	**4.8**	**4.7**	**36.3**	**32.7**	**2.6**	**2.2**	**30.0**	**21.2**	**2.7**	**3.2**	**16.3**	**10.3**	**3.6**	**2.3**
Belize	X	X	X	X	X	X	X	X	X	X	X	X	X	X	X	X
Costa Rica	18.5	28.1	0.0	0.0	57.3	48.7	6.8	1.6	24.1	16.8	3.2	0.0	10.8	18.8	7.9	0.8
Cuba	40.2	35.9	0.1	1.2	31.9	34.6	2.6	2.8	13.3	26.0	6.1	8.4	11.3	12.3	2.9	3.1
Dominican Rep	17.9	23.1	0.0	0.0	43.1	50.5	2.4	4.7	21.0	32.0	1.4	1.3	31.9	19.4	0.0	0.0
El Salvador	26.0	23.1	0.0	0.0	52.2	52.6	3.5	5.2	21.2	22.4	0.0	3.2	11.9	15.2	6.0	3.1
Guatemala	24.5	19.5	0.0	0.0	48.9	48.7	2.7	4.4	46.1	44.3	1.9	3.0	12.4	17.6	8.3	6.3
Haiti	18.5	38.5	0.0	0.0	65.4	48.2	8.0	6.2	24.6	19.1	0.0	1.3	5.7	11.3	0.3	0.0
Honduras	31.1	32.3	0.0	0.0	49.6	45.4	1.9	6.6	18.4	15.3	1.6	4.4	10.6	14.5	6.1	2.7
Jamaica	28.9	50.7	0.0	0.0	40.0	31.1	11.1	10.2	19.3	20.8	13.6	1.7	8.5	8.2	7.0	0.2
Mexico	39.4	43.3	5.6	5.5	36.2	31.8	2.5	1.9	33.0	20.2	2.5	2.8	17.5	9.8	3.5	2.3
Nicaragua	20.1	21.8	0.0	0.0	53.1	40.6	2.8	2.9	19.2	17.0	2.8	10.8	9.6	12.7	13.6	13.2
Panama	27.8	29.4	0.0	0.0	47.7	44.8	0.2	0.3	24.5	43.7	0.0	0.0	20.2	22.1	2.0	2.5
Trinidad and Tobago	85.0	65.2	7.4	2.9	11.0	23.6	1.3	2.7	9.7	20.9	0.0	0.0	2.3	5.4	1.3	0.9
SOUTH AMERICA	**34.4**	**36.2**	**6.9**	**7.4**	**38.3**	**37.6**	**2.7**	**2.7**	**33.6**	**32.4**	**4.6**	**3.8**	**12.3**	**12.7**	**5.6**	**3.8**
Argentina	25.8	30.1	0.3	0.3	36.2	32.8	2.7	2.5	33.5	29.0	6.8	7.7	20.3	23.8	6.4	2.2
Bolivia	24.2	21.1	0.0	5.2	50.6	49.4	6.3	7.7	42.3	40.7	2.6	0.9	18.4	27.4	2.1	0.0
Brazil	37.3	38.7	10.8	11.1	37.8	37.5	2.3	2.6	34.2	31.5	4.8	4.1	10.0	8.7	5.6	4.7
Chile	41.8	41.0	4.2	6.4	39.4	39.0	3.5	2.9	32.8	33.0	1.1	0.0	15.1	15.8	0.0	2.7
Colombia	30.1	31.7	1.9	2.2	40.4	43.0	3.9	3.8	35.5	38.7	2.2	1.8	12.0	12.3	5.1	5.1
Ecuador	17.4	17.2	0.0	0.0	48.6	50.9	4.4	3.8	34.7	33.7	6.5	5.1	14.6	9.6	8.2	1.8
Guyana	X	X	X	X	X	X	X	X	X	X	X	X	X	X	X	X
Paraguay	12.1	6.2	0.0	0.0	67.4	70.8	0.2	4.1	66.3	66.7	0.0	0.0	16.1	15.1	3.0	3.9
Peru	18.3	31.5	0.3	0.9	44.1	38.4	4.5	4.2	16.8	31.8	16.9	4.8	16.6	19.8	1.9	3.1
Suriname	X	X	X	X	X	X	X	X	X	X	X	X	X	X	X	X
Uruguay	17.1	22.0	0.1	0.1	41.9	36.2	0.9	2.2	19.3	30.9	9.6	12.5	19.0	21.3	8.6	6.5
Venezuela	43.4	42.8	10.0	10.8	35.6	36.5	2.3	1.8	33.3	34.3	1.6	0.1	7.1	9.0	7.7	2.9
ASIA	**49.1**	**51.8**	**9.8**	**11.0**	**19.8**	**18.1**	**2.2**	**1.8**	**15.7**	**13.4**	**3.6**	**3.7**	**14.0**	**15.7**	**5.3**	**4.6**
Afghanistan, Islamic State	X	X	X	X	X	X	X	X	X	X	X	X	X	X	X	X
Armenia, Rep	29.0	42.2	0.0	0.0	7.7	25.3	3.0	4.6	3.3	20.0	0.4	3.6	10.0	0.0	0.0	2.7
Azerbaijan	32.6	55.9	0.0	0.0	6.6	8.3	4.2	0.0	1.8	0.0	5.6	17.2	3.1	0.0	0.8	0.0
Bangladesh	49.2	49.2	0.4	0.4	18.4	18.1	1.7	2.6	11.9	10.1	7.7	5.8	14.5	18.5	1.5	2.0
Bhutan	X	X	X	X	X	X	X	X	X	X	X	X	X	X	X	X
Cambodia	X	X	X	X	X	X	X	X	X	X	X	X	X	X	X	X
China	66.2	61.1	15.2	14.6	8.8	8.2	0.5	0.2	5.9	4.2	4.1	4.9	13.4	18.0	4.9	3.8
Georgia	29.1	51.9	0.0	0.0	2.3	1.3	0.0	0.0	1.0	0.0	5.9	5.3	3.1	0.0	0.0	0.0
India	53.7	57.9	10.6	12.6	24.0	23.2	1.4	1.6	20.7	14.8	5.0	2.5	12.0	10.6	1.4	0.7
Indonesia	34.8	31.2	3.6	2.0	35.0	28.6	3.1	2.1	29.2	25.7	3.2	2.8	20.7	22.3	2.0	1.0
Iran, Islamic Rep	29.5	38.3	0.8	0.6	22.6	14.0	0.9	1.4	21.7	12.6	7.1	0.0	29.6	17.6	5.7	0.0
Iraq	27.2	23.9	0.0	0.0	45.2	50.1	2.2	2.6	43.0	47.5	0.0	0.0	11.8	15.0	0.0	0.0
Israel	23.4	29.6	0.7	0.0	34.9	41.1	6.7	11.7	27.5	28.8	1.1	0.9	15.4	7.7	4.6	4.5
Japan	42.7	47.5	11.2	14.2	25.1	22.1	2.8	1.9	20.5	17.7	3.2	3.1	13.9	13.2	11.7	10.2
Jordan	19.7	22.2	0.0	0.0	40.4	49.1	8.9	11.2	31.5	37.9	2.8	3.7	17.8	17.8	1.8	1.3
Kazakstan, Rep	43.4	67.8	4.4	0.0	9.2	6.4	1.5	0.0	6.5	0.0	3.7	12.7	2.4	0.0	0.0	0.0
Korea, Dem People's Rep	89.8	85.5	11.7	8.5	6.6	7.6	0.0	0.0	6.6	7.6	0.0	0.0	0.9	0.8	0.0	0.0
Korea, Rep	46.9	40.3	9.5	11.1	22.9	16.6	1.9	2.4	17.7	12.1	2.6	1.6	20.2	34.1	3.8	4.2
Kuwait	27.6	49.2	0.0	0.0	37.9	32.1	6.9	5.4	30.9	26.8	0.0	0.0	31.6	11.3	0.0	0.3
Kyrgyz Rep	25.9	49.7	0.0	0.0	5.9	1.6	4.1	0.0	0.0	0.0	14.7	30.5	9.8	0.0	0.0	0.0
Lao People's Dem Rep	X	X	X	X	X	X	X	X	X	X	X	X	X	X	X	X
Lebanon	26.7	2.5	0.0	0.0	45.2	74.6	6.0	6.5	39.2	68.1	0.0	0.0	21.0	6.4	1.6	0.0
Malaysia	40.8	41.1	0.8	0.2	35.2	40.8	5.2	4.6	29.9	36.2	2.0	0.0	8.2	8.5	4.3	4.1
Mongolia	X	X	X	X	X	X	X	X	X	X	X	X	X	X	X	X
Myanmar	65.2	61.2	0.0	0.0	26.7	33.9	1.8	2.3	24.9	31.7	0.0	0.0	4.8	2.9	1.6	0.6
Nepal	29.9	28.5	0.0	0.0	30.5	35.5	4.6	8.9	25.4	26.1	2.0	2.9	20.3	21.0	8.0	5.9
Oman	2.8	15.4	0.0	0.0	53.5	39.1	8.4	12.2	45.0	26.8	0.0	0.0	3.8	1.3	0.0	0.0
Pakistan	42.1	44.7	2.1	2.4	30.2	26.9	2.5	3.6	26.6	21.6	3.4	3.4	16.4	13.7	4.1	7.2
Philippines	32.3	40.4	1.3	7.2	42.7	25.0	4.8	5.0	34.7	16.5	1.9	12.4	11.2	17.4	7.9	3.8
Saudi Arabia	17.9	31.8	0.0	0.0	24.7	40.1	5.2	6.6	19.4	33.6	0.3	0.0	8.8	6.7	3.9	3.0
Singapore	33.3	33.5	0.8	0.6	52.1	46.9	30.5	23.0	21.6	24.0	0.0	0.0	3.6	4.5	0.2	5.6
Sri Lanka	14.6	13.3	0.0	0.1	56.0	61.6	8.2	9.8	46.2	49.5	0.6	0.0	15.7	18.6	5.5	2.6
Syrian Arab Rep	21.0	34.4	0.0	0.0	12.3	38.8	1.6	3.3	10.7	35.5	0.0	3.9	10.1	9.9	0.0	0.0
Tajikistan, Rep	21.0	64.0	0.0	0.0	38.3	0.7	0.2	0.0	37.8	0.0	13.9	24.6	5.3	0.0	0.0	0.0
Thailand	32.3	25.0	1.4	1.0	49.5	49.6	7.3	8.9	41.1	37.4	4.3	11.9	6.2	6.5	5.4	4.0
Turkey	31.7	29.0	6.9	6.5	25.1	20.8	2.5	0.7	21.5	18.7	5.5	4.7	32.1	41.8	2.3	1.2
Turkmenistan, Rep	1.8	41.6	0.0	0.0	5.6	17.0	0.0	0.0	5.5	0.0	1.5	20.3	1.0	0.0	0.0	0.0
United Arab Emirates	X	X	X	X	X	X	X	X	X	X	X	X	X	X	X	X
Uzbekistan, Rep	4.7	58.8	0.0	0.0	7.1	2.9	0.3	0.0	6.5	0.0	2.7	26.9	1.8	0.0	0.0	0.0
Vietnam	48.8	54.2	0.0	0.0	27.6	17.8	2.8	2.9	23.7	13.2	5.4	4.3	13.8	13.8	0.0	0.0
Yemen	X	X	X	X	X	X	X	X	X	X	X	X	X	X	X	X
OCEANIA	**35.3**	**37.8**	**6.0**	**6.3**	**37.9**	**37.7**	**5.8**	**4.0**	**28.7**	**30.2**	**2.3**	**2.6**	**12.3**	**12.6**	**6.0**	**5.7**
Australia	36.4	38.0	5.9	6.4	38.3	38.1	5.7	3.9	30.5	31.3	2.3	2.4	12.7	12.5	6.3	5.2
Fiji	X	X	X	X	X	X	X	X	X	X	X	X	X	X	X	X
New Zealand	29.7	36.2	6.6	5.9	35.7	35.0	6.8	4.7	18.7	23.2	2.4	3.7	10.4	13.1	4.1	8.9
Papua New Guinea	X	X	X	X	X	X	X	X	X	X	X	X	X	X	X	X
Solomon Islands	X	X	X	X	X	X	X	X	X	X	X	X	X	X	X	X

Production of Selected Minerals and Materials, 1995

Source: United States Geological Survey

	Bauxite {a} (Al content) (000 metric tons)	Iron Ore (Fe content) (000 metric tons)	Copper Ore (Cu content) (metric tons)	Silver Ore (Ag content) (metric tons)	Gold (Au content) (kilograms)	Sulfur (000 metric tons)	Salt (000 metric tons)	Nitrogen (ammonia) (000 metric tons)	Phosphorus (P2O5) (000 metric tons)	Potassium (potash) (000 metric tons)	Sand and Gravel (000 metric tons)	Hydraulic Cement (000 metric tons)
WORLD	27,250	554,846	10,000,000	14,600	2,250,000	54,300	189,000	91,600	40,100	24,700	X	1,421,342
AFRICA	X	X	X	X	X	X	X	X	X	X	X	X
Algeria	X	1,000	X	3	X	X	178	380	232	X	X	6,200
Angola	X	X	X	X	X	X	30	X	X	X	X	300
Benin	X	X	X	X	X	X	1	X	X	X	X	380
Botswana	X	X	21,029	X	86	X	208	X	X	X	X	X
Burkina Faso	X	X	X	X	6,000	X	7	X	X	X	X	X
Burundi	X	X	X	X	10	X	X	X	X	X	X	X
Cameroon	X	X	X	X	560	X	X	X	X	X	X	520
Central African Rep	X	X	X	X	700	X	X	X	X	X	X	X
Chad	X	X	X	X	X	X	X	X	X	X	X	X
Congo, Dem Rep	X	X	28,800	10	9,500	X	X	X	X	X	X	100
Congo, Rep	X	X	X	X	5	X	X	X	X	X	X	100
Côte d'Ivoire	X	X	X	X	3,200	X	X	X	X	X	X	500
Egypt	X	2,100	X	X	X	X	1,000	940	390	X	32,800	16,000
Equatorial Guinea	X	X	X	X	X	X	X	X	X	X	X	X
Eritrea	X	X	X	X	59	X	255	X	X	X	1,334	350
Ethiopia	X	X	X	X	4,500	X	5	X	X	X	1,600	611
Gabon	X	X	X	X	70	X	X	X	X	X	X	130
Gambia, The	X	X	X	X	X	X	X	X	X	X	X	X
Ghana	123	X	X	3	52,200	X	50	X	X	X	X	1,400
Guinea	3,600	X	X	X	7,863	X	X	X	X	X	X	X
Guinea-Bissau	X	X	X	X	X	X	X	X	X	X	X	X
Kenya	X	X	X	X	170	X	74	X	X	X	X	1,500
Lesotho	X	X	X	X	X	X	X	X	X	X	X	X
Liberia	X	X	X	X	500	X	X	X	X	X	X	X
Libya	X	X	X	X	X	X	12	200	X	X	X	2,300
Madagascar	X	X	X	X	500	X	30	X	X	X	X	60
Malawi	X	X	X	X	X	X	X	X	X	X	X	139
Mali	X	X	X	X	7,800	X	5	X	X	X	X	20
Mauritania	X	7,000	X	X	X	X	6	X	X	X	X	375
Mauritius	X	X	X	X	X	X	6	X	X	X	X	X
Morocco	X	40	13,000	330	X	X	175	X	X	X	X	6,500
Mozambique	3	X	X	X	900	X	40	X	X	X	X	20
Namibia	X	X	22,530	66	2,099	X	300	X	X	X	X	X
Niger	X	X	X	X	X	X	3	X	X	X	X	30
Nigeria	X	100	X	X	X	X	X	350	X	X	X	2,600
Rwanda	X	X	X	X	100	X	X	X	X	X	X	5
Senegal	X	X	X	X	X	X	120	X	600	X	X	590
Sierra Leone	70	X	X	X	50	X	100	X	X	X	X	X
Somalia	X	X	X	X	X	X	1	X	X	X	X	25
South Africa	X	19,806	199,600	174	523,820	509	313	600	1,087	X	X	9,071
Sudan	X	X	X	X	3,000	X	75	X	X	X	X	250
Swaziland	X	X	X	X	X	X	X	X	X	X	X	X
Tanzania	X	X	X	X	44	X	7	X	7	X	X	800
Togo	X	X	X	X	X	X	X	X	720	X	X	350
Tunisia	X	128	X	1	X	X	400	X	2,182	X	X	4,300
Uganda	X	X	X	X	X	X	5	X	X	X	X	130
Zambia	X	X	329,200	14	79	X	10	X	X	X	X	300
Zimbabwe	X	160	9,500	10	24,344	X	70	45	X	X	X	1,000
EUROPE	X	X	X	X	X	X	X	X	X	X	X	X
Albania	X	X	800	X	X	X	X	15	1	X	X	200
Austria	X	660	X	X	X	X	701	400	X	X	50,000	5,000
Belarus, Rep	X	X	X	X	X	X	219	500	X	3,210	X	1,235
Belgium	X	X	X	X	X	X	X	500	X	X	14,000	8,000
Bosnia and Herzegovina	19	52	X	X	X	X	50	1	X	X	750	150
Bulgaria	X	250	63,000	35	2,000	X	700	800	X	X	X	2,100
Croatia, Rep	1	X	X	X	X	X	28	300	X	X	3,000	1,700
Czech Rep	X	X	X	X	X	X	180	150	X	X	15,788	4,825
Denmark	X	X	X	X	X	X	576	X	X	X	37,500	2,000
Estonia, Rep	X	X	X	X	X	X	X	45	X	X	21,000	417
Finland	X	X	12,000	27	1,400	X	X	10	244	X	X	900
France	X	600	X	1	4,000	1,100	7,350	1,500	X	802	174,900	21,000
Germany	X	20	X	1	X	1,230	10,800	2,100	X	3,280	450,000	40,000
Greece	479	600	X	45	X	X	150	55	X	X	X	12,000
Hungary	275	X	X	X	X	X	X	230	X	X	3,200	3,000
Iceland	X	X	X	X	X	X	4	9	X	X	5,400	82
Ireland	X	X	X	15	X	X	X	370	X	X	7,500	1,500
Italy	23	X	X	12	X	X	3,400	600	X	X	125,000	35,000
Latvia, Rep	X	X	X	X	X	X	X	X	X	X	91	204
Lithuania, Rep	X	X	X	X	X	X	X	442	X	X	48	649
Macedonia, FYR	X	6	6,500	10	X	X	X	X	X	X	195	500
Moldova, Rep	X	X	X	X	X	X	X	X	6,381	X	X	49
Netherlands	X	X	X	X	X	X	3,500	2,500	X	X	X	3,400
Norway	X	1,430	6,800	X	X	X	X	300	X	X	X	1,400
Poland, Rep	X	X	383,600	1,000	X	2,440	4,000	1,500	X	X	2,000	13,884
Portugal	X	6	134,181	32	X	X	670	100	X	X	5,000	7,500
Romania	44	184	24,003	60	4,000	X	1,602	1	X	X	901	6,000
Russian Federation	968	X	591,000	700	132,170	4,000	2,000	7,500	3,000	2,800	X	36,400
Slovak Rep	X	230	500	X	X	X	70	250	X	X	X	2,500
Slovenia, Rep	X	X	X	X	X	X	8	X	X	X	3,000	1,000
Spain	X	900	5,000	135	6,000	702	3,400	360	X	650	X	25,000
Sweden	X	13,880	83,600	268	6,400	X	X	X	X	X	X	2,100
Switzerland	X	X	X	X	X	X	300	30	X	X	X	4,000
Ukraine	X	24,800	X	X	X	X	3,000	2,200	X	110	X	11,000
United Kingdom	X	X	X	X	X	X	7,100	1,000	X	582	104,000	12,500
Yugoslavia, Fed Rep	12	X	70,000	27	4,000	X	16	150	X	X	3,300	1,696

Data Table 15.4 continued

	Bauxite {a} (Al content) (000 metric tons)	Iron Ore (Fe content) (000 metric tons)	Copper Ore (Cu content) (metric tons)	Silver Ore (Ag content) (metric tons)	Gold (Au content) (kilograms)	Sulfur (000 metric tons)	Salt (000 metric tons)	Nitrogen (ammonia) (000 metric tons)	Phosphorus (P2O5) (000 metric tons)	Potassium (potash) (000 metric tons)	Sand and Gravel (000 metric tons)	Hydraulic Cement (000 metric tons)
NORTH AMERICA	X	X	X	X	X	X	X	X	X	X	X	X
Canada	X	24,651	728,680	1,195	150,273	9,010	10,893	3,500	X	9,010	240,189	10,722
United States	50	39,577	1,849,000	1,640	320,000	11,800	42,100	13,300	12,800	1,480	963,000	78,320
CENTRAL AMERICA	X	X	X	X	X	X	X	X	X	X	X	X
Belize	X	X	X	X	5	X	X	X	X	X	320	X
Costa Rica	X	X	X	X	500	X	47	X	X	X	1,500	990
Cuba	X	X	1,500	X	X	X	180	130	X	X	X	1,200
Dominican Rep	X	X	X	13	3,288	X	11	X	X	X	5,500	1,453
El Salvador	X	X	X	X	X	X	30	X	X	X	X	875
Guatemala	X	2	X	X	30	X	100	X	X	X	1,000	1,560
Haiti	X	X	X	X	X	X	X	X	X	X	1,500	50
Honduras	X	X	390	25	110	X	25	X	X	X	X	655
Jamaica	2,714	X	X	X	X	X	18	X	X	X	1,800	523
Mexico	X	5,540	331,900	2,400	20,292	2,880	7,670	2,100	180	X	157,692	23,971
Nicaragua	X	X	X	2	1,600	X	15	X	X	X	1,300	350
Panama	X	X	X	X	1,100	X	22	X	X	X	3,000	350
Trinidad and Tobago	X	X	X	X	X	X	X	1,696	X	X	X	600
SOUTH AMERICA	X	X	X	X	X	X	X	X	X	X	X	X
Argentina	X	<500	300	43	1,100	X	1,000	70	X	X	21,067	6,400
Bolivia	X	X	127	410	14,405	X	5	X	X	X	X	700
Brazil	2,190	120,900	41,000	155	72,000	X	3,100	940	700	223	X	25,500
Chile	X	5,119	2,488,000	1,032	39,180	X	3,000	X	3	50	300	3,000
Colombia	X	75,000	2,800	6	21,160	X	550	90	11	X	859	9,624
Ecuador	X	X	X	X	15,500	X	X	X	X	X	170	2,300
Guyana	525	X	X	X	11,800	X	X	X	X	X	X	X
Paraguay	X	X	X	X	X	X	X	X	X	X	2,000	570
Peru	X	4,900	380,700	1,908	56,500	X	238	90	12	X	900	2,100
Suriname	825	X	X	X	300	X	X	X	X	X	195	50
Uruguay	X	X	X	X	900	X	X	X	X	X	2,000	600
Venezuela	1,296	12,743	X	X	7,259	X	3,500	600	49	X	4,629	6,900
ASIA	X	X	X	X	X	X	X	X	X	X	X	X
Afghanistan, Islamic State	X	X	X	X	X	X	13	30	X	X	X	115
Armenia, Rep	X	X	1,000	X	100	X	50	X	X	X	X	200
Azerbaijan	9	83	X	X	X	X	20	X	X	X	X	200
Bangladesh	X	X	X	X	X	X	350	975	X	X	X	280
Bhutan	X	X	X	X	X	X	X	X	X	X	X	140
Cambodia	X	X	X	X	X	X	40	X	X	X	X	X
China	1,250	X	370,000	250	140,000	6,530	25,000	19,500	6,400	80	X	445,610
Georgia	X	X	1,000	X	500	X	30	X	X	X	X	100
India	1,200	37,800	63,000	40	2,300	X	9,500	7,713	338	X	X	70,000
Indonesia	225	197	443,618	112	62,800	X	670	2,850	2	X	X	16,300
Iran, Islamic Rep	25	4,500	100,000	60	650	890	936	700	X	X	X	16,300
Iraq	X	X	X	X	X	475	250	500	300	X	X	18,000
Israel	X	X	X	X	X	X	1,200	41	1,264	1,330	X	3,500
Japan	X	1	2,376	100	9,185	2,860	1,400	1,400	X	X	X	90,474
Jordan	X	X	X	X	X	X	25	X	1,655	1,070	X	4,000
Kazakstan, Rep	825	8,200	260,000	800	26,000	X	X	200	550	X	X	1,800
Korea, Dem People's Rep	X	5,100	16,000	50	5,000	X	600	600	164	X	X	17,000
Korea, Rep	X	106	5	258	13,000	X	770	470	X	X	1,718	55,130
Kuwait	X	X	X	X	X	X	45	325	X	X	X	2,000
Kyrgyz Rep	X	X	X	X	1,200	X	X	X	X	X	X	300
Lao People's Dem Rep	X	X	X	X	X	X	8	X	X	X	X	X
Lebanon	X	X	X	X	X	X	3	X	X	X	X	3,000
Malaysia	46	123	21,900	11	3,161	X	X	340	X	X	X	10,667
Mongolia	X	X	100,400	X	4,800	X	1	X	X	X	X	109
Myanmar	X	X	3,700	4	X	X	260	130	X	X	X	517
Nepal	X	X	2	X	X	X	7	X	X	X	X	220
Oman	X	X	X	X	X	X	X	X	X	X	6,500	1,400
Pakistan	2	X	X	X	X	X	952	1,450	5	X	X	8,586
Philippines	X	X	105,655	27	27,144	X	540	X	7	X	22,500	9,800
Saudi Arabia	X	X	925	18	8,080	2,200	X	2,000	X	X	X	16,000
Singapore	X	X	X	X	X	X	X	X	X	X	X	1,900
Sri Lanka	X	X	X	X	X	X	60	X	11	X	X	900
Syrian Arab Rep	X	X	X	X	X	X	130	67	477	X	4,200	6,000
Tajikistan, Rep	X	X	X	X	1,500	X	X	25	X	X	X	100
Thailand	X	17	X	X	X	X	481	X	3	X	X	26,500
Turkey	83	3,200	34,100	65	1,000	X	1,400	350	24	X	X	33,153
Turkmenistan, Rep	X	X	X	X	X	X	500	25	X	X	X	400
United Arab Emirates	X	X	X	X	X	X	X	250	X	X	X	6,000
Uzbekistan, Rep	X	X	45,000	X	75,000	X	X	1,100	X	X	X	3,500
Vietnam	X	X	X	X	X	X	375	52	145	X	X	7,500
Yemen	X	X	X	X	X	X	110	X	X	X	X	1,000
OCEANIA	X	X	X	X	X	X	X	X	X	X	X	X
Australia	10,664	88,653	437,000	920	253,504	X	8,480	433	1	X	45,000	6,000
Fiji	X	X	X	2	3,775	X	X	X	X	X	300	78
New Zealand	X	900	X	32	13,000	X	50	80	X	X	20,000	700
Papua New Guinea	X	X	212,737	65	52,635	X	X	X	X	X	X	X
Solomon Islands	X	X	X	X	1	X	X	X	X	X	X	X

Notes: a. Includes nepheline syenite ores from the Russian Federation and alunite ores from Azerbaijan converted to bauxite equivalents.

Sources and Technical Notes

Commercial Energy Production and Consumption, 1985–95

Source: United Nations Statistical Division (UN-STAT), *1995 Energy Statistics Yearbook* (UNSTAT, New York, 1997).

Energy data are compiled by UNSTAT, primarily from responses to questionnaires sent to national governments, supplemented by official national statistical publications and by data from intergovernmental organizations. When official numbers are not available, UNSTAT prepares estimates based on the professional and commercial literature.

Commercial energy production includes *total* energy production, solid, liquid, and gaseous fuels; and primary electricity production. *Solid fuels* include bituminous coal, lignite, peat, and oil shale burned directly. *Liquid fuels* include crude petroleum and natural gas liquids. *Gaseous fuels* include natural gas and other petroleum gases. *Primary electricity* refers to electricity generated by noncombustible energy sources and includes nuclear, wind, tidal, wave, solar, geothermal, and hydroelectric power sources. Primary electricity values are calculated to equate them with the amount of coal or oil required to produce an equivalent unit of thermal electricity and are expressed in joules. The conversion from kilowatt-hours to joules, assuming a thermal efficiency of the primary source of 100 percent, is 0.0036 petajoules per million kilowatt-hours. However, the efficiency, or the percentage of heat energy transformed into electrical energy, of nuclear power plants is estimated at an average of 33 percent, and geothermal plants at 10 percent. Hydroelectric, wave, wind, and solar power sources (which are mechanical as opposed to thermal sources) are assumed to be 100 percent efficient.

Electricity production data generally refer to gross production. Data for the Dominican Republic, Finland, France (including Monaco), Mexico, the United States, Zambia, and Zimbabwe refer to net production. Gross production is the amount of electricity produced by a generating station before consumption by station auxiliaries and transformer losses within the station are deducted. Net production is the amount of electricity remaining after these deductions. Typically, net production is 5 to 10 percent less than gross production. Energy production from pumped storage facilities is not included in gross or net electricity generation.

Electricity production includes both public and self-producer power plants. Public power plants produce electricity for many users. They may be operated by private, cooperative, or governmental organizations. Self-producer power plants are operated by organizations or companies to produce

electricity for internal applications, such as factory operations.

Total energy consumption includes *commercial energy* and *traditional fuels*. *Commercial energy* refers to apparent consumption and is defined as domestic production plus net imports, minus net stock increases, and minus aircraft and marine bunkers. Commercial energy consumption includes energy from solid, liquid, and gaseous fuels, plus primary electricity (see the definition above).

Traditional fuels include estimates of the consumption of fuelwood, charcoal, bagasse, and animal and vegetal wastes. Fuelwood and charcoal consumption data are estimated from population data and country-specific per capita consumption figures. These per capita estimates were prepared by the Food and Agriculture Organization of the United Nations (FAO) after an assessment of the available consumption data. Data were supplied by the answers to questionnaires or come from official publications by Bangladesh, Bhutan, Brazil, the Central African Republic, Chile, Colombia, Costa Rica, Cuba, Cyprus, El Salvador, The Gambia, Japan, Kenya, the Democratic People's Republic of Korea, the Republic of Korea, Luxembourg, Malawi, Mauritius, Nepal, Panama, Portugal, the former Soviet Union, Sri Lanka, Sweden, Thailand, and Uruguay. The conversion of fuelwood is based on 20 to 30 percent moisture content.

Similar estimates were prepared for coniferous fuelwood and for charcoal. Although the energy values of fuelwood and charcoal vary widely, UN-STAT uses standard factors of 0.33 metric ton of coal equivalent per cubic meter of fuelwood and 0.986 metric ton of coal equivalent per metric ton of charcoal.

Bagasse production is based on sugar production data in the *Sugar Yearbook* of the International Sugar Organization. It is assumed that 3.26 metric tons of fuel bagasse at 50 percent moisture are produced per metric ton of extracted cane sugar. The energy of a metric ton of bagasse is valued at 0.264 metric ton of coal equivalent.

One petajoule (1×10^{15} joules) is the same as $20,778 \times 10^{8}$ kilowatt-hours, 9.478×10^{-7} Quads, and 9.478×10^{11} British thermal units and is the equivalent of 163,400 "U.N. standard" barrels of oil or 34,140 U.N. standard metric tons of coal. The heat content of various fuels has been converted to coal-equivalent and then petajoule-equivalent values using country- and year-specific conversion factors. For example, a metric ton of bituminous coal produced in Argentina has an energy value of 0.843 metric ton of standard coal equivalent (7 million kilocalories). A metric ton of bituminous coal produced in Turkey has a 1991 energy value of 0.925 metric ton of standard coal equivalent. The original national production data for bituminous coal were multiplied by these conversion factors and then by 29.3076×10^{-6} to yield petajoule

equivalents. Other fuels were converted to coal-equivalent and petajoule-equivalent terms in a similar manner.

For additional information, refer to the UNSTAT *1995 Energy Statistics Yearbook*.

Electricity Production and Trade, 1985–95

Source: United Nations Statistical Division (UN-STAT), *1995 Energy Statistics Yearbook* (UNSTAT, New York, 1997).

Energy data are compiled by UNSTAT, primarily from responses to questionnaires sent to national governments, supplemented by official national statistical publications and by data from intergovernmental organizations. When official numbers are not available, UNSTAT prepares estimates based on the professional and commercial literature.

Electricity production, which encompasses *total*, *thermal*, *hydroelectric*, *geothermal*, and *nuclear* production, represents the amount of electricity output generated by each of the different sources in million kilowatt-hours. Figures generally refer to gross production. Data for the Dominican Republic, Finland, France (including Monaco), Mexico, the United States, Zambia, and Zimbabwe refer to net production. Gross production is the amount of electricity produced by a generating station before consumption by station auxiliaries and transformer losses within the station are deducted. Net production is the amount of electricity remaining after these deductions. Typically, net production is 5–10 percent less than gross production. Energy production from pumped storage is not included in gross or net electricity generation.

Total electricity production is the total amount of electricity produced, both from primary and secondary sources. *Thermal* electricity is generated from the heat produced by the burning of fossil and renewable fuels. *Hydroelectric* power is generated from the energy of water falling from a higher to a lower point. *Geothermal* refers to electricity produced using sources of heat from the earth's interior, except in some specified countries (see data table). *Nuclear* electricity is generated from the heat produced by nuclear fission.

Electricity production includes both public and self-producer power plants. Public power plants produce electricity for many users. They may be operated by private, cooperative, or governmental organizations. Self-producer power plants are operated by organizations or companies to produce electricity for internal applications, such as factory operations.

Import and *export trade* refer to the amounts of electric energy transferred to and from the country concerned, respectively.

One kilowatt-hour equals 3.6×10^6 joules, 3.41×10^{-15} Quads, and 3,413 British thermal units.

Data Table 15.3

Energy Balances, 1985–95

Source: International Energy Agency (IEA), *Energy Balances of Organisation for Economic Co-Operation and Development (OECD) Countries, 1960–95,* and *Energy Balances of OECD Countries, 1960–1995,* on diskette (OECD, Paris, 1997).

Data for OECD and Economic Commission for Europe (ECE) countries were compiled from information provided in IEA/OECD/UN-ECE Eurostat questionnaires. Data from other large and medium-sized energy consumers come mostly from individual country information. Data for the remaining countries were gathered from a variety of international organizations. WRI calculated the amount of individual energy-use sectors as a percentage of total final (energy) consumption for each country.

Total final consumption is the sum of consumption by the different sectors. Backflows from the petrochemical industry are not included. *Industry sector* includes the *iron and steel* industry, chemical industry, nonferrous metals basic industries, nonmetallic mineral products (e.g., glass, ceramics, cement, etc.), transport equipment, machinery, mining and quarrying, food and tobacco, paper, pulp and print, wood and wood products, construction, textile and leather, and any nonspecified industry. The *transportation sector* includes all fuel used for transportation except international marine bunkers. Fuel used for ocean, coastal, and inland fishing is not included. *Air transportation* includes both international civil aviation and domestic air travel. *Road transportation* includes all human and cargo transportation taking place on a nation's road network. *Agriculture* includes all agricultural activity, including ocean, coastal, and inland fishing. *Commercial and public services* include service sectors such as stores, repair shops, restaurants, etc. *Residential* includes energy use by residences. IEA reports that it can be difficult to accurately distinguish among the agriculture, commercial, and public services sectors, and that a total of the three is

more accurate than values for the individual sectors.

Data Table 15.4

Production of Selected Minerals and Materials, 1995

Source: United States Geological Survey (USGS), *Minerals and Materials Information CD-ROM* (USGS, Minerals Information Team, Reston, Virginia, 1997).

The work of the old U.S. Bureau of Mines, compiling data on the mineral resources of the world, continues through the work of the Minerals Information Team of the USGS. The team compiles data based on the review of the world's published literature and, often, through personal knowledge of particular industries and countries. Although these data are based on the best country information available, they are only as accurate and comprehensive as the information reported by companies, countries, and commodity organizations. Detailed commodity notes and sources are available from the USGS.

Bauxite is the primary ore from which aluminum is derived, although these data also contain the dry bauxite equivalents of the minerals nepheline syenite and alunite. To allow comparisons with other extraction activities, the bauxite equivalent is reported here in terms of its content of aluminum, which is 25 percent of the mass of bauxite. Not all bauxite is used for the production of aluminum, however; it can also be used in the production of such items as abrasives, chemicals, and refractories.

Iron ore is reported as the elemental iron contained in the production of iron ore, iron ore concentrates, and iron ore agglomerates and in principle contains no double-counting of ores traded rather than produced.

Copper ore is the world mine production in terms of the copper content of ores produced. Where possible, the copper content was calculated from actual analysis of the relevant ores or concentrates.

Silver ore is commonly produced as a byproduct of gold, copper, and other metals production, although it is also mined directly.

Gold production is based on the actual reported production of the element. It does not necessarily capture small-scale artisanal production nor pro-

duction that, to escape taxation, enters illegal channels.

Sulfur is produced from elemental deposits, from the production of other minerals, or as a byproduct of other industrial processes. It is counted here as produced in the country of origin if production is from native sulfur, pyrites, gypsum, byproducts from the extraction of crude oil and natural gas, or tar sands. It is counted as produced in the country of recovery if it is obtained from metallurgical operations, petroleum refineries, or spent oxides.

Salt here refers to sodium chloride, or common salt, and is derived from mines, oceans, and seas through evaporation and by the extraction of brines. It is used to season and preserve foods, as an essential raw material for the chemical industry, and for several other industrial uses.

Nitrogen is measured as the amount (82.2 percent) contained in anhydrous *ammonia* produced by combining nitrogen from the air with hydrogen (derived from several potential sources) and water. Ammonia, in turn, provides the essential input to a variety of nitrogen-based fertilizers that together provide more than 50 percent of the nitrogen required for the world's food and fiber production.

Phosphorus, another of the three essential elements for plant growth, is obtained primarily from phosphate rock and is measured in terms of the quantity of phosphorus pentoxide (P_2O_5) or its equivalent.

Potassium, the final of the three elements essential for plant growth, is derived from a variety of mined and manufactured salts.

Sand and gravel for construction are basic raw materials produced everywhere for local use. Because of the local nature of these resources, data on sand and gravel should be used with caution and can significantly understate the amount actually produced in a country. These data are presented here to illustrate the relative magnitude of reported production. Sand and gravel are used in the production of concrete, asphalt paving materials, road building, fill, concrete products, and in a variety of other applications.

Hydraulic cement is a product that can set underwater and is the dominant form of cement manufactured in the world. Its use in concrete and in masonry is critical to the construction industry. Portland and masonry cements are made by burning calcareous rocks such as limestone with lesser quantities of other materials.

C hapter 16

Atmosphere and Climate

Data Table 16.1
Emissions from Fossil Fuel Burning and Cement Manufacturing, 1995

Source: Carbon Dioxide Information Analysis Center

	Carbon Dioxide Emissions, 1995 (000 metric tons)						Per Capita Carbon Dioxide Emissions (metric tons) 1995	Bunker Fuels {a} (000 metric tons) 1995
	Solid Fuels	Liquid Fuels	Gaseous Fuels	Gas Flaring	Cement Manufacturing	Total Emissions		
WORLD	**9,016,712**	**8,342,675**	**4,179,833**	**233,479**	**687,927**	**22,714,561**	**3.9**	**485,806**
AFRICA	**274,078**	**269,355**	**100,416**	**73,386**	**27,932**	**745,595**	**1.1**	**25,326**
Algeria	3,243	22,134	47,222	15,578	3,089	91,267	3.3	1,411
Angola	0	1,667	322	2,460	149	4,602	0.4	2,561
Benin	0	443	0	0	189	634	0.1	59
Botswana	2,242	0	0	0	0	2,242	1.5	0
Burkina Faso	4	956	0	0	0	956	0.0	4
Burundi	18	198	0	0	0	213	0.0	18
Cameroon	4	3,880	0	0	259	4,144	0.3	48
Central African Rep	0	234	0	0	0	234	0.1	40
Chad	0	95	0	0	0	95	0.0	59
Congo, Dem Rep	854	1,194	0	0	50	2,099	0.0	476
Congo, Rep	0	1,048	7	167	50	1,268	0.5	33
Côte d'Ivoire	0	10,113	0	0	249	10,362	0.8	260
Egypt	2,451	55,205	26,055	0	7,973	91,684	1.5	5,108
Equatorial Guinea	0	132	0	0	0	132	0.3	0
Eritrea	X	X	X	X	X	X	X	X
Ethiopia	11	3,045	0	0	29	3,525	0.7	315
Gabon	0	1,894	1,583	0	65	3,543	3.3	418
Gambia, The	0	216	0	0	0	216	0.2	0
Ghana	7	3,342	0	0	698	4,045	0.2	161
Guinea	0	1,081	0	0	0	1,081	0.1	40
Guinea-Bissau	0	231	0	0	0	231	0.2	18
Kenya	253	5,683	0	0	747	6,683	0.3	172
Lesotho	X	X	X	X	X	X	X	X
Liberia	0	319	0	0	0	319	0.1	51
Libya	15	25,564	9,255	3,424	1,146	39,403	7.3	751
Madagascar	44	1,048	0	0	30	1,125	0.1	55
Malawi	44	612	0	0	69	725	0.1	37
Mali	0	454	0	0	10	465	0.0	51
Mauritania	15	2,865	0	0	187	3,067	1.4	70
Mauritius	176	1,315	0	0	0	1,491	1.3	861
Morocco	6,247	19,764	48	0	3,239	29,294	1.1	249
Mozambique	150	835	0	0	10	993	0.1	216
Namibia	X	X	X	X	X	X	X	X
Niger	458	645	0	0	15	1,118	0.1	48
Nigeria	150	29,217	8,563	51,493	1,296	90,717	0.8	2,301
Rwanda	0	484	0	2	3	491	0.1	29
Senegal	0	2,770	0	0	294	3,063	0.4	784
Sierra Leone	0	443	0	0	0	443	0.1	315
Somalia	0	0	0	0	12	11	0.0	0
South Africa	250,453	47,291	3,543	0	4,520	305,805	7.4	7,236
Sudan	0	3,375	0	0	125	3,499	0.1	139
Swaziland	454	0	0	0	0	454	0.5	0
Tanzania	15	2,026	0	0	399	2,440	0.1	158
Togo	0	572	0	0	174	744	0.2	0
Tunisia	238	8,849	3,818	261	2,143	15,308	1.7	586
Uganda	0	978	0	0	65	1,044	0.0	0
Zambia	795	1,462	0	0	149	2,404	0.3	110
Zimbabwe	5,738	3,495	0	0	498	9,735	0.9	0
EUROPE	**2,261,021**	**2,075,077**	**1,715,862**	**48,327**	**133,420**	**6,247,094**	**8.5**	**200,139**
Albania	176	1,550	22	0	100	1,847	0.5	0
Austria	12,439	29,184	15,165	0	2,492	59,280	7.4	627
Belarus, Rep	5,078	29,942	23,666	0	616	59,302	5.7	0
Belgium	33,449	42,099	24,281	0	3,986	103,816	10.3	15,224
Bosnia and Herzegovina	942	297	528	0	75	1,843	0.5	0
Bulgaria	28,594	17,613	9,442	0	1,046	56,697	6.7	861
Croatia, Rep	267	10,501	4,426	0	389	17,016	2.0	0
Czech Rep	77,113	19,591	12,941	0	2,404	112,049	10.9	0
Denmark	23,516	23,131	6,907	323	997	54,868	10.5	7,053
Estonia, Rep	0	3,243	1,198	0	47	16,444	0.0	51
Finland	23,351	20,485	6,731	0	448	51,014	10.0	1,938
France	58,913	202,821	67,887	0	10,464	340,085	5.9	19,756
Germany	353,543	309,623	150,990	1,011	19,932	835,099	10.2	23,472
Greece	32,943	37,263	99	3	5,980	76,284	7.3	13,894
Hungary	16,221	19,262	18,895	0	1,495	55,876	5.5	0
Iceland	209	1,554	0	0	41	1,803	6.7	344
Ireland	11,106	15,239	5,144	0	747	32,236	9.1	1,480
Italy	46,841	243,520	102,185	0	17,441	409,983	7.2	15,011
Latvia, Rep	993	6,141	2,081	0	101	9,318	3.7	0
Lithuania, Rep	1,074	9,208	4,206	0	324	14,814	4.0	0
Macedonia, FYR	X	X	X	X	X	X	X	X
Moldova, Rep	2,821	3,034	4,935	0	25	10,816	2.5	0
Netherlands	34,229	21,984	77,658	344	1,694	135,909	8.8	43,675
Norway	4,012	27,912	7,661	32,171	698	72,452	16.7	2,352
Poland, Rep	270,253	40,495	20,379	0	6,918	338,044	8.8	2,224
Portugal	15,521	32,668	0	0	3,737	51,926	5.3	3,074
Romania	40,817	37,501	39,784	0	2,990	121,092	5.3	0
Russian Federation	638,606	377,066	774,295	9,909	18,138	1,818,011	12.2	0
Slovak Rep	18,195	7,768	10,827	0	1,246	38,036	7.1	0
Slovenia, Rep	3,356	6,324	1,535	0	498	11,714	6.1	0
Spain	72,093	129,380	17,660	11	12,458	231,605	5.8	16,363
Sweden	10,790	31,195	1,557	0	1,046	44,591	5.1	4,734
Switzerland	348	31,488	5,023	0	1,993	38,853	5.4	3,781
Ukraine	214,919	68,095	149,715	0	5,481	438,211	8.5	0
United Kingdom	179,906	207,932	143,515	4,556	6,229	542,140	9.3	23,398
Yugoslavia, Fed Rep	X	X	X	X	X	X	X	X

	Carbon Dioxide Emissions, 1995 (000 metric tons)						Per Capita Carbon Dioxide	
	Solid Fuels	Liquid Fuels	Gaseous Fuels	Gas Flaring	Cement Manufacturing	Total Emissions	Emissions (metric tons) 1995	Bunker Fuels (a) (000 metric tons) 1995
NORTH AMERICA	**2,235,370**	**2,292,843**	**1,316,200**	**16,229**	**43,665**	**5,904,312**	**19.9**	**63,995**
Canada	93,626	180,961	151,796	4,021	5,343	435,749	14.8	4,507
United States	2,141,744	2,111,882	1,164,405	12,209	38,323	5,468,564	20.5	59,489
CENTRAL AMERICA	**23,952**	**356,500**	**73,921**	**5,102**	**16,526**	**477,045**	**3.6**	**4,210**
Belize	0	414	0	0	0	414	1.9	29
Costa Rica	0	4,741	0	0	493	5,232	1.5	0
Cuba	7	27,898	77	0	34	29,067	1.5	117
Dominican Rep	293	10,750	0	0	724	11,769	1.5	0
El Salvador	0	4,752	0	0	436	5,188	0.9	0
Guatemala	0	6,390	22	0	778	7,189	0.7	0
Haiti	0	612	0	0	25	638	0.1	0
Honduras	0	3,528	0	0	326	3,855	0.7	0
Jamaica	147	8,643	0	0	261	9,050	3.7	95
Mexico	23,358	257,158	61,830	3,544	11,945	357,834	3.9	1,480
Nicaragua	0	2,528	0	0	174	2,700	0.7	0
Panama	143	6,463	117	0	174	6,896	2.6	0
Trinidad and Tobago	0	3,430	11,824	1,558	299	17,111	13.3	788
SOUTH AMERICA	**76,695**	**454,710**	**160,974**	**26,187**	**28,774**	**747,331**	**2.4**	**12,454**
Argentina	3,572	59,767	56,334	6,600	3,189	129,464	3.7	1,004
Bolivia	0	5,276	2,928	1,923	349	10,475	1.4	0
Brazil	43,851	180,837	9,479	2,324	12,707	249,196	1.6	5,818
Chile	10,926	28,151	3,217	316	1,495	44,104	3.1	0
Colombia	15,246	38,670	8,075	739	4,796	67,524	1.9	0
Ecuador	0	19,009	506	1,969	1,146	22,633	2.0	788
Guyana	0	934	0	0	0	934	1.1	0
Paraguay	0	3,514	0	0	284	3,796	0.8	7
Peru	1,887	27,224	363	44	1,046	30,561	1.3	0
Suriname	0	2,125	0	0	25	2,151	5.0	0
Uruguay	4	5,078	0	0	299	5,379	1.7	385
Venezuela	1,209	83,253	80,073	12,271	3,438	180,243	8.2	4,400
ASIA	**3,960,971**	**2,800,139**	**772,034**	**64,248**	**434,181**	**8,270,648**	**2.3**	**168,266**
Afghanistan, Islamic State	15	824	322	22	57	1,238	0.1	15
Armenia, Rep	18	1,539	1,993	0	100	3,649	1.0	0
Azerbaijan	15	30,649	11,813	0	100	42,576	5.6	0
Bangladesh	0	7,493	13,304	0	140	20,932	0.2	37
Bhutan	59	110	0	0	70	238	0.1	0
Cambodia	0	498	0	0	0	498	0.0	0
China	2,489,036	447,004	34,394	0	222,049	3,192,484	2.7	3,133
Georgia	553	1,227	5,914	0	50	7,746	1.4	0
India	629,779	205,785	35,336	2,958	34,881	908,734	1.0	2,019
Indonesia	36,893	191,213	50,527	7,780	9,717	296,132	1.5	2,349
Iran, Islamic Rep	3,503	152,239	82,645	17,253	8,122	263,760	3.8	1,707
Iraq	0	83,902	6,035	96	8,969	99,001	4.9	0
Israel	16,232	28,301	44	0	1,744	46,320	8.4	1,854
Japan	331,731	630,868	119,076	0	45,084	1,126,753	9.0	36,574
Jordan	0	11,314	0	0	1,993	13,308	2.5	766
Kazakstan, Rep	165,682	34,064	20,837	0	897	221,478	13.2	0
Korea, Dem People's Rep	5,236	11,318	0	0	1,334	256,986	0.2	1,330
Korea, Rep	115,332	211,816	18,972	0	27,472	373,592	8.3	16,964
Kuwait	0	29,319	17,419	986	997	48,720	28.8	1,722
Kyrgyz Rep	2,045	1,795	1,473	0	149	5,463	1.2	0
Lao People's Dem Rep	4	308	0	0	0	308	0.1	0
Lebanon	502	11,344	0	0	1,495	13,341	4.4	513
Malaysia	6,555	58,855	30,455	5,422	5,315	106,604	5.3	784
Mongolia	6,793	1,612	0	0	54	8,457	3.4	0
Myanmar	172	3,800	2,788	14	258	7,031	0.1	0
Nepal	311	1,107	0	0	110	1,532	0.1	0
Oman	0	5,313	4,521	887	698	11,417	5.2	872
Pakistan	8,332	43,913	28,832	0	4,278	85,357	0.6	465
Philippines	5,980	50,296	0	0	4,883	61,159	0.9	1,942
Saudi Arabia	0	148,843	77,431	20,005	7,973	254,252	13.9	37,069
Singapore	110	62,614	0	0	947	63,669	19.1	35,479
Sri Lanka	4	5,434	0	0	448	5,888	0.3	1,301
Syrian Arab Rep	4	34,068	4,426	4,535	2,990	46,024	3.2	311
Tajikistan, Rep	66	410	3,213	0	50	3,741	0.7	0
Thailand	37,937	106,600	17,298	0	13,205	175,040	3.0	0
Turkey	63,929	73,522	11,945	0	16,520	165,917	2.7	1,385
Turkmenistan, Rep	0	12,271	15,865	0	199	28,334	7.0	0
United Arab Emirates	0	21,204	43,459	654	2,990	68,304	30.9	2,162
Uzbekistan, Rep	4,294	25,699	67,139	0	1,744	98,877	4.4	0
Vietnam	11,325	13,689	11	2,948	3,737	31,708	0.4	0
Yemen	0	13,912	0	0	498	14,411	1.0	473
OCEANIA	**184,625**	**94,051**	**40,425**	**0**	**3,427**	**322,535**	**11.3**	**11,417**
Australia	178,477	76,878	31,459	0	2,990	289,808	16.2	8,409
Fiji	51	645	0	0	39	736	1.0	169
New Zealand	5,657	12,622	8,808	0	349	27,440	7.7	2,682
Papua New Guinea	4	2,323	158	0	0	2,481	0.6	73
Solomon Islands	0	161	0	0	0	161	0.4	7

Notes: a. Bunker fuels are stored fuels to be used for ship or air transport.

Data in this table are reported as the mass of carbon dioxide emitted.

Data Table 16.2
Inventories of National Greenhouse Gas Emissions, 1989–94

Sources: Various

	Year	Carbon Dioxide Emissions (000 metric tons)				Methane Emissions from Anthropogenic Sources (000 metric tons)						Nitrous Oxide (000 metric tons)
		Fossil Fuels	Land Use Change	Industrial Processes {a}	Net CO2 Emissions {b}	Fossil Fuel Extraction	Fuel Combustion	Agriculture — Livestock	Agriculture — Other	Waste	Total Methane {c}	
WORLD												
AFRICA												
Côte d'Ivoire	1990	3,241	30,379	13	33,633	0	127	50	78	370	626	1
Egypt	1990	41,310	X	28,110	83,510 d	52	13	424	X	X e	489	X
Ethiopia	1992	2,336	13,393	130	15,859	15	340	974	171	28	1,597	5
Gambia, The	1993	206	1,648	X	1,854	X	2	13	8	7	30	0
Mauritius	1994	957	(208)	X	748	0	2	1	0	3	6	0
EUROPE												
Austria	1990	57,100	(15,000)	2,100	44,200 f	92	24	259	X	228	603	4
Belgium	1990	106,298	X	7,198	114,410 d	0	X	X	X	X	0	X
Bulgaria	1990	76,535	(5,801)	5,680	77,189	249	11	245	6	856	1,370	22
Czech Rep	1990	157,364	(2,265)	8,428	136,282 g	531	59	195	X	151	942	26
Denmark	1994	61,805	(2,600)	1,327	60,532	11	12	256	X	122	401	11
Estonia, Rep	1994	21,413	1,645	215	23,273	109	2	46	X	30	187	1
Finland	1994	57,500	(31,000) h	800	27,300	X i	16 j	92	X	135	247	11
France	1993	351,295	(37,189)	14,250	328,356	333	182	1,550	38	725	2,831	171
Germany	1993	886,000	(20,000)	25,200	891,200	1,460	130	1,688	X	1,917	5,203	191
Greece	1990	76,210	X	5,890	82,100 d	39	19	165	10	110	343	14
Hungary	1990	68,105	(4,467)	3,568	67,206	366	6	170	3	272	851	11
Iceland	1993	1,888	X	408	2,301 d	X	0	11	X	10	21	1
Ireland	1990	29,038	X	1,627	30,719 d	10	5	603	41	136	795	42
Italy	1990	401,350	(36,730)	27,591	392,211	348	66	1,541	319	1,611	3,901	120
Latvia, Rep	1990	22,606	(14,300)	371	8,677	2	2	111	X	44	159	2
Netherlands	1994	173,600	(1,700)	1,900	174,700	159	28	478	X	376	1,041	58
Norway	1994	30,682	(10,200) h	6,597	27,479	16	18	95	X	167	297	14
Poland, Rep	1992	360,988	X	10,603	371,591 d	793	29	702	1	941	2,474	50
Portugal	1990	38,686	X	3,462	42,148 d	2	14	163	13	35	227	11
Romania	1989	189,228	(2,925)	9,244	117,655 g	46		576	34	241	2,329	67
Russian Federation	1990	2,348,350	(587,200)	40,670	1,801,820	19,600 k	X l	4,900	100	2,400	27,360	225
Slovak Rep	1990	55,033	(4,451)	2,775	53,827	96	21	171	1	53	347	16
Spain	1990	209,425	(23,166)	17,696	204,156	695	76	772	115	491	2,151	94
Sweden	1994	53,081	(34,368) h	4,883	23,890	X i	34 j	202	X	100 j	336	25
Switzerland	1994	39,262	(5,150)	2,730	38,182	13	8	205	25	67	318	16
Ukraine	1990	668,360	(51,976)	31,780	648,164	6,220	60	2,235	15	930	9,460	25
United Kingdom	1994	542,689	(5,970)	8,373	545,605	808	91	1,116	X	1,862	3,877	94
NORTH AND CENTRAL AMERICA												
Canada	1994	451,835	X	25,019	483,558 d	1,695	40	964	X	815	3,514	111
United States	1994	5,103,000	(532,000)	23,083	4,594,083	7,630	945	8,558	638	10,400	28,171	359
Mexico	1990	312,906	89,148	X	402,053	753	X	1,804	35	386	2,977	X
SOUTH AMERICA												
Bolivia	1990	6,247	50,007	260	56,514	14	115 m	429	29	X	597	1
Brazil	1994	215,159	X	12,853	339,496 d	0	X	X	X	X	X	X
Ecuador	1990	18,878	13,736	1,150	33,764	21	20	281	108	64	555	1
Peru	1990	19,599	83,135	1,089	103,824	22	158	383	298	130	1,433	7
Venezuela	1990	107,334	80,612	2,867	190,813	1,827	12	853	98	221	3,170	454
ASIA												
Bangladesh	1990	74,727	(25,151)	X	110,860	80	190	520	473	74	1,335	3
China	1990	2,381,000	9,160	106,000	2,496,160	5,650	50	8,940	18,400	790	33,830	1,100
Indonesia	1990	116,881	(822,849)	33,769	(672,199)	527	316	864	2,039	X	3,746	2,769
Japan	1994	1,137,000	(90,000)	56,000	1,151,000	94	26	520	276	400	1,316 n	54 n
Kazakstan, Rep	1990	182,885	(90,000)	4,348	97,233	841	X	939	X	1,763	3,555	7
Mongolia	1990	13,970	18	220	14,208	9	5	301	X	15	329	0
Nepal	1990	913	X	83	996 d	84 k	X l	370	542	X	996	1
Oman	1992	303,633	X	4	303,641 o	0	X	X	X	1,518 o	1,518 o	X
Philippines	1990	38,245	84,202	3,286	168,444	8	220	315	559	138	1,290	8
OCEANIA												
Australia	1990	282,073	130,843	6,892	419,808	1,026	28	3,005	396	1,391	6,243	60
New Zealand	1994	24,749	(13,796)	2,680	13,633	23	8	1,436	X	423	1,895	19

Notes: a. Usually refers to cement production. b. Net emissions for some countries include sources of CO2 not listed. c. Total methane emissions for some countries include sources not listed. d. Total, not net, emissions. e. Waste is included under agriculture. f. Calculation of net emissions based on total emissions for 1992. g. Calculation of net emissions based on total emissions for 1993. h. 1990 figure. i. Emissions for fossil fuel extraction are included under fuel combustion. j. Includes fossil fuel extraction. k. Includes methane emissions from fuel combustion. l. Included under fossil fuel extraction. m. From land use and change. n. Methane and nitrous oxide emission reports are for 1993. o. 1993 data.

World CO₂ Emissions from Fossil Fuel Consumption and Cement Manufacturing, 1755–1995

ATMOSPHERE AND CLIMATE

Data Tables

Source: Carbon Dioxide Information Analysis Center

Year	Solid	Liquid	Gas	Cement Manufacturing	Gas Flaring	Total	Cumulative Total	Annual Per Capita Emissions (metric tons)
1755	11	0	0	X	X	11	55	X
1760	11	0	0	X	X	11	110	X
1765	11	0	0	X	X	11	165	X
1770	11	0	0	X	X	11	220	X
1775	15	0	0	X	X	15	293	X
1780	15	0	0	X	X	15	366	X
1785	18	0	0	X	X	18	458	X
1790	18	0	0	X	X	18	550	X
1795	22	0	0	X	X	22	660	X
1800	29	0	0	X	X	29	788	X
1805	33	0	0	X	X	33	953	X
1810	37	0	0	X	X	37	1,136	X
1815	44	0	0	X	X	44	1,341	X
1820	51	0	0	X	X	51	1,594	X
1825	62	0	0	X	X	62	1,880	X
1830	88	0	0	X	X	88	2,228	X
1835	92	0	0	X	X	92	2,664	X
1840	121	0	0	X	X	121	3,221	X
1845	158	0	0	X	X	158	3,913	X
1850	198	0	0	X	X	198	4,793	X
1855	260	0	0	X	X	260	5,928	X
1860	333	0	0	X	X	333	7,412	X
1865	436	0	0	X	X	436	9,343	X
1870	535	4	0	X	X	539	11,820	X
1875	685	4	0	X	X	689	15,026	X
1880	854	11	0	X	X	865	18,789	X
1885	1,000	15	4	X	X	1,015	23,636	X
1890	1,264	29	11	X	X	1,304	29,448	X
1895	1,440	40	7	X	X	1,488	36,453	X
1900	1,887	59	11	X	X	1,960	45,126	X
1905	2,330	88	18	X	X	2,433	56,217	X
1910	2,851	191	26	X	X	3,067	70,459	X
1915	2,873	224	33	X	X	3,129	86,683	X
1920	3,089	311	44	X	X	3,444	103,482	X
1925	3,085	454	66	X	X	3,605	120,359	X
1930	3,158	634	110	37	X	3,935	140,111	X
1935	2,972	1,205	220	33	X	4,433	158,527	X
1940	3,726	1,572	304	40	X	5,643	184,391	X
1945	3,004	1,803	432	26	X	5,265	212,750	X
1950	3,920	1,550	355	66	73	5,961	243,348	2
1951	4,137	1,755	421	73	81	6,467	249,815	3
1952	4,100	1,847	454	81	84	6,570	256,385	3
1953	4,122	1,953	480	88	81	6,731	263,116	3
1954	4,089	2,041	506	99	77	6,811	269,927	3
1955	4,426	2,290	550	110	95	7,471	277,398	3
1956	4,664	2,488	590	117	110	7,969	285,367	3
1957	4,800	2,616	652	125	106	8,295	293,662	3
1958	4,895	2,682	703	132	95	8,508	302,170	3
1959	5,064	2,895	784	147	92	8,984	311,154	3
1960	5,170	3,114	861	158	88	9,391	320,545	3
1961	4,943	3,316	931	165	88	9,442	329,987	3
1962	4,950	3,594	1,015	180	84	9,823	339,810	3
1963	5,119	3,858	1,099	187	92	10,354	350,165	3
1964	5,258	4,170	1,202	209	114	10,952	361,117	3
1965	5,353	4,474	1,286	216	132	11,457	372,574	3
1966	5,415	4,855	1,392	231	143	12,036	384,610	4
1967	5,305	5,218	1,502	238	191	12,454	397,064	4
1968	5,305	5,687	1,630	256	205	13,084	410,148	4
1969	5,448	6,134	1,784	271	245	13,883	424,031	4
1970	5,701	6,734	1,891	286	278	14,890	438,922	4
1971	5,701	7,130	2,030	308	322	15,488	454,409	4
1972	5,760	7,530	2,136	326	344	16,103	470,513	4
1973	5,789	8,207	2,228	348	403	16,975	487,488	4
1974	5,778	8,222	2,264	352	392	17,005	504,492	4
1975	6,123	7,808	2,283	348	341	16,902	521,395	4
1976	6,258	8,475	2,371	377	399	17,880	539,275	4
1977	6,485	8,753	2,367	396	381	18,386	557,661	4
1978	6,544	8,731	2,470	425	392	18,562	576,223	4
1979	6,896	9,285	2,616	436	366	19,595	595,818	4
1980	7,101	8,819	2,660	440	326	19,342	615,160	4
1981	6,998	8,321	2,697	443	264	18,719	633,879	4
1982	7,229	7,973	2,678	443	253	18,573	652,452	4
1983	7,247	7,918	2,686	458	231	18,540	670,992	4
1984	7,584	8,006	2,898	469	213	19,166	690,158	4
1985	8,152	7,951	3,012	480	209	19,800	709,959	4
1986	8,376	8,350	3,078	502	198	20,504	730,462	4
1987	8,563	8,387	3,309	524	187	20,969	751,431	4
1988	8,797	8,764	3,477	557	194	21,790	773,221	4
1989	8,918	8,900	3,602	572	183	22,178	795,399	4
1990	8,698	9,153	3,737	575	220	22,383	817,783	4
1991	8,468	9,548	3,774	590	256	22,636	840,419	4
1992	8,563	9,149	3,734	619	227	22,292	862,711	4
1993	8,336	9,153	3,811	649	231	22,178	884,889	4
1994	8,922	9,310	3,898	689	234	23,054	907,943	4
1995	9,307	9,409	4,177	707	234	23,838	931,781	4

Note: Mass of carbon dioxide.

Data Table 16.4
Atmospheric Concentrations of Greenhouse and Ozone-Depleting Gases, 1965–96

Source: Carbon Dioxide Information Analysis Center

Year	Carbon Dioxide (CO2) ppm	Carbon Tetra-chloride (CCl4) ppt	Methyl Chloro-form (CH3CCl3) ppt	CFC-11 (CCl3F) ppt	CFC-12 (CCl2F2) ppt	CFC-113 (C2Cl3F3) ppt	Total Gaseous Chlorine ppt	Nitrous Oxide (N2O) ppb	Methane (CH4) ppb
Preindustrial	280.0 a	0	0	0	0	0	0	285 a	700 a
1965	319.9	X	X	X	X	X	X	X	X
1966	321.2	X	X	X	X	X	X	X	X
1967	322.0	X	X	X	X	X	X	X	X
1968	322.9	X	X	X	X	X	X	X	X
1969	324.5	X	X	X	X	X	X	X	X
1970	325.5	X	X	X	X	X	X	X	X
1971	326.2	X	X	X	X	X	X	X	X
1972	327.3	X	X	X	X	X	X	X	X
1973	329.5	X	X	X	X	X	X	X	X
1974	330.1	X	X	X	X	X	X	X	X
1975	331.0	X	X	X	X	X	X	X	X
1976	332.0	X	X	X	X	X	X	X	X
1977	333.7	X	X	X	X	X	X	X	X
1978	335.3	88	58	139	257	X	1,457	298	X
1979	336.7	88	63	147	272	X	1,529	299	X
1980	338.5	90	71	158	289	X	1,622	299	X
1981	339.8	91	76	166	305	X	1,698	299	X
1982	341.0	93	82	175	325	26	1,871	301	X
1983	342.6	94	86	182	341	28	1,945	302	X
1984	344.3	95	89	190	355	31	2,024	303	X
1985	345.7	97	93	200	376	36	2,127	304	X
1986	347.0	98	97	209	394	40	2,222	305	1,600
1987	348.8	100	100	219	411	48	2,321	306	1,611
1988	351.3	101	104	231	433	53	2,432	306	1,619
1989	352.8	101	108	240	452	59	2,531	306	1,641
1990	354.0	102	111	249	469	66	2,626	307	1,645
1991	355.5	102	114	254	483	71	2,691	307	1,657
1992	356.3	101	118	260	496	77	2,762	308	1,673
1993	357.0	101	113	260	502	79	2,768	308	1,671
1994	358.9	101	108	261	509	81	2,774	309	1,666
1995	360.9	99	97	261	519	82	2,752	309	1,681
1996	362.6	99	89	261	522	82	2,731	310	1,670

Notes: a. Approximately. All estimates are by volume; ppm = parts per million; ppb = parts per billion; and ppt = parts per trillion.

Sources and Technical Notes

Data Table 16.1

CO₂ Emissions from Fossil Fuel Burning and Cement Manufacturing, 1995

Sources: All data are from Carbon Dioxide Information Analysis Center (CDIAC), Environmental Sciences Division, Oak Ridge National Laboratory, "1995 Estimates of CO₂ Emissions from Fossil Fuel Burning and Cement Manufacturing based on the United Nations Energy Statistics and the U.S. Geological Survey Cement Manufacturing Data," ORNL/CDIAC-25, NDP-030 (an Internet-accessible numerical database), available at: http://cdiac.ESD.ORNL.Gov/ndps/ndp030r6.html (Oak Ridge, Tennessee, September 1997).

These data from CDIAC represent a complete harmonized global data set of carbon dioxide (CO₂) emissions. Individual country estimates, based on more detailed information and a country-specific methodology, could differ. An experts meeting, convened by the Organisation for Economic Co-Operation and Development (OECD) in February 1991, recommended that when countries calculate their own emissions of CO₂, they use a more detailed method when these data are available (*Estimation of Greenhouse Gas Emissions and Sinks*, OECD, Paris, 1991). Such data are currently available for an increasing number of countries, but are still limited mostly to developed countries (see Data Table 16.2). CDIAC's method has the advantage of calculating CO₂ emissions from a single common data set available for all countries.

This table includes data on industrial additions to the CO₂ flux from *solid fuels*, *liquid fuels*, *gaseous fuels*, *gas flaring*, and *cement manufacturing*. CDIAC annually calculates emissions of CO₂ from the burning of fossil fuels and the manufacture of cement for most of the countries of the world. Estimates of total and per capita national *emissions* do not include *bunker fuels* used in international transport because of the difficulty of apportioning these fuels among the countries benefiting from that transport. Emissions from bunker fuels are shown separately for the country where the fuel was delivered.

CDIAC calculates emissions from data on the net apparent consumption of fossil fuels (based on the World Energy Data Set maintained by the United Nations Statistical Division) and from data on world cement manufacturing (based on the Cement Manufacturing Data Set maintained by the U.S. Geological Survey). Emissions are calculated using global average fuel chemistry and usage.

Although estimates of world emissions are probably within 10 percent of actual emissions, individual country estimates may depart more severely from reality. CDIAC points out that the time trends from a consistent, uniform time series should be more accurate than the individual values. Each year, CDIAC recalculates the entire time series from 1950 to the present, incorporating its most recent understanding and the latest corrections to the database. As a result, the carbon emissions estimate data set has become more consistent, and probably more accurate, each year.

Emissions of CO₂ are often calculated and reported in terms of their content of elemental carbon. For this table, their values were converted to the actual mass of CO₂ by multiplying the carbon mass by 3.664 (the ratio of the mass of carbon to that of CO₂).

Solid fuels, *liquid fuels*, and *gaseous fuels* are primarily, but not exclusively, coals, petroleum products, and natural gas, respectively. *Gas flaring* is the practice of burning off gas released in the process of petroleum extraction, a practice that is declining. During *cement manufacturing*, cement is calcined to produce calcium oxide. In the process, 0.498 metric ton of CO₂ is released for each ton of cement production. *Total emissions* consist of the sum of the CO₂ produced during the consumption of solid, liquid, and gaseous fuels, and from gas flaring and the manufacture of cement. *Per capita carbon dioxide emissions* are calculated by dividing the total emissions by the 1995 population of each country.

Combustion of different fossil fuels releases CO_2 at different rates. For the same level of energy consumption, burning oil releases about 1.5 times the amount of CO_2 released by burning natural gas; coal combustion releases about twice the CO_2 of natural gas.

It was assumed that approximately 1 percent of the coal used by industry and power plants was not burned and that an additional few percent were converted to nonoxidizing uses. Other oxidative reactions of coal are assumed to be of negligible importance in carbon budget modeling. CO_2 emissions from gas flaring and cement manufacturing production make up about 3 percent of the CO_2 emitted by fossil fuel combustion.

Data Table 16.2

Inventories of National Greenhouse Gas Emissions, 1989–94

Sources: Bangladesh: Bangladesh Climate Change Country Study, *Emission Inventory, Final Report* (Bangladesh Centre for Advanced Studies, 1996). Bolivia: Programa Nacional de Cambios Climaticos, *Inventario de Emisiones de Gases de Efecto Invernadero de Origen Antropogenico de Bolivia para el Año 1990* (Ministerio de Desarrollo Sostenible y Medio Ambiente, 1996). Brazil: *CO₂ Emissions from Energy Sector—Top-Down Approach*, Minesterio de Cienceo y Technologia. Available online at http://www.mct.gov.br/GABIN/CPMG/CLIMATE/PROGRAMA/ing/tab94.html (1997). China: Carbon Dioxide—National Conditions Analysis and Research Group of China Academy of Sciences, *No. IV Report of National Conditions, Opportunities, and Challenges—Goals of Economic Development and Study on Fundamental Development Strategy* (Science Press, Beijing, 1996); Methane—Wang Hanchen, National Environmental Protection Agency of 5.29 (NEPA, Beijing, 1997). Cote d'Ivoire: Ministère de l'Enseignement Superieur de la Recherche et de l'Innovation Technologique, *Emissions et Puits des Gaz a Effet de Serre en Cote d'Ivoire* (École Nationale Superieure des Travaux Publics, 1996). Ecuador: Ecuador Climate Change Country Study, *Modulo 4: Inventario Nacional de Emisiones Gaseosas que Producen el Efecto Invernador*, Borrador del Informe Final, Año 1990 (Ministerio de Energia y Minas, 1996). Egypt: El-Raey *et al.*, *Egypt: Inventory and Mitigation Options, and Vulnerability and Adaptation Assessment*, Interim Report on Climate Change Country Studies (1995). Available online at: http://www.gcrio.org/CSP/IR/IRegypt.html (1997). Ethiopia: Ethio–U.S. Country Study Project, *Greenhouse Gases Emission Inventory and Vulnerability, Adaptation, and Mitigation Assessment to Climate Change in Ethiopia Technical Report (Crop, Water Resources, Forestry, Grasslands and Livestock, and Energy Sectors)* (National Meteorological Services Agency, 1996). The Gambia: Bubu P. Jallow, *The 1993 Greenhouse Gas Emissions Inventory of The Gambia: A Synthesis Report* (National Climate Committee). Indonesia: U.S.–EPA Indonesia Country Study Program, *In-ventory of Greenhouse Gases Emissions and Sinks in Indonesia* (The State Ministry of Environment, 1996). Kazakstan: Kavalerchik *et al.*, *Kazakstan: Overall Approaches and Preliminary Results from Country Study*, Interim Report on Climate Change Country Studies (1995). Available online at: http://www.gcrio.org/CSP/IR/IRkazakh.html (1997). Kenya: Kenya Country Study on Climate Change, *Inventory of Greenhouse Gases (GHG) from Agricultural Activities, Second Progress Report* (1997). Mauritius: National Climate Committee: U.S. Country Study Programme Mauritius, *National Inventory of Greenhouse Gases (1990)*, Mauritius Meteorological Services Report No. 2 (Mauritius Meteorological Services, 1996). Mexico: Mexico Country Studies Project Team, *Mexico: Emissions Inventory, Mitigation Scenarios, and Vulnerability and Adaptation—Interim Report*, Country Study, Mexico. Available online at http:www.gcrio.org/CSP/IR/IRmexico.html (1997). Mongolia: U.S. Country Studies Program: Mongolia's Study Team, *Mongolia Greenhouse Gas Inventory 1990*, Mongolia's Country Studies Report on Climate Change, Volume 2 (Ulaanbaatar, 1996). Nepal: U.S. Country Studies Team—Nepal, *A Report on Inventory of Greenhouse Gases Emission for Nepal, Final Draft* (Integrated Methodical Research Centre and Associates [PVT] Ltd., 1997). Oman: Oman Country Studies Project Team, *National Emission Inventory of Greenhouse Gases* (Sultanate of Oman Ministry of Regional Municipalities and Environment, 1995). Peru: Peru Climate Change Country Study Team, *Peru's National Greenhouse Gas Inventory 1990* (Universidad Nacional de Ingenieria, 1996). Philippines: Philippine Country Study on Climate Change, *National Greenhouse Gas Inventory 1990* (PAGASA, 1996). Ukraine: Country Study on Climate Change in Ukraine, *Development of Greenhouse Gas Emissions Inventory, Final Report (Supplement)* (Agency for Rational Energy Use and Ecology, 1995). Venezuela: Venezuela Country Studies Team, *Venezuela Greenhouse Gas Emissions* (Ministry of Environment and Renewable Natural Resources). Available online at: http://www.gcrio.org/CSP/IR/gifs/VenTab1.gif (1997).

Australia, Austria, Belgium, Bulgaria, Canada, Czech Republic, Denmark, Estonia, Finland, France, Germany, Greece, Hungary, Iceland, Ireland, Italy, Japan, Latvia, Netherlands, New Zealand, Norway, Poland, Portugal, Romania, Russian Federation, Slovakia, Spain, Sweden, Switzerland, United Kingdom, and United States: Compiled by the Secretariat of the Climate Change Convention from national sources. Available online at: http://www.unfccc.de/fccc/emiss/file08.htm#emis94.

These inventories are detailed estimates of emissions and not inventories as the word is commonly understood. Estimates of other gas emissions at the national level have been shown to be highly labile due to changes in the understanding of the underlying data, changes in the methods used in estimation, and even changes in the extent of the phenomenon under study. Variations of 30 or 40 per-cent from one estimate of a particular year's emissions to a later estimate of the same year's emissions are not unheard of.

Carbon dioxide (CO₂) emissions from *fossil fuels* include emissions from combustion and other industrial processes. CO_2 emissions from *land use change* are estimates of the emissions associated with the clearing of land or increases in forest cover or forest biomass. *Industrial processes* refers to emissions from industry; most of these emissions result as a byproduct of cement manufacturing and steel production. *Net CO₂ emissions* sums energy use and negative or positive emissions from forest growth.

Methane emissions from anthropogenic sources: fossil fuel extraction includes methane released from venting and leakage from oil, gas, coal production, and distribution systems. *Fuel combustion* includes emissions from combustion of fuels for human use. In some countries this includes biomass. Under *agriculture*, emissions from *livestock* include enteric fermentation and animal waste. *Other* agricultural sources include wet rice agriculture, methane released from soils, and the burning of agricultural waste and grazing lands. *Waste* includes emissions from landfills. *Total methane* is the total of all sources, and for some countries, includes emissions from industrial processes and land use change.

Nitrous oxide (N₂O) is another potent greenhouse gas that is difficult to model. In descending order of importance, the primary sources of N_2O are agriculture, industry, and energy use for transport.

Data Table 16.3

World CO₂ Emissions from Fossil Fuel Consumption and Cement Manufacturing, 1755–1995

Source: Carbon Dioxide Information Analysis Center (CDIAC), Environmental Sciences Division, Oak Ridge National Laboratory, "Global CO₂ Emissions from Fossil-Fuel Burning, Cement Manufacture, and Gas Flaring: 1751–1995," prepared by Gregg Marland and Tom Boden (CDIAC), Bob Andres (University of Alaska-Fairbanks), and Cathy Johnston (University of Tennessee); and "1995 Estimates of CO₂ Emissions from Fossil Fuel Burning and Cement Manufacturing Based on the United Nations Energy Statistics and the U.S. Geological Survey Cement Manufacturing Data," ORNL/CDIAC-25, NDP-030 (an Internet-accessible numerical database), available at: http://cdiac.ESD.ORNL.GOV/ndps/ndp030r6.html (Oak Ridge, Tennessee, September 1995).

For years after 1950, CDIAC calculates world emissions from data on the global production of fossil fuels (based on the World Energy Data Set maintained by the United Nations Statistical Division), and from data on world cement manufacturing (based on the Cement Manufacturing Data Set maintained by the U.S. Geological Survey). Emissions are calculated using global average fuel chemistry and usage. These data account for all fuels including "bunker fuels" not accounted for in the totals in Data Table 16.1, which are also shown separately. For further information, see the Technical Notes for Data Table 16.1.

For years prior to 1950, estimates are based on CDIAC's historical database of national emissions.

Data Table 16.4

Atmospheric Concentrations of Greenhouse and Ozone-Depleting Gases, 1965–96

Sources: Carbon dioxide: Charles D. Keeling and T.P. Whorf, Carbon Dioxide Information Analysis Center (CDIAC), Environmental Sciences Division, Oak Ridge National Laboratory, "Atmospheric CO_2 Concentrations—Mauna Loa Observatory, Hawaii, 1958–1996" (revised August 1997), ORNL/CDIAC-25, NDP-001/R7 (an Internet-accessible numerical database), available at http://cdiac.ESD.ORNL.GOV/ftp/ndp001r7/ (Oak Ridge, Tennessee, September 1997). Other trace gases: CDIAC, Environmental Sciences Division, Oak Ridge National Laboratory, ORNL/CDIAC-25, DB-1001/R3 (an Internet-accessible numerical database), available at: http://cdiac.ESD.ORNL.GOV/ndps/alegage.html (ALE/GAGE/AGAGE Monthly Readings at Cape Grim, Tasmania), originally R.G. Prinn et al., "Atmospheric CFC-11 (CCl_3F), CFC-12 (CCl_2F_2), and N_2O from the ALE-GAGE Network," in T.A. Boden, et al., eds., *Trends '93: A Compendium of Data on Global Change* (ORNL/CDIAC-65, CDIAC, Oak Ridge, Tennessee, 1994), pp. 396–420.

The trace gases listed here affect atmospheric ozone, contribute to the greenhouse effect, or both. *Carbon dioxide (CO_2)* accounts for about half the increase in the greenhouse effect and is emitted to the atmosphere by natural and anthropogenic processes. See the Technical Notes for Data Tables 16.1 and 16.2 for further details.

Atmospheric CO_2 concentrations are monitored at many sites worldwide; the data presented here are from Mauna Loa, Hawaii (19° 32' North latitude, 155° 35' West longitude). Trends at Mauna Loa reflect global trends, although CO_2 concentrations differ significantly among monitoring sites at any given time. For example, the average annual concentration at the South Pole in 1988 was 2.4 parts per million (ppm) lower than at Mauna Loa.

Annual means disguise large daily and seasonal variations in CO_2 concentrations. The seasonal variation is caused by photosynthetic plants storing larger amounts of carbon from CO_2 during the summer than in the winter. Some annual mean figures were derived from interpolated data.

Data are revised to correct for drift in instrument calibration, hardware changes, and perturbations to "background" conditions. Details concerning data collection, revisions, and analysis are contained in C.D. Keeling et al., "Measurement of the Concentration of Carbon Dioxide at Mauna Loa Observatory, Hawaii," in *Carbon Dioxide Review: 1982*, W.C. Clark, ed. (Oxford University Press, New York, 1982).

Data for all other gases are from values monitored at Cape Grim, Tasmania (45° 41' South latitude, 144° 41' East longitude) under the Atmospheric Lifetime Experiment (ALE), Global Atmospheric Gases Experiment (GAGE), and Advanced GAGE (AGAGE). Although gas concentrations at any given time vary among monitoring sites, the data reported here reflect global trends. Cape Grim generally receives unpolluted air from the southeast and is the ALE/GAGE/AGAGE station with the longest, most complete dataset. Air samples were collected 4 times daily for ALE and 12 times daily for GAGE/AGAGE. The annual values shown here are averages of monthly values calculated by CDIAC. Missing values were interpolated.

Carbon tetrachloride (CCl_4) is an intermediate product in the production of CFC-11 and CFC-12. It is also used in other chemical and pharmaceutical applications and for grain fumigation. Compared with other gases, CCl_4 makes a small contribution to the greenhouse effect and to stratospheric ozone depletion.

Methyl chloroform (CH_3CCl_3) is used primarily as an industrial degreasing agent and as a solvent for paints and adhesives. Its contribution to the greenhouse effect and to stratospheric ozone depletion is also small.

CFC-11 (CCl_3F), CFC-12 (CCl_2F_2), and CFC-113 ($C_2Cl_3F_3$) are potent depletors of stratospheric ozone. Together, their cumulative effect may equal one fourth of the greenhouse contribution of CO_2.

Total gaseous chlorine is calculated by multiplying the number of chlorine atoms in each of the chlorine-containing gases (carbon tetrachloride, methyl chloroform, and the CFCs) by the concentration of that gas.

Nitrous oxide (N_2O) is emitted by aerobic decomposition of organic matter in oceans and soils, by bacteria, by combustion of fossil fuels and biomass (fuelwood and cleared forests), by the use of nitrogenous fertilizers, and through other processes. N_2O is an important depletor of stratospheric ozone; present levels may contribute one twelfth of the amount contributed by CO_2 toward the greenhouse effect.

Methane (CH_4) is emitted through the release of natural gas and as one of the products of anaerobic respiration. Sources of anaerobic respiration include the soils of moist forests, wetlands, bogs, tundra, and lakes. Emission sources associated with human activities include livestock management (enteric fermentation in ruminants), anaerobic respiration in the soils associated with wet rice agriculture, and combustion of fossil fuels and biomass (fuelwood and cleared forests). CH_4 acts to increase ozone in the troposphere and lower stratosphere; its cumulative greenhouse effect is currently thought to be one third that of CO_2, but on a molecule-for-molecule basis, its effect, ignoring any feedback or involvement in any atmospheric processes, is 11 to 30 times that of CO_2.

Acknowledgments

World Resources 1998–99 is the product of a unique international collaboration involving many institutions and individuals. Without their advice, support, information, and hard work, this volume could not have been produced.

We are especially grateful for the advice and assistance of our many colleagues at the World Resources Insitute (WRI), the United Nations Environment Programme (UNEP), the United Nations Development Programme (UNDP), and the World Bank. Their advice on the selection of material to be covered and their diligent review of manuscript drafts and data tables, often under pressure, have been invaluable.

Institutions

We wish to recognize and thank the many other institutions that have contributed data, reviews, and encouragement to this project. They include:

The Carbon Dioxide Information Analysis Center (CDIAC)
The Defense Meteorological Satellite Program (DMSP)
The Demographic and Health Surveys (DHS)
The European Environment Agency (EEA)
The Food and Agriculture Organization of the United Nations (FAO)
The Global Environmental Monitoring System of UNEP (GEMS)
The International Energy Agency (IEA)
The International Food Policy Research Institute (IFPRI)
The International Institute for Environment and Development (IIED)
The International Labour Office (ILO)
The International Species Information System (ISIS)
The National Aeronautics and Space Administration (NASA)
The National Oceanic and Atmospheric Administration (NOAA)
The Natural Resources Defense Council (NRDC)
The Organisation for Economic Co-Operation and Development (OECD)
The Organization of American States (OAS)
The Oxford Committee for Famine Relief (OXFAM)
The Population Reference Bureau (PRB)
The Ramsar Convention Bureau
The United Nations Centre for Human Settlements (Habitat)
The United Nations Children's Fund (UNICEF)
The United Nations Department of Economic and Social Information and Policy Analysis (UNDESIPA)
The United Nations Educational, Scientific, and Cultural Organization (UNESCO)
The United Nations Population Division
The United Nations Statistical Division (UNSTAT)
The United States Energy Information Administration (USEIA)
The United States Environmental Protection Agency (U.S. EPA)
The United States Geological Survey (USGS)
The World Conservation Monitoring Centre (WCMC)
The World Conservation Union (IUCN)
The World Health Organization (WHO)

Individuals

Many individuals contributed to the development of this volume by providing expert advice, data, or careful review of manuscripts. While final responsibility for the chapters rests with the *World Resources* staff, the contributions of these colleagues are reflected throughout the book. We are especially grateful to the writers who contributed boxes, background papers, regional profiles, and guest commentaries. All performed diligently and then endured patiently our numerous queries and often substantial editorial changes. Some of these outside authors have bylines in the chapters; others are acknowledged below. Many of our colleagues at the World Resources Institute contributed to the writing of this volume as well; they are acknowledged below.

Special thanks to Marion Cheatle of UNEP, Robert Watson of the World Bank, and Ralph Schmidt of UNDP, who coordinated access to pertinent experts at their agencies:

UNEP

Hussein Abaza, Uno Abrahamsen, Yinka Adebayo, Jacqueline Aloisi de Larderel, Alex Alusa, Ali Ayoub, Françoise Belmont, Hassane Bendahmane, Brenda Bender, Jaques Berney, Aiko Bode, Tore Brevik, Franklin Cardy, Uttam Dabholkar, Arthur L. Dahl, Joanne Fox-Przeworski, Hiremagalur Gopalan, Michael Graber, Midori Hatta, Christine Hogan, Mike Jansen, Sergei Khromov, Ji-Tae Kim, Isabella Masinde, Timo Maukonen, C. Mohanty, Elizabeth Maruma Mrema, Naomi Poulton, Walter Rast, Nelson Sabogal, Madhava Sarma, Bernard Schanzenbächer, Frits Schlingemann, Gerhart Schneider, Miriam Schomaker, Megumi Seki, Rajendra Shende, M. Short, Surendra Shrestha, Ashbindu Singh, Cheikh Sow, Janet Stevens, Agneta Sundén-Bylehn, Bai-Mass M. Taal, Peter Usher, Veerle Vandeweerd, Laura Williamson, James B. Willis, Ron Witt, Kaveh Zahedi, Hamdallah Zedan, Jinhua Zhang.

UNEP COLLABORATING CENTRES AND OTHER ORGANIZATIONS

Ayman A. Al-Hassan, Royal Scientific Society, Jordan; Clement Dorm-Adzobu, Network for Environment and Sustainable Development, Côte d'Ivoire; Mohamed Nabil Alaa El-Din, Arabian Gulf University, Bahrain; Ruben Mnatsakanian, Central European University, Hungary; Laszlo Pinter, International Institute for Sustainable Development (IISD), Canada; Marisabel Romaggi, University of Chile; Zhang Shigang, National Environmental Protection Agency, China; Leena Srivastava, Tata Energy Research Institute (TERI), India.

UNDP

Sakiko Fukuda-Parr, Luis Gomez-Echeverri, Frank Hartvelt, Selim Jehan, Thomas Johansson, Karen Jorgensen, Inge Kaul, Roberto Lenton, Peter Matlon, Ellen Morris.

THE WORLD BANK

Isabelle Alegre, Derek Byerlee, Miriam Claeson, Gloria Davis, Shelton Davis, Philippe Durand, François Falloux, François Gadelle, Yves Genevier, James Listorti, Magda Lovei, Kseniya Lvovsky, Richard Newfarmer, Thomas Novotny, Michel Petit, Robert Robelus, Tjaart W. Schillhorn van Veen, Andrew Steer, Robert E. Tillman, Cor P.W. van der Sterren, Hua Wang.

WRI

Karim Ahmed, Patricia Ardila, Matt Arnold, Christopher Bacon, Darryl Banks, Chip Barber, Theresa Bradley, J. Alan Brewster, Frank Dexter Brown, Jake Brunner, Dirk Bryant, Lauretta Burke, Liz Cook, Kathleen Courrier, Devra L. Davis, Rob Day, Daryl Ditz, Christine Elias, Paul Faeth, Katrine Fitzgerald, Tom Fox, Shirley Geer, Michelle Gottlieb, Allen Hammond, Julie Harlan, Norbert Henninger, Nels Johnson, Nancy Kete, Jonathan Lash, Jim MacKenzie, Kenton Miller, Daniel Nielsen, Mary Paden, Walter Reid, Robert Repetto, Frances Seymour, Nigel Sizer, Oretta Tarkhani, Lori Ann Thrupp, Dan Tunstall, Donna Wise, Deanna Madvin Wolfire, Changhua Wu.

Part I   Environmental Change and Human Health

PRINCIPAL AUTHORS

Chapter 1   *Leslie Roberts*
Chapter 2   *Carolina Katz* and *Gregory Mock*
Chapter 3   *Carolina Katz*

With contributions by Patricia Ardila, Jamie Bartram, Nancy Carson, Ulisses Confalonieri, Afzal Khan, Margie Patlak, and Kirk Smith.

This special section of *World Resources* is a collaborative effort of colleagues at numerous institutions around the world who contributed ideas, data, background papers, reviews, and attended planning meetings. Special thanks to several individuals who played a key role in shaping the report: Roberto Bertollini, Bonnie Bradford, Marion Cheatle, Ulisses Confalonieri, Carlos Corvalán, Devra L. Davis, Jeffrey Foran, Tord Kjellström, Roberto Lenton, Gordon McGranahan, Anthony McMichael, Walter Reid, Kirk Smith, Carolyn Stephens, and Robert Watson. The financial support provided by the Risk Science Institute of the International Life Sciences Institute (ILSI) helped make the health section possible.

U.S. AGENCY FOR INTERNATIONAL DEVELOPMENT (U.S. AID)

We wish to thank our colleagues at U.S. AID for their intellectual and financial support of this special section, as well as the comments on each chapter: John E. Borrazzo, Curt Grimm, David Hales, Gary Merritt, Sam Myers, John Tomaro.

ENVIRONMENTAL HEALTH PROJECT (EHP)

Andrew A. Arata, Pat Billig, Eugene Brantly, Karen Ramsey, Pandu Wijeyaratne.

SPECIAL ADVISORS

The section profited enormously from the insightful comments of our group of Special Advisors, who painstakingly reviewed every chapter. They include: Eugene Brantly, EHP; David C. Christiani, Harvard University School of Public Health; Paul Epstein, Harvard Center for Health and the Environment; Jeffrey A. Foran, ILSI Risk Science Institute; Duane J. Gubler, United States Centers for Disease Control and Prevention (CDC); Tord Kjellström, WHO; Wilfried Kreisel, WHO; Changsheng Li, Fraunhofer Institute of Atmospheric Environment; Gordon McGranahan, Stockholm Environment Institute (SEI); Anthony McMichael, London School of Hygiene and Tropical Medicine (LSHTM); Isabelle Romieu, Centro Panamericano de Ecología Humana y Salud; Ellen Silbergeld, University of Maryland Medical School; Kirk Smith, University of California, Berkeley; Jacob Songsore, University of Ghana; Carolyn Stephens, LSHTM.

REVIEWERS AND OTHER CONTRIBUTORS

We are grateful to the following individuals for their thoughtful comments on this special section: Arnold Aspelin, U.S. EPA; Oral Ataniyazova, National Academy of Sciences of Uzbekistan; John Balbus, George Washington University; Leslie Bernstein, University of Southern California/Norris Cancer Center; Martin Harold Birley, Liverpool School of Tropical Medicine; Aaron Blair, National Cancer Institute; Jerome Blondell, U.S. EPA; Martin Bobak, University College, London Medical School; Pierre Boileau, OECD; Sandy Buffett; Donald S. Burke, Walter Reed Army Institute of Research; Sandy Cairncross, LSHTM; Dara Carr, DHS; Lincoln Chen, Harvard Univeristy; Eric Chivian, Harvard Medical School; Rita R. Colwell, University of Maryland; Ralph Cooper, U.S. EPA; Angela Cropper, IUCN; Christopher De Rosa, Agency for Toxic Substances and Disease Registry; Elizabeth Economy, Council on Foreign Relations; Steven A. Esrey, UNICEF; Tony Fletcher, LSHTM; Theodore M. Fliedner, Global Advisory Committee on Health Research; Robert M. Friedman, The H. John Heinz III Center for Science, Economics, and Environment; Luz-Agusto Galvao, Pan American Health Organization (PAHO); Peter Gergen, Agency for Health Care Policy and Research; Bernard Goldstein, Rutgers University; H.R. Hapsara, WHO; Donald A. Henderson, The Johns Hopkins University; Polly Hoppin; Michael Horowitz, International Development Association (IDA); Bill Jobin, Blue Nile Associates; Robert Kavlock, U.S. EPA; Amy Kyle, University of California, Berkeley; Joseph LaDou, University of California-San Francisco; Phil Landrigan, Mount Sinai; James Le Duc, CDC; Stuart Levy,

Tufts University; Giovanni Lombardi, LSHTM; Alan Lopez, WHO; John Magistro, NOAA; Kathryn R. Mahaffey, U.S. EPA; B. Mansourian, WHO; Christopher McGahey, Associates in Rural Development, Inc.; Stephen S. Morse, Defense Advanced Research Projects Agency (DARPA); Christopher Murray, Harvard University; Chris Nielsen, Harvard University; Charles Normand, LSHTM; Wafaas Ofosu-Amaah; Horst Otterstader, PAHO; Ari Patrinos, U.S. Department of Energy (DOE); Jonathan A. Patz, The Johns Hopkins School of Public Health; Gerald Poje, National Chemical Safety and Hazard Investment Board; David Rall; Marilyn Roberts, University of Washington; David Satterthwaite, International Institute for Environment and Development (IIED); Bruce A. Sayers, DALY Review Group, Global Advisory Committee on Health Research; Jacob Scherr, NRDC; Susan M. Sieber, National Cancer Institute; Jacqueline Sims, WHO; Carl Smith, Foundation for Advancements in Science and Education (FASE); Gerald R. Smith, USGS; Ellen Spitalnik, U.S. EPA; Steve Stellman, American Health Foundation; M. A. Subramanian, WHO; Valerie Thomas, Princeton University; Ellis Turner, EHP; William Vorley, Leopold Center for Sustainable Agriculture; Diane Wagener, National Center for Health Statistics; John Walsh; James Wargo, Yale School of Forestry and Environment; Ellen Wasserman; William Waters, George Washington University; Wade Welshons, University of Missouri; John Wickham, Yale University; Jonathan Wiener, Duke Law School; Mary Wilson, Mount Auburn Hospital; Sheila K. Zahm, National Cancer Institute.

Environmental Health Indicators

PRINCIPAL AUTHOR

Robin P. White

With contributions by Carlos Corvalán, Allen Hammond, Carolina Katz, Eric Rodenburg, and Kirk Smith.

REVIEWERS AND OTHER CONTRIBUTORS

Marion Cheatle, UNEP; Christopher D. Elvidge, National Geophysical Data Center; Robert Engelman, Population Action International; Sakiko Fukuda-Parr, UNDP; David O. Hall, King's College, London; Mark Hereward, UNICEF; Selim Jahan, UNDP; Richard Jolly, UNDP; Jeanne X. Kasperson, Clark University; Masami Kojima, The World Bank; Magda Lovei, The World Bank; Walter Reid, WRI; A.E.C. Reitveld, WHO; Dieter H. Schwela, WHO; Dan Tunstall, WRI; Michael P. Walsh.

Part II   Global Environmental Trends

PRINCIPAL AUTHORS

Gregory Mock, Emily Matthews, and *Fred Powledge*

With contributions by Yvonne Baskin, Dirk Bryant, Lauretta Burke, Julie Harlan, Carolyn Knapp, Jim MacKenzie, Siobhan Murray, Christian Ottke, Elizabeth Pennesi, Carmen Revenga, Laura Tangley, and Robin P. White.

REVIEWERS AND OTHER CONTRIBUTORS

Population and Human Well-Being

Robert Engelman, Population Action International; Tom Fox, WRI; Carl Haub, PRB; Jay Moor, Habitat; Colin Rees, The World Bank; Walter Reid, WRI; Lori Ann Thrupp, WRI.

Feeding the World

Nikos Alexandratos, FAO; Pamela K. Anderson, Centro Internacional de Agricultura Tropical; Mark Andrew Bell, International Rice Research Institute (IRRI); Devra L. Davis, WRI; Tom Fox, WRI; Peter Hazell, IFPRI; Osamu Ito, IRRI; Dante de Padua, IRRI; Walter Reid, WRI; Mark Rosegrant, IFPRI; Morton Satin, FAO; Sara Scherr, IFPRI; Lori Ann Thrupp, WRI; Sami Zarqa, FAO.

Production and Consumption

Matthew Arnold, WRI; Rob Day, WRI; Margaret Flaherty, World Business Council for Sustainable Development (WBCSD); Walter Reid, WRI; Robert A. Rice, Smithsonian Migratory Bird Center; Nick Robbins, IIED; Helmut Schuetz, Wuppertal Institute.

The Global Commons

Duncan Brack, Royal Institute of International Affairs; Linda Doman, DOE; Tom Fox, WRI; Corinna Gilfillan, Friends of the Earth; Mary J. Hutzler, Energy Information Administration; Tom Land, U.S. EPA; Tanvi Nagpal, The World Bank; Walter Reid, WRI; Nelson Sabogal, UNEP; Michael Schomberg, World Energy Council; Rajendra Shende, UNEP; Robert Thresher, National Renewable Energy Laboratory; Lori Ann Thrupp, WRI.

Resources at Risk

Chip Barber, WRI; Ned Cyr, NOAA; Jean Marc Faures, FAO; Serge Garcia, FAO; Gregor Hodgson, Institute for the Environment and Sustainable Development Research Center; Stephan Schwartzman, Environmental Defense Fund; Kate Sebastian; Nigel Sizer, WRI; Laura Tangley; Ronan Uhel; Tony Whitten, The World Bank; Clive Wilkinson, Australian Institute of Marine Science.

Regions at a Glance

Adel Farid Abdel-Kader, Centre for Environment and Development for the Arab Region and Europe (CEDARE); Chris Anastasi, University of York; Abou Bamba, Network for Environment and Sustainable Development in Africa (NESDA); Winston Bowman, The Regional Environmental Center; Munyaradzi Chenje, India Musokotwane Environment Resource Centre for Southern Africa (IMERCSA); Christopher D. Elvidge, NOAA; Tom Fox, WRI; Edgar Gutierrez-Espeleta, University of Costa Rica; Johan Kuylenstierna, SEI; Ruben Mnatsakanian, Central European University; Laszlo Pinter, IISD; Walter Reid, WRI; Marisabel Romaggi, University of Chile; Ivelin Roussev, The Regional Environmental Center; Ram Manohar Shrestha, Asian Institute of Technology; Leena Srivastava, TERI; David Stanners, EEA; Donna Wise, WRI.

Part III Data Tables

REVIEWERS AND OTHER CONTRIBUTORS

Economic Indicators

Betty Dow, The World Bank; K. Sarawar Lateef, The World Bank; Saeed Ordoubadi, The World Bank; Eric Swanson, The World Bank.

Population and Human Development

Vittoria Cavicchioni, UNESCO; Joseph-Alfred Grinblat, United Nations Population Divison; Mark Hereward, UNICEF; Angela Martins-Oliveira, ILO; George Schieber, The World Bank.

Health

Valery Abramov, WHO; Jenny Barkway, WHO; Jennifer Bryce, WHO; Rachel Horner, WHO; Aminur R. Khan, United Nations Population Division; Magda Lovei, The World Bank; Suki McClatchey, WHO; Eduardo Netto, The Global Tuberculosis Programme; A.E.C. Rietveld, WHO; Sonja Schmidt, WHO; Dieter H. Schwela, WHO; Gerald R. Smith, USGS; Martin Wulfe, DHS.

Urban Data

Christine Auclair, Habitat; Joseph-Alfred Grinblat, United Nations Population Division; Jay Moor, Habitat.

Food and Agriculture

Jeff Tschirley, FAO.

Forests and Land Cover

Dirk Bryant, WRI; Robert Davis, FAO; Susan Iremonger, WCMC; Klaus Janz, FAO; Giovanni Preto, FAO.

Fresh Water

Simon Blyth, WCMC; Dirk Bryant, WRI; Christopher D. Elvidge, NOAA; Jean Marc Faures, FAO; Peter Gleick, The Pacific Institute; Peter Kristensen, National Environmental Research Institute; Tom Loveland, USGS EROS Data Center; Robert C. Lozar, Army Corps of Engineers; Walter Reid, WRI.

Oceans and Fisheries

Dirk Bryant, WRI; Adele Crispoldi, FAO; Serge Garcia, FAO; Richard Grainger, FAO; Brian Groombridge, WCMC; Maurizio Perotti, FAO.

Biodiversity

Dirk Bryant, WRI; Neil Cox, WCMC; Nathan Flesness, ISIS; Brian Groombridge, WCMC; Christine Hopkins, Australasian Species Management Program; Philip S. Miller, IUCN/SSC Conservation Breeding Specialist Group; Alan Mootnick, International Center for Gibbon Studies; James E. Paine, WCMC; Dwight Peck, Ramsar Convention Bureau; Anthony B. Rylands, Conservation International; Kevin Willis, American Zoo and Aquarium Association.

Compiling data on the estimated wild population of threatened animals was possible thanks to the input of more than 15 scientists around the world. These individuals are listed in the Sources and Technical Notes of Data Table 14.4.

Energy and Materials

Marilyn Biviano, USGS; Herman Haberman, UNSTAT; Gary Lam, UNSTAT; Grecia Matos, USGS.

Atmosphere and Climate

Thomas A. Boden, Carbon Dioxide Information Analysis Center.

PRODUCTION STAFF

A talented team of editorial, production, and publishing experts accomplished the enormous task of preparing this volume for printing. We thank them for their dedication, hard work, and high professional standards. In addition to the *World Resources* staff, they include:

Copyeditors: Michael Edington, Beth Rabinowitz
Proofreaders: Christine Schuyler, Anders Smith
Index: Enid Zafran, Indexing Partners
Design: Pamela Reznick, Reznick Design
Photographs: Theresa de Salis and Mark Edwards, Still Pictures

We are especially grateful to WRI librarians Beth Behrendt and Beth Harvey for assisting us with research and materials.

It has been a privilege to work with so many outstanding individuals throughout the world in producing *World Resources 1998–99*.

Leslie Roberts, Editor-in-Chief

The World Resources Institute (WRI) is an independent center for policy research and technical assistance on global environmental and development issues. WRI's mission is to move human society to live in ways that protect Earth's environment and its capacity to provide for the needs and aspirations of current and future generations. Because people are inspired by ideas, empowered by knowledge, and moved to change by greater understanding, WRI provides—and helps other institutions provide—objective information and practical proposals for policy and institutional change that will foster environmentally sound, socially equitable development.

WRI's particular concerns are with globally significant environmental problems and their interaction with economic development and social equity at all levels. WRI focuses on: the global commons, where the cumulative weight of human activities is undermining the integrity of environmental systems; U.S. policies, since the United States is the world's largest producer, consumer, and polluter, as well as a trend-setter for many nations; and developing countries, where natural resource deterioration is dimming development prospects and swelling the ranks of the poor and hungry.

In all of its policy research and work with institutions, WRI tries to build bridges between ideas and action, meshing the insights of scientific research, economic and institutional analyses, and practical experience with the need for open and participatory decisionmaking. In pursuit of its mission, WRI researches policy, gathers and disseminates information, strengthens institutions, builds technical capacities, and communicates information to government and private sector decisionmakers, NGOs, and educators. However diverse, these paths aim in the same direction. In short, WRI analyzes obstacles in the path to sustainability, recommends ways to surmount them, and promotes the understanding and implementation of these recommendations.

WRI's work is carried out by a 120-member interdisciplinary staff, strong in the social and natural sciences and augmented by a network of advisors, collaborators, international fellows, and partner institutions in more than 50 countries. WRI is an independent, not-for-profit corporation that receives financial support from private foundations, governmental and intergovernmental institutions, private corporations, and interested individuals.

World Resources Institute

1709 New York Avenue, N.W.
Washington, D.C. 20006 U.S.A.

WRI's Board of Directors:
Maurice F. Strong, *Chairman*
John Firor, *Vice Chairman*
Manuel Arango
Frances Beinecke
Robert O. Blake
Derek Bok
Bert Bolin
Robert N. Burt
David T. Buzzelli
Deb Callahan
Michael R. Deland
Sylvia A. Earle
José M. Figueres
Shinji Fukukawa
William M. Haney, III
Calestous Juma
Yolanda Kakabadse
Jonathan Lash
Jeffrey T. Leeds
Jane Lubchenco
C. Payne Lucas
William F. Martin
Julia Marton-Lefèvre
Matthew Nimetz
Paulo Nogueira-Neto
Ronald L. Olson
Peter H. Raven
Florence T. Robinson
Roger W. Sant
Stephan Schmidheiny
Bruce Smart
James Gustave Speth
Meg Taylor
Mostafa K. Tolba
Alvaro Umaña
Victor L. Urquidi
Pieter Winsemius

Officers:
Jonathan Lash, *President*
J. Alan Brewster, *Senior Vice President*
Walter V. Reid, *Vice President for Program*
Donna W. Wise, *Vice President for Policy Affairs*
Kenton R. Miller, *Vice President*
Marjorie Beane, *Secretary and Treasurer*

UNEP

United Nations Environment Programme

United Nations Avenue, Gigiri
P.O. Box 30552
Nairobi, Kenya

Executive Director
Klaus Töpfer

Deputy Executive Director
Reuben Olembo

Regional and Liaison Offices

Latin America and the Caribbean:
UNEP Regional Office for Latin America and the Caribbean
Boulevard de los Virreyes No. 155
Col. Lomas Virreyes, P.O. Box 10-793
11000 Mexico City, Mexico

Europe:
UNEP Regional Office for Europe
Geneva Executive Centre
15 Chemin des Anêmones, Case Postale 356
1219 Châtelaine, Geneva, Switzerland

Africa:
UNEP Regional Office for Africa
UNEP Headquarters
United Nations Avenue, Gigiri
P.O. Box 30552
Nairobi, Kenya

North America:
UNEP Regional Office for North America
Room DC2-0803
2 United Nations Plaza
New York, N.Y. 10017 U.S.A.

West Asia:
UNEP Regional Office for West Asia
1083 Road No. 425
Jufair 342, P.O. Box 10880
Manama, Bahrain

Asia and the Pacific:
UNEP Regional Office for Asia and the Pacific
United Nations Building
Rajadamnern Avenue
Bangkok 10200 Thailand

Cairo:
UNEP Arab League Liaison Office
31 Abdel Moneim Riad, Dokki, P.O. Box 212
Cairo, Egypt

Other Outposted Offices
International Register for Potentially Toxic Chemicals
Programme Activity Centre (IRPTC/PAC)
Geneva Executive Centre
15 Chemin des Anêmones, Case Postale 356
1219 Châtelaine, Geneva, Switzerland

UNEP Industry and Environment Programme Activity Centre (IE/PAC)
Tour Mirabeau
39-43 Quai Andre Citroen, F-75739
Paris Cedex 15, France

UNEP International Environmental Technology Centre (IETC)
Osaka Office
2-110 Ryokichi koen
Tsurumi-ku, Osaka 538, Japan

UNEP/Department of Humanitarian Affairs (DHA)
Geneva/Relief Coordination Branch
Palais des Nations
8-14 avenue de la Paix
1211 Geneva 10, Switzerland

The United Nations Environment Programme (UNEP) was established in 1972 and given by the United Nations General Assembly a broad and challenging mandate to stimulate, coordinate, and provide policy guidance for sound environmental action throughout the world. Initial impetus for UNEP's formation came out of the largely nongovernmental and antipollution lobby in industrialized countries. This interest in pollutants remains, but right from the early years, as perceptions of environmental problems broadened to encompass those arising from the misuse and abuse of renewable natural resources, the promotion of environmentally sound or sustainable development became a main purpose of UNEP.

From the global headquarters in Nairobi, Kenya, and seven regional and liaison offices worldwide, UNEP's staff of some 280 scientists, lawyers, administrators, and information specialists carry out UNEP's programme, which is laid down and revised every two years by a Governing Council of representatives from its 58 member states. These members are elected on a staggered basis for four years by the United Nations General Assembly.

UNEP's mission is to provide leadership and encourage partnership in caring for the environment by inspiring, informing, and enabling nations and peoples to improve their quality of life without compromising that of future generations. Broadly, UNEP's programme aims to stimulate action on major environ-

mental problems, promote environmentally sound management at both national and international levels by encouraging the application of assessment results, and make such actions and findings known to the public—from scientists and policymakers to industrialists and schoolchildren. The programme is run in cooperation with numerous other United Nations agencies, governments, intergovernmental organizations, nongovernmental organizations, and specialized institutions.

In recent years, UNEP has strengthened its regional delivery and adopted a more integrated approach. Activities are now grouped under five programme areas: sustainable management and use of natural resources; sustainable production and consumption; a better environment for human health and well-being; globalization and the environment; and global and regional servicing and support. The programme is implemented through three divisions: Programme; Environmental Information and Assessment; and Policy, Interagency, and External Affairs.

The Division of Environmental Information and Assessment works with a wide range of partners to keep under review and report on the state of the world environment, provide early warning of environmental threats, develop harmonised methodologies and tools for policy relevant assessments, improve access to information for environmental decision making, and enhance developing countries' capabilities to use information.

United Nations Development Programme

One U.N. Plaza
New York, New York 10017 U.S.A.

Administrator
James Gustave Speth

Bureau for Development Policy
Assistant Administrator and Director
Eimi Watanabe

Sustainable Energy and Environment Division
Director
Roberto Lenton

Through a unique network of 134 country offices, the United Nations Development Programme (UNDP) helps people in 174 countries and territories to help themselves, focusing on poverty eradication, environmental regeneration, job creation, and the advancement of women. In support of these goals, UNDP is frequently asked to assist in promoting sound governance and market development, and to support rebuilding societies in the aftermath of war and humanitarian emergencies.

UNDP's overarching mission is to help countries build their own national capacity to achieve sustainable human development, giving top priority to eliminating poverty and building equity.

In administering its programmes, UNDP draws on the expertise of developing country nationals and non-governmental organizations, the specialized agencies of the UN system, and research institutes in every field. Eighty-five percent of UNDP staff is based in the countries where people need help.

In 1996, core and non-core contributions and pledges to UNDP exceeded US$2 billion. Contributions to UNDP are voluntary, and come from nearly every government in the world. Importantly, recipient country governments cover more than half of total project costs through personnel, facilities, equipment, and supplies.

Eighty-seven percent of UNDP's core programme funds go to countries with an annual per capita GNP of US$750 or less. These countries are home to 90 percent of the world's extremely poor.

A *Human Development Report*, published yearly for UNDP since 1990 and drafted by a team of independent consultants, assists the international community in developing new, practical, and pragmatic concepts, measures, and policy instruments for promoting more people-oriented development.

Environment is one of the main themes for UNDP's 1997–2000 programming cycle. Environmental objectives will be included in almost all country programmes approved for this period, and all activities will be screened for their environmental impact. Programmes to build capacities for sustainable development and natural resource management are supported through work on food security, forests, water, energy, and urban development.

Together with the World Bank and the United Nations Environment Programme, UNDP is one of the managing partners of the Global Environment Facility (GEF). The GEF is a US$2 billion fund that helps countries translate global concerns into national action to help fight ozone depletion, global warming, loss of biodiversity, and pollution of international waters. UNDP is also one of six UN sponsors of a global programme on HIV/AIDS.

At the country level, the UNDP Resident Representative normally also serves as Resident Co-ordinator of the United Nations System's operational activities for development.

Headquartered in New York, UNDP is governed by a 36-member Executive Board, representing both developing and developed countries.

 **The World Bank**

The World Bank Group is a partner in opening markets and strengthening economies. Its goal is to improve the quality of life and expand prosperity for people everywhere, especially the world's poorest.

A first-rate financial standing and access to the world's capital markets enable the Bank to invest broadly in societies—from health, education, and the environment to infrastructure and policy reform.

The World Bank Group of institutions includes:

- The International Bank for Reconstruction and Development (IBRD), founded in 1944, is the single largest provider of development loans to middle-income developing countries and a major catalyst of similar financing from other sources. The IBRD funds itself primarily by borrowing on international capital markets.

- The International Development Association (IDA), founded in 1960, assists the poorest countries by providing interest-free credits with 35- to 40-year maturities. IDA is funded primarily by governments' contributions.

- The International Finance Corporation (IFC) supports private enterprises in the developing world through providing loan and equity financing, and through a range of advisory services.

- The Multilateral Investment Guarantee Agency (MIGA) offers investors insurance against noncommercial risk and helps developing country governments attract foreign investment.

- The International Center for the Settlement of Investment Disputes (ICSID) encourages the flow of foreign investment to developing countries through arbitration and conciliation facilities.

Over its 54-year history the World Bank has become a global partnership in which more than 180 countries have joined together for common goals: to improve the quality of life for people throughout the world and to meet the challenge of sustainable development.

The World Bank Group
1818 H Street, N.W.
Washington, D.C. 20433 U.S.A.

Index

Canned food, lead poisoning, 60
Carbamate pesticides, 43, *43*
Carbon dioxide concentration in atmosphere, 171
    climate change, impact of, 71–72
    data tables, 348
Carbon dioxide emissions, 63. *See also* Greenhouse gas
    emissions
    cement manufacturing, data tables, 344–45, 347
    consumption rates, correlation with, 39
    developed countries, 176
    developing countries, 176
    fossil fuel burning, data tables, 344–45, 347
    industrial emissions, 175
    Kyoto Protocol, 174–77
    motor vehicle emissions, 172–73
    parity with methane emissions, 100
    reduction of, 91–93, 171, 175, 177
    regions at a glance, 200–20
    season changes, impact on, 174
    temperature of atmosphere, impact on, 173
    trends, 170–71
Carbon monoxide emissions, China, 118
Carbon tax, 92–93
Carbon tetrachloride, atmospheric concentrations, data
    tables, 348
Carcinogens, 32–34. *See also* Cancer
    breast cancer, 102–04
    endocrine disruptors, *57*
    industrial chemicals, 54
    pesticides, *43,* 44–45, *45*
Cardiac disease. *See* Heart disease
Caribbean. *See* Latin America; *specific countries*
Carp, aquaculture production, 159
Cars. *See* Motor vehicles
Causes of death, 9–13. *See also* Mortality rates
Cement industries
    carbon dioxide emissions, data tables, 344–45, 347
    environmental impact, 52
    production, data tables, 338–39
Central America, 209–11. *See also* Latin America; *spe-
    cific countries*
Central Europe. *See also specific countries*
    blue-baby syndrome, 96
    pollution and life expectancy, 96–97
Ceramic industries, environmental impact, 52
Cereal. *See also specific cereal (e.g., Rice)*
    donations, data tables, 288–89
    price declines, 152
    production, data tables, 284–85
    regions at a glance, 200–20
    trade, data tables, 288–89
    yields, 152–53, 288–89
CFC-11, -12, and -113
    atmospheric concentrations, data tables, 348
CFCs. *See* Chlorofluorocarbons
Chagas disease, 25
    climate change, impact of, 70
    prevention strategies, 81–82
Channelization. *See* Navigation projects
Chavis, Benjamin, 99–100
Chemical hazards to health, 26–32, 101. *See also* Fertiliz-
    ers; Pesticides; *specific hazards*
    breast cancer, 102–04
    endocrine disruptors, 56–57
    industrial chemicals, 53–54
Chemical production, 51–52
Chernobyl accident, impact on health, 95
Childbirth. *See also* Pregnancy
    attended by trained personnel, data tables, 262–63
    birth rates, data tables, 246–47
    defects. *See* Birth defects
    low-birth-weight infants, 154, 256–57
    stillbirths, effect of indoor air quality, 66–67
Child mortality rates, 1. *See also* Infant mortality rates

data tables, 258–59
demographic regions, by, *2*
malnutrition, correlation with, 154
measles, 9
mother's education, impact of, 78
Senegal River region, 110
Children
    acute respiratory infections, 66–67
    diarrheal diseases, data tables, 268
    goiter, data tables, 256–57
    indicators of health, 256–57, 268
    lead exposure, 59, 60–61
    low-birth-weight infants, 154, 256–57
    malnutrition. *See* Malnutrition
    mortality rates. *See* Child mortality rates
    outdoor air quality, impact of, 64
    PCB exposure, 55
    pesticide exposure, 46
    school attendance, 149–50
    vulnerability to environmental hazards, *20*
    weight as indicator of health, 128, 256–57
China, 115–25
    air pollution, 116–120, 124
    aquaculture production, 159–60
    background, 115–16
    chronic diseases, 122
    coal production and consumption, 116–19, 124,
        170–71
    conservation laws, 123–24
    drinking water, 121–23
    economic reforms, 124
    enforcement of environmental laws, 123–24
    financial investment in environment, 124–25
    groundwater, 120–21
    indoor air quality, 118–20
    industrial wastewater, 120–22, 124
    infectious diseases, 121–23
    lead poisoning, 120
    motor vehicle use and emissions, 118, 172
    municipal wastewater, 120–21, 124
    outdoor air quality, 116–120
    particulate emissions, 124
    pollution control laws, 123–24
    public policy, 123–25
    respiratory diseases, 118–20
    sanitation, 123
    sulfur dioxide emissions, 124
    township-and-village enterprises, 121–22
    Trans-Century Green Plan, 124
    wastewater, 120–22, 124
    wastewater irrigation, 122
    water pollution, 120–22
    water shortages, 120
Chlordane. *See* Organochlorine pesticides; Persistent or-
    ganic pollutants
Chloride in European lakes, data tables, 308
Chlorine (gaseous), atmospheric concentrations, data
    tables, 348
Chlorofluorocarbons (CFCs), 32, 61
    black market trade, 178
    reduction of production and consumption, 177–79
Chlorophyll in European lakes, data tables, 308
Cholera
    climate change, impact of, 71
    morbidity rates, 260–61
    reemergence of, *22–23*
    Senegal River region, 113
    wastewater irrigation, impact of, 48–49
Chronic diseases. *See also specific disease (e.g., Cancer)*
    causes of death, 10–13
    China, 122
Cities. *See headings starting with Urban*
Civil wars. *See* Armed conflicts
Clean fuel, transition to, 67

Clean production, 53, 90
Climate change, 67–72. *See also* Global warming; Tem-
    perature changes
    air pollution, impact on, 69–70
    direct impacts, 67–70
    disease rates, effect on, 70–71
    ecological system disturbances, 68, 72
    indirect impacts, 70–72
    Kyoto Protocol, 174–77
    nutrition, effect on, 71–72
    overview, 67
    plant pests and diseases, effect on, 71–72
    rising sea levels, 68–69
    season changes, 174
    weather events, 68
"Closed-loop" processing cycles, 167
CO₂ emissions. *See* Carbon dioxide emissions
Coal consumption and emissions, 62–63, 67. *See also*
    Fossil fuels
    China, 116–17, 119, 124, 170–71
    heavy metal exposure, 58
    indicator of environmental health, 127
    life expectancy in Central Europe, impact on, 96
    particulate emissions, *64*
    reduction of pollution, 90–93
    sulfur dioxide emissions, *64*
Coal mining and production
    China, 116–17
    environmental impact, 52
Coastal waters. *See also* Oceans; Wetlands
    eutrophication, 47
    rising sea levels, 68–69
Coffee production and consumption, 165–66
Cold-related deaths, decline, 68
Columbia, flower industry, *43*
Commercial enterprises, energy balances, data tables,
    336–37
Commodity indexes and prices, World Bank, 240
Communicable diseases. *See* Infectious diseases
Community involvement. *See also* Preventive strategies
    disease prevention strategies, 75–78
    vector-borne disease prevention strategies, 81
Conservation. *See also* Recycling; Sustainable produc-
    tion
    biodiversity conservation, 100
    China, conservation laws, 123–24
    endangered species management programs, data ta-
        bles, 326–27
Consumption rates, 39
    biomass fuel-burning, 66
    chlorofluorocarbons, 177–79
    coal. *See* Coal consumption and emissions
    coffee, 165
    electricity, data tables, 332–33
    energy, generally. *See* Energy use
    fertilizers, 46–47, 286–87
    fish, 196, 314–15
    gasoline, data tables, 266–67
    paper consumption, 163–65
    pesticides, 41–42, 46
    population growth, impact of, 143
    salt consumption, data tables, 256–57
    trends, 161–69
    water, 188–89, 304–05
Contamination. *See* Air pollution; Soil degradation; Wa-
    ter pollution; *specific pollutant*
Contraceptive use, data tables, 262–63
Convention on Biological Diversity, 197
Conversion of land to agricultural use, 49–50, 152
Cookstove smoke, 66–67
Cooperation. *See* Multinational cooperation
Copper. *See also* Heavy metals
    production data tables, 338–39
Coral reefs, 193–95

Kerala State, education and health care policies, 150
motor vehicle use, 172
pesticide exposure, *45*
vector-borne disease prevention strategies, 81
Indicator maps, 221–24
Indicators of environmental health, 3–4, *4*, 127–30
air pollution, 129
air quality, 127–28
developed countries, 129
developing countries, 127–30
health hazards, 4, *4*, 94–95
maps, 5
nutrition, 128
ranking of developing countries, 128–29
refining of indicators, 129
twenty-first century issues, 94–95
water quality, 128
Indonesia
deforestation, 186
environmental performance ratings, 88
urbanization, 147
Indoor air quality, 65–67
acute respiratory infections, 25
asthma affected by, *30–31*
China, 118–20
developing countries, 66
disease prevention strategies, 80–81
health effects, generally, 66–67, 80
indicators of environmental health, 127–28
Industrial accidents, 54
Industrialization, 51–61. *See also* Production; *specific industry*
abatement of industrial pollutants, 87–88
Central and Eastern Europe, 96–97
chemical hazards, generally, 54
chemical production, 51
China, 115–16
chloroflurocarbons, 61
cleaner production, 53, 90
eco-efficiency strategies, 90, 167, *168*
energy balances, data tables, 336–37
energy efficiency, 167
environmental impact of selected industries, 52
environmental performance ratings, 88
factors promoting industrialization, 53
health impact, generally, 6–7, 87–90
heavy metal hazards, 58–61, 88
increase in, 161
injuries from industrial accidents, 54
material flows, 161–63
overview, 51–54
persistent organic pollutants, 54–58, *89*
Industrial wastewater
China, 120–22, 124
irrigation with. *See* Wastewater irrigation
treatment. *See* Wastewater treatment
Infant mortality rates
blue-baby syndrome, 47, 96
China, 116
data tables, 258–59
outdoor air quality, impact of, 64
parents' schooling, impact of, 15
poverty's impact on, 14
regions at a glance, 200–20
Senegal River region, 110
stillbirths, effect of indoor air quality, 66–67
Infectious diseases. *See also specific disease*
antibiotic resistance, *76–77*
biological hazards, 18–26
causes of death, 10–13
China, 116, 121–23
increase of, 150
irrigation, impact of, 47–49
land conversion to agricultural use, impact of, 49–50

morbidity rates, 260–61
Injuries
causes of death, 10–13
industrial accidents, 54
Insect-borne diseases, 24–25. *See also* Vector-borne diseases; *specific disease (e.g.,* Malaria)
climate change, impact of, 70
indicator of environmental health, 128
irrigation, impact of, 47
land conversion to agricultural use, impact of, 49–50
prevention strategies, 81–83
Rift Valley Fever, 112
Insecticides. *See* Pesticides
Integrated Pest Management (IPM), 85–86
Interdisciplinary research on environmental health, 95
International cooperation. *See* Multinational cooperation
International Coral Reef Initiative (ICRI), 195
International environmental justice, 99–101
International migration, 147–49
Intestinal schistosomiasis, 111–12
Investments. *See also* Foreign investments; Government expenditures
social investments, data tables, 250–51
Iodine deficiency, indicator of environmental health, 128
Iron, recycling, 162
Iron industries
environmental impact, 52
production data tables, 338–39
Irrigation, 86–87
health risks, generally, 47–49
improvements to prevent disease, 86–87
increase in irrigated land, 47
percentage of irrigated land, 157, 286–87
regions at a glance, 200–20
Senegal River development projects, 109–10, 113
soil degradation resulting from, 157
wastewater. *See* Wastewater irrigation
water-efficient systems, 189

J

Jamaica, coral reef damage, 194
Japan, PCB contamination, 55
Japanese encephalitis, impact of irrigation, 47

K

Kerala State, India, education and health care policies, 150
Kyansanur forest disease, 50
Kyoto Protocol, 174–77

L

Labor force. *See also* Workplace environment
fisheries and fishing industry, 196
growth, data tables, 244–45
international migration, 147–49
Lakes
ecosystem decline, 190–91
European lakes, water quality, data tables, 308
Great Lakes. *See* Great Lakes
nitrate levels, 180
Senegal River projects. *See* Senegal River
ultraviolet penetration, 183–84
Land, agricultural. *See* Agricultural land
Land area and use. *See also specific area or use (e.g.,* Agricultural land, Forests and woodlands)

cropland area, data tables, 286–87, 298–299
data tables, 298–299
domesticated land area. *See* Domesticated land area map, 222
watersheds, data tables, 309
Land conversion to agricultural use, 49–50, 152
Land cover, data tables, 291–302
Land distribution, data tables, 248–49
Land erosion. *See* Soil erosion
Landfills, paper disposal, 164
Latin America. *See also specific countries*
coffee production, 165–66
flower industry, pesticide use, *43*
HIV/AIDS morbidity rate, 151
Laws and regulations
ballast water discharges, 198
China, pollution control laws, 123–24
outdoor air quality, 63, 90
pesticides, 85
Leaded gasoline, 60
China, 118
data tables, 266–67
emissions as indicator of environmental health, 127, 129
health hazards, 1, 88–90
Lead exposure and poisoning, 59–61. *See also* Heavy metals
battery production and recycling, 60
canned food, 60
Central and Eastern Europe, 96
China, 120
paints, 61
pottery glazing, 60
Lead mining and processing, 60. *See also* Heavy metals
data tables, 266–67
Leather and tanning industries, environmental impact, 52
Leishmaniasis, impact of land conversion to agricultural use, 49–50
Leukemia, Chernobyl accident, 95
Libraries, data tables, 250–51
Life expectancy, 8
China, 115–16, 122
data tables, 246–47
demographic regions, by, *2*
Europe, East-West gap, 95, 96–98
regions at a glance, 200–20
trends, 142
Lifestyles
asthma affected by, *31*
breast cancer, impact on, 102
life expectancy in Eastern and Central Europe, impact on, 97
malaria prevalence in Amazon, impact on, *49*
Lindane. *See* Pesticides
Liquid fuels
carbon dioxide emissions, data tables, 344–45, 347
emissions, regions at a glance, 200–20
production and consumption, data tables, 332–33
Literacy, 144–45, 149–50
Liver cancer, China, 122
Livestock production
grain fed to livestock, data tables, 288–89
pasture land area, data tables, 298–299
Senegal River region, 113
Lobsters, biodiversity of regional seas, data tables, 316
Logging, 186
structure of forest industry, data tables, 292–93
Low-birth-weight infants, 154
data tables, 256–57
Lung cancer
China, 119
indoor air quality, effect of, 66
outdoor air quality, impact of, 64

smoke exposure, effect of, 67
Lymphoma, pesticide exposure, 45

M

Maize. *See also* Cereal
  yield, 152–53
Malaria, 24–25
  Brazilian Amazon, *48–49*
  climate change, impact of, 70
  indicator of environmental health, 128
  irrigation, impact of, 47
  land conversion to agricultural use, impact of, 49–50
  morbidity rates, *48–49,* 260–61
  prevention strategies, 81–83
  Senegal River region, 112
Males. *See* Gender
Mali, Senegal River development. *See* Senegal River
Malnutrition, 154–55
  burden of disease, 34
  data tables, 256–57
  poverty's impact on, *16–17,* 154–55
  reduction of, 154–55
  Senegal River region, 110, 112–13
Mammals
  endangered species management programs, data tables, 326–27
  marine mammals, biodiversity of regional seas, data tables, 316
  threatened species, data tables, 322–23
Mangroves
  data tables, 294–95
  destruction by aquaculture production, 159
Manufacturing. *See* Industrialization; Production; *specific industry*
Maps
  algal bloom sites, United States, 181
  bird species, percentage threatened, 197
  biomass fuel use, developing countries, 80
  China, 115
  demographic regions, *2*
  dengue fever risk, 26
  E coli O157 found, 21
  exposure to lead from gasoline, developed countries, 5
  health risks from environmental threats, developing countries, 5
  indicator maps, 221–24
  leaded gasoline use, 100
  malaria, 24
  malnutrition, *16*
  sea level rise, vulnerability to, 69
  Senegal River Basin, 108
  water supply, projected, 190
Marine fish
  aquaculture production, data tables, 314–15
  catch, data tables, 314–16
  catch, regions at a glance, 200–20
Marine mammals, biodiversity of regional seas, data tables, 316
Mass media campaigns, vector-borne disease prevention strategies, 81
Material flows, 161–63
  eco-efficiency strategies, 90, 167, *168*
Maternal education, impact on child mortality rates, 78
Maternal mortality rates, data tables, 258–59
Mauritania, Senegal River development. *See* Senegal River
Measles, 25–26
  child mortality rates, 9
  immunizations, data tables, 262–63
  morbidity rates, 260–61

Media campaigns, vector-borne disease prevention strategies, 81
Megacities, 146–47
Mekong River Basin, 191
Mercury exposure, *48. See also* Heavy metals
Metals. *See* Heavy metals; Mining; *specific metals*
Methane
  atmospheric concentrations, data tables, 348
  Kyoto Protocol, 174–77
  paper disposal in landfills, 164
  parity with carbon dioxide emissions, 100
Methemoglobinemia. *See* Blue-baby syndrome
Methyl chloroform, atmospheric concentrations, data tables, 348
Mexico, water supply and sanitation improvements, 80
Microorganisms, health hazards, 18–26
Migration, 147–49. *See also* Relocation and resettlement
Millet, 153. *See also* Cereal
Minerals. *See* Mining; *specific minerals (e.g.,* Copper)
Mining. *See also* Coal mining and production
  environmental impact, 52
  gold mining in Brazilian Amazon, *48*
  heavy metal exposure, 58
  hidden material flows, 161–62
  lead mining and processing, 60, 266–67
  production data tables, 338–39
Minorities, environmental racism, 99–101
Moldova, pesticide exposure, *45*
Molluscs and crustaceans
  aquaculture production, data tables, 314–15
  biodiversity of regional seas, data tables, 316
  trade balance, data tables, 314–15
Montreal Protocol on Substances that Deplete the Ozone Layer, 176–78
Morbidity rates, 13–14
  asthma, *30–31*
  breast cancer, 102
  Central and Eastern Europe, 96–97
  China, 116, 119
  cholera, 260–61
  climate change, impact of, 70–71
  HIV/AIDS, 150–51
  infectious diseases, 260–61
  malaria, *48–49,* 112, 260–61
  measles, 260–61
  polio, 260–61
  Rift Valley Fever, 112
  schistosomiasis, 47, 111–12
  tuberculosis, 25, *40,* 260–61
Mortality rates, 8–13
  causes of death, 9–13
  Central and Eastern Europe, 96–97
  children. *See* Child mortality rates
  China, 116, 119–20, 122
  cold-related deaths, decline, 68
  data tables, 258–59
  demographic regions, by, *2*
  estimation methods, *12*
  heat stress, impact of, 67–68
  HIV/AIDS, 151
  indoor air quality, effect of, 66–67
  infants. *See* Infant mortality rates
  maternal mortality rates, data tables, 258–59
  outdoor air quality, impact of, 63–64
  particulate emissions, effect of, *64*
  pesticide poisoning, 42–43
  poverty, effect of, 106
  regions at a glance, 200–20
  smoking, *33*
  sulfur dioxide emissions, effect of, *65*
  tuberculosis, 9, 25, *40*
Mosquito-borne diseases. *See* Insect-borne diseases; *specific disease (e.g.,* Malaria)
Motor vehicle emissions, 62–63, 172–73

China, 118
  particulate emissions, *64*
  reduction of, 90
Motor vehicle manufacturing, 161
  alternative fuel vehicles, 173
  "take-back" requirements, 168
Motor vehicles, 171–73
  emissions. *See* Motor vehicle emissions
  energy balances, data tables, 336–37
  energy use, 171
  increase in, 172
  manufacturing. *See* Motor vehicle manufacturing
  regions at a glance, 200–20
  urban households, data tables, 278–79
Multinational cooperation
  disease prevention, 82
  environmental health in twenty-first century, 94–95
  Kyoto Protocol, 174–77
  Montreal Protocol on Substances that Deplete the Ozone Layer, 176–78
  Senegal River projects, 109–10
Municipalities. *See* Urban *headings;* Urbanization
Municipal wastewater
  China, 120–21, 121, 124
  indicator of environmental health, 128
  irrigation with. *See* Wastewater irrigation
  treatment. *See* Wastewater treatment
Murders, urban population, data tables, 278–79

N

Nath, K.J., 105
Natural forests. *See also* Frontier forests
  data tables, 292–93
Natural resources. *See specific resource*
  degradation. *See* Degradation of environment
  scarcity. *See* Scarcity of resources
Navigation projects, 190–91
  Senegal River, 109–10
Nematicides. *See* Pesticides
Neurological damage
  PCB exposure, 55, *57*
  pesticide exposure, 44
Nigeria, wetlands ecosystem valuation, 193
Nighttime lights, map, 224
Nitrates
  contamination from fertilizers, 46–47
  watersheds, data tables, 309
Nitric oxide emissions, 180
Nitrogen
  European lakes, data tables, 308
  production data tables, 338–39
Nitrogen cycle, 179–81
Nitrogen dioxide emissions
  city pollution, data tables, 264–65
  indicator of environmental health, 127
Nitrous oxide, atmospheric concentrations, data tables, 348
Nitrous oxide emissions, 180
  China, 118
  Kyoto Protocol, 174–77
Non-Hodgkin's lymphoma, pesticide exposure, 45
Noncommunicable diseases. *See* Chronic diseases
Nonferrous metal industries, environmental impact, 52
Nontropical forests, data tables, 294–95
Nonwood fiber production, 164
North America, 206–08. *See also* Canada; United States
Nuclear energy
  Chernobyl accident, 95
  production, data tables, 334–35
Nuclear testing, site locations, 100
Nurses, percentage of population, data tables, 262–63

Nutrition. *See also* Malnutrition
  calorie supply, data tables, 256–57, 288–89
  climate change, impact of, 71–72
  data tables, 256–57, 288–89
  indicators of environmental health, 128
  trends, 154

O

Occupations. *See* Labor force; Workplace environment
Oceania, 218–20
Oceans
  biodiversity, data tables, 316
  coral reefs. *See* Coral reefs
  data tables, 313–18
  fish. *See* Marine fish
  regions at a glance, 200–20
Office equipment and supplies, recycling, 168
Official development assistance (ODA)
  data tables, 238–39
  regions at a glance, 200–20
Oil. *See also* Fossil fuels
  China, production and use, 116
  environmental impact of industries, 52
  transport sector, consumption, 172
Onchocerciasis. *See* River blindness
Oral rehydration therapy (ORT), 80
  data tables, 262–63
Organic produce, coffee, 166
Organochlorine pesticides, 42, 45, *45*
  breast cancer, effect on, 103
Organophosphate pesticides, *43*, 43–44, *45*
ORT (oral rehydration therapy), 80
  data tables, 262–63
Outdoor air quality, 63–65. *See also specific emissions*
  asthma affected by, *30*
  burden of disease, 34
  chemical hazards, 26–32
  China, 116–120
  city air pollution, data tables, 264–65
  health effects, generally, 63–65, 90
  history of pollution, 63
  indicators of environmental health, 127–29
  reduction of pollution, 90–93
  regulation, 63, 90
Overcrowding. *See also* Population density
  data tables, 278–79
  health, impact on, *1*
  tuberculosis morbidity rates, impact on, *40*
Ozone concentrations, China, 118
Ozone emissions, health effects, *65*
Ozone layer depletion, 32, 61, 177–79
  atmospheric concentrations of ozone-depleting
    gases, data tables, 348
  Montreal Protocol, 176–78

P

Packaging
  Germany's Packaging Ordinance, *164*
  manufacturer "take-back" requirements, 168
PAHs (polyaromatic hydrocarbons), Great Lakes, 55
Paints, lead-based, 61
Paper and pulp industries, 163–65
  data tables, 296–97
  environmental impact, 52, 164–65
Paper consumption, 163–65
Paper recycling, 164
Paraquat, *43*
Parasitic worms

health hazards, 18–26
  schistosomiasis. *See* Schistosomiasis
  wastewater irrigation, impact of, 48
Parental education
  infant mortality rates, impact on, 15
  maternal education, impact on child mortality rates,
    78
Parklands, data tables, 294–95
Particulate emissions
  China, 116–17, 119–20, 124
  city pollution, data tables, 264–65
  health effects, generally, *64*, 90
  indicator of environmental health, 127
  reduction of pollution, 90
  total suspended particulates. *See* Total suspended
    particulates
Pasture land area, data tables, 298–299
PCBs, 54–55, *57*. *See also* Persistent organic pollutants
  endocrine disruptors, *56–57*
Pelagic fish catch, data tables, 316
Perfluorocarbons (PFCs), Kyoto Protocol, 174–77
Persistent organic pollutants (POPs), 32, 54–58, *89*
  banning, 54
  endocrine disruptors, *56–57*
  exports and imports, 54–55
  future implications, 55–56
  Great Lakes, contamination, 55
Pesticides, 41–46. *See also* Persistent organic pollutants
  acute health effects, 42–44
  breast cancer, effect on, 103
  chronic health effects, *43*, 44–46
  consumption rates, 41–42, 46
  endocrine disruptors, *56–57*
  exports, 42, 44
  flower industry in Latin America, *43*
  future trends in use, 46
  health risks, 42–46
  immune system suppression, 44, *45*
  nonoccupational exposure, 43–45
  occupational exposure, *43*, 43–45
  protective clothing, 43, *43*
  reducing health risks, 85–86
  regulation of use, 85
Pests, plant. *See* Plant pests and diseases
Petroleum. *See* Oil
PFCs (perfluorocarbons), Kyoto Protocol, 174–77
Phaseouts
  asbestos, 53
  chlorofluorocarbons, 177–78
  halons, 178
  leaded gasoline, 60, 88–89
  ozone-depleting substances, 61, 176–78
  persistent organic pollutants, *89*
Philippines, postharvest losses of rice, 156
Phospates, watersheds, data tables, 309
Phosphorous, data tables, 308, 338–39
Physicians, percentage of population, data tables, 262–63
Plantations
  coffee, 165–66
  trees. *See* Forest plantations
Plant pests and diseases
  climate change, impact of, 71–72
  Integrated Pest Management (IPM), 85–86
  pesticides. *See* Pesticides
Plants
  bioinvasions, 198
  climate change, impact of, 174
  nitrogen cycle, 179–81
  pests and diseases. *See* Plant pests and diseases
  threatened species, data tables, 322–23
Plastics, recycling, 168
Plumbing, households without, 268
PM-10. *See* Particulate emissions
Poisoning

arsenic poisoning. *See* Arsenic poisoning
  lead poisoning. *See* Lead exposure and poisoning
  pesticide poisoning, 42–44
Poland, pollution and life expectancy, 96
Policy actions. *See* Preventive strategies; Public policy
Polio
  immunizations, data tables, 262–63
  morbidity rates, 260–61
Political disruption
  displaced persons, 148
  famines caused by, 155
  health, impact on, 97
  income inequities, impact of, 146
Polluter Pays Principle, 168
Pollution. *See* Air pollution; Soil degradation; Water pollution; *specific pollutant*
Polyaromatic hydrocarbons (PAHs), Great Lakes, 55
Polychlorinated biphenyls. *See* PCBs
Polychlorinated dioxins. *See* Persistent organic pollutants
Polyester, recycling, 168
POPs. *See* Persistent organic pollutants
Population
  age structure. *See* Age structure of population
  China, 115
  data tables, 244–45
  demographic regions, by, *2*
  density. *See* Population density
  growth. *See* Population growth
  income distribution by quintile, data tables, 246–47
  regions at a glance, 200–20
  trends, 141–51
  urban population, data tables, 274–77
Population density. *See also* Overcrowding
  data tables, 298–299
  map, 221
  urban residential density, data tables, 276–77
  watersheds, data tables, 309
Population growth, 37–39, 141–43
  Brazilian Amazon, 48
  data tables, 244–45
  demographic transition, 142–43
  implications, 143
  medium-variant projections, 141–42
  probability model, 143
  "social modernization," 142
  urban population, 146–47, 274–77
Postharvest losses, 155–56
Potassium production, data tables, 338–39
Pottery glazing, lead poisoning, 60
Potts, Sir Percival, 54
Poverty
  data tables, 248–49, 276–77
  disease prevention strategies, 75–78
  environmental risks, 17–18
  female-headed households in urban population, data
    tables, 276–77
  fuel use among impoverished, 81
  health, impact on, 14–18, 106–07
  Human Poverty Index, 145
  increase, 38–39, 145
  malnutrition and, *16–17*, 154–55
  trends, 145–46
  tuberculosis morbidity rates, impact on, *40*
  urban population, data tables, 276–77
Pregnancy. *See also* Childbirth
  anemia, data tables, 256–57
  contraceptive use, data tables, 262–63
  tetanus immunizations, data tables, 262–63
Preventive strategies
  acid rain, 183
  aquaculture pollution, 160
  bioinvasions, 198–99
  coffee production, 166

coral reef destruction, 195
corporate responsibility movement, *169*
diseases. *See* Disease prevention
eco-efficiency strategies, 90, 167, *168*
endangered species management programs, data tables, 326–27
fish stock management, 196
freshwater ecosystem decline, 191
malnutrition and hunger, 154–55
material use, 90, 162–63, 167, *168*
Montreal Protocol on Substances that Deplete the Ozone Layer, 176–78
nitrogen imbalance, 180–81
phaseouts. *See* Phaseouts
postharvest losses, 156
recycling. *See* Recycling
soil degradation, 158, 162
sustainable production. *See* Sustainable production
water scarcity, 189
Prior Informed Consent (PIC)
hazardous waste exports, 100–01
pesticides, 85
Production. *See also* Industrialization; *specific industry or specific product*
aquaculture production. *See* Aquaculture production
"closed-loop" processing cycles, 167
coal. *See* Coal mining and production
food production. *See* Food production
livestock production. *See* Livestock production
materials, data tables, 338–39
population growth, impact of, 143
sustainable production. *See* Sustainable production
trends, 161–69
Product stewardship, 167–68
Prostate cancer, endocrine disruptors, *57*
Protected areas
data tables, 320–21
forest ecosystems, data tables, 294–95
international protection systems, data tables, 320–21
national protection systems, data tables, 320–21
regions at a glance, 200–20
watersheds, data tables, 309
Protein supply, data tables, 288–89
Protozoa, health hazards, 18–26
Psychosocial effects on health, 95, 97
Publicity campaigns, vector-borne disease prevention strategies, 81
Public policy. *See also* Laws and regulations; Preventive strategies
antibiotic resistance, *76–77*
chemical hazards, 32
China, 116, 123–25
disease prevention, generally, 77–78, 83–84
environmental health in twenty-first century, 94–95
fuel use improvements, 81
pesticide use, 85
phaseouts. *See* Phaseouts
postharvest losses, 156
urbanization, consequences of, 147
vector-borne disease prevention, 81–82
water supply and sanitation improvements, 79–80, 82
Public services. *See also* Education; Health care services
energy balances, data tables, 336–37
government expeditures, 150
libraries, data tables, 250–51
Public transport, urban households, data tables, 278–79
Pulp industries. *See* Paper and pulp industries
Pulse production, data tables, 284–85
Purchase power parity, regions at a glance, 200–20

R

Racism, environmental, 99–101
Radiation, ultraviolet. *See* Ultraviolet radiation
Radios, households without, 268
Rainfall
acid rain. *See* Acid rain
agriculture, impact on, 71
air pollution, impact on, 70
disease rates, impact on, 70–71
Senegal River region, 108
Ramsar sites, watersheds, data tables, 309
Recycling, 162
battery recycling, lead exposure, 60
chlorofluorocarbons, 178
"closed-loop" processing cycles, 167
manufacturer "take-back" requirements, 168
paper, 164
plastics, 168
polyester, 168
Refineries
lead processing, 60, 266–67
petroleum, environmental impact, 52
Reforestation, 185
data tables, 292–93
Refrigerators, households without, 268
Refugees, 148
Regional profiles, 108–25
Regions at a glance, 200–20
Regulations. *See* Laws and regulations
Relocation and resettlement, 148
Senegal River region, 113
Reproductive abnormalities, endocrine disruptors, *56–57*
Reptiles
endangered species management programs, data tables, 326–27
threatened species, data tables, 324–25
Research studies
aquaculture production, 160
burden of disease studies, 32–34
chemical hazards, 30–32
environmental health in twenty-first century, 94–95
geographic information systems (GIS), 158
valuing of ecosystem services, 191–92
Reservoirs, Senegal River projects, 109–10
Resettlement. *See* Relocation and resettlement
Residences. *See* Household environment
Residential density, urban data tables, 276–77
Residential energy balances, data tables, 336–37
Respiratory diseases. *See also specific diseases (e.g.,* Lung cancer)
China, 118–20
indoor air quality, effect of, 66–67
outdoor air quality, impact of, 63–64
ozone emissions, *65*
particulate emissions, *64*
sulfur dioxide emissions, *65*
Rice. *See also* Cereal
crop intensification, 152–53
postharvest losses, 156
yield, 152–53
Rift Valley Fever, 112
Rising sea levels, 68–69
River blindness
climate change, impact of, 70–71
irrigation, impact of, 47
prevention strategies, 82
Rivers
annual flow, data tables, 304–05
dams, 190–91
ecosystem decline, 190–91
Mekong River Basin, 191

nitrogen depositions, 180
Senegal River projects, 108–14
watersheds, data tables, 309
Road transportation. *See* Motor vehicles
Root production, data tables, 284–85
Root yield, data tables, 288–89
Roundwood production and trade
data tables, 296–97
regions at a glance, 200–20
Rural population, regions at a glance, 200–20
Russia
pesticide exposure, *45*
tuberculosis morbidity and mortality rates, *40*

S

Salt
consumption data tables, 256–57
production data tables, 338–39
Saltwater
desalinated water production, data tables, 306–307
intrusion, Senegal River, 108–10
Sand production, data tables, 338–39
Sanitation
access to, data tables, 250–51
burden of disease, 34
China, 123
disease prevention strategies, 78–80, 82
disease rates, impact on, 9
indicator of environmental health, 128
Sawnwood production, data tables, 296–97
Scarcity of resources. *See also* Degradation of environment
deforestation. *See* Deforestation
fisheries, 195–96
food. *See* Food security
freshwater ecosystems, 190–91
migration, cause of, 148
trends, 185–99
water. *See* Water shortages
wood fiber, 164–65
Schistosomiasis
climate change, impact of, 70
irrigation, impact of, 47
morbidity rates, 47
Senegal River region, 110–12, 114
School attendance, 149–50
Seabirds, biodiversity of regional seas, data tables, 316
Seafood. *See* Fish; Molluscs and crustaceans
Seagrasses, biodiversity of regional seas, data tables, 316
Sea levels, rising, 68–69
Season changes, 174
Senegal, water supply improvements, 79
Senegal River, 108–14
background, 108
cholera, 113
development projects, 109–10
diarrheal diseases, 113
ecosystem changes in river basin, 110
future development, 113–14
health problems from environmental changes, 110–13
malaria, 112
malnutrition, 112–13
Rift Valley Fever, 112
schistosomiasis, 110–12, 114
social changes and conflict, 113
Sewage. *See* Municipal wastewater
Sewage systems, urban households, data tables, 278–79
Sewage treatment. *See* Wastewater treatment
Sharks, biodiversity of regional seas, data tables, 316
Ships, ballast water discharges, 198

Shrimp
    aquaculture production, 159–60
    biodiversity of regional seas, data tables, 316
Silver production, data tables, 338–39
Skin cancer, UV-B radiation, 61
Sleeping sickness, impact of climate change, 70
Smoke. *See also* Black smoke; Coal consumption and
    emissions; Particulate emissions
    cookstove smoke, 66–67
    wood smoke, 67
Smoking
    health hazards, 97
    mortality rates, *33*
Snails
    golden apple snail, 198
    schistosomiasis. *See* Schistosomiasis
SO₂ emissions. *See* Sulfur dioxide emissions
Social auditing, *169*
Social investments, data tables, 250–51
"Social modernization," 142
Social services. *See also* Education; Health care services
    government expeditures, 150
    libraries, data tables, 250–51
Socioeconomic characteristics of cities, data tables,
    276–77
Socioeconomic development
    corporate responsibility movement, *169*
    education, impact of, 149–50
    population growth, effect on, 142
Socioeconomic disruption
    climate change, impact of, 68
    health, impact on, 97
    income inequities, impact of, 146
    international migration, 149
    Senegal River region, 113
Soil, biological or chemical hazards, 19–24, 26–32
Soil degradation, 156–58
    acid rain, effect of, 178, 182
    nitrogen imbalance, 180
Soil erosion, 157–58, 161
    rising sea levels, impact of, 69
    United States, 162
Solar ultraviolet radiation. *See* Ultraviolet radiation
Solid fuels
    carbon dioxide emissions, data tables, 344–45, 347
    emissions, regions at a glance, 200–20
    health hazards, 80
    production and consumption, data tables, 332–33
Solid waste. *See also* Hazardous waste
    paper, 164
    urban households, data tables, 278–79
Sorghum, yield, 153
South America, 212–14. *See also specific countries*
    Hidrovia project, 191
Southeast Asia, urbanization, 39
Soviet Union (former). *See also* Russia
    HIV/AIDS morbidity rate, 151
Sparse trees and parklands, data tables, 294–95
Steel industries, environmental impact, 52
Stephens, Carolyn, 106–07
Sterility, pesticide exposure, 44
Stillbirths, effect of indoor air quality, 66–67
Stomach cancer, China, 122
Stoves
    cookstove smoke, 66–67
    environmental improvements, 80–81
Stratospheric ozone depletion. *See* Ozone layer depletion
Subsidies. *See* Financial aid and incentives
Sulfur dioxide emissions
    China, 117–18, 120, 124
    city pollution, data tables, 264–65
    developed countries, 183–84
    developing countries, 182–83
    health effects, *64–65*

indicator of environmental health, 127
reduction of pollution, 90
trading of emissions, 88, 175
trends, 181–84
Sulfur hexafluoride, Kyoto Protocol, 174–77
Sulfur production, data tables, 338–39
Surface water. *See also* Lakes; Rivers
    nitrate contamination from fertilizers, 46–47
    resources and withdrawals, data tables, 304–05
Sustainable cultivation, 162
    coffee, 166
Sustainable fishing, 196
Sustainable production, 166–69. *See also* Recycling
    corporate responsibility movement, *169*
    eco-efficiency strategies, 90, 167, *168*
    incentives, 168–69
    phases of progression toward, 166–67
    product stewardship, 167–68
    reshaping industry, 168–69
Synthetic xenoestrogens, effect on breast cancer, 103–04

T

Tanning industries, environmental impact, 52
Tanzania, fertility rates, 142
Taxation
    carbon tax, 92–93
    chlorofluorocarbon excise tax, United States, 178
    energy taxation, 91–93, *92*
Televisions
    households without, 268
    regions at a glance, 200–20
Temperature changes, 67–68. *See also* Global warming
    agriculture, impact on, 71
    air pollution, impact on, 69–70
    carbon dioxide emissions, impact of, 171
    disease rates, impact on, 70–71
Temperature profiles of atmosphere, 173–74
Terrestrial ecosystems, nitrogen imbalance, 180
Testicular cancer, endocrine disruptors, *57*
Tetanus immunizations, data tables, 262–63
Thailand
    aquaculture production, 159–60
    fertility rates, 142
    malnutrition, reduction of, 155
Thermal energy production, data tables, 334–35
Threatened and endangered species
    amphibians, data tables, 324–25
    bioinvasions, 197–99
    birds, 197, 322–23
    data tables, 322–25
    fish, data tables, 324–25
    mammals, data tables, 322–23
    management programs, data tables, 326–27
    plants, data tables, 322–23
    reptiles, data tables, 324–25
Threatened frontier forests, data tables, 294–95
Thyroid cancer, Chernobyl accident, 95
Toilets, flush, households without, 268
Total suspended particulates (TSP)
    China, 117, 120
    city pollution, data tables, 264–65
    indicator of environmental health, 127
Tourism, coral reef damage, 194
Toxaphene. *See* Persistent organic pollutants
Toxic algal blooms, 180–81, 194
Toxic waste. *See* Hazardous waste
Tractors, data tables, 286–87
Trade. *See also* Exports; Imports
    bioinvasions fostered by, 197–98
    cereal trade, data tables, 288–89
    chlorofluorocarbons, 178

coffee trade, 165–66
electricity trade, data tables, 334–35
fish, fish meal, molluscs and crustaceans, trade bal-
    ance, data tables, 314–15
free trade zones, 53
increase in global trade, 38
roundwood trade, data tables, 296–97
water markets, 189
wood trade, data tables, 296–97
Transportation. *See also headings starting with Motor ve-*
hicle
    energy balances, data tables, 336–37
    urban households, data tables, 278–79
Trash. *See* Solid waste
Trees. *See* Forests and woodlands
Trends in global environment, 138–224
    food production and security, 152–60
    global commons, 170–84
    population and human well-being, 141–51
    production and consumption, 161–69
    resources at risk, 184–99
Trichuris worms, impact of wastewater irrigation, 48
Tropical rainforests
    data tables, 294–95
    deforestation, 186
    wood pulp production, 163
Trucks. *See headings starting with Motor vehicle*
Tuberculosis (TB)
    immunizations, data tables, 262–63
    morbidity rates, 25, *40*, 260–61
    mortality rates, 9, 25, *40*
    urbanization, impact of, *40*
Tuber production, data tables, 284–85
Tuber yield, data tables, 288–89
Typhoid, 48–49, 122

U

Ultraviolet radiation, 61
    acid rain, combined impact of, 183–84
Undernourishment. *See* Malnutrition
United Church of Christ Commission for Racial Justice,
    99–100
United States
    air quality standards, 90
    ballast water discharge regulations, 198
    chlorofluorocarbon excise tax, 178
    emissions trading, 88, 175
    food waste, 156
    Great Lakes. *See* Great Lakes
    greenhouse gas emissions, 176
    HIV/AIDS morbidity rate, 151
    leaded gasoline phaseout, 60
    nitrogen oxide emissions, 183
    pesticide exposure, 44
    soil erosion, 162
    sulfur dioxide emissions, 182–83
    tuberculosis morbidity rates, *40*
    watershed protection and ecosystem valuation, 193
Urban agglomerations, data tables, 274–75
Urban characteristics, city level, data tables, 276–77
Urban environment, city level, data tables, 278–79
Urbanization, 39
    China, 115–16
    data tables, 273–81
    developing countries, 146
    environmental health in twenty-first century, 94–95
    implications of, 146–47
    megacities, 146–47
    outdoor air quality, 63
    population growth, 146–47, 274–77
    public policies, 147

rate of, 146–47
socioeconomic indicators, data tables, 276–77
tuberculosis increase, *40*
Urban population, 200–20
data tables, 274–77
growth, 146–47
Urban residential density, data tables, 276–77
Urinary schistosomiasis, 111–12
UV radiation. *See* Ultraviolet radiation

V

Vector-borne diseases, 24–25. *See also* Insect-borne diseases; *specific disease*
climate change, impact of, 70
irrigation, impact of, 86
land conversion to agricultural use, impact of, 49–50
prevention strategies, 81–83
Senegal River, 110–13
Vehicles. *See* Motor vehicles
Violence
murders in urban populations, data tables, 278–79
Wars. *See* Armed conflicts
Viral hepatitis, China, 122
Viruses, health hazards, 18–26
Vitamin A deficiency
data tables, 256–57
indicator of environmental health, 128

W

Wages, impact on industrialization, 53
War. *See* Armed conflicts
Waste
hazardous waste. *See* Hazardous waste
industrial wastewater. *See* Industrial wastewater
municipal wastewater. *See* Municipal wastewater
solid waste. *See* Solid waste
Waste of resources, 161–63. *See also* Consumption rates
food waste, 156
paper, 163–64
sustainable production. *See* Sustainable production
Wastewater. *See* Industrial wastewater; Municipal wastewater
Wastewater irrigation, 47–48, 86–87
China, 122
Wastewater treatment, 189

urban households, data tables, 278–79
Water-borne diseases, 19–24, 78–79
China, 121–22
climate change, impact of, 71
Water markets, 189
Water pollution
agricultural water pollution, *87*
aquaculture production causing, 160
arsenic poisoning in West Bengal, 105
biological hazards, 19–24, 78–79
burden of disease, 34
chemical hazards, 26–32
China, 116, 120–22
European lakes, data tables, 308
indicators of environmental health, 128
nitrate contamination from fertilizers, 46–47
paper and pulp industry, 164
scarcity of water, impact on, 189
Watersheds
data tables, 309
ecosystem valuation, 193
map, 224
Water shortages, 188–90
China, 120
health, effect on, 155
map, 223
Water storage, disease prevention strategies, 81
Water supply. *See also* Drinking water
agricultural water. *See* Agricultural water
consumption rates, 188–89, 304–05
desalinated water production, data tables, 306–307
disease prevention strategies, 78–80, 82
domestic water withdrawals, 188–89, 304–05
freshwater resources and withdrawals, 188–89, 304–05
groundwater. *See* Groundwater
indicator of environmental health, 128
industrial water withdrawals, 188–89, 304–05
internal renewable resources, data tables, 304–05
irrigation, impact of, 86
lakes. *See* Lakes
piped water, households without, 268
pollution. *See* Water pollution
regions at a glance, 200–20
rivers. *See* Rivers
Senegal River development projects, 109–10
shortages. *See* Water shortages
surface water. *See* Surface water
urban households, data tables, 278–79
watersheds. *See* Watersheds
withdrawals, 188–89
Weather events, 68. *See also specific events (e.g.,* Floods)

plant pests and diseases, effect on, 71
West Africa
Onchocerciasis Control Programme, 82
Senegal River, damming, 108–14
West Bengal, arsenic poisoning, 105
Wetlands
data tables, 309, 320–21
ecosystems, 190–91, 193
Wheat, 152–53. *See also* Cereal
Whooping cough immunizations, data tables, 262–63
Wildlife
chemical hazard studies, 30–32
endocrine disruptors, *56–57*
PCB exposure, 55
threatened species. *See* Threatened and endangered species
Wilkinson, Clive, 193
Wind patterns, impact on air pollution, 70
Woodlands. *See* Forests and woodlands
Wood production and trade, 200–20
data tables, 296–97
Wood smoke, 67
Workplace environment
air quality. *See* Indoor air quality
chemical hazards, 26–32
injuries from industrial accidents, 54
pesticide exposure, *43, 43–45*
World Bank commodity indexes and prices, 240
World heritage sites, data tables, 320–21
Worms. *See* Parasitic worms

X

Xenoestrogens, effect on breast cancer, 103–04

Y

"Yield plateau," 152–53
"Yield stagnation," 152–53

Z

Zinc. *See* Heavy metals
Zoos, endangered species management programs, data tables, 326–27

WRI Classroom Resources

WRI Teacher's Guides
These self-contained Teacher's Guides contain everything needed to teach multi-part lessons on a critical global issue including: suggestions for integrating the topics into civics, government, history, geography, mathematics, and science curriculums; step-by-step teaching strategies; student enrichment activities; student handouts and overhead transparency masters; and suggestions for further reading.

Published by Kendall-Hunt Publishing Co., Dubuque, Iowa

To order or to request more information, call 800-KH-BOOKS (542-6657).

Visit our Environmental Education Website at http://www.wri.org/wri/enved

WORLD RESOURCES 1998–99
READER SURVEY

TO REMAIN ON OUR MAILING LIST, PLEASE FILL OUT AND RETURN THIS SURVEY. THANK YOU.

About yourself

1. Your country of residence? _____

2. For what purpose do you use *World Resources*? (check all that apply)

    ____ for scholarly research
    ____ for policy research
    ____ to teach a class
    ____ to prepare a speech
    ____ to write an article
    ____ for access to basic environmental data
    ____ other _____

3. How do you use *World Resources*? (check all that apply)

    ____ read all sections thoroughly
    ____ read certain sections thoroughly
    ____ skim through or glance at
    ____ keep as a personal reference
    ____ place in a library
    ____ share with interested colleagues
    ____ leave unused on shelf
    ____ other _____

Your thoughts on overall content and presentation

4. How would you rate the report as a source of objective and impartial information?

    ____ always objective
    ____ usually objective
    ____ sometimes objective
    ____ rarely objective

5. If you are familiar with previous volumes of *World Resources*, please tell us which part(s) of *World Resources* you found most useful?

    ____ special focus (e.g., Urban Environment in *World Resources* 1996–97)
    ____ resource related chapters (e.g., Food and Agriculture, Population and Human Development, etc.)
    ____ data tables
    ____ not familiar with previous volumes

6. In the current volume which part(s) do you use *most often*?

    ____ Part I: Environmental Change and Human Health
    ____ Part II: Global Environmental Trends
        ____ Critical Trends
        ____ Regions at a Glance
    ____ Part III: Data Tables

7. In the current volume which part(s) do you use *least often*?

    ____ Part I: Environmental Change and Human Health
    ____ Part II: Global Environmental Trends
        ____ Critical Trends
        ____ Regions at a Glance
    ____ Part III: Data Tables

8. What type of companion materials to *World Resources* would be most useful to you?

    ____ data diskette
    ____ teachers' guide
    ____ slides of graphics/maps
    ____ other _____

9. I use the World Resources Institute (WRI) Web site to access the report.

    ____ no
    ____ yes
    ____ I don't have access to the Internet.

Your thoughts on the data tables

10. Are there tables you find particularly useful?

    ____ no
    ____ yes, specifically _____

11. Are there tables that you would like to be added?

    ____ no
    ____ yes, specifically _____

12. Are there tables you think should be omitted?

    ____ no
    ____ yes, specifically _____

13. In what format do you most often use the data tables?

    ____ in the report
    ____ on diskette
    ____ from the WRI Web site

14. I rely on the data tables in the *World Resources*:

    ____ as a primary source of data for my information needs
    ____ as one of many sources I rely on for my data needs (such as the World Bank, Internet, etc.)
    ____ because they are more easily accessible than other sources for data I need
    ____ other _____

Fold second and tape here.

If mailed outside the United States, please place in an envelope. Thank you.

Dr./Mr./Ms./Mrs. _____
Name _____
Position _____
Organization _____
Address _____
_____
City/State _____
Mail Code _____ Country _____

World Resources Report
World Resources Institute
1709 New York Avenue, N.W.
Washington, D.C. 20006
U.S.A.

15. We welcome any and all comments and suggestions concerning the *World Resources* series.

Fold First